INQUIZITIVE

InQuizitive is an adaptive online learning tool that is thoroughly informed by psychological research into how students learn.

InQuizitive is: Game-like

Game-like elements engage students and keep them working. Students gain or lose points by adjusting the confidence slider, progress through three levels in each chapter, and win bonus points for hot streaks and bonus questions.[1]

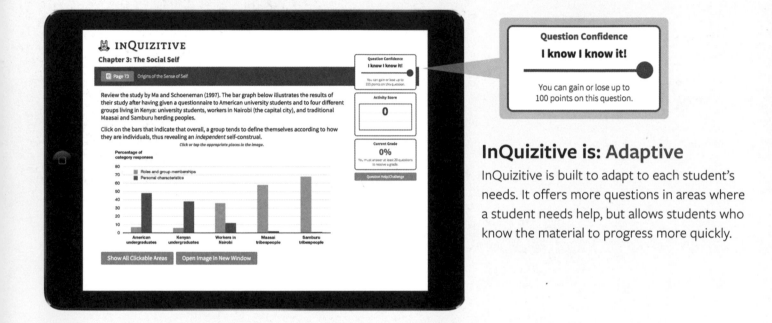

InQuizitive is: Adaptive

InQuizitive is built to adapt to each student's needs. It offers more questions in areas where a student needs help, but allows students who know the material to progress more quickly.

InQuizitive is: Motivating

InQuizitive guides students to the right answer after each response. This turns every question—even ones the students answer incorrectly—into a positive and motivating learning experience.[2]

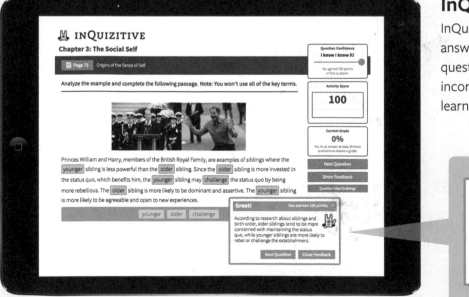

1 A study by Naceur and Schiefele (2005) found that information retention was more highly correlated with student interest than student ability.
2 To be maximally effective, a system also needs to turn failures into positive learning experiences (Gee, 2009).

Reducing Racial Disparities in the U.S. School System

A well-documented achievement gap is evident in the American educational system: Black students are more likely to be suspended or expelled and less likely to graduate than their White peers. Further studies have shown strong links between suspension rates and dropout rates, and between dropout rates and incarceration rates. In other words, disparities in the discipline of Black and White students can have lifetime implications. Racial bias among teachers may be part of the reason for these differences, but recent research shows that fostering empathy in teachers can reduce suspension rates among all racial groups.

Suspensions per Racial Group

Not only are Black students disproportionately likely to be suspended, but the Black-White racial disparity gets more extreme with more discipline.

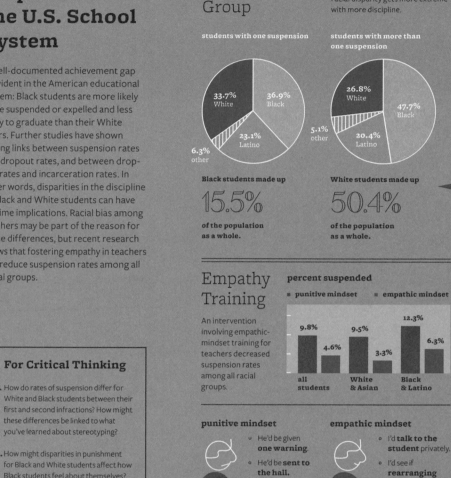

students with one suspension

- 36.9% Black
- 23.1% Latino
- 6.3% other
- 33.7% White

students with more than one suspension

- 47.7% Black
- 20.4% Latino
- 5.1% other
- 26.8% White

Black students made up

15.5%

of the population as a whole.

White students made up

50.4%

of the population as a whole.

Empathy Training

An intervention involving empathic-mindset training for teachers decreased suspension rates among all racial groups.

percent suspended

- ■ punitive mindset
- ■ empathic mindset

	all students	White & Asian	Black & Latino
punitive mindset	9.8%	9.5%	12.3%
empathic mindset	4.6%	3.3%	6.3%

punitive mindset
- He'd be given **one warning**.
- He'd be **sent to the hall**.
- He'd be **sent to the office**.

empathic mindset
- I'd **talk to the student** privately.
- I'd see if **rearranging desks** would help.
- I'd **try to understand** the problem and address it.

Sources: Suspensions per Racial Group: Civil Rights Data Collection, 2017; Empathy Training: Okonofua, Paunesku, & Walton, 2016.

New Closer Look infographics give students an inside view of experimentation in social psychology and helps them understand data and analysis for a range of topics like social class (diversity and inequality), politics and group polarization, research methodology, and the science of happiness. Each infographic ends with questions for critical analysis.

For Critical Thinking

1. How do rates of suspension differ for White and Black students between their first and second infractions? How might these differences be linked to what you've learned about stereotyping?

2. How might disparities in punishment for Black and White students affect how Black students feel about themselves? Incorporate what you've learned about attributional ambiguity, stereotype threat, and self-fulfilling prophecies.

Social Psychology

FIFTH EDITION

FIFTH EDITION

Social Psychology

Thomas Gilovich
Cornell University

Dacher Keltner
University of California, Berkeley

Serena Chen
University of California, Berkeley

Richard E. Nisbett
University of Michigan

W. W. Norton & Company · New York · London

W. W. Norton & Company has been independent since its founding in 1923, when William Ward
Mary D. Herter Norton first published lectures delivered at the People's Institute, the adult educat
New York City's Cooper Union. The firm soon expanded its program beyond the Institute, publish
brated academics from America and abroad. By midcentury, the two major pillars of Norton's pub
trade books and college texts—were firmly established. In the 1950s, the Norton family transferr
company to its employees, and today—with a staff of four hundred and a comparable number of
professional titles published each year—W. W. Norton & Company stands as the largest and olde
owned wholly by its employees.

EDITOR: Sheri Snavely
PROJECT EDITOR: Jennifer Barnhardt
EDITORIAL ASSISTANT: Eve Sanoussi
DEVELOPMENTAL EDITORS: Beth Ammerman and Emily Stuart
MANAGING EDITOR, COLLEGE: Marian Johnson
MANAGING EDITOR, COLLEGE DIGITAL MEDIA: Kim Yi
SENIOR PRODUCTION MANAGER: Sean Mintus
MEDIA EDITORS: Scott Sugarman and Kaitlin Coats
ASSOCIATE MEDIA EDITOR: Victoria Reuter
DIGITAL MEDIA PROJECT EDITOR: Danielle Belfiore
MEDIA EDITORIAL ASSISTANTS: Alex Trivilino and Allison Smith
EBOOK PRODUCTION MANAGER: Mateus Manço Teixeira
EBOOK PRODUCTION COORDINATOR: Lizz Thabet
MARKETING MANAGER, PSYCHOLOGY: Ashley Sherwood
DESIGN DIRECTOR: Jillian Burr
PHOTO EDITOR: Catherine Abelman
DIRECTOR OF COLLEGE PERMISSIONS: Megan Schindel
PERMISSIONS SPECIALIST: Bethany Salminen
COMPOSITION: Jouve
INFOGRAPHICS: Open, NY
MANUFACTURING: Transcontinental

Permission to use copyrighted material is included in the credits section of this book, which begins on page

Library of Congress Cataloging-in-Publication Data

Names: Gilovich, Thomas, author. | Keltner, Dacher, author. | Chen, Serena,
    author.
Title: Social psychology / Thomas Gilovich, Cornell University, Dacher
    Keltner, University of California, Berkeley, Serena Chen, University of
    California, Berkeley, Richard E. Nisbett, University of Michigan.
Description: Fifth Edition. | New York : W.w. Norton & Company, [2018] |
    Revised edition of the authors' Social psychology, 2016. | Includes
    bibliographical references and indexes.
Identifiers: LCCN 2018025284 | **ISBN 9780393624052 (hardcover)**
Subjects: LCSH: Social psychology.
Classification: LCC HM1033 .G52 2018 | DDC 302—dc23 LC record available at https://lccn.loc.gov/2018

W. W. Norton & Company, Inc., 500 Fifth Avenue, New York, NY 10110
wwnorton.com
W. W. Norton & Company Ltd., 15 Carlisle Street, London W1D 3BS
1 2 3 4 5 6 7 8 9 0

FIFTH EDITION

Social Psychology

Thomas Gilovich
Cornell University

Dacher Keltner
University of California, Berkeley

Serena Chen
University of California, Berkeley

Richard E. Nisbett
University of Michigan

W. W. Norton & Company · New York · London

W. W. Norton & Company has been independent since its founding in 1923, when William Warder Norton and Mary D. Herter Norton first published lectures delivered at the People's Institute, the adult education division of New York City's Cooper Union. The firm soon expanded its program beyond the Institute, publishing books by celebrated academics from America and abroad. By midcentury, the two major pillars of Norton's publishing program—trade books and college texts—were firmly established. In the 1950s, the Norton family transferred control of the company to its employees, and today—with a staff of four hundred and a comparable number of trade, college, and professional titles published each year—W. W. Norton & Company stands as the largest and oldest publishing house owned wholly by its employees.

EDITOR: Sheri Snavely
PROJECT EDITOR: Jennifer Barnhardt
EDITORIAL ASSISTANT: Eve Sanoussi
DEVELOPMENTAL EDITORS: Beth Ammerman and Emily Stuart
MANAGING EDITOR, COLLEGE: Marian Johnson
MANAGING EDITOR, COLLEGE DIGITAL MEDIA: Kim Yi
SENIOR PRODUCTION MANAGER: Sean Mintus
MEDIA EDITORS: Scott Sugarman and Kaitlin Coats
ASSOCIATE MEDIA EDITOR: Victoria Reuter
DIGITAL MEDIA PROJECT EDITOR: Danielle Belfiore
MEDIA EDITORIAL ASSISTANTS: Alex Trivilino and Allison Smith
EBOOK PRODUCTION MANAGER: Mateus Manço Teixeira
EBOOK PRODUCTION COORDINATOR: Lizz Thabet
MARKETING MANAGER, PSYCHOLOGY: Ashley Sherwood
DESIGN DIRECTOR: Jillian Burr
PHOTO EDITOR: Catherine Abelman
DIRECTOR OF COLLEGE PERMISSIONS: Megan Schindel
PERMISSIONS SPECIALIST: Bethany Salminen
COMPOSITION: Jouve
INFOGRAPHICS: Open, NY
MANUFACTURING: Transcontinental

Permission to use copyrighted material is included in the credits section of this book, which begins on page C-1.

Library of Congress Cataloging-in-Publication Data

Names: Gilovich, Thomas, author. | Keltner, Dacher, author. | Chen, Serena, author.
Title: Social psychology / Thomas Gilovich, Cornell University, Dacher Keltner, University of California, Berkeley, Serena Chen, University of California, Berkeley, Richard E. Nisbett, University of Michigan.
Description: Fifth Edition. | New York : W.w. Norton & Company, [2018] | Revised edition of the authors' Social psychology, 2016. | Includes bibliographical references and indexes.
Identifiers: LCCN 2018025284 | ISBN 9780393624052 (hardcover)
Subjects: LCSH: Social psychology.
Classification: LCC HM1033 .G52 2018 | DDC 302—dc23 LC record available at https://lccn.loc.gov/2018025284

W. W. Norton & Company, Inc., 500 Fifth Avenue, New York, NY 10110
wwnorton.com
W. W. Norton & Company Ltd., 15 Carlisle Street, London W1D 3BS

1 2 3 4 5 6 7 8 9 0

ABOUT THE AUTHORS

THOMAS GILOVICH is the Irene Blecker Rosenfeld Professor of Psychology and Co-Director of the Center for Behavioral Economics and Decision Research at Cornell University. He has taught social psychology for over 35 years and is the recipient of the Russell Distinguished Teaching Award at Cornell. His research focuses on judgment, decision making, and well-being. He is a member of the American Academy of Arts and Sciences and a fellow of the American Psychological Society, the American Psychological Association, the Society for Personality and Social Psychology, the Society of Experimental Social Psychology, and the Committee for Skeptical Inquiry.

DACHER KELTNER is the Thomas and Ruth Ann Hornaday Professor of Psychology and the Director of the Greater Good Science Center at the University of California, Berkeley. He has taught social psychology for the past 18 years and is the recipient of the Distinguished Teaching Award for Letters and Sciences. His research focuses on the prosocial emotions (such as love, sympathy, and gratitude), morality, and power. Other awards include the Western Psychological Association's award for outstanding contribution to research, the Positive Psychology Prize for excellence in research, and the Ed and Carol Diener mid-career award for research excellence in Social Psychology. He is a fellow of the American Psychological Association, the American Psychological Society, and the Society for Personality and Social Psychology. In 2008, the *Utne Reader* listed Dacher as one of the 50 visionaries changing the world.

SERENA CHEN is Professor of Psychology, the Marian E. and Daniel E. Koshland, Jr. Distinguished Chair for Innovative Teaching and Research, and the Director of the Berkeley Collegium at the University of California, Berkeley. She has taught social psychology for the past 20 years and is the recipient of the Distinguished Teaching Award from Berkeley's Social Science Division. Her research focuses on the social bases of the self and identity and on the intrapersonal and interpersonal consequences of social power and other hierarchy-related dimensions (e.g., social class, income inequality). She is a fellow of the Society of Personality and Social Psychology, American Psychological Association, and the Association for Psychological Science, as well as the recipient of the Early Career Award from the International Society for Self and Identity. The Association for Psychological Science also identified her as a Rising Star.

RICHARD E. NISBETT is the Theodore M. Newcomb Distinguished University Professor of Psychology at the University of Michigan and Research Professor at Michigan's Institute for Social Research. He has taught courses in social psychology, cultural psychology, cognitive psychology, and evolutionary psychology. His research focuses on how people reason and how reasoning can be improved. He also studies how people from different cultures think, perceive, feel, and act in different ways. He is the recipient of the Distinguished Scientific Contribution Award of the American Psychological Association and the William James Fellow Award of the American Psychological Society and is a member of the National Academy of Sciences and the American Academy of Arts and Sciences.

CONTENTS IN BRIEF

PREFACE

A FRESH PERSPECTIVE ON SOCIAL PSYCHOLOGY

Social psychology illuminates the nature of everyday social life. It's a science that offers novel insights into the foundations of moral sentiments, the origins of violence, and the reasons people fall in love. It provides basic tools for understanding racial bias and how we might curb it, how people persuade one another, why people trust and cooperate with each other, and how people rationalize their undesirable actions. Social psychology offers scientifically grounded answers to questions human beings have been thinking about since we started to reflect on who we are: Are we rational creatures? How can we find happiness? What is the proper relationship of the individual to the larger society? How are we shaped by the culture in which we are raised?

After decades of collective experience teaching social psychology, we decided at the turn of the twenty-first century to put pen to paper (or fingers to keyboard) and write our own vision of this fascinating discipline. It was an ideal time to do so. Many new developments in the field were reshaping social psychology. Exciting new research had revealed how different kinds of culture—country of origin, regional culture, social class—shape human thought, feeling, and action. Evolutionary theory was helping to guide how social psychologists study things such as homicide, morality, and cooperation. Social psychologists were making inroads into the study of the brain. Specific areas of interest to us—the self, judgment and decision making, emotion, relationships, and well-being—had emerged as well-defined areas of investigation that were producing important insights about human behavior. The lure of writing a textbook, and the challenge in doing so, was to capture all of these new developments and integrate them with the timeless classics of social psychology that make it such a captivating discipline.

It's a bit shocking to us to think that this is the fifth edition of the text; it seems like just yesterday when we first got together in Berkeley, California, to map out what an informative survey of social psychology might look like. Our work on all five editions has been deeply rewarding. Our fascination with the field, and our pride in being a part of it, has been rekindled and magnified with each edition. It is gratifying to have this book reach the minds of the next generation of social psychology students.

Whether students end up as teachers, health care providers, or talent agents or as software designers, forest rangers, or book editors, other people are going to be the center of their lives. All of us grow up dependent on the members of our nuclear family (and, in many cultural contexts, a larger extended family); we go through adolescence obsessed with our social standing and intensely focused on our prospects for romance and sexuality; and as adults we seek out others in the workplace, at clubs, in places of worship, and in our recreational activities. Social psychologists spend their professional lives studying this intense sociality, examining how we act, think, and feel in all of these social encounters—and *why* we act, think, and feel that way. Above all, we want our book to capture the fundamentally social nature of human life and to present the clever, informative, and sometimes inspiring methods that social psychologists have used to study and understand the social life around us.

In our teaching, we have found that many great studies in social psychology are simple narratives: the narrative of the person who felt compelled to harm another person in the name of science, the narrative of the clergyman who did not help someone in need because he was in a hurry, the narrative of the Southerner whose blood pressure rose when he was insulted in a hallway, the narrative of the young researcher who lived among hunter-gatherers in New Guinea to discover universal facial expressions. In our experience, teaching social psychology brings forth so many "Aha!" moments because of these stories that are embedded within, and inspire, our science.

SOCIAL PSYCHOLOGY, THE SCIENTIFIC METHOD, AND CRITICAL THINKING

These narratives are different, however, from others that try to capture something important about the human condition: the story of the tortoise and the hare, the tale of the boy who cried wolf, and the anecdote of the child down the street who "took candy from a stranger" and paid a high price for doing so. The tales we tell in this book are all grounded in empirical evidence. It's the scientific foundation of their claims that distinguish social psychologists from other astute observers of the human condition, such as novelists, playwrights, film directors, and parents, teachers, clergymen, and coaches. The methods of social psychology are every bit as important as the insights they reveal.

In fact, we believe that social psychology is unmatched as a means of teaching critical thinking. Accordingly, our text makes explicit the power of social psychology's methods and habits of thought for understanding the world and assessing the likely truth of what friends and the media tell us. To make sure students hone their critical thinking skills, we approach the subject matter of social psychology—and the *study* of social psychology—in several ways.

First, in Chapter 2, The Methods of Social Psychology, we present an overview of the most important elements of conducting research. We tie the methods of social psychology together by showing how many of them can be applied to a single problem: the nature of the "culture of honor." That chapter, and much of the rest of the book, is oriented toward providing the critical thinking skills that are the hallmark of social psychology. We show how the tools of social psychology can be used to critique research in the behavioral and medical sciences that students encounter online and in magazines and newspapers. More importantly, we show how the methods of social psychology can be used to understand everyday life and to figure out how to navigate new situations.

Second, our "Not So Fast" feature in each chapter highlights how easy it is to be fooled by the evidence we encounter in our lives and to draw conclusions that seem solid but in fact don't stand up to scientific scrutiny. They show how even the smartest among us can be misled by what we experience and what we read or hear unless we've learned some fundamental principles of the scientific method. Many of these lessons are reinforced at the end of each chapter with a set of open-ended "Think about It" questions that challenge students to think critically in the context of a research-related or real-life scenario.

Third, we embed discussions of methodological issues throughout the book in the context of many programs of research. This melds the content of social psychology with the principles that underlie research that can be used to understand ordinary events in people's lives.

Fourth, a new feature of this edition is a set of full-page infographics that examine social psychological topics of contemporary interest. These infographics give students an inside view of experimentation in social psychology and help them understand how to read data graphics and distill the takeaway points of research. We have tried to make sure that all our field's varied methods—such as archival analyses, randomized controlled experiments, neuroimaging studies, and participant observation—are represented and that the infographics shed light on important trends and questions in everyday life.

Much of the subject matter of social psychology—relationships, media, conformity, prejudice—readily engages the student's attention and imagination. The material sells itself. But in most social psychology textbooks, the presentation comes across as a list of unconnected topics—as one intriguing fact after another. As a result, students often come away thinking of social psychology as all fun and games. That's fine up to a point. Social psychology *is* fun. But it is much more than that, and we have tried to show how the highlights of our field—the classic findings and the exciting new developments—are part of a scientific study of human nature that can sit with pride next to biology, chemistry, and physics and that is worthy of the most serious-minded student's attention.

THE APPLICATION OF SOCIAL PSYCHOLOGY TO EVERYDAY LIFE

Possibly the easiest part of writing a social psychology textbook is pointing out the enormous applied implications of what the field has to offer. We do a great deal of this throughout the text. Each chapter begins with events in the real world that drive home the themes and wisdom of social psychology. For example, Chapter 3, The Social Self, begins with the story of Stefani Joanne Angelina Germanotta, who you and the world know as Lady Gaga. Chapter 6, Emotion, begins with the story of how Pixar director Pete Docter relied on the science of emotion to create the highly regarded film *Inside Out*.

Chapter 12, Groups, begins with the harrowing story of how Pelican Bay inmate Todd Ashker united different gangs in prison to lead a protest against solitary confinement. What better way for the student to ponder the findings of social psychology than by relying on them to understand current events? Interspersed throughout the text are Focus On boxes that profile real-world applications of the wisdom of social psychology—for example, in understanding how black uniforms make professional athletes more aggressive or how meditation might shift a person's brain chemistry.

To bring into sharper focus the relevance of social psychology to daily living, we have three applied mini-chapters, or modules, at the end of the book. These modules bring science-based insight to bear on three areas of great importance to just about everyone: the latest findings on health and how science-based, practical techniques can help us cope with stress during difficult times; the latest discoveries in the study of human intelligence and education; and a review of social psychological insights into how the legal system functions and how it can be improved. These modules constitute dramatic evidence of the relevance of social psychological findings to advancing human welfare.

NEW CONTENT IN THE FIFTH EDITION

The cumulative nature of science requires that revisions do justice to the latest discoveries and evolving views of the field. This new edition has much to offer in this regard.

Chapter	Changes in the Fifth Edition
1. An Invitation to Social Psychology	A new section called "The Uses of Social Psychology" has been added, covering social psychology and critical thinking, the uses and abuses of social media, and social psychology and the "good life."
2. The Methods of Social Psychology	We have added an extensive discussion of the issue that has commanded so much of the field's attention and sparked so much commentary—the replicability of research findings. Our discussion highlights the importance of replication, presents the results of research investigating the replication rate for prominent social psychological findings, and details why some failures to replicate are inevitable. Also new to this chapter is the infographic "Threats to Internal Validity."
3. The Social Self	We have incorporated additional theory and research on how the self influences and is influenced by the use of social media. In addition, we now include a section covering classic and recent research that reveals how shifts in construals and perspectives can play a critical role in effective self-regulation.
4. Social Cognition: Thinking about People and Situations	We have added a section that discusses the phenomenon of "fake news" and how influential it may be in shaping people's beliefs, as well as another section on "information bubbles" and how they can contribute to belief polarization. The latter section also contains some "quick tips" about what readers can do to burst their own information bubbles. A new infographic, "Overconfidence: A Pervasive Bias of Human Judgment," has been added as well.

Chapter	Changes in the Fifth Edition
5. Social Attribution: Explaining Behavior	We revised our discussion of the fundamental attribution error to highlight its significance to several recent trends in society, such as growing income inequality.
6. Emotion	We have added new material on the communication of emotion through emoji in social media, further advances in the understanding of how emotions guide moral judgment, and more tips for finding happiness. Additionally, this chapter features an infographic called "The Game of Happiness."
7. Attitudes, Behavior, and Rationalization	We continue to cover key findings and theories on the relationship between attitudes and behavior, honing our discussion of cognitive dissonance theory and the principles that determine whether and how people reduce dissonance. Dissonance is also illustrated through the infographic "How Cognitive Dissonance Can Make You Like What You Buy."
8. Persuasion	We continue to cover the latest in social psychological approaches to political ideology, as well as recent findings on barriers to persuasion. New topics include the role of social media in persuasion, particularly in the realm of political opinions.
9. Social Influence	We discuss new research showing how school bullying can be reduced by utilizing key members of social networks to change students' beliefs about prevailing norms about bullying.
10. Relationships and Attraction	In the domain of relationships, we continue to cover both classic and more contemporary approaches to understanding different types of relationships and a range of relationship processes, including commitment, self-concept change, and conflict. In terms of attraction, we have covered the latest thinking about mere exposure and proximity. An infographic called "(Don't Wanna Be) All By Myself: The Health Effects of Loneliness" has been added as well.
11. Stereotyping, Prejudice, and Discrimination	We now discuss the extent to which an analysis of Internet search traffic yields a different picture of the extent of strong racial prejudice compared with self-reports and other, more traditional data sources. An infographic, "Reducing Racial Disparities in the U.S. School System," has also been added to this chapter.
12. Groups	To our chapter covering the timeless study of groups we have added material on new approaches to collective intelligence, new thinking about power, and more work on social class. In addition, the chapter features an infographic, "Taking It to Extremes: Politics and Group Polarization."
13. Aggression	In our coverage of aggression, we consider new studies on movie violence and aggression, the neural underpinnings of social rejection, inequality, and sexual violence.
14. Altruism and Cooperation	We start Chapter 14 with a new story—that of the success of the film *Wonder Woman*—and cover new discoveries on religion and altruism and the cultural conditions that promote cooperation. An infographic called "How Selfish Are We?" is also featured.

In making these changes, we have preserved the approach in the previous editions that each chapter can stand alone and that chapters can be read in any order. We have done so stylistically by writing chapters that are complete narratives in their own right. Our chapters stand on their own theoretically as well, being organized around social psychology's emphasis on situationism, construal, and automaticity and highlighting important issues addressing what is universal about human behavior and what is variable across cultures. Although our table of contents suggests a particular order of covering the material, instructors will find it easy to present the topics in whatever order best suits their own preferences or needs.

ACKNOWLEDGMENTS

No book is written in a vacuum. Many people have helped us in the course of writing this text, starting with our families. Karen Dashiff Gilovich was her usual bundle of utterly lovable qualities that make the sharing of lives so enjoyable—and the difficulties of authorship so tolerable. Mollie McNeil was a steady source of kindness, enthusiasm, and critical eye and ear. Sebastian and Stella Chen-McDermott brought joy and inspiration daily, bringing to life so much of social psychology even in the context of their young lives. Sarah and Susan Nisbett were sounding boards and life-support systems. Mikki Hebl, Dennis Regan, and Tomi-Ann Roberts went well beyond the call of collegial duty by reading every chapter of early editions and providing us with useful commentary. John H. Bickford, Jr. was an indispensable resource as we worked to improve our LGBTQ coverage in the fourth and fifth editions, guiding us to the appropriate terminology and helping us create a more inclusive book. We are grateful to Beth Morling for providing invaluable advice regarding the revision of the research methods chapter and our discussion of the issues of replication in the fifth edition. In addition to giving us the considerable benefit of their good judgment and good taste, these reviewers also pointed out a few of our blind spots and saved us from an occasional embarrassing error.

Beth Ammerman, our talented developmental editor for the third edition, worked with us to create the new infographics for the fifth edition, and they would not have come together without her patience and insight. We'd like to thank Arianna Benedetti and Amanda Wang for researching the infographic topics and providing first-draft copy. Karen Blair, Alexander Czopp, Patrick Ewell, Jessica Remedios, and Heike Winterheld reviewed infographic ideas at every stage, and their feedback was invaluable in making these features engaging and relevant.

Maya Kuehn, Juliana Breines, and Anna Luerssen contributed the Think about It questions in each chapter and provided insightful reviews of the Not So Fast features and the test bank. Juliana and Anna also led the effort to revise and improve the test bank for the fourth and fifth editions. Jennifer Chmielewski authored the coursepack for our new edition, and Ashley Emmerich and Cornelius Sullivan contributed the InQuizitive questions.

We are indebted to Jon Durbin, Vanessa Drake-Johnson, and Paul Rozin for bringing us together on this project in the first place. And we owe enormous thanks to Sheri Snavely, who has steered us through chapter by chapter for all but the first edition. The book would not be where it is today without her insights, talent, and sense of humor, not to mention her well-timed and well-calibrated nudges. We would also like to thank Eve Sanoussi for her valuable photo suggestions and assistance in keeping the project on track, including keeping us and everyone at Norton sane when the inevitable difficulties of putting a four-author book together arise. We also owe a great deal to our developmental editor for the fifth edition, Emily Stuart, who literally read every line of every page with an eagle eye and a talented red marker. Thanks are also due to our tireless project editor Jennifer Barnhardt, photo editor Cat Ableman, and production manager Sean Mintus. Our media editors, Scott Sugarman and Kaitlin Coats, together with associate editor Tori Reuter, worked diligently to develop modern and high-quality media for our book, including the interactive instructors' guide, student eBook, InQuizitive adaptive assessment, and video. We also are grateful for the marketing efforts of Ashley Sherwood and the Norton travelers who have worked to make this book a success.

Our thanks to the following people for their helpful suggestions and close reading of various chapters and related support material over five editions:

Glenn Adams, *University of Kansas*

Frederic Agatstein, *Rhode Island College*

Craig Anderson, *Iowa State University*

Bob Arkin, *Ohio State University*

Clarissa Arms-Chavez, *Auburn University, Montgomery*

Angela J. Bahns, *Wellesley College*

Joan Bailey, *New Jersey City University*

Miranda Barone, *University of Southern California*

Doris Bazzini, *Appalachian State University*

Kristin Beals, *California State University, Fullerton*

Gordon Bear (retired), *Ramapo College of New Jersey*

Elliott Beaton, *University of New Orleans*

Frank Bernieri, *Oregon State University*

Anila Bhagavatula, *California State University, Long Beach*

John H. Bickford Jr., *University of Massachusetts Amherst*

Karen Blair, *St. Francis Xavier University*

Susan Boon, *Calgary University*

Juliana Breines, *The University of Rhode Island*

Tim Brock, *Ohio State University*

Jennifer Butler, *Case Western Reserve University*

Don Carlston, *Purdue University*

Sandra Carpenter, *University of Alabama*

Bettina Casad, *University of Missouri—St. Louis*

Clarissa Chavez, *Auburn University*

Nicholas Christenfeld, *University of California, San Diego*

Charlene Christie, *Oneonta College*

Eric Cooley, *Western Oregon University*

Alita Cousins, *Eastern Connecticut State University*

Karen Couture, *Keene State College*

Traci Craig, *University of Idaho*

Ken Cramer, *University of Windsor*

Chris Crandall, *University of Kansas*

Susan Cross, *Iowa State University*

Fiery Cushman, *Harvard University*

George Cvetkovich, *Western Washington University, Emeritus Faculty*

Alex Czopp, *Western Washington University*

Deborah Davis, *University of Nevada, Reno*

Chris De La Ronde, *Austin Community College*

Ken DeMarree, *The State University of New York, Buffalo*

Rachel Dinero, *Cazenovia College*

Pete Ditto, *University of California, Irvine*

Dan Dolderman, *University of Toronto*

John Dovidio, *Yale University*

David Duemler, *Lane Community College*

Richard P. Eibach, *University of Waterloo*

Scott Eidelman, *University of Arkansas, Fayetteville*

Naomi Eisenberger, *University of California, Los Angeles*

Ashley Emmerich, *University of Texas at San Antonio*

Renee Engeln, *Northwestern University*

Joyce Erlingher, *Washington State University*

Patrick Ewell, *Kenyon College*

Jack Feldman, *Georgia Institute of Technology*

Eli Finkel, *Northwestern University*

Marcia Finkelstein, *University of South Florida*

Madeleine Fugere, *Eastern Connecticut State University*

Amber Gaffney, *Humboldt State University*

Azenett Garza-Caballero, *Weber State University*

Daniel Gilbert, *Harvard University*

Omri Gillath, *University of Kansas*

Erinn Green, *University of Cincinnati*

Philippe Gross, *University of Hawaii*

Tay Hack, *Angelo State University*

Jon Haidt, *New York University—Stern*

Judith Harackiewicz, *University of Wisconsin, Madison*

Lisa Harrison, *California State University, Sacramento*

Todd Hartman, *University of Sheffield, United Kingdom*

Lora Haynes, *University of Louisville*

Steve Heine, *University of British Columbia*

Marlone Henderson, *University of Texas at Austin*

Edward Hirt, *Indiana University*

Zach Hohman, *Texas Tech University*

Gina Hoover, *Ohio State University*

Amy Houlihan, *Texas A&M, Corpus Christi*

Jane Huk, *University of Texas, Austin*

Matthew I. Isaak, *University of Louisiana at Lafayette*

Kareem Johnson, *Temple University*

Kimberly Kahn, *Portland State University*

Andy Karpinski, *Temple University*

Johan Karremans, *Radboud University*

Iva Katzarska-Miller, *Transylvania University*

Sulki Kim, *California State University, Fullerton*

Leslie Kirby, *Vanderbilt University*

Marc Kiviniemi, *University at Buffalo*

Stan B. Klein, *University of California, Santa Barbara*

Catalina E. Kopetz, *Wayne State University*

Maya Kuehn, *Facebook*

Ziva Kunda (deceased), *Waterloo University*

Marianne LaFrance, *Yale University*

Alan Lambert, *Washington University*

Jeff Larsen, *Texas Tech University*

Sadie Leder Elder, *High Point University*

Norman Li, *Singapore Management University*

Phoebe Lin, *Framingham State University*

Debra Lieberman, *University of Miami*

Anson (Annie) Long, *Indiana University of Pennsylvania*

Anna Luerssen, *Lehman College*

Debbie S. Ma, *California State University, Northridge*

Jon Maner, *Florida State University*

David Marx, *California State University, San Diego*

Doug McCann, *York University*

Connie Meinholdt, *Ferris State University*

Batja Mesquita, *University of Leuven*

Cynthia Mohr, *Portland State University*

Daniel Molden, *Northwestern University*

Margo Monteith, *Purdue University*

Beth Morling, *University of Delaware*

Mark Muravan, *University at Albany*

Mary Murphy, *Indiana University, Bloomington*

Todd Nelson, *California State University, Stanislaus*

Clark Ohnesorge, *Carleton College*

M. Minda Oriña, *St. Olaf College*

Bernadette Park, *University of Colorado*

Gerrod Parrott, *Georgetown University*

Ashby Plant, *Florida State University*

Jacqueline Pope-Tarrence, *Western Kentucky University*

Deborah Prentice, *Princeton University*

Mary Pritchard, *Boise State University*

Emily Pronin, *Princeton University*

David Rand, *Yale University*

Denise Reiling, *Eastern Michigan University*

Jessica Remedios, *Tufts University*

Jennifer Richeson, *Yale University*

Robert D. Ridge, *Brigham Young University*

Neal Roese, *Northwestern University—Kellogg*

Regina Roof-Ray, *Hartford Community College*

Alex Rothman, *University of Minnesota, Twin Cities Campus*

Abraham Rutchick, *California State University, Northridge*

Darcy Santor, *University of Ottowa*

Constantine Sedikides, *University of Southampton*

Sohaila Shakib, *California State University, Dominguez Hills*

Gregory P. Shelley, *Kutztown University*

J. Nicole Shelton, *Princeton University*

Jeff Sherman, *University of California, Davis*

Colleen Sinclair, *Mississippi State University*

Christine Smith, *University of Wisconsin—Green Bay*

Elizabeth R. Spievak, *Bridgewater State College*

Sue Sprecher, *Illinois State University*

Emily Stark, *Minnesota State University, Mankato*

Jeff Stone, *University of Arizona*

Justin Storbeck, *Queens College*

Michael Strube, *Washington University, St. Louis*

Cornelius Sullivan, *Fresno City College*

Kate Sweeny, *University of California, Riverside*

Lisa Szafran, *Syracuse University*

Lauren A. Taglialatela, *Kennesaw State University*

Charlotte Tate, *San Francisco State University*

Warren Thorngate, *Carleton University, Emeritus Professor*

Zakary Tormala, *Stanford University*

Jeanne Tsai, *Stanford University*

Jim Uleman, *New York University*

Naomi Wagner, *San Jose State University*

Nathan Westbrook, *California State University, Fullerton*

David Wilder, *Rutgers University*

Ben Wilkowski, *University of Wyoming*

Edward Witt, *Michigan State University*

Connie Wolfe, *Muhlenberg College*

Cor van Halen, *Radboud University*

Joseph Vandello, *University of South Florida*

Leigh Ann Vaughn, *Ithaca College*

Luis Vega, *California State University, Bakersfield*

Marcellene Watson-Derbigny, *Sacramento State University*

Aaron Wichman, *Western Kentucky University*

Heike Winterheld, *Washington University in St. Louis*

Matthew Woodward, *Western Kentucky University*

Nancy Yanchus, *VHA National Center for Organization Development*

Jennifer Yanowitz, *Utica College*

Janice Yoder, *Kent State University*

Jason Young, *Hunter College*

Randy Young, *Bridgewater College*

MEDIA AND PRINT RESOURCES FOR INSTRUCTORS AND STUDENTS

INQUIZITIVE
Cornelius Sullivan, *Fresno City College.* **Ashley Emmerich,** *University of Texas at San Antonio.*

InQuizitive helps your students learn through a variety of question types, answer-specific feedback, and game-like elements. It is assignable and gradable, and it gives you insights into the areas where your students need more help so you can adjust your lectures and class time accordingly. The fifth edition revision of InQuizitive for *Social Psychology* includes new questions that focus on the new Infographics, the "Not So Fast" critical thinking features, and areas that students typically find challenging, based on direct student feedback and user performance data.

INTERACTIVE INSTRUCTOR'S GUIDE
Heike Winterheld, *California State East Bay.*

The Interactive Instructor's Guide includes class activity and discussion ideas to engage students in both small and large class settings, new Concept Videos that connect key concepts to everyday scenarios, and "Beyond the Citation" Teaching Videos in which the authors talk to students about what conducting research is all about—including insider stories and unexpected findings.

TEST BANK
Anna Luerssen, *Lehman College.* **Joyce Ehrlinger,** *Washington State University.*

The Test Bank provides over 1,100 multiple choice and short answer questions that are classified by section, Bloom's taxonomy, and difficulty, making it easy for instructors to construct tests and quizzes that are meaningful and diagnostic. The Test Bank is available in Word, RTF, PDF, and *ExamView®* Assessment Suite format.

LECTURE AND "BEYOND THE TEXT" POWERPOINTS
Heike Winterheld, *California State East Bay.* **Tom Gilovich,** *Cornell University.* **Dacher Keltner,** *University of California, Berkeley.* **Serena Chen,** *University of California, Berkeley.*

This edition of the book features three sets of PowerPoints. Lecture PowerPoints follow the order of the text, feature images, and instructor notes, and are designed to be adaptable in order to fit the needs of each individual classroom. "Beyond the Text" PowerPoints were created by the authors to provide additional examples for use in their own courses. In addition, all of the art and tables from the textbook are available in PPT and JPEG formats.

COURSEPACK
Jennifer Chmielewski, *CUNY Graduate Center.* **Kimberly Mannahan,** *College of Coastal Georgia.*

Norton Coursepacks work within your existing Learning Management System to add rich, book-specific digital materials to your course—at no cost to your students. The Coursepack for *Social Psychology* is customizable and includes three additional quizzes per chapter: "Think about It" Quizzes that help students engage with their reading and apply the concepts they have learned, "Not So Fast" Quizzes that emphasize critical thinking and supplement the "Not So Fast" boxes from the book, and Chapter Review Quizzes.

CONTENTS

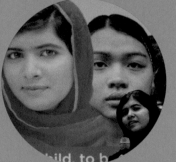

Social Psychology

FIFTH EDITION

Why have social attitudes toward sexual orientation changed over time?

Why are we quicker to blame a person's behavior on their dispositions than on situational influences?

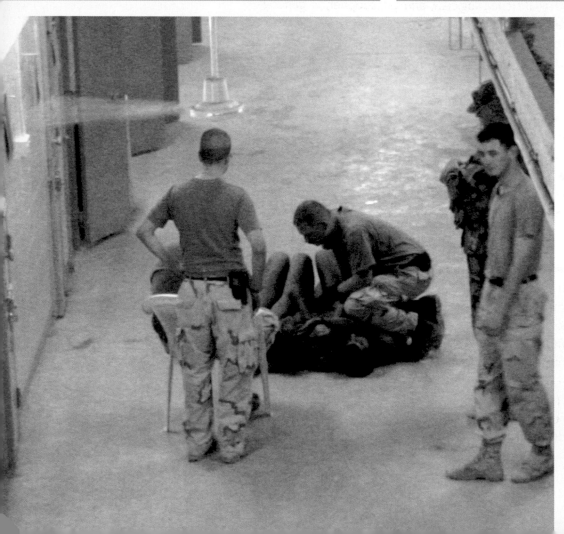

Why would people follow orders to mistreat others?

An Invitation to Social Psychology

ALAN TURING, A BRITISH MATHEMATICIAN, logician, and philosopher, is generally considered to be the founder of computer science. During World War II, Turing was head of Hut 8, the British government agency responsible for breaking the Enigma code of the German Navy, an accomplishment that contributed greatly to the Allied war effort.

In January 1952, when Turing was 39, he was arrested for "gross indecency," a term the British used for homosexual conduct. Turing was convicted of the charge and allowed to choose between imprisonment and chemical castration to reduce his libido and cause impotence. He chose the latter punishment, which involved the administration of female hormones. Turing attempted to come to the United States but was considered a security risk and not allowed to enter. Until 1974, the American Psychiatric Association held that homosexuality was a mental illness. On June 8, 1954, Turing was found dead from cyanide poisoning in his apartment. The death was ruled a suicide.

At the time of Turing's death, homosexuality was illegal in most U.S. states. It wasn't until 2003 that the U.S. Supreme Court reversed a previous decision and declared that homosexual conduct was permitted under the "due process" clause of the Fourteenth Amendment. Thereupon, all laws in the United States criminalizing homosexual acts became invalid.

Until 1994, homosexuality was a sufficient cause for discharge from the American military. President Clinton issued an order prohibiting discrimination against homosexual members of the armed forces, but also barring openly gay people who "demonstrate a propensity or intent to engage in homosexual acts" from serving in the armed forces. This "don't ask, don't tell" ruling was overturned in 2011 by President Obama, and openly gay, lesbian, and bisexual individuals can now serve in the armed forces.

For years, public opinion ran strongly against same-sex marriage until a recent and surprisingly rapid shift toward it. In 1996, a small minority of Americans favored gay marriage. Less than 20 years later, a solid majority supported the Supreme Court's decision to legalize marriage equality nationwide.

The American public went from viewing homosexuality as an illegal act and a mental illness possibly requiring surgical intervention to acceptance of marriage equality in scarcely more than a generation. This fact and many others concerning homosexuality in relation to social norms and individual psychology are the kinds of topics that deeply interest social psychologists.

Why was homosexuality seen as such a threat to people in modern Western societies? In many cultures, homosexuality never was considered abnormal or reprehensible or even particularly worthy of notice; in others it has been punishable by death since time immemorial. Why has homosexuality in women in virtually every society always been more tolerated than homosexuality in men? To what degree is same-sex attraction, or sexual orientation in general, influenced by social norms and institutional settings? How is it possible for an entire society to significantly change its attitudes toward a salient social issue in less than 20 years? What are the effects on sexual minorities of societal rejection versus the effects of acceptance? How and why do stereotypes of gay, lesbian, and bisexual people change over time? How do sexual-minority cultures and subcultures change over time, and what are the factors that influence such changes?

In this chapter, we explain what social psychology is and what social psychologists study. We also present some of the basic concepts of social psychology, especially the surprising degree to which social situations can influence behavior;

CHANGING ATTITUDES TOWARD HOMOSEXUALITY
Same-sex marriage is now legal in the United States, and adoption of children by same-sex couples is legal in many states. Openly gay, bisexual, and lesbian politicians, such as Tammy Baldwin, are being elected to national political office.

the role of construal, or the interpretive processes people use to understand situations; and how two different kinds of thinking—one rapid, intuitive, and nonconscious and the other slower, analytical, and conscious—both contribute to understanding what is happening in social situations. We also describe some relatively recent developments in social psychology that have changed the field—namely, the application of evolutionary concepts to human behavior, the use of the tools of neuroscience, and the discovery of some significant variations in human cultures that frequently lead people in diverse societies to respond to the "same" situation in very different ways. ∎

Characterizing Social Psychology

People have always sought explanations for human behavior. Stories, parables, and folk wisdom have been passed from generation to generation to explain why people do what they do and to prescribe behaviors to avoid or follow. Social psychologists go beyond folk wisdom and try to establish a scientific basis for understanding human behavior. **Social psychology** can be defined as the scientific study of the feelings, thoughts, and behaviors of individuals in social situations.

Why are people inclined to stereotype members of different groups? Why do people risk their lives to help others? Why do some marriages flourish and others fail? How do orderly crowds turn into violent mobs? These sorts of questions lie at the heart of social psychology, and careful research has provided at least partial answers to all of them. Some of the answers probably won't surprise you. For example, we tend to like people who like us, and the people we like generally have attitudes and interests that are similar to ours. When experimental findings reflect what our intuitions and folk wisdom say will happen, social psychologists go further, seeking to discover what lies behind the phenomenon in question. In contrast, other answers have been so counterintuitive that they surprised even the social psychologists who conducted the research. As you will see throughout this book, many of our most strongly held folk theories or intuitions fail to give complete answers to important questions, and others are just plain wrong. Social psychologists test these intuitions by devising studies and crafting experiments that reveal the causes of behavior in social situations.

Explaining Behavior

In April 2004, more than a year after the start of the war in Iraq, CBS broadcast a story that exposed American atrocities against Iraqi prisoners in the Abu Ghraib prison near Baghdad. CBS showed photos of naked prisoners with plastic bags over their heads, stacked up in a pyramid and surrounded by laughing American soldiers. Other photos showed hooded prisoners standing on narrow pedestals with their arms stretched out and electric wires attached to their bodies. CBS also reported that prisoners had been required to simulate sexual acts.

The reaction on the part of many Iraqis and others in the Arab world was to regard the soldiers' behavior as evidence that the United States had malevolent intentions toward Arabs (Hauser, 2004). Most Americans, too, were appalled at the abuse and ashamed of the behavior of the U.S. soldiers. Many people assumed

social psychology The scientific study of the feelings, thoughts, and behaviors of individuals in social situations.

"The test of learning psychology is whether your understanding of situations you encounter has changed, not whether you have learned a new fact."
—NOBEL PRIZE-WINNING PSYCHOLOGIST DANIEL KAHNEMAN

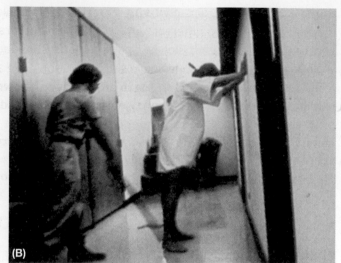

PRISON SITUATIONS AND INTIMIDATION
(A) Military guards at the Abu Ghraib prison in Iraq used torture, humiliation, and intimidation to try to obtain information from the prisoners. This included stripping them and making them lie naked in the prison corridors. (B) Such degradation echoes what happened in the Zimbardo prison study, as shown in this photo of a "guard" seeking to humiliate one of his prisoners at the simulated prison.

that the soldiers who had perpetrated these acts were bad apples—exceptions to a rule of common decency prevailing in the military and the general population.

Social psychologists, however, weren't so quick to make such an assumption. Indeed, 30 years before the atrocities at Abu Ghraib, Philip Zimbardo and his colleagues paid 24 Stanford University undergraduate men, chosen for their good character and mental health, to be participants in a study of a simulated prison (Haney, Banks, & Zimbardo, 1973). The researchers flipped a coin to determine who would be a "guard" and who would be a "prisoner." The guards wore green fatigue uniforms and reflective sunglasses. The prisoners wore tunics with nylon stocking caps and had a chain locked around one ankle. The "prison" was set up in the basement of the psychology department, and the researchers anticipated that the study would last 2 weeks. Right away, the guards turned to verbal abuse and physical humiliation, requiring the prisoners to wear bags over their heads, stripping them naked, and requiring them to engage in simulated sex acts. As a result, the study had to be terminated after 6 days because the behavior of the guards produced extreme stress reactions in several of the prisoners.

Zimbardo today maintains that the balance of power in prisons is so unequal that they tend to be brutal places unless the guards observe strict regulations curbing their worst impulses. Thus, at both Abu Ghraib and Stanford, "It's not that we put bad apples in a good barrel. We put good apples in a bad barrel. The barrel corrupts anything that it touches" (quoted in Schwartz, 2004). Some might contend that the soldiers in Iraq were only following orders and that, left to their own devices, they would not have chosen to behave as they did. That may be the case, but it then leads us to ask, Why did they follow such orders?

Social psychologists try to find answers to just such questions. They study situations in which people exert influence over one another, as well as the ways people respond to various attempts to influence them. Social psychologists are also interested in how people make sense of their world—how they decide what and whom to believe; how they make inferences about the motives, personalities, and abilities of other people; and how they reach conclusions about the causes of events. Social psychologists apply their knowledge to important questions concerning individuals and society at large: how to reduce stereotyping and prejudice in the classroom and workplace; how to make eyewitness testimony more reliable; how physicians can best use diverse sources of information to make a correct diagnosis; what goes wrong in airplane cockpits when there is an accident or near accident; and how businesses, governments, and individuals can make better decisions.

By the time you finish this book, you will have acquired a greater understanding of yourself and others. You will also have knowledge you can apply in your education, your career, and your relationships. Your reasoning and the quality of your life will improve accordingly.

The Power of the Situation

Kurt Lewin, the founder of modern social psychology, was a Jewish Berliner who fled Nazi Germany in the 1930s and became a professor at the University of Iowa and then at MIT. Lewin was knowledgeable about physics, and he applied a powerful idea from physics to an understanding of psychological existence. He believed that the behavior of people, like the behavior of objects, is always a function of the field of forces in which they find themselves (Lewin, 1935). To understand how fast a solid object will travel through a medium, for example, we must know such things as the viscosity of the medium, the force of gravity, and any initial force applied to the object. In the case of people, the forces are psychological as well as physical.

The field of forces in the case of human behavior is the situation, especially the social situation. Of course, a person's attributes are also important determinants of behavior, but these attributes always interact with the situation to produce the resulting behavior. The main situational influences on our behavior are the actions—and sometimes just the mere presence—of other people. Friends, romantic partners, even total strangers can cause us to be kinder or meaner, smarter or dumber, lazier or more hardworking, bolder or more cautious. They can produce drastic changes in our beliefs and behavior not only by what they tell us explicitly, but also by showing through their actions what we should think and do, by subtly implying that our acceptability as a friend or group member depends on adopting their views or behaving as they do. All these effects have been shown in numerous studies demonstrating the power of the situation.

The Milgram Experiment

One of the most striking demonstrations of the power of the situation is a classic experiment by psychologist Stanley Milgram (1963, 1974). Milgram advertised in the local newspaper for men to participate in a study on learning and memory at Yale University in exchange for a modest amount of money. (In subsequent experiments, women also participated; the results were similar.) When the volunteers—a mix of laborers, middle-class individuals, and professionals ranging in age from their 20s to their 50s—arrived at the laboratory, a man in a white lab coat told them they would be participating in a study about the effects of punishment on learning. There would be a "teacher" and a "learner," and the learner would try to memorize word pairs such as *wild/duck*. The volunteer and

KURT LEWIN
Lewin is generally considered the founder of modern social psychology. He emphasized the importance of situational factors external to the individual and showed that social psychologists could make use of experiments.

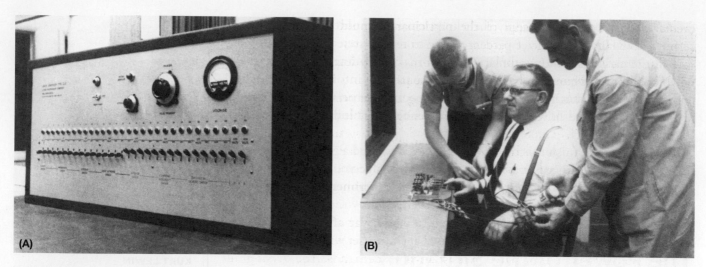

THE MILGRAM EXPERIMENT
To examine the role of social influence, Stanley Milgram set up a study in which participants believed they were testing a learner (actually a confederate) and punishing him with shocks when he gave the wrong answer. (A) Milgram's "shock machine." (B) The participant and experimenter attaching electrodes to the "learner" before testing begins.

another man, a somewhat heavyset, pleasant-looking man in his late 40s, drew slips of paper to determine who would play which role. But things were not as they seemed: the pleasant-looking man was actually an accomplice of the experimenter, and the drawing was rigged so that he was always the learner.

The participant "teacher" was then instructed to administer shocks—from 15 to 450 volts—to the "learner" each time the learner made an error. Labels under the shock switches ranged from "slight shock" through "danger: severe shock" to "XXX." The experimenter explained that the teacher was to administer shocks in ascending 15-volt magnitudes: 15 volts the first time the learner made an error, 30 volts the next time, and so on. The teacher was given a 45-volt shock so he would have an idea of how painful the shocks would be. What he didn't know was that the learner, who was in another room, was not actually being shocked.

Most participants became concerned as the shock levels increased and turned to the experimenter to ask what should be done, but the experimenter insisted they go on. The first time a teacher expressed reservations, he was told, "Please continue." If the teacher balked, the experimenter said, "The experiment requires that you continue." If the teacher continued to hesitate, the experimenter said, "It's absolutely essential that you continue." If necessary, the experimenter escalated to, "You have no other choice. You must go on." If the participant asked whether the learner could suffer permanent physical injury, the experimenter said, "Although the shocks may be painful, there is no permanent tissue damage, so please go on."

"Evil is obvious only in retrospect."
—GLORIA STEINEM

In the end, despite the learner's groans, pleas, screams, and eventual silence as the intensity of the shocks increased, 80 percent of the participants continued past the 150-volt level—at which point the learner mentioned that he had a heart condition and screamed, "Let me out of here!" Fully 62.5 percent of the participants went all the way to the 450-volt level, delivering everything the shock generator could produce. The average amount of shock given was 360 volts, *after* the learner let out an agonized scream and became hysterical.

Milgram and other experts did not expect nearly as many participants to continue to administer shocks as long as they did. A panel of 39 psychiatrists predicted that only 20 percent of the participants would continue past the 150-volt level and that only 1 percent would continue past the 330-volt level. Milgram's study and its implications are described in more detail in Chapter 9. For now, the important question is, What made the participants in Milgram's study engage in behavior that they believed was causing another person immense physical pain and, despite the experimenter's insistence, possible permanent harm as well? Milgram's participants were not heartless fiends. Instead, the situation was extraordinarily effective in getting them to do something that would normally fill them with horror. The experiment was presented as a scientific investigation—an unfamiliar situation for most participants. The experimenter explicitly took responsibility for what happened. (Adolf Hitler frequently made similar pledges during the years he marched his nation into a world war and the Holocaust.) Moreover, participants could not have guessed at the outset what the experiment involved, so they were not prepared to resist anyone's demands. And as Milgram stressed, the step-by-step nature of the procedure was undoubtedly crucial. If the participant didn't quit at 225 volts, then why quit at 255? If not at 420, then why at 435?

Seminarians as Samaritans

A classic experiment by John Darley and Daniel Batson (1973) demonstrates the power of the situation even more simply. These investigators asked students at the Princeton Theological Seminary about the basis of their religious orientation to determine whether particular students were primarily concerned with religion as a means toward personal salvation or were more concerned with religion for its other moral and spiritual values. After determining the basis of their religious orientation, the psychologists asked each young seminarian to go to another building to deliver a short sermon. The seminarians were told what route to follow to get there most easily. Some were told that they had plenty of time to get to the building where they were to deliver the sermon, and some were told that they were already late and should hurry. On the way to deliver their sermon—on the topic of the Good Samaritan, by the way—each of the seminarians passed a man who was sitting in a doorway with his head down, coughing and groaning and in apparent need of help.

It turned out that the nature of religious orientation was of no use in predicting whether the seminarians would offer assistance. But as you can see in **Figure 1.1**, whether seminarians were in a hurry or not was a very powerful predictor. The seminarians were pretty good Samaritans as a group—but only when they weren't in a rush.

The Fundamental Attribution Error

People are thus governed by situational factors—such as whether they are being pressured by someone or whether they are late—more than they tend to assume. At the same time, internal factors—the kind of person someone is—have much less influence than most people assume they do. You may be surprised by many of the findings reported in this book because most people

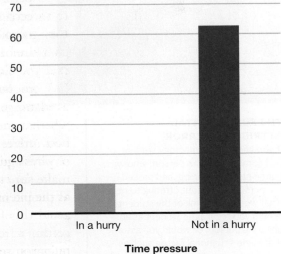

Percentage of seminarians offering help

Time pressure

FIGURE 1.1
THE POWER OF THE SITUATION AND HELPING
Princeton seminarians usually helped a "victim" if they were not in a hurry, but rarely helped if they were in a rush.
Source: Darley & Batson, 1973.

dispositions Internal factors, such as beliefs, values, personality traits, and abilities, that guide a person's behavior.

underestimate the power of the external forces that operate on an individual and tend to assume, often mistakenly, that the causes of behavior can be found mostly within the person.

Psychologists call internal factors **dispositions**—that is, beliefs, values, personality traits, and abilities that guide behavior. People tend to think of dispositions as the underlying causes of behavior, but that's not necessarily true. Seeing an acquaintance give a dollar to a beggar may prompt us to assume that the person is generous, but subsequent observations of the person in different situations might show that we had overgeneralized from a single act. Noticing a stranger in the street behaving angrily, we might assume that the person is aggressive or ill tempered. Such judgments are valid far less often than we think.

fundamental attribution error The failure to recognize the importance of situational influences on behavior, along with the corresponding tendency to overemphasize the importance of dispositions on behavior.

The failure to recognize the importance of situational influences on behavior, together with the tendency to overemphasize the importance of dispositions, was labeled the **fundamental attribution error** by Lee Ross (1977). Many findings in social psychology indicate that people should look for situational factors that might be affecting someone's behavior before assuming that the person has dispositions that match the behavior. As you read this book, you will become more attuned to situational factors and less inclined to assume that behavior can be fully explained by characteristics inherent in the individual. The ultimate lesson of social psychology is thus a compassionate one. Social psychology encourages us to look at another person's situation—to try to understand the complex field of forces acting on the individual—in order to fully understand the person's behavior.

Nudge, Don't Push

Kurt Lewin (1952) introduced the concept of "channel factors" to help explain why certain circumstances that appear unimportant on the surface can have great consequences for behavior, either facilitating it or blocking it. The term is also meant to reflect that such circumstances can sometimes guide behavior in a particular direction by making it easier to follow one path rather than another. The concept has been borrowed by behavioral economics, a new field at the intersection of social psychology and economics. Behavioral economists refer to the concept as "nudges"—small, innocuous-seeming prompts that can have big effects on behavior.

THE FUNDAMENTAL ATTRIBUTION ERROR
If you knew that a theology student had come across this person, who was coughing and groaning, and passed the person by without offering to help, what would you think of the student? Would you regard the student as an uncaring person, or would you assume that some situational factor, such as being late for an appointment, caused the student to rush past without stopping to help? If you're like most people, you would probably jump to an unfavorable conclusion about the student's personality.

Consider a study by Howard Leventhal and his colleagues on how to motivate people to take advantage of preventive care (Leventhal, Singer, & Jones, 1965). They attempted to persuade Yale students to get tetanus inoculations. To convince them that the inoculation was in their best interest, the researchers had them read scary materials about the number of ways a person could get tetanus (in addition to the proverbial rusty nail). To make sure they had the students' full attention, the team showed them photos of people in the last stages of lockjaw. But not to worry—the students could avoid this fate simply by going to the student health center at any time and getting a free inoculation. Interviews showed that most participants formed the intention to get an inoculation, but only 3 percent did so. Other participants were given a map of the Yale campus with a circle around the health center and were asked to review their weekly schedule and decide on a convenient time to visit the center and the route they would take to get there. Bear in mind that these were seniors who knew perfectly well where the health center was.

If you do not wish to take part in the retirement plan funded in part by the company, please indicate that by checking the box below. ☐	If you wish to take part in the retirement plan funded in part by the company, please indicate that by checking the box below. ☐

FIGURE 1.2
HOW TO HAVE A HAPPY RETIREMENT
If the box on your new employee form asks the question on the left, you are much more likely to be enrolled in the company's retirement plan than if the box asks the question on the right.

"If you are like most people, then like most people, you don't know you're like most people."
—SOCIAL PSYCHOLOGIST DAN GILBERT

Nevertheless, the nudge increased the percentage of students getting an inoculation ninefold, to 28 percent.

The tetanus shot nudge was employed in the Obama campaign's "Get Out the Vote" phone drive on election eve in 2008. Voters were asked, "Where will you be just before you vote?" And after the voter's answer, "What route do you plan to use to get there?" This procedure is now considered "best practice," and both Republicans and Democrats use it.

As we've noted, the nudge concept is central to behavioral economics. For example, economists have encouraged businesses to get as many of their employees as possible to participate in retirement plans in which the employer puts money away for the employee's retirement. Rather than have their employees "opt in" to their retirement programs by checking a box or signing a statement saying they wish to be enrolled in the retirement plan, employers create an easy channel for participation by having it be automatic. Employees must check a box or sign a statement saying they *don't* want the retirement plan; otherwise they are automatically enrolled (**Figure 1.2**). This trivial-seeming nudge creates far more participation (and far happier retirements) than when the nudge conspires against participation (Choi, Laibson, & Madrian, 2009; Madrian & Shea, 2001). And did you know that 99 percent of Austrians allow for harvesting their organs for transplant, whereas only 12 percent of Germans allow harvesting? Before you commit the fundamental attribution error, we hasten to tell you that Germans have to check a box if they want to have their organs harvested; Austrians have to check a box if they don't want their organs harvested.

← LOOKING BACK

Situations are often more powerful in their influence on behavior than we realize. Whether or not people are kind to others and whether or not they take action in their own best interest can depend on subtle aspects of the situation. We often overlook such situational factors when we try to understand our own behavior or that of others, and we often mistakenly attribute behavior to presumed dispositions (the fundamental attribution error).

The Role of Construal

Look at **Figure 1.3**. Do you see a white triangle? Most people do, but in fact there is no white triangle. We construct a triangle in our mind out of the *gaps* in the picture. The gaps are located just where they would be if a triangle were laid over

FIGURE 1.3
GESTALT PRINCIPLES AND PERCEPTION
When viewing this figure, known as the Kanizsa triangle, people fill in the empty spaces in their mind and perceive a white triangle.

GESTALT PRINCIPLES IN ART
In his *Slave Market with Disappearing Bust of Voltaire*, Salvador Dali confronts the viewer with the bust of the French philosopher Voltaire (at center of painting). But on closer inspection, Voltaire's head consists of the gap in the wall behind the two Dutch women in the marketplace (what artists refer to as "negative space") and his face consists of the women themselves.

"We don't see things as they are; we see them as we are."
—ANAIS NIN

the outlined triangle and a portion of each of the three circles. That makes a good, clear image, but it's entirely a creation of our perceptual apparatus and our background assumptions about the visual world. Both the perceptual process and the assumptions are automatic and nonconscious—that is to say, we're not consciously aware of them. Now look at *Slave Market with Disappearing Bust of Voltaire*, the above painting by surrealist artist Salvador Dali. Dali was a master at using the mind's tendency to construct meaningful figures from the gaps in an image. He created a number of well-known double images—pictures that could be perceived in two different ways, as in this painting.

Interpreting Reality

Our perceptions normally bear a resemblance to what the world is really like, but perception requires substantial interpretation on our part and is subject to significant bias under certain conditions. What we see is not necessarily what is actually there but what is plausible—what makes a good, predictable "figure" in light of the stored existing representations we have of the world and in light of the context in which we encounter something. German psychologists in the early part of the twentieth century convincingly argued for this view in the case of visual perception. The theoretical orientation of those psychologists centered on the concept of *gestalt*, German for "form" or "figure." The basic idea of **Gestalt psychology** is that objects are perceived not by means of some passive and unbiased perception of objective reality, but by active, usually nonconscious

Gestalt psychology Based on the German word *gestalt*, meaning "form" or "figure," an approach that stresses the fact that people perceive objects not by means of some automatic registering device but by active, usually nonconscious interpretation of what the object represents as a whole.

interpretation of what the object represents. The belief that we see the world directly, without any complicated perceptual or cognitive machinery "doctoring" the data, is referred to by philosophers and social psychologists as "naive realism" (Pronin, Gilovich, & Ross, 2004; Ross & Ward, 1996).

What's true for visual perception is even truer for judgments about the social world. Our judgments and beliefs are actively constructed from perceptions and thoughts. They are not simple readouts of reality. In his study of obedience (discussed earlier), Milgram manipulated his participants' understanding of the situation they found themselves in by lulling them with soothing interpretations of events that were designed to throw them off the scent of anything that could be regarded as sinister. A "study participant" who had "chosen" to be in the "experiment" was "learning" a list of words with "feedback" that was given by the real participant in the form of electric shock. A *participant* is someone who is acting freely; *learning* is a normal activity that often depends on *feedback*, generally an innocuous form of information. All this was taking place in the context of an *experiment*, a benign activity carried out by trustworthy scientists. Participants in the Milgram experiment weren't simply registering what the situation was; they were interpreting it in ways that the experimenter was encouraging.

Our **construal** of situations and behavior refers to our interpretation of them and to the inferences, often nonconscious, that we make about them. Whether we regard people as free agents or victims, as freedom fighters or terrorists, as migrant workers or illegal aliens, will affect our perceptions of their actions. And our perceptions drive our behavior toward them.

Schemas

How do we know how to behave in different kinds of situations? For example, suppose you're riding on an uncrowded train and someone asks you to give up your seat so she can sit. What prompts you to respond in a particular way? Do you refuse, ask for an explanation, pretend not to hear, or promptly surrender the seat? For that matter, how do you know how to behave in even the most ordinary situations, such as attending a college seminar?

First umpire: "I call 'em as I see 'em."
Second umpire: "I call 'em as they are."
Third umpire: "They ain't nothin' till I call 'em."

construal One's interpretation of or inference about the stimuli or situations that one confronts.

"Without a profound simplification the world around us would be an infinite, undefined tangle that would defy our ability to orient ourselves and decide upon our actions.... We are compelled to reduce the knowable to a schema."
—NOVELIST PRIMO LEVI

SCHEMAS
A fast food restaurant and a fancy restaurant.

schema A knowledge structure consisting of any organized body of stored information that is used to help in understanding events.

stereotype A belief that certain attributes are characteristic of members of a particular group.

Although it usually seems as though we understand social situations immediately and directly, we actually depend on elaborate stores of systematized knowledge to understand even the simplest and most "obvious" situation. These knowledge stores are called **schemas**, generalized knowledge about the physical and social world, such as what kind of behavior to expect when dealing with a minister, a sales clerk, a professor, or a panhandler and how to behave in a seminar, at a funeral, at a McDonald's or a four-star restaurant, or when riding on a crowded or empty subway. There is even a schema—alleged to be universal—for falling in love. Schemas capture the regularities of life and lead us to have certain expectations we can rely on so we don't have to invent the world anew all the time.

Stereotypes

Much work in social psychology has been dedicated to the study of **stereotypes**—schemas that we have for people of various kinds. Research on stereotyping examines the content of these person schemas and how they are applied and sometimes misapplied in order to facilitate—or derail—the course of interaction. We tend to judge individuals based on particular person schemas we have—stereotypes about a person's nationality, gender, religion, occupation, neighborhood, or sorority. Such summaries may be necessary to function efficiently and effectively, but they're often unfounded. They can be applied in the wrong way and to the wrong people, and they can be given too much weight in relation to more specific information we have about a particular person (or would have if we didn't assume that the stereotype is all we need to know). The frequently pernicious role of stereotypes is the subject of an entire chapter of this book (Chapter 11).

STEREOTYPES AND CONSTRUAL
Stereotypes are schemas about people of a certain kind. We construe people in light of the stereotypes they call up. Would you be surprised to know that the fellow in this picture is a wealthy lawyer who plays polo and frequents trendy bars in Manhattan? None of these things is true, and you relied on your stereotypes to prevent you from entertaining those possibilities.

← **LOOKING BACK**

Although our understanding of situations often seems to be the result of a direct, unmediated registration of meaning, our comprehension of even the simplest physical stimulus is the result of construal processes that make use of well-developed knowledge structures. Such structures are called schemas when they summarize commonly encountered situations, and they are called stereotypes when they describe different types of people.

Automatic vs. Controlled Processing

How would you react if you saw a stranger at an airport carrying a backpack, looking agitated, and sweating profusely? In the post-9/11 world, you might fear that such a person might be carrying a bomb and that you could become a victim of a terrorist attack. The mind processes information in two ways when you encounter a social situation. One is automatic and nonconscious, often based on emotional factors, and the other is conscious and systematic and more likely to be controlled by deliberative thought. Often, emotional reactions occur before conscious thought takes over. Thus, your fearful reaction to the person with the backpack might automatically kick in without any special thought on your part. But when you start thinking systematically, you realize that he might have just come in from the summer heat, that he might be agitated because he's late for his flight, and that there's no reason to suspect he might be carrying a bomb or threatening your safety in any way.

Automatic and controlled processing can result in quite different attitudes in the same person toward members of outgroups (Devine, 1989a, 1989b; Devine, Monteith, Zuwerink, & Elliot, 1991; Devine, Forscher, Austin, & Cox, 2012; Devine, Plant, Amodio, Harmon-Jones, & Vance, 2002). People with low expressed prejudice toward an outgroup may nevertheless reveal feelings toward people in that outgroup that are almost as prejudiced as those of people who confess to explicit disliking of the group. For example, experimenters asked some white participants to read words stereotypically associated with African-Americans (for example, jazz, busing) and then read a brief description of someone whose race was not specified. Those participants were more likely to report that the individual was hostile than were participants who hadn't read such words. And this was true whether or not they were willing to express anti-black attitudes in a questionnaire—in other words, whether or not they were openly prejudiced. The judgments of the "unprejudiced" people were found to be just as prejudiced as their explicitly prejudiced counterparts when it came to nonconscious processing of information.

In general, automatic processes give rise to *implicit* attitudes and beliefs that can't be readily controlled by the conscious mind; and controlled, conscious processing results in *explicit* attitudes and beliefs that we're aware of—though these may become implicit or nonconscious over time. It's important to recognize, too, that participants in this experiment weren't necessarily dissembling when they reported being unprejudiced. They likely were genuinely unaware of the extent of the bias that was revealed by the implicit measures of attitude.

AUTOMATIC PROCESSING
People often react quickly to frightening situations so that they can take immediate action to save themselves from danger. The girl is handling the snake under the supervision of her teacher, but an automatic reaction is still visible. If the girl were to come across a snake in the grass, she would probably have a stronger automatic fear reaction.

"If you press me to say why I loved him, I can say no more than because he was he, and I was I."

—FRENCH RENAISSANCE ESSAYIST MICHEL DE MONTAIGNE

A variety of social categories, not just race, have considerable impact on judgments and behavior. Other easily discernible personal features, such as gender and age, also tend to trigger stereotypes that a person uses in forming judgments about other people, even when the person is unaware that these social categories have influenced the judgment in question (Blair, Judd, & Fallman, 2004; Brewer, 1988; Macrae, Stangor, & Milne, 1994).

Types of Nonconscious Processing

Social psychologists have shown that much of our cognitive activity is hidden from us. In solving problems, sometimes we're well aware of the relevant factors we're dealing with and the procedures we're using to work with them. For example, when we solve a math problem ("Take half the base, multiply it by the height and . . ."), we generally know exactly what formula we're using. But these sorts of cognitive processes—where we are conscious of most of what is going on in our head—are rarer than you might think. Often we can't correctly explain the reasons for our judgments about other people, our understanding of the causes of physical and social events, or what led us to choose one job applicant over another (or one romantic partner over another, for that matter).

In one experiment making this point about awareness, researchers asked customers in a mall to evaluate the quality of four pairs of nylon stockings laid out in a row on a table (Nisbett & Wilson, 1977). Customers were four times as likely to give the highest rating to the last pair of stockings they examined as to give it to the first pair of stockings. Yet in response to whether the position of the stockings had influenced their judgments about quality, they were astonished that the questioner could think they might have been influenced by such a trivial, irrelevant factor!

Often we can't even identify some of the crucial factors that affect our beliefs and behavior. John Bargh and Paula Pietromonaco presented words on a computer screen for one-tenth of a second (Bargh & Pietromonaco, 1982). Some participants were exposed to words with a hostile meaning and some to neutral words. The participants then read about a man named Donald, whose behavior was ambiguous as to whether it could be construed as hostile. ("A salesman knocked at the door, but Donald refused to let him enter.") Participants exposed to the hostility-related words rated Donald as being more hostile than did participants exposed to the neutral words. Immediately after reading the paragraph, participants were unable to distinguish words they had seen from those they hadn't seen and didn't even know that words had been flashed at all.

By now there have been hundreds of demonstrations of influences on important judgments and behavior which people are unaware of.

- When people are surrounded by greenery, they are less aggressive than when in an environment with lots of red in it (Kuo & Sullivan, 2001).
- When people read a persuasive communication in a room with a fishy smell, they are less likely to be persuaded by it than if there is no distinctive smell present or if there is an unpleasant smell that isn't fishy (Lee & Schwarz, 2012). (This works, though, only in cultures where dubious propositions are described as "fishy.")
- And here's something you can try for yourself. Have a conversation with someone in which you deliberately change your body position from time to time. Fold your arms for a couple of minutes. Shift most of your weight to one side. Put one hand in a pocket. Watch what your conversation partner does after each change and try not to giggle when your partner mimics your body language. "Ideomotor mimicry" is something we engage in quite nonconsciously. When people don't do it, the encounter can become awkward and unsatisfying.

You will read countless examples in this book of the effects of various stimuli and situations that exert their effects without our conscious awareness. Indeed, if the effects in a given study were consciously produced, you wouldn't have to read about it in this book; you would already know about it.

TYPES OF NONCONSCIOUS PROCESSING
We subconsciously imitate other people's body language. This is called "ideomotor mimicry."

Functions of Nonconscious Processing

Why does so much mental processing take place outside of our awareness? Partly, it's a matter of efficiency. Conscious processes are generally slow and can run only serially—one step at a time. Automatic processes are typically much faster and can operate in parallel. When we recognize a face as belonging to a fourth-grade classmate, we have done so by processing numerous features (forehead, eyes, chin, coloring, and so on) holistically and in a fraction of a second. Recognizing each feature one step at a time would leave us hopelessly mired in computation. And it's quite handy to be able to drive a car on autopilot while enjoying the scenery or carrying on a conversation. (You may sometimes have been startled to realize that you've reached your destination without being completely aware of how you got there.)

We're not conscious of many of the stimuli that influence us, and we're not fully aware of the cognitive processes that underlie our judgments and behaviors. A very important implication of nonconscious processing is that research on human behavior should not normally depend on people's verbal reports about why they believe something or why they engaged in a particular behavior. Instead, social psychologists have to craft experiments to isolate the true causes of people's behavior.

← LOOKING BACK

Much of our behavior and many kinds of construal processes occur without our awareness, sometimes without awareness of even the stimuli to which we are responding. We tend to overestimate how accessible our mental processes are to our consciousness.

Evolution and Human Behavior: How We Are the Same

Why do human beings generally live in family groups, assign roles to people on the basis of age and gender, enjoy sharing food, adorn their bodies, classify flora and fauna, and have rites of passage and myths? Evolution may explain such behaviors (Conway & Schaller, 2002).

Evolutionary theory has been around for about 150 years, ever since Charles Darwin published *On the Origin of Species*. Darwin discovered many modifications in animal and plant characteristics that had occurred over time in the Galápagos Islands. Evolutionary theory has proved invaluable in understanding why organisms of all kinds have the properties they do and how they come to have them. The key idea is that a process of **natural selection** operates on animals and plants, so that adaptive traits—those that enhance the probability of survival and reproduction—are passed on to subsequent generations. Organisms that die before they reproduce may be unlucky or may possess characteristics that are less than optimal in their particular environment. And when these organisms don't reproduce, they don't pass on such nonadaptive characteristics (through their genes) to a new generation. Those that do survive and reproduce give their genes a chance to live on in their offspring, along with the possibility that their characteristics will be represented in at least one more generation. Disadvantageous characteristics are selected against; characteristics better adapted to the environment are selected for.

Darwin himself assumed that natural selection operates for behavioral inclinations, just as it does for physical characteristics such as size, coloring, or susceptibility to parasites. In addition, that many of our traits and behaviors are found in all human groups is consistent with the idea that much of what we share is at least partly the result of natural selection and is encoded in our genes. Recent developments in evolutionary theory and comparative biology, together with anthropological findings and studies by psychologists, have shown that the theory of evolution can be quite helpful in explaining why people behave the way they do.

natural selection An evolutionary process that molds animals and plants so that traits that enhance the probability of survival and reproduction are passed on to subsequent generations.

The Evolution of Man. Cartoon by Wilbur Dawbarn, www.cartoonstock.com.

Human Universals

One fact that's consistent with evolutionary theory is that many human behaviors and institutions are universal, or very nearly so (Schaller, Simpson, & Kenrick, 2006). In the process of human evolution, we've acquired basic behavioral tendencies, much as we've acquired physical features like bipedalism (walking upright on two legs), that help us adapt to the physical and social environment.

Table 1.1 contains a list of reputed universals. Two things are worth noting about the practices listed in the table, aside from their alleged universality. One is that

TABLE 1.1 UNIVERSAL BEHAVIORS, REACTIONS, AND INSTITUTIONS

Sex, Gender, and the Family

Copulation normally conducted privately	Sexual jealousy	Sexual regulation
Live in family (or household)	Marriage	Husband usually older than wife
Sexual modesty	Division of labor by gender	Males more physically aggressive
Females do more child care	Mother-son incest unthinkable	Incest prevention and avoidance
Preference for own kin	Sex differences in spatial cognition	

Social Differentiation

Age statuses	Classification of kin	Leaders
Ingroup distinguished from outgroup	Division of labor by age	

Social Customs

Baby talk	Pretend play	Group living
Dance	Rites of passage	Law (rights and obligations)
Dominance/submission	Taboo foods	Feasting
Practice to improve skills	Body adornment	Property
Hygienic care	Death rites	Rituals
Magic to sustain and improve life	Etiquette	Taboo utterances
Magic to win love	Gossip	Toys
Decorative art	Food sharing	

Emotion

Childhood fear of strangers	Wariness around snakes	Rhythm
Facial expressions of fear, anger, disgust, happiness, sadness, and surprise	Envy	Melody

Cognition

Aesthetics	Anthropomorphism of animals	Myths
Belief in supernatural, religion	Medicine	Taxonomy
Classification of flora and fauna	Language	Narrative

Source: Compiled by Donald Brown, 1991; appearing in Pinker, 2002.

humans share some of these characteristics with other animals, especially the higher primates. These include facial expressions, dominance and submission, food sharing, group living, greater aggressiveness on the part of males, preference for own kin, and wariness around snakes. The other, even more striking aspect of Table 1.1 is that the number of universals we share with other animals is quite small.

The bulk of Table 1.1 represents a number of behaviors and institutions that appear to be effective adaptations for highly intelligent, group-living, upright-walking, language-using animals that are capable of living in almost any kind of ecology. These universals are compatible with an evolutionary interpretation (we are a particular kind of creature, qualitatively different from any other, with many adaptations so effective that they have become wired into our biology). But some theorists believe that some of these commonalities can be accounted for as simply the result of our species' superior intelligence. For example, every human group figures out for itself that incest is a bad idea and that classification of flora is useful.

Group Living, Language, and Theory of Mind

Group living contributed to survival in ages past. Groups provided protection from predators and greater success in hunting game and finding foraging areas. The ability to produce and understand language has enabled people to live in groups and convey not only emotions and intentions to others, but also beliefs, attitudes, and complex thoughts.

There is strong evidence that infants are born with their brain "prewired" to acquire language, perhaps because of its importance to humans living together in groups (Pinker, 1994). Normal children learn language at developmental stages that are almost identical from one culture to another. At birth, all infants can produce the full range of possible sounds (phonemes) that exist in the totality of languages spoken anywhere on Earth, and they babble all these sounds in the crib. Language acquisition consists of dropping all the "wrong" phonemes—the ones that are not used by the child's particular language. Thus, children can learn to speak any language, depending on where they grow up; they can learn to speak their native language perfectly well even if they grow up with deaf parents who never speak at all; and twins can sometimes develop their own unique language in the crib, a language that follows rules of grammar in the same way

UNIVERSAL FACIAL EXPRESSIONS

Chimpanzees and humans express dominance and submission, anger and fear, through similar facial expressions.

formally recognized languages do (Pinker, 1994, 2002). These findings indicate that there are general, inherited propensities to develop grammatical language.

Just as evolution has prepared humans to live together in groups and to communicate to promote survival and reproduction, it also may have provided humans with a "theory of mind"—the ability to recognize that other people have beliefs and desires. Children recognize before the age of 2 that the way to understand other people's behavior is to understand their beliefs and desires (Asch, 1952; Kuhlmeier, Wynn, & Bloom, 2003; Leslie, 2000; Malle, Moses, & Baldwin, 2001). By the age of 3 or 4, theory of mind is sophisticated enough that children can recognize when other people's beliefs are false (Wellman, 1990).

Some of the most powerful evidence for a biologically based theory of mind comes from studying people who, through a genetic defect or physical or chemical trauma before or after birth, seem not to have a theory of mind or to have only a weak version of one. Such a claim has been made about people with *autism*, a disorder characterized by the inability to adequately communicate with others and interact with them. Autistic individuals have more difficulties comprehending others' desires or beliefs, including the fact that others' beliefs might be false (Perner, Frith, Leslie, & Leekam, 1989). Autistic children can have normal or even superior intellectual functioning, but less comprehension of people's beliefs and desires, than children with Down syndrome, whose general intellectual functioning is far below normal. It seems plausible that evolution has provided us with a kind of understanding that is too universally essential to leave to chance or laborious trial-and-error learning. Given the importance of accurately understanding other people's beliefs and intentions, it would not be surprising that a theory of mind comes prewired.

Evolution and Gender Roles

Why is polygyny (one man with several wives) more common than polyandry (one woman with several husbands)? Why do women tend to care more than men about a potential partner's financial prospects? The evolutionary approach provides a possible answer to such questions in its theory of **parental investment**. In almost all mammalian species, the two sexes have different costs and benefits associated with the nurturing of offspring, largely because the number of offspring a female can have over the course of her lifetime is limited. The value of each child to her is therefore relatively high—her investment in each is great. And it's in the interest of her genes to see to it that each infant grows to maturity; therefore her mate's ability to support her is very important. For males, however, a nearly unlimited number of offspring is theoretically possible because so little energy is involved in creating them. A male can walk away from copulation and never see his mate or offspring again. Even if the male stays with the female and their offspring, however, his investment in the offspring is less than that of the female. The economic resources of a female with whom he has reproduced are therefore of less consequence to him. Evolution thus provides one way of looking at many seemingly universal tendencies related to gender roles and child rearing.

GENDER ROLES OFTEN DIFFER Men and women have different roles in most societies. Women are more likely to be involved in nurturance activities. Each child produces a relatively greater benefit for women, who are limited in the number of children they can have over a lifetime. Men are not limited for number of offspring, and their inclusive fitness is more dependent on the resources they can generate.

parental investment The evolutionary principle that costs and benefits are associated with reproduction and the nurturing of offspring. Because these costs and benefits are different for males and females, one gender will normally value and invest more in each child than will the other.

Avoiding the Naturalistic Fallacy

Evolutionary theory as applied to human behavior is controversial. The claim that there are biologically based differences between women and men in behaviors related to mate choice is particularly objectionable to some people. Such notions are controversial in part because they follow a long history of mistaken claims about biological differences that have been used to legitimize and perpetuate male privilege (Bem, 1993).

Evolutionary claims about human behavior can also lead people to assume, mistakenly, that biology is destiny—that what we are biologically predisposed to do is what we inevitably will do and perhaps even should do. This claim—that the way things are is the way they should be—is known as the **naturalistic fallacy**, and it has no logical foundation. We are predisposed to do many things that we can overcome. Virtually all human societies are plagued by violence in everyday life, for example, but the incidence of it over the past few centuries has declined astronomically. The chances of being murdered in various parts of England, for example, declined from the thirteenth century to the twentieth by factors ranging from 10 to 100 (Pinker, 2011); and the most horrendous forms of torture, such as breaking all the bones in a person's body on the rack, are no longer practiced in Europe. Civilization can be regarded as the never-ceasing attempt to modify much of what comes naturally, reducing the extent to which human life, as seventeenth-century philosopher Thomas Hobbes put it, is "poor, nasty, brutish, and short."

Just because a theory can be misused is no reason to reject the theory in all its aspects. While we should not reject evolutionary ideas out of hand, caution about evolutionary claims is essential.

Social Neuroscience

Evolutionary approaches to the study of social behavior alert us to the fact that everything humans do or think involves biological processes in the brain and body that have been shaped by natural selection. In recent years, social psychologists have begun to examine the biological grounding for all behavior: the brain. There is a new field focusing on the neural underpinnings of social behavior called *social neuroscience.*

The brain is considered by many to be the most complex living system in the universe, with 100 billion neurons organized into at least 50 distinct regions. One of the chief tools social psychologists use to understand the brain's role in social behavior is a technology known as functional magnetic resonance imaging (fMRI). When a person is talking with another person or perhaps making a moral judgment or experiencing fear or outrage, blood flows to the areas of the brain that are activated by the social stimulus. Scientists can take a picture of the brain that detects this blood flow, thus showing which brain regions are involved in the social behavior of interest.

As the new field of social neuroscience has matured, it has revealed just how social the human brain is (Lieberman, 2013). Older regions of the brain that we share with other mammals appear to be involved in nonconscious, automatic reactions to our social environment. For example, the amygdala, an

naturalistic fallacy The claim that the way things are is the way they should be.

"The human brain is the most complex and orderly arrangement of matter in the universe."
—ISAAC ASIMOV

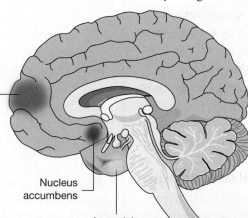

Prefrontal cortex

Nucleus accumbens

Amygdala

FIGURE 1.4
A SIDEWAYS VIEW OF THE BRAIN
Toward the middle of the brain are regions involved in emotion, such as the amygdala and the nucleus accumbens. Those regions project to areas of the prefrontal cortex (PFC), which is involved in decision making and more controlled cognition.

almond-shaped region of the brain colored yellow in **Figure 1.4**, is involved in gut feelings, especially those of a fearful nature, about salient stimuli we encounter in the environment—strangers, threatening images, people from adversarial groups (Cunningham & Brosch, 2012; Ochsner & Lieberman, 2001). Near the amygdala is another old, mammalian region of the brain known as the nucleus accumbens, colored red in Figure 1.4. This area is rich with dopamine receptors (dopamine is the chemical associated with reward) and projects to the prefrontal cortex, where we process complex thoughts and emotions. The nucleus accumbens is thought of as the brain's "reward circuit"; it signals to the individual in quick, automatic fashion what is rewarding in the environment, be it the smile of a stranger, the opportunity to have delicious ice cream, or support from a friend (Haber & Knutson, 2010).

What is unique about the human brain when compared with the brains of other mammals is the size of our neocortex, which consists of the layers of neurons on top of older regions of the brain, such as the amygdala. Significant areas of the neocortex are involved in reasoning, abstract thought, and memory. At the same time, social neuroscientists have demonstrated that regions of the neocortex are involved in social behavior. For example, different regions of the prefrontal cortex are involved in self-awareness (Wagner, Haxby, & Heatherton, 2012) and moral judgment (Greene, 2014). There is also an empathy network of the neocortex that enables us to feel the feelings of others (Singer & Klimecki, 2014) and a mentalizing network that enables us to understand other people's mental states, intentions, desires, and beliefs (Lieberman, 2007, 2013). Yet another region of the neocortex is activated both when we're rejected socially and when we're esteemed by others (Muscatell & Eisenberger, 2012).

"Young man, go to your room and stay there until your cerebral cortex matures."

These advances by social neuroscientists set the stage for answers to intriguing questions, such as why gaining power so often leads to its abuse or why people experience a warm glow when they cooperate with others. These discoveries have also provided a window into the development of social behavior by tracing physical changes in the brain. For example, it turns out that a region of the brain that alerts people to danger is poorly developed until early adulthood (Decety & Michalska, 2010). This late development of an important brain region may help explain why adolescents take greater risks (in how they drive, for instance) than people in their mid-20s and beyond.

Neuroscience not only tells us which areas of the brain function most when certain kinds of activities are taking place. It also informs us about how the brain, the mind, and behavior function as a unit and how social factors influence each of these components at the same time.

← LOOKING BACK

Evolutionary theory informs our understanding of human behavior, just as it does our understanding of the physical characteristics of plants and animals. The many universals of human behavior suggest that some of these behaviors may be prewired—especially language and theory of mind. Differential parental investment of males and females may help us understand certain differences between women and men. Although misunderstandings and misapplications of evolutionary ideas sometimes make people suspicious of it, the theory has important implications for the field of social psychology. Social neuroscience is helping us to understand what happens in the brain in different kinds of social situations.

Culture and Human Behavior: How We Are Different

CULTURAL DIFFERENCES IN PREFERENCES
Every culture has its distinctive preferences, sometimes incomprehensible to the members of other cultures, such as the popularity of cotton candy in America. Some preferences are more central or important than food preferences—for example, independence vs. interdependence.

The most important legacy of evolution for human beings is not the way it constrains behavior, but rather the great flexibility it allows for adaptation to different circumstances. The enormous range of behaviors that people exhibit is tied to the fact that humans, together with rats, are the most successful of all the mammals in our ability to live in virtually every type of ecosystem. Our adaptability and the range of environments we have evolved in have resulted in extraordinary differences between human cultures. Depending on the prevailing culture, humans may be more or less likely to cooperate with each other, to assign different roles to men and women, or to try to distinguish themselves as individuals. Moreover, different cultures vary in what they deem morally wrong and how they punish transgressions.

Cultural Differences in Social Relations and Self-Understanding

Until fairly recently, psychologists regarded cultural differences as being limited primarily to differences in beliefs, preferences, and values. Some cultures regard the world as having been created by a supernatural force, some by impersonal natural forces, and some don't ponder the question much at all. The French like to eat fatty goose liver, the Chinese like to eat chicken feet, Americans like to eat cotton candy—and each group can have trouble appreciating the tastes preferred by the other groups. These differences, while interesting, are not the sort of thing that would make anyone suspect that fundamentally different psychological theories are needed to account for the behavior of people in different societies.

Recent research, however, shows that cultural differences go far deeper than beliefs and values. In fact, they extend all the way to the level of fundamental forms of self-conception and social interaction and even to the perceptual and cognitive processes people use to develop new thoughts and beliefs (Henrich, Heine, & Norenzayan, 2010). Many of these differences are discussed throughout the book, but one set of interrelated tendencies is particularly central, and we introduce it here.

To get a feel for this set of tendencies, think about the following propositions. How plausible do you find each one?

- People have substantial control over their life outcomes, and they much prefer situations in which they have choice and control to those in which they do not.
- People want to achieve personal success. They find that relationships with other people can sometimes make it harder to attain their goals.
- People want to be unique, to be different from other people in significant respects.
- People want to feel good about themselves. Excelling in some ways and being assured of their good qualities by other people are important to personal well-being.
- People like their relationships with others to be based on mutuality and equality, but if some people have more power than others, most people prefer to be in the superior position.
- People believe that the same rules should apply to everyone; individuals should not be singled out for special treatment because of their social role or personal attributes. Justice is, or should be, blind.

Hundreds of millions of people are reasonably well described by these propositions, but those people tend to be found in particular parts of the world—namely, Western Europe and many of the present and former nations of the British Commonwealth, including the United States, Canada, and Australia. These societies tend to be highly **independent** (or **individualistic**) **cultures** (Fiske, Kitayama, Markus, & Nisbett, 1998; Hofstede, 1980; Hsu, 1953; Markus & Connor, 2013; Markus & Kitayama, 1991; Triandis, 1995). Westerners think of themselves as distinct social entities, tied to each other by bonds of affection and organizational memberships to be sure, but essentially separate from other people and having attributes that exist in the absence of any connection to others. They tend to see their associations with other people, even their own family members, as voluntary and subject to termination once those associations become sufficiently troublesome or unproductive (**Table 1.2**).

independent (individualistic) culture A culture in which people tend to think of themselves as distinct social entities, tied to each other by voluntary bonds of affection and organizational memberships but essentially separate from other people and having attributes that exist in the absence of any connection to others.

TABLE 1.2 INDEPENDENT VS. INTERDEPENDENT CULTURES

Independent Cultures	Interdependent Cultures
Conception of the self as distinct from others, with attributes that are constant	Conception of the self as inextricably linked to others, with attributes depending on the situation
Insistence on ability to act on one's own	Preference for collective action
Need for individual distinctiveness	Desire for harmonious relations within group
Preference for achieved status based on accomplishments	Acceptance of hierarchy and ascribed status based on age, group membership, and other attributes
Conviction that rules governing behavior should apply to everyone	Preference for rules that take context and particular relationships into account

But these characterizations provide a poor description of most of the world's people, particularly the citizens of East Asian countries such as China (Triandis, McCusker, & Hui, 1990), Japan (Bond & Cheung, 1983), and Korea (Rhee, Uleman, Lee, & Roman, 1995), as well as people from South Asian countries such as India (Savani, Markus, & Conner, 2008), people from the Middle East (Greenberg, Eloul, Markus, & Tsai, 2012), people from many Latin American countries (de Oliveira & Nisbett, 2017; Gabrielidis, Stephan, Ybarra, Pearson, & Villareal, 1997), and people from Eastern Europe (Grossmann & Kross, 2010). These societies represent more **interdependent** (or **collectivistic**) **cultures**. People in such cultures don't have as much freedom or personal control over their lives, and they don't necessarily want or need it (Sastry & Ross, 1998).

Such differences between people in independent and interdependent societies have important implications for the nature of their personal goals and strivings, values, and beliefs, as **Box 1.1** illustrates. Success is important to East Asians, but in good part because it brings credit to the family and other groups to which they belong, rather than merely as a reflection of personal merit.

Personal uniqueness is not very important to interdependent peoples and may in fact be undesirable. In an experiment by Kim and Markus (1999), Korean and American participants were offered a pen as a gift for being in a study. Several of the pens were of one color and one pen was of another color. Americans tended to choose the unique color and Koreans the common color. Being unique and being better than others are not so important for interdependent people to feel good about themselves; moreover, feeling good about themselves is itself not as important a goal as it is for Westerners and other independent peoples (Heine, Lehman, Markus, & Kitayama, 1999).

Interdependent people tend not to expect or even value mutuality and equality in relationships; on the contrary, they're likely to expect hierarchical relations to be the rule (Hsu, 1953; Triandis, 1987, 1995). They tend not to be universalists in their understanding of social norms; instead, they believe in different strokes for different folks. Justice should keep her eyes wide open, paying attention to the particular circumstances of each case that comes before her.

To the extent that culture influences deep patterns of thinking and feeling—a central theme in this book—we would expect these influences to be reflected in differences in a person's brain—for example, the density of neurons in a region that supports culture-related thought. And indeed, culture appears to shape the human brain. In one recent study, 265 Chinese participants had images of their brains taken and then completed measures of how independent ("I do whatever I believe is right") or interdependent ("I regularly sacrifice for the group") they were (Wang, Peng, Chechlacz, Humphreys, & Sui, 2017). Those participants who were more independent actually showed denser gray matter (increased cell bodies of neurons) in the ventromedial prefrontal cortex, which supports attention and thought about the self, and the dorsolateral prefrontal cortex, which is thought to support thoughts of self-agency.

Some Qualifications

Much of the early research on the distinction between independence and interdependence focused on comparing Western countries with East Asian ones, but there appear to be variations of interdependence and independence in other cultures as well. For example, in Latino-American cultures more than in

---

interdependent (collectivistic) culture A culture in which people tend to define themselves as part of a collective, inextricably tied to others in their group and placing less importance on individual freedom or personal control over their lives.

Among traditional Kenyan tribespeople, the individualist is "looked upon with suspicion.... There is no really individual affair, for everything has a moral and social influence."
—JOMO KENYATTA (1938), FIRST PRESIDENT OF INDEPENDENT KENYA

BOX 1.1 ▶ FOCUS ON CULTURE

Dick and Jane, Deng and Janxing

The first page of a reader for American children from the 1930s shows a little boy running with his dog. "See Dick run," the primer reads. "See Dick run and play." The first page of a Chinese reader from the same era shows a little boy sitting on the shoulders of a bigger boy. "Big Brother loves Little Brother," reads the text. "Little Brother loves Big Brother." The difference between what the American child and the Chinese child of the 1930s were exposed to on the first day of school says much about the differences between their worlds. The American child is taught to orient toward action and to be prepared to live in a world where control and individual choice are normal. The Chinese child is more likely to be taught to be attuned to relationships. To Westerners, it makes sense to speak of the existence of the person apart from any group. To East Asians (Chinese, Japanese, and Koreans, for example) and to many of the world's other peoples, the person exists only as a member of a larger collective—family, friends, village, corporation. People are related to one another like ropes in a net, completely interconnected and having no real existence without the connections (Munro, 1985).

ATTENTION TO ACTION VS. RELATIONSHIPS (A) The *Dick and Jane* readers of the United States emphasize action and individualism, as shown here with the drawing of Dick running and the words "See Dick. See Dick run." (B) East Asian readers are more likely to emphasize relationships, as seen in this Chinese reader in which two boys walk down the street with their arms around each other. The text says, "Xiao Zhiang is a very nice boy. He is my best friend. We always study together and play together. We have a lot of fun together."

Asian-American cultures, interdependence involves what is called *familialism*, a social value defined by interpersonal warmth, closeness, and support (Sabogal, Marin, Otero-Sabogal, VanOss Marin, & Perez-Stable, 1987). Latinos who feel a great sense of familialism enjoy greater well-being and stronger relationships, but they also experience greater stress, in particular when faced with moving away from family—for example, to attend a faraway college (Campos, Ullman, Aguilera, & Dunkel Schetter, 2014).

Recent research has also extended the independence/interdependence framework to the understanding of another kind of culture—social class—which captures the degree of wealth, education, and occupational prestige a person enjoys. Within many cultures, there are social class differences in independence

FAMILIALISM AND LATIN CULTURES
Familalism—close contact with extended family, who provide strong emotional and material support—is particularly characteristic of Hispanic people.

versus interdependence (Stephens, Markus, & Phillips, 2014). Working-class people in modern societies are more interdependent than middle-class individuals. Working-class people have more interactions with their families than middle-class individuals do (Allan, 1979); their parenting styles emphasize conformity and obedience more than those of middle-class individuals (Kohn, 1969); and they value personal uniqueness less than middle-class individuals do.

A study by Stephens and her colleagues provides a striking example of the different values placed on uniqueness (Stephens, Markus, & Townsend, 2007). The researchers asked people how they would feel if a friend bought a car just like one they themselves had recently bought. Middle-class people were likely to report that they would be disappointed because they like to be unique; working-class people were more likely to say they would be very happy to share that similarity with a buddy. Middle-class people also appear to care much more about exercising choice than do working-class people. Middle-class people were found to like an object that they had chosen better than one they were given; the reverse was true for working-class people (Stephens, Fryberg, & Markus, 2011).

It's important to bear in mind that it's probably not accurate to put any society entirely in one box or another, to say that some are independent in all respects and others are interdependent in all respects. The American South, for example, is more interdependent than much of the rest of the country in that family connections and community ties tend to be more important (Vandello & Cohen, 1999). However, the South has been described as more tolerant of character quirks and various kinds of social deviance than other regions of the country—clearly individualistic tendencies (Reed, 1990).

As a final qualification, researchers have found that the same person can have a relatively independent orientation in some situations (such as competing in a debate tournament) and a relatively interdependent orientation in others (such as singing in a choir; Gardner, Gabriel, & Lee, 1999; Kühnen & Oyserman, 2002).

Culture and Gender Roles

Earlier, the discussion focused on some aspects of gender roles that seem to be universal. But gender roles vary greatly around the world and, as already noted, can even vary within subcultures in the same country. Male dominance is one of the most variable aspects of gender roles. In hunter-gatherer societies, the predominant male role is to hunt; the predominant female role is to gather plants. Despite the sharp demarcation of gender roles, such societies are relatively gender-egalitarian. In fact, the social structures are characterized by weak hierarchies in general; leaders have little power over others. Many Western cultures are also relatively gender-egalitarian, especially Northwestern European countries and most especially Scandinavian countries. For example, women constitute almost half the membership of the Parliament in Sweden. Relative status of women in the rest of the world ranges from the Scandinavian extreme of equality to near-slavery conditions for women.

The kinds of sexual relations that are considered normal and appropriate also vary enormously. Overwhelmingly, polygyny (one man with several wives) and serial monogamy are the most common practices among the world's subcultures—and that may have been the case for thousands of years. The traditional American ideal of lifetime monogamy is a rarity. The United States is considered decidedly prudish by many Western Europeans, for whom extramarital affairs are commonplace. On the other hand, in certain cultures, women (and sometimes even men) who are suspected of having extramarital affairs are put to death. Indeed, a woman who is raped might be expelled from the family circle or even killed. Gay and lesbian people in some societies may be put to death. Until just a generation or so ago, gays and lesbians in certain European countries were routinely sentenced to prison. In contrast, in some Native American cultures, bisexual men were admired as being "two-spirit" people. And in yet other cultures, homosexual behavior is so unremarkable that there is no term for either the practice or the type of person who engages in it.

It's a matter of some disagreement among social scientists whether the different sexual mores (norms) that characterize various cultures are merely arbitrary or whether most of them have economic or other practical roots. An example of an economic explanation concerns farmers in Nepal and Tibet who practice a form of polyandry: one wife with many husbands who are brothers. This system serves the economic goal of keeping scarce agricultural land in one family and

CULTURE AND GENDER ROLES
Women constitute almost 50 percent of politicians in Scandinavia. Their representation goes all the way to the top. (A) Jóhanna Sigurðardóttir, prime minister of Iceland (2009–2013). (B) Erna Solberg, prime minister of Norway (2013–present). (C) Mari Kiviniemi, prime minister of Finland (2010–2011). (D) Helle Thorning-Schmidt, prime minister of Denmark (2011–present).

(A)

(B)

(C)

(D)

produces just one set of related heirs per generation. A similar purpose was served by primogeniture, a common rule in Western Europe that only the firstborn male could inherit land. Otherwise, estates would be broken up into ever-smaller units, and the original power of the landowning family would dwindle away to the status of ordinary peasants.

In this book, we frequently return to discussions of gender. Women and men differ in the way they understand themselves, as well as in their emotions and motivations. But these diverse patterns are far from being constant across cultures. There are many ways of constructing gender.

Culture and Evolution as Tools for Understanding Situations

Both evolution and culture affect how people see the world and behave within it. The two together are complementary ways of understanding social relations. For the first hundred thousand years or so of human existence, our ancestors were largely concerned with the necessities of surviving, reproducing, and nourishing their young in a fundamentally social environment. Such challenges may have resulted in the evolution of prewired inclinations toward certain behaviors and ways of thinking. But such inclinations are tools that can be applied flexibly or not at all. And many, if not most, of these tools are highly modifiable by culture (Sperber, 1996). Different ecologies and economies placed people in situations that varied markedly from one another and in turn produced different social systems and practices.

Evolution has given us the capacity for an astonishingly wide range of behaviors. Whether a society develops a particular prewired inclination or not may depend on how adaptive the behavior is for the ecological, economic, and cultural circumstances people find themselves in (Sperber, 1996). Far from making us rigidly programmed automatons, evolution has equipped us with a large repertoire of tools for dealing with the enormous range of circumstances that humans confront. Our circumstances and our high intelligence determine which tools we develop and which tendencies we try to override.

← LOOKING BACK

People in some cultures are characteristically individualistic, or independent, whereas people in many other societies are more likely to be collectivistic, or interdependent. Individualism involves defining the self as having attributes that exist apart from one's relations with other people. Those who are more interdependent define themselves in terms of their relations with others. These differences have important implications for many of the most important phenomena of social psychology. Gender roles and sexual mores are examples of behaviors that differ widely from one culture to another. Evolution and culture both make important contributions to understanding human social behavior. Evolution predisposes us to certain behaviors, but culture determines which behaviors are likely to be developed in particular situations.

The Uses of Social Psychology

When you decided to take this course, you knew you were going to learn some interesting things about human behavior. You may have even hoped that the knowledge would be helpful in your daily life. Indeed it will. But you will gain more from this course than you might have anticipated.

Social Psychology and Critical Thinking

Many of your college courses teach not only facts and methods of research, but also how to reason. Mathematics courses, for example, teach rules of logic. Literature courses teach how to read a text closely to derive intended meanings that may not be obvious on the surface. Such reasoning tools can be applied broadly in everyday professional and personal life.

It's our belief that there is no better way to improve critical thinking than by studying social psychology. Courses in social psychology present a great deal of information about scientific methods. Unlike most other sciences, though, social psychology presents those methods in the context of common everyday events. This makes it easier to learn to apply them very broadly to daily problems.

Take, for example, statistics. The examples used in statistics courses typically concern agricultural plots, IQ tests, and other phenomena not drawn from ordinary life, which means that statistics courses by themselves have a limited impact on critical reasoning (Nisbett, 2015). When knowledge about statistics is applied to everyday life, however, the gain for reasoning in general is very great. People will come to apply statistical heuristics, or rules of thumb, to choices they make each day, to understanding the behavior of other people, and to scientific claims they encounter in the media. The same is true of many methodological concepts such as the need for control groups.

Two of the authors of this book have written a great deal about how to improve critical thinking (Belsky & Gilovich, 1999; Gilovich, 1991; Nisbett, 2015; Nisbett, 2017; Nisbett, Fong, Lehman, & Cheng, 1987; Nisbett & Ross, 1980). Much of what they have shown to be effective is achieved to a substantial extent in a social psychology course. But we believe that even more can be done to improve critical thinking skills by engaging you in exercises that make use of the scientific tools you will develop by reading about research on particular topics. To bring home lessons in critical reasoning, we highlight in each chapter various ways of applying critical tools to everyday life events.

Good reasoning principles are essential to understanding the world. But they aren't enough. Almost as important as having good reasoning principles

USING SOCIAL PSYCHOLOGY
The potential uses of social psychology are boundless. Examples include how to structure work or study groups (such as the one pictured here) to maximize performance, how to combat bullying in schools, how to reduce prejudice and discrimination, and how to craft a public service campaign.

SOCIAL MEDIA: USES AND ABUSES
Through social media, we have almost limitless access to information from and about other people and current events. This can make us informed or misinformed, happy or unhappy, depending on how we make use of it.

is making sure that the information we are reasoning about is accurate. Unfortunately, much of the information available to us is distorted or flat-out wrong. This is partly because our techniques for getting information are flawed. We are often content with inadequate or mistaken information, hastily obtained or obtained by means of cognitive processes that are error-prone. Information provided to us by others can be misleading or false—sometimes intentionally so. To help you develop better critical thinking skills, at many places in the book we point to mistaken procedures for obtaining and interpreting information made available to us by friends and family, the media (including social media), and the Internet. We also propose techniques for ensuring that information about important matters is the most accurate possible.

Uses and Abuses of Social Media

Today there are over 1.9 billion people on Facebook, 1 billion of whom are active users who have logged into Facebook sometime in the past month. As of April 2016, over 40 billion photos had been shared on Instagram worldwide. It is estimated that people share 6 billion emoji a day worldwide. Social media have been pivotal to recent political protests, from the Arab Spring to the upheaval in Myanmar, and have been central to the dynamics of every election campaign around the world.

It doesn't surprise social psychologists that these relatively new platforms are so widely used, for we are a hypersocial species that will connect and communicate through whatever medium we have available to us. But the density and prevalence of social media—Facebook, Instagram, Snapchat, Reddit, and Tumblr, to name a few—raise the overarching question of what our social lives and selves are like online. Throughout this book, we will draw on the social psychology of social media to seek answers to this question. We will consider, for example, when too much Facebook use might get you down, what your identity is like online, and how our attitudes and behaviors are influenced by new communication technologies.

Social Psychology and the Good Life

THE GOOD LIFE
Social psychology has provided us with lots of clues about what makes us happy and what makes us unhappy—clues that just living don't necessarily provide.

What draws people to social psychology is its relevance to their lives. In the past 20 years, social psychologists have turned their attention to one of the most personally relevant questions people have been asking for centuries: What is happiness? The answer to this question matters more than you might imagine. A wealth of studies find that feeling happy is associated with greater marital satisfaction, heightened creativity and productivity, and more robust physical health. Seeking to understand what makes us happy isn't just narcissistic navel-gazing; the quest has wide-ranging and important implications for the kinds of lives we will lead.

How, then, might you find happiness? The answers to this question are myriad and nuanced and depend critically on what stage of life you are in, your cultural background, and your upbringing. But hundreds of studies from social psychology offer some wisdom you might consider in your pursuit of the good life. You'll learn that certain things we might assume would influence our happiness profoundly—money, for example, and getting old—don't shape our well-being as much as we might think. You'll also learn about simple practices that have been shown to boost happiness, such as being generous, expressing gratitude to others, and valuing experiences over material objects.

The good life also requires that you learn how to handle the stress that comes with being overwhelmed by the circumstances that you face. Regrettably, people are experiencing more stress today than they did 30 years ago (S. Cohen & Janicki-Deverts, 2012). And stress, especially when it is chronic, can have extraordinary costs for your health, increasing the likelihood of disease and even damaging your DNA. In light of this, we will present scientifically tested ideas about how to handle stress in your personal life—practices such as learning how to distance yourself a bit from your problems, avoiding rumination and unnecessary worry, and practicing mindful meditation.

← LOOKING BACK

In addition to learning many useful facts about human behavior, this course will substantially improve your critical thinking, will help you to make the most of your use of social media, and will detail many ways to improve the quality of your life.

Chapter Review

SUMMARY

Characterizing Social Psychology

- *Social psychology* is the scientific study of the feelings, thoughts, and behaviors of individuals in social situations.

The Power of the Situation

- Social psychology emphasizes the influence of situations on behavior. People often find it difficult to see the role that powerful situations can play in producing their own and others' behavior and so are inclined to overemphasize the importance of personal dispositions in producing behavior. These two tendencies together are called the *fundamental attribution error*.

The Role of Construal

- Social psychology also focuses on the role of *construal* in understanding situations. People often feel that their comprehension of situations is direct, without much mediating thought. In fact, even the perception of the simplest objects rests on substantial inference and the complex cognitive structures that exist for carrying it out.
- The primary tool people use for understanding social situations (and physical stimuli, for that matter) is the *schema*. Schemas are stored representations of numerous repetitions of highly similar stimuli and situations. They tell us how to interpret situations and how to behave in them. *Stereotypes* are schemas of people of various kinds—police officers, Hispanics, yuppies. Stereotypes serve to guide interpretation and behavior, but

they can often be mistaken or misapplied, and they can lead to damaging interactions and unjust behaviors.

Automatic vs. Controlled Processing

- People's construals of situations are often largely automatic and nonconscious. As a consequence, people are sometimes in the dark about how they reached a particular conclusion or why they behaved in a particular way.
- People perceive many things nonconsciously and have little access to cognitive processes, in part because they have no need for conscious access to these things.

Evolution and Human Behavior: How We Are the Same

- The evolutionary perspective focuses on practices and understandings that are universal and seem to be indispensable to social life, suggesting that humans are prewired to engage in those practices. *Natural selection* has operated on human behaviors just as it has on physical traits.
- Some evolutionary theorists talk about universal characteristics that are cognitive in nature, including language, which appears at the same stage of development in all cultures, and theory of mind, which also develops early in normal people of all cultures. Some have argued that some differences between males and females may be explained by the differential *parental investment* required of the two sexes.
- Prewiring does not imply lack of modifiability. Human behavior is highly susceptible to being changed. To assume that humans have a genetic predisposition to behave in particular ways does not mean it is right to behave in those ways. Believing that because things are a particular way means they should be that way is to commit the *naturalistic fallacy*.

Culture and Human Behavior: How We Are Different

- Behaviors and meanings can differ dramatically across cultures. Many of these differences involve the degree to which a society is *independent*, or *individualistic* (characterized by fewer social relationships of a looser sort), or whether it is *interdependent*, or *collectivistic* (characterized by many relationships of a highly prescribed nature). These differences influence conceptions of the self and the nature of human relationships, as well as basic cognitive and perceptual processes.
- Gender roles and sexual mores differ enormously across cultures. Even within the West, gender and sexual practices diverge significantly. Theorists differ in how

strongly they believe that this variability is arbitrary versus rooted in economic factors or some other aspect of the objective situation confronting the culture.

The Uses of Social Psychology

- Scientific methods, when applied to everyday life events, provide reasoning skills that are very widely applicable. This text focuses on maximizing gains to critical thinking and learning how to make optimal use of social media.

THINK ABOUT IT

1. How does social psychology differ from related disciplines, such as personality psychology and sociology? How might a social psychologist, in contrast to researchers in other disciplines, try to understand the atrocities at Abu Ghraib?

2. What does the Milgram experiment on obedience demonstrate about the power of the situation? What features of the experimental situation might have increased the likelihood that participants would continue to shock the learner even after the learner showed signs of pain?

3. Why are schemas so important for social interaction? What is your schema for being a student in a classroom? What might happen if you didn't have that schema?

4. When trying to understand people's thoughts, feelings, and motivations, why don't researchers just ask them? What does research on automatic versus controlled processing tell us about people's awareness of their own mental states?

5. How does evolution help explain social behavior? What are some types of behaviors that seem most likely to be explained by evolution, and what behaviors seem less likely?

6. What is the naturalistic fallacy, and why is it so important to avoid when considering evolutionary explanations?

7. How do Western and Eastern countries differ in their beliefs about the role of the self in relation to the group? How might these beliefs lead to different behaviors in an academic setting?

8. Are evolutionary and cultural explanations for behavior compatible? How might these two perspectives complement each other when it comes to explaining gender differences in mate selection?

The **answer guidelines** for the think about it questions can be found at the back of the book . . . 👉

ONLINE STUDY MATERIALS

Want to earn a better grade on your test?

Go to **INQUIZITIVE** to learn and review this chapter's content, with personalized feedback along the way.

Is there a regional culture of honor where people are more accepting of crimes that have been committed to protect one's honor?

What are the benefits of conducting a longitudinal study spanning decades?

The Methods of Social Psychology

RETAIL BUSINESS OWNERS ACROSS THE NORTHERN and Southern United States received the following letter from a job applicant who described himself as a hardworking 27-year-old man who was relocating to the potential employer's town. Among a set of appropriate qualifications listed in the letter, the applicant described one rather striking blemish on his record:

> There is one thing I must explain, because I feel I must be honest and want no misunderstandings. I have been convicted of a felony, namely manslaughter. You will probably want an explanation for this before you send me an application, so I will provide it. I got into a fight with someone who was having an affair with my fiancée. . . . One night this person confronted me in front of my friends at the bar. He told everyone that he and my fiancée were sleeping together. He laughed at me to my face and asked me to step outside if I was man enough. I was young and didn't want to back down from a challenge in front of everyone. As we went into the alley, he started to attack me. He knocked me down, and he picked up a bottle. I could have run away and the judge said I should have, but my pride wouldn't let me. Instead I picked up a pipe that was laying in the alley and hit him with it. I didn't mean to kill him, but he died a few hours later at the hospital.

Some business owners who received the letter replied and complied with the applicant's requests, providing a job application, the name of a contact person, or a phone number to call. Some even sent a personal note along with their response.

OUTLINE

DEFENDING ONE'S HONOR
Duels, like the one depicted here between Aaron Burr and Alexander Hamilton, were practiced in the United States well into the nineteenth century. They were called "affairs of honor."

In truth, however, the applicant was a fictional character created by two social psychologists in a carefully planned study (Cohen & Nisbett, 1997). The investigators measured the degree to which potential employers responded to the applicant's inquiry. If there was a note, the researchers rated how sympathetic it seemed—how encouraging it was and whether it mentioned an appreciation for the applicant's candor.

Cohen and Nisbett found some distinct patterns in the replies. Retailers from the South complied with the applicant's requests more than retailers from the North. And the notes from Southern business owners were much warmer and more sympathetic than those from the North. One Southern retailer wrote in her letter:

As for your problem of the past, anyone could probably be in the situation you were in. It was just an unfortunate incident that shouldn't be held against you. Your honesty shows that you are sincere. . . .

I wish you the best of luck for your future. You have a positive attitude and a willingness to work. Those are the qualities that businesses look for in an employee. Once you get settled, if you are near here, please stop in and see us.

No letter from a Northern employer was remotely as sympathetic.

Why were the Southerners seemingly so accepting of murder? You will find out in this chapter. More important, you will learn *how* the investigators found out. In addressing this question, the investigators employed most of the methods at the disposal of social psychologists—methods that deepen our understanding of human behavior and, in so doing, give us some tools to benefit society. ■

The Value of Social Psychology Research

Why do social psychologists conduct research? Why is it useful to read about it? First and foremost, dealing effectively with many of today's most pressing problems—climate change, growing income inequality, biases against minority students in schools, sexual harassment—can be informed by findings from social psychology.

But even beyond helping people to deal with critical societal challenges, social psychological research can provide us with a clearer understanding of less weighty elements of our everyday lives. To be sure, we can get along perfectly well in everyday life without the benefit of findings from social psychology. Our everyday lives can be reasonably predictable: most of the situations we find ourselves in are similar to other familiar situations, and our observations about how people behave in those situations are accurate enough to allow us to get by with some confidence in the correctness of our predictions.

But many situations—dating, interviews, political discussions with a friend—contain surprises and pitfalls that social psychology research can help us anticipate and avoid. And even in familiar situations, our ideas about how people are likely to behave can be mistaken. Chapters 4, 5, and 12 describe some of these mistaken beliefs about social behavior and how those beliefs get formed.

Our opinions about *why* we behave as we do can also be mistaken (Nisbett & Wilson, 1977). As discussed in Chapter 1, many of the factors that influence our behavior are hidden from us: they aren't available in conscious, verbal form, but rather occur in nonconscious, nonverbal forms that aren't accessible to introspection. Fortunately, social psychology research can give us insight into the reasons not just for other people's behavior but for our own as well.

To see how social psychology research can illuminate even familiar aspects of human behavior and its causes, take a look at **Box 2.1** (see p. 40). Make your own guesses about the outcomes of the research described, and then see how accurate your guesses are by looking at p. 42. When you have to predict the results of studies and *then* find out what they were, you avoid the **hindsight bias**, the tendency to believe that you could have predicted some outcome that you've learned about—when in fact you couldn't have predicted it accurately.

Once we hear some new fact, it's easy to think of reasons why it might be true. Coming up with those reasons can leave us with the feeling that we could have predicted the outcome when often we couldn't have. Psychologists have demonstrated this hindsight bias by telling some people a fact and asking them if they would have predicted it and not telling other people about the fact and asking for their predictions. It's very common that the people kept in ignorance make incorrect predictions, but those told the fact are confident they could have predicted it correctly (Bradfield & Wells, 2005; Fischhoff, Gonzalez, Lerner, & Small, 2005; Guilbault, Bryant, Brockway, & Posavac, 2004).

hindsight bias People's tendency to be overconfident about whether they could have predicted a given outcome.

← LOOKING BACK

Social psychology research shows us that some of our beliefs about how people behave are mistaken. Our beliefs about the reasons for our own behavior can also be mistaken. Social psychology findings sometimes seem obvious, but often only *after* we know what they are. The hindsight bias mistakenly convinces us that we would have known the correct answer if we had been asked to predict the finding.

How Social Psychologists Test Ideas

Social psychologists use a wide variety of methods to test hypotheses about human behavior. As you read about these methods in this chapter and see them applied elsewhere in the book, keep in mind that their underlying logic is crucial for getting at the truth of propositions about social behavior. Even if you can't conduct a study to test a particular proposition because resources are insufficient or because it would be unethical, thinking through how you *would* test a given idea can lead you to new ideas that, on reflection, might surpass your initial speculation. Such an exercise is called a *thought experiment*, and it's one of the most useful critical-thinking skills you'll learn from reading this book. To conduct a thought experiment, you need to speculate about the results you might obtain

"The scientific method itself would not have led anywhere, it would not even have been born without a passionate striving for clear understanding."
—ALBERT EINSTEIN,
OUT OF MY LATER YEARS

BOX 2.1 ▶ FOCUS ON INTUITIVE SOCIAL PSYCHOLOGY

Predicting Research Results

Try to predict how people would behave in each of these situations. Put a check by the answer you believe to be correct before you see the right answer. If you don't commit yourself in that way, you'll be vulnerable to the hindsight bias. (See p. 42 for answers.)

1. Does familiarity breed liking or contempt? Would you be likely to prefer (a) a song you had heard many times on the radio or (b) one you had heard less often?

2. Suppose some people were persuaded to lie about their beliefs about a certain matter. Would those people be more inclined to adjust their beliefs in the direction of the lie if paid (a) a small amount of money, (b) a large amount of money, or (c) no money at all?

3. Suppose you knew that an acquaintance wanted a favor from you that was somewhat inconvenient for you to grant. Would you like him better if (a) he refrained from asking you the favor, (b) he asked you to do the favor and you complied, or (c) he asked you to do the favor and you regretfully turned him down?

4. Suppose you got a friend to think seriously for a few minutes about the inevitability of death. Would those thoughts likely make her feel (a) more helpless, (b) less favorably inclined toward her fellow human beings, or (c) more patriotic?

5. Suppose male college students were asked to grade an essay written for an English class, and a picture of the female student who allegedly wrote the essay was attached to the essay. Would the grade be higher if (a) she was very pretty, (b) she was average looking, (c) she was quite plain looking, or (d) the student grading the essay was about as good looking as the person who allegedly wrote the essay?

6. Suppose people were asked to choose between an option with substantial potential gain but also substantial risk and another option that entails less potential gain but also less risk. Would people be more likely to choose the risky option if (a) they considered the choice by themselves or (b) they considered the choice in discussion with a small group; or (c) would it make no difference?

7. Suppose you offered a reward to some nursery school children if they would draw with some special colored markers, and all the children who were offered the reward drew with them. Would these children be (a) more likely to play with the markers at a subsequent time than the children who were never offered the reward but got one anyway, (b) less likely, or (c) equally likely?

8. Suppose you asked a group of people to report 6 instances when they behaved in an assertive fashion, another group to report 12 instances when they behaved in an assertive fashion, and a third group to report 6 instances of some other behavior altogether, such as instances of introverted behavior. Which group would later report that they were most assertive: (a) the group asked for 6 instances of assertive behavior, (b) the group asked for 12 instances of assertive behavior, (c) the group asked about some other behavior; or (d) would it make little difference what the group was asked?

---

under two different sets of circumstances to develop more precise hypotheses about the phenomenon in question. Although no substitute for actually collecting data, a thought experiment can help to clarify your assumptions and general conceptual understanding of the phenomena in question.

A **hypothesis** is a prediction about what will happen under particular circumstances, especially in a research study. A **theory** is a set of related propositions intended to describe some phenomenon or aspect of the world. In speaking casually, people sometimes say that something is "just a theory," meaning it's a notion largely unsupported by facts. In science, including social science, theories generally have support in the form of empirical data, and they often entail predictions that would be surprising except in light of the theory. In the history of science, many theories have led to a greater understanding of natural phenomena or to important real-life consequences. Evolutionary theory is supported by an enormous number of facts as well as nonintuitive predictions that have been confirmed by empirical observation. Bacterial adaptation to drugs, for example, is well understood in terms of evolutionary theory.

hypothesis A prediction about what will happen under particular circumstances.

theory A set of related propositions intended to describe some phenomenon or aspect of the world.

An example of a hypothesis born of a social psychology theory is the prediction that when people work hard to acquire something (a consumer product, a new job, or admission to an exclusive club) and it turns out to be disappointing, they will be motivated to find hidden benefits in what they acquired. Such a hypothesis, which can be tested in a variety of ways, is an example of the sort of hypotheses that are generated by *dissonance theory*, the theory that people like their thoughts to be consistent with one another and will do substantial mental work to achieve such cognitive consistency. Hypotheses are tested by studies, which examine predictions about what will happen in particular concrete contexts. Thus, theories are more general than hypotheses, which are in turn more general than the findings derived from the studies that test them.

Observational Research

The first step in scientific research is often just looking at a phenomenon in a systematic way, with a view to understanding what's going on and coming up with hypotheses about why things are as they are. Charles Darwin was first and foremost a great observer of natural life, and his observations of finches in the Galápagos Islands, as well as all manner of other species during his five and a half years on the *Beagle*, led to his theory of evolution by natural selection.

Social psychologists likewise learn a great deal from observation. One such method of research, used by both psychologists and cultural anthropologists, is called *participant observation* and involves observing some phenomenon at close range. An anthropologist may live with a group of people for a long time, noting what they do and coming up with guesses—sometimes inspired by conversations with the people being studied—about why those people behave in certain ways or have certain beliefs.

In the 1950s, social psychologists Roger Barker and Herbert Wright (1954) studied how children in a U.S. Midwestern town interacted with their surroundings. They followed children around as they delivered the morning paper, went to school, played kick the can, did their homework, and went to church suppers. The study revealed a great deal about the way the children interacted with their environment, the opportunities and constraints that came with their environment, and the factors that molded their characters.

Social psychologists often observe social situations in a semiformal way, taking notes and interviewing participants. Observations can be misleading, however, so any tentative conclusions gleaned from observation should ideally be tested using other methods.

Archival Research

One type of research can be conducted without ever leaving the library or one's computer. Researchers can look at evidence found in *archives* of various kinds, including census reports, police records, sports statistics, newspaper articles, and databases containing ethnographic (anthropological) descriptions of people in different cultures. For example, for their research on cultures of honor, Nisbett (1993) and his colleagues

"Science and everyday life cannot and should not be separated."
—ROSALIND FRANKLIN, BRITISH SCIENTIST WHOSE WORK PAVED THE WAY FOR THE DISCOVERY OF DNA

OBSERVATIONAL METHODS
The evolutionary psychologist and human behavioral ecologist Lawrence Sugiyama is shown here, with bow and arrow, involved in a particularly active form of participant observation.

1. Familiarity, in general, breeds liking. The more a person has been exposed to a stimulus, within broad limits, the more the person likes it. See Chapter 10.

2. People are more persuaded by the lies they tell if they are paid nothing or a small amount than if they are paid a lot. See Chapter 7.

3. We like people more if we do them a favor. See Chapters 7 and 9.

4. When people are reminded of their own mortality, they focus on the values they hold most dear, such as religion and love of country. See Chapter 7.

5. Males give higher grades to females who are good looking. See Chapter 10.

6. There's no general answer to the question of whether people are more likely to prefer risk when they discuss things in a group. They prefer risk more if that was their initial inclination before discussion and less if caution was their initial inclination. See Chapter 12.

7. Rewarding children for doing something they would do anyway makes them less interested in doing it. Contracts are likely to turn play into work. See Chapter 7.

8. People report that they're more assertive if they're asked to think of a few instances of assertiveness rather than if they're asked to think of many. It's easier to come up with a few instances than many, and people use the effort it was necessary to expend as an indicator of what they are really like. If it seems hard to come up with examples, they'll rate themselves as less assertive than if it's easy. See Chapter 4.

studied FBI reports of homicides and found, as they had anticipated, that homicides were more common in the U.S. South than in the North. The FBI reports also included the circumstances of the homicides—murders committed in the context of another felony (such as while robbing a convenience store) versus murders that are crimes of passion (such as in the context of a love triangle). In another study, Nisbett and Cohen (1996) analyzed the various types of murders and discovered that in the South, the most common kinds of homicide involved some type of insult—for example, barroom quarrels and cases of sexual infidelity. Indeed, other kinds of homicide not involving personal honor are actually less common in the South, leading a Southern sociologist (Reed, 1981) to say that you're safer in the South than in the North if you stay out of the wrong bars and bedrooms!

Surveys

One of the most common types of study in social psychology involves simply asking people questions. *Surveys* can be conducted using either interviews or written questionnaires. The participants can be a small collection of students or a large sample of the national population. When the investigator is trying to discern the beliefs or attitudes of some group of people—freshmen at a particular university, say, or Hispanics living in Canada—*representative sampling* is important. The people in the survey must be representative of the population as a whole, which is best achieved by selecting potential respondents randomly. The only way to obtain a random sample is to give everyone in the population an equal chance of being chosen. If the university has a directory of students, a random sample can be obtained by finding out the total number of freshmen (say, 1,000), deciding how many to interview (say, 50), and then selecting every twentieth name from the directory and asking those people to participate in the survey (**Figure 2.1**). (Such a sample isn't technically random because the directory is likely to be organized alphabetically and every twentieth name is chosen systematically rather than randomly. But the procedure is a reasonable approximation because there's unlikely to be anything systematically associated with every twentieth name.)

Convenience sampling, such as contacting people as they enter the library or e-mailing fraternity and sorority members, is not random. A convenience sample may be *biased* in some way; that is, it might include too many of some kinds of people and too few of others. Information based on biased samples is sometimes worse than no information at all. One famous example from the history of public-opinion polling comes from a survey conducted by the *Literary Digest*, involving more than a million respondents. The *Literary Digest* erroneously predicted that the Republican Alf Landon would defeat Franklin Delano Roosevelt in the 1936 U.S. presidential election. In fact, the election was one of the most dramatic landslides in history: Landon carried only two states. How could the survey have been so far off? The sample was biased because it was drawn from telephone directories and automobile registrations. In 1936, wealthy people were more likely to own phones and cars than were poorer people, and they were also more likely to vote Republican.

You've undoubtedly seen the results of reader surveys in various magazines. Two-thirds of *People* magazine readers who went on a vegan diet say they lost weight. Three-quarters of the readers of *Outside* magazine say that sex is more enjoyable outdoors. Sixty percent of respondents in a *Slate* poll claim they are happier after going to church than if they stay home and watch a football game on Sunday. Actually, all three results are fictitious and you should ignore each claim. In fact, you should ignore all claims like these even if they aren't made up, because the people who take the time to respond to such polls are likely to be different from those who do not respond and therefore are unlikely to represent the population as a whole. For example, readers of *People* who have lost weight may be more likely to respond to a survey about weight loss than those who haven't lost weight. The criterion that everyone be equally likely to be included in the sample is clearly not met, upping the odds that the survey results are misleading.

Nisbett and Cohen (1996) used surveys to try to find out why U.S. Southerners were more likely to commit homicide. One possibility was that Southerners were simply more accepting of violence. But when the investigators looked at published national surveys of attitudes toward violence, they found few regional differences. For example, Southerners were no more likely than Northerners to agree with the sentiment that "an eye for an eye" justifies retaliation, and Southerners were actually more likely to agree that "when a person harms you, you should turn the other cheek and forgive him." However, the researchers found that Southerners were more likely to favor violence in response to insults and to think that a man would be justified to fight an acquaintance who "looks over his girlfriend and talks to her in a suggestive way." Southerners were also more likely to approve of violence in response to threats to home and family, thinking, for example, that "a man has a right to kill a person to defend his house." The investigators also found that Southerners were more approving of violence in socializing children: they were more likely to say that spanking was a reasonable way to handle a child's misdeeds and more likely to say that they would encourage a child to beat up someone who was bullying him.

In trying to explain this acceptance of violence in specific contexts, Nisbett and Cohen sought out anthropologists and historians. Several sources suggested that the South might be a "culture of honor." The U.S. North was settled by farmers from England, Holland, and Germany. Farmers in general are peace-loving folks; there's little reason for them not to be. The U.S. South was settled by herding peoples from the edges of Great Britain—Scottish, Irish, and Scotch-Irish from Ulster. Herding peoples throughout the world tend to be tough guys. They need to be because they can lose their livelihood—their herd—in an instant. They cultivate a stance of being ready to commit violence at the merest hint that they might not be able to protect themselves, their homes, and their property. A man has to retaliate violently if insulted in order to establish that he is not to be trifled with. Parents teach their children not to fear violence and to

Population
Group you want to know about
(e.g., U.S. college students)

Random samples
are likely to capture the proportions of given types of people in the population as a whole (i.e., U.S. college students).

Convenience samples
can produce proportions that are severely skewed away from the actual proportions in the population as a whole.

FIGURE 2.1
RANDOM SAMPLING AND CONVENIENCE SAMPLING

PROBLEMS WITH CONVENIENCE SAMPLES
Convenience sampling can produce results that are wide of the mark. The biggest presidential poll of the 1936 election predicted that Alf Landon would be the winner.

correlational research Research that involves measuring two or more variables and assessing whether there is a relationship between them.

experimental research In social psychology, research that randomly assigns people to different conditions, or situations, and that enables researchers to make strong inferences about why a relationship exists or how different situations affect behavior.

third variable A variable, often unmeasured in correlational research, that can be the true explanation for the relationship between two other variables.

self-selection In correlational research, the situation in which the participant, rather than the researcher, determines the participant's level of each variable (for example, whether they are married or not, or how many hours per day they spend playing video games), thereby creating the problem that it could be these unknown other properties that are responsible for the observed relationship.

know how to protect themselves. This historical hypothesis guided the rest of Nisbett and Cohen's research.

In addition to the fringes of Britain, herding has traditionally been much more common in the Mediterranean countries than in northern Europe, and those countries in general have always been cultures of honor (the Corsican Napoleon and the Sicilian Mafia are examples). In Greek mythology (or perhaps in Greek history, we don't really know), Paris of Troy took beautiful Helen from her husband, Menelaus of Sparta, provoking a war of ten years' duration. "The face that launched a thousand ships" likely wouldn't have caused so many northern European vessels to set sail.

Correlational Research

One of the most important distinctions among different types of research is between correlational research and experimental research. In **correlational research**, psychologists measure two or more variables and examine whether a relationship exists between them. **Experimental research** goes a step further, enabling investigators to make strong inferences about *why* a relationship exists or how different situations affect people's behavior.

CORRELATION DOES NOT ESTABLISH CAUSATION Looking for correlations is an important way to begin a line of inquiry. However, once established, a correlation requires further exploration. Does variable 1 causally influence variable 2, or is it the other way around—reverse causation? Or does some **third variable** influence both? In correlational research, we can never be sure about causality.

For example, *U.S. News and World Report* reported in 2013 that casual sex worsens college students' mental health. The article reported that students who have more casual sex encounters tend to have poorer mental health than those who have fewer. But casual sex might be associated with loneliness, and we know that lonelier people have poorer mental health than people who don't report that they're lonely. So a third variable—loneliness—might be causing students to engage in more casual sex and might worsen their mental health. In that case, casual sex might not in fact be causing poorer mental health, rather a third variable is causing both. It's even possible that the causal direction runs the opposite way from what is suggested in the headline. Poorer mental health may cause people to seek out casual sex as a way of feeling less unhappy.

Correlational research usually can't provide convincing evidence that there is a causal relationship because of the possibility of **self-selection**; that is, the investigator has no control over a particular participant's level, or score, on a given variable—for example, whether the participant grew up in poverty or opulence, has an IQ of 100 or 130, or follows the teachings of Jesus, Mohammed, or Buddha. In effect, the participants have "chosen" their level on *all* variables—those that are measured and those that aren't. For example, in the study reported by *TIME*, the researchers didn't assign people to be married or not; they either were or weren't. And the researchers didn't know what other qualities each participant brought in addition to marital status—a sunny or gloomy disposition, good or bad physical health, an easygoing or high-maintenance personality. These various qualities are simply measured (or not); not assigned by the researcher.

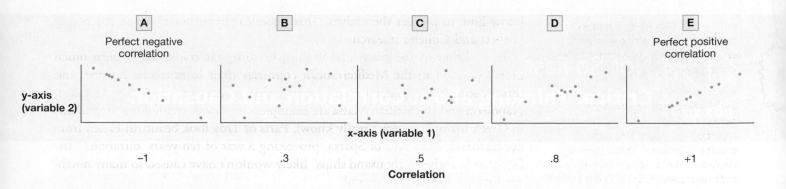

**FIGURE 2.2
SCATTERPLOTS AND
CORRELATIONS**

In correlational research, investigators can look at only the degree of relationship between two or more variables. The strength of a relationship between variables can range from 0, meaning that the variables have no relationship at all, to 1 (or +1), meaning that the higher the level on one variable, the higher the level on the other—without exception. (If being higher on one variable is perfectly associated with being lower on the other, the correlation is –1.) By convention, a correlation of .1 indicates a weak relationship, a correlation of .3 a moderate relationship, and a correlation of .5 or higher a strong relationship. **Figure 2.2** shows what are called scatterplots. Variable 1 is on the x-axis (horizontal), and variable 2 is on the y-axis (vertical). Each dot represents a study participant for whom there is a score on both variables: a score on variable 1 and a score on variable 2. Panel A shows a perfect negative correlation: the higher the level on variable 1, the lower the level on variable 2, without exception. Panel E shows a perfect positive correlation: the higher the level on variable 1, the higher the level on variable 2, without exception.

Panel B in Figure 2.2 shows a correlation of .3—a moderate relationship between the two variables—which could correspond, for example, to the correlation between a person's percentage of body fat and the degree of risk for cardiovascular illness. Both the marked spread of the dots (their scatter) and the relatively shallow slope of the line that best fits the scatterplot show that the association is relatively weak.

Panel C in Figure 2.2 shows a correlation of .5—a strong relationship—which is approximately the degree of association between height and weight. Panel D in Figure 2.2 shows a correlation of .8—a very strong relationship. This is about the degree of correlation between a person's score on the math portion of the SAT on a first testing occasion and the same person's score a year later. Whether strong or weak, correlations establish only that there is an association between variables, not that one variable exerts a causal influence on the other.

Scientific findings reported in the media are often based on correlational research. It's crucial to recognize the limits of such findings. They're often interesting, and they might *suggest* a particular causal connection, but by no means can correlational studies establish causation. To further develop your critical thinking abilities, try your hand at interpreting the correlational results in **Box 2.2** (see p. 46).

THE VALUE OF CORRELATIONAL FINDINGS Correlational studies can point investigators to possible causal hypotheses about some aspect of the world. Moreover, correlational studies are sometimes a researcher's best option when an experimental study would be difficult or unethical to conduct. Random assignment

Not So Fast:
Critical Thinking about Correlation and Causation

BOX 2.2

The following items are the findings of numerous correlational studies for which scientists or the media have implied a causal connection. To be a good consumer of correlational research, you need to be able to evaluate such causal claims carefully. For each of the findings in the list, consider alternatives to the stated or implied causal relationship—namely, that A causes B. Might it actually be the case that B causes A? Or that some variable C causes both?

1. *TIME Magazine* reported that attempts by parents to control the size of portions their children eat will cause the children to become overweight (June 23, 2008, p. 102). If the parents of overweight children stop controlling their portions, will the children get thinner?

2. Countries whose citizens have higher average IQs have higher average wealth. Does being smarter make a country richer?

3. People who attend church have lower mortality rates than those who do not (Schnall et al., 2008). Does religion make people live longer?

4. People who have a dog are less likely to be depressed. If you give a dog to a depressed person, will the person become happier?

5. States with abstinence-only sex education have higher homicide rates. Does abstinence-only sex education cause aggression? If students in those states receive more informative sex education, will the homicide rate go down?

6. Intelligent men have better sperm, meaning higher sperm count and greater motility (Arden, Gottfredson, Miller, & Pierce, 2008). Does this suggest that attending college, which makes people smarter, also improves sperm quality?

7. People who smoke marijuana are subsequently more likely to use cocaine than people who do not smoke marijuana. Does marijuana use cause cocaine use?

(Some possible responses to the causality claims are presented on pp. 56–57.)

is a requirement of a well-designed experiment, but researchers can't randomly assign people to the levels of certain variables (such as socioeconomic status, intelligence, and gender). Unfortunately, even if it seems possible that a causal relationship exists, correlational studies don't normally indicate which variable may be causing the other, nor do they reveal whether some third variable is at work driving the association between the two variables being studied. Consider the following example: people who watch the local evening news—with reports of murders, fires, and other newsworthy mayhem—see more danger in the world than people who don't. The most obvious explanation is that seeing dangers on TV makes people feel more at risk. But could it be that people who are already anxious watch the local news to justify their fearfulness? Or is there some third variable at play? For example, elderly people may have more anxiety about their lives and may have more time to watch TV. This study could be refined so that it potentially rules out the latter hypothesis by showing that older adults are not more likely to watch TV than younger people, nor do they tend to be more anxious about their lives than younger people. But ruling out an alternative hypothesis isn't normally sufficient to prove that a given relationship is causal. As more and more alternative explanations are tested and rejected, however, it becomes more and more plausible that the hypothesized causal relationship is indeed valid.

Some insight into the nature and meaning of a correlational result can be obtained by conducting a **longitudinal study**, which involves collecting measures at different points in time. For example, an investigator might measure how many hours teenagers devote each week to playing violent video games and then examine incarceration rates and other measures of criminal behavior in adulthood. A correlation between video game use in adolescence and criminality in adulthood cannot establish that playing such games leads to a life of crime—there can be a hidden third variable that's responsible for the relationship. But it does rule out one direction of causality: nothing that happens when a person is 30 can affect anything the person did when younger.

Experimental Research

The best way to be sure about causality is to conduct an experiment. Experimental research requires an independent variable and a dependent variable. The **independent variable**, which the scientist manipulates, is presumed to be the cause of some particular outcome called the **dependent variable**, which is measured. In experiments, the researcher determines what the independent variable will be and what the levels for that variable will be. Dependent variables can be measured in many ways, including verbal reports (such as statements about degree of anger or anxiety); behavior (helping or not, getting an inoculation or not); physiological measures (heart rate or stress monitoring, such as cortisol levels); or neural measures (increased activity in certain brain areas).

The great power of experiments comes from exposing participants to different levels of the independent variable by **random assignment**, which ensures that participants are as likely to be assigned to one condition as to another. It guarantees that, on average, except for the manipulation of the independent variable, there should be no systematic differences across experimental groups. There will be roughly as many men as women in each condition, as many liberals as conservatives, as many athletes as nonathletes. Random assignment thus rules out the possibility of self-selection biases in samples; the experimenter has done the selecting. Also critical to experiments is a carefully crafted **control condition**, which is comparable to the experimental condition in every way except that it lacks the one ingredient hypothesized to produce the expected effect on the dependent variable.

As an example of a carefully designed experiment, let's reconsider two findings: U.S. Southerners are more likely to commit homicide in situations where there has been an insult, and Southerners are more likely to believe that violence is an appropriate response to an insult. Both of these findings are correlational: Southernness is associated with insult-related homicides, and Southernness is associated with the belief that violence is an appropriate response to an insult.

To study further whether Southerners actually do react more aggressively to an insult, Cohen and his colleagues conducted a series of experiments (Cohen, Nisbett, Bowdle, & Schwarz, 1996). The participants were all middle-class male

LONGITUDINAL STUDIES
Jackie, Sue, and Lynn (above) are three participants in *Up*, a series of documentary films by Michael Apted tracing the development of 14 British people from various socioeconomic backgrounds. New material for this longitudinal study has been collected every seven years since 1964, starting when the participants were 7 years old.

longitudinal study A study conducted over a long period of time with the same participants.

independent variable
In experimental research, the variable that is manipulated; it is hypothesized to be the cause of a particular outcome.

dependent variable
In experimental research, the variable that is measured (as opposed to manipulated); it is hypothesized to be affected by manipulation of the independent variable.

random assignment Assigning participants in experimental research to different conditions randomly, so they are as likely to be assigned to one condition as to another, with the effect of making the types of people in the different conditions roughly equal.

control condition A condition comparable to the experimental condition in every way except that it lacks the one ingredient hypothesized to produce the expected effect on the dependent variable.

HONOR EXPERIMENTS

Researchers had U.S. Southern and Northern male students walk down a hallway where an accomplice shoved the student and called him an asshole. Southern students responded with more anger, as well as higher increases in their testosterone levels (Cohen, Nisbett, Bowdle, & Schwarz, 1996).

students at the University of Michigan; some were Southerners and some were Northerners. All of them believed they were participating in a study on the effects of time constraints on judgments of various kinds. After filling out a questionnaire, they were asked to take it down a long, narrow hallway lined with filing cabinets and leave it on a table at the end.

As some participants walked down the hall, another student stood in the hallway with a file drawer pulled out. For the participant to pass by, the student had to push the drawer in and move out of the way. Moments later, when the participant returned down the same hallway, the student had to get out of the participant's way again. This time the student slammed the drawer shut, pushed into the participant's shoulder, and said, "Asshole." (He then quickly exited behind a door labeled Photo Lab to avoid a physical confrontation.) Subjects in a control condition simply left the questionnaire on the table without incident. (The participants were, of course, randomly assigned to one or the other condition.) The study therefore had two independent variables: one involving a manipulated variable (insulted versus control) and one involving a nonmanipulated, "correlational" variable (Northerner versus Southerner).

Several dependent variables were examined after the insult either did or did not take place. First, observers noted the participants' immediate reactions after the insult. Insulted Southerners usually showed a flash of anger; insulted Northerners were more likely to shrug their shoulders or to appear amused. Second, participants were asked to read a story in which a man made a pass at another man's fiancée and then to provide an ending to the story. Southerners who had been insulted were much more likely to provide a violent ending than Southerners who hadn't been insulted, whereas the endings provided by Northerners were unaffected by the insult. Third, the participants' level of testosterone, the hormone that mediates aggression in males, was tested both before and after the insult. The level of testosterone increased for Southerners who had been insulted, but it did not increase for Southerners who hadn't been insulted or for Northerners, whether insulted or not.

Fourth, participants were asked to walk back down the narrow hallway, and this time another assistant to the experimenter walked toward the participant. This assistant was very tall and muscular and his instructions were to walk down the middle of the hall, forcing the participant to dodge out of his way. The dependent variable was how far away the participant was when he finally swerved out of the assistant's way. The investigators thought that the insulted Southerners would be put into such an aggressive mood that they would play "chicken" with the assistant, waiting until the last moment to swerve aside. And indeed they did. Northerners, whether insulted or not, swerved aside at a distance of about 5 feet (1.4 meters) from the assistant. Southerners, who are known for their politeness, stood aside at around 9 feet (2.75 meters) if not insulted, but pushed ahead until 3 feet away (less than 1 meter) if they had been insulted.

This study was not an experiment in the full sense. Only one of the independent variables was created by random assignment—namely, whether the participant was insulted or not. The other independent variable was status as a Southerner or Northerner. Thus, part of the study was correlational. The basic finding was that something about Southernness predisposes college men to respond aggressively to insults, but the study doesn't indicate what the causally relevant aspect of Southernness is.

In many cases, however, experimental research can establish a causal relationship between two variables. Recall from Chapter 1 the study in which Darley and Batson (1973) found that seminary students in a hurry were less likely to offer aid to a victim. In that experiment, the main independent variable was whether or not the student was in a hurry, and the dependent variable was whether or not the student stopped to help the victim. The seminary students were randomly assigned to either the "late" condition or the control ("not late") condition. This random assignment ensured that participants in the two conditions were, on average, the same kind of people, and, in so doing, minimizes the chance that any hidden third variable is responsible for the obtained results. In this case, random assignment ensures that it was something related to being late that caused such a large proportion of seminarians in the late condition to fail to help the apparent victim.

Although experimental research can provide answers to questions about causality that are left unclear by purely correlational research, experiments are not without their limits. One limit, alluded to earlier, is that sometimes an experiment is simply not possible or wouldn't be ethical to conduct. We wouldn't want to assign 10-year-old children to watch lots of violent TV over a long period of time, for example. And we couldn't randomly assign some people to be married and others to remain single. Nonetheless, causality can sometimes be established in important domains like these. One way to get closer to establishing causality in such situations is by taking advantage of natural experiments. In a **natural experiment**, events occur that the investigator believes to have causal implications for some outcome. For example, we might measure people's happiness before and after they get married. It turns out that people are happier after marriage than they were before (Argyle, 1999). These findings are hardly decisive, but they strongly suggest that married people are happier *because* they are married—not that they are married because they are cheerful.

Another example of a natural experiment occurred when television was first introduced in the United States. It didn't come to all regions of the country at the same time; some communities had TV and others didn't. Whether or not a community received television was not determined by the community itself (and hence any results could not be attributed to self-selection). This natural experiment therefore allowed investigators to draw relatively strong conclusions about the impact of TV on people's habits and opinions.

natural experiment A naturally occurring event or phenomenon having somewhat different conditions that can be compared with almost as much rigor as in experiments where the investigator manipulates the conditions.

← LOOKING BACK

Social psychologists study phenomena by observational methods, archival research involving records of various kinds, and surveys in which people are asked questions. The validity of surveys typically depends on using respondents who are randomly sampled from the population they represent. Correlational research, in which the investigator establishes whether there is a relationship between two variables, suffers from the problem that individuals being studied have "chosen" their level on each variable rather than being assigned a level by the investigator. Experimental research manipulates an independent variable and observes the effects of the manipulation on a dependent variable.

"Science walks forward on two feet, namely theory and experiment. Sometimes it is one foot which is put forward first, sometimes the other, but continuous progress is only made by the use of both."
—ROBERT MILLIKAN,
NOBEL PRIZE IN PHYSICS, 1946

The Criteria of Sound Research

All research is not created equal. Just because someone has conducted a study doesn't mean you should accept the results as fact. What sets a well-designed study apart from a flawed one? In an experiment, random assignment and a carefully designed control group can go a long way toward eliminating potential problems. But in designing any study, researchers also need to consider carefully certain types of validity and reliability, as well as the statistical significance of their findings.

External Validity in Experiments

The previous section pointed out the weaknesses of correlational research, but experimental studies can have weaknesses, too. Sometimes experiments can be so removed from everyday life that it can be hard to know how to interpret them (Aronson, Ellsworth, Carlsmith, & Gonzalez, 1990). **External validity** is an indication of how well the results of a study pertain to contexts outside the conditions of the laboratory. When researchers are unable to generalize the results to real-life situations, there is poor external validity. When the purpose of the research is to be directly relevant to events in the outside world, external validity is critical. For example, if researchers are investigating whether watching violence on TV makes children more aggressive, the TV programs the children see in the study should resemble real TV shows, and the types of aggressive behavior examined should be behavior that children might actually engage in.

Poor external validity isn't always a problem. Milgram's study of obedience (discussed in Chapters 1 and 9) had poor external validity in the sense that few people in our society are ever placed in a situation where an authority figure commands them to harm another person. Nevertheless, Milgram's study illuminates why such things have happened in the world and will likely happen again.

As in Milgram's study, researchers sometimes deliberately strip down a situation to its bare essentials to make a theoretical point that would be hard to make in real-world circumstances. To find out how familiarity with a stimulus affects its attractiveness, Robert Zajonc (1968) and his colleagues showed fictitious Turkish words and fake Chinese characters to Americans, presenting some of them many times and some of them only a few times (**Figure 2.3**). The more times participants saw a given stimulus, the more they thought the stimulus referred to something good. The experiment had poor external validity because the experimental situation was unlike something anyone would ever encounter in real life. But the simplicity of the situation and the initial unfamiliarity of the foreign words and characters ensured that it was the sheer number of repetitions of the words that affected their attractiveness and not something else about the stimuli. In research like Zajonc's, where the purpose is to clarify a general idea or theory, external validity is not essential.

One of the best ways to ensure external validity is to conduct a field experiment. Similar conceptually to a laboratory experiment, a **field experiment** takes place in the real world, usually with participants who are unaware they are involved in a research study at all. An example would be an experiment in which researchers study the reactions of people who are asked to give up their seats on an uncrowded bus or train.

external validity How well the results of a study generalize to contexts outside the conditions of the laboratory.

field experiment An experiment conducted in the real world (not a lab), usually with participants who are not aware they are in a study of any kind.

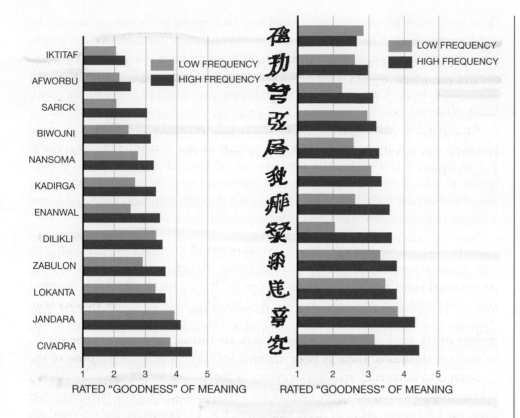

FIGURE 2.3
EXTERNAL VALIDITY

In this study, researchers presented fictitious Turkish words and made-up Chinese characters to participants a varying number of times. After the presentation, the participants were asked to guess how positive the meaning was for each word or character. Words and characters that were presented many times were more likely to be regarded as referring to something positive. Although this study has poor external validity because nobody in real life would be in such a situation, it was a good test of the hypothesis that mere familiarity with a stimulus makes it more attractive.

Source: Adapted from Zajonc, 1968.

In the field experiment described at the beginning of this chapter, Cohen and Nisbett (1997) examined the reactions of business owners to a letter allegedly written by a job applicant who had been convicted of a felony. The felony in question was either a motor vehicle theft or, in the version you read, a homicide in the context of a love triangle. The dependent variable was the degree of responsiveness to the applicant's letter, ranging from no response at all to sending an encouraging letter and an application form. Southern retailers were much more encouraging than Northern retailers of the man convicted of homicide. The experiment provides, in a field setting, evidence that Southern norms concerning violence in response to an insult are more accepting than Northern norms. Because there was no difference in the reactions of Southerners and Northerners to the letter that mentioned a theft, we know that Southerners are not simply more forgiving of crimes generally. Thus, the theft letter constitutes a control condition in this field experiment. And because the participants were potential employers who believed they were responding to a real applicant, the experiment's external validity is much higher than it would be if the participants had been asked to assess fictional job applicants in a laboratory setting.

Internal Validity in Experiments

Whatever the goal of an experiment, internal validity is essential. **Internal validity** refers to the likelihood that only the manipulated variable—and no other external influence—could have produced the results. The experimental situation is held constant in all other respects, and participants in the various experimental conditions don't differ at all, on average, before they come to the laboratory. You'll remember the easy way to avoid the possibility that participants will differ

internal validity In experimental research, confidence that only the manipulated variable could have produced the results.

from each other in some unanticipated way that might influence the results: by randomly assigning them to the various experimental conditions—for example, by flipping a coin to determine the condition for each participant. Random assignment ensures that the participants in one condition will not be different, on average, from those in the other conditions—and this is essential for establishing internal validity.

An experiment lacks internal validity when there is a third variable that could plausibly account for any observed difference between the different conditions. For example, if Darley and Batson asked their hurried and unhurried participants to take different routes to where they were to deliver their talks on the Good Samaritan, it could be something about the different routes they took, not whether they were in a hurry, that was responsible for their results.

Internal validity also requires that the experimental setup seem realistic and plausible to the participants. If participants don't believe what the experimenter tells them or if they don't understand something crucial about the instructions or the nature of the task they are to perform, then internal validity will be lacking and the experimenter can have no confidence in the results. In such cases, participants aren't responding to the independent variable as conceptualized by the experimenter, but to something else entirely.

Researchers can help ensure that their experimental design meets the criteria for internal validity by interviewing participants who have served in pilot studies, or preliminary versions of the experiment. Pilot study participants are generally told the purpose of the experiment and what the investigators expected to find. Pilot participants can often provide useful information about how well the experiment is designed when they are brought in as consultants, so to speak, in the debriefing.

Reliability and Validity of Tests and Measures

Reliability refers to the degree to which a measure gives consistent results on repeated occasions or the degree to which two measuring instruments (such as human observers) yield the same or very similar results. If you take an IQ test twice, do you get roughly the same score (test-retest reliability)? Do two observers agree in how they rate the charisma of a world leader or the kindness or a classmate (inter-rater reliability)? Reliability is typically measured by correlations between 0 and 1. As a rule of thumb, ability tests such as IQ tests are expected to have test-retest reliability correlations of about .8 or higher. Personality tests, such as verbal measures of extraversion, are expected to have that level of reliability or somewhat lower. People's degree of agreement about the kindness or charisma of another person would likely show a correlation of at least .5.

Measurement validity refers to the correlation between a measure and some outcome the measure is supposed to predict. For example, IQ test validity is measured by correlating IQ scores with grades in school and with performance in jobs. If IQ scores predict behavior that requires intelligence, we can safely infer that the test is a valid measure of intelligence. Validity coefficients, as they are called, typically do not exceed .5. Personality tests rarely correlate with behavior in a given situation more than about .3. This result is surprising to most people, who expect that a measure of extraversion should predict quite well a person's behavior at a party, and a measure of aggression should predict quite well a person's behavior in a hockey game.

"Inquiry is fatal to certainty."
—WILL DURANT, PHILOSOPHER

reliability The degree to which the particular way researchers measure a given variable is likely to yield consistent results.

measurement validity The correlation between a measure and some outcome the measure is supposed to predict.

BOX 2.3 ▶ FOCUS ON CRITICAL THINKING

Regression to the Mean

An important and frequently misunderstood statistical regularity is known as "regression to the mean": the tendency for extreme scores on one variable to be followed by, or to accompany, less extreme scores on another. This is a completely general point. Extreme scores on any variable are farther away from the mean of a distribution of scores, and scores close to the mean of nearly all distributions are more common than extreme scores farther from the mean. This pattern is visible in **Figure 2.4**, which shows a *normal distribution*, sometimes called a bell curve. Many types of variables are distributed in this fashion: IQ, physical height, income level, annual corn yield in Iowa, number of mistakes per day in the manufacturing of glass jars. These variables are distributed in that way because every score has a chance component: the luck of the genetic draw, the particular weather conditions last year in Iowa. Scores get to be extreme because of particular patterns of chance events that are rare and unlikely to be repeated. Extremely tall fathers have sons who are typically closer to the mean, and extremely tall sons, in turn, tend to have fathers who are closer to the mean. The rookie of the year in baseball typically doesn't do as well his second year. Your unhappiest day is likely to be followed by one that's not so unhappy. When you go to the doctor with a bad cold, you'll likely get better even if all the doctor does is say "hello." The reason is that you probably went when your symptoms were close to their peak intensity and therefore had no place to go except down—in other words, back toward the mean of your health distribution. (This isn't true, of course, for progressive diseases such as arthritis or cardiovascular problems.)

An interesting application of the concept of regression to the mean was noted by Daniel Kahneman in his attempt to improve the training of Israeli pilots (Kahneman & Tversky. 1973b). Kahneman told the instructors that a general principle of learning is that people benefit more from positive feedback, which informs them about what they're doing right, than they do from negative feedback. The instructors insisted that the principle didn't apply to pilot training: when they praised an unusually good maneuver, the novice pilot typically performed worse the next time around. Moreover, if they shouted at the pilot for a particularly bad performance, the pilot nearly always performed better the next time around. But of course, the instructor could say nothing at all and get the same results simply due to regression to the mean: a particularly good performance would typically be worse the next time a maneuver was tried, and a particularly bad performance would typically be better the next time around. Once they understood this idea, the instructors got better results, and novice pilots had a more pleasant training experience.

Regression to the mean, at its core, is probabilistic. The reason the rookie of the year did so well is that the stars aligned just right for him. He was in perfect health and had no injuries. There were no family or girlfriend problems, and his team had just gotten the best coach in the league. The odds are against such a terrific pattern the next year.

Regression to the mean is an extremely important concept to have in your critical thinking toolbox. Once you have it firmly in mind, you'll see it crop up constantly as you observe and think about human behavior and about all kinds of other events having a chance component. Before jumping to conclusions about a pattern that might seem meaningful, ask yourself, "Might this just be another example of regression to the mean?"

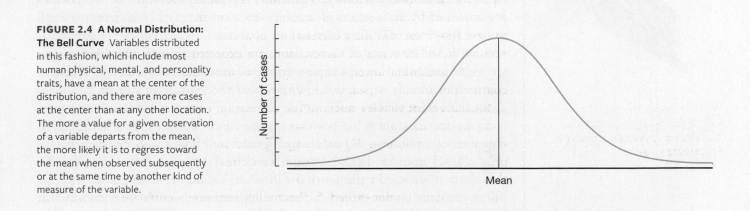

FIGURE 2.4 A Normal Distribution: The Bell Curve Variables distributed in this fashion, which include most human physical, mental, and personality traits, have a mean at the center of the distribution, and there are more cases at the center than at any other location. The more a value for a given observation of a variable departs from the mean, the more likely it is to regress toward the mean when observed subsequently or at the same time by another kind of measure of the variable.

Statistical Significance

When researchers obtain an empirical result—such as observing a correlation between two variables or finding that some independent variable affects a dependent variable in an experiment—they can test the relationship's statistical significance. **Statistical significance** is a measure of the probability that a given result could have occurred by chance alone. By convention, a finding achieves statistical significance if the probability of obtaining that finding by chance is less than 1 in 20, or .05, though the required probability can vary. Statistical significance is primarily determined by two factors: (1) the size of the difference between groups in an experiment or the size of a relationship between variables in a correlational study and (2) the number of cases on which the finding is based. The larger the difference or relationship and the larger the number of cases, the greater the statistical significance. All the findings reported in this book are statistically significant (though not all are based on large effects). There are many nuances to determining whether a finding is statistically significant, nuances you can learn more about in a statistics course.

Replication

One of the ways in which science is different from other modes of inquiry is the importance placed on replication. **Replication** involves the reproduction of research results by the original investigator or by someone else. If a result is genuine or valid, it should be possible for scientists to replicate it.

Some results do not replicate: attempts to duplicate the procedures of the study don't succeed in producing the same results, calling the results into question. Sometimes the original investigator can show that the replication attempt was not carried out correctly, and the original investigator (or someone else) may show that the original result is again found when the study is done properly. Sometimes, it's just by chance that a replication attempt fails: every result, including an attempted replication, has a certain probability of being an error. Other times, the replication attempt fails because the original result itself was a fluke or the methods that produced it were not precise or sound. And sometimes (thankfully, very rarely) a reported result is the product of outright fraud, where an investigator simply makes up samples of data to support a favored hypothesis.

Scientific controversy is often generated by failures to replicate (sometimes accompanied by accusations of incompetence on the part of different investigators). These debates usually result in consensus about whether a particular finding should be accepted or not. In this way, science is self-correcting. Errors are made and initial interpretations may be faulty, but over time the scientific community usually manages to winnow out the claims we can be confident about from those that are not as solid.

In recent years, there has been increasing concern that many scientific findings do not replicate—in fields ranging from cell biology to neuroscience to drug efficacy research. In 2015, Brian Nosek and dozens of other psychologists published an article in the journal *Science* reporting on attempts to replicate 100 psychology studies (Open Science Collaboration, 2015). They found that depending on the criterion used, only 36–47 percent of the original studies were successfully replicated.

As you can imagine, the article received a great deal of press coverage and was greeted with alarm and dismay by psychologists. The findings received heavy

statistical significance A measure of the probability that a given result could have occurred by chance.

replication Reproduction of research results by the original investigator or by someone else.

Threats to Internal Validity

An investigator wants to be sure, after a study is run, that any observed difference in the dependent variable was caused by the manipulated difference in the independent variable. That can only happen when the design of the experiment is such that the study has high **internal validity**. Various shortcomings of experimental design can threaten internal validity and thereby call into question whether any variation in the dependent variable is in fact due to variation in the independent variable—whether the conclusion the investigator would like to draw is valid.

For Critical Thinking

1. Debriefing participants at the end of a study can be a useful way for researchers to determine whether the study might suffer from which of the five threats to internal validity described here?

2. Members of two student organizations study a word list while listening to music. The psychology honor society studies while classical music is played, and the running club while techno music is played. The researcher then compares the two groups' performance on a memory test. What are the threats to internal validity in this study? What steps could have been taken to eliminate them?

Common Threats to Internal Validity

Selection bias
Assignment to conditions is not random but systematic, meaning that different kinds of people are in the different conditions and that may be the reason for the observed difference, not the manipulated variable itself.

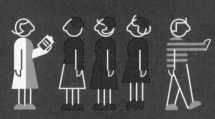

Differential attrition
If many more people "drop out" from one condition than another, the people who stay in the more taxing or upsetting condition are likely to be different from those in the other condition, thus undermining random assignment.

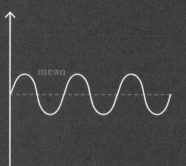

Regression to the mean
If people are in a study because they're extreme on the variable of interest, they are likely to become less extreme even if nothing is done. Therefore, a "treatment" can seem effective even when it is of no value. To combat this problem, the subjects in the treatment and control conditions should be equally extreme (by means of random assignment).

Experimenter/ rater bias
If the dependent measure has an element of subjectivity and the rater knows the hypothesis or what condition the subject or object of judgment was in, the rater may make biased judgments. The most common solution is to make the rater "blind."

Expectancy/ Hawthorne effects
Participants can be biased by their expectations about the purpose of the experiment and act in a way that confirms them. The most common solution is to make the experiment "double blind," so that neither the raters nor the participants know what the study is designed to test and/or what condition the participant is in.

1. It could be that parents try to control the size of portions their children eat if the children are already overweight. If so, the direction of causation is the reverse of that hypothesized by *TIME Magazine*. It could also be the case that families with more stress in their lives have more controlling parents and more overweight children, but there is no causal connection between the two. Instead, a third variable, associated with stress, accounts for the correlation.

2. It could be that wealthier countries have better education systems and hence produce people who get higher IQ scores. In that case, wealth causes intelligence, rather than the other way around. In fact, we have good reason to believe that the correlation between IQ and wealth holds because of causality working in both directions: greater intelligence leads to greater wealth, and greater wealth leads to greater intelligence (in part through better educational systems).

3. It could be that healthier people engage in more social activities of all kinds, including going to church. If so, the direction of causation runs opposite to the one implied. Or it could be that good social adjustment—a third variable—causes people both to engage in more social activities and to be healthier.

4. It could be that people who are depressed are less likely to do anything fun, like getting a pet. If so, the direction of causation is opposite to the one implied. (But in fact, giving a pet to a depressed person does improve the person's mood.)

open science Practices such as sharing data and research materials with anyone in the broader scientific community in an effort to increase the integrity and replicability of scientific research.

criticism from some quarters (Gilbert, King, Pettigrew, & Wilson, 2016). The most prominent concern was that many of the attempted replications utilized procedures that differed substantially from the original studies and thus weren't replications at all. For example, a study asking Israelis to imagine the consequences of military service was "replicated" by asking Americans to imagine the consequences of a honeymoon (Gilbert, King, Pettigrew, & Wilson, 2016). A study that looked at Americans' attitudes toward African-Americans was repeated, but with Italian respondents, not Americans. In cases where the original authors endorsed the methods used by replicators, the rate of successful replication was four times greater than for studies whose original authors did not endorse the methods used in the replication.

Other systematic efforts to reproduce the results of findings reported in behavioral science journals have yielded higher replication rates, on the order of 78–85 percent (Camerer et al., 2016; Klein et al., 2014). These rates may not be high enough for comfort, though they are higher than what is found in some other sciences. Failures to replicate are more common at the frontier of any field, as investigators try to push the envelope of what is known and there is less guidance from established theory and preexisting findings. Failures to replicate are less common for mainstream research that is more anchored in existing theory and findings.

Note that in social psychology, some failures to replicate are nearly inevitable because of the very nature of the subject matter. For example, research conducted in the early part of this century found that exposing people to images of the American flag made them more politically conservative (Carter, Ferguson, & Hassin, 2011). More recent studies have failed to find an effect of "priming" people with the flag (Klein et al., 2014). When the initial studies were conducted, Republican George W. Bush was in the White House, a president and an administration marked by the tragic events of 9/11 and an aggressive military response to those events. But the political atmosphere changed after Barack Obama was elected president in 2008, and this may have changed the associations many people had to the U.S. flag, altering the very psychology that led to the original reported effects.

To be sure, some failures to replicate are due to the shoddy work by the original investigators, which led to a reported result that was never, in fact, true or valid. In those cases, investigators who report failed attempts to replicate do a great service to everyone by setting the record straight. Social psychologists' concerns about recent failures to replicate a number of high-profile findings has led to changes in research practices that are designed to reduce the number of reports of invalid "findings." Foremost among these changes has been an increase in the sample sizes generally used in research. With small sample sizes, it's easier to obtain apparently significant results that are, in fact, just "flukes." Another remedy has been the insistence that investigators report the results of all measures and all experimental conditions run in their studies. If an investigator obtains statistically significant results on one measure, but not on several other measures that, theoretically, should yield similar results, there's reason to worry that the one significant result may be a fluke (a "false positive" error). Having to report the results of all measures rather than highlighting a subset of measures serves as a safeguard against such errors. More generally, adopting the practice of **open science** whereby investigators are encouraged or required to share their methods and data with any interested party makes it easier to check whether reported findings hold up to closer scrutiny and to conduct replications that are most informative.

In this textbook, we have tried to be scrupulous about noting when the evidence about a given point is mixed, usually due to replication failures or to the existence of similar studies that produced a different result. There are no guarantees in any science. Social psychology is an ever-evolving field. It's a safe bet that some of the findings reported in this textbook (not a large number, we suspect) will turn out to be mistaken or misleading.

← LOOKING BACK

External validity refers to how well the results of a study generalize to contexts outside the laboratory. Internal validity refers to the extent to which investigators can know that only the manipulated variable could have produced the results. Reliability refers to the degree to which different measuring instruments or the same instrument at different times produces the same values for a given variable. Measurement validity refers to the extent to which a measure predicts outcomes that it is supposed to measure. Statistical significance is a measure of the probability that a result could have occurred by chance. Replication of results increases our confidence in them.

Ethical Concerns in Social Psychology Research

Most people would want to conduct research geared to changing people's attitudes only if they believed the direction of change was for the better. We wouldn't support research that might have the effect of encouraging people to engage in unhealthy or dangerous behaviors. For this reason, research conducted at universities that has the potential for harm has to be approved by an **institutional review board (IRB)**, a committee that examines research proposals and makes judgments about their ethical appropriateness. An IRB includes at least one scientist, one nonscientist, and one person who is not affiliated with the institution. If some aspect of the study's procedures is deemed overly harmful, that procedure must be changed before the research can be approved. Prior to 2018, all psychological research conducted with federal funds had to be submitted to an IRB. Now an investigator need not be required by their institution's IRB to obtain prior approval if a study involves only a manifestly "benign intervention," such as ordinary interviews and surveys, ability and personality tests, economic games, decision making, and research on conformity to group norms.

Research may be allowed even if it makes people uncomfortable or embarrassed or causes physical pain, as long as the research is deemed sufficiently likely to yield scientific information of significant value and the discomfort or harm to the participants is not too great. For example, the Milgram studies on obedience (1963, 1974) were conducted before IRB committees existed. Today, Milgram's proposal would be thoroughly examined by an IRB, and it's not clear whether it would be approved. On the one hand, there is no question that Milgram's research made some participants extremely uncomfortable; their psychological distress was manifest to observers. On the other hand, many (if not most) people would consider the knowledge gained to be enormous. It's impossible to think

5. It could be that states that are poorer are more likely to have higher homicide rates, and states that are poorer are more likely to have abstinence-only sex education. Indeed, both are true. So there may be no causal connection at all between sex education and homicide. Rather, a third variable, such as poverty or something associated with it, may be causally linked to both, thereby accounting for the correlation.

6. It could be that better physical health—a third variable—helps people to be smarter and helps sperm to be of better quality. Or some other factor could be associated with both intelligence and sperm quality, such as drug or alcohol use. So there might be no causal connection between intelligence and sperm quality.

7. It could be that people who take any kind of drug are more sensation seeking than other people and therefore engage in many kinds of stimulating behavior that are against the law. Smoking marijuana may not cause cocaine use, and cocaine use may not cause marijuana use. Rather, some third factor, such as sensation seeking, may influence both.

institutional review board (IRB) A committee that examines research proposals and makes judgments about the ethical appropriateness of the research.

about Nazi Germany the same way after learning the results of the Milgram studies. We can no longer blithely assume that ordinary, decent people would refuse to obey commands that are patently harmful. Different IRBs would undoubtedly reach different conclusions about the admissibility of the Milgram experiments today. What do you think? Would you permit research like Milgram's to be conducted?

Informed consent—the participant's agreement to participate after learning about all relevant aspects of the procedure—is required for that small fraction of social psychology research that poses the possibility of significant harm. However, for certain types of studies, known as **deception research**, it's not possible to obtain informed consent from the participants. Darley and Batson (1973) couldn't have told their seminary participants that the stated reason for their need to hurry was bogus and the apparent victim was actually a confederate who was merely pretending to be hurt as part of the experiment. Informed consent would have defeated the purpose of the study. Even in deception research, moreover, participants are generally told about the goals of the research project afterward, during **debriefing**. The debriefing session serves an important educational purpose: it informs participants about the broad questions being addressed, the specific hypotheses being tested, and why the results might have social value. Debriefing can also be helpful to the investigators by letting them know whether, say, the procedures are stressful or upsetting to the participants and need to be changed, or whether participants are interpreting the stimuli used in the experiment as the investigator intended and whether they find the procedures meaningful.

When asked their opinion about what they were put through, deceived participants generally understand the reasons and often say they learned more, and enjoyed the study more, than subjects who were not deceived or made uncomfortable (Smith & Richardson, 1983). For example, participants in the insult condition of the Cohen study actually reported that they learned more and had a better time than participants in the control condition.

When participants have been deceived or made uncomfortable, experimenters owe them a full accounting of what was done, what aspects of the procedure involved deception, why they were made uncomfortable, what the experiment was intended to examine, and what the potential value to society the research might provide.

← LOOKING BACK

Psychology research that poses a significant possibility of harm is submitted to an institutional review board. Minor harm to participants is sometimes allowed when the potential gain in knowledge is considered great enough.

Basic and Applied Science

The practice of scientific research is of two broad types: basic and applied. **Basic science** (or basic research) is concerned with trying to understand some phenomenon in its own right, rather than using a finding to solve a particular real-world

---

informed consent A person's signed agreement to participate in a procedure or research study after learning all of its relevant aspects.

deception research Research in which the participants are misled about the purpose of the research or the meaning of something that is done to them.

debriefing In preliminary versions of an experiment, asking participants directly if they understood the instructions, found the setup to be reasonable, and so on. In later versions, debriefing is used to educate participants about the questions being studied.

basic science Science or research concerned with trying to understand some phenomenon in its own right, with a view toward using that understanding to build valid theories about the nature of some aspect of the world.

problem. Basic scientific studies are conducted with a view toward using the findings to build valid theories about the nature of some aspect of the world. For example, social psychologists investigating people's obedience to an authority figure in the laboratory are doing basic science, attempting to understand the nature of obedience and the factors that influence it. They're not trying to find ways to make people less obedient to dubious authorities, though they may hope their research is relevant to such real-world problems.

Applied science (or applied research) is concerned with solving a real-world problem of importance. An example of applied research in social psychology would be a study of how to make preteens less susceptible to cigarette advertising. (One way is to make them aware of the motives of tobacco companies and the companies' cynical desire to get teens to do something that is not in their best interest.)

There is a two-way relationship between basic and applied research. Basic research can give rise to theories that can lead to **interventions**, or efforts to change certain behaviors. For example, social psychologist Carol Dweck and her colleagues found that people who believe that intelligence is a matter of hard work study harder in school and get better grades than people who believe that intelligence is a matter of genes—you're either intelligent or not, and you can't do much to change it (Dweck, Chiu, & Hong, 1995). Her basic research on beliefs about intelligence on school performance prompted her to design an intervention with minority junior high students. She told some of them that their intelligence was under their control and gave them information about how working on school subjects actually changes the physical nature of the brain (Blackwell, Trzesniewski, & Dweck, 2007; Henderson & Dweck, 1990). Those students worked harder and got better grades than students who were not given such information.

The direction of influence can also go the other way: applied research can produce results that feed back into basic science. For example, applied studies during World War II on how to produce effective propaganda led to an extensive program of basic research on attitude change. That program, in turn, gave rise to theories of attitude change and social influence that continue to inform basic science and to generate new techniques of changing attitudes in applied, real-world contexts.

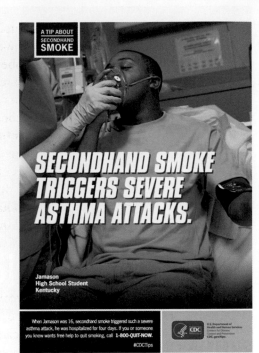

A TIP ABOUT
SECONDHAND
SMOKE

SECONDHAND SMOKE TRIGGERS SEVERE ASTHMA ATTACKS.

Jamason
High School Student
Kentucky

When Jamason was 16, secondhand smoke triggered such a severe asthma attack, he was hospitalized for four days. If you or someone you know wants free help to quit smoking, call **1-800-QUIT-NOW**.

#CDCTips

CDC   U.S. Department of Health and Human Services Centers for Disease Control and Prevention CDC.gov/tips

APPLIED RESEARCH
Social psychology research can be undertaken to solve real-world, applied problems, such as how to persuade people not to smoke.

applied science Science or research concerned with solving important real-world problems.

intervention An effort to change a person's behavior.

← **LOOKING BACK**

Basic science attempts to discover fundamental principles; applied science attempts to solve real-world problems. There is an intimate relationship between the two: basic science can reveal ways to solve real-world problems, and applied science aimed at solving real-world problems can give rise to the search for basic principles that explain why the solutions work.

Chapter Review

SUMMARY

The Value of Social Psychology Research

- Research by social psychologists teaches people how to interpret and predict the outcomes of various social experiences. Study results and findings help people understand their own behavior and that of others.

How Social Psychologists Test Ideas

- Social psychologists often use *participant observation*, placing themselves in real situations to understand a social phenomenon better and helping them plan research that will test the hypotheses developed in observational settings.
- Social psychologists use *archives* for information that helps them understand social phenomena; such records include census reports, police records, newspaper accounts, and historical and ethnographic records.
- *Surveys* ask people questions. *Random sampling* is essential for accurately describing the attitudes or behavior of a particular population, such as students at a certain university, residents of a town, or the population of a country as a whole.
- *Correlational research* examines relationships between variables, such as between age and support for welfare reform. Correlations can vary in strength from –1 to +1.
- The problem of *self-selection* in correlational research occurs when the investigator is unable to choose the level of any variable for participants. Consequently, it's impossible to know if something associated with one of the measured variables is causing the correlation between two variables or if one of the variables is causing the other.

- In *experimental research*, the investigator manipulates different levels of the *independent variable* (the variable about which a prediction is made) and measures the effect of different levels on the *dependent variable*.

The Criteria of Sound Research

- *External validity* refers to how closely the experimental setup resembles real-life situations. The greater the external validity, the more it is possible to generalize from the results obtained to real-life settings.
- *Field experiments* test hypotheses experimentally in real-life situations rather than in the laboratory. Field experiments automatically have external validity.
- *Internal validity* refers to the likelihood that only the manipulated variable accounts for the results, rather than some extraneous factor such as participants' failure to understand instructions.
- When *debriefing* study participants, investigators may ask pretest participants to assess various aspects of the experiment to make sure that the experiment is perceived as intended. Debriefing also refers to the investigator's explanation of the purpose of the experiment after the study is over.
- *Reliability* refers to the extent to which participants receive the same score when tested with a conceptually similar instrument or when tested at different times.
- *Measurement validity* is the degree to which some measure predicts what it is supposed to, such as the degree to which an IQ test predicts school grades.
- *Statistical significance* is a measure of the probability that a result could have occurred by chance.
- *Replication* involves repeating a study to determine whether the findings can be duplicated.

Ethical Concerns in Social Psychology Research

- *Institutional review boards* are committees that review research procedures to make sure that the privacy and safety of participants are protected.
- *Informed consent* refers to the willingness of participants to take part in a study based on information presented to them before the study begins, including the procedures they will undergo and any possible risks. Informed consent is not always possible, as when an experiment involves deception, in which participants are misled about the purposes of a study.

Basic and Applied Science

- *Basic science* is research conducted for the purpose of understanding phenomena in their own right. *Applied science* is research intended to solve real-world problems.

THINK ABOUT IT

1. After reading this chapter, do you think it's important for students of social psychology to have a basic understanding of research methods? Why or why not?

2. Recall from Chapter 1 the experiment on nonconscious processing in which participants read a persuasive message in a room with either a fishy smell, an unpleasant smell that was not fishy, or no distinctive smell (Lee & Schwartz, 2012). The researchers measured the degree to which each participant was persuaded by the message and discovered that participants were least likely to be persuaded in the presence of a fishy smell (there was something "fishy" about the message). In this experiment, what was the independent variable? What was the dependent variable?

3. Suppose a group of researchers hypothesized that finding your romantic partner physically attractive contributes to feelings of satisfaction in your relationship. To evaluate this hypothesis, the researchers asked 100 participants to complete a survey that included questions assessing their current relationship satisfaction, as well as ratings of how physically attractive they believed their partner to be. The researchers found that the more physically attractive participants rated their partners, the more satisfied they tended to be in their relationship. In this fictitious study, did the researchers employ a correlational or an experimental design? How do you know?

4. Consider the hypothetical study in question 3 again. The researchers found a relationship between perceptions of partner physical attractiveness and relationship satisfaction. With these data, can the researchers conclude that perceiving your partner as physically attractive causes you to become more satisfied in your relationship? Are there other potential explanations for these findings?

5. In Chapter 3, you will learn about research on the self, including self-esteem. Suppose the scatterplot below displays the relationship between self-esteem and academic success. How might you interpret this graph? Is the correlation between these two variables positive or negative? Try guessing the correlation coefficient.

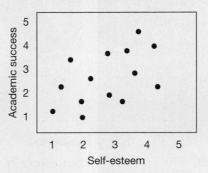

6. In this textbook, you will learn about various studies evaluating social psychological phenomena using functional magnetic resonance imaging (fMRI), which measures activation in the brain while the participant lies immobile in a large metal tube. For example, researchers may measure brain activation while participants experience a social rejection or may look at how brain activation during a stressful experience is affected if a close friend holds the participant's hand. How would you characterize the external validity of such research?

The answer guidelines for the think about it questions can be found at the back of the book . . . ☞

ONLINE STUDY MATERIALS

Want to earn a better grade on your test?

Go to **INQUIZITIVE** to learn and review this chapter's content, with personalized feedback along the way.

Why would a famous athlete need to engage in self-protective behaviors?

How might hardships faced during childhood shape one's social self in adulthood?

Do children who play sports have higher self-esteem than those who do not?

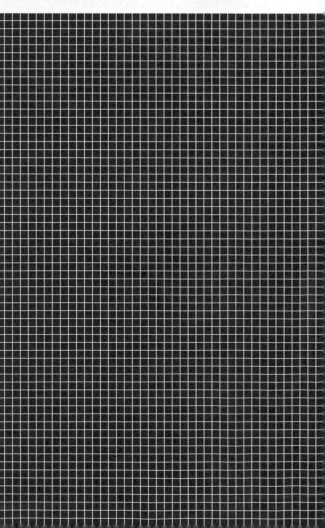

The Social Self

ON MARCH 28, 1986, IN NEW YORK CITY, Cynthia and Joseph Germanotta welcomed their first daughter, Stefani Joanne Angelina Germanotta, into the world. It didn't take long for Cynthia and Joe to discover that Stefani was artistically gifted. Stefani was playing the piano by ear by the age of 4, and soon she was also singing, songwriting, and acting. By her early teens, Stefani had a voice teacher and took acting lessons while starring in local plays. But her creativity and talents weren't always celebrated. What was seen as gifted to some was seen as odd and eccentric, even "freakish," to many of her peers, leaving Stefani to struggle with bullying, ostracism, and deep feelings of insecurity through much of her adolescence and early adulthood.

Nonetheless, Stefani endured these challenges and, by early 2008, at the age of 22, she released her debut album, *The Fame*, and the person now known worldwide as Lady Gaga was born. Lady Gaga has achieved international fame as a singing, songwriting, and performing powerhouse. Indeed, she is one of the best-selling musical artists of all time and has won countless awards for her musical achievements, including 6 Grammy Awards and 13 MTV Video Music Awards.

Yet in the eyes of many people, and undoubtedly herself, Lady Gaga is far more than a singer and performer. She is a Golden Globe–winning actress, a practicing Christian, and a passionate advocate for LGBT rights. She is a widely photographed and lauded fashion icon. She is a rape survivor. She's someone who has battled anorexia, bulimia, and depression. She is a philanthropist, providing support for many causes, such as relief efforts after the 2010 Haiti earthquake and Hurricane Sandy in 2012. She is the founder of an influential nonprofit organization, the

Lady Gaga—pictured here receiving an award for her musical accomplishments, showing her unique fashion sense, and campaigning for Hillary Clinton during the 2016 presidential race—has many different selves.

"A man has as many social selves as there are individuals who recognize him. As many different social selves as there are distinct groups about whose opinions he cares."
—WILLIAM JAMES

Born This Way Foundation, that advocates youth empowerment and anti-bullying, among other youth-related issues. The list goes on.

Lady Gaga provides a treasure trove of examples to illustrate the concept of the self in social psychology. Revealing how profoundly social the self is, she has spoken widely and openly about the ways that the social obstacles and pain she endured as a child have shaped who she is today. Her fans see her as a symbol of self-acceptance and self-confidence—what social psychologists call self-esteem. And her many personas show how, like Lady Gaga, most of us have many sides to who we are and think of ourselves in many different ways—as a hard-working student, a loyal friend, a chocolate aficionado, an awkward dancer, a romantic, a skilled procrastinator, an aspiring writer. In this chapter, we draw a portrait of the self as it is constructed, maintained, and negotiated in the social environment. ■

The Nature of the Social Self

In his book *The Principles of Psychology* (1890), William James introduced many concepts about the self that inspire research to this day. One of his most enduring contributions is reflected in the title of this chapter, "The Social Self." James coined the term *the social me* to refer to what we know about ourselves from social relationships. James's term reflects his conviction that the self is not something to be distinguished from the social world but rather is a social entity through and through. Who a person is in one social context (with soccer buddies) is often not the same as who the person is in another social environment (with a romantic partner). Recall from Chapter 1 that there are cultural differences in the self-conceptions that people hold dear. In this chapter, we explore cultural and other key social origins of the self. As James articulated over a century ago, our sense of who we are is forged in large part by our interactions with others.

The Accuracy of Self-Knowledge

Before we explore the social underpinnings of the self, it's reasonable to ask how we figure out who we are. The Ancient Greek admonition to "know thyself" implies that a major source of self-knowledge is, well, ourselves. Indeed, our self-understanding is largely a product of construal processes—our making sense of our experiences, proclivities, preferences, attributes, and so on. Researchers like Dan McAdams (2008) even argue that people weave intricate stories about themselves. If self-knowledge is based in considerable part on our construals, what does that say about the accuracy of self-knowledge? That is, if you wanted to find out who someone really is, who would you ask?

Most of us assume that the best person to ask is in fact the person we want to know about (Pronin, Kruger, Savitsky, & Ross, 2001). After all, this person has privileged access to self-relevant information, such as past experiences, not to mention current thoughts, feelings, and intentions (Epley & Dunning, 2006). Yet we're also quick to recognize that people can sometimes possess a startling lack of self-insight. Recall the research described in Chapter 1 in which Nisbett and Wilson (1977) discovered that people can readily provide explanations for their behaviors that are not in fact accurate. Someone might say that she picked her favorite nightgown because of its texture or color, when in fact she picked it out because it was the last one she saw. Even our ability to report accurately on more important decisions—such as why we chose job candidate A over job candidate B, why we like Joe better than Jack, or how we solved a particular problem—can be wide of the mark (Nisbett & Wilson, 1977).

Sometimes our lack of self-insight can be a self-protective measure: there are certain things many of us would rather not know about ourselves. But much of the time, we draw inaccurate conclusions about the self because we don't have access to certain mental processes, such as those that lead us to prefer objects we looked at last (Wilson, 2002; Wilson & Dunn, 2004). Such mental processes are nonconscious, occurring outside of our awareness, leaving us to generate alternative, plausible accounts for our preferences and behaviors instead.

Given such roadblocks, how can a person gain accurate self-knowledge? Vazire and Mehl (2008) tackled this question over a series of studies. In one study, they asked participants to rate how accurate they think people are at assessing how much they themselves perform 25 different behaviors (for example, reading, singing, watching TV). They also asked participants how accurate they think people are at predicting how often *other* people they know well perform these behaviors. For every single behavior, the participants rated the accuracy of self-predictions to be greater than the accuracy of predictions about others—in other words, there was a widespread assumption that each of us is our own best expert.

In a subsequent study, however, the same researchers again had participants report on their enactment of the 25 behaviors. They also recruited "informants"—close friends, parents, and romantic partners of the participants—to report on the participants' enactments of the behaviors. Then, over a 4-day period, with participants wearing a device that records the ambient sounds of their daily lives, Vazire and Mehl measured the actual frequency of participants' behaviors. Contrary to the assumption that we know ourselves the best, they found that the reports of close others are as accurate as our own in anticipating our actual behavior.

But there's more to the story. Interestingly, ratings made by the self and ratings made by close others *independently* predicted the self's behavior; that is, both the self and others have at least some accurate insight into who one is. But a closer inspection of the findings showed that there are certain aspects of a person that are uniquely known to the self and certain aspects that are uniquely known to others (Vazire, 2010; Vazire & Carlson, 2011). Because we have greater information than others do about our inner states (such as our thoughts and feelings), we are better judges of our internal traits (being optimistic or pessimistic, for instance). Other people, though, have better information for judging our external traits by observing our overt behavior (such as whether we are boisterous or outspoken).

Vazire and colleagues further point out that motivational forces might also be at play. As we will explore in depth later in this chapter, most people want to think highly of themselves, so when it comes to traits to which we attach a lot of value, such as creativity, other people tend to know us better than we know ourselves—because their judgments are less likely to be tainted by the desire to arrive at favorable assessments of the self.

The Organization of Self-Knowledge

Regardless of its accuracy, there's no question that most of us have an enormous pool of self-knowledge. Collectively, all this self-knowledge is stored in our memories in some fashion, and it's capable of being retrieved, elaborated on, and used as a source of information and continuity as well as comfort or dismay.

Social psychologists assume that self-knowledge is stored in memory in cognitive structures known as self-schemas. Built from past experience, **self-schemas** represent people's beliefs and feelings about themselves, both in general and in particular kinds of situations (Greenwald, 1980; Markus, 1977; Markus & Wurf, 1987). Consider the domain of conscientiousness. Each of us has a self-schema, stored in memory, representing our beliefs and feelings about how conscientious (or not) we are. These beliefs and feelings are based on our experiences in situations where conscientiousness was relevant (such as studying for exams or remembering a sibling's birthday). Like the schemas we have about personality traits, other people, situations, and objects, the schemas we have about ourselves serve as more than simple storehouses of self-knowledge. They also perform an organizing function by helping us navigate, and make sense of, all the information that bombards us every day.

In one of the earliest studies of self-schemas, Hazel Markus (1977) hypothesized that if self-schemas exist, then a person who has a self-schema in a particular domain (for example, a schema about how extraverted she is) should process information in that domain more quickly, retrieve evidence consistent with the schema more rapidly, and readily reject information that contradicts the schema. To test these hypotheses, Markus first identified participants who labeled themselves as either quite dependent or quite independent. She labeled the participants who rated themselves closer to the extremes of dependence and independence as "schematic." She also identified "aschematic" participants, those who rated themselves moderately on this dimension and for whom neither dependence nor independence was important to their self-definition.

Several weeks later, the participants rated how well a series of traits presented on a computer screen described them. The

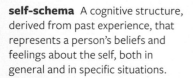

self-schema A cognitive structure, derived from past experience, that represents a person's beliefs and feelings about the self, both in general and in specific situations.

"I don't know anybody here but the hostess—and, of course, in a deeper sense, myself."

schematic participants judged schema-relevant traits as true or not true of themselves much more quickly than aschematic participants, suggesting that people are particularly attuned to information that maps onto an existing self-schema. Also, when asked to do so, the schematic participants were able to generate many more behaviors consistent with the schema-relevant traits, suggesting that past actions and experiences supporting the self-schema are abundant in memory and come readily to mind. Finally, the schematic participants were more likely to refute feedback from a personality test that contradicted their self-schemas, such as independent participants being told they were actually dependent. In short, regardless of their accuracy, self-schemas serve as a basic unit of organization for self-knowledge and influence our interpretations and judgments of ourselves and the social world.

← LOOKING BACK

The notion that the self is fundamentally social has long been recognized. As the immediate or broader social context shifts, so, too, may the nature of the self. Self-knowledge is derived in large part from construal processes, is limited by what people have access to, and can be distorted by motivational forces. Self-knowledge is stored in memory in cognitive structures known as self-schemas.

Origins of the Sense of Self

What are the building blocks of self-construals? A social psychologist would posit that a sense of self comes primarily from specific ways the social situation shapes the self. The social situation can be as concrete as the presence of a close friend or a more academically successful classmate. It can also be rather abstract and diffuse, such as norms conveyed by key institutions in one's culture or by members of an important social group, such as one's gender group.

Family and Other Socialization Agents

We learn what attitudes and behaviors are socially appropriate from parents, siblings, teachers, peers, and other "socialization agents." This process happens directly, as when parents insist that their children share, take turns, and say "thank you," and indirectly, as when teachers model appropriate behaviors. By encouraging certain behaviors and providing opportunities for particular activities, socialization agents influence the personality traits, abilities, and preferences we come to think of as our own. Imagine a woman whose Jewish parents took her to synagogue every week as a child, insisted she take Hebrew lessons, and made sure she had a Bat Mitzvah ceremony. Because of this upbringing, it's not surprising that, as an adult, being Jewish became central to this woman's sense of self. **Box 3.1** (see p. 68) provides another illustration of how family—in particular, siblings—can profoundly influence the nature of the self.

Another way that family and other socialization agents shape the self is captured by the notion that we come to know ourselves by imagining what

UPBRINGING SHAPES THE SELF
Being raised in a Jewish family undoubtedly influences how the girl in the above photo, shown at her Bat Mitzvah ceremony, defines herself.

BOX 3.1 ▶ FOCUS ON EVOLUTION

Siblings and the Social Self

What do most U.S. presidents, English and Canadian prime ministers, Oprah Winfrey, Bette Davis, and all of the actors who have portrayed James Bond (except Daniel Craig) have in common? What do Virginia Woolf, Ben Franklin, Charles Darwin, Mohandas Gandhi, Vincent Van Gogh, and Madonna have in common? The first group are firstborns. The second are later-borns. What does birth order have to do with a person's sense of self? According to Frank Sulloway (1996, 2001), a great deal. Sulloway has looked at sibling dynamics from an evolutionary perspective and arrived at a "born-to-rebel" hypothesis. Across species, Sulloway theorizes, sibling conflict, especially when resources are scarce, is frequent, widespread, and occasionally deadly. Sand sharks devour one another before birth in the oviducts of the mother until one well-fed young shark emerges. Once a blue-footed booby drops below 80 percent of its body weight, its siblings exclude it from the nest, or worse, peck it to death. Infant hyenas are born with large canine teeth, which they often use to deadly effect on their newly born siblings. Even in humans, young siblings engage in frequent conflict, up to one squabble every 5 minutes (Dunn & Munn, 1985).

Humans have evolved adaptations, or solutions, to threats to survival, and one such adaptation involves a means of resolving sibling conflict. According to the principle of diversification, siblings develop different personality traits, abilities, and preferences within the same family so that they can peacefully occupy different niches.

Throughout most of development, older siblings are larger and more powerful and often act as surrogate parents. They are invested in the status quo, which benefits them. ("Things were fine until you came along.") In contrast, younger siblings, with the "establishment" niche already occupied by their older sibling, develop in ways that make them inclined to challenge the family status quo. In a review of 196 studies of personality and birth order, Sulloway found that older siblings tend to be more assertive and dominant and more achievement oriented and conscientious. These traits are consistent with older siblings' more assertive, powerful role in the family. In contrast, younger siblings tend to be more agreeable, and they are likely to be more open to

novel ideas and experiences. This social self emerges as younger siblings learn to coexist with their more dominant older siblings (which accounts for their elevated agreeableness) and as they find imaginative ways to carve out their own niche in the world (which accounts for their increased openness to experience).

SIBLING DIFFERENCES Firstborns like Prince William (top) are often more responsible and more likely to support the status quo than younger siblings like Prince Harry, who often are more mischievous, more open to novel experiences, and more likely to rebel against authority.

---

reflected self-appraisal A belief about what others think of one's self.

others think of us. The sociologist Charles H. Cooley (1902) coined the phrase "looking-glass self" to refer to the idea that other people's reactions to us—their approval or disapproval—serve as a mirror of sorts. That is, self-knowledge is derived in part from **reflected self-appraisals**, our beliefs about others' reactions to us. Throughout our lives, we experience overt or subtle reactions and appraisals from others. For example, your parents praise your accomplishments; a romantic partner makes light of your fears; a teacher assigns you a challenging task; your peers laugh heartily at your jokes. Reactions and appraisals like these convey that you're competent, neurotic, have potential, or are funny. In short, we see ourselves partly through the eyes of those around us.

The idea that we gain self-knowledge through reflected self-appraisals might seem to suggest that we have little say in how we see ourselves. But the key concept here is that we internalize how we *think* others perceive us, not necessarily how they *actually* see us. In fact, our reflected self-appraisals often don't correlate highly with the way other people evaluate us (Felson, 1993; Kenny & DePaulo, 1993; Shrauger & Schoeneman, 1979; Tice & Wallace, 2005). For example, far more people think they are shy than are actually perceived as shy by others (Zimbardo, 1990).

Figuring out how, and to what degree, reflected self-appraisals influence a person's sense of self can be tricky. For example, Amy's view of herself as a clumsy person could stem from her perception that her family and friends see her this way and convey that impression to her. But it's also possible that her view of herself as clumsy has been detected by other people who then convey that impression back to her. The way we view ourselves often affects the perceptions of other people, who then reflect those views back to us in a kind of echo chamber (Felson, 1993; Kenny & DePaulo, 1993).

Situationism and the Social Self

In many a film depicting the social lives of teenagers, you see the teenage characters adapting who they are to the people around them. Surrounded by their studious classmates, they readily compare homework notes and share gripes about the difficult test they had to take; in the presence of the "cool kids," they convey nonchalance about their schoolwork. The chameleon-like nature of the teenagers in such films hits at a deeper and more universal truth: that our social self shifts from one situation to another. This notion that the social self changes across different contexts is consistent with the principle of *situationism*, and it's supported by abundant empirical evidence.

ASPECTS OF THE SELF THAT ARE RELEVANT AND DISTINCTIVE IN THE SOCIAL CONTEXT Students who are rebellious and free-spirited in the dorm will shift to a more sober and conventional demeanor around parents or professors. Someone who sees herself as relaxed and outspoken when with her close friends may be shy and inhibited when interacting with a group of new acquaintances. Markus and Wurf (1987) coined the term **working self-concept** to refer to the idea that only a subset of a person's vast pool of self-knowledge is brought to mind in any given context—usually the subset that's most relevant or appropriate in the current situation. Thus, for example, notions of the self related to relationships are likely to be the mind's prime focus with a romantic partner, whereas notions of the self related to competition are likely to be at the forefront during an important sports match.

William McGuire and Alice Padawer-Singer (1978) proposed that we also tend to highlight what makes us unique or distinctive in a given situation. To test this hypothesis, they asked sixth-graders at different schools to describe themselves.

"Oh would some power the gift give us, To see ourselves as others see us."
—ROBERT BURNS

working self-concept A subset of self-knowledge that is brought to mind in a particular context.

CONTEXT AND SENSE OF SELF
In the HBO original series *Girls*, the character Shoshanna Shapiro, played by actress Zosia Mamet, moves to Japan for a job. Here she is depicted walking around town in her newfound home, showing clear signs that her sense of self (including her fashion sense) has shifted to fit the context.

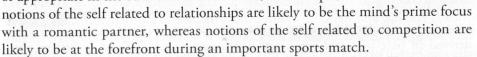

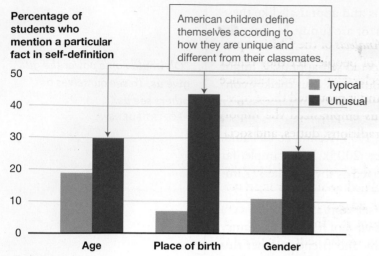

Percentage of students who mention a particular fact in self-definition

American children define themselves according to how they are unique and different from their classmates.

Typical
Unusual

Age   Place of birth   Gender

FIGURE 3.1

DISTINCTIVENESS AND THE SENSE OF SELF

Source: Adapted from McGuire & Padawer-Singer, 1978.

On average, children wrote 12 statements referring to their recreational activities, attitudes, friends, and school activities. As it turned out, the children defined themselves according to how they differed from their classmates (**Figure 3.1**). Thirty percent of the children who were especially young or old compared with their classmates (that is, six months from the most common age of their classmates) mentioned their age in their self-definition, whereas only 19 percent of the other children did. Forty-four percent of the children who were born outside the United States mentioned this biographical fact, whereas only 7 percent of those born in the United States mentioned that fact about themselves. Twenty-six percent of the children of the minority gender in their class mentioned their gender as part of their self-definition compared with 11 percent of the majority gender (see also Cota & Dion, 1986). At least in the Western world, what's most central to identity is what makes a person distinct.

MALLEABILITY AND STABILITY Most of us would readily agree that our sense of self shifts depending on the social context. Yet we also experience a sense of continuity in the self, the feeling that we have a stable, core self. How can we reconcile what appear to be dueling notions of malleability (something that can be shaped) and stability in the self?

There are several paths of reconciliation. First, although one's working self-concept varies across situations, there are nevertheless core aspects of self-knowledge that are likely to be what a person thinks of first when thinking about the self (Markus, 1977). Thus, although Jiang Yun may see herself as painfully shy around members of the opposite sex but outgoing with her girlfriends, she sees herself as a good listener no matter whom she is around. For LGBT people, who frequently face the decision of whether or not to disclose their LGBT status, their sexual-minority identity is likely to be a core, cross-situationally noticeable aspect of the self (Cain, 1991).

Second, a person's overall pool of self-knowledge remains relatively stable over time, providing a sense of self-continuity even as different pieces of self-knowledge come to the fore in different contexts (Linville & Carlston, 1994). Thus, your belief that you're lazy may not be part of your working self-concept in a job interview, but it's nonetheless stored in memory, ready to be retrieved when you're lounging around watching TV instead of doing the laundry.

Finally, although a person's sense of self may shift depending on the context, it's likely that these shifts conform to a predictable, stable pattern (Chen, Boucher, & Tapias, 2006; English & Chen, 2007; Mischel & Shoda, 1995). Take a person who sees herself as confident around her friends but as insecure around her overly critical mother. Although this person's sense of self clearly shifts according to the social context, it's not as if she's confident around her friends one day and insecure around them the next. In other words, the malleability in this individual's self is itself *stable*. Whenever she is around her friends, she sees herself as confident, whereas being around her mother reliably shifts her self-concept to include being insecure. In short, the social self is defined by two truths: it is malleable, shifting from one context to another, but it also has core components that persist across contexts.

Culture and the Social Self

The American Declaration of Independence and the *Analects* of the Chinese philosopher Confucius have shaped the lives of billions of people. Yet they reflect radically different ideas about the social self. The Declaration of Independence prioritized the rights and freedoms of the individual, and it protected those rights and liberties from infringement by others. Confucius emphasized the importance of knowing one's place in society, of honoring traditions, duties, and social roles, and of thinking of others before the self.

The differences reflected in these documents run deep in the cultures that people inhabit. In Western societies, people are concerned about their individuality, about freedom, and about self-expression. Our adages reflect this: "The squeaky wheel gets the grease." "If you've got it, flaunt it." In Asian cultures, homilies and folk wisdom encourage a different view of the self: "The empty wagon makes the most noise." "The nail that stands up is pounded down." Hazel Markus, Shinobu Kitayama, and Harry Triandis have offered far-reaching theories about how cultures vary in the social selves they encourage and how these different conceptions of the self shape the emotions we feel, the motivations that drive us, and our ways of perceiving the social world (Markus & Connor, 2013; Markus & Kitayama, 1991; Triandis, 1989, 1994, 1995).

INDEPENDENT AND INTERDEPENDENT SELF-CONSTRUALS As discussed in Chapter 1, many Western cultures, especially those of northwestern Europe and former British colonies, such as Canada, the United States, Australia, and New Zealand, promote an *independent self-construal*. In these societies, the self is an autonomous entity that is distinct and separate from others (**Figure 3.2A**). It's important for people to assert their uniqueness and independence, and the focus is on internal causes of behavior. These imperatives lead to a conception of the self in terms of traits that are stable across time and social context.

In contrast, most other cultures in the world, notably those of East Asia, Eastern Europe, and Latin America, foster *interdependent self-construals*, in which the self is fundamentally connected to other people (**Figure 3.2B**). The imperatives are to find a place within the community and to fulfill appropriate roles. There is close attention to social contexts and a recognition of the shifting demands

> "We hold these truths to be self-evident, that all men are created equal, that they are endowed by their Creator with certain unalienable rights, that among these are Life, Liberty, and the pursuit of Happiness."
> —DECLARATION OF INDEPENDENCE

> "A person of humanity wishing to establish his own character, also establishes the character of others."
> —CONFUCIUS

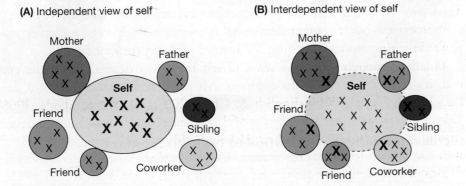

FIGURE 3.2
VIEWS OF THE SELF
(A) In the independent view of the self, the self is construed as a distinct, autonomous entity, separate from others and defined by distinct traits and preferences. (B) In the interdependent view of the self, the self is construed as connected to others and defined by duties, roles, and shared preferences and traits.

of situations on behavior. These concerns lead to a conception of the self as something embedded within social relationships, roles, and duties. This kind of self-construal is prevalent in many East Asian cultures (Markus & Kitayama, 1991), as well as in many Eastern European cultures (De Freitas et al., 2017; Realo & Allik, 1999; Tower, Kelly, & Richards, 1997), South Asian cultures (Dhawan, Roseman, Naidu, Thapa, & Rettek, 1995; Savani, Markus, & Conner, 2008), African cultures (Ma & Schoeneman, 1997), and Latin American cultures (Sanchez-Burks, Nisbett, & Ybarra, 2000).

In short, an independent self-construal promotes an inward focus on the self, whereas an interdependent self-construal encourages an outward focus on the social situation. Research shows that this difference in focus is reflected in the stories that members of different cultures construct about themselves. Cohen and Gunz (2002) asked Canadian and Asian students (a mixture of students from Hong Kong, China, Taiwan, Korea, and various South and Southeast Asian countries) to tell stories about ten different situations in which they were the center of attention—for example, being embarrassed. Canadians were more likely than Asians to reproduce the scene from their original point of view, looking outward from their own perspective. Asians were more likely to imagine the scene as an observer might, describing it from a third-person perspective. We might say that Westerners tend to experience and recall events from the inside out—with themselves at the center, looking out at the world. Easterners are more likely to experience and recall events from the outside in—starting from the social world, looking back at themselves as an object of attention. Westerners play the lead in their personal narratives; non-Westerners are more likely to be just one among many cast members. **Figure 3.3** provides another illustration of how Westerners and East Asians differ in the degree of attention they pay to the social context.

FIGURE 3.3
CULTURAL DIFFERENCES IN ATTENTION TO THE SOCIAL CONTEXT
In this study, American and Japanese participants were shown a series of cartoons with either a Caucasian boy (for Americans) or an Asian boy (for Japanese) in the center, surrounded by four other people who were the same in all the pictures (Masuda et al., 2008). In some cartoons, the emotional expression of the boy (for example, happy) matched the emotional expressions on the faces of the surrounding people (happy). In other cases, as in the two pictures shown here, there was a mismatch in the emotional expressions of the boy (for example, angry) versus the others (happy). The researchers found that when judging an individual's emotions, the Japanese are more likely to take into account the emotions of others in the surrounding social context.

WHO ARE YOU? The common belief among Westerners that they are self-contained is shown by simply asking them to describe themselves. Kuhn and McPartland (1954) invented a simple "Who Am I?" exercise that asks people to list 20 statements that describe who they are. Americans' self-descriptions tend to be context-free responses referring to personality traits ("I'm friendly," "hard-working," "shy") and personal preferences ("I like camping"). The responses of people from interdependent cultures tend to refer to relationships with other people or groups ("I am Jan's friend") and are often qualified by context ("I am serious at work"; "I am fun-loving with my friends") (Cousins, 1989; Ip & Bond, 1995; Markus & Kitayama, 1991).

Ma and Schoeneman (1997) gave the Who Am I? test to American university students and to four different groups living in Kenya: university students, workers in Nairobi (the capital city), and traditional Maasai and Samburu herding peoples. Kenya was for decades a colony of Great Britain, and city dwellers, especially those who are educated, have had a great deal of exposure to Western culture. Kenyan students have been exposed still more to Western culture and are being educated in a Western tradition. In contrast, traditional African tribespeople have had very little contact with Westerners.

Figure 3.4 shows how differently these four African groups view themselves. Traditional Maasai and Samburu define themselves in terms of their family, property, and position in the community. Tribespeople are constantly made aware of their roles and status in relation to family members and other groups (Mwaniki, 1973). Kenyan students, on the other hand, are far more likely to mention personal characteristics. Kenyan students, in fact, differ only slightly from American students. Workers in Nairobi are in between the tribespeople and the students. These findings illustrate that different self-construals can emerge even among those who ostensibly live within the same "culture." That is, culture is made up of more than just one's country of residence. One's occupation, educational institution, religion, race, social class—each of these can exert cultural influences of its own, shaping self-construals in more independent or

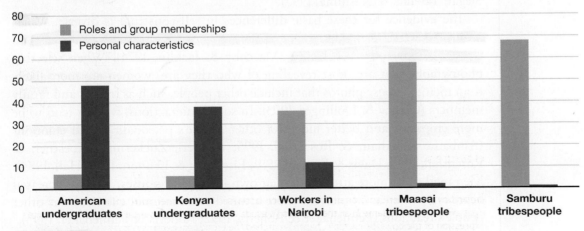

Percentage of category responses

FIGURE 3.4
SELF-CHARACTERIZATION IN FOUR AFRICAN GROUPS
The results from this study suggest that Westernization is associated with the development of a more independent self-construal.
Source: Ma & Schoeneman, 1997.

BOX 3.2   FOCUS ON CULTURE AND NEUROSCIENCE

Culture and the Social Self in the Brain

As we saw in our discussion of reflected appraisals and the brain, when people are asked to judge themselves with respect to various trait dimensions, a certain region of the brain known as the medial prefrontal cortex is particularly active (Heatherton et al., 2006). This suggests that this part of the frontal lobe is involved in processes that represent self-knowledge. Zhu and his colleagues conducted a study using an interesting twist on this paradigm to ascertain whether many of the cultural differences in self-construal discussed in this chapter would be reflected in differences in neural activation (Zhu, Zhang, Fan, & Han, 2007). They had Chinese participants and Western Europeans rate the applicability of different traits to themselves, their mothers, and another unrelated person. For members of both cultures, considering the

applicability of the traits to themselves produced activation in the medial prefrontal cortex. But for Chinese participants, activation in this same region was also observed when participants were thinking about whether the traits characterized their mothers. For the Westerners, there was, if anything, a relative deactivation of the medial prefrontal cortex when they thought about their mothers. These findings seem to suggest that for people with interdependent self-construals, the same region of the brain represents the self and mother; they are merged within the brain. In contrast, for those with independent self-construals, the self and mother are quite distinct, all the way down to which neurons are activated in the brain.

interdependent directions. **Box 3.3** expands on the example of social class differences in self-construal, first noted in Chapter 1. Gender is yet another example of a cultural divide that has implications for self-construals.

Gender and the Social Self

In a review of the literature on the self-concept and gender, Susan Cross and Laura Madson (1997) gathered evidence indicating that women in the United States tend to construe the self in more interdependent terms than men do—that is, in terms of connection to others. In contrast, men in the United States tend to prioritize difference and uniqueness, construing the self in more independent terms. The same gender differences are found among the Japanese (Kashima, Siegal, Tanaka, & Kashima, 1992).

The evidence for these basic differences in self-construal is diverse. When women describe themselves, they are more likely than men to refer to social characteristics and relationships (Maccoby & Jacklin, 1974). When selecting photographs that are most revealing of who they are, women are more likely than men to choose photos that include other people, such as friends and family members (Clancy & Dollinger, 1993). In social interactions, women tend to be more empathic and better judges of other people's personalities and emotions (Ambady, Hallahan, & Rosenthal, 1995; Bernieri, Zuckerman, Koestner, & Rosenthal, 1994; Davis & Franzoi, 1991; Eisenberg & Lennon, 1983; Hall, 1984). Men tend to be more attuned to their own internal responses, such as increased heart rate, whereas women are more attuned to situational cues, such as other people's reactions (Pennebaker & Roberts, 1992; Roberts & Pennebaker, 1995).

Where do these gender differences in self-construal come from? Socialization processes are one influential source. Parents raise girls and boys differently. For example, parents tend to talk with their girls more than with their boys about emotions and being sensitive to others (Fivush, 1989, 1992). The friendships that people

BOX 3.3 | FOCUS ON CULTURE

Social Class Shapes the Social Self

Stephens and her colleagues propose that life in different social class subcultures in the United States promotes the elaboration of distinct construals of the self (Stephens, Markus, & Phillips, 2014). Living in relatively higher-class environments, with their more abundant resources, safer neighborhoods, greater access to education, higher job security, and so on, affords people with the opportunity, if not the mandate, to develop selves that reflect the U.S. cultural ideal of independence. This independent self-construal emphasizes choice, freedom from constraint, the pursuit of opportunities, and self-expression. In contrast, the culture of lower-class individuals in the United States is characterized by fewer resources, less safe neighborhoods, limited access to education, and tenuous job security. In such circumstances, the Stephens team argues, it makes sense that people would develop selves that are more sensitive to the social context, to the constraints in the environment, and to their dependence on others. Among lower-class individuals, a more socially responsive, interdependent kind of self-construal is promoted. Do such class differences matter?

Because the norms and values of many U.S. institutions reflect the ideal of independence, people who hold an independent self-construal and think and behave accordingly are at an advantage—and one that serves to perpetuate social class differences. For example, in most American schools, administrators and teachers reward behavior associated with an independent self-construal, such as standing out from the pack (Stephens, Fryberg, Markus, Johnson, & Covarrubias, 2012). It's hardly surprising, then, that students whose social class promotes an independent self-construal have better academic achievement outcomes than those raised in a social class that encourages interdependence.

Researchers have begun to explore ways to promote the growth and development of lower-class individuals and, accordingly, help close the social class achievement gap. Stephens, Hamedani, and Destin (2014) studied a group of incoming first-generation college students (students who do not have parents with four-year degrees and who are disproportionately in the lower class) and a group of continuing-generation students (those who have at least one parent with a four-year degree). Both groups listened to one of two panels of first-generation and continuing-generation junior- and senior-year students sharing stories about their college experiences. Panelists in one condition described the ways their social class backgrounds had had both positive and negative effects, emphasizing the importance of using strategies that take into account their different social class status. Panelists in the other condition also shared stories about their college experiences but did not highlight the role of their social class.

Remarkably, the typical academic achievement gap seen between first- and continuing-generation students was eliminated among students exposed to the difference-education panel. The data suggest that the elimination of this gap occurred because the intervention increased the likelihood that first-generation students would seek out resources (such as e-mailing a professor for help) and, as a result, improved their grades. More research is of course needed, but findings like these at least raise the possibility that even relatively simple interventions can help level the playing field for individuals who tend to hold an interdependent self-construal, yet are faced with situations tailored to reward independence. Social class shapes the nature of the social self, but does not have to determine life outcomes.

CLASS DIFFERENCES AND THE SOCIAL SELF Higher- and lower-class individuals often inhabit very different environments, as shown by these photos of an upper-class neighborhood on the left and a lower-class neighborhood on the right.

form from the earliest ages also influence gender differences in self-construal. Starting at age 3 and continuing through the primary school years, girls and boys tend to play in gender-segregated groups that reinforce and amplify the differences in self-construal (Maccoby, 1990). Girls tend to focus on cooperative games that are oriented toward interpersonal relationships (for example, mother and child). Boys tend to emphasize competition, hierarchy, and distinctions among individuals. As adults, gender-specific roles further amplify these differences. For example, even today, Western women tend to take on most of the responsibilities for raising children, which calls on interdependent tendencies. These gendered roles are portrayed in the media as well, which tend to showcase men in positions of power and agency and women in more nurturing roles.

These aspects of socialization tend to reinforce and enhance biological differences between the sexes that make females more inclined to be nurturing and males more inclined to be competitive and aggressive. And you may recall from Chapter 1 that some cultures maximize these predispositions well beyond what is characteristic of a hunter-gatherer culture, whereas others minimize them, some to the point of near-zero temperamental differences.

Social Comparison

Sometimes people actively seek out information about themselves through comparison with other people. This is the central tenet of **social comparison theory**, an influential and enduring theory in social psychology put forward by Leon Festinger in the 1950s (Festinger, 1954; see also Suls & Wheeler, 2000; Wood, 1996). The theory maintains that when people have no objective standard by which to evaluate their traits or abilities, they do so largely by comparing themselves with others. Whether you are "physically strong" can be determined fairly objectively by simple tests of strength. But to be "honest" or "morally upright," dimensions that are not so easy to quantify objectively, is to be more honest and morally upright than others.

Festinger noted, however, that there is no point in comparing yourself with Neil DeGrasse Tyson or Serena Williams, nor is it very helpful to compare yourself with total novices. To get an accurate sense of how good you are at something, you need to compare yourself with people who have roughly your level of skill. Numerous studies have shown that people are indeed especially drawn to comparisons with similar others (Kruglanski & Mayseless, 1990; Strickhouser & Zell, 2015; Suls, Martin, & Wheeler, 2002). We like to feel good about ourselves, though, so our search for similar targets of comparison tends to be biased toward people who are slightly inferior to, or worse off than, ourselves. This is ironic because it puts us in the position of saying, "Compared with people who are slightly worse at tennis than I am, I'm pretty good!" or "Compared with people who are almost as conscientious as I am, I'm pretty darn conscientious!" These sorts of *downward* social comparisons help us define ourselves favorably, giving a boost to our self-esteem (Aspinwall & Taylor, 1993; Helgeson & Mickelson, 1995; Lockwood, 2002).

But if we only engage in downward social comparison, we sacrifice opportunities for improvement. In fact, when our focus is on improving ourselves, we tend to forgo the self-esteem benefits of downward social comparison and engage in *upward* social comparison instead (Sedikides & Hepper, 2009). For example, in one study that examined the social comparisons made by a group of ninth-graders, researchers found that students usually chose to compare their grades

social comparison theory The idea that people compare themselves to other people to obtain an accurate assessment of their own opinions, abilities, and internal states.

"It is not enough to succeed. Others must fail."
—GORE VIDAL

SOCIAL COMPARISONS
It's not informative to compare your intelligence or athletic skill to someone renowned for brilliance, such as Neil DeGrasse Tyson, or celebrated for tennis-playing ability, like Serena Williams.

with those of someone who had slightly better grades than they did, presumably with the hope that one day they might get higher grades themselves (Blanton, Buunk, Gibbons, & Kuyper, 1999).

In today's social media–crazed world, we can find ourselves bombarded with social comparison "opportunities." Pictures of your friend's happy romantic relationship pop up on your Facebook feed. Your smartphone pings to let you know that your neighbor has just shared a stunning video of her exotic vacation. A former classmate tweets that his company just landed a prestigious new account. You wouldn't be alone if such events made you wonder: Why am I not in a relationship? Is my relationship as perfect as other people's relationships? Was my last vacation really that much fun? How more or less successful am I? This self-doubt raises the question of whether exposing yourself to all of this social media is good or bad for you.

Researchers have begun to tackle this question. In one study, Verduyn and colleagues (2015) text-messaged participants five times a day over a 6-day period, prompting them to fill out a survey upon receiving each text. The survey asked participants to make a series of ratings, including their current affective well-being (how positive or negative they felt), their amount of passive use of Facebook since the last text (for example, scrolling through their news feed), their amount of active use of Facebook since the last text (for example, posting and sharing links), and finally, in an effort to measure social comparison, their current feelings of envy. The findings suggest that passive (but not active) Facebook use makes one feel less upbeat and that this is due in part to feelings of envy, presumably triggered by comparing one's own life with the images of other people's lives splashed all over one's Facebook feed. Results like these point to social media as a potentially major social influence on construals and evaluations of the self.

The social self originates from a variety of sources. Socialization agents—by virtue of what they teach us, what they encourage in us, how they react to us—help define who we are. The current situation matters as well: the social self shifts from one context to another. A person's cultures (country of residence, gender, race, social class) shape the social self in profound ways, leading to defining the self in more independent terms, with an emphasis on uniqueness and autonomy, or in more interdependent terms, with an emphasis on connection to others. Finally, the social self is shaped by comparisons with other people.

Self-Esteem

In 1987, California Governor George Deukmejian signed Assembly Bill 3659 into law. The bill allocated an annual budget of $245,000 for a self-esteem task force, charged with two goals: understanding the effects of self-esteem on drug use, teenage pregnancy, and high school dropout rates; and elevating the self-esteem of schoolchildren. The initiative was based on the assumption that strengthening self-esteem would help cure society's ills.

Several findings would seem to support this assumption. People with low self-esteem are less satisfied with life, more hopeless, and more depressed (Crocker & Wolfe, 2001), and they are less able to cope with life's challenges, such as the social and academic demands of college (Cutrona, 1982). They tend to disengage from tasks following failure (Brockner, 1979), and they are more prone to anti-social behavior and delinquency (Donnellan, Trzesniewski, Robins, Moffitt, & Caspi, 2005). Raising self-esteem, the thinking was, just might produce healthier, more resilient children and a better society in the long run. Much of the data that the California legislators relied on was correlational in nature, which means we can't conclude that self-esteem had a *causal* effect on any of the other variables. Regardless, the topic of self-esteem has attracted considerable attention by social psychologists.

Defining Self-Esteem

self-esteem The overall positive or negative evaluation people have of themselves.

Self-esteem refers to the overall positive or negative evaluation people have of themselves. Researchers usually evaluate self-esteem with simple self-report measures like the scale in **Table 3.1.** As you can see from this scale, self-esteem represents how we feel about our attributes and qualities, our successes and failures, and our self in general. People with high self-esteem feel quite good about themselves. People with low self-esteem feel ambivalent about themselves; they tend to feel both good and bad about who they are. People who truly dislike themselves are rare and are typically found in specific clinical populations, such as severely depressed individuals.

Trait self-esteem is a person's enduring level of self-regard across time. Studies indicate that trait self-esteem is fairly stable: people who report high trait

TABLE 3.1 SELF-ESTEEM SCALE

Indicate your level of agreement with each of the following statements by using the scale below.

0 Strongly Disagree	1 Disagree	2 Agree	3 Strongly Agree

_____ 1. At times I think I am no good at all.

_____ 2. I take a positive view of myself.

_____ 3. All in all, I am inclined to feel that I am a failure.

_____ 4. I wish I could have more respect for myself.

_____ 5. I certainly feel useless at times.

_____ 6. I feel that I am a person of worth, at least on an equal plane with others.

_____ 7. On the whole, I am satisfied with myself.

_____ 8. I feel I do not have much to be proud of.

_____ 9. I feel that I have a number of good qualities.

_____ 10. I am able to do things as well as most other people.

To determine your score, first reverse the scoring for the five negatively worded items (1, 3, 4, 5, & 8) as follows: 0 = 3, 1 = 2, 2 = 1, 3 = 0. Then add up your scores across the 10 items. Your total score should fall between 0 and 30. Higher numbers indicate higher self-esteem.

Source: M. Rosenberg, 1965.

---

self-esteem at one point in time tend to report high trait self-esteem many years later; people who report low trait self-esteem at one point tend to report low trait self-esteem later (Block & Robins, 1993).

State self-esteem refers to the dynamic, changeable self-evaluations a person experiences as momentary feelings about the self (Heatherton & Polivy, 1991). Much as your working self-concept changes from one context to the next, so, too, can your state self-esteem. When people experience a setback, their self-esteem is likely to take a dive—especially among those who have low self-esteem to begin with (Brown & Dutton, 1995). For example, when college students watch their beloved college football team lose, their feelings of personal competence often drop (Hirt, Zillman, Erickson, & Kennedy, 1992). And children of average intelligence have lower self-esteem when they're in a classroom with academically talented children rather than with children who have lower academic abilities (Marsh & Parker, 1984). Self-esteem also shifts during different stages of development. As males move from early adolescence (age 14) to early adulthood (age 23), their self-esteem tends to rise. During the same period, females' self-esteem tends to fall (Block & Robins, 1993).

Success and failure in different domains do not affect everyone equally. Some people attach more importance to doing well in some domains (such as popularity, academics, physical appearance, or moral virtue) than others. According to Jennifer Crocker's **contingencies of self-worth** model, people's self-esteem rises

"Life is not easy for any of us. But what of that? We must have perseverance and above all confidence in ourselves. We must believe that we are gifted for something and that this thing must be attained."
—MARIE CURIE

contingencies of self-worth A perspective maintaining that people's self-esteem is contingent on the successes and failures in domains on which they have based their self-worth.

ELEVATING SELF-ESTEEM
People in the self-esteem movement feel it is important for all children to have high self-esteem so that they will be happy and healthy. They have encouraged teachers to make every child a VIP for a day and coaches to give medals or trophies to every child who plays on a team, whether the team wins or loses.

sociometer hypothesis The idea that self-esteem is an internal, subjective index or marker of the extent to which a person is included or looked on favorably by others.

"Who so would be a man must be a nonconformist. Hitch your wagon to a star. Insist on yourself; never imitate. The individual is the world."
—RALPH WALDO EMERSON

"Men resemble the times more than they resemble their fathers."
—ARAB PROVERB

and falls with successes and failures in the domains in which they have staked their self-worth. In other words, self-esteem goes up when you do well in areas that matter to you, but drops when you stumble in these areas. In a test of this prediction, researchers studied the self-esteem of University of Michigan students who had applied to graduate school (Crocker, Sommers, & Luhtanen, 2002). They asked students to fill out a self-esteem questionnaire every day that they received an acceptance or rejection response from a graduate school. Not surprisingly, students had higher self-esteem on days when they received an acceptance and lower self-esteem on days when they received a rejection. But these effects were much larger for those students whose self-esteem was highly dependent on academic competence. These findings suggest that it's probably wise for people to stake their self-worth in a wide range of areas—perhaps on academic achievement, but also on the strength of their friendships and family relationships, their ability to play a particular sport or musical instrument, their concern for the feelings of others, and so on—rather than put all their eggs in one basket. Indeed, studies suggest that to the extent we derive our self-worth from multiple domains that are distinct from one another, the more likely we are to avoid feeling devastated by a setback in any one domain (Linville, 1987; Showers, 1992).

Social Acceptance and Self-Esteem

Several of the domains that define people's self-worth (for example, social approval) are highly social in nature. In his **sociometer hypothesis**, Mark Leary maintains that self-esteem is primarily a readout of our likely standing with others; that is, self-esteem is an internal, subjective index of how well we are regarded by others and hence how likely we are to be included or excluded by them (Leary, Tambor, Terdal, & Downs, 1995). Throughout most of evolutionary history, Leary reasons, we couldn't go it alone; therefore, we needed a way to quickly assess how we were doing socially. Our feelings of state self-esteem constitute just such an assessment.

Leary notes that those things that make us feel good about ourselves—feeling likable, competent, physically attractive, and morally upright—are precisely those things that make others accept us (or reject us if we fall short). High self-esteem indicates that we are thriving in our relationships; low self-esteem suggests that we are having interpersonal difficulties. In this sense, low self-esteem is not something to be avoided at all costs; rather, it provides useful information about when we need to attend to and shore up our social bonds.

Culture and Self-Esteem

Many East Asian languages have no word or phrase for self-esteem. The Japanese have a term now, but like the Japanese rendering for *baseball*—namely, *beisoboru*—the word for *self-esteem* is simply borrowed from English: *serufu esutiimu*. The fact that it was Westerners who invented the term *self-esteem* reflects a long-standing concern in the West with the value of the individual. During the Enlightenment period in the eighteenth century, Western Europeans began to prioritize individuality, freedom, and rights—ideas that would weave their way into the U.S. Constitution (Baumeister, 1987; Seligman, 1988; Twenge, 2002).

Today, the emphasis on self-esteem in the West is higher than ever. Bookstores are filled with books about the importance of having a strong sense of self-worth. Modern American parents want to raise independent and confident children—not the obedient children of 50 years ago (Remley, 1988). Independent cultures foster higher levels of self-esteem than interdependent cultures. Compared with the world's more interdependent peoples—from Japan to Malaysia to India to Kenya—Westerners report higher self-esteem and a more pronounced concern with evaluating the self (Markus & Kitayama, 1991; Schmitt & Allik, 2005). It's not that people who define the self in more interdependent terms feel bad about themselves. Rather, they're more concerned with other ways of feeling good about themselves—for example, they're motivated toward self-improvement and commitment to collective goals (Crocker & Park, 2004; Heine, 2005; Norenzayan & Heine, 2004). Interestingly, as people from interdependent cultures are increasingly exposed to the West, the independent emphasis on self-worth rubs off on them and their self-esteem rises. As shown in **Figure 3.5**, as Asians become more immersed in Canadian life, they become more like Canadians in general with respect to self-esteem (Heine & Lehman, 2003).

What is it about independent and interdependent cultures that creates these differences? A situationist hypothesis would be that people from Western cultures create social interactions that enhance self-esteem. Consistent with this notion, studies have found that situations described by Japanese as common daily experiences are seen as less conducive to high self-esteem—by both Japanese and Americans—than daily situations in the United States (Kitayama,

"So, when he says, 'What a good boy am I,' Jack is really reinforcing his self-esteem."

"Independence is happiness."
—SUSAN B. ANTHONY

"America is a vast conspiracy to make you happy."
—JOHN UPDIKE

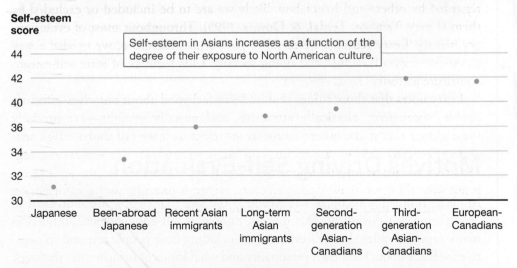

Self-esteem score

Self-esteem in Asians increases as a function of the degree of their exposure to North American culture.

Cultural sample

FIGURE 3.5
CULTURAL CHANGE AND SHIFTS IN SELF-ESTEEM
The graph represents a number of groups. Japanese are those who live in Japan. Been-abroad Japanese are those who have spent time in a Western culture. Recent Asian immigrants are those who moved to Canada within the last seven years (prior to the study). Long-term Asian immigrants have lived in Canada for more than seven years. Second-generation Asian-Canadians were born in Canada but their parents were born in Asia. Third-generation Asian-Canadians were born in Canada, and their parents were born in Canada, but their grandparents were born in Asia. European-Canadians are Canadians whose ancestors were Europeans.
SOURCE: Adapted from Heine & Lehman, 2003.

Markus, Matsumoto, & Norasakkunkit, 1997). For example, Japanese people are more often encouraged to engage in "assisted" self-criticism than Americans are. Japanese math teachers and sushi chefs critique themselves in sessions with their peers—not the sort of activities that tend to build self-esteem, however beneficial they might be to skill development. Situations Americans reported as typical, by contrast, are seen by both Americans and Japanese to be more esteem enhancing. For example, Americans are more often praised for their achievements than Japanese people are.

Cultural differences in the emphasis on promoting self-esteem versus improving the self can have important consequences for how people respond to failures and setbacks. Steven Heine and his colleagues asked Canadian and Japanese students to take a so-called creativity test and then gave them false performance feedback (Heine et al., 2001). Some were told they had performed well, while others were told they had performed badly. The experimenters then gave the participants the opportunity to work on a similar task. The Canadians worked longer on the second task if they had succeeded at the first; the Japanese worked longer if they had failed. The Canadians thus avoided being reminded of failure, and the Japanese used the occasion to improve.

CULTURE AND SELF-ESTEEM
Japanese students are encouraged to focus on how they can improve more so than how to feel good about themselves, an emphasis that may help explain cultural differences in levels of self-esteem.

MOTIVATIONS BEHIND SELF-EVALUATION
Everyone spends some time evaluating their abilities and skills, but different motives can drive these evaluations. Whereas the man scrutinizing himself in the mirror seems to be taking a self-critical stance toward himself, others evaluate the self through rose-colored glasses.

self-enhancement The desire to maintain, increase, or protect one's positive self-views.

← LOOKING BACK

Self-esteem refers to the positive or negative evaluation people have of themselves. Trait self-esteem is fairly stable, whereas state self-esteem fluctuates across different situations. People have different contingencies of self-worth, domains in which they invest their self-esteem. These lead to rises or declines in self-esteem when they succeed or fail, respectively, in these domains. According to the sociometer hypothesis, self-esteem is a gauge of a person's standing with others and thus a useful potential warning about the possibility of rejection. People who construe the self in more interdependent terms are less concerned with feeling positively about their attributes than are modern Westerners, who define the self in more independent terms. Defining the self in interdependent terms is also associated with being more likely to seek opportunities for self-improvement.

Motives Driving Self-Evaluation

Implicit in our discussion of self-esteem is the fact that people are motivated to view themselves positively. This motive, known as self-enhancement, influences many processes related to self-evaluation, including how people respond to negative feedback about their own personality and what kinds of information they seek out. Another important motivating factor in evaluating oneself is self-verification.

Self-Enhancement

Suppose you just found out that your romantic interest in a coworker is not reciprocated, or you recently received a less than stellar performance appraisal at work. Naturally, you're going to feel bad about yourself and will probably try to find ways to feel better. In other words, there will be a need for self-enhancement.

the desire to maintain, increase, or protect positive views of the self (Leary, 2007; Sedikides & Gregg, 2008). To satisfy this very powerful motive, people use various strategies.

SELF-SERVING CONSTRUALS As we've already discussed, most people—or at least most Westerners—tend to view themselves positively. In fact, when asked to indicate how they compare with others on various dimensions, people exhibit a pronounced **better-than-average effect**; they think they are above average in popularity, kindness, fairness, leadership, and so on (Alicke & Govorun, 2005). And it will probably not surprise you to learn that most people think they are above-average drivers. A majority of drivers interviewed *while hospitalized for being in an automobile accident* rated their driving skill as closer to "expert" than to "poor" (Preston & Harris, 1965; Svenson, 1981).

Why are people so upbeat about themselves? Part of the answer has to do with how people interpret what it means to be kind, fair, athletic, or even a good driver. That is, self-serving interpretations of these kinds of traits are one means of pursuing self-enhancement. As Nobel Prize–winning economist Thomas Schelling once stated:

> Everybody ranks himself high in qualities he values; careful drivers give weight to care, skillful drivers give weight to skill, and those who think that, whatever else they are not, at least they are polite, give weight to courtesy, and come out high on their own scale. This is the way that every child has the best dog on the block. (Schelling, 1978, p. 64)

David Dunning and his colleagues have shown that people form just these sorts of self-serving interpretations, or construals, of what it means to be, say, artistic, athletic, or agreeable and that such construals are an important part of the better-than-average effect. They have found, for example, that people are more likely to think they are significantly above average in ambiguous traits that are easy to construe in multiple ways (artistic, sympathetic) than in unambiguous ones that are not (tall, punctual). Also, when people are given precise instructions about how they should interpret what it means to be, for instance, artistic or athletic, the better-than-average effect shrinks in size (Dunning, Meyerowitz, & Holzberg, 1989).

People also take advantage of another type of ambiguity that allows them to think highly of themselves: the ambiguity concerning which behaviors or characteristics "count" in determining what someone is like. People tend to judge *other* people—how kind, outgoing, or athletic they are—by the way they are on average, and yet they define *themselves* in terms of how they behave when they're at their best. If people (unknowingly) juggle the standards for what constitutes "talented," "considerate," or "agreeable," it should come as no surprise that they think of themselves as above average (Williams & Gilovich, 2012; Williams, Gilovich, & Dunning, 2012).

SELF-AFFIRMATION Affirmations are another strategy people can use to maintain a positive view of themselves (Steele, 1988). **Self-affirmation theory** focuses on people's efforts to maintain an overall sense of self-worth when they're confronted with feedback or events that threaten a valued self-image, such as getting a poor test grade or learning that they're at risk for a certain illness. Under these circumstances, people can maintain an overall sense of self-worth by affirming themselves in a domain unrelated to the threatened domain. For instance, if you learn

better-than-average effect The finding that most people think they are above average on various personality trait and ability dimensions.

NOT THAT ONE WHERE ALL THE WOMEN ARE STRONG, ALL THE MEN ARE GOOD-LOOKING & THE CHILDREN ARE ABOVE AVERAGE AGAIN.

STAHLER 6/24

© 2014 Jeff Stahler/Dist. by Universal UClick for UFS

THE BETTER-THAN-AVERAGE EFFECT
The humor of the above cartoon lies in the fact that most people are inclined to see themselves (and people connected to them) as above average, rather than mediocre.

self-affirmation theory The idea that people can maintain an overall sense of self-worth following psychologically threatening information by affirming a valued aspect of themselves unrelated to the threat.

of threatening health information, you can restore the blow to your self-esteem by reminding yourself of, say, your artistic abilities or your close friendships.

There is much empirical evidence that self-affirmation is effective (McQueen & Klein, 2006; Sherman & Cohen, 2006). Moreover, self-affirmations have been shown to do more than simply help people maintain a general sense of self-worth. Self-affirmations also help minimize a wide range of defensive, and potentially harmful, behaviors people exhibit when faced with threat, such as the tendency to attribute responsibility to themselves when they succeed but to deny responsibility when they fail (Sherman & Cohen, 2006). (For more discussion, see Chapter 5.) Another defensive maneuver people show in response to a threat to self-esteem is putting down members of stereotyped groups (Fein & Spencer, 1997). This behavior is less likely to occur if people affirm a valued aspect of themselves prior to evaluating stereotyped group members. In the domain of health awareness, studies have shown that after affirming the self, people are more receptive to troubling, but potentially useful, health information, resulting in a greater likelihood of actually engaging in healthy behaviors (Sherman, Nelson, & Steele, 2000).

SELF-ENHANCEMENT AND WELL-BEING In light of the fact that people tend to employ various strategies to view themselves in a positive light, we may wonder whether having a truly honest and accurate understanding of oneself instead might be better for a person's mental health and happiness.

In a provocative line of work, Shelley Taylor and Jonathon Brown challenged this position. They argue that self-knowledge often includes positive illusions about the self—that we are funnier, smarter, or warmer than we really are— and that such illusions, far from being detrimental, actually enhance well-being (Taylor & Brown, 1988, 1994; Updegraff & Taylor, 2000). Dozens of studies, carried out with Europeans and North Americans, have shown that people who are well adjusted are more prone to various illusions about the self compared with those who suffer from low self-esteem and unhappiness.

In a laboratory context, Taylor and her colleagues examined whether positive illusions about the self have good or bad biological consequences in stressful situations (Taylor, Lerner, Sherman, Sage, & McDowell, 2003). Participants who were more likely to hold positive illusions about themselves (high self-enhancers) and participants who were less likely to hold positive illusions about themselves (low self-enhancers) faced several stress-inducing tasks (such as counting backward by sevens from 9,095), during which their biological responses to stress were recorded. The results showed a healthier set of coping responses among high self-enhancers compared with low self-enhancers. For instance, high self-enhancers exhibited lower baseline levels of cortisol (the stress hormone) and less arousal of their autonomic nervous system during the stressful tasks.

Other researchers have questioned the notion that positive illusions consistently promote good adjustment and health, arguing instead that accurate rather than false self-beliefs foster well-being and other positive outcomes (Colvin & Block, 1994; Colvin & Griffo, 2008). They cite research showing that people who rate themselves more favorably than others do (that is, people who self-enhance) are seen by others as narcissistic (John & Robins, 1994). Other studies demonstrate that people who hold relatively accurate views of themselves, in that their ratings of themselves are similar to others' ratings of them, are judged by others more positively than are people who self-enhance (Colvin, Block, & Funder, 1995).

Perhaps the greatest challenge to Taylor and Brown's thesis about the benefits of positive illusions comes from cross-cultural research. This work demonstrates that East Asians are less likely than Westerners to approve of positive illusions about the self (Heine, Lehman, Markus, & Kitayama, 1999; Kitayama, Markus, Matsumoto, & Norasakkunkit, 1997). In one study, Japanese college students were less likely than American students to assume they were better than average in important abilities, such as academic talent (Markus & Kitayama, 1991). Such cross-cultural evidence suggests that positive illusions do not automatically enhance well-being. They often do so for Westerners because a positive view of the self is a cherished cultural value in the West. In contrast, personal well-being for East Asians appears to be more closely tied to interdependent values, such as fulfilling social roles and expectations. This finding is consistent with an interdependent self-construal (Suh, Diener, Oishi, & Triandis, 1998).

So are self-enhancing tendencies adaptive or not? Do they benefit the individual? At present, the answer appears to be: it depends. For example, Robins and Beer (2001) showed that students who entered college with self-enhancing beliefs about their academic ability reported higher average levels of self-esteem and well-being over a four-year period relative to their non-enhancing peers. However, self-enhancement tendencies were associated with a downward trajectory over the four-year period for both self-esteem and well-being. In essence, although self-enhancement was linked to greater self-esteem and well-being in the short term, the advantages linked to self-enhancement eroded over time. The safest conclusion to draw at this point is that self-enhancement provides a number of benefits, but it can be taken too far and exact significant costs.

Self-Verification

Although a wealth of evidence indicates that self-enhancement is a powerful motive that drives our pursuit of self-evaluation, we don't always want to see ourselves through rose-colored glasses. The truth, at least our version of it, also matters. According to **self-verification theory**, sometimes we strive for stable, subjectively accurate beliefs about ourselves rather than invariably favorable ones (Swann, 1990). Stable and accurate self-views make us more predictable to ourselves and others, which helps interactions with others go more smoothly. More concretely, we strive to get others to confirm or verify our preexisting beliefs about ourselves. For example, if you see yourself as extraverted, self-verification theory would predict that you will seek to get others to see you as extraverted as well. This holds true even for negative self-views: if you truly believe you are, say, socially awkward, getting others to see this subjective truth bolsters your feelings of coherence and predictability.

People engage in a number of self-verification strategies. They selectively attend to and recall information that is consistent with (and therefore verifies) their views of themselves. People with negative self-views, for example, spend more time studying negative rather than positive feedback about themselves; they remember negative feedback better; and they prefer to interact with others who are likely to provide negative rather than positive feedback (Swann & Read, 1981; Swann, Wenzlaff, Krull, & Pelham, 1992).

People also choose to enter into relationships that maintain consistent views of the self. These sorts of preferences guarantee that their personal lives will probably confirm their self-views. In a study of intimate bonds, romantic partners

self-verification theory The theory that people sometimes strive for stable, subjectively accurate beliefs about themselves because such self-views give them a sense of coherence and predictability.

"We accept the love we think we deserve."
—STEPHEN CHBOSKY, *THE PERKS OF BEING A WALLFLOWER*

Consider what the following decisions have in common: applying only to highly selective law schools; ignoring the physical therapy your doctor prescribed; pursuing a career in art instead of accounting; asking one of the most popular girls on campus out on a date. Each decision involves an assessment of your traits and abilities and a decidedly favorable assessment. We've learned how strong the desire for self-enhancement tends to be (especially among members of Western cultures) and how adept people are at satisfying that desire. But while it is tempting to assume that the desire for self-enhancement alone accounts for people's inflated self-assessments, other, nonmotivational factors may in fact be at play.

One example of a cognitive barrier to accurate self-assessment is the simple fact that sometimes people don't have access to all the information required to appraise their traits and abilities accurately. Of course, we don't have access to nonconscious processes, but we may also lack basic knowledge related to the trait or ability in question. Kruger, Dunning, and their colleagues offer a particularly clear example of this deficiency, what they call the double curse of incompetence

(Dunning, Heath, & Suls, 2004; Kruger & Dunning, 1999). The curse is that incompetent people—that is, those who tend to perform well below their peers in a given domain—are deficient not only in the skills needed to perform better, but also in the very knowledge necessary for accurately recognizing their incompetence. We all know of students who walk out of an exam room certain they've aced the test, only to find out a few days later that they bombed it. The skills and knowledge that would have led to a better test score are pretty much the same skills and knowledge required for having a more accurate prediction of how they did on the test in the first place.

So before concluding that someone's overly flattering self-assessment is a clear sign of a hefty appetite for self-enhancement, it's important to consider other, less motivational sources of flawed self-appraisal. We mentioned just one of these sources—lacking the skills and knowledge needed to make more accurate self-assessments in the first place—but

other possibilities exist. For example, in an effort to be polite, other people tend to provide us with overly positive estimates of our abilities and traits. To the extent that's true, we can scarcely be blamed for overestimating our abilities and the attractiveness of our personality.

The broader lesson here is that a certain explanation for our own and other people's behaviors can jump out as obvious and in fact may sometimes be correct. However, we should also consider the possibility that the behavior in question may have additional, less obvious causes.

who viewed each other in a congruent fashion—that is, whose perceptions of each other were in agreement with their self-views—reported more commitment to the relationship, even when one partner viewed the other in a negative light (Swann, De La Ronde, & Hixon, 1994).

Can both self-enhancement and self-verification motives be at play? Sure. Self-enhancement seems to be most relevant to our emotional responses to feedback about ourselves, whereas self-verification determines our more cognitive assessment of how valid that feedback is (Swann, Griffin, Predmore, & Gaines, 1987). To test this hypothesis, the Swann team gave participants with negative or positive self-beliefs negative or positive feedback. In terms of participants' evaluations of the accuracy and competence of the feedback—that is, the quality of the information—self-verification prevailed. Those with negative self-beliefs

IDENTITY CUES AND SELF-VERIFICATION
We create self-confirming social environments through the clothes we wear, hairstyles, jewelry, tattoos, and other identity cues. Left: A high school student wears his varsity jacket off the field, signaling his identity as an athlete. Right: Girls signal their youth and trendiness by donning Harajuku-inspired fashion while hanging out in the Harajuku district of Tokyo.

found the negative feedback most accurate, whereas participants with positive beliefs rated the positive feedback as most accurate. All participants, however, felt good about the positive feedback and disliked the negative feedback. Our quest to verify our sense of ourselves, then, guides our assessment of the validity of self-relevant information, while our desire to think favorably about ourselves guides our emotional reactions to the same information.

> ← **LOOKING BACK**
>
> Self-evaluative activities such as seeking out evaluative feedback about ourselves can be driven by different motives, such as self-enhancement and self-verification. Self-enhancement strategies include self-serving construals and self-affirmations. When self-verification is our priority, we seek out appraisals and relationship partners that confirm our preexisting self-views, and we display cues that increase the likelihood that others will see us as we see ourselves.

Self-Regulation: Motivating and Controlling Behavior

Self-regulation refers to the processes by which people initiate, alter, and control their behavior in pursuit of their goals—whether the goal is doing well in school, being a good friend, or getting in better shape (Carver & Scheier, 1982;

self-regulation Processes by which people initiate, alter, and control their behavior in the pursuit of goals, including the ability to resist short-term rewards that thwart the attainment of long-term goals.

Higgins, 1999; Muraven & Baumeister, 2000). Given that successful goal pursuit often requires resisting temptations, self-regulation also involves the ability to prioritize long-term goals (getting into graduate school) by forgoing short-term immediate rewards (a weeknight out on the town). Let's take a look at what social psychologists have discovered about self-regulation.

Self-Discrepancy Theory

One influential perspective on self-regulation is captured in a theory proposed by Tory Higgins (1987). According to **self-discrepancy theory**, people hold beliefs about not only what they *are actually* like, but also what they would *ideally* like to be and what they think they *ought* to be. Your **actual self** is the self you believe you are; your **ideal self** represents your hopes and wishes; and your **ought self** represents your duties and obligations.

According to self-discrepancy theory, ideal and ought beliefs serve as self-guides, motivating people to regulate their behavior in order to close the gap between their actual self and their ideal and ought standards. When people feel that they're failing to live up to these standards—in other words, when they perceive a discrepancy between their actual self and either their ideal or ought self—there are predictable emotional consequences. Specifically, discrepancies between the actual and the ideal self produce dejection-related emotions, and discrepancies between the actual and the ought self give rise to agitation-related emotions. Here are two examples. When the judges disparage Sameer's singing ability at an *American Idol* audition, the discrepancy between his actual self (a poor singer) and his ideal self (a rock star) arouses dejection-related emotions, such as disappointment and shame. When Mina loses patience with her ailing grandmother (actual self), she may feel agitation-related emotions, such as guilt and anxiety, if her ought self includes being a patient and loving granddaughter.

Ideal and ought standards are associated with two fundamentally different approaches to goal pursuit. When people regulate their behavior with respect to ideal self standards, they have a **promotion focus**, or a focus on attaining positive outcomes (Higgins, 1996). By contrast, when people regulate their behavior with respect to ought self standards, they have a **prevention focus**, a focus on avoiding negative outcomes. So, imagine you have the chance to hang out with someone you've had a crush on for a while. A promotion focus would nudge you to focus on what you can do to get the person to reciprocate your feelings, whereas a prevention focus would have you thinking about what you can do to avoid looking like a fool.

Lots of evidence supports Higgins's account of how ideal and ought selves can have different emotional, motivational, and behavioral consequences. When people are subtly prompted to think about how they might approximate their ideal self—for example, by reading personality trait terms that capture their ideal self—they generally exhibit elevated cheerful emotions (Higgins, Shah, & Friedman, 1997; Shah & Higgins, 2001) and heightened sensitivity to positive outcomes (Brendl, Higgins, & Lemm, 1995). But if they think they will never become their ideal self, they experience dejection-related emotions, such as depression and shame, and show reduced physiological arousal. In contrast, associations to a person's ought self, and any deviation from it, activates agitated emotions (such as guilt or panic), elevated physiological arousal, avoidant behavior, and sensitivity to negative outcomes (Strauman & Higgins, 1987).

self-discrepancy theory A theory that behavior is motivated by standards reflecting ideal and ought selves. Falling short of these standards produces specific emotions: dejection-related emotions in the case of actual-ideal discrepancies and agitation-related emotions in the case of actual-ought discrepancies.

actual self The self that people believe they are.

ideal self The self that embodies people's wishes and aspirations.

ought self The self that is concerned with the duties, obligations, and external demands people feel they are compelled to honor.

promotion focus Self-regulation of behavior with respect to ideal self standards; a focus on attaining positive outcomes through approach-related behaviors.

prevention focus Self-regulation of behavior with respect to ought self standards; a focus on avoiding negative outcomes through avoidance-related behaviors.

As you might expect, Westerners are more likely to have a promotion focus. They are more interested in attaining personal goals and more likely to feel that their own efforts are sufficient to achieve them. East Asians are more likely to exhibit a prevention focus. They are more concerned with the possible negative consequences of their actions for their relations with others (Lee, Aaker, & Gardner, 2000; Uskul, Sherman, & Fitzgibbon, 2009).

Shifts in Construals and Perspectives

When people pursue a goal with a promotion versus prevention focus, the goal itself is construed in two fundamentally different ways—obtaining a positive outcome or avoiding a negative one. Shifts in one's construal, or perspective, are central to a number of other theories on self-regulation. Many of these theories focus on how people control the impulse to engage in behaviors that undermine their goals. How do you resist the impulse to go out with your friends the night before a big exam? How about stopping yourself from having another scoop of ice cream when you're trying to lose weight?

In the early 1970s, Walter Mischel and colleagues studied such questions in a well-known program of research involving, of all things, marshmallows (Mischel, Ebbesen, & Zeiss, 1972; Mischel, Shoda, & Rodriguez, 1989). In the classic marshmallow paradigm, preschool children were left in a room with a tempting marshmallow and given one of two options: they could have the one marshmallow (small reward) immediately simply by ringing a bell to summon the experimenter, or they could have two marshmallows (large reward) if they waited for the experimenter to return 15 minutes later. So, go for the small reward now, or control yourself so as to get a bigger reward later? Sound familiar? Go out with your friends to have a fun night now, or resist so you can do better on your exam tomorrow?

It turns out that one way to exert self-control in such situations is to shift how you construe the tempting reward—whether it be a marshmallow, ice cream, or night out on the town. This cognitive strategy is what enabled some of the children in Mischel's studies to resist the small, immediate reward in the service of the larger one later. Rather than construe the object before them as a marshmallow in all its sweet and mouth-watering delight, some of the children viewed the marshmallow in "cooler," less arousing terms, visualizing it as a decidedly non-mouth-watering cotton ball or cloud (Metcalfe & Mischel, 1999; Mischel & Ayduk, 2004). If you're trying to resist a temptation in the here and now (going out with your friends), it helps to focus less on its arousing, inviting features (great music, laughter) and more on its unappealing facets (spending money, losing much-needed sleep).

Construals of a situation can vary in other ways as well. Yaacov Trope and colleagues (Liberman, Trope, & Stephan, 2007; Trope & Liberman, 2010) have argued that events, goals, behaviors, and so forth, can also vary in how high level or low level they are. High-level construals focus on abstract, global, and essential features, whereas low-level construals emphasize salient, incidental, and concrete details. In other words, high-level construals involve seeing the "forest," whereas low-level construals put the spotlight on the "trees." It's higher-level construals that tend to facilitate self-control. The idea is that higher-level construals, compared with lower-level ones, increase people's appreciation of the

SELF-CONTROL AND CONSTRUALS
If the young girl views the marshmallow in "cooler" terms, such as in terms of something that resembles a cloud or cotton ball, rather than construing the marshmallow in "hotter" terms, such as in terms of its yummy, mouth-watering qualities, she'll have a better shot at resisting gobbling up the marshmallow while she waits for the researcher to return so that she can get two marshmallows instead.

consequences that their choices and behaviors have for their long-term goals. In other words, high-level construals place the emphasis on people's larger goals and values. For example, in a high-level construal (when you're focusing on the forest, not the trees), you think about what that extra scoop of ice cream means for your dieting and health goals, whereas in a low-level construal (when your focus is on the trees), you're focused on the pleasing taste and smooth texture of that ice cream (Fujita, 2011; Fujita, Trope, Liberman, & Levin-Sagi, 2006).

Automatic Self-Control Strategies

Exercising self-control may sound like a conscious, deliberate endeavor. But there's quite a lot of evidence that self-regulation efforts can operate automatically, without our even realizing it.

Researchers have distinguished between goal intentions, which simply specify a goal one wants to achieve (I intend to be kinder to my roommate), from **implementation intentions**, which specify how one will behave to achieve a goal under particular circumstances. Implementation intentions follow an *if-then* format—for example, "If my roommate makes a snarky remark, then I'll just ignore it." So the "if" refers to some kind of cue, and the "then" refers to a behavior that will follow the cue to achieve the larger goal (in this case, being kinder to a roommate) (Gollwitzer & Sheeran, 2006). There's no question that to achieve a goal we must form an intention, but research shows that forming multiple, smaller *implementation intentions* related to the same goal increases our likelihood of goal attainment. In the typical study of implementation intentions, participants are randomly assigned to either form an implementation intention or not. Take, for example, a group of students who all share the goal of completing a paper. Those who are randomly assigned to the implementation intention condition are asked to form an implementation intention by indicating a specific point in time ("Saturday afternoon") and specific place ("in my dorm room") when they will engage in the goal-directed behavior ("work on my paper"). Students in the other group are not asked to form an implementation intention but simply have the general goal of completing the paper. When level of goal completion (completing the paper) is then assessed, students who formed an implementation intention show higher rates of goal completion. Such if-then implementation intentions help you reach your goals by putting you on the lookout for whatever cue is specified ("if it's Saturday afternoon") and making you likely to automatically enact the goal-directed behavior ("then I will work on my paper") (Gollwitzer & Oettingen, 2016).

The effectiveness of implementation intentions has been documented across a wide range of goals and domains—doing well in school, being healthy, succeeding at work. Stern and West (2014) recently tested whether the formation of implementation intentions might even make stressful social interactions more pleasant, such as ones involving people of different races. What they found was that forming implementation intentions for such interactions—intentions that specify an anxiety-reducing behavior when feeling uncomfortable—increased the likelihood of a successful interaction. The lesson here seems to be that the next time you anticipate an anxiety-provoking interaction (your next interview), you might form an if-then plan for this interaction that specifies what you will do (perhaps remind yourself of your amazing credentials) whenever your heart starts to race.

implementation intention An "if-then" plan to engage in a goal-directed behavior ("then") whenever a particular cue ("if") is encountered.

Let's take one more example. Suppose you're trying to eat a healthier diet (long-term goal), but you're faced with a plate of freshly baked cookies (temptation). Surely the alluring properties of the cookies will put thoughts about eating healthily on the back burner, right? Fishbach, Friedman, and Kruglanski (2003) showed that quite the opposite can happen: the cookies may actually make you think more about your goal to eat healthily. The idea is that temptations (unhealthy foods) may become linked in memory to your goal (eating well), so that when temptations are brought to mind, so, too, are thoughts of healthy eating. And the connection between the two can occur automatically. What's more, the Fishbach team found that bringing goals to mind first has the effect of *diminishing* thoughts about temptations. Thus, being faced with temptations reminds us of our goals, and thinking about our goals puts temptations out of mind. But before deciding you can abandon all deliberate efforts to resist temptations, note that the effects found in this research apply mainly to people for whom the goal is very important and who have had substantial past success resisting goal-interfering temptations.

← LOOKING BACK

Self-regulation refers to how people go about initiating, changing, and controlling their behavior in pursuit of goals. Goal-directed actions can be motivated by standards in the form of ideal and ought selves. Such actions can be either promotion focused or prevention focused. People tend to experience dejection-related emotions when they fall short of their ideal standards, and they experience agitation-related emotions when they fail to meet their ought standards. Self-regulation can be facilitated by "cooler" and higher-level construals of tempting, short-term rewards. People may have unintentional self-control strategies, such as implementation intentions and automatic behavioral tendencies to approach goals and avoid temptations.

Self-Presentation

Alexi Santana entered Princeton University as a member of the class of 1993. His academic performance was impressive, he excelled in track, and he was admitted to one of Princeton's most exclusive eating clubs. He dazzled his dormmates with tales of being raised on a sheep farm in the wild canyons of southern Utah and with his unusual habits, such as preferring to sleep on the floor and routinely arising at dawn.

The only trouble was that Alexi Santana was actually James Hogue, a 34-year-old drifter and former track star from Kansas City. Hogue had been convicted and served time for various crimes, including check forging and bicycle theft. He had gotten into Princeton thanks to a fraudulent application and had earned the admiration of his peers based on a completely fabricated identity. In the documentary film *Con Man*, Jessie Moss showed that Hogue had had a pattern of assuming false identities.

SELF-PRESENTATION
James Hogue attended Princeton University on an academic scholarship under the assumed name of Alexi Santana. He constructed a false identity for himself as a self-educated 18-year-old from Utah. Hogue was arrested for forgery, wrongful impersonation, and falsifying records at Princeton.

self-presentation Presenting the person we would like others to believe we are.

face The public image of ourself that we want others to believe.

self-monitoring The tendency to monitor one's behavior to fit the current situation.

SELF-MONITORING
This couple is probably engaging in a considerable degree of self-monitoring, altering their behavior to fit the specific demands of first-date situations like this one.

Hogue's story (or is it Santana's?) is an extreme version of a basic truth: our social self is often a dramatic performance in which we try to project a public self consistent with our hopes and aspirations. This public self is one that we actively create in our social interactions and that is shaped by the perceptions of other people and the perceptions we want others to have of us (Baumeister, 1982; Mead, 1934; Schlenker, 1980; Shrauger & Schoeneman, 1979). The public self is concerned with **self-presentation**—presenting the person we would like others to believe we are. Another term for this concept is *impression management*, which refers to how we attempt to control the particular impressions other people form about us.

Sociologist Erving Goffman inspired the study of self-presentation with his keen observations about how we stake out our identity in the public realm (Goffman, 1959, 1967). Goffman relied on naturalistic observations of how people behave in public settings. He observed patients in mental institutions, noting how they seemed to ignore many rules of self-presentation, such as making unflattering comments about others and failing to observe common social courtesies. Goffman wrote an entire chapter on what he called response cries, like "Oops!," that we resort to after committing social gaffes and feel deeply embarrassed. These linguistic acts help reestablish social order when we have violated the rules of self-presentation and show how committed we are to preserving the self we want others to accept.

Such observations led Goffman to form what has been called a dramaturgic perspective on the social self. Social interaction can be thought of as a drama of self-presentation, in which we attempt to create and maintain an impression of ourselves in the minds of others (Baumeister, 1982; Brown, 1998; Goffman, 1959; Leary & Kowalski, 1990; Schlenker & Leary, 1982). Critical to this drama, in Goffman's terms, is **face**, the public image of ourselves that we want others to have. For instance, one person may want to be seen as a gifted, temperamental artist; another might want to give the impression of being an object of romantic interest to many people. Social interactions are the stage on which we play out these kinds of claims, regardless of how true they may be. Much like a play, the social drama of self-presentation is highly collaborative. We depend on others to honor our desired social identities, and others likewise depend on us to honor their face claims.

Goffman's insights have shaped the study of the social self in several ways. For example, the concept of self-monitoring derives in part from Goffman's work (Gangestad & Snyder, 2000; Snyder, 1974, 1979). **Self-monitoring** refers to the tendency to monitor one's behavior to fit the demands of the current situation. High self-monitors carefully scrutinize situations and, like actors, shift their self-presentation and behavior according to the people and situation. In contrast, low self-monitors are more likely to behave according to their own traits and preferences, regardless of the social context.

(A) (B)

This suggests admirable candor and honesty. However, one study showed that patients in a psychiatric hospital scored low on a self-monitoring scale, suggesting that effective social functioning requires participation in some degree of strategic self-presentation (Snyder, 1974).

Self-Handicapping

One of the complexities of strategic self-presentation is that people often don't live up to the public self they're trying to portray. For example, your claim about being the next great American writer will eventually be put to the test when you submit your prose for publication; your claim about being a great triathlete will eventually face the truth of the stopwatch. The obvious drawback of the public self is that we might not live up to it, and we risk embarrassing ourselves when that happens. To protect the self in these circumstances, we engage in various self-protective behaviors.

Self-handicapping is the tendency to engage in self-defeating behavior to protect the self in public and prevent others from making unwanted inferences based on poor performance (Arkin & Baumgardner, 1985; Deppe & Harackiewicz, 1996; Hendrix & Hirt, 2009; Hirt, McCrea, & Kimble, 2000; Jones & Berglas, 1978). Think of how often people engage in self-destructive behaviors when their public selves are on the line. Students sometimes irrationally put too little effort into studying for an exam. A person may act too casually at a job interview or say shockingly inappropriate things on a first date. Why do we engage in such self-defeating behaviors? In Goffman's view, these actions provide an explanation for possible failure, thereby protecting the desired public self if failure does occur. If you don't do as well as expected on an exam, there's no threat to your claim about your academic talents if you have the excuse of not having prepared for the exam in the first place. Of course, some "self-handicap" claims are bogus. Classrooms are filled with students who act as though they haven't studied hard when

self-handicapping The tendency to engage in self-defeating behavior in order to have an excuse ready should one perform poorly or fail.

BOX 3.5 ▶ FOCUS ON HEALTH

Dying to Present a Favorable Self

You might assume that self-presentation is always a good thing. Erving Goffman himself wrote about how people's strategic self-presentation and their honoring of other people's public claims are essential ingredients of harmonious communities. But self-presentational concerns can sometimes be dangerous to our health (Leary, Tchividjian, & Kraxberger, 1994). Many practices that promote health are awkward or embarrassing and pose problems for our public identity. As a consequence, we avoid them. We sacrifice physical health to maintain a public identity defined by composure and aplomb. In one study, for example, 30–65 percent of respondents reported embarrassment when buying condoms (Hanna, 1989). Embarrassment could deter sexually active teenagers from buying condoms, thus increasing their risk of sexually transmitted diseases and unwanted pregnancies. Similarly, the

fear of embarrassment at times prevents obese individuals from pursuing physical exercise programs or taking needed medications (Bain, Wilson, & Chaikind, 1989).

In other instances, we engage in risky behavior to enhance our public image and identity. Concerns about others' impressions of us and concerns about our physical appearance are good predictors of excessive sunbathing, which increases the likelihood of skin cancer (Leary & Jones, 1993). Moreover, adolescents typically cite social approval as one of the most important reasons for starting to drink alcohol and smoke cigarettes (Farber, Khavari, & Douglass, 1980). And the same need for an enhanced public image motivates many cosmetic surgeries, which carry with them a variety of health risks.

---

in fact they did. The phenomenon is so common that students at Dartmouth College have given the people who do it a name: "sneaky bookers."

In one of the first experiments testing self-handicapping, male participants were led to believe that they were either going to succeed or going to have difficulty on a test they were scheduled to take (Berglas & Jones, 1978). Participants were given the chance to ingest one of two drugs: the first would enhance their test performance, and the second would impair it. Participants who felt they were likely to fail the test preferred the performance-inhibiting drug, even though it was likely to diminish their chances of success. Apparently, people would sometimes rather fail and have a ready excuse for it than go for success and have no excuse for failure.

Presenting the Self Online

As of late 2016, Facebook reported over 1.23 billion daily active users. When you add to the tally all the other possible forms of social media, that's a whole lot of social life happening online. What does self-presentation in the online social world look like? Given that most of the information on social networking sites, such as Facebook, is provided by the users themselves, there is ample opportunity for people to manage others' impressions of them. Do people tend to present themselves authentically online, posting accurate information about who they are, what they've accomplished, their beliefs, and their likes and dislikes? Or do people take advantage of the opportunity that social networking sites offer to convey especially positive self-images?

Self-presentation researchers have begun to tackle these questions. In one study, researchers had observers rate the personality traits (including extraversion, neuroticism, and openness) of 236 American and German users of online social networking sites—Facebook in the United States and similar sites called StudiVZ and SchuelerVZ in Germany—based on the information provided on

Brian Cox ✔
@ProfBrianCox

Ultra-naïve positivist-ish, although science can't explain the existence of antipositivists

SOCIAL MEDIA PROFILES AND THE SELF
Public presentation of the self often occurs online, such as in the social media profile pictured above.

their profile pages (Back et al., 2010). Observers' ratings were compared with an accuracy criterion made up of an average of users' own ratings of their personality and the ratings of four well-acquainted friends. Users were also asked to provide ratings reflecting who they would ideally like to be. Would you expect observer ratings to correlate more highly with the users' own and friends' ratings, thus suggesting that people present themselves relatively accurately online, or with users' ideal self ratings, suggesting instead that people try to present themselves in an ideal light online? You may be surprised to learn that the findings supported the former view: that online, people tend to present their offline selves fairly accurately, a conclusion bolstered by other studies as well (Waggoner, Smith, & Collins, 2009).

Why would people present themselves accurately online when it seems so easy, not to mention tempting, to paint a positive image of the self online? Recall that although self-enhancement motives are robust (particularly among members of Western cultures), other self-evaluative motives may prevail at times. In particular, online self-presentations may be driven as much or more by self-verification motives, the desire to be known by others as they truly are (Swann, 1990), and crafting accurate online profiles of the self would serve that need. A less flattering explanation is that overly favorable online presentations of the self often need to withstand offline scrutiny. You can probably relate to having offline interactions with people who have read your profile, making it difficult (or at least awkward) to post blatantly inaccurate statements about yourself online. But perhaps surprisingly, research suggests that while we may present our personality and other attributes (such as our occupation) fairly accurately online, we are less likely to do so when it comes to our physical attributes, such as height, weight, and age (Toma & Hancock, 2010). This may be because of the vital role that physical appearance plays in attraction (see Chapter 10).

← LOOKING BACK

Self-presentation involves people's efforts to get others to form particular impressions of them. These strategies are more characteristic of high self-monitors, people who change their behavior based on the situation in which they find themselves. Low self-monitors attend more to their own preferences and dispositions, with little regard for the situation or what others think. People may engage in self-defeating behaviors, or self-handicapping, to have an excuse available should they fail or perform poorly. Self-presentation is also relevant in online social networking, where it appears that people are more inclined to provide accurate information about some aspects of themselves, such as their personality traits, and less accurate information about other aspects of themselves, such as their physical features.

Chapter Review

SUMMARY

The Nature of the Social Self

- The self is fundamentally social, and it shifts according to changes in the social situation.
- *Self-schemas*, organizing structures that help guide the construal of social information, represent a person's beliefs and feelings about the self, both in general and in specific situations.

Origins of the Sense of Self

- Socialization by family members and other important people is one of the foundations of the social self. *Reflected self-appraisals* are beliefs about what others think of one's social self.
- The social self is shaped by the current situation in many ways, and different selves are evoked in different situations.
- The social self is profoundly shaped by whether people live in independent or interdependent cultures.
- Women generally emphasize their relationships and define themselves in an interdependent way; men generally emphasize their uniqueness and construe themselves in an independent way.
- People rely on *social comparisons* to learn about their own abilities, attitudes, and personal traits.

Self-Esteem

- Trait self-esteem is a stable part of one's identity, whereas state self-esteem changes according to different contextual factors.

- Self-esteem is defined by particular domains of importance, or *contingencies of self-worth*, and by being accepted by others.
- Self-esteem is more important, and is higher, in Western cultures than in East Asian cultures.

Motives Driving Self-Evaluation

- The motives for self-evaluation include the desire for *self-enhancement* and *self-verification*.
- The motivation to think well of oneself guides the maintenance of relationships that let people make favorable social comparisons and that provide the opportunity to bask in the successes of relationship partners.
- Having a stable set of self-beliefs gives people a sense of coherence and predictability.

Self-Regulation: Motivating and Controlling Behavior

- *Self-discrepancy theory* investigates how people compare their *actual self* to both their *ideal self* and their *ought self* and the emotional consequences of such comparisons.
- When people regulate their behavior with respect to ideal self standards, they have a *promotion focus* for attaining positive outcomes. When people regulate their behavior with respect to ought self standards, they have a *prevention focus* for avoiding negative outcomes.
- Self-control can be facilitated by construals that focus on "cooler" features of a tempting stimulus and by higher-level, abstract construals of the situation.
- Self-control strategies can be implemented automatically, such as when behavior unfolds automatically as specified in an implementation intention or when long-term goals automatically spring to mind when people face temptations that can thwart these goals.

Self-Presentation

- *Self-presentation* is related to the public self; people present themselves the way they want others to see them. *Face* refers to the image people want others to have about them. *Self-monitoring* ensures that a person's behavior fits the demands of the social context.
- People protect their public self through *self-handicapping*, behavior that can excuse a poor performance or a failure.
- Self-presentation happens online, just as it does in face-to-face interactions. Different motives can guide online self-presentation, including the desire for others to see the self accurately.

THINK ABOUT IT

1. According to research on the accuracy of self-knowledge, for what qualities are we the best judges of ourselves? For what qualities are others superior judges of us? How does motivation contribute to this asymmetry?

2. Josie is a 13-year-old girl who thinks she's a funny person, and her friends and family generally think Josie is funny too. How would Cooley's notion of the "looking-glass self" explain how Josie's sense of herself as funny developed? Bearing in mind that Josie is an adolescent, what does research suggest is likely occurring in her brain when she thinks about her self-views?

3. How might a female undergraduate's working self-concept regarding her gender shift during a day on campus as she attends her advanced math class (in which she is the only female), has a low-key lunch with a friend, and attends her gender studies class? Will her frequently shifting self-concept undermine her sense of having a coherent self?

4. How do people's daily experiences in their contingent versus noncontingent domains affect their state self-esteem? Over time, how might these experiences translate to trait self-esteem?

5. Do people from Eastern cultures generally feel worse about themselves than people from Western cultures? How do researchers interpret self-reported self-esteem differences between cultures?

6. Should people be more likely to display the better-than-average effect for their own intelligence before or after learning how intelligence is measured in scientific research? How do construals contribute to this process?

7. If you're fairly sure you are scatterbrained, but a friend tells you that you're organized and focused, what will your cognitive reaction likely be? What will your emotional reaction likely be? Which motive—self-enhancement or self-verification—drives which set of reactions?

8. Suppose two friends both have an actual self that is relatively happy and a potential self that is extremely happy (happier than their actual self). If this discrepancy in happiness leads one friend to experience agitation and the other friend to experience dejection, what does this tell you? What theory would this evidence support?

The **answer guidelines** for the think about it questions can be found at the back of the book . . . 👉

ONLINE STUDY MATERIALS

Want to earn a better grade on your test?

Go to **inquizitive** to learn and review this chapter's content, with personalized feedback along the way.

What makes us sometimes trust people we shouldn't?

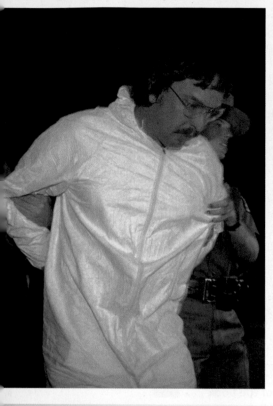

What determines whether we think of foreign travel as "expanding our horizons" versus "walking around in another country"?

How might the labels applied to immigrant workers affect our views of immigration?

CHAPTER 4

Social Cognition: Thinking about People and Situations

EARLY IN THE MORNING ON JUNE 28, 1993, New York State troopers on Long Island's Southern State Parkway noticed a Mazda pickup truck with no license plates. When they motioned for the driver to pull over, he sped off, leading them on a 25-minute chase that ended when the Mazda slammed into a utility pole. After arresting the driver, the officers noticed a foul odor emanating from under a tarp in the back of the truck. When the tarp was removed, the officers discovered the badly decomposed body of a 22-year-old woman. Subsequent investigation implicated the driver, Joel Rifkin, in the murders of 16 other women, making him the most prolific serial killer in New York State history.

Those who knew Rifkin expressed shock at the news. One neighbor told reporters, "When I would come home at 1 or 2 in the morning, if I saw the garage light on, I'd feel safe because I knew Joel was around." A second neighbor said he was "simply a gentle young man." Classmates asserted he was "not the kind of guy who would do something like this."

As this story makes clear, social judgments can have serious consequences. Mistaking a serial killer as someone who's "gentle" and "safe" can be a lethal error. More generally, effective action requires sound judgment about other people and the world around us. "How will my professor react if I ask for more time?" "Are they developing nuclear weapons?" "Can I trust my boyfriend?"

This chapter's discussion of social cognition—and sources of error in judgments about the social world—proceeds in five parts, each focusing on a critical aspect of social judgment: (1) Our judgments are only as accurate as the quality of the information on which they are based, and the information available to us in everyday life is not always representative or complete. (2) The way information is presented, including the order in which it is presented and how it is framed, can affect the judgments we make. (3) We don't just passively take in information. We often actively seek it out, and a pervasive bias in how we do so can distort the conclusions we reach. (4) Our preexisting knowledge and mental habits can influence how we construe new information and thus substantially influence judgment. (5) Two mental systems, reason and intuition, underlie social cognition, and their complex interplay determines the judgments we make. ■

Studying Social Cognition

The field of social cognition involves the study of how people think about the social world and arrive at judgments that help them interpret the past, understand the present, and predict the future. One of the earliest and most fundamental principles of social psychology is the construal principle introduced in Chapter 1: if we want to know how a person will react in a given situation, we must understand how the person interprets that situation.

The story that opened this chapter does more than testify to the importance of the social judgments we make in everyday life. It also highlights the fact that our judgments are not always flawless. We trust some people we shouldn't. We make some investments that turn out to be unwise.

Errors in judgment are informative to psychologists because they provide particularly helpful clues about how people think about others and make inferences about them. The strategy of scrutinizing mistakes has a long tradition in psychology. Perceptual psychologists study illusions because they help reveal general principles of perception. Psycholinguists study speech errors to learn about speech production. Mistakes can reveal a great deal about how a system works by showing its limitations. Thus, researchers interested in social cognition have often explored the limitations of everyday judgment.

The Information Available for Social Cognition

Understanding other people depends on accurate information. But sometimes we have only fragmentary information on which to base our assessments; sometimes the available information is misleading; sometimes the way we acquire information biases the conclusions we reach. Each of these circumstances presents special challenges to achieving an accurate understanding of others.

Minimal Information: Inferring Personality from Physical Appearance

A lack of sufficient information on which to base a sound judgment rarely stops people from making judgments about a person or situation. Consider how quickly we form impressions of complete strangers based on the briefest glances. The term *snap judgment* exists for a reason. In a telling empirical demonstration of how quickly we can make judgments about others, Janine Willis and Alex

Todorov (2006) showed participants a large number of faces and had them rate how trustworthy, competent, likable, aggressive, or attractive each person seemed. Some participants were given as much time as they wanted to make each rating, and their trait judgments were used as the "gold standard" of comparison—the most telling impressions an individual could form based solely on photographs. Other participants were also asked to rate the photos, but after seeing each face for only a second, half a second, or a tenth of a second. As it turned out, hurried trait judgments corresponded remarkably well with the more reflective assessments. A great deal of what we conclude about people based on their faces is determined almost instantaneously. In fact, the correlation between judgments made at leisure and those made in a tenth of a second was almost as high as the correlation between judgments made at leisure and those made in a full second.

PERCEIVING TRUST AND DOMINANCE What is it that people think they see in brief glances at another person's face? To find out, Todorov and his colleagues had participants rate a large number of photographs of different faces on the personality dimensions people tend to mention spontaneously when describing faces (Todorov, Said, Engell, & Oosterhof, 2008). When they looked at how all these judgments correlated with one another, they found that two dimensions stand out. One is a positive-negative dimension, involving such assessments as whether someone is seen as trustworthy or untrustworthy, aggressive or not aggressive. The other dimension centers around power, involving assessments such as whether someone seems confident or bashful, dominant or submissive. It appears, then, that people are set to make quite important judgments about others: whether they should be approached or avoided (dimension 1), and whether they're likely to be top dog or underdog (dimension 2). Todorov used computer models to generate faces that represent various combinations of these two dimensions, including faces that are more extreme on each trait dimension than would ever be encountered in real life (**Figure 4.1**). In these faces, you can see the hypermasculine features, such as a very pronounced jaw, that make someone look dominant, and the features, such as the shape of the eyebrows and eye sockets, that make someone look trustworthy.

If you look at the faces that are seen as trustworthy and not dominant, you'll notice that they tend to look like baby faces. Indeed, extensive research by Leslie Zebrowitz and her colleagues has shown that adults with such baby-faced features as large round eyes, a large forehead, high eyebrows, and a rounded, relatively small chin are assumed to possess many of the characteristics associated with the very young (Berry & Zebrowitz-McArthur, 1986; Zebrowitz & Montepare, 2005). They are judged to be relatively weak, naive, and submissive, whereas adults with small eyes, a small forehead, and an angular, prominent chin tend to be judged as strong, competent, and dominant.

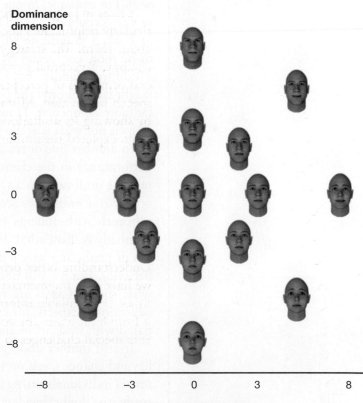

FIGURE 4.1
JUDGING FACES
These computer-generated faces show variations on the two independent dimensions of trustworthiness (x-axis) and dominance (y-axis).
Source: Adapted from Todorov et al., 2008.

It makes sense that we consider adults with baby faces to be relatively harmless and helpless. The renowned ethologist Konrad Lorenz (1950/1971) speculated that the cuteness of the young in many mammalian species triggers a hardwired, automatic reaction that helps ensure the young and helpless receive adequate care. The automatic nature of our response to infantile features makes it more likely that we would overgeneralize and come to see even adults with such features as trustworthy and friendly. These assessments have dramatic consequences: baby-faced individuals receive more favorable treatment as defendants in court (Zebrowitz & McDonald, 1991), but they have a harder time being seen as appropriate for "adult" jobs, such as banking (Zebrowitz, Tenenbaum, & Goldstein, 1991).

THE ACCURACY OF SNAP JUDGMENTS How accurate are the snap judgments we make about people based on their appearance or very brief samples of their behavior? Are people with baby faces, for example, really more likely to be weak or submissive? Are the facial features people associate with different personality traits valid cues to those traits? Are brief samples of people's behavior—psychologists call them "thin slices" of behavior—reliable guides to what they're really like?

Note that sometimes it's as important to know what other people *think* someone is like as it is to know that person's true characteristics. In those cases, the pertinent question boils down to how well snap judgments predict more considered consensus opinion. And the evidence indicates that they predict rather well. For example, in one study, participants were shown, for 1 second, pictures of the Republican and Democratic candidates in U.S. congressional elections and asked to indicate which candidates looked more competent. Those judged to be more competent by most of the participants won 69 percent of the races (Todorov, Mandisodza, Goren, & Hall, 2005). These judgments of competence might lack validity: the person judged to be more competent might not actually be more competent. However, what matters in predicting the outcome of elections is not what is really true, but what the electorate believes to be true.

In another line of research, participants were shown thin slices of professors' performance in the classroom (three 10-second silent video clips) and asked to rate the professors on a variety of dimensions, such as how anxious, competent, active, and warm they seemed. These relatively quick assessments correlated significantly with students' evaluations of their professors at the end of the semester (Ambady & Rosenthal, 1993). In other words, the quick reactions did a decent job of predicting later judgments based on exposure to much larger samples of behavior. But we still don't know that these reactions are valid with respect to what the professors are really like—how competent they might be judged by educational experts, for example, or how well their students do on exams compared with students in another professor's class.

In still another study, participants were able to determine sexual orientation at beyond chance levels on the basis of 10-second clips of gay, lesbian, and heterosexual individuals sitting in a chair (Ambady, Hallahan, & Conner, 1999). (Their study cast doubt, incidentally, on the concept of "gaydar.")

The available evidence thus indicates that there is often some validity even to impressions based on extremely brief exposure to other people's behavior. Nevertheless, it's probably unwise to put too much confidence in our snap judgments, because in general they contain only a kernel of truth (Pound, Penton-Voak, & Brown, 2007; Zebrowitz, Voinescu, & Collins, 1996). But they do provide a kernel.

Misleading Firsthand Information: Pluralistic Ignorance

Some of the information we have about the world, including our immediate impressions of others, comes to us through direct experience. The rest comes to us secondhand, through gossip, the mass media, biographies, textbooks, and so on. In many cases, information collected firsthand is more accurate because it has the advantage of not having been filtered by someone else, who might slant things in a particular direction. But firsthand experiences can also be deceptive, as when we fail to pay close attention to information about events that occur before our eyes or when we misconstrue their true meaning. Our firsthand experience can also be unrepresentative, as it tends to be, for example, when judging what the students at a given university are like based on the one or two encountered during a campus tour or when judging what "the locals" in a foreign country are like from the few we encounter at hotels or museums.

Some of the firsthand information we acquire about people is inaccurate because it's intended to be. People often mislead us by acting in ways that don't reflect their true attitudes or beliefs. One especially noteworthy example is the phenomenon of **pluralistic ignorance**, which occurs whenever people act in ways that conflict with their private beliefs because of a concern for the social consequences. It's embarrassing to admit you didn't understand a lecture when you suspect that everyone else did, so you act like you aren't befuddled. However, when everyone follows that logic, they all mislead one another about the true group norm.

Pluralistic ignorance is particularly common in situations where "toughness" is valued and people are afraid to show their kinder, gentler impulses. Gang members, for example, have been known privately to confess their objections to brutal initiation procedures and the lack of concern for human life, but they're afraid to say so because of the fear of being ridiculed by their peers. The result is that few of them realize how many of their fellow gang members share their private reservations (Matza, 1964).

INFANTILE FEATURES IN YOUNG MAMMALS
Do you find these baby animals cute? Do you feel warmth and compassion toward them? You should. Psychologists and ethologists argue that the features associated with the very young in virtually all mammalian species trigger emotions that encourage caregiving and hence survival.

pluralistic ignorance Misperception of a group norm that results from observing people who are acting at variance with their private beliefs out of a concern for the social consequences; those actions reinforce the erroneous group norm.

DRAWING STRONG CONCLUSIONS FROM LIMITED INFORMATION
We often form strong impressions of what something is like, such as the students at this university, based on the few people we happen to meet during a brief visit.

More recently, Nicole Shelton and Jennifer Richeson (2005) examined another form of pluralistic ignorance, one with profound implications for interactions between members of different ethnic groups. The researchers predicted that people might worry that someone from another ethnic group would not be interested in talking to them. Initiating conversation would therefore seem risky, something they might want to avoid out of fear of being rejected. As a result, no opening gesture is made and no contact is established. When Shelton and Richeson asked students a series of focused questions to probe this issue, they found that although the students generally attributed their own failure to initiate contact to their fear of rejection, they assumed that the other person didn't initiate contact because of a lack of interest in establishing friendships across ethnic lines. And when both people assume the other isn't interested, neither one makes the effort to become friends.

Misleading Firsthand Information: Self-Fulfilling Prophecies

self-fulfilling prophecy The tendency for people to act in ways that bring about the very thing they expect to happen.

In early January of 1981, Joseph Granville, financial writer and author of the *Granville Market Letter*, wrote that the stock market was headed for a steep decline and advised his readers to "sell everything." Remarkably, stocks tumbled the very next day in what was then the biggest day of trading in the history of the New York Stock Exchange. Had Granville seen something that other analysts missed? Or did his advice lead to a sell-off that helped cause the very decline he predicted? This question highlights another way in which firsthand information can be misleading: we can fail to notice that our own behavior has brought about what we're seeing. This phenomenon is called the **self-fulfilling prophecy**: our expectations lead us to behave in ways that elicit the very behavior we expect from others. If we think someone is unfriendly, we're likely to offer something of a cold shoulder ourselves, which is likely to elicit the very coldness we anticipated.

The most famous demonstration of the impact of self-fulfilling prophecies is a study in which researchers told elementary school teachers that aptitude tests indicated that several of their students could be expected to "bloom" intellectually in the coming year (Rosenthal & Jacobson, 1968). In reality, the students so described were chosen randomly. Nevertheless, the expectation that certain students would undergo an intellectual growth spurt set in motion a pattern of student-teacher interaction that led those students to score higher on IQ tests administered at the end of the year (Jussim, 1986; Smith, Jussim, & Eccles, 1999).

SELF-FULFILLING PROPHECIES
A teacher who believes a student is capable is likely to act toward the student in ways that bring out the best in that student, thereby confirming the teacher's initial belief.

In another notable study, Saul Kassin, Christine Goldstein, and Ken Savitsky (2003) had some students commit a mock crime (stealing $100 from a locked laboratory cabinet) and other students simply visit the scene of the crime. These students were then questioned by student interrogators who were led to believe they were likely to be guilty or innocent. The interrogators who thought their suspects were likely to be guilty asked more incriminating questions and generally conducted more vigorous and aggressive interrogations. This in turn led these suspects to act more defensively, which made them appear guilty to a group of observers who listened to tapes containing only the suspects' comments (with the interrogators' questions removed). When the interrogators thought someone was guilty, he or she acted in ways that elicited apparent evidence of guilt.

Note that if a prophecy is to be self-fulfilling, some mechanism must be at work to translate a person's expectation into action that would then confirm the prophecy. In the study of teachers' expectations, the mechanism was the teachers' behavior. They gave the alleged "bloomers" more attention and encouragement and challenged them with more difficult material. This helped these students to later score higher on IQ tests, thus fulfilling the prophecy. Not all prophecies have that link. Someone might think you're rich, but that belief wouldn't make it so. In fact, some prophecies can even be self-negating, as when a driver believes that "nothing bad can happen to me" and therefore drives recklessly (Dawes, 1988).

Misleading Secondhand Information

Do you believe that global warming is caused by humans? That Walt Disney was anti-Semitic? That your roommate's father is a good parent? Opinions like these are based to a large extent on secondhand information. Few of us have any first-hand knowledge of the links between industrialization and climatological data. None of us knows firsthand what Walt Disney thought about Jews. And for most people, knowledge of their roommate's father is limited to whatever stories the roommate has told about him.

What are some of the variables that influence the accuracy of secondhand information? What factors reduce the reliability of secondhand information, and when do these factors come into play?

IDEOLOGICAL DISTORTIONS People who transmit information often have an ideological agenda—a desire to foster certain beliefs or behaviors—that leads them to accentuate some elements of a story and suppress others. Sometimes such motivated distortion is relatively "innocent": the person relaying the message fervently believes it but chooses to omit certain inconvenient details that might detract from its impact. As U.S. Undersecretary of State Dean Acheson remarked when preparing President Harry Truman for a 1947 speech, sometimes it is necessary to be "clearer than the truth."

Of course, not all distortions are so innocent. People often knowingly provide distorted accounts for the express purpose of misleading. In American politics, Republicans and Democrats call attention to all kinds of misleading statistics to make the other party look bad. In areas of intense ethnic strife, such as Yemen, the Congo, Gaza, and Kashmir, all sides wildly exaggerate their own righteousness and inflate tales of atrocities committed against them (even though the reality is often bad enough).

DISTORTIONS IN THE SERVICE OF ENTERTAINMENT: OVER-EMPHASIS ON BAD NEWS One of the most pervasive causes of distortion in secondhand accounts is the desire to entertain. On a small scale, this happens in the stories people tell one another,

"Here it is—the plain, unvarnished truth. Varnish it."

sometimes embellished to make them more interesting. Being trapped in an elevator with 20 people for an hour is more intriguing than being trapped with 6 people for 15 minutes. So we round up, generously. On a larger scale, the desire to entertain distorts the messages people receive through the mass media. One way print and broadcast media can attract an audience is to report—indeed, overreport—negative, violent, and sensational events. Bad news tends to be more newsworthy than good news—or, as the news world puts it, "If it bleeds, it leads."

The media do indeed provide a distorted view of reality, without necessarily intending to. In the world as the media present it, 80 percent of all crime is violent; in the real world, only 20 percent of reported crimes are violent (Center for Media and Public Affairs, 2000; Marsh, 1991; Sheley & Askins, 1981). In addition, news coverage of crime doesn't correlate with the rise and fall of the crime rate. There is just as much coverage during the best of times as there is during the worst of times (Garofalo, 1981; Windhauser, Seiter, & Winfree, 1991). The world presented in film and television dramas is even more violent than TV news coverage (Gerbner, Gross, Morgan, & Signorielli, 1980). As a result, it's scarcely surprising that although the crime rate in the United States is much lower than it was 20 years ago, most people think it has increased.

EFFECTS OF THE BAD-NEWS BIAS The bad-news bias can lead people to believe they are more at risk of victimization than they really are. Investigators have conducted surveys that ask people how much television they watch and their impressions of the prevalence of crime: "How likely do you think it is that you or one of your close friends will have their house broken into during the next year?" "If a child were to play alone in a park each day for a month, what do you think that child's chances are of being the victim of a violent crime?"

Such studies have consistently found a positive correlation between the amount of time spent watching TV and the fear of victimization. As with all correlational studies, however, this finding by itself is difficult to interpret. Perhaps there is something about the kind of people who watch a lot of television, besides their viewing habits, that makes them feel vulnerable. To address this problem, researchers have collected data from a variety of other measures (income, gender, race, residential location) and examined whether the findings hold up when these other variables are statistically controlled. An interesting pattern emerges. The correlation between TV viewing habits and perceived vulnerability is substantially reduced among people living in low-crime neighborhoods, but it remains strong among those living in high-crime areas (Doob & MacDonald, 1979; Gerbner et al., 1980). People who live in dangerous areas and don't watch much TV feel safer than their neighbors who watch a lot.

Thus, the violence depicted in TV programs can make the world appear to be a dangerous place, especially when the televised images resonate with what people see in their own environment.

JUST HOW FAKE IS THE NEWS? People from both ends of the political spectrum in the United States have recently taken to accusing some in the news

TV VIOLENCE AND BELIEF IN VICTIMIZATION
Viewing crime shows such as *Blue Bloods* makes people feel unsafe. People who don't watch much TV feel safer than those living in the same neighborhood who do watch TV frequently.

BOX 4.1 | FOCUS ON NEWS, POLITICS, AND SOCIAL MEDIA

Burst Your Bubble

Were you astonished when Donald Trump won the presidency in 2016? Were you surprised when Mitt Romney didn't win the presidency in 2012? If your answer to either of these questions is yes, you may be living in a news bubble not entirely of your own making. Once you click on a few stories or commentaries with a heavily liberal or conservative bias, the Internet will then supply you with large amounts of ideologically congruent news and opinion pieces. Thus, in the 2016 U.S. presidential campaign, supporters of Hillary Clinton received news that was mostly favorable to her and unfavorable to Donald Trump, allowing many of them to remain unaware of the grievances of working-class and middle class white voters who were decisive in handing a victory to Trump. In the 2012 presidential campaign, Romney supporters, inundated primarily with news that was in line with their views, felt that although Romney was behind in the polls, the enthusiasm of his supporters greatly exceeded that of Obama supporters. Romney himself was so convinced that he would win that he allegedly did not prepare a concession speech and had to wing it once the results were clear.

When the only information we receive is that which serves to support our preexisting viewpoints, we're not getting the full picture about current events. And the more people become trapped in news bubbles, the more intractable become the nation's political divisions and the more confident people become that those on the other side are tremendously misguided and are consuming fake and biased news (Westfall, Van Boven, Chambers, & Judd, 2015).

Fortunately, there are a number of Internet applications that can help burst your bubble. One such application, "Escape Your Bubble," seeds your Facebook feed with views opposite to your own. Another application, "Outside Your Bubble," brings you comments from across the political spectrum and strips them of partisan venom, rephrasing them as neutral observations so that you can assess them objectively rather than rejecting them simply on the basis of their tone. These and other applications will ensure you get news and opinions that differ from your own.

"That was Brad with the Democratic weather. Now here's Tammy with the Republican weather."

media of chronically making false statements. Is fake news a real thing? Absolutely. And it's not just a recent phenomenon: think about the various conspiracy theories and hoaxes that have been reported by the media throughout modern history. But how big a problem is fake news today? It's hard to answer this question definitively, as comprehensive data that bear on it are not easy to come by. And although the truthfulness of some news stories, such as the claim that Pope Francis endorsed Donald Trump during the 2016 U.S. presidential campaign, are relatively easy to verify or disprove, other stories and claims are murkier and may be exaggerated rather than outright lies. Meanwhile, social media can magnify the impact of any fake or hyperbolic news story because it provides a ready means to spread news widely and quickly—although recent findings suggest that social media's role in inflating the impact of fake news during the 2016 U.S. presidential election may have been more modest than many people assumed (Allcott & Gentzkow, 2017). The bottom line is that it can be difficult for the average consumer of news to discern truth from fiction.

However, the core mission of journalism is still to discover and disseminate the truth, making it likely that the willful spreading of misinformation is more the exception than the rule. But it's not necessary for a news outlet to lie to try

WikiLeaks CONFIRMS Hillary Sold Weapons to ISIS... Then Drops Another BOMBSHELL!

CUES TO FAKERY
Extreme improbability is one cue that a news item is fake; being sent the item on social media is another reason to exercise some skepticism.

to influence public opinion in the direction of its own biases. The choice of experts to quote is one way to influence the reader's (or viewer's) judgment. Liberal newspapers are more likely to quote liberal sources, and conservative newspapers are more likely to quote conservative sources. In the most reliable outlets, deliberate errors in reporting the facts are rare. But selective reporting of sources can have a big impact on the conclusions that a reader, listener, or viewer is likely to reach.

Anchors on cable news shows often ask their guests leading questions, praise responses they like, and rebut those they don't like. Some anchors fail to correct any factual errors or misrepresentations by a politician or "expert" who appears on the show if the error in question fits the show's ideological leanings. Because of these tendencies, if you consume liberal papers and TV shows to the exclusion of conservative ones, your views will probably be tugged in a liberal direction, whereas if your news diet is made up exclusively of conservative papers and TV shows, your views will probably be guided in a conservative direction. In the media age we live in, and a highly partisan one at that, it's hard to resist the influence of the slanted secondhand reports we receive of what's going on in the world. It's therefore all the more important to be on the lookout for such biases and to try to get information from multiple sources to get a variety of viewpoints.

← LOOKING BACK

The quality of our judgments derives in part from the quality of the information on which our judgments are based. Sometimes we have very little information at our disposal, as when we have to make snap judgments about other people based only on physical appearance and small samples of their behavior. Research indicates that when people make snap judgments, they tend to agree with one another to a remarkable degree. The information available for closer examination may suffer from a number of potential biases. Even firsthand information can be biased, as when people behave in ways that don't reflect their true attitudes or when people act in ways that elicit from others the very behavior they were expecting. Information received secondhand can also lead to errors, as when communicators distort information in the interest of profit or ideology. This may account for the heightened fear that accompanies exposure to the media's overreporting of negative, violent, and sensational news stories and for the news reports that are frequently biased, even though they may not contain any outright misstatements of fact.

How Information Is Presented

To understand the powerful impact of how information is presented, we can start by considering the marketing and advertising of products. In the modern world of material abundance, companies often produce more than enough to satisfy the needs of society, and they find it useful to further stimulate "need" so that there will be a larger demand for their products. By manipulating the messages people receive about various products through marketing, producers hope to influence consumers' buying impulses. The key to successful marketing, in turn, is not simply the selection of *what* information to present, but *how* to present it. Countless studies have demonstrated that slight variations in the presentation of information—*how* it is presented and even *when* it is presented—can have profound effects on people's judgments.

Order Effects

How happy are you with your life in general? How many dates have you been on in the past month? If you're like most people, there may have been some connection, but often not a strong one, between your responses to the two questions. After all, there is more to life than dating. Indeed, when survey respondents were asked these two questions in this order, the correlation between their responses was .32, only a slight relationship. But when another group was asked the two questions in the opposite order, the correlation between their responses was twice as strong: .67. Asking about their recent dating history in the first question made them very aware of how that part of their life was going, which then had a notable impact on their assessment of their happiness generally (Strack, Martin, & Schwarz, 1988; see also Haberstroh, Oyserman, Schwarz, Kiihnen, & Ji, 2002; Tourangeau, Rasinski, & Bradburn, 1991).

Results such as these provide striking confirmation of something many people grasp intuitively—that the order in which items are presented can have a powerful influence on judgment. This is why we worry so much about whether we should go first or last in any kind of performance—interviewing for a job, say, or giving a classroom presentation. Sometimes the information presented first exerts the most influence, a phenomenon known as a **primacy effect**. Other times the information presented last has the most impact, a phenomenon known as a **recency effect**. These two are collectively referred to as *order effects*.

As a rough general rule, primacy effects most often occur when the information is ambiguous, so that what comes first influences how the later information is interpreted. Consider a study in which Solomon Asch (1946) asked people to evaluate a hypothetical individual described by the following terms: intelligent, industrious, impulsive, critical, stubborn, and envious. The individual was rated favorably, no doubt because of the influence of the two very positive terms that began the list—*intelligent* and *industrious*. A second group read the same trait adjectives in the opposite order and formed a much less favorable impression, because the first two descriptive terms—*stubborn* and *envious*—are negative. Thus, there was a substantial primacy effect. Traits presented at the beginning of the list had more impact than those presented later on. Etiquette books (and your parents) are right: first impressions are crucial. Note that all the traits in Asch's experiment have different shades of meaning, and how each is construed depends on the information already encountered. Take the word *stubborn*. When it follows positive traits, such as *intelligent* and *industrious*, people interpret it charitably, as steadfast or determined. However, when it follows *envious*, it is seen more negatively, as closed-minded or rigid (Asch & Zukier, 1984; Biernat, Manis, & Kobrynowicz, 1997; Hamilton & Zanna, 1974).

Recency effects, in contrast, typically result when the last items come more readily to mind. Information remembered obviously receives greater weight than

primacy effect A type of order effect: the disproportionate influence on judgment by information presented first in a body of evidence.

recency effect A type of order effect: the disproportionate influence on judgment by information presented last in a body of evidence.

information forgotten, so later items sometimes exert more influence on judgment than information presented earlier.

Framing Effects

framing effect The influence on judgment resulting from the way information is presented, such as the order of presentation or the wording.

Order effects are a type of **framing effect**: the way information is presented, including the order of presentation, can "frame" the way it's processed and understood. Asking survey respondents first about how many dates they've had recently frames the question about life in a way that highlights the importance of one's dating life to overall well-being.

Order effects are a type of "pure" framing effect: the frame of reference is changed by reordering the information, even though the content of the information remains exactly the same. Consider the (probably apocryphal) story of the monk whose request to smoke while he prayed was met with a disapproving stare by his superior. When he mentioned this to a friend, he was told: "Ask a different question. Ask if you can pray while you smoke." The request is the same in both versions. But there is a subtle difference in the frame of reference. The latter presupposes smoking; the former doesn't.

SPIN FRAMING Framing effects aren't limited to the order in which information is presented. *Spin framing* is a less straightforward form of framing that varies the content, not just the order, of what is presented. A company whose product is of higher quality than competing products will introduce information that frames the consumer's choice as one of quality. Another company whose product has a lower price will feature information that frames the consumer's choice as one of savings.

Participants in political debates use spin framing to highlight some aspects of the relevant information and not others. Thus, we hear advocates of different positions talk of "pro-choice" versus "pro-life," "illegal aliens" versus "undocumented workers," even "torture" versus "enhanced interrogation." The power of such terms to frame, or spin, the relevant issues led the United States in 1947 to change the name of the War Department to the more benign-sounding Defense Department. More recently, people have been encouraged to view dubious assertions as "alternative facts."

Politicians (and some polling organizations with a political mission) engage in spin framing when they conduct opinion polls to gather support for their positions. People are more likely to say they are in favor of repealing a "death" tax than an "inheritance" tax. And asking people whether they are in favor of "tax relief" is almost guaranteed to elicit strong support because the very word *relief* implies that taxes are a burden from which relief is needed (Lakoff, 2004). Because it's so easy to slant public opinion in a given direction, it's important to check the source of the poll and to be mindful of the exact wording of the questions. As former Israeli Prime Minister Shimon Peres noted, opinion polls are "like perfume—nice to smell, dangerous to swallow."

SPIN FRAMING
Describing these people as "illegal aliens" creates a more unfavorable impression than describing them as "undocumented workers."

POSITIVE AND NEGATIVE FRAMING Nearly everything in life is a mixture of good and bad. Ice cream tastes great, but it's full of saturated fat. Loyalty is a virtue, but it can make a person blind to another's faults. The mixed nature of

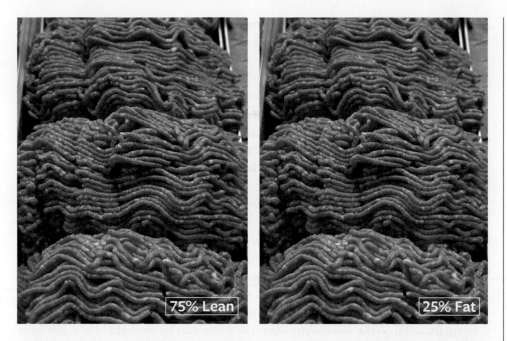

75% Lean   25% Fat

most things means that they can be described, or framed, in ways that emphasize the good or the bad, with predictable effects on people's judgments. A piece of meat described as 75 percent lean seems more appealing than one described as 25 percent fat (Levin & Gaeth, 1988); people feel much safer using a condom described as having a 90 percent success rate than one described as having a 10 percent failure rate (Linville, Fischer, & Fischhoff, 1993). Notice that the exact same information is provided in each frame; only the focus is different. Also note that there is no "correct" frame. It is every bit as valid to state that a piece of meat is 75 percent lean as it is to state that it is 25 percent fat.

These sorts of framing effects can influence judgments and decisions of the greatest consequence, even among individuals with considerable expertise on the topic in question. In one study, for example, over 400 physicians were asked whether they would recommend surgery or radiation for patients diagnosed with a certain type of cancer (McNeil, Pauker, Sox, & Tversky, 1982). Some were told that of 100 previous patients who had the surgery, 90 lived through the postoperative period, 68 were still alive after a year, and 34 were still alive after 5 years. Eighty-two percent of these physicians recommended surgery. Others were given exactly the same information, but framed in different language: that 10 died during surgery or the postoperative period, 32 had died by the end of the first year, and 66 had died by the end of five years. Only 56 percent of the physicians given the information in this form recommended surgery.

Because negative information tends to attract more attention and have greater psychological impact than positive information (Baumeister, Bratslavsky, Finkenaur, & Vohs, 2001; Rozin & Royzman, 2001), information framed in negative terms tends to elicit a stronger response. The results just described reflect that tendency: Ten people dying sounds more threatening than 90 out of 100 surviving.

Temporal Framing

Suppose one of your friends e-mails you today and asks if you can come over next Saturday morning at 9:00 to help him move. You're free that day and he's a good friend, so of course you say yes. Now suppose that on a Saturday morning at 8:30, your friend e-mails to ask if you can come over in half an hour and help him move. It's cold out and you still feel sleepy, so you write back that you're not feeling well—or maybe you don't write back at all, pretending you never saw the e-mail. Why were you so eager to help when asked a week in advance, but so reluctant when asked on the day in question?

You probably have had similar feelings of being at odds with a decision made by an earlier version of yourself. Your earlier self might have thought it was a good idea to take an extra-heavy course load this semester, but now your present self is frazzled and sleep deprived. How could you have thought this would be a good idea?

Why does something often seem like a brilliant idea at one time and a terrible idea at another? The key to understanding this type of disparity is to recognize that we think about actions and events within a particular time perspective—a *temporal frame*—belonging to the distant past, the present moment, the immediate future, and so on.

According to **construal level theory**, the temporal perspective from which people view events has important and predictable implications for how they construe them (Fiedler, 2007; Liberman, Sagristano, & Trope, 2002; Trope & Liberman, 2003, 2010, 2012). Any action or event can be thought of at a low level of abstraction, rich in concrete detail—for example, chewing your food, carrying a friend's couch up the stairs, or giving a panhandler a dollar. But actions and events can also be thought of at a higher level of abstraction, rich in meaning but stripped of detail—dining out, helping a friend, or being generous (recall the discussion in Chapter 3 about the role of high-level, abstract versus low-level concrete construals in self-control). It turns out that we tend to think of distant events, those from long ago or far off in the future, in abstract terms and tend to think of events close at hand in concrete terms. Next week you'll be dining out, but right now you're chewing your food. Next month you'll help a friend move, but later this afternoon you'll be carrying your friend's chair up the stairs.

This difference in construal has important implications for what people think and how they act in their everyday lives, and it explains many inconsistent

construal level theory A theory about the relationship between temporal distance (and other kinds of distance) and abstract or concrete thinking: psychologically distant actions and events are thought about in abstract terms; actions and events that are close at hand are thought about in concrete terms.

TEMPORAL DISTANCE AND CONSTRUAL
When an event is far in the future, we think of it in broad, abstract terms (for example, exploring foreign lands); when an event is close at hand, we think about it in narrower, more concrete terms (for example, packing for the trip).

preferences. Decisions that sound great in the abstract are sometimes less thrilling when fleshed out in all their concrete detail, so we regret making some commitments. You think of a heavy course load a year from now as "furthering my education," or "expanding my horizons." That sounds great, so you accept the challenge. But when the time comes, you experience the heavy course load as "studying" or "spending time in the library," which is less inspiring, so you question your earlier decision to take on this burden. In contrast, sometimes decisions are more enticing at the concrete level and less desirable at the abstract level, producing the opposite sort of inconsistency. At the abstract level you might have sworn that you'd stick to your diet no matter what (because you don't want to "pig out"), yet when you're standing in front of the buffet, you find it easy to indulge (because you're only "sampling the different options").

← LOOKING BACK

The way information is presented can affect judgment. Primacy effects occur when information presented first has more impact than information presented later, often because the initial information influences the way later information is construed. Recency effects occur when information presented later is better remembered and thus has more impact. People are also susceptible to how information is framed. Sometimes people deliberately spin information so as to influence our judgment by changing our frame of reference. The temporal framing of an event—whether it will occur soon or far in the future—also influences how we think of it; far-off events are construed in more abstract terms, and imminent events are construed more concretely.

How We Seek Information

Suppose a friend gives you several potted plants for your dorm room or apartment and says, "I'm not sure, but they might need frequent watering. You should check that out." How would you go about checking? If you're like most people, you would water them often and see how they do. What you would *not* do is give a lot of water to some, very little to the others, and compare the results.

Confirmation Bias

When evaluating a proposition (a plant needs frequent watering; a generous allowance spoils a child; Hispanics highly value family life), people more readily, reliably, and vigorously seek out evidence that would support the proposition rather than information that would contradict the proposition. This tendency is known as the **confirmation bias** (Klayman & Ha, 1987; Skov & Sherman, 1986).

In one study that examined the confirmation bias, Jennifer Crocker asked one group of participants to determine whether working out the day before an important tennis match makes a player more likely to win (Crocker, 1982). Another group was asked to determine whether working out the day before a match makes a player more likely to *lose*. Both groups could examine any of four types of information before coming to a conclusion: the number of players in a

confirmation bias The tendency to test a proposition by searching for evidence that would support it.

sample who worked out the day before and won their match, the number of players who worked out and lost, the number of players who didn't work out the day before and won, and the number of players who didn't work out and lost. In fact, all four types of information are needed to make a valid determination. You have to calculate and compare the success rate of those who worked out the day before the match with the success rate of those who didn't. If the first ratio is higher than the second, then working out the day before increases the chances of winning.

But participants tended not to seek out all the necessary information. Instead, as **Figure 4.2** makes clear, participants exhibited the confirmation bias: they were especially interested in examining information that could potentially confirm the proposition they were investigating. Those trying to find out whether practicing leads to winning were more interested in the number of players who practiced and won than those trying to find out whether practicing leads to losing—and vice versa (Crocker, 1982).

This tendency to seek confirming information can lead to all sorts of false beliefs, because we can find supportive evidence for almost anything (Gilovich, 1991; Shermer, 1997). Are people more likely to come to harm when there is a full moon? There will certainly be many months in which hospital ERs are unusually busy during the full moon. Do optimistic people live longer? You can probably think of some very elderly people who are unusually upbeat. But evidence consistent with a proposition is not enough to draw a firm conclusion, as there might be even more evidence against it—more days with empty ERs during the full moon,

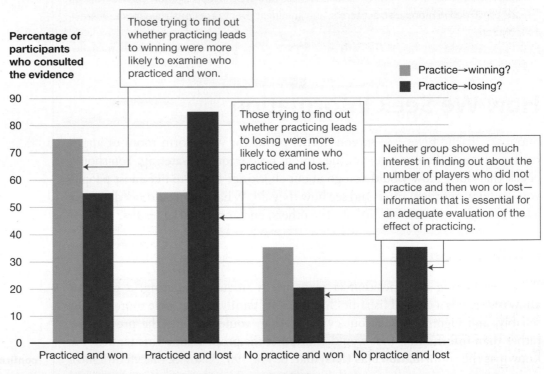

FIGURE 4.2
THE CONFIRMATION BIAS
Light green bars represent the responses of participants trying to determine whether practicing the day before a tennis match makes a player more likely to win. Dark green bars represent the responses of participants trying to find out whether practicing the day before makes a player more likely to lose.
Source: Adapted from Crocker, 1982.

Overconfidence: A Pervasive Bias of Human Judgment

The overconfidence bias, the tendency for individuals to have greater confidence in their judgments and decisions than their actual accuracy merits, is one of the most pronounced and consistent biases documented by psychologists. If people were perfectly "calibrated," their accuracy would match their confidence. They would be 100% accurate when they are 100% confident, 70% accurate when they are 70% confident, and so forth. But people's confidence frequently exceeds their accuracy, and this bias appears in numerous areas, including physical ability, test performance, and general knowledge.

"Heavier than air flying machines are impossible."
Lord Kelvin, president of British Royal Society, 1895

"They couldn't hit an elephant at this dist— ..."
last words of General John Sedgwick before being shot by Confederate fire in the U.S. Civil War Battle of Spotsylvania, 1864

Classic Overconfidence Study

In a classic study of overconfidence, people answered 20 two-alternative general-knowledge questions and judged the probability that each answer was correct. The white line indicates perfect correspondence between accuracy and expressed confidence. The pink line depicts participants' average accuracy rates for particular levels of confidence. The fact that the pink line lies below the white line indicates that participants were more confident than they were accurate.

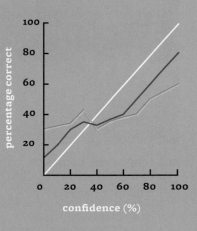

— perfect correspondence
— actual results

Are You Overconfident?

To answer the following questions, give a range that you're 90% sure covers the true value. For example, you probably don't know the exact length of the Nile, but give a range of lengths that you're 90% sure the true value falls within. That is, there's only a 5% chance that the Nile is shorter than x and only a 5% chance that it is longer than y. The correct answers are at the bottom of the page.

1. **Length of Nile River** (x to y miles)
2. **Martin Luther King's age at death** (x to y years)
3. **Number of countries in European Union** (x to y countries)
4. **Number of books in Old Testament** (x to y books)
5. **Diameter of the Moon** (x to y miles)
6. **Weight of a 787 airplane** (x to y tons)
7. **Year Mozart was born** (x to y years)
8. **Gestation period of Asian elephant** (x to y days)
9. **Shortest air distance from London to Tokyo** (x to y miles)
10. **Deepest known point in Earth's oceans** (x to y feet)

Forecasting Study

In a long-term forecasting study, experts and undergraduate students assessed the probability of various events, such as whether the Apartheid system in South Africa would become more entrenched, stay the same, or end (three possible answers to each question). These assessments were then compared with what actually happened. The yellow and purple lines depict participants' average accuracy rates for different levels of confidence. The experts did better than the undergraduates, but they were still highly overconfident.

— perfect correspondence
— experts
— undergraduates

answer key: 1) 4,187; 2) 39; 3) 28; 4) 39; 5) 2,160; 6) 130; 7) 1756; 8) 645; 9) 5,959; 10) 36,198

Sources: Quotations and overconfidence test: Adapted from Russo & Shoemaker, 1990; Classic study Koriat, Lichtenstein, & Fischhoff, 1980; Experts/nonexperts study: Tetlock, 2005.

more pessimists living long lives. The danger of the confirmation bias, then, is that if we look mainly for one type of evidence, we are likely to find it. To truly test a proposition, we must seek out the evidence against it as well as the evidence for it.

In the social realm, the confirmation bias can lead people to ask questions that shape the answers they get, thereby providing illusory support for the very thing they're trying to find out. In one telling study, researchers asked one group of participants to interview someone and determine whether the target person was an extravert; another group was asked to determine whether the target person was an introvert (Snyder & Swann, 1978). Participants selected their interview questions from a list provided. Those charged with determining whether the target was an extravert tended to ask questions that focused on sociability ("In what situations are you most talkative?"). Those charged with determining whether the target was an introvert tended to ask questions that focused on social withdrawal ("In what situations do you wish you could be more outgoing?"). Of course, if you ask people about times when they are most sociable, they are likely to answer in ways that will make them seem relatively outgoing, even if they aren't. And if you ask about their social reticence, they will almost certainly answer in ways that make them seem relatively introverted—again, even if they aren't. In a powerful demonstration of this tendency, the investigators tape-recorded the interview sessions, edited out the questions, and then played the responses to another, uninformed set of participants. These latter participants rated those who had been interviewed by someone testing for extraversion as more outgoing than those who had been interviewed by someone testing for introversion.

SEARCHING FOR EVIDENCE THAT FITS OUR BELIEFS
People who deny the reality of global warming often seize on episodes like these to support their skepticism ("Would we have weather like this if the planet were really getting warmer?"). Those who are worried about climate change are likely to seize on them to support *their* view ("This is precisely the extreme weather we can expect as a result of climate change").

It's easy to see how the confirmation bias, in concert with all the information available on the Internet, can result in highly polarized beliefs. If you want to find out whether the Trump campaign colluded with Russia's KGB and search the Internet for confirmatory information, you'll find quite a bit. Or if you're curious about whether President Barack Obama had Trump Tower bugged during the 2016 presidential campaign, a confirmatory search will turn up some evidence of that, too. *Some* evidence is out there in apparent support of even the most outlandish propositions. That's why a balanced search for both confirmatory and disconfirmatory information is essential to sound judgment. But as we have seen, people don't recognize the need to seek out information from all sides of an issue, and doing so is made even harder by the fact that modern technologies create "information bubbles" where confirmatory information is shared by members of like-minded communities.

One study examined which sites people visited, "liked," and forwarded on Facebook (Quattrociocchi, Scala, & Sunstein, 2016). The investigators identified people for whom 95 percent of their "likes" were for posts that embraced various conspiracy theories (for example, that there is no link between HIV and AIDS, but powerful forces want people to believe there is) and people for whom 95 percent of their "likes" were for posts that embraced scientific claims (for example, the discovery of gravitational waves). The investigators found that the more these individuals favored one type of post over the other, the more their *friends* tended to be highly polarized as well, and the more often these individuals responded to the occasional post that challenged their beliefs by going to (or returning to) posts that reinforced their beliefs. To have an ideological position is to be surrounded, especially in today's world, by information that supports that position.

Motivated Confirmation Bias

People can fall prey to the confirmation bias even when they have no particular motivation to confirm a particular outcome. You may not care whether a given type of plant needs a lot of water, but if someone suggests that it does, you will evaluate that suggestion by looking disproportionately at evidence that might confirm it.

But some of the time, of course, people are motivated to deliberately search for evidence that supports their preferences or expectations. Someone who wants a given proposition to be true may sift through the relevant evidence with special vigor to uncover information that confirms its validity. In such cases, information that supports what a person wants to be true is readily accepted, whereas information that contradicts what the person would like to believe is subjected to critical scrutiny and often discounted (Dawson, Gilovich, & Regan, 2002; Ditto & Lopez, 1992; Druckman & Bolsen, 2011; Gilovich, 1983, 1991; Kruglanski & Webster, 1996; Kunda, 1990; Pyszczynski & Greenberg, 1987; Slothuus & de Vreese, 2010).

In one notable examination of this type of motivated confirmation bias, proponents and opponents of capital punishment read about studies of the death penalty's effectiveness as a deterrent to committing a crime (Lord, Ross, & Lepper, 1979). Some read state-by-state comparisons purportedly showing that crime rates are not any lower in states with the death penalty than in states without the death penalty, but they also read about how crime rates within a few states decreased as soon as the death penalty was put in place. Other participants read about studies showing the exact opposite: state-by-state comparisons that made the death penalty look effective and before-and-after comparisons that made it look ineffective. Those who favored the death penalty interpreted the evidence, whichever set they were exposed to, as strongly supporting their position. Those opposed to the death penalty thought the evidence warranted the opposite conclusion. Both sides jumped on the problems associated with the studies that contradicted their positions, but they readily embraced the studies that supported them. Their preferences tainted how they viewed the pertinent evidence.

← LOOKING BACK

Efforts to acquire needed information are often compromised by two pronounced types of confirmation bias. One type occurs when we look for evidence consistent with propositions or hypotheses we wish to evaluate. To evaluate a proposition satisfactorily, however, it's necessary to examine evidence both for it and against it. The other type of confirmation bias occurs when we want a given proposition to be true; we seek out and embrace evidence that confirms our beliefs or preferences and explain away evidence that contradicts them.

Top-Down Processing: Using Schemas to Understand New Information

Understanding the world involves the simultaneous operation of bottom-up and top-down processing. **Bottom-up processing** takes in relevant stimuli from the outside world, such as text on a page, gestures in an interaction, or sound patterns at a cocktail party. At the same time, **top-down processing** filters and interprets bottom-up stimuli in light of preexisting knowledge and expectations. The meaning of stimuli is not passively recorded; it is actively *construed*.

Preexisting knowledge is necessary for understanding. What we know about human nature and about different social contexts allows us to determine, for example, whether another person's tears are the product of joy or sadness. What we know about norms and customs enables us to decide whether a gesture is hostile or friendly. Our preexisting knowledge, furthermore, is not filed away bit by bit. It is organized in coherent configurations, or schemas, in which related information is stored together. For example, information about Hillary Clinton, 2016 Democratic candidate for president, is tightly connected to information about Hillary Clinton, Wellesley graduate; Hillary Clinton, former First Lady; and Hillary Clinton, former secretary of state (Bartlett, 1932; Markus, 1977; Nisbett & Ross, 1980; Schank & Abelson, 1977; Smith & Zarate, 1990). We have schemas for all sorts of things, such as a fast-food restaurant chain (so-so food, bright primary colors for decor, limited choices, cheap), a party animal (boisterous, drinks to excess, exuberant but clumsy dancer), and an action film (good guy establishes good guy credentials, bad guy gains the upper hand, good guy triumphs and bad guy perishes in eye-popping pyrotechnical finale).

The Influence of Schemas

The various schemas we possess affect our judgments in many ways: by directing our attention, structuring our memories, and influencing our interpretations (Brewer & Nakamura, 1984; Hastie, 1981; Taylor & Crocker, 1981). Without schemas, our lives would be a buzzing confusion. But schemas can also sometimes lead us to mischaracterize the world.

ATTENTION Attention is selective. We can't focus on everything, and the knowledge we bring to a given situation enables us to direct our attention to what's most important and largely ignore everything else. The extent to which our schemas and expectations guide our attention was powerfully demonstrated by an experiment in which participants watched a videotape of two teams of three people, each passing a basketball back and forth (Simons & Chabris, 1999). The members of one team wore white shirts, and the members of the other team wore black shirts. The researchers asked each participant to count the number of passes the members of one of the teams made. Forty-five seconds into the action, a person wearing a gorilla costume strolled into the middle of the action. Although a large gorilla might seem hard to miss, only half the participants noticed it! The participants' schemas about what is likely to happen in a game of catch directed their attention so intently to some parts of the videotape that they failed to see a rather dramatic stimulus they weren't expecting.

bottom-up processing "Data-driven" mental processing, in which an individual forms conclusions based on the stimuli encountered in the environment.

top-down processing "Theory-driven" mental processing, in which an individual filters and interprets new information in light of preexisting knowledge and expectations.

© 2005, Daniel J. Simons

MEMORY Because schemas influence attention, they also influence memory. We are most likely to remember stimuli that have captured our attention. Indeed, memory has been described as "attention in the past tense" (Goleman, 1985).

Researchers have documented the impact of schemas on memory in a great many experiments (Fiske & Taylor, 1991; Hastie, 1981; Hirt, 1990; Stangor & McMillan, 1992). In one study, students watched a videotape of a husband and wife having dinner together (Cohen, 1981). Half of them were told that the wife was a librarian, the other half that she was a waitress. The students later took a quiz that assessed their memory of what they had witnessed. The central question was whether their memories were influenced by their stereotypes (schemas about particular groups in society) of librarians and waitresses. The researchers asked them, for example, whether the woman was drinking wine (librarian stereotype) or beer (waitress stereotype) and whether she had received a history book (librarian) or romance novel (waitress) as a gift. The tape had been constructed to contain an equal number of items consistent and inconsistent with each stereotype.

Did the participants' preexisting knowledge influence what they recalled? It did indeed. Students who thought the woman was a librarian recalled librarian-consistent information more accurately than librarian-inconsistent information; those who thought she was a waitress recalled waitress-consistent information more accurately than waitress-inconsistent information. Information that fits a preexisting schema often enjoys an advantage in recall (Carli, 1999; Zadny & Gerard, 1974).

CONSTRUAL Schemas influence not only what information we focus on and remember, but also the way we interpret, or construe, that information (DeCoster & Claypool, 2004; Loersch & Payne, 2011). To understand how this works, meet Donald, a fictitious person who has been used as a stimulus in numerous experiments on the effect of prior knowledge on social judgment:

> Donald spent a great amount of his time in search of what he liked to call excitement. He had already climbed Mt. McKinley, shot the Colorado rapids in a kayak, driven in a demolition derby, and piloted a jet-powered boat—without knowing very much about boats. He had risked injury, and even death, a number of times. Now he was in search of new excitement. He was thinking, perhaps, he would do some skydiving or maybe cross the Atlantic in a sailboat. By the way he acted one could readily guess that Donald was well

EXPECTATIONS GUIDE ATTENTION
Because people don't expect to see a gorilla in the middle of a game of catch, only half the participants who watched this video saw it. Schemas can be so strong that they prevent us from seeing even very dramatic stimuli we don't expect to see.

aware of his ability to do many things well. Other than business engagements, Donald's contacts with people were rather limited. He felt he didn't really need to rely on anyone. Once Donald made up his mind to do something it was as good as done no matter how long it might take or how difficult the going might be. Only rarely did he change his mind even when it might well have been better if he had. (Higgins, Rholes, & Jones, 1977, p. 145)

In one early study featuring Donald as the stimulus, students participated in what they thought were two unrelated experiments (Higgins, Rholes, & Jones, 1977). In the first, they viewed a number of trait words projected on a screen as part of a perception experiment. Half the participants were shown the words *adventurous, self-confident, independent,* and *persistent* among a set of ten traits. The other half were shown the words *reckless, conceited, aloof,* and *stubborn.* After completing the ostensible perception experiment, the participants moved on to the second study on reading comprehension, in which they read the short paragraph about Donald and rated him on a number of trait scales. The investigators were interested in whether the words that participants encountered in the first experiment would lead them to apply different schemas and thus affect their evaluations of Donald.

ADVENTUROUS OR RECKLESS?
Recent exposure to concepts like "self-confident" and "independent" makes people more likely to see this young person eating insects as "adventurous." Exposure to concepts like "conceited" and "stubborn" encourages seeing her as "reckless."

As the investigators expected, participants who had previously been exposed to the words *adventurous, self-confident, independent,* and *persistent* formed more favorable impressions of Donald than did those who were shown the less flattering words. Thus, participants' schemas about personality traits like adventurousness and recklessness influenced the kind of inferences they made about Donald.

The broader point is that information that is most accessible in memory can influence how we construe new information. This is most likely to occur when the stimulus, like many of Donald's actions, is ambiguous (Trope, 1986). In such cases, we must rely more heavily on top-down processes to compensate for the inadequacies of the information obtained from the bottom up.

priming The presentation of information designed to activate a concept and hence make it accessible. A prime is the stimulus presented to activate the concept in question.

BEHAVIOR We've seen how schemas influence our attention, memory, and construal. Can they also influence behavior? Absolutely. Studies have shown that certain types of behavior are elicited automatically when people are exposed to stimuli in the environment that bring to mind a particular action or schema (Loersch & Payne, 2011; Weingarten et al, 2016). Such exposure is called **priming** a concept or schema.

subliminal Below the threshold of conscious awareness.

In one study, participants played a simplified game of blackjack in which a computer dealt them two cards and they had to decide whether to bet that the sum of their two cards would exceed the sum of two cards that would soon appear for the "dealer" (the computer) or whether they wanted to pass and go to the next round. If they decided to bet, they won 5 points if their cards were higher than the dealer's and lost 5 points if they were lower. On some trials, the word *gamble* or *wager* was **subliminally** presented right before the participants made their decisions; on other trials, the word *fold* or *stay* appeared. Even though the primes were presented too quickly for participants to consciously perceive them, participants were more likely to bet on trials preceded by the word *gamble* or *wager* than on trials preceded by the word *fold* or *stay* (Payne, Brown-Iannuzzi, & Loersch, 2016).

Other studies of this sort found that priming participants with dollar signs increased their betting on a laboratory slot machine (Gibson & Zielaskowski, 2013) and that activating the goal of achievement led people to persevere longer at difficult tasks (Bargh, Gollwitzer, Lee-Chai, Barndollar, & Trotschel, 2001; Weingarten et al., 2016). Moreover, playing German music in a liquor store appears to boost sales of German wine at the expense of French wine, whereas playing French music appears to boost sales of French wine—even if customers don't realize what type of music is being played (North, Hargreaves, & McKendrick, 1999).

Which Schemas Are Activated and Applied?

In the librarian/waitress study described earlier, there is little doubt about which schema participants applied to the information in the videotape. The experimenter informed them that the woman was a librarian (or waitress), and they viewed the videotape through the lens of their librarian (or waitress) schema. In real life, however, the situation is often more complicated. You might know that besides being a librarian, the woman is a triathlete, a Republican, and a gourmet cook. Which schema (or combination of schemas) is likely to be thought of, or activated?

RECENT ACTIVATION Schemas can be brought to mind, or activated, in various ways. Recent activation of a schema is one of the most common determinants of which schemas get activated. If a schema has been brought to mind recently, it tends to be more accessible and hence ready for use (Ford & Kruglanski, 1995; Herr, 1986; Sherman, Mackie, & Driscoll, 1990; Srull & Wyer, 1979, 1980; Todorov & Bargh, 2002).

In the "Donald" study described earlier, for example, recent exposure to trait adjectives such as *adventurous* or *reckless* influenced participants' impressions of Donald (Higgins et al., 1977). By exposing participants to words implying adventurousness or recklessness, the researchers were trying to prime participants' schemas for those traits. Of course, exposure to stimuli other than words can activate schemas. People's judgments and behavior have been shown to be influenced by schemas primed by features of the surrounding environment, such as the objects in a room or the color of the walls (Aarts & Dijksterhuis, 2003; Kay, Wheeler, Bargh, & Ross, 2004); cultural symbols, such as a country's flag (Carter, Ferguson, & Hassin, 2011; Ehrlinger et al., 2011; Hassin, Ferguson, Shidlovsky, & Gross, 2007); feedback from one's own body (Epley & Gilovich, 2001; Jostmann, Lakens, & Schubert, 2009; Priester, Cacioppo, & Petty, 1996); even a passing smell (Holland, Hendricks, & Aarts, 2005).

FREQUENT ACTIVATION AND CHRONIC ACCESSIBILITY You may have noticed that people differ in the schemas they tend to use when evaluating others. Employers at high-tech firms are often concerned with whether job candidates are smart, sales managers with whether employees are persuasive, and those involved in the entertainment business with whether an actress or actor has charisma. As these examples illustrate, the role of the evaluator and the context in which a target person is encountered often influence which traits or schemas are used. But sometimes it's simply a matter of habit. If a person uses a particular schema frequently, it may become chronically accessible and therefore likely to

THE INFLUENCE OF CHRONICALLY ACCESSIBLE SCHEMAS ON PERCEPTION AND JUDGMENT
Certain schemas, such as "hipster" or "techie," are used a lot and therefore are highly available and readily applied to new stimuli.

be used still more often in the future (Higgins, King, & Mavin, 1982). A frequently activated schema functions much like a recently activated one: its heightened accessibility increases the likelihood that it will be applied to understanding a new stimulus.

CONSCIOUSNESS OF ACTIVATION: NECESSARY OR NOT? Carefully conducted interviews with participants at the end of many priming experiments have found that few, if any, of them suspected that there was any connection between the two parts of the study—the initial priming phase and the subsequent judgment phase. This finding raises the question of how conscious a person must be of a stimulus for it to effectively prime a given schema. Research suggests a clear-cut answer: we don't need to be conscious of the stimulus at all. A great many studies have shown that stimuli presented outside of conscious awareness can prime a schema sufficiently to influence subsequent information processing (Bargh, 1996; Debner & Jacoby, 1994; Devine, 1989b; Draine & Greenwald, 1998; Ferguson, 2008; Ferguson, Bargh, & Nayak, 2005; Greenwald, Klinger, & Liu, 1989; Klinger, Burton, & Pitts, 2000; Lepore & Brown, 1997; Welsh & Ordonez, 2014). Thus, schemas can be primed even when the presentation of the activating stimuli is subliminal (**Box 4.2**).

EXPECTATIONS Sometimes people apply a schema because of a preexisting expectation about what they will encounter (Hirt, MacDonald, & Erikson, 1995; Sherman et al., 1990; Stangor & McMillan, 1992). The expectation activates the schema, and the schema is then readily applied. If the expectation is warranted, it saves considerable mental energy. For example, applying a "haggling" schema to a given commercial transaction allows us to dismiss the stated price without much thought or anxiety, and it frees us to make a counteroffer. Misapplying the haggling schema, however, can lead to the embarrassment of making a counteroffer when haggling is not appropriate. Expectations thus influence information processing by priming the schema, and the schema is readily applied at the slightest hint that it is applicable.

← LOOKING BACK

Knowledge structures, or schemas, play a crucial role in judgment. Schemas influence judgment by guiding attention, influencing memory, and determining how information is construed. Schemas can also directly influence behavior. Schemas are particularly likely to exert an influence if they have been recently activated (and hence primed) or are habitually used, and we needn't be aware of the recent or chronic activation of a schema for it to exert its effects. Schemas normally allow us to make judgments and to take action quickly and accurately, but they can also mislead.

"I know too well the weakness and uncertainty of human reason to wonder at its different results."
—THOMAS JEFFERSON

Reason, Intuition, and Heuristics

Suppose you were offered a chance to win $10 by picking, without looking, a red marble from a bowl containing a mixture of red and white marbles. You can make your selection from either of two bowls: a small bowl with 1 red marble and

BOX 4.2   **FOCUS ON** EVERYDAY LIFE

Subtle Situational Influence

Words, sights, sounds, and other stimuli can influence how we act, for good or for ill, even when we're not consciously aware of them. Consider the following findings.

- Want to make your employees be more creative? Have them work in a green or blue environment—and be sure they don't work in a red environment (Lichtenfeld, Elliot, Maier, & Pekrun, 2012; Mehta & Zhu, 2009).

- Green, as in environmental greenery, can help reduce violence. People living in public housing surrounded by greenery commit fewer violent crimes than people in nearby public housing surrounded by concrete (Kuo & Sullivan, 2001b).

- Want to get lots of hits on your dating profile? Wear a red shirt in your profile photo or at least put a red border around your picture. Both men and women are considered sexier when dressed in red or just surrounded by red (Elliot et al., 2010).

- Want taxpayers to support education bond issues? Lobby to make schools the primary voting location. Want to get the voters to outlaw late abortion? Lobby to have voters cast their ballots in churches. The associations people have to the buildings that serve as polling stations influence how they vote (Berger, Meredith, & Wheeler, 2008).

- Want people to pay more consistently for the office coffee they consume by putting the agreed-upon fee in the "honest box"? On the wall near the box, put up a poster of anything with eyes (even a symbolic stick-figure face). A nonconscious sense of being observed makes people more likely to be on their best behavior (Bateson, Nettle, & Roberts, 2006; Haley & Fessler, 2005).

- Want someone to be deeply concerned about the threat posed by climate change? Have them fill out a survey about carbon emissions in an especially hot room. People take the threat of global warming more seriously when they are feeling uncomfortably warm themselves (Risen & Critcher, 2011).

This list might remind you of the stand-up comic who follows a rapid-fire series of one-liners with the statement, "I've got a million of these." And indeed, social psychologists have offered no shortage of demonstrations of the influence of incidental stimuli on people's behavior. The most obvious implication of this research is that we can influence people's behavior by attending to the details of their surrounding physical environment. A less obvious implication is that if we want to free ourselves of these kinds of influences, we should try to consider important propositions and potential courses of action in a number of different settings, if possible. That way, incidental stimuli associated with the different environments are likely to cancel each other out, resulting in more sound judgments and decisions.

---

9 white marbles or a large bowl with 9 red marbles and 91 white marbles. Which bowl would you choose?

If you're like most people, you might experience some conflict here. The rational thing to do is to select the small bowl because it offers better odds: 10 percent versus 9 percent (**Figure 4.3**). But there are 9 potential winning marbles in the large bowl and only 1 in the other. The greater number of winning marbles gives many people a gut feeling that they should select from the large

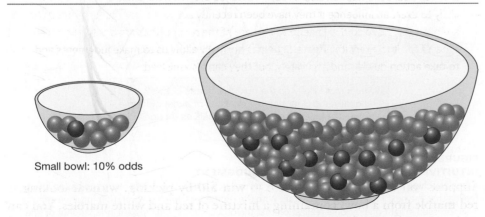

Small bowl: 10% odds

Large bowl: 9% odds

FIGURE 4.3
INTUITION AND REASON
Even though a small bowl with just 1 red marble and 9 white ones provides a better chance of choosing a winning (red) marble, people often select the larger bowl, with more red marbles and many more white marbles, knowing full well that they're giving themselves lower odds of winning, thereby letting intuition override reason.

bowl, regardless of the objective odds. Indeed, in one experiment, 61 percent of those who faced this decision chose the larger bowl, even though that bowl gave them lower odds of winning (Denes-Raj & Epstein, 1994).

These results show that we're often "of two minds" about certain problems. Indeed, a great deal of research suggests that our responses to stimuli are guided by two systems of thought analogous to intuition and reason (Epstein, 1991; Evans, 2007; Kahneman & Frederick, 2002; Sloman, 2002; Stanovich & West, 2002; Strack & Deutsch, 2004). The intuitive system operates quickly and automatically, is based on associations, and performs many of its operations simultaneously—*in parallel*. The rational system is slower and more controlled, is based on rules and deduction, and performs its operations one at a time—*serially*.

The rapid, parallel nature of the intuitive system means that it virtually always produces some output—an "answer" to the prevailing problem—and does so very quickly. That output is sometimes overridden by the output of the slower, more deliberate rational system. For instance, if you had to predict the outcome of the next coin flip after witnessing five heads in a row, your intuitive system would quickly tell you that six heads in a row is rare and that you should therefore bet on tails. But then your rational system might remind you of a critical feature of coin flips that you may have learned in a statistics or probability course: the outcomes of consecutive flips are independent of each other—the odds are always 50-50—so you should ignore what happened on the earlier flips (**Figure 4.4**).

Note that several things can happen with the output of these two systems: (1) The two systems can agree. For example, you might have a good feeling about one job candidate over another (the intuitive system), and that candidate's qualifications might fit your rule to "always go with the person with more experience" (the rational system). (2) As in the coin-flip example, the two systems can disagree, and the message from the rational system can override the message from the intuitive system. (3) Finally, the intuitive system can produce a response that "seems right" and can do so with such speed that the rational system is never engaged. In that case, you simply go with the flow—that is, with the quick output of the intuitive system.

The rest of this chapter focuses on the latter pattern, drawing from Amos Tversky and Daniel Kahneman's work on the heuristics of judgment. Their work

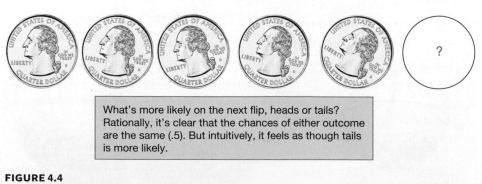

What's more likely on the next flip, heads or tails? Rationally, it's clear that the chances of either outcome are the same (.5). But intuitively, it feels as though tails is more likely.

FIGURE 4.4
INTUITIVE PROCESSING AND MISTAKEN JUDGMENT
When watching a series of coin flips and seeing several heads in a row, nearly everyone has an intuitive feeling that the next flip is going to be a tail. With the right education, however, that intuitive impulse is suppressed in light of a rational realization that the outcomes of coin flips are independent of one another, and the chances of heads on the next flip are the same as they always are, 50-50.

has had a great impact—not only in psychology, but also in economics, management, law, medicine, political science, and statistics (Gilovich, Griffin, & Kahneman, 2002; Kahneman, Slovic, & Tversky, 1982; Tversky & Kahneman, 1974). Tversky and Kahneman have argued that the intuitive system automatically performs certain mental operations—assessments of how easily something comes to mind or of how similar two entities are—that powerfully influence judgment. They refer to these mental operations as **heuristics**: mental shortcuts that provide serviceable, if usually rather inexact, answers to common problems of judgment. They yield answers that feel right and therefore often forestall more effortful, rational deliberation.

Tversky and Kahneman have argued that although these heuristics generally serve us well, they sometimes distort our judgments. Our intuitive system generates an assessment relevant to the task at hand and suggests what may seem like a perfectly acceptable answer to the problem. But without a deeper, more considered analysis, important considerations might be ignored and our judgments systematically biased. Let's examine how such biases can arise in the context of two of the most important and extensively researched heuristics: the availability heuristic and the representativeness heuristic. We rely on the **availability heuristic** when we judge the frequency or probability of some event by how readily pertinent instances come to mind. We use the **representativeness heuristic** when we try to categorize something by judging how similar it is to our conception of the typical member of the category.

The Availability Heuristic

Which Midwestern state has more tornadoes each year: Nebraska or Kansas? Even though they both average the same number, you, like most people, may have answered Kansas. If so, then you were guided by the availability heuristic. For most people, thinking about the frequency of tornadoes in Kansas immediately brings to mind the one in the classic film *The Wizard of Oz.*

We can't prevent ourselves from assessing the ease with which we can think of examples from Nebraska and Kansas, and once we've made such assessments, they seem to give us our answer. It's easier to think of a tornado in Kansas (even though it was fictional) than one in Nebraska, so we conclude that Kansas

heuristics Intuitive mental operations, performed quickly and automatically, that provide efficient answers to common problems of judgment.

availability heuristic The process whereby judgments of frequency or probability are based on how readily pertinent instances come to mind.

representativeness heuristic The process whereby judgments of likelihood are based on assessments of similarity between individuals and group prototypes or between cause and effect.

THE AVAILABILITY HEURISTIC People often judge the likelihood of an event by how readily pertinent examples come to mind. (A) While tornadoes occur with equal frequency in both Nebraska and Kansas, people tend to think they are more common in Kansas because of familiarity with (B) *The Wizard of Oz,* in which a tornado in Kansas whisks Dorothy and her dog Toto to the land of Oz.

(A)

(B)

probably has more tornadoes. The implicit logic seems compelling: if examples can be quickly recalled, there must be many of them. Usually that's true. It's easier to think of male CEOs of Fortune 500 companies than female CEOs, successful Russian novelists than successful Norwegian novelists, and instances of German military aggression than Swiss military aggression—precisely because there are more male CEOs, more successful Russian novelists, and more instances of German military aggression. The availability heuristic, therefore, often serves us well. The ease with which relevant examples can be brought to mind—how available they are—is often an accurate guide to overall frequency or probability.

Often, but not always. Certain events may simply be more memorable or retrievable than others, making availability a poor indicator of true number or probability. Nebraska has as many tornadoes as Kansas, but none is as memorable as the one in *The Wizard of Oz*. In an early demonstration of the availability heuristic, Kahneman and Tversky (1973a) asked people whether there are more words that begin with the letter *r* or more words that have *r* as the third letter. A large majority thought more words begin with *r*, but in fact more words have *r* in the third position. Because words are stored in memory in some rough alphabetical fashion, words that begin with *r* (*rain, rowdy, redemption*) are easier to recall than those with *r* as the third letter (*nerd, harpoon, barrister*). The latter words, although more plentiful, are harder to access.

BIASED ASSESSMENTS OF RISK One area where the availability heuristic can lead to trouble in everyday life harks back to the earlier discussion of negative information being overreported in the news. If people assess their risk by how easily they can bring to mind various hazards, they will be especially worried about those hazards they hear a lot about in the media and not as worried about hazards that receive less attention, even if the latter are equally (or more) lethal (Slovic, Fischoff, & Lichtenstein, 1982).

For example, do more people die each year by homicide or by suicide? As you've surely noticed, homicides receive much more media coverage, so most people think they are more common. In reality, suicides outnumber homicides in the United States by a ratio of 3 to 2. Are people more likely to die by accident or from disease? Statistics indicate that disease claims more than 16 times as many lives as accidents, but because accidents (being more dramatic) receive disproportionate media attention, most people erroneously consider them responsible for about as many deaths as disease.

People typically overestimate the frequency of dramatic events that claim the lives of many people at once. Deaths due to plane crashes, earthquakes, and tornadoes are good examples. In contrast, people underestimate the commonness of silent individual deaths, such as those resulting from emphysema and stroke. **Table 4.1** lists the most overestimated and underestimated hazards.

BIASED ESTIMATES OF CONTRIBUTIONS TO JOINT PROJECTS Another example of how the availability heuristic can distort everyday judgment involves the dynamics of joint projects. People sometimes work together on a project and then afterward decide who gets the bulk of the credit. Suppose you work with someone on a class project and turn in a single paper. Whose name is listed first? What if you and an acquaintance are hired to write a computer program for a lump-sum payment. How do you split the money?

Now that you know about the availability heuristic, you might expect that people would tend to overestimate their own contributions to such projects

TABLE 4.1 BIASED ASSESSMENTS OF PERCEIVED CAUSES OF DEATH	
Most Overestimated	**Most Underestimated**
Motor vehicle accidents	Diabetes
Tornadoes	Lightning
Flood	Stroke
All cancers	Asthma
Fire	Emphysema
Homicide	Tuberculosis

Source: Adapted from Slovic, Fischoff, & Lichtenstein, 1982.

(Kruger & Savitsky, 2009; Ross & Sicoly, 1979; Savitsky, Adelman, & Kruger, 2012; Schroeder, Caruso, & Epley, 2016). After all, we devote a lot of energy and attention to our own contributions, so they should be more available than the contributions of everyone else. In one early test of this idea, married couples were asked to apportion responsibility for various tasks or outcomes in their daily life: how much each contributed to keeping the house clean, maintaining the social calendar, starting arguments, and so on (Ross & Sicoly, 1979). The respondents tended to give themselves more credit than their partners did. In most cases, when the estimates made by the two participants were summed, they exceeded the logically allowable maximum of 100 percent. (In our favorite example, a couple was asked to estimate their relative contributions to making breakfast. The wife said her share was 100 percent, on the reasonable grounds that she bought the food, prepared it, set the table, cleared the table, and washed the dishes. The husband estimated his contribution to be 25 percent—because he fed the cat!)

OVERESTIMATING THE FREQUENCY OF DRAMATIC DEATHS
People tend to overestimate the likelihood of dramatic causes of death that kill many people at once, such as building fires. Because these catastrophes receive a great deal of coverage in the media, they come to mind easily when we consider the relative risk of different hazards.

How do we know it's the availability heuristic rather than a motivational bias that gives rise to this phenomenon? In other words, maybe people overestimate their contributions simply because they want to see themselves, and have others see them, in the most favorable light. This would certainly be the logical conclusion if the effect held true only for positive items. But the investigators found that the overestimation of a person's own contributions held for negative outcomes (such as starting arguments) as well as positive outcomes (such as taking care of the house), making it clear that availability plays a large role in this effect.

AVAILABILITY'S CLOSE COUSIN: FLUENCY Just as examples of some categories are easier to think of than others, some individual stimuli are easier to process

fluency The feeling of ease (or difficulty) associated with processing information.

than others. Psychologists use the term **fluency** to refer to the ease (or difficulty) associated with information processing. A clear image is easy to process, or fluent. An irregular word (like *imbroglio*) is hard to process, or disfluent.

The subjective experience of fluency, much like the subjective sense of availability, influences all sorts of judgments people are called on to make (Jacoby & Dallas, 1981; Oppenheimer, 2008). For example, we judge fluent names to be more famous, fluent objects to be more prototypical members of their categories, and common adages that rhyme to be more valid and truthful than those that don't (Jacoby, Woloshyn, & Kelley, 1989; McGlone & Tofighbakhsh, 2000; Whittlesea & Leboe, 2000). Fluency also influences the perceived difficulty of a task that's being described. When the font (typeface) of a recipe is hard to read, people assume the dish would be hard to cook (Song & Schwarz, 2008).

In addition to such direct effects on judgment, fluency appears to influence *how* people process relevant information. A feeling of disfluency while processing information leads people to take something of a "slow down, be careful" approach to making judgments and decisions. Researchers have examined this tendency using the Cognitive Reflection Test (Frederick, 2005). In one study, the test was printed in either a normal, **highly readable font** or a degraded, *hard-to-read font*. Performing well on the Cognitive Reflection Test requires stifling an immediate gut feeling to get the correct answer to each question. For example: "A bat and ball cost $1.10 in total. The bat costs $1 more than the ball. How much does the ball cost?" You need to think beyond the immediate response of 10 cents to arrive at the correct response of 5 cents ($0.05 + $1.05 = $1.10). Participants gave more correct answers when the questions were presented in a degraded, and hence disfluent, font (Alter, Oppenheimer, & Epley, 2013; Alter, Oppenheimer, Epley, & Eyre, 2007). The difficulty of merely reading the question caused them to slow down, giving their more analytical, reflective cognitive processes a chance to catch up with their immediate intuitive response.

The Representativeness Heuristic

We sometimes find ourselves wondering whether someone is a member of a particular category. Is he gay? Is she a Republican? In making such assessments, we automatically assess the extent to which the person in question *seems* gay or Republican. In so doing, we rely on what Kahneman and Tversky (1972) have dubbed the representativeness heuristic. Instead of focusing on the true question of interest—"Is it likely that this person is a Republican?"—we ask, "Does this person seem like a Republican?" or "Is this person similar to my prototype of a Republican?" The use of the representativeness heuristic thus reflects an implicit assumption that a member of a given category ought to resemble the category prototype (that, say, Republicans are fiscally and socially conservative and have conventional tastes in films, music, and fashion.

The representativeness heuristic can be useful in making accurate judgments about people and events. Group members often resemble the group prototype (after all, the prototype must come from somewhere). The degree of resemblance between person and group can thus be a helpful guide to group membership. The strategy is effective to the extent that our prototype of that category has some validity and the members of the category cluster around the prototype—that is, are at least similar to the prototype if not exactly the same.

But even when the prototype has some validity, the representativeness heuristic can create difficulties if we rely on it exclusively. The problem is that a strong sense of resemblance can blind us to other potentially useful sources of information. One source of useful information, known as **base-rate information**, concerns our knowledge of relative frequency of the members of a given category. How many members of the category in question are there relative to the members of all other categories? The individual in question is more likely to be a Republican if the local population includes a lot of Republicans. But a strong sense of representativeness sometimes leads us to ignore base-rate likelihood, which could (and should) be put to good use.

THE RESEMBLANCE BETWEEN MEMBERS AND CATEGORIES: BASE-RATE NEGLECT Many studies have documented this tendency to ignore or underutilize base-rate information when assessing whether someone belongs to a particular category (Ajzen, 1977; Bar-Hillel, 1980; Ginosar & Trope, 1980; Tversky & Kahneman, 1982). In one of the earliest studies, Kahneman and Tversky (1973b)

THE REPRESENTATIVENESS HEURISTIC
(A) Images like this can give people a specific sense of what a representative Republican is like. (B) But many Republicans aren't at all like the stereotype, so we can be surprised when we learn that a person who doesn't fit the stereotype is a Republican.

base-rate information
Information about the relative frequency of events or of members of different categories in a population.

asked participants to consider the following description of Tom W., supposedly written during Tom's senior year in high school by a psychologist who based his assessment on Tom's responses on personality tests. The participants were also told that Tom is now in graduate school.

> Tom W. is of high intelligence, although lacking in true creativity. He has a need for order and clarity and for neat and tidy systems in which every detail finds its appropriate place. His writing is rather dull and mechanical, occasionally enlivened by somewhat corny puns and by flashes of imagination of the sci-fi type. He has a strong drive for competence. He seems to have little feel and little sympathy for other people and does not enjoy interacting with others. Self-centered, he nonetheless has a deep moral sense. (Kahneman & Tversky, 1973b, p. 238)

One group of participants ranked nine academic disciplines (including computer science, law, and social work) in terms of the likelihood that Tom chose them as his field of specialization. A second group ranked the nine disciplines in terms of how similar they thought Tom was to the typical student in each discipline. A final group did not see the description of Tom; they merely estimated the percentage of all graduate students in the United States who were enrolled in each of the nine disciplines.

How should the participants assess the likelihood that Tom would choose each discipline for graduate study? They should certainly assess how similar Tom is to the type of person who pursues each field of study—that is, they should consider how representative Tom is of the people in each discipline. But representativeness is not a perfect guide. Some of the least lawyerly people study law, and some of the least people-oriented individuals pursue social work. Therefore, any additional useful information should also be considered, such as the proportion of all graduate students in each field (or base-rate information). Clearly, Tom is more likely to be in a field that has 1,000 students on campus than one that has 10. A savvy judgment, then, would somehow combine representativeness with an assessment of the popularity of each field.

Table 4.2 lists the rankings of the nine disciplines by each of the three groups of participants—those assessing likelihood, similarity, and base rate. Notice that the rankings of the *likelihood* that Tom chose to study each of the disciplines are virtually identical to the rankings of Tom's *similarity* to the students in each discipline. In other words, the participants' responses were based entirely on how much the description of Tom resembled the typical student in each field. By basing their responses exclusively on representativeness, the participants failed to consider the other useful source of information: base-rate frequency. As you can also see from Table 4.2, the likelihood rankings didn't correspond at all to what the participants knew about the overall popularity of each of the fields. Useful information was ignored.

It's important to note, however, that although it's common to neglect base-rate information, it isn't inevitable (Bar-Hillel & Fischhoff, 1981). Certain circumstances encourage the use of base-rate information. It's particularly helpful if the base-rate information has some causal significance to the task at hand (Ajzen, 1977; Tversky & Kahneman, 1982). For example, if you were given a description of an individual's academic strengths and weaknesses and were asked to predict whether the person passed an exam, you would certainly take into account the fact that 70 percent of the students who took the exam failed (that the base rate

TABLE 4.2 THE REPRESENTATIVENESS HEURISTIC

Participants ranked nine academic disciplines in terms of the likelihood that
Tom W. chose that particular field, the perceived similarity between Tom W. and the
typical student in that field, or the number of graduate students enrolled in that field.

Discipline	Likelihood	Similarity	Base Rate
Business administration	3	3	3
Computer science	1	1	8
Engineering	2	2	5
Humanities and education	8	8	1
Law	6	6	6
Library science	5	4	9
Medicine	7	7	7
Physical and life sciences	4	5	4
Social science and social work	9	9	2

Source: Adapted from Kahneman & Tversky, 1973B.

of failure was 70 percent). Note that the base rate has causal significance in this case: the fact that 70 percent of the students failed means that the exam was difficult, and the difficulty of the exam is part of what *causes* a person to fail. People use the base rate in such contexts because its relevance is obvious. When the base rate is not causally relevant, as in the Tom W. experiment, its relevance is less obvious. If twice as many people major in business as in the physical sciences, it would be *more likely* that Tom W. is a business major, but it wouldn't *cause* him to be a business major. The relevance of the base rate is thus less apparent.

THE RESEMBLANCE BETWEEN CAUSE AND EFFECT The representativeness heuristic also affects people's assessments of cause and effect (Downing, Sternberg, & Ross, 1985; Gilovich & Savitsky, 2002). For example, people are predisposed to look for and accept causal relationships in which "like goes with like." Big effects are thought to have big causes, small effects to have small causes, complicated effects to have complicated causes, and so on. This assumption is often valid. Being hit with a small mallet typically produces a smaller bruise than being hit with a large mallet. Resolving the complicated mess in the Middle East will probably require complex, sustained negotiation, not some simple suggestion that has yet to be made. But sometimes small causes create big effects, and vice versa: tiny viruses give rise to devastating diseases like Ebola and AIDS; splitting the nucleus of the atom releases an awesome amount of energy.

Health and medicine are areas in which the impact of representativeness on judgments of cause and effect is particularly striking. Many people think you should avoid milk (or other dairy products) if you have a cold and give up potato chips if you have acne. Why? Because milk seems representative of phlegm, and the greasiness of potato chips seems representative of the oily skin that often accompanies acne. For centuries, Western physicians believed that yellow

Not So Fast:
Critical Thinking about Representativeness and the Regression Effect

To cut back on illegal driving practices (such as speeding, running red lights, and driving in bus lanes), local authorities in the United States and many other countries have been installing more and more safety cameras at especially hazardous locations. Some people have complained that it's just a way for municipalities to increase revenue from the fines they charge for violations. But others passionately maintain that these cameras have increased road safety. One group estimated that safety cameras in the United Kingdom save over 100 lives a year and result in over 4,000 fewer collisions (PA Consulting Group, 2005).

Alas, the purported safety benefit is substantially overstated. It fails to take into account a statistical phenomenon that plagues sound judgment in all walks of life: the regression effect. The **regression effect** is the statistical tendency, when any two variables are imperfectly correlated, for extreme values of one of them to be associated with less extreme values of the other. Tall parents tend to have tall kids, but not as tall as the parents themselves. Extremely attractive people tend to marry attractive partners, but not as attractive as they are themselves. Students with the worst scores on the midterm tend to do badly on the final, but not as badly as they did initially.

What does this have to do with traffic safety? Cameras are installed where they are most needed—in locations where there have been a large number of recent collisions. Given that the number of accidents at one time is imperfectly correlated with the number of accidents afterward, locations where there were an unusually large number of accidents are likely to have fewer accidents afterward, regardless of the presence of safety cameras. When the regression effect is taken into account, the best estimate is that safety cameras in the UK save 24 lives a year, not over 100. They work, in other words, but not as well as they *seem* to work.

People often fail to see the regression effect for what it is and instead conclude that they've encountered some important phenomenon (like an exaggerated effect of safety cameras). Psychologists refer to this as the **regression fallacy**. If you're a sports fan, for example, you've probably heard of the *Sports Illustrated* jinx. The idea is that appearing on the cover of *Sports Illustrated* is bad luck: it's often followed by an unfortunate outcome, such as an injury, the end of a winning streak, or a loss in a key game or match. Of course it is! People appear on the cover of *Sports Illustrated* precisely when they're at their peak, and so, on average, they will tend not to do as well in the near future. It's pure statistical regression, not a jinx.

The lesson for research should be clear. We're often most interested in helping people who are most in need, such as those who have been depressed for a long time and finally seek treatment, individuals whose arthritis has become unbearable, or students sent to the counselor's office for classroom disruption. Because these people are at such a low point, they are likely to experience improvement, whether or not their problems are addressed. That can make it tricky to assess the effectiveness of any treatment they receive. Among other things, the regression effect reinforces the importance of conducting research with a suitable control group: it allows researchers to determine whether the improvement seen in the treatment group is greater than that in the control group.

Why do people so often overlook the regression effect and commit the regression fallacy? One explanation is that regression runs counter to the representativeness heuristic. The most representative outcome for an athlete pictured on the cover of *Sports Illustrated* is success, not failure; the most representative outcome for someone who is extremely depressed is further sadness, not an uptick in mood. Because the mind makes predictions based on representativeness, we often find results that regress toward the mean surprising, and we invent explanations to make sense of the surprise.

regression effect The statistical tendency, when two variables are imperfectly correlated, for extreme values of one of them to be associated with less extreme values of the other.

vegetables were good for people with jaundice (which turns the skin yellow). To be sure, people are affected by what they eat—they gain weight by eating lots of fat and sugar and develop an orange tint to the skin by consuming too much carotene.

Sometimes, however, we take this belief that "you are what you eat" to magical extremes. In one experiment, college students were asked to make inferences about the attributes of members of (hypothetical) tribes (Nemeroff & Rozin,

1989). One group read about a tribe that ate wild boar and hunted sea turtles for their shells, a second group read about a tribe that ate sea turtles and hunted wild boar for their tusks. The students' responses indicated that they assumed the characteristics of the food would "rub off" on the tribe members. Members of the turtle-eating tribe were considered better swimmers and more generous; those who ate wild boar were thought to be more aggressive and more likely to have beards.

Another area where representativeness affects causal judgments is the realm of pseudoscientific belief systems. Consider, for example, the case of astrological signs and representative personality traits. A central tenet of astrology is that an individual's personality is influenced by the astrological sign under which the person was born. And the personalities said to characterize individuals of a certain astrological sign tend to resemble the features we associate with that sign's namesake. For example, people whose astrological sign is Leo (the lion) are said to be proud; people whose astrological sign is Aries (the ram) are supposedly quick-tempered and headstrong; Capricorns (the goat) are hardworking and down-to-earth; Virgos (the virgin) are modest and retiring; and so on. The personality profiles that supposedly accompany various astrological signs have been shown time and again to have absolutely no validity (Abell, 1981; Schick & Vaughn, 1995; Zusne & Jones, 1982). Why, then, is astrology so popular? Part of the reason is that astrology takes advantage of people's use of the representativeness heuristic. Each of the personality profiles has some superficial appeal because each draws on the intuition that like goes with like. Who is more inclined to be vacillating than a Gemini (a Twin)? Who is more likely to be fair and balanced than a Libra (the Scales)?

"For what it's worth, next week all your stars and planets will be in good aspect for you to launch an invasion of England."

The Joint Operation of Availability and Representativeness

The representativeness and availability heuristics sometimes operate in tandem. For example, a judgment that two things belong together—that one is representative of the other—can make an instance in which they do occur together readily available, that is, easy to bring to mind as evidence that the two things belong together. The joint effect of these two heuristics can thus create an **illusory correlation** between two variables, or the belief that they are correlated when in fact they are not. A judgment of representativeness leads us to expect an association between the two entities, and this expectation in turn makes instances in which they are paired unusually memorable.

A classic set of experiments by Loren and Jean Chapman (1967) highlights how readily people form illusory correlations and how consequential they can be. The Chapmans were struck by a paradox observed in the practice of clinical psychology. Clinicians often claim that they find so-called projective personality tests helpful in making clinical diagnoses, but systematic research has shown most of these tests to be completely lacking in validity. Projective tests require people to respond to unstructured and ambiguous stimuli, such as the famous Rorschach inkblots, thus "projecting" their personalities onto what they see. Why would intelligent, conscientious, and well-trained clinicians believe that

ILLUSORY CORRELATION IN CLINICAL JUDGMENT
Clinicians have been shown to "see" connections between responses to projective tests—like the Rorschach test shown here—and various pathological conditions. These illusory correlations are the product of the joint influence of availability and representativeness.

such tests can diagnose mental or emotional problems when they cannot? Why, in other words, do some clinicians perceive an illusory correlation between their clients' conditions and their clients' responses on such tests?

To find out, the Chapmans first asked numerous clinicians about which of their clients' specific test responses tended to indicate the presence of which specific pathological conditions. Much of their work focused on the Draw-a-Person Test, in which the client draws a picture of a person and the therapist interprets the picture for signs of various psychopathologies. The clinicians reported that they observed many connections between particular drawings and specific conditions—drawings and pathologies that seem, intuitively, to belong together. People suffering from paranoia, for example, were thought to be inclined to draw unusually large or small eyes. People excessively insecure about their intelligence were thought to be likely to draw a large (or small) head.

To investigate these illusory correlations further, the Chapmans gathered a sample of 45 Draw-a-Person pictures: 35 drawn by psychotic patients in a nearby hospital and 10 drawn by graduate students in clinical psychology. They then attached a phony statement to each picture that supposedly described the condition of the person who drew it. Some came with the description "is suspicious of other people," others with the description "has had problems of sexual impotence," and so on. The researchers were careful to avoid any correlation between the nature of the drawings and the condition attached to each one. For example, "is suspicious of other people" appeared just as often on pictures with average eyes as on pictures with large or small eyes.

These pictures (with accompanying pathologies) were then shown to college students who had never heard of the Draw-a-Person Test. Although the study was carefully designed so there was no connection between the pictures and specific conditions, the students nonetheless "saw" the same relationships reported earlier by the clinical psychologists. To the students, too, it seemed that prominent eyes were likely to have been drawn by individuals who were suspicious of others. This finding suggests, of course, that the clinical psychologists were not detecting any real correlations between pathological conditions and responses on the Draw-a-Person Test. Instead, they were "detecting" the same nonexistent associations that the undergraduate students were seeing—illusory correlations produced by the availability and representativeness heuristics working together. Certain pictures seem representative of specific pathologies (for example, prominent eyes and being suspicious of other people), and therefore instances in which the two are observed together (a suspicious individual drawing a person with large eyes) are particularly noteworthy and memorable.

In a final study, the Chapmans asked another group of students to indicate the extent to which various conditions (suspiciousness, impotence, dependence) "called to mind" different parts of the body (eyes, sexual organs, mouth). Tellingly, their responses matched the correlations reported by the earlier groups of clinicians and students. In addition to highlighting the joint influence of availability and representativeness, these findings exemplify a much broader point about human judgment: when associations or propositions seem plausible, people often believe them, regardless of the evidence.

Two mental systems guide our judgments and decisions: one akin to intuition and the other akin to reason. The intuitive system operates quickly and automatically, while the rational system tends to be more deliberate and controlled. These systems can lead to the same judgments or to opposite judgments—or the intuitive system may produce a satisfying judgment so quickly that the rational system is never engaged. The quick assessments made by the intuitive system are often based on heuristics, which can sometimes bias judgment. The availability heuristic may lead to biased assessments of risk and biased estimates of people's contributions to joint projects. The representativeness heuristic may result in neglecting base-rate information and lead to mistaken assessments of cause and effect. When these two heuristics operate together, they can lead to an illusory correlation between two variables.

Chapter Review

SUMMARY

Studying Social Cognition

- By studying errors in judgment, psychologists can understand how people make judgments and learn what can be done to avoid mistakes.

The Information Available for Social Cognition

- Sometimes people make judgments on the basis of very little information, such as making personality judgments based on physical appearance.
- Mistaken inferences can arise from *pluralistic ignorance*, which tends to occur when people are reluctant to express their misgivings about a perceived group norm; their reluctance in turn reinforces the false norm.
- People's judgments can seem to them more accurate than they really are because of the *self-fulfilling prophecy*. More specifically, people can draw mistaken inferences about others that seem valid because they act in ways that elicit the very behavior they were expecting—behavior that wouldn't have happened otherwise.
- Information received secondhand often does not provide a full account of what happened, instead stressing certain elements at the expense of others.
- Negative information is more likely to be reported than positive information, which can lead people to believe they are more at risk of various calamities than they actually are.

How Information Is Presented

- The way information is presented, such as the order of presentation, can affect judgment. A *primacy effect* arises when the information presented first is more influential because it affects the interpretation of subsequent information. A *recency effect* arises when information presented last is more influential, often because it is more available in memory.
- Order effects are a type of *framing effect*. Other framing effects involve a change of the language or structure of the information presented to create a desired effect.
- The temporal framing of an event can also influence how it is interpreted. Far-off events are construed in more abstract terms, whereas imminent events are construed more concretely.

How We Seek Information

- People tend to examine whether certain propositions are true by searching for information consistent with the proposition in question. This *confirmation bias* can lead people to believe things that aren't true because evidence can generally be found to support even the most questionable propositions.
- People are sometimes motivated to find evidence supporting a preexisting conclusion and so they do so disproportionately, coming to the conclusion that their preferred conclusion is more valid than it really is.

Top-Down Processing: Using Schemas to Understand New Information

- Schemas influence the interpretation of information. They are important *top-down* tools for understanding the world, as opposed to the *bottom-up* processing of information from the world.
- Schemas guide attention, memory, and the construal of information, and they can directly prompt behavior.
- Being exposed to certain stimuli (such as a plastic shovel) often has the effect of *priming* the concepts with which they're associated (the beach), making those concepts momentarily more accessible.
- In general, the more recently and the more frequently a schema has been activated, the more likely it is to be applied to new information. Conscious awareness of a schema is not required for it to have an influence.

Reason, Intuition, and Heuristics

- People have two systems for processing information: an intuitive system and a rational system. Intuitive responses are based on rapid, associative processes, whereas rational responses are based on slower, rule-based reasoning.
- *Heuristics* are mental shortcuts that provide people with sound judgments most of the time, although they sometimes lead to errors in judgment.

- People use the *availability heuristic* when judging the frequency or probability of some event by how readily relevant instances come to mind. It can cause people to overestimate their own contributions to group projects, and it can lead to faulty assessment of the risks posed by memorable hazards.
- The sense of *fluency* people experience when processing information can influence the judgments they make about it. Disfluent stimuli lead to more reflective thought.
- People use the *representativeness heuristic* when trying to categorize something by judging how similar it is to their conception of the typical member of a category or when trying to make causal attributions by assessing how similar an effect is to a possible cause. Sometimes this leads people to overlook highly relevant considerations, such as *base-rate information*—how many members of the category there are in a population.
- Operating together, availability and representativeness can produce potent *illusory correlations*, which result from thinking that two variables are correlated, both because they resemble each other and because the simultaneous occurrence of two similar events stands out more than that of two dissimilar events.

THINK ABOUT IT

1. How valid are snap judgments? Do brief exposures to a person's physical appearance or "thin slices" of the individual's behavior provide meaningful information about what that person is really like? What are possible consequences of snap judgments?

2. What role might pluralistic ignorance play in the problem of binge drinking on college campuses? What could school administrators do to reduce pluralistic ignorance in this context?

3. How does the desire to entertain tend to bias the kinds of stories that are reported most frequently in the media? What effects might this bias have on people's beliefs about the world?

4. If you were developing an advertising campaign for a fitness class, what kinds of framing strategies might you use to increase the chances of people signing up for the class? In particular, consider spin framing, positive and negative framing, and temporal framing.

5. Suppose you're about to go on a blind date when a mutual friend warns you that your date can be a little cold and unfriendly. According to research on the confirmation bias, how might this information influence the impression you ultimately form about your date?

6. Research on priming suggests that it is possible for a stimulus to activate a schema even if a person is not consciously aware of the stimulus. Can you think of ways that you might be able to use priming to influence others' behavior?

7. Imagine you're working on a group project with three other students and you are all asked to indicate your individual contribution to the project, relative to the other group members' contributions, in the form of a percentage. If you were to sum the individual percentages reported by each group member, would you expect it to add up to roughly 100 percent? Why or why not?

The **answer guidelines** for the think about it questions can be found at the back of the book . . . 👉

ONLINE STUDY MATERIALS

Want to earn a better grade on your test?
Go to **inQuizitive** to learn and review this chapter's content, with personalized feedback along the way.

Why do we attribute Bill Gates' achievements to his intelligence instead of his advantages?

Why do we dwell on decisions we could have made?

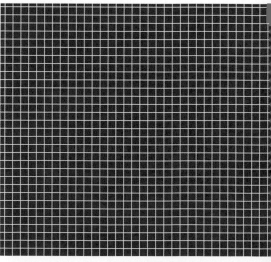

Why would an Olympic athlete be more satisfied with winning third place than second?

Social Attribution: Explaining Behavior

UNTIL OCTOBER 2017, BILL GATES WAS THE RICHEST PERSON IN THE WORLD (HE'S NOW THE SECOND RICHEST). Having dropped out of Harvard at the ripe old age of 19, he started a company called Microsoft (you might have heard the name). Why was he able to invent tremendously creative and powerful software at such a young age and build such a hugely successful company? Most people would say he must be one of the smartest people who ever lived. But Bill Gates himself would not say that.

Instead, Gates would tell you that in 1968, when he was in eighth grade, his parents were well-off enough to enroll him in a private school called Lakeside (Gladwell, 2008). Lakeside happened to have a time-sharing computer terminal that linked the school's computer club (at a time when few colleges, let alone high schools, had computer clubs) to a mainframe computer in downtown Seattle. Back then, most computers still required a clumsy punch-card system for data entry; but Lakeside's terminal, like those today, used a more efficient keyboard system. Gates became one of a handful of teenagers in the world who were able to do real-time programming in 1968.

Gates's luck continued. Though Lakeside soon ran out of money to pay for expensive computer time, by coincidence, one of the founders of a company called Computer Center Corporation (CCC) had a son at Lakeside and offered the Lakeside Computer Club free programming time in exchange for testing the company's software. CCC went bankrupt shortly thereafter, but by then Gates and his friends had managed to persuade a local firm, Information Sciences, Inc. (ISI), to give them free computer time as payment for helping the firm develop a payroll

BILL GATES
(A) A fledgling entrepreneur. (B) The man today, primarily a philanthropist.

program. Gates by this time was spending 20–30 hours a week programming. Gates also established a connection with the University of Washington, which happened to have one computer that was free for the little-used period from 3 a.m. to 6 a.m. Living close to the university, he could sneak out of bed at night and walk to the computer center.

The next fortuitous event was that ISI needed programmers who were familiar with their particular type of software. Gates and his pals fit the bill, and they went to work under the supervision of a brilliant master of programming. By the time he got to Harvard, Gates had spent many thousands of hours programming—likely more than any freshman anywhere. Bill Gates was a brilliant guy, but he couldn't have started Microsoft at 19 if he hadn't had such unusually fortunate experience with programming beginning when he was 13.

This difference between the explanations—or "causal attributions"—of the observer (that's you) and the actor (Bill Gates) is commonplace. The observer is inclined to attribute actions, especially highly distinctive ones, to properties of the actor, such as personality traits and abilities. The actor is more inclined to attribute the same action to situational factors. People make causal attributions because they need to draw inferences about others (and themselves) in order to make predictions about future behavior.

This chapter examines how people explain the behavior of those around them and the effect of these explanations on the judgments they make about other people. We'll also explore how people understand the causes of their own behavior, as well as the way their understanding influences both their immediate emotional experience and their subsequent behavior. These are the concerns of **attribution theory**, the study of how people understand the causes of events. ■

attribution theory A set of concepts explaining how people assign causes to the events around them and the effects of these kinds of causal assessments.

Inferring the Causes of Behavior

In class one day, you listen as a student gives a long-winded answer to a question from your professor. When the student is finally finished, your professor says, "Good point" and moves on. You can't help wondering, "Did the professor really think it was a good point, or was she just trying to encourage student

participation? Or was she trying to boost her standing on ratemyprofessors.com?" The way you answer these questions—the way you construe the meaning of the professor's behavior—explains her particular action. It also helps make sense of many of her other actions in the course, such as whether she consistently praises students' opinions in general. And your attributions may also affect your own behavior toward your professor in the future.

Causal attribution is the construal process people use to explain both their own and others' behavior. Understanding causal attributions is crucial to understanding everyday social behavior because we all make causal attributions many times a day, and the attributions we make can greatly affect our thoughts, feelings, and future behavior.

causal attribution Linking an event to a cause, such as inferring that a personality trait is responsible for a behavior.

The Pervasiveness and Importance of Causal Attribution

When you ask someone out for a date but are rebuffed ("Sorry, but I already have plans"), you don't simply take the response at face value. You wonder whether the person actually has something else going on or is just giving you the brush-off. Similarly, when you get an exam back, you're not simply delighted or dejected about the grade you received. You make an attribution. If the grade is a good one, you might decide that this is another example of how smart and hardworking you are, or you might attribute the grade to luck or easy grading. If the grade is a bad one, you might decide you're not so good at this subject, or you might decide that the test was unfair.

Concluding that someone won't go out with you because she's busy leads to an entirely different set of emotional reactions than concluding that she finds you unappealing. And attributing a bad grade on an exam to a lack of ability leads to unhappiness and withdrawal, whereas attributing failure to a lack of effort often leads to more vigorous attempts to study harder and more effectively in the future. Indeed, systematic research on causal attribution has shown that people's explanations have tremendous consequences in a number of areas, including health and education.

Explanatory Style and Attribution

Social and personality psychologists have examined the impact of attributions on academic and professional success by relating a person's explanatory style to long-term performance. **Explanatory style** refers to a person's habitual way of explaining events, and it's assessed along three dimensions: internal/external, stable/unstable, and global/specific. To assess explanatory style, researchers ask participants to imagine six different good events that might happen to them ("You do a project that is highly praised") and six bad events ("You meet a friend who acts hostilely toward you") and to provide a likely cause for each (Peterson & Barrett, 1987). The participants then say whether each cause (1) is due to something about them or something about other people or circumstances (internal/external), (2) will be present again in the future or not (stable/unstable), and (3) is something that influences other areas of their lives or just this one (global/specific). An explanation that mentions an *internal* cause implicates the self ("There I go again"), but an *external* cause does not ("That was the pickiest set of questions I've ever seen"). A *stable* cause implies that things will never change ("I'm just not good at this"), whereas an *unstable* cause implies that things may improve ("The cold medicine I was taking made me groggy"). Finally, a *global* cause is something that affects many areas of life ("I'm stupid"), while a *specific* cause applies to only a few ("I'm not good with names").

Researchers typically combine the three dimensions of internal/external, stable/unstable, and global/specific to form an overall explanatory style index, which is then correlated with an outcome of interest, such as students' GPAs. A tendency to explain negative events in terms of internal, stable, and global causes is considered a pessimistic explanatory style, and it's related to a variety of undesirable life outcomes. For example, students with a pessimistic explanatory style tend to get lower grades than those with a more optimistic style (Peterson & Barrett, 1987).

Explanatory style has also been shown to relate to people's physical health. A person's explanatory style as a young adult has been found to predict physical health later in life (Peterson, Seligman, & Vaillant, 1988; see also Peterson, 2000). The study in question took advantage of the fact that members of Harvard's graduating

explanatory style A person's habitual way of explaining events, typically assessed along three dimensions: internal/external, stable/unstable, and global/specific.

"A pessimist sees the difficulty in every opportunity; an optimist sees the opportunity in every difficulty."
—SIR WINSTON CHURCHILL

EXPLANATORY STYLE AND ACADEMIC SUCCESS
How people explain their academic successes and failures ("I'm not good at this," vs. "The questions were picky") has implications for students' long-term success in school.

BOX 5.1   FOCUS ON WELL-BEING

The Sunny Side of the Street

Buoyed by the finding that optimism predicts better health decades later, other investigators have asked whether prompting people to practice optimism can lead to increased happiness (Layous, Chancellor, & Lyubomirsky, 2014; Lyubomirsky & Layous, 2013). In this intervention-oriented work, researchers translate abstract concepts such as optimism into everyday practices. In one study, for example, participants in an optimism-enhancing condition wrote about what their best possible future life would look like if everything were going well in their personal and professional lives (Boehm, Lyubomirsky, & Sheldon, 2011). This act of practicing optimism led Western European college students to report greater happiness one month later (although this practice, it should be noted, had no effect on East Asian students). In related work, participants were asked to identify signature strengths they possess (for example, having courage, a strong sense of justice) and apply that strength to their daily lives during the ensuing week. In another condition, participants were asked each day to think about three good things in their lives. Thinking about a signature strength and reminding oneself of the good things in life each day are close cousins of developing an optimistic view of the future. These practices, compared to a control condition in which participants journaled each day for a week about their past, led to increased happiness and reduced depression over a period of six months (Seligman, Steen, Park, & Peterson, 2005).

Three Good Things in My Life

1.

2.

3.

Jot these three things down.
You'll be glad you did!

classes from 1942 to 1944 took part in a longitudinal study that required them to complete a questionnaire every year and submit medical records of periodic physical examinations. Using the medical records, judges scored each person's physical health on a 5-point scale, where 1 means the person was in good health and 5 means the person was deceased. This was done for all participants when they reached the ages of 25, 30, 35, and so on. The physical health of the men at each of these ages was then correlated with their explanatory style as young men, which was assessed by having judges score the descriptions they gave in 1946 of their most difficult experiences during World War II. Optimistic explanatory style during younger adulthood was a significant predictor of good physical health in later life.

The optimistic tendency to make external, unstable, and specific attributions for failure presumably makes us less prone to despair and encourages more of a can-do outlook that promotes such behaviors as exercising regularly and visiting the doctor—behaviors that can lead to a longer, healthier life (**Box 5.1**).

ATTRIBUTIONS ABOUT CONTROLLABILITY Other researchers, led by Bernard Weiner and Craig Anderson, have also shown that people's attributional style has a powerful effect on long-term outcomes. These investigators emphasize whether an attribution implies that a given outcome is controllable. For example, attributions for failure that imply controllability—a lack of effort or a poor strategy—make it easier to persevere because we can always try harder or try a new strategy

(Anderson, 1991; Anderson & Deuser, 1993; Anderson, Krull, & Weiner, 1996). If we view outcomes as beyond our control, on the other hand, it's tempting to simply give up—indeed, it may often seem rational to do so.

Research inspired by this framework has shown that people can be trained to adopt more productive attributional tendencies for academic outcomes—in particular, an inclination to attribute failure to a lack of effort—and that doing so has beneficial effects on subsequent academic performance (Dweck, 1975; Forsterling, 1985). The effects are both substantial and touching. Blackwell, Trzesniewski, and Dweck (2007) report tough junior high school boys crying when made to realize that their grades were due mainly to a lack of effort rather than a lack of brains. Making people believe they can exert control over events that they formerly believed to be beyond their control restores hope and unleashes the kind of productive energy that makes future success more likely (Crandall, Katkovsky, & Crandall, 1965; Dweck & Reppucci, 1973; Peterson, Maier, & Seligman, 1993; Seligman, Maier, & Geer, 1968; Weiner, 2010).

PRODUCTIVE ATTRIBUTIONAL STYLE
Franklin Delano Roosevelt was elected U.S. president for four terms. FDR's optimistic attributional style undoubtedly contributed to his being one of the most successful political figures in U.S. history, despite having a severe physical handicap.

GENDER AND ATTRIBUTIONAL STYLE Such training programs might be put to good use in undoing some inadvertent attributional training that occurs in elementary school classrooms and that may give rise to a troubling gender difference in attributional style. Research shows that boys are more likely than girls to attribute their failures to lack of effort, and girls are more likely than boys to attribute their failures to lack of ability (Dweck, 1986; Dweck, Davidson, Nelson, & Enna, 1978; Lewis & Sullivan, 2005; Ryckman & Peckham, 1987; Whitley & Frieze, 1985).

Carol Dweck and her colleagues have found that this difference results in part from teachers' feedback patterns in fourth-grade and fifth-grade classrooms (Dweck et al., 1978). The researchers found that although girls, on average, outperform boys in school, negative evaluation of girls' performance was almost exclusively directed at intellectual inadequacies ("This is not right, Lisa"). In contrast, almost half of the criticism of boys' work referred to nonintellectual factors ("This is messy, Bill"). Positive evaluation of girls' performance was related to the intellectual quality of their performance less than 80 percent of the time; for boys, it was 94 percent of the time. From these data, Dweck and her colleagues argue that girls learn that criticism means they may lack intellectual ability, whereas boys learn that criticism may just mean they haven't worked hard enough or paid enough attention to detail. Similarly, girls are likely to come to suspect that praise may be unrelated to the intellectual quality of their performance, whereas boys learn that praise means their intellectual performance was excellent (Good, Rattan, & Dweck, 2012).

When Dweck and her colleagues performed an experiment in which they gave both boys and girls feedback—either the kind girls typically receive or the kind boys typically receive—they found that *both* genders tended to view subsequent failures accordingly, either as a reflection of their lack of ability or as a reflection of their lack of effort and attention to detail (Dweck et al., 1978). Therefore, whatever other reasons there may be for boys routinely taking credit for their successes and dismissing their failures and for girls' more modest attributions, these patterns are reinforced by the treatment they receive in the classroom (Espinoza, Areas da Luz Fontes, & Arms-Chavez, 2014).

People differ in their explanatory styles; that is, they differ in whether they tend to make attributions that are external or internal, stable or unstable, global or specific. Attributional style predicts academic success as well as health and longevity. Belief in the controllability of outcomes is important, and beliefs about the controllability of academic outcomes can be altered by training. Boys and girls often learn to draw different conclusions about academic outcomes. Boys receive feedback indicating that success is due to ability and failure is due to insufficient effort or to incidental factors, whereas girls receive feedback indicating the reverse.

The Processes of Causal Attribution

Does she really like me, or is she just pretending she does because she's after my best friend? Does that salesman really believe the turbo boost is essential to performance, or is he just saying that to get a bigger commission? Is that guy really that selfish, or is he just under a lot of pressure? These types of questions run through our heads every day. How we answer them—how we assess the causes of observed or reported behavior—is not capricious; rather, our assessments follow predictable patterns that serve several purposes. They help us understand the past, illuminate the present, and predict the future. Only by knowing the cause of a given event can we grasp the true meaning of what has happened and anticipate what's likely to happen next.

For example, our perception of how much control another person has over his or her actions is one important factor in how we judge that person. When a person offers an excuse for problematic behavior, it typically yields more sympathy and forgiveness if the excuse involves something beyond the person's control ("I had a flat tire") than if it involves something controllable ("I needed to take a break") (Weiner, 1986). Gay and lesbian people are viewed more favorably by those who believe they are "born that way" rather than choosing their sexual orientation (Haider-Markel & Joslyn, 2008; Whitely, 1990).

When we're trying to figure out the cause of something, a particularly important question is whether an outcome is the product of something within the person (that is, an internal, or dispositional, cause) or a reflection of something about the context or circumstances (an external, or situational, cause). Ever since Kurt Lewin pointed out that behavior is always a function of both the person and the situation (see Chapter 1), theories of attribution have focused on how people assess the relative contributions of these two types of causes (Heider, 1958; Hilton & Slugoski, 1986; Hilton, Smith, & Kim, 1995; Jones & Davis, 1965; Kelley, 1967; Medcoff, 1990).

Frequently, the distinction between internal and external causes is straightforward. You might win the pot in your weekly poker game because you're a better player than everyone else (internal cause), or maybe you simply were lucky and got the best cards (external cause). In other contexts, the distinction isn't as clear. We might say that someone became a rock-and-roll guitarist because of a deep love of the instrument

"If we're being honest, it was your decision to follow my recommendation that cost you money."

(internal cause) or because of the desire for fame and fortune (external cause). But aren't love of the instrument and desire for fame both inner states? Why is the desire for fame and fortune considered an external cause? The answer is that loving to play the guitar is not something shared by most people, so it tells us something characteristic and informative about the person and is therefore personal, or internal. Many people, however, seem to find the prospect of fame attractive. (Why else would there be so many reality TV shows?) And even more find the prospect of wealth attractive. Doing something to achieve fame and fortune, then, tells us little about the person in hot pursuit of either. So in this case, it makes sense to refer to the cause as something impersonal, or external. Determining whether certain actions are the product of internal versus external causes thus requires assessments of what most people are like and what most people are likely to do.

Attribution and Covariation

When scientists attempt to nail down the cause of some phenomenon, they try to isolate the one cause that seems to make a difference in producing the effect. In other words, they try to identify the cause that seems always to be present when the effect or phenomenon occurs and always seems to be absent when the phenomenon does not occur. For example, to determine whether ulcers are caused by a bacterium, a medical researcher might determine whether people who are given the bacterium develop ulcers and whether people with ulcers improve after taking an antibiotic to fight the bacterium.

To a considerable degree, this is also how people assess causality in their everyday lives (Cheng & Novick, 1990; Fiedler, Walther, & Nickel, 1999; Forsterling, 1989; Hewstone & Jaspers, 1987; Kelley, 1973; Nisbett & Ross, 1980; White, 2002). When your friend states that she likes her statistics class, you automatically try to figure out why: Is she a math person? Is the class taught by a great professor? What does your friend say about other math classes or about her classes in general? What do other students in her statistics class say about it?

In assessing causality, people use what attribution theorists have dubbed the **covariation principle** (Kelley, 1973). We try to determine what causes—internal or external, symptomatic of the person in question or applicable to nearly everyone—"covary" with the observation or effect we're trying to explain. Psychologists believe that three types of covariation information are particularly significant: consensus, distinctiveness, and consistency.

1. **Consensus** refers to what most people would do in a given situation. Does everyone behave the same way in that situation, or do few other people behave that way? Is your friend one of a precious few who likes her statistics class, or do most students like the class? All else being equal, the more an individual's reaction is shared by others (when consensus is high), the less it says about that individual and the more it says about the situation.

2. **Distinctiveness** refers to what an individual does in different situations. Is a particular behavior unique to a specific situation, or does the person react the same way in many situations? Does your friend seem to like all math classes or even all classes in general, or does she just like her statistics class? The more someone's reaction is confined to a particular

---

"The logic of science is also that of business and life."
—JOHN STUART MILL

"The whole of science is nothing more than refinement of every-day thinking."
—ALBERT EINSTEIN

covariation principle The idea that behavior should be attributed to potential causes that occur along with the observed behavior.

consensus A type of covariation information: whether most people would behave the same way or differently in a given situation.

distinctiveness A type of covariation information: whether a behavior is unique to a particular situation or occurs in many or all situations.

situation (when distinctiveness is high), the less it says about that individual and the more it says about the specific situation.

3. **Consistency** refers to what an individual does in a given situation on different occasions. Is the behavior the same now as in the past, or does it vary? Does your friend have favorable things to say about today's statistics class only, or has she raved about the course all semester? The more an individual's reaction varies across occasions (when consistency is low), the harder it is to make a definite attribution either to the person or to the situation. The effect is likely due to some less predictable combination of circumstances. When consistency is high and an individual's reaction does not vary much across occasions, it's easier to make a definite attribution either to the person or to the situation.

A *situational attribution* is called for when consistency, consensus, and distinctiveness are all high. When everyone else taking your friend's statistics class likes it too, when your friend claims to like few other math classes, and when she has praised the class all semester, there must be something special about that class. In contrast, a *dispositional attribution* is called for when consistency is high but consensus and distinctiveness are low. When few other students like the statistics class, when your friend claims to like all math courses, and when she has raved about the statistics class all semester, her fondness for the course must reflect something about her.

When psychologists have given research participants these three types of covariation information and asked them to attribute a reported effect to a particular cause, they do indeed use the logic of covariation (Forsterling, 1989; Hewstone & Jaspers, 1983; Hilton et al., 1995; McArthur, 1972; White, 2002). They make situational attributions when consensus, distinctiveness, and consistency are high and make dispositional attributions when consistency is high but consensus and distinctiveness are low. The only surprising finding is that people are sometimes only modestly influenced by consensus information. They respond to whether or not everyone laughed at the comedian, but rather mildly. This reflects a common tendency to focus more on information about the person (distinctiveness and consistency) at the expense of information that speaks to the influence of the surrounding context (consensus).

Discounting, Augmentation, and Counterfactual Thinking

The judgments people make aren't always based on what's actually happened; sometimes they are based on what people *imagine* would happen under different situations or if a different individual were involved. For example, in considering the high rates of obedience in Milgram's experiment (see Chapters 1 and 9), you might try to imagine what you would do if you were a participant. You might find it difficult to imagine administering so much electric shock to the victim (the "learner"). In other words, you might believe that a change in the participant—in particular, if *you* were the participant—would lead to a change in the outcome. Hence, you would conclude that it must have been the person

consistency A type of covariation information: whether an individual behaves the same way or differently in a given situation on different occasions.

COVARIATION AND ATTRIBUTION
If your roommate laughs at Ali Wong but doesn't laugh at many other comedians on TV (high distinctiveness), and if most people you know laugh at Ali Wong (high consensus), and if both your roommate and most other people you know almost always laugh at an Ali Wong performance (high consistency), you're going to think your roommate laughs at Ali Wong because of the situation, namely, because it's an Ali Wong performance. If your roommate laughs at pretty much every comic on the tube (low distinctiveness) every time he sees one (high consistency), and, of course, you know that's not true of everyone you know (low consensus), you're going to think that your roommate laughs at any comedian because he's a pushover for comedians; in other words, he has a disposition to like comedians.

(or rather the people who delivered so much shock), not the situation, that was responsible for the behavior.

THE DISCOUNTING AND AUGMENTATION PRINCIPLES Sometimes the information available to us suggests that there could be multiple causes responsible for a given behavior. A young man interviews for a job and seems quite personable. Did he seem personable because that's the way he really is or because he was just putting on a good face for the interview?

In circumstances like these, the **discounting principle** says that our confidence that a particular cause is responsible for a given outcome will be reduced (discounted) if there are other plausible causes that might have produced that same outcome (Kelley, 1973). Either a sunny disposition or the desire to land a job is sufficient to make someone act personably in an interview. By pure logic, then, we can't make a confident attribution. But we supplement the pure logic with our knowledge of what people are like. That knowledge tells us that nearly everyone would act in a personable manner to get the job offer, so we can't be confident that the applicant's disposition is all that sunny. We thus discount the possibility that what we've seen (a personable demeanor) tells us something about the person involved (he's personable) because we imagine that nearly everyone would act similarly in that context.

Extending that logic just a bit leads to a complementary **augmentation principle**, by which we can have greater (augmented) confidence that a particular cause is responsible for a given outcome if other causes are present that we imagine would produce a *different* outcome. Typically, we can be more certain that a person's actions reflect what that person is really like if the circumstances would seem to discourage such actions. If someone advocates a position despite being threatened with torture for doing so, we can safely conclude that the person truly believes in that position.

THE INFLUENCE OF WHAT ALMOST HAPPENED In making causal assessments, we sometimes consider whether a given outcome is likely to have happened if the circumstances were slightly different. Our attributions are thus influenced not only by our knowledge of what has actually happened in the past, but also by **counterfactual thinking** (thoughts *counter* to the facts)—considerations of what might have, could have, or should have happened "if only" a few minor things were done differently (Johnson, 1986; Kahneman & Tversky, 1982; Roese, 1997; Roese & Olson, 1995). "If only I had studied harder" implies that a lack of effort was the cause of a poor test result. "If only the Democrats had nominated a different candidate" implies that the candidate, not the party's principles, was responsible for defeat.

Because our attributions influence our emotional reactions to events, our counterfactual thoughts should do so as well. An emotional reaction tends to be more intense if the event almost didn't happen—a phenomenon known as **emotional amplification**. Would you feel worse, for example, if someone you loved died in a plane crash after switching her assigned flight at the last minute or after sticking with her assigned flight? Most people say that a last-minute switch would make the loss harder to bear because of the thought that it "almost" didn't happen. In general, the pain or joy we derive from any event tends to be proportional to how easy it is to imagine the event not happening.

So what determines whether a counterfactual event seems like it "almost" happened? Some of the most common determinants are time and distance. Imagine,

---

discounting principle The idea that people will assign reduced weight to a particular cause of behavior if other plausible causes might have produced it.

augmentation principle The idea that people will assign greater weight to a particular cause of behavior if other causes are present that normally would produce a different outcome.

counterfactual thinking Thoughts of what might have, could have, or should have happened "if only" something had occurred differently.

"Of all sad words of tongue or pen, the saddest are these, 'It might have been.'"
—JOHN GREENLEAF WHITTIER, NINETEENTH-CENTURY QUAKER POET AND ABOLITIONIST

emotional amplification An increase in an emotional reaction to an event that is proportional to how easy it is to imagine the event not happening.

for example, that someone survives a plane crash in a remote area and then tries to hike to safety. Suppose he hikes to within 75 miles (120 kilometers) of safety before dying of exposure. How much should the airline pay his relatives in compensation? Would your estimate of the proper compensation change if he'd made it to within a quarter of a mile (402 meters) to safety? It would for most people.

In one study, those who were led to believe he died a quarter mile from safety recommended an average of $162,000 more in compensation than those who thought he died 75 miles away (Miller & McFarland, 1986). Because he almost made it (within a quarter mile), his death seems more tragic and thus more worthy of compensation.

This psychology of coming close leads to a kind of paradox in the emotional reactions of Olympic athletes to winning a silver or bronze medal instead of the gold. An analysis of the smiles and grimaces that athletes exhibited on the medal stand at the 1992 Summer Olympics in Barcelona, Spain, revealed that second-place silver medalists seemed to be less happy than the third-place bronze medalists they had outperformed (Medvec, Madey, & Gilovich, 1995). This finding was replicated at the 2004 Olympics in Athens, Greece (Matsumoto & Willingham, 2006). Since when is bronze better than silver? The reversal of reasonable expectations about medals stems from silver medalists being consumed by what they did not receive (the coveted gold medal), whereas bronze medalists focus on what they did receive (a medal). Indeed, analyses of the athletes' comments during post-event interviews confirmed the suspected difference in their counterfactual thoughts. Silver medalists were more focused on how they could have done better "if only" a few things had gone differently, whereas bronze medalists were more inclined to state that "at least" they received a medal. Second place

COUNTERFACTUAL EMOTIONS ON THE OLYMPIC PODIUM (BARCELONA, 1992)
The happy athlete on the right won the bronze medal. The unhappy one on the left won the silver medal. The happy bronze medal winner is undoubtedly comparing the result with a failure to win a medal at all. The gloomy silver medalist is probably contemplating how close she came to the gold.

THE ANGUISH OF WHAT MIGHT HAVE BEEN
It's especially upsetting when someone dies who was not supposed to be in a particular situation. (A) The matador José Cubero, known as Yiyo, died in the bullring after substituting at the last minute for another bullfighter. (B) In the Israeli army, soldiers are forbidden to trade missions, no matter how compelling the circumstances. The reasoning is that if a soldier dies on a mission that he was not supposed to go on, the family will feel even greater anguish at his "needless death," and the soldier who should have gone may feel guilt over still being alive.

can thus be a mixed blessing. The triumph over many can get lost in the defeat by one.

THE INFLUENCE OF EXCEPTIONS VS. ROUTINES Another determinant of how easy it is to imagine an event not happening is whether it resulted from a routine action or a departure from the norm. In one study that examined this idea, participants read about a man who was severely injured when a store he happened to be in was robbed (Miller & McFarland, 1986). In one version of the story, the robbery took place in the store where the man typically shopped. In another version, the robbery took place in a store he decided to visit for "a change of pace." When participants considered how much the victim should be compensated for his injuries, those who thought the injuries were sustained in an unusual setting recommended over $100,000 more than those who thought the injuries occurred in the victim's usual store. The injuries were presumably more tragic because it was so easy to imagine the counterfactual event that would have left the man unharmed.

← LOOKING BACK

A primary aspect of causal attribution involves assessing how much the person or the situation is responsible for a given event. People make such assessments by employing the logic of covariation. We consider the distinctiveness and consistency of a person's behavior, as well as whether others would have behaved similarly (consensus). We also rely on our psychological insight to make attributions. When someone stands to gain from a particular behavior, we attribute the behavior to what the person stands to gain and not to the person's underlying disposition. But when someone behaves in a way that conflicts with self-interest, we are inclined to attribute the behavior to the person's disposition. Counterfactual thoughts about events that almost occurred influence our causal attributions and emotional reactions to events that did occur.

Errors and Biases in Attribution

The attributions people make are sometimes less than fully rational. Our hopes and fears sometimes color our judgment; we sometimes reason from faulty premises; and we're occasionally misled by information of questionable validity. In other words, our causal attributions are occasionally subject to predictable errors and biases. Indeed, since the initial development of attribution theory in the late 1960s and early 1970s, social psychologists have made considerable progress in illuminating some of the pitfalls of everyday causal analysis.

The Self-Serving Attributional Bias

One of the most consistent biases in causal assessments is one you have no doubt noticed time and time again: people are inclined to attribute their failures and other bad events to external circumstances, but to attribute their successes and other good events to themselves—that is, they're subject to a **self-serving attributional bias** (Carver, DeGregorio, & Gillis, 1980; Greenberg, Pyszczynski, & Solomon, 1982; Mullen & Riordan, 1988). Students, for example, tend to make external attributions for their failures ("The test questions were ambiguous"; "The professor is a sadist") and to make internal attributions for success ("My hard work paid off"; "I'm smart"). Research shows that professors do the same thing when their manuscripts are evaluated for possible publication (Wiley, Crittenden, & Birg, 1979). "Of course they accepted this brilliant paper." "They obviously sent this to reviewers who are morons." (But note, as we're sure we don't have to tell you, that papers by the authors of this textbook really are rejected only because of theoretical bias, unfair evaluation procedures, or the simple narrow-mindedness of reviewers.)

Consider your favorite athletes and their coaches. How do they explain their wins and losses, their triumphs and setbacks? Richard Lau and Dan Russell (1980) examined newspaper accounts of the postgame attributions of professional athletes and coaches and found that attributions to one's own team were much more common for victories than for defeats. In contrast, attributions to external elements (bad calls, bad luck, and so on) were much more common for defeats than for victories. Overall, 80 percent of all attributions for victories were to aspects of one's own team, but only 53 percent of all attributions for defeats were to one's own team. Only 20 percent of attributions for victories were to external elements, whereas 47 percent of attributions for defeats were to external elements (see also Roesch & Amirkhan, 1997).

You've no doubt observed this tendency to attribute success internally and failure externally (**Box 5.2**, see p. 152), and it's easy to explain why it happens: people are prone to a self-serving bias in their attributions because doing so makes them feel good about themselves (or at least prevents them from feeling bad about themselves). The self-serving attributional bias, then, is a motivational bias—motivated by the desire to maintain self-esteem. What could be simpler?

Actually, things are not so simple. Even a completely rational person, unaffected by motivations to feel good, might make the same pattern of attributions and be justified in doing so (Wetzel, 1982). After all, when we try to succeed at something, any success is usually at least partly due to our efforts and thus warrants our taking some of the credit. Failure, on the other hand, usually occurs *despite* our efforts and therefore requires looking elsewhere, perhaps externally, for its cause. A fully rational individual, then, might exhibit an apparently self-serving pattern of attribution because success is generally so much more tightly connected than failure to our intentions and effort.

To see this pattern more clearly, consider experimental paradigm that reliably elicits the self-serving attributional bias (Beckman, 1970). Participants tutor a student who is having difficulty mastering some material. (In some of these studies the participants are real teachers, and in others they're college students.) After an initial round of tutoring, the student is assessed and

self-serving attributional bias The tendency to attribute failure and other bad events to external circumstances and to attribute success and other good events to oneself.

"Success has a thousand fathers; failure is an orphan."
—OLD SAYING

"There might have been some carelessness on my part, but it was mostly just good police work."

"First, I'd like to blame the Lord for causing us to lose today."

BOX 5.2   FOCUS ON DAILY LIFE

Self-Serving Attributions

It's easy to find self-serving attributional bias in various public documents. When corporations send end-of-year letters to their shareholders, how do you think they account for their corporation's triumphs and tribulations? One study found that CEOs claimed credit for 83 percent of all positive events and accepted blame for only 19 percent of all negative events (Salancik & Meindl, 1984). Or consider the accident reports motorists file with their insurance companies after being involved in an auto accident. The externalizing here can be downright comic. "The telephone pole was approaching; I was attempting to swerve out of its way when it struck my car" was how one motorist explained his mishap. "A pedestrian hit me and went under my car," stated another (MacCoun, 1993).

These data, of course, require a disclaimer. Unlike the more controlled laboratory studies of the self-serving attributional bias, the corporate reports and insurance forms are for public consumption. Perhaps the authors of these reports don't really believe what they're saying; they're just hoping others will swallow it. These examples should thus be taken as illustrations of the self-serving attributional bias, not as solid evidence for it. The real evidence comes from the more carefully controlled studies described in the text.

found to have done poorly. A second round of tutoring follows and then an additional assessment. For half the participants, the student's performance on the second assessment remains poor; for the other half, the student shows marked improvement. Such studies typically reveal that the teachers tend to take credit if the student improves from session to session, but they tend to blame the student if the student continues to perform poorly. In other words, people make an internal attribution for success (improvement) but an external attribution for failure (continued poor performance).

It may seem as if the teachers are trying to feel good about themselves and are making less than rational attributions to do so. But that's not necessarily the case. Suppose researchers programmed a computer, devoid of any feelings and hence having no need to feel good about itself, with software that employed the covariation principle. What kind of attributions would it make if the programmers gave the computer these inputs? (1) The student did poorly initially, (2) the teacher redoubled efforts or changed teaching strategy (as most people do after an initial failure), and (3) the student did well or poorly in the second session. The computer would then look for a pattern of covariation between the outcome and the potential causes that would tell it what sort of attribution to make. When the student failed both times, there would be no correlation between the teacher's efforts and the student's performance (some effort at time 1 and poor performance by the student; increased effort at time 2 and continued poor performance). Because an attribution to the teacher couldn't easily be justified, the attribution would be made to the student. When the student succeeded the second time, however, there would be an association between the teacher's efforts and the student's performance (some effort at time 1 and poor performance; increased effort at time 2 and improved performance). An attribution to the teacher would therefore be fully justified.

As this example indicates, we shouldn't be too quick to accuse others of making self-serving attributions just to make themselves feel good. It can be difficult to tell from the pattern of attributions alone whether someone has made an attribution to protect self-esteem; such a pattern could be the result of a purely rational analysis.

"We permit all things to ourselves, and that which we call sin in others, is experience for us."
—RALPH WALDO EMERSON, *EXPERIENCE*

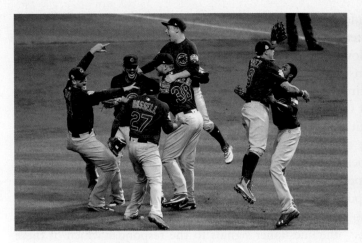

The Fundamental Attribution Error

Try to recall your initial thoughts about the individuals who delivered the maximum level of electric shock in Milgram's studies of obedience (again, see Chapters 1 and 9). The participants had to deliver more than 400 volts of electricity to another person, over the victim's protests, as part of a learning experiment (Milgram, 1963, 1974). Nearly two-thirds of all participants followed the instructions. In this case, a straightforward application of the covariation principle would lead to a situational attribution, not an inference about the participants' character or personality. Because virtually all participants delivered a high level of shock in the face of protests by the "learner," and nearly two-thirds were willing to deliver everything the machine could produce (that is, consensus was high), their behavior doesn't say much about the individual people involved, but rather speaks to something about the situation that made their behavior (surprisingly) common.

If you're like most people, however, you formed a rather harsh opinion of the participants, thinking of them as unusually cruel and callous, perhaps, or as unusually weak. If so, your judgments reflect a second way that everyday causal attributions often depart from the general principles of attributional analysis. There seems to be a pervasive tendency to see people's behavior as a reflection of the kind of people they are, rather than as a result of the situation they find themselves in.

As discussed in Chapter 1, the tendency to attribute people's behavior to elements of their character or personality, even when powerful situational forces are acting to produce that behavior, is known as the **fundamental attribution error** (Ross, 1977). It's called "fundamental" because the problem being solved (figuring out what someone is like from a sample of behavior) is so basic and essential and because the tendency to think dispositionally (to attribute behavior to the person while ignoring important situational factors) is so common and pervasive.

EXPERIMENTAL DEMONSTRATIONS OF THE FUNDAMENTAL ATTRIBUTION ERROR Social psychologists have devised a number of experimental paradigms to examine the fundamental attribution error (Gawronski, 2003; Gilbert & Malone, 1995; Lord, Scott, Pugh, & Desforges, 1997; Miller, Ashton, & Mishal, 1990; Miller, Jones, & Hinkle, 1981; Vonk, 1999).

Remarkably, people will sometimes attribute to personal dispositions another person's behavior even if they themselves have elicited that person's behavior. To illuminate this point, let's consider some studies in which experimenters have

SELF-SERVING ATTRIBUTIONAL BIAS
Athletes tend to attribute their success to internal causes like their talents and hard work, but attribute their failures to external causes like bad officiating and bad luck.

fundamental attribution error The failure to recognize the importance of situational influences on behavior, along with the corresponding tendency to overemphasize the importance of dispositions on behavior.

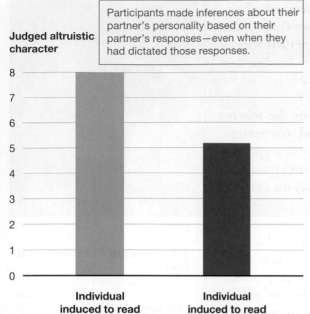

Judged altruistic character

Participants made inferences about their partner's personality based on their partner's responses—even when they had dictated those responses.

FIGURE 5.1
PERCEIVERS "LEARN" FROM BEHAVIOR THEY ELICITED FROM ANOTHER PERSON
This graph shows participants' average trait ratings of individuals that *they themselves* had directed to respond in an altruistic or selfish manner. Higher numbers indicate greater assumed altruism.
Source: Adapted from Van Boven et al., 1999.

ATTRIBUTIONS TO ABILITY
We tend to attribute people's success in life to their inner qualities, like talent and hard work, even when other causes, like family connections and early opportunities, have played a strong role.

randomly assigned participants to one of two roles: questioner or responder (Gilbert & Jones, 1986; Van Boven, Kamada, & Gilovich, 1999). The questioner's job is to read a series of questions to the responder, who then answers with one of two entirely scripted responses. Thus, the responders' answers are not their own and shouldn't be considered informative about their true personalities. The added twist in these studies is that the questioners themselves, following instructions from the experimenter, indicate to the responders which of the two responses to read. Thus, the questioners are determining the responders' behavior. For example, in response to the question, "Do you consider yourself to be sensitive to other people's feelings?" the questioner signals to the responder which of these two answers to give: "I try to be sensitive to others' feelings all the time. I know it is important to have people one can turn to for sympathy and understanding. I try to be that person whenever possible" (altruistic response) or "I think there are too many sensitive, 'touchy-feely' people in the world already. I see no point in trying to be understanding of another if there is nothing in it for me" (selfish response).

After reading a list of these questions to the responders and eliciting a particular response, the questioners in one such study rated the responders on a set of personality traits: trustworthiness, greediness, and kindheartedness (Van Boven, Kamada, & Gilovich, 1999). The investigators found that the questioners drew inferences about the responders—even though they themselves had directed the responders to answer as they did! Responders led to recite mainly altruistic responses were rated more favorably than those led to recite mainly selfish responses (**Figure 5.1**). Note that this occurred even though the responders could have (and may have) tried through tone of voice to distance themselves from the responses they had to give.

THE FUNDAMENTAL ATTRIBUTION ERROR AND PERCEPTIONS OF THE ADVANTAGED AND DISADVANTAGED An inferential problem we face in our daily lives is deciding how much credit to give to those who are succeeding in life and how much blame to direct at those who are not. How much praise and respect should we give to successful entrepreneurs, film stars, and artists? And to what degree should we hold the impoverished accountable for their condition? The discussion thus far about the fundamental attribution error suggests that people tend to assign too much responsibility to the individual for great accomplishments and terrible mistakes and not enough responsibility to the particular situation, broader societal forces, or pure dumb luck.

An ingenious study by Ross, Amabile, & Steinmetz (1977) shows that we can sometimes fail to see clearly the advantages some people enjoy in life and the disadvantages others must overcome. Participants took part in a quiz-game competition, much like the television show *Jeopardy*. Half of them were assigned the role of questioner and the other half the role of contestant. The questioner's job was to think of challenging, but not impossible, general-knowledge questions ("Who were the two coinventors of calculus?" "Who played the role of Victor Laszlo in the film *Casablanca*?"), and the contestant would try to answer the questions (see answers on p. 156).

From a self-presentation standpoint, the questioners had a tremendous advantage. It was relatively easy for them to come off well because they could focus on whatever personal knowledge they happened to have and ignore their various pockets of ignorance. The contestants, however, suffered from the disadvantage of having to field questions about the questioners' store of knowledge, which typically didn't match their own.

If participants were thinking logically, they should correct for the relative advantages and disadvantages enjoyed by the questioners and contestants, respectively: any difference in the questioners and contestants' apparent knowledge and intelligence could easily be explained by their roles. But that was not what happened. Predictably, the hapless contestants failed to answer many of the questions correctly. The contestants came away quite impressed by the questioners' abilities, rating the questioners' knowledge and intelligence more highly than their own. And when the quiz game was later reenacted for a group of observers, they, too, rated the questioners' general knowledge more highly than that of the contestants (**Figure 5.2**). Notice that the only people not fooled by the questioners' performance were the questioners themselves, who rated their own general knowledge and intelligence as roughly equal to the average of the student body. The questioners knew they had skipped over yawning gaps in their knowledge base in order to come up with whatever challenging questions they could offer.

The quiz-game study has profound relevance to everyday life (Ross et al., 1977). Organizational psychologist Ronald Humphrey set up a laboratory microcosm of a business office (Humphrey, 1985). He told participants he was interested in "how people work together in an office setting." All participants witnessed a random procedure whereby some of the participants were selected to be "managers" and to assume supervisory responsibilities, while others were selected to be mere "clerks" who followed orders. Humphrey gave the managers time to study manuals describing their tasks. While they were studying them,

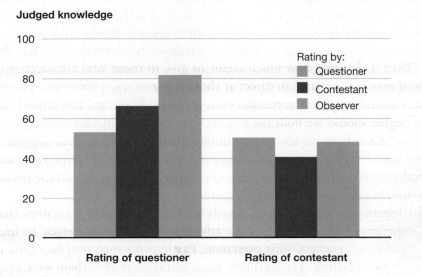

Judged knowledge

FIGURE 5.2
ROLE-CONFERRED ADVANTAGE AND DISADVANTAGE
The bars show ratings of the general knowledge of the questioner and contestant in the quiz-show experiment. Participants thought the questioners were more knowledgeable than the contestants, even though they knew they had been randomly assigned to their roles and that the questioners had a much easier task.
Source: Adapted from Ross et al., 1977.

Answers to Quiz-Show Game Questions p. 154

Isaac Newton and Gottfried von Leibnitz; Paul Henreid.

the experimenter showed the clerks the mailboxes, filing system, and so on. The newly constructed office team then went about their business for 2 hours. The clerks were assigned to work on a variety of low-skilled, repetitive jobs and had little autonomy. The managers, as in a real office, performed reasonably high-skill-level tasks and directed the clerks' activities.

At the end of the work period, managers and clerks rated themselves and each other on a variety of role-related traits, such as leadership, intelligence, capacity for hard work, assertiveness, and supportiveness. For all these traits, managers rated their fellow managers more highly than they rated their clerks. For all but the capacity for hard work, clerks rated their managers more highly than they rated their fellow clerks. And bear in mind that these attributions were made by people who knew their jobs were assigned by the proverbial flip of a coin. Studies like these serve as a caution about rushing to judgment when it comes to the successes and failures we see in everyday life. If we're ever tempted to heap scorn on those who haven't succeeded, we should remember the fundamental attribution error—and the unfortunate office clerks—and ask ourselves whether there are subtle, but powerful situational forces responsible for what we've observed.

Causes of the Fundamental Attribution Error

Why are people so quick to see someone's actions as a reflection of the person's inner traits and enduring character? A tendency so strong and so pervasive is probably the result of several causes acting jointly. Indeed, social psychologists have identified several psychological processes that appear to be responsible for the fundamental attribution error.

MOTIVATIONAL INFLUENCE AND THE BELIEF IN A JUST WORLD One reason we're likely to attribute behavior to people's traits and dispositions is that dispositional inferences can be comforting. The twists and turns of life can be unsettling. A superbly qualified job candidate may be passed over in favor of a mediocre applicant with the right connections. A selfless Good Samaritan may be stricken with cancer and experience an agonizing death. Such events cause anxiety, and we're tempted to think such things couldn't happen to us. But we can minimize such threats by attributing them to something about those who suffer from them, rather than to fate or chance (Burger, 1981; Walster, 1966).

just world hypothesis The belief that people get what they deserve in life and deserve what they get.

More broadly, by thinking that people "get what they deserve" or that "what goes around comes around," we can reassure ourselves that nothing bad will happen to us if we are the right kind of person living the right kind of life. Thus, we tend to attribute behavior and outcomes to dispositions in part because there is a *motive* to do so.

Social psychologists maintain that this motive lies behind what's called the **just world hypothesis**—the belief that people get what they deserve in life (Lambert, Burroughs, & Nguyen, 1999; Lerner, 1980; Lipkus, Dalbert, & Siegler, 1996; Nudelman & Shiloh, 2011). Victims of rape, for example, are often viewed as responsible for their fate (Abrams, Viki, Masser, & Bohner, 2003; Bell, Kuriloff, & Lottes, 1994), as are victims of domestic abuse (Summers & Feldman, 1984). This insidious tendency reaches its zenith in the claim that if no defect in a

"The employees have to assume a share of the blame for allowing the pension fund to become so big and tempting."

BOX 5.3

Not So Fast:
Critical Thinking about the Fundamental Attribution Error

Recent hurricanes Harvey, Irma, and Maria caused tremendous damage. But the most deadly hurricane occurred in 2005 when Hurricane Katrina devastated the city of New Orleans. People across the United States and around the world were surprised that thousands of residents stayed in the city rather than evacuate—costing the lives of nearly 1,500 of them and leading to a harrowing several days for many more. Why would so many people have stayed and risked their lives rather than evacuate, as they were told to do by numerous authorities and media sources? Viewers were puzzled because they thought of staying as *choosing* to stay. As Secretary of Homeland Security Michael Chertoff put it, "Officials called for a mandatory evacuation. Some people chose not to obey that order. That was a mistake on their part." Michael D. Brown, head of the Federal Emergency Management Agency (FEMA) at the time (who ended up losing his job as a result of his handling of the federal response to the hurricane), echoed the same sentiment when he stated that " . . . a lot of people . . . chose not to leave."

But how many really "chose" to stay? It's not hard to detect the influence of the fundamental attribution error here when we consider that those who stayed behind were poorer, probably didn't own a car, had minimal access to news, and had weaker social networks and therefore less opportunity to discuss the situation and how to deal with it. If you don't have a car

to get you out of the city, don't have the money to pay for lodging wherever you flee, and are less likely to hear about the gravity of the threat from friends, family, or the media, you might very well end up, as they did, staying put and sticking it out.

The influence of the fundamental attribution error is even more obvious in the results of a survey that asked relief workers from around the country (doctors, counselors, firefighters, police officers) to provide three words to describe those who evacuated in advance of the hurricane and those who stayed behind. Those who left were most often described as "intelligent," "responsible," and "self-reliant," whereas those who stayed behind were described as "foolish," "stubborn," and "lazy" (Stephens, Hamedani, Markus, Bergsieker, & Eloul, 2009). Being taken in

by the fundamental attribution error is easy to do here because the raw facts are that some people left and some stayed, and the fortunes of those who left tended to be much better than those of the people who stayed behind. The dispositional explanations come easily when it's just those facts that command our attention. It takes some effort to look further and see the background influences that made it so much easier for some people to evacuate than others.

There's a general lesson from the Katrina tragedy and our mistaken causal attributions for the deaths of so many: we shouldn't be so fast to make dispositional attributions for others' behavior; we should hold off until we've made a serious attempt to assess the situation confronting them.

THE FUNDAMENTAL ATTRIBUTION ERROR AND HURRICANE KATRINA Some people had ready means of escape from Katrina and some did not. Commenters typically ignored such differences when explaining the "choice" to evacuate in advance of the hurricane's arrival.

victim's manifest character or past actions can be found, the tragic affliction must be due to some flaw or transgression in a "past life" (Woolger, 1988). Research also shows that people tend to "derogate the victim"—that is, they disparage the character of those who suffer unfortunate experiences that are completely beyond their personal control (Jones & Aronson, 1973; Lerner & Miller, 1978; Lerner & Simmons, 1966). Moreover, they choose to believe that "since I'm a good person, I don't have to worry that I will suffer the terrible fate of that bad person."

PERCEPTUAL SALIENCE AND CAUSAL ATTRIBUTIONS In assessing someone's behavior, what influences whether a potential cause springs to mind? One important determinant is how much the cause stands out perceptually, or how *salient* it is (Lassiter, Geers, Munhall, Ploutz-Snyder, & Breitenbecher, 2002; Robinson & McArthur, 1982; Smith & Miller, 1979). Features of the environment that more readily capture our attention are more likely to be seen as potential causes of an observed effect. And because people are so noticeable and interesting, they tend to capture our attention much more readily than other aspects of the environment. Situations, if attended to at all, may be seen as mere background to the person and his or her actions. This is particularly true of various social determinants of a person's behavior (customs, social norms) that are largely invisible. Attributions to the person, then, have an edge over situational attributions in everyday causal analysis because people are usually more salient than situations.

The importance of perceptual salience in our causal attributions has been demonstrated in many ways. In one study, participants watched a videotape of a conversation between two people (Taylor & Fiske, 1975). Some participants saw a version that showed only one of the individuals; others saw a version that showed both people equally well. When the participants assigned responsibility for setting the tone of the conversation, those who could see only one person assigned more responsibility to that individual than those who could see both people in the conversation equally well.

ATTRIBUTION AND COGNITION Perceptual salience explains some instances of the fundamental attribution error better than others. It explains the results of the quiz-show study, for example, because the decisive situational influence—that the questioner could avoid areas of ignorance but the contestant could not—was invisible and therefore had little impact on people's judgments. But what about the studies in which participants directed another person to give a particular answer and then went ahead and assumed that the person's true nature had been revealed by that answer? Here the situational constraints were far from invisible. Why didn't the participants discount appropriately, decide that the person's answer was perfectly well accounted for by the situational constraint of being assigned to give that answer, and thus refrain from making any inference about the person at all? The answer is that the cognitive machinery people draw on when using the discounting principle doesn't work that way.

Research by Dan Gilbert (1989, 2002) makes it clear that we make attributions for people's behavior in a way that stacks the deck in favor of the fundamental attribution error. Gilbert argues that when we observe someone's behavior, we automatically characterize the person as having a disposition corresponding to the behavior observed. Someone doing something kind is instinctively thought of as kind; someone doing something cruel is reflexively thought of as cruel. The representativeness heuristic discussed in the previous chapter does this work for us. Only on reflection do we consider the context of the behavior, and it's often too little and too late: our assumption that the behavior is dispositional rather than situational has been made, and revising it is effortful and therefore typically insufficient. Indeed, sometimes an adjustment to consider the context is neglected altogether. In short, the situation is secondary and often slighted in the process as we attempt to establish a causal explanation.

Ample evidence supports Gilbert's contention that we rapidly and automatically characterize other people based on their behavior (Carlston & Skowronski,

1994; Moran, Jolly, & Mitchell, 2014; Moskowitz, 1994; Newman, 1993; Todorov & Uleman, 2003; Uleman, 1987; Winter & Uleman, 1984). Then, only later do we consciously ponder what we know about the prevailing situational constraints and adjust our initial dispositional inference if it seems warranted. This analysis suggests that when we are tired, unmotivated, or distracted, we should be more likely to commit the fundamental attribution error (or to make a larger error) because the adjustment process that considers the situational context is shortened or skipped.

In one study that supports this analysis, participants watched a videotape, without the sound, of a young woman engaged in a conversation with another person. The woman appeared anxious throughout: "She bit her nails, twirled her hair, tapped her fingers, and shifted in her chair from cheek to cheek" (Gilbert, 1989, p. 194). Gilbert told half the participants that the woman was responding to a number of anxiety-inducing questions (about her sexual fantasies or personal failings, for example). He told the other participants that she was responding to questions about innocuous topics (world travel or great books, for example). Gilbert predicted that all participants, regardless of what they were told about the content of the discussion, would immediately and automatically assume that she was an anxious person. Those told she was discussing anxiety-producing topics, however, would take that into account and adjust their initial characterization, concluding that maybe she was not such an anxious person after all. Those told she was discussing a series of bland topics would not make such an adjustment and would conclude that she was an anxious person.

So far, this is just a standard attribution experiment. But Gilbert added a twist. He gave another two groups of participants the same information he gave the first two, but he had these groups memorize a list of words while watching the videotape. Gilbert reasoned that this extra demand on their attention would make them less able to carry out the deliberative stage of the attribution process in which they would (ordinarily) adjust their initial characterization of the person to account for situational constraints. If so, then those who thought the woman was discussing anxiety-provoking topics should nevertheless rate her as being just as anxious as those who were told she was discussing innocuous topics. As **Figure 5.3** indicates, that's just what happened. When participants were busy memorizing a list of words, they didn't have the cognitive resources needed to adjust their initial impression, so they rated the woman as being just as anxious when they thought she was discussing anxiety-provoking topics as when discussing innocuous topics. This demonstration is important because many things in life may rob us of the cognitive resources needed to carry out the correction phase of attributional analysis in which we take into account situational constraints (Geeraert, Yzerbyt, Corneille, & Wigboldus, 2004).

CONSEQUENCES OF THE FUNDAMENTAL ATTRIBUTION ERROR Does it matter that we're susceptible to the fundamental attribution error? Indeed it does. We make the error many times a day, and the results can be unfortunate.

THE INFLUENCE OF PERCEPTUAL SALIENCE ON CAUSAL ATTRIBUTIONS
People who are more salient—bigger, more brightly lit, more distinctively dressed—are typically seen as more influential in outcomes.

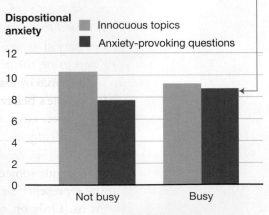

Observers who were kept busy by having to memorize a list of words did not correct their initial, automatic impression that the person was dispositionally anxious and did not take into account the nature of the material being discussed.

Dispositional anxiety

Innocuous topics
Anxiety-provoking questions

Not busy   Busy
Participants were . . .

FIGURE 5.3
ADJUSTING AUTOMATIC CHARACTERIZATIONS
Observers had to judge how generally anxious a person was who appeared anxious while discussing either innocuous or anxiety-provoking topics.
Source: Adapted from Gilbert, 1989.

Here's just one example: People, including employers and college admissions officers, often assume they can learn a lot about a person's traits and abilities from a 30-minute unstructured interview. But interviews reveal only the person's *apparent* traits and abilities in a *single situation*. In fact, the validity of the unstructured interview is close to nil: the correlation between judgments based on interviews and the subsequent judgments based on performance on the job or in school is only .10 (Hunter & Hunter, 1984).

A more accurate prediction of future performance would require information based on a wide array of situations: letters summarizing experience with the candidate in a range of situations, reports of previous job performance, high school GPA (which in turn is based on performance in everything from labs to homework to writing assignments and exams). Such information is far from infallible, but it often predicts future behavior with reasonable accuracy. Correlations between these types of "input" information and later outcomes are typically much higher than for interviews, on the order of .30–.50. Relying on one or two interviews is a setup for disappointment; employees are hired and students admitted who aren't as terrific as initially thought, and more deserving people are passed up.

If the fundamental attribution error is so pervasive and consequential, why are we so susceptible to it and so unaware of it? For one thing, we're not very good at assessing the validity of our own judgments. We can explain after the fact almost any failure of prediction, and we do it so effectively that we're prevented from seeing our errors. Suppose, for example, you were the interviewer who hired Jane, who didn't work out very well. "True, but she had some personal problems that came up shortly after she was hired." Or "Jane's boss was the real problem; it would be hard for anyone working for her to be successful." Choosing Jane automatically prevented you from finding out that other candidates for that job might have been more satisfactory.

A second reason for the pervasiveness of the fundamental attribution error is that we often see a given individual only in particular kinds of situations. You see Rachel only at parties, when she seems nice and fun to be around, but you don't know about the trials she inflicts on her roommates. You see Professor Jones only in his statistics classroom, where he seems stiff and boring and none too pleasant, but you don't see him being kind, funny, and helpful with his student advisees, let alone with his kids. Such errors sometimes cause no harm, but sometimes they do; and it's difficult to trace the error back to the fact that dispositional inferences were formed on the basis of limited or biased information.

THE FALLIBILITY OF INTERVIEWS
We tend to assume far more accuracy and utility for interviews than is really the case. The 30-minute interview—for college, medical school, executive positions, the Peace Corps, and so on—has almost no predictive validity.

The Actor-Observer Difference in Causal Attributions

It may have occurred to you that the degree to which you're oriented toward the person versus the situation depends on whether you're engaged in the action yourself or just observing someone else. In the role of "actor," you're usually more interested in determining what kind of situation you're dealing with than assessing what kind of person you are. In the role of "observer," in contrast, you're often primarily interested in determining what kind of person you're dealing with. By this logic, actors should be more likely than observers to make situational attributions for a particular behavior—to see their own behavior as caused by the situation, when observers of the very same behavior are more likely to focus on the actor's dispositions. Indeed, there's considerable evidence for just such a difference (Gioia & Sims, 1985; Jones & Nisbett, 1972; Pronin, Lin, & Ross, 2002; Saulnier & Perlman, 1981; Schoeneman & Rubanowitz, 1985; Watson, 1982; see Malle, 2006, for a dissenting voice).

In one of the most straightforward demonstrations of this **actor-observer difference** in attribution, participants had to explain why they chose the college major that they did or why their best friends chose the major that they did. When the investigators scored the participants' explanations, they found that participants more often referred to characteristics of the person when explaining someone else's choice than they did when explaining their own choice. They typically focused on the specifics of the major when explaining their own choice. You might attribute your own decision to major in psychology, for instance, to the facts that the material is fascinating, the textbooks beautifully written, and the professors dynamic and accessible. In contrast, you might attribute your friend's decision to major in psychology to "issues" he needs to work out (Nisbett, Caputo, Legant, & Maracek, 1973).

This phenomenon has significant implications for human conflict, both between individuals and between nations. Married couples, for example, often squabble over attributional differences. John may blame a late meeting or unusually heavy traffic to explain why an errand didn't get done, whereas his husband may be more inclined to argue that he's lazy, inattentive, or "just doesn't care." Similarly, at the national level, the United States is likely to explain the stationing of its troops in so many locations across the globe as a necessary defense against immediate and future threats. Other countries may be more inclined to see it as a manifestation of U.S. "imperialism."

Like the fundamental attribution error, the actor-observer difference has no single cause. Several factors give rise to it. First, assumptions about what needs explaining can vary for actors and observers. When asked, "Why did you choose the particular college that you did?" you (here the actor who chose a particular college) might reasonably interpret the question to mean "Considering you are who you are, why did you choose the particular college that you did?" The person (you) is taken as a given and therefore need not be included as part of the explanation. This is much like Willie Sutton's explanation of why he robbed banks: "Because that's where the money is." He takes it as given that he's a crook and thus interprets the question as one about why he robs *banks* rather than gas stations. Notice, in contrast, that when you're asked about someone else and are hence the observer ("Why did your roommate choose his particular college?"), the nature of the person can't be taken as a given, so it's reasonable to invoke the roommate's dispositions in offering an explanation (Kahneman & Miller, 1986; McGill, 1989).

Second, the perceptual salience of the actor and the surrounding situation is different for the actor and the observer (Storms, 1973). Because, as we noted earlier, people tend to make attributions to potential causes that stand out—are perceptually salient—it makes sense that actors tend to attribute their behavior to the situation, while observers tend to attribute that same behavior to the actor.

actor-observer difference A difference in attribution based on who is making the causal assessment: the actor (who is relatively inclined to make situational attributions) or the observer (who is relatively inclined to make dispositional attributions).

Third, actors and observers differ in the amount and kind of information they have about the actor and the actor's behavior (Andersen & Ross, 1984; Jones & Nisbett, 1972; Prentice, 1990; Pronin, Gilovich, & Ross, 2004). Actors know what intentions influenced them to behave in a certain way; observers can only guess at those intentions. Actors are also much more likely to know whether a particular action is typical of them or not. (In the attribution language used earlier, the actor is in a much better position to know if the behavior is *distinctive* and thus merits a situational rather than a dispositional attribution.)

← LOOKING BACK

Our attributions are subject to predictable errors and biases. We often exhibit a self-serving attributional bias, attributing success to the self and failure to the situation. We exhibit the fundamental attribution error when we attribute behavior to a person's dispositions rather than to the situation, even when there are powerful situational factors that we ought to consider. Actors are more likely than observers to attribute behavior to the situation, whereas observers are more likely than actors to attribute behavior to the actor's dispositions.

Culture and Causal Attribution

Much of what psychologists know about how people understand the behavior of others is undoubtedly universal. People everywhere are likely to engage in counterfactual thinking, imagining outcomes that might have occurred as an aid in understanding what did happen. People everywhere probably prefer to maintain the view that they live in a just world. All people undoubtedly perceive the causes of their own behavior somewhat differently than they perceive the causes of other people's behavior. But there are also some basic differences in how people from different cultures understand the causes of behavior. Some of these differences can be anticipated on the basis of what has been discussed already about cultural differences in perception and in characteristic social relations.

Cultural Differences in Attending to Context

Most of the world's people tend to pay more attention to social situations and the people who are involved in them than Westerners do. The kinds of social factors that are merely background for North Americans appear to be more salient to people from other cultures (Hedden et al., 2000; Ji, Schwarz, & Nisbett, 2000). Recall from Chapters 1 and 3 that Westerners generally define themselves in terms of their relationships with others less often than other people throughout the world do. Westerners think about themselves more in the context of personal goals, attributes, and preferences, whereas non-Westerners think about themselves more in terms of the social roles they occupy and their obligations to other people and institutions. Non-Westerners therefore have to pay more attention to others and to the details of the situations they find themselves in because effective action typically requires coordinating their actions with those of other people.

Asians and Westerners do indeed differ in how much attention they give to context, even when perceiving inanimate objects. Kitayama, Duffy, Kawamura, and Larsen (2002) demonstrated this difference in a study with Japanese and American participants (**Figure 5.4**). After examining a square with a line drawn at the bottom, the participants went to another part of the room and saw a square of a different size; they had to draw either a line of the same length as the original or a line having the same length *in relation to* the original square. The Americans were better at the absolute judgment, which required ignoring the context, whereas the Japanese were better at the relative judgment, which required paying attention to the context.

Hedden and his colleagues used functional magnetic resonance imaging (fMRI) to examine activation of the frontoparietal area of the brain, which is associated with difficult perceptual judgments (Hedden, Ketay, Aron, Markus, & Gabrieli, 2008). There was more activity in that region when participants had to do the task that did not come as naturally to them: for East Asians when they made judgments about absolute line length and thus had to *ignore* the context, and for Westerners when they made proportional judgments and thus had to *attend to* the context.

Causal Attribution for Independent and Interdependent Peoples

Given the pronounced difference between Asians' and Westerners' attention to context, it should come as no surprise to learn that Asians are more inclined than Westerners to attribute an actor's behavior to the situation rather than to the person's dispositions. For example, attributions for the outcomes of sports events are not the same in independent cultures as they are in interdependent cultures. Coaches and players on sports teams in the United States tend to see positive outcomes as the result of the abilities of individual players and the actions of coaches

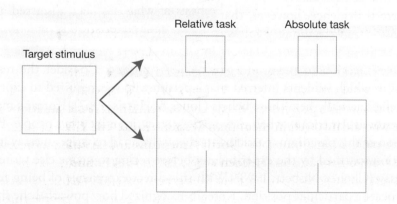

FIGURE 5.4
SENSITIVITY TO CONTEXT AND THE FRAMED LINE TASK
After seeing the target stimulus, participants were asked to draw a vertical line at the bottom of an empty square. In the relative task, the line must be drawn in the same *proportion* to the square as it was originally. In the absolute task, the new line must be exactly the same length as the original line. Japanese participants performed better at the relative task and Americans performed better at the absolute task.
Source: Adapted from Kitayama et al., 2002.

("We've got a very good keeper in Bo Oshoniyi, who was defensive MVP of the finals last year") (Lau & Russell, 1980). In contrast, the attributions of Hong Kong coaches and players are more likely to refer to the other team and the context ("I guess South China was a bit tired after having played in a quadrangular tournament") (Lee, Hallahan, & Herzog, 1996).

Culture and the Fundamental Attribution Error

Is it reasonable to assume that the fundamental attribution error occurs in all cultures? After all, nearly everyone wishes to live in a just world; other people and their dispositions are everywhere more salient than the situation and therefore capture attention more readily than the situation; and all people have the same basic cognitive machinery. The error does indeed seem widespread. For example, the finding that people assume that a speech or an essay by another person represents that person's own opinion on the topic, even when the position advocated in the speech or essay was assigned, has been demonstrated in many societies, including China (Krull et al., 1996), Korea (Choi & Nisbett, 1998), and Japan (Kitayama & Masuda, 1997).

There is evidence, however, that the fundamental attribution error is more widespread and pronounced for Westerners than for Easterners. Westerners pay little attention to situational factors in circumstances in which Asians pay considerable attention to them and grant their influence. Consider the results of studies in which students inferred that a person who was required to express certain beliefs actually held those beliefs (Jones & Harris, 1967). Koreans make the same error as Americans when they read essays written by other people. But in a variation of this paradigm, participants themselves had to write an essay favoring a position specified by the experimenter before seeing someone else write a similar essay (Choi & Nisbett, 1998). With this direct experience of being required to advocate a particular position, Koreans recognized how powerful the situation was and therefore made no assumption about the attitudes of a target individual they subsequently observed. American participants, in contrast, learned nothing from the experience of being pressured to write what they did. They were just as likely as control participants to assume that the coerced targets believed what they said.

Koreans are also more likely to appreciate the implications of consensus information. They recognize that if many people behave in a particular way in a given situation, then the situation is probably the main determinant of behavior (Cha & Nam, 1985). Americans' attributions tend to be less influenced by consensus information. Finally, there is evidence that Asians are less likely to make an initial dispositional inference in circumstances where such inferences are made by the great majority of Westerners. Na and Kitayama (2011) presented participants with information about a person that could be expected to lead them to make an inference about the person's personality. For example, the statement "She checked twice to see if the gas was on in the stove before she left" might lead a participant to infer that the person was *careful*. When participants were later shown a picture of the person along with the word *reckless*, the American participants exhibited a pattern of brain activity associated with surprise, but the Korean participants did not. Thus, Asians are not just more likely to notice situational cues that might correct a dispositional inference; they might also be less likely to make a dispositional inference in the first place.

There are also differences in attributional tendencies among American subcultures. Puerto Rican children use fewer traits when describing themselves than Anglo-American children (Hart, Lucca-Irizarry, & Damon, 1986), and they are less likely to use traits to describe other people's behavior (Newman, 1991). Zarate, Uleman, and Voils (2001) found that Mexican-Americans and Mexicans were also less likely than Anglo-Americans to make trait inferences.

Priming Culture

In today's world of highly mobile populations, many people have spent significant parts of their lives in both independent and interdependent societies. Their experiences provide psychologists with an opportunity to better understand cultural influences on attribution. For example, Hong Kong has been the location for several fruitful cultural studies because the British governed Hong Kong for 100 years. The culture there is substantially Westernized, and children learn English when they are quite young, sometimes at the same time that they learn Cantonese.

People in Hong Kong, it turns out, can be encouraged to think in either an interdependent way or an independent way by being presented with images that suggest one culture or the other. Hong, Chiu, and Kung (1997) showed some participants the U.S. Capitol building, a cowboy on horseback, and Mickey Mouse. They showed other participants a Chinese dragon, a temple, and men writing Chinese characters using a brush. They also showed a control group of participants neutral pictures of landscapes. The investigators then showed all participants animated cartoons of an individual fish swimming in front of a group of other fish, behind the group, joining the group, departing from the group, and so on. They had the participants explain why the individual fish was behaving in these various ways. Participants who previously saw the American pictures gave more reasons relating to motivations of the individual fish and fewer explanations relating to the other fish or to the context than participants who saw the Chinese pictures. Participants who saw the neutral pictures gave explanations that were in between those of the other two groups.

Other natural experiments are made possible by the fact that many people living in North America are of Asian descent and think of themselves as partly Asian and partly Western. In one study, researchers asked Asian-American participants to recall either an experience that made their identity as an American apparent to them or an experience that made their Asian identity salient (Peng & Knowles, 2003; see also Benet-Martinez, Leu, Lee, & Morris, 2002). They then showed the participants a group of highly abstract cartoon vignettes suggesting physical movement, such as an object falling to the bottom of a container of liquid, and had them rate how much they thought the object's movement was due to dispositional factors (shape, weight) versus contextual factors (gravity, friction). Participants who had their American identity primed rated causes internal to the objects as being more important, compared with participants who had their Asian identity primed.

It's also possible to prime religious concepts and affect the degree to which attributions are dispositional. Research shows that Protestants are more concerned than Catholics with the state of their souls, and they are more likely to make internal, dispositional attributions for behavior (Li et al., 2011). When Protestants are primed to think about the soul, this increases their internal attributions still further. The same manipulation has no effect on the attributions of Catholics (Li et al., 2011).

Social Class and Attribution

So far in this section, we've looked at how people from different countries and from diverse ethnic and religious backgrounds vary in their tendencies to attribute behavior to situational versus dispositional causes. Recent studies find that another form of culture—social class—influences attribution in important ways. **Social class** refers to the amount of wealth, education, and occupational prestige individuals and their families enjoy. Families with higher socioeconomic status enjoy greater wealth, education, and occupational prestige than those from less privileged backgrounds. And it turns out that within a particular culture or ethnicity, people from different levels on the socioeconomic ladder arrive at very different causal explanations for events.

Michael Kraus and his colleagues have found that lower-class or working-class individuals resemble individuals from interdependent cultures in their attributional tendencies (Kraus, Piff, & Keltner, 2009). The investigators had

social class The amount of wealth, education, and occupational prestige individuals and their families have.

participants make attributions for positive life events (getting into a desired graduate program) and negative life experiences (suffering a health problem). Lower- and working-class participants were more likely to invoke situational causes, whereas those higher up the socioeconomic ladder tended to invoke dispositional causes. When the investigators showed participants a person with a particular facial expression (smiling, sad, or angry) surrounded by people with the same or different expressions, those lower on the socioeconomic ladder were more likely to be swayed by the emotions of the faces in the surrounding context (also see Figure 3.3). The lower-class participants were less likely to rate a smiling target as happy when the other faces were frowning, for example. Investigators believe that these class differences are found because, similar to Asians, lower-class people live in a world where attention to other people is more essential for effective functioning than it is for higher-class people.

Why are some people richer than others? Class-related differences in attribution extend to how people from different class backgrounds explain why some people are rich and some are poor. Kraus and Keltner (2013) asked participants to offer explanations for why some people rise in society and others remain in the lower rungs of the class hierarchy. Wealthy participants were likely to endorse the belief that a person's standing in society is determined by genetic factors and a person's temperamental inclination to succeed or fail. Working class individuals are more likely to cite situational factors. Another study in this investigation found that upper-class individuals' tendency to attribute a person's lot in life to genetically based, biological factors led them to advocate for harsher punishments for students who have been found cheating and for citizens who have violated the law.

Dispositions: Fixed or Flexible?

Do Asians, Catholics, and people of lower social class think like "social psychologists," putting greater emphasis on situational determinants of behavior, whereas Westerners, Protestants, and people of higher social class think like "personality psychologists," putting more emphasis on dispositional determinants? Not quite. It may be more accurate to say that everyone is inclined to think in both of these ways. We know that Asians and Westerners both understand their fellow human beings in terms of the so-called Big Five personality dimensions of extraversion, neuroticism, agreeableness, conscientiousness, and openness to experience. These dimensions play almost as big a role in judging people's personalities, including their own personality, for Asians as they do for Westerners (Cheung et al., 2001; McCrae, Costa, & Yik, 1996; Piedmont & Chase, 1997; Yang & Bond, 1990).

Norenzayan, Choi, and Nisbett (1999), however, asked Korean and American college students a number of questions intended to tap their theories about the causes of behavior and found that although Koreans and Americans rated the importance of personality the same, the Koreans reported situations to be more important than did the Americans. The Norenzayan team also asked their participants several questions about their beliefs regarding how fixed or flexible personality is, including whether it is something about a person that can't be altered much or whether it can be changed. The Koreans considered personalities to be more changeable than the Americans did. The belief in the flexibility of personality is, of course, consistent with the view that behavior is substantially influenced by external factors.

The idea that personality is changeable is also consistent with the view—much more characteristic of interdependent people than independent people—that abilities can be changed by environmental factors and through sustained effort (Dweck, 1999; Dweck, Chiu, & Hong, 1995; Dweck, Hong, & Chiu, 1993). American students spend much less time studying than Asian students do (Stevenson & Stigler, 1992). The belief in the value of effort to overcome inadequacy is deeply rooted in the cultures of China, Korea, and Japan. Not surprisingly, Asian-Americans are more academically successful than European-Americans. Moreover, their occupational success far exceeds what would be expected on the basis of SAT/ACE scores.

← LOOKING BACK

People in interdependent cultures pay more attention to social context than Westerners do. Asians as well as Westerners are susceptible to the fundamental attribution error, but Westerners are more susceptible to it. For individuals reared in both interdependent and independent cultures, it is possible to prime the different ways of perceiving and attributing behavior. Social class also influences attributional tendencies: lower- and working-class people are more likely to attend to the surrounding circumstances, whereas middle- and upper-class people tend to make dispositional attributions. Protestants, whose concerns focus on the soul, are more likely to make dispositional attributions than Catholics.

Beyond the Internal/External Dimension

Everyday causal analysis often requires people to determine whether a given action is mainly due to something about the person involved or to the surrounding situational context. But this person/situation question is not the only one we ask, and it's not the whole story about everyday causal analysis. We often ask ourselves additional questions about someone's behavior to arrive at a more nuanced understanding of its meaning and to enable us to make more refined predictions about future behavior. In particular, we're often interested in understanding a person's intentions (Heider, 1958; Jones & Davis, 1965; Malle, 1999, 2004).

Think of it this way: people engage in causal analysis to make the world more predictable—to find the "glue" that holds all sorts of varying instances of behavior together. Sometimes that glue is a trait in the person—for example, her kindness explains her long hours at the soup kitchen, her unfailing politeness to everyone in the residence hall, and her willingness to share her notes with others in her class. At other times the glue is provided by knowing someone's intentions—for example, the long hours in the library, the ingratiating behavior toward the professor, and the theft of another student's notes all come together and make sense if we know that the individual has a particularly strong desire to get good grades (Malle, Moses, & Baldwin, 2001; Searle, 1983). One study found that across a wide range of circumstances, people explain intentional actions by referring to the actor's reasons (Malle, 2001). Reasons for action, of course, are many and varied, but the overwhelming majority of the reasons offered to

UNDERSTANDING OTHERS' INTENTIONS
We often try to understand other people's behavior by discerning their beliefs and desires. We might understand Texas Senator Ted Cruz's appearance at this rally, for example, by assuming that he wants to get elected, and he believes that winning over Jewish voters will help him do so.

explain behavior fall into two classes: desires and beliefs. Why did the senator endorse an amendment banning the burning of the American flag? Because she *wants* to be reelected, and she *believes* she needs to appease her constituents. Why does the neighbor put up with his wife's abusive insults? Because he doesn't *want* to be alone, and he *believes* no one else would be interested in him.

← LOOKING BACK

When we want to understand a person's intentions, the attributional question we are most inclined to ask concerns the *reason* for the person's behavior. Understanding a person's reasons for a particular action, in turn, often requires understanding the person's beliefs and desires.

Chapter Review

SUMMARY

From Acts to Dispositions: Inferring the Causes of Behavior

- People constantly search for the causes of events, and their attributions affect their behavior.
- People have different *explanatory styles*, which tend to be stable over time. A pessimistic style, attributing good outcomes to external, unstable, and local causes and bad outcomes to internal, stable, and global causes, is associated with poor health, poor performance, and depression.

The Processes of Causal Attribution

- The *covariation principle* is involved in making attributions. When a person engages in a given behavior across many situations and other people tend not to engage in that behavior, it's reasonable to attribute the behavior to the person. When the person engages in the behavior only in a particular situation and most others in the same situation also exhibit the behavior, it's reasonable to attribute the behavior to the situation.
- The ability to imagine what others would likely do in a given situation allows people to make use of the *discounting principle* and the *augmentation principle*. If situational constraints could plausibly have caused an observed behavior, people discount the role of the person's dispositions. If strong forces were present that would typically inhibit the behavior, but the behavior occurs anyway, they assume that the actor's dispositions were particularly powerful.
- *Counterfactual thoughts* can powerfully affect attribution. People often imagine what the outcome would have been like "if only" something had occurred differently. Joy or pain in response to an event is amplified when counterfactual thinking encourages the thought that things might have turned out differently.

Errors and Biases in Attribution

- People's attributions are not always rational. People sometimes attribute events to causes that flatter themselves beyond what the evidence calls for, thus exhibiting the *self-serving attributional bias*.
- The *fundamental attribution error* is the tendency to attribute behavior to real or imagined dispositions of the person and to neglect influential aspects of the situation confronting the person. Even when it ought to be obvious that the situation is a powerful influence on behavior, people often attribute behavior to presumed traits, abilities, and motivations.
- One cause of the fundamental attribution error is the *just world hypothesis*: thinking that people get what they deserve and that bad outcomes are brought about by bad or incompetent people.
- Another cause of the fundamental attribution error is the tendency for people and their behavior to be more salient than situations.
- A final cause of the fundamental attribution error is the tendency for attributions to be made in a two-step process. People typically characterize others immediately and automatically in terms consistent with their behavior, and only later, or perhaps not at all, do they adjust this initial characterization to account for the impact of prevailing situational forces.
- There are *actor-observer differences* in attributions. In general, actors tend to attribute their behavior much more to situations than observers do, partly because actors can usually see the situations they confront better than observers can.

Culture and Causal Attribution

- There are marked cultural differences in susceptibility to the fundamental attribution error. Interdependent people are less likely to make the error than independent people, in part because their tendency to pay attention to context encourages them to look to the situation confronting the actor.
- When bicultural people are primed to think about one culture or the other, they make causal attributions consistent with the culture that is primed.
- Lower-class individuals, like people from interdependent cultures, tend to make more situational attributions compared with middle-class and upper-class individuals.

Beyond the Internal/External Dimension

- Much of the time, people are concerned with more than just whether to attribute behavior to the situation versus the person. They're interested in discerning the intentions and reasons that underlie a person's behavior.

THINK ABOUT IT

1. Carla is the last person to be picked for dodgeball teams in her gym class. She thinks to herself, "Jeez, no one wants me for their team. I'm terrible at dodgeball. In fact, I'm terrible at all sports. No matter how much I work out or how hard I try, I'm never going to get any better." What are the three attribution dimensions that make up a person's explanatory style? Describe where Carla falls on these three dimensions. Overall, what is Carla's explanatory style? How do you know?

2. Can you think of a time when you committed the fundamental attribution error? What happened? Why do you think you made this mistake?

3. Curtis, a busy guy with good taste in music, has a friend who raves about a new band. Curtis wants to know whether it's worth his time to listen: Is the band actually awesome (an external attribution) or is his friend not all that discerning about music (an internal attribution)? Curtis recalls that his friend raves about the band every time he listens to them, although none of their other friends rave about the band, and his friend raves about every band. Describe the three components of the covariation principle, and explain how each one applies in this scenario. Based on this information, what should Curtis conclude? Is the band awesome or does his friend simply love all music?

4. Imagine you are single and decide to go to a speed-dating event, in which you will have a series of 5-minute dates with many people. You really care about getting to know what your dates are like. Given this situation, which types of behaviors would strongly signal the type of person your date is? What types of behaviors might you discount, that is, chalk up to the demands of the speed-dating situation? Apply the augmentation and discounting principles in your analysis.

5. Can you think of other aspects of our identity (besides culture, religion, or social class) that might influence the types of attributions we make? How so?

6. Mary, Travis, and Hussein stand to receive their awards at the National Spelling Bee. Mary, who won first place, receives her trophy with a smile on her face. The second-place winner, Travis, covers his face with his hands and sobs. Eventually, he politely receives his award despite the tears. When Hussein's name is called for the third-place prize, he grins and excitedly claims his award. Using what you learned in this chapter, explain Mary, Travis, and Hussein's (perhaps surprising) reactions to their respective prizes.

The **answer guidelines** for the think about it questions can be found at the back of the book . . . ☞

ONLINE STUDY MATERIALS

Want to earn a better grade on your test?

Go to **INQUIZITIVE** to learn and review this chapter's content, with personalized feedback along the way.

What explains the enduring popularity of risky sports like skateboarding in America?

How do we communicate romantic attraction?

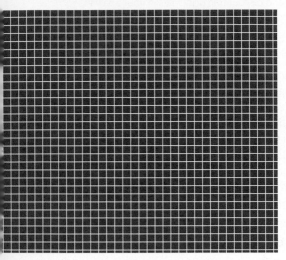

How might our emotions guide our perceptions of the world?

Emotion

AFTER THE SUCCESS OF his movie *Up*, Pixar director Pete Docter was searching for a subject for his next film. What captured his imagination was something very close to home: the emotions his own daughter was experiencing in her transition to adolescence. Adolescence is a notoriously emotional time when the joys and easy delights of childhood are replaced by the anxieties and pressures that come with the social and sexual dynamics of the adolescent years. His daughter's experiences gave Docter the idea of portraying his new subject—emotions themselves—as characters in a movie.

To better understand his new subject, Docter immersed himself in the science of emotion you are about to study. Intrigued by the dramatic possibilities of portraying how emotions work in the human mind, he asked such questions as: How many emotions are there? How do emotions shape how we perceive the world? Why do we feel sadness? The science of emotion became the bedrock of his new film, *Inside Out*.

Inside Out is about the emotional turmoil that an 11-year-old girl, Riley, experiences as she moves from Minnesota to San Francisco. It is a traumatic move, one that requires Riley to leave behind her best friend, idyllic moments of ice skating with her parents, and the passion of her childhood—her hockey team. Along with human characters you would typically find in a movie, *Inside Out*'s plot is also driven by the characters inside Riley's mind—her emotions. There are five, to be precise: anger, disgust, fear, joy, and sadness.

Inside Out dramatizes two central insights about emotion. The first is that emotions guide how we construe the social world—the "Inside" of *Inside Out*. The five emotions depicted in the film vie for control over a console in Riley's mind, and

PETE DOCTER
Academy award-winning Disney-Pixar director Pete Docter drew upon the science of emotion in making his hit movie *Inside Out*.

"We all know that emotions are useless and bad for our peace of mind and our blood pressure."
—B. F. SKINNER

emotion A brief, specific response, both psychological and physiological, that helps people meet goals, including social goals.

once in charge, if only for a second or two, they guide how Riley construes her present circumstances. For example, in one scene, when Riley's dad offers to walk with her to her first day of school, the voice of disgust rises to provide an evaluation of how mortifying it would be to be seen with her dad. These emotions also guide how Riley thinks about the past. In one of the more poignant scenes in the film, Riley's current sadness adds a blue tint to her joyous, yellow-hued memories of her childhood in Minnesota.

A careful viewing of *Inside Out* illustrates a second overarching idea about emotion: emotions guide our social behavior in immediate and powerful ways—the "Out" of *Inside Out*. Anger drives Riley's behavior when she competes fiercely on the ice rink or storms upstairs during a fight with her parents. Even sadness prompts thoughtful and wise action, guiding Riley to comfort her imaginary friend when he has lost the wagon they had played in during Riley's childhood. If you watch the film carefully, you will see how artfully Docter shows that fleeting emotional shifts in Riley's mind quickly lead to behaviors that fit the present context. Emotions give rise to action.

Inside Out's artistic portrayal of the central insights of the science of emotion counters traditional ideas of emotions as enemies of rationality and disruptive of cooperative social relations. Rather, emotions guide how we perceive and act on the world around us.

This chapter explores the science that so informed *Inside Out*. In doing so, we will seek answers to several enduring questions: In what ways are emotions universal, and in what ways do they vary across cultures? What roles do emotions play in social relationships? How do emotions influence reasoning? And finally, what is happiness? Before tackling these questions, we first attempt to define emotion—not a simple task. ■

Characterizing Emotion

Light is something everybody can see but is hard to define. The same is true of emotions. When you experience cold feet before giving a presentation in class, what is that experience of fear like? When you are awestruck by coastal redwoods over 350 feet tall, what makes up those feelings of the sublime? What happens when a stranger's kindness moves you to tears? What are emotions, and, critically, how do they differ from other kinds of feeling states, such as moods and more general feelings of, say, well-being or despair?

Emotions can be defined as brief, specific, subjective responses to challenges or opportunities that are important to our goals. Usually an emotion lasts only for seconds or minutes. Facial expressions of emotion typically last between 1 and 5 seconds (Ekman, 1992). Many physiological responses that accompany emotion—sweaty palms, tearing up, blushing, goosebumps—tend to last only dozens of seconds or minutes. In contrast, *moods*, such as feeling irritable or blue, can last for hours and even days. Emotional disorders, including depression and generalized anxiety, last for weeks, months, or years.

Emotions are also specific. They arise in response to specific people and events, most typically in our immediate social environment—the politician whose rhetoric infuriates you, the kind friend whose act of generosity fills you with gratitude, the ill relative whose demise saddens you. Philosophers call the focus of an emotional experience its "intentional object." When you're angry, you usually have a very clear sense of what you're angry about (say, the cutting remark of a rival). By contrast, other feeling states, such as moods and disorders, are more diffuse, and it isn't always clear what they're about.

Why do we have emotions? What functions might these brief, specific states serve? One answer is that they help us interpret our surrounding circumstances (Oatley, 2004). Any situation can be construed in multiple ways, thereby eliciting a variety of behaviors. When at a party, you might attend to a new acquaintance's awkward attempts to mix with your friends, the blowhard in the corner singing his own praises, or signs of conflict that might require your deft intervention. Emotions prioritize which events you attend to in the environment, influence how much weight you assign them, determine how to reason about them, and even affect whether you deem them right or wrong.

A second purpose emotions serve is to prompt us to act (Frijda, 1986). Without emotions, we would be lost in thought. When you see a friend suffering, it is feelings of sympathy that spur altruistic action (Eisenberg et al., 1989). Fear shifts the body's physiology—it raises blood pressure, for example—in ways that enable you to flee peril quickly and effectively (Levenson, Ekman, & Friesen, 1990). Even an emotion like anger, which might appear to produce maladaptive outbursts and temper tantrums, more typically produces specific actions that remedy injustice. For example, in studies of protestors who demonstrate against low wages, unemployment, discrimination, and police violence, it is the experience of anger that consistently predicts whether an individual will join a march or sign a petition (van Zomeren, Postmes, & Spears, 2008). Anger even appears to drive protests against injustice in nonhuman primates. In one study, two capuchin monkeys sat next to each other and traded tokens with an experimenter in exchange for food (Brosnan & de Waal, 2003). When both received cucumbers from the experimenter, they each performed the task calmly and

EMOTIONS AND ACTIONS
(A) This angry-looking monkey shows a classic threat display, signaling aggressive intentions. (B) This demonstrator shows a similar pattern of expressive behavior, signaling anger at the injustice she is protesting.

contentedly. However, when one received a more desirable grape, nearly half the monkeys who still received only the bland cucumbers refused to exchange tokens for food, and many threw their cucumbers in angry protest. In this way, emotions, even anger, motivate specific actions that advance our goals.

For over 2,000 years, philosophers and other observers of the human condition have been wary of emotions, seeing them as enemies of reason and the source of maladaptive social behavior (Oatley, 2004). But more recent scientific findings lead to a much different view. Brief, fleeting experiences of emotion enable us to respond effectively to the specific challenges and opportunities we face, especially those involving other people (van Kleef, de Dreu, & Manstead, 2010). Gratitude motivates us to reward others for their generosity. Guilt prompts us to make amends when we have harmed someone. Anger impels us to right social wrongs and restore justice. Of course, not every episode of emotion has positive results; outbursts of anger, for example, can end friendships, lead to incarceration, and even start wars. But in general, emotions motivate and guide appropriate goal-directed behavior that supports stronger and smoother social relationships.

← LOOKING BACK

Emotions are brief, specific, subjective experiences that help people meet their (often social) goals. Emotions guide our behavior and lead to action, enabling us to respond to the threats and opportunities we perceive in the environment.

Emotional Expression: Universal and Culturally Specific

An evolutionary approach entails a view of emotions as adaptive reactions to survival-related threats and opportunities (Ekman, 1992; Nesse, 1990; Tooby & Cosmides, 1992). Thus, we might expect emotions to be universal.

In contrast, a cultural approach assumes that emotions are strongly influenced by the values, roles, institutions, and socialization practices that vary across cultures (Mesquita, de Leersnyder, & Boiger, 2016; Oatley, 1993). As a result, people in different cultures might be expected to express their emotions in different ways.

Scientific studies of emotional expression provide support for both perspectives. The ways we express emotions are both universal and subject to cultural differences.

Darwin and Emotional Expression

The science of emotional expression begins with Charles Darwin's musings about where emotions come from. After his travels aboard the HMS *Beagle*, Darwin published *The Expression of Emotions in Man and Animals* in 1872, detailing his

"How much more grievous are the consequences of anger than the causes of it."
—MARCUS AURELIUS, *MEDITATIONS*

"Nothing's either good or bad but thinking makes it so."
—WILLIAM SHAKESPEARE, *HAMLET*

BOX 6.1

Not So Fast:
Critical Thinking about
The Validity of Narratives about the Causes of Emotions

Emotions often drive a search for understanding, explanation, and meaning. We feel ourselves falling in love and in our delirium seek an explanation for why. We feel anger at work and try to put together a story that accounts for our strong feelings. In therapy, which over 60 million Americans have tried, people often construct narratives that explain the deep causes of their current emotional struggles.

Soliciting narratives from people of their understanding of the causes of their emotions is a widely used method in the science of emotion. In these studies, participants are asked to think about a past emotional experience and explain why it happened. This research has helped emotion scientists to pinpoint specific construals that give rise to different, but closely related, emotions. For example, the experience of guilt centers around harm done to another person, whereas the experience of shame results from the sense that we have failed to live up to expectations about who we should be (Tangney, Miller, Flicker, & Barlow, 1996). People report that other people's unfair actions are a driving cause of anger, while it is situational causes that tend to be a driving cause of sadness (Smith & Ellsworth, 1985). But do the stories we tell about the causes of our emotions correspond to their actual causes?

To be sure, when you ask someone to give a causal account of an emotional experience, their narrative will get a lot right. When someone tells you why they felt awe when sitting on the rim of the Grand Canyon, their vivid description of the sights, smells, and sounds of the canyon likely correspond to the actual causes of the experience of awe. Nevertheless, there is good reason to suspect that people's verbal accounts will miss

NARRATIVES AND EMOTION UNDERSTANDING Research finds that people become attracted to other individuals in highly arousing situations, such as walking across this suspension bridge. Yet it is highly unlikely that they would explain such feelings of warmth in terms of being aroused on a harrowing suspension bridge.

important influences on their emotional experience (Parkinson & Manstead, 1992). For example, our narrative accounts of emotion rarely refer to certain contextual factors that are known to influence people's emotions, such as the time of day, the day of the week, the level of air pollution, the sight of nearby green spaces, the presence of people of high or low status, and regional levels of income inequality (for example, Moskowitz, 2010; Oishi, 2014; Rusting & Larsen, 1998; Sugiyama, Leslie, Giles-Corti, & Owen, 2008). You wouldn't tell a friend that you are angry because it's 11 a.m. on Tuesday or because the smog index is high; such explanations don't fit our cultural theories of emotion. Nor would you say that you fell in love with your boyfriend because he lived near you,

you often bumped into him in the hallway, and he enjoys high status among your peers (all documented causes of attraction, as you will learn in Chapter 10). Were you to explain your love for your boyfriend in this fashion, you'd not only offend him, you'd likely be seen by others as strange or cold. The more general lesson is that a variety of complex processes, many of them automatic, give rise to emotional experience. The verbal accounts we offer for why we feel the way we do articulate only some of those processes. Therefore, self-reports like those solicited in narrative recall studies cannot always be trusted. People are quite accurate when reporting *what* they are feeling; but their accounts of *why* they feel that way should be treated with some skepticism.

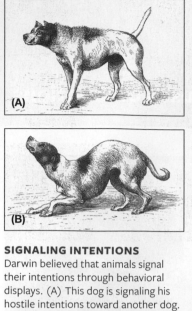

SIGNALING INTENTIONS
Darwin believed that animals signal their intentions through behavioral displays. (A) This dog is signaling his hostile intentions toward another dog. (B) This dog signals submission to another dog. Remind you of any other species? Our own, for instance?

CHARLES DARWIN
In addition to developing the theory of evolution, Darwin studied emotional expressions in humans and nonhuman species. He sought to document that human emotional expressions have parallels in other species and are universal to people of all cultures.

evolutionary perspective on emotional expression. In making his case, Darwin proposed what he called the "principle of serviceable associated habits," or the idea that the expressions of human emotion we observe today derive from actions that proved useful in our evolutionary past. For example, the observable signs of anger—the furrowed brow and display of teeth, the tightened posture and clenched fists, the fierce growl—are vestiges of threat displays and attack behavior observed in our mammalian relatives and once useful in adversarial encounters in our evolutionary past.

Darwin's detailed analysis generated three hypotheses about emotional expression that suggest universality. First, Darwin reasoned that because all humans have used the same 30–40 facial muscles to communicate similar emotions in our evolutionary past, people in all cultures should communicate and perceive emotion in a similar fashion. Second, Darwin reasoned that because humans share an evolutionary history with other mammals, most recently primates, our emotionally expressive behaviors should resemble those of other species. In support of this thesis, Darwin drew fascinating parallels between human emotion and the behaviors of animals in the London Zoo. Third, Darwin argued that blind individuals, lacking the rich visual input a culture provides about how to display emotion, will still show expressions similar to those of sighted people because the tendency to express emotions in specific ways has been encoded by evolutionary processes.

The Universality of Facial Expression

Interested in the universality of emotional expression, Darwin asked British missionaries living in other cultures whether they had observed expressions not seen in contemporary Victorian England. The missionaries could come up with no such expressions. That evidence is anecdotal, but some 100 years later, the question of universality was pursued more systematically by Paul Ekman and Wallace Friesen, as well as Carroll Izard (Ekman, Sorenson, & Friesen, 1969; Izard, 1971; Tomkins, 1962, 1963).

CROSS-CULTURAL RESEARCH ON EMOTIONAL EXPRESSION To test Darwin's universality hypothesis, Ekman and Friesen took more than 3,000 photographs of people, including a sample of actors, as they portrayed anger, disgust, fear, happiness, sadness, and surprise (Ekman et al., 1969). They then presented photos of these expressions to people in Japan, Brazil, Argentina, Chile, and the United States, who selected from six emotion terms the one that best matched the feeling the person appeared to be showing in each photo. Across these five cultures, accuracy rates were in the 70–90 percent range for the six emotions. If participants couldn't read the emotions with any accuracy and had been merely guessing, they would have succeeded only 16.7 percent of the time. These findings seemed to provide strong evidence that emotions are indeed universal.

Critics of Ekman and Friesen, however, were unconvinced, and they noted a fundamental flaw in this study: the participants had all been exposed to Western media and therefore might have learned how to identify the expressions through that exposure.

The investigators thus faced a stiff challenge: to find a culture that had little or no exposure to Westerners or to Western media. To accomplish this goal, Ekman traveled to Papua New Guinea to study the Fore (pronounced *FOR-ay*), an isolated hill tribe living in preindustrial, hunter-gatherer-like conditions. The Fore who participated in Ekman's study had seen no movies or magazines, didn't speak English or pidgin (a combination of English and a native language), had never lived in Western settlements, and had never worked for Westerners. After getting approval for his study from the local witch doctor, Ekman devised an emotion-appropriate story for each of the six emotions. For example, the sadness story was: "The person's child had died, and he felt sad." For adult participants, he presented photos of three different expressions, along with a story that matched one of the expressions, and asked them to match the story to the appropriate expression (Ekman & Friesen, 1971). Here chance guessing would have yielded an accuracy rate of 33 percent. Children in the study had to select from two photos to match an expression to a story (in this case, chance guessing would be 50 percent). The Fore adults achieved accuracy rates ranging from 68 to 92 percent in judging the six emotions; the children achieved accuracy rates ranging from 81 to 98 percent.

Ekman also videotaped the posed expressions of Fore participants as they imagined being the person in the six emotion-specific stories, then presented these clips to American college students, who selected from six emotion terms the one that best matched the Fore's pose (**Figure 6.1**). The students labeled the posed expressions of the Fore with above-chance accuracy for each emotion except fear. Over 90 subsequent studies have confirmed these results, finding that people from cultures that differ in religion, political structure, economic development, and independence versus interdependence nevertheless agree a great deal in how they label the photos depicting happiness, surprise, sadness, anger, disgust, and fear (Ekman, 1984, 1993; Elfenbein & Ambady, 2002, 2003; Izard, 1971, 1994).

EMOTIONAL EXPRESSION IN OTHER ANIMALS Darwin's second claim—that our emotional expressions resemble those of our mammalian relatives—has

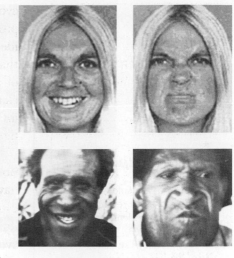

**FIGURE 6.1
RECOGNIZING FACIAL EXPRESSIONS OF EMOTION**
Groups of Americans and Fore tribe members in New Guinea both reliably judged the emotions expressed in these photos at higher rates of accuracy than expected by chance. This study demonstrated that facial expressions of emotion have been shaped by evolution and are universal.
Source: Adapted from Ekman, Sorenson, & Friesen, 1969.

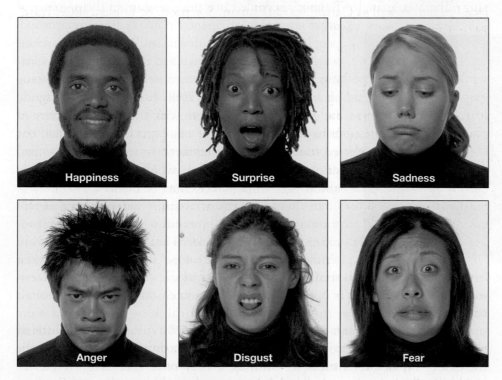

SIX UNIVERSAL FACIAL EXPRESSIONS OF EMOTION

ORIGINS OF OUR EMOTIONAL EXPRESSIONS
These chimpanzees demonstrate two facial expressions that resemble those of humans. (A) The silent bared-teeth display, like a smile. (B) The relaxed open-mouth display, like a laugh.

helped explain their origins in humans. For example, chimps show threat displays and emit whimpers that are remarkably similar to our own displays of anger and sadness. When interacting in a friendly fashion, nonhuman primates show the "silent bared-teeth display" that resembles our smile, and when playing and wrestling, they exhibit the "relaxed open-mouth display," the predecessor to the human laugh (Preuschoft, 1992). Similarly, many of the brief sounds humans use to communicate emotion—shrieks, laughs, cries, growls, and the "mmms" when eating delicious food—resemble the emotion-related calls of other primates (Cordaro, Keltner, Tshering, Wangchuk, & Flynn, 2016).

Understanding the parallels between human and nonhuman expression has also helped reveal why we express embarrassment as we do. Participants in these kinds of studies have been led to experience embarrassment in various ways. In one of the most mortifying, participants had to watch themselves on videotape sing "The Star-Spangled Banner" (recorded in a prior session) in the presence of other research participants. When feeling embarrassed, people shift their gaze down, smile in a self-conscious way, move their head down and to the side, thus exposing their neck, and often touch their face or shrug their shoulders (Harris, 2001; Keltner, 1995). Why do we express embarrassment with this specific pattern of behavior? Cross-species comparisons reveal that our expression of embarrassment resembles appeasement displays in other mammals, which short-circuit conflict and trigger affiliation (Keltner & Buswell, 1997).

SOCIAL BENEFITS OF EMBARRASSMENT
President Kennedy shows classic signs of embarrassment and remorse, including the head movements, downward gaze, and nervous face touching. Although conveying regret, this display causes others to trust the individual more.

In humans, embarrassment signals remorse for social transgressions, prompting forgiveness and reconciliation after the individual has violated a social norm (Miller & Leary, 1992). One study found that when strangers encounter someone who shows embarrassment or blushes visibly, as opposed to displaying no emotion or other emotions such as pride, they trust that stranger more and think he or she has a more upstanding character (van Dijk, de Jong, & Peters, 2009). Another study found that people will even give more lottery tickets to such an individual, thereby increasing his or her chances of winning a cash prize (Feinberg, Willer, & Keltner, 2012).

EMBARRASSMENT, APPEASEMENT, AND MAINTAINING SOCIAL BONDS
To maintain harmonious social relations, humans often exhibit behaviors that are reminiscent of appeasement displays in nonhuman species. (A) This woman shows the typical elements of an embarrassment display—downward gaze, head movements down and to the side, a compressed smile, and face touching—that trigger others to forgive. (B) The chimp on the right is the alpha male, who is deliberately ignoring a subordinate in the middle, who bows for him and pant-grunts loudly, which is the chimpanzee's expression of low status. Photograph by Frans de Waal.

Well-timed displays of embarrassment can serve people well. Early in his presidency, John F. Kennedy approved a disastrous attempt to overthrow Cuban dictator Fidel Castro. He immediately took public ownership of the failure and apologized for his poor leadership. President Kennedy's approval ratings, already high, spiked following his apology and his honest and open signs of embarrassment.

EMOTIONAL EXPRESSION AMONG THE BLIND Recent studies of pride and shame bring together Darwin's ideas about cross-species similarities, universality, and the expressions of emotion by those born without eyesight. Pride is the feeling associated with gaining status through socially valued actions. The emotion is reliably signaled with dominance-related behaviors seen in other mammals: expansive posture, chest expansion, head movements up and back, and upward arm thrusts (Tracy & Robins, 2004). And the emotion appears to be universal: When Jessica Tracy and Richard Robins traveled to Burkina Faso, in Africa, they found that a remote tribe there could readily identify displays of pride from photos (Tracy & Robins, 2007).

Studies of blind individuals have shown that their expressions of emotion are remarkably similar to those of sighted people. Tracy and Matsumoto (2008) analyzed the emotional expressions of sighted and blind Olympic athletes from 37 countries just after they had either won or lost a judo competition. Congenitally blind athletes, who made up part of the sample, had received no visual input from their culture about how to express emotion nonverbally. Sure enough, after victory, both sighted and blind athletes, including those blind from birth, expressed pride with smiles and by tilting their head back, expanding their chest, and raising their arms in the air. After losing, both groups of athletes lowered their head and slumped their shoulders in shame.

Cultural Specificity of Emotional Expression

Although there does appear to be a great deal of universality in how people express emotion across cultures, when anthropologists began writing about the emotional lives of people in different cultures, they noticed cultural variations in emotional expressions. In one well-known study, the Utku Inuit of Alaska (colloquially referred to as Eskimos) were never seen by visiting anthropologists to express anger (Briggs, 1960). Even when visiting Europeans stole their canoes or acted rudely, the Inuit showed no anger. How can we begin to understand such cultural variation in emotional reactions and emotional expression?

CULTURE AND FOCAL EMOTIONS Cultures seem to be defined by particular emotions. Tibet is a compassionate culture, Mexico a proud one, and Brazil an affectionate, flirtatious one. Batja Mesquita proposes that cultures vary in their **focal emotions**, those that are relatively common in the everyday lives of the members of a culture and are experienced and expressed with greater frequency and intensity (Mesquita et al., 2016). For example, anger appears to be a more focal emotion in cultures that value honor: sexual slurs and insults to the family are highly charged events that trigger more anger than in cultures that don't prioritize honor (Rodriguez Mosquera, Fischer, & Manstead, 2000, 2004).

Consider embarrassment and shame. These emotions convey modesty and an appreciation of others' opinions—core concerns in interdependent cultures. Indeed, recent studies have confirmed that shame and embarrassment are focal emotions in more interdependent cultures. In China, a highly interdependent culture, there are at least 113 words to describe shame and embarrassment, far exceeding the 25 or so synonyms in the English language (Li, Wang, & Fischer, 2004).

The degree to which an emotion is focal is also evident in expressive behavior. In the study of Olympic athletes we considered earlier, athletes from interdependent cultures, such as China and Japan, showed more intense shoulder shrugs of shame in response to losing than did athletes from independent cultures, such as the United States (Tracy & Matsumoto, 2008).

CULTURE AND IDEAL EMOTIONS Why do some emotions become focal in a particular culture? Jeanne Tsai and her colleagues have offered one answer in their *affect valuation theory* (Tsai, 2007; Tsai, Knutson, & Fung, 2006). They argue that emotions that promote important cultural ideals are valued and will tend to play a more prominent role in the social lives of individuals. For example, in the United States, excitement is greatly valued because it enables people to pursue a cultural ideal of independent action and self-expression. In contrast, many East Asian cultures attach greater value to feelings of calmness and contentedness because these emotions make it easier for individuals to fit into harmonious relationships (Kitayama, Karasawa, & Mesquita, 2004).

These cultural differences in which emotions are most valued translate into variations in emotional behavior. Americans, for example, are more likely than East Asians to participate in exciting but risky recreational practices (such as mountain biking); to advertise consumer products with broad smiles of excitement; to get addicted to excitement-enhancing drugs (cocaine); to express preferences for upbeat, exciting music rather than soothing, slower songs; and to read children's books that feature highly excited protagonists (Tsai, 2007). In responding to emotional stimuli, people from independent cultures are more likely to show intense smiles of excitement (Tsai & Levenson, 1997). Executives, university leaders, and politicians in the West tend to display bigger, more intense smiles in the photos they put out to the public than do those in East Asian cultures (Tsai et al., 2016).

These descriptions of cultural variations are averages, of course. You probably know (or may be) someone of East Asian ancestry who loves to bungee-jump or

focal emotion An emotion that is especially common within a particular culture.

BOX 6.2 ▶ **FOCUS ON** NEW SOCIAL MEDIA

Focal Emotions Expressed in Emoji

It is estimated that people send over 6 billion emoji each day in their online communications. Most people use some kind of emoji to communicate each day, whether they are texting, commenting on Facebook, or sharing photos on Instagram. Why do we send emoji? To be sarcastic? To be humorous? To express a thought or feeling we think we can't convey as well with words? Actually, according to recent studies, the answer is rather straightforward: we send emoji—the most popular being iconic representations of emotion, such as the heart or smiley face—to express how we feel about what is being communicated online (Lo, 2008). You might share a heart emoji to convey affection and gratitude for the support someone has shown online or a laughter emoji to convey your amusement at what someone has shared.

Recently, a team at Facebook led by illustrator Matt Jones and one of this textbook's authors, Dacher Keltner, helped design a set of science-based emoji that express human emotions that have been studied in the recent scientific literature. In this project, Jones produced emoji-like drawings based on Charles Darwin's descriptions of emotions as well as findings characterizing the facial and head movements that express emotions such as awe, love, and sympathy (Keltner, Tracy, Sauter, Cordaro, & McNeil, 2016). A design team at Facebook then produced animated emoji from these sketches called Finch emoji. **Table 6.1** shows three examples of Jones' drawings of an emotion and the corresponding animated Finch emoji.

Do people from different countries vary in terms of which emotions they share through Facebook with the Finch emoji? **Figure 6.2** shows two maps of emoji usage representing the sharing of the love and sympathy Finch emoji from over 120 million individuals across 122 nations during one month in 2012. Countries in more purple colors are those in which the emotion in question

TABLE 6.1		
Emotion	Matt Jones Drawing	Finch Emoji
Awe		
Love		
Sympathy		

was more likely to be shared than other emotions, meaning that that emotion might be thought of as a focal emotion in the culture. The citizens of countries depicted in pinker colors shared less of that emotion compared with other emotions.

Though the love emoji was the most commonly shared emoji overall, some countries' citizens shared it more than others. Stereotypes hold that certain Mediterranean cultures such as Italy are known for romance and that Brazil is a highly affectionate, passionate culture. Love might be thought of as a focal emotion in these countries. Figure 6.2A supports those claims.

Now take a look at Figure 6.2B, the sympathy map. One can't help but be struck by the contrast between the United States—known for its high proportion of people in prison and high rates of violent crime—where the sympathy emoji wasn't shared as much, and Canada—a stereotypically peaceful and considerate country—where the emoji was shared a lot.

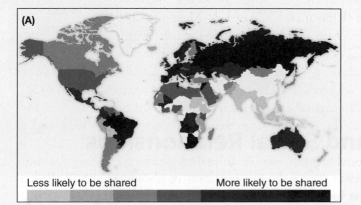

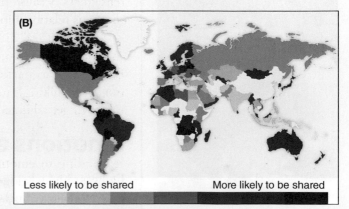

FIGURE 6.2 Love and Sympathy Maps (A) Love map. (B) Sympathy map.

CULTURE AND THE VALUING OF EMOTION
People in the United States have been found to engage in thrilling and dangerous recreational practices, such as skateboarding, because of the value they place upon feeling excited.

display rule A culturally specific rule that governs how, when, and to whom people express emotion.

NEUTRALIZING EXPRESSIONS
In accordance with the display rules of poker, this woman masks any feelings about her cards with a neutral poker face.

jump into the mosh pit at a rock show. And you probably also know someone of U.S. or European ancestry who'd rather read poetry or listen to Haydn or Schubert than ride a mountain bike or go cliff diving. But these notable average differences in emotional behavior, Tsai maintains, derive from the value placed on excitement in the West and contentment in the East. It's these differences in value that lead people from many parts of the world to be bemused by American excitability. Indians, for example, sometimes refer affectionately to Americans as "dogs"—because they're always saying "Wow, wow!"

CULTURE AND DISPLAY RULES Various cultures differ in their **display rules**—culturally specific rules that govern how, when, and to whom people express emotion (Ekman & Friesen, 1969). People can *de-intensify* their emotional expression—for example, suppress the urge to laugh at a friend fumbling a romantic quest. People can *intensify* their expression—smile widely upon taking the first bite of yet another culinary disaster concocted by a roommate, for instance. They can *mask* their negative emotions with a polite smile. And they can *neutralize* their expression with a poker face.

Here's one example of how culturally specific display rules shape emotional expression. In many Asian cultures, it's inappropriate to speak of personal enthusiasms; and in these cultures, people may also de-intensify their expressions of pleasure at personal success. Across dozens of cultures, people from interdependent cultures report being more likely to suppress positive emotional expression than people from independent cultures and to temper their experience of positive emotion with negative emotions (Matsumoto, Keltner, Shiota, O'Sullivan, & Frank, 2008; Mesquita & Leu, 2007; Schimmack, Oishi, & Diener, 2002).

← LOOKING BACK

Darwin inspired dozens of studies finding that human emotional expression is universal, is seen in other species, and is evident in those blind from birth. At the same time, cultures vary in the emotions that are focal, having richer vocabularies for those emotions and expressing them more in their nonverbal behavior. People of different cultures vary in the emotions they value. And cultures differ in how they regulate emotions with specific display rules, the rules governing how and when to express emotions.

Emotions and Social Relationships

Eadweard Muybridge was one of the most innovative photographers in the history of the art, known for his cold, analytical photos of Yosemite and human bodies in motion. To pay his bills, he ran a rare bookstore with his brother during the Gold Rush era in San Francisco. On one trip back East in search of rare books, the driver of Muybridge's stagecoach lost control and Muybridge was hurled out of the coach, smashing headfirst into a tree. After the accident, he seemed like a different man. Although his language and reasoning abilities remained intact, he became remote, aloof, and cold. He had trouble in his family life, at work, and in feeling like part of society.

What caused Muybridge's social difficulties? Social neuroscience provides one answer. We now know that Muybridge damaged his orbitofrontal cortex, a region of the frontal lobes right behind the eye sockets. People who damage this area lose the ability to rely on their emotions to act in ways that fit their current situation, and as a result, their relations with their spouses, children, friends, and work colleagues often go awry. The difficulties these patients endure tell us that our emotions act like a language that guides our social interactions; they are the "grammar" of social relationships (Eibl-Eibesfeldt, 1989; van Kleef, 2009). Our fleeting expressions of emotion are more than just momentary readouts of how we feel; they coordinate our interactions with others—whether playing on a team, reconciling with a friend, soothing a distressed child, or flirting (**Box 6.3**, see p. 186). Knowing how others feel provides critical information to guide our own socially savvy action. In fact, studies find that at every stage of life, people who are aware of their own feelings and those of other people fare better in their social relationships: they have more friends at age 5, get along better with romantic partners in their 30s, and do better at work in the middle of life (Brackett, Rivers, & Salovey, 2011; English, John, & Gross, 2013; Mayer, Barsade, & Roberts, 2008).

In this section, we follow the sad tale of Eadweard Muybridge to detail how emotions enable strong social relationships.

EMOTIONS IN PERSONAL RELATIONSHIPS
Emotions often determine the quality and stability of romantic relationships. If this couple can maintain the humor and mirth and other positive emotions throughout their relationship they will be less likely to separate.

Promoting Commitment

After his accident, Muybridge struggled with his commitment to the welfare of others. He felt distant from his wife, Flora. He never developed an attachment to his young son. Successful, long-term relationships require that we solve what economist Robert Frank refers to as the "commitment problem": our long-term relationships require that we sacrifice for others even when we are tempted to do otherwise (Frank, 1988). When we consider how common divorce is (see Chapter 10), it's clear that this is no simple task. Lacking the ability to feel the appropriate emotions, Muybridge felt little commitment to the people around him.

Emotions help solve the commitment problem in two ways. First, the expression of certain emotions signals our commitment to others' well-being. For example, a timely expression of sympathy indicates that we are concerned about the person's welfare and will make sacrifices on his or her behalf if need be. Second, emotions can motivate us to put aside our own self-interest and act in ways that prioritize the welfare of others. Feelings of guilt can be painful, but they often lead us to do things—apologize, make amends, sacrifice—that benefit others (Schaumberg & Flynn, 2012). Anger can be profoundly unpleasant, but it can motivate us to defend someone who has been wronged, even at great cost to ourselves (Fehr & Gächter, 2002).

It turns out that there's a chemical that fosters commitment in long-term relationships. Oxytocin is produced in the hypothalamus and released into the brain and bloodstream. In nonhuman species, oxytocin promotes commitment, or what is called pair bonding, the preference for one mate over desirable

BOX 6.3 ▶ FOCUS ON ROMANCE

Flirtation

Flirting is the pattern of behavior—both verbal and nonverbal, conscious and at times nonconscious—that communicates attraction to a potential romantic partner. Researchers David Givens (1983) and Timothy Perper (1985) spent hundreds of hours in singles bars, charting the flirtatious behaviors that predict romantic encounters. They found that in the initial attention-getting phase, men roll their shoulders and engage in exaggerated motions to show off their physical size, raising their arms to let others admire their well-developed pecs and washboard abs. Women smile coyly, preen, flip their hair, and walk with arched back and swaying hips. In the recognition phase, the potential romantic partners lock their gaze on each other, expressing interest by raised eyebrows, singsong voices, and laughter. In the touching phase, the potential romantic partners move close, and they create opportunities to touch with provocative brushes of the arm, pats on the shoulder, or not-so-accidental bumps against one another. Finally, in the keeping-time phase, the potential partners express

FLIRTING Can you tell from the woman's nonverbal language what she is trying to convey?

and assess each other's interest by lining up their actions. When they are mutually interested, their glances, gestures, and laughter mirror each other's, and their shoulders and faces align.

---

alternatives. When scientists give montane voles, who do not display pair bonding, an injection of oxytocin, they stay close to a sexual partner, even when desirable voles are placed nearby (Williams, Insel, Harbaugh, & Carter, 1994).

In experiments with humans, social psychologists have administered oxytocin via a nasal spray to some participants and a saline solution (the control) to others and compared the effects. When administered oxytocin, people are more generous and cooperative, they look more consistently at other people's faces, and they score higher on tests of empathy (Bartz, 2016). You might think that oxytocin could be a solution to today's political problems—just give political adversaries a whiff of oxytocin and their animosity might subside. Alas, it's not so simple. Carsten de Dreu and his colleagues have shown that oxytocin largely promotes commitment and generosity toward one's own group, but can actually enhance biases against outgroups (de Dreu et al., 2010). You may also be wondering whether oxytocin might help with commitment problems closer to home, namely in romantic relationships. Here the answer is more promising. One experiment found that couples solved their conflicts more constructively after having inhaled oxytocin (Ditzen et al., 2009).

THE EFFECT OF OXYTOCIN ON COMMITMENT
Research demonstrating that oxytocin promotes commitment and love might have had something to do with the development of the new perfume Pheromax, whose selling feature is the oxytocin it includes in its chemical makeup.

Coordinating Actions with Others

One of the first signs of Muybridge's social difficulties was his struggles at work. In his bookstore, he had trouble keeping promises, honoring contracts, and even engaging in polite exchanges with customers. Expressing emotions in timely ways and knowing the emotions of others is necessary for coordinating our collaborative actions with others. Before infants can tell their parents what they like and don't like, they rely on their smiles, coos, and laughs to express delight to their parents for things they have done that are pleasing. The same is true in our adult social lives: smiles, laughs, warm pats on the back, and interested vocalizations are ways we express our approval of what others are doing (van Kleef, 2009).

Consider the coordinating function of emotions by examining another modality of expression: touch. A deftly placed touch can encourage people or dissuade them from inappropriate behavior. A tactile expression of gratitude or love rewards others for actions we find desirable. In one study demonstrating this idea, a toucher and a touchee sat at a table with a black curtain between them, preventing all communication other than touch between the two (Hertenstein, Keltner, App, Bulleit, & Jaskolka, 2006). The toucher attempted to convey different emotions by making contact with the touchee for 1 second on the forearm, for example, smoothly stroking the arm to convey compassion or lightly clasping and shaking the arm a bit to convey gratitude. Upon being touched, the touchee selected which emotion had been communicated from a list of emotion terms. As you can see in **Figure 6.3**, participants could reliably communicate love, sympathy, and gratitude with brief tactile contact, all emotions that convey commitment and provide rewarding experiences to others.

Other research shows how the right kind of touch can prompt people to act collaboratively. For example, Michael Kraus and his colleagues coded all the touches—high fives, fist bumps, head slaps, and bear hugs—that basketball teammates in the NBA engaged in during one game at the beginning of the 2008 season (Kraus, Huang, & Keltner, 2010). Each player touched his teammates for only about an average of 2 seconds during the game. Still, teams who touched more early in the season played better later in the season, even when controlling for how well the team was playing in the game in which the touch was coded, how much money the players were making, and the preseason expectations for the team. Naturally, this study was not a pure experiment in the sense that players were randomly assigned to touch their teammates or not, and this weakens the inferences to be drawn from its results. But its results converge

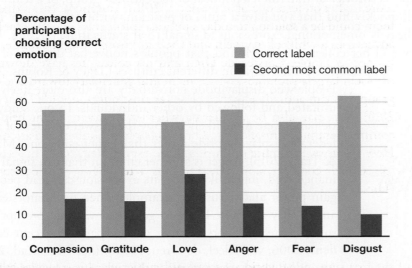

FIGURE 6.3
COMMUNICATING EMOTION THROUGH TOUCH
With a brief touch to the forearm, participants in this study could reliably communicate different emotions to a stranger.
Source: Adapted from Hertenstein et al., 2006.

TOUCH AND COOPERATION ON THE BASKETBALL COURT
Athletic teams in which teammates touch each other more play better. In 2000, the USA basketball team celebrated the Olympic gold medal with many kinds of touch.

with an intriguing study of touch promoting collaboration in the classroom. In the study, teachers were randomly assigned to touch some students in a friendly fashion and to not touch others (Guéguen, 2004). Students who were touched were much more likely to go to the chalkboard to solve a difficult problem the teacher had assigned.

Knowing Our Place in Groups

Like many people with damaged frontal lobes, Eadward Muybridge became an outcast, with little sense of connection to others. He cared little for social outings. He stopped dressing in accord with the fashion of his times. And, lacking the guidance of emotions, he had little sense of his place in society.

Certain emotions help us feel part of larger social collectives. The best example of this is the emotion of awe, the feeling of being in the presence of something vast that transcends our understanding of the world (Keltner & Haidt, 2003). We often feel awe in highly collective situations—at political rallies, sporting events, concerts, artistic events, and dance performances. Many stimuli that elicit awe—music, inspiring leaders, art, and religious rituals—are central to the core values and institutions of a culture (Van Cappellen & Rimé, 2014). And studies find that compared with experiences of other positive emotions, brief experiences of awe—for example, watching an awe-inspiring nature video or taking a stroll amid tall trees or standing near a replica of *T. rex*—increase people's sense of belonging with others. People feeling awe are more likely to define themselves in terms of collective traits ("I am an environmentalist") and report feeling embedded in stronger, more interconnected social networks (Bai et al., 2017; Shiota, Keltner, & Mossman, 2007).

Emotions not only help us identify with certain groups; they also enable us to find our place, or status, within social groups. Join just about any kind of group—a sorority or fraternity, a political or recreational group, or a team—and you'll quickly find that you have a rank, or position, within that group. People rely heavily on emotional expressions to signal their status in hierarchies. Jessica Tracy and her colleagues have found that people's nonverbal displays of pride signal that person's elevated status in different cultures (Tracy & Robins, 2007).

People who display pride nonverbally are also more likely to be imitated and followed by other individuals. In one study, participants were more likely to copy the answer on a test of a confederate displaying pride rather than other emotions (Martens & Tracy, 2013). Anger is another emotion that can signal dominance, and, much like pride, its expression can lead people to gain power and status. For example, when negotiators express anger, they are more likely to get their way and prompt more subordinate behaviors in their counterparts (Sinaceur & Tiedens, 2006; van Kleef, de Dreu, Pietroni, & Manstead, 2006). An old adage of trial lawyers is that when you have the law on your side, you should argue the law; when you have the facts on your side, you should argue the facts; and when you have neither on your side, you should pound the table!

"I brought out the meekness in others."

Emotions are the grammar of our social interactions. Emotions serve to communicate our commitment to others and build trust. Our emotional expressions, such as touch, serve as rewards in interactions and help coordinate behavior between people. Emotions help us know our place within groups.

Emotions and Understanding the Social World

Many of our most important decisions—what job to take, whom to marry, which neighborhood to live in—rely on gut feelings. Philosophers have long argued that this is not a good thing. Our emotions, according to this line of thought, are less sophisticated than our logic and higher reasoning and can lead to rash, misguided decisions (Oatley, 2004). The metaphors we use to describe our feelings betray this belief about emotion: we speak of emotions as forms of insanity ("I'm madly in love") and disease ("I'm sick with envy") rather than forms of clarity and health. Perhaps we are better off when reason is the master of our passions.

It certainly is true that emotions bias how we see the world. But psychologists have made the case that this is often, and even typically, a good thing. Emotions prioritize the information we should focus on and factor into our decisions and actions (Oatley & Johnson-Laird, 2011). Sometimes this leads to problematic biases; but often emotions guide perception, reasoning, and judgment in ways that enable quick and adaptive responses to challenges and opportunities in the environment (Lerner, Li, Valdesolo, & Kassam, 2015).

Emotions Influence Perception

After the death of a loved one, bereaved individuals often experience recurring and profound sadness. For many months, and very often longer, their perceptions are imbued with the qualities of sadness: a piece of music may trigger recollections of a first date; a room or object in the house will prompt memories of the past; a falling leaf may elicit thoughts about the shortness of life. The idea that emotions influence perception is found in color-based metaphors that portray emotions as lenses through which we perceive our circumstances—sadness is blue, anger makes us see red, happiness has us looking at the world through rose-colored glasses.

We perceive events, in other words, in ways that are consistent with the emotions we're currently feeling (Oatley & Johnson-Laird, 2011). To explore this idea empirically, researchers in one study had participants listen to uplifting music by Mozart or melancholy music by Mahler (Niedenthal & Setterlund, 1994). Feeling either happy or sad, participants then completed a lexical decision task, judging whether strings of letters were words or nonwords. When feeling happy, participants were quicker to identify happy words (such as *delight*) than sad words (*weep*) or positive words unrelated to happiness (*calm*). When

"Reason is and ought to be the slave of passion."
—DAVID HUME, SCOTTISH PHILOSOPHER

ANGER AND PERCEIVED THREAT
Police officers are known to experience high levels of stress, which interferes with sleep and can lead to irritability, frustration, and anger. There are some who believe that it is this anger that can lead police officers to misinterpret tense encounters with civilians, sometimes leading to tragic results.

"The only thing we have to fear is fear itself—nameless, unreasoning, unjustified terror which paralyzes needed efforts to convert retreat into advance."
—FRANKLIN DELANO ROOSEVELT

feeling sad, participants were quicker to identify the sad words than the happy words or the negative words unrelated to sadness (*injury*).

Emotions can also influence broader judgments, such as our sense that our circumstances are fair or safe or that they're unfair or dangerous. In one study conducted two months after the 9/11 terrorist attacks, participants were asked to write about how the attacks had made them either angry or frightened. Those primed to feel fear not only judged future terrorist attacks to be more likely than participants primed to feel anger, but also reported that they themselves were more likely to be victimized by different threats, such as dying in a flu epidemic (Lerner & Gonzalez, 2005; Lerner, Gonzalez, Small, & Fischhoff, 2003). Fear can lead us to exaggerate the sense of danger around us.

Studies of anger also highlight the problematic influence emotions can have on perception. When we experience frustration at school or at work and return to our friends and loved ones at the end of the day, we may be quicker to perceive potential affront and hostile intent in others' actions. In one study that brings this notion to life, participants first wrote about a memory that made them feel either angry, disgusted, or sad (Baumann & DeSteno, 2010). Then they briefly viewed a photograph of a man who was holding either a gun or a neutral object. Anger, but not disgust or sadness, made participants more likely to identify the neutral object as a gun, but not misidentify the gun as a neutral object. Anger primes us to perceive threat and aggression.

Emotions Influence Reasoning

People tend to assume that positive emotions prompt simplistic or lazy thinking. Think of any highly creative person—such as Vincent van Gogh, Virginia Woolf, Toni Morrison, or Charles Darwin—and you're likely to imagine that their creative acts were produced during moments of struggle, tension, somberness, and even despair.

Alice Isen (1987, 1993) argued that this view of creativity is wrong and that happiness, or being in a good mood more generally, prompts people to reason in ways that are flexible and creative. In her studies, Isen induced positive emotion in her participants with trivial events. She gave them little bags of candy or made sure that they would find a dime she had placed in their path. These subtle ways of making participants feel good produced striking changes in their reasoning. When given one word (such as *carpet*) and asked to generate a related word, people feeling positive emotions came up with more novel associations (*fresh* or *texture*) than people in a neutral state, who tended to produce more common responses (such as *rug*). Participants in a good mood categorized objects in more inclusive ways, rating fringe members of categories (like *cane* or *purse* as an example of clothing) as better members of that category than people in a neutral state, whose categories tended to be more narrowly defined. These effects of positive emotion have important social consequences: negotiators in a positive mood are more likely to reach an optimal agreement that incorporates the interests of both sides, because positive moods allow opponents to think flexibly about the positions and interests of the other side (Carnevale & Isen, 1986).

Building on these findings, Barbara Fredrickson has advanced her **broaden-and-build hypothesis**. Here the central idea is that whereas negative emotions narrow our attention on the details of what we are perceiving, positive emotions broaden our patterns of thinking in ways that help us expand our understanding of the world and build our social relationships (Fredrickson, 1998, 2001). In research inspired by this hypothesis, participants led to feel positive emotions (for example, by watching amusing films) thought of a wider range of ways to respond to different situations than participants feeling negative emotions or a neutral state. When asked to pick one of two figures in the bottom row of **Figure 6.4** to match the target stimulus in the top row, participants feeling positive emotion chose the less obvious choice—the one that is similar in its global arrangement (the three triangles) rather than the one that is similar in specific details (the four squares). These broadening patterns of thought extend to ways of thinking about others that build stronger ties. For example, people feeling positive emotion rate themselves as more similar to outgroup members, and they see themselves as sharing deeper similarities with their romantic partners (Fredrickson, 2001; Waugh & Fredrickson, 2006).

Emotions Influence Moral Judgment

Near the end of a legal trial, judges in the United States often caution jurors to put aside their emotions when deciding on the guilt or innocence of the defendant, sentence length, and punitive damages. In light of what we have learned thus far, this recommendation would seem to be at best unrealistic: emotions have powerful, automatic influences on perception and reasoning, influences that can't simply be set aside. This recommendation also ignores the essential role that emotions play in our moral judgments (Haidt, 2001). To begin to appreciate this role, read the following scenario, and decide whether you think the actions of the protagonists are right or wrong:

> Mark and Julie are brother and sister. They are traveling together in France on a summer vacation from college. One night they're staying alone in a cabin near the beach. They decide it would be interesting and fun if they tried making love. At the very least it would be a new experience for each of them. Julie was already taking birth control pills, but Mark uses a condom, too, just to be safe. They both enjoy making love, but they decide not to do it again. They keep that night as a special secret, which makes them feel even closer to each other.

When asked whether such actions are wrong, nearly all college students immediately say yes, typically with pronounced disgust (Haidt, 2001). They're in good company. All cultures around the world view incest as immoral (Brown, 1991). When pressed to explain why Julie and Mark's encounter is wrong, people may reason that it is dangerous to inbreed, only to remember that Julie and Mark are using contraception. They may contend that each would be hurt emotionally, but recall that it was clearly specified that Julie and Mark weren't harmed in any way by the event. Eventually, when all possible reasons have been refuted, people typically say, "I can't explain why, I just know this is wrong." Jonathan Haidt

broaden-and-build hypothesis The idea that positive emotions broaden thoughts and actions, helping people build social resources.

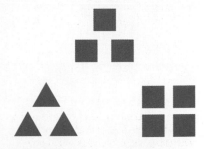

FIGURE 6.4
GLOBAL AND LOCAL DECISION TASK
Participants feeling positive emotion tend to choose the three-triangle figure rather than the four-square figure as most resembling the three-square figure.

labels this kind of firm insistence upon a moral conviction in the absence of reason "moral dumbfounding."

The way people respond to this scenario illustrates the central thesis of Haidt's **social intuitionist model of moral judgment**. The central idea is that our moral judgments are the product of fast, emotional intuitions, like the gut feeling that incest is wrong, which then influence how we reason about the issue in question (Haidt, 2001). We feel our way to our moral judgments, in other words; we don't reason our way there. Reason often *follows* our immediate gut feeling, serving merely to justify the moral conviction we arrived at intuitively or emotionally.

Neuroscientist and philosopher Joshua Greene and his colleagues have provided an illustrative demonstration of Haidt's social intuitionist model of moral judgment (Greene, 2013; Greene, Sommerville, Nystrom, Darley, & Cohen, 2001). They presented participants with morally compelling scenarios and asked for quick decisions about what to do while their brains were scanned using fMRI. Some of the moral dilemmas were likely to engage mainly impersonal, rational calculation. An example is the well-known "trolley dilemma," in which the participant imagines a runaway trolley headed for five people who will be killed if it proceeds on its present course. The only way to save them is to hit a switch that will turn the trolley onto another set of tracks, where, unfortunately, one person is located and will die as result of the switch. The participant is asked whether it is appropriate to hit the switch and save the five lives at the cost of the one. Most participants answer yes with only a little hesitation.

Other scenarios were more emotionally evocative. For example, in the "footbridge dilemma," five people's lives are again threatened by a trolley, but in this case the participant is asked to imagine standing next to a very heavy stranger on a footbridge over the trolley tracks. The participant is told that pushing the stranger off the bridge and onto the tracks would kill the stranger, but his dead body would cause the train to veer off its course and thus save the lives of the five. (The stranger's own weight, it is explained, is insufficient to send the trolley off the track.) You probably noticed that, at the core, the two options in the trolley and footbridge dilemmas are the same—one death or five? But in the footbridge dilemma, the action is highly emotional: participants must imagine using their own hands to push the stranger to his death. In keeping with Haidt's social intuitionist model, the personal moral dilemmas like the "footbridge dilemma" activated regions of the brain that are involved in emotional processing, whereas nonmoral dilemmas and impersonal moral dilemmas like the "trolley dilemma" activated brain regions associated with working memory and deliberative reasoning.

What, then, are our emotion-based moral intuitions? To account for many of them, Haidt has proposed his **moral foundations theory**, a theory that draws upon analyses of different cultural practices as well as evolutionary arguments about the "moral" responses observed in primates. Haidt and colleagues have built from those ideas to make the case that much of our moral psychology rests on five "foundations" (or domains) that are supported by different emotional reactions (Graham et al., 2013; Haidt, 2012; Haidt & Joseph, 2004). The *Care/harm* foundation centers on concern for the suffering of others, especially vulnerable individuals. The moral intuitions underlying people's concerns with care and harm are triggered by signs of vulnerability and pain, and they elicit prosocial emotions like sympathy that orient us to enhancing the welfare of others, often at personal cost. The foundation of *fairness/cheating* focuses on concerns that others act in a just fashion and is triggered by unfair acts—scamming, deceiving, failing to reciprocate a generous act, or taking more than what one deserves. Anger is the quintessential emotion associated with violations of fairness: it fuels our passion for justice. *Loyalty/betrayal* pertains to the commitments we make to groups. It's the foundation for strong, cohesive social collectives, and it evokes emotions like group pride (loyalty) or rage (betrayal). *Authority/subversion* is about finding one's place in social hierarchies. Our intuitions about authority and respect are grounded, as we have seen, in the experience of emotions like embarrassment, shame, fear, pride, and awe. Finally, *purity/degradation* centers on avoiding dangerous diseases and contaminants and, more metaphorically, socially impure ideas or actions. Disgust is the emotion at the core of such intuitions.

When we encounter people who violate the rules specified by any of these moral foundations, specific emotions arise that guide our initial judgments of right and wrong (Greene & Haidt, 2002; Haidt, 2003; Horberg, Oveis, & Keltner, 2011). After the initial gut feeling is under way, people rely on more deliberative processes—assessments of costs and benefits, causal attributions, considerations of prevailing social norms—to arrive at a final moral judgment of right or wrong. We've already seen how this theory accounts for judgments related to harm. But consider another moral foundation, the concern for purity. Disgust is the emotion that arises in response to threats to purity, as we saw earlier with people's reaction to incest. Studies have shown that feelings of disgust intensify judgments that "impure" acts are morally wrong. For example, people who feel high levels of disgust about a behavior—such as smoking or eating meat—more strongly condemn the act as immoral (Rozin & Singh, 1999). Even when the original cause of the emotion has nothing to do with the action being judged, disgust still leads to more extreme moral condemnation of impure acts. For example, after being induced to feel disgust through viewing repulsive images in film or smelling noxious scents, participants will condemn with greater severity someone who's left sweat on an exercise machine (Horberg, Oveis, Keltner, & Cohen, 2009) or individuals from groups that might be construed as "impure"—namely, gay men (Dasgupta, DeSteno, Williams, & Hunsinger, 2009; Inbar, Pizarro, & Bloom, 2012).

Haidt maintains that moral foundations theory can help us understand the so-called "culture wars" between political liberals and conservatives over issues like abortion, gun rights, same-sex marriage, and climate change. Surveys of tens of thousands of participants reveal that liberals and conservatives look at the world through different moral lenses. If you study **Figure 6.5** (see p. 194), you'll see that liberals attach a bit more importance to harm and fairness than conservatives do, whereas conservatives attach greater importance to authority, loyalty, and purity than liberals do. It may surprise you (especially if you're liberal) that conservative morality is broader, involving concerns about harm and fairness (though less than liberals in these categories) as well as about authority, loyalty, and purity.

These differences help explain why liberals and conservatives diverge on important issues of our day. Consider the debate over climate change. Liberals are more likely than conservatives to believe that by burning fossil fuels, humans have caused an increase in the Earth's temperature, which in turn is causing the loss of species, more extreme weather, rising sea levels, and economic and political instability. How might moral foundations theory account for the difference in liberals' and conservatives' concern about climate change? Matthew Feinberg and Robb Willer note that climate change is most often framed in public discourse, including public service announcements and newspaper editorials, as

MORAL FOUNDATIONS AND THE CULTURE WARS
Part of the acrimony associated with the "culture wars" in the United States, depicted here in the clash between anti-Trump protesters and Trump supporters on the Berkeley campus of the University of California, derives from the fact that liberals and conservatives differ in the weight they place on the moral foundations of authority, in-group loyalty, and purity.

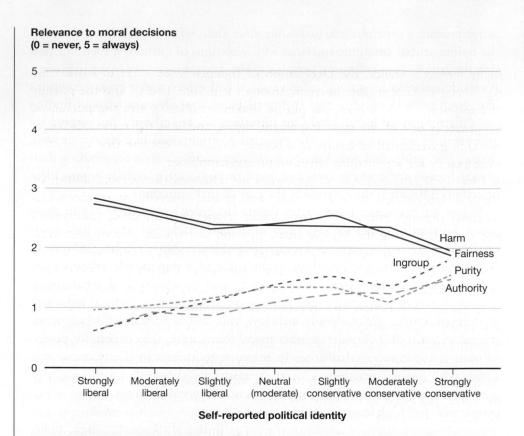

Relevance to moral decisions
(0 = never, 5 = always)

Harm
Fairness
Ingroup
Purity
Authority

Strongly liberal — Moderately liberal — Slightly liberal — Neutral (moderate) — Slightly conservative — Moderately conservative — Strongly conservative

Self-reported political identity

FIGURE 6.5
MORAL FOUNDATIONS THEORY
Liberals and conservatives endorse different moral foundations.
Source: Adapted from Graham, Haidt, & Nosek, 2009, Fig. 1.

being about harm (to vanishing species) and care (of natural lands and oceans), a framing that is likely to be more compelling to liberals (Feinberg & Willer, 2013). When conservatives are given arguments for pro-environment policy changes that are not framed in terms of harm and care but rather couched in the language of purity (and are accompanied by purity-violating images of toxic clouds, dirty drinking water, and forests covered in garbage), they express pro-environment attitudes comparable to those expressed by liberals.

Interestingly, there's an asymmetry between liberals and conservatives in their understanding of the importance that the other group attaches to the different moral foundations (Haidt, 2012). Conservatives tend to be aware that liberals value fairness and avoidance of harm more than they themselves do and that liberals value the other moral foundations less. But liberals generally fail to realize that conservative views are often the result of their emphasis on the values of authority, loyalty, and purity.

← LOOKING BACK

Emotions prioritize certain interpretations of the environment over others and shape how we think in profound ways. Emotions influence how we perceive the world, guiding what we focus on and how we categorize the stimuli we encounter. When fearful, for example, we exaggerate the perils, risks, and uncertainties around us. Emotions also shape how we reason. Positive emotions broaden and build thought patterns, producing more creative thinking. Emotions are also powerful intuitions that feed into our moral judgments, shaping our views about punishment and wrongdoing and what we deem right and wrong.

Happiness

In its second sentence, the Declaration of Independence refers to inalienable rights that all citizens should enjoy, among them "life, liberty, and the pursuit of happiness." This well-known phrase makes a radical point: the pursuit of happiness is one of the most important rights, and it is the responsibility of the U.S. government to ensure that people are free to exercise that right. But what exactly are we pursuing when we pursue happiness?

Over time, the meaning of happiness has changed (McMahon, 2006). In classical Greek times, about 2,500 years ago, people believed that happiness was achieved through ethical behavior—being temperate, fair, kind, courageous, and dutiful. During the Middle Ages, a period of frequent plagues and wars, people thought that happiness was found in the afterlife, in communion with God when the soul was liberated from the turmoil of Earthly life. Philosophers of the eighteenth-century Enlightenment encouraged people to seek happiness in hedonistic experiences and in actions that advanced the well-being of many (the idea of the greater good). As psychologists have turned their attention to the scientific study of happiness, they, too, have uncovered variations in its meaning. For Americans, personal achievement is a main pathway to happiness; for East Asians, harmonious interactions and the fulfillment of duties are regarded as the surest pathways to the good life (Kitayama, Karasawa, & Mesquita, 2004; Yuchida & Kitayama, 2009).

Psychologists believe that happiness has two distinct, measurable components (Diener, 2000). The first is life satisfaction, or how well you think your life is going in general. Life satisfaction is based on summary evaluations of your life. The second is emotional well-being, which refers to the balance of positive and negative emotions at any moment in time over a given length of time. Emotional well-being is based purely on the quality of your moment-to-moment feelings. A recent review of hundreds of studies reveals that this mixture of life satisfaction and emotional well-being—happiness—matters a great deal in many areas of life (Lyubomirsky, King, & Diener, 2005). For example, being happy is associated with being creative and productive at work. It is also connected to better health, as evidenced by less physical pain, better sleep, and stronger cardiovascular and immune systems. Happiness may even increase life expectancy. One study found that nuns who at age 20 reported greater happiness in the personal narratives they wrote as they entered the convent were more likely to live into their 80s and 90s than nuns who reported being less happy in young adulthood (Danner, Snowdon, & Friesen, 2001).

In light of these considerations, let's address two time-honored questions: Do we know what makes us happy? How should we pursue happiness?

Knowing What Makes Us Happy

Can we reliably predict what will make us happy? One would hope so, because such predictions matter. We burn the midnight oil at work because we assume that professional success will bring sustained joy and satisfaction. We choose a career, vacation, or romantic partner because we believe the one we chose will bring more happiness than those we rejected. And we're often right. We know we're more likely to be happier if we have a partner who's kind rather than cruel, if we add salted caramel sauce to our ice cream rather than pickled artichoke hearts,

HAPPINESS AT WORK
Studies show that having healthy social relationships and meaningful work are two of the most important determinants of happiness. Having them both—as do these individuals, who appear to be enjoying one another and their work—can be especially conducive to happiness.

and if we vacation in awe-inspiring Yosemite rather than war-torn Yemen. But these accurate assessments aside, there is a growing body of empirical research that indicates that we're not always so good at predicting what will make us happy.

In research on what they call **affective forecasting**, Daniel Gilbert and Timothy Wilson have documented a variety of biases that undermine our attempts to predict what will make us happy (Gilbert, Brown, Pinel, & Wilson, 2000). One study examined the expected impact of breaking up with a romantic partner and compared it with its actual impact (Gilbert, Pinel, Wilson, Blumberg, & Wheatley, 1998). Students who had not experienced a romantic breakup, called "luckies," reported on their own overall happiness and then predicted how unhappy they would be two months after a breakup. The researchers compared this estimate with the happiness of people who had recently broken up, labeled "leftovers." As **Figure 6.6** shows, leftovers were almost as happy as luckies, but luckies predicted they would be much *less* happy two months after a breakup (labeled "predicted leftovers" in Figure 6.6) than actual leftovers actually were. Although some breakups are indeed devastating, and divorce has many costs, people tend to overestimate how much a romantic breakup would diminish their life satisfaction down the line.

A variety of biases interfere with people's attempts to predict their future happiness. One is **immune neglect** (Gilbert et al., 1998). We are often remarkably resilient in responding to painful setbacks, largely because of what Gilbert and Wilson call the "psychological immune system," which enables us to get beyond stressful experiences and trauma. Just as our biological immune system protects us from toxins and disease, our psychological immune system protects us from psychological distress. We have a great capacity to find the silver lining, the humor, the potential for insight and growth in the face of painful setbacks and traumatic experiences; and these "immune-related" processes allow us to return to satisfying lives in the face of negative experiences. However, when estimating the effects of traumatic events like breakups or failures at work, we fail to consider these processes, how effectively they will take hold, or how quickly they

affective forecasting Predicting future emotions, such as whether an event will result in happiness or anger or sadness, and for how long.

immune neglect The tendency for people to underestimate their capacity to be resilient in responding to difficult life events, which leads them to overestimate the extent to which life's problems will reduce their personal well-being.

"Nothing in life is as important as you think it is at the moment you are thinking of it."
—PSYCHOLOGIST AND NOBEL LAUREATE DANIEL KAHNEMAN

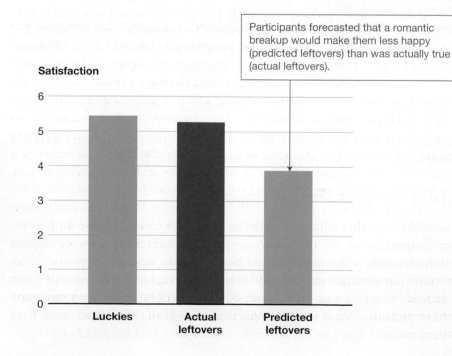

Participants forecasted that a romantic breakup would make them less happy (predicted leftovers) than was actually true (actual leftovers).

FIGURE 6.6
DO WE KNOW WHAT MAKES US HAPPY?
This study demonstrated the accuracy of participants in their judgments of how happy they would be following a romantic breakup. The results were consistent with their claims about biased affective forecasting.
Source: Adapted from Gilbert et al., 1998.

will exert their effects. As a consequence, we inaccurately predict our future happiness.

Another reason people sometimes have difficulty predicting what will make them happy is due to a bias known as **focalism**: we focus too much on the most immediate and most central (or "focal") elements of significant events, such as our initial despair upon learning a romantic partner is leaving us, and we fail to consider how other aspects of our lives will influence how happy we are (Wilson, Wheatley, Meyers, Gilbert, & Axson, 2000). We tend to assume that once a particular event happens—for example, acing the GREs or landing a dream job—we will be truly and enduringly happy. What we forget to consider is that after those exam scores arrive or after we have the career we've always wanted, many other events—such as health problems, conflicts with our spouse, or difficulties with our children—will also influence our happiness. Consider this telling example: When people from the Midwest were asked whether they'd be happier if they lived in sunny California, the average response was a big yes. But when survey researchers ask residents of California and the Midwest how happy they are, there's no noticeable difference (Schkade & Kahneman, 1998). We think we'd be happier in California because we focus on the weather and the beaches, but most Californians spend little time at the beach, and it's hard to focus on the weather when your boss is making demands on you, your child is acting up in school, or a loved one had a worrisome X-ray result.

Much as our predictions about what will make us happy in the future are sometimes biased, so, too, are our recollections of past pleasures. To explore this possibility, Barbara Fredrickson and Daniel Kahneman (1993) had participants watch a series of pleasurable film clips, such as a comedy routine or a puppy playing with a flower. While doing so, the participants rated the intensity of their second-by-second experience of pleasure by moving a dial back and forth. Then, after the film clips ended, they provided an overall assessment of how pleasurable it was to watch the clips. The researchers correlated these general, retrospective assessments with the specific, moment-to-moment ratings to find out how immediate experiences of pleasure relate to people's subsequent recollections of how much enjoyment they had.

This study and others like it have documented two factors that influence recollections of pleasure—and a third that, surprisingly, has very little influence. First, the *peak moment* of pleasure during the course of an event—the most delicious bite of a dessert, the most beautiful sunset during an island vacation, the most gratifying compliment received during a family gathering—strongly predicts how much pleasure you'll remember later. Second, how you feel at the *end* of the event also strongly predicts your overall experience of pleasure. So try to make sure that the last few moments of a first date you've enjoyed are especially good. Similarly, it's wise for a teacher to end a lecture with an inspiring conclusion, a provocative question, or a good joke. And by all means, don't spend the last day of your vacation running around buying gifts for friends back home; take care of that earlier, and do something especially fun before heading to the airport. Something that has surprisingly little impact on people's subsequent overall assessments is the *length* of the pleasurable experience in question—an effect known as **duration neglect**. Whether a massage lasts 20 minutes or an hour or whether a first date lasts 1 hour or 10 has very little effect on our recollections of pleasure. What matters most is quality of the experience at its peak and at the end.

focalism A tendency to focus too much on a central aspect of an event while neglecting the possible impact of associated factors or other events.

duration neglect Giving relative unimportance to the length of an emotional experience, whether pleasurable or unpleasant, in judging and remembering the overall experience.

The Pursuit of Happiness

If people's theories about what makes them happy are sometimes misguided, are there things that science can tell us about the most reliable contributors to happiness? What are some principles to follow in the pursuit of happiness?

One answer may seem obvious but warrants mention: happiness is often found in being with other people. Relationships of all kinds—romantic partnerships, friendships, family connections, neighborhood ties, and links to teammates, fellow activists, or parishioners—tend to lift people's spirits (Lyubomirsky, 2007). Religious engagement is associated with greater happiness, probably in part because such involvement leads to a sense of community and trust in others (Helliwell & Putnam, 2004). Social bonds bring personal happiness. This doesn't mean that you have to be around people all the time or live the life of an extravert. A few close friendships can do the trick. Just be sure to avoid isolation (Baumeister & Leary, 1995).

A second answer concerns money. Is it really true that "money doesn't buy happiness," or do people who believe that, as the actress Bo Derek maintains, "simply don't know where to shop?" There is an enormous body of research on this question, and the evidence indicates that money will bring you some happiness, but perhaps not as much as you might expect. In one survey of over 400,000 U.S. residents, people who made more money reported greater life satisfaction, and the poorest respondents were the least happy and the most likely to suffer from sadness, divorce, and health problems (Kahneman & Deaton, 2010). Thus, money does matter in terms of overall satisfaction with life. But only up to a point; for someone making $75,000 a year, making more money had little influence on emotional well-being or negative and positive emotions. Some have argued that the lifestyle changes brought about by making more money, such as longer commutes and diminished time with friends, undermine emotional well-being (Frank, Levine, & Dijk, 2014; Myers, 2001). So yes, a basic level of economic success is important to life satisfaction, but making a great deal of money does not seem to increase the quality of people's moment-to-moment emotional experience.

A third way to increase your happiness is to practice gratitude, which the philosopher Adam Smith believed to be a key to the functioning of healthy societies. Try to appreciate from time to time the many things you've received from other people, like the opportunity to learn, to do meaningful work, or to express your ideas. In one experiment, participants were randomly assigned to either write about an experience in the past or write a letter of gratitude to someone close to them (Boehm, Lyubomirsky, & Sheldon, 2011). At a one-month follow-up, participants who had written a letter of gratitude were happier than those in the control condition.

A fourth recommendation is to follow the conventional wisdom, backed up by empirical research, that it's better to give than to receive. Elizabeth Dunn and her colleagues tested this idea by asking participants to rate how happy they were and then giving them either $5 or $20 to spend by the end of the day (Dunn, Aknin, & Norton, 2008). Some were told to spend the money on themselves; others were told to spend it on someone else. Those required to spend the money on others reported greater happiness during a follow-up assessment at the end of the day compared with those told to spend the money on themselves. This finding has since been

"The duties of gratitude are perhaps the most sacred of those which the beneficent virtues prescribe to us."
—ADAM SMITH, *THE THEORY OF MORAL SENTIMENTS*, 1759

CAUSES OF UNHAPPINESS
One of the consistent enemies of happiness is driving in cars and getting stuck in traffic jams, such as this one.

The Game of Happiness

Among the emotions, happiness is one of the most highly valued, especially in Western societies. This premium placed on happiness extends beyond the fact that being happy simply feels good. Happiness is also associated with occupational success, better physical health, and density of social networks. Fortunately, scientists have identified various strategies that can help increase happiness. Here are ten empirically based tips that are simple and concrete enough to be implemented in the span of a single day.

For Critical Thinking

1. How many of these tips do you regularly practice? What keeps you from doing the others more frequently?
2. Before reading these ten tips, what would you have guessed makes people happy? How do your intuitions compare to what these ten tips suggest?

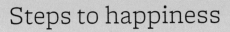

Steps to happiness

You today

1.

Take 30 minutes and write down what you are grateful for in your life.

2.

Take a moment once a week to express your appreciation for your romantic partner or a friend, noting something specific this person does that you are grateful for.

3.

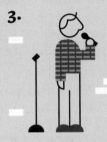

Do something that makes you laugh with a friend or romantic partner— see a movie or a comedy show, share a series of funny GIFs.

4.

Go for a walk somewhere that makes you feel awe—in a great part of a city or in a natural setting.

5.

If you have 10 dollars to spare, give it to a charity whose work is important to you.

6.

Take 10 minutes a week to sit quietly, breathe deeply, and focus on feelings of kindness toward one person you are close to.

7.

Take 10 minutes a day for four days and write about your life goals and your "best possible self," the person you aspire to be, in 5 years.

8.

If you have some spare money and are contemplating buying something, instead of buying a consumer product, use the money to create an experience —dinner with a friend, an outing to a park or museum.

9.

Take 10 minutes to think about a present difficulty in your life and imagine what a dear friend would say to you as a form of support. Take in the feelings of self-compassion.

10.

Get off your smartphone and Facebook and go out with friends.

A happier future you

BOX 6.4   FOCUS ON POSITIVE PSYCHOLOGY

Nirvana in the Brain

Ever since the Buddha found enlightenment when meditating under a bo tree 2,500 years ago, billions of people have turned to meditation to find peace and happiness. There are many kinds of meditation practices, but they share certain principles. They encourage you to mindfully slow your breathing to a steady rhythm with deep exhalations, which reduces stress-related cardiovascular arousal. Many meditation practices encourage a mindful attention to different sensations in your body. They likewise encourage a calm, nonjudgmental awareness of your thoughts and feelings. And many meditation practices, such as those popularized by the Dalai Lama, encourage training the mind in loving kindness and compassion. Here the meditator extends warm feelings of compassion to family members, friends, loved ones, strangers, the self, and ultimately adversaries, to encourage a more compassionate stance toward fellow human beings.

Does meditation work? Neuroscientist Richard Davidson has been seeking a rigorous answer to that question (Davidson & Begley, 2012). In one line of work, he has studied practitioners of Tibetan Buddhism, who spend as much as 4 or 5 hours a day quietly meditating. Upon scanning the brain of one monk, he found that his resting brain showed levels of activation in the left frontal lobes—regions of the brain involved in positive emotion—that were literally off the charts. In another task, Davidson blasted the monk with a loud burst of white noise, which for most people activates an ancient and powerful startle response, the strength of which is a good indicator of how stressed out the person is. The monk didn't even blink.

These benefits can be enjoyed by most people, not just monks who have devoted their lives to the practice of meditation.

MEDITATION AND HAPPINESS French Tibetan Buddhist Monk Matthieu Ricard practices various contemplative meditations for hours a day and, in different tests by Richard Davidson, has been shown to have a remarkably "happy" brain.

Davidson, Jon Kabat-Zinn, and their colleagues had software engineers train in the techniques of mindfulness meditation, with the aim of developing the ability to accept without judgment their thoughts and feelings and the practice of loving kindness toward others (Davidson et al., 2003). Six weeks later, the participants showed increased activation in the left frontal lobes. They also showed enhanced immune function, evident in the size of the immune response in the skin when given a flu shot. In similarly motivated work, researchers have found that practicing mindfulness meditation, with a focus on being mindful of breathing and extending loving kindness to others, boosts happiness several weeks later (Fredrickson, Cohn, Coffey, Pek, & Finkel, 2008).

replicated in a worldwide study involving 136 cultures (Aknin et al., 2013). To experience greater happiness, these studies indicate, we would be well served by sharing, giving to charity, volunteering, or surprising others with gifts.

You're not likely to spend all your money on others, of course. What about the money you spend on yourself? Do some types of expenditures lead to more happiness than others? There's an easy answer to this question, which is our fifth recommendation in the pursuit of happiness: focus a bit more on experiences and a bit less on material possessions. The results of both consumer surveys and laboratory experiments indicate that if you're conflicted about whether to buy a material good (an attractive coat, a 3D TV) or to finance a personal experience (such as tickets to a concert or a trip to Mexico), you're generally better off opting for the experience (Carter & Gilovich, 2010; Van Boven, Campbell, & Gilovich, 2010). When people are asked to recall their most significant material purchase and most significant experiential purchase over the past five years, they report that the experiential purchase brought more joy, was a source of more enduring satisfaction, and was more clearly "money well spent." Why is this so? One reason is that we quickly adapt or habituate to the material good (the new smartphone is fun for a while but soon it feels no different from the old one), but the experience lingers. It lives on in the memories we cherish, in the stories we tell, and in the very sense of who we are.

Finally, try to cultivate experiences that can lead to awe. Research indicates that even brief experiences of awe produced, say, by watching awe-inspiring films, reading stories about extraordinary experiences, being around inspiring people, or taking 10 minutes to get outdoors into natural beauty all boost people's happiness (Gordon et al., 2017; Rudd, Vohs, & Aaker, 2012). One reason for this boost is that awe leads to an expanded sense of time; experiences of awe make people feel less oppressed by the time crunch that is such a common element of today's life (Rudd et al., 2012). Brief experiences of awe also attenuate certain thoughts—especially thoughts of entitlement and the concern with material consumption—that diminish personal happiness (Piff, Dietze, Feinberg, Stancato, & Keltner, 2015). In your search for happiness, then, you may want to put down this book for a moment and take a look at the awe-inspiring things around you—the sky outside, an approaching thunderstorm, a beautiful stand of trees, the petals of the flowers on a nearby table, even the strength of the materials in the building that's keeping you warm.

NATURE, HEALTH, AND WELL-BEING
Walking in nature is a consistent booster of happiness, awe, and good health.

← LOOKING BACK

Happiness consists of overall life satisfaction and moment-to-moment emotional well-being (or the ratio of daily positive to negative emotions). It's sometimes hard to predict the extent of our future happiness; we tend to focus on certain "focal" factors while neglecting other, less focal elements that will nonetheless powerfully influence how happy we'll be. We are also biased in our recollection of past pleasures, focusing on the peak and endpoint of an experience. We can cultivate happiness by pursuing social connection, practicing gratitude, giving to others, focusing on experiences rather than material objects, and seeking out experiences of awe.

Chapter Review

SUMMARY

Characterizing Emotion

- The experience of emotion is generally brief, lasting only seconds or minutes; moods often last for hours or days.
- Emotions guide how we perceive the world and how we act in response to challenges and opportunities in the environment.

Emotional Expression: Universal and Culturally Specific

- Universal aspects to emotion are based on evolutionary factors; emotions enable people to respond quickly and effectively to threats and opportunities related to survival.
- People in different cultures facially express happiness, surprise, sadness, anger, disgust, and fear in similar ways.
- Cultures vary in *focal emotions*, which are common in everyday experience.
- There are cultural differences in which emotions are highly valued and in the *display rules* that govern how emotions are expressed.

Emotions and Social Relationships

- Emotions help solve the "commitment problem," enabling people to express sincere commitment and to behave in ways that benefit others' well-being, thus strengthening social relationships. The chemical oxytocin, circulating throughout the blood, contributes to building commitment and trust.
- Emotional expressions in the face, voice, and touch trigger reactions in others, thus coordinating interactions like flirtation or attachments between parents and children.
- The experience and expression of certain emotions, like awe, pride, and anger, enable people to know their status within social groups.

Emotions and Understanding the Social World

- Emotions influence how people perceive information. Fear, for instance, makes people more attuned to threats in the environment.
- The *broaden-and-build hypothesis* holds that positive emotions broaden thoughts and actions, prompting people to see greater similarities between themselves and others, thereby building stronger relationships.
- According to the *social intuitionist model of moral judgment*, people have fast, emotional intuitions about right or wrong, then rely on reason to make moral judgments. *Moral foundations theory* offers five evolved, universal moral domains in which specific emotions guide moral judgments.

Happiness

- Happiness is described as the combination of life satisfaction and emotional well-being, the tendency to experience more positive emotions than negative emotions. Happiness is associated with stronger relationships, increased creativity, and better health.
- *Affective forecasting* involves predictions about how life events will influence happiness. People often fail to predict how much an emotional experience, such as breaking up from a romantic relationship, will affect them.
- *Focalism* is narrowly focusing on how a single event will influence future happiness, while not considering other events.
- People can cultivate happiness by being grateful, practicing generosity, and focusing on experiences rather than purchasing material goods.

THINK ABOUT IT

1. Humans appear to have a coordinated display of embarrassment that resembles appeasement signals in other species. What does this tell us about the function of embarrassment? Why do you feel embarrassed when you trip and fall in a full lecture hall? What effects should your display of embarrassment have on your classmates?

2. The relationship between culture and emotion is complex. Say you're seated at a wedding reception with an older European-American man, who tells you that East Asians never get excited. How would you explain to him that he's mistaken by drawing on the concepts of ideal emotions and display rules?

3. Much communication today occurs via electronic text rather than face-to-face, whether in an online chat or text message, an e-mail, or a post on a social media site. Given what you know about the importance of emotions for social relationships, why do you think people frequently use emoticons and emojis in these communications? What social functions do they perform?

4. Suppose you just got into a huge fight with your parents on the phone and are feeling angry. You call up your romantic partner to talk about the fight, but just end up fighting with your partner. Using what you know about emotion's effects on perception, how would you explain this second fight and perpetuated mood states more generally?

5. If you were working as a canvasser collecting signatures for a petition to ban same-sex marriage, what strategies could you use to increase your signature count, given what you know about moral foundations theory and the effects of disgust on moral judgment?

6. Would winning several million dollars in the lottery make you happier? What does research on affective forecasting predict? What does the research on money and happiness have to say? How should you spend your winnings to maximize happiness?

The answer guidelines for the think about it questions can be found at the back of the book . . . ☞

ONLINE STUDY MATERIALS

Want to earn a better grade on your test?
Go to **INQUIZITIVE** to learn and review this chapter's content, with personalized feedback along the way.

Why were Americans more patriotic after the 9/11 attacks on the World Trade Center?

AMERICA ONE NATION UNDER GOD

How can we convince other people to change their behavior?

What can someone's bodily movements tell us about their emotions?

Attitudes, Behavior, and Rationalization

THROUGHOUT AMERICA'S LONG AND PAINFUL military involvement in Vietnam—a conflict that split the nation into "hawks" and "doves," consumed the energies of three administrations, and ultimately cost the lives of 58,000 U.S. soldiers—the government put a positive spin on the enterprise. But despite the government's many positive pronouncements about the war effort, many government officials had doubts. Their reservations often surfaced when key decisions needed to be made, such as whether to increase the number of U.S. soldiers stationed in South Vietnam or whether to initiate a bombing campaign against North Vietnam.

Lyndon Johnson, the U.S. president responsible for the largest buildup of American troops in Vietnam, used an interesting tactic to deal with those in his administration who had begun privately to express such reservations (Halberstam, 1969). Johnson would send the doubters on a "fact-finding" mission to Vietnam, nearly always accompanied by a group of reporters. This might seem like a risky move on Johnson's part, because if any of these doubters expressed their concerns to the press, the administration's policies would be undermined. Johnson knew, however, that they wouldn't express their dissent publicly and, moreover, when confronted by criticism of the war by reporters, would actually be put in the position of publicly *defending* administration policy. This public endorsement, Johnson reasoned, would serve to lessen their doubts and help transform them into advocates. Known as an unusually savvy politician, President Johnson was using some very clever psychology—psychology we'll explore in this chapter—to win support for his Vietnam policy.

Johnson's strategy highlights some important questions about the consistency between attitudes and behavior, especially whether the consistency between the

PUBLIC ADVOCACY AND PRIVATE ACCEPTANCE
Despite continuing problems in fighting the Vietnam War, U.S. President Lyndon Johnson publicly declared that things were going well and insisted that his advisers and cabinet members publicly express their support and confidence. (A) U.S. Secretary of Defense Robert McNamara had reservations about the war that may have been alleviated by the constant necessity of defending it. Here he is shown briefing the press on U.S. air attacks. (B) To bolster morale, Johnson himself spoke to American troops in South Vietnam while U.S. General William Westmoreland, South Vietnamese General Nguyen Van Thieu, South Vietnamese Premier Nguyen Coo Ky, and U.S. Secretary of State Dean Rusk looked on.

two is the result of attitudes influencing behavior or behavior influencing attitudes. Both types of influence occur. Attitudes influence behavior: those with strong pro-environment attitudes are more likely to vote Green or Democratic than Republican. But behavior influences attitudes as well: environmentally minded individuals who drive gas-guzzling cars tend to convince themselves that automobile exhaust contributes very little to air pollution or global warming—or that they don't drive that much anyway.

Which is stronger: the effect of attitudes on behavior or the effect of behavior on attitudes? It's a difficult question to answer, but decades of research on the topic have shown that the influence of attitudes on behavior is a bit weaker than most people suspect, and the influence of behavior on attitudes is much stronger than most suspect. So President Johnson was right: get skeptics to publicly endorse the policy, and they will be skeptics no longer.

This chapter examines what social psychologists have learned about the consistency between attitudes and behavior. The chapter also examines two "consistency theories" that explain why people tend to maintain consistency among their attitudes and between their attitudes and behavior. ■

Components and Measurement of Attitudes

Let's start with the basics: What are attitudes, and how are they measured? Attitudes can have multiple components, and researchers use a variety of different methods to measure them.

Three Components of Attitudes

attitude An evaluation of an object in a positive or negative fashion that includes three components: affect, cognition, and behavior.

An **attitude** is an evaluation of an object along a positive-negative dimension. At their core, then, attitudes involve *affect* (emotion)—how much someone likes or dislikes an object, be it a politician, a landscape, an athletic shoe, a dessert, or oneself. Nearly every object triggers some degree of positive or negative emotion, which constitutes the affective component of the attitude somebody has toward it (Bargh, Chaiken, Raymond, & Hymes, 1996; Cacioppo & Berntson, 1994; Fazio, Sanbonmatsu, Powell, & Kardes, 1986; Zanna & Rempel, 1988).

But attitudes also involve *cognitions*— thoughts that typically reinforce a person's feelings (Breckler, 1984; Eagly & Chaiken, 1998; Zimbardo & Leippe, 1991). These include knowledge and beliefs about the object, as well as associated memories and images. Your attitude about a favorite city, for example, includes knowledge about its history and its most appealing neighborhoods and landmarks, as well as the special times you've spent there.

OBJECTS TRIGGER EMOTIONS
Like most objects, this image of a tropical beach likely triggers some degree of emotion—presumably positive emotion for most of us.

Finally, attitudes are associated with specific *behaviors* (Fishbein & Ajzen, 1975). Most generally, the affective evaluation of good versus bad is connected to a behavioral tendency to either approach or avoid (Harmon-Jones, Price, & Harmon-Jones, 2015). Put differently, attitudes alert us to rewarding objects we should approach and to costly or punishing objects we should avoid (Ferguson & Bargh, 2008; Ferguson & Zayas, 2009). When specific attitudes are primed— brought to mind, even unconsciously—people are more likely to behave in ways consistent with the attitude (Chen & Bargh, 1999). Neuroscientific studies indicate that our attitudes activate particular brain regions, areas of the motor cortex, that support specific actions (McCall, Tipper, Blascovich, & Grafton, 2012; Preston & de Waal, 2002). When you see a young child crying or a scrumptious hot fudge sundae, your mind prepares your body for the action of caretaking or consumption.

Measuring Attitudes

Attitudes are most commonly determined through simple self-report measures, such as survey questions. When researchers want to know how participants feel about members of other groups, their romantic partners, a public figure, and so on, they usually just ask them. To do so, they often rely on a Likert scale, named after psychologist Rensis Likert, its inventor. A **Likert scale** lists a set of possible answers with anchors on each extreme—for example, 1 = strongly disagree, 7 = strongly agree. So, for example, to assess attitudes toward the use of cell phones while driving, researchers might have participants respond on a scale of 1 to 7, where 1 is the least favorable answer ("It's never acceptable") and 7 is the most favorable ("It's always acceptable"). You've probably responded to many of these kinds of queries. Yet when it comes to many complex attitudes—such as your attitude toward capital punishment, environmentalism, or hedge fund managers—responses to these sorts of simple scales are likely to miss some important elements.

Consider the following questions: How much do you value freedom? How strongly do you feel about the need to reduce discrimination? How important is a less polluted environment? If an investigator asked these questions of a random selection of individuals, chances are most responses on a Likert scale would be very positive. But surely people differ in the strength and depth of their attitudes

Likert scale A numerical scale used to assess people's attitudes; a scale that includes a set of possible answers with labeled anchors on each extreme.

toward these issues. How can social psychologists better capture these other dimensions of attitudes?

One approach is to measure the *accessibility* of the attitude—how readily it comes to mind (Fazio, 1995; Fazio & Williams, 1986). To do so, researchers track the time it takes a person to respond to an attitude question—known as the person's **response latency**. Someone who takes less than a second to respond affirmatively to a question such as "Do you approve of how the president is handling the economy?" is likely to have a stronger attitude on this topic than somebody who takes several seconds to respond. In a study conducted five months before Ronald Reagan and Walter Mondale squared off in the 1984 U.S. presidential election, for example, Fazio and Williams (1986) measured how long it took participants to indicate their attitude toward Reagan. Those who responded quickly to the attitude question showed greater consistency between their attitude and how they ultimately voted compared with those who responded relatively slowly.

A second way to assess the strength and importance of someone's attitude is to determine the *centrality* of the attitude to the person's belief system (Krosnick & Petty, 1995). To evaluate attitude centrality, researchers measure a variety of attitudes within a domain and calculate how strongly each one is linked to the others. To illustrate, a researcher might ask your opinions about abortion, stem cell research, fracking, same-sex marriage, sex education in high school, drug legalization, and taxation. If your attitude on a specific topic is very important to you, it should be consistent with your attitudes about certain other issues. For example, if abortion is a defining issue for you, then your view on abortion is likely to be strongly correlated with your attitudes about stem cell research and sex education and perhaps even with your attitudes about same-sex marriage and taxation.

Other ways of measuring attitudes don't rely on explicit self-reports. Investigators often use **implicit attitude measures** when there is reason to believe that people may be unwilling or unable to report their true feelings or opinions (Cameron, Brown-Iannuzzi, & Payne, 2012). Chapter 11, on stereotypes and prejudice, discusses in some detail two widely used implicit measures: affective priming and the implicit association test (IAT; Greenwald, McGhee, & Schwartz, 1998). With both of these measures, people don't realize that their attitudes are being examined. Implicit measures let researchers tap *nonconscious attitudes*—that is, people's immediate evaluative reactions they may not be aware of or that may conflict with their consciously endorsed attitudes. Researchers also sometimes use nonverbal measures, such as degree of physical closeness, as signals of positive attitudes toward others.

Finally, physiological indicators, such as the increased heart rate and sweaty palms associated with fear, can capture people's attitudes. **Box 7.1**, for example, describes how patterns of brain activity recorded from the surface of the scalp reflect the relative strength of positive and negative attitudes (Ito, Larsen, Smith, & Cacioppo, 1998).

response latency The amount of time it takes to respond to a stimulus, such as an attitude question.

implicit attitude measure An indirect measure of attitudes that doesn't involve a self-report.

← **LOOKING BACK**

Attitudes can have three components: affect, cognition, and behavior. Researchers have developed many ways to measure attitudes, including explicit self-reports, implicit indices, and physiological measures.

BOX 7.1	FOCUS ON NEUROSCIENCE

Is the Bad Stronger Than the Good?

At the core of our attitudes is a positive or negative response to an attitude object—an old friend's voice, a roommate's messy pile of dishes, the smell of freshly cut grass. Pioneering research by neuroscientist Joseph LeDoux has found that one part of the brain, the amygdala, is central to this initial, core component of our attitudes (LeDoux, 1989, 1993, 1996). After receiving sensory information about a stimulus from the thalamus, the almond-shaped amygdala then provides information about the positive or negative valence, or value, of the object. This evaluation occurs, remarkably, before the mind has categorized the object in question. Thus, even before we fully know what an object is, we have a gut feeling about it. When the amygdala is damaged, animals no longer have appropriate evaluations of objects: they eat feces, attempt to copulate with members of other species, and show no fear of threatening stimuli such as snakes or dominant animals.

LeDoux's research raises an interesting question: Are our quick positive and negative evaluations of stimuli comparable with respect to their strength? Reviews by Shelley Taylor (1991), Paul Rozin and Edward Royzman (2001), Roy Baumeister and his colleagues (Baumeister, Bratslavsky, Finkenauer, & Vohs, 2001), and John Cacioppo and Wendi Gardner (1999) have all yielded the same answer: negative evaluations are stronger than positive evaluations. It would certainly make evolutionary sense for an organism to be more vigilant about avoiding harm than seeking pleasure, to be more watchful for danger signs than for cues to opportunity. Food or mating opportunities not pursued today might be realized tomorrow; if a predator is not avoided today, there is no tomorrow. A pronounced negativity bias might therefore increase the chances of survival.

Consider a few generalizations supporting the conclusion that the bad is stronger than the good. Negative stimuli, such as frightening sounds or noxious smells, elicit more rapid and stronger physiological responses than positive stimuli, such as delicious tastes. Losing $20 is more painful than winning $20 is pleasurable.

CONTAMINATION The presence of cockroaches on food spoils a delicious meal. (Note that the meal does not make the cockroaches suddenly seem appetizing.)

Negative trauma, such as the death of a loved one or sexual abuse, can change a person for a lifetime; positive events don't appear to have equivalent effects. Or consider Rozin's observation about contamination: the briefest contact with a cockroach will spoil a delicious meal, but the inverse—making a pile of cockroaches delicious by spicing it up with your favorite foods—is unimaginable (Rozin & Royzman, 2001).

In related work, Tiffany Ito, John Cacioppo, and their colleagues presented participants with positively valenced pictures—pizza or a bowl of chocolate ice cream, for instance; and negatively valenced slides—such as photos of a mutilated face or a dead cat (Ito et al., 1998). As they did so, they recorded the participants' brain activity on the scalp and studied brain regions known to be involved in evaluative responses to stimuli. They discovered a clear negativity bias in evaluation: the negative stimuli generated greater brain activity than the positive or neutral stimuli. In this context, it seems that the bad is indeed stronger than the good.

Predicting Behavior from Attitudes

Most academic discussions of how well attitudes predict behavior begin with a remarkable study conducted by the sociologist Richard LaPiere in the early 1930s (LaPiere, 1934). LaPiere spent two years touring the United States with a young Chinese couple, visiting numerous hotels, camping grounds, restaurants, and cafés. Although prejudice and discrimination against Chinese individuals were common at the time, LaPiere and his traveling companions were denied service by only one of the 250 establishments they visited, leading LaPiere to wonder if maybe anti-Chinese prejudice wasn't so strong after all.

ATTITUDES DON'T ALWAYS PREDICT BEHAVIOR

This bar in Pattaya Beach, Thailand, displays a sign declaring "No Arab to sit down here." The bar owners may indeed intend to block Arabs from their establishment, but if an Arab walked into the bar with some friends, would the owners really forbid the person from sitting down?

To find out, LaPiere wrote to all of the establishments they had visited and asked whether their policy was to serve "Orientals." About 90 percent of the respondents said they wouldn't—a figure stunningly inconsistent with what LaPiere had actually experienced during his earlier tour. This result was unfortunate in human terms because it indicated that anti-Chinese prejudice was indeed rather robust. But it was also unfortunate from the perspective of psychological science because it suggested that attitudes don't predict behavior very well. To a scientific discipline that had treated attitudes as powerful determinants of people's behavior, this news was surprising—and rather unsettling.

Note that this inconsistency wasn't some fluke. Many studies conducted over the next several decades yielded similar results. As a much-cited review in the 1960s of the existing literature on attitudes and behavior concluded: "The present review provides little evidence to support the postulated existence of stable, underlying attitudes within the individual which influence both his verbal expressions and his actions" (Wicker, 1969, p. 75).

Most people find this result surprising because everyday life provides lots of evidence that attitudes and behavior often *do* go together. People who picket abortion clinics have anti-abortion attitudes. People who show up at the local bowling alley have positive attitudes toward the sport. Families with lots of kids usually have favorable attitudes about children. Evidence of a tight connection between attitudes and behavior is all around us. But such evidence indicates only that if people behave a certain way, they probably have positive feelings about that behavior. It doesn't mean that those with a positive attitude toward a given behavior will necessarily behave in a manner consistent with that attitude. What's not so obvious in everyday life are the many instances of, say, people with positive attitudes about bowling who don't bowl or people with favorable attitudes about kids who don't have children.

There are many reasons for failing to act on our attitudes. And once we're aware of all these reasons, the finding that attitudes so often fail to predict behavior may no longer seem so surprising. Furthermore, an awareness of these reasons gives us a better understanding of *when* attitudes are likely to be highly predictive of behavior and when they aren't (Glasman & Albarracín, 2006; Kruglanski et al., 2015).

Attitudes Can Conflict with Other Powerful Determinants of Behavior

Think about the relationship between a person's attitudes about dieting and actual success in sticking to a diet. Would you expect a strong relationship? Probably not. Eating less is determined by so many things other than a person's attitude about dieting, including eating habits, individual physiology, and whether a roommate happens to be pigging out at the moment—not to mention the person's attitudes about things like ice cream, doughnuts, and french fries. What's true about attitudes toward dieting is true about attitudes in general. They all compete with other determinants of behavior. The situationist message of social psychology (and of this book) suggests that attitudes don't always win out over these other determinants, and hence attitudes aren't always tightly connected to behavior.

One potent determinant of a person's actions that can weaken the relationship between attitudes and behavior is that person's understanding of the prevailing norms of appropriate behavior. You might be dying to share your hilarious commentary about the movie with the guy next to you in the theater, but let's hope you refrain from doing so because you recognize it just isn't done and others—probably including the guy next to you!—would disapprove. Similarly, the hotel and restaurant owners in LaPiere's study may have wanted to turn away the Chinese couple, but refrained from doing so out of concern for how it would look and the scene it might cause.

Introspecting about the Reasons for Our Attitudes

Consider your attitude toward someone to whom you're attracted. Why are you attracted to that person? A number of answers likely spring to mind: "She's cute." "She's ambitious." "He's fun to be with." Sometimes, however, it's not so easy to know exactly why we like someone. It may not be because of specific, readily identifiable attributes; we may simply share some indescribable chemistry. Suppose this is the case and you're asked to come up with reasons why you like your romantic partner. Like most people, you'll probably focus on what is easy to identify, easy to justify, and easy to capture in words—and thus miss the real, but hard-to-articulate, reasons for your attraction. Why does this matter? It turns out that coming up with the (wrong) reasons for an attitude you have can mislead you about what your attitude actually is.

In one test of this phenomenon, Timothy Wilson and his colleagues asked students about the person they were dating. Participants in one group simply gave an overall evaluation of their relationship. Those in another group listed the reasons they felt the way they did and then gave an overall relationship evaluation. The researchers contacted the participants again nine months later and asked about the status of their relationship. The attitudes of participants in the first group, who evaluated the relationship without considering their reasons, were much more accurate predictors of their current relationship status than the attitudes of participants who had introspected about their reasons for liking their partner (Wilson, Dunn, Bybee, Hyman, & Rotondo, 1984). Thinking about why we like someone can mislead us in terms of our true, full attitude toward that person, making the attitude we report after generating reasons not a very good predictor of our subsequent behavior.

Wilson has found that introspecting about the reasons for our attitudes about all sorts of things can undermine how well those attitudes guide our behavior. The cause in all cases is the same: introspection may lead us to focus on the easiest-to-identify reasons for liking or disliking something at the expense of the *real* reasons for our likes and dislikes.

INCONSISTENT ATTITUDES Attitudes may not be good predictors of behavior because people often have attitudes that conflict with one another. Elliot Spitzer, disgraced former governor of New York, had campaigned on the importance of high ethical standards among public officials and vowed to "change the ethics of Albany." Following reports that he was a frequent customer in a high-priced prostitution operation, he resigned. Did he think his involvement with prostitutes was wrong but did it anyway, or did he view participation in the sex trade as ethically acceptable?

Does this mean that introspection is always (or even typically) harmful? Should we always just go with our gut? Not at all. In deciding whether to launch a military campaign, for example, it's imperative for analysts to exhaustively consider the reasons for and against the campaign. Also, the real reasons for our attitudes are sometimes perfectly easy to identify and articulate, and in those cases introspection produces no rift between the things we *think* are guiding us and those that actually are. The contaminating effect of introspection is limited to those times when the true source of our attitude is hard to pin down, as when the basis of an attitude is largely affective (emotional). In such cases, a cognitive, thoughtful analysis is likely to seize on seemingly plausible but misleading cognitive reasons. When the basis of an attitude is primarily cognitive, however, the search for reasons tends to yield the real reasons, and introspection isn't likely to mislead us about our true attitude or diminish the relationship between our attitude and behavior (Millar & Tesser, 1986; Wilson & Dunn, 1986). Thus, examining your reasons for enjoying a certain artist's work may cause a rift between your expressed attitude and your subsequent behavior, but analyzing why you prefer one digital camera over another probably won't create such a gap.

The Mismatch between General Attitudes and Specific Targets

Typically, the attitudes people express are about general categories, such as the environment, pushy people, French cuisine, or global trade. But the attitude-relevant behavior that researchers typically assess has a more specific focus: donating to Greenpeace, reacting to a specific pushy individual, ordering steak frites, or picketing a meeting of the World Trade Organization. Given this mismatch between general attitudes and specific behaviors, no wonder attitudes don't always predict behavior particularly well.

Studies have shown that highly specific attitudes typically do a better job of predicting specific behaviors, and general attitudes typically do a better job of predicting how a person behaves "in general" (Ajzen, 1987). In LaPiere's study, for example, the attitudes expressed by the various merchants were rather general: whether they would serve Orientals. But the behavior assessed was directed at one specific Chinese couple with a specific demeanor and dressed in a specific fashion. Perhaps the results would have been different if LaPiere had asked the merchants whether they would serve a well-dressed, pleasant Chinese couple. If you want to predict a specific type of behavior accurately, you have to measure people's attitudes toward that specific behavior.

The broader point here is that what most people usually think of as attitudes about different classes of people, places, things, and events are often expressions of attitudes about a prototypical example of a given category. So if we encounter a specific situation or person who doesn't fit the prototype, our behavior probably won't reflect our stated attitude. Our general attitude doesn't apply to *that* particular person. Consider a study in which male college students expressed their attitudes about gay men (Lord, Lepper, & Mackie, 1984). The researchers also elicited from each student his stereotype of the "typical" gay man. Two months later, a different experimenter asked the participants if they would be willing to show some visiting students around campus. One of the visitors, "John B.," was described in such a way that the participants would think he was gay. For half the participants, the rest of the description of John B. was crafted to fit their own

GENERAL ATTITUDES AND SPECIFIC TARGETS
A person with a generally positive attitude about science may not participate in rallies and marches associated with the March for Science movement that was launched in 2017. But someone with more specific attitudes about the importance of science to the health and well-being of the world's population is more likely to join in a rally, like this person marching in a rally in Washington, DC.

individualized stereotype of a gay man; for the other half, it wasn't. The investigators found that the students' willingness to show John B. around campus—their behavior—was strongly predicted by their attitudes about gay men (those with positive attitudes said they were willing; those with negative attitudes said they were not), but only if John B. matched their prototype of a gay individual. If John B. didn't fit their image of a gay man, their attitudes about gay people didn't predict their behavior (their willingness to show him around campus).

← LOOKING BACK

Attitudes can be surprisingly weak predictors of behavior. The reasons are that attitudes sometimes conflict with social norms about appropriate behavior; examining the reasons for our attitudes can cause confusion about our true feelings; and general attitudes sometimes don't correspond to the specific action being predicted in a given situation.

Predicting Attitudes from Behavior

Many young people resent being sent to church, temple, mosque, or other religious service and often complain, "Why do I have to go? I don't believe any of this stuff." Many of them are told, "It doesn't matter if you believe it. What's important is that you continue with your studies and your prayers." Some resist to the very end and abandon all religious rituals and practices the minute their parents give them permission to opt out. But a remarkable number stick with it and eventually find themselves genuinely holding some of the very religious convictions they once resisted. Over time, mere outward behavior can give way to genuine belief.

The previous section presented the first part of the story about the connection between attitudes and behavior: attitudes can predict behavior, but not as strongly as most people suspect. The second part of the story, as illustrated by the religion example just described, is that behavior can powerfully influence attitudes. Social psychology research over the past half-century has repeatedly shown that people tend to bring their attitudes in line with their actions. How is it that our behavior has such a strong influence on our attitudes? A number of important theories seek to explain this relationship. Referred to collectively as *cognitive consistency theories*, they maintain that the impact of behavior on attitudes reflects the powerful tendency we have to justify or rationalize our behavior and to minimize any inconsistencies between our attitudes and actions. We focus here on the most influential of these theories: cognitive dissonance theory.

BEHAVIOR CAN INFLUENCE ATTITUDES
Many people who consider themselves environmentalists nonetheless drive gas-guzzling SUVs. Driving a vehicle that isn't fuel efficient can lead those who are concerned about the environment to convince themselves that there isn't much connection between fuel efficiency and air pollution or climate change.

Cognitive Dissonance Theory

cognitive dissonance theory The theory that inconsistency between a person's thoughts, sentiments, and actions creates an aversive emotional state (dissonance) that leads to efforts to restore consistency.

"It is our choices... that show what we truly are, far more than our abilities."
—J.K. ROWLING, *HARRY POTTER AND THE CHAMBER OF SECRETS*

Leon Festinger's **cognitive dissonance theory** is one of the most significant theories in the history of social psychology (Festinger, 1957). Festinger maintained that people are troubled by inconsistency between their thoughts, sentiments, and actions and that they'll expend psychological energy to restore consistency. More specifically, he thought that an aversive emotional state—dissonance—is aroused whenever people experience inconsistency between two cognitions. And when the cognitions are about our own behavior ("I just failed to live up to my promise"), we're troubled by the inconsistency between our cognitions and our behavior as well. This unpleasant emotional state motivates efforts to restore consistency—typically by changing the cognition to make it more consistent with the behavior.

What constitutes cognitive inconsistency, and under what conditions does it arise? What are the different ways that people try to get rid of inconsistency? Festinger's theory has inspired a tremendous amount of research aimed at answering such questions. To get a better sense of the kinds of inconsistency people find troubling, as well as a flavor for the diverse phenomena cognitive dissonance theory can explain, let's look at some of the classic experiments on the subject.

DECISIONS AND DISSONANCE A mere moment's reflection tells us that all hard decisions cause some feelings of dissonance. Because the decision is hard, the rejected alternative must have some desirable features, the chosen alternative must have some undesirable features—or both. Because these elements are inconsistent with the decision made, the result is dissonance (Brehm, 1956). If you move to Los Angeles from a small town in the Midwest in pursuit of good weather, you'll enjoy the sun, but the hours spent in traffic will probably produce dissonance. According to Festinger, once you've made an irrevocable decision to move to L.A., you'll exert effort to reduce this dissonance. You'll rationalize. You'll tell yourself and your friends how much you've learned from the audiobooks you play in your car during your long commute.

Many experiments have documented this tendency for people to rationalize their decisions. In one study, researchers interviewed bettors at a racetrack, some just before and some just after placing their bets (Knox & Inkster, 1968). The investigators reasoned that the act of placing a bet and irrevocably choosing a particular horse would cause the bettors to reduce the dissonance associated with the chosen horse's negative features (doesn't do well on a wet track) and the positive features of the competing horses (the perfect distance for one horse, the best jockey on another). Dissonance reduction should be reflected in greater confidence on the part of those interviewed right *after* placing their bets, once rationalization has set in. Indeed, bettors who were interviewed right before they placed their bets gave their horses, on average, a "fair" chance of winning; those interviewed after they had placed their bets gave their horses, on average, a "good" chance to win. One participant provided some extra commentary that illustrates the process of dissonance reduction especially well. Having been

interviewed while waiting in line (before placing his bet), he approached another member of the research team after placing his bet and said, "Are you working with that other fellow there? Well, I just told him that my horse had a fair chance of winning. Will you have him change that to a good chance? No, by God, make that an excellent chance." Similar findings have been reported in studies of elections: voters express greater confidence in their candidates when interviewed after they've voted than when interviewed right beforehand (Frenkel & Doob, 1976; Regan & Kilduff, 1988).

Festinger argued that dissonance reduction takes place only after an irrevocable decision has been made—that is, a decision that can't be undone. He maintained, for example, that "there is a clear and undeniable difference between the cognitive processes that occur during the period of making a decision and those that occur after the decision has been made. Reevaluation of alternatives in the direction of favoring the chosen or disfavoring the rejected alternative . . . is a post-decision phenomenon" (Festinger, 1964, p. 30).

The evidence from the betting and election studies supports Festinger's contention. But this seems at odds with other things we know about people. One of humankind's distinguishing characteristics is the ability to anticipate the future. If, in the process of making a decision, we see blemishes associated with what is emerging as our favorite option, why not start the process of rationalization beforehand, to minimize or eliminate dissonance altogether (Wilson, Wheatley, Kurtz, Dunn, & Gilbert, 2004)?

Indeed, more recent research suggests that the same sorts of rationalization and distortion that occur after people make a decision also subconsciously take place *before* they make the decision. Whether choosing restaurants, vacation spots, consumer goods, or political candidates, once people develop a slight preference for one option over the others, they distort subsequent information to support their preference (Brownstein, 2003; Brownstein, Read, & Simon, 2004; Russo, Meloy, & Medvec, 1998; Simon, Krawczyk, & Holyoak, 2004). Thus, the small size of a particular Italian restaurant tends to be rated as a plus by those leaning toward Italian food ("It's nice and intimate") but as a minus by those leaning toward a burger joint ("We won't be able to talk without everyone overhearing us"). So Festinger was right in maintaining that decisions evoke dissonance and then dissonance reduction, but these processes seem to occur more broadly than he anticipated; they take place both before and after decisions are made.

EFFORT JUSTIFICATION The element of dissonance theory that rings most true to many people is the idea that if you pay a high price for something—in dollars, time, or effort—and it turns out to be disappointing, you'll probably experience dissonance. As a result, you're likely to devote mental energy to justifying what you've done; this tendency is known as **effort justification**. This sort of *sweet lemons rationalization* ("It's really not so bad") can be seen in many contexts.

RATIONALIZING DECISIONS, REDUCING DISSONANCE
After placing a bet at the track, as here at the Kentucky Derby, people are likely to concentrate on the positive features of the horse they bet on and downplay any negatives. This rationalization process gives them greater confidence in the choice they made.

effort justification The tendency to reduce dissonance by justifying the time, effort, or money devoted to something that turned out to be unpleasant or disappointing.

LEON FESTINGER
In studying how people bring their attitudes in line with their behavior, Leon Festinger developed cognitive dissonance theory.

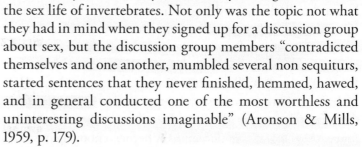

Those who don't have pets often suspect that pet lovers exaggerate the pleasure they get from their animals to offset all the early morning walking, poop scooping, and furniture wrecking. And those who choose not to have children suspect that sleep-deprived, overtaxed parents are fooling themselves when they say that nothing in life brings greater joy (Eibach & Mock, 2011).

Researchers explored the role of dissonance reduction in such situations in an early study in which female undergraduates signed up for an experiment thinking it involved the opportunity to join an ongoing discussion group about sex (Aronson & Mills, 1959). When they arrived, however, the students were told that not everyone can speak freely and comfortably about such a topic, so potential participants had to pass a screening test to join the group. Those assigned to a control condition simply read aloud a list of innocuous words to the male experimenter. Those assigned to a "mild" initiation condition read aloud a list of mildly embarrassing words, such as *prostitute*, *petting*, and *virgin*. Finally, those in a "severe" initiation group read aloud a list of obscene words and a passage from a novel describing sexual intercourse.

All participants were then told they had passed the screening test and could join the group. The group was meeting that very day, but participants were told that because everyone else in the discussion group had been given a reading assignment beforehand, it was best if they just listened in on the discussion. Then, through headphones in a nearby cubicle, they heard a very boring discussion of the sex life of invertebrates. Not only was the topic not what they had in mind when they signed up for a discussion group about sex, but the discussion group members "contradicted themselves and one another, mumbled several non sequiturs, started sentences that they never finished, hemmed, hawed, and in general conducted one of the most worthless and uninteresting discussions imaginable" (Aronson & Mills, 1959, p. 179).

The investigators predicted that the discussion would be boring and disappointing to all the participants, but that it would produce dissonance only for those who had undergone a severe initiation to join the group. The cognition "I suffered to get into this group" is inconsistent with the cognition "This group is worthless and boring." One way for the participants in the severe initiation condition to reduce dissonance would be to convince themselves that the group and the discussion weren't so boring after all. Indeed, when the experimenters asked participants at the end of the study to rate the quality of the discussion they listened to, those in the severe initiation condition rated it more favorably than those in the other two conditions (**Figure 7.1**).

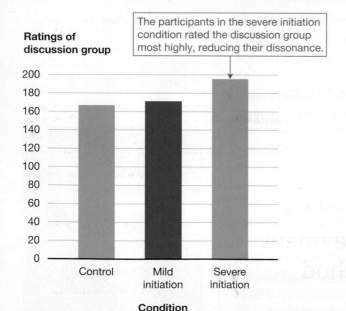

Ratings of discussion group

The participants in the severe initiation condition rated the discussion group most highly, reducing their dissonance.

Condition: Control, Mild initiation, Severe initiation

FIGURE 7.1
GROUP INITIATION AND LIKING FOR THE GROUP
This graph shows the different ratings of a discussion group by participants who experienced no initiation (the control condition), a mild initiation, or a severe initiation to join the group.
Source: Adapted from Aronson & Mills, 1959.

The need to justify "costly" behavior influences people in other areas of life as well. When people pay for consumer goods in ways that feel costly (think cash or check), they end up being more committed to the product and to the company from which they bought it than when they pay in ways that feel less costly

How Cognitive Dissonance Can Make You Like What You Buy

Cognitive dissonance isn't just a laboratory phenomenon. As consumers, businesses, and marketers can attest, it also has widespread influence in real-world contexts, including product choice, consumer satisfaction, and brand loyalty. When a product is more difficult to acquire, people often justify the extra effort by evaluating the product more positively.

The IKEA Effect

In these studies, some participants assembled IKEA boxes and Lego sets, and then all participants indicated how much they would pay for their own product, a prebuilt product, or someone else's finished product.

How much is the IKEA piece worth to you on a scale of $0-$1?

self-built **$0.78**

other-built **$0.48**

Lego Study

	prebuilt set		participant-built set	
$0.32		$0.26	$0.84	$0.42
bid on own set		bid on partner's set	bid on own set	bid on partner's set

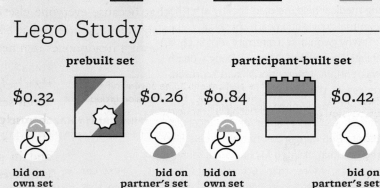

Pain as a Function of Payment Method

Participants in this study rated how much subjective pain they felt and the emotional attachment they felt toward a mug when paying for it with either cash (for which the loss of money is more vivid and concrete) or a credit card (abstract).

How painful is it to pay for a mug on a scale of 0–5:

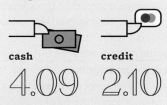

cash **4.09** credit **2.10**

What minimum price would you sell the mug for?

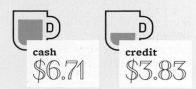

cash **$6.71** credit **$3.83**

For Critical Thinking

1. From the perspective of self-perception theory, why would people evaluate a product differently if they build it themselves? If they pay for it with cash versus credit?

2. What are some potential implications of effort justification in other consumer industries, such as restaurant/dining, travel, and entertainment?

Sources: The IKEA Effect: Norton, Mochon & Ariely, 2012; Pain as a Function of Payment Method: Shah, Eisenkraft, Bettman, & Chartrand, 2016.

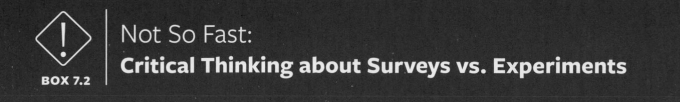

! BOX 7.2

Not So Fast:
Critical Thinking about Surveys vs. Experiments

Chun Hsien "Michael" Deng, a 19-year-old student at Baruch College in New York City, was excited about joining the school's Pi Delta Psi fraternity. Like everyone else in the pledge class, he went on a weekend retreat to the Pocono Mountains, in Pennsylvania, with the more senior members of the fraternity. While there, he and his fellow pledges were subjected to a "gauntlet"-like hazing ritual in which he was blindfolded and required to negotiate a path while being knocked repeatedly to the ground. Michael suffered a major brain trauma from this hazing ritual, and because his fraternity brothers were slow in seeking medical help, he died shortly after his eventual arrival at a nearby hospital.

Why would a fraternity do such a thing? To be sure, Michael Deng's death was entirely unintentional, and representatives of the national Pi Delta Psi organization condemned the actions of the Baruch College chapter in no uncertain terms. But dangerous hazing rituals like the one that claimed Michael's life remain common. More than 60 students are known to have died in incidents like this in the United States since 2005, at least 10 of them in initiations by a single national fraternity. Why do fraternities continue to engage in such practices?

Cognitive dissonance theory provides one answer. Having pledges undergo a painful initiation ritual can make them, once they've gone through it, more dedicated to the fraternity. After all, it may be hard for someone to walk away from an organization after paying such a stiff price to become a member. Doing so would likely cause a lot of dissonance, which could be reduced by deciding that the fraternity is a wonderful organization, one that is sure to make college a golden time.

FRATERNITY HAZING AND COMMITMENT Fraternities try to increase the commitment of members by having them undergo difficult and embarrassing initiation rituals like the one shown here.

How can we establish that efforts to reduce that dissonance really do lie at the heart of fraternity hazing? Stated differently, how can we determine whether fraternities that have more severe initiations do indeed cultivate more loyalty and enthusiasm among their members? One approach would be to survey members of various fraternities to evaluate their commitment to their fraternity. We could also find out about their initiation practices and have judges, unaware of the purpose of the study, rate them for severity. Do the fraternities with the most severe initiations have the most committed members?

Unfortunately (and we hope you've anticipated this), such a survey-based finding wouldn't be informative. It might mean, as dissonance theorists would expect, that undergoing a difficult initiation makes a person feel compelled to embrace the fraternity's virtues. But the finding might instead be the result of the best, most desirable fraternities having the "luxury" of subjecting their pledges to severe initiations. Maybe it's just that people wouldn't tolerate a severe initiation to get into a less attractive fraternity. This is the correlation versus cause problem; it plagues many empirical studies, and savvy consumers of research findings know to anticipate it (see Chapter 2). Only a true experiment—wherein people are randomly assigned to either, say, a "mild initiation" versus "severe initiation" condition—could tell us with great confidence whether more painful initiations lead to greater group loyalty than less painful ones.

(think debit or credit cards) (Shah, Eisencraft, Bettman, & Chartrand, 2016). And when people have to assemble a product (think IKEA) before they can enjoy it, they end up enjoying it more (as long as the assembly is successful and doesn't result in a torrent of cursing) (Norton, Mochon, & Ariely, 2012).

INDUCED COMPLIANCE AND ATTITUDE CHANGE Cognitive dissonance theory can also explain what often happens as a result of **induced (forced) compliance**—that is, when people are induced to behave in a manner that's inconsistent with their beliefs, attitudes, or values. Most people will feel some discomfort with the mismatch between the way they've been induced to behave and their attitudes. One way to deal with the inconsistency—the easiest and most likely way, given that the behavior can't be taken back—is for people to change their original attitudes. This was the idea behind President Johnson's strategy, described in the chapter opening: when skeptics publicly defended the administration's position, the inconsistency between their private reservations and their public comments should lead them to dispel their doubts.

In the first experiment to demonstrate the power of induced compliance to shift people's attitudes, Leon Festinger and Merrill Carlsmith (1959) had participants in a control condition engage in what can only be described as experimental drudgery for an hour (loading spools on a tray over and over, turning pegs on a pegboard one-quarter turn at a time). Immediately afterward, these participants were asked to rate how much they enjoyed the experiment. They gave quite low ratings. No surprise there.

Participants in two other conditions also engaged in the boring task but were subsequently told that the experiment involved how performance on a task is influenced by expectations about it beforehand. These participants were then led to believe they were in a control, "no expectation," condition, but that other subjects were told beforehand the study was either very interesting or boring. Looking rather sheepish, the experimenter then explained that the next participant was about to show up and needed to be told the study was interesting. This was usually done, the experimenter explained, by a confederate posing as a participant. But the confederate was absent, putting the experimenter in a bit of a jam. Would you, the experimenter asked, play the role usually performed by the confederate and tell the next participant that the experiment is interesting? The experimenter offered the participant either $1 or $20 for doing so.

Nearly every participant agreed to the request. In this "play within a play," the true participants believed they were confederates. What was most important to the experiment, and what was readily apparent to the participants, was that they had just been induced to behave in a way that was inconsistent with their true attitude: they lied by saying that a mind-numbingly boring study was interesting. Festinger and Carlsmith predicted that this act would produce dissonance for those participants paid only $1 for the assignment. Their words were inconsistent with their beliefs, and $1 wasn't enough to justify the lie. In contrast, those paid $20 would not have any need to rationalize because the reward was substantial and the lie was of little consequence. To reduce their dissonance, participants in the $1 condition would rationalize their behavior by changing their attitude about the task they had performed. If they convinced themselves the task was interesting after all, their lie wouldn't really be a lie. Consistent with these predictions, when participants in the $1 condition later evaluated their experience, they rated the monotonous tasks more favorably than those in

induced (forced) compliance
Subtly compelling people to behave in a manner that is inconsistent with their beliefs, attitudes, or values in order to elicit dissonance and therefore a change in their original attitudes and values.

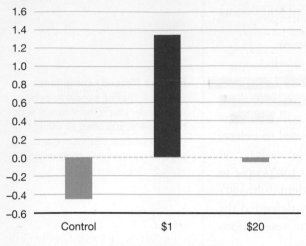

Ratings of enjoyment of tasks

FIGURE 7.2
INDUCED COMPLIANCE AND ATTITUDE CHANGE
Saying something we don't believe, and doing so with little justification ($1 instead of $20), produces dissonance. To reduce this dissonance, in this study the participants in the $1 condition rated the boring task more favorably than participants in the other two conditions, thereby providing some justification for their behavior (they did really lie). Ratings of task enjoyment were made on a −5 (extremely dull and boring) to +5 (extremely interesting and enjoyable) scale.
Source: Adapted from Festinger & Carlsmith, 1959.

the other conditions. Only the participants in the $1 condition rated the activities above the neutral point (**Figure 7.2**).

One takeaway message from this study is that if you want to persuade people to do something (such as take schoolwork seriously, protect the environment, or refrain from using foul language) and you want them to internalize the broader message behind the behavior, you should use the smallest amount of incentive or coercion necessary to get them to do it. In other words, don't go overboard with the incentives. If the inducements are too big, people will justify their behavior accordingly—"it was worth it for the payoff" (like participants in Festinger and Carlsmith's $20 condition)—and they won't have to rationalize their behavior by coming to believe in the broader purpose or philosophy behind it. But if the inducements are just barely sufficient (as in the $1 condition), their need to rationalize will tend to produce attitude change in line with their behavior.

INDUCED COMPLIANCE AND EXTINGUISHING UNDESIRED BEHAVIOR The flip side of this idea involves the use of mild versus severe punishments; this is illustrated by experiments using what is known as the "forbidden toy" paradigm (Aronson & Carlsmith, 1963; Freedman, 1965; Lepper, 1973). In one such study, a researcher showed nursery school children a set of five toys and asked them to say how much they liked each one. He then said he would have to leave the room for a bit, but would be back soon. In the meantime, each child was free to play with any of the toys except his or her second-favorite. Half the kids were told not to play with the forbidden toy because the experimenter would "be annoyed" if they did. This was the "mild threat" condition. In the "severe threat" condition, if the kids played with the forbidden toy, the experimenter "would be very angry" and "would have to take all the toys and go home and never come back again."

While the experimenter was gone, each child was covertly observed, and none played with the forbidden toy. The investigators predicted that not playing with the forbidden toy would produce dissonance, but only for the children in the mild threat condition. For all children, not playing with the toy would be inconsistent with the fact that it was highly desirable, but for those who received the severe threat, the severity of the threat justified not playing with the toy. For children who received only a mild threat, there would be no such justification, producing dissonance, and they would likely resolve the inconsistency by devaluing the toy, convincing themselves it wasn't so great after all.

To find out whether these predictions were correct, the children had to reevaluate all five toys when the experimenter returned. As expected, those in the severe threat condition either didn't change their opinion of the forbidden toy or liked it even more than before (**Figure 7.3**). In contrast, many of those in the mild threat condition viewed the toy less favorably. Thus, the threat of severe punishment will keep children from doing something you don't want them to do; but they will still, later on, want to do it. The threat of mild punishment—if it's just enough of a threat to keep them from doing it—can bring about psychological change, such that they'll no longer be tempted to do what you don't want them to do. Contrary to the old adage, you should spare the rod.

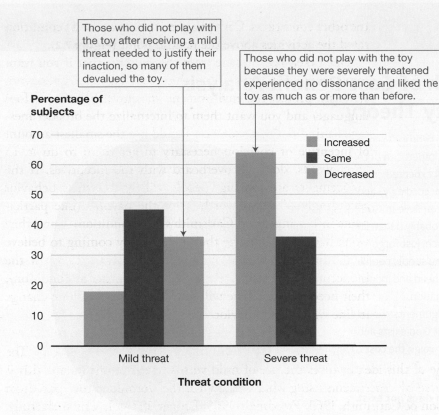

Those who did not play with the toy after receiving a mild threat needed to justify their inaction, so many of them devalued the toy.

Those who did not play with the toy because they were severely threatened experienced no dissonance and liked the toy as much as or more than before.

Percentage of subjects

- Increased
- Same
- Decreased

Threat condition

FIGURE 7.3
DEVALUING THE FORBIDDEN TOY
For this study, the graphs show the percentages of children in the mild and severe threat conditions whose opinion of the forbidden toy increased, stayed the same, or decreased.
Source: Adapted from Aronson & Carlsmith, 1963.

When Does Inconsistency Produce Dissonance?

Festinger's original insight was that holding two inconsistent cognitions triggers dissonance. But what constitutes inconsistency? And what's so jarringly unpleasant about inconsistency? These questions lead us to wonder which situations are likely to cause dissonance and which ones aren't.

Eliot Aronson offered an answer. A given inconsistency will arouse dissonance, Aronson argued, if it implicates our core sense of self (Aronson, 1969; Sherman & Gorkin, 1980). People like to think of themselves as rational, morally upright, worthy individuals, and anything that challenges such assessments tends to produce dissonance (Kouchaki & Gino, 2016). Expending great effort to join a boring group calls into question our wisdom and rationality; telling another student that a tedious task is interesting challenges our integrity.

To understand the sorts of cognitions that might challenge our sense of our good judgment and personal character, it's useful to think about when *someone else's* actions make us question *that person's* character and also to think of the justifications someone else could offer that would *prevent* us from questioning that person's judgment or moral fiber. Suppose you ask a tech-savvy friend to help you with a computer problem, but he says no. How harshly would you judge him? The answer probably depends on several factors. First, you wouldn't blame him if he couldn't have acted otherwise—for example, if he was at work and his boss wouldn't let him leave. He had no choice. Second, you probably wouldn't blame him much if he could justify his actions; perhaps he had to study for a really important exam. He *could* have helped out—he had some choice in the matter— but it's clear that doing so would have been really costly for him. Third, you'd probably judge him more or less harshly in rough proportion to how much harm resulted from his failure to help. You'd (understandably) think worse of him if you ended up failing a course because of it than if you were simply prevented

BOX 7.3 FOCUS ON INTELLECTUAL HISTORY

Pascal's Wager: The Birth of Cost-Benefit Analysis and Cognitive Consistency Theory

In a single stroke Blaise Pascal, the seventeenth-century French mathematician and Catholic philosopher, gave an impetus to both modern cost-benefit analysis (comparing the total expected costs and benefits of different options and choosing accordingly) and cognitive consistency theory. Why should people believe in God? *Benefit*: If God exists and we believe in God, we'll probably behave in such a way to guarantee eternal life. *Cost*: Not much, just forgoing a few guilty pleasures and avoiding some sins. Why should people *not* believe in God? *Benefit*: Not much, just going ahead and indulging in those pleasures and sins. *Cost*: Eternal damnation.

Anyone who accepts the logic of these arguments would agree that it would be foolhardy not to wager that God exists and choose to believe in God. The benefits clearly outweigh the costs.

Payoff Matrix for Pascal's Wager

	God exists	God does not exist
Belief in God	+∞ (infinite gain)	-1 (finite loss)
Disbelief in God	-∞ (infinite loss)	+1 (finite gain)

BLAISE PASCAL

The problem, however, is that logically concluding that it pays to believe in God may not be enough to make a person truly believe. Pascal recognized that some people will say, "Try as I might, I simply cannot believe. What can I do?" As a solution, Pascal appealed to a version of what we would now call cognitive consistency theory, advising nonbelievers to behave as believers do: pray, light candles, attend church. If they behaved in such a way, Pascal reasoned, their beliefs would change to be consistent with their behavior. Problem solved. (But note that although Pascal was on to something very important about people's need for cognitive consistency, scholars such as Voltaire and Diderot had no difficulty spotting and articulating logical flaws in Pascal's argument for believing in God.)

---

from checking Facebook or surfing the Internet. Finally, you wouldn't blame him much if you'd never told him just how badly you needed his help; after all, he had no way to foresee the harm his refusal might cause.

This analysis of when we hold other people responsible for their actions helps us understand when we will hold *ourselves* responsible for our behavior and experience dissonance as a result. Specifically, this analysis suggests that we ought to experience dissonance whenever we act in ways that are inconsistent with our core values and beliefs and (1) the behavior was freely chosen, (2) the behavior wasn't sufficiently justified, (3) the behavior had negative consequences, and (4) the negative consequences were foreseeable.

FREE CHOICE The critical role of freedom of choice was first demonstrated (and replicated many times) in a study in which college students were offered either $0.50 or $2.50 to write an essay in favor of a state law banning communists from speaking on college campuses (Linder, Cooper, & Jones, 1967). (Since the original experiment was done in the mid-1960s, both payments seem low now;

for comparable amounts today, it would be reasonable to multiply by a factor of 8: $4 and $20, respectively.) Because the law was at variance with the U.S. Constitution's guarantee of freedom of speech, nearly all students were opposed to it, and their essays thus conflicted with their true beliefs. For half the participants, their freedom to agree (or decline) to write such an essay was emphasized. For the other half, it was not. There was no dissonance effect among participants for whom their freedom to agree or decline was *not* emphasized. Indeed, those paid $2.50 later expressed attitudes more in favor of the ban than those paid $0.50 (presumably because writing the essay was associated with the good feelings that accompany the larger reward). In the free-choice group, however, the standard dissonance effect was obtained: those paid $0.50 changed their attitude more than those paid $2.50.

INSUFFICIENT JUSTIFICATION This last experiment, like all the induced-compliance studies (including Festinger and Carlsmith's original $1/$20 study), also demonstrates the role of insufficient justification in arousing dissonance. If a person's behavior is justified by a powerful incentive of some sort, even behavior that dramatically conflicts with the person's beliefs won't produce dissonance. Those paid $2.50 (about $20 today) for writing an essay that was inconsistent with their true beliefs felt no pressure to change their attitudes because their behavior was justified by the large cash payment. Those paid only $0.50 (about $4 today) had no such justification and thus felt the full weight of their behavioral inconsistency.

NEGATIVE CONSEQUENCES If nothing of consequence results from actions that are at variance with our attitudes and values, it's easy to dismiss them as trivial. Indeed, studies show that people experience dissonance only when their behavior results in harm of some sort. One such study, using Festinger and Carlsmith's paradigm, induced participants to tell someone (who was actually an associate working with the researchers) that a boring experiment was very interesting by offering either a small or a large incentive for doing so (Cooper & Worchel, 1970). Half the time, the confederate appeared convinced that the boring task was going to be interesting, and half the time the confederate clearly remained unconvinced: "Well, you're entitled to your own opinion, but I don't think I've ever enjoyed an experiment, and I don't think I'll find this one much fun." Note that there were no negative consequences when the person appeared unconvinced: no one was deceived. So, if negative consequences are necessary for the arousal of dissonance, the standard dissonance effect should occur only when the person is convinced and the participant feels like a deceiver. That's exactly what happened: the boring task was rated more favorably only by participants who were offered little incentive to lie to another person and the person appeared to believe the lie.

FORESEEABILITY We typically don't hold people responsible for harm they've done if the harm wasn't foreseeable. If a dinner guest who is allergic to peanuts becomes ill after eating a dish with peanut sauce, we don't hold the host responsible if the guest never informed the host of the allergy. As this example suggests, it may be the *foreseeability of the negative consequences of our actions that generates* cognitive dissonance. Negative consequences that aren't foreseeable don't threaten a person's self-image as a moral and decent person, so they shouldn't arouse dissonance.

Supporting this reasoning are experiments in which participants are induced to write an essay in favor of a position to which they are opposed (for example, that the size of the freshman class at their university should be doubled). If any negative consequences of such an action (the essays will be shown to a university committee charged with deciding whether to implement the policy) are made known to the participants after the fact, there's no dissonance and hence no attitude change in the direction of the essay they wrote. But if the negative consequences were either foreseen (participants knew beforehand that their letters would be shown to the committee) or foreseeable (they knew ahead of time that their letters *might* be shown to such a committee), the standard dissonance effect was obtained (Cooper, 1971; Goethals, Cooper, & Naficy, 1979).

Self-Affirmation and Dissonance

If dissonance results from threats to people's sense of themselves as rational, competent, and moral beings, it follows that they can ward off dissonance not only by dealing directly with the specific threat itself, but also indirectly by taking stock of their other qualities and core values. As we learned in Chapter 3, Claude Steele and his colleagues have argued that this sort of self-affirmation is a common way for people to cope with threats to their self-esteem (Cohen & Sherman, 2014; Correll, Spencer, & Zanna, 2004; McQueen & Klein, 2006; Steele, 1988). "Sure, I might have violated a friend's confidence, but I'm very empathetic when other people are having difficulties." "I know I drive an SUV, but no one attends church services more regularly than I do." By bolstering themselves in one area, people can tolerate a bigger hit in another.

Recent research has examined how self-affirmation can assuage the need to reduce dissonance in a situation that will be familiar to many

AFFIRMING THE SELF, WARDING OFF DISSONANCE
This pro-environment couple may ward off any dissonance that might get aroused by their choice to drive an SUV by reminding themselves how devoted they are to their church and its good works.

of us. Imagine you're having a conversation with someone—a coworker, friend, family member—and in the course of the conversation the person makes a prejudicial remark with which you strongly disagree. Do you confront the person or let the remark pass? Let's be honest: we often let remarks like this slide because confrontation is uncomfortable and can have interpersonal costs (Czopp & Ashburn-Nardo, 2012). But for those of us who think it's important to confront prejudice, not doing so arouses dissonance, and we start rationalizing our failure to act. And that's exactly what researchers have shown: people who value confronting prejudice but fail to do so end up evaluating the person making the prejudicial remark more favorably—and even reduce the importance they place on confronting prejudice in the first place (Rasinski, Geers, & Czopp, 2013). There's good news though. These researchers also showed that a simple self-affirmation intervention—giving nonconfronters a few minutes to make a list of their positive characteristics—eliminated the need to reduce the dissonance arising from their failure to confront.

Is Dissonance Universal?

We have discussed cognitive dissonance as if it were a cross-culturally universal phenomenon. Is it? Research on this question has yielded some interesting answers. Using the free-choice, self-affirmation paradigm, researchers asked all the participants in a study to choose between two objects (CDs, in this case) to see if they would exhibit the dissonance effect by rationalizing their decision as the correct one. The researchers, however, first gave some participants self-affirmation in the form of positive feedback on a personality test (Heine & Lehman, 1997). The participants were Japanese and Canadian, and the researchers wanted to see if the dissonance effect was the same in people from these two different cultures. The results for the Canadians were similar to those in earlier studies: they showed a substantial dissonance effect in the control condition, finding previously unnoticed attractions in the chosen CD and previously unnoticed flaws in the unchosen one, but no dissonance effect if they had received positive feedback about their personalities. The Japanese participants, in contrast, were unaffected by the self-affirmation manipulation. More striking still, they showed no dissonance effect in *either* condition, which led the researchers to conclude that dissonance might be a phenomenon unique to Westerners. But using an induced-compliance paradigm, researchers in another study persuaded participants to do something they didn't want to do and found dissonance effects for Japanese participants—if they were led to think that other students were observing their behavior (Sakai, 1981).

As we have emphasized throughout this book, East Asians, along with many other people in the world, are more attuned than Westerners are to other people and their reactions. If East Asians exhibit dissonance effects in the induced-compliance paradigm because they question their actions when others are observing them, then they should also show dissonance effects in the free-choice paradigm if they are led to think about other people's possible reactions to their choice.

This outcome was demonstrated in a study in which investigators had participants choose between two CDs under one of two circumstances (Kitayama, Snibbe, Markus, & Suzuki, 2004). For some participants, hanging right in front of them at eye level was the poster shown in **Figure 7.4** (see p. 226), allegedly a prop from an unrelated experiment. But in actuality, the researchers wanted to see whether the schematic faces in the poster might prime the concept of "social others," thereby prompting the Japanese participants to show a dissonance effect. And that's what happened: in the standard free-choice condition, the Japanese showed no evidence of dissonance reduction, but in the poster condition they did. American participants actually showed the same or even slightly less dissonance reduction in the poster condition than in the standard condition.

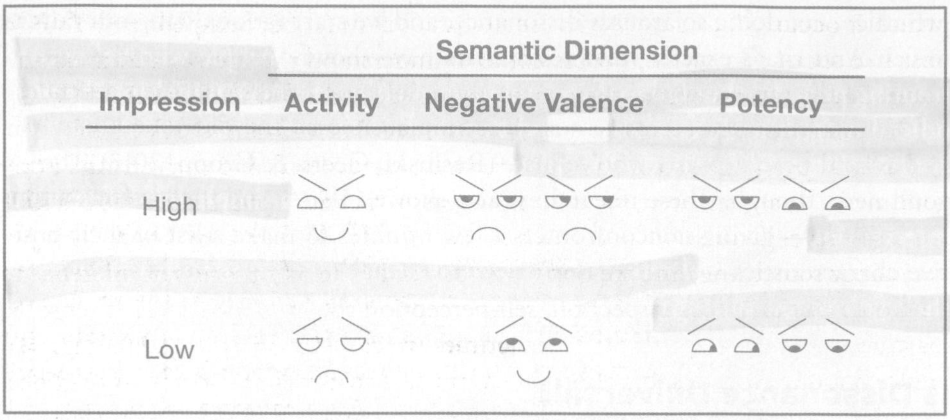

	Semantic Dimension			
Impression	Activity	Negative Valence		Potency
High				
Low				

FIGURE 7.4
CULTURE AND PRIMING
This is the poster used by researchers to prime the idea of "social others." The labels were included simply to make the poster look like part of another, unrelated experiment.
Source: Adapted from Kitayama et al., 2004.

Another research team observed a similar effect of social priming when they had participants choose a CD either for themselves or for a friend (Hoshino-Browne, Zanna, Spencer, & Zanna, 2004). Euro-Canadians, as well as Asian-Canadians who only weakly identified themselves as Asians, showed much larger dissonance effects when choosing for themselves than when choosing for a friend; but Asian-Canadians who strongly identified themselves as Asians showed much larger dissonance effects when choosing for a friend than when choosing for themselves.

← LOOKING BACK

Behavior can have a powerful influence on attitudes, largely because people like their attitudes to be consistent with their behavior. Inconsistency between cognitions, values, or actions usually produces cognitive dissonance. We can reduce dissonance by changing our attitudes to be in line with our behavior. Dissonance is more pronounced when the inconsistency implies that the self is deficient in some way. Therefore, when we can affirm the self somehow, we are less susceptible to dissonance. Different circumstances arouse dissonance in people of different cultures.

Self-Perception Theory

Like all prominent theories that have been around for a long time, cognitive dissonance theory has faced many theoretical challenges, and there have been numerous critiques. One critique, however, stands out above all others in its impact: Daryl Bem's self-perception theory (Bem, 1967, 1972). The theory began as an alternative account of all of the cognitive dissonance findings, but it has important implications for self-understanding more generally, and it offers novel explanations for many real-life choices and behaviors.

Inferring Our Own Attitudes

self-perception theory The theory that people come to know their own attitudes by looking at their behavior and the context in which it occurred and inferring what their attitudes must be.

According to Bem's **self-perception theory**, people don't always come to know their own attitudes by introspecting about what they think or how they feel about something. Rather, they often look outward, at their behavior and the context in which it occurred, and *infer* what their attitudes must be. Self-perception works just like social perception. People come to understand themselves and their attitudes in the same way that they come to understand others and their attitudes.

At first this idea seems bizarre—as implausible as the old joke about two behavioral psychologists who've just finished having sex: one turns to the other and says, "That was great for you, how was it for me?" The theory feels wrong on a gut level because we're convinced that sometimes we "just know" how we feel about something, and we don't need to engage in any process of inference to find out. But on closer inspection, self-perception theory makes a lot of sense, in part because Bem concedes that sometimes we can just analyze our thoughts to figure out our attitudes. It's only when our prior attitudes are "weak, ambiguous, and uninterpretable," he argues, that "the individual is functionally in the same position as an outside observer" (Bem, 1972, p. 2).

This caveat is helpful. Most of us can remember times when we figured out how we felt about something by examining our behavior. "I guess I was hungrier than I thought," you might say after downing a second bacon cheeseburger. The key question, then, is whether the inference process that is the focus of self-perception theory applies only to such trivial matters as these or whether the process operates when we grapple with attitudes of substance, such as working on a political campaign or choosing to buy a particular car.

Bem's account of dissonance effects is quite simple. He argues that people aren't troubled by any unpleasant state of arousal like dissonance; they merely engage in a rational inference process. They don't *change* their attitudes; rather, they infer what their attitudes must be. People value what they have chosen more after having chosen it because they infer that "If I chose this, I must like it." People form tight bonds to groups that have unpleasant initiation rituals because they reason that "If I suffered to get this, I must have felt it was worth it." And people who have little incentive to tell someone a task is interesting come to view the task more favorably because they conclude that "There's no other reason I would say this is interesting if it wasn't, so it really must be."

In support of this explanation, Bem showed that when *observer-subjects* (participants who only observe a situation versus actually experiencing it for themselves) read descriptions of dissonance experiments and are asked what attitude a participant would have had, the observer-subjects replicate the attitudes of the actual participants (Bem, 1967, 1972). They assume, for example, that a person who was paid only $1 to say that working on a boring task was interesting would have more favorable attitudes toward the task than a person paid $20. Bem reasoned that if the observers come up with the same inferences about attitudes as the attitudes reported by the actual participants, there's no reason to assume the participants themselves arrived at their beliefs because they were motivated to reduce dissonance.

Reconciling the Dissonance and Self-Perception Accounts

As already noted, cognitive dissonance theory states that the inconsistency between behavior and prior attitudes or values produces an unpleasant physiological state that motivates people to reduce the inconsistency. If there's no unpleasant psychological arousal, there's no attitude change. Self-perception theory, in contrast, contends that no arousal is involved: people coolly and rationally

infer what their attitudes must be in light of their behavior and the context in which it occurred. Therefore, any decisive test to determine which of the two theories is more accurate should focus on whether people experience arousal in the standard dissonance paradigms (for example, the induced-compliance paradigm) and in similar everyday situations.

Considerable evidence indicates that, as dissonance theory predicts, acting at variance with our true beliefs does indeed generate arousal (Elliot & Devine, 1994; Galinsky, Stone, & Cooper, 2000; Harmon-Jones, 2000; Norton, Monin, Cooper, & Hogg, 2003; Waterman, 1969). Dissonance arousal has been detected with explicit, self-report measures (Elliot & Devine, 1994), as well as with more implicit measures, such as recordings of the electromyographic (EMG) activity of facial muscles associated with arousal (Martinie, Oliver, Milland, Joule, & Capa, 2013). And there's evidence that efforts to dispel such arousal and restore consistency motivates the types of attitude change found in dissonance experiments (Harmon-Jones, Brehm, Greenberg, Simon, & Nelson, 1996). It thus appears that dissonance theory is the proper account of the phenomena observed in these experiments (and their real-world counterparts), not self-perception theory.

But self-perception theory and the studies Bem offered in support of his theory capture some important aspects of how the mind works. In fact, a consensus has emerged among social psychologists that dissonance reduction processes and self-perception processes both occur, and both of them influence people's attitudes and broader views of themselves. Dissonance reduction processes are activated when behavior is inconsistent with preexisting attitudes that are clear-cut and of some importance. Self-perception processes, in contrast, are invoked when behavior conflicts with attitudes that are relatively vague or of less import (Chaiken & Baldwin, 1981; Fazio, Zanna, & Cooper, 1977).

This consensus view might make it seem as if self-perception processes are relegated to the trivial fringe of social life. They aren't. Substantial research has made it clear that a surprising proportion of our attitudes *are* rather weak and ambiguous. Although self-perception processes typically influence unimportant attitudes more than important ones, at times they do influence important attitudes—and important subsequent behavior. For example, studies have shown that we exhibit the self-perception process—inferring our own attitudes by observing our behavior—when it comes to such important areas as whether we're likely to contribute to the public good (Freedman & Fraser, 1966; Uranowitz, 1975), whether we're likely to cheat to reach a goal (Dienstbier & Munter, 1971; Lepper, 1973; see **Box 7.4**, p. 230), our judgments of the precise emotion we're feeling and how strongly we feel it (Dutton & Aron, 1974; Schachter & Singer, 1962), our assessments of our own personality traits (Schwarz et al., 1991), and whether we truly enjoy an activity we have engaged in our entire life (Lepper & Greene, 1978).

In addition, the crux of self-perception theory—that we use whatever cues we have available to us to figure out what we think and how we feel, including knowledge of the surrounding context and how we've acted—fits with a tremendous amount of recent evidence that our thoughts and feelings are affected by, even grounded in, our physical states and bodily movements. This area of inquiry, on "embodied" cognition and emotion, is currently being pursued in many areas of psychology.

The Embodied Nature of Cognition and Emotion

A variety of physical actions are associated with different psychological states. When we're happy, we tend to smile; if we don't like something, we're inclined to push it away; and if we agree with something, we nod our head up and down. This is the behavioral component of attitudes discussed earlier: the motor actions of smiling, pushing, and nodding *are important parts of* our attitudes. As a result, if we're induced to make the bodily movements associated with certain attitudes, beliefs, or emotions, we might come to have, or find it easier to have, those very attitudes, beliefs, or emotions. In other words, in figuring out what we think, feel, or believe, we draw on whatever cues are available to us—including what our body is doing—without being consciously aware that we are doing so.

In one early demonstration of this effect, Gary Wells and Richard Petty (1980) had students ostensibly test a set of headphones by moving their heads up and down or side to side while listening to radio editorials. When later asked about the viewpoints advocated in the editorials, the students indicated that they agreed with them more if they'd listened to them while nodding their heads up and down than if they'd listened while shaking their heads from side to side.

Other researchers have explored the implications of our tendency to push away things we find aversive and pull toward us things we find appealing (see Chapter 1). Because extending the arm is closely associated with negative stimuli (things we want to push away) and flexing the arm is associated with positive stimuli (things we want to pull toward us), being induced to make these bodily movements can have predictable effects on attitudes. In one study, John Cacioppo, Joseph Priester, and Gary Berntson (1993) showed college students a series of 24 Chinese ideographs while they were either pressing down on a table (arm extension) or lifting up on a table from underneath (arm flexion). The students evaluated

EMBODIED COGNITION AND EMOTION
This runner's pride at winning the race is easily discerned from his outstretched arms, a physical embodiment of pride seen across cultures.

BOX 7.4 FOCUS ON EDUCATION

The Overjustification Effect and Superfluous Rewards

If you dropped in on a family dinner in a foreign country and heard a parent tell a child she had to eat her *pfunst* before she could eat her *pfeffatorst*, you'd immediately conclude that the youngster didn't like *pfunst* but loved *pfeffatorst*. Things people do only to get something else are typically things they don't particularly like. But what happens if the child actually likes *pfunst*? Because the parents are making her eat *pfunst* in order to have the privilege of eating *pfeffatorst*, she might decide maybe *pfunst* isn't so great after all.

Self-perception theory makes just such a prediction, and this tendency to devalue those activities we perform, even if they are pleasing, in order to get something else is known as the *overjustification effect* (Lepper, Greene, & Nisbett, 1973). The initial justification for performing the pleasing activity (eating *pfunst*) is evident: we would do it because it's inherently rewarding—this is the intrinsic reason we do it. But we also do it because there's an external payoff (eating *pfeffatorst*)—this is the extrinsic reason. Because the extrinsic reason would be sufficient to produce the behavior, we might discount the intrinsic reason and conclude that we don't much like the activity for its own sake.

Particularly intriguing evidence for the overjustification effect comes from a study of children's choice of activities in school. Investigators showed two attractive drawing activities to elementary school children. In one condition, the researchers told the children they could first do one drawing activity and then the other. In a second condition, they were told they *must* do one activity *in order to* do the other. (In both conditions, the experimenters counterbalanced which activity came first.) For several days after this initial drawing session, the experimenters put out both drawing activities during the school's free-play period and covertly observed how long the children played with each activity. Those who earlier had simply drawn first with one and then the other played with both activities equally often. But those who earlier had used one *in order to* use the other tended to avoid the former (Lepper, Sagotsky, Dafoe, & Greene, 1982). Their intrinsic interest in the first drawing activity had been undermined.

The overjustification effect has important implications for how rewards should be used in education and raising children. It's common practice, for example, to reward children for reading books, getting good grades, or practicing the piano. That's fine if the child wouldn't otherwise read, study, or practice. But if the child has some interest in these activities to begin with, the rewards might put that interest in jeopardy. In one powerful demonstration of this danger, researchers introduced a set of novel math games into the free-play portion of an elementary school curriculum. As **Figure 7.5** shows, the children initially found the games interesting, as indicated by the amount of time they played with them at the outset of the experiment (baseline phase). Then, for several days afterward, the investigators instituted a "token-economy" program whereby the children could earn points redeemable for prizes by playing with the math games. The more they played, the more points they earned. The token-economy program was effective in increasing how much the children played the games (green bar in the treatment phase). But what happened when the token-economy program was terminated and the children no longer earned points for playing the games? Would they still play with them as much? As the blue bar indicates, they did not. Having once received rewards for these activities, the children came to see the math games as something

the ideographs presented while they flexed their arms more favorably than those presented while they extended their arms (see also Chen & Bargh, 1999; Epley & Gilovich, 2004; Friedman & Forster, 2000). Effects like these challenge the idea (as self-perception theory does) that our attitudes, knowledge, and beliefs are stored as abstract propositions or representations in the brain. They support an alternative view that our attitudes and beliefs, and even the most abstract concepts, are partly "embodied" in the physical movements associated with those attitudes, beliefs, or concepts (Barsalou, 2008; Niedenthal, Barsalou, Winkielman, Krauth-Gruber, & Ric, 2005). Part of the attitude of disapproval or the belief that we don't like something is represented in the physical act of pushing away. Even our understanding of sentences like "He raced down the corridor" is grounded in the physical act of running. When people read such a sentence, motor regions associated with running become ever so slightly activated, and when they read "Raymond picked up the Easter egg," brain areas involved in

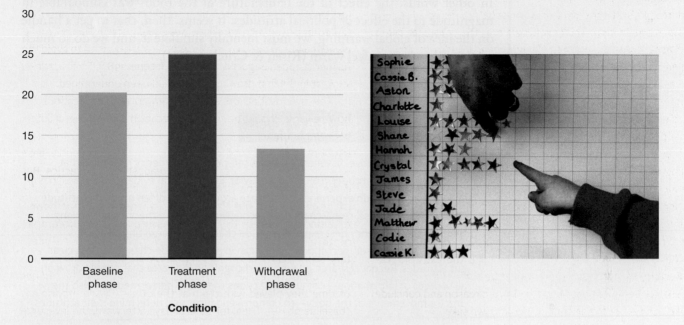

Time spent playing with math games (in minutes)

Condition: Baseline phase, Treatment phase, Withdrawal phase

FIGURE 7.5 The Effects of Superfluous Rewards This graph shows the amount of time elementary school children spent playing math games originally (baseline phase), when they received rewards for playing them (treatment phase), and afterward (withdrawal phase).
SOURCE: Adapted from Greene et al., 1976.

to do only to get a reward, and their original interest was diminished (Greene, Sternberg, & Lepper, 1976).

Such findings don't imply that giving out rewards is always a bad thing. People aren't always intrinsically motivated, and when they aren't, rewards are often the best way to get them to do something they would not otherwise do. Rewards can also be administered in ways that minimize their negative impact. For instance, rewards can be performance contingent, or based on how well someone performs. These have been shown to be less likely to decrease interest in an activity than task-contingent rewards, which are simply based on doing a task or not (Deci & Ryan, 1985; Sansone & Harackiewicz, 2000).

grasping become activated (Speer, Reynolds, Swallow, & Zacks, 2009). This explains why people who have had Botox injections (which smooth out wrinkles in the face by immobilizing facial muscles) have a harder time processing sentences containing emotion. Without being able themselves to mimic the emotional expressions as they are reading, the very concepts of sad, angry, and so on, are a bit harder to access and comprehend (Havas, Glenberg, Gutowski, Lucarelli, & Davidson, 2010).

Thus, the seemingly abstract, cognitive act of comprehension isn't always abstract. To understand something—whether an abstract proposition, a sentence of text, or a possible future state of the world (like cars being self-driven)—people must mentally "try it on," or simulate it. And what our body is doing or how it's feeling can facilitate or impede the act of simulation, influencing what we think and feel. Consider the finding that people believe more in the reality of global warming and see it as a more serious threat on hotter days than on cooler days (Li, Johnson, & Zaval, 2011; Risen & Critcher, 2011). In one study, participants were inside a laboratory where the thermostat was set to either 81 or 73 degrees Fahrenheit. Respondents in the warmer room expressed greater belief in global warming. The effect was strong enough that conservatives in a warm room expressed the same concern about the problem as liberals in a cold room. In other words, the effect of the temperature of the room was comparable in magnitude to the effect of political attitudes. It seems, then, that to get a handle on the idea of global warming, we must mentally simulate it, and we do so much more easily when we feel warm (Risen & Critcher, 2011).

← LOOKING BACK

In contrast to cognitive dissonance theory, self-perception theory maintains that people infer their attitudes from their behavior. Experimental evidence, however, has shown that people do experience dissonance arousal and it often motivates attitude change. Nevertheless, researchers have reconciled these two theories by showing that dissonance theory best explains attitude change for preexisting clear-cut attitudes, whereas self-perception theory can explain attitude change for less clear-cut attitudes. Recent research on embodied cognition indicates that people draw on all sources of information—not just the actions they have performed, but also the precise movements of the body—to comprehend ideas and determine their attitudes.

Beyond Cognitive Consistency to Broader Rationalization

The core of dissonance theory is the idea that people find cognitive inconsistency uncomfortable and therefore try to find ways to relieve the discomfort. Other kinds of tension, of course, can also produce uneasiness, and social psychologists have advanced theories about how we respond to these other sources of discomfort. One deals with the uneasiness that arises when thinking about the problems associated with the broader sociopolitical system to which we are committed. Another deals with the extreme anxiety—indeed, the terror—that can accompany thinking about the inevitability of death.

System Justification Theory

Chapter 3 discusses our need to think well of ourselves, or what some have called ego justification motives (Jost, Banaji, & Nosek, 2004; Jost & van der Toorn, 2012). Chapter 11 discusses our need to think well of the groups to which we belong, or group justification motives. But beyond the desire to think highly of our own talents or to take pride in being, say, a Canadian, a Christian, or a conservative, we want to think highly of the larger sociopolitical system we are part of—we want to see it as fair, just, and desirable (Jost & Banaji, 1994; Jost et al., 2004).

Social psychologists who have studied these tendencies recognize that social and political systems don't serve everyone's needs equally. Those who benefit the most from a given system, such as the wealthier and more powerful people in society, have both a psychological motive and an economic incentive to defend the system. People who don't benefit from the system (or are even disadvantaged by it) obviously don't have an economic incentive to defend the system, but they do have a psychological incentive to do so. According to **system justification theory**, believing that the world is or should be fair, combined with abundant evidence of inequality, can generate a fair amount of ideological dissonance. Extolling the virtues of the prevailing system is typically an easier way of reducing that dissonance than bringing about effective change. Protest is hard; justification is easy.

Common observations that seem to support system justification theory are the fact that many women report that they deserve lower pay than men doing the same work (Hogue, DuBois, & Fox-Cardamone, 2010; Jost, 1997; Major, 1994; O'Brien, Major, & Gilbert, 2012) and the fact that low-income groups in the United States don't necessarily support more egalitarian economic policies over the status quo (Fong, 2001; Jost, Pelham, Sheldon, & Sullivan, 2003; Rodriguez-Bailon et al., 2017). Some of the most interesting support for the system justification perspective comes from studies that look at compensatory stereotypes, or beliefs that those who occupy less privileged roles in a society nonetheless derive a number of compensatory benefits: "Low-income people may be poor, but they're happier than the wealthy." "Women may not have much power, but they're nicer, warmer, and more socially connected than men." These stereotypes give ideological support to the status quo, making people more accepting of current gender roles and more accepting of the broader sociocultural status quo (Jost & Kay, 2005; Kay & Jost, 2003).

SYSTEM JUSTIFICATION
To defend the prevailing sociopolitical system to which they belong, economically disadvantaged people often defend their own disadvantage. For example, sometimes women, such as the nurse shown here, report feeling they deserve to make less money than their male counterparts doing the same work.

system justification theory The theory that people are motivated to see the existing sociopolitical system as desirable, fair, and legitimate.

Terror Management Theory

Humans may be the only organisms who know with certainty that they will die. For many people, thinking about the inevitability of their own death—really pondering it and letting it sink in—brings on a level of anxiety that verges on debilitating. **Terror management theory (TMT)** specifies what people do to deal with the potentially crippling anxiety associated with the knowledge of death, in order to get on with their life.

The most common approach is denial—to maintain that it's only the physical body and this particular earthly existence that will come to an end. Many people, all around the world, believe they will go on living in some form after life on Earth is over. But beyond this common form of what has been called "the denial of death" (Becker, 1973), people can derive some solace from believing that although they personally will cease to exist, many of the things they value will live on. For many, this sort of indirect immortality is achieved by thinking about their parental role. They won't live on, but their children and grandchildren will. This viewpoint may explain why men who are reminded of the inevitability of their own death express an interest in having more children (Wisman & Goldenberg, 2005).

terror management theory (TMT) The theory that people deal with the potentially crippling anxiety associated with the knowledge of the inevitability of death by striving for symbolic immortality through preserving valued cultural worldviews and believing they have lived up to the culture's standards.

TMT further emphasizes that people try to achieve symbolic immortality by thinking of themselves as connected to a broader culture, worldview, and set of values. We will certainly die at some point, but many of the things we value most—our country; freedom and democracy; Christianity, Judiasm, Buddhism, or Islam; or even our alma mater or favorite sports team—will live on long after we ourselves do. To the extent that people are closely connected to such institutions, they symbolically live on along with them. Indeed, people tend to vigorously embrace their broader worldview and cultural institutions when reminded of their own inevitable death.

But to live on, even symbolically, with a broader cultural institution, we must be a member "in good standing" with the institution—or at least think we are. It's only when we feel good about who we are that we can feel meaningfully connected to the institutions and worldviews we care about and thus feel a sense of symbolic immortality. Terror management theory therefore maintains that we should be especially concerned with striving to achieve and maintain high self-esteem when our mortality is brought to mind, or made salient.

"The future's uncertain and the end is always near."
—THE DOORS, "ROADHOUSE BLUES"

Terror management theorists have tested their ideas by subjecting participants to manipulations intended to make their mortality salient. The most common manipulation is to have participants write out responses to two directives: "Briefly describe the emotions that the thought of your own death arouses in you" and "Jot down, as specifically as you can, what you think will happen to *you* as you physically die." In other studies, participants have been asked to fill out surveys in front of a funeral home—a location associated with death—or they've been shown pictures of fatal car accidents.

Consistent with the tenets of TMT, mortality salience manipulations have been shown to make people more hostile to those who criticize their country (Greenberg et al., 1990), more committed to their ingroups and more hostile to outgroups (Dechesne, Greenberg, Arndt, & Schimel, 2000; Greenberg et al., 1990), more eager to punish those who challenge prevailing laws and established procedures (Rosenblatt, Greenberg, Solomon, Pyszczynski, & Lyon, 1989), and more reluctant to use cultural artifacts such as a crucifix or the U.S. flag for a mundane, utilitarian purpose (Greenberg, Simon, Porteus, Pyszczynski, & Solomon, 1995). Making death salient, in other words, makes people want to uphold the values of the institutions they identify with and that will live on after them.

MORTALITY SALIENCE AND NATIONALISM
This outpouring of nationalist sentiment during this multi-denominational prayer service at Yankee Stadium following the 9/11 attacks on the World Trade Center and the Pentagon may have been partly fueled by the very salient reminder of our own mortality the attacks provided.

It isn't hard to think of potential political implications of terror management concerns. For example, in the run-up to the 2004 U.S. presidential election, survey respondents gave their opinions about either the Democratic challenger, John Kerry, or the incumbent Republican, George W. Bush (Landau, Solomon, Greenberg, Cohen, & Pyszczynski, 2004). Some participants responded after their mortality was made salient, and others did so after writing about their experience with dental pain. Because Bush, as the incumbent president, was the head of the country and was seen by many as the leader of the fight against al-Qaeda and other terrorist organizations, the investigators predicted that survey respondents would be more favorable to Bush and less favorable to Kerry after a mortality salience manipulation. As **Figure 7.6** indicates, this prediction was confirmed.

There's also support for TMT's contention that mortality salience increases striving for self-esteem (Arndt, Schimel, & Goldenberg, 2003; Kasser & Sheldon, 2000; Taubman-Ben-Ari, Florian, & Mikulincer, 1999). In one study, participants in one condition read an essay stating that the scientific consensus on reports of near-death experiences—such as feelings of leaving and looking down at one's body—is that such sensations are expected, given the makeup of the brain, and they don't suggest in any way the existence of life after death (Dechesne et al., 2003). Participants in another condition read an essay arguing that such reports point to the plausibility of some sort of life after death. Next, all participants received favorable feedback about themselves from unreliable sources, such as horoscopes, and then rated the source's validity. Those who read the essay that cast doubt on life after death rated the feedback as more valid than those who read the essay that encouraged belief in an afterlife. In other words, if we can believe there is life after death, we needn't be so concerned with living on symbolically, so the need for self-esteem is reduced.

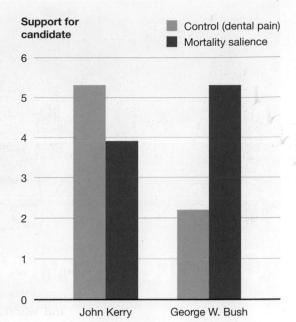

FIGURE 7.6
MORTALITY SALIENCE AND SUPPORT FOR CANDIDATES IN THE 2004 U.S. PRESIDENTIAL ELECTION
Survey respondents reported their attitudes toward presidential candidates John Kerry and George W. Bush either under normal survey conditions or after a mortality salience manipulation.
Source: Adapted from Landau et al., 2004.

← LOOKING BACK

The tendency to rationalize goes beyond our attempts to resolve personal cognitive inconsistencies. We are motivated to see the broader sociopolitical system in which we live as fair and just and good. We're also motivated to deal with the anxiety that comes from being reminded of our mortality, and we often do so by adhering more closely to our worldviews and finding ways to boost our self-esteem.

Chapter Review

SUMMARY

Components and Measurement of Attitudes

- An *attitude* is an evaluation of an object along a positive-negative dimension; it includes three core components: affect (emotion), cognition (thoughts and knowledge), and behavior (the tendency to approach or avoid the object).
- Attitudes can be measured with self-report *Likert scales*. Their strength or importance can be assessed with *response latencies* that capture attitude accessibility (how readily the attitude can become active in an individual's mind). Attitude linkage measures gauge attitude centrality (how closely an attitude is correlated to attitudes about other issues). *Implicit attitude measures* tap into attitudes people are unaware they have or may be unwilling to report.

Predicting Behavior from Attitudes

- It can be hard to predict behavior from attitudes because attitudes can conflict with other powerful determinants of behavior; the reasons underlying our attitudes can be difficult to pinpoint; and attitudes and behaviors may be at different levels of generality.

Predicting Attitudes from Behavior

- Behavior can have substantial effects on attitudes. Cognitive consistency theories emphasize how much people value consistency between their various attitudes and between their attitudes and behavior.
- *Cognitive dissonance theory* is based on the idea that people experience dissonance, or discomfort, when attitudes and behavior are inconsistent. To reduce the dissonance, people try bringing their attitudes in line with their behavior.
- After making a difficult choice between two objects or courses of action, people engage in dissonance reduction by finding new attractions in the chosen alternative and previously undetected flaws in the unchosen alternative.
- People engage in *effort justification* when they exert effort toward some goal and the goal turns out to be disappointing. They justify their expenditure of energy by deciding the goal is truly worthwhile.
- *Induced (forced) compliance* leads to a need to reduce dissonance. When induced to argue for a position at variance with their true attitudes, those who are poorly compensated feel they must justify their behavior and typically do so by changing their attitudes to align better with their behavior.
- Inconsistency between attitudes and behavior should produce dissonance only when there is free choice (or the illusion of it) to engage in the behavior, when there is insufficient justification for the behavior, when the behavior has negative consequences, and when the consequences were foreseeable.
- People can offset or reduce the negative effects of psychological inconsistency, and of threats to self-identity and self-esteem more generally, by engaging in self-affirmation: affirming other important elements of identity, such as values.
- Dissonance is apparently universal, but there are cultural differences in the conditions that prompt people to experience it. The Japanese tend to experience post-decision dissonance only when asked to think about what another person would choose.

Self-Perception Theory

- *Self-perception theory* is based on the premise that people change their attitudes to align with their behavior because they observe their behavior and the circumstances in which it occurs and then infer, just as an observer might, what their attitudes must be.
- Whereas self-perception may play a role in generating the effects in some dissonance experiments, evidence indicates that there is often a motivational component as well. Self-perception appears to account for attitude change when attitudes are weak or unclear to begin with, and more motivated dissonance reduction is invoked when attitudes are more strongly held.
- Bodily sensations are often incorporated into people's judgments about an object or appraisal of a situation.

Beyond Cognitive Consistency to Broader Rationalization

- According to *system justification theory*, people are motivated to justify the broader sociopolitical system of which they are a part. One way is through stereotypes that play up the advantages of belonging to relatively disadvantaged groups, such as the belief that the poor are happier than the rich.

- The certainty of mortality can elicit paralyzing anxiety. *Terror management theory* maintains that people often cope with this anxiety by striving for symbolic immortality through their offspring and through their identification with institutions and cultural worldviews that live on after their own death.

THINK ABOUT IT

1. Consider an attitude object you feel strongly about, something you love or something you hate. Maybe you're passionate about soccer. Perhaps you are staunchly opposed to capital punishment. Describe this attitude along the three elements of affect, cognition, and behavior.

2. Suppose you're an attitude researcher and want to assess participant attitudes about the institution of marriage. Describe three methods you might use in your assessment.

3. You have two close friends who you like very much, Tanya and Amanda. Unfortunately, Tanya can't stand Amanda. This makes your life difficult, as the three of you can never spend time together without Tanya getting irritated. Based on what you learned about cognitive dissonance theory, how might you go about getting Tanya to like Amanda more?

4. Although we readily assume that attitudes relate in meaningful ways to behavior, research suggests they don't always match up. Consider the dentist as the attitude object. Why might attitudes toward the dentist not necessarily predict behavioral responses to the dentist?

5. Suppose you're choosing between two vacation spots you think are equally amazing: Greece and Costa Rica. You have to pick one and elect to go to Costa Rica. Following your decision, Costa Rica starts to sound even more fantastic—zip-lining, cloud forests, and incredible wildlife. In contrast, Greece seems a little less special, it's expensive, and the beaches aren't really that nice. Describe a cognitive dissonance account of this change in your attitude following the decision.

6. Although your son already likes vegetables, you want him to eat even more vegetables. You decide to pay him $1 to spend at the toy store for every portion of vegetables he eats. Given what you learned about self-perception theory, is this a good approach? Why or why not?

The **answer guidelines** for the think about it questions can be found at the back of the book . . . ☞

ONLINE STUDY MATERIALS

Want to earn a better grade on your test?
Go to **INQUIZITIVE** to learn and review this chapter's content, with personalized feedback along the way.

What characteristics made Martin Luther King, Jr. such a credible source of persuasion?

Why are some campaigns more effective at changing behavior than others?

Why are we more likely to support social causes endorsed by celebrities?

CHAPTER

8

Persuasion

IN 1985, "DON'T MESS WITH TEXAS" bumper stickers began appearing on cars in Texas, beginning the launch of what turned out to be the most successful anti-littering campaign ever conducted in the United States. The campaign, commissioned by the Texas Department of Transportation, was aimed at reducing the cost of picking up roadside litter. Research showed that the main culprits were young, male truck drivers. Aware of the demographic they were targeting, the advertising team had an epiphany. Since most Texans associated the word *litter* with a group of puppies or kittens, a campaign on "littering" wasn't going to work. The campaign needed a motto that would resonate with the likes of the rough-and-tumble males who thought nothing of throwing their empty beer cans out their truck windows. The slogan "Don't Mess with Texas" was born.

The slogan not only fit the sensibilities of the target demographic; it also capitalized on a well-known fact—enormous Texan pride. The team astutely recruited well-known masculine icons to disseminate the anti-littering message. Members of the Dallas Cowboys, singers such as Willie Nelson and Lyle Lovett, and the actor Matthew McConaughey were among the first to participate. The spokespersons for the campaign did not plead; instead, rugged football players looked sternly into the camera as they crushed beer cans, threw them into the garbage, and proclaimed: "Don't mess with Texas!"

The "Don't Mess with Texas" campaign is a legendary success story in the world of advertising. It's also a story about the psychology of persuasion—how to influence people's attitudes and behaviors. The campaign's success suggests that large numbers of people can be persuaded—something we have seen throughout

Don't mess with Texas®

"The object of oratory alone is not truth, but persuasion."
—THOMAS BABINGTON MACAULAY

"Men are not governed by justice, but by law or persuasion. When they refuse to be governed by law or persuasion, they have to be governed by force or fraud, or both."
—GEORGE BERNARD SHAW

history. Charismatic leaders such as Nelson Mandela, Martin Luther King, Jr., and Mohandas (Mahatma) Gandhi have stirred the masses and brought about radical social change, even when lacking significant institutional power or money. And in 2014, the "Ice Bucket Challenge," a promotional strategy aimed at combating the neurodegenerative condition ALS, became a craze that spread worldwide. In addition to raising awareness about the disease, the campaign persuaded people to donate, ultimately taking in over $115 million, which funded groundbreaking research.

People, however, can be remarkably resistant to persuasion. Many well-designed, well-funded efforts to encourage people to practice safe sex, stop using drugs, or improve their diet have failed (Aronson, Fried, & Stone, 1991). People can be stubbornly resistant to changing their minds, even when their health or economic well-being is affected. This chapter will examine both of these truths: we can be markedly susceptible to persuasion but also impressively resistant to it. ■

Dual-Process Approach to Persuasion

Over 90 percent of the scientific community believe that people are the cause of the warming of the Earth's atmosphere and that global warming will likely yield catastrophic events—hurricanes that dwarf Irma, rising sea levels that will place parts of the U.S. South and many tropical islands under water, rampant wildfires, and the disappearance of thousands of species. It's also clear that each of us can do many things to cut our own carbon emissions, a primary source of global warming. Here are just a few:

- We can drive our cars less and rely more on bikes or public transportation.
- We can fly less often to our vacation destinations.
- We can eliminate red meat from our diet (you'd be surprised how much that can help).
- We can use energy-efficient light bulbs, toilets, heating systems, and solar panels—all of which right now cost more than the conventional options but will yield many benefits in the long run.
- We can turn off computers and lights when not in use.
- We can buy local produce or grow our own food (which helps reduce carbon emissions because trucking isn't required to deliver the food).

Imagine you're leading a public service campaign to persuade people to adopt these habits. Doing so might not be as difficult as, say, getting people to change their sexual practices to curb AIDS, which some African countries tried with limited success. Still, there are plenty of barriers to modifying attitudes and behavior related to cutting carbon emissions. People would have to alter old habits (driving their cars), give up strong preferences (double cheeseburgers), and adjust their daily routine (taking extra time to use public transportation or bike to work). What kind of campaign would you design? The literature on persuasion suggests that there is no simple, one-solution-fits-all means of persuasion. Instead, social psychologists propose that there are two basic ways to persuade people, or two "routes" to persuasion.

Elaboration Likelihood Model

In the 1980s, Richard Petty and John Cacioppo developed the **elaboration likelihood model (ELM)** to explain how people change their attitudes in response to persuasive messages (Petty & Cacioppo, 1979, 1984, 1986; for related theorizing, see Chaiken, 1980; Chaiken, Liberman, & Eagly, 1989). The core idea is that people in certain contexts process persuasive messages rather mindlessly and effortlessly and on other occasions deeply and attentively. Does this notion of dual processes sound familiar? It should. It's analogous to the distinction we made in Chapter 4 between automatic and controlled processing. When applied to persuasion, the key insight is that some types of persuasive appeals will be more effective when the target audience is largely on "autopilot," and other types will be more effective when the target audience is alert and attentive. Indeed, the very name "elaboration likelihood model" captures the idea that in trying to predict whether a persuasive message will be effective, it's essential to know whether the target audience is likely to "elaborate"—think deeply about—the message or process it mindlessly.

According to the ELM, the **central route** to persuasion occurs when people think carefully and deliberately about the content of a persuasive message (**Figure 8.1**). They attend to the logic and strength of the arguments and evidence presented in the message; they rely on relevant information of their own—experiences, memories, and knowledge—to evaluate the message. Whether or not all of this high-effort thinking, or elaboration of the message, leads to attitude change, there's a careful sifting of the arguments and evidence presented.

Through the ELM's **peripheral route**, people primarily attend to peripheral aspects of a message—relatively superficial, easy-to-process features of a communication that are tangential to the persuasive information itself. A peripheral cue might be the apparent expertise, credibility, or attractiveness of the person communicating a persuasive message. To be sure, some of these peripheral cues, such as the communicator's expertise or credibility, can be a form of evidence when processed

elaboration likelihood model (ELM) A model of persuasion maintaining that there are two different routes to persuasion: the central route and the peripheral route.

central route A route to persuasion wherein people think carefully and deliberately about the content of a persuasive message, attending to its logic and the strength of its arguments, as well as to related evidence and principles.

peripheral route A route to persuasion wherein people attend to relatively easy-to-process, superficial cues related to a persuasive message, such as its length or the expertise or attractiveness of the source of the message.

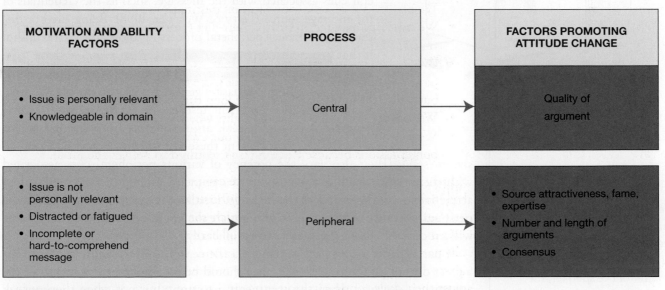

FIGURE 8.1
DUAL-PROCESS APPROACH TO PERSUASION
According to Petty and Cacioppo's elaboration likelihood model, there are two routes to persuasion: a central route and a peripheral route. The routes are engaged by different levels of motivation and ability to attend to the message, and different types of persuasive appeals are more effective through one route than through the other. Any persuasion variable, such as a source's expertise, can bring about attitude change through either or both central and peripheral routes to persuasion.

in a deliberate, thoughtful fashion. But when persuasion occurs through the peripheral route, the person is swayed by these cues without engaging in much thought.

In the peripheral route, people rely on relatively simple heuristics, or rules of thumb that guide them in how to respond to a persuasive message. Thus, a person's attitude toward red meat might change simply because "an expert says it's bad to eat it," "there are many arguments against eating it," or "a lot of people don't eat it." Or a peripheral cue might change a person's emotional reaction to the attitude object (the focus of the persuasive appeal), leading to a change in attitude on this basis alone. If the source of a message is attractive, for instance, this might make the person feel more positively about the attitude object simply by eliciting general feelings of liking or attraction that rub off on the object itself.

The Roles of Motivation and Ability

What determines whether we will engage in central or peripheral processing in response to a persuasive message? Two factors matter: motivation and ability (see Figure 8.1). In terms of our *motivation* to devote time and energy to a message: when the message has personal consequences—it bears on our goals, interests, or well-being—we're more likely to go the central route and carefully work through the arguments and relevant information. In terms of our *ability* to process the message in depth: when we have sufficient cognitive resources and time, we're able to process persuasive messages more deeply; in general, the more we know, the more thoughtfully we're able to scrutinize a persuasive message (Eagly & Chaiken, 1993; Petty & Cacioppo, 1986).

In contrast, when ability is low—for example, the arguments in a persuasive message are being presented too quickly or are hard to comprehend—we're more apt to rely on easy-to-process, peripheral cues associated with the message, such as the credentials of the message source (Petty & Wegener, 1998). Being tired or distracted also makes peripheral processing more likely. The upshot is that for persuasion to occur via the central route, we have to be both motivated and able to engage in more in-depth processing. If either is lacking, persuasion generally relies on peripheral cues.

In a typical experiment testing the ELM, researchers first generate strong and weak arguments for an attitude issue or object. They then present these arguments as part of a persuasive message. They also vary the potency of various peripheral cues associated with the message, such as the number of arguments offered or the credibility or attractiveness of the source of the message. Finally, they vary a factor, such as the personal relevance of the issue, to manipulate the likelihood that the participants will process the message centrally or peripherally.

If participants process the message via the central route because the issue has a great deal of personal relevance, they should be sensitive to the strength of the arguments—swayed when the arguments are strong but not when they're weak (Eagly & Chaiken, 1993; Petty & Cacioppo, 1986). In contrast, participants who are low in motivation or ability (or both) would be unlikely to discern the strength of the arguments because they're only noticing peripheral cues of the message. So whether or not they change their attitudes is less affected by argument strength.

"You're right. It does send a powerful message."

"Of the modes of persuasion furnished by the spoken word there are three kinds. The first kind depends on the personal character of the speaker; the second on putting the audience into a certain frame of mind; the third on the proof, provided by the words of the speech itself."
—ARISTOTLE

BOX 8.1

NOT SO FAST:
Critical Thinking about External Validity

In 1990, the rock band Judas Priest was tried for contributing to the suicide deaths of Ray Belknap and James Vance. Prosecutors alleged that the men had been led down the path to suicide by the subliminal message "Do it" that the band had embedded into one of its songs. Can subliminal messages have such powerful effects? Can they be the basis of a nonconscious, peripheral route to persuasion?

Subliminal stimuli—stimuli presented below conscious awareness—can activate certain concepts and even shape everyday thoughts, feelings, and actions (Dijksterhuis, Aarts, & Smith, 2005). Consider a laboratory experiment in which participants saw pictures of a target person immediately after being subliminally presented with a pleasant image (such as a child playing with a doll) or an unpleasant one (such as a bloody shark). Upon later evaluation of the target person, those who were subliminally exposed to positive images provided more favorable evaluations than those exposed to negative images (Krosnick, Betz, Jussim, & Lynn, 1992).

In another study, participants were told not to drink anything for 3 hours before coming to the experiment (Strahan, Spencer, & Zanna, 2002). Upon arrival, half the participants were allowed to quench their thirst and half were kept thirsty. All of them were then subliminally primed, some with words related to thirst (*thirst, dry*) and some with neutral words (*pirate, won*). They were then allowed to drink as much as they wanted of each of two beverages. Thirsty participants who were primed with thirst-related words drank significantly more than thirsty participants primed with neutral words. (As expected, the primes had no influence on those who weren't thirsty.)

Findings like these are provocative and attest to the potential influence of subliminal messages on our decisions and behaviors. But are they cause for alarm? Do we need to be on constant alert for the possibility that advertisers, political campaign managers, or rock bands might try to alter our behavior with messages we aren't consciously aware of having seen? Maybe not. Recall Chapter 2's discussion of internal and external validity. Laboratory experiments of subliminal persuasion score high on internal validity, but considerably lower on external validity. In other words, the outside world and the lab differ in a number of important ways that make subliminal effects weaker in daily life.

The focus of the persuasion attempt in the lab is typically something people have no firm opinion about, such as a new sports drink. It's one thing to shift attitudes and behavior with respect to neutral stimuli; it's another thing entirely to shift attitudes and behavior with respect to more familiar, psychologically significant stimuli—such as getting Republicans to vote for a Democratic candidate.

In addition, the subliminal message in lab studies is presented right before assessment of the target attitude or behavior, and the participants encounter no competing messages in the interim. That's almost never the case in the real world. A subliminal command to "Drink Coke" could conceivably motivate people to leave their seats to get a drink; but once in the lobby, surrounded by all sorts of messages, they might be as likely to drink Pepsi as Coke or even get a candy bar.

In fact, no studies have ever demonstrated that subliminal stimuli induce people to do something they are opposed to doing. There's no reason to believe that being subliminally primed with the words "Do it" would lead those not already accustomed to the idea of suicide to kill themselves. The relevant lesson is that while experiments can shed light on potential attitudes and behaviors (while revealing a lot about how the mind works in the process), broad conclusions about the likelihood of a behavior or outcome occurring in daily life require a thoughtful consideration of the external validity of the body of experimental evidence.

SUBLIMINAL ADVERTISING In a television ad run by the Republicans during the 2000 U.S. presidential election, the word *RATS* was quickly flashed on the screen in a subliminal attack on Al Gore, the Democratic candidate, and his Medicare plan.

Given this reasoning, consider one study that varied the strength of the arguments, the personal relevance of the issue, and a peripheral cue: the expertise of the person delivering the persuasive message. Participants read either eight weak arguments or eight strong arguments in support of implementing a policy to require a comprehensive exam for all graduating seniors at their university (Petty, Cacioppo, & Goldman, 1981). Personal relevance was manipulated by telling the participants the policy would be initiated either the following year, meaning they would have to take the exam, or in ten years (presumably well after the students' graduation). Finally, source expertise was varied: half the participants were told the arguments were generated by a local high school class, and half were told the arguments were generated by the "Carnegie Commission on Higher Education," allegedly chaired by a Princeton University professor.

Take a look at **Figure 8.2A**. Higher values along the vertical y-axis indicate more favorable attitudes toward the comprehensive exam, whereas lower values indicate less favorable attitudes. You can see that when the message was personally relevant to the students—that is, when the exam was to be implemented the next year and these students would have to take it—they were motivated to pay attention to the strength of the arguments. But for students for whom the message was *not* personally relevant—they wouldn't have to take the test themselves—the strength of the arguments didn't matter as much. These participants noticed, and were mainly influenced by, the expertise of the source—whether the arguments

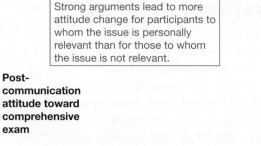

Strong arguments lead to more attitude change for participants to whom the issue is personally relevant than for those to whom the issue is not relevant.

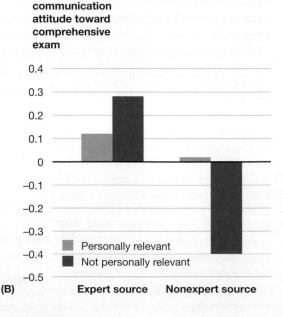

The expertise of the source of the communication, in contrast, matters more for participants to whom the issue is not personally relevant, suggesting that they mainly attend to peripheral aspects of the message.

FIGURE 8.2
CENTRAL OR PERIPHERAL ROUTE TO PERSUASION
Attitude change can be brought about by (A) strong arguments when people are motivated and by (B) the expertise of the source of the persuasive message when people aren't motivated.
Source: Adapted from Petty & Cacioppo, 1986.

were produced by a high school class or by a professorial committee (**Figure 8.2B**). Students who would theoretically have to take the test the following year were far less influenced by whether or not the source was an expert and more persuaded by strong than by weak arguments. In short, high personal relevance led participants to be persuaded by the strength of the arguments (the central route to persuasion), whereas a lack of personal relevance led participants to be persuaded by the expertise of the source (the peripheral route to persuasion).

It's worth noting, though, that persuasion variables, such as argument strength and source expertise, are not tied to a single persuasion route. In fact, the variables can play multiple roles, influencing persuasion through either the central or the peripheral route, depending on the circumstances (Chen & Chaiken, 1999; Petty, 1997; Petty & Briñol, 2008). For example, the expertise of the person delivering a persuasive message is often easy to discern and may therefore easily change someone's attitude without engaging a thoughtful response—persuasion via the peripheral route. But if someone is highly motivated and has the ability to think carefully, source expertise could function as an argument whose strength is carefully evaluated, such as with someone who's more apt to be convinced by an argument delivered by an expert source than by a nonexpert. This results in more mindful attitude change—persuasion via the central route. Source expertise can also affect persuasion through the central route by influencing the thoughts people generate about the issue at hand (Chaiken & Maheswaren, 1994; Tormala, Briñol, & Petty, 2007). For example, people may be more likely to think of supportive evidence if the source is an expert.

The upshot remains that there are two basic routes to persuasion—one involving systematic elaboration of the persuasive arguments, the other characterized by less effortful processing of relatively superficial cues. So is one route more effective than the other? Well, for long-lasting attitude change, persuasion through the central route is preferable. Through this route, people will attend to a message carefully and elaborate on it more deeply, increasing the chance of integrating the arguments into their belief system. The end result is attitude change that is more enduring, more resistant to persuasion, and more predictive of future behavior (Eagly & Chaiken, 1993; Mackie, 1987; Petty, Haugtvedt, & Smith, 1995). By contrast, for immediate acquiescence of an audience not very motivated or attentive, the peripheral route is the way to go.

← LOOKING BACK

The elaboration likelihood model describes two ways of processing persuasive messages. When motivation and ability are high (such as when the issue is personally relevant and there are minimal distractions), persuasion is likely to occur through the central route, whereby people are persuaded on the basis of a careful, systematic analysis of a message, such as the strength of its arguments. When motivation and ability are low, on the other hand, attitude change tends to occur through the peripheral route, whereby people are persuaded by easy-to-process cues, such as the sheer number of arguments or the attractiveness of the message source.

The Elements of Persuasion

Now that you have a sense of the different ways people can process a persuasive message, let's take a look at specific elements that influence whether a persuasive attempt works or not. Many of the studies in this area were inspired by research that Carl Hovland and his colleagues conducted at Yale University in the 1940s and 1950s (Hovland, Janis, & Kelley, 1953). These researchers broke down persuasion into three elements, or three W's of persuasion: (1) the "who," or source of the message; (2) the "what," or content of the message itself; and (3) the "to whom," or intended audience of the message.

Source Characteristics

Spokespeople for social causes are often rich, famous, and good-looking. For example, actor Matt Damon is cofounder and spokesperson for Water.org, an organization devoted to getting clean water to impoverished countries. Famous actress and singer-songwriter Demi Lovato has lent her name and influence to many social causes, among them the promotion of health and well-being. What are the effects of having such striking spokespeople? Questions about who delivers a persuasive message have to do with **source characteristics**. Let's take a look at some of the most deeply researched of these characteristics.

ATTRACTIVENESS George Clooney, the handsome, award-winning actor, has spoken up on behalf of many causes, among them the humanitarian crisis in Darfur, Sudan. Glamorous celebrities often appear in commercials, singing the praises of a particular consumer product or brand. They're also the faces of public service announcements, urging kids to read, stay in school, or avoid drugs. One could argue that relying on the beautiful and famous in these campaigns makes no sense—after all, what does beauty and charisma have to do with, say, the merits of a cause or the quality of a product? But as we've discussed, attractive communicators can promote attitude change through the peripheral route. For example, we tend to like physically attractive people (see Chapter 10), and for good or ill, this simple fact makes us more likely to accept the attitudes they endorse.

Research shows that attractive sources are particularly persuasive when the message isn't personally important to the people hearing it and when those people don't have much knowledge in the domain; in other words, the attractiveness of a source is especially persuasive under circumstances that sway people to focus on peripheral cues (Chaiken, 1980; Petty, Cacioppo, & Schumann, 1983; Wood & Kallgren, 1988). This doesn't mean that finding an attractive person to deliver a persuasive message is a waste of time when your audience is apt to be thinking about the message carefully. Attractive sources can lead to persuasion through the central route by, for example, increasing the favorability of people's effortful thinking about the position being endorsed. In short, it's hard to go wrong with having someone attractive deliver your persuasive message.

CREDIBILITY Credible sources are expert and trustworthy. Advertisers try to take advantage of this. For example, there's no shortage of ads for toothpaste, aspirin, and other health-related products that cite testimonials from doctors, known for their expertise and trustworthiness. More generally, the sheer credibility of a message's source can sway opinions under circumstances that

PERSUASION AND CELEBRITY ENDORSEMENTS
Demi Lovato is pictured here at the United Nations headquarters celebrating International Day of Happiness, part of a worldwide movement to increase recognition that happiness and well-being are as important to progress as economic growth.

source characteristics
Characteristics of the person who delivers a persuasive message, such as attractiveness, credibility, and certainty.

promote the peripheral route to persuasion, such as when the topic is of low personal relevance to the audience or the audience is distracted (Kiesler & Mathog, 1968; Petty et al., 1981; Rhine & Severance, 1970). And when the audience happens to be highly motivated and able to think carefully, source credibility can be taken as a strong argument in favor of moving toward the position the credible source is endorsing. Martin Luther King, Jr.'s credibility as a leader of the civil rights movement undoubtedly served as a strong argument in persuading people to join the movement.

What about all the noncredible messengers who crowd the airwaves these days—the crackpots maintaining that the Holocaust never happened or that AIDS is not caused by sexual contact? Do these messages fall on deaf ears? An early study unfortunately suggests otherwise (Hovland & Weiss, 1951). Participants first rated the likelihood that a nuclear submarine would be built in the near future (at the time, they didn't exist). Five days later, participants read an essay about the imminence of nuclear submarines and were told the essay was written either by the highly credible physicist Robert Oppenheimer, the "father of the atomic bomb," or by a noncredible journalist who worked for *Pravda*, the propaganda newspaper of the former Soviet Union. As you might expect, the Oppenheimer essay led to greater attitude change than the essay by the less credible *Pravda* writer, even though the content of the essay was exactly the same.

Much more surprising, however, was that four weeks later, participants who had read the essay by the *Pravda* writer, although unmoved initially, actually shifted their attitudes toward the position he advocated. This came to be known as the **sleeper effect**—that is, messages from unreliable sources exert little influence initially but over time have the potential to shift people's attitudes (Pratkanis, Greenwald, Leippe, & Baumgardner, 1988). The idea is that over time, people dissociate the source of the message from the message itself. You hear some irresponsible guy on talk radio arguing that the government is preparing to ban the sale of handguns. Initially, you discount the message because of the messenger's lack of credibility. But over time, the message has a chance to influence your views because you have dissociated the source of the message from its content. Down the road, the idea may not seem entirely far-fetched.

Notice, here, that we're talking about how the ineffectiveness of a noncredible source can fade over time, allowing a message from a noncredible source to shift attitudes down the road. So how about a highly credible source linked to a weak message? The weakness of the message will surely hurt persuasion initially, but could the message get dissociated from the credible source over time so that persuasion is ultimately effective in the longer run solely because of the source's credibility? Indeed it can. Recent studies document this new form of sleeper effect whereby you get delayed persuasion by a credible source who is initially linked to a weak message but down the road is dissociated from it (Albarracin, Kumkale, & Poyner-Del Ventro, 2017).

CREDIBILITY AND PERSUASION
Martin Luther King, Jr., is pictured here during the March on Washington in August 1963 as he is about to give his "I Have a Dream" speech. His credibility, due to his leading role in the civil rights movement and having repeatedly put his life on the line, undoubtedly contributed to his ability to persuade.

"Every time a message seems to grab us, and we think, 'I just might try it,' we are at the nexus of choice and persuasion that is advertising."
—ANDREW HACKER

sleeper effect An effect that occurs when a persuasive message from an unreliable source initially exerts little influence but later causes attitudes to shift.

CERTAINTY Imagine there are two online reviews of a new restaurant. One of the reviews comments, "This is absolutely the best Italian meal you'll ever have." The other review comments, "I don't know, but I kinda feel like maybe this could be the best Italian meal you'll ever have." If you're like most people, you'd be far more inclined to try the restaurant if you read the first review. This simple example illustrates that sources who express their views with certainty and confidence tend to be more persuasive. This is because people generally judge certain and confident sources to be more credible, and as we've seen, source credibility is persuasive.

By and large, then, if your goal is to persuade someone, it wouldn't be a bad idea to express confidence in your viewpoint (Akhtar & Wheeler, 2016; Karmarkar & Tormala, 2010; Tenney, MacCoun, Spellman, & Hastie, 2007). Research conducted in various real-world contexts supports this idea. For example, studies of jurors show that people judge how credible eyewitnesses are based on the confidence they express when they give their testimony (Wells, Ferguson, & Lindsay 1981). This is true despite the fact that the actual association between eyewitness confidence and accuracy is rather weak (Kassin, 1985). In a similar vein, people regard financial advisers who express high confidence in their stock forecasts as more knowledgeable than those who express less confidence, and the more confident advisers are accordingly chosen more often by clients (Price & Stone, 2004).

Message Characteristics

message characteristics Aspects, or content, of a persuasive message, including the quality of the evidence and the explicitness of its conclusions.

What are the **message characteristics** that make a persuasive appeal most effective? By now you should be able to anticipate the answer from the perspective of the Elaboration Likelihood Model (ELM): it depends on the audience's motivation and ability to process the message.

MESSAGE QUALITY As you saw in Figure 8.1, high-quality messages are more persuasive in general, especially for people who are strong in motivation and ability. Messages are of higher quality when they appeal to core values of the audience (Cacioppo, Petty, & Sidera, 1982); when they're straightforward, clear, and logical; and when they articulate the desirable consequences of taking the actions suggested by the message (Chaiken & Eagly, 1976; Leippe & Elkin, 1987).

More attitude change will result if the conclusions are explicit in the message (Hovland, Lumsdaine, & Sheffield, 1949): "Here's the take-away message." And it's usually a good idea to pointedly refute the opposition, thereby giving the receiver of the message material to use in arguing against any opposing messages (Hass & Linder, 1972; Petty & Wegener, 1998). Finally, messages are more persuasive when sources argue against their own self-interest. For example, Walster, Aronson, and Abrahams (1966) found that a message delivered by a prison inmate advocating longer prison sentences was more persuasive than a message in which the same prisoner argued for shorter sentences. When someone argues for a position contrary to obvious self-interest, the source of the message is seen as more sincere. A real-world example of this might be the case of Patrick Reynolds, whose anti-smoking advocacy is likely seen as more sincere by the mere fact that it goes against his own self-interest (he is the heir to the second-largest tobacco company in the United States).

ARGUING AGAINST SELF-INTEREST
Patrick Reynolds, the grandson and heir of the late R. J. Reynolds (founder of the second-largest tobacco company in the United States), is shown speaking to students about the dangers of smoking. He watched his father and older brother both die of emphysema and lung cancer brought on by cigarette smoking. His anti-smoking speeches have high credibility given his family history and the fact that his arguments, if effective, would ultimately reduce his inheritance.

VIVIDNESS When information is vivid—colorful, interesting, and memorable—it tends to be more effective. In fact, vivid but misleading information can often

BOX 8.2 | FOCUS ON POP CULTURE

Lie to Me

The popular TV show *Lie to Me*, which ran from 2009 to 2011, was based on the research of social psychologist Paul Ekman, who did the early studies of the universality of facial expression (see Chapter 6). Lying, of course, is one of the most challenging acts of persuasion: to get someone to believe the opposite of what you actually believe. Ekman, Bella DePaulo, and others have discovered certain clues to discern whether someone is lying or telling the truth. When people lie, they are more likely to show speech hesitations, face touches, micro-expressions of negative emotion, leg jiggles, speech dysfluencies (such as scrambled word order), sudden rises in the pitch of the voice, and increased eye contact (DePaulo, Lanier, & Davis, 1983; Ekman, O'Sullivan, Friesen, & Scherer, 1991; Mehrabian & Williams, 1969; Riggio & Friedman, 1983). Yes, *increased* eye contact. Liars exploit the conventional belief that people can't look you in the eye when they're lying.

How good are people at catching liars? It turns out that most folks are surprisingly inept at this important task. Ekman and his colleagues have presented videotapes of people lying and telling the truth to thousands of people (Ekman & O'Sullivan, 1991). Participants simply had to indicate whether each person was lying or telling the truth. Whereas chance guessing would yield accuracy rates of 50 percent, people were correct, on average, only 57 percent of the time. This same research yielded interesting answers about who's particularly good at catching liars. What's your guess? Contrary to what you might expect, those sages of the human character—judges, clinicians, and psychological scientists—proved no better than the average person. The one group that shone in their ability to catch liars was Secret Service agents, probably because they get sound training in the social psychology of lying just discussed.

---

trump more valid and relevant information that's not as flashy. In a study showing that vivid information conveyed by a personal narrative with emotional punch can be more persuasive than statistical facts, the researchers first assessed attitudes toward welfare (Hamill, Wilson, & Nisbett, 1980). In one condition, participants then read a vivid, gripping story about a woman who was a lifetime welfare recipient. The story was based on one that former U.S. President Ronald Reagan told to great effect about a "welfare queen," a lifetime recipient of welfare who exploited the system to enjoy a life of comfort and leisure. In another condition, participants read facts about welfare: that the average time on welfare was two years, and only 10 percent of recipients received welfare for four years or more. In a third condition, participants read both the vivid narrative and the facts. In this condition, it should have been clear that the case was not typical of welfare recipients in general. Which message led to more attitude change? Participants changed their attitudes more if they heard the vivid story—even when they also had the cold statistics. The facts did little to alter their attitudes.

Vivid images abound in the media, and their power is evident in the **identifiable victim effect**. Vivid, flesh-and-blood victims are often more powerful sources of persuasion than abstract statistics (Collins, Taylor, Wood, & Thompson, 1988; Shedler & Manis, 1986; Taylor & Thompson, 1982). People are more willing to donate to a cause when an appeal is made on behalf of an identifiable individual than on behalf of anonymous or statistical victims (Jenni & Loewenstein, 1997; Small, Loewenstein, & Slovic, 2007). Recognizable

identifiable victim effect The tendency to be more moved by the vivid plight of a single individual than by a more abstract number of people.

"The death of a single Russian soldier is a tragedy. The death of a million soldiers is a statistic."
—JOSEPH STALIN

THE IDENTIFIABLE VICTIM EFFECT
People are more inclined to be persuaded to act on behalf of a cause by portrayals of clearly identifiable victims, such as the children in this compelling ad for UNICEF.

victims are more apt to elicit feelings of empathy, thereby leading to a willingness to donate to worthy causes (Kogut & Ritov, 2005; Ritov & Kogut, 2011). The identifiable victim effect has limitations, however. For example, Kogut (2011) has shown that in cases where it's possible to blame a victim for his or her plight, making the person identifiable can actually breed negative perceptions of the victim and decrease rather than increase aid.

FEAR Suppose you want to persuade people to act in order to avoid some dire outcome. Should you try to frighten your audience about just how terrible the outcome would be, or should you avoid such fear tactics? Let's return to our hypothetical campaign to reduce carbon emissions. Should you scare the daylights out of people with images of wildfires and flooded coastal areas, or should you expose your audience to tamer fare? The ELM offers somewhat competing notions regarding fear and persuasion. On the one hand, intense fear could disrupt the careful, thoughtful processing of the message, thus reducing the chances of long-lasting attitude change. On the other hand, the right kind of fear might heighten people's motivation to attend to the message, thus increasing the likelihood of enduring attitude change (Calanchini, Moons, & Mackie, 2016).

What does the evidence say? In general, it's advisable to make ad campaigns frightening, but make sure they include clear, concrete information about what steps to take to address the source of the fear (Boster & Mongeau, 1984). Supporting this recommendation, Howard Leventhal and his colleagues tried to change smoking habits in one of three ways. They showed some participants a graphic film of the effects of lung cancer, which included footage of a lung operation in which the blackened lung of a smoker was removed. They gave other participants a pamphlet with instructions about how to quit smoking. A third group saw the film and read the pamphlet (Leventhal, Watts, & Pagano, 1967). Participants who only viewed the scary film reduced their smoking more than those who just read the bland instructions. In this case, fear was persuasive. But participants exposed to both the film and the pamphlet decreased their smoking the most. **Figure 8.3** presents participants' self-reports of their daily smoking behavior a month after the intervention. In short, it appears that fear-eliciting persuasive messages that provide information that can be acted on can be highly effective (Leventhal, 1970; Leventhal et al., 1967; Robberson & Rogers, 1988).

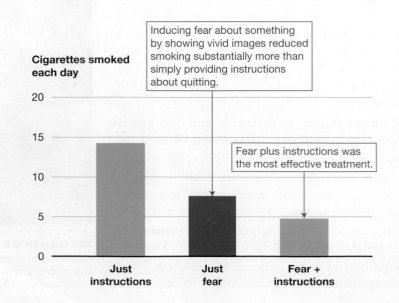

FIGURE 8.3
FEAR AND PERSUASIVE MESSAGES
Fear, especially when paired with instructions on how to respond to the fear, is likely to lead to attitude change.
Source: Adapted from Leventhal et al., 1967.

CULTURE Not surprisingly, it's important to tailor a message to fit the norms, values, and outlook of the cultural group of your audience. Thus, the message content in the media of independent and interdependent cultures often differs substantially. Marketing experts Sang-pil Han and Sharon Shavitt analyzed the advertisements in American and Korean news magazines and women's magazines (Han & Shavitt, 1994). They found that the American ads emphasized benefits to the individual ("Make your way through the crowd"), whereas Korean ads focused on benefits to collectives ("We have a way of bringing people closer together"). In experimental studies that manipulated the content of advertisements, these researchers found that the individual-oriented ads were more effective with American participants and that the collective-oriented ads were more effective with Korean participants. Related arguments have been made with regard to upper-class individuals, who tend to define themselves in more independent terms, compared with lower-class individuals, who define themselves in more interdependent terms (Carey & Markus, 2016). Persuasive messages that appeal to independence may be more effective among higher-class individuals, whereas messages conveying interdependent themes may be more effective among lower-class individuals.

Along related lines, recall the discussion in Chapter 3 about cultural differences in motivational orientation. Whereas Westerners tend to pursue their goals with a promotion orientation, focusing on the positive outcomes they hope to achieve, East Asians are more inclined to pursue their goals with a prevention orientation, focusing on the negative outcomes they hope to avoid (Lee, Aaker, & Gardner, 2000). What do such differences imply for how best to frame a persuasive appeal aimed at Westerners versus East Asians? In one study, researchers

(A) (B)

MESSAGE CHARACTERISTICS AND TARGETING
Persuasive messages are generally targeted to collective concerns in interdependent cultures and individual concerns in independent cultures. Similarly, messages may vary at different times within the same society or culture. (A) During World War II, U.S. Army posters stressed collective concerns. (B) In recent times, army recruitment posters highlight individual characteristics cultivated by military service, such as individual strength.

recruited participants from a British university who identified themselves as white British or of East Asian origins (for example, Chinese, Korean) and presented them with a persuasive appeal about the importance of flossing one's teeth (Uskul, Sherman, & Fitzgibbon, 2009). The appeal was framed in terms of either the benefit of flossing or the cost of not flossing. The white British participants were more persuaded by the gain-framed message, whereas the East Asian participants were more swayed by the loss-framed message.

Audience Characteristics

audience characteristics
Characteristics of those who receive a persuasive message, including need for cognition, mood, and age.

The work on culture and persuasion illustrates a broader idea: it's important to match the characteristics of the persuasive message to characteristics of the intended audience. In fact, researchers have discovered a range of **audience characteristics** that can influence whether a persuasive message is likely to be effective. Let's consider some of these.

NEED FOR COGNITION People differ in their need for cognition, the degree to which they like to think deeply about things (Cacioppo, Petty, Feinstein, & Jarvis, 1996). Those with a strong need for cognition like to think, puzzle, ponder, and consider multiple perspectives on issues. This is the kind of person you might observe on the subway reading *Scientific American* or working through sudoku puzzles on their smartphone. People with a weaker need for cognition don't find thought and contemplation that much fun. As you might imagine, people with a high need for cognition are more persuaded by high-quality arguments and are relatively unmoved by peripheral cues of persuasion (Cacioppo, Petty, & Morris, 1983; Haugtvedt & Petty, 1992; Luttrell, Petty, & Xu, 2017). By contrast, people who have a lower need for cognition are persuaded more by easier-to-process, peripheral cues.

MOOD As anyone who's ever tried to win the heart of another can attest, it's easier to persuade when the person you're trying to woo is in the right mood. It's no wonder that sometimes people go to great lengths to create a particular mood in an audience they're trying to sway. Hitler staged enormous rallies for his most important speeches, surrounded by bold Nazi banners, awesome displays of military strength, soaring music, and thousands of supporters chanting and saluting in unison. His intent was to stir the emotions of his audience to make them more receptive to his ideas. Studies have found that people exposed to persuasive messages while eating or listening to beautiful music are more apt to change their attitudes (McGuire, 1985).

PERSUASION AND MOOD
The mood of an audience can affect whether a message will lead to attitude change. In Germany in the 1930s, Adolf Hitler staged rallies, like this Hitler Youth rally, to create a mood of strength and unity that would encourage people to support his ideas.

The effects of mood on persuasion can also be more nuanced. Duane Wegener and Richard Petty suggest that persuasive efforts tend to be successful when the mood of the message matches the mood of the audience. More pessimistic, counterattitudinal messages (arguing against the prevailing attitude of the audience) tend to prompt greater message processing in sad or depressed people, whereas uplifting, optimistic, proattitudinal messages prompt greater message processing in happy people (Bless

BOX 8.3 **FOCUS ON** DAILY LIFE

The Timing of Persuasive Attempts Matters

Whether you're trying to persuade your parents to help you finance a new car, nudge your romantic partner to take a job offer in a nearby city, or win a debate with a classmate about gun control, it's important to consider the three W's of persuasion: "who" (source characteristics), "what" (message characteristics), and "to whom" (audience characteristics). But what about the *"when"* of persuasion—that is, the timing of your persuasive attempt? Social psychologist Robert Cialdini has made a compelling case for the importance of the moments *before* a persuasive attempt. Sure, it can't hurt if you're attractive and come off as likable and credible or if your message is brimming with convincing arguments, but Cialdini (2016) argues that what transpires in the pocket of time right before you deliver your persuasive message can determine whether you succeed or fail to persuade. Cialdini uses the term *pre-suasion* to refer to this approach.

The driving idea behind pre-suasion is that what people are paying attention to just prior to encountering a persuasive appeal is critical. You want to sell someone a product? Channel attention to the most favorable feature of that product and diminish attention to rival brands. You want to convince the public to support a war effort? Focus their attention on the suffering that would occur if we didn't intervene rather than on the questionable nature of the facts about the enemy. You want to convince people to bike to work more often? Direct their attention to vivid media images of horrific car accidents. And so forth.

Cialdini outlines a variety of psychological principles and processes that account for why attention is so important to effective persuasion, but the novel insight here isn't that attention matters. What's new are the many and often quite subtle ways we can direct people's attention one way or another in those "privileged moments" right before people are even aware that an attempt to persuade is coming.

Cialdini gives the example of a company trying to get people to try a new soft drink. The traditional approach to persuasion would have the company hiring a celebrity to endorse the drink, citing compelling statistics on the appealing flavor of the drink, and perhaps commissioning commercials likely to appeal to the target audience. But a pre-suasion approach would focus on what you might do before a consumer is even presented with the persuasive attempt to get them to taste or buy the new drink. Researchers Bolkan and Andersen (2009) tackled this very question. They got people to think of themselves as "adventurous" simply by asking them if they saw themselves as "somebody who is adventurous and likes to try new things" (almost 100 percent of those asked responded affirmatively) right before asking them for their e-mail address so they could be sent instructions on how to get a free sample of the new drink. This led to an over two-fold increase in the percentage of people who gave their e-mails (76 percent) compared with when the simple "how adventurous are you?" question was not asked (33 percent). The lesson here? Don't just focus on what you do during a persuasive attempt. It's worth considering the precious moments right before.

---

et al., 1996; Wegener & Petty, 1994; Wegener, Petty, & Smith, 1995). Other work shows that inducing people to feel guilt can increase their compliance to a persuasive appeal—such as an appeal to engage in pro-environment behavior—so long as the message conveys how such behavior helps to repair the environment. In other words, guilt seems to lead to enhanced persuasion so long as the communication offers people a way to alleviate some of their guilt (Graton, Ric, & Gonzalez, 2016).

AGE Who is more likely to be persuaded by messages, younger people or older people? As you might have guessed, it's younger people (Sears, 1986). This finding has great real-world significance. For example, one source of former President Reagan's political success was the overwhelming support he received from the 18–25 age-group, the same demographic group that backed President Obama in overwhelming numbers 28 years later in the 2008 U.S. presidential election. This young age-group can be quite malleable when it comes to political allegiances.

Another real-world application of the age effect in persuasion has to do with relying on children as witnesses in legal cases. In child abuse cases, for instance, how seriously the courts should consider the testimony of young children is a major issue in light of the fact that their attitudes can be readily altered by clever attorneys interested in winning a case, not at getting at the truth (Loftus, 1993, 2003). A further problem concerns the extent of advertising directed at young children. Given that advertising can shape people's attitudes and does so more for the young than for the old, the immense amount of advertising directed at children 16 and younger is a serious concern.

Let's return again to the example of changing people's everyday habits to reduce carbon emissions. How might the literature on persuasion help you design a campaign? Perhaps the most important lesson is to tailor your message to your audience. Certain people—including those for whom global warming is personally relevant, who know quite a bit about the crisis, and who have a high need for cognition—are likely to go through the central route to persuasion, responding to the deeper substance of the message. For people like this, there is no substitute for high-quality messages, ones that are logical and clear, that make subtle rather than heavy-handed recommendations, and that appeal to clear consequences and values.

For many other people, and in many contexts, the peripheral route to persuasion is probably a better bet. For example, the peripheral route is likely to be more effective for younger audiences, for those who know less about global warming, and for people who don't think global warming is relevant to their lives. For such audiences, you might resort to attractive or credible message sources or vivid messages.

← LOOKING BACK

The three elements of persuasion are characteristics of the message's source, the content of the message itself, and the intended audience. In general, attractive, credible, and confident sources are effective at persuasion. Messages containing strong (versus weak) arguments will be more persuasive, especially through the central route of attitude change. Messages with vivid or fear-inducing content can also be quite persuasive, as can messages that are framed in ways that are culturally relevant. Audience characteristics include mood and age.

Metacognition and Persuasion

Beyond the "who, what, and to whom" elements of a persuasive message, a number of social psychologists have begun to examine how **metacognition**—the thoughts we have about our thoughts—can influence attitude change (Briñol & DeMarree, 2012; Petty, Briñol, Tormala, & Wegener, 2007). The idea is that we have primary cognitions, the thoughts themselves, as well as secondary cognitions, reflections on the thoughts we just had. So, for example, in thinking about your attitude toward reducing carbon emissions, you're likely to think about the origins of carbon emissions and their effects on the environment. Accompanying these primary cognitions, though, could be secondary cognitions: for example, assessments of how confident you are in your knowledge about carbon emissions, the ease with which facts about carbon emissions come to mind, or how clear the facts seem to you. Growing research suggests that such secondary cognitions can have their own persuasive impact.

metacognition Secondary thoughts that are reflections on primary thoughts (cognitions).

The Self-Validation Hypothesis

One of the most extensively researched metacognitions has to do with the feeling of confidence (or lack thereof) we have in our reactions to a persuasive appeal. The **self-validation hypothesis** maintains that feeling confident about our thoughts validates those thoughts, making it more likely that we'll be swayed in their direction (Petty, Briñol, & Tormala, 2002). When we have doubts about our thoughts, we might disregard the thoughts entirely or even end up endorsing an opposing attitude (Briñol & Petty, 2009; Tormala, Petty, & Briñol, 2002). For example, we might have a number of arguments against posting the Ten Commandments in the city courthouse, but coming up with these counterarguments is so hard that we end up accepting the idea ("Maybe freedom of speech is more important than separation of church and state"). In this example, we can see that how easily thoughts come to mind affects our confidence in these thoughts. How confident we feel about our thoughts can also arise from our perceptions of the accuracy of a thought or just from how clear a thought is in our mind (Petrocelli, Tormala, & Rucker, 2007). We have greater confidence—and are thus more apt to be persuaded—when we perceive our thoughts to be easily brought to mind, accurate, and clear.

In an early test of the self-validation hypothesis, Richard Petty and his colleagues designed another study in which university participants read a persuasive message arguing in favor of a new campus policy that would require all seniors to take a comprehensive exam before they graduate, and then recorded whether their thoughts in response to the message were favorable or unfavorable (Petty et al., 2002). Participants were then led to feel confidence or doubt by recalling a situation in the past when they had experienced either confidence or doubt. In the condition where participants had recalled an episode of confidence, those who had previously generated mostly favorable thoughts about the comprehensive exam reported more favorable attitudes toward this issue—in other words, they were more persuaded—than those with mostly unfavorable thoughts about the exam. What about the participants who recalled a time of doubt? Their attitudes toward the comprehensive exam were not predicted by the favorability or unfavorability of their thoughts about the exam. That is, they didn't rely on their thoughts to come up with their attitudes toward the senior comprehensive exam—presumably because those thoughts were shrouded in doubt. Thus, just as the self-validation hypothesis would predict, the favorability or unfavorability of one's thoughts influenced persuasion only when they were associated with a feeling of confidence.

Embodiment and Confidence

How confident (or not) we feel about the thoughts we have in response to a persuasive appeal can also come from nonverbal sources—for example, from whether our posture is upright or slouching, our tone of voice confident or uncertain. In other words, attitudes can be partly "embodied." Recall, for example, the study from Chapter 7 in which participants who listened to radio editorials while nodding their heads up and down expressed more agreement with the editorials compared with participants who were shaking their heads side to side while listening (Wells & Petty, 1980).

"What's come over Heisenberg? He seems to be certain about _everything_ these days."

self-validation hypothesis The idea that feeling confident about our thoughts validates those thoughts, making it more likely that we'll be swayed in their direction.

EMBODIMENT AND CONFIDENCE Nodding the head up and down while reading a persuasive message can result in more persuasion compared with shaking the head—but only when the message is made up of strong arguments. When the arguments are weak, leading people to have mostly unfavorable thoughts about the persuasive topic, nodding the head can boost confidence in these thoughts and actually lead to less persuasion compared with shaking the head.

The idea behind this research is that nodding and shaking the head can affect attitudes because they are peripheral cues of agreement and disagreement. But the self-validation hypothesis suggests another mechanism to account for findings like these: bodily movements can signal varying degrees of thought confidence, and it's this confidence that determines whether or not persuasion occurs.

Briñol and Petty (2003) found support for this novel prediction in a study in which participants listened to either strong or weak arguments in favor of a consumer product (headphones) while nodding or shaking their heads. The expectation was that strong arguments about the quality of the headphone would elicit primarily favorable thoughts about the product, whereas weak arguments would elicit mostly unfavorable thoughts. This was indeed the case, but how did the participants' head movements factor in? As you might expect, nodding while listening to the strong arguments led to greater confidence in the mostly favorable thoughts participants generated, leading to more favorable attitudes toward the headphones. In the weak arguments condition, however, students who nodded their heads were actually *less* persuaded than those who shook their heads side to side. This may seem surprising in light of the idea that nodding one's head is a sign of agreement, but the self-validation hypothesis accounts for this counterintuitive finding: namely, nodding led students to feel greater confidence in the unfavorable thoughts they had in response to the weak arguments they were listening to, leading them to feel less favorable toward the headphones. The broad take-home point here is that it's important to understand people's thinking about their thoughts to have a fuller understanding of the dynamics of persuasion.

← **LOOKING BACK**

Metacognitions—the thoughts people have about their own thinking—can influence responses to a persuasive appeal. The confidence people have in the validity of their thoughts is a primary example of a metacognition. Growing evidence indicates that when thought confidence is high, persuasion in the (favorable or unfavorable) direction of one's thoughts is more likely to occur.

The Media and Persuasion

We live in a media-saturated world. A 2011 compilation of studies found that every day, on average, the American adult watches 4.34 hours of TV and video, surfs the Internet for 2.47 hours, listens to 1.34 hours of radio, and reads newspapers or magazines for 0.44 hour (eMarketer, 2011). These figures have only increased over time. A more recent report indicates that U.S. adults spend, on average, 12 hours, 7 minutes a day consuming media (eMarketer, 2017). All told, over half the waking hours of most Americans are spent taking in various types of broadcast, online, and print media. This far exceeds the time spent in face-to-face social interaction with friends and family.

The Power of the Media

How powerful are the media in actually shaping our attitudes? Documenting the effects of the media on people's attitudes is no simple task. Researchers have done some experiments, but more typically they've relied on surveys in which people report which programs and ads they've seen. The investigator then examines whether those exposed to certain programs or ads hold opinions that are closer to the advocated positions than the opinions of people who have less exposure to the same media. Retrospective self-reports, however, are notoriously fallible. If participants say they have seen some ad, or say they have not, how can researchers be sure? How can they be sure viewers saw the ad under the same conditions? Most importantly, what about self-selection effects? For example, highly motivated citizens are more likely to tune in to political ads than less motivated citizens (Iyengar, 2004). Any apparent effect of an ad campaign is confounded by these differences in political motivation.

Regardless of these difficulties, many studies attest to the power of the media to influence people's tastes, opinions, and behavior. Interestingly, recent data suggest that the power of broadcast media doesn't just arise from the fact that it reaches a wide audience; it's also the sheer awareness of each person in the audience of this broad reach (Shteynberg, Bramlett, Fles, & Cameron, 2016). That is, when people perceive that they're attending to a stimulus (for example, a televised political speech) simultaneously with many others—a phenomenon known as *shared attention*—they're inclined to process the stimulus more deeply, resulting in persuasion via the ELM's central route.

In addition, researchers are increasingly paying attention to the role of social media in persuasion. Consider the use of social media platforms like Facebook. Although many people use Facebook primarily for social and entertainment purposes, this platform provides a forum for people to express their opinions on political candidates, parenting practices, current events, restaurants, and so on. Facebook and other social media platforms also serve as a source of news for many people, a fact that became especially well-known during and after the 2016 U.S. presidential election due to accusations of the Russian government using social media to meddle in the election. Regardless of the precise ways that people use social media, platforms like Facebook expose us to others' opinions, and growing evidence suggests that such exposure can sway our opinions and behavior (Baek, 2015; Diehl, Weeks, & Gil de Zúñiga, 2016; Greenwood, Sorenson, & Warner, 2016). So even though social media might not be the first thing that comes to mind when you think about persuasive arenas, persuasion may well be occurring more subtly while people are using such forms of media for other purposes.

The Media and Conceptions of Social Reality

Some researchers have pointed to a more indirect, but arguably more profound and unsettling influence of the media: shaping our very conception of social reality (Eibach, Libby, & Gilovich, 2003). For example, even if specific advertisements don't succeed at getting us to buy specific products, they could still sway us to believe that personal happiness lies in materialistic pursuits. Television and film portrayals of U.S. society can be misleading about, for example, actual levels of racial or socioeconomic diversity in a given region or country. And political ads may not get us to vote for a particular candidate, but they may lead us to conclude that the country is going downhill.

AGENDA CONTROL IN FILMS
Sofia Coppola's film *The Beguiled* featured a cast lacking in racial diversity. Coppola was criticized for not including the African-American character who appeared in the book on which the film was based. Such biased media portrayals can result in misleading portraits of the world.

agenda control Efforts of the media to select certain events and topics to emphasize, thereby shaping which issues and events people think are important.

Political scientist Shanto Iyengar and social psychologist Donald Kinder refer to this effect of the media as **agenda control**: media of all types substantially contribute to shaping the information we think is broadly true and important. For example, the prominence given to certain issues in the news media—crime, traffic congestion, or economic downturns—is correlated with the public's perception that these issues are important (Cialdini, 2016; Dearing & Rogers, 1996; Iyengar & Kinder, 1987). In one experiment, viewers in one condition saw three news stories dealing with U.S. dependence on foreign energy sources; in another condition, six such stories; and in a final condition, no stories like this (Iyengar & Kinder, 1987). When exposed to no news about dependence on foreign energy, 24 percent of the viewers cited energy as one of the three most important problems facing the country. This percentage rose to 50 percent for the participants who saw three stories on the subject and 65 percent for those who saw six stories. Therefore, a politician in office should hope that news reports focus on things that are going well at the time, and a politician who wishes to defeat the incumbent should hope that the media focus on things that are not going well (**Box 8.4**).

George Gerbner and his colleagues have explored the agenda control thesis by coding the content of television programs and looking at the attitudes of heavy TV viewers (Gerbner, Gross, Morgan, & Signorielli, 1986). It should come as no surprise that the world depicted on most TV shows scarcely resembles social reality. On prime-time programs, for example, males outnumber females by a factor of 3 to 1; and recent analyses of popular films from 2007 to 2012 find that women have only about 25 percent of the speaking roles (Smith, Choueiti, Scofield, & Pieper, 2013). Ethnic minorities, young children, and older adults are also underrepresented. Crime is wildly more prevalent per unit of time on prime-time shows than in the average American's real life. And heavy TV viewers—those who watch 5 hours or more per day—construe social reality much like the reality they see on the screen. They tend to endorse more racially prejudiced attitudes, assume that women have more limited abilities than men, and overestimate the prevalence of violent crime. These findings could, of

BOX 8.4   FOCUS ON THE MEDIA

The Hostile Media Phenomenon

Accusations of media bias in coverage of the U.S. presidential race have been commonplace throughout modern history. For example, Richard Nixon maintained that the media were run by an elite Jewish clique. During his run for president in 2008, John McCain claimed the media were treating Barack Obama uncritically, in biased fashion, reacting to him as if he were a rock star rather than looking critically at his political agenda. Meanwhile, his running mate, Sarah Palin, derided the "lame-stream media" for having what she perceived as a consistent "liberal bias." Accusations of media bias, from both sides of the aisle, were particularly heated and frequent during the 2016 presidential campaign. Such accusations have continued since Trump took office, such as ones that arose about media coverage of Trump's controversial comments in the wake of the 2017 white supremacy protests in Charlottesville, VA. And, of course, since he assumed office, President Trump has regularly derided even the mainstream media as presenting "fake news."

The thesis that the media are ideologically biased regularly leads to the publication of best-selling books that appeal to liberals and conservatives alike. An entire organization, Fairness and Accuracy in Reporting (FAIR; www.fair.org), is devoted to documenting bias in the media (showing, for instance, that conservatives are more likely to appear as experts on such news shows as *Nightline*).

Research by Robert Vallone, Lee Ross, and Mark Lepper (1985) suggests that we all tend to believe the media are biased against our preferred causes. According to these researchers, most people believe they see the world in a reasonable, objective fashion—a fallacy known as naive realism (see Chapter 1). Thus, any media presentation that attempts to present both sides of an issue is going to be perceived as biased by both sides of any controversy. This basic tendency to perceive the media as hostile is a regularity in the political theater of presidential politics, as well as a common feature of our perception of the media. In one telephone survey conducted 3 days before the 1980 U.S. presidential election, among Jimmy Carter supporters who felt the media had favored one candidate in its coverage, 83 percent thought it favored Reagan. In contrast, for Reagan supporters who felt the media had been biased, 96 percent felt the media had favored Carter. One thing we can all agree on: the media are biased!

President Trump ✔
@POTUS

Follow ∨

If the people of our great country could only see how viciously and inaccurately my administration is covered by certain media! -DJT

6:28 AM - 29 Mar 2017

PERCEIVED BIAS IN THE MEDIA
The hostile media phenomenon is arguably stronger than ever in today's political and media climate. Accusations of bias on the part of mainstream media seem to accompany reports of any controversial event or issue. The leader of our country himself regularly tweets about such bias against him.

course, be the result of self-selection; perhaps more prejudiced, cynical, and uninformed people watch more TV in the first place. But the results are still worth pondering.

← **LOOKING BACK**

Most people believe that the media are quite effective in directly influencing public opinion. But this influence may often be indirect. The greatest effects of the media seem to involve influencing conceptions of reality and exerting agenda control, making people feel that certain issues are particularly important.

Resistance to Persuasion

Despite the degree to which we're immersed in media of different kinds on a daily basis, several reviews suggest that the media have only a small effect on what we buy, whom we vote for, and whether or not we adopt healthier habits (McGuire, 1985). Why? Part of the answer lies in the fact that many of the important principles of social psychology—such as the influence of our perceptual biases, previous commitments, and prior knowledge—serve as sources of independent thought and significant forces of resistance in the face of persuasive attempts.

Attentional Biases and Resistance

The U.S. Office of the Surgeon General issued a report in 1964 linking smoking to lung cancer. This presumably incontrovertible evidence about the related health risks would logically have both smokers and nonsmokers shifting their attitude about smoking. And yet, following the release of the report, 40 percent of smokers found the document to be flawed, compared with 10 percent of nonsmokers. We all like to think we absorb data and information in relatively unbiased fashion (Pronin, Gilovich, & Ross, 2004). If we learn that a particular practice or habit is dangerous to our health, we should alter our attitude accordingly. But our minds sometimes respond selectively to information in a way that maintains our initial point of view. Let's break this down into two concepts: selective attention and selective evaluation.

Several studies indicate that people are inclined to *attend selectively* to information that confirms their original attitudes (Eagly & Chaiken, 1998; Hart et al., 2009; Sweeney & Gruber, 1984). We tune in to information that reinforces our attitudes, and we tune out information that contradicts them. In one study, students who either supported or opposed the legalization of marijuana listened to a message that advocated legalization (Kleinhesselink & Edwards, 1975). The message contained 14 arguments: 7 were strong and difficult to refute (and thus clearly appealing to the pro-legalization

students), and 7 were silly and easy to refute (and thus very attractive to the anti-legalization students). The students heard the message through earphones accompanied by a continual static buzz. To combat this problem, students could press a button to eliminate the buzz for 5 seconds.

As you might have anticipated, the pro-legalization students pushed the button more often when the speaker was delivering the strong arguments in favor of legalization. They wanted to hear the information that would reinforce their own viewpoint. The anti-legalization students, in contrast, were more likely to push the button while the speaker was offering up the easy-to-refute arguments in favor of legalization. They wanted to hear the weakness of the pro arguments, thereby reinforcing their anti-legalization position.

During presidential elections, people are more inclined to subscribe to and read newspapers, blogs, and websites that support their preferred candidate and avoid those that support the opposition. Such selective attention in turn forms the basis of algorithms that drive the results of people's Internet searches, as well as the content of their social media feeds, leading to the creation of echo chambers (Quattrociocchi, Scala, & Sunstein, 2016; Stroud, 2010). It's this phenomenon that made Donald Trump's presidential victory a shock to many liberals, whose social media feeds, in the days leading up to the election, suggested that Clinton would likely triumph.

Social scientists of all stripes have discussed the tendency people have to evaluate information—such as the credibility of a source or the soundness of an argument—in ways that support their existing beliefs and values (Kahan, 2012; Kahan, Braman, & Jenkins-Smith, 2011). Someone who believes that the importance of climate change is exaggerated is likely to see more flaws in an article urging steps to combat global warming than is someone who believes that climate change is a defining issue of the times.

Peter Ditto and his colleagues have shown that selective evaluation extends to evidence that violates cherished beliefs about one's personal health. Patients who receive unhealthy diagnoses are more likely to downplay both the seriousness of the diagnosis and the validity of the test that produced it (Ditto, Jemmott, & Darley, 1988). In one study, Ditto and Lopez (1992) gave undergraduates a test of a fictitious medical condition, a deficiency that was supposedly associated with pancreatic disorders later in life. The test was simple: put saliva on a piece of yellow paper and observe whether it changes color in the next 20 seconds. In the deficiency condition, participants were told that if the paper remained yellow, they had the medical condition; in the no-deficiency condition, participants were told that if the paper changed to a dark green, they had the medical condition. You won't be surprised to know the paper remained yellow throughout the study.

Clearly, participants in the deficiency condition would be motivated to see the paper change color, and they should be disturbed by the evidence confronting them—the paper remaining yellow. And indeed, as shown in **Figure 8.4** (see p. 262), these participants took almost 30 seconds longer than those who got more favorable evidence to decide that their test was finished, repeatedly dipping the paper in saliva to give it every possible opportunity to turn green. Given our tendency to selectively attend to and evaluate incoming messages in ways that confirm our preexisting attitudes, it's no surprise that media effects can be weak in producing attitude change. Most messages, it would seem, end up mainly preaching to the choir.

"When I believe in something, I'm like a dog with a bone."
—MELISSA McCARTHY

SELECTIVE FRAMING
Like selective evaluation of evidence that supports or contradicts one's attitude, people can also frame the same issue—in this case, gun control—in a selective manner. People in favor of gun control frame guns as the main reason for gun-related deaths, whereas those opposed to gun control frame the problem in terms of those who shoot the guns.

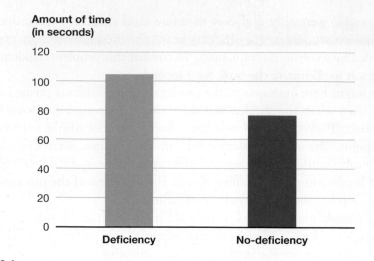

Amount of time (in seconds)

FIGURE 8.4
SELECTIVE EVALUATION
People who are personally motivated will be more skeptical of information that challenges cherished beliefs.
Source: Adapted from Ditto & Lopez, 1992.

PUBLIC COMMITMENT AND RESISTANCE
When people commit to a position on an issue publicly, this can increase their resistance to attempts to persuade them otherwise.

thought polarization hypothesis The hypothesis that more extended thought about a particular issue tends to produce a more extreme, entrenched attitude.

Previous Commitments and Resistance

Many persuasive messages fail because they can't overcome the target audience's previous commitments. Antidrug campaigns are aimed at decreasing habitual drug-taking behavior, which is embedded in a way of life and a community of friends centered around drugs. Some forces of resistance to change may be even more formidable than habits—genetics, for example. Research reveals that our political allegiances are passed from parent to child to a degree and seem to be part of our DNA (**Box 8.5**). Ads that try to get people to shift their political allegiances must, in effect, convince voters to abandon these deep commitments.

There's also evidence that public commitments, declarations of one's attitude around a given issue in a public setting, make people resist attitude change. (In addition, public commitments might make people resistant to conformity; see Asch's line judgment studies in Chapter 9.) In some studies, when participants made public commitments to their attitudes—as people do every day when discussing politics and social issues with their friends—they were more resistant to subsequent counterattitudinal messages than control participants (Kiesler, 1971; Pallak, Mueller, Dollar, & Pallak, 1972).

Why do public commitments increase our resistance to persuasion? One basic reason is that it's hard to back down from such endorsements without losing face, even when evidence is presented against the position we publicly embraced. A less obvious reason is that public commitments engage us in more extensive thoughts about a particular issue, which tends to produce more extreme, entrenched attitudes. Abraham Tesser labeled this idea the **thought polarization hypothesis**. To test his hypothesis, Tesser measured participants' attitudes about social issues, such as legalizing prostitution (Tesser & Conlee, 1975). He then had them think for a few moments about the issue. When they stated their opinions about the same issue a second time, they routinely gave stronger ratings; both opponents and proponents became polarized.

BOX 8.5 ▶ FOCUS ON BIOLOGY

The Genetic Basis of Attitudes

One of the deepest sources of our commitment to strong attitudes and resistance to persuasive messages is our genes. Work by Abraham Tesser (1993) indicates that our opinions and beliefs are in part inherited. He examined the attitudes of monozygotic (identical) twins, who share 100 percent of their genes, and those of dizygotic (fraternal) twins, who share 50 percent of their genes. For most of the viewpoints surveyed, the identical twins' attitudes were more similar than those of fraternal twins. This was true, for example, for opinions about the death penalty, jazz, censorship, divorce, and socialism. Moreover, researchers found that the more heritable attitudes were also more accessible, less susceptible to persuasion, and more predictive of feelings of attraction to a stranger who had similar attitudes. Of course, there is no gene for attitudes about censorship or socialism; the hereditary transmission must occur through some element of temperament, such as impulsivity, a preference for risk taking, or a distaste for novelty (which might make a person dislike jazz but be more tolerant of censorship).

More recent research by James Fowler and his colleagues found that genes account not only for politically relevant attitudes, as Tesser documented, but also for political participation (Fowler, Baker, & Dawes, 2008). They found that identical twins were more likely to resemble each other than were fraternal twins in sharing party affiliations and in their likelihood of voting in an election. No wonder it's often hard to shift people's political opinions and voting preferences and behavior; doing so would require changing a basic part of who they are.

Similarly, the repeated expression of attitudes has been shown to lead to more extreme positions in a variety of domains, including viewpoints about particular people, artwork, fashions, and football strategies (Downing, Judd, & Brauer, 1992; Judd, Drake, Downing, & Krosnick, 1991; Tesser, Martin, & Mendolia, 1995). But a caveat is in order here. Increased thought about an attitude object can lead to more moderate attitudes for people who previously had little motivation to think about the issue or little preexisting knowledge about it (Judd & Lusk, 1984).

Knowledge and Resistance

As you learned in reading about the ELM approach to persuasion, prior knowledge makes people engage with persuasive messages through the central route, thereby leading them to scrutinize those messages carefully. People with a great deal of knowledge are more resistant to persuasion; their beliefs and habits (and sometimes emotions) are tied up with their attitudes, and thus their point of view tends to be fixed. This insight has been repeatedly borne out in the experimental literature (Haugtvedt & Petty, 1992; Krosnick, 1988; Lydon, Zanna, & Ross, 1988; Zuwerink & Devine, 1996).

In a study of attitudes about environmental preservation, Wendy Wood (1982) divided students into two groups: those who were pro-preservation and knew a lot about the issue and those who were pro-preservation but knew less about the subject. She exposed these two groups to a message opposed to environmental preservation. Those with a lot of knowledge about the environment changed their stance only a little bit, as they counterargued a great deal in response to the message, relying on what they already knew and strongly believed about the issue. In contrast, the less knowledgeable students shifted their attitudes considerably toward the anti-preservation message.

Attitude Inoculation

Thus far, we've looked at how people's belief systems—their biases and preexisting knowledge—make them resistant to persuasion and attitude change. Social psychologists have discovered some techniques that can be used to strengthen these tendencies.

McGuire developed one such technique, which found inspiration in a rather unusual source: inoculation against viruses. When we receive an inoculation, we're exposed to a weak dose of the virus. This small exposure stimulates our immune system, which is then prepared to defend against larger doses of the virus. McGuire believed that resistance to persuasion could be encouraged in a similar fashion by **attitude inoculation**—small attacks on our beliefs that would engage our preexisting attitudes, prior commitments, and background knowledge and thereby counteract a larger attack (McGuire & Papageorgis, 1961).

In his studies on attitude inoculation, McGuire first assessed participants' endorsements of different cultural truisms to confirm a preexisting attitude, such as "It's a good idea to brush your teeth after every meal if at all possible" or "The effects of penicillin have been, almost without exception, of great benefit to mankind" (McGuire & Papageorgis, 1961). More than 75 percent of the participants checked 15 on a 15-point scale to indicate their agreement with truisms like these.

Then came the intervention. McGuire and Papageorgis exposed participants to a small attack on their belief in the truism. In the toothbrushing case, they might read, "Too frequent brushing tends to damage the gums and expose the vulnerable parts of the teeth to decay." In some conditions, the researchers had the participants refute that attack by offering arguments against it; this was the attitude inoculation, akin to a small dose of a virus stimulating the immune system. In other conditions, the researchers had participants consider arguments in support of the truism. Then, at some time between 1 hour and 7 days later, the participants read a three-paragraph, full-scale attack on the truism. **Figure 8.5** presents data that attest to the immunizing effectiveness of attitude inoculation.

attitude inoculation Small attacks on people's beliefs that engage their preexisting attitudes, prior commitments, and background knowledge, enabling them to counteract a subsequent larger attack and thus resist persuasion.

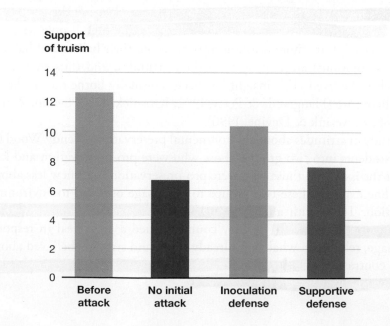

FIGURE 8.5
ATTITUDE INOCULATION
This study showed that using preexisting attitudes, commitments, and knowledge to come up with counterarguments against an initial attack on an attitude makes people more resistant to persuasion in the face of a subsequent attack (third bar) compared with when there was no initial attack (second bar), or when they initially generated supportive arguments in favor of their attitude (fourth bar).
Source: Adapted from McGuire & Papageorgis, 1961.

Applied to a real-life situation, like a smoking prevention program, the idea would be to present people with pro-smoking arguments from peers and advertisements, such as "Smoking is about freedom and maturity," then encourage them to make counterarguments. The hope would be that counterarguing in response to an initial attack would inoculate them, thus making them more resistant to future inducements to smoke. Inoculation techniques would seem to be very useful in today's context given how widely available and easily accessible "fake news" and other forms of misinformation are (van der Linden, Leiserowitz, Rosenthal, & Maibach, 2017).

← LOOKING BACK

People can resist persuasive messages by selectively attending to and evaluating information that confirms their original attitudes and beliefs and ignoring or criticizing contradictory information. Attitudes tied up with considerable prior knowledge can be highly resistant to change. Attitude inoculation can make people resist persuasive attempts, because the small attacks give them the chance to muster arguments to use when faced with stronger attacks on their beliefs and attitudes.

Chapter Review

SUMMARY

Dual-Process Approach to Persuasion

- The *elaboration likelihood model* hypothesizes that there are two routes to persuasion. A person's motivation and ability to think carefully and systematically about the content of a persuasive message determine which route is used.
- When using the *central route* to persuasion, people attend carefully to the message, and they consider relevant evidence and underlying logic in detail. People are especially likely to go through this route when motivation is high (the issue has personal consequences) and ability is high (they have a lot of knowledge in the domain). With the central route, people are sensitive to the quality of the persuasive arguments, leading them to be more persuaded when the arguments are strong but not when they are weak.
- In the *peripheral route* to persuasion, people pay attention to superficial aspects of the message. They use this route when they have little motivation (the issue has no bearing on their outcomes) or ability to attend to its deeper meaning (they have little knowledge or are distracted). With this route, people are persuaded by easy-to-process cues, such as the attractiveness and credibility of the message source or the mere length of the persuasive message.

The Elements of Persuasion

- The elements of a persuasive attempt are the source of the message ("who"), the content of the message ("what"), and the audience of the message ("to whom").

- Sources that are attractive, credible, and confident tend to be persuasive. Although a noncredible source is unlikely to induce immediate attitude change, a *sleeper effect* may occur, in which attitude change happens gradually and the message has become dissociated from its source.
- Vivid messages are usually more persuasive than matter-of-fact ones. An example is the *identifiable victim effect*, whereby messages with a single identifiable victim are more compelling than those without such vivid imagery. Messages that instill fear in the audience can also be effective, as long as they include information about the courses of action one can take to avoid the feared outcome.
- Advertisements in independent cultures emphasize the individual, and those in interdependent societies emphasize the collective.
- Characteristics of the audience affect whether a message is persuasive; they include the need for cognition (how deeply people like to think about issues), mood, and age.

Metacognition and Persuasion

- *Metacognition*, people's thoughts about their thinking, can play a powerful role in persuasion.
- The *self-validation hypothesis* states that when people have greater confidence in their thoughts, they are more persuaded in the (favorable or unfavorable) direction of their thoughts.
- Bodily movements, such as head nodding or shaking, can indicate the level of confidence people have in their thoughts about an attitude issue or object.

The Media and Persuasion

- Documenting the effects of media on persuasion can be methodologically challenging, but there is no question that the media can shape opinions, tastes, and behavior to some degree.
- The media are most effective in *agenda control*, shaping what people think about by controlling, for example, the number and kinds of stories presented on various issues.

Resistance to Persuasion

- People can be resistant to persuasion because of pre-existing biases, commitments, and knowledge. They selectively attend to and evaluate information according to their original attitudes, tuning in to what supports their prior attitudes and beliefs and tuning out whatever contradicts them.

- Public commitment to a position helps people resist persuasion. Just thinking about an attitude object can produce *thought polarization*, movement toward extreme views that can be hard to change.
- People with more knowledge are more resistant to persuasion because they can counterargue messages that take an opposite position to what they know and believe.
- Resistance to persuasion can be encouraged through *attitude inoculation*, exposing people to weak arguments against their position and allowing them to generate arguments against that opposing view.

THINK ABOUT IT

1. A new boutique coffeehouse just opened in your neighborhood featuring coffee sustainably sourced from small organic farms around the world. Design two ads for the coffeehouse, one using the central route to persuasion and one using the peripheral route. How do your ads differ?

2. Describe the three elements of a persuasive appeal, and give two examples of each element that influence persuasiveness.

3. Suppose you are part of a global advertising team responsible for creating ads for oatmeal in both South Korea and the United States. Design an ad for each country, and explain why you designed the ads the way you did.

4. What is the self-validation hypothesis? What aspects about our thoughts, besides the positive-negative direction and number of thoughts we have on a topic, influence whether or not we are persuaded by them?

5. Tyrell and his girlfriend, Shea, have very different views on capital punishment: he opposes it, while she supports it. Even after Tyrell presents evidence that capital punishment is both financially wasteful and ineffective at preventing crime, Shea does not change her views. Using what you know about resistance to persuasion, how might Shea be staving off Tyrell's attempts to persuade her?

The **answer guidelines** for the think about it questions can be found at the back of the book . . . ☞

ONLINE STUDY MATERIALS

Want to earn a better grade on your test?

Go to **INQUIZITIVE** to learn and review this chapter's content, with personalized feedback along the way.

267

How do strict social norms influence children?

How does religion influence how people think, feel, and act?

Why are tattoos viewed so differently today than they were in decades past?

Social Influence

IN 1980, YOU'D HAVE BEEN MORE LIKELY to see a woman smoking a cigar than sporting a tattoo. Back then, tattoos were rarely seen on anyone besides sailors and prison inmates. Now you wouldn't be surprised to see architects, accountants, doctors, judges, even professors with tattoos. According to a 2016 study, three in ten adults have at least one tattoo (Harris Poll, 2016).

The growing popularity of tattoos over the past few decades reflects the power of social influence. The many people who paid for permanent markings on their body didn't suddenly sense the virtues of body art on their own; they influenced one another. The influence was sometimes implicit ("Look at that cool arrow Jill has on her ankle") and sometimes explicit ("Check out our fraternity letters on my triceps; you should get them too").

Social influence takes many forms. It contributes to prison guards abusing inmates (see Chapter 1), schoolchildren failing to stop a bully, and soldiers suppressing their fear and charging into battle. Sometimes people consciously decide to copy others or comply with requests; other times they just go along, unaware they're being influenced. The power of social influence can be seen in studies of how much people in different social networks influence each other. You are 40 percent more likely to suffer from obesity if a family member or friend is obese. You're also 20 percent more likely to be obese if a *friend* of your friend is obese and 10 percent more likely if a friend of a friend of a friend is obese. This pattern, which seems to hold through three degrees of connection in social networks, has been demonstrated in studies of drinking behavior, smoking, and general levels of happiness. If a friend of your friend is happy, you're more likely to be happy too (Christakis & Fowler, 2013; Ejima, 2017).

A SOCIAL INFLUENCE NETWORK

This depiction shows how happiness clusters among friends, spouses, and siblings in a sample of participants in Framingham, Massachusetts. Each point represents a participant (circles for women, squares for men), and the lines between each point represent their relationship (black for siblings, red for friends and spouses). The color of each point represents that person's happiness level: blue for the least happy participants, yellow for the most happy, and green for those in between. You can readily see that the most and least happy people cluster together.

Source: Fowler & Christakis, 2008, © The BMJ.

This effect is partly due to shared genes and partly to what is called homophily, the tendency for people to associate disproportionately with people who are like them (see Chapter 10). However, not all these social network effects result from homophily and genetics. Some are the result of social influence. In one telling experiment, someone canvassed residents door-to-door and encouraged them to vote. The canvassing influenced not just the person at the door, but other household members as well (Nickerson, 2008). Another study examined whether participants in a game where money was at stake cooperated with one another or focused on their narrow self-interest (Fowler & Christakis, 2010). Everyone played many rounds of the game, with each participant randomly assigned to a different four-person group each round. The investigators found that whether a person was altruistic on, say, round 3 had been influenced by how selfish or altruistic that person's groupmates had been on round 2. But that person was also influenced by what her round 2 groupmates had experienced with *their* groupmates on round 1. Because the participants were strangers randomly assigned to different groups, the results must have been due to social influence, not homophily or genetics. Thus, some types of behavior truly are contagious.

The topic of social influence highlights an important theme first raised in Chapter 1: many elements of a situation can profoundly affect behavior. In examining social influence, this chapter discusses a number of "situationist classics" in social psychology—experiments that have become well known, in both the field of psychology and the broader culture, for revealing how seemingly inconsequential details of a social situation can have powerful effects on behavior. ■

SOCIAL INFLUENCE AND FASHION

Social influence affects what we do and say and how we present ourselves to others. (A) In the 1940s, tattoos were rarely seen on anyone other than sailors and soldiers. (B, C) Today, tattoos are common on both men and women.

What Is Social Influence?

Social influence refers to the many ways people affect one another. It involves changes in behavior or attitudes that result from the comments, actions, or simply the presence of others. Other people routinely try to influence us—a friend's pressure to go out drinking, an advertiser's efforts to get us to adopt the latest fashion, a charity's plea for money, or the attempts of a parent, politician, or priest to shape our moral, political, or religious values. And we ourselves often try to influence others, as when we unconsciously smile at someone for actions we like, frown at someone for behavior we dislike, or deliberately try to coax a friend into doing us a favor. Effective interactions with others require knowing when to yield to their attempts to influence us and when—and how—to resist. Effective social interaction also demands that we exercise some skill in our own attempts to influence others.

Social psychologists distinguish among several types of social influence. The most familiar form of influence is **conformity**, defined as changing one's behavior or beliefs in response to some real (or imagined) pressure from others. As noted earlier, the pressure to conform can be implicit, as when you decide to toss out your loose-fitting jeans in favor of those with a tighter cut (or vice versa) simply because other people are doing so. But conformity pressure can also be explicit, as when members of a peer group pointedly encourage one another to smoke cigarettes, try new drugs, or push the envelope on the latest extreme sport.

When conformity pressure is sufficiently explicit, it blends into another type of social influence called **compliance**, which is when a person responds favorably to an explicit request by another person. Compliance attempts can come from people with some power over you, as when your boss asks you to run an errand, or they can come from peers, as when a classmate asks to borrow your notes. Compliance attempts from powerful people often aren't as nuanced and sophisticated as those from peers because they don't have to be. (Think how much easier it would be for your professor to persuade you to loan her $20 than it would be for the person who happens to be sitting next to you in the classroom.) Another type of social influence, **obedience**, occurs when a more powerful person, an authority figure, issues a demand (rather than a request), to which the less powerful person submits.

Conformity

If you went back in time to the 1930s and visited any commuter train station, you would notice a number of similarities to today's commuting scene, as well as a few obvious differences. One important similarity is that most people would keep to the right so that collisions and inconvenience are kept to a minimum. But two important differences would stand out: nearly all the commuters in the 1930s were men, and nearly all of them wore hats. The transition from a predominantly male workforce in the 1930s to today's more gender-egalitarian workplace was the product of all sorts of social influences, many of them intentional and hard fought. But what about the hats? Was their disappearance over the years deliberate? If so, who did the deliberating? It's hard to resist the conclusion that this trend was much more mindless—that most people simply copied the clothing choices of everyone else.

social influence The many ways people affect one another, including changes in attitudes, beliefs, feelings, and behavior resulting from the comments, actions, or even the mere presence of others.

conformity Changing one's behavior or beliefs in response to explicit or implicit pressure (real or imagined) from others.

compliance Responding favorably to an explicit request by another person.

obedience In an unequal power relationship, submitting to the demands of the person in authority.

"Be regular and orderly in your life like a bourgeois, so that you may be violent and original in your work."
—GUSTAVE FLAUBERT, NINETEENTH-CENTURY FRENCH NOVELIST

CONFORMITY PRESSURES IN DAILY LIFE
Conformity to what others are doing can be seen in these comparative images of commuters during the 1930s and commuters today. Nearly all the earlier commuters wore hats on their way to work, but very few do so now.

Is the tendency to go along with others a good thing or a bad thing? In today's Western society, which prizes autonomy and uniqueness, the word *conformity* seems negative to most people. If someone called you a conformist, for instance, you probably wouldn't take it as a compliment. To be sure, some types of social influence *are* bad, such as going along with a crowd to pull a harmful prank or drive a vehicle while intoxicated. Other types of conformity, however, are neither good nor bad, such as conforming to the norm of wearing very loose pants (as in the 1990s) or tighter pants (as in the 2000s).

Still other types of conformity are clearly beneficial. Conformity eliminates potential conflict and makes human interaction much smoother, and it allows us not to have to think so much about every possible action. Conformity plays a big part, for example, in getting people to suppress anger; to pay taxes; to form lines at the theater, museum, and grocery store; and to stay to the right side of the sidewalk or roadway (in the United States anyway). Would any of us really want to do away with those conformist tendencies? Indeed, evolutionary psychologists and anthropologists have argued that a tendency to conform is generally beneficial. We are often well served by doing what others are doing, unless we have a good reason not to (Boyd & Richerson, 1985; Henrich & Boyd, 1998).

Automatic Mimicry

Perhaps the most subtle form of conformity is our tendency to mindlessly imitate other people's behavior and movements. It's often said that yawning and laughter are contagious, but a great deal of other behavior is contagious as well. Like it or not, we're all nonconscious copycats: we all mimic those around us.

The tendency to reflexively mimic the posture, mannerisms, expressions, and other actions of those around us has been examined experimentally. In one study, undergraduates took part in two 10-minute sessions in which each of they, along with another participant, described various photographs from popular magazines, such as *Newsweek* and *Time* (Chartrand & Bargh, 1999). The other participant was, in reality, a confederate of the experimenter, and there was a different confederate in each of the two sessions. The confederate in one session frequently rubbed his or her face, whereas the confederate in the other session continuously shook his or her foot. As the participant and confederate went about their business of describing the various photographs, the participant was surreptitiously videotaped. The videotapes were taken of the participants only—the confederates weren't visible on the tape—so the experimenters watching the tapes could not have been affected by knowledge of what movement—face rubbing or foot shaking—the confederates were doing. As predicted, the participants tended to mimic (conform to) the behavior exhibited by the confederate. The participants shook their feet more often in the presence of a foot-shaking confederate and rubbed their faces more often when next to a face-rubbing confederate (**Figure 9.1**).

"I don't know why. I just suddenly felt like calling."

REASONS FOR MIMICRY Why do we mindlessly copy the behavior of other people? There appear to be two reasons. William James (1890) provided the first explanation by proposing his principle of **ideomotor action**, whereby merely thinking about a behavior makes performing that behavior more likely. Simply thinking about eating a bowl of ice cream, for example, makes us more apt to open the freezer, take out the carton, and dig in. The thought that we might type the wrong letter on the keyboard makes us more prone to typing that very letter (Wegner, 1994; Wegner, Ansfield, & Pilloff, 1998). The principle of ideomotor action is based on the fact that the brain regions responsible for perception overlap with those responsible for action. When this principle is applied to mimicry, it means that when we see others behave in a particular way, the idea of that behavior is brought to mind (consciously or otherwise) and makes us more likely to behave that way ourselves.

The second reason we reflexively mimic others is to facilitate smooth, gratifying interaction and, in so doing, to foster social connection. People tend to like those who mimic them more than those who don't, even when they're unaware of being mimicked (Chartrand & Bargh, 1999). What's more, people who have been mimicked tend to engage in more prosocial behavior (behavior intended to help others) immediately afterward, such as donating money to a good cause or

ideomotor action The phenomenon whereby merely thinking about a behavior makes performing it more likely.

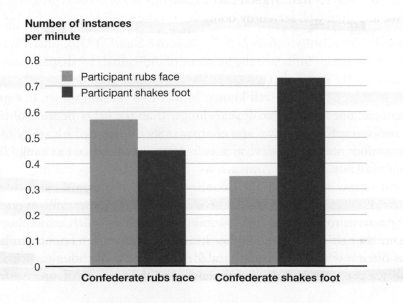

Number of instances per minute

[Bar graph with legend:]
- Participant rubs face
- Participant shakes foot

[Y-axis: 0 to 0.8 in increments of 0.1]
[X-axis categories: Confederate rubs face, Confederate shakes foot]

FIGURE 9.1
UNCONSCIOUS MIMICRY

This graph shows the average number of times per minute participants performed an action (face rubbing, foot shaking) while in the presence of someone performing that action or not, demonstrating that people tend to mindlessly mimic the behavior of those around them.
Source: Adapted from Chartrand & Bargh, 1999.

IDEOMOTOR ACTION AND CONFORMITY
Seeing others behave in a particular way sometimes makes us nonconsciously mimic their postures, facial expressions, and behavior. Before the signing of the 1995 Middle East Peace Accord, U.S. President Bill Clinton, Israeli Prime Minister Yitzhak Rabin, Egyptian President Hosni Mubarak, and King Hussein of Jordan all adjusted their ties, as Yasser Arafat, who was not wearing a tie, looked on.

leaving a larger tip for the person who mimicked them (van Baaren, Holland, Kawakami, & van Knippenberg, 2004; van Baaren, Holland, Steenaert, & van Knippenberg, 2003). Studies have shown that our tendency to mimic others is particularly strong when we feel a need to affiliate with others and when the others in question are well liked (Chartrand & Bargh, 1999; Lakin & Chartrand, 2003; Leighton, Bird, Orsini, & Heyes, 2010; Stel et al., 2010). Mimicry seems to be a helpful first step toward goodwill and harmonious interaction.

Informational Social Influence and Sherif's Conformity Experiment

Sometimes people conform to one another a bit more consciously, as illustrated by an early conformity experiment by Muzafer Sherif (1936). Sherif was interested in how groups influence the behavior of individuals by shaping how reality is perceived. He noted that even our most basic perceptions are influenced by frames of reference. In the well-known Müller-Lyer illusion shown in **Figure 9.2**, for example, one vertical line appears longer than the other because of how the lines are "framed" by the two sets of arrows. Sherif designed his study to examine how other people can serve as a *social* frame of reference to change our perception of reality.

Sherif's experiment was built around what's called the autokinetic illusion—the sense that a stationary point of light in a completely dark environment is moving. Ancient astronomers first noted this phenomenon, which occurs because in complete darkness there are no other stimuli, or frames of reference, to help the viewer discern where the light is located. Perhaps, Sherif thought, other people in the same completely dark space would serve as a social frame of reference that

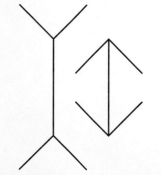

FIGURE 9.2
THE MÜLLER-LYER ILLUSION
The framing of the vertical lines by the arrows affects how the viewer perceives their lengths. Even though the two vertical lines are exactly the same length, the one on the left appears longer than the one on the right because of its outward-pointing "fins" at the top and bottom, as opposed to the inward-pointing fins at the top and bottom of the line on the right.

would influence the viewer's perceptions of the light's movement. To start off, Sherif put individual participants in a darkened room alone, presented them with a stationary point of light on trial after trial, and had them estimate how far it "moved" each time. Some people thought, on average, that the light moved very little on each trial (say, 2 inches), and others thought it moved a good deal more (say, 8 inches).

Sherif's next step was to bring several participants into the room together and have them call out their estimates. He found that people's estimates tended to converge over time. Those who individually had thought the light moved a fair amount soon lowered their estimates; those who individually had thought the light moved very little soon raised theirs (**Figure 9.3**). Sherif argued that everyone's individual judgments quickly fused into a group norm, and that norm influenced how far participants reported seeing the light move. A follow-up experiment reinforced his interpretation: when participants came back for individual testing up to one year later, their judgments still showed the influence of their group's earlier responses (Rohrer, Baron, Hoffman, & Swander, 1954).

Social psychologists typically interpret the behavior of Sherif's participants to be the result of **informational social influence**—the reliance on other people's comments and actions as an indication of what's likely to be correct, proper, or effective (Cialdini & Goldstein, 2004; Deutsch & Gerard, 1955). We want to be right, and the opinions of other people can be a useful source of information to draw on. (Remember this concept of *informational* social influence, as we will soon contrast it in depth with another type of social influence.) The tendency to draw on other people's comments, actions, and opinions as useful sources of information is most pronounced when we're uncertain about what is factually correct or are in unfamiliar situations and are uncertain about how to behave. For example, we're more likely to conform to others' views on subjects we have only vague ideas about, such as

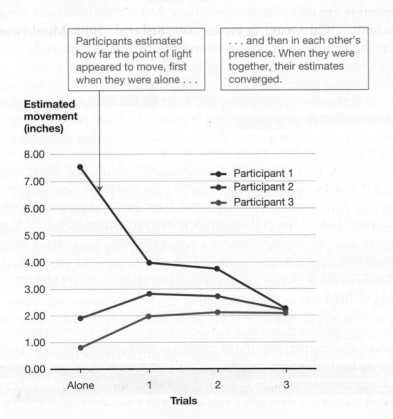

Participants estimated how far the point of light appeared to move, first when they were alone . . .

. . . and then in each other's presence. When they were together, their estimates converged.

Estimated movement (inches)

8.00
7.00
6.00
5.00
4.00
3.00
2.00
1.00
0.00

Alone   1   2   3

Trials

Participant 1
Participant 2
Participant 3

informational social influence The influence of other people that results from taking their comments or actions as a source of information about what is correct, proper, or effective.

FIGURE 9.3
INFORMATIONAL SOCIAL INFLUENCE
Sherif's conformity experiment used the autokinetic illusion to assess group influence. Participants' estimates tended to become more similar over time.
Source: Adapted from Sherif, 1936.

macroeconomic policy, than on familiar topics, such as how much more fun it would be to vacation in Northern Italy versus North Korea. And we're more likely to conform to what others are doing when we are in a foreign country than when we are in the familiar environment of our own country.

Note that the task Sherif asked his participants to perform was about as ambiguous as it gets, so informational social influence was strong. The light, in fact, didn't move at all—it just appeared to move. The uncertainty of the light's movement left the participants open to the influence of others. (See also Baron, Vandello, & Brunsman, 1996; Levine, Higgins, & Choi, 2000; Tesser, Campbell, & Mickler, 1983.)

Normative Social Influence and Asch's Conformity Experiment

You might be wondering: What's the big deal here? It makes sense that participants conformed to one another's judgments. After all, there was in fact no right answer, and participants couldn't have felt confident in their own estimates. Why *not* rely on others? If this is your reaction, then you're thinking just like another pioneer of conformity research, psychologist Solomon Asch. Asch thought that Sherif's experiment, although informative about a certain type of conformity, didn't address situations in which there is a clear conflict between an individual's own judgment and that of the group. Sherif's findings don't apply, for example, to the experience of knowing you've had too much to drink to drive safely while your peers are urging you to get behind the wheel ("Come on. Don't be a wimp, you'll be fine"). Asch predicted that in a case of clear conflict between a person's own position and the viewpoint of the group, there would be far less conformity than that observed by Sherif. He was right. The reduced rate of conformity, however, was not what made Asch's experiment one of the most famous in the history of psychology. What made his study so well known was how often participants actually *did* conform, even when they thought the group's viewpoint was completely crazy (Levine, 1999; Prislin & Crano, 2012).

In this famous experiment (Asch, 1956), eight male students were gathered together to perform a simple perceptual task: determining which of three lines was the same length as a target line (**Figure 9.4**). Each person called out his judgment publicly, one at a time. The task was so easy that the experience was uneventful, boring even—at first.

On the third trial, however, one participant found that his private judgment was at odds with the expressed opinions of everyone else in the group. He was the only true participant in the experiment; the seven others were confederates instructed by Asch to respond incorrectly. The confederates responded incorrectly on 11 more occasions before the experiment was over. The question was how often the participant would forsake what he knew to be the correct answer and conform to the incorrect judgment given by everyone else. Here there was no ambiguity as there was in Sherif's experiment: the right answer was clear. (When participants in a control group made these judgments by themselves, with no social pressure, they almost never made a mistake.)

As Asch predicted, there was less conformity in his study than in Sherif's, but the rate of caving in to the group was still surprisingly high. Three-quarters of the participants conformed to the group's incorrect answer at least once. Overall,

SOLOMON ASCH
A pioneer of conformity research, Asch studied the effect of normative social influence.

Test lines   Target line

FIGURE 9.4
NORMATIVE SOCIAL INFLUENCE
Participants in Asch's conformity study had a difficult time understanding why everyone appeared to be seeing things incorrectly. Even though it was clear to them what the right answer was, they ended up going along with the erroneous majority a third of the time.
Source: Adapted from Asch, 1956.

participants conformed on a third of the critical trials. These results aren't simply surprising; they are disturbing as well. We like to think of people, ourselves especially, as sticking to what we think is right rather than following the herd (Pronin, Berger, & Molouki, 2007). In addition, we worry about people abandoning the dictates of their own conscience to follow others into wrongheaded or potentially destructive behavior.

There is undoubtedly some *informational* social influence, discussed in the previous section, at work in Asch's experiment: the incorrect judgments called out by the majority were for lines that were only 0.5–0.75 inch off the correct answer, so some participants may have questioned their own judgment and regarded the confederates' responses as reliable sources of information. However, control participants who were not subject to social pressure got the answer right nearly 100 percent of the time, so there wasn't much uncertainty about the correct response. Thus, informational social influence was not the main cause of conformity. The primary reason people conformed was to avoid standing out negatively in the eyes of the group (**Box 9.1**, see p. 278). Social psychologists refer to this kind of influence as **normative social influence**—the desire to avoid being criticized, disapproved of, or shunned (Deutsch & Gerard, 1955).

People are often reluctant to depart from the norms of society, or at least the norms of the groups they care most about, because they fear the social consequences (Cialdini, Kallgren, & Reno, 1991). The normative social pressures in Asch's experiment were sufficiently intense that the participants found themselves in a wrenching dilemma: "Should I say what I truly think it is? But what would everyone else think if I gave a different response? They all agree, and they all seem so confident. Will they think I'm nuts? Will they interpret my disagreement as a

normative social influence The influence of other people that comes from the desire to avoid their disapproval and other social sanctions (ridicule, barbs, ostracism).

BOX 9.1 ▶ FOCUS ON HEALTH

Bulimia and Social Influence

Why do so many young women engage in binge eating and then purging by vomiting or using laxatives? The phenomenon is relatively new. This sort of behavior, an eating disorder known as bulimia, was virtually unheard of until about 45 years ago. Has it become more common because the fashion industry and media have persuaded women to want to be thinner than is natural or healthy (see Chapter 10)? Is it because body image and self-esteem have worsened?

Such factors may play a role in the current epidemic of bulimia, but another factor is simple social influence. Christian Crandall (1988) studied sorority women at a large university and found that the more bulimic a woman's friends were, the more bulimic she was likely to be. As Crandall learned, this relationship wasn't because bulimic women discovered each other and became friends. Early in the school year, when the students had known one another for only a short time, there was no association between the level of a woman's bulimia and that of her friends. But over the course of the year, women in established friendship groups (not different, newly formed groups) came to have similar levels of bulimia.

Crandall studied two sororities and found two slightly different patterns of influence. In one sorority, women who differed in their level of bulimic activity from the average level in their sorority were less likely to be popular. Crandall inferred from this that there was an "appropriate," or normative, level of bulimia in that sorority, and deviations from it *in either direction* were punished by rejection. In the other sorority, more binge eating (up to quite a large amount) was associated with more popularity. In that sorority, Crandall concluded, there was pressure toward considerable binge eating, and those most inclined to binge were rewarded with acceptance and popularity. The lesson, once again, is that social influence is everywhere, even influencing whether or not we're likely to suffer from chronic medical conditions.

THINNESS AND SOCIAL INFLUENCE When some members of a sorority engage in binge eating and purging to stay thin, pressures on other members of the sorority to do likewise can be intense.

---

slap in the face? But what kind of person am I if I go along with them? What the #@!$% should I do?"

To get an idea of the intensity of the participants' dilemma, imagine the following scenario. As part of a discussion of Asch's experiment, your social psychology professor shows an image of the target line and the three test lines and reports that although the right answer is line B, the confederates all say it's C. As your professor begins to move on, one student raises his hand and announces with conviction, "But the right answer *is* C!"

What would happen? Probably everyone would chuckle, making the charitable assumption that the student was trying to be funny. But if the student continued to insist that the confederates' answer was correct, the chuckles would turn to awkward, nervous laughter, and everyone would turn toward the professor in an implicit plea to "make this awkward situation go away." In subsequent lectures, people might avoid sitting by the nonconformist, and lunch invitations, dating opportunities, and offers to join a study group would likely diminish as well. Negative social repercussions like these are what Asch's participants likely felt they risked if they departed from the majority's response. Perhaps it's no surprise, then, that participants so often chose not to take the risk and conformed to the majority response (Janes & Olson, 2000; Kruglanski & Webster, 1991; Levine, 1989; Schachter, 1951).

Factors Affecting Conformity Pressure

Several generations of researchers have examined a number of variables that influence the tendency to conform. These include the characteristics of the group; the surrounding context, including cultural influences; and the task or issue at hand. (See **Box 9.2** on p. 280 for another determinant of people's readiness to conform.) This research has provided a clearer understanding of when people are especially likely to conform and when they're less likely to do so. Both informational and normative social influences are powerful forces: as either one intensifies, so does the rate of conformity.

GROUP SIZE It's probably no surprise that people are more likely to conform to a bigger group. What *is* surprising, perhaps, is that the effect of group size levels off pretty quickly (**Figure 9.5**). Research using Asch's paradigm, for example, has shown an increase in conformity as the size of the group increases, but only to a group size of three or four; after that, the amount of conformity levels off (Campbell & Fairey, 1989; Gerard, Wilhelmy, & Conolley, 1968; Insko, Smith, Alicke, Wade, & Taylor, 1985; Rosenberg, 1961).

When we consider informational social influence, it makes sense that the larger the number of people who express a particular opinion, the more likely that opinion has merit as a source of information—but only to a certain point. The validity of a consensus opinion increases only if the individual opinions are independent of one another. The more people there are, the less likely it is that their views are independent; therefore, additional consenting opinions don't offer any additional real information.

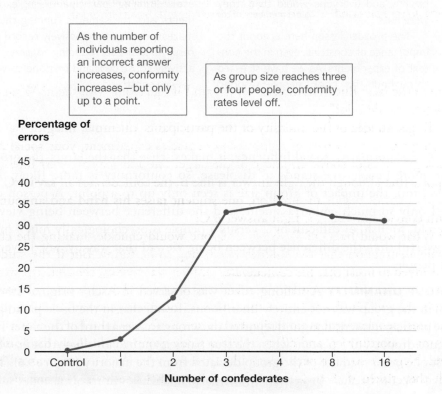

As the number of individuals reporting an incorrect answer increases, conformity increases—but only up to a point.

As group size reaches three or four people, conformity rates level off.

FIGURE 9.5
THE EFFECT OF GROUP SIZE ON CONFORMITY
As the number of people in a majority increases, so does the tendency to conform, but only up to a unanimous majority of three or four. After that, conformity levels off.
Source: Adapted from Asch, 1951.

BOX 9.2

Not So Fast:
Critical Thinking about Conformity and Construal

A common reaction upon learning about Asch's experiment is to think, "Wow, if people conform that much to a group of strangers, imagine how much they'd conform to the judgments of those they care about and have to continue to deal with in the future!" Indeed, it is true that normative social influence is diminished in situations, like Asch's, where people care less about others' judgments because everyone is a stranger and they all assume they'll never see one another again (Lott & Lott, 1961; Wolf, 1985).

Yet there are other, more subtle aspects of Asch's procedure that can lead to *more* conformity than usually occurs in daily life. Participants in Asch's experiment faced a double whammy. First, they had to confront the fact that everyone else saw things differently than they did. Second, they had no basis for understanding *why* everyone else saw things differently. ("Could I be mistaken? No, it's as plain as day. Could they be mistaken? I don't see how, because they're not any farther away than I am and it's so clear. Are they unusual? No, they don't look much different from me or anyone else.")

If we can pinpoint a reason for why our opinions are different ("They don't see things the way I do because they're wearing distorting glasses"), both informational influence and normative social influence are lessened. Informational social influence is reduced because the explanation for the difference of opinion can diminish the group's impact as a source of information ("They're biased"). Normative social influence is reduced because we can assume that those in the majority are aware of why we differ from them. For instance, if we have different views on some burning political issue of the day, those we disagree with might think we're biased, selfish, or have different values, but at least they won't think we're crazy. In Asch's situation, in contrast, the participants faced the reasonable fear that if they departed from everyone else's judgment, their behavior would look truly bizarre, and everyone would think they were nuts.

The broader lesson here is about the importance of construal, even in the context of experiments. As we have stressed throughout this book, people respond not to the objective situations they face, but to their subjective interpretations of those situations. Participants in Asch's study were in a situation in which it was unusually hard to develop a compelling interpretation of what was going on. It's hard to act independently and decisively when things have stopped making sense, so it may be a mistake to assume that Asch's participants would conform even more outside the psychology lab (Ross, Bierbrauer, & Hoffman, 1976).

To understand the real meaning of any experiment, it's important to pay attention to how the participants might have interpreted the instructions, procedures, and stimuli they faced. The same is true for experimenters. They must pay attention to the meaning the participants are apt to give their experience in the lab in order to design studies that constitute truly informative tests of their hypotheses. Running participants in experiments isn't the same as running rats in mazes: people don't passively record and respond to the surrounding context; they actively construe it and respond to what they've construed.

As for normative social influence, it makes sense that the larger the group, the more people one stands to displease, so conformity is more likely. But here, too, the impact of group size is seen only up to a point. A person can feel only so much embarrassment, and the difference between being viewed as odd, foolish, or difficult by 2 versus 4 people is psychologically much more powerful than the difference between being viewed that way by, say, 12 versus 14 people.

GROUP UNANIMITY A striking effect was observed in Asch's original studies when the group was not entirely unanimous. Recall that in the basic paradigm, the participant went along and reported the wrong answer a third of the time. That figure dropped to 5 percent when the true participant had an ally—that is, when just one other member of the group deviated from the majority (**Figure 9.6**). This effect occurs because the presence of an ally weakens both informational social influence ("Maybe I'm not crazy after all") and normative social influence ("At least I've got someone to stand by me"). This effect suggests a powerful tool for protecting independence of thought and action: if you expect to be pressured to conform and want to remain true to your beliefs, bring along an ally. Indeed, an important subtext of Asch's research is just how hard it can be to go it alone. People can stand up to misguided peers, but they usually need some help. Being the lone dissenter can be agonizingly difficult.

Note that the other person who breaks the group's unanimity doesn't need to offer the correct answer—just something that departs from the group's answer. Suppose the right answer is the shortest of the three lines, and the majority claims it's the longest. If the fellow dissenter states that it's the middle line, it still reduces the rate of conformity even though the participant's own view (that it's the shortest line) hasn't been reinforced. What matters is the break in unanimity. This fact has important implications for free speech. It suggests that we might want to tolerate loathsome and obviously false statements ("The Holocaust never happened"; "The World Trade Center attacks were a government hoax") not because what is said has any value, but because it liberates *other people* to make atypical remarks that *are* of value. The presence of voices, even bizarre or patently wrongheaded voices, that depart from conventional opinion frees the body politic to speak out and thus can foster productive political discourse.

ANONYMITY If standing up to a misguided majority is hard, what happens when people can register dissent without calling attention to themselves? In other words, what happens when the response is anonymous? Anonymity eliminates normative social influence and therefore should substantially reduce conformity. Indeed, when the true participants in Asch's paradigm are allowed to write their judgments on a piece of paper instead of having to say them aloud for the group to hear, conformity drops dramatically. When nobody else is aware of your judgment, there is no need to fear the group's disapproval.

This effect highlights an important distinction between the impact of informational and normative social influence. Informational social influence, by guiding how we come to see the issues or stimuli before us, leads to **internalization**, or the private acceptance of the position advanced by the majority (Kelman, 1958). We don't just mimic a particular response—we adopt the group's perspective. Normative social influence, in contrast, often has a greater impact on public compliance than on private acceptance. That is, to avoid disapproval, we sometimes do or say one thing but continue to believe another.

EXPERTISE AND STATUS Suppose you were a participant in Asch's experiment, and the other participants who were inexplicably stating what you thought was the wrong answer were all former major-league batting champions. If you proceeded on the assumption that a player can't lead the league in hitting without exceptional eyesight, you'd probably grant the group considerable authority and go along with the group's opinion. In contrast, if the rest of the group were all wearing thick eyeglasses, you'd be less apt to take their opinions seriously.

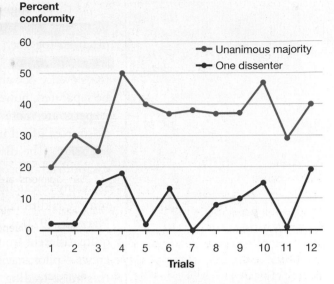

FIGURE 9.6
THE EFFECT OF GROUP UNANIMITY ON CONFORMITY
The tendency for people to go along with a misguided majority drops precipitously once there's a break in the majority, when there is just one other person willing to dissent.
Source: Adapted from Asch, 1956.

"If there is any principle of the Constitution that more imperatively calls for attachment than any other it is the principle of free thought—not free thought for those who agree with us but freedom for the thought that we hate."
—OLIVER WENDELL HOLMES

internalization Private acceptance of a proposition, orientation, or ideology.

As this thought experiment illustrates, the expertise and status of the group members powerfully influence the rate of conformity. Expertise and status often go together, because we grant greater status to those with expertise, and we often assume (not always correctly) that those with high status are experts (Koslowsky & Schwarzwald, 2001). To the extent that these characteristics can be separated, however, expertise primarily affects informational social influence. Experts are more likely to be right, so we take their opinions more seriously as sources of information. Status, in contrast, mainly affects normative social influence. The disapproval of high-status individuals can hurt more than the disapproval of people we care less about.

Many researchers have examined the effect of expertise and status on conformity (Cialdini & Trost, 1998; Crano, 1970; Ettinger, Marino, Endler, Geller, & Natziuk, 1971). One of the most intriguing studies of status used a paradigm quite different from Asch's. Torrance (1955) gave the members of navy bombing crews—pilot, navigator, and gunner—a number of reasoning problems, such as this horse-trading problem:

> A man bought a horse for $60 and then sold it for $70. He later repurchased the horse for $80 and then, changing his mind yet again, sold it for $90. How much money did he make on his series of transactions? (For the correct answer, see page 284.)

The crew then had to report one answer for the whole group. Torrance monitored the group's deliberations and found that if the pilot (who generally held the highest status) originally came up with the correct solution, the group eventually reported it as their answer 91 percent of the time. If the navigator offered the correct answer, the group ended up reporting the correct answer 80 percent of the time. But if the lowly gunner offered the correct answer, the group offered it up only 63 percent of the time. The opinions of higher-status individuals thus tend to carry more weight (Foushee, 1984).

CULTURE As we emphasize throughout this book, people from interdependent cultures are much more concerned about their relationships with others and about fitting into the broader social context than people from independent cultures. People reared in interdependent cultures are therefore likely to be more susceptible to both informational social influence (they consider the actions and opinions of others very telling) and normative social influence (they consider the high regard of others very important). Thus, people from interdependent cultures might be expected to conform more than those from independent cultures.

Evidence supports this contention. An analysis of the results of 133 experiments using the Asch paradigm in 17 countries found that conformity does indeed tend to be greater in interdependent countries (Bond & Smith, 1996). The individualism that is highly valued in American and Western European societies has given individuals in those independent cultures a greater willingness to stand apart from the majority.

EXPERTISE, STATUS, AND SOCIAL INFLUENCE
When the United States was preparing to invade Iraq to unseat Saddam Hussein and secure his putative weapons of mass destruction in March 2003, the government sent Secretary of State Colin Powell to speak to the delegates of the United Nations because he had great credibility. Powell presented the case for the U.S. government's contention that Iraq had weapons of mass destruction, hoping to convince the delegates of the need to invade Iraq.

TIGHT AND LOOSE CULTURES Michele Gelfand and her colleagues have pursued a distinction between cultures that overlaps somewhat with the independence-interdependence dimension but differs enough that it deserves a name of its own: tightness versus looseness (Gelfand et al., 2011). Conformity to social norms lies at the heart of this construct. Some cultures, which Gelfand calls "tight," have strong norms regarding how people should behave and don't tolerate departure from those norms. Other cultures are "loose": their norms aren't as strong, and their members tolerate more deviance.

In a highly ambitious study, the Gelfand team examined a number of variables in 33 nations (Gelfand et al., 2011). They found that compared with loose nations, tight nations are more likely to have governments that are autocratic or dictatorial, to punish dissent, to have sharp controls on what can be said in the media, to have more laws and higher monitoring to ensure that the laws are obeyed, and to inflict more punishment for disobedience. If a nation was tight on one of these dimensions, it tended to be tight on all; if it was loose on one, it tended to be loose on all. Tight countries include India, Germany, People's Republic of China, South Korea, Japan, Austria, Portugal, Britain, Turkey, and Italy. Loose countries include Greece, Hungary, Israel, the Netherlands, Ukraine, New Zealand, and Brazil. You probably guessed that the United States is relatively loose, which it is—on the whole. But there's great variation across America's 50 states on almost everything, including how tight or loose they are. California, Nevada, and Maine are rather loose, whereas Mississippi, Kansas, and Texas are rather tight (Harrington & Gelfand, 2014).

Gelfand and her colleagues surveyed people in each of the 33 countries, asking them about the appropriateness of arguing, crying, laughing, singing, flirting, reading a newspaper, and several other behaviors in each of 15 different social situations or places, such as a doctor's office, a restaurant, and a movie theater (Gelfand et al., 2011). The tighter the nation's laws and norms, the fewer behaviors were allowed in these various situations. The researchers also asked people if their country had many social norms, whether others would strongly disapprove if someone acted inappropriately, and so forth. Citizens in tighter nations pointed to tighter constraints.

TIGHT VS. LOOSE CULTURES
(A) As this picture of Chinese girls lined up for school illustrates, some cultures are relatively tight; they have strong norms about how people should behave and tolerate very little leeway in deviating from those norms. (B) Other cultures are relatively loose; their norms aren't as stringent, as this more chaotic line indicates.

Why are some nations tight and some loose? The Gelfand team found that tighter nations tend to have higher population densities, fewer natural resources, unreliable food supplies, less access to safe water, greater risk of natural disasters, more territorial threats from neighbors, and a higher prevalence of pathogens (Gelfand et al., 2011). It appears, then, that behavioral constraints are associated with, and perhaps partly caused by, ecological constraints.

GENDER If there are cultural differences in conformity behavior, should we expect gender differences as well? Perhaps. There are significant differences in how various cultures socialize boys and girls, but they have one thing in common: they all sex-type to some degree. Women are raised to value interdependence and to nurture important social relationships more than men are, whereas men are raised to value autonomy and independence more than women are. So we might expect women to be more subject to social influence and thus to conform more than men do.

Reviews of the literature on gender differences in conformity have shown that women tend to conform more than men—but only a bit (Bond & Smith, 1996; Eagly, 1987; Eagly & Carli, 1981; Eagly & Chrvala, 2006). The difference in conformity tends to be greatest when the situation involves face-to-face contact, as in Asch's original study. However, the difference also seems to be strongly influenced by the specific content of the issue at hand. As we have seen, people tend to conform when they're confused by the events unfolding around them or the topic under discussion. For instance, if you're like most people, you know more about sandwiches than the periodic table, so you're less likely to conform to other people when they assert that the most important ingredient in a good sandwich is horseradish than when they assert that the atomic number of beryllium is 62.

Analyses of the specific contexts in which men and women differ in the tendency to conform reveal just this effect: that you are more likely to conform in areas where you feel less confident (Sistrunk & McDavid, 1971). Thus, women tend to conform more in stereotypically male domains (on questions about geography or deer hunting, for instance), whereas men tend to conform more in stereotypically female domains (such as questions about child rearing or relationship advice). It should be no surprise, then, that overall, women and men tend to differ in conformity, but only slightly.

The Influence of Minority Opinion on the Majority

There was a time in the United States when people owned slaves, when women weren't allowed to vote, and when children worked long hours for scandalously low pay in unhealthy conditions. But small groups of abolitionists, suffragettes, and child welfare advocates saw things differently than their peers. They worked tirelessly to change public opinion about each of these issues—and they succeeded. In each case the broader public changed its views, and important legislation was passed. Minority opinion became the majority opinion. One of the most dramatic examples of minority influence in the West is quite recent. Over the past 20 years, the acceptance of same-sex marriage has gone from a small minority to a majority today.

Examples like these are reminders that although conformity pressures can be powerful, majority opinion doesn't always prevail. It's possible to resist conformity pressure, and minority voices are sometimes loud enough to change the prevailing norms. How do minority opinions come to influence the majority? Are the sources of influence the same as those that majorities bring to bear on minorities?

In the first experimental examination of these questions, Serge Moscovici and his colleagues had groups of participants call out whether a color was green or blue (Moscovici, Lage, & Naffrechoux, 1969). The border between blue and green isn't always clear, but the critical stimuli the participants saw were ones that, when tested alone, participants nearly always thought were blue (99 percent of the time). The experimenter showed participants these stimuli in a setting in which they could hear one another's responses, including those of a minority group of respondents (confederates of the study) who all responded alike. When the confederates varied their responses randomly between "green" and "blue," the participants said "green" after the confederates did so only 1 percent of the time, about the same as when participants responded alone. But when the confederates responded with "green" consistently, the participants responded with "green" 8 percent of the time.

The influence of the consistent minority showed up in other ways as well. When the participants thought the study was over, the experimenter introduced them to a second investigator. This second investigator showed participants a series of blue-green colors and recorded where each participant, individually, thought blue left off and green began. Those who had earlier been exposed to a consistent minority now identified more of these stimuli as green; their sense of the border between blue and green had shifted. Thus, when the minority opinion was consistent, it had both a direct effect on participants' responses in the public setting and a latent effect on their subsequent private judgments.

Further investigations of minority influence have shown that minorities have their effect primarily through informational social influence rather than through normative social influence (Moscovici, 1985; Nemeth, 1986; Wood, Lundgren,

> *"Give me a firm place to stand and I will move the world."*
> —ARCHIMEDES OF SYRACUSE

MINORITY INFLUENCE ON THE MAJORITY
Minority opinions can influence the majority through consistent and clear messages that persuade the majority to systematically examine and reevaluate its opinions. (A) British suffragette Emmeline Pankhurst presented her views in favor of women's right to vote to an American crowd in 1918. (B) Rosa Parks refused to give up her seat at the front of a bus in Montgomery, Alabama, in December 1955. Her actions resulted in a citywide bus boycott that eventually led the U.S. Supreme Court to declare that segregation was illegal on the city bus system. (C) Harvey Milk was the first openly gay person to be elected to public office in California. His activism contributed to the much greater support for the civil rights of gay and lesbian individuals that we see today.

Ouellette, Busceme, & Blackstone, 1994). People in the majority are typically not terribly concerned about the social costs of stating their opinion out loud—they have the majority on their side and normative social influence is minimized. But they might wonder why the minority keeps stating its divergent opinion. This can lead the majority to consider the stimulus more carefully, resulting in a level of scrutiny and systematic thought that can produce genuine change in attitudes and beliefs. Thus, majorities typically elicit more conformity, but it is often of the public compliance sort. In contrast, minorities typically influence fewer people, but the nature of the influence is often deeper and results in true private attitude change (Maass & Clark, 1983).

← LOOKING BACK

Conformity can be a response to implicit or explicit social pressure, and it can be the result of automatic mimicry, informational social influence, or normative social influence. Group size influences conformity, but it appears to reach maximum effect at around four people. Unanimity is also crucial in conformity, and a single ally can help an individual hold out against the group. People conform more to those with high status or expertise, and they conform more when they must express their opinions publicly rather than register them in private. People from interdependent cultures conform more than people from independent cultures, and women conform slightly more than men. Conformity pressures notwithstanding, minorities often make an impact, primarily through informational social influence.

Compliance

You need a favor from a friend. How should you ask? You're trying to raise funds for a favorite charity. How should you go about getting people to donate their hard-earned money? Your first job out of college is in sales. How do you get people to sign on the dotted line? These are all questions about compliance: getting people to comply with something you want. Coming from the other direction, how can you avoid being influenced by the compliance attempts of others? What techniques should you watch out for? Social psychologists have studied different strategies for eliciting compliance, and their research findings help explain how—and how effectively—these strategies work (Cialdini, 2008, 2016; Goldstein, Martin, & Cialdini, 2008).

There are three basic types of compliance approaches: those directed at the head, those directed at the heart, and those based on the power of norms (which, given the impact of informational and normative influences, appeal to both the head and the heart). People can be led to comply with requests because they see good reasons for doing so, because their emotions compel them to do so, or because everyone else is doing so. Of course, these types of influence aren't always neatly separable, and many compliance efforts are a blend of the three.

Reason-Based Approaches

We often make decisions by weighing the pros and cons—by tabulating the reasons for and against different options and choosing the one with the most favorable balance of good and bad. Some attempts to influence other people are targeted at changing their decision calculus. Reason-based approaches aim to convince people that they would be better off choosing a particular course of action.

NORM OF RECIPROCITY When someone does something for us, we usually feel compelled to do something in return. Indeed, all societies that have ever been studied possess a powerful **norm of reciprocity**, according to which people are expected to provide benefits for those who provided benefits for them (Fiske, 1991; Gouldner, 1960). This norm also exists in many bird and mammal species. When one monkey removes parasites from another's back, the latter typically returns the favor, thus helping cement the social bond between them.

When someone does you a favor, you have a tacit obligation to agree to any reasonable request that person might make in turn. To fail to respond is to violate a powerful social norm and run the risk of social condemnation (Cotterell, Eisenberger, & Speicher, 1992). Indeed, the English language is rich in derogatory terms for those who don't uphold their end of the bargain: *sponge, moocher, bum, deadbeat, ingrate, parasite, bloodsucker, leech*. If you do a favor for someone, that person will probably agree to a reasonable request you subsequently make, to avoid being seen as a moocher. This may be why restaurant customers often leave larger tips when the server gives them a piece of candy (Strohmetz, Rind, Fisher, & Lynn, 2002).

The influence of the norm of reciprocity in getting someone to comply was demonstrated in a simple experiment in which two people were asked to rate a number of paintings, supposedly as part of a study of aesthetics (D. Regan, 1971; see also Burger, Sanchez, Imberi, & Grande, 2009; Whatley, Webster, Smith, & Rhodes, 1999). One was a real participant; the other was a confederate of the experimenter. In one condition, the confederate returned from a break with two sodas and offered one to the participant. "I asked (the experimenter) if I could get myself a Coke, and he said it was OK, so I bought one for you, too." In another condition, the confederate returned empty-handed. Later, the confederate asked the participant for a favor. He explained that he was selling raffle tickets; the prize was a new car, and he'd win $50 if he sold the most tickets. He then proceeded to ask if the participant was willing to buy any tickets for 25 cents apiece: "Any would help, the more the better." (To make sure all participants had the means to purchase some tickets, they had already been paid—in quarters—for participating in the study.)

In a testament to the power of the norm of reciprocity, participants who earlier had been given a soda by the confederate bought twice as many raffle tickets as those who had not (or those who had been given a soda by the experimenter, to control for the possibility that simply receiving a

norm of reciprocity A norm dictating that people should provide benefits to those who benefit them.

"All contacts among men rest on the schema of giving and returning the equivalent."
—GEORG SIMMEL, GERMAN SOCIOLOGIST

"There is no duty more indispensable than that of returning a kindness."
—CICERO

RECIPROCITY AND GROOMING AMONG MAMMALS
Reciprocity helps promote group living and reduce aggression, as evidenced by grooming in macaques. They abide by the rule "You scratch my back and I'll scratch yours." Macaque A is more likely to groom macaque B than a random other macaque if macaque B has previously groomed macaque A.

soda, and perhaps being in a good mood as a result, is what had increased compliance).

Thus, doing a favor for someone creates an uninvited debt that the recipient is obligated to repay. Businesses and other organizations often try to take advantage of this pressure by preceding their request with a small gift. Insurance agents give out calendars or return-address labels. Marketers who want us to complete a survey send it along with a dollar. Cult members offer a flower before giving their pitch. Sometimes our hearts can sink when we see these gifts coming, and we often go to great lengths to avoid them, recognizing the obligations they bring.

THE RECIPROCAL CONCESSIONS (DOOR-IN-THE-FACE) TECHNIQUE Robert Cialdini, social psychology's most innovative contributor to the literature on compliance, has explored a novel application of the norm of reciprocity. The inspiration for his research on the subject is best introduced in his own words:

> I was walking down the street when I was approached by an eleven- or twelve-year-old boy. He introduced himself and said that he was selling tickets to the annual Boy Scouts circus to be held on the upcoming Saturday night. He asked if I wished to buy any at five dollars apiece. Since one of the last places I wanted to spend Saturday evening was with the Boy Scouts, I declined. "Well," he said, "if you don't want to buy any tickets, how about buying some of our big chocolate bars? They're only a dollar each." I bought a couple and, right away, realized that something noteworthy had happened. I knew that to be the case because: (a) I do not like chocolate bars; (b) I do like dollars; (c) I was standing there with two of his chocolate bars; and (d) he was walking away with two of my dollars. (Cialdini, 1984, p. 47)

Cialdini's experience with the Boy Scout led him to articulate a general compliance technique whereby people feel compelled to respond to a concession by making a concession themselves (Cialdini et al., 1975; Feeley, Anker, & Aloe, 2012; O'Keefe & Hale, 1998, 2001; Reeves, Baker, Boyd, & Cialdini, 1991). First, you ask someone for a very large favor that will certainly be refused, and then you follow that request with one for a more modest favor that you are really interested in receiving. The idea is that the drop in the size of the request will be seen as a concession; the person being asked will feel compelled to match that concession to honor the norm of reciprocity. The most available concession the person can make is to comply with the asker's second request.

Another way of looking at this **reciprocal concessions technique** is that the first favor is so large and unreasonable that the target inevitably refuses, slamming the door in the face of that request but keeping it open just a crack for the subsequent, smaller request to get through. Accordingly, it's also known as the *door-in-the-face technique*.

Cialdini demonstrated the power of this technique in a field study in which members of his research team posed as representatives of the "County Youth Counseling Program" and approached students around campus. They asked individual students if they would be willing to chaperone a group of juvenile delinquents on a trip to the zoo. Not surprisingly, the overwhelming majority, 83 percent, refused. But the response rate was much different for a second group of students who had first encountered a much larger request. They were first asked whether they would be willing to counsel juvenile delinquents for 2 hours

reciprocal concessions technique A compliance approach that involves asking someone for a very large favor that will certainly be refused and then following that request with one for a smaller favor (which tends to be seen as a concession the target feels compelled to honor).

a week for the next two years! Not surprisingly, all of them refused, at which point they were asked about chaperoning the trip to the zoo. Fifty percent of these students agreed to chaperone—triple the rate of the other group (Cialdini et al., 1975). A series of carefully crafted follow-up studies revealed that the pressure participants felt to comply to what was perceived as a concession (chaperone one trip to the zoo rather than provide counsel for the next two years) was responsible for the dramatic increase in compliance. Accordingly, this technique doesn't work when the two requests are made by different individuals. In that case, the second, smaller request isn't seen as a concession, but rather an entirely separate request by a different person, so the person being asked doesn't feel the same obligation.

THE FOOT-IN-THE-DOOR TECHNIQUE All of us perform certain actions because they're consistent with our self-image. Environmentalists take the time to recycle, even when sorely tempted to toss a bottle or can into the trash, because that's part of what it means to be an environmentalist. Skiers rise early to tackle fresh snow, even when they really want to hit the snooze button on the alarm clock, because that's what real skiing enthusiasts do. It's logical, therefore, that if requests are crafted to appeal to a person's self-image, the likelihood of compliance is increased.

One way to appeal to a person's self-image is to employ what's known as the **foot-in-the-door technique** (Burger & Guadagno, 2003; Dillard, Hunter, & Burgoon, 1984; Freedman & Fraser, 1966; Souchet & Girandola, 2013). It starts with a small request to which nearly everyone complies, thereby allowing the person making the request to get a foot in the door. This person then follows up with a larger request involving the real behavior of interest. The idea is that the initial agreement to the small request will lead to a change in the target person's self-image as someone who does this sort of thing or who contributes to such causes. That person then has a reason for agreeing to the subsequent, larger request: "It's just who I am."

In an early test of this technique, the investigators knocked on doors in a residential neighborhood and asked one group of homeowners if they would be willing to have a large billboard sign bearing the slogan "Drive Carefully" installed in their front yard for one week (Freedman & Fraser, 1966). They were shown a picture of the sign: it was large and unattractive, so not surprisingly, only 17 percent agreed to the request. Another group of residents was approached with a much smaller request—to display in a window of their home a 3-inch-square sign bearing the phrase "Be a Safe Driver." Virtually all of them agreed with the request. Two weeks later, when this group was asked to display the billboard in their yard (receiving the very same request as those in the first group), a staggering 76 percent of them agreed to do so.

You've probably heard politicians oppose a piece of legislation—not because there's anything wrong with the legislation itself, but because they think it might create a "slippery slope" leading to the passage of more questionable legislation

foot-in-the-door technique A compliance approach that involves making an initial small request with which nearly everyone complies, followed by a larger request involving the real behavior of interest.

THE FOOT-IN-THE-DOOR TECHNIQUE
After getting the customer to agree to a test drive, it may be easier for the salesperson to close the deal and have her buy the car.

later on. Research on the foot-in-the-door technique suggests that there is merit to this concern. Human behavior, like a ball rolling down a sloping plane, is subject to momentum. Getting people started on something small often makes it easier to get them to do much bigger things down the road. We'll see just how powerful these slippery slopes can be when we discuss the most famous studies in all of social psychology later in this chapter.

Emotion-Based Approaches

Cognitive, or reason-based, approaches aim at the head and, as we have seen, can be very effective in obtaining compliance. Affective, or emotion-based, approaches aim at the heart, and they, too, are powerful tools for eliciting compliance.

POSITIVE MOOD Suppose you want to ask your dad for a new computer, a new amplifier for your guitar, or simply to borrow the family car for a road trip. When would you ask? When he's just come home from work in a foul mood, cursing his boss and his suffocating job? Or after he's just landed a promotion and a big raise? It doesn't take an advanced degree in psychology to know that it's better to request a favor when the person's in a good mood (Andrade & Ho, 2007). A positive mood makes people feel expansive and charitable, so they're more likely to agree to reasonable requests. Even little children know to wait before asking someone for a favor until that person seems cheerful.

The wisdom of this approach has been verified in countless experiments. In one study, participants received a telephone call from someone who claimed to have spent her last dime on this very ("misdialed") call; she asked if they would dial a specified number and relay a message (Isen, Clark, & Schwartz, 1976). In one condition, shortly before receiving the call, participants were given a free sample of stationery to put them in a positive mood. In another condition, participants did not receive a free sample before the call. When the request was made of those without the free sample, only 10 percent complied. But the compliance rate shot up dramatically among participants who received the request a few minutes after receiving the gift. The compliance rate then declined gradually as the delay between receiving the gift and hearing the request increased (**Figure 9.7**).

A positive mood tends to increase compliance for two main reasons. First, our mood colors how we interpret events. We're more likely to view requests for favors as less intrusive and less threatening when we're in a good mood. We're more inclined to give others the benefit of the doubt. For instance, when you're in a good mood, you're more likely to consider someone who asks to borrow your class notes to be a victim of circumstance who could get back on track with a little help rather than an irresponsible or lazy person who doesn't deserve to be bailed out (Carlson, Charlin, & Miller, 1988; Forgas, 1998a, 1998b; Forgas & Bower, 1987).

POSITIVE MOOD AND REQUESTS When people are in a good mood, they are more likely to agree to requests. Those attending this benefit for the charitable organization Pencils of Promise (and getting to shake Usher's hand) are therefore more likely to ᵇate money to support the charity's ᵗˢ to build schools and expand ᵃⁿᵃl opportunities around the

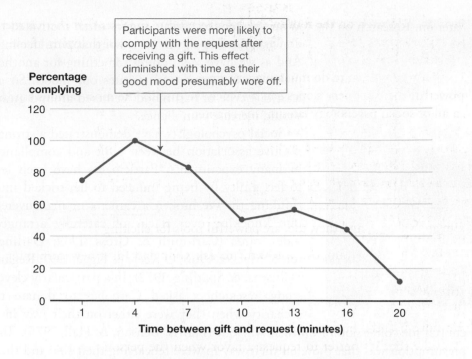

Percentage complying

Participants were more likely to comply with the request after receiving a gift. This effect diminished with time as their good mood presumably wore off.

Time between gift and request (minutes)

FIGURE 9.7
POSITIVE MOOD AND COMPLIANCE
In this study, being in a good mood boosted participant compliance, with the effect slowly wearing off with the passage of time.
Source: Adapted from Isen, Clark, & Schwartz, 1976.

The second reason a positive mood tends to increase compliance involves what's known as mood maintenance. Pardon the tautology, but it feels good to feel good, and we typically want that feeling to last as long as possible (Clark & Isen, 1982; Wegener & Petty, 1994). One way to sustain a good mood is to do something for another person (Dunn, Aknin, & Norton, 2008). Stated differently, one way to wreck a good mood is to turn down a request for a favor and invite all sorts of self-recrimination: "What kind of heartless person am I?"

Several studies have shown that wanting to maintain a good mood is an important component of the impact of a positive mood on compliance. In one experiment, some of the participants were first given cookies, which put them in a good mood; the others weren't given cookies. All of them were then asked (by someone other than the person who provided the cookies) if they'd be willing to assist with an experiment by serving as a confederate. Half the participants were told the job of confederate would involve *helping* the "true" participant in the experiment, and the other half were told it would involve *hindering* the participant. Having received a cookie (and being in a good mood) increased the compliance rate when the task involved helping the participant, but not when it involved hindering the participant. Helping another person promotes feeling good; hurting someone doesn't. Thus, while being in a good mood increases compliance, it does not do so when the act of compliance would undermine that good mood.

NEGATIVE MOOD If a good mood increases compliance, does a bad mood decrease it? It surely can (your dad is less likely to lend you the family car when he's mad at his boss), but even the slightest introspection reveals that certain types of bad moods are actually likely to *increase* compliance, not decrease it. Some people know this and use it to their advantage. Suppose, for example, your girlfriend was flirting with a classmate of yours, and you point out the offense. Would that be a good time to ask her for something? You bet it would!

NEGATIVE STATE RELIEF
Oskar Schindler (in the center) saved the lives of 1,200 Polish Jews during the Holocaust. Initially driven by the desire for easy profits, he took over a Jewish factory and ran it with cheap Jewish labor. Perhaps in a desire for negative state relief or from sheer humanitarianism, he used the millions he made from the cheap labor to bribe officials to save those who were slated for death. He is pictured here in Tel Aviv with some of those he saved and their descendants.

negative state relief hypothesis The idea that people engage in certain actions, such as agreeing to a request, to relieve their negative feelings and feel better about themselves.

"The best way to get people to do something is to tell them that their neighbors are already doing it."
—JOSHUA GREENE, PSYCHOLOGIST

When people feel guilty, they're often motivated to do whatever they can to get rid of that awful feeling. And as we have seen, doing something for another makes us feel good and elevates our mood. So at least one type of bad mood, centered around guilt, should increase compliance.

Social psychologists have demonstrated a strong, positive association between guilt and compliance in many experiments. Participants have been led to feel guilty by being induced to lie, tricked into thinking they've broken a camera, or maneuvered into knocking over stacks of carefully arranged index cards (Carlsmith & Gross, 1969; Darlington & Macker, 1966; O'Keefe & Figgé, 1997; Regan, Williams, & Sparling, 1972). In a particularly clever study, researchers asked Catholics to donate to a charity when they were either on their way into church for confession or on their way out (Harris, Benson, & Hall, 1975). The presumption was that those on their way in were rehearsing their sins and thus feeling guilty; those on their way out had done penance for their sins and were no longer plagued by guilt. As predicted, those solicited on the way in to church gave more money than those solicited on the way out.

Other types of bad moods, not just those produced by guilt, can also increase compliance. In one study, watching an adorable lab rat get "accidentally" jolted with an intense shock led participants to donate more money to charity than those who hadn't seen the unfortunate event (J. Regan, 1971). And in general it seems that bad moods sometimes increase compliance in part because we simply don't want to feel bad, and helping others makes us feel better, so we jump at the chance to brighten our mood. This is the **negative state relief hypothesis** in action, which says that taking an action to benefit someone else, especially when it's for a good cause, is one way to make ourselves feel better (Cialdini, Darby, & Vincent, 1973; Cialdini & Fultz, 1990; Cialdini et al., 1987). We often help others, in other words, to help ourselves.

A final word about the impact of moods, good and bad, on compliance. Investigators in Israel have found that if parole judges had just finished a meal before hearing a prisoner's plea for release from prison, there was a two-thirds chance they would vote for parole (Danziger, Levav, & Avnaim-Pesso, 2011). Cases that came up just before lunch, however, when the judges were hungry and presumably crankier, had precisely a zero chance for parole. A full stomach makes a difference, so hit your dad up for the car keys after dinner, not before.

Norm-Based Approaches

Adolescent girls exposed to pregnant peers are more likely to become pregnant themselves (Akerlof, Yellen, & Katz, 1996); planning for retirement is greatly influenced by coworkers' plans (Duflo & Saez, 2003); and student drinking is connected to student perceptions of how much other students drink (Lewis & Neighbors, 2004). The tendency to conform to people around us can be harnessed to achieve compliance with explicit requests or implicit suggestions.

Norm-based approaches to compliance are based on the power of social norms. They appeal to both the head and the heart.

EFFECTIVE NORM-BASED APPEALS Letting people know what others are doing can be used to advance the public good. Consider a norm-based approach to energy use that was instituted in California (Schultz, Nolan, Cialdini, Goldstein, & Griskevicius, 2007). Researchers left hang-tags on people's doors indicating their average daily residential energy use (in kilowatt-hours), as well as that of their neighbors. The effect of this simple intervention was clear-cut and immediate: those who consumed more energy than average altered their habits to significantly reduce their energy use.

What about the households that used *less* energy than average? Did telling them that their neighbors tended to be less conscientious make them more wasteful? Yes, it did. But the investigators had a simple remedy at hand that preserved the decrease in energy use among the energy wasters while avoiding increased energy use by the energy savers. The usage information given to half the households was accompanied by a small sign of approval or disapproval: a happy face for those who had used relatively little energy and a sad face for those who had used more than average. The signal of approval to the former was enough to maintain the superior conservation efforts of those who might otherwise have slacked off after hearing that their neighbors used more energy than they did (**Figure 9.8**). Used wisely, providing information about norms can be a powerful tool to promote energy conservation: giving consumers information about norms reduces energy consumption by the same amount as does raising the price of energy 10–20 percent.

Telling people about social norms is likely to be most effective when the information is surprising (when people have misunderstood the norm), such as when people overestimate the popularity of destructive behavior or underestimate the popularity of constructive behavior. Student drinking is a case in point. On campuses across the United States, students think that binge drinking is much

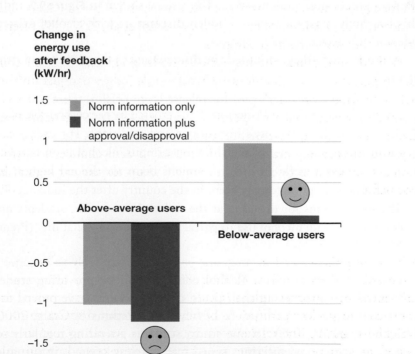

FIGURE 9.8
USING NORMS TO CONSERVE ENERGY
In this study, telling above-average energy consumers how much energy they use and how much the average household uses significantly reduced energy consumption (bars on the left). Providing this information to below-average energy consumers led to significantly greater energy consumption, unless it was accompanied by a simple symbol of approval (bars on the right).
Source: Adapted from Schultz et al., 2007.

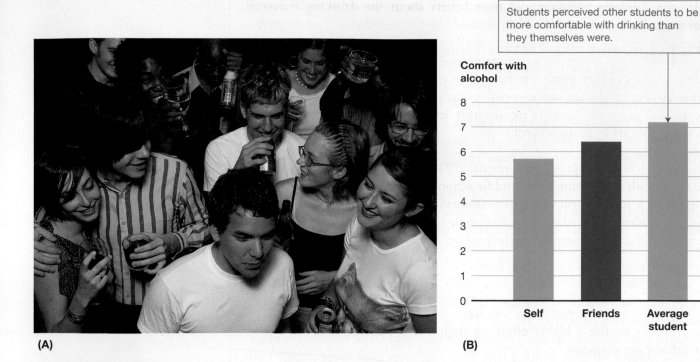

Students perceived other students to be more comfortable with drinking than they themselves were.

(A)

(B)

FIGURE 9.9
PLURALISTIC IGNORANCE
(A) University students believe drinking alcohol is more popular among their peers than it really is. Because of this belief, they censor their own reservations about drinking, thus furthering the illusion that alcohol is so popular.
(B) These results show student ratings of their own and others' comfort with campus drinking habits at Princeton University.
Source: Part B adapted from Prentice & Miller, 1993.

more common than it actually is and that "teetotaling" or moderate drinking is much less common than it is (Perkins, Haines, & Rice, 2005). These beliefs represent examples of pluralistic ignorance (discussed in Chapter 4). In one study, Deborah Prentice and Dale Miller (1993) examined the discrepancy between private attitudes and public norms about alcohol use at Princeton University. Prentice and Miller asked Princeton undergraduates how comfortable they felt about campus drinking habits, as well as the comfort level of both their friends and the average undergraduate. If the students were suffering from pluralistic ignorance, they would indicate that they were less at ease with drinking than they supposed most students were. The results, shown in **Figure 9.9**, indicate that this is exactly what happened. Hidden discomfort with alcohol existed side by side with perceived popular support.

Prentice and Miller attributed the discrepancy to the visibility of drinking on campus:

> The alcohol situation at Princeton is exacerbated by the central role of alcohol in many of the university's institutions and traditions. For example, at the eating clubs, the center of social life on campus, alcohol is on tap 24 hours a day, 7 days a week. Princeton reunions boast the second highest level of alcohol consumption for any event in the country after the Indianapolis 500. The social norms for drinking at the university are clear: students must be comfortable with alcohol use to partake of Princeton social life. (Prentice & Miller, 1993, p. 244)

Efforts to stem excessive alcohol consumption by providing students with accurate information about their peers' drinking habits have proved to be quite effective (Neighbors, Larimer, & Lewis, 2004; Perkins & Craig, 2006; Schroeder and Prentice, 1998). In one study, students attending regularly scheduled club or organizational meetings typed into wireless keypads information about their own drinking behavior and their beliefs about the drinking habits of their peers (LaBrie, Hummer, Neighbors, & Pedersen, 2008). Their aggregate responses were immediately projected for all to see, giving everyone information about actual drinking behavior on campus—and correcting widespread misunderstandings of how much and how often other students drink. In follow-up online surveys conducted one and two months later, students who received this information reported drinking significantly less than they had previously and less than students in a control group.

Similar norm-based approaches have been used to combat harassment and bullying in schools (Paluck & Shepherd, 2012; Shepherd, & Paluck, 2015). In one study, half of a group of 56 middle schools in New Jersey were randomly assigned to a social norm treatment condition in which a randomly selected group of students was asked to model opposition to the kinds of conflict and harassment that were common at their school (for example, speaking out when one student taunted or viciously teased another). The other schools served as controls. Disciplinary reports declined in the treatment schools by 30 percent relative to the control schools. As you might expect, some students were more effective than others at modeling anti-harassment norms, with the more popular students having a bigger effect on their peers' beliefs about what sorts of conflicts are common or acceptable at their school (Paluck, Shepherd, & Aronow, 2016).

DESCRIPTIVE AND PRESCRIPTIVE NORMS In preparing norm-based compliance appeals, it's important to be aware that there are two kinds of norms. **Descriptive norms** are simply descriptions of what is typically done. **Prescriptive norms**, often called *injunctive norms*, are what one is supposed to do. Descriptive norms correspond to what *is*; prescriptive norms correspond to what *ought to be*. University administrators often say that students should get 8–9 hours of sleep each night (prescriptive norm), but most students sleep much less (descriptive norm).

To increase compliance, the two norms should not be placed in conflict with each other. A common mistake is to try to strengthen the pull of the prescriptive norm by stating how infrequently it is followed. "Isn't it a shame that so few people . . ." vote in elections, eat a healthy diet, get screened for cancer—you name it. Making such an appeal seems sensible, but note that it highlights the unfortunate reality—the descriptive norm—as much or more than the prescriptive norm you want to promote (Sieverding, Decker, & Zimmermann, 2010; Stok, de Ridder, de Vet, & de Wit, 2014). By saying what a shame it is that so few people vote, you're pointing out that few people vote. Given the power of descriptive norms, such information can actually make people *less* likely to vote, not more likely. Indeed, those involved in get-out-the-vote campaigns now realize, thanks to research by social psychologists, that it's more effective to emphasize how many people vote, not how few (Gerber & Rogers, 2009).

descriptive norm The behavior exhibited by most people in a given context.

prescriptive norm The way a person is supposed to behave in a given context; also called *injunctive norm*.

DESCRIPTIVE AND PRESCRIPTIVE NORMS IN CONFLICT
By telling people they shouldn't remove petrified wood from the Petrified National Forest (prescriptive norm), park officials are communicating that stealing wood is something people do (descriptive norm). This can increase the very action—theft—the authorities want to prevent.

Researchers conducted an ingenious investigation of this approach in the Petrified Forest National Park in Arizona, where visitors sometimes take samples of petrified wood home with them as souvenirs (Cialdini et al., 2006). If everyone took samples, of course, there would soon be no Petrified Forest to visit. To examine the most effective ways to deal with the problem, the investigators rotated different warning signs at various locations in the park. One sign included the usual emphasis on the severity of the problem, stating, "Many past visitors have removed petrified wood from the park, changing the state of the Petrified Forest," accompanied by photographs of visitors taking wood. An alternative sign was framed positively: "The vast majority of past visitors have left the petrified wood in the park, preserving the natural state of the Petrified Forest," with accompanying pictures of visitors admiring and photographing a piece of petrified wood. The investigators placed specially marked pieces of wood along trails near these signs and monitored how many of them were stolen over the course of the experiment. In a remarkable demonstration of the importance of aligning prescriptive and descriptive norms, the theft rate was over four times lower when the signs emphasized how *few* people take wood from the park.

← LOOKING BACK

Reason-based approaches induce compliance by providing good reasons for people to agree to a request. The norm of reciprocity compels people to benefit those who have benefited them. In the reciprocal concessions (door-in-the-face) technique, people who have refused a large request are then induced to agree to a smaller request. In the foot-in-the-door technique, people comply with a small request and then are induced to grant a larger request. Emotion-based approaches also can lead to compliance. People who are in a positive mood are more likely to comply with a request in order to maintain their good mood. In contrast, according to the negative state relief hypothesis, people who feel guilty or sad are also likely to comply with a request in order to feel better. Norm-based approaches capitalize on people's tendencies to look to others for guidance. People are responsive to both descriptive and prescriptive norms, but it is important that norm-based appeals do not pit the two against each other.

Obedience to Authority

The study of when and why people obey the commands or instructions of someone in authority has been dominated by the most famous set of social psychology experiments ever conducted—those of Stanley Milgram (previously discussed in Chapters 1 and 5). Milgram's experiments are so well known, in fact, that the social psychologist Lee Ross says they "have become part of our society's shared intellectual legacy—that small body of historical incidents, biblical parables, and classic literature that serious thinkers feel free to draw on when they debate about human nature or contemplate human history" (Ross, 1988, p. 101).

The Setup of the Milgram Experiments

Milgram's research on obedience began as an investigation of conformity. Milgram was interested in whether the kind of pressures observed in Asch's conformity experiment were powerful enough to lead people to do something far more significant than report an incorrect line length. He wondered what would happen if he asked participants to deliver electric shocks whenever a subject performing a task (in reality the experimenter's confederate) responded incorrectly. Would participants conform to the example set by other obedient participants, even when doing so involved hurting another human being?

STANLEY MILGRAM
Using a shock generator that looked real but was actually just a prop, Milgram studied whether participants would continue to obey instructions and deliver electric shocks to a learner, even when they thought the learner was in grave distress.

This is an interesting question, but Milgram never pursued it. The reason is that he first needed to obtain data from a control group to determine the willingness of participants to deliver electric shocks in the first place, when there was no pressure to conform (Evans, 1980). And that's where he got his surprising result—one that radically changed his research agenda. A large percentage of participants were willing to do something they thought was hurting another person, even when there was no group of other participants leading the way.

Recall from Chapter 1 the basic procedure of Milgram's experiments. After responding to a newspaper ad, participants showed up for an experiment on learning. The setup was rigged so the participant was always assigned to the role of the "teacher" and the confederate to the role of the "learner." The teacher's job was to administer an electric shock every time the learner—a genial, middle-aged man who was strapped into a chair with his arm attached to a pretend shock generator—made a mistake by reporting the wrong word from a list of word pairs (such as *glove/book, grill/detergent, anvil/pope*). Teachers

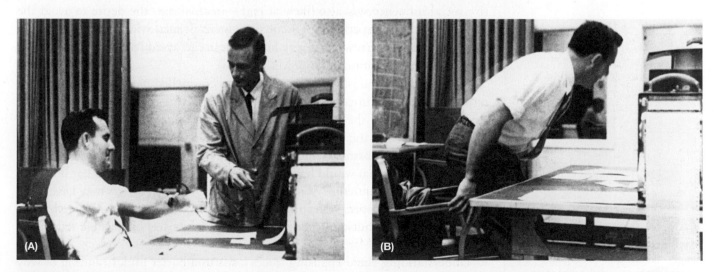

THE MILGRAM EXPERIMENT
Participants were led to believe that the shock generator had 30 levels of shock, ranging from "slight shock" to "danger: severe shock" to "XXX."
(A) A participant being given a sample shock of 45 volts (this was the only real shock in the experiment). (B) A participant standing up to ask the experimenter if he could stop the experiment.

were briefly strapped to the chair themselves and given a 45-volt shock so they would know the shocks were painful. The teacher started off by delivering 15 volts after the learner's first mistake, then increased the shock in 15-volt increments after each subsequent mistake. As the mistakes accumulated, participants found themselves required to deliver 255, 300, and 330 volts of electricity—all the way up to 450 volts. (In reality, no electric shock was delivered to the learner.) If a participant expressed reservations or tried to terminate the experiment, the experimenter would respond with a carefully scripted set of responses: "Please continue," "The experiment requires that you continue," "It is absolutely essential that you continue," and "You have no other choice; you must go on."

The great surprise in these studies was how many participants continued to obey the experimenter's orders and deliver the maximum level of shock to the confederate (**Box 9.3**). In the *remote-feedback version* of the experiment, in which the learner was in an adjoining room and could not be heard except when he vigorously pounded on the wall after a shock of 300 volts, 66 percent of the participants continued the learning experiment and delivered the maximum shock of 450 volts. In the *voice-feedback version*, the participants could hear a series of increasingly desperate pleas by the learner—including screaming that he had a heart condition—until finally, ominously, he became silent. Despite the many cues that the learner was suffering, 62.5 percent of the participants delivered the maximum shock (Milgram, 1965, 1974).

Opposing Forces

Milgram's participants were caught in an agonizing conflict. On the one hand were forces compelling them to complete the experiment and continue delivering shock (Reeder, Monroe, & Pryor, 2008). Among these forces was a sense of fair play: they had agreed to serve as participants, they had already received payment for doing so, and they felt they now had to fulfill their part of the bargain. Some were probably also motivated by the reason they'd agreed to participate in the first place: to advance science and the understanding of human behavior. Normative social influence was also likely at play—in this case, the desire to avoid the disapproval of the experimenter or anyone else associated with the study. Closely related to this concern was the very human desire to avoid "making a scene" and upsetting others (Goffman, 1966; Miller, 1996).

On the other hand, several powerful forces compelled participants to want to terminate the experiment. Foremost among these was the moral imperative to stop the suffering of the learner (Burger, Girgis, & Manning, 2011). Participants may have felt a specific desire not to hurt the genial man they had met earlier, as well as a more abstract reluctance to hurt others. Some were also probably concerned about what would happen if something went wrong. "What if he dies or is permanently injured?" "Will there be a lawsuit?" Still others may have wondered about the prospect of having to walk out with the learner after everything was over and the resulting embarrassment they might feel or possible retaliation from the learner.

Understanding these opposing forces leads to a better understanding of why participants responded the way they did and why the whole experience was so stressful. How might the rate of obedience change if the strength of these opposing forces were modified (Blass, 2000, 2004; Miller, 1986)? This is exactly the

reactance theory The idea that people reassert their prerogatives in response to the unpleasant state of arousal they experience when they believe their freedoms are threatened.

BOX 9.3 | **FOCUS ON** POSITIVE PSYCHOLOGY

Resisting Social Influence

People don't always conform, comply, and obey. They sometimes engage in heartening, even heroic, acts of independence—refusing to go along with misguided peers, defying the illegitimate demands of a commanding officer, or blowing the whistle on unethical business practices. What enables people to hold their ground, follow their conscience, and resist being influenced by others?

The pressure to give in to others can be offset by the tendency to resist attempts to restrict freedom of action or thought. According to **reactance theory**, people experience an unpleasant state of arousal when they believe their free will is threatened, and they often act to reduce this discomfort by reasserting their prerogatives (Brehm, 1956). If your parents tell you you mustn't dye your hair, does your desire to dye it diminish or increase? Reactance theory predicts that the moment you feel your freedom is being taken away, it becomes more precious and your desire to maintain it increases.

Once motivated to resist, what factors might increase someone's ability to stand firm? One important variable is practice. In Milgram's obedience studies, many participants wanted to disobey and even tried to do so, but they weren't very good at it (Milgram, 1963, 1974). Maybe if they had been trained to disobey when the situation called for it, they would have done a better job. There is evidence that the Christians who tried to save Jews during the Holocaust tended to be people who had a history of helping others, either as part of their job or as volunteers. Those who helped the most often didn't have any higher regard for their Jewish neighbors than those who helped less; they were simply more practiced in reaching out and providing aid.

Another way to increase the ability to resist social influence is to have an ally. In Asch's conformity experiment, having just one additional person who departed from the majority was enough to reduce conformity rather dramatically (Asch, 1956). Indeed, the most important lesson of Asch's research is just how difficult it can be to be the *lone* holdout. People also need to be wary of potentially slippery slopes. The stepwise procedure in Milgram's experiments may have played an important role in the surprising levels of obedience observed in those studies. It's often easiest to resist influence from the start, rather than giving in and hoping to put a stop to things later on. As the Catholic Church teaches, "Avoid the near occasion of sin."

It's important to keep in mind, too, that many social influence attempts are based on appeals to emotion, as we discussed earlier. A particularly effective strategy for dealing with emotion-based approaches is simply to put off a response. If there is a "first law" of emotional experience, it is that emotions fade and moods change. Therefore, the compulsion to give in because you are caught up in a particular emotion can be diminished simply by waiting to respond. After the initial feelings dissipate, you can then decide whether to comply with a request on the merits of the idea, not on the basis of a bad mood or an intense emotional state.

RESISTING SOCIAL INFLUENCE
In the fall of 2017, the "Me Too" movement erupted, norms and awareness shifted, and many people who previously turned a blind eye toward or stayed silent about efforts to cover up wrongdoing suddenly refused to do so. Many people did so in the face of considerable pressure from their harassers and employers not to step forward.

IN TOUCH WITH THE LEARNER
In a "touch-proximity" version of Milgram's original experiment, participants were required to force the learner's hand onto the shock plate, which reduced the participants' obedience rates.

question Milgram tried to answer through a comprehensive series of studies in which he conducted important variations on his original studies.

TUNING IN THE LEARNER Milgram directed his initial efforts at increasing the forces that compelled people to want to terminate the experiment and stop hurting the learner. These forces were all triggered by an awareness of the learner's suffering, so Milgram tried to increase them by making the learner more prominent—or, in his words, by "tuning in the learner." Participants spontaneously tried to do the opposite—that is, to deal with their own discomfort by tuning *out* the learner, sometimes literally turning away from him in their chair. As already noted, in the remote-feedback version of the experiment, the teacher (the participant) could neither see nor hear the learner (except for one episode of vigorous pounding), and in the voice-feedback version, the learner was still not in view, but he and his vigorous protests were clearly audible, and the teacher was constantly aware of him. In subsequent variations of the experiment, Milgram introduced the *proximity version*, in which the learner received his shock in the same room where the teacher delivered it, from only 1.5 feet away, as well as a *touch-proximity version*, in which the teacher was required to force the learner's hand onto the shock plate (a sheet of insulation supposedly kept the teacher from being shocked, too). **Figure 9.10** shows the effect of these manipulations. As the learner became more and more present and "real," the teachers found it increasingly difficult to deliver the shocks, and obedience rates diminished.

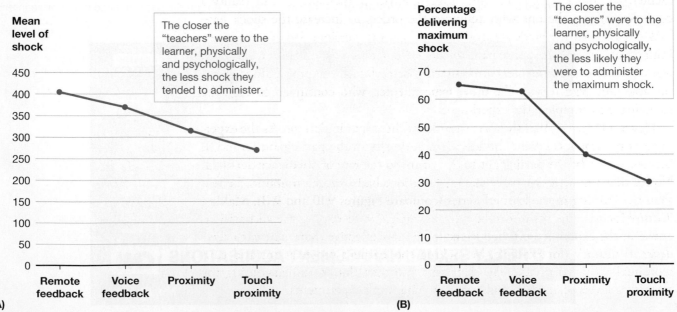

(A)

(B)

FIGURE 9.10
TUNING IN THE LEARNER
The effect of Milgram's experimental manipulations that made the learner more and more salient on (A) the mean level of shock participants delivered and (B) the percentage of participants who delivered the maximum amount of shock. As the "signal" coming from the learner got stronger, obedience declined.
Source: Adapted from Milgram, 1965.

One lesson to be drawn from this experiment is chilling: the more removed we are from others, the easier it is to hurt them. Consider, for example, military combat, which is often no longer hand-to-hand. A mere push of a button can release a Hellfire missile from a Predator drone and strike a target a continent away. The remoteness of the victims in such cases makes the harm done to them abstract, so the emotional consequences of aggression are weakened dramatically, and people find it easier to harm others than they would if they had any kind of direct contact with the victims. Or consider how much more remote our communications are online rather than face-to-face. The indirectness of online communication has been cited as one reason for the prevalence of cyberbullying (Kowalski, Giumetti, Schroeder, & Lattanner, 2014).

TUNING OUT THE VICTIM
Missiles can be fired from drone (pilotless) aircraft by a person located thousands of miles away. This distance can make the harm more abstract, making orders to fire less likely to be questioned.

TUNING OUT THE EXPERIMENTER Another way Milgram influenced the rate of obedience was to strengthen or weaken the "signal" coming from the experimenter, thereby strengthening or weakening the forces encouraging participants to complete the experiment. In the standard version of the study, the experimenter was present in the same room, right next to the participant. In an *experimenter-absent version*, the experimenter gave the initial instructions alongside the participant, but then left the room and issued all subsequent orders over the telephone. By physically removing himself from the scene, the experimenter lost much of his influence, and participants were less likely to obey.

Another way to diminish the experimenter's power is to alter the experimenter's authority. In one version, for example, instead of an authoritative experimenter, an "ordinary person" (seemingly another participant, but in reality a confederate) was the one who delivered the orders to increase the shock level each time the learner made a mistake. In still another version, two experimenters initially instructed the participant to shock the learner. At one point, however, one of the two experimenters announced that he found the proceedings objectionable and argued with the other experimenter, who continued to urge the participant to complete the experiment.

Figure 9.11 (see p. 302) shows the results of these manipulations. As the experimenter became less salient and less of an authority in the participant's mind, it became easier for the participant to defy him, so the rate of obedience declined. Notice that this series of experimental variations had a more pronounced effect than the "tuning in the learner" series (compare Figures 9.10 and 9.11). Making it *easier* for participants to disobey (for example, by decreasing the authority or power of the experimenter) thus seems to be more effective than increasing their *desire* to disobey (for example, by making the learner's protestations and pain more real). This distinction provides an important clue to understanding the surprising levels of obedience observed in Milgram's experiments.

Would You Have Obeyed?

Nobody anticipated the widespread levels of obedience Milgram observed. A group of psychiatrists predicted that fewer than 1 percent of all participants—a pathological fringe—would continue until they delivered the maximum amount

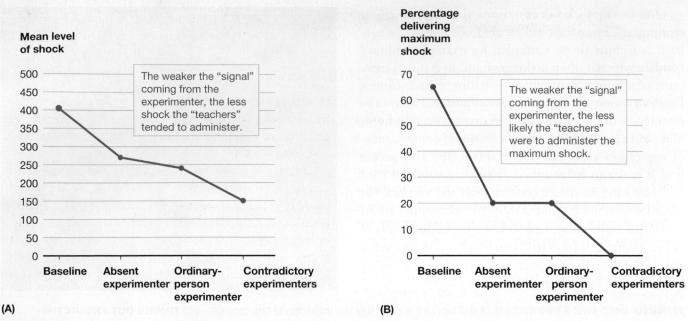

Mean level of shock

> The weaker the "signal" coming from the experimenter, the less shock the "teachers" tended to administer.

(A) Baseline / Absent experimenter / Ordinary-person experimenter / Contradictory experimenters

Percentage delivering maximum shock

> The weaker the "signal" coming from the experimenter, the less likely the "teachers" were to administer the maximum shock.

(B) Baseline / Absent experimenter / Ordinary-person experimenter / Contradictory experimenters

FIGURE 9.11
TUNING OUT THE EXPERIMENTER
The effect of Milgram's experimental manipulations that made the experimenter less and less salient on (A) the mean level of shock participants delivered and (B) the percentage of participants who delivered the maximum amount of shock. As the "signal" coming from the experimenter got weaker, obedience declined.
Source: Adapted from Milgram, 1965.

of shock. This failure of prediction is matched by an equally noteworthy failure of after-the-fact insight: the vast majority of people believe, even after hearing the basic results and all the study variations, that they themselves would never deliver very high levels of shock. Thus, although Milgram's experimental variations shed light on when and why people engage in such surprising behavior, they don't provide a fully satisfying explanation, or else we would be more likely to accept that we ourselves might obey in the same situation. As Lee Ross put it, the experiments do not pass a critical "empathy test" (Ross, 1988). They don't lead us to empathize fully with the obedient participants and take seriously the possibility that we would also obey to the end—as most participants did. A truly satisfying explanation might not convince us that we would *surely* obey, but it should at least convince us that we *might* act that way.

Milgram's work is often mentioned in discussions of how people sometimes obey the directives of malevolent government officials and engage in sadistic, demeaning torture, such as that observed at Abu Ghraib, or commit hideous crimes against humanity, such as those witnessed during the Holocaust in Nazi Germany, in the "ethnic cleansing" in Bosnia, or in the massacres in Cambodia, Rwanda, or Darfur. Explanations of such incomprehensible cruelties vary along an "exceptionalist-normalist" continuum. The exceptionalist thesis is that such crimes are perpetrated only by "exceptional" people—that is, exceptionally sadistic, desperate, or ethnocentric people. Many Germans were virulent anti-Semites. The Serbs harbored long-standing hatred and resentment against the Bosnians. The Rwandan Hutus had a score to settle with the Tutsis. The normalist thesis, in contrast, is that most people are capable of such destructive obedience, and given the right circumstances, almost anyone would commit such acts (**Box 9.4**).

Milgram's research, of course, is typically taken to support the normalist position. Milgram himself certainly took this position. When Morley Safer on the

BOX 9.4   **FOCUS ON** TODAY

Would Milgram Get the Same Results Now?

Milgram's studies were done in the early 1960s. But that was then, this is now. If you conducted Milgram's experiments today, would you get the same results? Some argue that today's more intense media coverage of such events as domestic spying by the U.S. National Security Agency, along with constant claims of "fake news" by President Trump, have made people less trusting of authority and thus less likely to obey instructions to harm another individual. Perhaps, but that's a difficult idea to test because ethical concerns make it impossible to replicate Milgram's experiments today. All psychological research must now be approved by an institutional review board (IRB), whose responsibility is to make sure any proposed research wouldn't cause undue stress to the participants or harm them in any way (see Chapter 2). Few, if any, IRBs would approve a direct replication of Milgram's experiments.

Jerry Burger, at Santa Clara University in California, did the next best thing by conducting a near-replication of Milgram's basic experiment to investigate whether the tendency to obey authority has changed since Milgram's time (Burger, 2009; Burger, Girgis, & Manning, 2011). Burger identified a critical moment in the original proceedings when disobedience was most likely: right after the participant had (supposedly) delivered 150 volts of electric shock and the learner protested and demanded to be released. It was something of a now-or-never moment: four out of five of Milgram's participants who didn't stop at this point never stopped at all.

Burger saw an opportunity. It would be ethically unacceptable to put people through the stress of deciding between disobeying the experimenter and administering 300 or 400 volts of electricity. But the procedure isn't so stressful—and is thus more ethically acceptable—up to the 150-volt level. Until that point, Milgram's learner hadn't protested, so the pain caused by the shocks (the participants would presume) can't be that bad. Burger therefore sought and received permission from Santa Clara's IRB to replicate Milgram's basic experiment up to that point only.

The results were essentially the same as those obtained by Milgram himself. In Burger's study, 70 percent of the participants were willing to administer the next level of shock (165 volts) after hearing the learner's protest. This compares with 82 percent of Milgram's participants—not a statistically significant difference. Men and women were equally likely to continue past the critical 150-volt level. Today, people seem to react to pressure to obey the same way they did more than 50 years ago.

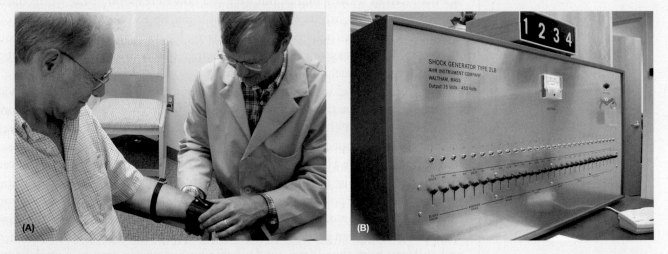

REVISITING MILGRAM (A) In Burger's 2009 near-replication of the original Milgram experiments from the 1960s, participants faced the same conflict over whether to administer increasing levels of shock (up to 165 volts) to the learner or to call a halt to his suffering by refusing to continue. (B) Burger used the same type of bogus shock generator used by Milgram.

CBS TV show *60 Minutes* asked whether he thought something like the Holocaust could happen in the United States, Milgram offered this opinion:

> I would say, on the basis of having observed a thousand people in the experiment and having my own intuition shaped and informed by these experiments, that if a system of death camps were set up in the United States of

the sort we had seen in Nazi Germany, one would be able to find sufficient personnel for those camps in any medium-sized American town. (Quoted in Blass, 1999, p. 955)

Let's take a closer look.

THEY TRIED BUT FAILED One reason people think they would never behave like the average participant in Milgram's studies is that they misunderstand exactly how the average participant behaved (Ross, 1988). People conjure up images of participants casually going along with the experimenter's commands, increasing the shock level from trial to trial, and being relatively inattentive to the learner's situation. Indeed, Milgram's experiments have often been described as demonstrations of "blind" obedience.

But that's not what happened. Participants didn't blindly obey. Nearly all tried to disobey in one form or another. Nearly everyone called the experimenter's attention to the learner's suffering in an implicit plea to stop the proceedings. Many stated explicitly that they refused to continue (but nonetheless went on with the experiment). Some got out of their chair in defiance, only to sit back down moments later. Most participants tried to disobey, but they weren't particularly good at it. As Ross pointed out, "the Milgram experiments have less to say about 'destructive obedience' than about ineffective and indecisive *disobedience*" (Ross, 1988, p. 103).

This distinction is critical. Most of us have had the experience of having good intentions but not being able to translate those intentions into effective action. For instance, maybe you've *wanted* to speak up more forcefully and effectively against racist or sexist remarks, but were too slow to respond or the words didn't come out as forthrightly as you intended. Or maybe you've *wanted* to reach out to someone who was being ignored at a party, but you were distracted by your own social needs. Most of us can relate to being good-hearted but ineffective, but most of us can't relate to being uncaring.

A chilling parallel to the behavior of Milgram's participants is the behavior of some of the German soldiers called on to execute Polish Jews during World War II (Browning, 1992). Members of German Reserve Police Battalion 101 were mostly men who hoped to avoid the inevitable violence of the war by volunteering for police duty in Hamburg. After the invasion of Poland, however, they were reassigned to serve as military police in occupied Poland. Most of their duties consisted of routine police work. But on July 13, 1942, the men were roused from their barracks before dawn and taken to the outskirts of the village of Józéfow, where they were given gruesome orders: to round up all the Jewish men, women, and children from the village, send all able-bodied young men to a work camp, and shoot the rest.

Most were shocked and repelled by their orders. Many resisted. But their resistance, like that of Milgram's participants, was feeble. Some kept busy with petty errands or moved to the back of the battalion, hoping to avoid being called on. Others took part in the roundup but then refrained from shooting if no one was watching. Still others fired but missed intentionally. What they *didn't* do was state assertively that they wouldn't participate or that what they were being asked to do was wrong. They tried to find an easy way to disobey, but there was no easy way—and so they obeyed. (Of course, many of the acts of genocide during the Holocaust were perpetrated by individuals who, unlike most of the soldiers in Reserve Police Battalion 101, fully embraced what they were doing.)

In the case of Milgram's experiments, participants had trouble halting the proceedings partly because the experimenter wasn't playing by the normal rules of social life. The participants offered reasons for stopping the experiments, but the experimenter largely ignored those reasons, making minimally responsive statements such as "The experiment requires that you continue." Participants were confused and uncertain about how to act. As we noted in our earlier discussion of conformity, people tend not to act decisively when they lack a solid grasp of the events happening around them. What should you do when told to deliver electric shock to "teach" someone who's no longer trying to learn anything, at the insistence of an authority figure who seems unconcerned about the learner's predicament? How do you respond when events have stopped making sense?

These questions have important implications for those real-world instances of destructive obedience with which we should be most concerned. Many of the most hideous episodes of genocide, for example, have occurred right after large-scale social upheaval. Without reliable norms of appropriate behavior, people are less able to muster the confidence necessary to take decisive action to stop such atrocities.

RELEASE FROM RESPONSIBILITY The inability of Milgram's participants to stop the experiment meant they were trapped in a situation of terrible conflict and stress. Although they knew what was happening should not continue, they didn't know how to bring it to an end. They were therefore desperate for anything that would reduce their stress. Fortunately for the participants (but unfortunately for the learner, if he really had been receiving electric shock), the experimenter provided something to reduce their stress by taking responsibility for what was happening. When participants asked, as many did, "Who is responsible for what happens here?" the experimenter responded, "I am responsible." Participants seized on this assertion as a justification for their actions, and the stress they were experiencing was significantly reduced.

Of course, the cover, or "out," the experimenter provided worked only because participants viewed the person taking responsibility as a legitimate authority. People generally don't let just anyone take responsibility and then assume that everything is okay. Suppose you're approached by a strange character on campus who says, "Quick, help me set fire to the administration building; I'll take full responsibility." You certainly would refuse to pitch in. In Milgram's experiments, however, participants believed they could legitimately transfer responsibility to the experimenter because he was a representative of science; in nearly all the variations, the experimenter was affiliated with Yale University, a respected institution (although obedience was still high when the experimenter operated out of a storefront in downtown Bridgeport, Connecticut). These aspects of the situation made it easier for participants to reduce their own stress over what was happening by assuming that the experimenter knew better and was ultimately responsible for what happened.

The cover provided by authorities has implications for some of history's worst acts of destructive obedience. In Nazi Germany, in Rwanda, and at Abu Ghraib, the demands to obey were issued by authority figures who either explicitly took responsibility or whose position supported an assumption of responsibility. And such claims of responsibility have nearly always been legitimized by some overarching ideology. Whether based on nationalism, religious ideology, or ethnic

"I'd rather be a free man in my grave / Than living as a puppet or a slave."
—REGGAE LEGEND JIMMY CLIFF

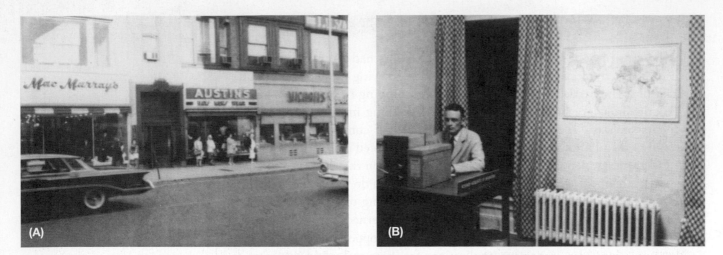

LEGITIMIZING THE EXPERIMENT
To see how participants would react if the experiment were not conducted at Yale and the authority seemed less legitimate, Milgram had them report to (A) a fictitious business called Research Associates of Bridgeport, located above a storefront in downtown Bridgeport, and (B) inside a seedy office. Obedience rates declined somewhat but remained high even under these conditions.

identity, every example of organized aggression has been draped in a seemingly legitimizing ideology that seeks to present otherwise hideous actions in a way that makes them seem morally appropriate (Staub, 1989; Zajonc, 2002).

STEP-BY-STEP INVOLVEMENT It's also important to remember that the participants in Milgram's experiments didn't deliver 450 volts of electric shock right away. Instead, each participant first administered only 15 volts to the learner. Who wouldn't do that? That's feedback, not punishment. Then 30 volts. No problem there either. Then 45, 60, 75—each step a small one. Once participants started down this path, though, it was hard to stop, and they administered more and more shock. Indeed, the increments were so small that if a certain level of shock seemed like too much, why wouldn't the previous level also have been too much (Gilbert, 1981)?

The step-by-step nature of participants' obedience in these experiments is a powerful reason why so many administered as much electric shock as they did. Most of us have had the experience of gradually getting in over our heads in this way. We may tell a "little white lie"—but one that sets in motion a cascade of events that requires more and more deception. (Many a TV sitcom plot rests on this very sequence.) Our behavior often creates its own momentum, and it's hard to know in advance where that behavior will lead. Milgram's participants can certainly be forgiven for not foreseeing how everything would unfold. Would any of us have seen it any more clearly?

The parallels between this element of Milgram's procedure and what happened in Nazi Germany are striking (**Box 9.5**). German citizens weren't asked, out of the blue, to assist with or condone the deportation of Jews, Gypsies, gay people, and communists to the death camps. Instead, the rights of these groups were gradually stripped away. Certain business practices were restricted, then travel constraints were imposed, and then citizenship was narrowed; only later were people loaded into boxcars and sent to the death camps. Of course, the step-by-step process in Nazi Germany is no excuse for the atrocities committed, but the Nazis would doubtless have had a much harder time getting so many people to comply if they had started with the last step.

BOX 9.5   FOCUS ON HISTORY

Step by Step to Genocide

Anti-Jewish laws and policies of the German government before and during World War II are listed below. Notice the gradual nature of their severity.

1. April 1, 1933
Boycott of Jewish businesses is declared.

2. April 7, 1933
Law for the Restoration of the Professional Civil Service authorizes the dismissal of most non-Aryan civil servants (especially those with Jewish parents or grandparents).

3. September 22, 1933
Reestablishment of the Reich Chamber of Culture leads to the removal of non-Aryans from organizations and enterprises related to literature, the press, broadcasting, music, and art.

4. September 15, 1935
The Reich Citizenship Law defines citizens of the Reich as only those who are of German or kindred blood.

5. September 16, 1935
The Law for the Protection of German Blood and German Honor forbids marriage between Jews and nationals of German or kindred blood and declares marriages conducted in defiance of this law void, forbids relations outside of marriage between Jews and nationals of German or kindred blood, and forbids Jews from employing in their household female nationals of German or kindred blood who are under age 45.

6. November 16, 1936
Jews are prohibited from obtaining passports or traveling abroad, except in special cases.

7. April 1938
Jews are forced to register with the government all property valued at 5,000 marks or more.

8. July 25, 1938
The Fourth Decree of the Reich Citizenship Law terminates the licenses of Jewish physicians as of September 30, 1938.

9. September 27, 1938
The Fifth Decree of the Reich Citizenship Law allows Jewish legal advisers to attend professionally only to the legal affairs of Jews.

10. October 5, 1938
Jewish passports and ration cards are marked with a J.

11. January 1, 1939
All Jews are required to carry a special ID card.

12. July 1940
Purchases by Jews are restricted to certain hours and stores; telephones are taken away from Jews.

13. September 19, 1941
Jews are forced to display the Jewish badge prominently on their clothing and with few exceptions are not allowed to use public transportation.

14. October 14, 1941
Massive deportation of German Jews to concentration camps begins.

15. October 23, 1941
Jewish emigration is prohibited.

16. January 20, 1942 (the Wansee Conference)
Nazi leaders decide that 11 million Jews (every Jew in Europe) are to be killed.

← LOOKING BACK

As Milgram's experiment exemplifies, many factors contribute to people's willingness to obey leaders who demand immoral behavior. Several elements of the situation may make obedience easier to understand: a person's attempts to disobey are often blocked; the person in authority often takes responsibility for what happens; and once the obedience begins, there is typically no obvious stopping point. But when circumstances lead the individual to be tuned in to the victim, obedience decreases substantially. When circumstances lead the individual to tune out the person in authority, obedience is even more greatly reduced, suggesting that it's more effective to make it *easier* for participants to disobey than it is to increase their *desire* to disobey.

Chapter Review

SUMMARY

What Is Social Influence?

- There are three types of *social influence*. *Conformity* involves a change in a person's attitudes or behavior in response to explicit or implicit pressure from others. *Compliance* involves going along with explicit requests made by others. *Obedience* is submitting to the demands of a person in authority.

Conformity

- Mimicry is the conscious or nonconscious imitation of someone else's behavior. People sometimes conform because of *informational social influence*: they view the actions of others as informative about what is correct or proper. People also conform because of *normative social influence*: they conform with others to avoid disapproval and other social sanctions.
- Conformity pressure depends on group characteristics. The larger the size, the greater the group's influence, but only up to about four people. Unanimous groups exert more pressure to conform than those with even a single dissenter. The greater the expertise and status of the group members, the greater their influence.
- People from interdependent cultures are more likely to conform than people from independent cultures. Women tend to conform more than men, but both men and women conform more in domains in which they have less knowledge.
- The direction of influence is not always from the majority to the minority. Sometimes minority influence can

be substantial, especially when the minority expresses consistent views.

Compliance

- Reason-based approaches to compliance include invoking the *norm of reciprocity* by doing a favor for someone who then feels obligated to do a favor for you in return or by making a concession and using the *reciprocal concessions technique* (door-in-the-face technique) to get the target person to make a concession as well. With the *foot-in-the-door technique*, a person first gets someone to agree to a small request before making a more substantial request.
- Emotion-based approaches to compliance include getting the targeted person in a good mood, which is likely to increase compliance because of mood maintenance and because of the influence of the good mood on how the request is interpreted.
- Compliance may also result from a desire for *negative state relief* because an act of compliance may reduce guilt or sadness.
- Norm-based approaches to compliance take advantage of the tendency to look to others for guidance about how to behave. *Descriptive norms* indicate how people actually behave in specific contexts, and *prescriptive norms* indicate how people should behave in various situations. To get people to adhere to a prescriptive norm, the two should not be pitted against each other.

Obedience to Authority

- The study of obedience has been dominated by the Milgram experiments, which demonstrated the surprising willingness of most people to go along with the seemingly harmful demands of an authority.
- Participants in obedience studies are caught in a conflict between two opposing forces: normative social influence and moral imperatives. The balance between these forces shifts toward the former when participants tune out the learner and tune in the experimenter. It shifts toward the latter when participants tune out the experimenter and tune in the learner.
- Although Milgram's results strike nearly everyone as wildly counterintuitive, they can be rendered less surprising by considering that most participants made (ineffective) attempts to terminate the experiment, the experimenter took responsibility for what was happening (thus alleviating the participants' sense of responsibility for what they were doing), and the participants were caught on a "slippery slope" because of the stepwise nature of the demands.

THINK ABOUT IT

1. What two reasons appear to explain why people so often mimic one another?

2. Suppose your dining hall is having a contest, and you have to guess how many gumballs are in a giant jar (the closest guess wins). You and a few friends walk up to the gumball jar and tell your guesses to the volunteer running the contest. Your friends all say their guesses out loud, and you go last. You find yourself increasing your gumball estimate to be closer to those of your friends. How could each type of social influence (normative and informational) have affected your guess? How could you reduce the normative social influence in this situation?

3. In the battle for LGBTQ rights, what kind of social influence can minority LGBTQ groups exert on the majority? Should their goal be to engage public support or private internalization and acceptance of their arguments among members of the majority?

4. Suppose you want to increase voting rates among the millennial generation (people born in the 1980s and 1990s). Describe one reason-based approach, one emotion-based approach, and one norm-based approach you could use to do so.

6. In the context of the Milgram experiment, give an example of "tuning in the learner" and an example of "tuning out the experimenter," and explain how each one affects obedience rates.

The **answer guidelines** for the think about it questions can be found at the back of the book . . . 👉

ONLINE STUDY MATERIALS

Want to earn a better grade on your test?

Go to **INQUIZITIVE** to learn and review this chapter's content, with personalized feedback along the way.

What determines relationship satisfaction later in life?

Why do people get married?

How do dating apps like Tinder affect our offline mate preferences?

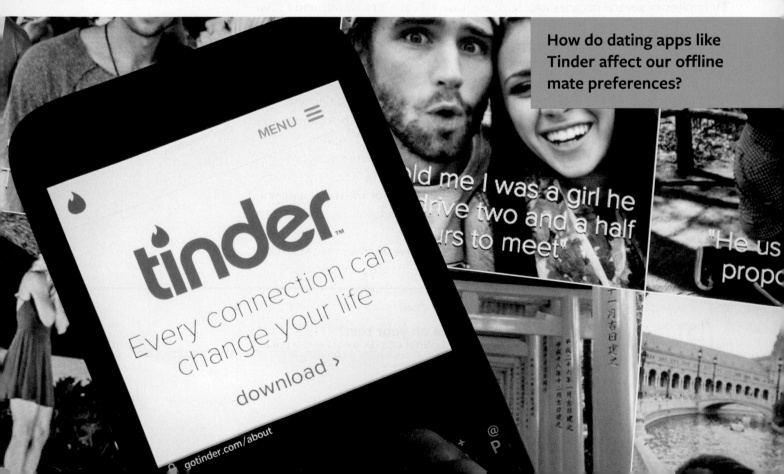

MENU ☰

tinder™

Every connection can change your life

download ›

gotinder.com/about

Relationships and Attraction

IN THE PILOT EPISODE OF THE popular television series *Modern Family*, viewers meet Claire and Phil, parents in a household that—although modern in terms of clothing, language, and technology—isn't really different from the conventional TV families of several decades ago, such as those in *Leave It to Beaver* and *I Love Lucy*. Claire and Phil are both white, have been married for 16 years, and have three biological children. Phil is the sole breadwinner. Chaos ensues as the oldest daughter, Hayley, brings home her first boyfriend.

We then meet Jay, a gruff 50-something-year-old with a well-concealed heart of gold; his beautiful young Colombian wife of 6 months, Gloria; and her son from a previous marriage, Manny. More chaos ensues as people keep assuming Jay is Gloria's father and Manny declares his love for a girl out of his league.

Next we meet Cam and Mitchell, a gay couple, as they return to Los Angeles with their newly adopted Vietnamese infant daughter, Lily. Still more chaos, this time centered on which of the two men is best suited for the more feminine sides of raising a child and how they should break the news of the adoption to Mitchell's apparently not-so-accepting family.

When Cam and Mitchell arrive at a family gathering, we discover that Mitchell's family consists of all the other characters we met earlier. Claire is his sister, and Jay is their dad. This makes Gloria, although younger, Claire and Mitchell's stepmother and 10-year-old Manny their stepbrother. Modern indeed.

The series captures the complications that can arise in the extended families of varying compositions so common in today's world. What can *Modern Family* tell us about relationships and attraction? For one thing, it shows that human beings can

MODERN FAMILY
As this hit TV show illustrates, families can be quite diverse, and people form all sorts of romantic bonds.

find themselves romantically attracted to all kinds of people: people of the same or different sex, people from different races or cultures, and people spanning a considerable age range. It also shows us that many different kinds of relationships can, despite the usual difficulties of being in an intimate relationship with another individual, be healthy, happy, and meet the needs of the individuals involved.

This chapter explores a broad range of enduring relationships—with parents, friends, and romantic partners and with members of the same and opposite sex. We focus mainly on interpersonal relationships, attachments in which bonds of family or friendship, or love or respect or hierarchy, tie together two or more individuals over an extended period of time. We consider what social psychologists have to say about attraction, about the initial stage of a relationship, and about the characteristics of established relationships. ■

Characterizing Relationships

In studying relationships, researchers face certain challenges that aren't as common in other areas of social psychology (Finkel & Eastwick, 2008; Gonzalez & Griffin, 1997; Karney & Bradbury, 1995). For example, many studies of relationships can't be true experiments with random assignment of participants to different conditions, because, of course, researchers can't assign individuals to certain relationships or conditions within a relationship. This kind of research must grapple with the methodological problem of self-selection, which occurs whenever investigators are unable to assign participants to the conditions being compared (see Chapter 2). When participants "select" their own condition, researchers can't know with complete confidence whether an observed difference between two conditions is a reflection of the different experiences of the people in those conditions or if it's simply that different types of people gravitate to each of the two conditions. Researchers must rely on longitudinal methods to examine the dynamics that unfold over time in preexisting relationships.

Here's an example. Couples who make a special effort to celebrate their wedding anniversary may be less likely to get divorced than couples who don't. But is the failure to celebrate an anniversary a cause of discord, or is it that people who aren't getting along don't do it? Despite these methodological challenges, the social psychology literature on relationships is flourishing, revealing fundamental truths about the bonds we form with one another.

The Importance of Relationships

Many people from Western cultures define themselves in independent, individualistic terms, focusing on how they are different and separate from others. Nevertheless, human nature is profoundly social, and a person's identity and sense of self are shaped by social relationships (see Chapter 3). Indeed, human beings (and many other kinds of animals) have what appears to be a biological need for belonging in relationships.

It's self-evident that humans have biologically based needs for food, oxygen, warmth, and safety. Without food, air, or water, we die. Roy Baumeister and Mark Leary claim that the same is true of relationships: we have a need to be embedded in healthy relationships (Baumeister & Leary, 1995). These researchers offer a number of arguments to support their claim that we all have a biological need—not just a desire—to belong.

ARGUMENTS FOR THE NEED TO BELONG Baumeister and Leary highlight the evolutionary basis of our tendency to seek out relationships. Relationships help individuals and their offspring to survive, thus increasing the likelihood of passing on one's genes. Long-term romantic bonds evolved to facilitate reproduction and to raise offspring, who are vulnerable and dependent for many years (Diamond, 2003; Ellis, 1992). Parent-offspring attachments help ensure that infants and children will survive until they can function independently (Bowlby, 1982). Friendship evolved as a means for non-kin to cooperate, thereby avoiding the perils of competition and aggression (Trivers, 1971).

If relationships have an evolutionary basis, then they can be expected to have universal features. Similar kinds of dynamics should exist between romantic partners, parents and children, siblings, and friends in different cultures around the world. Indeed, pioneers in the field of human ethology, who studied hunter-gatherer groups in their natural environments, documented patterns of social behavior that do appear to be universal, including caregiving between mother and child, wrestling between siblings, flirtation by young people who are courting, affection between romantic partners, and dominance displays between adolescent males (Eibl-Eibesfeldt, 1989).

Baumeister and Leary also note that if the need to belong is truly a need, then that need should be able to be satisfied. When we are thirsty or hungry, we drink or eat—but only to a point, just until we have satisfied the need. The same appears to be true of our social lives. Consider friendship. In Western European cultures, college students tend to restrict their meaningful interactions to, on average, about six friends (Wheeler & Nezlek, 1977). It seems that we satisfy our

"No more fiendish punishment could be devised, were such a thing physically possible, than that one should be turned loose in society and remain absolutely unnoticed by all the members thereof."
—WILLIAM JAMES

need for friendship with a limited number of close friends, and once that need is satisfied, we don't continue to seek other relationships.

EVIDENCE FOR THE NEED TO BELONG Far-ranging evidence supports the need to belong in nonhumans and humans alike. In a classic series of experiments, Harry Harlow (1959) raised baby rhesus monkeys without contact with other rhesus monkeys but with access to two "mother surrogates"—props vaguely resembling monkeys. One prop was covered in cloth, where the monkeys could go for comfort when feeling threatened; the other was made out of wire that could provide milk when the monkeys were hungry (**Figure 10.1**). The monkeys preferred the mother who could provide comfort to the one that could provide food. Still, those raised with these mothers, but otherwise in isolation, were in no way normal when they reached adolescence. As adolescents, they were highly fearful, couldn't interact normally with their peers, and engaged in inappropriate sexual behaviors—for example, attacking potential mates or failing to display typical sexual positions during copulation.

There's ample evidence for the need to belong in humans as well. Data suggest that mortality rates are higher for divorced, unmarried, and widowed individuals (Kaplan & Kronick, 2006; Lynch, 1979). Suicide rates are also higher for single and divorced individuals (Rothberg & Jones, 1987), as are crime rates (Baumeister & Leary, 1995). A recent synthesis of nearly 150 studies found that the increase in odds of survival associated with having strong social relationships is comparable, if not larger, to the increase in the odds of survival associated with various factors already directly linked to survival such as stopping smoking and being lean rather than obese (Holt-Lunstad, Smith, & Layton, 2010).

According to the so-called marriage benefit, married people fare better than unmarried ones on various indicators of well-being (Gove, Style, & Hughes, 1990; Ross, Mirowsky, & Goldsteen, 1990). This appears to extend to gay and lesbian relationships, as seen in a survey in which partnered gay men and lesbians scored higher on well-being than their non-partnered counterparts (Wienke & Hill, 2009). Having support from others also contributes to good health, strengthening the cardiovascular, immune, and endocrine systems (Feeney & Collins,

FIGURE 10.1
SOCIAL ISOLATION LEADS TO SOCIAL IMPAIRMENTS
The rhesus monkeys in Harlow's classic experiments, provided with mother surrogates in the form of props resembling monkeys but otherwise reared in isolation, showed significant social deficiencies in adolescence.

THE UNIVERSALITY OF RELATIONSHIPS
(A, B) Siblings in different cultures all play, support, and fight with each other, although the specific kinds of play, support, and conflict may vary according to the culture. (C) Parents in different cultures show similar kinds of attachment behaviors, including patterns of touch and eye contact.

2015; Oxman & Hull, 1997; Uchino, Cacioppo, & Kiecolt-Glaser, 1996). Studies like these aren't immune from methodological and other critiques (see DePaulo, 2015; Kalmijn, 2017; Luhmann, Hofmann, Eid, & Lucas, 2012), and some research highlights the benefits of being single, not in a romantic relationship (DePaulo, 2007; Girme, Overall, Faingataa, & Sibley, 2016). But overall, the evidence is overwhelming that social relationships of varying kinds can, and frequently do, confer psychological and physical benefits (Robles, Slatcher, Trombello, & McGinn, 2014; Slatcher & Selcuk, 2017).

Different Ways of Relating to Others

This chapter focuses on interpersonal relationships, such as those between friends and between romantic partners, but it's important to understand some distinctions among the different types of relationships. After all, most of us would agree that we behave in pretty different ways with a romantic partner, with friends

THE NEED TO BELONG
There is an evolutionary basis for the need to belong. Not only do elephant parents feed and protect young elephants, but they teach them appropriate social behavior that enables them to live in groups. If the young elephants grow up without adults, they are likely to become antisocial and aggressive and have difficulty living in groups.

communal relationship
A relationship in which the individuals feel a special responsibility for one another and give and receive according to the principle of need. Such relationships are often long term.

COMMUNAL RELATIONSHIPS IN DIFFERENT CULTURES
Communal relationships are especially common in East Asian and Latin American societies. Here, two young Japanese friends show a level of closeness and affection that may be less common in less communal societies.

exchange relationship
A relationship in which individuals feel little responsibility toward one another; giving and receiving are governed by concerns about equity and reciprocity. Such relationships are usually short term.

from our ultimate Frisbee team, with a professor, with a minister or rabbi, and with our supervisors at work (Fiske, 1992; Moskowitz, 1994).

COMMUNAL AND EXCHANGE RELATIONSHIPS As economic growth has advanced in the past few decades, millions of young people have left their towns and villages and moved to large cities. For many young people, a quiet village life of friends and family has been replaced by one of interacting mostly with strangers and bosses with whom they have little personal connection. How best to think about these changes in psychological terms?

Margaret Clark and Judson Mills argue that two fundamentally different types of relationships—communal relationships and exchange relationships—arise in different contexts and are governed by different norms (Clark, 1992; Clark & Mills, 1979, 1993, 2012). In a **communal relationship**, the individuals feel a special responsibility for one another and often expect their relationship to be long term. Communal relationships are based on a sense of "oneness" and a family-like sharing of common identity (Clark & Aragon, 2013; Fiske, 1992). In these relationships, individuals give and receive according to the principle of need—that is, according to which person in the relationship has the most pressing need at any given time (Park, Troisi, & Maner, 2010). Prototypical examples of communal relationships are ones between family members and between close friends—the kinds of relationships that are the social fabric of communal life in small villages.

An **exchange relationship**, in contrast, is trade based and often short term, and the individuals feel no special responsibility for one another's well-being. In exchange relationships, giving and receiving are governed by concerns about equity (you get what you put into the relationship) and reciprocity (what you receive is about equal to what you give). Examples of exchange relationships are interactions with salespeople and bureaucrats or with workers and supervisors in a business organization.

Societies differ widely in which approach—communal or exchange—they generally prefer. People in East Asian and Latin American societies are inclined to take a communal approach to many situations in which people in European and Commonwealth countries would be inclined to take an exchange approach. Consider the question of how businesspeople would treat an employee who had put in 15 good years of service, but over the past year had fallen down on the job and was unlikely to get back on track. East Asians tended to feel that the company had an obligation to treat the employee more like a family member and keep him on the payroll. Western businesspeople were more likely to feel that the relationship was contractual, or exchange based, and thus the employee should be let go. There are differences among Western nations, however: people from Catholic countries are more likely to take a communal stance than people from Protestant countries, and the same difference is found among Catholics and Protestants even within the United States (Sanchez-Burks, 2002, 2004).

REWARDS AND THE SOCIAL EXCHANGE THEORY OF INTERPERSONAL RELATIONSHIPS The distinction between communal and exchange relationships notwithstanding, many social psychologists believe that even the most intimate relationships are based, to a certain extent, on rewards. Indeed, one of

(Don't Wanna Be) All By Myself: The Health Effects of Loneliness

Humans are social animals who depend on interpersonal relationships and communities to survive. Extensive evidence has been found for the negative health effects of loneliness, characterized by a feeling that the desired level of social connection is not being met by the quantity and quality of one's relationships. Recent studies also show that, in the United States and elsewhere, the prevalence of loneliness is growing. Meanwhile, advances in technology have enabled people to connect with others with greater ease and speed than ever before.

For Critical Thinking

1. A person directly connected to a lonely individual is more likely to become lonelier in the future. What are some possible explanations for this finding?

2. Do you ever use social media to strengthen your existing relationships? Do you ever use social media instead of fostering your existing relationships? What differs between these two uses of social media?

Loneliness Is Bad for You

The effect of social isolation on mortality is greater than the effect of obesity or physical inactivity and comparable with that of smoking.[1]

Loneliness is contagious. People directly connected to a lonely person are

52%

more likely to be lonely, and they grow lonelier over time.[2]

Loneliness is cyclical. Lonely people tend to have fewer friends over time.[2]

35% of U.S. adults aged 45 or older are lonely

45% of them have been lonely for at least 6 years.[3]

43%

of U.S. adults 60 years or older feel lonely.[4]

Loneliness is associated with an increased risk of physical decline and death.[4]

Does Using Social Media Make You Lonelier?

Displacement hypothesis: Social media use replaces offline, face-to-face interactions, thus increasing loneliness.

Stimulation hypothesis: Online interactions strengthen existing relationships and help fend off loneliness.

Both hypotheses have been supported, suggesting that the way people use the internet (passively vs. actively), as well as their motives for using it (to avoid social anxiety associated with face-to-face interactions vs. to enhance existing social connections), lead to different outcomes in terms of loneliness.[5]

1. Holt-Lunstad, Smith, & Layton, 2010; 2. Cacioppo, Fowler, & Christakis, 2009; 3. Wilson & Moulton, 2010; 4. Perissinotto, Stijacic Cenzer, & Covinsky, 2012; 5. Nowland, Necka, & Cacioppo, 2017.

social exchange theory A theory based on the idea that how people feel about a relationship depends on their assessments of its costs and rewards.

comparison level Expectations people have about what they think they deserve or expect to get out of a relationship.

comparison level for alternatives Expectations people have about what they can get out of available, alternative relationships.

equity theory The idea that people are motivated to pursue fairness, or equity, in their relationships. A relationship is considered equitable when the benefits are proportionate to the effort both people put into it.

the most widely accepted principles of interpersonal relationships has the virtue of simplicity: people like and gravitate toward those who provide them with rewards. The rewards don't have to be tangible or immediate, and they don't have to come from direct interaction; rather, according to this reward framework, people tend to like those who make them feel good (Clore & Byrne, 1974; Lott & Lott, 1974).

Here's how you can test the reward principle yourself. Think of all your friends, and ask yourself whether this principle helps explain why you like each of them. Often rewards are easy to identify. You like one friend because you can count on him to share your heartaches as well as your joys, and another friend because she's hilarious and brings levity and laughter to your time with her. To take a specific example, research on friendships between heterosexual women and gay men reveals the rewards such relations offer: they enable each party to get perspectives on dating and mating from a friend who they know doesn't have a romantic or sexual agenda (Russell, DelPriore, Butterfield, & Hill, 2013).

Two influential theories specify how rewards shape our relationships. **Social exchange theory** posits that humans, in seeking to maximize their own satisfaction, seek out rewards in their interactions with others, and they are willing to pay certain costs to obtain those rewards (Kelley & Thibaut, 1978; Rusbult, 1983). Typically, people prefer interactions or relationships in which the rewards exceed the costs. On the flip side, if rewarding interactions aren't available and an individual has access only to relationships in which the costs exceed the rewards, that person is likely to seek out those interactions in which the costs exceed the rewards by the smallest amount.

How do we evaluate the rewards and costs of different relationships? Social exchange theory details how people rely on certain standards to do so (Finkel, Simpson, & Eastwick, 2017). One such standard is known as the **comparison level**—the expectations people have about what they expect to get out of a relationship. People who have a high comparison level expect a lot from their relationships. Another standard is the **comparison level for alternatives**, which reflects the outcomes people think they can get out of alternative relationships (Broemer & Diehl, 2003; Thibaut & Kelley, 1959). If you have plenty of attractive suitors knocking at your door, you're likely to have a pretty high comparison level for alternatives. Both of these standards vary from one person to another and help explain why, for example, a person chooses to stay in an abusive relationship that most people would have ended long ago (this person has a very low comparison level) or why an individual never seems to be able to stay in a relationship for more than a few months (this person may have a high comparison level for alternatives).

Though social exchange theory says that we generally seek out relationships in which the rewards exceed the costs, we don't want the rewards to outweigh the costs by too much. A second theory, **equity theory**, helps us understand how the combination of too many rewards and too few costs in a relationship can be unattractive: it simply feels unfair. This theory maintains that people are motivated to pursue fairness, or equity, in their relationships, such that the ratio of rewards to costs is similar for both partners (Hatfield & Rapson, 2012; Walster, Walster, & Berscheid, 1978). In other words, both partners ought to receive roughly what they put into a relationship. Thus, for instance, a relationship can feel equitable even if one person gets more out of it than the other, as long as that person tends to put in more effort.

It should be noted that some aspects of social exchange theory apply mostly to people who live in individualistic, egalitarian cultures, where independence, individuality, and equality are valued. In collectivist cultures, where the group rather than the individual is valued, there are good reasons to suspect that equity isn't so commonly the goal and that hierarchy and imbalance are more acceptable, sometimes actually more desirable.

Attachment Styles

Attachment theory was first advanced by John Bowlby, an early advocate of an evolutionary approach to human behavior (Bowlby, 1982; Hazan & Shaver, 1994; Mikulincer & Shaver, 2003; Rholes & Simpson, 2015). The central thesis of Bowlby's theory is that our early attachments with our parents and other caregivers shape our relationships for the rest of our lives.

attachment theory The idea that early attachments with parents and other caregivers can shape relationships for a person's whole life.

Bowlby noted that, unlike many mammals, human infants are born with few survival skills. Being extremely vulnerable, babies require several years to reach even a limited amount of independence, and they survive by forming intensely close attachments to parents or parental figures. Evolution has given infants a variety of traits that promote parent-offspring attachments, including the heartwarming smiles, laughs and coos, as well as the facial features that evoke love and devotion (Berry & McArthur, 1986; McArthur & Baron, 1983). Likewise, evolution has given parents a variety of traits that promote attachment—most notably, strong feelings of parental love and protective instincts toward their offspring (Fehr, 1994; Fehr & Russell, 1991; Hazan & Shaver, 1987, 1994; Hrdy, 1999).

Early in development, children rely on their parents for a sense of security, which allows them to explore the environment and to learn. A child's confidence in the secure base the parents provide stems in part from the parents' availability and responsiveness to the child's ever-shifting emotions. Over time, children develop internal "working models" of themselves and of how relationships function based on their parents' availability and responsiveness to them (Baldwin, Keelan, Fehr, Enns, & Koh-Rangarajoo, 1996; Bowlby, 1969, 1973, 1980; Collins & Read, 1994; Sherman, Rice, & Cassidy, 2015). Internal working models of the self reflect individuals' beliefs about their lovability and competence. Internal working models of how relationships work reflect indi-

"Ezra, I'm not inviting you to my birthday party, because our relationship is no longer satisfying to my needs."

viduals' beliefs about other people's availability, warmth, and ability to provide security. These working models, Bowlby claimed, originate early in life and shape our relationships from cradle to grave, giving rise to distinct styles of attachment.

Inspired by Bowlby's ideas, Mary Ainsworth classified the attachment patterns of infants according to how they responded to separations and reunions with their caregivers, both in the laboratory and in the home (Ainsworth, 1993; Ainsworth, Blehar, Waters, & Wall, 1978). Using an experimental procedure that came to be known as "the strange situation," Ainsworth had infants and

THE STRANGE SITUATION
In Ainsworth's experimental situation, she was able to measure infants' attachment styles to their caregivers. (A) A mother takes her infant to an unfamiliar room with interesting toys. While the infant explores the room and plays with the toys, a stranger enters and the mother leaves. (B) When the mother returns to the room, she picks up and comforts the infant if the infant is upset that she has left the room. (C) The mother then puts the infant down, and the infant is free to return to playing with the toys, or the infant might react by crying and protesting the separation.

their caregivers enter an unfamiliar room containing many interesting toys. The infant explored the room and began to play with some of the toys with the caregiver present. Infants who were securely attached were comfortable moving away from their caregivers to explore a novel environment—with the occasional glance back at the caregiver to make sure things were okay. These children felt safe when the caregiver was present even though they weren't in contact with their caregiver. After a few minutes, a stranger walked in. The stranger remained in the room, and the caregiver quietly left. Returning after 3 minutes, the caregiver greeted and comforted the infant if the infant was upset. The separation typically caused all infants to be distressed. But securely attached infants had caregivers who, as assessed by outside observers, responded quickly and reliably to their distress cries.

Infants who showed anxious attachment were generally distressed when placed in novel environments, even when their caregiver was in the room. These caregivers weren't as reliable in their responses to their infants—sometimes intruding on the child's activities and sometimes not, in an unpredictable fashion. Anxiously attached infants were less comforted by contact with their caregiver when the caregiver returned after an absence. Caregivers who rejected their infants frequently generally had children with an avoidant attachment style. In a strange situation, the avoidant child tended to be the least inclined to seek out the caregiver and might even reject attention when it was offered.

ATTACHMENT TYPES OR DIMENSIONS? In the late 1980s, Cindy Hazan and Phillip Shaver published a paper that changed the landscape of social psychology research on relationships (Hazan & Shaver, 1987). They had the insight that the theoretical ideas about attachment being used to understand the infant-caregiver relationship could shed light on the dynamics of relationships between adults. In other words, it could be fruitful to study how adults are attached to and behave with their various relationship partners through the lens of attachment theory.

That idea seems plausible. It's common for adults to protest separations from family, friends, and romantic partners, just as infants often protest being separated from a caregiver. Adults also seek comfort and support from relationship partners, and the security they get from their relationships helps them feel safe to venture forth into the world. Building on this key insight, Hazan and Shaver developed adult equivalents of each of the three attachment types Ainsworth had identified in her work with infants: secure, avoidant, and anxious-ambivalent (**Figure 10.2**).

Over the years, countless research participants have been presented with the three paragraphs shown in Figure 10.2 and asked to choose the one that best describes their relationships. By virtue of their choice, respondents are assumed to be a certain type of person: securely attached, avoidantly attached, or anxious-ambivalently attached. Research taking this "attachment types" approach has yielded numerous findings in support of the basic idea that there are parallels between the relationships adults form with one another and the bonds they as infants formed with their caregivers. For example, secure people report seeking support from their romantic partners more than either anxious-ambivalent or avoidant people, can more readily retrieve trust-related, positive relationship memories, and deal with trust violations of their partners in a more constructive manner (Girme, Overall, Simpson, & Fletcher, 2015; Mikulincer, 1998; Simpson & Rholes, 2017).

Before long, however, adult attachment researchers began to question whether thinking about attachment in terms of types, or categories, overlooks important variations within categories (Bartholomew & Horowitz, 1991; Brennan, Clark, & Shaver, 1998; Collins & Read, 1990). These days, although some researchers continue to rely on categorical measures of attachment or find it convenient to refer to people as being of a certain attachment type, the emerging consensus is that people's various attachment styles are more accurately represented in terms of dimensions instead of more rigid types (Fraley, Hudson, Heffernan, & Segal, 2015).

The two dimensions that have been shown to capture most of the variation in attachment are referred to as anxiety and avoidance (Fraley, Waller, & Brennan, 2000). The **anxiety dimension of attachment** refers to the amount of fear a person feels about rejection and abandonment within close relationships. The **avoidance dimension of attachment** refers to whether a person is comfortable with intimacy and dependence in primary adult relationships or finds them aversive to a degree. The individual who scores low on both of these dimensions is, in the language of attachment types, the prototypical securely attached person—someone who isn't anxious about rejection or abandonment, who is comfortable with intimacy, and who seeks closeness to and support

anxiety dimension of attachment A facet of attachment that captures the degree to which a person is worried about rejection and abandonment by relationship partners.

avoidance dimension of attachment A facet of attachment that captures the degree to which a person is comfortable with intimacy and dependence on relationship partners.

Secure
I find it relatively easy to get close to others and am comfortable depending on them and having them depend on me. I don't often worry about being abandoned or about someone getting too close.

Avoidant
I am somewhat uncomfortable being close; I find it difficult to trust them completely, difficult to allow myself to depend on them. I am nervous when anyone gets close, and often, love partners want me to be more intimate than I feel comfortable being.

Anxious-ambivalent
I find that others are reluctant to get as close as I would like. I often worry that my partner doesn't really love me or won't stay with me. I want to merge completely with another person, and this desire sometimes scares people away.

FIGURE 10.2
THREE ATTACHMENT TYPES
The three adult attachment types were inspired by the identification of three different types of attachment in infants: secure, avoidant, and anxious-ambivalent.

from relationship partners. As opposed to simply finding, say, that someone is anxious-ambivalent in terms of attachment style, attachment dimensions help researchers capture the degree of anxiety—variation that corresponds to meaningful differences in how the person thinks, feels, and behaves in close relationships.

STABILITY OF ATTACHMENT STYLES Regardless of whether we think of attachment in terms of types or dimensions, a central principle of attachment theory is that internal working models of attachment are established early and are relatively stable throughout a person's life. The attachments you form as a child shape the way you relate as an adult to your romantic partners, your children, and your friends. Evidence supports this provocative thesis: important early life events are associated with later attachment styles. In a 40-year longitudinal study of women who graduated from college in 1960, Klohnen and Bera (1998) found that those who classified themselves as avoidant at age 52 had also reported greater conflict in the home 31 years earlier at age 21. What's more, individuals classified as secure, avoidant, or anxious at age 1 tend to be similarly classified in early adulthood (Fraley & Spieker, 2003). A more recent study showed that the observed quality of adolescents' interactions with their parents at age 15 predicted their self-reported attachment security ten years later (Dinero, Conger, Shaver, Widaman, & Larsen-Rife, 2008).

As you might expect, a secure attachment style predicts more positive life outcomes (Cooper, Shaver, & Collins, 1998). Securely attached people report the greatest relationship satisfaction (Shaver & Brennan, 1992). In a four-year longitudinal study, secure participants were less likely to have experienced a romantic breakup (25.6 percent) during that time than avoidant participants (52.2 percent) or anxious participants (43.6 percent). In the Klohen and Bera study, secure women were more likely to be married at age 52 than avoidant women (82 percent versus 50 percent) and to report fewer marital problems. Though attachment-related processes and outcomes have been mostly documented in heterosexual relationships, recent research suggests that, by and large, they operate in a similar manner in same-sex romantic relationships (Mohr, Selterman, & Fassigner, 2013).

If you've become concerned while reading this that your future relationships are doomed because you've had some negative relationship experiences that have left you feeling insecurely attached, don't despair. Although attachment theorists assume that people's early experiences shape their relationships throughout life, and there is evidence pointing to some degree of stability in attachment styles, attachment styles are not rigid or fixed for life.

First, there's the question of whether people tend to have the same attachment style across all their relationships—with parents, friends, siblings, and romantic partners. Mark Baldwin and his colleagues asked undergraduates to list ten important relationships in their lives and then had them indicate the attachment style (secure, anxious-ambivalent, or avoidant) that best characterized them in each relationship (Baldwin et al., 1996). Rather than having the same attachment style across all, or even most, of their relationships, more than 50 percent of participants characterized themselves as having all three attachment styles across their ten relationships. In other words, people have multiple kinds of attachment working models stored in their memories, and any of these can be activated in the many relationships in their adult life (Chen, Boucher, & Tapias, 2006).

BOX 10.1 FOCUS ON CULTURE

Building an Independent Baby in the Bedroom

If you are a white, middle-class North American, odds are you slept by yourself in your own bedroom as a child. And that probably seems perfectly normal to you. Normal, maybe, but common? Definitely not. There are few cultures in the world where such a sleeping arrangement is customary. In an article titled "Who Sleeps with Whom Revisited," Shweder, Jensen, and Goldstein (1995) describe the sleeping arrangements of people in many of the world's cultures. The sleeping arrangements predict fairly well how independent and individualistic a given culture is. In Japan, most children sleep with their parents until they are adolescents. In the non-Western, developing world, it is virtually unheard of for very young children *not* to sleep with their parents, and such a practice would be regarded as a form of child abuse. Even in the United States, where you might expect to find lower rates of children sleeping in their parents' bed, 55 percent of African-American children less than 1 year of

age sleep with a parent every night, and 25 percent of African-American children ages 1–5 sleep with a parent. In a white, predominantly blue-collar community in Appalachian Kentucky, 71 percent of children between the ages of 2 months and 2 years were found to sleep with their parents, and 47 percent of children between 2 and 4 years of age did as well.

This study reveals the extent to which interdependent and independent self-construals permeate social behavior. In more interdependent cultures, young children are much more likely to sleep side by side with their parents than in independent cultures. While psychologists can only speculate about the effects these patterns of sleep have on attachment patterns, we might expect secure attachments in independent cultures to be characterized by greater independence and autonomy than secure patterns in interdependent cultures.

Consistent with the idea that we have multiple working models of attachment, numerous studies have shown that different attachment styles can be momentarily primed or activated—in effect, leading a person to respond in, for example, a securely attached manner even if that person is avoidant in most relationships (Baldwin et al., 1996; Jakubiak & Feeney, 2016; McClure, Bartz, & Lydon, 2013; Mikulincer, Shaver, Gillath, & Nitzberg, 2005).

A second question is whether a person's attachment style within one given relationship is stable across time. The evidence described earlier points to some degree of stability, but it's a moderate degree at most (Fraley, Vicary, Brumbaugh, & Roisman, 2011). Overall, given that most people appear to have different attachment styles with different relationship partners, and given that the stability of attachment style within any particular relationship is a matter of degree, it's likely that there's room for change in a person's attachment style even within a specific relationship (Arriaga, Kumashiro, Simpson, & Overall, 2018).

Finally, it's worth noting that the findings described here about attachment apply most readily to modern Western cultures (Morelli & Rothbaum, 2007). In cultures that place less value on autonomy, infants who are left in a room without their mother may be more fearful about exploring the environment, and the reunion with their mother may be much more turbulent. This observation doesn't imply that such children are "insecurely attached." Instead, it means they've been socialized to be interdependent with others, especially family members, making them less inclined to go off and explore on their own. For more discussion of cultural differences in attachment, see **Box 10.1**.

Relationships are essential to daily social functioning, and a feeling of belonging is a biological need. In communal relationships, generally long term, people are concerned with each other's needs; in contrast, exchange relationships, generally short term, are governed by concerns over equity and reciprocity. According to social exchange theory, people want interactions in which rewards exceed costs; satisfaction with rewards and costs also depends on what people expect to get out of a current relationship or an alternative one. Equity theory maintains that people are most satisfied when the ratio of rewards to costs is about equal for both partners in a relationship. Childhood attachments influence adult relationships as well as personal well-being. Although people are often viewed as being a certain attachment type, attachment is more accurately described in terms of dimensions, with room for variation.

Attraction

As we have seen, forming relationships is instinctive and necessary to our health and well-being. But why are we drawn to some people as friends or romantic partners and not to others? Although we generally know *whether* we like someone, we are often at a loss to explain *why*. To be sure, we know we like people who are kind to us, make us laugh, share our values, and so on. But these obvious influences notwithstanding, sometimes we're drawn to certain people and mildly put off by others for reasons we can't explain.

What are the most powerful determinants of whether we will like someone? What is the underlying basis of good or bad "chemistry"? And, in particular, what leads two people to be romantically attracted to each other? In this section, we'll consider several answers to these questions.

Proximity

Who are your best friends on campus? Are they the people who were on your hall freshman year? Are they the ones you encountered most often in class? Are they your peers on an intramural team, drama club, or college newspaper? Something that *has* to influence whether people become friends or lovers is simple physical proximity. And, in fact, the most enduring friendships are forged between people whose paths cross frequently.

STUDIES OF PROXIMITY AND ATTRACTION A number of studies have demonstrated that proximity matters in terms of who becomes friends and romantic partners (Preciado, Snijders, Burk, Stattin, & Kerr, 2011). One of the first, and most imaginative, studies was conducted at MIT in the 1940s in a married student housing project known as Westgate West, built for returning American servicemen and their families after World War II (Festinger, Schachter, & Back, 1950). The housing project consisted of 17 ten-unit apartment buildings that were isolated from other residential areas of the city. The incoming students were randomly assigned to their residences, and few of them knew one another beforehand. **Figure 10.3** shows the layout of the Westgate West apartment houses.

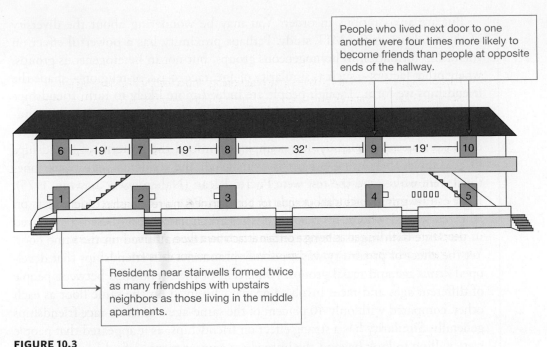

People who lived next door to one another were four times more likely to become friends than people at opposite ends of the hallway.

Residents near stairwells formed twice as many friendships with upstairs neighbors as those living in the middle apartments.

FIGURE 10.3
THE EFFECT OF PHYSICAL PROXIMITY ON FORMING FRIENDSHIPS
The location and layout of the married student apartments influenced the extent to which residents formed friendships with one another.
Source: Adapted from Festinger, Schachter, & Back, 1950.

The investigators asked each resident to name the three people in the housing project with whom they socialized most often. The effect of proximity was striking: two-thirds of those the respondent listed as friends lived in the same building as the respondent, even though only 5 percent of the residents of Westgate West lived in the respondent's building. More striking still was the pattern of friendships *within* each building. Even though the physical distance between apartments was quite small—19 feet between the doorways of adjacent apartments and 89 feet between those at the ends of each hallway—41 percent of those living in adjacent apartments listed each other as friends, compared with only 10 percent of those living at opposite ends of the hallway.

Proximity presumably leads to friendship because it facilitates chance encounters. If so, then pure physical distance should matter less than **functional distance**—the influence of an architectural layout to encourage or discourage contact between people. The MIT study shows just how important functional distance is. As Figure 10.3 indicates, the stairs are positioned such that upstairs residents will encounter the occupants of apartments 1 and 5 much more often than the occupants of the middle apartments. And indeed, the residents of apartments 1 and 5 formed twice as many friendships with their upstairs neighbors as those living in the middle apartments. Notice also that the residents of apartments 2 and 7 were just as far apart as the residents of apartments 1 and 6 and reside directly above one another. But the stairs that pass the door of apartment 1 make it and apartment 6 vastly closer from a functional perspective. No wonder residents of apartments 1 and 6 were 2.5 times more likely to become friends than the residents of apartments 2 and 7. Thus, it's functional distance more than physical distance that is decisive. Proximity promotes friendship because it (literally) brings people together.

"Despite the fact that a person can pick and choose from a vast number of people to make friends with, such things as the placement of a stoop or the direction of a street often have more to do with determining who is friends with whom."
—WILLIAM WHYTE,
THE ORGANIZATION MAN

functional distance The influence of an architectural layout to encourage or inhibit certain activities, including contact between people.

But are any cautions in order? You may be wondering about the diversity of the residents in the MIT study. Perhaps proximity has a powerful effect on friendship formation in homogeneous groups, but not in heterogeneous groups, where other factors—such as similarity of age, race, class, or religion—shape the friendships we form. Though people are indeed more likely to form friendships with others who are similar to them, the largest effects of proximity on friendship formation have actually been found between people of *different* races, ages, or social classes. One study, for example, examined the patterns of friendships in a Manhattan housing project in which half the residents were black, one-third were white, and the rest were Puerto Rican (Nahemow & Lawton, 1975). Each ethnic group included people of all ages. Proximity had strong effects on who befriended whom: 88 percent of those designated as a "best friend" lived in the same building as the respondent, and nearly half lived on the same floor. Yet the effect of proximity was especially pronounced in friendships that developed *across* age and racial groups: 70 percent of the friendships between people of different ages and races involved people who lived on the same floor as each other, compared with only 40 percent of the same-age and same-race friendships generally. Similarity has a strong effect on friendships, as it appeared that people were willing to look beyond the immediate environment to find friends of their own age and race. But proximity is especially powerful across differences, as the friendships with people of a different age or race tended to be those that fell in the residents' laps.

THE MERE EXPOSURE EFFECT Part of the reason proximity has such a big influence on friendship is simply that it makes contact more likely: you're not going to become friends with someone you haven't met. But simple contact isn't the whole story. Robert Zajonc has offered compelling evidence for another reason that proximity leads to liking: the **mere exposure effect**—the notion that the more you are exposed to something, the more you tend to like it (Zajonc, 1968). This may strike you as implausible. After all, what about all those songs on the radio that become more irritating each time you hear them? And why are there sayings like "Familiarity breeds contempt"?

In fact, researchers have generated a great deal of evidence for the mere exposure effect (Bornstein, 1989; Montoya, Horton, Vevea, Citkowicz, & Lauber, 2017; Zajonc, 1968). Some of the most striking (though less convincing) evidence is correlational. There is a remarkably strong correlation between how frequently people are exposed to various items (words, fruits, cities, chemical elements) and how much they like those items. For example, there is a strong correlation between people's preference for various letters in the English alphabet and how often those letters appear in the language (Alluisi & Adams, 1962). It's hard to imagine that the English language contains so many *e*'s or *r*'s just because people like those letters; it's more plausible that people like them because they are exposed to them so often.

In an experimental demonstration of the mere exposure effect, Zajonc (1968) created a stimulus set of Turkish words that were unfamiliar to his participants, such as *kadirga*, *afworbu*, and *lokanta*. Different words within this set were then shown to participants 0, 1, 2, 5, 10, or 25 times. Afterward, the participants indicated the extent to which they thought each word referred to something good or bad. The more times participants saw a given word, the more they assumed it referred to something good. Zajonc replicated this experiment using college

mere exposure effect The idea that repeated exposure to a stimulus, such as an object or a person, leads to greater liking of the stimulus.

THE INFLUENCE OF MERE EXPOSURE ON LIKING
Many famous landmarks that are beloved and respected today initially elicited anything but reverence. (A) When the Eiffel Tower was completed in Paris in 1889, to commemorate the French Revolution's centennial, a group of artists and intellectuals, including Alexandre Dumas, Guy de Maupassant, and Émile Zola, signed a petition calling it "useless and monstrous" and "a disgraceful column of bolts." (B) Likewise, San Francisco's Transamerica building, completed in 1972, received negative reactions at first; renowned *San Francisco Chronicle* columnist Herb Caen angrily suggested knitting a giant tea cozy to cover the spire.

yearbook photos as stimuli and had subjects judge how much they thought they would like the person. Within face-to-face and online social interactions, people become more attracted to strangers as they interact with them more frequently (Reis, Maniaci, Caprariello, Eastwick, & Finkel, 2011). **Box 10.2** (see p. 329) expands on the growing social psychology literature on online dating.

Perhaps the most intriguing test of the mere exposure effect was done with albino rats (Cross, Halcomb, & Matter, 1967). One group of rats was raised in an environment where selections of Mozart's music played for 12 hours each day. A second group was exposed to an analogous schedule of music by Schoenberg. The rats were then placed individually in a test cage that was rigged so that the rat's presence on one side of the cage would trip a switch that caused previously unheard selections of Mozart to be played and the rat's presence on the other side would generate new selections of Schoenberg. The rats were thus able to "vote with their feet" and express a preference for the quintessentially classical music of Mozart or the modern, atonal compositions of Schoenberg. The results support the mere exposure effect: rats raised on a musical diet of Mozart moved significantly more often to the side of the cage that caused Mozart to be played, whereas those raised on a diet of Schoenberg moved to the side that caused Schoenberg's music to be played (**Figure 10.4**, see p. 328). (Rats in a control condition with no initial exposure to music later exhibited a preference for—you guessed it, Mozart; maybe twenty-first century rats will have developed a taste for Schoenberg.)

This early research inspired over 100 studies that have explored the conditions in which one is most likely to observe the mere exposure effect (Montoya et al., 2017). Here's one question you may be asking: Is there a limit to the number of

"I don't like that man. I must get to know him better."
—ABRAHAM LINCOLN

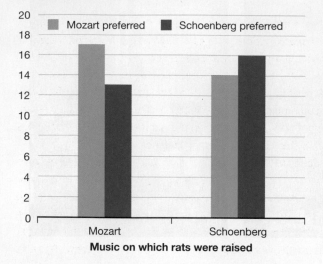

Average amount
of time rats spent
on Mozart and
Schoenberg sides
of the cage (minutes)

**FIGURE 10.4
REPEATED EXPOSURE AND
MUSICAL PREFERENCE**
Exposure leads to liking. In this study,
exposure to Mozart's music led to a
preference for Mozart, and likewise for
Schoenberg.
Source: Adapted from Cross, Halcomb, & Matter, 1967.

exposures that produces the mere exposure effect, after which the effect disappears or reverses? Will you continue to like a photo of yourself more if you see it 50 times? 75 times? 200 times? Across different studies, exposure to different kinds of stimuli, such as paintings, photographs, words, and ideographs, tends to increase liking up to about 35 presentations of the stimulus, after which the liking of the stimulus begins to decline.

You may also be wondering whether the mere exposure effect is stronger for some kinds of stimuli than for others. If you look at an image of da Vinci's *Mona Lisa* over and over again, will you like it more? What about photos of people's faces? Or phrases in your native tongue? Attesting to the robustness of the mere exposure effect, studies examining this question find that with increased exposure, we like paintings, photographs, geometric shapes, and both meaningful and meaningless words more. There are, however, two exceptions: the mere exposure effect doesn't apply to auditory stimuli, such as brief sounds or musical pieces; nor does it work with stimuli that you initially dislike. Looking over and over again at a photo of someone you find repugnant won't lead you to like the individual more.

At this point, we hope you're asking, *Why* does mere repeated exposure lead to liking? One explanation is that people find it easier to perceive and cognitively process familiar stimuli: the processing of familiar stimuli is more "fluent." And because people find the experience of fluency inherently pleasurable, those positive feelings make the stimuli more appealing (Reber, Schwarz, & Winkielman, 2004; Winkielman & Cacioppo, 2001; see also Chapter 4).

Zajonc offered a second interpretation. Upon repeated exposure to a stimulus without any negative consequences resulting from the encounter, we learn to associate the stimulus with the absence of anything negative and thus form a comfortable, pleasant attachment to it. Mere repeated exposure leads to attraction, in other words, because it reinforces that comfortable, pleasant feeling. This conditioning process helps organisms distinguish stimuli that are "safe" from those that aren't (Zajonc, 2001). Thus, the more often people are exposed to something, the more they tend to like it.

Similarity

Another important determinant of attraction is similarity: people tend to like other people who are similar to themselves (Byrne, Clore, & Smeaton, 1986; Caspi & Herbener, 1990). After all, "Birds of a feather flock together." Not that friends agree about everything, of course. But some areas of common ground are more important than others. Agreement on core political values, for example, is likely to have more of an impact on whether you like someone than whether you root for the same baseball team or agree on the best musical artists from the past decade.

STUDIES OF SIMILARITY AND ATTRACTION The impact of similarity on attraction has been documented in many ways. For example, there is a robust tendency for people to become romantically involved with people who are similar in terms of their social class, educational level, and religious background (Schwartz, 2013). When you think about it, this finding isn't all that surprising,

BOX 10.2   FOCUS ON SOCIAL MEDIA

Forming Relationships Online

The topic of online dating is important to consider in any contemporary discussion of romantic relationships. Attitudes toward online dating have grown considerably more favorable over time (Paumgarten, 2011). In fact, recent data suggest that over one in five new romantic relationships now begin online (Rosenfeld & Thomas, 2010) and that close to 50 percent of singles in the United States engage in some form of online dating (Gelles, 2011).

The advent of online dating has raised countless interesting and potentially important questions for the scientific study of attraction and relationships (Finkel, Eastwick, Karney, Reis, & Sprecher, 2012). Do people misrepresent themselves online (Toma, Hancock, & Ellison, 2008)? Does online dating lead to more dating across racial and ethnic group boundaries or do people show ingroup racial and ethnic preferences in their online dating behavior (Jakobsson & Lindholm, 2014)? How well do social psychology principles of attraction, such as similarity and proximity, fare in terms of leading to successful online matches (Finkel et al., 2012)? Do relationships that start out online differ from relationships started in person in terms of their longevity, quality, and trajectory (Cacioppo, Cacioppo, Gonzaga, Ogburn, & VanderWeele, 2012)?

Ravi Bapna and colleagues recently conducted a field experiment aimed at understanding something else: what impact an anonymity feature—namely, the ability to search others' profiles without leaving any visible record of having done so—has on how people search for matches and how many matches they get (Bapna, Ramaprasad, Shmueli, & Umyarov, 2016). In their randomized field experiment, they teamed up with a major North American online dating website to randomly select 50,000 out of 100,000 new users of the website who would get the ability to look at others' dating profiles anonymously, without leaving a trace. The remaining 50,000 new users, who made up the control group, did not have this anonymity feature enabled.

You probably have some intuition, perhaps even firsthand experience, about what having the anonymity feature does to online dating behavior and outcomes. The researchers reasoned that the anonymity feature may lead to more disinhibited search behavior, thereby increasing the number and diversity of profiles people view, and it may also reveal people's true preferences because it can be conducted at minimal to no social cost. The end result of such processes could be more matches. However, when people search others' profiles anonymously, leaving no trace that they have done so, they are no longer leaving any signal of interest. And it is precisely such signaling—even the relatively weak signal of simply having viewed someone's profile—that often initiates communication between online daters, which is a necessary step for finding a match. From this perspective, then, anonymous searching may hinder achieving matches.

Bapna and colleagues defined a match as a sequence of three or more messages between a pair of users. They found that although participants in the anonymity condition did view more profiles than their control counterparts, they ended up having fewer matches, which was partly accounted for by the fact that these participants sent out fewer signals of interest. Because people are often nudged to initiate communication precisely when they learn that someone is interested in them, anonymous participants received fewer attempts from others to initiate communication, which is the first step in finding a match.

Such findings are just the beginning. The literature on this subject is still young, and with the ever-growing popularity of online dating, there's no doubt that more research aimed at understanding the processes and outcomes associated with it will follow suit.

ONLINE DATING Pictured here is an ad for the dating app Tinder.

because people who come from similar backgrounds in terms of class or religion or education are more likely to encounter each other and, as we have learned, through such proximity and exposure become attracted to one another. Importantly, though, in the past couple of decades there has been a marked rise in interreligious and interracial romantic relationships (Rosenfeld, 2008).

"We are so in sync. I was just about to ask you for a divorce."

Similarity in personal characteristics also predicts romantic attraction. In one study, the members of 1,000 engaged couples—850 of whom eventually married—rated themselves on 88 characteristics (Burgess & Wallin, 1953). When researchers compared actual couples' ratings with those of "random couples" created by pairing individual members of different couples, they found that on 66 of 88 characteristics, the average similarity of the engaged couples was greater than the similarity of "random couples." Furthermore, the members of engaged couples were never more *dissimilar* than the "random couples" on any characteristic. The similarity of engaged couples was strongest for demographic characteristics (such as social class) and physical characteristics (such as health and physical attractiveness; **Box 10.3**). Similarity was less strong—but still present—for personality characteristics (such as leadership and sensitivity), although other studies find that married couples do exhibit stronger similarity in certain core personality characteristics, such as extraversion and genuineness (Buss, 1984). Moreover, interracial and interethnic couples tend to be more similar to each other in terms of their personality traits than are couples of the same race and ethnicity. People may compensate for dissimilarity on one dimension by seeking out greater similarity on others (Rushton & Bons, 2005).

A second type of evidence that supports the link between similarity and attraction comes from studies in which individuals are thrown together for an extended period of time. In one study, Theodore Newcomb recruited male college transfer students, who did not know each other beforehand, to live for a year, rent free, in a large house in exchange for filling out surveys a few hours each week (Newcomb, 1956, 1961). In response to one of the survey questions, the students indicated how much they liked each of their housemates. To an increasing degree over the course of the 15-week study, as students got to know one another better and better, their liking for other students was predictable based on how similar they were (see also Griffitt & Veitch, 1974).

Another type of evidence supporting the proposition that people are attracted to those who are similar to themselves comes from the "bogus stranger" paradigm (Byrne, 1961; Tan & Singh, 1995). In these experiments, participants are given the responses to attitude or personality questionnaires supposedly filled out by someone else (but really created by the experimenter to show a given level of similarity to the participants' own responses). After reading the responses of the bogus stranger, the participants rated him or her on several dimensions, including their liking of the person in question. In study after study of this type, the more similar the stranger is to the participant, the more the participant likes that stranger.

"Jack Sprat could eat no fat. His wife could eat no lean. And so between them both you see, they licked the platter clean."
—MOTHER GOOSE NURSERY RHYME

DON'T OPPOSITES ATTRACT? Although most people accept the idea that similarity fosters attraction, **complementarity**, or the idea that opposites attract, is also intuitively compelling: individuals with different characteristics should complement each other and thus get along well. It does seem that, say, a person who is quiet might get along with someone who likes to talk. The yin and yang of two divergent personalities seems like it *ought* to create a successful unity.

Upon closer inspection, however, it should seem clear that the effect of complementarity on attraction will be more limited than that of similarity. Unlike

complementarity The tendency for people to seek out others with characteristics that are different from, and complement, their own.

BOX 10.3   FOCUS ON DAILY LIFE

Do Couples Look More Alike over Time?

Many people claim that not only do the two people in a couple tend to look like each other, but they look more alike the longer they've been together. There are many reasons why this might be so. People who live together may adopt similar styles of dress and grooming. They might have similar diets, which could contribute to making them look more alike over time, influencing skin tone, for example, or the health of their teeth. They obviously live in the same region of the country, and because of climatic factors, they may acquire the same suntan and a similar pattern of wrinkles.

Perhaps most interesting from a psychological perspective, couples also experience many of the same emotions. At the extreme ends, the death of a child devastates both parents; winning the lottery brings elation to both. More generally, a downbeat household is typically one in which both members are unhappy; an upbeat household is one in which both are happy. Eventually, a lifetime of experiencing similar emotions may have similar effects on the face and physical bearing of each member of the couple. For example, a happy lifetime tends to produce crow's feet around the eyes, while an unhappy one tends to leave creases around the outside of the mouth.

Robert Zajonc and his colleagues found that there is indeed truth to this idea. They enlisted the help of 12 married couples to see whether they came to look more alike over time (Zajonc, Adelmann, Murphy, & Niedenthal, 1987). The couples, all of whom were 50–60 years of age, provided both current photos of themselves and photos taken during their first year of marriage, about 25 years earlier. The photos were cropped to remove extraneous identifying information, leaving just the head and shoulders. Judges who were unaware of who was married to whom were then asked to assess how much each of the men resembled each of the women (for both the current and the older photos).

The couples looked significantly more alike roughly 25 years into their marriage than they did as newlyweds. To check for the possibility that older people as a whole are simply more alike, the Zajonc team established a set of control couples by randomly pairing members of different couples with one another and then assessing the similarity of these "random couples." Contrary to the notion that older people are generally more homogeneous in appearance, there was no tendency for the random couples to converge in appearance over time, though, as noted, this tendency was evident among actual couples. Thus, not only do we seek mates who are similar to ourselves in personality and background; we also become even more similar in appearance over time.

PHYSICAL SIMILARITY Over time, the members of a couple tend to look like each other, perhaps because of initial physical similarities, but also because of shared living conditions, diet, and emotional experiences.

similarity, there is no reason to expect that complementary attitudes (for example, vis-à-vis abortion), beliefs (for example, about the existence God), or physical characteristics (short versus tall) will lead to attraction. The complementarity hypothesis really makes sense only for those traits for which one person's needs can be met by the other person's difference (Levinger, 1964). People who are dependent can have their needs taken care of by a partner who is nurturing. But someone who is a hard worker probably won't want to be with someone who is lazy, and someone who values honesty isn't likely to associate with a habitual liar. Thus, we might expect to find complementarity in such traits as dependence-nurturance or introversion-extraversion, but not in such traits as honesty, optimism, or conscientiousness. In general, the evidence for the complementarity hypothesis when it comes to personality traits is mixed, with some supporting and some inconsistent findings (Antill, 1983; Boyden, Carroll, & Maier, 1984; Neimeyer & Mitchell, 1988; Wagner, 1975).

It's worth noting, though, that complementarity may be a stronger force in predicting attraction when it comes to social status. We derive social status, or respect and esteem, from several sources, including our family's class background, our educational achievement, and the prestige of our work (Anderson, Hildreth, & Howland, 2015). The complementarity hypothesis suggests an intriguing possibility: perhaps we become attracted to individuals who enjoy elevated status in a domain where we ourselves are lacking, such as, say, family background, but who themselves are lacking in domains where we excel, such as, say, education achieved. This idea is known as the *status exchange hypothesis*: romantic attraction increases when two individuals complement each other in terms of their social status by offering each other elevated status, through romantic partnership, where they themselves are lacking. Empirical evidence supports the status exchange hypothesis. Christine Schwartz and her colleges examined the family class background (based on the parents' educational achievement) and the participant's own educational achievement in 7,398 couples who married between 1968 and 2013 (Schwartz, 2013). In this study, like others, there was a strong tendency for people to marry individuals of similar family class backgrounds and personal educational achievement—another nod to the power of similarity in predicting attraction. But at greater rates than expected by chance, individuals in a couple complemented each other's social status: it was the individual who hailed from a modest family class background, but who had personally achieved high levels of education, who married someone who came from a more distinguished family class background but who had achieved less in education.

Thus, similarity appears to be the rule and complementarity the exception, except when it comes to social status. Even when two people seem to represent a perfect example of complementarity, they are likely to complement each other on only one or two features of their personalities. Their other characteristics are likely to be similar or unrelated.

Physical Attractiveness

"There are many more obscure, miserable, and impoverished geniuses in the world than underappreciated beauties."
—JERRY ADLER, *NEWSWEEK*

Not surprisingly, one of the most powerful determinants of interpersonal attraction is physical attractiveness. Who are the people who get the most attention at parties, the gym, or the checkout line at the campus bookstore? Attractive people have an advantage in winning other people's attention and affection. Because a person's physical appearance is so visible—and visible so *immediately*—it affects our instantaneous, gut reaction to someone we meet for the first time. Although we can learn to appreciate someone's keen intelligence and strong moral fiber, that usually takes some time. Beauty is obvious right away. Partly for this reason, research indicates that a person's looks play an even more important role in interpersonal attraction than you might expect. (See **Box 10.4** on p. 334 for different perspectives on the basis of perceptions of beauty.)

Before considering the relevant findings, it's worthwhile—and bracing, for those of us who aren't so attractive—to keep in mind some important caveats. First, although certain features are deemed attractive by most people, there's considerable variability in what individuals find attractive. Social psychologist Elaine Walster, a pioneer in the study of attraction, conducted an informal study in which she asked people on her campus if anyone had ever told them they were good-looking or told them they weren't. The researchers deliberately surveyed the least attractive and most attractive people they encountered. All of the most unattractive people said there were people who thought they were good-looking, and all of the most attractive people said there were people who considered them ugly (E. H. Walster, personal communication, December 2, 2017).

BEAUTY SHARES MANY QUALITIES ACROSS DIFFERENT ETHNICITIES
Across different ethnicities, physical attractiveness is influenced by facial symmetry, skin, and signs of youth in women, and it comes with many social benefits, from better salaries to greater interest in others.

Second, although people like people who are physically attractive, the reverse is also true: people find those they like more attractive than those they don't like (Kniffin & Wilson, 2004). How attractive we find someone to be initially can grow based on how much we come to like that person. Third, happy couples tend to perceive each other as physically attractive even if other people don't see them that way (Murray, Holmes, & Griffin, 1996). Fourth, although some people are considered good-looking throughout their lives, physical attractiveness is less stable than most of us think (Zebrowitz, 1997). People who are unattractive in their teens sometimes bloom in young adulthood, while the looks of the kings and queens of the high school prom often fade. And finally, an extensive literature finds that, independent of how physically attractive a person is, if that individual chooses to engage in more friendly behaviors—nice eye contact, warm smiles, physical proximity, engaged talk, and even affirmative language—strangers and potential romantic partners will find that person more attractive (Montoya, Kershaw, & Prosser, in press).

BENEFITS OF BEING ATTRACTIVE The most frequently observed finding about the impact of physical attractiveness—and the least surprising—is that attractive individuals are more popular as friends and potential romantic partners than their less attractive counterparts. This effect has been shown in studies that correlate various indicators of popularity, such as dating frequency and friendship ratings, with physical attractiveness (Berscheid, Dion, Walster, & Walster, 1971; Feingold, 1984); in investigations where blind dates are later asked how attracted they are to their partners (Walster, Aronson, Abrahams, & Rottman, 1966); and in studies of online and speed dating in which participants indicate how attracted they are to people they can see in photographs or in brief face-to-face encounters (Alterovitz & Mendelsohn, 2009; Asendorpf, Penke, & Back, 2011; Eastwick & Finkel, 2008; Luo & Zhang, 2009).

"Look your best—who said love is blind?"
—MAE WEST

But attractive folks benefit in other areas as well. An essay supposedly written by an attractive author is typically evaluated more favorably than one written by an unattractive author (Cash & Trimer, 1984). And men are more likely to come to the aid of an injured female if she is good-looking (West & Brown, 1975). Other studies have shown that each 1-point increase (on a 5-point scale) in physical attractiveness is worth about $2,000 in additional annual salary—closer to $3,500 in current inflation-adjusted dollars (Frieze, Olson, & Russell, 1991; Hamermesh & Biddle, 1994). Stated another way, people who are better-than-average looking can expect to earn nearly a quarter of a million dollars more during their careers than their less attractive counterparts (Hamermesh, 2011).

BOX 10.4 ▷ **FOCUS ON** AESTHETICS

The Basis of Beauty

What makes the Golden Gate Bridge so aesthetically pleasing? Why do mathematicians describe certain proofs as beautiful or elegant? And why are pandas and harp seals considered more adorable than mollusks and vultures? Thinkers throughout the ages have pondered and argued about the nature of aesthetic beauty. Those who have taken the *objectivist view*, a view ancient Greeks especially favored, argue that beauty is inherent in the properties of objects that produce pleasant sensations in the perceiver. Within this perspective, properties of the stimulus such as balance, proportion, symmetry, and contrast produce feelings of beauty. Other scholars, those who subscribe to the *subjectivist view*, argue that "beauty is in the eye of the beholder," and therefore the search for general laws of beauty is futile.

Psychologists have recently offered a third view, one that attributes aesthetic pleasure to perceptual and cognitive fluency, or how easily information can be processed (Reber, Schwarz, & Winkielman, 2004). Some objects are more easily identified than others (perceptual fluency), and some are more easily interpreted, defined, and integrated into existing knowledge (cognitive fluency). The core idea is that the more fluently an object is processed, the more positive the aesthetic experience is for the viewer. This argument is compelling because people do indeed experience pleasure when processing fluent stimuli. Electromyography (EMG) recordings of people's faces reveal more activation of the so-called smiling muscle (zygomaticus major) when they are exposed to fluent stimuli rather than disfluent stimuli (Winkielman & Cacioppo, 2001).

Another critical part of the argument is that all the features that objectivists regard as inherently pleasing—symmetry, contrast, and so on—tend to increase perceptual fluency. Symmetrical patterns are processed efficiently, and symmetrical faces are considered particularly good-looking—as are symmetrical structures like the Eiffel Tower, the Chrysler Building, and the Golden Gate Bridge. Objects characterized by high contrast can be recognized quickly, and studies have found that high-contrast stimuli are judged to be particularly attractive, such as flowers, goldfinches, and photographs taken by Ansel Adams (Reber, Winkielman, & Schwarz, 1998). The fluency perspective is broader than those classic features of beauty and maintains that *anything* that increases the fluent processing of an object ought to increase its aesthetic appeal. Thus, for example, previous exposure to a stimulus makes it easier to process, and mere repeated exposure leads to greater liking.

But if simple stimuli are processed more fluently than complex stimuli, how does this explain people's aesthetic appreciation of complex stimuli such as Beethoven's Symphony No. 9 or the ceiling of the Sistine Chapel? What seems to be particularly appealing is "simplicity in complexity." Processing a simple image fluently isn't necessarily all that satisfying, but a complex image or sound pattern made accessible by some underlying structure often yields the greatest sensation of aesthetic pleasure.

The fluency perspective on aesthetic beauty thus occupies a middle ground between the objectivist and subjectivist views. Beauty is indeed in the eye of the beholder, but not in the sense that it is completely arbitrary and variable from person to person. Rather, beauty lies in the processing experience of the beholder.

AESTHETIC ASSESSMENTS Symmetrical stimuli are easy to process (they're fluent), and, like fluent stimuli in general, tend to be experienced as aesthetically pleasing. The symmetry of the Golden Gate Bridge may be one reason it's regarded as one of the most beautiful bridges in the world.

In addition, jurors often give attractive defendants a break (Efran, 1974); even when convicted, attractive criminals receive lighter sentences from judges (Gunnell & Ceci, 2010; Stewart, 1980). In one study, for example, participants recommended prison sentences that were 86 percent longer for unattractive defendants than for attractive ones (Sigall & Ostrove, 1975). Crime may not pay, but the wages are clearly better for those who are good-looking.

THE HALO EFFECT Being attractive not only benefits people in terms of how they are treated. Attractive people also benefit from a **halo effect**, the common belief (accurate or not) that people who are appealing to look at have a host of positive qualities beyond their physical appearance. Thus, people may try to date, mate, and affiliate with those who are physically attractive not only because of their looks but also because of many other attributes they're thought to have. In experiments that require people to make inferences about individuals' personality based solely on photographs, good-looking men and women were judged to be happier, more intelligent, and more popular and to have more desirable personalities, higher incomes, and more professional success (Dion, Berscheid, & Walster, 1972; Eagly, Ashmore, Makhijani, & Longo, 1991; Feingold, 1992b). The only consistently negative inferences about physically attractive individuals are that they are immodest and less likely to be good parents (Dion et al., 1972). Attractive women are sometimes also seen as vain and materialistic (Johnson, Podratz, Dipboye, & Gibbons, 2010).

halo effect The common belief (accurate or not) that attractive individuals possess a host of positive qualities beyond their physical appearance.

The attractiveness halo appears to vary in predictable ways across different cultures. In independent cultures such as the United States, physically attractive people are assumed to be more dominant and assertive. In interdependent cultures such as Korea, attractive people are thought to be more generous, sensitive, and empathic than unattractive individuals (Wheeler & Kim, 1997).

Is there any validity to these beliefs? Given the preferential treatment good-looking people often receive, it would be surprising if that treatment didn't have any impact on their behavior and their sense of themselves. Indeed, physically attractive people seem to be somewhat happier, less stressed, and more satisfied with their lives, and they perceive themselves as having greater control over what happens to them (Diener, Wolsic, & Fujita, 1995; Umberson & Hughes, 1987).

Physically attractive people also behave differently in social interactions, and in ways that generate more favorable impressions in others. In one study, the experimenters rated all participants for physical attractiveness. Participants then had 5-minute telephone conversations with a member of the opposite sex (Goldman & Lewis, 1977). Even though participants couldn't see their conversation partners, they still rated the more attractive individuals as more likable and socially skilled than less attractive counterparts. In a related study, male participants had a get-acquainted phone conversation with a woman whom they were led to believe, through viewing a photo provided by the experimenter, was attractive or unattractive (Snyder, Tanke, & Berscheid, 1977). The females in the chosen photos were quite attractive for half the participants and unattractive for the others. When only the woman's recorded comments from the conversations were played to other participants who weren't shown the woman's photo, and thus had no preconceptions about her

"The secret to looking good is to be good-looking."

"Not to worry—I'm going to put our best-looking people on the job."

appearance, a rather stunning result emerged. They rated the woman who had talked to a man who *thought* she was attractive as being warmer and more socially poised than the woman who had talked to a man who thought she was unattractive. Studies like these reveal how being attractive leads to easier, rewarding social encounters, which in turn instill in good-looking people the confidence and social skills that bring about more rewarding interactions in the future (Langlois et al., 2000; Reis et al., 1982).

THE ROLE OF GENDER Attractiveness is more important in determining women's life outcomes than men's. Women deemed unattractive at work have more negative experiences than similarly unattractive men (Bar-Tal & Saxe, 1976). And physical attractiveness matters more for women, and for gay men, than it does for heterosexual men when it comes to popularity, dating prospects, and even marriage opportunities and satisfaction in marriage (Meltzer, McNulty, Jackson, & Karney, 2014; Peplau et al., 2009).

Beauty, therefore, can translate into power for women. Barbara Fredrickson and Tomi-Ann Roberts (1997) have argued that these kinds of external rewards for beauty encourage women's preoccupation with their own attractiveness, even coaxing them to adopt a kind of outsider's perspective on their physical selves. This can be costly in terms of their satisfaction with who they are and even how well they do academically and professionally.

THE UNIVERSALITY OF PHYSICAL ATTRACTIVENESS What do people who are considered attractive look like? What features set them apart from everyone else? These questions might seem impossible to answer. After all, doesn't it depend on who's doing the evaluating—on the unique preference of each person as well as the more general tastes of the prevailing culture or historical era?

Yes, of course. As noted earlier, there is considerable variation from one person to the next in terms of specific physical preferences (Beck, Ward-Hull, & McLear, 1976). There's also substantial variation in preferences between cultures and subcultures and across historical periods (Darwin, 1871; Fallon, 1990; Ford & Beach, 1951; Hebl & Heatherton, 1997; **Box 10.5**). But such variations don't mean that all determinants of physical attractiveness are arbitrary or subject to the whims of fashion. People in Western cultures widely agree on who is attractive and who isn't (Langlois et al., 2000). And they aren't alone: people from different cultures and subcultures tend to share their assessments (Cunningham, Roberts, Barbee, Druen, & Wu, 1995; Rhodes et al., 2001). Asians, blacks, and whites, for example, share roughly the same opinions of which Asian, black, and white faces they find attractive (Bernstein, Lin, & McClellan, 1982; Maret, 1983; Perrett, May, & Yoshikawa, 1994; Thakerar & Iwawaki, 1979).

Moreover, infants prefer to look at attractive faces. Experimenters have shown infants as young as 3 months slides of two human faces side by side. Adults had previously judged one of the faces as attractive and the other as unattractive. The slides were typically shown to the infant for 10 seconds. Infants showed a clear preference for attractive over unattractive faces, with the time the infant spent looking at each one serving as an indicator of the infant's preference (Langlois, Ritter, Roggman, & Vaughn, 1991; Slater et al., 1998). By the end of the first year, when infants' behavioral repertoires are more advanced, they are more inclined to play contentedly with

BOX 10.5 | FOCUS ON HEALTH

The Flight to Thinness

Today, much of the world—particularly the United States—is obsessed with thinness. It's an unhealthy obsession and has been blamed for the alarming increase in such eating disorders as bulimia and anorexia nervosa in young women (Brumberg, 1997). Society's current preference for thin women is actually something of an anomaly, given the historical preference for a heavier figure. Heaviness was not always viewed as negatively as it is now. Just consider this claim by the eighteenth-century French gourmand Brillat-Savarin: "To acquire a perfect degree of plumpness . . . is the life study of every woman in the world" (Shapin, 2006).

The modern trend toward thinness has been documented in a number of ways. Researchers examined photographs of women appearing in *Vogue* and *Ladies' Home Journal* over the course of the twentieth century, computing the relative size of the women's busts and waists. The bust-to-waist ratio declined markedly across this time span, indicating a turning away from a more voluptuous standard of female beauty (Silverstein, Perdue, Peterson, & Kelly, 1986). Analyses of *Playboy* centerfolds and Miss America contestants over the latter half of the twentieth century have revealed a similar trend toward slenderness (Garner, Garfinkel, Schwartz, & Thompson, 1980; Wiseman, Gray, Mosimann, & Ahrens, 1992).

To try to make sense of both the historical norm and the current norm, Judith Anderson examined the preferred female body type in 54 cultures (Anderson, Crawford, Nadeau, & Lindberg, 1992). She and her colleagues found a relationship between body-weight preferences and the reliability of the food supply across cultures. In cultures with a relatively uncertain food supply, moderate-weight to heavyset women were considered more desirable. But in cultures with very reliable supplies of food, a thin body type was generally preferred. And it's hard to imagine a culture with a more stable food supply and a more pronounced infatuation with slender bodies than that of the United States today.

The ongoing obsession with thinness also appears to be characterized by some misperceptions. In one telling study, male and female undergraduates were shown a series of nine drawings of body types ranging from very thin to very heavy (Fallon & Rozin, 1985). The participants had to identify the body types along a continuum that represented (1) their own current body type, (2) the body type they would most want to have, (3) the body type they thought would be most attractive to the opposite sex, and (4) the body type of the opposite sex that they personally found most attractive (this time, of course, on a set of drawings of the opposite sex). The male students, on average, thought that their current body type was precisely as heavy as the ideal body type. Moreover, they also believed that their current body type was the most attractive to female students (although the women actually preferred a more slender male physique than the men anticipated). The results were different for the female students. The women judged themselves to be heavier than their own ideal and also heavier than what they thought would be most attractive to men. The most disturbing finding was that the women believed that the most attractive body type to men was much more slender than the ideal the men actually preferred. An unfortunate pair of "thought bubbles" spring immediately to mind: a woman standing next to a man worrying that "I'd feel more comfortable around him if only I lost a few pounds," while the man is simultaneously thinking, "She looks great, but she would look even better if she'd gain a few pounds."

PREFERRED BODY TYPES Although most modern American women wish to be thin, for centuries the standard of female beauty was a heavier figure with more curves. (A) Renoir's *Nude Woman Seated* (1876). (B) Renoir's *Blond Bather* (1919). (C) Marilyn Monroe (1950s). (D) Model Gigi Hadid.

PREFERRED FACIAL FEATURES
(A) Queen Nefertiti, of prebiblical times, was considered physically attractive in her time—and is in ours. Her clear skin, widely spaced and large eyes, small nose and chin, full lips, and high eyebrows are features deemed attractive in all eras. (B) These same features can be found in many people considered very attractive today, such as Angelina Jolie.

reproductive fitness The capacity to pass one's genes on to subsequent generations.

an adult stranger who is attractive than with one who is unattractive.

EVOLUTION AND ATTRACTION What are the features that adults across cultures find physically attractive? Important attempts to address this question have been guided by evolutionary theorizing and have focused on romantic or sexual attraction. The central idea is that we've evolved to prefer people whose physical features signify health or, more generally, **reproductive fitness**—the capacity to pass one's genes to subsequent generations. By mating with reproductively fit individuals, people maximize the chances of their own genes being passed on.

Following the evolutionary thesis, we should not be attracted to people whose physical characteristics might indicate vulnerability to disease or reproductive problems. Thus, we might steer clear of people with facial features that are too unusual—for example, eyes placed so close together that the person looks like a cyclops or so far apart that the person looks like an alien. At the extremes, such features could reflect genetic problems or indicate that something has gone wrong during early development—both of which could make the person's offspring poor evolutionary prospects.

There's evidence that people do indeed find unusual facial features unattractive and that they are drawn to "average" faces (**Figure 10.5**). Photographic and computer technology can be used to create a composite (or average) face out of any number of individual faces (Langlois & Roggman, 1990; Said & Todorov, 2011). People typically consider such composite faces of both men and women as more attractive than the average individual face in the set of faces from which they were constructed. This effect is stronger as more individual faces are put into the composite, which makes it less likely to possess unusual features typical

FIGURE 10.5
ATTRACTION TO AVERAGE FACES
In this study, the researchers created average faces by dividing an individual face into small squares. (A) Each square's number was on a shade of gray. (B) They averaged the shades of gray across two photos to create an averaged configuration of two faces and continued averaging even more individual faces with the newly created face. Faces that are closest to average are judged to be more attractive.
Source: Adapted from Langlois & Roggman, 1990.

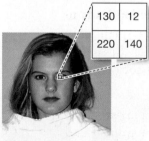

(A)

(B)

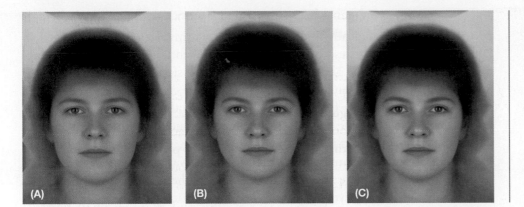

(A) (B) (C)

ATTRACTION TO EXAGGERATED FEATURES
In this study, the researchers made three different kinds of composite faces: (A) a face created by averaging 60 faces, (B) a face created by averaging only the 15 most attractive of these faces, and (C) a face created by calculating the differences between the first two composites and then exaggerating these differences by 50 percent. Participants found the exaggerated face to be the most attractive.
Source: Adapted from Perrett et al., 1994.

of individual faces. To a significant extent, then, the more average, or typical, a face is, the more attractive it is.

Another factor that plays an important role in judgments of physical attractiveness is bilateral (two-sided) symmetry, particularly in the human face (Scheib, Gangestad, & Thornhill, 1999; Thornhill & Gangestad, 1993). Departures from symmetry typically result from conditions that might signal low reproductive fitness, such as injuries to an organism in utero (before birth; Polak, 1993) and infectious diseases experienced by the mother during pregnancy (Livshits & Kobyliansky, 1991). Bilaterally symmetrical adults tend to have fewer respiratory and intestinal infections than their less symmetrical peers (Thornhill & Gangestad, 2005). Bilateral symmetry thus seems to serve as a signal of an organism's ability to resist disease and is therefore sought out by potential mates, human and nonhuman alike. Bilaterally symmetrical individuals in a variety of animal species have been shown to have an advantage in attracting mates (Markow & Ricker, 1992).

Gender Differences in Mate Preferences

Any discussion of the evolutionary basis of attraction leads to the question, Do men and women look for different qualities in a mate? Let's examine the evidence for such gender differences and how they are explained by evolutionary and sociocultural perspectives.

INVESTMENT IN OFFSPRING Evolutionary psychologists claim that evolution gave rise to different preferences in women and men because of the different investments each sex typically makes in offspring. It is incontrovertible that women invest more in offspring than men. For conception, the egg that women provide (one of only 200–250 they will produce in their lifetime) contains both genetic material and nutrients the developing embryo needs in the initial stages of life. Men, by contrast, provide sperm, which contributes primarily genetic material and little else and is something the average man produces on the order of hundreds of millions each day. After conception, of course, in utero development takes place entirely within the woman, taxing her physiologically and preventing her from

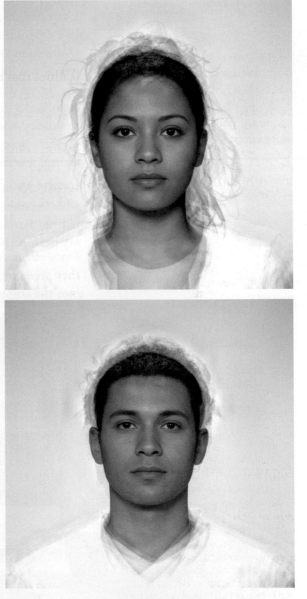

AGGREGATED FACES
In an increasingly multicultural society, the typical face in many countries will mix the attributes of many ethnicities.

conceiving another child for at least nine months. During that time, her male partner is able—biologically—to conceive a large army. (It's estimated that 1 in 200 men alive today are descendants of the twelfth-century Mongol leader Genghis Khan, who conquered 12 million square miles of Asia and Europe and impregnated thousands of women along the way.) After the child is born, an extended period of nursing and care further taxes the woman and reduces her fertility, thus further increasing the time until she's capable of producing additional offspring.

Given these differences in investment in offspring, women ought to be more selective in their choice of mates. Or stated the other way, men would be expected to be more indiscriminate than women. This hypothesis conforms to both the historical record and to everyday observation: in virtually all societies in which this issue has been systematically studied, the average man appears ready to jump into bed much more quickly and with a much wider range of potential partners than the average female. (Note that in the world's oldest profession, prostitution, it's nearly always a man making the payment.) In keeping with these observations, in a cross-cultural study with over 16,000 participants from societies all over the globe, men and women were asked, "Ideally, how many different sexual partners would you like to have?"— over various time intervals ranging from one month to the rest of their lives. For every time interval and in all regions of the world, men expressed a desire for a greater number of sexual partners (Schmitt, 2003). Similar trends are observed in studies of the sexual inclinations of gay men, who express a greater interest in having lots more partners than lesbian or heterosexual women do and less interest in monogamy (Peplau & Fingerhut, 2007).

WHAT DO MEN WANT? WHAT DO WOMEN WANT? In heterosexual relations, what do men find attractive in a mate? And if women are indeed more discriminating than men, what do women find attractive in a mate? From an evolutionary perspective, if men are to reproduce successfully, they need to find mates who are fertile. But how does one spot a fertile woman? There are no direct cues, but because women experience a relatively narrow window of lifetime fertility (the biological clock), there's at least one reasonably good indirect cue—youth. Men should thus be drawn to younger women and the cues associated with youth: smooth skin, lustrous hair, full lips, and a figure in which the waist is much narrower than the hips (Singh, 1993).

The key reproductive facts for women are much different. Although the quality of a man's sperm tends to decline a bit in older age, men typically continue to be fertile throughout life, so there is less evolutionary pressure for women to be attracted to youthful men. Instead, given the demands of nine months of pregnancy and years of breast-feeding, a critical task for women in our ancestral past was to secure a mate who had resources and who could be counted on to invest those resources in their children. According to evolutionary psychologists, then, women should be attracted to men who either possess material

"*It is a truth universally acknowledged, that a single man in possession of a good fortune, must be in want of a wife.*"
—JANE AUSTEN,
PRIDE AND PREJUDICE

"Will he ever be able to produce revenue again?"

resources or the characteristics associated with acquiring them: ambition, industriousness, social status, and physical strength.

This proposed asymmetry in mate selection (men and women seeking each other out and being attracted to one another for different reasons) has been examined systematically in studies of personal ads and online dating sites in the United States, Canada, India, and Brazil (Alterovitz & Mendelsohn, 2009; Camposa, Ottab, & Siqueira, 2002; Gustavsson, Johnsson, & Uller, 2008). These studies reveal an overwhelming tendency for men to seek youth and beauty and to offer material resources and for women to seek resources and accomplishment and to offer youth and beauty. (For more extensive evidence, see Feingold, 1990, 1992a.) It's noteworthy that similar patterns are observed in the ads of gay men, who put more emphasis on physical attractiveness as a quality they seek in a potential partner than lesbians do (Hatala & Prehodka, 1996).

This asymmetry in mate selection also emerged in a survey of over 10,000 participants from 37 different cultures (Buss, 1989, 1994). Respondents were from the West (Germany and the Netherlands); industrialized regions in non-Western countries (Shanghai, China, and Tehran, Iran); and more rural societies (the Gujarati Indians and South African Zulus). Notably, when asked what they look for in a mate, both men and women in *all* cultures rated kindness and intelligence more highly than either physical attractiveness or earning potential, as do gay men and lesbians (Lippa, 2007). Nevertheless, just as evolutionary psychologists would predict, men in nearly every culture rated physical attractiveness as more desirable in a mate than women did. And in *every* culture, men preferred marriage partners who were younger than they were. Women consistently preferred partners who were older than they were and consistently assigned greater importance than men did to various indicators of a potential mate's ability to provide material resources, such as having "good financial prospects," "social status," and "ambition-industriousness."

CRITIQUES AND EXTENSIONS OF EVOLUTIONARY THEORIZING ON GENDER DIFFERENCES IN MATE PREFERENCES The empirical evidence on human gender differences in mate preferences, like all controversial findings, has been subject to illuminating critiques. In the study examining 37 cultures, participants indicated their hypothetical preferences for what they look for in a mate. But do people actually act on such preferences in real relationships? An evolutionary account would predict that attractive women should marry high-status, wealthy men. Such a result, though, could be explained not by evolution but by other dynamics of attraction we have already considered. For example, perhaps attractive women enjoy elevated status themselves (a benefit of attractiveness) and pair up with more attractive and high-status men (a similarity effect). The challenge for the evolutionary perspective, then, is to show that attractive women pair up with high-status men independent of such benefits of attractiveness and similarity effects, selecting these men instead because of the material resources they can offer. To test the possibility that such pairings may be due to attractiveness and similarity effects, Elizabeth McClintock gathered ratings of attractiveness and status (socioeconomic standing) from individuals in 500 dating, 500 cohabiting, and 500 married couples (McClintock, 2014). What she found was that more attractive women and men did indeed personally enjoy greater socioeconomic standing (a benefit of attractiveness) and that attractive and high-status women *and* men paired off with more attractive and high-status partners (a similarity

"I love a cute guy walking down the street checking me out. . . . I have blonde shoulder-length hair, a nice toushie [sic], and brown bedroom eyes."

"I am looking for someone to spoil. To be blunt I work for an investment firm and I make quite a bit of money. I am looking for a sweet, cute girl/woman to take care of financially."
—PERSONAL ADS FROM CRAIGSLIST

effect). Importantly, once these benefits of attractiveness and similarity effects were controlled for, there was no evidence for the claim that attractive women pair off with higher-status men for the resources they provide.

A second critique of the evolutionary approach to mate preferences is more theoretical in nature: To what extent is an evolutionary perspective actually supported by the results from the 37 cultures study? This isn't an easy question to answer. Though there was consistency among the available data, nearly all the research results can be explained in other ways, without reference to reproductive fitness or any biologically based male/female differences. One influential alternative account, from Alice Eagly and Wendy Wood, maintains that because men have, on average, greater physical size and strength and don't experience the restrictions of pregnancy and nursing, a division of labor has emerged in which men across cultures are usually engaged in work outside the home and women are the primary caretakers of children (Eagly & Wood, 1999; Wood & Eagly, 2002, 2015). This division of labor has allowed men to have disproportionate control over material resources in virtually all cultures. Thus, being relatively vulnerable economically, women might be more concerned than men are with material needs, and finding mates with resources is one way of meeting those needs—rather than a choice motivated by a need to find a mate who will provide for any offspring, as the evolutionary perspective would have it.

If this line of thinking is true, then in societies where the two genders have relatively equal power and control over material resources, there shouldn't be as much emphasis for women on finding a mate with status and economic resources. In a reanalysis of the data from the 37 cultures study, Wood and Eagly (2002) found just this pattern. The greater the gender equality in a society (as indicated by United Nations data on income differential, the proportion of women in the national legislature, and so on), the less importance women placed on earning capacity in a potential mate. It should be noted that gender equality didn't affect how much importance men placed on women's attractiveness, however. In more recent, similar research, Zentner and Mitura (2012) found that in cultures with greater gender inequality, such as Turkey and Mexico, the usual pattern of men seeking beautiful mates and women seeking mates with resources was more pronounced; but in cultures with greater gender equality, such as the United States, Finland, and Republic of the Philippines, the usual pattern of men seeking beautiful mates and women seeking mates with resources was less pronounced.

FURTHER EVOLUTIONARY INSIGHTS: PHYSIOLOGICAL INFLUENCES ON MATE PREFERENCES In response to the critiques we have just reviewed, evolutionary psychologists have sought to link mate preferences more directly to biologically based processes, examining whether the hypothesized preferences women might express for symmetrical, masculine, high-status, attractive men would be stronger when women are most biologically likely to reproduce—that is, when they are ovulating (for a critical review, see Wood, Kressel, Joshi, & Louie, 2014).

In one study, the researchers had women during various phases of their menstrual cycle sniff (no kidding) a number of T-shirts that had earlier been worn by a group of men whose degrees of facial bilateral symmetry varied (Gangestad & Thornhill, 1998; Thornhill & Gangestad, 1999; Thornhill et al., 2003). As the investigators anticipated, the T-shirts of the facially symmetrical men were judged to have a better aroma than those of less symmetrical men—but only by those women who were close to the ovulation phase of their menstrual cycle and thus the most biologically prepared for reproduction at that time. It's unlikely that anyone without the help of evolutionary theory would ever have predicted or sought to test such an association.

There is evidence that women's preferences may also change in other ways as a function of the phase of their menstrual cycle. For example, it has been argued that the strong jaw of particularly masculine-looking male faces is also a sign of good genes. But women actually tend to rate slightly feminized male faces as most attractive (Perrett et al., 1998)—*except* when they are ovulating and the chances of conception are highest. Near ovulation, their preferences tend to shift toward more masculinized faces (Penton-Voak et al., 1999; **Figure 10.6**).

Where a woman is in her menstrual cycle also appears to influence the behavior of the men around her. In one study, men were asked to smell the T-shirts worn by women at different points in their cycles (Miller & Maner, 2010). Those exposed to the scent of a woman near ovulation had higher levels of testosterone—a hormone known to lead to status-enhancing behavior that might be more likely to attract women—than those exposed to a woman's scent at other phases of her cycle.

Studies like these, which assess changes in judgments of attractiveness across biologically meaningful conditions, provide the strongest evidence to date that the evolutionary approach to human attraction has merit (for a critique, see

50% more feminized ⟵ Original   Original ⟶ 50% more masculinized

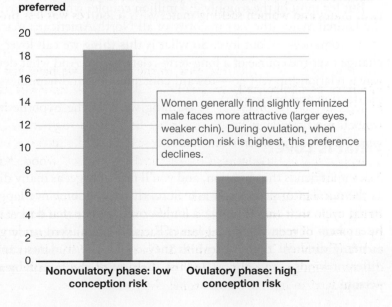

Mean feminization preferred

Women generally find slightly feminized male faces more attractive (larger eyes, weaker chin). During ovulation, when conception risk is highest, this preference declines.

Nonovulatory phase: low conception risk

Ovulatory phase: high conception risk

FIGURE 10.6
MALE ATTRACTIVENESS TO WOMEN DURING THE MENSTRUAL CYCLE

In this study, women selected the one face they thought was most attractive from photos varying from 50 percent masculinized to 50 percent feminized. The graph shows that the women tended to select somewhat feminized faces overall, but the mean degree of feminization of the selected face was less for women who were at a stage in their cycle when the chance of pregnancy was high.

Source: Adapted from Penton-Voak et al., 1999.

Wood et al., 2014). These studies take us far beyond simple empirical demonstrations of male and female differences that most people have already observed in their daily lives and speak to the insights yielded by an evolutionary perspective and the controversies it has generated.

← LOOKING BACK

Proximity causes people to have direct encounters, and mere exposure leads to liking. People are more inclined to be attracted to those who are similar to themselves, because they validate one's beliefs and values. Physically attractive individuals are more popular with members of the opposite sex, are evaluated more positively, and tend to have better social skills. Certain elements of physical attractiveness may indicate reproductive fitness—the individual's ability to reproduce. Interesting evidence and debate has emerged surrounding the contentions that there are gender differences in mate preferences—namely, that women may prefer high-status men who can provide ample resources to a relationship and that men express a stronger preference for physical attractiveness and youth.

Romantic Relationships

Throughout history and across many different cultures, the reasons for marrying have varied dramatically (Coontz, 2005). In hunter-gatherer societies, parents married their children off to members of neighboring tribes. This practice had the effect, whether intended or not, of ensuring more cooperative trading relationships between groups; it also reduced the likelihood of genetic problems that can stem from inbreeding within one's own tribe. For much of Western European history as well, marriages were arranged by parents to consolidate ties with other families, thereby ensuring that property and wealth stayed within the families. In some cultures today, arranged marriages are still common.

But for most of the roughly 2.3 million couples who get married each year in the United States (the vast majority of all North Americans marry), marriage is about romance—about love. So what is this thing we call love? How does love change over the course of a long-term relationship? And what determines which way a relationship will go—toward contentedness and happiness or toward dissatisfaction and breakup?

What Is Love?

Ask some friends this question, and you'll probably get as many different answers as the number of people you ask. Sure, there'll be some overlapping sentiments in the responses, but there'll be a lot less overlap than you'd have thought. When researchers Beverley Fehr and James Russell (1991) asked undergraduates to list as many different types of love as they could, the students came up with 216 different kinds—and almost half of these were mentioned by more than one person!

MARRIAGE ACROSS CULTURES
Wedding ceremonies vary in their specific styles and formats according to cultural practices, but they are held throughout the world. Here are ceremonies in (A) South India, (B) Scotland, and (C) Jilin, China.

Most social psychology studies account for multiple varieties of love, but researchers typically organize them into three broad categories: companionate love, compassionate love, and romantic love (Berscheid, 2010; Reis & Aron, 2008; Sternberg, 1986). *Companionate love* is the love we typically experience with friends and family members—people we generally trust, share activities and interests with, and like to be around. *Compassionate love* is akin to a communal relationship, with bonds that focus on monitoring and responding to another person's needs, such as how a mother looks out for her child's well-being or how a spouse might put his partner's needs above his own. But it's *romantic love* we're referring to when we say we're "in love" with someone. This is the love that we're moved by in poetry and epic romance novels, that we laugh about in romantic comedies, that we search for on dating websites. Romantic love is the love associated with intense emotion and sexual desire, which is why it's sometimes referred to as *passionate love*. What do we know about this kind of love?

One prominent feature of romantic love is its time course. Early in romantic love relationships, partners experience powerful, at times all-consuming, feelings of passion, or sexual arousal, for each other. The intensity of romantic passion is expressed in a host of metaphors that capture its single-mindedness and loss of control: lovers feel "knocked off their feet," "hungry" for each other, and "mad" or "crazy" with desire (Lakoff & Johnson, 1980). These feelings of passion are registered in specific patterns of touch, cuddling, and sexual behavior and fluctuate for women with rising levels of certain sex hormones, especially estrogen (Konner, 2003). (See Box 10.7, on p. 354, for more on biological bases of love.)

It's important to note that people feel this early passion uniquely for one preferred romantic partner. Eli Finkel and Paul Eastwick pioneered the speed-dating approach to the study of early desire (Finkel & Eastwick, 2008). In their research, a dozen or so young heterosexual women and a dozen or so young heterosexual men arrived at the lab and engaged in a series of rapid-fire, 2-minute get-acquainted conversations with all the members of the opposite sex. After each interaction, the participants rated their sexual desire and feelings of chemistry for each other. The researchers found that when one person felt unique desire and chemistry for another, those feelings were often reciprocated (Eastwick, Finkel, Mochon, & Ariely, 2007). Speed-daters who felt chemistry for many other people actually generated little desire or chemistry in others. Apparently, people can detect whether another's interest in them is targeted or promiscuous.

Surveys indicate that when two people spend increasing amounts of time together, early passion ebbs and a second element of the romantic relationship becomes more prominent—a deep sense of intimacy (Acevedo & Aron, 2009; Sprecher & Regan, 1998). Couples feel increased comfort and security from the sense of being close to and knowing each other better. With increasing intimacy, romantic partners include their partner's perspectives, experiences, and characteristics more and more into their own self-concept (Aron & Aron, 1997; Aron, Aron, & Allen, 1989; Aron & Fraley, 1999). In one study of this second phase, married couples first rated 90 trait adjectives for how accurately they described themselves and their spouse (Aron, Aron, Tudor, & Nelson, 1991). After a brief distracter task, participants viewed each trait on a computer screen and indicated as quickly as possible whether the trait was "like me" or "not like me." As you can see in **Figure 10.7**, participants were faster to identify traits on which they were similar to their spouse and slower to ascribe traits to themselves that their partner didn't also possess. With increasing intimacy, it's almost as if the two partners become one.

An Investment Model of Commitment

Of course, we've all known people—maybe even ourselves!—who seem unable to commit to romantic relationships. One approach to understanding why some romantic partners remain committed to their relationships while others don't is provided by Caryl Rusbult's **investment model of commitment** (Rusbult, 1980,

investment model of commitment A model of interpersonal relationships maintaining that three determinants make partners more committed to each other: relationship satisfaction, few alternative partners, and investments in the relationship.

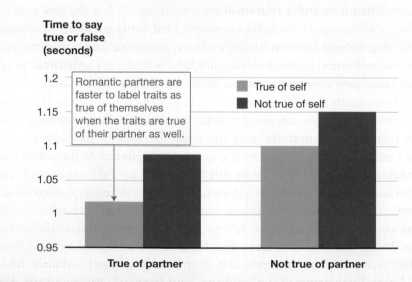

FIGURE 10.7
CONSTRUING CLOSE OTHERS AS WE CONSTRUE OURSELVES
When we fall in love, does our identity merge with that of our partner? In exploring this question, the researchers in this study had romantic partners label traits as true or not true of the self. Some traits were also true of the partner; others weren't.
Source: Adapted from Aron et al., 1991.

1983; Rusbult, Agnew, & Arriaga, 2012). According to the model, influenced by social exchange theory (described earlier), once partners have a romantic bond, three determinants make them more committed to each other: satisfaction, the relative absence or poor quality of alternative partners, and investments in the relationship.

The first and perhaps most obvious determinant of enduring commitment is *satisfaction*, based on the partners' evaluation of the rewards and costs associated with their relationship. One of the strongest indicators of romantic satisfaction in long-term relationships is how much partners feel they get out of the relationship (Cate, Lloyd, Henton, & Larson, 1982). Interestingly, recent work suggests that people base their commitment to a relationship more on their expected future satisfaction in the relationship than their current satisfaction (Baker, McNulty, & Vanderdrift, 2017; Lemay, 2016). In other words, people have beliefs (accurate or not) about how satisfied they are likely to be in their relationship down the road, and these beliefs impact their current relationship commitment.

But neither current satisfaction in a relationship nor beliefs about future satisfaction in it tell the whole commitment story. Whether or not *alternative partners* are available is another strong contributor to the enduring commitment a partner feels. The fewer options a romantic partner has outside the relationship, the more committed that partner tends to feel, and the more likely that partner is to remain in the relationship. For example, in questionnaire studies, romantic partners who report few potential alternative partners are less likely to break up later (White & Booth, 1991).

The third determinant of commitment is the magnitude of the *investments* the couple puts into the relationship. People are more likely to remain in a relationship if they have invested heavily in it. Investments can include the time, effort, caring, and love expended, as well as the shared memories, mutual friends, and shared possessions that are part of having a life together. Just as it's hard to walk away from a business venture into which one has invested substantial time and money, it's difficult to end a relationship into which one has poured a lot of time and energy. Indeed, for committed romantic partners, the self is literally invested in the relationship in the sense that both people come to mentally view themselves as a single unit with their partners, using the plural pronoun *we* to refer to themselves (Agnew, Van Lange, Rusbult, & Langston, 1998).

Recent findings suggest that one person's investment in a relationship not only increases that person's own commitment to the relationship but also increases the partner's investment in the relationship. In one experiment, one group of participants listed various ways their romantic partners invested in their relationship, including a specific example that was particularly meaningful and important. Participants in this group subsequently reported greater commitment to their relationships relative to control participants, who either listed only the investments they themselves made or didn't list any at all (Joel, Gordon, Impett, MacDonald, & Keltner, 2013). Participants in the first group also reported more gratitude. It was this gratitude that accounted for their own subsequent higher commitment to the relationship after thinking about their partners' investments.

In empirical tests of Rusbult's investment model, participants indicated every six months or so their level of agreement with statements tapping commitment,

THE INVESTMENT MODEL OF COMMITMENT
This model maintains that commitment to a relationship depends on satisfaction with the relationship, the presence and quality of alternatives to the relationship, and investments in the relationship.

TABLE 10.1 MEASURING THE COMMITMENT DETERMINANTS IN ROMANTIC RELATIONSHIPS

Determinant	Sample Item
Satisfaction	"Our relationship does a good job of fulfilling my needs for intimacy."
Alternative partners	"People other than my partner are appealing."
Investments	"I feel very involved in our relationship—like I've put a great deal into it."
Commitment level	"I am committed to maintaining my relationship with my partner."

Source: Adapted from Rusbult, Martz, & Agnew, 1998.

as well as ones capturing the three determinants of commitment: satisfaction, alternative partners, and investments (Rusbult, Martz, & Agnew, 1998). Examples of these statements are shown in **Table 10.1**. The level of partner agreement for each of the three determinants of commitment early on predicted whether a couple stayed together or broke up down the road.

How exactly, then, does commitment promote relationship longevity? Is it enough to simply be committed? If only it were that easy. Rather, research shows that commitment is linked to longer-lasting relationships because it encourages behaviors that are good for the relationship, such as sacrifice and forgiveness. To illustrate, Finkel and his colleagues have shown that higher commitment is associated with forgiving a romantic partner's mistakes (Finkel, Rusbult, Kumashiro, & Hannon, 2002). Other researchers have found that commitment is also linked to greater self-sacrifice in couples, as when one partner agrees to move to an undesirable city for the sake of the other partner's job or when one partner gives up meat because it offends a vegan spouse (Van Lange, Agnew Harinck, & Steemers, 1997).

Relationship Dissatisfaction

It's widely known that roughly half of first marriages in the United States end in separation or divorce (Martin & Bumpass, 1989; Myers, 2000). Less widely known is the finding that marriages are less satisfying today than they were 30 years ago (Finkel, Cheung, Emery, Carswell, & Larson, 2015; Glenn, 1991; Myers, 2000). Marital conflict stimulates adrenal and pituitary stress responses, which are known to cause cardiac problems and inhibit immune system protections (Kiecolt-Glaser, Malarkey, Cacioppo, & Glaser, 1994). In addition, unhappy marriages can leave a disturbing legacy: children of divorced parents experience more personal, academic, and romantic difficulties, both during childhood and later in adulthood (Amato & Keith, 1991; Wallerstein, Lewis, & Blakeslee, 2000). Given that romantic dissatisfaction is so widespread and has such far-reaching effects, learning about what predicts romantic dissatisfaction and divorce is important.

PREDICTORS OF DISSATISFACTION AND DIVORCE One way to understand unhappy romantic relationships is to ask whether certain kinds of people or specific circumstances make marital dissatisfaction or divorce more likely. Does the kind of person you marry matter? What about the social class or age of the two people?

To answer these questions, researchers relate measures of marital satisfaction to measures of personality and background. They have learned, first, that personality matters. Neurotic people, who tend to be anxious, tense, emotionally volatile, and melancholy have less happy romantic relationships and are more likely to divorce (Karney & Bradbury, 1997; Karney, Bradbury, Fincham, & Sullivan, 1994; Kurdek, 1993). Similarly, people with low self-esteem (Cavallo, Holmes, Fitzsimons, Murray, & Wood, 2012; Murray, Holmes, Griffin, Bellavia, & Rose, 2001; Murray, Holmes, MacDonald, & Ellsworth, 1998) and people who are highly sensitive to rejection (Ayduk, Gyurak, & Luerssen, 2008; Downey & Feldman, 1996) have greater difficulties in intimate relationships. Moreover, romantic partners and friends who are sensitive to rejection respond with greater hostility when feeling rejected by intimate others (Ayduk, Downey, Testa, Yen, & Shoda, 1999; Downey, Feldman, & Ayduk, 2000). This hostility is often directed at others, but may be directed at the self as well (Breines & Ayduk, 2015).

"I hope when I grow up I'll have an amicable divorce."

Certain demographic factors also predict problems in romantic relationships. Most notably, individuals from lower socioeconomic backgrounds are more likely to divorce (Williams & Collins, 1995). Socioeconomic status (SES) refers to a combination of educational background, income, and occupational prestige (see Chapters 3 and 5). Lower SES is apt to introduce into the relationship financial difficulties and the burdens of finding gratifying and stable work, some of the primary reasons that marriages break up (Berscheid & Reis, 1998).

In terms of the age of couples, people who marry at a younger age are more likely to divorce. Of several possible explanations for this finding, here are two: younger people may not be as effective at being long-term committed partners, and people who marry young may not be as successful at choosing the right partners.

THE FOUR MOST HARMFUL BEHAVIORS As romantic partnerships mature, they revolve more and more around conversations and emotional exchanges about children, finances, and intimacy. Are there certain patterns of communication that indicate a relationship is in trouble? John Gottman and Robert Levenson pioneered an approach to study this question—one that identifies the specific emotions and patterns of communication that predict dissatisfaction and, ultimately, the termination of heterosexual, gay, and lesbian relationships (Gottman & Levenson, 1992, 1999; Levenson & Gottman, 1983).

Gottman and Levenson videotaped married couples engaged in intense conversations in the laboratory and then studied the videos carefully for clues to romantic dissatisfaction. In a "conflict discussion task," partners talked for 15 minutes about an issue they both recognized as a source of intense conflict in their relationship, and they tried their best to resolve it. The researchers studied those interactions and coded them for anger, criticism, defensiveness, stonewalling (resisting dealing with problems), contempt, sadness, and fear, as well as several positive behaviors, including affection, enthusiasm, interest, and humor.

HARMFUL RELATIONSHIP BEHAVIORS
The conversational behavior of the romantic couple pictured here suggests that the couple may be dissatisfied with their relationship.

Frequency of contempt expressions shown in a 15-minute conversation

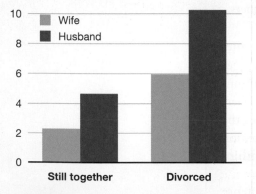

**FIGURE 10.8
CONTEMPT AND MARITAL DISSATISFACTION**
In this study, married partners who expressed contempt in a brief conversation about a source of conflict were more likely to be divorced 14 years later, compared with couples who exhibited less contempt. Feeling contempt is clearly toxic for a relationship.
Source: Adapted from Gottman & Levenson, 1999.

In one long-term study using these techniques, Gottman and Levenson (1999) followed the marriages of 79 couples from one city over many years. Based on their observations, they identified "the Four Horsemen of the Apocalypse"—that is, the four negative behaviors that are most harmful to relationships: criticism, defensiveness, stonewalling, and contempt.

The researchers found, just as you would expect, that married individuals who continually criticize and find fault with their partners have less satisfying marriages. The same is true of people who are prone to stonewalling and avoidance. Romantic partners are also in trouble when they are unable to talk openly and freely about their difficulties without getting defensive—refusing to consider the possibility that something they are doing might contribute to the conflict. In contrast, the more couples disclose to each other about how they are feeling, the better it is for the relationship (Collins & Miller, 1994).

And finally, contempt, the emotion felt by one person looking down on another, is particularly toxic to maintaining romantic bonds. **Figure 10.8** shows how frequently couples were observed to express contempt and whether they stayed together or eventually got divorced (Gottman & Levenson, 1999). The couples who eventually divorced expressed more than twice as much contempt as the couples who stayed together.

Gottman and Levenson's studies are susceptible to the problem of self-selection mentioned earlier. Without being able to select participants for each condition, it is difficult to tell which variable is caused by the other: Do married couples get divorced because they express contempt and other negative emotions, or do they express these emotions because their relationship is already on rocky ground? Additional findings by Gottman and Levenson indicate the former—that negative communication patterns may in fact contribute directly to divorce. In another study of the 79 couples mentioned earlier, the researchers used measures of the four toxic behaviors (criticism, defensiveness, stonewalling, and contempt) early in the relationship to predict who would stay together and who

BOX 10.6

Not So Fast:
Critical Thinking about the Variable Being Measured

Most newlyweds are happy with each other; however, as the harsh reality of a 50 percent divorce rate shows, many don't stay that way. Is there any way to predict which couples are likely to thrive over the long term and which ones are headed for trouble? If so, would it be better to ask the newlyweds directly what they think of each other, or would an indirect, implicit measure be better?

To find out, a group of investigators asked 135 newlywed couples to rate their relationship on a number of scales, such as good/bad and satisfied/dissatisfied (McNulty, Olson, Meltzer, & Shaffer, 2013). They also administered an implicit measure of how much the partners liked each other by flashing a picture of their partner very briefly (a third of a second) before showing them pictures of positive and negative items (such as flowers and spiders). The participants indicated, as quickly as possible, whether the items pictured were positive or negative, and the investigators used the extent to which their partner's photo speeded up participants' responses to the positive words and slowed down their responses to the negative words as an indirect measure of how much they liked their partner. The investigators then checked in with the newlyweds every six months for the next four years and asked how satisfied they were with their relationship.

The indirect measure did a very good job of predicting relationship satisfaction down the road. The more positive they felt about each other as newlyweds by that measure, the more satisfied they were four years later. The explicit measure was worthless. Participants' conscious assessments of how good/bad or satisfied/unsatisfied they felt about their relationship as newlyweds was not related to how they felt down the road. It seems that people's automatic, nonconscious attitudes can reveal a lot about what's really going on inside, but explicit assessments don't really reveal anything. As the investigators put it in the title of their paper, "Though they may be unaware, newlyweds implicitly know whether their marriage will be satisfying" (McNulty et al., 2013).

Not so fast. Things aren't always as they seem, and the phrase "may be unaware" is a telling hedge. What this study shows is that this particular *measure* of the newlyweds' explicit attitudes are a poor predictor of the course of their relationship. It doesn't mean their explicit attitudes generally are a poor predictor. Maybe this measure doesn't really capture their explicit attitudes. After all, if you had concerns about the person with whom you'd just tied the knot—"I worry about his drinking"; "Is she going to end up looking like her mother?"—you might be unwilling to express that in a survey. And maybe that's why the explicit measure didn't predict subsequent relationship satisfaction.

The broader point here is that we are fundamentally interested in the relationship between *variables* (sexual orientation and self-esteem, for instance), but we are restricted to working with *measures* of those variables (what someone says about their sexual orientation, the size of a person's signature). We can get into trouble and draw the wrong conclusion when we confuse a variable with just one *measure* of that variable.

---

would be divorced 14 years later. Remarkably, based on these four measures gathered from a 15-minute conversation, they could predict with 93 percent accuracy who would get divorced (Gottman & Levenson, 2000).

DANGEROUS ATTRIBUTIONS Certain construal tendencies—the way we interpret things—are also related to the weakening of romantic bonds. One of these tendencies is blame. Bradbury, Karney, and their colleagues have looked at the relationship between romantic partners' causal attributions (what they tend to attribute events and behaviors to) and their relationship satisfaction (Bradbury & Fincham, 1990; Karney & Bradbury, 2000; McNulty & Karney, 2001). These researchers have found that dissatisfied, distressed couples make attributions that cast their partner and their relationship in a negative light; that is, they attribute rewarding, positive events in their relationships to unstable causes that are specific, unintended, and selfish. For example, distressed partners might interpret an unexpected gift of flowers as the result of a whim, particular to that day, and anticipate the gift to be followed by some selfish request from their partners. Happier couples, on the other hand, tend to attribute the same positive events to stable causes that are general, intended, and selfless. A satisfied romantic partner thus might attribute a gift of flowers to her partner's enduring kindness. Similarly, happier partners attribute negative events—the forgotten anniversary or sarcastic comment—to specific and unintended causes, whereas distressed partners attribute the same kinds of negative events to stable and global causes and see their partners as blameworthy and selfish.

Creating Stronger Romantic Bonds

Now that we've identified some of the most common trouble spots in relationships, let's turn to the kinds of things you might do to build healthier romantic bonds. As you can gather from the previous discussion, you might be wise to avoid highly anxious, rejection-sensitive, neurotic individuals when choosing a partner; to minimize criticism, defensiveness, stonewalling, and contempt in your interactions; and to try to interpret your partner's actions in a praiseworthy fashion. Social psychologists have begun to make progress in identifying other things that may contribute to healthier romantic relationships.

CAPITALIZING ON THE GOOD Are there healthy patterns of conversation that foster more satisfying bonds? Shelly Gable and her colleagues believe it's particularly important to capitalize on the good: to share what's good in your life with your partner and to engage with the other's good news (Gable, Gonzaga, & Strachman, 2006; Gable, Reis, Impett, & Asher, 2004; Reis et al., 2010). In their research, these investigators found that individuals reported greater relationship satisfaction if they tended to receive active, constructive "capitalization" from their significant others—when their partners responded to their good news with engaged enthusiasm (Gable et al., 2004). For example, at the news of a partner's forthcoming art show, the actively constructive partner might ask questions about what pieces to show and whom to invite—questions that reveal an active engagement in such an important development in the partner's life.

BEING PLAYFUL Courtship and the early phases of a relationship involve unusual levels of fun: late-night dancing, candlelit exchanges of poetry, weekend getaways, and other exhilarating activities. The later stages, especially when children are involved, become focused on less inherently enjoyable activities—diaper changing, house cleaning, bill paying, and chauffeuring children to soccer practice. It's not surprising that having children, while bringing many joys, typically leads to a drop in romantic satisfaction (Myers, 2000). In fact, married partners typically don't return to their previous level of satisfaction until the children leave home. (This point is nicely made in an exchange between a priest, a rabbi, and a minister on when life begins: the priest says at conception, the rabbi says at birth, and the minister says when the dog dies and the last child goes away to college.)

Keeping an element of playfulness alive in a relationship can help. Experimental work by Art Aron and his colleagues attests to the benefits of a bit of exhilarating silliness in a marriage (Aron, Norman, Aron, McKenna, & Heyman, 2000). In their study, spouses who had been married for several years engaged in one of two tasks. In a playfully arousing condition, partners were tied together at the knees and wrists with Velcro straps, and they were required to move a soft

"A baby is an inestimable blessing and bother."
—MARK TWAIN

"Laughter is more important than tears."
—TONI MORRISON

KEYS TO GOOD RELATIONSHIPS
(A) Shared laughter and play are vital to healthy relationships. (B) Open communication and disclosure during conflicts are more helpful than stonewalling.

ball positioned between their heads across a long mat. In the other condition, each partner had to push a ball alone to the middle of the mat with a stick. Spouses reported significantly higher marital satisfaction after engaging in the novel, amusing joint task, compared with participants in the other condition and with a baseline assessed earlier. Unusual, playful activities are fun and exciting— and spouses often misattribute their excitement about the activities to their feelings about their partner, thereby enhancing both partners' satisfaction with the relationship. Laughter often comes with play, and research suggests that shared laughter also bodes well for relationship well-being (Kurtz & Algoe, 2015).

LOOKING ON THE BRIGHT SIDE Sandra Murray and her colleagues suggest that a tendency to idealize one's romantic partner is another important ingredient in a satisfying intimate bond (Murray & Holmes, 1993, 1997; Murray, Holmes, Dolderman, & Griffin, 2000; Neff & Karney, 2002). In one study (Murray et al., 1996), married couples and dating partners rated themselves and their partners on 21 traits related to virtues (such as being understanding and patient), desirable attributes within romantic relationships (such as being easygoing and witty), and faults (such as being critical or distant). The researchers compared the participants' ratings of their partners' virtues and faults with their ratings of their satisfaction in the relationship. Those who idealized their romantic partners—that is, rated their partners higher on positive traits than the partners did themselves— were more satisfied with their relationships. Individuals also reported greater relationship satisfaction when their partners idealized them. A different research team examined heterosexual cohabiting couples and lesbian, gay, and heterosexual married couples and found that for all four types of couples, viewing one's romantic partner in an idealized fashion was linked to greater satisfaction with the relationship (Conley, Roesch, Peplau, & Gold, 2009).

In other studies, investigators have explored precisely *how* people idealize their romantic partners. In one case, people were asked to write about their partners' greatest fault (Murray & Holmes, 1999). Satisfied partners were more likely

> *"Love to faults is always blind, Always is to joy inclined, Lawless, winged, and unconfined, And breaks all chains from every mind."*
> —WILLIAM BLAKE

BOX 10.7 ▶ FOCUS ON NEUROSCIENCE

This Is Your Brain in Love

As the work of Sandra Murray and her colleagues suggests, the mind does amazing things when in love, turning faults into charming idiosyncrasies, for example (Murray & Holmes, 1999). What does your brain do during love? Recently, neuroscientists and relationship researchers have joined forces to answer this question, and their answers are both intuitive and surprising. In these studies, fMRI images record the brain's pattern of activation while a person looks at a picture of a romantic partner or is in the throes of feeling intense love (Fisher, Aron, & Brown, 2006). Not surprisingly, these neuroimaging methods reveal that romantic love is associated with activation in reward regions of the brain (the ventral striatum)—regions rich with receptors for oxytocin (which promotes trust and love; see Chapter 6) and dopamine (which promotes approach-related behavior).

What may surprise you, though, is that romantic love also deactivates the amygdala, a region of the brain associated with the perception of threat. It appears that in the throes of love, the brain disables your ability to see what is threatening or dangerous about the new love. This finding may help your parents understand why you might fall in love with someone who doesn't quite live up to their standards. Your brain simply isn't reacting to potential signs of risk in your new love—the fondness for motorcycles, the disregard for conventional society. These findings also shed light on what the brain might be doing as you turn your partner's faults and flaws (which in others might activate the amygdala) into pleasing virtues, as the Murray team found.

---

to engage in two forms of idealization. First, they were more apt to see virtue in their partners' faults. For example, an individual might write that the partner was melancholy but that the melancholy quality gave the partner a depth of character that was incomparably rewarding. Second, satisfied partners were more likely to offer "yes, but" refutations of the fault. For instance, a satisfied individual might write that the partner didn't like to hold down a steady job, but at least that gave the partner more time to help out at home. (For a possible neuroscientific explanation, see **Box 10.7**.)

Love and Marriage across Cultures

To a degree that can be hard for modern Westerners to comprehend, some of our generalizations about love and marriage don't apply to most of the world's cultures, nor did they even apply to most Western cultures until relatively recently. Although romantic love seems to exist in almost every culture, it has generally not been regarded as a prerequisite to marriage (Dion & Dion, 1993). The more typical pattern is a marriage arranged by parents. A young man's parents and a young woman's parents come to an agreement about the suitability of the pair for each other, and they announce the marriage transaction to their children. Just like it sounds, the term *transaction* often applies in a very economic sense: the prospective bride's parents provide a dowry, or, somewhat less often, the groom's parents pay a "bride price." These sorts of transactions are common today in much of South, East, and Southeast Asia and in much of Africa.

Arranged marriages avoid some of the pitfalls of marrying for romantic love, including mismatches between the couple's socioeconomic status and religion, two factors associated with relatively high rates of divorce. In an arranged marriage, the in-laws are more apt to be respectful of one another—a stance perhaps less common when the in-laws, usually having not known each other previously, are brought together for reasons having nothing to do with mutual regard or existing respect for one another's families. Finally, the lack of expectation that there should be romantic love in the first place avoids the natural, gradual transformation of romantic into a more companionate form of love that can serve as a source of disappointment and discontent.

← LOOKING BACK

Love comes in different varieties, and the kind of love experienced in romantic relationships is just one of these. One's commitment to a relationship is influenced by how satisfying the relationship is, the relative absence or poor quality of alternative partners, and one's investments in the relationship. Personality and demographic factors predict unhappiness in marriage, as do toxic behaviors like criticism, defensiveness, stonewalling, contempt, and blame. Research on relationships by social psychologists is yielding important insights about successful and rewarding relationships, in which partners capitalize on the good, choose to be playful, and see each other in a flattering light.

Chapter Review

SUMMARY

Characterizing Relationships

- The need to belong is biologically based, as evident in the evolutionary benefits and universality of human relationships and the negative consequences that result from their absence.
- In long-term *communal relationships*, people feel responsible for each other; in short-term *exchange relationships*, people are concerned with equity and reciprocity.
- *Social exchange theory* is based on the idea that how people feel about a relationship depends on their assessments of its costs and rewards and what they believe alternative relationships can offer.
- According to *attachment theory*, early attachments with parents and other caregivers shape relationships for a person's whole life. The two dimensions of attachment are anxiety (fear of rejection) and avoidance (discomfort with intimacy). Attachment style is relatively stable and has wide-ranging effects on a person's well-being throughout life.

Attraction

- Proximity, the sheer closeness of contact, leads to attraction and liking. Liking can be influenced by the *functional distance* created by the architectural layout of a living arrangement that encourages social contact. This is partly explained by the *mere exposure effect*, the tendency to like a stimulus the more frequently it is encountered.
- Similarity influences attraction because people like others who resemble them in their class background, recreational preferences, and core values and beliefs. There is little evidence that opposites attract, except when one partner's need can be fulfilled by the other's difference.
- Physically attractive people are more popular with the opposite sex, earn more money, and receive lighter sentences for crimes. Because of the *halo effect*, they are believed to have many positive qualities that go beyond their physical appearance. Physical appearance affects the lives of women more than men.
- *Reproductive fitness* is the capacity to pass one's genes on to future generations, and people seek mates with characteristics, such as the ability to resist disease, that enhance the likelihood of reproductive success.
- Evolutionary psychologists believe that parental investment leads men to prefer women whose physical appearance indicates they will be fertile and leads women to be attracted to men who can provide for them and their children.

Romantic Relationships

- Romantic relationships, an important part of social life, are essential for well-being and physical health.
- There are many kinds of love, including companionate love, compassionate love, and romantic love.
- According to the *investment model of commitment*, three determinants make partners more committed to each other: satisfaction, few alternative partners, and investments in the relationship.
- Commitment is linked to longer-lasting relationships because it increases relationship-promoting behaviors such as forgiveness and self-sacrifice.
- Predictors of relationship dissatisfaction and divorce include disparities in personality and socioeconomic status, marrying too young, communication issues, and behavioral problems, such as criticism, defensiveness, stonewalling, contempt, and blame.
- In healthy relationships, couples work on strengthening their bond by capitalizing on the good events in their lives, being playful, and looking on the bright side by seeing each other's positive attributes.
- In many cultures around the world, marriages are arranged by the parents, which may have some advantages that Westerners don't generally realize.

THINK ABOUT IT

1. The need to belong is thought to be a fundamental human drive, similar to physical drives like hunger. When people have their need to belong satisfied, they are unlikely to pursue this drive further. Given this premise, who is more likely to call up a friend to make plans: Betty, who's been spending lots of quality time with her children lately, or Blanche, who tends to stay home by herself?

2. Sean and Mitch are just starting a relationship, but they seem to have different expectations about what each one deserves from a romantic partner. Sean thinks that if his partner doesn't treat him extremely well, then that romantic partner is just not worth his time because there are better guys out there. Mitch, on the other hand, has been in several bad relationships and puts up with just about anything from a partner because he's deeply afraid of being alone. How would you describe Sean and Mitch's respective comparison levels and comparison levels for alternatives? What might the consequences of these levels be?

3. Jenny feels comfortable relying on and being close to her immediate family members, and she seeks extremely intimate, clingy romantic relationships but keeps her distance from her friends, not disclosing much to them or counting on them. How would you analyze her attachment styles? How would you describe her working models?

4. Robert has a crush on Marilyn, but she doesn't seem to know he exists. What can Robert do to make himself more attractive to Marilyn, based on the principles of proximity and similarity?

5. Suppose Alice wants to try an experiment about the halo effect of physical attractiveness on an online dating website. She sets up two profiles for herself, making the content of the profiles identical except for her picture. On one profile, she uses a beautiful photo of herself as her profile photo, but on the other profile, she uses a horrible photo of herself. How might men respond to these two profiles, and how might Alice be expected to respond to them in turn?

6. How can the investment model of commitment help explain why people stay in long-term abusive relationships? How might an abusive partner manipulate the factors that contribute to commitment to make an abuse victim stay in the relationship?

The **answer guidelines** for the think about it questions can be found at the back of the book . . . ☞

ONLINE STUDY MATERIALS

Want to earn a better grade on your test?

Go to **INQUIZITIVE** to learn and review this chapter's content, with personalized feedback along the way.

Why has violence and mistreatment toward African-Americans persisted in the United States?

How much are people's identities derived from the groups to which they belong?

How does the success of the Obamas or Oprah challenge negative perceptions of people of color?

Stereotyping, Prejudice, and Discrimination

PARENTS OFTEN DREAD THE DAY WHEN THEY have to have "the conversation" with their child. For many parents, the conversation entails an awkward discussion about sex, birth control, sexually transmitted diseases, perhaps even the existence of sexual predators. For elderly parents talking to an adult child, the conversation might be about "do not resuscitate" orders and directives about what to do with their bodies when they die.

But for African-American parents, the conversation is so much more wrenching and urgent. They have to tell their children how to act when they are stopped by the police (Gandbhir & Foster, 2015). And they have good reason to teach them about *when,* not *if,* because African-Americans, particularly African-American males, are stopped by police far more often than people of other races. One study of the New Jersey State Police found that African-Americans accounted for 42 percent of the drivers stopped by police even though they accounted for only 15 percent of verified violations (Brown & Jantzi, 2010).

The conversation for African-American parents focuses on the unpleasant truth that their children cannot expect to be treated the same as white children. Police officers will treat them with greater suspicion, sometimes with greater hostility, and, disturbingly often, with greater force—even deadly force. The many deaths of black men at the hands of the police—Tamir Rice, Trayvon Martin, Philando Castile, Eric Garner, Michael Brown, Jr., Freddie Gray, and many others—that have given rise to the Black Lives Matter movement make this particular conversation an unfortunate necessity for conscientious black parents.

The need for such conversations and for community workshops designed to teach black youth how to live safely in twenty-first-century America (Ross, 2017) speak to the issues we discuss in this chapter—stereotypes, prejudice, and discrimination and what can be done to deal with these facets of the human condition. Why is it that some individuals, all part of the same human family, are treated so differently than others because of their skin color, gender, religion, ethnic origin, sexual orientation, or even their age or occupation?

"The conversation," along with the troubles it reflects, takes place against a background of indisputable progress. Slavery still exists in some pockets of the world but is no longer a sanctioned, state-sponsored enterprise. The world is now more multicultural than ever, with members of different races, ethnicities, and religions living and working alongside one another more peacefully and productively than ever before. In 2008, and again in 2012, the United States elected its first African-American president, a triumph that nearly all pioneers of the Civil Rights Movement said they never thought they'd see in their lifetime. As Martin Luther King, Jr., famously noted in 1965, "The arc of the moral universe is long, but it bends toward justice."

Despite such progress, however, the origins of the Black Lives Matter movement make it abundantly clear that the human tendencies to stereotype, harbor prejudice, and engage in discrimination are still with us. So, too, do the actions of white supremacist Dylan Roof, who, on June 17, 2015, stormed into Emanuel African Methodist Episcopal Church in South Carolina and, hoping to start a race war, killed nine African-American worshippers. Beyond the United States, Sunni and Shia Muslims are at each other's throats in numerous hotspots in the Middle East, and the prospects for peace between Israelis and Palestinians seem as remote as ever. Recent conflicts in Syria, Yemen, Darfur, Rwanda, Somalia, and Ukraine show that intergroup enmity continues to be a distressingly common component of the human condition. And although the legalization of same-sex marriage in many European countries and the United States is a sign of genuine improvement in civil rights, gays and lesbians continue to face discrimination—daily and worldwide. Women in nearly all countries continue to earn less than men doing comparable work, elderly people are often dismissed as incompetent, and people who are not good-looking have challenges that their more attractive peers never face. Stereotyping, prejudice, and discrimination are still all around us. As Martin Luther King also noted, "Human progress is neither automatic nor inevitable." ∎

Theoretical Perspectives

The pervasiveness of stereotypes and the persistence of ethnic, religious, and racial animosity challenge us to understand the underlying causes of intergroup tension. Where do stereotypes, prejudice, and discrimination come from? Why do they persist? What can be done to eliminate or reduce their impact?

Any serious attempt to address these questions must begin with the recognition that there will likely never be a single, comprehensive theory of the causes of stereotyping, prejudice, or discrimination. Their causes are many and varied, and any satisfactory account of these intertwined phenomena must incorporate numerous elements. This chapter focuses on three general perspectives that shed light on these issues. The *economic perspective* identifies the roots of intergroup hostility in competing interests that can set groups apart from one another. The *motivational perspective* emphasizes the psychological needs that lead to intergroup conflict. The *cognitive perspective* traces the origin of stereotyping to the same cognitive processes that enable people to categorize, say, items of furniture into distinct classes of chairs, couches, and tables. This perspective takes into account the frequent conflict between people's consciously held beliefs and values and their quick, reflexive, sometimes subconscious reactions to members of other groups.

Note that these three perspectives are exactly that—*perspectives*, not sharply defined categories. They're also not competing accounts, but complementary elements of a more complete analysis. These three elements often influence one another. Take, for example, victims of genocide. Jews, expatriate Chinese, and Armenians have all been the victims of genocide. The reasons in each case were partly economic, as these groups were richer than many others in their countries. The economic element may have driven the cognitive element, which caused people to perceive these minority groups as fundamentally different from themselves. The cognitive element in turn may have fed into the motivational element of anger over the wealth obtained by prominent members of these minority groups. It would be a mistake, however, to assume that these processes necessarily happen in a precise order; for example, seeing these minority groups as different from the mainstream might have made it easier for people to notice and resent their wealth and to focus their attention on the members of these groups who were wealthy. Certainly, the three elements tend to be tightly intertwined. Nevertheless, the distinctions between the economic, motivational, and cognitive perspectives is useful for the purpose of organizing and thinking clearly about the varied causes of stereotyping, prejudice, and discrimination—and about ways that intergroup conflict might be reduced. In this chapter, we'll examine each of these perspectives in turn. But first let's take a closer look at the nature of intergroup bias.

Characterizing Intergroup Bias

Do you believe that Asians are conscientious, Italians are temperamental, Muslims are fanatical, or that Californians are "laid back"? Such beliefs are examples of **stereotypes**—beliefs that certain attributes are characteristic of members of particular groups. Stereotyping is a way of categorizing people (Lee, Jussim, & McCauley, 1995). A stereotype can be positive or negative, largely true or entirely false. It involves thinking about a person not as an individual, but as a member of a group, and projecting your beliefs about the group onto that person.

Certain stereotypes have some truth to them and others don't. Consider the old joke that heaven is a place where you have an American house, a German car, French food, British police, an Italian lover, and everything is run by the Swiss. Hell, on the other hand, is a place where you have a Japanese house, a French car, British food, German police, a Swiss lover, and everything is run by the Italians. The Swiss bureaucracy is indeed more widely praised than the Italian's, and automobile magazines rave more about what's rolling off the assembly lines at BMW and Audi than at Peugeot and Renault. Some stereotypes are accurate. But is there really any reason to be especially wary of German police? There certainly was during the 1930s and 1940s, but has German law enforcement been unusually harsh or corrupt since then? Maybe, maybe not. Are Italian lovers preferable to Swiss? You make the call.

"I speak French to my ambassadors, English to my accountant, Italian to my mistress, Latin to my God and German to my horse."
—FREDERICK THE GREAT OF PRUSSIA

stereotype A belief that certain attributes are characteristic of members of a particular group.

SEEDS OF INTERGROUP BIAS
(A) The stereotype of African-Americans being more likely than other groups to break the law, combined with anti-black sentiment, can lead to discriminatory behavior, such as police officers pulling over African-American drivers in wildly disproportionate numbers. (B) The stereotype linking Islam with extremism can lead to negative reactions toward Muslims and Islamic institutions. (C) The Trump administration created the Victims of Immigration Crime Engagement (VOICE) office to publicize the plight of victims of crimes committed by undocumented immigrants, thereby highlighting immigrant crime but not the same crimes committed by U.S. citizens.

Stereotypes about Swiss administrators, German police, or Italian lovers are not what concern most social psychologists, however (Judd & Park, 1993). They've focused instead on those stereotypes that are most likely to lead to pernicious forms of prejudice and discrimination.

Prejudice refers to an attitudinal and affective response toward a group and its individual members. Negative attitudes generally get the most attention, but it's also possible to be positively prejudiced toward a group. Prejudice involves *prejudging* others because they belong to a specific category. **Discrimination** refers to favorable or unfavorable *behavior* directed toward members of a group. It involves unfair treatment of others, based not on their individual character or abilities, but strictly on their group membership.

Roughly speaking, stereotyping, prejudice, and discrimination refer to the beliefs, attitudes, and behaviors, respectively, that drive negative relationships between groups. The three often go together. People are more inclined to injure those they hold in low regard. But these components of intergroup bias don't *have* to occur together. For example, it's possible (and common) to be prejudiced but not engage in discrimination, if only to avoid social or legal repercussions. On the flip side, a person can also discriminate without prejudice. Jewish parents sometimes say they don't want their children to marry outside the faith, not because they have a low opinion of other groups, but because they're concerned about assimilation with non-Jews and its implications for the future of Judaism. Thus, ingroup favoritism can arise even when there isn't any hostility toward different outgroups. Sometimes, of course, statements such as "I have nothing against them, but . . ." are merely cover-ups of underlying bigotry. At other times, they are doubtless sincere and don't reflect any bad intent—but they can cause insult and injury nonetheless (Gaertner, Iuzzini, Witt, & Orina, 2006; Lowery, Unzueta, Knowles, & Goff, 2006).

Contemporary Prejudice

Throughout much of the world, norms about how different groups are viewed and treated have changed. In Western countries in particular, it's illegal to engage in many forms of discrimination that were common half a century ago, and it's not socially acceptable to express the sorts of prejudices and stereotypes that were common (and brazenly open) until relatively recently. These changes have caused some people to be conflicted between what they truly think and feel and what they think they *should* think and feel (or what they believe is prudent to say or do publicly). For many people, the changes have also created a conflict between competing beliefs and values (such as a belief in equal treatment for all but also a desire to make up for past injustice toward racial minorities with affirmative action). Similarly, people might experience a conflict between abstract beliefs and gut-level reactions (such as a belief that one should feel the same toward all people but also some hard-to-shake resistance to that belief). In addition, as research has shown, some people's responses to members of other groups are nonconscious and automatic and may differ considerably from their more thoughtful and explicit beliefs and attitudes. These kinds of conflicts have inspired social psychologists to develop new theories to explain this modern, more constrained, more conflicted sort of prejudice (Dovidio, 2001).

This shift in theoretical approaches is particularly noteworthy with respect to race relations in the United States. Some have argued that old-fashioned racism has largely disappeared in the United States but has been supplanted by a subtler, more modern counterpart (Kinder & Sears, 1981; McConahay, 1986; Sears, 1988; Sears & Henry, 2005; Sears & Kinder, 1985; see also Haddock, Zanna, & Esses, 1993 on homophobia; and Swim, Aiken, Hall, & Hunter, 1995 on sexism). In one example of this theoretical shift, **modern racism** is defined as a rejection of explicitly racist beliefs—for example, that black people are morally inferior to white people—while nevertheless feeling animosity toward African-Americans or being highly suspicious of them and uncomfortable dealing with them.

Sam Gaertner and Jack Dovidio (1986; Dovidio & Gaertner, 2004) have led the way in exploring the conflicts and inconsistencies that often accompany modern racism. They note that many people hold strong egalitarian values that lead them to reject prejudice and discrimination, yet they also harbor unacknowledged negative feelings and attitudes toward minority groups that stem from ingroup favoritism and a desire to defend the status quo (Kteily, Sidanius, & Levin, 2011; Sidanius & Pratto, 1999). Whether these individuals will express prejudice or discriminate depends on the situation. If they can't identify a justification or "disguise" for discriminatory action, their responses will conform to their egalitarian values. But if they sense, even nonconsciously, that a suitable rationalization is available, the modern racist's prejudices will emerge.

In an early test of this idea, white participants were in a position to aid a white or black person in need of medical assistance (Gaertner & Dovidio, 1977; see also Dovidio, Smith, Donella, & Gaertner, 1997; Saucier, Miller, & Doucet, 2005). If the participants thought they were the only one who could help, they came to the aid of the black person somewhat more often (94 percent of the time) than the white person (81 percent). But when they thought other people were present and their own inaction could be justified on nonracial grounds ("I thought somebody else with more expertise would intervene"), they helped the black person much less often than the white person (38 percent versus 75 percent). In situations such as this, the prejudice or discrimination is "masked," and the individual remains comfortably unaware

---

prejudice An attitude or affective response (positive or negative) toward a group and its individual members.

discrimination Favorable or unfavorable treatment of individuals based on their membership in a particular group.

modern racism Prejudice directed at racial groups that exists alongside the rejection of explicitly racist beliefs.

of any racist impulses. Thus, modern racism shows itself in subtle ways. The modern racist would never join the Ku Klux Klan but might consistently give black passersby a wider berth. Such a person might never utter a racist word, but might insist that "discrimination against blacks is no longer a problem in the United States" (this statement is an item on the Modern Racism Scale; McConahay, 1986).

In another study, white participants evaluated black and white applicants to college (Hodson, Dovidio, & Gaertner, 2002). Participants all had scores on the Attitudes toward Blacks Scale that indicated that they were either high or low in explicit prejudice toward blacks. All participants rated white and black applicants the same when the applicants either excelled on all relevant dimensions (such as SAT scores and grade point average) or were below average on all dimensions. But when the applicants excelled on certain dimensions (for example, high SAT scores) and were below average on others (for example, low GPA), the ratings of prejudiced and unprejudiced participants diverged: the prejudiced participants rated the black applicants less favorably than did the unprejudiced participants. Here, prejudiced participants could defend their responses as nondiscriminatory by claiming that the dimensions on which the black applicants fell short were more important than those on which they excelled.

Theories of contemporary prejudice, such as the theory of modern racism, are important because while they track the undeniable progress that's been made in how members of historically marginalized or stigmatized groups are treated, they also uncover subtle forms of prejudice and discrimination that still persist and need to be combated. None of this, however, should blind us to the fact that old-fashioned, virulent intergroup hatred and discrimination are still disturbingly common. There's nothing "modern" about ISIS and other Islamic extremist groups killing "apostates" and claiming that they're serving Allah when they do so. Nor is there anything modern about the fact that in some U.S. states, on the night that Barack Obama was elected president in 2008, there were more Internet searches for "[n-word] president" than "first black president" (Stephens-Davidowitz, 2017).

"Benevolent" Racism and Sexism

Statements like "Some of my best friends are_____" (fill in the blank) or "I'm not sexist; I love women!" illustrate a common conviction that stereotypes must be negative to be harmful. In fact, however, many of our "isms"—racism, sexism, ageism, heterosexism—can be ambivalent, containing both negative and positive features (Czopp, Kay, & Cheryan, 2015; Czopp & Monteith, 2006; Devine & Elliot, 1995; Ho & Jackson, 2001). Someone might believe, for example, that Asians are less warm and more rigid than whites—and at the same time believe they are more intellectually gifted. Similarly, someone might believe that women are less intelligent than men—and at the same time believe that women are kinder and have better social skills.

In their work on ambivalent sexism, Peter Glick and Susan Fiske (2001a, 2001b) interviewed 15,000 men and women in 19 nations and found that "benevolent" sexism (a chivalrous ideology marked by protectiveness and affection toward women who embrace conventional roles) often coexists with hostile sexism (dislike of nontraditional women and those viewed as usurping men's power). Glick and Fiske argue that even these seemingly positive stereotypes aren't benign.

Ambivalent and benevolent sexist or racist attitudes may be particularly resistant to change. The favorable features of such beliefs enable the stereotype holder to deny any prejudice. (Think of the trucker who romanticizes women so much he decorates his mud flaps with their likeness.)

By rewarding women and minorities for conforming to the status quo—for acting in ways that are in keeping with the stereotypes about them—benevolent sexism and racism inhibit progress toward equality. In other words, those who hold ambivalent attitudes tend to act positively toward members of outgroups only if those members fulfill their idealized image of what such people should be like—say, the happy housewife or the dutiful staffer bringing coffee. Members of the outgroup who deviate from the stereotype tend to be treated with hostility (Lau, Kay, & Spencer, 2008). Furthermore, benevolent sexism can be just as damaging as hostile sexism. In one study, for example, women treated in a paternalistic manner (a kind of benevolent sexism) did not perform as well on a series of intellectual tests because of the self-doubts aroused by the treatment they received (Dardenne, Dumont, & Bollier, 2007).

Measuring Attitudes about Groups

The most straightforward way to assess how people feel about various groups is, of course, to ask them. Researchers have done so in two ways. First, they've provided survey respondents with a list of trait adjectives and asked them to indicate which ones they believe characterize members of different groups—the elderly, the wealthy, Latinos, and so on (Dovidio, Brigham, Johnson, & Gaertner, 1996; Katz & Braly, 1933). Second, researchers have developed various self-report questionnaires that ask respondents about their attitudes and beliefs about members of different groups, including the Attitudes toward Blacks Scale (Brigham, 1993), the Modern Racism Scale (McConahay, Hardee, & Batts, 1981), the Fraboni Scale of Ageism (Fraboni, Saltstone, & Hughes, 1990), and the Sexual Prejudice Scale (Chonody, 2013).

But surveys of people's attitudes toward certain groups can't always be trusted because respondents may not think it's acceptable to express what they really feel or because what people report verbally is only a part of their stance toward members of other groups, and there may be other beliefs or feelings beneath the surface. Given that so many forms of prejudice are ambivalent, uncertain, or hidden—even from the self—they're not easily tapped through self-report (Crandall & Eshleman, 2003). Social psychologists have therefore developed more subtle self-report measures (Fiske & North, 2015) and created a number of indirect, non-self-report measures of prejudice and stereotyping. We discuss two types here: the implicit association test and different types of priming procedures. (For overviews of a wider set of implicit measurement procedures, see Gawronski & Payne, 2010; Wittenbrink & Schwarz, 2007.)

THE IMPLICIT ASSOCIATION TEST (IAT) Anthony Greenwald and Mazarin Banaji (1995) pioneered a technique called the **implicit association test (IAT)** for revealing subtle, nonconscious prejudices, even among those who sincerely believe they are bias-free. Here's how the technique works. A series of words or pictures are presented on a computer screen, and the respondent presses a key with the left hand if the picture or word conforms to one rule and another key with the right hand if it conforms to another rule. Before you read further, either

implicit association test (IAT)
A technique for revealing nonconscious attitudes toward different stimuli, particularly groups of people.

Not So Fast:
Critical Thinking by Finding the Proper Comparison

BOX 11.1

Suppose you want to see whether gender stereotypes bias a teacher's judgments of student work. How would you find out? Researchers have generally used a straightforward approach: They've given essays to groups of participants, telling some of them that the essay was written by, say, John, and others that it was written by Jane. They have then had participants assess its quality. Of course, it's important for the researchers to choose the names assigned to the essay carefully. Comparing the ratings of an essay supposedly written by Adolf with those of an essay written by Jennifer wouldn't work, because there's so much baggage associated with the name Adolf. How do researchers ensure that the names are comparable? One way is to choose pairs of male and female names that are as similar as possible—Michael and Michelle, Paul and Paula, Robert and Roberta, and so on. This is precisely what researchers interested in gender bias have done, and what they have found is abundant evidence of sexism. The very same essay tends to be rated more favorably when it's attributed to a male student rather than to a female student (Goldberg, 1968). What could be more straightforward and telling?

It turns out that these studies are not so straightforward and informative after all. In fact, when you try to create pairs of male and female names that are as similar as possible, you can easily end up with a set of male names that people tend to like more than the female names. The higher ratings given to essays purportedly written by Paul or Robert may not be because

they're thought to be written by men, but because they're thought to be written by people with more desirable names. These studies, in other words, may showcase *nameism* rather than sexism (that is, in this example people may tend to like the names Paul or Robert more than the names Paula or Roberta). In fact, when the male and female names are equated in terms of how much participants like them as names, and not by how similar they are in other ways (length, phonemic overlap, and so on), there is no effect of the gender of the purported author on how favorably an essay is evaluated (Kasof, 1993).

Does this mean there's no sexism when it comes to evaluating a person's performance? Of course not. It just means there may be no sexism when it comes to the evaluation of essays. And that shouldn't be surprising. Girls are known to perform better than boys in school, especially when it comes to reading and writing, so their work in this context at least is less likely to suffer from negative stereotyping. But there are other areas in which sexist stereotypes might indeed undermine the evaluation of a woman's performance. Historically, for example, it was thought that women didn't have the same musical talent as men, and their performance during auditions for premier orchestras appeared to validate that assessment. But when orchestra directors had musicians audition behind a screen so the performers couldn't be seen, there was a sharp rise in the percentage of women deemed worthy of positions in the world's most esteemed orchestras (Goldin & Rouse, 2000).

Moreover, although there may not be any sexism on the part of *individuals* evaluating essays written by men and women, there might nevertheless be *societal* sexism when it comes to how names are created. Nearly all pairs of very similar male and female names—Paul and Pauline, Donald and Donna—result from the female name being derived from the male name. Society is apparently more tolerant of derivative female names than derivative male names. That's a different kind of sexism, but it's sexism nonetheless.

What's especially noteworthy about the research in this area is that the very strategy the investigators used to rule out an alternative interpretation of their results opened the door to an alternative interpretation! What could be more sensible—more seemingly scientific—than to choose male and female names that were as alike as possible? Who would have thought that doing so would threaten the validity of the study? Research like this serves as a reminder that knowledge is hard won. It also serves as a reminder that selecting the proper comparison is not always as easy as it seems. Should I pair Jack's essay with one supposedly written by Jane or by Joan? Or, in other studies, should I have participants in the control group complete their questionnaires right after they've finished reading the instructions, as those in the experimental group did, or, since the experimental group had more to read, after the same amount of time has passed? Making the right call can be the difference between an experiment that's informative and one that's misleading.

FIGURE 11.1
THE IMPLICIT ASSOCIATION
TEST: TRY IT OUT ON YOURSELF
The IAT examines whether we group
words (or images) depicting members
of particular groups with words (or
images) stereotypically associated with
those groups faster than we do with
words that contradict the stereotypes
associated with those groups.

First, as you read each word in the column below, tap your left index finger if it is either a
female name or a "weak" word, and tap your right index finger if it is either a male name or
a "strong" word.

Martha
Vigorous
Jason
Small
David
Powerful
Karen
Delicate
Gloria
Feather
Tony
Mighty
Matthew
Wispy
Rachel
Robust
Amy
Fine
George
Flower
Betsy
Stout
Charlene
Iron

Now repeat the procedure, but as you read each word, tap your left index finger if it is
either a female name or a "strong" word, and tap your right index finger if it is either a male
name or a "weak" word.

Did you find yourself tapping faster as you read the words the first time or the second?

try a noncomputerized version of the task in **Figure 11.1** or see whether you hold
any implicit stereotypes or prejudice toward a variety of groups by taking some
of the IATs online at https://implicit.harvard.edu/implicit/research/.

Greenwald and Banaji argued that respondents would be faster to press one
key for members of a particular group and words stereotypically associated with
that group than they would to press the same key for members of that group
and words that *contradict* the stereotype associated with that group. It's easy to
respond quickly when members of a group and the attributes associated with
them are signaled with the same key rather than different keys.

The same general procedure is used to assess implicit prejudice (rather than
stereotyping). In this case, participants press one key for both positive words and
photos of people in one group, and another key for both negative words and people
in another group. Participants then repeat the procedure with the pairings of the
two groups and the positive/negative words switched. A nonconscious prejudice
toward older people, for example, would be captured by a difference between the
average time it takes to respond to old faces/positive words and the average time it
takes to respond to old faces/negative words. Someone with negative views toward
older adults would take longer to respond to old faces/positive words than they
would to old faces/negative words (Nosek, Greenwald, & Banaji, 2005).

Millions of people have taken the IAT online. Among other results, researchers
have found that both young and older individuals show a pronounced prejudice

in favor of the young over the old, and about two-thirds of white respondents show a strong or moderate prejudice for white over black (Nosek, Banaji, & Greenwald, 2002). About half of all black respondents also show some prejudice in favor of white faces.

Although the test has its critics (Blanton & Jaccard, 2008; Oswald, Mitchell, Blanton, Jaccard, & Tetlock, 2013; Roddy, Stewart, & Barnes-Holmes, 2010), there's evidence that IAT responses correlate with other indirect measures of prejudice (Lane, Banaji, Nosek, & Greenwald, 2007; Rudman & Ashmore, 2007). In one study, participants in a brain-imaging machine viewed pictures of black faces and white faces. The participants' earlier IAT responses to black faces were significantly correlated with heightened neural activity in the amygdala (a brain center associated with fear and emotional learning) in response to the black faces. Their scores on a more traditional, conscious measure of prejudice, the Modern Racism Scale, were not correlated with this difference in neural activity, suggesting that the IAT assessed an important component of attitudes that participants were unable or unwilling to articulate (Phelps et al., 2000).

An important question, however, is whether a person's responses on the IAT are predictive of behavior that's more significant than pressing computer keys (Amodio & Devine, 2006; Brendl, Markman, & Messner, 2001; Greenwald, Poehlman, Uhlmann, & Banaji, 2009; Karpinski & Hilton, 2001). In one study addressing this question, participants interacted with a white experimenter, took the IAT, and then interacted with a black experimenter. The participants' IAT scores predicted the discrepancy between how much they spoke to the white versus the black experimenter, how often they smiled at the white versus the black experimenter, and the number of speech errors and hesitations they exhibited when interacting with the white versus the black experimenter (McConnell & Leibold, 2001).

PRIMING AND IMPLICIT PREJUDICE Social psychologists have also used **priming** (mental activation) procedures (see Chapter 4) to measure prejudices that individuals might not know they have or that they may wish to deny. The logic is simple. If I show you the word *butter* and then ask you to tell me, as quickly as you can, whether a subsequent string of letters is a word, you'll recognize that *bread* is a word more quickly than you'll recognize that *car* is a word because of your preexisting association between bread and butter. Similarly, if you associate nuns with virtue and charity, you're likely to respond quickly to positive terms (*good, benevolent, trustworthy*) after seeing a picture of a nun. But if you have negative associations to nuns—say, you see them as strict, rigid, or cold—you're likely to respond more quickly to negative terms (*mean, unhappy, unbending*) after seeing a picture of a nun.

As shown in **Figure 11.2**, an implicit measure of prejudice can thus be derived by comparing a person's average reaction time to real and made-up words preceded by faces of members of a given category (compared with "control" trials, in which positive and negative words are preceded by faces of people not in that category). As discussed later in this chapter, numerous studies using these priming methods have shown that people who are sure they aren't prejudiced against blacks nonetheless respond more quickly to negative words preceded by pictures of black faces and more slowly to positive words preceded by pictures of black faces (Banaji, Hardin, & Rothman, 1993; Bessenoff & Sherman, 2000; Dijksterhuis, Aarts, Bargh, & van Knippenberg, 2000; Dovidio, Kawakami, & Gaertner, 2002; Fazio & Hilden, 2001; Friese,

priming The presentation of information designed to activate a concept (such as a stereotype) and hence make it accessible. A prime is the stimulus presented to activate the concept in question.

Hofmann, & Schmitt, 2008; Gawronski, Cunningham, LeBel, & Deutsch, 2010). And one shouldn't assume that people are lying when they deny such prejudices: they may simply not have conscious access to many of their true attitudes and beliefs.

A variant of this sort of priming procedure, the **affect misattribution procedure (AMP)**, doesn't measure how *quickly* people respond to a stimulus after a given prime, but how people *evaluate* that stimulus (Payne, Cheng, Govorun, & Stewart, 2005). In the AMP, subjects are shown a picture of a member of a particular target group—a Muslim, a transgender individual, a hedge fund manager—which is immediately followed by a neutral or unfamiliar image: say, a belt buckle or a Chinese pictograph. The key question is whether the feelings associated with the target group (for example, Muslims) transfer to the subjects' evaluations of the subsequent, otherwise neutral image (for example, Chinese pictographs). If a person has negative associations to Muslims, the average rating of Chinese pictographs that follow the presentation of the image of a Muslim should be lower than the average rating of pictographs that follow non-Muslim faces. Responses on the AMP have been shown to be related to political attitudes, other measures of racial bias, and significant personal habits like smoking and drinking (Greenwald, Smith, Sriram, Bar-Anan, & Nosek, 2009; Payne, et al., 2005; Payne, Govorun, & Arbuckle, 2008; Payne, McClernon, & Dobbins, 2007).

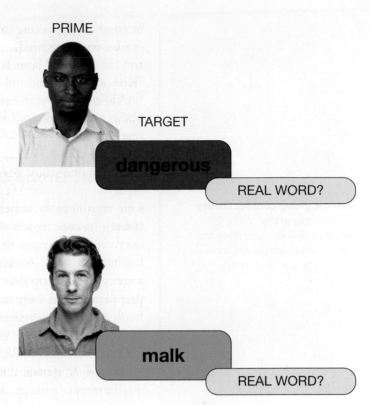

**FIGURE 11.2
AN AFFECTIVE PRIMING PARADIGM**
People are faster to identify real words (rather than made-up words) after seeing pictures of members of a given group if they associate those real words with that group. In this example, someone with negative associations about black people would be faster to recognize "dangerous" as a real word after seeing a picture of a black person's face.

affect misattribution procedure (AMP) A priming procedure designed to assess people's implicit associations to different stimuli, including their associations to various ethnic, racial, occupational, and lifestyle groups.

← LOOKING BACK

In much of today's Western world, prejudice and discrimination are frowned upon. This trend has led to an explicit rejection of prejudiced attitudes that nonetheless can be accompanied by subtle and often nonconscious discriminatory behavior. The schism between what people consciously maintain and how they sometimes feel or act has led to the development of various indirect measures of beliefs and attitudes about different groups. These include the implicit association test and priming procedures, which measure the degree to which different groups trigger positive or negative associations.

The Economic Perspective

Not surprisingly, some of the most intense intergroup tensions arise between groups that vie for the same limited resource. Israelis and Palestinians claim ownership of much of the same small strip of land, and, to put it mildly, they have difficulty getting along. Immigrants to the United States, especially those from Mexico and Central America, face some of the harshest discrimination from those U.S. citizens who see them as threats to their own jobs. Filipino, Sri Lankan, and African guest workers in rich Gulf countries like Qatar and the United Arab Emirates have been known to quarrel with one another and to "stick to their own kind." These observations highlight the core tenets of the economic perspective on prejudice and discrimination: groups develop prejudices about each other and discriminate against one another when they compete for material resources.

Realistic Group Conflict Theory

realistic group conflict theory
A theory that group conflict, prejudice, and discrimination are likely to arise over competition between groups for limited resources.

One version of the economic perspective has been called **realistic group conflict theory** because it acknowledges that groups sometimes confront real conflict over economic issues (Esses, Jackson, & Bennettt-AbuAyyash, 2010; LeVine & Campbell, 1972). According to this theory, prejudice and discrimination often arise from competition over limited resources. The theory predicts, correctly, that prejudice and discrimination should increase under conditions of economic difficulty, such as recessions and periods of high unemployment (King, Knight, & Hebl, 2010; Krosch & Amodio, 2014; Rodeheffer, Hill, & Lord, 2012; Vaughn, Cronan, & Beavers, 2015). When there's less to go around or when people are afraid of losing what they have, competition intensifies.

The theory also predicts that prejudice and discrimination should be strongest among groups that stand to lose the most from another group's economic advance. For example, working-class white Americans exhibited the most anti-black prejudice in the wake of the Civil Rights Movement (Simpson & Yinger, 1985; Vanneman & Pettigrew, 1972). Blue-collar jobs were most at risk once millions of black Americans were allowed to compete more freely for entry-level manufacturing jobs in companies from which they had previously been excluded. Similarly, Donald Trump's efforts during the 2016 presidential campaign to depict immigrants as threats to American jobholders resonated most strongly among white voters in communities experiencing hard times economically (Cohn, 2016; see also Filindra & Pearson-Merkowitz, 2013).

Realistic group conflict theory has been expanded to address the fact that groups often compete not just for material resources, but over ideology and cultural supremacy as well (Esses et al., 2010; Stephan, Ybarra, & Morrison, 2009). Groups fight over whose God should be worshipped, what values should be taught, and what should (and shouldn't) be allowed to be shown on television and posted on the Internet. The theory also specifies some of the ways group conflict plays out. First of all, a pronounced **ethnocentrism** develops—that is, the other group is vilified and one's own group is glorified. Anyone who has ever played pickup basketball knows this phenomenon well. An opponent whose antics seem intolerable instantly becomes more likable once that person becomes a teammate. More generally, people in the outgroup are often thought of in stereotyped ways and are treated in a manner normally forbidden by one's moral code. At the same time, loyalty to the ingroup intensifies, and a "circle the wagons" mentality develops. For example, in the wake of the 9/11 terrorist attacks on the World Trade Center, many people reported that individuals across different ethnic and racial groups in the United States seemed to pull together more than they had beforehand. In an experimental investigation of this tendency, telling white students that the attacks were directed at all Americans, regardless of race and class, served to reduce prejudice toward African-Americans (Dovidio et al., 2004).

ethnocentrism Glorifying one's own group while vilifying other groups.

The Robbers Cave Experiment

A group of researchers explored the ethnocentrism that results from intergroup competition in one of social psychology's classic studies. In 1954, Muzafer Sherif and his colleagues carried out an ambitious experiment far from the confines of the psychology laboratory (Sherif, Harvey, White, Hood, & Sherif, 1961). Twenty-two fifth-grade boys were taken to Robbers Cave State Park in southeastern Oklahoma (so named because the outlaws Belle Starr and Jesse James supposedly hid there). The boys had signed up for a two-and-a-half-week summer camp experience that, unbeknownst to them, was also a study of intergroup relationships. The research team spent over 300 hours screening boys from the Oklahoma City area to find 22 who were not unusual in any way: none had problems in school, all were from intact, middle-class families, and there were no notable ethnic group differences among them. The boys, none of whom knew each other beforehand, were divided into two groups of 11 and taken to separate areas of the park. Neither group even knew of the other's existence—initially.

COMPETITION AND INTERGROUP CONFLICT In the first phase of the experiment, the two groups independently engaged in activities designed to foster group unity (pitching tents, preparing meals) and took part in such common camp activities as playing baseball, swimming, and putting on skits. Cohesion developed within each group, and one group of boys named themselves the Eagles and the other named themselves the Rattlers.

In the second phase, the Eagles and Rattlers were brought together for a tournament. Each member of the winning team would receive a medal and a highly coveted pocketknife (a reward researchers would certainly not hand out to young boys today). Members of the losing team would get nothing. The tournament lasted five days and consisted of such activities as baseball, touch football, tug-of-war, cabin inspections, and a treasure hunt. The competitive nature of the tournament was designed to encourage each group to see the other as an obstacle to obtaining the reward and hence as a foe. And that's exactly what happened.

> "Without knowledge of the roots of hostility we cannot hope to employ our intelligence effectively in controlling its destructiveness."
> —GORDON ALLPORT, AMERICAN PSYCHOLOGIST

COMPETITION IN THE ROBBERS CAVE EXPERIMENT
Two groups of fifth-graders participated in a study that demonstrated intergroup competition and cooperation. (A) During an early phase of the study, the two groups competed against each other, as in this tug-of-war contest. (B) This competition led to numerous acts of aggression—they raided each other's cabins, called one another names, and stole things from one another, as shown here with the Rattlers showing off a pair of pants they stole from a member of the Eagles.
Source: Adapted from Sherif et al., 1961.

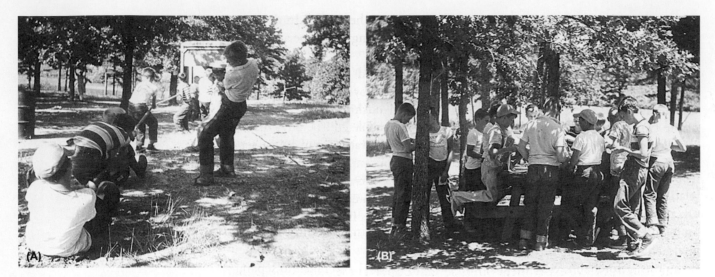

COOPERATION IN THE ROBBERS CAVE EXPERIMENT
To study ways of diminishing intergroup conflict, Sherif and his research team engineered a number of crises that could be overcome only if the two groups worked together. (A) Here the boys pulled a stalled truck, something that could be done only if everyone pitched in. (B) Working together on these superordinate goals led the two groups of boys to set aside their differences and become friends.
Source: Adapted from Sherif et al., 1961.

From the very first competitive encounter, and with increasing frequency throughout the tournament, the two groups hurled insults at each other, calling those in the other group "bums," "cowards," "stinkers," and so on. Although such terms may be tame by today's trash-talking standards, they are clearly not terms of endearment, and they differed markedly from the self-glorifying and congratulatory comments the boys made about members of their own group. Expressions of intergroup hostility, moreover, weren't limited to words. The Eagles captured and burned the Rattlers' flag, which naturally led to a retaliatory theft of the Eagles' flag. Food fights broke out in the dining area, they raided each other's cabins, and they issued challenges to engage in physical fights.

REDUCING INTERGROUP CONFLICT THROUGH SUPERORDINATE GOALS
The third and final part of the experiment is in many ways the most important, because it dealt with how to reduce the conflict between the two groups. On seven occasions over the next two days after the competition was over, the two groups were simply brought together in various noncompetitive settings to see whether their hostility would dissipate. It didn't. Simple contact between the two groups just led to more name-calling, jeering, food fights, and insults.

Given that simple noncompetitive contact failed to reduce hostility between the two groups, the investigators next tried confronting the boys with a number of crises that could be resolved only through the cooperative efforts of both groups. For example, the water supply to the camp was disrupted, and the entire length of pipe from the reservoir to the campgrounds had to be inspected to find the source of the problem—a task made much more manageable if the boys in both groups were assigned to inspect different segments of the line together. In another example, a truck carrying supplies for a campout at a distant area of the park mysteriously "broke down" and the boys were instructed to try to get it running again. The investigators left a large section of rope near the truck, hoping the boys might try to pull the truck to get it started. One of the boys said, "Let's get our tug-of-war rope and have a tug-of-war against the truck." In doing so, members of both groups intermingled throughout the length of rope and pulled it together.

Relations between the two groups quickly showed the effects of these **superordinate goals**—goals that could only be achieved by both groups working together. Name-calling abruptly dropped off and friendships between members of the two groups developed. When the study was completed, the boys insisted that everyone return to Oklahoma City on the same bus rather than on the separate buses on which they had arrived. And when the bus pulled over at a roadside diner, the Rattlers (who had won $5 in an extra competitive event held after the main tournament) decided to spend their money on malted milks for everyone, Eagles included. (Yes, $5 could buy a lot of malted milks in 1954.) The hostility produced by five days of competition was erased by the joint pursuit of common goals. In short, a happy ending (see **Box 11.2**, see p. 374).

The Robbers Cave experiment offers several important lessons. One is that neither differences in background nor differences in appearance nor a prior history of conflict are necessary for intergroup hostility to develop. All that's required is that two groups enter into competition over rewards that only one can attain. Another lesson is that competition against outsiders often increases group cohesion. This tendency is often exploited by political demagogues who invoke the threat of outside enemies to try to stamp out dissension or deflect attention from problems or conflict within the group itself. The final lesson points to how intergroup conflict can be diminished. To reduce the hostility between certain groups, policy makers should think of ways to get them to work together to fulfill common goals. Simply putting adversaries together "to get to know one another better" is usually not enough (Bettencourt, Brewer, Croak, & Miller, 1992; Brewer & Miller, 1988; Stephan & Stephan, 1996; Wilder, 1986). It's the pursuit of bigger, shared, superordinate goals that keeps everyone's eyes on the prize and away from troublesome subgroup distinctions. We'll return to the subject of how to reduce intergroup

superordinate goal A goal that transcends the interests of any one group and can be achieved more readily by two or more groups working together.

INTEGRATION OF THE MILITARY
The integration of different racial and ethnic groups has been remarkably successful in the U.S. military, where soldiers cooperate to accomplish the shared goal of defending the nation.

BOX 11.2 | FOCUS ON EDUCATION

The "Jigsaw" Classroom

School classrooms can often be competitive places where students try to outdo one another for the top grades. Not the type of environment that is most conducive to building intergroup harmony and acceptance. But what would happen if the classroom were made less competitive? Might a more cooperative learning environment improve academic performance and intergroup relations in integrated settings?

Social psychologist Elliot Aronson developed a cooperative learning procedure to find out. When the public school system in Austin, Texas, was integrated in 1971, the transition was not smooth. A disturbing number of physical confrontations took place between black, Hispanic, and white children, and the atmosphere in the classrooms was not what proponents of integration had hoped it would be. The superintendent of schools invited Aronson to do something to improve matters. Mindful of the lessons of the Robbers Cave experiment, Aronson wanted to institute procedures that would unite students in the common goal of mastering a body of material, rather than competing for the highest grades and the teachers' attention. He and his colleagues came up with something called the "jigsaw" classroom (Aronson, Stephan, Sikes, Blaney, & Snapp, 1978; Aronson & Thibodeau, 1992).

In the jigsaw classroom, students are divided into small groups of about six students. Every effort is made to balance the groups in terms of ethnicity, gender, ability level, leadership, and so on. The material on a given topic is then divided into six parts, and each student is required to master one part (and only one part) and teach it to the others. For a lesson on Russian President Vladimir Putin, for example, one student might be responsible for the history of the Soviet Union, another for the history and workings of the KGB, a third for Putin's childhood, a fourth for the current political and economic situation in Russia, and so on. By dividing the material in this way, Aronson ensured that no student could learn the entire lesson without help from peers. Each student's material must, like the pieces of a jigsaw puzzle, fit together with all the others for everyone in the group to learn the whole lesson.

The students' dependence on one another dampens the usual competitive atmosphere and encourages them to work cooperatively toward a common goal. To the extent that the groups are ethnically heterogeneous, members of different ethnic groups gain the experience of working together as individuals rather than as representatives of particular ethnic groups.

The effectiveness of this approach has been assessed in field experiments comparing students in jigsaw classrooms with those in classrooms that teach the same material in the usual fashion. These studies have typically found that students in the jigsaw classrooms like school more and develop more positive attitudes toward different ethnic groups than students in traditional classrooms (Roseth, Johnson, & Johnson, 2008; Slavin, 1995).

Thus, the lessons learned from the Robbers Cave experiment—that intergroup hostility can be diminished by cooperative activity directed at a superordinate goal—have profound practical significance. A simple classroom procedure derived from these lessons—one that can be used in conjunction with traditional, more individualistic classroom exercises—can boost academic performance and facilitate positive racial and ethnic relationships.

hostility later in this chapter when we discuss efforts—derived from more than just the economic perspective—to reduce stereotyping, prejudice, and discrimination.

← LOOKING BACK

Consistent with the economic perspective, prejudice can arise from conflict between groups over limited resources. The Robbers Cave experiment serves as an instructive model of this sort of conflict, showing how otherwise friendly boys could turn into enemies when placed in groups competing for a limited resource. The hostility between the groups evaporated when they had to cooperate to achieve superordinate goals of value to both groups.

The Motivational Perspective

Hostility between groups, it turns out, can develop even in the absence of competition. In the Robbers Cave experiment, there were signs of increased ingroup solidarity when the two groups first learned of each others' existence—*before* they were engaged in, or even knew about, the organized competition. Midway through phase 1 of the experiment, when the two groups were still being kept apart, they were allowed to get within earshot of each other. The mere fact that another group existed made each set of boys take their own group membership more seriously. Both groups quickly became territorial, referring to the baseball field as "*our* diamond" rather than "the diamond" and a favorite swimming spot as "*our* swimming hole." Soon after learning about each other's existence, both groups wanted to "run them off" and "challenge them."

The fact that these developments took place before any competition had been arranged indicates that intergroup hostility can develop merely because another group exists. The existence of group boundaries among any collection of individuals, then, can be sufficient to initiate group discrimination. The motivational processes that lead to this sort of hostility have been explored in a telling research paradigm.

The Minimal Group Paradigm

People's readiness to adopt an "us versus them" mentality has been extensively documented in experiments using the **minimal group paradigm** pioneered by Henri Tajfel (Tajfel & Billig, 1974; Tajfel, Billig, Bundy, & Flament, 1971; see also Ashburn-Nardo, Voils, & Monteith, 2001; Yamagishi, Mifune, Liu, & Pauling, 2008). Tajfel's lifelong interest in intergroup dynamics can be traced to his own experiences as a young man. Because of restrictions on Jewish higher education in Poland, Tajfel emigrated to France to study at the Sorbonne. When World War II broke out, he volunteered to serve in the French Army, which he did for a year before being taken prisoner. He spent the rest of the war in a German prisoner of war camp, fully aware that if his captors had thought of him as Jewish rather than French, he would have shared the same fate as everyone else in his immediate family, none of whom survived the war.

In his research, Tajfel created groups based on arbitrary and seemingly meaningless criteria and then examined how the members of these so-called "minimal groups" behaved toward one another. The participants first performed a rather trivial task and were then divided into two groups, ostensibly on the basis of their responses. In one such task, for example, participants had to estimate the number of dots projected briefly on a screen. Some participants were told they belonged to a group of "overestimators" and others that they belonged to a group of "underestimators." In reality, the participants were randomly assigned to the groups, and they learned only that they were assigned to a particular group; they never learned who else was in their group or who was in the other group. Thus, what it meant to be part of a "group" was boiled down to the bare minimum— the category was arbitrary and members of each group did not know who the others members were.

After learning their group membership, the participants were taken to separate cubicles and asked to assign points, redeemable for money, to pairs of their

minimal group paradigm An experimental paradigm in which researchers create groups based on arbitrary and seemingly meaningless criteria and then examine how the members of these "minimal groups" are inclined to behave toward one another.

TABLE 11.1 AWARDING POINTS IN THE MINIMAL GROUP PARADIGM									
Ingroup	18	17	16	15	14	13	21	11	10	9
Outgroup	3	5	7	9	11	13	15	17	19	21

fellow participants. They were shown multiple pairings of preassigned point values, where one amount would go to a participant who was in the group they were in (the ingroup) and the other amount to a participant in the outgroup. See **Table 11.1** for an example: if you assign a member of the ingroup 18 points, then the member of the outgroup gets only 3 points, as shown in the first column; if you assign the member of the ingroup 17 points (the second column), then the member of the outgroup gets 5 points; and so on. Participants assigning points didn't know the individual identity of those to whom they were awarding points; all they knew was the other participants' group membership. In this way, the investigators could determine whether participants assigned points equally to members of the ingroup and outgroup; whether they instead maximized the total point payout regardless of group membership; or whether they maximized the points given to the ingroup *over the outgroup*, even if the ingroup could have gotten more points through other choices that would have given the outgroup more points as well.

In Table 11.1, for example, someone who chooses 13 and 13 would appear to be interested in equality; someone who chooses 9 for the ingroup member and 21 for the outgroup member would appear to be interested in handing out the greatest number of points overall; and someone who chooses 18 for the ingroup member and 3 for the outgroup member would appear to be interested in maximizing the *relative* advantage of the ingroup over the outgroup, even though the ingroup could have gotten more in the pairing that gives the ingroup 21 points—but also gives the outgroup a more generous amount of points at 15.

Numerous experiments have shown that a majority of participants are interested more in maximizing the *relative* gain for members of their ingroup over the outgroup than they are in maximizing the absolute gain for their ingroup. A moment's reflection reveals just how extraordinary this is. The participants don't know who the ingroup and outgroup members are; the points awarded are never for themselves; and, of course, the basis for establishing the two groups is utterly meaningless. Yet participants still tend to favor their minimal ingroup. In fact, they're willing to do so at a cost to the ingroup, which earns fewer points when the focus is on "beating" the other group rather than on maximizing their group's absolute gain. The ingroup favoritism that emerges in this context demonstrates how easily we slip into thinking in terms of *us* versus *them* (Brewer & Brown, 1998). And if history has taught us anything, it is that the us/them distinction, once formed, can have enormous—and enormously unfortunate—implications.

Social Identity Theory

Studies using the minimal group paradigm have shown the pervasiveness and persistence of ingroup favoritism, but what does it have to do with the motivational perspective on prejudice? Might it not reflect a purely cognitive tendency

"Cruelty and intolerance to those who do not belong to it are natural to every religion."
—SIGMUND FREUD

SOCIAL IDENTITY THEORY
People derive their sense of identity not only from their individual accomplishments but also from those of the groups to which they belong.
(A) These delegates at the U.S. Republican National Convention identify with the Republican Party. (B) These individuals derive part of their identity from belonging to the community of surfers.

to divide the world into categories of *us* and *them*? Just as all children quickly learn to distinguish the self from all others, might we not also all learn to distinguish "my side" from the "other side"?

Much of the psychology behind ingroup favoritism might very well reflect these kinds of cognitive tendencies. The us/them distinction may be one of the basic cuts people make in organizing the world. Still, the ingroup favoritism observed in the minimal group situation can't be the product of cognition alone. For that we need a motivational theory—a theory to explain why, once the us/them distinction is made, we treat those we consider "us" better than those we consider "them." Some divisions into *us* and *them* have the kind of material or economic implications discussed earlier, which often provide motivation enough for people to treat ingroup members better than outgroup members. But not all motivations are economic, and certainly no meaningful economic implications are present in the ingroup/outgroup division in the minimal group paradigm. To explain that sort of ingroup favoritism, a different motivational perspective is needed.

The most widely recognized theory that attempts to explain the ubiquity of ingroup favoritism is **social identity theory**, which is based on the idea that our self-esteem comes not only from our personal identity and accomplishments, but also from the status and accomplishments of the various groups to which we belong (Tajfel & Turner, 1979; see also Spears, 2011; Stroebe, Spears, & Lodewijkx, 2007). Being "an American" is an element of the self-concept of most Americans, and with it may come the pride associated with, say, the Bill of Rights, U.S. economic and military clout, and the accomplishments of American scientists, industrialists, athletes, and entertainers. With it, too, may come the shame associated with the country's history of slavery and its treatment of Native Americans. Similarly, being a gang member, a professor, a film buff, or a surfer means that our identity and esteem are intimately tied up with the triumphs and shortcomings of our fellow gang members, academics, film buffs, and surfers.

social identity theory The idea that a person's self-concept and self-esteem derive not only from personal identity and accomplishments, but also from the status and accomplishments of the various groups to which the person belongs.

BOOSTING THE STATUS OF THE INGROUP Because our self-esteem is based in part on the status of the various groups to which we belong, we may be tempted to boost the status and fortunes of these groups and their members. Therein lies a powerful cause of ingroup favoritism: doing whatever we can to feel better about the ingroup leads us to feel better about ourselves. Evidence supporting this idea comes from studies that have assessed participants' self-esteem after they've had an opportunity to exhibit ingroup favoritism in the minimal group situation, such as the one described earlier where participants awarded pairs of points to "overestimators" or "underestimators." As expected, those who had been allowed to display ingroup favoritism had higher self-esteem than those who hadn't had a chance to boost their own group at the expense of another (Lemyre & Smith, 1985; Oakes & Turner, 1980). Other research has shown that people who take particularly strong pride in their group affiliations (such as feeling particularly proud to be an American) are more prone to ingroup favoritism when placed in a minimal group situation (Crocker & Luhtanen, 1990). And people who are highly identified with a particular group react to criticism of the group as if it were criticism of the self (McCoy & Major, 2003).

BASKING IN REFLECTED GLORY Social identity theory also receives support from the everyday observation that people go to great lengths to announce their affiliation with a group when that group is doing well. Sports fans, for example, often chant, "We're number 1!" after a team victory. But what does "*We're number 1*" mean? It's a rare fan indeed who does anything other than cheer their team, heckle referees, or taunt opposing players. Yet countless fans want to be connected to the effort when the outcome is a victory. After a loss, not so much.

Robert Cialdini refers to this tendency to identify with a winning team as **basking in reflected glory**. He investigated the tendency by recording how often students wore their school sweatshirts and T-shirts to class after their football team had just won or lost a game. As expected, students wore the school colors significantly more often following victory than after defeat. Cialdini and his colleagues also tabulated students' use of first-person versus third-person references. It's no surprise to learn that, as a general rule, "we" won, whereas "they" lost (Cialdini et al., 1976). As social identity theory predicts, the triumphs and failings of the groups with which we affiliate affect our self-esteem—even when

"Victory finds a hundred fathers but defeat is an orphan."
—COUNT GALEAZZO CIANO,
THE CIANO DIARIES (1945)

basking in reflected glory Taking pride in the accomplishments of other people in one's group, such as when sports fans identify with a winning team.

BASKING IN REFLECTED GLORY
Sports fans, like these Ohio State students, passionately identify with their team and feel joyous when the team wins and dejected when it loses. To connect themselves to the team, fans often wear team jerseys to the game and even to class or work the next day if the team wins.

the group is simply a favorite sports team (Hirt, Zillman, Erickson, & Kennedy, 1992). We therefore have an incentive to identify with such groups when they do well but to distance ourselves from them when they lose.

DENIGRATING OUTGROUPS TO BOLSTER SELF-ESTEEM To bask in reflected glory is to use ingroup identity to enhance self-esteem. But does denigrating outgroups also boost self-esteem? Does criticizing another group make people feel better about their own group—and hence themselves? Indeed it does.

In one study, researchers threatened the self-esteem of half the participants by telling them they had just performed poorly on an intelligence test; the other half were told they had done well (Fein & Spencer, 1997). The participants then watched a videotaped interview of a job applicant. The video made it clear to half the participants (none of whom was Jewish) that the candidate was Jewish, but not to the other half. Participants later rated the job candidate (see **Figure 11.3**). Participants whose self-esteem had been threatened rated the candidate negatively if they thought she was Jewish; participants whose self-esteem was not threatened did not (Figure 11.3A). In addition, the participants whose self-esteem had been threatened and had "taken it out" on the Jewish candidate experienced an increase in their self-esteem from the time they received feedback on the IQ test to the end of the experiment (Figure 11.3B). It appears that denigrating members of outgroups can indeed bolster self-esteem.

Lisa Sinclair and Ziva Kunda explored a related way that outgroups are strategically used to enhance self-esteem. In this study, non-black participants were either praised or criticized by a white or black male doctor (Sinclair & Kunda, 1999). The investigators predicted that the participants would be motivated to cling to the praise they received but to challenge the criticism and that they'd use the race of their evaluator to help them do so. In particular, the investigators predicted that participants who received praise from a black doctor would tend to think of him more as a doctor (a prestigious occupation) than as a black man,

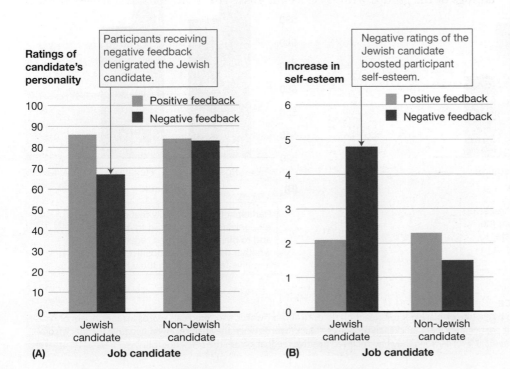

FIGURE 11.3
BOLSTERING SELF-ESTEEM
(A) The average ratings of a job candidate's personality, depending on whether the candidate was Jewish or non-Jewish after the person doing the rating had received positive or negative feedback. The results demonstrate that feeling down on oneself (a rater who had received negative feedback) can make a person more likely to denigrate the outgroup (rate the Jewish candidates more poorly). (B) Raters who had received negative feedback and subsequently denigrated the outgroup received a boost in self-esteem from doing so.
Source: Adapted from Fein & Spencer, 1997.

ALTERNATIVE CONSTRUALS
Do you see this person mainly as a man? A doctor? A black man? A black doctor? How you see him may depend on how each construal contributes to your self-esteem.

whereas those who were criticized by a black doctor would tend to think of him more as a black man than as a doctor.

The participants performed a lexical decision task right after getting feedback from the doctor (Sinclair & Kunda, 1999). The researchers flashed a series of words and nonwords on a computer screen and had the participants indicate, as fast as they could, whether each string of letters was a word. Some of the words were related to the medical profession (for example, *hospital*, *prescription*) and some were associated with common stereotypes of blacks at that time (*rap*, *jazz*). Sinclair and Kunda reasoned that if the participants were thinking of their evaluator primarily as a doctor, they would recognize the medical words faster; if they were thinking of their evaluator primarily as a black man, they would recognize the words related to the black stereotype faster.

As **Figure 11.4** shows, that's exactly what happened. Participants were particularly fast at recognizing words associated with the black stereotype when they'd been criticized by the black doctor and slow to recognize those words when they were praised by the black doctor (Figure 11.4A). The reverse was true for the medical words (Figure 11.4B). Participants were fast at recognizing medical words when they'd been praised by the black doctor and slow to do so when criticized by the black doctor. When the black doctor criticized them, in other words, participants saw him as a black man—and when he praised them, they saw him as a doctor.

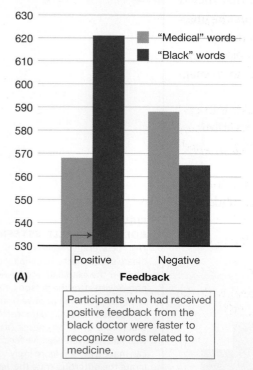

Participants who had received positive feedback from the black doctor were faster to recognize words related to medicine.

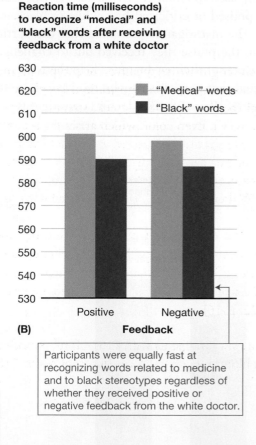

Participants were equally fast at recognizing words related to medicine and to black stereotypes regardless of whether they received positive or negative feedback from the white doctor.

FIGURE 11.4
SELF-ESTEEM AND RACIAL PREJUDICE
Participants were either praised or criticized by a white or black doctor. Reaction times to "black" words and "medical" words after criticism or praise by white doctors were virtually the same, but participants were quicker to recognize "black" words when they had received negative feedback from the black doctor and quicker to recognize "medical" words when they had received positive feedback from the black doctor.
Source: Adapted from Sinclair & Kunda, 1999.

Social identity theory also maintains that group memberships are part of every individual's identity. If so, then people will often be motivated to denigrate outgroup members not just when they personally are under threat, but when their *groups* are. Studies confirm this prediction. When white Americans or Canadians are made aware of the changing racial demographics of their country, they express more negative attitudes toward minority groups, increased implicit pro-white bias, and less interest in affiliating with members of non-white groups (Craig & Richeson, 2014; Outten, Schmitt, Miller, & Garcia, 2012). This, of course, was a much discussed element of the 2016 presidential election: the part of the electorate who felt they were losing ground economically and culturally were thought to be most receptive to Donald Trump's harsh rhetoric about immigration.

← LOOKING BACK

Consistent with the motivational perspective on stereotyping, prejudice, and discrimination, people are inclined to favor ingroups over outgroups, even when the basis of group membership is trivial. Part of the reason is that people identify with their groups and feel good about themselves when they feel good about their groups. Threats to self-esteem also result in the denigration of outgroup members.

The Cognitive Perspective

From the cognitive perspective, stereotyping is inevitable. It stems from the ubiquity and necessity of categorization. People categorize nearly everything, both natural (bodies of water—creek, stream, river) and artificial (cars—sports car, sedan, SUV). Even color, which arises from continuous variation in electromagnetic wavelength, is perceived as distinct categories.

All of this categorizing has a purpose: it simplifies the task of taking in and processing the incredible volume of stimuli surrounding us. The American journalist Walter Lippmann, who is credited with coining the term *stereotype*, stated:

> The real environment is altogether too big, too complex, and too fleeting, for direct acquaintance. We are not equipped to deal with so much subtlety, so much variety, so many permutations and combinations. . . . We have to reconstruct it on a simpler model before we can manage with it. (Lippmann, 1922, p. 16)

Stereotypes provide us with those simpler models that allow us to deal with the "great blooming, buzzing confusion of reality" (Lippmann, 1922, p. 96).

Stereotypes and the Conservation of Cognitive Resources

If stereotypes are useful schemas that enable us to process information efficiently, then we should be more inclined to use them when we're overloaded, tired, or mentally taxed in some way—in other words, when we're in need of a shortcut.

Several experiments have demonstrated exactly that (Kim & Baron, 1988; Macrae & Bodenhausen, 2000; Macrae, Hewstone, & Griffiths, 1993; Pratto & Bargh, 1991; Stangor & Duan, 1991; Wigboldus, Sherman, Franzese, & van Knippenberg, 2004).

In one intriguing study, participants were more likely to invoke stereotypes when tested at the low point of their circadian rhythm. "Morning people," when tested at night, tended to invoke a common stereotype and conclude, for example, that a person charged with cheating on an exam was guilty if he was an athlete. "Night people," when tested in the morning, were more inclined to conclude that a person charged with dealing drugs was guilty if he was black (Bodenhausen, 1990). Thus, people are more likely to fall back on stereotypes when they lack mental energy. Not surprisingly, then, people have also been shown to stereotype others more when they're intoxicated with alcohol and their mental capacities are low (Bartholow, Dickter, & Sestir, 2006).

If the use of stereotypes conserves intellectual energy, then using them should free up extra cognitive resources that can be applied to other mental tasks. In one test of this idea, participants performed two tasks simultaneously (Macrae, Milne, & Bodenhausen, 1994). On one task, they formed an impression of a (hypothetical) person described by a number of trait terms presented on a computer screen (for example, *rebellious*, *dangerous*, *aggressive*). The other task involved monitoring a tape-recorded lecture about Indonesia and then taking a quiz on the content of the lecture. For half the participants, the trait terms were accompanied by a stereotype associated with those terms (such as skinhead); for the other half, the trait terms were presented alone. The key questions were whether presenting participants with the stereotype would help them later recall the trait terms they'd seen and, more importantly, whether being prompted to stereotype would also release extra cognitive resources that could be devoted to the lecture on Indonesia.

As the experimenters anticipated, the use of stereotypes made the first task easier and thereby freed up cognitive resources that allowed them to perform better on the second task (**Figure 11.5**). Those given a stereotype not only remembered

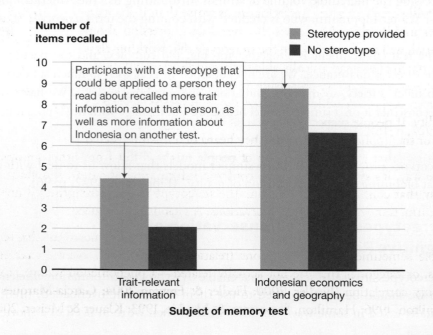

FIGURE 11.5
CONSERVING COGNITIVE RESOURCES
Providing participants with an applicable stereotype makes it easier for them to recall stereotypically consistent information, thereby conserving mental energy for use in performing other tasks, such as the quiz on Indonesia.
Source: Adapted from Macrae, Milne, & Bodenhausen, 1994.

the relevant trait information better, but also performed better on the test on Indonesia (Macrae, Milne, et al. 1994).

Construal Processes and Biased Assessments

Not every member of a given category conforms to the group stereotype. So while relying on stereotypes can save time and effort, it can also lead to mistaken impressions and unfair judgments about individuals.

Social psychologists have produced countless demonstrations of this point. A simple and particularly unsettling example comes from an early study by John Darley and P. H. Gross (1983). They had students watch a videotape of a fourth-grader named Hannah. One version of the video reported that Hannah's parents were professionals and showed her playing in an obviously upper-middle-class area. Another version reported that Hannah's parents were working class and showed her playing in a rundown environment.

The next part of the video showed Hannah answering questions involving math, science, and reading. Her performance was ambiguous; she answered some difficult questions well but also seemed distracted and flubbed easier questions. The researchers asked the students how well they thought Hannah would perform in relation to her classmates. Those who saw an upper-middle-class Hannah estimated she would perform better than average, while those who saw working-class Hannah assumed she would perform worse than average.

What's especially sad is that these assumptions about a student's performance based solely on her social class are grounded in fact (Jussim, 2012). On average, upper-middle-class children perform better in school than working-class children. Therefore, given an ambiguous performance by a child, we might reasonably anticipate her long-term academic success would be greater if she's upper middle class than if she's working class.

The reason is that working-class Hannah starts life with two strikes against her. People will expect and demand less of her and will perceive a given performance as worse than if she were upper middle class. Moreover, the mistaken impression about Hannah will tend to reinforce the stereotype that working-class children are less academically able than middle-class children.

Biased information processing is especially harmful when the stereotypes on which it's based are completely lacking in validity. If people suspect—because of something they've been told or the implications of a joke they heard or a misinterpreted statistic—that a particular group of people might differ from other groups in some way, it's shockingly easy to construe information about an individual in a way that confirms that suspicion. The stereotype is then strengthened due to "confirmation" by the biased observations. A vicious cycle indeed.

"Why is it we never focus on the things that unite us, like falafel?"

DISTINCTIVENESS AND ILLUSORY CORRELATIONS As we noted in Chapter 4, people sometimes "see" correlations (relationships) between events, characteristics, or categories that are not actually related—a phenomenon referred to as illusory correlation (Fiedler, 2000; Fiedler & Freytag 2004; Garcia-Marques & Hamilton, 1996; Hamilton, Stroessner, & Mackie, 1993; Klauer & Meiser, 2000;

Shavitt, Sanbonmatsu, Smittipatana, & Posavac, 1999). Illusory correlations can arise for many reasons, with some being simply the result of how we process unusual or distinctive events.

Distinctive events capture our attention. We would notice if a student came to a lecture wearing a clown outfit—or nothing at all. Because we attend more closely to distinctive events, we're also likely to remember them better, and as a result they may become overrepresented in our memory. These processes have important implications for the kinds of stereotypes that are commonly associated with minority groups. By definition, minority groups are distinctive to most members of the majority, so minority group members stand out. In addition, negative behaviors, such as robbing, assaulting, and murdering are (fortunately) much less common than positive behaviors, such as saying thank you and obeying traffic signs, so negative behaviors are distinctive as well. Negative behavior on the part of minority group members is therefore doubly distinctive and doubly memorable. Minority groups are therefore vulnerable to being stereotyped as more likely to engage in negative behavior than they actually are.

David Hamilton and Robert Gifford (1976) explored the impact of **paired distinctiveness**—the pairing of two distinctive events that stand out because they occur together—in an experiment that examined the formation of such illusory correlations from scratch. Participants were presented with information about the actions of members of "group A" or "group B." Those were the only group labels they received; these were not existing groups they were familiar with, such as theater arts majors, Native Americans, or heterosexual or transgender individuals. They learned, for example, that "John, a member of group A, visited a sick friend in the hospital" and "Bill, a member of group B, always talks about himself and his problems." Mimicking real life, most of the actions by members of each group were positive (69 percent, to be exact). Thus, there was no correlation between group membership and the likelihood of positive or negative behavior. But two-thirds of the actions they read about described the actions of someone in group A, thus making A the majority group.

When later asked to remember who did what, participants overestimated how often the negative behaviors were performed by a member of the minority group. They also rated members of the minority group less favorably. Even though participants knew nothing about these two arbitrary "groups" beforehand, and even though they were exposed to the same ratio of positive and negative actions on the part of both groups, they came away thinking that the smaller group did more bad things (**Figure 11.6**). A distinctiveness-based illusory correlation became lodged in participants' minds; that is, they "detected" false correlations based on the distinctiveness of minority group members and the distinctiveness of negative behaviors.

Subsequent research has shown that beliefs in such illusory correlations can be formed on the basis of a single instance of unusual behavior by someone from a minority group. If you've seen few Polynesians in your life, for instance, but you see a Polynesian curse at the bank teller serving your line, you might be tempted to conclude that something about being Polynesian was at least part of the reason ("I guess that's just the way they are"). Of course, if a member of your own ethnic group behaved that way, you probably wouldn't consider ethnicity

paired distinctiveness The pairing of two distinctive events that stand out even more because they occur together.

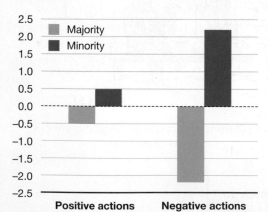

FIGURE 11.6
DISTINCTIVENESS AND ILLUSORY CORRELATION
Distinctive events, such as negative actions by members of minority groups, tend to stand out and exert a disproportionate influence on judgments. In this study, participants attributed more of the negative behaviors to the minority group than the members of that group were actually responsible for.
Source: Adapted from Hamilton & Gifford, 1976.

PAIRED DISTINCTIVENESS
(A) When we see unusual actions performed by people we rarely encounter (such as, for Westerners, these Vietnamese children), we tend to won-der whether "those people" are fond of that type of activity, and a link between the two is often formed. (B) When the same actions are performed by types of people we encounter frequently (such as, for Westerners, a child from the United States), we don't draw any conclusions about "those people."

as a possible explanation ("Every group has some jerks") (Risen, Gilovich, & Dunning, 2007). Members of your group do plenty of obnoxious things as well as wonderful things, but being a member of your own group doesn't normally count as an explanation for any specific behavior.

EXPECTATIONS AND BIASED INFORMATION PROCESSING To stereotype is to overgeneralize. But of course, people don't generalize everything they witness to the same degree. Some acts (an epileptic seizure, for example) discourage gen-eralization from the individual to the group no matter who the actor is; other behaviors (such as rudeness) invite it. In general, people are more likely to gener-alize behaviors and traits they already suspect may be typical of the group's mem-bers. This is another way in which stereotypes can be self-reinforcing. Actions that are consistent with an existing stereotype are noticed, deemed significant, and remembered, whereas actions that are at variance with the stereotype may be ignored, dismissed, or quickly forgotten (Bodenhausen, 1988; Kunda & Thagard, 1996; von Hippel, Sekaquaptewa, & Vargas, 1995).

Stereotypes also influence how the details of events are interpreted. In a strik-ing demonstration of this effect, white participants watched a videotape of a heated discussion between two men, one black and one white, and were asked to code the behavior they were watching into one of several categories, such as "Gives information," "Playing around," or "Aggressive behavior" (Duncan, 1976; see also Dunning & Sherman, 1997; Kunda & Sherman-Williams, 1993; Plant, Kling, & Smith, 2004; Sagar & Schofield, 1980). At one point in the video, one of the men shoved the other. For half the participants, a black man shoved the white man; for the other half, the white man did the shoving. The race of the

> "Stereotypic beliefs about women's roles, for example, may enable one to see correctly that a woman in a dark room is threading a needle rather than tying a fishing lure, but they may also cause one to mistak-enly assume that her goal is embroidery rather than cardiac surgery."
> —DAN GILBERT

person made a difference in how the action was interpreted. When perpetrated by a white man, the incident tended to be coded as more benign (as "Playing around," for example). When perpetrated by a black man, it was coded as a more serious action (such as "Aggressive behavior").

These results are remarkable because the participants saw the shove with their own eyes. The influence of stereotypes can be even greater when the episode is presented to people secondhand and is therefore more open to being construed in different ways. In one study, for instance, participants listened to a play-by-play account of a college basketball game and were told to focus on the exploits of one player in particular, named Mark Flick (Stone, Perry, & Darley, 1997). Half the participants saw a photo of Mark that made it clear he was African-American and half saw a photo that made it clear he was white. When participants rated Mark's performance, their assessments reflected commonly held stereotypes about black and white basketball players. Those who thought Mark was African-American rated him as more athletic and as having played better; those who thought he was white rated him as having hustled more and as having played a more savvy game.

Studies like these demonstrate that people don't evaluate information even-handedly. Instead, information that's consistent with a group stereotype typically has more impact than information that's inconsistent with it. This is yet another way that even inaccurate stereotypes can stay alive and even grow in strength.

SELF-FULFILLING PROPHECIES Stereotypes can also be reinforced by self-fulfilling prophecies: that is, people act toward members of certain groups in ways that encourage the very behavior they expect to see from those groups. For example, thinking that members of a particular group are hostile, a person might act toward them in a guarded manner, thereby eliciting a coldness that's then taken as proof of their hostility (Shelton & Richeson, 2005). A teacher who believes members of a specific group lack intellectual ability may give them less attention in class, thereby increasing the chances that they'll fall behind their classmates. As Robert Merton, who coined the term *self-fulfilling prophecy*, once said, "The specious validity of the self-fulfilling prophecy perpetuates a reign of error. For the prophet will cite the actual course of events as proof that he was right from the very beginning" (Merton, 1957, p. 423).

The damage that can be done by self-fulfilling prophecies was powerfully illustrated in an experiment in which white undergraduates interviewed both black and white men pretending to be job applicants (Word, Zanna, & Cooper, 1974). The interviews were monitored, and the researchers discovered that the students (the white interviewers) unwittingly treated black and white applicants differently. When the applicant was black, the interviewer tended to sit farther away, to hem and haw throughout the session, and to terminate the proceedings earlier than when the applicant was white. That is not the type of environment that inspires smooth interview performance.

Sure enough, the second phase of the experiment showed just how difficult it had been for the black applicants. Interviewers were trained to treat *a new set of* applicants, all of whom were white, the way that either the white or the black applicants had been treated earlier. These interviews were tape-recorded and later rated by independent judges. These new applicants, who had been interviewed in the way the black applicants had been interviewed earlier, were evaluated more negatively than those who'd been interviewed in the way the white

"Oppression has no logic—just a self-fulfilling prophecy, justified by a self-perpetuating system."
—GLORIA STEINEM

applicants had been interviewed earlier. In other words, by placing black applicants at a disadvantage by treating them differently, the white interviewers confirmed their negative stereotypes of blacks. Similar results have been obtained in interview studies of gay and lesbian job applicants (Hebl, Foster, Mannix, & Dovidio, 2002).

EXPLAINING AWAY EXCEPTIONS If every rule has an exception, the same is true for stereotypes. Groups known for their intellectual talents nonetheless include a few dolts. Groups renowned for their athletic abilities are sure to include a klutz or two. Even if a stereotype is largely accurate, there's almost certain to be examples that contradict it. Of course, if the stereotype is completely invalid, counterexamples will be even more plentiful. What happens when people discover evidence that disagrees with their view? Do they abandon their stereotypes or hold them less confidently?

The way people respond to disconfirmation of their stereotypes varies according to their emotional investment in the stereotype, whether the stereotype is specific to the person who holds it or is widely shared, and numerous other factors. One thing is clear, however: people don't give up their stereotypes easily. As numerous studies have demonstrated, people evaluate disconfirming evidence in a variety of ways that have the effect of reducing its impact. An understanding of these processes provides some insight into one of the most vexing questions about stereotypes—namely, why they so often persist in the face of evidence that would seem to contradict them.

Although we generalize when we stereotype, no one expects perfectly consistent behavior from members of a given group. Groups thought to be dishonest, lazy, or carefree are thought to be dishonest, lazy, or carefree *on average*, or at least more dishonest, lazy, or carefree than other groups; not all members are expected to behave in those ways all the time. This loophole lets people remain unmoved by apparent disconfirmations of their stereotypes, because anyone who acts at variance with the stereotype is simply walled off into a category of "exceptions." Psychologists refer to this tendency as **subtyping** (Queller & Smith, 2002; Richards & Hewstone, 2001; Weber & Crocker, 1983). Sexists who believe that women are passive and dependent and should stay home to raise children are likely to subtype assertive, independent women who choose not to have children as "militant" or "strident" feminists, thereby leaving their stereotype of women largely intact. Similarly, racists who maintain that African-Americans can't excel outside of sports and entertainment are likely to remain untroubled by the likes of, say, Barack Obama ("He's half white") or U.S. Senator Kamala Harris ("Her father was born in Jamaica and her mother in India"). To the racist mind, they're merely the "exceptions that prove the rule." (Incidentally, if you've ever wondered how an exception can prove a rule—it can't. The expression uses the word *prove* in its less common meaning: to test, as in, "proving grounds.")

Subtyping reflects a more general truth: people treat evidence that supports a stereotype differently from evidence that refutes it. People tend to accept supportive evidence at face value, whereas they often critically analyze and discount contradictory evidence. One way they do this, in keeping with the self-serving attributional bias (see Chapter 5), is by attributing behavior consistent with a stereotype to the dispositions of the people involved and attributing behavior inconsistent with a stereotype to external causes (Crocker, Hannah, & Weber, 1983; Deaux & Emswiller, 1974; Kulik, 1983; Swim & Sanna, 1996; Taylor &

subtyping Explaining away exceptions to a given stereotype by creating a subcategory of the stereotyped group that can be expected to differ from the group as a whole.

EXPLAINING AWAY EXCEPTIONS
People who hold stereotypes of ethnic groups sometimes dismiss examples of individuals who don't conform to the stereotype as exceptions or members of relatively rare subtypes.

CONCRETE AND ABSTRACT CONSTRUALS DURING THE PALIO COMPETITION
Fans of the Palio Competition in Ferrara, Italy, tended to see positive actions by members of their team in abstract, meaningful terms and negative actions in concrete, less meaningful terms. They did just the opposite for the positive and negative actions of members of the opposing team, making it easier for them to continue to think more positively of their own team than their opponents.

Jaggi, 1974). An anti-Semite who believes that Jews are "cheap" is likely to dismiss a Jewish person's acts of philanthropy as reflecting a desire for social acceptance but to interpret any pursuit of self-interest as being a reflection of some "true" Jewish character. Thus, episodes consistent with a stereotype reinforce its perceived validity; episodes that are inconsistent with the stereotype are deemed insignificant (Pettigrew, 1979).

We also treat supportive and contradictory information differently by varying how concretely or abstractly we evaluate the actions of people from different groups. Almost any action can be construed at different levels of abstraction (Vallacher & Wegner, 1987; see Chapters 3, 5, and 8). For example, if you see a person lifting someone who has fallen, you could describe the action concretely as exactly that—as lifting. Alternatively, you could say, more abstractly, that the person was "helping" the fallen individual. More abstractly still, you might say the person was being "helpful" or "altruistic." These different levels of abstraction carry different connotations. The more concrete the description ("lifting"), the less it says about the person involved; the more abstract the description ("altruistic"), the more it says about the person.

These differences in concrete versus abstract construal were examined in a study that took place during the annual *palio* competition in Ferrara, Italy (Maass, Salvi, Arcuri, & Semin, 1989). The *palio* are horse-racing competitions that have taken place in various Italian towns since the thirteenth century (with a brief interruption during the time of the Black Plague). Pitting teams from different districts, or *contrade*, against one another, the races take place in the context of an elaborate festival in which residents of each *contrada* root for their team. In the weeks leading up to the *palio*, feelings of intergroup competition run high.

Before one such *palio* competition, the researchers showed the residents of two *contrade*, San Giorgio and San Giacomo, a number of sketches depicting a member of their own team or of the rival team engaged in an action. The *contrada* membership of the person depicted was established simply by having the color of the protagonist's shirt match that of one *contrada* or another. Some of the sketches portrayed desirable actions (such as helping someone), and some portrayed undesirable actions (such as littering). After inspecting each sketch, the participants described what it depicted, and their responses were scored for level of abstraction.

The results revealed a clear bias (**Figure 11.7**). Participants maintained positive views of their own group by describing negative actions of members of their own

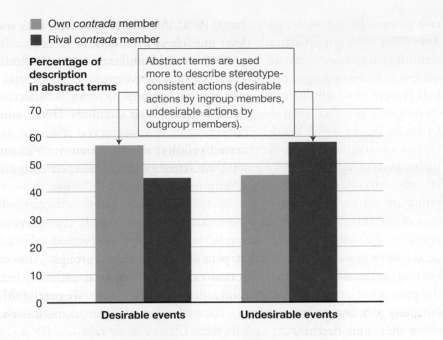

Own *contrada* member
Rival *contrada* member

Percentage of description in abstract terms

Abstract terms are used more to describe stereotype-consistent actions (desirable actions by ingroup members, undesirable actions by outgroup members).

Desirable events   Undesirable events

FIGURE 11.7
STEREOTYPES AND THE ENCODING OF BEHAVIOR
People encode events consistent with their preexisting stereotypes (both positive events associated with the ingroup and negative events associated with the outgroup) at a more abstract, and therefore more meaningful, level than events that are inconsistent with preexisting stereotypes. This graph shows the percentage of abstract (versus concrete) terms used to describe desirable and undesirable actions by members of the ingroup and outgroup. Abstract terms consist of state verbs or trait terms (*hates, hateful, loves, loving*), and concrete terms consist of descriptive and interpretive action verbs (*hits, hurts, lifts, aids*).
Source: Adapted from Maass et al., 1989.

group on a more concrete level—a low level of abstraction—so the individual was less implicated in the action ("The guy from my *contrada* dropped a piece of paper"). But participants maintained their less favorable views of the other group by describing negative actions of members of the other group at a high level of abstraction ("The guy from your *contrada* is a litterer"). They did precisely the opposite for positive actions. ("The guy from my *contrada* is very kind. The guy from your *contrada* lifted the little kid on his shoulders.") This asymmetry feeds the tendency to perceive the ingroup in a favorable light. Abstractly evaluating events that fit one's stereotypes lends them greater import; concretely evaluating events that violate one's preferences or expectations renders them less consequential.

Accentuation of Ingroup Similarity and Outgroup Difference

There's an apocryphal story about a man who owned a farm near the Russian–Polish border. Over the course of European history, the farm had gone back and forth under the rule of each country many times. After the most recent boundary was drawn, the farmer was uncertain whether he lived in Poland or Russia. To settle the issue, the farmer saved up to have a proper survey conducted and his national identity established. When the survey was finished, the farmer, scarcely able to contain his anticipation, asked, "Well, do I live in Russia or Poland?" The surveyor replied that although remarkably near the border, the entire farm was located in Poland. "Good," the farmer stated, "I don't think I could take those harsh Russian winters."

The point of the story, of course, is that although an arbitrary national border can't affect the weather at a fixed location, arbitrary categorical boundaries can have significant effects on the way we perceive things. Indeed, research has shown that merely dividing a continuous distribution into two groups leads people to see less variability within each group and more variability between the two groups. In one study, participants were divided into two arbitrary groups. They then filled out an attitude questionnaire twice—once to record their own attitudes and once to record how they thought another ingroup member or outgroup member might respond. Participants consistently assumed that their beliefs were more similar to those of another ingroup member than to those of an outgroup member, even though the basis of group membership was arbitrary (Allen & Wilder, 1979; Wilder, 1984).

The remarkable thing about this result is *not* that people assume more similarity between members within a group than across groups. That makes sense. After all, why categorize members into groups in the first place if the members of each group are not, on average, more similar to one another than they are to the members of the other group? What *is* remarkable, and potentially troubling, is that people make such assumptions even when the groups are formed arbitrarily or on the basis of a dimension (such as skin color, age, or body weight) that has no bearing on the attitude or behavior under consideration. In these circumstances, the pure act of categorization distorts judgment. Also, the more people think of outgroup members as homogeneous, the more likely they are to spout prejudices about them and discriminate against them (Brauer & Er-rafiy, 2011).

THE OUTGROUP HOMOGENEITY EFFECT Think of a group to which you do not belong: Islamic fundamentalists, reality TV participants, heroin addicts, Tesla owners. It's tempting to think of such groups as a unitary *they*. We tend to call to mind an image of such groups in which all members think alike, act alike, even look alike. We also tend to assume that the members of an outgroup are more similar to one another than those of us in our ingroup are. *They* all think, act, and look alike. *We*, on the other hand, are a remarkably varied lot. This tendency is called the **outgroup homogeneity effect**. The effect can be seen in different perspectives on Latin America. Anglo-Americans often lump all "Latinos" together, regardless of whether they're from Mexico, Nicaragua, Puerto Rico, or Chile. Meanwhile, Chileans, Puerto Ricans, Nicaraguans, and Mexicans see a great many important differences between the residents of their countries (Huddy & Virtanen, 1995).

One study examined the outgroup homogeneity effect by showing Princeton and Rutgers students a series of videos of other students making decisions, such as whether to listen to rock or classical music or whether to wait alone or with other participants during a break in an experiment (Quattrone & Jones, 1980). Half the participants were told the students on the video were from Princeton; half were told they were from Rutgers. Afterward, the participants estimated the percentage of students at the same university who would make the same choices as those they had seen on the video. The results indicated that the participants assumed more similarity among outgroup members than among ingroup members. Princeton students who thought they had witnessed the behavior of a Rutgers student were willing to generalize that behavior to other Rutgers students. In contrast, Princeton students who thought they had witnessed the behavior of a Princeton student were less willing to generalize. The opposite was true for Rutgers students. People see more variability of habit and opinion among members of the ingroup than they do among members of the outgroup (Quattrone & Jones, 1980; see also Bartsch, Judd, Louw, Park, & Ryan, 1997; Linville, Fischer, & Salovey, 1989; Ostrom & Sedikides, 1992; Park & Judd, 1990; Read & Urada, 2003; Simon et al., 1990).

outgroup homogeneity effect The tendency for people to assume that within-group similarity is much stronger for outgroups than for ingroups.

It's easy to understand why the outgroup homogeneity effect occurs. For one thing, we typically have much more contact with members of our own ingroup than with outgroup members, so we have more opportunity to encounter evidence of divergent opinions and habits among ingroup members. Indeed, sometimes *all* we know about an outgroup is what its stereotypical characteristics are reputed to be. But having more interactions with the ingroup is only half the story. The *nature* of the interactions we have with ingroup and outgroup members is likely to be different as well. Because we share the same group membership, we don't treat an ingroup member as a representative of a group. It's the person's individual likes, dislikes, talents, and shortcomings that are front and center. Not so with outgroup members. We often treat an outgroup member merely as a representative of a group, so the person's unique characteristics recede into the background. If we think members of that group are all alike, we're more inclined to behave toward all of them in the same way—thereby eliciting the same kind of behavior from all of them.

The expression "they all look alike" finds support in research that examines people's ability to distinguish faces of members of their own and other races. White people are better at recognizing white faces, black people are better at recognizing black faces, Hispanics are better at recognizing Hispanic faces, and both the young and the old are better at recognizing faces from their own age-group (Devine & Malpass, 1985; Platz & Hosch, 1988; Wright & Stroud, 2002). This **own-race identification bias** appears to result from the fact that people interact with members of their own race as individuals, without thinking about race, and so the individual features of the person in question are processed more deeply. When interacting with someone from another race, part of one's attention is drawn to the person's race, taking away from the processing of the person's individuating characteristics (Hugenberg, Miller, & Claypool, 2007).

own-race identification bias
The tendency for people to be better able to recognize and distinguish faces from their own race than from other races.

Automatic and Controlled Processing

Some of the cognitive processes that give rise to stereotyping and prejudice are deliberate, mindful, and conscious—in other words, controlled. Subtyping ("He doesn't count because...") is often a conscious process (Devine & Baker, 1991; Kunda & Oleson, 1995; Weber & Crocker, 1983). Other cognitive processes, however, give rise to stereotyping and prejudice rapidly and automatically, without much conscious attention and elaboration. This is particularly likely to be the case for distinctiveness-based illusory correlations and the outgroup homogeneity effect discussed earlier.

In the past 30 years, researchers have explored the interplay of automatic and controlled processes (see Chapter 4) and how they collectively influence the way people react to members of different groups (Bodenhausen, Macrae, & Sherman, 1999; Devine & Monteith, 1999; Fazio & Olson, 2003; Sherman et al., 2008; Sritharan & Gawronski, 2010; Wittenbrink, 2004). This research has shown that our reactions to different groups of people are, to a surprising degree, guided by quick and automatic mental processes that we can override but not eliminate. The findings also highlight the common discrepancy between our immediate, reflexive reactions to outgroup members and our more reflective responses.

Patricia Devine (1989b) examined the joint operation of these automatic and controlled processes by investigating the schism that exists for many people between their knowledge of racial stereotypes and their own beliefs and attitudes toward those same groups. More specifically, Devine sought to demonstrate that what separates prejudiced and nonprejudiced people is not their knowledge of derogatory stereotypes, but whether they resist those stereotypes. To carry out her investigation, Devine relied on the distinction between controlled processes, which we direct more consciously, and automatic processes, which we do not consciously control. The activation of stereotypes is typically an automatic process; thus, stereotypes can be triggered even if we don't want them to be. Even a nonprejudiced person will, under the right circumstances, access an association between, say, Muslims and fanaticism, blacks and criminality, and WASPs and emotional repression, because those associations are present in our culture. Whereas a bigot will endorse or employ such stereotypes, a nonprejudiced person will employ more controlled cognitive processes to discard or suppress them—or at least try to.

To test these ideas, Devine selected groups of high- and low-prejudiced participants on the basis of their scores on the Modern Racism Scale (Devine, 1989b). To show that these two groups don't differ in their automatic processing of stereotypical information—that is, that the same stereotypes are triggered in both high-prejudiced and low-prejudiced people—she presented each participant with

SHARED STEREOTYPES
Nearly everyone, prejudiced or not, shares common stereotypes (that they may or may not try to suppress). In these photos, you may have associated the basketball with the black man, the computer with the Asian student, and the explosion with the Muslim, even though they weren't aligned in this presentation.

a set of words, one at a time, so briefly that the words could not be consciously identified. Some of them saw neutral words (*number, plant, remember*) and others saw words stereotypically associated with blacks (*welfare, jazz, busing*). Devine hypothesized that although the stereotypical words were presented too briefly to be consciously recognized, they would nonetheless prime the participants' stereotypes of blacks. To test this hypothesis, she presented the participants with a written description of an individual who acted in an ambiguously hostile manner (a feature of the African-American stereotype). In one incident, for example, the person refused to pay his rent until his apartment was repaired. Was he being needlessly belligerent or appropriately assertive? The results indicated that he was seen as more hostile—and more negative overall—by participants who had earlier been primed by words designed to activate stereotypes of blacks (words such as *jazz*, it's important to note, that are not otherwise connected to the concept of hostility). Most importantly, this result was found equally for prejudiced and nonprejudiced participants. Because the words activated their stereotypes unconsciously, the nonprejudiced participants were unable to suppress the automatic processing of stereotypical information.

To demonstrate that prejudiced and nonprejudiced people differ primarily in their *controlled* cognitive processes, if not in their automatic cognitive processes, Devine next asked her participants to list characteristics of black Americans (Devine, 1989b). As predicted, the prejudiced participants listed many more negative characteristics stereotypically associated with blacks than did nonprejudiced participants. Thus, even though both prejudiced and nonprejudiced people may know the same negative stereotypes of black Americans (as shown in the first part of Devine's study), those who are prejudiced believe them and are sometimes willing to voice those beliefs, whereas those who are not prejudiced reject them.

Other studies of people's automatic reactions to members of stigmatized groups are quite disturbing. In a study by Keith Payne (2001), participants had to decide as quickly as possible whether an object depicted in a photo was a handgun or a hand tool, such as pliers. Each photograph was immediately preceded by a picture of either an African-American face or a white face. The participants (all of whom were white) were faster to identify a weapon as a weapon when it was preceded by an African-American face and faster to identify a hand tool as a hand tool when it was preceded by a white face (**Figure 11.8**, see p. 394).

Do these results mean that the white participants exhibited automatic *prejudice* toward African-Americans? In other words, was the recognition of handguns facilitated by African-American faces because the white participants have negative attitudes about both handguns and African-Americans? Or are these results due to automatic *stereotyping*? In other words, is the facilitation caused by a stereotypical association between handguns and African-Americans that is activated even in people who don't actually hold prejudiced attitudes toward African-Americans?

The good news (limited, perhaps, but good news nonetheless) is that it appears to be the latter. Charles Judd, Irene Blair, and Kristine Chapleau (2004) replicated Payne's experiment with four types of stimuli that varied in whether they were viewed positively or negatively and whether they were stereotypically associated with African-Americans. Specifically, the stimuli associated with African-Americans consisted of pictures of handguns (negative) and sports equipment (positive), and the stimuli not associated with African-Americans consisted of pictures of insects (negative) and fruit (positive). Judd and his colleagues found that

**FIGURE 11.8
STEREOTYPES AND
CATEGORIZATION**
In this study, culturally shared stereotypes of African-Americans led white
participants to identify handguns more
quickly if they had been primed by an
African-American face and hand tools
more quickly if they had been primed
by a white face.
Source: Adapted from Payne, 2001.

African-American faces facilitated the recognition of both positive and negative
stereotypical items (handguns and sports equipment), but not the nonstereotypi-
cal items (insects and fruits), regardless of whether they were positive or negative.

A similar conclusion emerges from studies with even more chilling implications
for the everyday lives of African-Americans
(**Box 11.3**, p. 397). This research was inspired
by the tragic death of Amadou Diallo, a black
West African immigrant who in 1999 was
shot 19 times by police officers who later said
they thought, incorrectly, that he was reaching for a gun—a tragedy echoed in many of
the shootings of African-Americans that have
given birth to the Black Lives Matter movement. In these studies, participants watch
a video game in which, at unpredictable
moments, a target individual—sometimes
white, sometimes black—pops up out of
nowhere holding either a gun or some other
object (Correll, Park, Judd, & Wittenbrink, 2002; Correll, Urland, & Ito, 2006;
Ma & Correll, 2011; Payne, 2006). Participants are instructed to "shoot" by
pressing one key if the person is holding a gun and to press a different response
key if he is not. Because participants are instructed to respond as quickly as possible, they are bound to make occasional mistakes. And, as **Figure 11.9** shows,
they tend to treat black and white targets differently. In this study, participants
made both types of mistakes—shooting an unarmed target and not shooting
an armed target—equally often when the target individual was white. But for
black targets, participants were much more likely to make the mistake of shooting if the target was unarmed than failing to shoot if the target was armed. This
effect is especially pronounced when the background (for example, on a darkened street) is itself threatening (Correll, Wittenbrink, Park, Judd, & Goyle,
2011) and when the black individuals depicted in the video game have more

**THE DIRE COST OF
STEREOTYPING AND REACTING
AUTOMATICALLY**
White police officers in New York City
attempted to question Amadou Diallo,
a black West African immigrant who
had gone outside his apartment building to get some air and who seemed to
fit the description of the serial rapist
they were looking for. Diallo ran up the
steps of his building and then reached
inside his jacket for what police
believed was a gun but was actually his
wallet. Reacting out of fear that Diallo
was about to start firing a weapon, the
four policemen fired 41 shots, striking the innocent Diallo 19 times and
killing him.

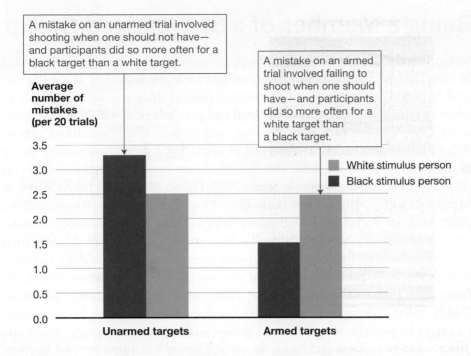

A mistake on an unarmed trial involved shooting when one should not have—and participants did so more often for a black target than a white target.

A mistake on an armed trial involved failing to shoot when one should have—and participants did so more often for a white target than a black target.

Average number of mistakes (per 20 trials)

White stimulus person
Black stimulus person

Unarmed targets   Armed targets

FIGURE 11.9
AUTOMATIC STEREOTYPING AND PREJUDICE
Participants were shown images of an armed or unarmed individual who appeared suddenly on a computer screen. They were told to respond as quickly as possible by pressing one button to "shoot" an armed individual and another button if the individual was unarmed.
Source: Adapted from Correll et al., 2002

stereotypical African features (Ma & Correll, 2011). Notably, the same effect was obtained in a follow-up experiment with African-American participants. This effect has also been observed in participants' decisions about whether to "shoot" men or women wearing an Islamic headdress (Unkelbach, Forgas, & Denson, 2008).

Prolonged experience with these sorts of shoot/don't shoot decisions, either through laboratory exposure or real-world police training and experience, seems to diminish the tendency to shoot unarmed blacks more than unarmed whites, but the reaction time differences (faster to decide to shoot an armed black person and not to shoot an unarmed white person) tend to persist (Correll et al., 2007; Glaser, 2014; Payne, 2006; Plant & Peruche, 2005; Plant, Peruche, & Butz, 2005).

← LOOKING BACK

Consistent with the cognitive perspective, stereotypes help us make sense of the world and process information efficiently, freeing us to use cognitive resources for other work. But they can also cause us to make many errors, as when we form distinctiveness-based illusory correlations. Stereotypes also influence how events are interpreted, and they endure because people act toward members of certain groups in ways that encourage the very behavior they expect (self-fulfilling prophecies). Our expectations of what a group of people is like can lead us to process information in ways that make stereotypes resistant to disconfirmation, as we explain away information that violates a stereotype and subtype members of a group who don't fit the stereotype. We also tend to see outgroup members as more homogeneous than they actually are. Stereotypes can result from both automatic and controlled processing. Even people who don't express prejudicial views may reflexively respond to individuals on the basis of their unconscious stereotypes and prejudices.

Being a Member of a Stigmatized Group

So far, this chapter has focused on the perpetrators of prejudice—who, it should be clear by now, can be presumed to include all of us. But what about the victims of prejudice—members of stigmatized groups? They pay an unfair price in terms of numerous indicators of material and psychological well-being—health, wealth, employment prospects, housing options, and longevity, among others. What's more, members of stereotyped or stigmatized groups are usually aware of the stereotypes others hold, and this awareness can have negative effects on them as well (Crocker, Major, & Steele, 1998; Herek, 1998; Inzlicht, Aronson, & Mendoza-Denton, 2009; Jones et al., 1984; Pinel, 1999; Shelton, Alegre, & Son, 2010; Shelton, Richeson, & Salvatore, 2005). These effects include increased stress, diminished psychological well-being, greater incidence of diseases such as hypertension and diabetes, and greater engagement in unhealthy behavior such as smoking, poor nutrition, and missing doctor appointments (Meyer & Frost, 2013; Pascoe & Smart Richman, 2009; Schmitt, Branscombe, Postmes, & Garcia, 2014). We focus here on three burdens that come with knowing others might be prejudiced against one's group: attributional ambiguity, stereotype threat, and the psychological costs of concealing one's identity.

Attributional Ambiguity

To function effectively, people need to understand the causes of events happening around them. But this understanding is threatened for members of stigmatized groups because they can't always tell whether their experiences have the same causes as those of members of the ingroup or the majority or whether their experiences are instead the result of prejudice. They suffer from attributional ambiguity—not knowing the underlying causes of what they experience: "Did my officemate get the promotion instead of me because I'm Latino?" "Would the state trooper have pulled me over if I were white?" Questions like these can be distressing even when it comes to positive outcomes: "Did I get that fellowship because I'm African-American?" When someone has to wonder whether an accomplishment is the product of an affirmative action policy, it can be difficult to completely "own" it and reap the full measure of pride it would ordinarily afford.

In one study that examined this type of attributional predicament, African-American and white students received flattering or unflattering feedback from a white student in an adjacent room (Crocker, Voelkl, Testa, & Major, 1991). Half the participants were led to assume that the white student could see them through a one-way mirror, and half thought they couldn't be seen because a blind covered the mirror. Whether or not they could be seen had no effect on how white students reacted to the feedback, but it did affect how black students reacted. When black students thought the other person could *not* see them—and therefore didn't know their race—their self-esteem went down from the unflattering feedback and was boosted by the positive feedback. When they thought the other person *could* see them, in contrast, their self-esteem was not injured by the bad news (presumably because they did not know whether to attribute the negative feedback to their own failings or to the other's prejudice), nor was it enhanced by the good news (presumably because they did not know whether to attribute the positive feedback to their own skill or to the other's condescension). This study indicates that members

BOX 11.3   FOCUS ON THE LAW

Stereotypical Facial Features and the Death Penalty

The election of Barack Obama as the 44th president of the United States highlights the often ambiguous nature of race. Although the child of a white mother and black father, Obama is almost always referred to as the first African-American president, not the first biracial president. This is no doubt a legacy of the "one-drop rule": historically, individuals were considered black if they had any trace of black ancestry at all. Various Southern states used this standard to back the notorious Jim Crow laws that enforced racial segregation and restricted the rights of blacks. But now that society has moved beyond the one-drop rule, we are left with the difficult issue of "who counts" as black, white, Asian, Hispanic, and so on. Indeed, many biologists question whether racial categories make any sense at all—that is, whether race really exists (Bamshad & Olson, 2003).

The psychology behind the one-drop rule notwithstanding, race-based judgments about others often differ in intensity depending on how much a person's physical features conform to a stereotype. African-American faces with more stereotypically African features (darker skin, fuller lips, more flared nostrils) elicit prejudiced reactions more readily than faces with less stereotypical features (Livingston & Brewer, 2002; Ma & Correll, 2011). Furthermore, both black and white individuals with more stereotypically African features are assumed to have traits associated with common stereotypes of African-Americans (Blair, Judd, Sadler, & Jenkins, 2002). In the most consequential manifestation of this tendency, both black and white convicts with stereotypically African features tend to receive harsher sentences than those with less stereotypically African features (Blair, Judd, & Chapleau, 2004), and blacks accused of capital crimes are more likely to end up on death row if they have stereotypically African features (Eberhardt, Davies, Purdie-Vaughns, & Johnson, 2006). Moreover, testifying to the utility of the motivational perspective on stereotyping and prejudice, people are more likely to categorize ambiguous faces as black when they are primed with thoughts of economic scarcity (Krosch & Amodio, 2014; Rodeheffer, Hill, & Lord, 2012).

of stigmatized groups live in a less certain world, not knowing to what cause they can attribute their experience.

Stereotype Threat

An extensive program of research initiated by Claude Steele and his colleagues highlights a second difficulty for members of stigmatized groups (Steele, 1997; Steele, Spencer, & Aronson, 2002). Their performance can be impaired by **stereotype threat**, the fear that they will confirm the stereotypes others have about them and their group. In one study, researchers examined the effect on women's math test scores of bringing to mind the stereotype that women don't perform as well as men in mathematics (Spencer, Steele, & Quinn, 1999). In one condition, participants were told there was no gender difference on a particular test they were about to take. Other participants were told that there was a gender difference in favor of men. As **Figure 11.10** (see p. 398) shows, men and women performed equivalently when they thought there was no gender difference on the test, but women performed worse than men when they thought there was a gender difference.

It's not necessary to blatantly invoke stereotype threat for it to have an effect. Michael Inzlicht and Talia Ben-Zeev (2000) had female undergraduates take a math test in the company of either two other women or two men—they did not say a word about any gender differences on the test. Nonetheless, those who took the test with other women got 70 percent of the problems correct on average. Those who took the test with men got 55 percent correct on average.

stereotype threat The fear of confirming the stereotypes that others have about one's group.

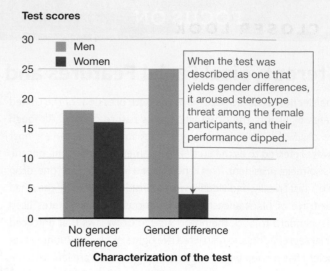

Test scores

When the test was described as one that yields gender differences, it aroused stereotype threat among the female participants, and their performance dipped.

Men
Women

No gender difference   Gender difference
Characterization of the test

**FIGURE 11.10
STEREOTYPE THREAT AND PERFORMANCE**
This study shows the performance of men and women on a math test when they thought the test tapped gender differences and when they did not.
Source: Adapted from Spencer et al., 1999.

In another study, Claude Steele and Joshua Aronson examined the sensitivity to stereotype threat on the part of African-American students (Steele & Aronson, 1995). Playing on a stereotype that questions blacks' intellectual ability, they gave black and white college students a difficult verbal test taken from the Graduate Record Exam. Half the students were led to believe that the test could measure their intellectual ability, and half were told that the investigators were in the early stages of developing the test and that nothing could be learned about intellectual ability from the participants' scores. This information had no effect on the performance of white students. In contrast, the African-American students did as well as the white students when they thought it was the test that was being tested, but they performed much worse than the white students when they thought their intellectual ability was being tested. Again, a blatant manipulation was not required to produce a significant effect on the performance of African-Americans: even without directly priming any stereotypes about African-Americans' intellectual performance, the African-American students still felt the effects of that pervasive stereotype, and it affected their scores accordingly. In a follow-up study, it was enough simply to have participants indicate their race at the top of the page to cause African-American students' performance to be worse than in a control condition in which they did not indicate their race (Steele & Aronson, 1995).

It seems that no one is safe from stereotype threat. Another research team showed that the math performance of white males deteriorated when they were reminded of Asian proficiency in math (Aronson et al., 1999). And in a particularly clever experiment, Jeff Stone and his colleagues had college students perform a laboratory golf task described as a measure of "natural athletic ability," "sports intelligence," or "sports psychology" (Stone, Lynch, Sjomeling, & Darley, 1999). White and black students performed equally well in the "sports psychology" condition. But black students performed significantly worse when it was described as a test of "sports intelligence," and white students performed worse when it was described as a test of "natural athletic ability." In still another telling study, Asian-American women did worse on a math test than control participants when their gender was made salient, but better than control participants when their race was highlighted (Shih, Pittinsky, & Ambady, 1999).

Reducing Racial Disparities in the U.S. School System

A well-documented achievement gap is evident in the American educational system: Black students are more likely to be suspended or expelled and less likely to graduate than their White peers. Further studies have shown strong links between suspension rates and dropout rates, and between drop-out rates and incarceration rates. In other words, disparities in the discipline of Black and White students can have lifetime implications. Racial bias among teachers may be part of the reason for these differences, but recent research shows that fostering empathy in teachers can reduce suspension rates among all racial groups.

For Critical Thinking

1. How do rates of suspension differ for White and Black students between their first and second infractions? How might these differences be linked to what you've learned about stereotyping?

2. How might disparities in punishment for Black and White students affect how Black students feel about themselves? Incorporate what you've learned about attributional ambiguity, stereotype threat, and self-fulfilling prophecies.

Suspensions per Racial Group

Not only are Black students disproportionately likely to be suspended, but the Black-White racial disparity gets more extreme with more discipline.

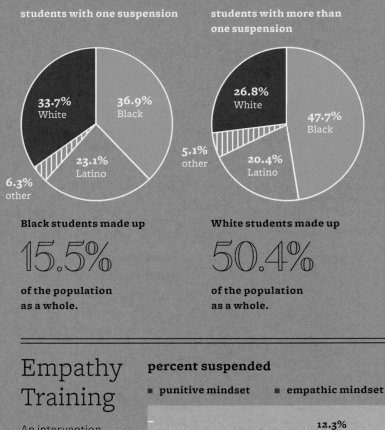

students with one suspension

- 33.7% White
- 36.9% Black
- 23.1% Latino
- 6.3% other

students with more than one suspension

- 26.8% White
- 47.7% Black
- 20.4% Latino
- 5.1% other

Black students made up

15.5%

of the population as a whole.

White students made up

50.4%

of the population as a whole.

Empathy Training

An intervention involving empathic-mindset training for teachers decreased suspension rates among all racial groups.

percent suspended

- ■ punitive mindset
- ■ empathic mindset

	all students	White & Asian	Black & Latino
punitive mindset	9.8%	9.5%	12.3%
empathic mindset	4.6%	3.3%	6.3%

punitive mindset

- He'd be given **one warning**.
- He'd be **sent to the hall.**
- He'd be **sent to the office.**

empathic mindset

- I'd **talk to the student** privately.
- I'd see if **rearranging desks** would help.
- I'd **try to understand** the problem and address it.

Sources: Suspensions per Racial Group: Civil Rights Data Collection, 2017; Empathy Training: Okonofua, Paunesku, & Walton, 2016.

Stereotype threat appears to undermine performance in a number of ways. Stereotype threat leads to increased arousal, which can directly interfere with performance on complex tasks (see Chapter 12; Ben-Zeev, Fein, & Inzlicht, 2005) and serve as a source of distraction that interferes with concentration on the task at hand (Cheryan & Bodenhausen, 2000). Furthermore, knowing that one's group is "suspect" in the eyes of others tends to elicit negative thinking (Cadinu, Maass, Rosabianca, & Kiesner, 2005). This can both directly undermine performance and lead individuals to "play it safe" by being more obsessed with avoiding failure than striving for success (Seibt & Forster, 2004). In accordance with the idea that stereotypes affect health, stereotype threats to women's math performance have been shown to increase physiological markers of increased stress (John-Henderson, Rheinschmidt, & Mendoza-Denton, 2015).

Although all people are vulnerable to some type of stereotype threat based on their group memberships, Steele (1997) maintains that the vulnerability of African-Americans has particular potential for damage. Stereotype threat can result in poorer overall academic performance, which undermines confidence, rendering the individual still more susceptible to stereotype threat. This vicious cycle can result in "disidentification" from academic pursuits, as students who feel the threat most acutely often opt out of academics altogether and identify other areas in which to invest their talent and energy and from which to derive their self-esteem. The same process appears to play a role in the underrepresentation of women in STEM (science, technology, engineering, and mathematics) fields (Deemer, Lin, & Soto, 2015; Walton, et al., 2015). Fortunately, social psychologists have developed a number of low-cost, highly effective interventions that can help deal with the debilitating effects of stereotype threat in schools (see Application Module 3).

The Cost of Concealment

Australia is known for its powerhouse Olympic swimming teams, but no Aussie swimmer has had a bigger hold on the country's imagination than Ian Thorpe. Nicknamed "the Thorpedo" for the speed and grace with which he cut through the water, Thorpe won five Olympic gold medals in his career. Throughout his career, Thorpe was dogged by rumors that he was gay, rumors he steadfastly denied. "You know, I'm a little bit different to what most people would consider being an Australian male. That doesn't make me gay. I mean I'm straight, so people want to claim me as part of a minority group and put labels on you and that's not what I'm about, and I don't understand why people are like that" (Magnay, 2002). After retiring from swimming, however, Thorpe announced during a television interview that he was in fact gay.

Sadly, Ian Thorpe's experience is not unusual. Members of stigmatized groups throughout history have often felt compelled to hide their true identity. LGBTQ individuals have often chosen to remain "in the closet," light-skinned blacks have sometimes tried to "pass" as white, and many older adults get plastic surgery, tummy tucks, and toupees in an effort to hide their true age. The ubiquity of such underground experiences makes one wonder what sort of toll they exact.

A big one, it turns out. Physically, the concealment of sexual orientation is associated with cardiovascular stress, and gay men who conceal their sexual orientation show more rapid progression of HIV symptoms (Cole, Kemeny, Taylor, & Visscher, 1996; Pérez-Benítez, O'Brien, Carels, Gordon, & Chiros, 2007).

Psychologically, being "out of the closet" is associated with a variety of indicators of better mental health, including reduced depression, less anger, and higher self-esteem (Legate, Ryan, & Weinstein, 2012; Miranda & Storms, 1989; Ross, 1990; Szymanski, Chung, & Balsam, 2001).

Concealment can also take a cognitive toll. In one study, researchers Clayton Critcher and Melissa Ferguson instructed half the participants to conceal their sexual orientation during a mock interview while the control participants were free to say whatever they wanted (Critcher & Ferguson, 2013). The investigators predicted that the act of concealment would be mentally taxing, making them less able to perform well on subsequent tasks. Indeed, across several experiments, they found that those asked to conceal their sexual orientation did less well on tests of spatial ability, self-control, and physical stamina. Concealing an important part of oneself is demanding, and meeting those demands can have unfortunate consequences down the road.

← LOOKING BACK

Victims of stereotyping can suffer attributional ambiguity, not knowing whether others' feedback on their performance is genuine or based on their group membership. They can suffer from stereotype threat, performing worse than they would otherwise because they are afraid of confirming a stereotype that exists about their group. Members of some minority groups feel compelled to try to cover up their minority status, an effort that can exact a physical and psychological toll.

Reducing Stereotypes, Prejudice, and Discrimination

This chapter began with a discussion of the progress that's been made in intergroup relations in the United States and across much of the globe—and how much farther we must go to achieve true equality of opportunity for everyone. What has contributed to the improvements we've witnessed thus far, and what principles can we draw on to advance even more?

Many factors, including specific legal interventions and broad economic developments, have brought about improved relations between LGBTQ and straight people, blacks and whites, Latinos and Anglos, and numerous other groups. One factor that is both cause and consequence of these developments is the increased daily interactions between members of different groups. When people interact frequently, it becomes easier to see people as individuals, rather than representatives of particular groups. As Barack Obama said in his 2008 inaugural address, "As the world grows smaller, our common humanity shall reveal itself."

Individual Approaches to Prejudice Reduction

What, then, are the most effective ways to make "our common humanity" clear to one and all? Some efforts to improve intergroup relations are didactic: they use the media or school programs to promote acceptance of outgroups or to convince individuals that their peers frown on the endorsement of unfounded or overly broad stereotypes, the expression of prejudice, and the perpetuation of discrimination. These efforts are often met with resistance because people don't hold their beliefs and prejudices in isolation; they belong to social groups that pressure them back to their old ways of thinking. Nevertheless, laboratory studies aimed at convincing participants that the prevailing norms favor outgroup tolerance have been shown to be effective in reducing stereotypes of stigmatized groups, at least in the short term (Monteith, Deneen, & Tooman, 1996; Stangor, Sechrist, & Jost, 2001). Outside the laboratory, school reading programs designed to promote greater acceptance of outgroups have also enjoyed some success (Clunies-Ross & O'Meara, 1989; Hughes, Bigler, & Levy, 2007). In one study, for example, British schoolchildren were randomly assigned, during story hour over a six-week period, to listen to and discuss stories about friendships between disabled and nondisabled children or to stories unrelated to disabilities. The children who read about disabled children later expressed more favorable attitudes and a greater willingness to interact with the disabled (Cameron & Rutland, 2006). Venturing further still from the laboratory, a year-long field experiment in Rwanda found that a radio soap opera could be effectively used to heal the scars of ethnic conflict (in this case, between the Hutus and Tutsis). Rwandans who were exposed to the soap opera were more open to intermarriage between Hutus and Tutsis and more in favor of putting the past trauma behind them compared with those exposed to a control soap opera (Paluck, 2009).

Intergroup Approaches to Prejudice Reduction

Until the late stages of World War II, soldiers in the U.S. Army were racially segregated. Black soldiers were relegated to combat support roles such as cooks, quartermasters, and grave diggers. Segregation remained official army policy until 1948, but in 1944, black soldiers who volunteered for combat duty were allowed to fight alongside white soldiers in battalions consisting of one all-black platoon and three all-white platoons. Concerned about the influence of this (modest) integration policy on morale, the army commissioned a survey of white soldier's attitudes. The results were striking: Those who actually served in (semi) integrated units expressed little resistance to the idea of fighting alongside their black countrymen—a sentiment that was not shared by white soldiers who remained in entirely segregated battalions (Stouffer, Suchman, DeVinney, Star, & Williams, 1949).

contact hypothesis The proposition that prejudice can be reduced by putting members of majority and minority groups in frequent contact with one another.

These results led to early optimism about the **contact hypothesis**, the idea that prejudice would be reduced if members of minority and majority groups were in frequent contact with one another. But it turns out that simple contact between different groups is not a magic solution to the problem of intergroup conflict. Numerous studies examined the effect of the U.S. Supreme Court's desegregation decision in *Brown v. the Board of Education of Topeka* (1954) on race relations in American schools, and the results were not encouraging. One review of the literature found that a majority of the studies observed an *increase* in prejudice after schools were integrated (Stephan, 1986).

Not an encouraging finding, to be sure, but given what we learned from the Robbers Cave study, not a surprising finding either. After all, simply bringing the Rattlers and Eagles together did not reduce the animosity between the two groups. As that study suggested and subsequent research has confirmed, contact between different groups is likely to be more positive and more productive if certain conditions are met. First, the groups need to have equal status. If one group feels superior and the other resentful, then harmonious, productive interactions are not likely to be the norm. Second, as in the Robbers Cave study, productive intergroup interactions can occur if the different groups have a shared goal that requires mutual cooperation (a superordinate goal), thereby promoting a common ingroup identity (Gaertner & Dovidio, 2000, 2009; Nier, Gaertner, Dovidio, Banker, & Ward, 2001; West, Pearson, Dovidio, Shelton, & Trail, 2009). That's no doubt a big part of why racial integration of the military and later the acceptance of gay and lesbian soldiers have proceeded relatively smoothly. Soldiers face a common, deadly enemy and must depend on one another for their very survival. Sports teams also face a common foe, and many people have noted that sports have also been effective in tearing down barriers between groups. In one notable study, Kendrick Brown and his colleagues examined the racial attitudes of white athletes at 24 colleges and universities in the United States and found a positive correlation between their attitudes toward blacks and the percentage of minority players they had on their high school teams. But testifying once again to the importance of interdependent action, this was only true for athletes in true team sports like basketball and soccer, not in largely individual sports like swimming and track (Brown, Brown, Jackson, Sellers, & Manuel, 2003). And as we saw in Box 11.2, making school assignments more cooperative and interdependent promotes more favorable attitudes between different ethnic and racial groups.

A third condition that's been shown to be important for promoting positive intergroup relations is community support: a community's broader social norms must support intergroup contact. If children of different races, religions, and ethnicities go to school with one another but their parents send them begrudgingly and rarely miss an opportunity to speak ill of the "other" children, the students themselves are unlikely to reach out across group boundaries. On the other hand, merely knowing that someone in one's group is friends with a member of an outgroup—which strengthens perceived social support for contact with the outgroup—is sufficient to reduce stereotyping and outgroup denigration (Wright, Aron, McLaughlin-Volpe, & Ropp, 1997). Finally, intergroup contact should encourage one-on-one interactions between members of the different groups. Doing so puts each person's identity as an individual in the foreground and downplays a person's group membership.

An analysis of numerous studies of the effect of desegregation, involving tens of thousands of students in over 25 countries, found that when most of these conditions are met, contact between members of different groups does indeed tend to be effective in reducing prejudice (Pettigrew & Tropp, 2000, 2006, 2008). In a different study, university students who were assigned roommates of a different race reported reduced anxiety about cross-race interactions and registered a significant improvement on implicit measures of attitudes toward the other group (Shook & Fazio, 2008).

The Dimensions of Productive Intergroup Contact

When groups with a history of animosity and conflict have one-on-one contact with one another under conditions of equal status, interdependence, and supportive social norms, three important changes appear to take place that together reduce prejudice. First, people begin to see members of the outgroup as

BOX 11.4 ▶ **FOCUS ON** APPLIED SOCIAL PSYCHOLOGY

Conflict Remediation

Research by social psychologists on the contact hypothesis has inspired numerous efforts to reduce intergroup hostility by bringing together people from groups with a history of conflict. For example, programs have been designed to improve relations between Israelis and Palestinians. Seeds of Peace, for example, is a program that brings groups of Israeli and Palestinian teenagers to the United States for a three-week summer camp experience in which they (like the Robbers Cave participants) tackle a variety of challenges that can only be met if everyone cooperates. Campers are also encouraged to "make one friend" with someone from the other group of kids.

Do these types of coexistence programs work? To find out, Juliana Schroeder and Jane Risen surveyed four sets of Seeds of Peace campers, 279 in all, before camp began, as it ended, and more than nine months later (Schroeder & Risen, 2014).

The participants described their attitudes toward the Israelis and Palestinians they met at camp and toward Israelis and Palestinians in general, and they indicated whether they had made any friends from the other group at camp. The researchers found that living together for three weeks led to attitudes at the end of camp that were more mutually favorable, and more favorable toward each other's ethnic group, than they were at the beginning.

Some of this positive feeling ebbed when the teenagers returned to their homes in the Middle East. But not all of it: attitudes more than nine months later were still more favorable than they had been at the beginning of camp. The investigators also found that forming a friendship with someone from the other group was a significant predictor of favorable attitudes after the teenagers had gone back to their normal lives.

SEEDS OF PEACE When Israeli and Palestinian teenagers are brought together for a three-week residential summer camp experience in which they complete a variety of interdependent tasks, their attitudes toward each other, and toward Israelis and Palestinians in general, tend to improve.

individuals rather than as stereotyped, undifferentiated members of a social category, a process psychologists refer to as personalization (Brewer & Miller, 1984). Personalization makes it easier for people to empathize with outgroup members and to think of them as similar to themselves (Ensari, Christian, Kuriyama, & Miller, 2012). Second, in this kind of one-on-one contact, a person's positive feelings for particular outgroup members start to generalize to the outgroup as a whole. That happens when the outgroup members one interacts with are seen as typical of the group in question (that is, the individual members are not subtyped as exceptions) and when the individual members' behavior is not construed in a way that reinforces previous stereotypes about the group (Brown & Hewstone, 2005). Finally, positive intergroup sentiments are solidified when members of both groups come to think of themselves as sharing a common identity (Gaertner, Dovidio, Guerra, Hehman, & Saguy, 2016). Members of sports teams come to think of themselves primarily as teammates, not as white or black teammates. Members of integrated military units come to think of themselves first and foremost as soldiers, not as Muslim, Christian, or Jewish soldiers. This is the "common humanity" that Barack Obama referred to—something that's most likely to "reveal itself" when people of different backgrounds come together with equal status to work on shared goals.

← LOOKING BACK

Contact between members of different groups can go a long way toward reducing group stereotypes and intergroup hostility. Intergroup contact is especially beneficial when members of different groups interact as equals, work together to try to accomplish common goals, and come together on a one-on-one basis, as well as when these interactions are supported by broader societal norms.

Chapter Review

SUMMARY

Theoretical Perspectives

- Three approaches to studying stereotyping, prejudice, and discrimination are the economic perspective, the motivational perspective, and the cognitive perspective.

Characterizing Intergroup Bias

- *Stereotypes* are generalizations about groups that are often applied to individual group members. *Prejudice* involves either a positive or a negative attitude and emotional response to members of a group. *Discrimination* is favorable or unfavorable treatment of an individual because of the person's membership in a specific group.
- Blatant, explicit racism has declined in much of the world in recent times. But *modern racism* is still prevalent, whereby people consciously hold egalitarian attitudes while nonconsciously having negative attitudes and exhibiting more subtle forms of prejudice.
- "Benevolent" racism and sexism consist of attitudes the individual thinks of as favorable toward a group but that have the effect of supporting traditional, subservient roles for members of disadvantaged groups.
- The *implicit association test (IAT)* measures nonconscious attitudes by comparing reaction times when outgroup pictures (or words) and positive items are in the same response category versus when outgroup pictures (or words) and negative items are in the same category. Other implicit measures involve *priming* with a picture of a member of some group right before the participant must either identify different words or rate different stimuli; speeded response times to negative words and delayed response times to positive words reveal negative prejudice, as do lowered ratings of immediately following stimuli.

The Economic Perspective

- One version of the economic perspective is *realistic group conflict theory*, the theory that group conflict, prejudice, and discrimination are likely to arise over competition between groups for limited resources, whether material/economic or cultural/ideological.
- The classic Robbers Cave experiment put two groups of boys in competition at a camp, and soon they were expressing open hostility toward each other. When the groups were brought together in noncompetitive situations where they had to cooperate to achieve shared *superordinate goals*, the hostility dissipated.

The Motivational Perspective

- According to the *motivational perspective*, poor intergroup relations can result simply because there *are* two groups, and an us/them opposition results. This occurs in the *minimal group paradigm*, where members of arbitrarily defined groups favor their fellow group members over members of the other group.
- *Social identity theory* attempts to explain ingroup favoritism, maintaining that self-esteem is derived in part from group membership and group success.

The Cognitive Perspective

- The *cognitive perspective* focuses on stereotypes, which are a form of categorization. People rely on them all the time, but especially when they are tired or overburdened.
- Several construal processes lead to inaccurate stereotypes. People engage in biased information processing, seeing aspects of other groups that confirm common stereotypes and failing to see facts that are inconsistent with them.
- Distinctive groups (because they are in the minority) are often associated with distinctive (rare) behaviors. This *paired distinctiveness* results in attributing false characteristics or tendencies to such groups, creating illusory correlations.
- Erroneous stereotypes can also be unknowingly maintained through self-fulfilling prophecies, when people act toward members of certain groups in ways that encourage the very behavior they expect.
- Contradictory evidence about group members may not change people's ideas about a group because people often consider such evidence an exception that proves the rule. Behavior consistent with a stereotype tends to be attributed to the dispositions of the group members, whereas behavior that is inconsistent with a stereotype is often attributed to the situation.
- People tend to code favorable evidence about ingroup members more abstractly and the same sort of evidence about outgroup members less abstractly and more concretely. The reverse is true for unfavorable evidence.

- People tend to assume that outgroups are more homogeneous than ingroups, leading to the *outgroup homogeneity effect.*
- People sometimes respond to outgroup members reflexively, relying on automatic processes whereby they reveal their prejudice even without being aware of it. Often these automatic reactions can be corrected by conscious, controlled processes.

Being a Member of a Stigmatized Group

- Members of stigmatized groups suffer from attributional ambiguity. They have to ask themselves whether others' negative or positive behavior toward them is due to prejudice or to some factor unrelated to their group membership.

- The performance of members of stigmatized groups can be impaired by *stereotype threat*, the fear that they will confirm others' stereotypes.
- Members of minority groups are sometimes tempted to try to hide their minority group status, an effort that is associated with physical and psychological costs.

Reducing Stereotypes, Prejudice, and Discrimination

- According to the *contact hypothesis*, contact between members of different groups can reduce intergroup hostility, especially if the contact involves one-on-one interactions between individuals of equal status, if it encourages the cooperative pursuit of superordinate goals, and if it is supported by the prevailing norms in each group.

THINK ABOUT IT

1. Is it possible for people to be prejudiced without being aware of it? How have researchers addressed this question, and what evidence have they found?

2. Suppose every year, the male CEO of a small company always asks a female employee to take care of organizing the company's holiday party. When one female employee asks the CEO why he always gives this task to women, he says that women are better party planners than men. Is this an example of sexism? Why or why not? What adverse effects might the CEO's positive stereotype regarding women's party planning ability have on the female employees?

3. Describe the Robbers Cave experiment and outline three important points this study revealed about intergroup relations.

4. Imagine that a conversation about race relations in the United States develops during a family dinner. One of your relatives argues that given how ubiquitous stereotypes are, prejudice and discrimination are inevitable. Using research from the

cognitive perspective, and controlled and automatic processing in particular, how would you respond to this assertion? Are prejudice and discrimination inevitable? Under which conditions are they more likely to emerge?

5. Suppose a woman named Taylor was applying for a job at an accounting firm, and applicants had to complete a math test as part of the onsite interview process. If Taylor met her older male interviewer just prior to taking the math test and he (inappropriately) exclaimed, "You're Taylor? I was expecting, well, a man . . . ," what impact might that have on Taylor's test performance, interview performance, and eventual likelihood of getting the job?

6. Suppose you are a social psychologist and have been hired to help reduce prejudice and discrimination among students of different races, classes, cultures, and sexual orientations in a school system. What might you suggest in addressing this concern?

The **answer guidelines** for the think about it questions can be found at the back of the book . . . ☞

ONLINE STUDY MATERIALS

Want to earn a better grade on your test?

Go to **INQUIZITIVE** to learn and review this chapter's content, with personalized feedback along the way.

407

Why might group decisions have worse consequences than independent thinking?

Is solitary confinement inhumane?

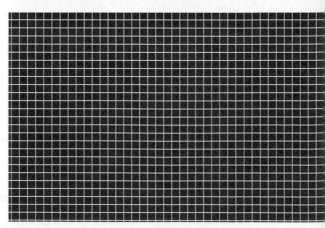

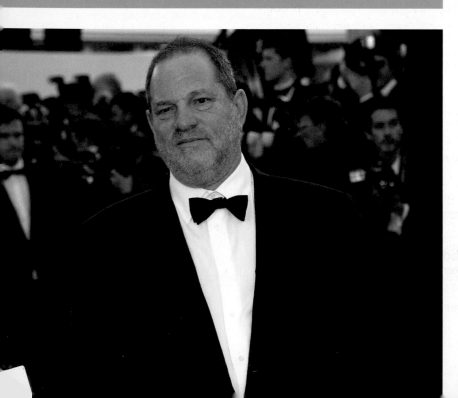

Why would a famous Hollywood producer abuse their position of power?

Groups

TODD ASHKER, A CONVICTED MURDERER, spent over 20 years in the Security Housing Unit, or SHU, in Pelican Bay, a maximum-security prison in fog-filled Crescent City, in Northern California. The idea behind the SHU was to isolate gang members from other gang members (Ashker was a member of the Aryan Brotherhood). In solitary confinement in the SHU, Ashker spent 23 hours a day by himself in a windowless cell about the size of a parking space, often staring at the walls for hours. He could exercise 1 hour a day, by himself, in a moldy, enclosed space, with no clear view of the sky. He could see no other prisoners and received his meals through a slot in the door to his cell. When his family or friends were permitted to visit, he was not allowed to touch them.

When social psychologist Craig Haney first interviewed a sample of SHU prisoners, he found the effects of solitary confinement to be devastating: 70 percent of SHU prisoners showed signs of impending nervous breakdown, 40 percent suffered from hallucinations, and 27 percent had suicidal ideation. One SHU inmate summed it up aptly: "I would rather have gotten the death penalty."

In the despair of solitary confinement, Ashker did something extraordinary: he formed a group with the leaders of rival gangs in cells nearby. Desperate for human contact, prisoners began calling out to one another when in the exercise room. In a series of conversations, the leaders of the rival gangs talked about their parents and grandparents, their children and spouses, their neighborhoods and pasts. They talked about the profound suffering produced by solitary confinement. Moved by these conversations, Ashker and his neighbors called for a truce between the rival gangs. And on July 8, 2013, Ashker led a hunger strike that, through informal word of mouth, involved over 30,000 prisoners in California,

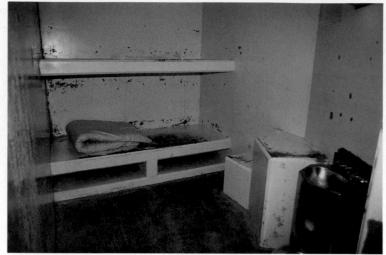

THE IMPORTANCE OF GROUP LIFE
A prison cell (right) and the exercise area (left) in the Security Housing Unit at Pelican Bay.

"No man is an island, entire of itself; every man is a piece of the continent, a part of the main."
—JOHN DONNE, ENGLISH POET

all protesting solitary confinement as a violation of the Eighth Amendment of the Constitution, which prohibits the use of cruel and unusual punishment.

Ashker's efforts inspired a team of lawyers to sue the state of California to free prisoners from solitary confinement in the SHU. The case involved several social psychologists, including an author of this book, who relied on findings you are learning about to make the case that solitary confinement is indeed cruel and unusual punishment: humans have a drive-like need to belong and connect (see Chapter 10); in fact, isolation, exclusion, and rejection activate the pain centers of the brain much as physical harm does, and when humans are deprived of touch, their stress system can go on overdrive. In 2015, the case was settled in favor of the prisoners, and over 2,000 prisoners across California were moved out of solitary confinement.

There are many lessons to be learned from Todd Ashker's experience of solitary confinement. When we are denied the chance to connect and be in groups, we suffer in profound ways. Our humanity is found in group life. ■

The Nature and Purpose of Group Living

What happened to Todd Ashker in the SHU at Pelican Bay speaks to our fundamentally social nature. Humans and all large primates (except orangutans) live in groups, so group life must provide advantages. Today it's recognized that our capacity to form groups has helped us meet many of the challenges of survival and the reproduction of our genes: in groups we provide care for our extremely vulnerable offspring, find protection from predators, enjoy increased efficiency in acquiring and sharing food, and bolster our defense against aggressors. These benefits of group living are so crucial to survival that we have a psychological need to be with others and belong to groups (Baumeister & Leary, 1995; Correll & Park, 2005).

But what, exactly, is a group? This is not an easy question to answer, since there are so many types of groups, and they don't always share many features. The members of a baseball team are clearly a group, but most people wouldn't consider the members of a large lecture course to be a group. Similarly, most people would say that the individuals riding together in an elevator aren't a group. But suppose the elevator breaks down, and those inside must figure out how to escape or summon help. Most would say that the people in the elevator now seem more like a real group. But why?

A group has been described as "a collection of individuals who have relations to one another that make them interdependent to some significant degree" (Cartwright & Zander, 1968, p. 46). Thus, the people in the functioning elevator don't make up a group because they're not interdependent. But once the elevator breaks down and they must decide on joint action (or whether to take joint action), they become interdependent and hence more of a group. There are degrees of interdependence, of course, and therefore degrees of "groupness" (McGrath, 1984). The members of a family are more of a "real" group than are participants in a seminar, and seminar attendees, in turn, are more of a group than are students in a large lecture course. By this reasoning, a nation's citizens make up something of a group, but they are less of a group than the members of a tribe or band, who interact more often and are more directly dependent on one another.

This chapter explores how groups function, how they make decisions, and how group decision making can go wrong. It also examines how people achieve positions of leadership within a group, as well as the effects of power on people. Finally, the chapter explores how orderly groups can devolve into unruly mobs when its members' personal identities are diminished.

Social Facilitation

Let's begin by considering one of the simplest questions about social life: What effect does the presence of other people have on individual performance? Does the presence of others typically help or hinder performance, or does it have no effect at all? To address these questions, let's consider them in more personal and vivid terms. Suppose you're by yourself as you try to perfect a skill—practicing a chord progression on the guitar, mastering a tricky dance move, or working through the intricacies of conjugating French verbs. You feel you're making progress when someone—a perfect stranger, your mother, or even, say, Amy Schumer or W. Kamau Bell—takes a seat nearby and proceeds to observe. What does this other person's presence do to your performance? Does it give you the energy and focus necessary to bring your performance to new heights? Or do you become so nervous and distracted that your performance suffers?

Initial Research

Norman Triplett (1898) is often credited with being the first person to experimentally examine the effect of other people's presence on human performance. Triplett was a bicycling enthusiast (or "wheelman," as they were known at the time). After reviewing speed records put out by the Racing Board of the League of American Wheelmen, Triplett noticed that the fastest times were recorded when cyclists competed directly against one another on the same track at the same time. Slower speed records were obtained when cyclists raced alone against the clock. This observation led Triplett to hypothesize that the presence of others tended to facilitate human performance.

Triplett realized, however, that cycling records did not offer the best test of his hypothesis, so he conducted what is widely considered social psychology's first experiment (Triplett, 1898). He invited a group of 40 children to his laboratory and had them turn a fishing reel as fast as they could. Each child did so on six trials. On three of the trials, the child was alone; on the other three trials, another child was alongside doing the same thing. Under these more controlled conditions, Triplett found that the children tended to turn the reel faster when in the presence of another child engaged in the same activity. The presence of others appeared to facilitate their performance. Research on this subject thus came to be known as **social facilitation** research.

A number of subsequent experiments reinforced Triplett's findings and extended them in two important ways. First, the same effects were obtained when the others were not doing the same thing (that is, not "coacting"), but were merely present as an audience of passive observers (Gates, 1924; Travis, 1925). Second, the same effect was also observed in a vast number of animal species, indicating that the phenomenon is quite general and fundamental. For example, animals as diverse as dogs, fish, armadillos, opossums, and frogs have been shown to eat more when in the presence of other members of the same species than when alone (Boice, Quanty, & Williams, 1974; Platt & James, 1966; Platt, Yaksh, & Darby, 1967; Ross & Ross, 1949; Uematsu, 1970). Ants dig more earth (Chen, 1937), fruit flies do more preening (Connolly, 1968), and centipedes run faster through mazes (Hosey, Wood, Thompson, & Druck, 1985) when together than when alone. For both humans and other animals, then, the presence of others seems to facilitate performance.

But numerous exceptions emerged soon after Triplett's original findings. Floyd Allport (1920), for example, asked undergraduate students to refute philosophical arguments as best they could in a 5-minute period. The students provided higher-quality refutations when working alone than when working in the presence of another student. The presence of others has also been shown to inhibit performance on arithmetic problems, memory tasks, and maze learning (Dashiell, 1930; Pessin, 1933; Pessin & Husband, 1933). And the presence of other members of the same species has sometimes been found to inhibit the performance of nonhuman species (Allee & Masure, 1936; Shelley, 1965; Strobel, 1972).

Resolving the Contradictions

For a time, then, it seemed that the best generalization available about the effect of the presence of others on performance was that it sometimes helps and sometimes hurts—not a terribly satisfying answer. It's about as helpful as an expert saying we might be headed for another economic crash, but then again, we might not. Although that may be all you'd expect from someone trying to predict which

social facilitation Initially a term for enhanced performance in the presence of others; now a broader term for the effect, positive or negative, of the presence of others on performance.

"The bodily presence of another contestant participating in the race serves to liberate latent energy not ordinarily available."

—NORMAN TRIPLETT

SOCIAL FACILITATION AND COMPETITION
Performance is typically enhanced in the presence of others when the activity is well learned, as cycling is for Vincenzo Nibali, of Italy, shown here entering Paris as the winner of Le Tour de France 2014.

way the economy is going, you probably want more from researchers studying a simpler process like social facilitation.

ZAJONC'S THEORY OF MERE PRESENCE Nearly 70 years after Triplett's discovery, social psychologist Robert Zajonc offered an elegant theory to account for the divergent findings on this topic. Zajonc (1965) argued that the presence of others, indeed the *mere* presence of others, tends to facilitate performance on simple or well-learned tasks, but it hinders performance on difficult or novel tasks. Even more importantly, Zajonc's theory explained *why* the presence of others has these effects.

Zajonc's theory has three components (**Figure 12.1**). First, the mere presence of others makes us more aroused. Other people are dynamic and unpredictable stimuli, capable of doing almost anything at any time. We therefore need to be alert, or aroused, in their presence so we can react to what they might do.

Second, arousal tends to make us more rigid and narrowly focused, in the sense that we become even more inclined to do what we're already automatically inclined to do. In the language Zajonc used, arousal makes us more likely to make a **dominant response**. Think of it like this: in any situation, you can respond in a variety of ways, arranged in a hierarchy according to their likelihood of occurrence. Whatever you're most inclined to do in that situation is at the top of the hierarchy and is thus the dominant response. When aroused, Zajonc argued, people are even more inclined to make that dominant response.

The third component of Zajonc's theory specifies that the increase in dominant response tendencies leads to the facilitation of performance on simple tasks and the inhibition of performance on complex tasks. For easy or well-learned tasks, the dominant response is likely to be the correct response. In fact, that's tantamount to what it means for a task to be easy or well learned. Thus, the presence of other people, by facilitating the dominant response, facilitates the correct response and improves performance. In contrast, for difficult or novel tasks, the dominant response is not likely to be the correct response. Again, that's what it

ROBERT B. ZAJONC

dominant response In a person's hierarchy of possible responses in any context, the response that person is most likely to make.

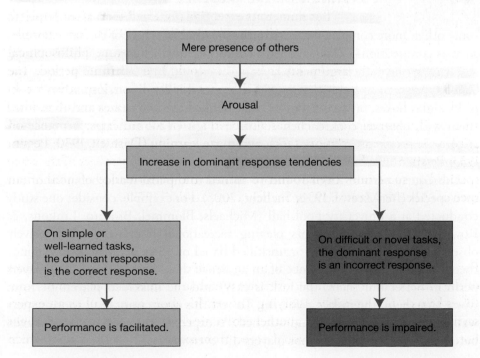

FIGURE 12.1
ZAJONC'S MODEL OF SOCIAL FACILITATION
The presence of others (indeed, their mere presence) increases arousal and facilitates dominant response tendencies. This improves performance on easy or well-learned tasks but hinders performance on difficult or novel tasks.

means for a task to be difficult or novel. Thus, the presence of others facilitates an *incorrect* response and hinders performance.

TESTING THE THEORY Zajonc's theory synthesized the diverse findings that existed at the time and has been tested in a number of studies across species. For example, Zajonc and his colleagues placed cockroaches in the start box of one of two mazes and then shone a light at the start box (Zajonc, Heingartner, & Herman, 1969). Cockroaches instinctively flee from light and head toward a dark area; in this case, the cockroaches would try to reach the dark goal box. In the simple maze (a "runway"), getting to the darkened chamber was easy. The cockroach needed only to do what it does instinctively: run directly away from the light (its dominant response). In contrast, getting to the darkened chamber in the complex maze was more of a challenge: the cockroach had to do more than follow its instincts and flee from the light; it had to execute a turn. Two features of this setup were especially important. First, because cockroaches invariably run from light, doing so is clearly their dominant response. Second, Zajonc created two different conditions: in one, the dominant response led to the goal (the simple maze); in the other, it did not (the complex maze).

Zajonc had the cockroaches run one of these two mazes either alone or with another cockroach. He predicted that cockroaches running the simple maze would get to the goal box more quickly when together than when alone, but that those running the complex maze together would take longer to reach the chamber. That's exactly what happened: the presence of another cockroach facilitated performance on the simple maze but hindered performance on the complex maze (**Figure 12.2**).

COACTING VS. MERE PRESENCE To show that the *mere* presence of another cockroach has these effects—as opposed to some other, more complex factor than the presence of others of the same species, such as competition—Zajonc added a condition in which the cockroach ran the maze not with another cockroach running alongside, but with other cockroaches merely present as a passive "audience." To create this condition, Zajonc built a set of Plexiglas boxes, or "grandstands," that flanked the two mazes and then filled them with observer cockroaches. Again, as Figure 12.2 indicates, the presence of the observing cockroaches facilitated performance on the simple maze but inhibited performance on the complex maze.

Subsequent tests of Zajonc's theory turned to the real-world behavior of our own species (Ben-Zeev, Fein, & Inzlicht, 2005). For example, consider one study conducted at a university pool hall (Michaels, Blommel, Brocato, Linkous, & Rowe, 1982). College students playing recreational pool were unobtrusively observed and deemed skilled or unskilled based on their performance. Zajonc's theory predicts that the presence of an audience should make the skilled players perform better (for them, the task is easy) and the unskilled players perform worse (for them, the task is difficult). To test this prediction, the experimenters walked up to the pool tables and watched. As expected, the good players did even better than before, and the poor players did even worse.

RUBES®   **By Leigh Rubin**

"Why cockroaches give lousy surprise parties."

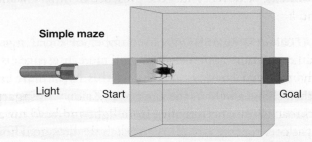

Simple maze

Light   Start   Goal

Complex maze

In the **simple maze**, the cockroach need only follow its dominant response and run directly away from the light to get to the goal.

In the **complex maze**, the cockroach's dominant response does not easily lead it to the goal. The cockroach must execute a turn.

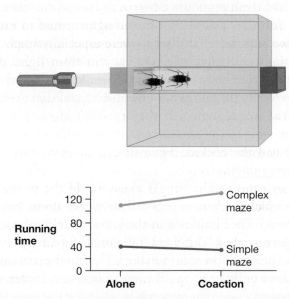

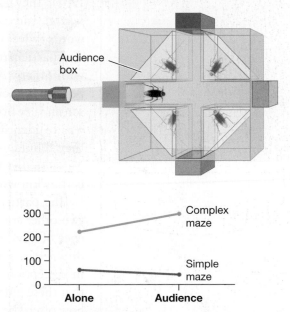

Audience box

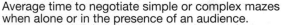

Average time (in seconds) taken by cockroaches to negotiate simple or complex mazes when alone or alongside another cockroach.

Average time to negotiate simple or complex mazes when alone or in the presence of an audience.

FIGURE 12.2
SOCIAL FACILITATION IN ANOTHER SPECIES
For cockroaches, as for humans, the presence of others increases dominant response tendencies, leading to better performance on easy tasks (in this case the simple maze) and worse performance on difficult tasks (the complex maze).
Source: Adapted from Zajonc et al., 1969.

Mere Presence or Evaluation Apprehension?

Zajonc's theory has stood the test of time, with many studies finding that the presence of others tends to facilitate performance on easy tasks and hinders performance on difficult tasks (Thomas, Skitka, Christen, & Jurgena, 2002). One element of Zajonc's theory, however, has been disputed: whether it is the *mere* presence of other people that increases arousal. When most people reflect on why they would be aroused in the presence of others, it's not just their presence that seems decisive. Instead, it's **evaluation apprehension**—a concern about looking bad in the eyes of others, about being evaluated—that seems to be important (Blascovich, Mendes, Hunter, & Salomon, 1999; Cottrell, Wack, Sekerak & Rittle, 1968; Seta & Seta, 1992). Several studies have purported to show that it is only when subjects feel they are being evaluated that they

evaluation apprehension People's concern about how they might appear in the eyes of others, or be evaluated by them.

show arousal and consequent facilitation on easy tasks and impairment on difficult tasks.

TESTING FOR EVALUATION APPREHENSION A number of social psychologists have argued that evaluation apprehension, not mere presence, is the critical element underlying social facilitation. To test this hypothesis experimentally, there must be three conditions: one with the subject performing alone, one with the subject performing in front of an evaluative audience, and one with the subject performing in front of an audience that cannot evaluate the subject's performance. In one such study, the investigators cleverly built "from scratch" a response hierarchy in their participants so they'd know exactly what the dominant and subordinate responses were (Cottrell et al., 1968). They gave the participants a list of ten nonsense words (such as *nansoma*, *paritaf*, and *zabulon*), and had them pronounce two of the ten words once, two words twice, two words 5 times, two words 10 times, and two words 25 times. The participants were thus much more familiar with some of the words than with others. After this initial training phase of the experiment, the test phase began. Participants were told that these same words would be flashed on a screen very briefly (some so briefly they might not be visible) and that their task was to identify each word as it was shown. If they couldn't identify a word, they should guess. Unbeknownst to the participants, none of the target words was actually shown, and they were reduced to guessing on every trial (this task is thus known as a *pseudorecognition test*).

The participants performed this task either (1) alone, (2) in the presence of two other students who watched the proceedings attentively, or (3) in the presence of blindfolded "observers." The blindfolds in the latter, mere presence condition were supposedly to prepare the blindfolded individuals for an experiment in perception, but in reality their purpose was to make it clear to the participants that these individuals could not evaluate them. The researchers were interested in how often the participants gave a dominant response by guessing the most familiar word (those they had pronounced 25 times) and how this rate varied across the three conditions. The results, shown in **Figure 12.3**, highlight the importance

FIGURE 12.3
EVALUATION APPREHENSION AND SOCIAL FACILITATION
This graph shows the average number of dominant responses made by participants who were responding alone, next to a blindfolded audience (who therefore couldn't monitor or evaluate their performance), or next to an attentive audience (who could evaluate their performance). Participants were more likely to exhibit dominant responses in the presence of an attentive audience, but not a merely present, blindfolded audience.
Source: Adapted from Cottrell et al., 1968.

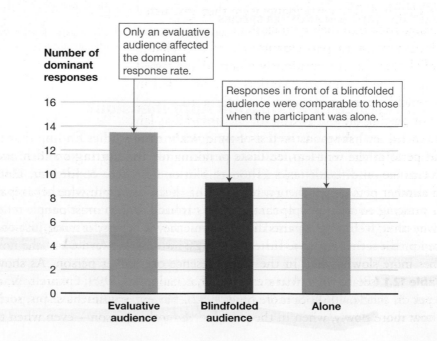

Number of dominant responses

Only an evaluative audience affected the dominant response rate.

Responses in front of a blindfolded audience were comparable to those when the participant was alone.

| Evaluative audience | Blindfolded audience | Alone |

of evaluation apprehension. Participants performing in front of an evaluative audience made more dominant responses than those performing alone; those performing in front of a blindfolded audience did not. Thus, the audience that couldn't evaluate what was going on had no effect on performance. This experiment seems to demonstrate rather conclusively that it's the concern about others as a source of evaluation, and not their mere presence, that's responsible for social facilitation.

TESTING FOR MERE PRESENCE More careful scrutiny, however, gives rise to doubts about the results of the experiment just described. More specifically, although participants in the alone condition were alone in an objective sense (no one else was physically present), they may not have been *psychologically* alone. After all, they were in an experiment, one in which they were asked to perform a strange task. It seems likely that they might feel apprehensive about the prospect of their performance being surreptitiously recorded (which it was). Thus, the alone condition used in this study may not have been a "true" alone condition. To adequately test Zajonc's theory, then, it is essential to create a condition in which participants *feel* that they are truly alone.

In an ingenious experiment, Hazel Markus (1978) showed that the mere presence of another person, in the absence of any concern about that person being evaluative, is indeed sufficient to create arousal that facilitates performance on an easy task and impairs performance on a difficult task. When participants arrived individually for the experiment, they were told to go into an adjoining room to wait for the other participants to arrive. While there, they had to put on the necessary attire for the experiment: take off their own shoes, put on a pair of lab socks over their own socks, put on a pair of oversized lab shoes, and put on a similarly oversized lab coat. The participants did all this and waited, in vain, for the "other participants" to arrive. In reality, there were no other participants. After 10 minutes, the experimenter reappeared and stated that the other participants were apparently not coming, and the experiment would have to be scratched. The participants were then instructed to change back into their own clothes.

Unbeknownst to participants, all of this changing of clothes was surreptitiously observed and timed through a one-way mirror. Markus was interested in how quickly participants could perform the novel tasks of putting on and taking off the unfamiliar lab coat, socks, and shoes, as well as how quickly they could perform the well-learned tasks of taking off and putting on their own, very familiar, shoes. Participants did this in one of three conditions: alone, with another person watching attentively, or in the mere presence of a repairman working on a piece of apparatus with his back to the participant.

Even though the participants did not think they were "performing," Zajonc's theory predicts that they should change their own clothes faster and the novel clothes more slowly when in the mere presence of another person. As shown in **Table 12.1** (see p. 418), that's exactly what happened. Participants took off and put on their own shoes more quickly, and the experimenter's shoes, socks, and coat more slowly, when in the presence of another person—even when the

DOMINANT RESPONSES AND SOCIAL FACILITATION
People tend to do better on well-learned tasks but worse on difficult or poorly mastered tasks in the presence of others. Presumably, the children who know the material well will do better on these standardized tests in the presence of other test takers because their dominant responses will be correct. But children who don't know the material well will be more likely to give incorrect answers in the presence of others.

TABLE 12.1	SOCIAL FACILITATION AND THE EFFECT OF AN AUDIENCE		
	Alone	Merely present audience	Attentive audience
Well-learned tasks (own shoes)	16.5 seconds	13.5 seconds	11.7 seconds
Novel tasks (lab shoes, socks, and coat)	28.8 seconds	32.7 seconds	33.9 seconds

Source: Adapted from Markus, 1978.

other person had his back turned and was unable to observe. Thus, when a true alone condition is included, an effect of the mere presence of someone else can be observed. Note again that the effects were stronger for an attentive audience than for a merely present audience, but that's not a problem for the theory. It just means that evaluation apprehension can add to a person's arousal and thus intensify the effect of mere presence. These results and those of similar investigations strongly support Zajonc's theory that the mere presence of another does indeed have an effect on performance (Platania & Moran, 2001; Schmitt, Gilovich, Goore, & Joseph, 1986).

Beyond Social Facilitation

social loafing The tendency to exert less effort when working on a group task in which individual contributions cannot be monitored.

One hundred years of research on social facilitation has made it clear that the mere presence of others is sufficient to increase arousal and thus facilitate performance on well-learned tasks and inhibit performance on novel tasks. It's also clear, however, that people are complex stimuli and that their presence can have a variety of effects that overlay the influence of mere presence that we just examined. People are often very concerned about making a good impression, and their evaluation apprehension can intensify arousal and lead to more pronounced social facilitation effects.

One phenomenon that runs counter to the standard social facilitation effects is what social psychologists call **social loafing**, the tendency to exert less effort when working on a group task in which individual contributions cannot be monitored (Hoeksema-van Orden, Gaillard, & Buunk, 1998; Karau & Williams, 1995; Plaks & Higgins, 2000; Price, Harrison, & Gavin, 2006; Williams, Harkins, & Latané, 1981). If you and your friends have to move a couch up a flight of stairs, for example, you might be tempted to coast a bit and hope that your friends' more vigorous efforts will get the job done. In these situations, people often loaf because their contributions are not seen as crucial to the success of the effort and because their individual contributions—and hence they themselves—can't be assessed.

SOCIAL LOAFING
When their contributions cannot be individually monitored, people have a tendency to loaf, working less hard than they would otherwise and relying on the efforts of others to get the job done.

Even the most minimal group situation—the mere presence of a single other person—can influence performance, as can concerns about being evaluated. The presence of others is arousing, and arousal accentuates a person's existing performance tendencies. Easy tasks are made easier, and difficult tasks are made more difficult.

Group Decision Making

When people come together in groups, one of the most important things they do is make decisions. Groups that can't decide what to do or how to act don't function well. They wallow, bicker, backstab, and often split apart. You won't be surprised to know, then, that social psychologists have spent considerable energy studying how groups make decisions and what makes those decisions better or worse (Kerr, MacCoun, & Kramer, 1996; Laughlin, Hatch, Silver, & Boh, 2006; Levine & Moreland, 1990, 1998; Rose, 2011; Sommers, 2006).

Much of the research on group decision making has been guided by the assumption that decisions made by groups are typically better than decisions made by individuals. The thinking is that many heads are better than one. And indeed, when groups and individuals are presented with problems for which there are precise, factual answers, groups are more likely than the average individual to come up with the correct solution (Laughlin & Ellis, 1986).

Yet in many contexts, group decisions are no better than those made by individuals. The key to understanding such contexts is to recognize that although arriving at a best possible solution to a problem may be the *group's* most important goal, it may not be the most important goal for any of the individual group members. Individuals may be more concerned with how they will be judged by everyone else, how they can avoid hurting someone's feelings, and how they can dodge responsibility if things go wrong. When people get together to make group decisions, some predictable social psychological processes unfold that can undermine the stated goal of arriving at the best possible choice.

Groupthink

In informal settings where social harmony is all-important and the costs of making an incorrect decision are not great, it's hardly surprising that group pressure to be agreeable can lead to defective decision making. But what happens when life and death are literally at stake and the incentives to "get it right" are high? In those contexts, surely people wouldn't go along with faulty reasoning merely to preserve group harmony or to avoid embarrassment, would they? In fact, they would—and they often do.

Irving Janis carefully analyzed a number of decisions made at the very highest levels of the U.S. government and found evidence of just this sort of faulty, and

"[When people] come together . . . they may surpass, collectively and as a body, the quality of the few best. . . . When there are many who contribute to the process of deliberation, each can bring his share of goodness and moral prudence."
—ARISTOTLE

often calamitous, group decision making (Janis, 1972, 1982; see also Esser, 1998). Here are a few of the fiascos Janis studied:

- The Kennedy administration's decision to foster the overthrow of Fidel Castro's regime by depositing a group of CIA-trained Cuban refugees on the beaches of Cuba's Bay of Pigs but failing to provide air cover. (The refugees were captured in short order, thus humiliating the United States internationally, both for its role in trying to undermine a sovereign nation and for initially denying its involvement in the affair.)
- The Johnson administration's decision to increase the number of American soldiers fighting in Vietnam. (This policy failed to advance U.S. objectives in the region and substantially increased the number of lives lost.)
- The conclusion by the U.S. naval high command that extra precautions were not needed at Pearl Harbor despite warnings of an imminent attack by the Japanese. (This had severe repercussions on December 7, 1941, the "day of infamy," when the Japanese destroyed a large part of the U.S. Pacific Fleet at the Pearl Harbor naval base in a surprise attack.)

groupthink Faulty thinking by members of highly cohesive groups in which the critical scrutiny that should be devoted to the issues at hand is subverted by social pressures to reach consensus.

Janis attributed these disastrous decisions to **groupthink**, a kind of faulty thinking by highly cohesive groups in which the critical scrutiny that should be devoted to the issues at hand is subverted by social pressures to reach consensus. Other investigators have made the same claim about more recent disasters, such as the ill-fated launches of the space shuttles *Challenger* and *Columbia* and other consequential government decisions (Esser & Lindoerfer, 1989; Glanz & Schwartz, 2003; Rose, 2011).

SYMPTOMS AND SOURCES OF GROUPTHINK According to Janis, groupthink is the compromised decision making of a group, fueled by a shallow examination of information, a narrow consideration of alternatives, and a sense of invulnerability or moral superiority (Janis, 1972). Especially under the direction of a strong leader, groups may discourage others from coming forward with dissenting ideas and assessments, ignore or reject alternative viewpoints, and end up overly confident about the wisdom and moral correctness of their proposed solutions. Thus, the very source of a group's potentially superior decision making—the airing of differing opinions and the presentation of varied facts and perspectives—never comes into play (**Figure 12.4**).

The historical record shows that social psychological forces have had a hand in numerous instances of faulty decision making. Less clear, however, is whether these psychological processes cluster together to produce a recognizable condition of groupthink (Henningsen, Henningsen, Eden, & Cruz, 2006). Do such conditions as cohesiveness, insularity, and high stress tend to occur together, or are they separate variables that each might lead to groupthink in separate ways? And are symptoms of groupthink *essential* ingredients of this sort of faulty decision making? Questions like these have not been adequately resolved, and the evidence gathered to test Janis's thesis has been mixed (Aldag & Fuller, 1993; Rose, 2011; Tetlock, Peterson, McGuire, Chang, & Feld, 1992). Nonetheless, his observations have been useful in identifying social factors that can lead to calamitous decisions, as well as factors that can improve group decision making.

For example, strong, directive leaders who make their preferences known sometimes intimidate even the most accomplished group members and stifle

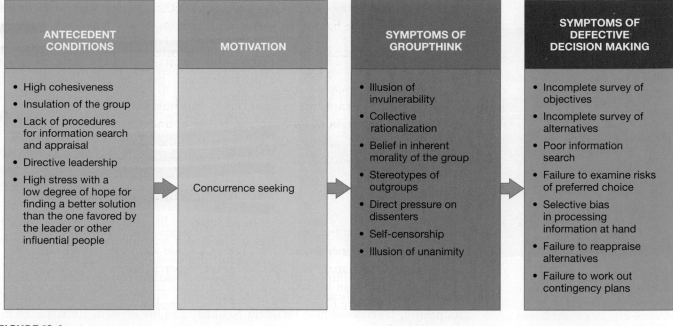

FIGURE 12.4
ELEMENTS OF JANIS'S GROUPTHINK HYPOTHESIS
Certain conditions lead decision-making groups to be excessively concerned with seeking consensus, which detracts from a full, rational analysis of the existing problem.
Source: Adapted from Janis & Mann, 1977, p. 132.

vigorous discussion (Hildreth & Anderson, 2016; McCauley, 1998). Also, just as Janis contends, at times the issue that must be decided is so stressful that groups seek the reassurance and comfort of premature or illusory consensus. In addition, both strong leaders and the drive to find consensus breed **self-censorship**, the decision to withhold information or opinions. Janis reports that Arthur Schlesinger, a member of President Kennedy's inner circle during the Bay of Pigs deliberations, was ever afterward haunted

> for having kept so silent during those crucial discussions in the Cabinet Room. . . . I can only explain my failure to do more than raise a few timid questions by reporting that one's impulse to blow the whistle on this nonsense was simply undone by the circumstances of the discussion. (Quoted in Janis, 1982, p. 39)

Some of the participants in that fiasco have written that the pressures to agree with the flawed plan were so great because the group was newly created, and the participants were reluctant to step on each other's toes. In contrast, by the time that same group came together to deliberate over subsequent crises, they had been around the block with one another and were more willing to offer and accept criticism without worrying so much about threatening their relationship with the group.

PREVENTING GROUPTHINK In light of the perils of groupthink, Janis offers several ideas for improving group deliberations (see also Lu, Yuan, & McLeod, 2012). Freer, more vigorous discussion is likely to take place, for example, if group leaders refrain from making their opinions or preferences known at the

self-censorship Withholding information or opinions in group discussions.

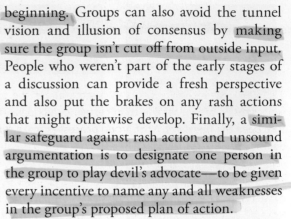

PREVENTING GROUPTHINK
John F. Kennedy's cabinet met during the Cuban missile crisis to try to resolve the impasse with the Soviets over Soviet missiles in Cuba. They took steps to avoid groupthink by encouraging vigorous debate and making recommendations based on unbiased analysis.

group polarization The tendency for group decisions to be more extreme than those made by individuals; whatever way the group as a whole is leaning, group discussion tends to make it lean further in that direction.

"It's agreed, then, that we move forward on the philodendron."

beginning. Groups can also avoid the tunnel vision and illusion of consensus by making sure the group isn't cut off from outside input. People who weren't part of the early stages of a discussion can provide a fresh perspective and also put the brakes on any rash actions that might otherwise develop. Finally, a similar safeguard against rash action and unsound argumentation is to designate one person in the group to play devil's advocate—to be given every incentive to name any and all weaknesses in the group's proposed plan of action.

In addition to his analysis of foreign policy fiascos, Janis also examined a number of highly successful decisions, including the Kennedy administration's handling of the Cuban missile crisis, and claimed that the deliberations leading to these successful decisions were not marked by symptoms of groupthink. Janis noted how President Kennedy and his advisers, embarrassed by the Bay of Pigs disaster, took steps to ensure that all future policies would be evaluated more thoroughly from then on. In the case of the Cuban missile crisis, the president frequently excused himself from the group so as not to constrain the discussion. He also brought in outside experts to critique his advisers' analysis and tentative plans, and he appointed specific individuals (his brother, Robert Kennedy, and Theodore Sorensen) to act as devil's advocates (see **Box 12.1** for other behaviors that make for smarter group decision making). These safeguards seem to have paid off because the negotiations that kept Soviet missiles out of Cuba were one of the enduring highlights of the tragically short Kennedy administration.

Group Polarization

Today's headlines of acrimonious elections, gridlock in Congress, the culture wars over immigration and abortion, and protests on college campuses suggest that we are living in a time of profound discord. Might basic group processes have something to do with the social divisions we are experiencing? One contributor to such social divisions is **group polarization**, whereby group decisions tend to be more *extreme* than those made by individuals. Whatever way the majority of the individuals are leaning, group discussion tends to make them lean even further in that direction (Esteban & Schneider, 2008; Myers & Bishop, 1971; Zuber, Crott, & Werner, 1992).

In one study, for example, French students expressed their opinions about President Charles de Gaulle (a French general during World War II) and about Americans, first individually and then again after having discussed them in groups. The results? Their initially positive sentiments toward de Gaulle became even more positive, and their initially negative sentiments toward Americans became even more negative (Moscovici & Zavalloni, 1969). It appears that we are more likely to hear "ugly American" from a group of foreigners than from a collection of individual foreigners.

BOX 12.1	FOCUS ON WORK

Social Determinants of Collective Intelligence

The study of groupthink is largely a story about the poor decisions groups are vulnerable to in certain conditions. This literature begs the question, What group processes make for smarter decision making? Anita Woolley and Thomas Malone have been seeking answers to this very question. In one early study in this research program, small groups of students engaged in a variety of well-tested decision-making tasks (Woolley, Chabris, Pentland, Hashmi, & Malone, 2010). The groups of participants reasoned through practical intelligence tasks, such as identifying what five things a person would need to survive alone in the desert. They tackled tasks requiring logical reasoning. They engaged in open-ended brainstorming. Each group's scores on these tasks were tallied to yield a score of the group's collective intelligence. What dynamics raised a group's collective intelligence? One hypothesis might be that it just takes one really smart person to lift the intelligence of a group's decision making. This proved not to be the case. How well each individual did on decision-making tasks prior to the study had no influence on the collective intelligence of that person's group. Instead, groups that had more empathic individuals, as assessed in an emotion recognition task prior to the study, had higher collective intelligence scores. Also, groups that practiced effective turn-taking as they deliberated, where each member had the chance to voice ideas freely, scored higher in their collective intelligence. Groups led by one domineering person prone to monologues and decrees proved to be less intelligent. And finally, as the proportion of women in the group rose, so, too, did the team's collective intelligence, presumably because women are more likely to engage in social behaviors—empathic listening, effective turn-taking, more open-ended discussion—that promote collective intelligence.

Why does group discussion lead to more extreme positions by group members? Why is it that individuals in a group don't simply conform to the group average instead of moving the group in one direction or the other? Research indicates that two causes work in concert to produce group polarization. One involves the persuasiveness of the information brought up during group discussion; the other involves people's tendency to try to claim the "right" position among the various opinions within the group. Let's consider each explanation in turn.

THE "PERSUASIVE ARGUMENTS" ACCOUNT When trying to decide on a course of action, people consider the merit of different arguments. It stands to reason that when people are predisposed to favor one course of action in a given situation, they can think of more and better arguments for that action. Of course, any one person in the group is unlikely to think of *all* the arguments in favor of one alternative or the other. So, when the issue is discussed by the group, each person is likely to be exposed to new arguments. This expanded pool of arguments, in turn, is likely to be skewed in favor of the action the people were predisposed to.

The net result, then, is that group discussion tends to expose the average person to even more arguments in favor of the position that the average person was already inclined to take. This exposure serves to strengthen those initial inclinations, and group polarization happens. This explanation suggests that personal, face-to-face discussion is not necessary to produce group polarization. All that's needed is exposure to the pool of arguments that true group discussion tends to elicit. Several studies have tested this idea by having participants read the arguments of other group members in private so that they are exposed to the arguments without knowing who in the group might have advanced them. In support of the persuasive arguments interpretation,

RISK TAKERS
The value placed on risk taking is reflected in the widespread admiration of bold entrepreneurs who took big chances and ended up reshaping entire industries. Vera Wang altered the land-scape of bridal fashion and Steve Jobs transformed the world of computers, music, and communications.

these studies have shown that reading others' arguments is indeed sufficient to produce group polarization (Burnstein, Vinokur, & Trope, 1973).

THE "SOCIAL COMPARISON" INTERPRETATION Another process that encourages group polarization is the very human tendency to compare ourselves with others. "Am I as smart as most people here?" "Do my neighbors all drive better cars than I do?" "Am I getting as much out of life as everyone else?" Consider how these sorts of comparisons might lead to group polarization. For example, when evaluating an issue for which people are inclined to take risks (for example, a career choice early in life), people are likely to think they're more tolerant of risk than the average person. In this case, riskiness is valued, and people like to think of themselves as having more than an average amount of a valued trait. On the other hand, when considering an issue for which people are inclined to be cautious (investing money that belongs to a beloved relative), most people are likely to think they are more prudent or risk averse than the average person. People tend to think, in other words, that they are farther out on the correct side of the opinion distribution on most issues.

What happens when everyone in a group is inclined to make the same choice—say, a risky choice—and are also inclined to think of themselves as more likely than average to take risks? Many people will inevitably find that their tolerance of risk is closer to average than they thought—perhaps even below average. This realization leads some individuals to attempt to show that they are in fact more risk tolerant than average. The group as a whole, then, becomes a bit riskier on those issues for which a somewhat risky approach initially seemed warranted. Similarly, the group would become a bit more conservative on those issues for which a somewhat cautious approach seemed warranted. In other words, the desire to distinguish oneself from others by expressing a more extreme opinion in the "right" direction leads predictably to the group polarization effect. As one journalist put it, "People are always trying to outdo one another; if everyone in a group agrees that men are jerks, then someone in the group is bound to argue that they're assholes" (Kolbert, 2009, p. 112).

Taking It to Extremes: Politics and Group Polarization

Group polarization, the tendency for group members to embrace more extreme positions after discussing an issue, can be intensified when the group consists largely of like-minded individuals. Such was the focus of a 2007 study on conservative versus liberal political views in the United States. The results showed clear-cut group polarization: after deliberating with ideologically similar others, liberals became even more liberal and conservatives became even more conservative. Moreover, the political beliefs within each group became increasingly similar.

For Critical Thinking

1. Elaborate on the findings of the group polarization study using what you have learned about *confirmation bias, conformity,* and *social identity theory.*

2. What are some implications of group polarization in contexts such as courtroom juries, hiring committees, and university classrooms and departments?

Polarization on Hot-Button Issues

In this study, residents of relatively liberal Boulder, Colorado, and relatively conservative Colorado Springs had 15-minute discussions about climate change, affirmative action, and same-sex civil unions with people from their own community. Before and after the discussions, participants rated their views on the topics on a 1–10 scale. The graph shows participants' average ratings for the three topics.

Overall Polarization among Groups

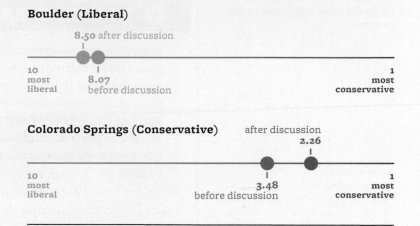

Boulder (Liberal)

8.50 after discussion

10 most liberal

8.07 before discussion

1 most conservative

Colorado Springs (Conservative)

after discussion 2.26

10 most liberal

3.48 before discussion

1 most conservative

Polarization of U.S. Political Views

Group polarization has broader implications for the political climate. As people seek out homogeneous social environments, they are increasingly exposed only to views that resemble their own, which pushes their views further toward the extremes.

2004

70% of Republicans were **more conservative** than the median Democrat.

68% of Democrats were **more liberal** than the median Republican.

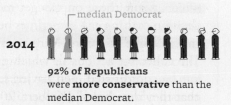

2014

92% of Republicans were **more conservative** than the median Democrat.

94% of Democrats were **more liberal** than the median Republican.

Soures: Colorado study: Schkade, Sunstein, & Hastie, 2007; U.S. political views: Pew Research Center, 2014.

THE DANGERS OF GROUPTHINK
Postmortem analyses of the decision to invade Iraq in 2003 identified examples of apparent groupthink on the part of those responsible for the decision.

The social comparison interpretation can be tested by doing just the opposite of what was done to test the persuasive arguments account: expose people to everyone else's positions without conveying the content of any of the arguments for or against one position or another. As predicted, in one experiment when people were told only about others' positions and not provided any arguments or reasons underlying those positions, the group polarization effect was observed (Teger & Pruitt, 1967). But the group polarization effect in this experiment was weaker than usual, as would be expected if both persuasive arguments and social comparison contribute to the effect.

← LOOKING BACK

Groupthink can lead to defective decision making as people in highly cohesive groups censor their reservations, reject alternative viewpoints, and succumb to group pressures. To avoid this problem, the group should encourage the airing of all viewpoints, leaders should refrain from stating their opinions at the outset, and someone should be designated to play devil's advocate. Group decision making can also lead to group polarization, in which group decisions tend to be more extreme than those made by individuals due to the force of persuasive arguments and social comparison.

Leadership and Power

Social hierarchies are a natural part of group life. So are leaders and people who are led. When children as young as 2 join their first groups—their packs of friends in preschool—some quickly rise to the top rungs of status. When middle-school children form groups of friends at summer camp, they quickly identify the leaders and those who are more likely to follow (Savin-Williams, 1977). Even in the egalitarian confines of a college dorm, hallmates within the first week of living together agree on who are the floor leaders and who are not (Anderson, John, Keltner, & Kring, 2001).

Groups quickly evolve into hierarchies because having leaders helps solve some of the problems inherent in group living (Anderson & Brown, 2010). The allocation of resources can give rise to intense conflict between group members, and a social hierarchy provides rules for dividing up resources that, although often unfair (those on top get more), can dampen or avoid that strife. Group decision making can sometimes be unmanageably complex, and hierarchies provide a shared notion of who guides group discussion and how decisions are made. The collective actions in which groups engage demand that individual behaviors be coordinated, and having leaders helps get the group going and provides needed order. Finally, group life often requires that individuals sacrifice their own interests to benefit the group, and leaders (especially charismatic leaders) can help motivate selfless action.

That leaders and hierarchies are an inevitable part of group life leads us to two important questions: Who rises to positions of leadership? And what happens to leaders once they're in positions of power?

Characteristics of Leaders

How do people rise to positions of leadership in social hierarchies? The influential Italian philosopher Niccolò Machiavelli offered his hypotheses in *The Prince*, the most influential book ever written on the nature of leadership. His thesis, formulated amid the turmoil of sixteenth-century Italy, is that people rise to positions of leadership by being deceptive, by pitting competitors against one another, and by coercion, fear, and manipulation rather than directness, honesty, and inspiration (Machiavelli, 1532/2003). This strategy can be effective in short-term encounters—for example, if you have to negotiate a single deal (Gunnthorsdottir, McCabe, & Smith, 2002). But on balance, studies find that people who adhere to the Machiavellian philosophy of power actually report feeling less powerful in their work and personal lives than other people (Anderson, John & Keltner, 2012).

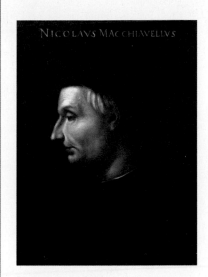

LEADERSHIP CHARACTERISTICS
Influential Italian statesman Niccolò Machiavelli.

Actually, one of the most important determinants of leadership is skillful expertise relevant to the goals of the group; there is simply no substitute for having specific talents that enable the group to achieve its goals (Anderson & Brown, 2010; French & Raven, 1959). The emergency room nurse who has the most adroit and timely skills in surgery will rise in the ranks at that hospital; the software engineer who knows how to write the best code will rise in today's tech world. Cameron Anderson and Gavin Kilduff have found that groups tend to choose quickly as leaders those individuals who demonstrate knowledge and skill in tasks that are central to the group's identity and goals (Anderson & Kilduff, 2009). When leaders have the knowledge and skill that enable better group performance, everyone benefits.

Of course, leadership is not based on expertise, knowledge, and technical skill alone. Groups are more likely to be effective if they're cohesive and have a sense of unity and common cause—when they function smoothly together and the whole is greater than the sum of the parts. Thus, individuals who have the social skills to build strong, cooperative relations among group members also increase their chances of rising to positions of leadership. In summer camps, the more socially dynamic, outgoing children tend to become leaders (Savin-Williams, 1977). In college dorms and in the workplace, individuals who are socially engaged and adept at building and maintaining relationships are more likely to achieve status and reach positions of leadership (Anderson et al., 2001; Judge, Bono, Hies, & Gerhardt, 2002). And emotionally intelligent people, who can read the moods and needs of others, tend to be effective managers (Côté & Miners, 2006). Even in our close primate relatives, the socially skilled chimpanzees and bonobos who build strong alliances, negotiate conflicts between subordinates, and ensure just allocations of resources are the ones who acquire and maintain elevated positions of rank in their primate hierarchies (de Waal, 1986).

Finally, alongside expertise and social skills, someone who can provide rewards to the group is more likely to rise to a leadership role. Studies show that individuals who share resources with others are more likely to rank highly in social hierarchies (Anderson & Brown, 2010; Willer, 2009). Our tendency to grant authority to the more generous group members is another example of how leadership often comes to those whose traits and talents promise to benefit the group as a whole.

The Elements of Power

When people assume leadership positions, they experience many changes: more responsibility and the challenge of managing people with diverse needs and interests, but also increased wealth and prestige, the respect of colleagues, and that great intangible that so many in history have lusted after—power. And with power, a person's behavior is likely to change in many ways, sometimes in ways we wouldn't expect.

To understand the influence of power on social behavior, it's important to describe it more carefully. **Power** is usually defined as the ability to control one's own outcomes and those of others; it's also described as the freedom to act and to be free of constraints (Fiske, 1993). In the most general sense, your power is about your capacity to influence others and make a difference in the world (Keltner, 2016). Power is related to three other kinds of social rank—status, authority, and dominance—but it's not synonymous with them. **Status** is the result of an evaluation of social attributes that produces differences in respect and prominence among group members (French & Raven, 1959). It's possible to have power without status (think of a dictator or a corrupt politician) and to have status without power (think of a religious leader in a slow-moving line at the Department of Motor Vehicles). **Authority** is power that derives from institutionalized roles or formalized positions within a hierarchy (Weber, 1947). But power, of course, can exist in the absence of formal roles (such as within informal social groups). **Dominance** is behavior enacted with the goal of acquiring or demonstrating power. Yet power can be attained without any attempt to establish dominance (as with leaders who attain their positions through their efforts to create goodwill among group members).

power The ability to control one's own outcomes and those of others; the freedom to act.

status The outcome of an evaluation of attributes that produces differences in respect and prominence.

authority Power that derives from institutionalized role or arrangements.

dominance Behavior enacted with the goal of acquiring or demonstrating power.

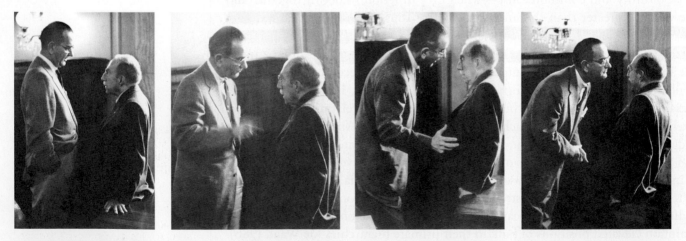

POWER AND INTIMIDATION
High-power people often feel less constrained by social rules about appropriate behavior than people of lower rank. President Lyndon Johnson approaches Senator Theodore Green more closely than is generally socially acceptable, touches his arm, and leans in close to his face as he seeks to intimidate him into voting the way Johnson wants him to.

The Influence of Power on Behavior

Many chapters of human history are defined by astonishing abuses of power, such as the horrifying genocides perpetrated by Hitler, Stalin, Mao Zedong, Pol Pot, Idi Amin, Saddam Hussein, and Bashar al-Assad. This impulsive, often immoral side to power is reflected in such time-honored sayings as "Power corrupts" and "Money [a source of power] is the root of all evil." And it begs for an explanation from social psychology.

The **approach/inhibition theory** of power offers one account of how simply having power can lead to its abuse (Keltner, Gruenfeld, & Anderson, 2003). If, as noted earlier, power involves a lack of constraint and the freedom to act as one wishes, when people experience elevated power, they should be less concerned about the evaluations of others and more inclined to engage in behavior that satisfies their goals and desires (Guinote, 2007, 2017; Guinote & Chen, 2018). In contrast, reduced power is associated with increased constraint and a vulnerability to the actions of others. As a result, the experience of diminished power should make a person more vigilant and careful in making judgments and decisions and more inhibited with respect to taking action. In effect, power gives the green light to an individual to pursue personal goals and desires. Reduced power is more like a yellow light: caution is in order.

The approach/inhibition theory of power makes two core predictions. The first concerns the influence of power on how people perceive others. High-power individuals, inclined to go after their own goals, are predicted to be

approach/inhibition theory
A theory maintaining that high-power individuals are inclined to go after their goals and make quick (and sometimes rash) judgments, whereas low-power individuals are more likely to constrain their behavior and pay careful attention to others.

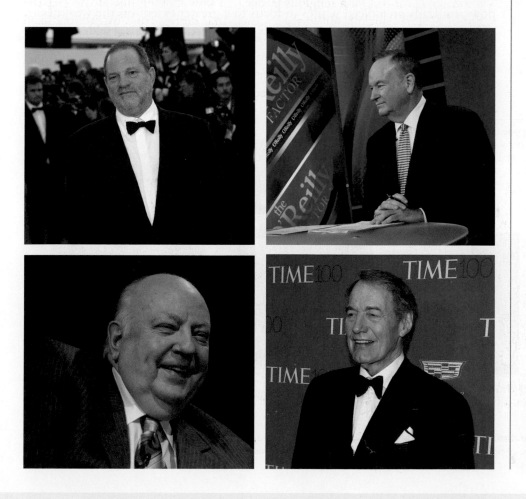

ABUSES OF POWER
As the approach/inhibition theory of power maintains, being in a position of power can lead people, such as the powerful men shown here (film producer Harvey Weinstein, Fox News host Bill O'Reilly, former talk show host and television journalist Charlie Rose, and the late Fox News Chairman and CEO Roger Ailes), to ignore many of the usual constraints on behavior and to act in ways that promote their desires.

less careful and systematic in how they assess others (Brauer, Chambres, Niedenthal, & Chatard-Pannetier, 2004). Consistent with this hypothesis, high-power individuals are more likely to stereotype others rather to than carefully attend to individuating information about them (Fiske, 2010). High-power people are also less accurate judges of others' emotions (Gonzaga, Keltner, & Ward, 2008).

One dramatic demonstration of the empathy failures associated with elevated power was provided by Joseph Magee and his colleagues (Magee, Galinsky, Inesi, & Gruenfeld, 2006). These investigators first induced people to feel relatively powerful or powerless by having them recall a time when they exerted control over another person or when someone else exerted control over them. Participants then performed a simple perspective-taking task: drawing the letter *E* on their forehead so that someone across from them could read it. This task requires the participant to take the other person's perspective and draw the *E* in reverse. As you can see in **Figure 12.5**, participants feeling a surge of power were much less likely to draw the *E* in a way that took the other person's perspective into account. Power reduces the ability to take the perspective of others (Galinsky, Rucker, & Magee, 2016).

The empathy deficits produced by power can have unfortunate consequences. Theresa Vescio and her colleagues have found that powerful men who stereotype female employees by focusing exclusively on their weaknesses tend to grant female employees fewer resources (Vescio, Gervais, Snyder, & Hoover, 2005), evaluate them more negatively, and anticipate less success by female employees than by male employees (Vescio, Snyder, & Butz, 2003). In a similar vein, feeling powerful leads prejudiced whites to focus to a greater extent on the weaknesses of black employees relative to other employees (Vescio, Gervais, Heidenreich, & Snyder, 2006).

"Power is like drinking gin on an empty stomach. You feel dizzy, you get drunk, you lose your balance."
—POPE FRANCIS

"Power is the ultimate aphrodisiac."
—HENRY KISSINGER, FORMER U.S. SECRETARY OF STATE

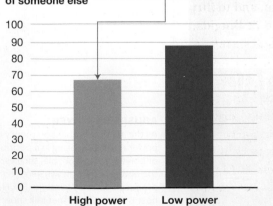

Percentage of participants who drew *E* from the perspective of someone else

When feeling powerful, participants were less likely to draw a reversed *E* on their forehead so that it was easy for another person to read.

FIGURE 12.5
POWER AND EMPATHY FAILURES
This study showed how power diminishes one's capacity to consider the perspective of others.
Source: Magee et al., 2006.

These findings likely converge with your own observations that powerful individuals often appear somewhat out of touch, whereas the powerless seem more clued in. But are there costs to the heightened vigilance that low-power individuals maintain as they carefully attend to others? There are indeed. The experience of diminished power makes people less flexible in their thoughts and less able to shift their attention to meet the varied demands of the task at hand (Smith & Trope, 2006). For example, Pamela Smith and her colleagues induced people to feel elevated power or diminished power by priming them with low- or high-power words (*obey, dominate*) or having them recall an experience of low or high power (Smith, Jostmann, Galinsky, & van Dijk, 2008). Participants then worked on a variety of cognitive tasks. In one task, words were flashed one at a time on a computer screen, and participants indicated whether a current word on the screen matched the word presented two trials earlier. In another, the Stroop task, participants had to name the color of the ink (red, for example) in which a word (*sedan*, for example) was written—a task made more difficult on trials in which the word itself referred to a color different from the font color (*blue*). Performance on these tasks requires considerable cognitive flexibility and control. In the Stroop task, for example, the participant must ignore the meaning of the word when naming the color of the ink in which it is written. As predicted, participants randomly assigned to feel relatively powerless proved less effective in performing these cognitive tasks. The vigilant and narrowed focus that comes with a sense of reduced power can diminish an individual's ability to think flexibly and creatively.

The second core element of approach/inhibition theory is the prediction that power should make people behave in less constrained and sometimes more inappropriate ways. Take sex, for example. Do you think it's mainly CEOs, politicians, and rock stars who exhibit sexually inappropriate behavior? Think again. Social psychologists have found that just giving people the faintest whiff of power—for example, by having them recall an experience when they had power or having them read power-related words (priming them with ideas of power)—can lead them to act in sexually assertive and potentially problematic ways. People who have a good deal of power, as well as individuals who are primed with feelings of power, are more likely to touch others and approach them closely, to have sexual ideas running through their minds, to feel attraction for a stranger, to overestimate another's sexual interest in them, and to flirt in an overly forward fashion (Kunstman & Maner, 2011; Rudman & Borgida, 1995). In one survey of 1,261 employees, the higher an individual's rank in the organization, the more likely he or she was to report having had sexual affairs when married (Lammers, Stapel, & Galinsky, 2011). Power differences are almost always involved when men sexually harass women (and less typically men) at work with patterns of inappropriate comments, sexually forward behaviors, and coercion and threat (Cortina & Berdahl, 2008). More generally, power frees the individual from being concerned about the constraints of sexual norms and enables more disinhibited sexual behavior (Lammers & Maner, 2016). Power would indeed appear to be the ultimate aphrodisiac—but mainly for the person feeling powerful.

Perhaps most unsettling are studies showing that elevated power is associated with increased antisocial behavior. At work it's the more powerful who are more likely to interrupt and swear at others (Pearson & Porath, 1999). It's

"Nearly all men can stand adversity, but if you want to test a man's character, give him power."
—ABRAHAM LINCOLN

"The fundamental concept in social science is Power, in the same sense that Energy is the fundamental concept in physics. . . . The laws of social dynamics are laws which can only be stated in terms of power."
—BERTRAND RUSSELL

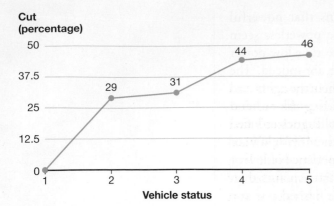

Cut (percentage)

50 — 46

37.5 — 44

25 — 29 · 31

12.5

0

1 2 3 4 5

Vehicle status

FIGURE 12.6
POWER AND UNETHICAL BEHAVIOR

Power can lead to more impulsive behavior, as in this study where driving a fancy car led drivers to be more likely to cut illegally in front of a pedestrian. Source: Piff et al., 2012.

"I'm not a machine, Deborah. I can't just turn my greed on and off."

wealthy white teenagers who are more likely to shoplift than poorer students of color (Blanco et al., 2008). Power even produces more antisocial behavior in how people drive. Paul Piff and his colleagues had a confederate stand at an edge of a marked crosswalk on a busy street abutting a university campus in California (Piff, Stancato, Côté, Mendoza-Denton, & Keltner, 2012). In California, it is state law for the driver to give the right of way to the pedestrian. Piff and colleagues then kept track of which cars stopped for the pedestrian and which did not, noting the status of the car on a 5-point scale (where 1 is lowest in status and 5 is highest). As you can see in **Figure 12.6**, drivers of the fancy cars stopped 46.2 percent of the time; drivers of the low-status cars always obeyed the law.

It's important to bear in mind that the consistent effect of power is that it disinhibits. As the great presidential biographer Robert Caro observed, "Power reveals." Power encourages people to express their underlying inclinations, both good and bad. In one study that illustrates this idea, Serena Chen and her colleagues preselected participants who were either self-interested and exchange oriented or more compassionate and communally oriented (Chen, Lee-Chai, & Bargh, 2001). Each participant was then randomly assigned to a high-power or low-power position in a clever, subtle manner: high-power participants were seated in a snazzy leather professorial chair during the experiment; low-power people were seated in a plain chair. Participants were then asked to complete a long questionnaire with the help of another participant, who was late. Consistent with the idea that power amplifies the expression of preexisting tendencies, the high-power communally oriented participants performed the lion's share of the task. In contrast, the more self-interested participants with high power acted in a more self-serving fashion, leaving more of the task for the other participant (see also Gordon & Chen, 2013). The same difference was not found between low-power communal versus exchange participants. The effects of power, then, depend on who holds it. Power corrupts the corruptible.

← **LOOKING BACK**

Individuals are more likely to become leaders if they have knowledge and skills that help a group get along and reach its goals. Power is the freedom from constraints to act and the ability to control one's own outcomes and those of others. Knowledgeable, outgoing, and socially adept people tend to assume positions of leadership within a group. Power tends to make people less careful in their thoughts about others and more impulsive in their behavior.

Deindividuation and the Psychology of Mobs

Consider the following quite similar reactions to two very different events in San Francisco. The first involved the tragic circumstances surrounding the murders of Mayor George Moscone and Supervisor Harvey Milk, San Francisco's first openly gay supervisor, in 1978. On November 27 of that year, Milk's political rival Dan White shot and killed both Moscone and Milk in City Hall. In a rather swift trial, White's lawyers argued that he was minimally responsible for his deeds because of severe depression. His lawyers claimed that his depression led him to subsist on a junk-food diet, which further "diminished his capacity" to distinguish right from wrong. These tactics, ridiculed in the press as the "Twinkie defense," were nonetheless effective. Instead of a first-degree murder conviction, White was found guilty of the lesser charge of voluntary manslaughter and faced a maximum sentence of eight years in prison. With good behavior, he would be eligible for parole in less than five years. (White ended up serving a little over five years, but 22 months after his release from prison, he committed suicide.)

The verdict infuriated members of San Francisco's gay community. Many thought the verdict would have been more severe if a supervisor other than Harvey Milk had been slain. The evening of the verdict, gay activists organized a peaceful protest march, but events quickly got out of hand. It began with several demonstrators smashing the glass windows and doors of City Hall. Over the pleas of rally organizers urging calm, the crowd began to chant, "Kill Dan White! Get Dan White!" Vandalism and violence soon intensified. When police moved in to quell the disturbance, a battle ensued. The demonstrators threw rocks and bottles at police, set fire to numerous police cars, and looted nearby stores. They were met with a strong police response. In the end, 12 police cars were gutted by fire, 20 police officers were injured, and 70 demonstrators needed medical attention. Eight people were arrested. As unfortunate and destructive as the rioting was, it nevertheless strikes most people as understandable. However

THE PSYCHOLOGY OF MOBS
(A) Upon learning of the killing of Harvey Milk and George Moscone by Dan White, large crowds of demonstrators gathered to mourn their passing.
(B) When Dan White was given a light sentence in his trial for the murder, demonstrators again took to the streets, this time rioting and setting cars on fire in protest of what they saw as a travesty of justice.

much they might disapprove, most observers would not think of the rioters' actions as bizarre: the rioters were lashing out against a justice system they thought had failed.

Now consider the striking similarity to the violence that erupted in the same city three years later in response to a very different kind of event: the San Francisco 49ers' *victory* over the Cincinnati Bengals in Super Bowl XVI, a victory that earned the city its first professional championship in any sport. Within minutes of the game's conclusion, giddy fans poured out of homes and bars and into the streets to celebrate. At first it was all harmless, celebratory stuff—horns blared, beer was chugged, champagne was sprayed. As the evening wore on, however, events took a more sinister turn, eventually echoing what had transpired in the aftermath of the Dan White verdict. Bonfires were started in an intersection and atop a car. When police tried to restore order, they were met with a barrage of stones, bricks, and bottles. Before the streets were cleared, 8 police officers and 100 others were treated for injuries, and 70 arrests were made.

Deindividuation and the Group Mind

These two events in San Francisco's history, as well as a great many similar events around the world, challenge us to understand how large groups of people can transform into unruly mobs. How do peaceful gatherings spin out of control and become violent? Why do law-abiding citizens, when immersed in a crowd, engage in acts of destruction they would never commit alone? How can we understand the psychology of "the mob"?

Social psychologists have addressed these questions in the context of examining the *emergent properties of groups*—behaviors that emerge only when people are in groups. People do things in groups that they would never do alone. Indeed, we often hear people say that a group has "a mind of its own." As a result, the behavior of large groups of people is more than the sum of the behavioral tendencies of its individual members. You might dance, sing, and play air guitar at a rock concert with all your friends, but you wouldn't likely do that if the band were playing a private concert just for you.

One of the first people to offer an extensive analysis of the psychology of the mob was a nineteenth-century French sociologist, Gustav Le Bon. Le Bon thought that people tended to lose their higher mental faculties of reason and deliberation when they were in large groups: "By the mere fact that he forms part of an organised crowd, a man descends several rungs in the ladder of civilization" (1895, p. 52). For Le Bon, this descent stems from the collection of individual, rational minds giving way to a less self-reflective "group mind."

Social psychologists have expanded on Le Bon's ideas by examining how the thought patterns of individuals change when they come together in large groups and how these changes make them more susceptible to group influence. Most of the time, we feel individuated—that is, we feel individually identifiable by others, we consider ourselves individually responsible for our actions, and we are concerned with the propriety and future consequences of our behavior. But as a

> *"Whoever be the individuals that compose it, however like or unlike be their mode of life, . . . their character, or their intelligence, the fact that they have been transformed into a crowd puts them in possession of a sort of collective mind."*
> —GUSTAV LE BON

EMERGENT PROPERTIES OF GROUPS
Some behaviors surface only when people are part of a group and submerge their individual identities into the group. The people in this flash mob converged at this spot after receiving e-mails telling them when and where to gather. Their actions reflect the fact that they are in a group—behavior that would be highly unlikely if each of them were there alone.

number of social psychologists have noted, we often experience a loss of individual identity—a sense of **deindividuation**—when we're in a large group (Diener, 1980; Zimbardo, 1970). When in large crowds, we sometimes feel "lost in the crowd," caught up in what's happening in the moment, with a diminished sense of responsibility for our actions.

A Model of Deindividuation

Philip Zimbardo (1970) proposed a theoretical model of deindividuation that specifies how certain conditions create the kind of psychological state that promotes the impulsive and often destructive behaviors observed in mobs (**Figure 12.7**). Perhaps the most important of these conditions are the anonymity individuals enjoy by blending in with a large group and the diffusion of responsibility that occurs when there are many people to share the blame. These conditions, along with the arousal, heightened activity, and sensory overload that often accompany being immersed in a large group, lead to the internal state of deindividuation. The deindividuated state is characterized by diminished self-observation and self-evaluation and a lessened concern with how others evaluate us.

Thus, a deindividuated person is less aware of the self, more focused on others and the immediate environment, and hence more responsive to behavioral cues from others—for good or for bad. Being in a deindividuated state lowers the threshold for engaging in actions that are typically inhibited. People are more likely to engage in a host of impulsive behaviors, both because there is more of a "push" to do so (because of increased arousal and the presence of many other impulsive people to imitate) and because the constraints that usually "pull" them back from such actions are weakened (because of a lessened sense of personal evaluation and responsibility).

What emerges is the kind of impulsive, irrational, emotional, and occasionally destructive behavior characteristic of mobs. This kind of behavior often creates its own momentum and is less responsive to stimuli that might, if a person were alone, bring it under control. Thus, Zimbardo's model of deindividuation is not an account of mob violence per se. Instead, it is a theoretical analysis

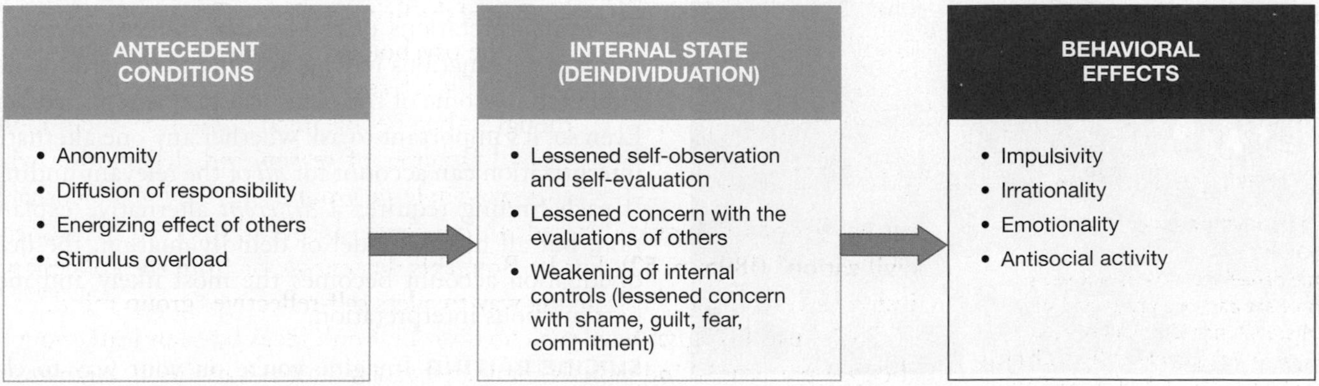

deindividuation A reduced sense of individual identity accompanied by diminished self-regulation that can come over people when they are in a large group.

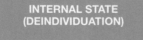

ANTECEDENT CONDITIONS	INTERNAL STATE (DEINDIVIDUATION)	BEHAVIORAL EFFECTS
• Anonymity • Diffusion of responsibility • Energizing effect of others • Stimulus overload	• Lessened self-observation and self-evaluation • Lessened concern with the evaluations of others • Weakening of internal controls (lessened concern with shame, guilt, fear, commitment)	• Impulsivity • Irrationality • Emotionality • Antisocial activity

FIGURE 12.7
A THEORETICAL MODEL OF DEINDIVIDUATION
Certain conditions lead to an internal state of deindividuation, which in turn leads to impulsive behaviors that in other situations would be kept under control.
Source: Adapted from Zimbardo, 1970.

Deindividuation and the Psychology of Mobs · **435**

DEINDIVIDUATION AND RIOTING
When people are in a group and angry, they may let go of self-control and give in to impulses to wreak havoc. Normally law-abiding citizens merge into this crowd and break windows and smash cars with little thought to personal responsibility or the law.

of crowd-induced *impulsive* behavior—behavior that because of its very impulsivity often turns violent (Spivey & Prentice-Dunn, 1990).

One implicit element in the model is that people often find the impulsivity that accompanies deindividuation to be liberating. Zimbardo argues that people go through much of their lives in a straitjacket of cognitive control. Living under such constraints can be tiresome and stifling, so people sometimes yearn to break free and act more impulsively. In support of this idea, Zimbardo notes that virtually all societies try to safely channel the expression of this yearning by scheduling occasions when people are encouraged to "let loose." We see this in harvest rites in agrarian cultures, carnivals in religious societies, galas and festivals throughout history, and, perhaps, in the mosh pits and use of intoxicants at modern rock concerts.

Testing the Model

It should be noted at the outset that the psychology of the mob and other emergent properties are extremely difficult to study. People are on their best behavior when they enter a scientific laboratory, and it's difficult to create a situation where they will act impulsively and destructively. Also, there are ethical constraints against putting people in situations where aggressiveness and acts of destruction are likely. Therefore, some of the most informative research on the subject takes place out in the world and not in the lab (for exceptions, see Lea, Spears, & de Groot, 2001; Postmes & Spears, 1998).

This research also involves relatively few controlled experiments. Instead, it often involves the examination of archives—data originally gathered with no thought to its relevance to deindividuation. Investigators use these records to search for predicted correlations between various antecedent conditions and resultant behaviors.

Because these empirical tests are not controlled experiments, they don't control for, or rule out, various alternative interpretations of the results. Indeed, you might think of explanations having nothing to do with deindividuation for some of the empirical results reported here. Even so, it's important to ask whether any one alternative interpretation can account for *all* of the relevant findings. If each finding requires a *different* alternative explanation, but all fit the model of deindividuation, the deindividuation account becomes the most likely and most parsimonious interpretation.

SUICIDE BAITING Imagine you're on your way to class when you notice a disturbance up ahead. When you get closer, you find that everyone is looking up at the top floor of a high-rise dormitory. Apparently, a student is halfway out an open window and threatening to jump. What do you do? Try to stop the tormented person from jumping? Call for help?

DEINDIVIDUATION AND IMPULSIVE BEHAVIOR
At many rock concerts, in the spirit of deindividuated joy, people will crowd surf over their fellow concertgoers.

Hard as it may be to believe, people occasionally do just the opposite—they engage in suicide baiting, urging the person to jump. Is suicide baiting more likely when many people are gathered below? In other words, are people more likely to engage in suicide baiting when they feel deindividuated?

To answer these questions, researchers examined 15 years of newspaper accounts of suicidal jumps and averted jumps (Mann, 1981). They found 21 instances of attempted suicide, and suicide baiting occurred in 10 of them. They then analyzed the data to determine whether two variables associated with deindividuation—the cover of darkness and the presence of a large group of onlookers—were related to whether suicide baiting occurred. Quite remarkably, suicide baiting was more than twice as likely when the crowd size exceeded 300. Also, suicide baiting was more than four times as likely if the episode took place after 6 p.m. As people feel more anonymous, either by being lost in a large crowd or under the cloak of darkness, they are more inclined to egg on a potential suicide.

It's possible to question some of the details of these analyses—for example, why the cutoffs were set at 300 people and 6 p.m. It's also possible to suggest alternative interpretations: for example, the larger the group, the more likely it is to contain a psychopath who starts the baiting. However, the data are nevertheless consistent with the idea that variables leading to deindividuation also lead to antisocial behavior.

THE CONDUCT OF WAR Wars have always been a part of what English novelist and scientist C. P. Snow calls the "long and gloomy history of man." The conduct of warfare, however, has varied enormously from culture to culture and epoch to epoch. For example, warfare practices vary in their ferocity. At the high end are beheadings, ritualistic torture, and the systematic slaughter of civilian noncombatants. At the very low end would be what Tom Wolfe (1979) has described as single-combat warfare: the David and Goliath battles in which the warring parties each select a single warrior to do battle with each other. The losing side pays a price in territory or some other form of wealth, but less damage is done to both groups.

Is the brutality of warfare related to deindividuation? The theory predicts that it should be. It should be easier for people to let go of the usual prohibitions against barbarity when they feel anonymous and unaccountable for their actions. To determine whether such a relationship exists, the warfare practices of 23 non-Western cultures were investigated (Watson, 1973). The researchers examined each culture to see whether its warriors were deindividuated before battle (for example, by wearing masks or war paint) and how aggressively they waged war (whether they tortured the enemy, whether they fought to the death in all battles, and so on). As predicted, there was a strong correlation between deindividuation and aggressiveness in warfare. Among those cultures whose warriors changed their appearance before battle, 80 percent were deemed particularly aggressive; among those cultures whose warriors did not change their appearance, only 13 percent were deemed especially aggressive. When warriors are disguised in battle, they fight more ferociously. (On the other hand, the ancient Celts were in the habit of fighting

WARFARE AND DEINDIVIDUATION
Warriors in tribes that deindividuate themselves before battle by wearing war paint and war masks tend to engage in more brutal warfare practices.

naked, and they were ferocious fighters that the Romans were terrified to face. Of course, whether to consider nakedness an increase in individuation or a decrease isn't clear.)

HALLOWEEN MAYHEM For Americans, one of the most familiar occasions for uninhibited and impulsive behavior is Halloween night. The destructive acts that occur on that holiday range from mild episodes of egg throwing to much more serious hooliganism. One group of social psychologists decided to take advantage of the Halloween atmosphere to conduct an ambitious test of the role of deindividuation in antisocial behavior (Diener, Fraser, Beaman, & Kelem, 1976). They set up research stations in 27 homes throughout the city of Seattle and monitored the behavior of over 1,000 trick-or-treaters. At each participating house, the children were told they could take one piece of candy from a large bowl sitting on a table in the entrance to the house. Next to the bowl of candy was a bowl filled with coins. The experimenter then excused herself from the scene and covertly monitored the children's actions from afar. Would the children take just their allotted single piece of candy, or would they take more—and perhaps even some coins?

The investigators examined the influence of two variables connected to deindividuation. First, the children arrived either individually or in groups, and the investigators expected those in groups to feel more anonymous and therefore be more likely to transgress. Second, the experimenter purposely "individuated" a random sample of children arriving both alone and in groups; before departing, she asked each child his or her name and address and then repeated this information aloud for emphasis. Individuating the children—that is, identifying them by name so they'd no longer feel anonymous—was predicted to inhibit any temptation to transgress.

As **Figure 12.8** shows, both variables had the anticipated effect. The children who arrived in groups were much more likely to transgress than those who were alone, regardless of whether they were anonymous or not. Children who were anonymous were much more likely to transgress than those who were individuated, regardless of whether they were alone or in groups. Putting these two findings together, the children in anonymous groups were the most likely to transgress.

Self-Awareness and Individuation

If "losing ourselves" in a crowd and becoming deindividuated makes us more likely to behave impulsively, it stands to reason that being especially self-aware and self-conscious would have the opposite effect. Anything that focuses attention on the self, such as being in front of a camera, seeing ourselves in a mirror, or wearing a name tag, may lead to **individuation** and make us particularly inclined to act carefully and in accordance with our sense of propriety. This is just what **self-awareness theory** predicts. When people focus their attention on themselves, they become more concerned with self-evaluation and how their current behavior conforms to their own standards and values (Duval & Wicklund, 1972).

individuation An enhanced sense of individual identity produced by focusing attention on the self, which generally leads people to act carefully and deliberately and in accordance with their sense of propriety and values.

self-awareness theory A theory maintaining that when people focus their attention inward on themselves, they become concerned with self-evaluation and how their current behavior conforms to their internal standards and values.

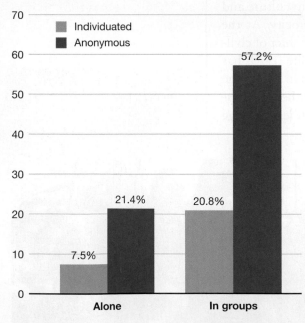

Percentage transgressing

FIGURE 12.8 DEINDIVIDUATION AND TRANSGRESSION
In this study, the percentage of trick-or-treaters who transgressed was affected by whether they had been asked to give their name (individuated condition) or not (anonymous condition) and whether they were alone or in a group.
Source: Adapted from Diener et al., 1976.

BOX 12.2

Not So Fast:
Critical Thinking about Correlated Trends

If you look up statistics on the number of people regularly attending their church, temple, or mosque each year over the past quarter century and tally up instances of especially brutal episodes of violence each year over that same time span (beheadings, suicide bombings, torture), you'll observe a high correlation between the two. Why? Has increased religious fervor encouraged a dehumanization of religious outgroups? Has exposure to gruesome images of this sort of violence led people to seek solace in religion?

Perhaps both are true, and by this point in the book we hope you've learned not to jump to any one conclusion on the basis of a simple correlation. But there's another

possibility: the two may have absolutely nothing to do with each other, and their correlation reflects the basic fact that both religiosity and episodes of violence have increased over this time period. The number of people attending religious services has gone up over this period simply because the world population has gone up. Beheadings and bombings have gone up for all sorts of geopolitical reasons. The broader point is that whenever *any* two variables have increased over time, there will be a substantial year-to-year correlation between them. Thus, if you look up the number of search requests for, say, Ryan Gosling or Kate Upton over the past five years and the number of

search requests for jihad (or the number of bombings for that matter), you'll find a positive correlation between the two. Both have been going up during that time, so they *have* to be correlated.

Statisticians refer to any systematic increase or decrease over time as a *secular trend* (from the late Latin word for "age" or "span of time"), and the lesson here is that it's important to be especially cautious about interpreting a significant correlation involving two such trends. Again, correlation does not equal causation. It may have no more meaning than the correlation between the yearly sales of salted caramel ice cream and legalized marijuana (both of which have been growing substantially in recent years).

STUDIES OF SELF-AWARENESS Many experiments have shown that people do indeed act in ways that are more consistent with their attitudes and values when they've been made self-conscious by being placed in front of a mirror or an attentive audience (Duval & Lalwani, 1999; Froming, Walker, & Lopyan, 1982; Scheier, Fenigstein, & Buss, 1974). In one study, college students were asked to solve a series of anagrams and told to stop when a bell sounded. In a control condition, nearly three-quarters of them fudged a bit by continuing to work beyond the bell. But in a condition that caused participants to be made self-aware by working in front of a mirror, fewer than 10 percent

INDIVIDUATION AND SELF-AWARENESS
Anything that focuses attention on the self and individual identity is likely to lead to heightened concern with self-control and propriety. Name tags on these people at a business conference can encourage a sense of individuation and, most likely, restrained behavior.

cheated (Diener & Wallbom, 1976). Although most students *say* that cheating is a bad thing, it appears to take some self-awareness to get them to act on that belief. Note that because being in a state of self-awareness is the flip side of feeling deindividuated, all of these experiments that support self-awareness theory also provide indirect support for the model of deindividuation.

A clever study in a work setting provides yet more evidence that self-awareness promotes behavior that is more in keeping with personal standards

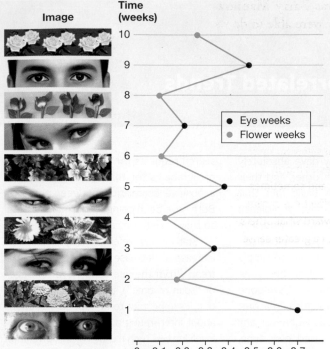

Image

Time (weeks)

Pounds paid per liter of milk consumed

● Eye weeks
● Flower weeks

FIGURE 12.9
SELF-AWARENESS AND SOCIALLY APPROPRIATE BEHAVIOR IN THE OFFICE
People gave more money to cover the expense of milk when made self-aware by images of people looking at them.
Source: Bateson et al., 2006

spotlight effect People's conviction that other people are paying attention to them (to their appearance and behavior) more than they actually are.

(Bateson, Nettle & Roberts, 2006). In many offices, it's common to have a regularly offered goody, be it coffee, snacks, or tea, with an "honest box" next to it, in which people donate to cover the cost of the refreshment. The trouble, though, is that people are prone to exploit such a public good. In Melissa Bateson's Department of Psychology at the University of Newcastle, the distribution of coffee ran according to such an honor system, where people were free to contribute whatever they wanted for milk. You can see the results in **Figure 12.9**. When Bateson and colleagues placed an image of flowers on a wall near the coffee dispenser, her work colleagues on average gave 15 pence for every liter of milk. When an image of a person's eyes stared at them as they contributed, prompting greater self-awareness, their donations jumped considerably, rising to 70 pence when it was that of a stern-looking male (at bottom). Self-awareness prompts more socially appropriate behavior.

SELF-CONSCIOUSNESS AND THE SPOTLIGHT EFFECT
The inverse relationship between self-consciousness and deindividuation raises the question of how self-conscious people typically are in the normal course of events. There are pronounced individual differences, of course, in how focused people are on themselves and in how much they believe that others are focused on them as well (Fenigstein, Scheier, & Buss, 1975). But there is also reason to believe that the typical level of self-consciousness is fairly high, particularly when others are around. People begin to feel deindividuated only in the presence of a large crowd. This is why, as noted earlier, it has been assumed that people enjoy feeling deindividuated; it's a welcome break from the usual self-conscious state.

Evidence that people are indeed prone to a high level of self-consciousness comes from research on the **spotlight effect**—people's conviction that other people are paying attention to their appearance and behavior more than is actually the case. People who make an insightful comment in a group discussion, for example, believe that others will notice their comment and remember it better than other people actually do. People who suffer an embarrassing mishap, such as triggering an alarm in a public building or stumbling while entering a lecture hall, think others are judging them more harshly than they actually are (Epley, Savitsky, & Gilovich, 2002; Fortune & Newby-Clark, 2008; Gilovich, Kruger, & Medvec, 2002; Gilovich, Medvec, & Savitsky, 2000; Savitsky, Epley, & Gilovich, 2001).

In one of the clearest demonstrations of the spotlight effect, participants who arrived individually for an experiment were asked to put on a T-shirt sporting a picture of the pop singer Barry Manilow. Despite obvious signs of displeasure, everyone did so. They then reported to another room down the hall where, upon entering, they found a group of fellow students filling out questionnaires. After leaving the room moments later, the participants had to estimate the percentage of those other students who would be able to recall the person pictured on the T-shirt. As predicted, the participants overestimated how much they had stood out in their new shirt. They estimated that roughly half the other students would be able to identify that it was Barry Manilow pictured on their shirt, when in fact only about one-quarter were able to do so (Gilovich et al., 2000).

← LOOKING BACK

Research on deindividuation has shown that the diminished sense of self-awareness that sometimes occurs when we are immersed in large groups makes us more likely to get caught up in ongoing events and encourages impulsive, and sometimes destructive, actions. Research on self-awareness and the spotlight effect has shown how carefully we typically monitor our own behavior with an eye toward what others might think and how our awareness of self encourages us to act with a greater sense of propriety.

Chapter Review

SUMMARY

The Nature and Purpose of Group Living

- Human beings, like all large primates except the orang-utan, are group-living animals who influence, and must get along with, others.

Social Facilitation

- *Social Facilitation* refers to the positive or negative effect that the presence of others has on performance. Arousal from the presence of others increases people's tendency to do what comes naturally. On easy tasks, people are predisposed to respond correctly, so the presence of others facilitates performance on easy tasks; on new or hard tasks, when they're not predisposed to respond correctly, the presence of others hinders performance by making people more likely to respond incorrectly.
- The mere presence of others leads to social facilitation effects, and other factors, including *evaluation apprehension*, can intensify these effects.
- *Social loafing* is the tendency to exert less effort on a group task when individual contributions cannot be monitored.

Group Decision Making

- *Groupthink* refers to the faulty thinking by members of cohesive groups, in which critical decision-making scrutiny is undermined by social pressures to reach consensus. Groupthink has been implicated in the faulty decision making that has led to various policy fiascos.

- Group decision making is affected by how cohesive a group is, how directive its leader is, and by ingroup pressures that can lead to the rejection of alternative viewpoints and to *self-censorship*, the tendency to refrain from expressing reservations in the face of apparent group consensus.
- Group discussion can create *group polarization*; initial leanings tend to be made more extreme by group discussion.
- Group polarization can result when group discussion exposes members to more persuasive arguments in favor of a consensus opinion than they would have thought of themselves; it can also result from social comparison, when people compare their opinions with those of others.

Leadership and Power

- Power involves control and the freedom to act. It derives from interpersonal sources, such as a person's position of authority or expertise, as well as individual factors, such as the ability to engage with others socially and build strong alliances.
- People with knowledge and skills that help group members get along and help the group reach its goals are generally more likely to become leaders.
- According to *approach/inhibition theory*, people in elevated positions of power look at the environment in terms of how they can satisfy their personal desires and act in disinhibited ways, sometimes leading to excesses and abuses.

Deindividuation and the Psychology of Mobs

- Large groups sometimes transform into unruly mobs; the anonymity and diffusion of responsibility people feel in large groups can lead to a mental state of *deindividuation*, in which they are less concerned with the future, with normal societal constraints on behavior, and with the consequences of their actions.
- The deindividuated state of getting lost in the crowd contrasts with how people normally feel, which is individually identifiable. *Self-awareness theory* maintains that focusing attention on the self leads people to a state of individuation, marked by careful deliberation and concern with how well their actions conform to their moral standards.
- People tend to overestimate how much they personally stand out and are identifiable to others, a phenomenon known as the *spotlight effect*.

THINK ABOUT IT

1. Open-plan offices, where large communal desks are used in place of private rooms or cubicles, are becoming increasingly popular. From the perspective of Zajonc's social facilitation theory, do you think open-plan offices are likely to facilitate or hinder performance and productivity? Why or why not? How might it depend on the type of work being conducted?

2. Can you think of any examples in your own life where group-think has taken place? What factors contributed to groupthink in these situations? What kinds of safeguards could you put in place in similar future situations to promote better decision making?

3. Suppose your company is trying to decide whether to make a risky new hire. Individually, most of the members of the hiring team lean toward hiring the candidate, as it could substantially increase revenues if it works out. When the hiring team gets together to discuss the potential hire, how might you predict that the attitudes of the individuals in the group will shift? What decision is likely to be made?

4. In *The Prince*, Machiavelli argued that people gain power through deception, manipulation, coercion, and the use of fear tactics. How does this perspective compare with research findings about who rises to power?

5. Do you think it's accurate to say that power corrupts? Why or why not? What factors influence the extent to which power leads to prosocial versus antisocial behavior?

6. What does research on deindividuation show about why crime rates are so high on Halloween?

7. How could you use your knowledge of self-awareness theory to reduce cheating behavior on a test that relies on the honor system?

The **answer guidelines** for the think about it questions can be found at the back of the book . . .

ONLINE STUDY MATERIALS

Want to earn a better grade on your test?

Go to **INQUIZITIVE** to learn and review this chapter's content, with personalized feedback along the way.

What would motivate a person to attack a human rights advocate?

How did peaceful relations between two ethnic groups dissolve into the Rwandan genocide?

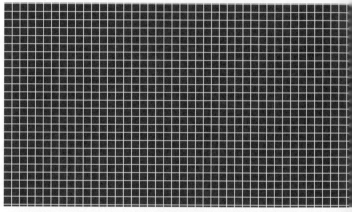

Can Internet activism reduce the prevalence of sexual violence?

Aggression

ON THE EVENING OF APRIL 6, 1994, JEAN-BAPTISTE and Odette, Rwandan husband-and-wife physicians, were enjoying a drink with a friend while listening to the radio. Just after 8 p.m., they heard that the plane carrying Rwanda's President Juvenal Habyarimana, a Hutu, had been shot down near Kigali, Rwanda's capital. Odette knew there was going to be trouble. Her husband was a Hutu just like the president, but Odette was a Tutsi. Though the Tutsis and Hutus shared language, religion, and a history of living together, in her lifetime Odette had witnessed several massacres of her people at the hands of the Hutus. She was worried that the killing of the president would fuel anti-Tutsi sentiment among the majority Hutus.

Tragically, she proved to be right. In the 100 days that followed the incident, Hutus would massacre approximately 800,000 Tutsis and moderate Hutus (Gourevitch, 1998). Many of the massacres were carried out by militiamen known as the *interahamwe*. They set up roadblocks throughout Rwanda, pulled Tutsis from their cars, and killed them. In small Rwandan towns, Hutus turned on their Tutsi neighbors, brutally killing them with machetes. Hutu schoolteachers massacred their Tutsi students. Even Tutsis taking sanctuary in churches were slaughtered. Throughout the rolling hills of Rwanda, flocks of crows and buzzards flew above areas where massacres had taken place.

Regrettably, massacres like the Rwandan genocide are a recurring part of history, and they are not limited to the past. The 2016 elections in Uganda led rival factions to murder dozens of their counterparts and burn hundreds of family homes. And today the world has been witness to the Rohingya genocide in Myanmar, in which fanatical Buddhist monks have instigated the massacre of Muslims living in that country.

OUTLINE

Situational Determinants of Aggression

Construal Processes and Aggression

Culture and Aggression

Evolution and Aggression

Conflict and Peacemaking

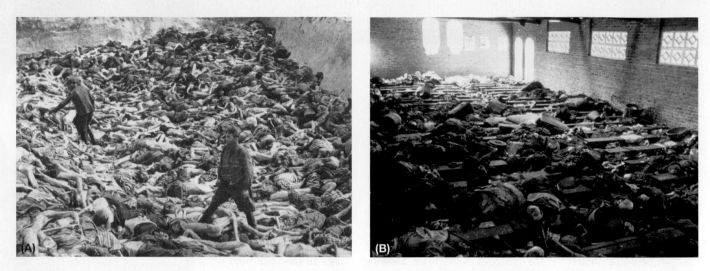

GENOCIDE
In addition to the mass murders by the Nazis, genocide has also occurred in the former Yugoslavia, in Cambodia, in Rwanda, and in Sudan, among other places. (A) An open grave of 10,000 naked bodies was found at the Bergen-Belsen concentration camp when the British liberated the camp in April 1945. (B) A church in Nitarama, Rwanda, holding the remains of 400 Tutsis killed by the Hutu *interahamwe* was discovered by a United Nations team in September 1994.

How do social psychologists make sense of such genocides and other forms of violence considered in this chapter—school shootings, homicide, rape, and the violence in families? How do situational factors produce aggression, and how does a person's construal of complex situations give rise to violence? Just as importantly, what factors promote group conflict—and what factors can pave the way for peace? ■

Situational Determinants of Aggression

One thing that's so striking about the massacres in Rwanda and elsewhere is how quickly peaceful, stable relations between groups can turn to aggression. Just as the right ecological conditions can transform a healthy forest into a roaring inferno, the right mix of situational factors can give rise to violence, whether between different ethnic or religious groups, adolescent males encountering each other on a Friday night, alt-right and antifa (that is, anti-fascist) protestors on college campuses, or children on grade-school playgrounds.

Explanations of aggression vary according to whether the behavior is hostile or instrumental. **Hostile aggression** refers to behavior motivated by feelings of anger and hostility, where the primary aim is to harm another, either physically or psychologically. Clearly, the genocide in Rwanda emerged in part for purely hostile reasons: Hutus seeking revenge on Tutsis out of anger about past grievances. **Instrumental aggression**, in contrast, refers to behavior that is intended to harm another in the service of motives other than pure hostility. People harm others, for example, to gain status, to attract attention, to acquire wealth, and to advance political and ideological causes. Over and above the anger and resentment felt by many Hutus, the genocide in Rwanda also had clear political motives: the Hutus were seeking to displace the more powerful Tutsis, who held many of the most important government positions. Many acts of aggression involve a mix of hostile and instrumental motives. A football player who intentionally harms

hostile aggression Behavior intended to harm another, either physically or psychologically, and motivated by feelings of anger and hostility.

instrumental aggression Behavior intended to harm another in the service of motives other than pure hostility (such as attracting attention, acquiring wealth, or advancing political or ideological causes).

BOX 13.1 | FOCUS ON GENES AND ENVIRONMENT

Nature or Nurture? It's Both

Many biological factors predispose people to act aggressively, ranging from the levels of testosterone in the blood to the density of neural connections in the frontal lobes (White, 1997; Yudko, Blanchard, Henne, & Blanchard, 1997). Research by Avshalom Caspi, Terrie Moffitt, and their colleagues indicates that aggression might best be thought of as the interaction of situational factors and genetically based individual differences (Caspi et al., 2002). They tested for the two forms of the monoamine oxidase A (MAOA) gene. Monoamine oxidase is an enzyme that metabolizes certain neurotransmitters in the synapses in the brain, allowing for smooth communication between neurons. In nonhuman species, individuals with a defective, short form of the MAOA gene have been shown to be more aggressive, suggesting that this version of the gene might also predict aggressive behavior in humans. Caspi and his colleagues identified men with this defective short form of the gene (37 percent of their sample) and those with the long form of the gene. To examine the influence of situational factors, they also identified men who had or hadn't been mistreated by their parents as children—one of the most potent factors in a person's childhood that can lead to violent behavior in adulthood.

Overall, the defective MAOA gene alone didn't affect whether the boys committed violent crimes (rape, assault, robbery) by age 26. This finding suggests that by itself, a genetic predisposition doesn't determine whether an individual will engage in aggression. But the combination of the short form of the MAOA gene *and* a family environment of physical abuse led boys to be three times more likely to have been convicted of a violent crime by age 26 than the boys who had the defective gene but had *not* been mistreated. Although those with the gene for low MAOA activity who had also suffered mistreatment were only 12 percent of the population in the study, they were responsible for 44 percent of the group's convictions for violent crime. Another way of putting it is that 85 percent of the boys with the short form of the MAOA gene who were severely mistreated engaged in some form of antisocial behavior. The important lesson of this telling study is that nature typically requires nurture to shape behavior.

---

another might do so out of aggressive emotion (hostile aggression) or for a variety of instrumental reasons, such as to foster a reputation for fearlessness, to help his team win, or to make the kind of plays that secure a place on the team or that earn a lucrative contract.

It's tempting to believe that aggression is largely the province of aggressive people—the bullies, sociopaths, and criminal personalities among us. There's certainly a grain of truth to this belief, but social psychology shows how a situational perspective is crucial to an adequate understanding of aggression. For example, scientists have discovered that certain genes may predispose people to aggression, but these genes increase the likelihood of aggressive action only in certain circumstances (**Box 13.1**). The important point is that situations give rise to or release people's aggressive tendencies. Let's explore some of the situational factors that might lead to violence.

Hot Weather

The opening line of Spike Lee's classic movie *Do the Right Thing* comes from a radio newscaster who says, "It's hot out there, folks." It's early in the morning, and the main characters, wearing T-shirts and shorts, are already uncomfortable and sweating profusely. By the end of the day, tensions between African-Americans and Italian-Americans escalate, and a race riot ensues.

People have long believed that moods and actions are closely tied to the weather. Perhaps the most widely assumed connection is between heat and aggression. We think of angry people as "boiling over," "steamed," or "hot under

HEAT AND AGGRESSIVE ACTION
In Spike Lee's movie *Do the Right Thing,* a confrontation between whites and blacks begins in a restaurant on a very hot day and escalates into a race riot.

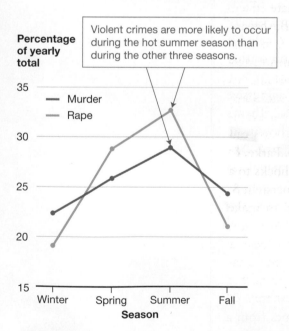

Percentage of yearly total

Violent crimes are more likely to occur during the hot summer season than during the other three seasons.

— Murder
— Rape

Season: Winter, Spring, Summer, Fall

FIGURE 13.1
SEASONAL EFFECTS ON VIOLENT BEHAVIOR
Do the hot months of summer make people more aggressive? Various studies of aggressive behaviors throughout different months of the year indicate that they do.
Source: Adapted from Anderson, 1989, p. 82.

the collar." Indeed, anger literally raises the temperature of the body because of accelerated heart rate and increased distribution of blood to certain areas, such as the hands.

Are people more aggressive when it's hot outside? As early as the nineteenth century, people noted that violent crime rates were higher in southern France and southern Italy, where the temperatures are hotter, than in northern France and northern Italy. Of course, other factors—such as levels of unemployment, per capita income, ethnic composition, the proportion of young men in the population, or average age—might also have produced these regional differences.

But Craig Anderson has provided evidence that higher-than-normal temperatures alone are associated with higher rates of violent crime (Anderson, 1987, 1989). Anderson examined the crime rates of 260 U.S. cities during the year 1980. For each city, he identified the number of days when the temperature exceeded 90 degrees Fahrenheit. The number of hot days (above 90 degrees) was a strong predictor of elevated violent crime rates but not nonviolent crime rates, even when controlling for the city's level of unemployment, per capita income, and average age of its citizens (Anderson, 1987).

People in the United States are also more violent during hot months, such as July and August, than during cooler months, such as January and February. (The one exception is December, when violent crime rates also rise—so much for holiday good cheer.) In **Figure 13.1**, you can see that the incidence of murder and rape increases during the summer months. Moreover, one of the cleverest studies of heat and aggression found that as the weather gets hotter, major league baseball pitchers are more likely to hit batters with a pitch (Reifman, Larrick, & Fein, 1991). This is especially true when the pitcher's teammates have been hit by the opposing pitcher earlier in the game (Larrick, Timmerman, Carton, & Abrevaya, 2011). This effect can't be attributed to the heat's effect on the pitcher's ability to control the pitch: neither wild pitches nor walks go up with the temperature (Kenrick & MacFarlane, 1984).

These findings point to an additional consequence of climate change: as Earth's temperature rises, we might expect to see increases in violence throughout the world. Recently, scientists have addressed this possibility, and the results provide one more reason to be concerned about climate change. For example, over the past 55 years, with every rise in annual temperature of 1 degree Celsius, there are 7.5 more assaults and homicides per 100,000 people in the United States, after controlling for such variables as inequality, poverty, and rates of incarceration (Anderson & DeLisi, 2011). Solomon Hsiang and his colleagues looked at data for the past 50 years and found that during what are known as El Niño years in tropical countries, when the weather is especially hot and dry, the likelihood of civil conflict rises dramatically (Hsiang, Meng, & Cane, 2011).

What is it about hot weather that makes people more aggressive? The connection between aggressive behavior and heat may be associated with what the ambient temperature does to people's emotions. One explanation involves people's attributional processes (see Chapter 5). People are aroused by the heat, but they are often unaware of the extent to which hot weather is the source of their arousal. When they encounter circumstances that prompt anger—say, a discourteous driver or an irritating romantic partner—they attribute their arousal to that person, and this misplaced annoyance gives rise to amplified feelings of anger, which can lead to aggression.

Media Violence

The average American adolescent spends about 9 hours a day viewing content on computers, handheld devices, and television screens (Rideout, 2015). These visual media are saturated with images of aggression. By age 12, the average viewer of American TV has seen about 100,000 acts of violence—from car crashes on reality police shows, to murders and beatings on weekly crime or courtroom dramas, to dead bodies on the nightly news. Social media such as Facebook and Instagram further expose people to images of violence, such as the shooting of Philando Castile, which was streamed on Facebook Live, or the killing of Eric Garner by police officers, which went viral on social media. Does the violence portrayed in the media make people more aggressive? Every year, concerned citizens urge the entertainment industry to stop depicting so much violence. Are their concerns warranted? Does scientific research unambiguously link violent media depictions to real-life aggressive behavior?

Researchers have explored this question by examining the immediate effects of media violence on aggression (Anderson, Shibuya, Ihori, Swing, Bushman, et al., 2010). In these studies, participants typically view aggressive films and then have an opportunity to act in an aggressive fashion, such as by administering a shock to a confederate of the researcher who was acting confrontational. In these types of controlled experiments with appropriate comparison conditions, exposure to media violence does indeed make people more aggressive. For example, watching aggressive films has been found to make juvenile delinquents confined in a minimum-security prison more aggressive (Leyens, Camino, Parke, & Berkowitz, 1975), to make male college students apply more intense shocks to a female confederate when made to feel angry (Donnerstein, 1980; Donnerstein & Berkowitz, 1981), and, when the videos were violently pornographic, to make males more strongly endorse aggression against women (Allen, Emmers-Sommer, Gebhardt, & Giery, 1995). Still other studies have found that media violence is especially likely to lead to aggression when viewers identify with the perpetrator of violence in the film or view the violence as justified—that is, when it is perpetrated against "bad people" (Leyens & Picus, 1973; Leyens, Cisneros, & Hossay, 1976).

But before concluding that media violence causes aggression, let's consider a couple of limitations of these lab studies. First, the measures of aggression, such as applying electric shock to a confederate, may have little to do with real-world violence—murder, rape, assault, genocide, and hate crimes. Another limitation is that these studies have captured only the short-term effects on aggression after exposure to violent media and haven't addressed the possibility of more enduring effects.

"I pray thee good Mercutio, let's retire;
The day is hot, the Capulets abroad.
And, if we meet, we shall not 'scape a brawl,
For now, these hot days, is the mad blood stirring."
—SHAKESPEARE, *ROMEO AND JULIET*

One more recent study suggests some caution in concluding that exposure to media violence in the real world leads to actual acts of aggression outside of the lab. In this study, researchers examined whether the rate of violent crime tends to rise or fall on dates surrounding the theatrical release of blockbuster films with especially violent content, such as *Hannibal* or *Passion of the Christ* (Dahl & Dellavigna, 2009). Contrary to what you might expect, when viewership of violent films in theaters rose, violent crimes actually dropped that day. For every million additional viewers of violent films, there was a 1.1–1.3 percent drop in violent crimes during the day in question, and viewership of violent films was especially likely to be associated with reduced violent crime during the evening and early-morning hours of the day when viewership was high. The authors explain this result in two ways: First, people who are most likely to commit violent crimes—young men—are particularly drawn to violent films and are of course less likely to engage in acts of aggression when sitting in a theater seat and engaged with watching the movie. This account explains the decrease in crime during the hours of 6 p.m. to midnight, when the movies are showing. Second, to explain the even larger drop in the crime rate from midnight to 6 a.m., the authors note that the time spent in the theater is a time some violent individuals would be drinking alcohol, a contributor to aggression. Being in the theater at a key point in the evening therefore sends them down a more benign path that night than they might otherwise travel. In general, then, it does seem that viewing media violence increases aggressive tendencies, with interesting counterexamples such as the study we just considered.

Violent Video Games

About 85 percent of American teenagers play video games regularly, averaging about 13 hours of play a week (Anderson & Bushman, 2001; Gentile, 2009). Boys spend more time playing on average (just over 16 hours a week) than girls (about 9 hours). Some 8 percent of all American children spend an average of 24 hours a week with video games. This level of video game playing shows symptoms of addiction—playing gives these kids a high, and they feel withdrawal symptoms when they don't play.

Eric Harris and Dylan Klebold were two such kids, aficionados of video games—and violent games specifically—who played hour after hour. Their favorite game was *Doom*. Harris, in fact, created a custom version of *Doom* in which two shooters, armed with extra weapons and unlimited ammunition, would gun down group after group of helpless victims. Tragically, on April 20, 1999, Harris and Klebold's real-life actions mirrored their violent video game world. The two teenagers took several guns and massive amounts of ammunition to their school, Columbine High School, in Littleton, Colorado. There they killed 12 of their classmates and a teacher, as well as injuring another 23 students, before killing themselves.

Are violent video games the cause of this kind of violence? Certainly they're not the only cause, and the video game industry vehemently denies any relationship between playing video games and violent behavior. In a May 12, 2000, interview on CNN, Doug Lowenstein, then president of the Interactive Digital Software Association, stated, "There is absolutely no evidence, none, that playing a violent video game leads to aggressive behavior." Yet research by Craig Anderson and Brad Bushman and their colleagues indicates otherwise (Anderson et al., 2017; Anderson & Bushman, 2001).

VIOLENT VIDEO GAMES AND THE COLUMBINE MASSACRE
(A) This is an image from a violent video game. The correlation between playing such games and aggressive thoughts and behavior documented in lab studies may play out in real life. (B) Harris and Klebold obsessively played the violent video game *Doom*, and some speculate that may have contributed to the boys' decision to plant bombs and shoot their classmates at Columbine High School in Littleton, Colorado. Here, cameras in the school cafeteria on April 20, 1999, show Harris and Klebold armed with guns, getting ready to shoot their fellow students, huddled beneath the tables.

In one illustrative study, 43 undergraduate women and men with an average amount of experience playing video games were randomly assigned to play one of two games (Bartholow & Anderson, 2002). Some played *Mortal Kombat*, in which the player chooses a character and attempts to kill six other characters, winning points for each violent death. Others played *PGA Tournament Golf*, in which players complete 18 holes of simulated golf, choosing appropriate clubs and shots best suited to the simulated wind conditions and the layout of sand traps and trees. All participants played several rounds of one of these games against a confederate of the researchers. When participants lost, the confederate punished them with an unpleasant, loud burst of white noise. When participants won, they returned the favor, punishing the confederate with white noise. Participants who had played *Mortal Kombat* gave longer and more intense bursts of white noise to their competitor than those who had played the golf game.

There have been over 100 studies on the effects of playing violent video games (Anderson et al., 2017). Some were experiments, like the one just described. Others were longitudinal studies examining whether the amount of violent video games a child plays predicts levels of aggression months later (Anderson et al., 2008). Anderson and his colleagues have documented five unsettling reactions associated with playing violent video games. Playing these games appears to (1) increase aggressive behavior; (2) reduce prosocial, positive behavior; (3) increase aggressive thoughts; (4) increase aggressive emotions, especially anger; and (5) increase blood pressure and heart rate, two physiological responses associated with fighting. These effects were observed in children and adults, both men and women, in the United States, several European countries, and Japan.

Social Rejection and Aggression

Along with the possibility that playing violent video games increases aggressive behavior, the Columbine massacre prompted considerable reflection in the United States about other causes of the shooting spree. Another question that was raised was whether social rejection contributed to the violence: Harris and Klebold felt rejected by the more popular students at school, and

BOX 13.2

Not So Fast:
Critical Thinking about Third Variables and False Associations

In light of extensive research showing the increased numbers of young people watching violent TV shows and movies and playing violent video games, you might be tempted to make a gloomy prediction: violent behavior must be rising dramatically among young people. Not so. While it's clear that kids are exposed to more violence in the media and are playing more violent video games than in the past, empirical analyses find that rates of violent behavior by young people are actually declining.

What's going on? How can the association between exposure to violence and aggression observed in society be the opposite of what's been documented in the lab? Critics of the longitudinal studies linking media and violent video game exposure to aggression later in life have brought into focus what they call the third-variable critique. Recall from Chapter 2 that in correlational research, such as the studies of media violence and aggression, researchers must take into account variables that weren't measured but that might be responsible for the observed association between two variables. For

example, if you find the amount of ice cream people eat is associated with the likelihood of violent behavior, you'd wisely attribute such an association to a third variable described in this chapter: hot weather. People eat more ice cream and engage in more violent behavior when it's hot (the third variable), so the apparent relationship between eating ice cream and violence is false—produced by some other cause.

What unmeasured variables, then, might produce the association between media exposure to violence in childhood and later aggressive behavior? Chris Ferguson and his colleagues have noted a few such variables (Ferguson & Kilburn, 2010). In the studies of interest, researchers rarely if ever control for how depressed the child is, and depression is known to predict both aggressive behavior and the consumption of media violence. Further, rarely do studies measure aggressive behavior in the child's peer group, yet kids who hang around aggressive peers are almost certainly more likely to play violent video games and to engage in aggressive behavior. When these unmeasured

variables—the depression of the child and the aggression of the peer group—are controlled for, the association between playing the games and subsequent aggression is reduced significantly (Ferguson, San Miguel, & Hartley, 2009).

Let's consider another unmeasured variable that's typically not assessed: the level of violence in the family. It's well established that a violent family atmosphere—where cruel comments, harsh punishment, and physical and emotional abuse are daily occurrences—is one of the strongest predictors of children acting out in aggressive ways. And a violent family environment is also associated with the tendency to consume violent media. Yet few, if any, studies have measured the degree to which the family environment is hostile, leaving open the possibility that this might be responsible for the observed association between playing violent video games and later aggression. (The same point can be made, of course, about violent TV shows and movies.) As always, controversy and criticism pave the way for more rigorous science and sharper answers to the questions that matter.

their shooting rampage was viewed by many as a reaction to being bullied and ostracized. Following the massacre, the U.S. Department of Education issued a report endorsing this hypothesis, concluding that school shooters like Harris and Klebold tend to feel rejected by their peers. Of course, it's clear that social rejection by itself wasn't a sufficient cause of their behavior, and many accounts of the tragedy emphasize the underlying pathologies of both boys (Cullen, 2009).

How might social rejection contribute to aggression on the scale of the Columbine massacre? Geoff MacDonald and Mark Leary (2005) have proposed an answer. Given human beings' profound dependence on others for food, shelter, and defense, being socially rejected from the group was akin to a death warrant throughout most of the long course of human evolution. Because of the many evolutionary advantages to being integrated into groups, MacDonald and Leary argue that social rejection came to activate a threat defense system that involves fight-or-flight, cardiovascular arousal. This arousal includes the release of the stress hormone cortisol, feelings of distress and pain, and, most relevant to the current discussion, defensive aggressive tendencies. Early in primate evolution, this threat defense system was attuned to cues of physical aggression, such as a predator's attack, and it enabled our ancestors to fare well in aggressive encounters. As humans evolved, social cues—overhearing gossip, spotting a sneer or contemptuous eye roll, or detecting a superior's critical tone of voice—became some of the triggers of this threat defense system.

SOCIAL ISOLATION AND AGGRESSIVE BEHAVIOR
In 2012, Adam Lanza fatally shot 20 first-graders and 6 teachers at Sandy Hook Elementary School, in Newtown, Connecticut. His social circumstances echo those of Harris and Klebold, perpetrators of the Columbine massacre. Lanza immersed himself in violent chat rooms and video games on the Internet. Throughout his life he experienced profound rejection and isolation, remaining holed up in his room for three continuous months before the shooting took place.

Dozens of studies have clarified how social rejection sets in motion feelings that can lead to aggression. For example, people who feel rejected report higher levels of chronic physical pain and physical ailments (MacDonald & Leary, 2005). People who feel rejected because of their gender, race, or social class tend to show elevated levels of threat-related physiology, such as increased blood pressure or higher levels of the stress hormone cortisol (Eliezer, Major, & Mendes, 2010; Jamieson, Koslov, Nock, & Mendes, 2013; John-Henderson, Rheinschmidt, Mendoza-Denton, & Francis, 2014).

To study experimentally the painful consequences of rejection, Kip Williams developed an ingenious ball-tossing paradigm, which may remind you of the politics involved in playing four square on your grade-school playground. One participant plays a ball-tossing game with two confederates. At a predetermined time in the experiment, the two confederates stop throwing the ball to the participant and throw it back and forth to each other for 5 minutes. Sure enough, being rejected in this game triggers feelings of distress, shame, and self-doubt in the participant and initiates a submissive, slouched posture (Williams, 2007).

In a neuroimaging study conducted by Naomi Eisenberger and her colleagues, participants thought they were playing a computerized version of the ball-tossing game with two other people. In actuality, the actions of the other two "people" had been programmed by the experimenter (Eisenberger, Lieberman, & Williams, 2003). When the participant experienced this virtual form of rejection, fMRI images revealed that a region of the brain (the dorsal anterior cingulate cortex) that processes physically painful stimuli lit up (Eisenberger, 2015). Subsequent studies have found that reliving a romantic breakup also activates this region of the brain (Kross, Berman, Mischel, Smith, & Wager, 2011). Taken together, these findings show that social rejection does activate a threat defense system.

Social rejection also increases the likelihood of aggression. People who report a chronic sense of rejection are more likely to act aggressively in their romantic relationships, even resorting to physical abuse (Dutton, 2002). In experimental work, Jean Twenge and her colleagues have found that people who were led to imagine a lonely, socially rejected future were more likely than control participants to administer unpleasant noise blasts to strangers who had nothing to do with the participant's rejection (Twenge, Baumeister, Tice, & Stucke, 2001). Putting these findings together, MacDonald and Leary have argued that social rejection is a root cause of the school shootings that are tragically an all-too-common feature of the contemporary landscape in the

United States and other countries, such as Scotland, Germany, and Norway (Leary, Kowalski, Smith, & Phillips, 2003). When assessing this last possibility, that social rejection gives rise to school shootings like those at Columbine and Sandy Hook, it's important to remember that many other factors are likely at play, from family dynamics to genetic tendencies (see Box 13.1), and that much of the evidence linking social rejection to actual violence is correlational, not causal.

Income Inequality

We've seen that short-term factors, such as hot weather and exposure to violent media, can lead to higher levels of aggression, and social conditions such as an individual's experience of social rejection or family violence can as well. Increasingly, social psychologists are turning their attention to whether more enduring conditions in a person's life influence levels of aggression, such as the presence of parks and green spaces in the neighborhood or prevailing economic conditions. Let's consider one such economic factor: society's level of income inequality, or the degree to which the wealthy differ from the poor in their yearly income and net wealth. Some countries are characterized by high economic inequality: the highest-paid professionals—CEOs, lawyers, and financial managers—have vastly more annual income than the average worker. The United States is characterized by *extreme* inequality. As you can see in **Figure 13.2**, income inequality in the United States is higher than in every European country and is exceeded by only a few countries, such as the Republic of the Philippines, Venezuela, and South Africa.

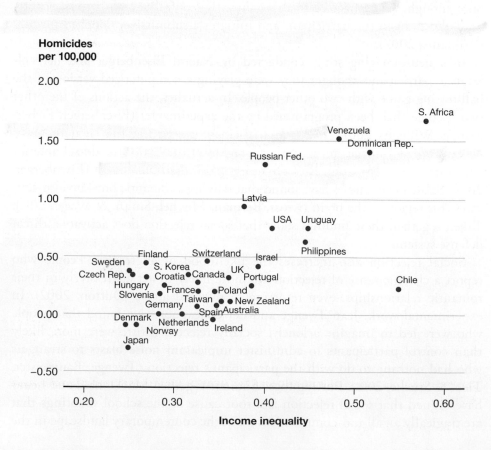

FIGURE 13.2
INCOME INEQUALITY AND HOMICIDE RATES
Homicides are more likely in countries where there is greater income inequality between the rich and the poor.
Source: Adapted from Elgar & Aitken, 2011.

BOX 13.3 ▶ FOCUS ON THE ENVIRONMENT

Green Neighborhoods Make More Peaceful Citizens

The current environmental movement was inspired by philosophers Henry David Thoreau and Ralph Waldo Emerson, who were known as transcendentalists. These writers found great calm and peace in being out in the woods. Their writings inspired a young naturalist, John Muir, whose experiences as a young man in the Sierra Nevada mountains of California led him to found the Sierra Club and lobby on behalf of state and national parks, which he helped create.

Social psychologists have recently begun to examine how easy access to nature and green spaces influences our psychological health. Recent experiments have found, for example, that a walk in the woods (as opposed to a walk through a town) enables adults to perform better on a measure of concentrated attention (Berman, Jonides, & Kaplan, 2008). Experiences in nature are the best predictor, compared with other recreational activities, of calming down from the stress of work (Korpela & Kinnunen, 2009). In geographical regions where people have greater access to beautiful green spaces, people tend to report greater happiness and good will toward others (Green & Keltner, 2017).

These findings raise a question: Might green spaces decrease neighborhood violence? Social psychologist Frances Kuo thinks so. In one line of research, Kuo studied police reports of violence occurring near 98 low-rise buildings that are part of the Ida Wells housing project in Chicago (Kuo & Sullivan, 2001). Some of the buildings were surrounded by trees and lawns, others by asphalt and a lack of greenery. The residents in these 98 buildings came from similar backgrounds, were enduring similar levels of unemployment and economic hardship, and had been randomly assigned to the buildings they lived in. Kuo discovered that the likelihood of violent crime was lower near apartments surrounded by green spaces. In experimental research, Kuo allowed children with attention deficit disorder, who are more prone to aggressive acts, to go for a walk of comparable length and physical exertion in one of three places: a green park, a quiet neighborhood, or noisy downtown Chicago (Taylor & Kuo, 2009). She found that children scored better on a measure of concentration only after the walk in the park. Green spaces seem to calm people's minds, enabling them to concentrate more effectively and better handle the frustrations of daily living.

BEING OUTDOORS AND PHYSICAL AND MENTAL HEALTH Urban areas that include green spaces encourage greater calm and civility and less aggression.

Is economic inequality associated with increased violence? To explore this question, researchers measured the degree of inequality, indicated by differences between the relatively wealthy in a society (usually the top 20 percent) and the relatively poor (usually the bottom 20 percent) in various regions of the world (Wilkinson & Pickett, 2009). They then looked at whether regional inequality—by country, state, or county—correlates with the prevalence of different kinds of violence. Indeed it does. In countries characterized by high economic inequality, such as Venezuela, South Africa, and the United States, the average citizen is much more likely to be murdered, assaulted, or raped than in countries with less economic inequality, such as Japan, Ireland, and Norway (see Figure 13.2 for the relationship between inequality and homicide). In addition, children in countries with greater income inequality are more likely to experience conflict with their peers and to report being victims of bullying.

This pattern emerges as well when states within the United States are classified according to their levels of economic inequality. Rates of homicide, for example, are higher in states with relatively high inequality (such as Louisiana and California) than in those with lower inequality (such as Utah and Wisconsin). On an even smaller scale, inequality also seems to play a role in determining which neighborhoods are more violent: there are higher rates of violence in urban neighborhoods in the United States with high income inequality than in neighborhoods with lower income inequality (Morenoff, Sampson, & Raudenbush, 2001).

Why might income inequality give rise to aggression? Social psychologists have provided several explanations. Wilkinson and Pickett (2009) found that the powerful feelings of social rejection that those at the bottom experience in unequal societies can trigger violence, a claim supported by our earlier discussion of social isolation and rejection.

Another possibility is that inequality undermines feelings of well-being, trust, and goodwill among people, which can give rise to frustration, anger and, ultimately, aggression, as we will explore in the next section. Consistent with this idea, researchers have found that during times of growing economic inequality in a country, citizens are less happy, experience greater physical pain, and feel less trusting of others (Daniels, Berkman, & Kawachi, 2000; Oishi, Kesebir, & Diener, 2011). These feelings, in turn, wear down the social fabric and so may increase the likelihood of aggression.

Finally, evolutionary psychologists Martin Daly, Margot Wilson, and Shawn Vasdev (2001) offer another possibility, contending that inequality throws males into more intense competition for economic resources and access to mates, two sources of conflict that often motivate murder and other crimes.

← LOOKING BACK

Many situational factors contribute to the likelihood of aggressive behavior. These include hot weather, violence in the media, violent video games, social rejection, and economic inequality.

Construral Processes and Aggression

We've seen that some circumstances encourage aggression. Situations, however, do nothing by themselves to incite aggression; it is how people construe situations that matters. Most people who live in extremely hot environments, see lots of violent images in movies or in video games, or encounter social rejection and income inequality do so without acting aggressively. Let's explore how particular construals of such states as feeling excessively hot and being socially isolated might lead to aggressive behavior.

Anger

For centuries, social theorists have known that anger leads to aggression. Leonard Berkowitz has offered a detailed theoretical account of the role of construal in the relationship between anger and aggression. He argues that any unpleasant stimulus can trigger a fight-or-flight response of anger. This is true of more obvious causes of aggression, such as being exposed to violent images in the media, living in a neighborhood defined by income inequality and poverty, and being insulted, as well as such factors as physical discomfort, hunger, and feelings of shame and depression (Berkowitz, 1989, 1993). Once angry, people are more likely to think things are unfair, to perceive others as having more combative intentions, and to imagine ways of inflicting harm (DeSteno, Petty, Wegener, & Rucker, 2000; Huber, Van Boven, Park, & Pizzi, 2015; Keltner, Ellsworth, & Edwards, 1993). This line of thinking helps clarify when aspects of a situation will lead to anger and aggression. For instance, sometimes hot weather doesn't trigger anger (it could very well prompt relaxation in the hammock instead) and thus won't lead to aggressive behavior. Other times, though, the discomfort of extreme heat will stimulate anger, thereby making people more prone to acting aggressively.

In one provocative test of this theory, Berkowitz examined how anger and the presence of weapons combine to make people more aggressive. Today weapons are everywhere, and they are a source of intense political debate. Worldwide, roughly 650 million guns are in the hands of civilians (Small Arms Survey, 2011). The same survey found that in the United States there are nearly 89 guns for every 100 citizens. According to Berkowitz, though, the presence of guns will lead to aggression only when combined with experiences of anger. To test his hypothesis, Berkowitz had male participants work on a series of intellectual problems with a male confederate, taking turns "evaluating each other's performance" by delivering shocks for performances that needed improvement (Berkowitz & LePage, 1967). The participants worked on the problems first and then were shocked by the confederate. Unknown to the participants, the confederate delivered shocks based on whether the participants had been assigned to a neutral condition or an anger condition (not based on their actual performance). The confederate shocked those assigned to the neutral condition just one time and those assigned to the anger condition seven times. The participant then watched the confederate work on the problems and provided feedback to the confederate. The participant did so under one of three conditions. In a "no object" condition, no objects were near the shock machine. In a "neutral object" condition, badminton rackets and shuttlecocks were near the shock machine. In a "gun" condition, a revolver and

BOX 13.4 ▷ FOCUS ON SPORTS

The Effect of Uniform Color on Aggression

The tendency to act more aggressively when a weapon is nearby reinforces a core lesson of social psychology—the situationist message that seemingly small changes in the environment (such as the presence of a weapon) can have a substantial impact on behavior. This tendency also raises the question of whether other environmental cues might foster or inhibit aggression. For example, might the clothes people wear influence how they behave, including whether they behave aggressively? Is it possible that the menacing black shirts worn by Hitler's S.S. (*Schutzstaffel*) made it easier for them to brutalize the populace of conquered lands?

Support for such a possibility comes from research on the effect of uniform color on aggressiveness in professional sports (Frank & Gilovich, 1988). The investigators began by examining the penalty records of all teams in American professional football (the NFL) and ice hockey (the NHL) from 1970 to 1985. As shown in **Figure 13.3**, the black-uniformed teams consistently ranked near the top in penalties every year.

As pronounced as this tendency might be, however, it can't predict whether wearing black actually causes players to be more aggressive. There are two other possibilities. First, because of some negative stereotypes involving the color black (such as black being the typical dress of movie villains), players in black uniforms may look more intimidating even if they play no differently than players on other teams who aren't wearing black. Thus, players in black uniforms may be more likely than others to be penalized for marginal infractions. Second, the finding may simply be a selection effect; that is, the general managers of certain teams, believing that aggressiveness pays off in victories, may both recruit particularly aggressive players and, incidentally, give them black uniforms to foster an aggressive image.

The latter interpretation, however, can be ruled out. By a convenient twist of fate, several teams switched uniforms from non-black to black during the period under investigation, and all experienced a corresponding increase in penalties. One team, the NHL's Pittsburgh Penguins, changed uniform colors in the middle of a season, so the switch wasn't accompanied by any changes in players, coaches, or front-office personnel. Nevertheless, the Penguins averaged 8 penalty minutes in the blue uniforms they wore before the switch and 12 penalty minutes in the black uniforms they wore after—a 50-percent increase.

Follow-up laboratory experiments have provided support for both perceptions of aggressiveness and actual aggressiveness of players dressed in black. Thus, the tendency for black-uniformed teams to draw so many penalties appears to be the joint effect of a bias on the part of referees and a tendency for players wearing black to act more aggressively (Frank & Gilovich, 1988).

But does wearing black always make people more aggressive? Probably not. The effect seems to be limited to contexts that are already associated with confrontation and aggression. The black clothing worn by Catholic clerics and Hasidic Jews, for example, may not make them any more aggressive, but the black shirts worn by Hitler's S.S. might very well have contributed to their brutality.

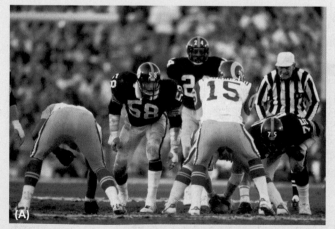

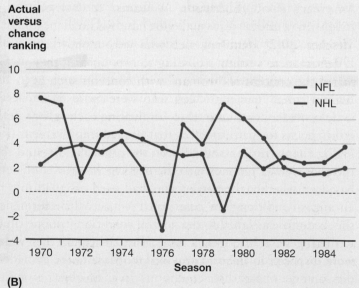

FIGURE 13.3 Uniform Color and Aggression (A) The Pittsburgh Steelers, wearing black uniforms, were known for their aggressive play. (B) Points on the graph of penalty records represent the difference between the average ranking of the black-uniformed teams and the average to be expected based on chance alone (dotted horizontal line at 0). Source: Adapted from Frank & Gilovich, 1988.

a shotgun lay near the shock machine—rather unusual experimental props, to say the least. As you can see in **Figure 13.4**, the presence of guns made participants more aggressive only when they were also angered by the confederate's actions (that is, after being shocked seven times in the anger condition). In further support of the point that the presence of guns alone does not trigger aggression, a more recent study found that hunters don't become more aggressive when presented with images of guns, probably because they construe guns as objects for recreation and fun rather than for violence (Bartholow, Anderson, Carnagey, & Benjamin, 2005).

Dehumanization

Acts of aggression often go hand-in-hand with a particularly dangerous construal process known as **dehumanization**, the attribution of nonhuman characteristics to other people (Haslam & Loughnan, 2014). Studies of escalating conflict and genocide regularly find that dehumanization fuels extreme violence. During the Rwandan genocide, the Hutus referred to the Tutsis as "cockroaches." The Nazis described the Jews as "lice." During the eighteenth-century slave trade, Europeans referred to the Africans they captured, sold, and killed as "brutes" and "beasts." Hate crimes against gay men are often justified with dehumanizing rhetoric. One of the fastest-growing targets of violent hate crimes—the homeless—are frequently dehumanized as animals. Even in more peaceful times, dehumanization arises in more subtle forms. You might hear a political pundit refer to an "infestation" of undocumented immigrants (who are further dehumanized by being referred to as "illegals" or "aliens") or a candidate he doesn't like as "robotic."

Dehumanization can unleash aggression for the simple reason that it's easier to harm people when they seem less human, less like ourselves. For example, dehumanization plays a role in bullying behavior (Haslam & Loughnan, 2014) and in condoning police violence against African-Americans (Goff, Eberhardt, Williams, & Jackson, 2008). In a study of sexual violence, Rudman and Mescher (2012) identified men who were more likely to dehumanize women according to how quickly they paired the concept of "woman" with concepts such as "animal" and "instinct." Men who were more likely to dehumanize women in this way reported that they would harass women sexually, that if no one would ever find out about it they would force a woman to have sex, and that women on occasion deserve to be raped.

One factor that increases the likelihood of dehumanization is loyalty to valued social groups. When we feel strongly committed to a group, whether a political party, an ethnic group, or a sports team, we are more disposed to dehumanize outgroup members. In one survey of over 180 groups in developing countries, tribes characterized by powerful ingroup loyalty and a strong sense of "we feeling" were more likely to dehumanize other tribes and act in violent fashion against them (Cohen, Montoya, & Insko, 2006).

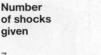

Number of shocks given

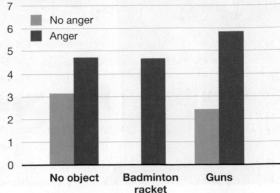

**FIGURE 13.4
ANGER, WEAPONS, AND AGGRESSION**
When people are angry and in the presence of weapons, they behave more aggressively.
Source: Adapted from Berkowitz & LePage, 1967.

dehumanization The attribution of nonhuman characteristics and denial of human qualities to groups other than one's own.

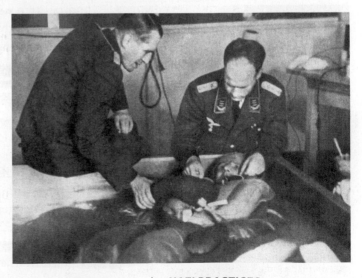

NAZI PRACTICES
The pain experiments the Nazis performed on Jews during the Holocaust are an extreme example of dehumanization.

THE PSYCHOLOGY OF SHOOTING SPREES
Elliot Rodger killed 6 people and injured 14 more near the campus of the University of California, Santa Barbara. His violence was fueled by a hatred of women and disgust at interracial couples.

Shockingly, even rather benign feelings of social connection to some people increase the likelihood of dehumanizing others. Here the thinking is that although feeling socially connected brings us closer to people within our group, it creates greater distance from those who are different from us, making dehumanization more likely. In one study guided by this idea, students who were asked to recall a time of feeling connected to another person attributed less human-like mental states, such as empathy and moral concern, to outgroups such as the wealthy or the poor (Waytz & Epley, 2012). In a clever extension of this work, when participants reported their attitudes while sitting next to a friend (thus feeling socially connected) as opposed to sitting next to a stranger, they were more likely to dehumanize non–U.S. citizens who were detained for security reasons and to more strongly endorse forms of torture such as waterboarding and the application of electric shock (Waytz & Epley, 2012).

Distancing from the Causes of Aggression

How might we avoid the pernicious tendencies associated with anger and dehumanization? One recommendation comes from the work of Ethan Kross and Ozlem Ayduk (2017), who propose that getting some distance from anger makes people more peaceful in contexts that might otherwise trigger aggression. Any experience of anger can be recalled from the original point of view, as it was initially experienced, or from a distance (Ayduk & Kross, 2008). To view our anger from a distance, we could, for example, think of the frustrating event as just one moment in time or as a single episode within a much longer relationship or even as if it were part of a movie or novel. Construing potentially angering situations in each of these ways allows us to attain some distance from our feelings, and research suggests that doing so is a good thing.

In one study, participants were asked to think about a time that had made them angry (Ayduk & Kross, 2008). Half of them were told to immerse themselves in the experience and vividly feel it in the present moment. The other half, those in the distance condition, were told to look at the experience from a distance, as if they were watching themselves in a movie. Those participants who distanced themselves from their anger showed less fight-or-flight increases in blood pressure and reported a greater sense of calm. In a similar vein, when people look at conflicts from a more distant perspective by imagining what the situation will be like a year from now (as opposed to taking an immersed, here-and-now point of view), they tend to blame others less and are more forgiving (Hyunh, Yang, & Grossmann, 2016).

Remarkably, when you ask people why they are upset, referring to them in the third person rather than the second person evokes less negative emotion. For example, if we ask Jennifer, "Why are you upset?" she will experience more negative emotion than if we ask her, "Why is Jennifer upset?" (Grossmann & Kross, 2014). Both experience and research indicate that it's easier for people to reason calmly about other people's problems than their own. When people use

NEGATIVE CHARACTERIZATIONS
During wartime, dehumanization can be found in all kinds of publications. This is a page from a 1938 Nazi children's book. The picture's caption reads: "Just look at these guys! The louse-infested beards! The filthy, protruding ears, those stained, fatty clothes . . . Jews often have an unpleasant sweetish odor. If you have a good nose, you can smell the Jews."

their own names to think about the self, it prompts them to take an observer's perspective—to think about themselves as though they were someone else (albeit another person whose inner thoughts and feelings they have privileged access to). This practice often provides them with the psychological distance needed to calmly reason through stressful situations and come up with wiser solutions for them.

← LOOKING BACK

People's construals of situations can be crucial in determining whether they act aggressively. When any kind of stimulus triggers anger, we're more likely to act aggressively. Our tendency to dehumanize others can fuel aggression. We aren't prisoners of such hostile construals, however. When we step back from them and look at what's making us angry from a distance, we become less hostile and more calm.

Culture and Aggression

Anthropologists have long noted dramatic cultural variation in the expression of aggression. People in some cultures have been observed to be unusually kind, peaceful, and cooperative. Alaskan Inuits, for example, have been described as rarely expressing anger or aggression and as remarkably kind in their actions with others. People in other cultures have been portrayed as violent, belligerent, and aggressive. Among the Yanomami, who live in the Amazon region, aggression is encouraged in children, intratribal fighting with spears and knives is a weekly source of injury and death, and rape and war are considered an intrinsic

CULTURAL DIFFERENCES IN AGGRESSIVE EXPRESSION
(A) The Alaskan Inuits rarely express anger or aggression. (B) The Yanomami encourage aggression in their children and are known for their violent raids against their enemies.

part of human nature (Chagnon, 1997). Their fitting name for themselves is "the fierce people." These qualitative observations are backed up by quantitative data: there are dramatic cultural variations in every kind of aggression, including bullying, assault, murder, and rape.

What accounts for such variation? A cultural perspective holds that certain values, as well as habitual ways of construing the self and others, make members of one culture more aggressive and violent than others. Social psychologists have developed ways of examining cultural differences in aggressive behavior in the laboratory in order to better understand them.

The Culture of Honor

culture of honor A culture defined by its members' strong concerns about their own and others' reputations, leading to sensitivity to insults and a willingness to use violence to avenge any perceived wrong.

In a **culture of honor**, which is prevalent in the U.S. South (see Chapter 2), men tend to be more concerned than people in other cultures about their reputation for toughness, machismo, and their willingness and ability to avenge a wrong or insult. These concerns give rise to firm rules of politeness and other ways people recognize the honor of others, thus lending stability to social relationships and reducing the risk of violence. The downside of the concern with honor is that it makes people particularly sensitive to slights and insults, thereby leading them to respond with violence to protect or reestablish their honor.

As you'll recall from Chapter 2, Richard Nisbett and Dov Cohen (1996) have shown that when their honor is slighted, Southerners are more likely than Northerners to respond with aggression. In archival research, Nisbett and his colleagues found that murders in the context of another felony case were about equally common in the North, South, and Southwest; but murders that occurred as a result of an argument or perceived insult were far more common in the South and Southwest than in the North (**Figure 13.5**).

To examine participants' sensitivity to slights and insults, Cohen and his colleagues exposed Southerners and Northerners to an insult in the context of a

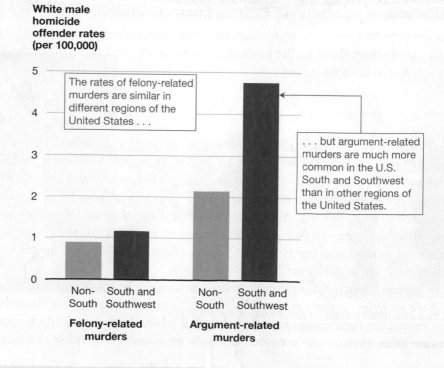

FIGURE 13.5
HOMICIDE AND THE CULTURE OF HONOR
Argument-related homicide rates point to a sensitivity to slights and insults that characterizes a culture of honor in the South and Southwest.
Source: Adapted from Nisbett & Cohen, 1996, p. 21; based on data from Fox & Pierce, 1987.

laboratory study. An accomplice of the experimenter bumped into the subject and called him an "asshole" (Cohen, Nisbett, Bowdle, & Schwarz, 1996). Insulted participants from Southern states showed more anger in their facial expressions than did insulted Northerners. The insulted Southerners' testosterone and cortisone levels increased significantly more than those of insulted Northerners. Following the insult, the Southerners shook another person's hand more firmly and refused to move out of the way of an imposing confederate walking toward them down a narrow hallway. Additionally, in a later field experiment, Cohen and Nisbett (1997) found that some Southern employers actually expressed a good deal of warmth toward a potential job applicant who confessed to having been convicted of manslaughter after defending his honor.

Where did this regional difference in the importance attached to honor come from? Why is honor-related homicide more common in the South? Could it just be the hot weather? It's not likely, because honor-related homicides are actually more common in the relatively cool mountain regions of the South (Kentucky, Arkansas) than in the relatively hot agricultural lowlands (Mississippi, Alabama). Could it be the brutal history of slavery? Again, it's not likely, and for the same geographical reason: Homicide is more common in the highlands, where slavery was relatively uncommon, than in the lowlands, where slavery was ubiquitous.

Nisbett and Cohen (1996) argue that the culture of honor in the South is a variant of a cultural perspective found worldwide among people who earn their living by herding animals. Herders are susceptible to losing their entire wealth in an instant if someone steals their cows, pigs, or sheep. Farmers, in contrast, are susceptible to no such rapid and catastrophic loss, at least not at the hands of another person. The vulnerability of the herder means he has to develop a tough exterior and make it clear he's willing to take a stand against the slightest threat, even an insult or a joke at his expense. This difference fits the pattern of violence in the United States because the North was founded primarily by farmers from England, Germany, and the Netherlands, whereas the South was founded primarily by Scottish and Irish settlers (and especially the Scotch-Irish of Northern Ireland, Celtic peoples who had herded, rather than farmed, since prehistoric times). Thus, the people in the Southern highlands, where the herding culture continued to be a major economic activity until quite recently, were more likely to be violent than those in the lowlands, where settlers had taken advantage of the rich soil to become farmers.

Culture and Sexual Violence

In 1990, Nobel Prize–winning economist Amartya Sen estimated that there were 100 million missing women in the world (Sen, 1990). Women, holding constant their country of origin and class background, are more likely to enjoy a longer life expectancy than men, so a given population should include more women than men. But in some countries, particularly those where women have less status than men, women are underrepresented in the population because of premature death due to patterns of negligence and violence—hence the estimate of "missing" women (Kristof & WuDunn, 2009).

In certain countries, for example, female infanticide is practiced. In addition, in those societies, parents are less likely to immunize their daughters than their sons or to take their daughters to the hospital when they are sick. As a result, girls are more likely to die early deaths due to preventable or curable sicknesses.

RAPE IS A COMMON METHOD OF VIOLENCE DURING WAR Maomi Thomas, age 16 and pictured here, was raped amidst the violence in the Democratic Republic of Congo.

rape-prone culture A culture in which rape tends to be used as an act of war against enemy women, as a ritual act, or as a threat against women to keep them subservient to men.

SEXUAL VIOLENCE ON CAMPUS The continuing prevalence of sexual violence prompted a new federal investigation of 55 American universities and colleges for failing to take appropriate measures in responding to sexual attacks on campus.

Bride burning, the practice of punishing a young woman for her family's failure to confer a sufficient dowry on the groom's family in marriage, claims the lives of several thousand young women in India every year. The sexual trafficking of young girls into a life of prostitution, widespread throughout the world, claims the lives of thousands of girls each year, some as young as age 8. Some of these girls are sold by their own families.

Less deadly forms of sexual violence are common in virtually every country. For example, in the United States, 50–80 percent of women have been sexually harassed, having been stalked, catcalled, or made the target of obscene comments at work or over the phone (Fairchild & Rudman, 2008). Moreover, approximately 10–20 percent of adolescent and young-adult females report having been sexually assaulted by someone they are dating (Black et al., 2011), and one in every five women have been raped (Fisher, Cullen, & Turner, 2000; Statistics about sexual violence, 2015).

One of the most disturbing and common acts of violence against women is rape, the coercive forcing of sex by one person (usually male) on another (typically female). Rape is often used as an instrument of terror during war, as it was in the genocides in Bosnia, Rwanda, and Darfur and when ISIS took over large tracts of land in Iraq and Syria. But acts of rape aren't limited to the madness of war. According to the organization UN Women (2011), sexual violence and rape are disturbingly common. A survey of 86 countries found that, on average, about 20 percent of women experience sexual violence or rape in a romantic relationship at some time in their lives. In some countries, this rarely happens; for example, only 2.7 percent of women in Cambodia reported such an experience. In other countries, the statistics are staggering; in Ethiopia, 58.6 percent of women reported experiencing at least one episode of sexual violence in an intimate relationship. Sexual violence has enormous long-term costs. Compared with women who haven't been traumatized by sexual violence, women who have are twice as likely to experience major episodes of depression and are more likely to commit suicide (Krahé, 2017).

What makes rape more prevalent in certain cultures than in others? And how can such a question be tackled empirically? Peggy Reeves Sanday (1981, 1997) relied on archival records to study the cultural determinants of rape. She read descriptions provided by historians and anthropologists of 156 cultures dating back to 1750 BCE and continuing to the 1960s. Looking carefully for references to rape in these accounts, Sanday identified what she called **rape-prone cultures**, which made up 18 percent of the cultures studied. In these cultures, men used rape as an act of war against enemy women; as a ritual act, such as part of a wedding ceremony or an adolescent male's rite of passage to adulthood; and as a threat against women to keep them subservient

to men. In 35 percent of the other cultures, rape was present or observed, but not used in such ritualistic and systematic ways as in rape-prone cultures. And we note, sadly, that it would be no surprise if these figures actually *underestimated* the prevalence of rape-proneness across cultures. They are based largely on anthropologists' observations, and rape is one of the most difficult acts to observe and a taboo subject in many cultures.

The cultures where rape was particularly prevalent were defined by two qualities. First, rape-prone cultures were more likely to have high levels of violence generally, a history of frequent warfare, and an emphasis on machismo and male toughness. Second, in keeping with the idea that rape is a means of subordinating women, rape was more prevalent in cultures in which women had lower status. Women in rape-prone cultures were found to be less likely than in other cultures to receive education and participate in political decision making. Where rape was uncommon, women were more empowered and more likely to be granted equal status with men. Additionally, studies find that with rising economic equality, violence perpetrated by romantic partners against women declines (Archer, 2006).

Consider the Mbuti Pygmies, who are an indigenous group in the Congo region of Africa, as an illustration of these findings (Turnbull, 1965). The Mbuti Pygmies are a (reportedly) nearly rape-free society, and there is minimal interpersonal violence and fighting. This culture attaches great prestige to the raising of children and values women's contribution to group well-being. Though women and men assume different duties, they have equal standing, and women and men participate equally in political decision making.

GENDER EQUALITY IN A RAPE-FREE CULTURE
The Mbuti Pygmies, in the Congo region of Africa, are known for their low levels of violence against women.

Evolution and Aggression

For many people, the word *evolution* brings to mind a violent struggle for survival and the opportunity to reproduce—the "nature red in tooth and claw," to quote from Tennyson's poem "In Memoriam." As we've emphasized at several points in this book, evolutionary theory is more than just a theory of competition and violence; it's helped illuminate all manner of social behaviors, from romantic attraction to empathic concern for others. Nevertheless, just as popular views of evolution would have it, an evolutionary perspective *has* proved helpful in understanding some of the origins of aggression.

Violence in Stepfamilies

Literature is full of tales of wicked stepparents who abuse their children. In the animal kingdom, "step-relations" seem similarly prone to violence. To take one example, when male lions acquire a new mate, they routinely kill all of that female's cubs from her prior matings. Evolutionary psychologists Margo Wilson and Martin Daly argue that these tendencies in our mammalian relatives have left their trace in human nature (Daly & Wilson, 1996; Wilson, Daly, & Weghorst, 1980).

Natural selection, Daly and Wilson maintain, rewards those parents who devote resources to their own offspring. All the behaviors related to parental care, from filial love to breast-feeding, assist the survival of our own offspring, thereby increasing **inclusive fitness**—our own survival plus that of children carrying our genes. But parental care is costly, as any parent of a newborn knows; it requires time, effort, and material resources. It's been estimated that hunter-gatherers typically don't become net contributors of food and other resources until around the age of 21. (Your parents should be so lucky!) In evolutionary terms, parental expenditures are offset by the gains of having offspring—namely, the survival of their genes. Stepparents, in contrast, incur the same costs with no enhancement of their inclusive fitness, since they don't share genes with their stepchildren.

Survey results consistently indicate that relationships between stepparents and stepchildren tend to be more distant and conflicted, as well as less committed and satisfying, than between parents and their genetic offspring (Hobart, 1991). Crime statistics are even more sobering. Daly and Wilson (1996) found that in the United States, children who are younger than age 2 are 100 times more likely to be abused to the point of death by stepparents than by genetic parents, and in

inclusive fitness According to evolutionary theory, the fitness of an individual is based on reproductive success and the passing of one's own genes and those of relatives to future generations.

MISTREATED STEPCHILDREN
Literature and fairy tales abound with tales of stepchildren treated badly by their stepmothers. (A) Cinderella becomes the scullery maid for her stepmother and stepsisters. (B) Hansel and Gretel are sent out to die in the forest at the urging of their stepmother.

Canada, they are 70 times more likely to be killed by stepparents than by genetic parents. These findings hold, it's important to note, even when controlling for a variety of contributing causes, such as poverty, age of the mother, length of time the couple has lived together, and number of children in the home. In a study of a South American hunter-gatherer people, 43 percent of children raised by a mother and stepfather died before their fifteenth birthday; that's more than twice the rate of death (19 percent) of children raised by two genetic parents. (This statistic doesn't imply that the stepchildren were killed; but at the very least, they were more likely to have been denied resources, such as food and physical care, that were made available to genetic offspring.)

Gender and Aggression

When we hear about school shootings or teen violence or when we read about rape or genocide, it's almost always true that these acts of aggression are committed by young men. Physical aggression is, in fact, from early childhood to old age, among the most marked gender differences in behavior. In the United States, 99 percent of all people arrested for rape, 88 percent of those arrested for murder, 92 percent arrested for robbery, and 87 percent arrested for aggravated assault are men (Kimmel, 2004). As early as age 2, boys are more physically aggressive than girls (Archer, 2009). Men are also overwhelmingly the victims of violence. For example, men are 20 times as likely to kill other men as women are to kill other women (Daly & Wilson, 1988).

Women, of course, are also aggressive, but in different ways. Women seem to exceed men in what's known as relational aggression or emotional aggression; they are more likely to gossip, form alliances, and practice exclusion and social rejection to hurt others (Coie et al., 1999; Dodge & Schwartz, 1997; McFayden-Ketchum, Bates, Dodge, & Pettit, 1996). Many female readers will remember with a wince the vicious ways girls can behave toward one another in middle school, talking behind people's backs and tarnishing reputations. And with the rise of Internet

A SCENE FROM THE MOVIE
MEAN GIRLS
Although men commit most of the acts of physical aggression, women are more likely to engage in relational or emotional aggression.

use, it shouldn't be surprising that female adolescents are also more likely to be the target of cyberbullying and the spreading of malicious rumors (U.S. Department of Education, 2015). Obviously, this kind of aggression can be extremely hurtful.

Most striking and well documented, though, is the tendency for men to engage in more physical violence than women. Evolutionary psychologists, including John Archer, have sought to understand these striking gender differences in aggression in terms of access to reproductive opportunities (Archer, 2009; Daly & Wilson, 1988). Their theorizing builds on the concept of parental investment (see Chapter 1). According to this thinking, women invest more in their offspring than men and thus are less likely to desert their offspring and seek other reproductive opportunities. Men, in contrast, are evolutionarily freer to go outside the primary relationship and compete with other men for access to mates. Within this competition, high-status, more aggressive men are more successful than low-status men in terms of reproductive success, or number of offspring. By contrast, reproductively healthy women who want to pass on their genes are, almost without exception, able to do so and therefore don't have the same need to be physically aggressive.

Throughout evolutionary history, the basic difference in reproductive opportunities led males to evolve characteristics and strategies for outcompeting other males for mates. Physical aggression is one such strategy, and it accounts for the evolution of that trait, as it serves males well in competing with other males. For example, surveys from cultures around the world reveal that men are 7.6 percent taller than women, 25 percent heavier, and 1.5 times physically stronger (Archer, 2009). Male physical prowess evolved for aggressive encounters with other men, and indeed, today bigger men tend to engage in more aggressive behaviors (DeWall, Bushman, Giancola, & Webster, 2010). Another advantage of male size and strength is for protecting mates and offspring against animal predators and other humans.

According to evolutionary psychologists, nonverbal signals of size and strength evolved in males so they could negotiate their rank in status hierarchies in order to gain privileged access to mates. Cues of physical strength include a broader chin, a deeper voice (which correlates with physical size), and even facial hair—all of which have evolved, the thinking goes, for men to signal strength to other males and enjoy elevated status and preferential access to mating opportunities (Archer, 2009; Cheng, Tracy, Ho, & Henrich, 2016).

The evolutionary approach helps explain the increases in muscle mass, facial hair, and other signs of physical development during puberty in young men. Higher levels of testosterone are associated with higher levels of aggression. For example, juvenile delinquents have higher levels of testosterone than college students (Banks & Dabbs, 1996). Members of rowdier fraternities also have higher testosterone levels than members of more responsible fraternities (Dabbs, 2000). Social psychologists have also found that testosterone promotes status-related behaviors in competitive settings (Mehta & Josephs, 2010). Two general patterns of results suggest that testosterone probably served men well in the competition for mates (Mehta, Mor, Yap, & Prasad, 2015; Schultheiss, 2013). First, men who have higher levels of testosterone tend to exhibit more dominant, assertive behaviors that presumably help them achieve higher status. (In women, the hormone estradiol, which converts to testosterone in the body, has a similar effect.) Second, men who care a lot about power and status show increased testosterone (in women, increased estradiol) after winning competitions.

Some cultural theorists have a very different take on these striking gender differences in aggressive behavior. These theorists believe that men are more aggressive not primarily because of evolutionary patterns but because men are socialized into roles that encourage physical aggressiveness. Parents, teachers, media sources, and social institutions systematically (but often unwittingly) cultivate more aggressive tendencies in men. Consider, for example, how young boys are treated from the earliest stages of life. When parents see a video of an infant looking startled, the parents are likely to say that the infant is angry if it's a boy. If the same infant is said to be a girl, the parents say that the infant is fearful (Condry & Condry, 1976). Mothers talk more about emotions with their daughters than with their sons, and such conversations may cultivate greater empathy in women (Fivush, 1991). The one emotion mothers don't tend to talk more about with their daughters is anger, which mothers are more likely to mention in labeling the emotions of their sons. Thus, starting very early in life, anger and aggressive reactions are made more salient to young boys than to young girls. Given that anger is a primary determinant of aggression, this socialization process might account for at least some of the gender differences we're discussing.

Combining the evolutionary and cultural approaches to male aggression, Jennifer Bosson and Joseph Vandello have proposed that as a consequence of both evolutionary and socialization processes, a man's gender identity is significantly tied up in his physical strength, toughness, and fierceness. However, according to their **precarious manhood hypothesis**, many factors—competition, status contests, being the target of male violence, shifting economic conditions, the loss of a job—can render a man's gender identity relatively uncertain (Vandello & Bosson, 2013). According to this hypothesis, male gender identity is more vulnerable than women's gender identity, and as a result, men need to resort to risky and often aggressive actions to continually prove their manhood.

Empirical studies show that people do indeed believe that manhood is precarious (Bosson & Vandello, 2011). For example, in one study participants read proverbs that portrayed the insecure nature of manhood ("manhood is hard won and easily lost") or the same proverbs phrased to focus on the uncertain nature of womanhood ("womanhood is hard won but easily lost"). Participants significantly more often endorsed the proverbs portraying precarious manhood.

As the precarious manhood hypothesis would have it, men, aware of their more vulnerable gender identity, should be more sensitive to threats to their manhood and thus more likely to resort to risky and often aggressive behaviors to prove themselves. For some readers this may be reminiscent of high school bravado—the dangerous acts young men routinely engage in, challenging each other physically, provoking fights, climbing water towers, driving recklessly. (We've been told by physicians in the Southwest that the only people who show up in hospitals with rattlesnake bites are inebriated young men!) In one study, men first either braided a bunch of ropes or braided the hair of a wig, the latter being a more feminine task and a threat to stereotypical notions of masculinity (Bosson & Vandello, 2011). All participants then put on boxing gloves and struck

EVOLUTIONARY THEORY AND PHYSICAL APPEARANCE
According to evolutionary theorists, someone like Don Draper in the TV series *Mad Men* could be expected, on the basis of his physical appearance, to have many mates.

precarious manhood hypothesis The idea that a man's gender identity of strength and toughness may be lost under various conditions and that such a loss can trigger aggressive behavior.

BOX 13.5 ▶ **FOCUS ON** MENTAL HEALTH

The Cold-Hearted Psychopath

Cold-hearted killers are stock figures in violent films. The inspiration for these characters is a clinical category known as antisocial personality disorder, or psychopathy. Psychopaths, usually male, are prone to extreme patterns of violence and make up a significant number of individuals in prison for violent offenses (Hare, 1991). A long-standing assumption is that psychopaths have profound empathy deficits, lacking any feeling for those they harm.

Research reveals a more nuanced picture, suggesting that while psychopaths are as adept as the average person in *understanding* the emotions of others, they have deficits in *responding* emotionally to the suffering of others. The most systematic study of psychopathy has been conducted by James Blair and his colleagues (Blair, Mitchell, & Blair, 2005). These researchers have found that psychopaths cognitively understand the emotions of others quite well. For example, when shown photos of facial expressions of emotion, psychopaths do as well as appropriate comparison participants in identifying emotions from the face. They also prove to be quite capable at assessing the mental states of other people; they can reliably infer what other people are thinking. They do show empathic deficits in their responses to others' sadness, however. Show a photo of a sad face to the average adult, and that person will respond with a galvanic skin response, a measure of the sweat response in the palms that indicates a physiological reaction to the other person's suffering. By contrast, psychopaths

show no such physiological response to the sadness of others, but they do show such galvanic skin responses to other emotionally evocative images, such as images of guns. The results of the Blair research indicate that psychopaths understand quite well the emotions and mental states of others, but they lack any feeling for them, most notably their suffering.

THE PSYCHOPATH IN MOVIES In *No Country for Old Men*, Javier Bardem plays the psychopathic hitman Anton Chigurh, whose lack of emotion in causing pain illustrates the finding that psychopaths often respond with little empathy to the suffering of others.

a punching bag. Men who had braided hair hit the bag much harder than those who had braided ropes.

These findings suggest a link between precarious manhood and violence against gay people (here, too, almost exclusively perpetrated by men). In laboratory studies, men whose manhood has been threatened express more distance from gay people and greater aggression toward them (Bosson & Vandello, 2011).

← LOOKING BACK

Evolutionary theory predicts that stepparents would be more likely than genetic parents to behave in violent ways toward children, and they are. Males tend to be more aggressive than females partly because such behavior can help them attain status and gain access to females. Females tend to be more relationally or emotionally aggressive than males. Cultural theorists believe that socialization processes contribute to gender differences in aggression. Recent studies on precarious manhood bring these two lines of theorizing together, helping to explain why threats to the sense of manhood can trigger violence in men.

Conflict and Peacemaking

This chapter began with an account of the Rwandan genocide, a story that seems to repeat itself with discouraging regularity in human history. In the aftermath of that genocide, Rwandans went through a process of reconciliation, following principles similar to those used in post-apartheid South Africa to help blacks and whites move beyond a history of oppression and violence to a more just, peaceful society. In Rwanda, formal court proceedings convicted several leaders of the genocide. In informal "truth and reconciliation" gatherings in Rwandan villages, Hutu perpetrators apologized to the relatives of their victims, who were given a public arena to air their rage. By most accounts, Rwanda is today a stable and peaceful society. Although tensions and bitterness persist, levels of aggression and conflict between the Hutus and Tutsis are low.

What does social psychology have to say about transitions between conflict and reconciliation? Some empirically tested insights point to the power of construal as a source of both conflict and peacemaking.

Misperception and Polarization

The frenzied rush toward genocide in Rwanda was stirred by a manifesto known as the Hutu Ten Commandments, which was published in a widely read newspaper, the *Kangura*, and broadcast by local radio stations. The Hutu Ten Commandments warned of the threat posed by the Tutsis, insisting that Tutsi women were secret agents bent on Hutu demise, that Hutu men who married or employed Tutsi women were traitors, and that Hutus who did business with a Tutsi were enemies of the Hutu people. These and other rumors and fears led Hutus to form deadly misperceptions about the Tutsis that helped fuel the genocide. Such misperceptions of another group, often of a dehumanizing nature, are commonly promoted in wartime propaganda and in the rhetoric that accompanies international crises and serve to readily justify aggression. (This is why so many people were so concerned about efforts by the Trump administration to collect and publicize a weekly list of crimes committed by immigrants in the Unites States; Fossett, 2017.)

Efforts such as these encourage the tendency on the part of adversaries to see their conflict as a fight between good and evil (Bar-Tal, 1990). They come to think of their own group as moral and good and the other side as immoral and evil (Brewer & Kramer, 1985). Adversaries routinely assume that their opponents' interests are the exact opposite of their own, such that any gain for one side means a loss for the other (Plous, 1985). In the political arena, opposing partisans will tend to see their party as patriotic and their opponents as lacking in this virtue (Iyengar, Sood, & Lelkes, 2012).

These kinds of construals can lead to two problematic outcomes that fuel social conflict. First, they lead people to believe that conflicts are polarized, that on all sorts of issues people fall into one of two opposing camps; this tendency causes people to overlook the common ground they so often share. Lee Ross and his colleagues surveyed people on opposite sides of ideological conflicts over such issues as abortion and the death penalty, as well as enemies embroiled in geopolitical conflicts like those in Northern Ireland and the Middle East (Ross & Ward, 1995). The researchers had members of both sides report on their own attitudes and estimate the attitudes of their opponents (Robinson, Keltner, Ward, & Ross, 1995). They found that group members systematically overestimated the extremity of their opponents' attitudes; that is, they assumed that the other side was made up of fanatical extremists and that the conflict was very polarized, when in fact many people on the other side were more moderate in their convictions.

Given this tendency, it should not come as a surprise that survey data from the past 30 years consistently find that people in the United States overestimate the differences between Republicans and Democrats (Westfall, Van Boven, Chambers, & Judd, 2015). This tendency to polarize is particularly true for people who hold more extreme political views and is particularly salient when disputes are framed as conflicts between "opposing groups" (Van Boven, Judd, & Sherman, 2012). The media have become more polarized as well, as evident in the rise of negative media campaigns during elections and the move away from news shows that cover both sides of an issue to cable shows that masquerade as "news" programs but in reality are opinion shows that advocate one ideological perspective (Iyengar & Hahn, 2009; Iyengar, Sood, & Lelkes, 2012).

The second problematic outcome that misconstruals of one's opponents can lead to is a bias known as **reactive devaluation**, the tendency of opposing sides in a dispute to attach little value to any offer made by their counterpart in a negotiation. The mere fact that the other side makes a concession is enough to reduce the attractiveness of the proposal (Ross & Stillinger, 1991). In other words, "You're my enemy, so if you made this proposal, it must not be in my interests or morally sound." To explore this tendency, researchers measured student protestors' attitudes about their university's proposal about its investments in companies doing business in South Africa during the height of student protests against apartheid in the 1980s (Ross & Stillinger, 1991). Before the university adopted the plan, when students were considering its merits in the abstract, the students felt it was a significant and positive move. But after the plan was adopted and it was no longer an abstract proposal, students evaluated it much less favorably. The mere fact that "the other side" (the university administration) was known to have adopted the plan was enough to make students regard it with suspicion. When parties to a conflict react in this way, it can be difficult indeed to reach a satisfactory resolution.

Simplistic Reasoning and Rhetoric

In the heat of conflict, group members are prone to misperceive their opponents' intentions and to distrust their actions and proposed resolutions rather than think about them in a nuanced way. Psychologist Phil Tetlock (1981) has found that this kind of simplistic reasoning is reflected in simplistic rhetoric as well, which in turn can escalate conflicts.

Tetlock notes that adversaries can reason and speak to each other in either a relatively complex fashion or a simple fashion. The complexity (or simplicity) of a position in a conflict is defined by two qualities: (1) the level of differentiation, or the number of principles and arguments in the position; and (2) the level of integration, or the connections drawn between the different principles and arguments. Those taking complex positions in conflicts consider many arguments and principles, even opposing ones, and draw many connections between them. Simpler positions involve fewer arguments (very few arguments from the other side especially) and few connections between the arguments and information

reactive devaluation Attaching less value to an offer in a negotiation once the opposing group makes it.

BOX 13.6 ▶ **FOCUS ON** CULTURE

Moral Murders?

Alan Fiske and Tage Rai, in their book *Virtuous Violence*, have gone so far as to say that most murders are committed by people who feel they're acting morally (Fiske & Rai, 2014). The perpetrators feel that what they're doing is just and right. Hundreds of thousands of European Protestants were killed by Catholics to end what Catholics believed was a heresy that presented a mortal challenge to the true faith. Hundreds of thousands of Catholics were murdered by Protestants to rid the world of people who willingly supported what Protestants thought of as a manifestly evil institution. The Nazis' killing of Jews was carried out in service to a moral obligation to rid the country of "vermin" who had been deliberately undermining the fatherland for decades. Stalin killed millions of Russians because they were venal capitalists blocking the path to a communist Utopia. Mao Zedong and Pol Pot killed untold numbers of their compatriots in China and Cambodia, respectively, for the same reason.

Most family feuds and tribal conflicts are seen by their participants as having moral motives: "We must defend the family honor." "They killed one of ours, it would be cowardly and wrong not to kill one of theirs." Many more soldiers have fought for love of tribe or country than for blood lust. Loyalists of ISIS (Islamic State of Iraq and Syria) behead enemies in service to what they see as the moral obligation to hasten the coming of the world caliphate.

Even the murder of one person by another over a quarrel or a perceived injustice can be rationalized by a spirit of self-righteousness: "The victim deserved to die because of what he did to me." Members of a group will sometimes kill one of their own because of transgressions against the group's moral code, as in stonings for adultery or stranglings for slander.

None of this implies that such actions are objectively moral, but rather that the actors subjectively feel that their behavior will make the world a better place. Fiske and Rai (2014) maintain that if we fail to recognize the self-perceived morality of people who are willing to kill on a massive scale, we're likely to misunderstand their motives and make serious mistakes in our conduct toward them. For example, governments often assume that if they simply build a strong enough war machine, they'll defeat insurgents fighting in what they believe is a sacred cause. Such insurgent groups have been known to shock their enemies by winning the day against a force ten times larger than their own, something they're able to pull off because of the great moral commitment and fervor they have for their cause.

The Burning of Rich.ᵈ Woodman, Geo. Stevens, Wᵐ Maynard, Alex.ʳ Hosman, Tho. Wood, Margery Morris, Jaˢ Morris, Mʳˢ Ashdowne, Mʳˢ Gloves & Mʳˢ Burges, at Lewes in Sussex.

MASS KILLINGS THROUGH HISTORY Queen Mary of England, who earned the nickname "Bloody Mary," restored Catholicism in England and during her reign executed numerous Protestants, including these ten Protestant martyrs portrayed in this etching.

---

being considered. For example, a complex position either for or against single-payer health care would involve many principles (such as ideas about the right to health care and a commitment to preventive care) as well as many factual arguments (such as health care savings, income tax consequences of single-payer coverage, and consideration of other countries that have single-payer coverage). A complex position on this issue would also include various connections between these principles and arguments (such as how single-payer coverage would influence the market and availability of qualified doctors). On the other hand, a simple position either for or against single-payer health care might be that it should be accepted in order to honor the fundamental right to health care or that it is unacceptable for the government to control a realm of society that free markets are better suited to address.

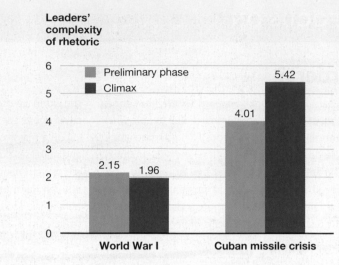

FIGURE 13.6
CONFLICT AND THE COMPLEXITY OF RHETORIC
In international crises, leaders who speak in ways that are more complex, taking into consideration the other side's views, are more likely to avoid escalating conflicts.
Source: Adapted from Suedfeld & Tetlock, 1977.

How does the complexity or simplicity of reasoning influence group conflict? To answer this question, Tetlock and his colleagues coded the complexity of politicians' reasoning from their speeches and interviews (Tetlock, 1981). They found that politicians are more simplistic and extreme when combating opponents and wooing potential voters on the campaign trail, but then become more complex once elected, when dealing with the give-and-take of policy making. In another study, researchers examined the complexity of political leaders' rhetoric during two crises: the buildup to World War I in 1914 and the 1962 Cuban missile crisis, in which U.S. President John F. Kennedy and Soviet Premier Nikita Khrushchev averted a nuclear encounter (Suedfeld & Tetlock, 1977). **Figure 13.6** shows that between the preliminary phase of the conflict and the climax that led to World War I, the complexity of the political leaders' rhetoric decreased. In the Cuban missile crisis, which was successfully resolved, the complexity of the leaders' rhetoric increased between the preliminary phase of the conflict and the climax.

Communication and Reconciliation

Often in the heat of conflict or in the aftermath of aggression, adversaries stop communicating and separate from one another. Politicians fighting over a budget deal hunker down with their own party, formulating strategy intended to cut their opponents out of the deal. Warring nations expel diplomats and end formal communication. In divorce proceedings, the husband and wife are told not to communicate with each other, no matter how benign their intentions. Moreoever, in today's world of websites, talk shows, cable TV, and news sharing on social media platforms, people all too readily become immersed in echo chambers of opinion populated by likeminded individuals.

As a result of these tendencies, adversaries are less likely to look at issues from perspectives other than their own. How do we get out of our cultural bubbles and counteract these isolationist trends? One solution is to actively imagine other people's perspectives. To document the benefits of taking different perspectives

THE CAMP DAVID PEACE ACCORDS
Although the communication in 1978 was painful and filled with conflict, it led to a lasting peace between Israel and Egypt. Shown here are U.S. President Jimmy Carter (in center), Israeli Prime Minister Menachem Begin, and Egyptian President Anwar Sadat.

on social conflict, Ethan Kross and Igor Grossmann (2012) had student participants talk about two heated political issues and what the future would look like if their preferred candidate in the 2008 U.S. presidential election (McCain versus Obama) were to lose. They did so after being instructed either to immerse themselves in their own point of view, as people so often do during conflict, or to reflect on this political future from the perspective of someone in Iceland, thus taking on an outsider's view of the polarizing political issues of the day. Participants who looked at the conflicts of the day from a different, more distant perspective were more likely to humbly recognize the limitations of their own knowledge, were more convinced that the conflicts of the day would change, reported less extreme attitudes, and were more likely to join a bipartisan political discussion group that brought together students of contrasting political views.

The tendency to avoid adversaries and immerse oneself only in one's own perspective also flies in the face of a potent tool for reducing conflict: face-to-face communication (Frank, 1988). Numerous empirical studies find that simply allowing adversaries to communicate reduces levels of competition and aggression and increases the chances of finding satisfying resolutions to many kinds of conflict (Thompson, 2005). Communication helps reduce the misperceptions of opponents and paves the way for peacemaking and cooperation.

As adversaries communicate, they often show a powerful tendency to reconcile, to make amends for hurtful words and harmful acts, and to return to more peaceful relations. Though we tend to avoid communication with adversaries, reconciliation is in our nature as well. Even our primate relatives exhibit instinctual tendencies toward reconciliation (de Waal, 1996). For example, in the heat of conflict, chimpanzees display submissive postures and vocalizations, actions that trigger conciliation behaviors such as grooming, open-handed gestures, and even embraces. Humans resort to more complex reconciliation behaviors—confessions, apologies, signs of remorse—that may trigger forgiveness, leading to reduced feelings of revenge and increased acceptance of the other person (McCullough, 2008).

A PICTURE OF RECONCILIATION
This conciliatory photograph shows Jean Pierre Karenzi, a perpetrator, and Viviane Nyiramana, a survivor of the Rwandan genocide, 20 years later. They express their feelings in the following statements. *Karenzi*: "My conscience was not quiet, and when I would see her I was very ashamed. After being trained about unity and reconciliation, I went to her house and asked for forgiveness. Then I shook her hand. So far, we are on good terms." *Nyiramana*: "He killed my father and three brothers. He did these killings with other people, but he came alone to me and asked for pardon. He and a group of other offenders who had been in prison helped me build a house with a covered roof. I was afraid of him—now I have granted him pardon, things have become normal, and in my mind I feel clear." (Quoted in Hugo & Dominus, 2014.)

"The quality of mercy is not strained.

It droppeth as the gentle rain from heaven

Upon the place beneath. It is twice blest:

It blesseth him that gives and him that takes."

SHAKESPEARE, *THE MERCHANT OF VENICE*

Studies of reconciliation by social psychologists have led to an innovative approach adopted by the criminal justice system in the United States, Australia, and other countries (McCullough, 2008). In many jurisdictions, the perpetrator and victim of crimes are usually separated (often for very good reason) and denied any opportunity to communicate and reconcile. As an alternative to this approach, in programs focused on restorative justice, professionals who are trained in both counseling and the law mediate conversations between perpetrators and victims. The offender takes responsibility for the crime (something the offender often resists confessing to in a courtroom); the offender tries to "undo" the crime through apology, acts of reparation, or both; and the offender and victim are encouraged to engage in a respectful dialogue. As difficult as these conversations may sound, they are often highly effective. Victims of crime who participate in restorative justice programs report many fewer thoughts of revenge than comparison individuals do, and they're more than twice as likely to forgive the offender and say that the criminal justice system is fair (Sherman & Strang, 2007).

Moving toward a Less Violent World?

We began this chapter by pointing out that people the world over have witnessed horrific levels of violence in the past 100 years in the form of wars and genocides. But despite the dispiriting news we hear daily, psychologist Steven Pinker has offered a very different perspective on our current times (Pinker, 2007, 2011). He argues that we are enjoying one of the least aggressive, most cooperative periods in human history. The data he draws on to make his claim are broad in scope. For example, people are dramatically less likely to die in today's wars as opposed to those in the past. Gone are the days in Europe when soldiers marched to their death in orderly rows, stepping over the bodies of comrades in previous rows mowed down by musket and cannon fire.

Murder rates have also fallen precipitously in every European culture that has been analyzed, as well as former European colonies in the Western and Southern Hemispheres. In fifteenth-century England, the annual murder rate was 24 per 100,000 people; in 1960 England, it was 0.6 per 100,000. The "enhanced interrogation" techniques used by the United States at various times since the 9/11 terrorist attacks have drawn criticism from many quarters; but several hundred years ago, much more brutal torture was the norm, and it was often a form of public entertainment. Enhanced interrogation in the Spanish Inquisition often meant breaking every bone in the suspected heretic's body with iron bars or roasting him slowly in an oven in the shape of a bull.

How do we explain such broad cultural shifts in violence and today's more humane treatment of our foes? Pinker believes that the printing press and video camera have played a role. If everyone can read, everyone can be exposed to arguments against war and violence. Literacy and numeracy have made us smarter (Flynn, 1987), and in general, more intelligent people will choose to handle their conflicts without violence. Images of the horrors of genocide and the devastation wrought by modern weaponry can lead to a revulsion that can chill the march to war. Armed conflict has come to seem an obviously terrible solution to any problem.

The world has become substantially more interconnected: our interests are more intertwined with those of people from other communities and nations. Globalization has made businesses multinational. Solutions to climate change and many other environmental problems will require treaties that involve many countries. Many college campuses in the United States and Canada draw students from all over the world. People communicate with others in distant lands over the Internet, especially on social media platforms, and through Skype. People are much more likely to marry and form friendships with people from different backgrounds. This expanding interdependence has given rise to greater cooperation among nations, states, and communities (Wright, 2000). Cooperation, Pinker argues, has short-circuited our more aggressive tendencies, thereby leading to behavior that is more prosocial.

← **LOOKING BACK**

Several construal biases, including dehumanization, misperceiving common ground, and simplistic reasoning and rhetoric, can escalate group conflict. Reconciliation processes can be a powerful tool for increasing peacemaking tendencies during and in the aftermath of conflict.

Chapter Review

SUMMARY

Situational Determinants of Aggression

- Hostile aggression is motivated by anger and hostility and has the primary aim of harming others, either physically or psychologically. Instrumental aggression is behavior intended to harm others to achieve a goal.
- Hot weather affects levels of aggressive behavior and violence. Hotter cities have higher rates of violent crime, and more violence occurs during hot months than during cool months.
- Media violence has been shown to promote aggressive acts in real life. Watching violent TV shows can lead to more aggressive behaviors in the short run, as can playing violent video games.
- Social rejection and isolation are powerful triggers of aggressive tendencies.
- Income inequality at the level of nation, state, county, neighborhood, and social context strongly predicts aggression of just about every kind.

Construal Processes and Aggression

- Anger-related thoughts of blame and revenge, as well as patterns of fight-or-flight responses, make people more likely to respond aggressively when prompted by cues, such as the presence of weapons.
- Extreme forms of violence, such as genocide and rape, are often accompanied by *dehumanization*, in which people deny others their basic human nature and the unique attributes that differentiate humans from other things. Group loyalty also predicts increases in dehumanization.

- People can modify their tendencies toward anger, dehumanization, and aggression by looking at frustrating issues or conflicts from a distance.

Culture and Aggression

- People in some cultures, including the U.S. South, are especially likely to adhere to a *culture of honor*; they are inclined to respond to insults and actions that convey malicious intent with violence or threats of violence. Such cultures exist where there is a history of herding, with the associated risks of losing all wealth.
- In *rape-prone cultures*, levels of violence tend to be high in general, and rape is used as a weapon in battle. Rape is also used as a ritual act and as a threat to keep women subservient to men. Cultures with fewer incidences of rape tend to grant women equal status.

Evolution and Aggression

- Evolutionary theory provides a perspective on family violence, such as stepchildren being more subject to abuse than genetic offspring, who can carry on the genetic line.
- Violent and aggressive actions are generally committed by men more than women. Women are more likely to resort to relational aggression such as gossip and ostracism to hurt others emotionally.
- The evolutionary perspective explains that men are more likely to harm other men than women harm women because they face a fiercer competition for mates.
- In a recent synthesis of evolutionary and cultural approaches to male violence, researchers have proposed the *precarious manhood hypothesis*: a man's gender identity is variable and vulnerable, which makes men more reactive to threats to their identity and more likely to behave aggressively to prove their manhood.

Conflict and Peacemaking

- Groups in conflict tend to misperceive the other side as extremist and social conflicts as polarized. They believe their own side is moral and reactively devalue concessions of the other side.
- Complex reasoning involving more evidence and integration of ideas than simplistic reasoning promotes peacemaking in international conflicts.
- Getting distance to one's own views, as well as communication and reconciliation, are powerful ways to reduce conflict.

THINK ABOUT IT

1. Describe the culture of honor, and provide two pieces of evidence that support this characterization. What might be the origin of these cultural tendencies?

2. According to the research described in this chapter, what kinds of attitudes and behaviors are more likely among men who dehumanize women?

3. Suppose you're the warden at a prison and can select the temperature setting for the master prison thermostat, but the thermostat doesn't have enough settings, forcing you to choose between an uncomfortably cold setting and an uncomfortably hot setting. Which should you choose, and why?

4. Sometimes people respond to social rejection with physical aggression. How does the fundamental nature of our need for social connectedness help explain this tendency?

5. Suppose a friend said to you, "Well, men are just biologically hardwired to be more aggressive than women." How would you respond? What nuances might this perspective miss?

6. What kinds of strategies have been shown to be most effective for reducing conflict and promoting peace, and why?

The **answer guidelines** for the think about it questions can be found at the back of the book . . . 👉

ONLINE STUDY MATERIALS

Want to earn a better grade on your test?

Go to **INQUIZITIVE** to learn and review this chapter's content, with personalized feedback along the way.

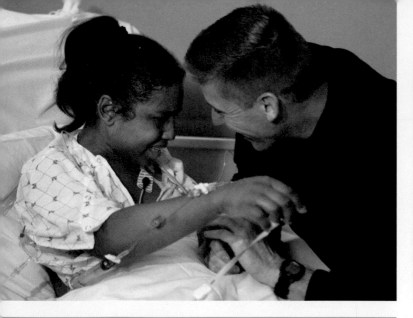

Why do some people donate their organs to strangers?

Why do we sometimes ignore people in need of help?

How do movies like *Wonder Woman* promote altruism among audiences?

Altruism and Cooperation

WONDER WOMAN WAS ORIGINALLY published as a comic book in 1941, the creation of Harvard psychologist William Marston. It took 76 years for *Wonder Woman* to make it to the silver screen, and the results were groundbreaking. The film featured a female superhero, a rarity in film (*Wonder Woman* was preceded by six *Superman* movies and eight *Batman* movies). Further, it was directed by a woman, Patty Jenkins, during a time when only 7 percent of Hollywood directors were women. The film was praised by reviewers and fans alike and made over $700 million at the box office worldwide.

Wonder Woman tells the story of Diana, princess of the Amazons, raised on the Greek-like island Themyscira. As a young girl, Diana is inspired by the female warriors on the island and persuades her protective mother, Queen Hippolyta, to let her train to become a warrior. Through physical prowess and force of will, she becomes the greatest of warriors and is soon put to the test. When an American pilot crashes his plane into the sea off her island, she rescues him and shortly thereafter fights German soldiers who have landed in pursuit. Upon hearing of the Great War in Europe (World War I), she travels there to save innocent lives, knowing that an encounter with her arch nemesis, Ares the God of War, awaits. With her signature protective bracelets and magic lasso, Wonder Woman takes down four German spies in a London alley, fearlessly charges through bullets and German soldiers in intense battle, and, in the climax of the film, destroys Ares. Each heroic act is inspired by strong protective feelings and a faith in the good of people. The message couldn't be clearer: when it comes to courage and physical heroism, women are just as capable as men, a message Marston hoped would inspire young girls and women in their pursuit of equality.

For all that's unique about the film, *Wonder Woman* also touches on deep truths about altruism that you'll learn about in this chapter. First, we have strong emotions—empathic concern or sympathy—that drive us to acts of altruism. Throughout the film, Wonder Woman is moved to help out of the "sacred duty to defend others" and "to give." Second, altruism isn't blind; it's more likely to be directed toward some people than others. In the film, Wonder Woman has particularly powerful emotional responses to young children, mothers, the injured, and the vulnerable. Third, in spite of strong inclinations to help those in need, there are often powerful situational constraints upon altruistic action. In the film, it's Wonder Woman's own mother who tries to prevent her from pursuing the life of a warrior. Sexist beliefs and the conventions of the era depicted in the film conspire to try to constrain Wonder Woman's heroic tendencies (but fail to do so). Finally, altruism is something that can be cultivated; it's shaped by culture. In the film, Wonder Woman is raised in a culture in which courage and sacrifice are taught as the default orientation to living in the world.

Humans have long created stories, myths, legends, and religious fables depicting and promoting altruism, courage, and heroism. *Wonder Woman* is yet another example of a story that highlights such nobler human tendencies. Let's turn to social psychology's own story about altruism and its close relative, cooperation. ■

Altruism

Wonder Woman's acts of courage and kindness occur in combat and war, when her life is truly on the line. Such acts of altruism during war are strikingly common. Even during the unspeakable violence of the Rwandan genocide, discussed in Chapter 13, individuals engaged in inspiring acts of concern for others. For example, Paul Rusesabagina, a Hutu, was the acting manager of the Mille Collines, the most prestigious hotel in the capital city of Kigali. As the massacres unfolded, he hid over a thousand people (both Tutsis and moderate Hutus) at the hotel. Each day, the Hutu *interahamwe* (militia) would arrive and demand to take some of the Tutsis away. And each day Rusesabagina would plead and ply them with beer and money to prevent further massacres. Around the clock he frantically called and faxed influential contacts, appealing for their help. Often risking his own life and those of his children and wife, he pleaded and schemed tirelessly for the survival of his guests.

Rusesabagina's actions are clear examples of **altruism**—prosocial behavior that benefits others without regard to consequences for oneself. Altruistic acts arise out of feelings of compassion that lead us to behave in ways that benefit others who are suffering, often at a cost to ourselves. At the same time, although most of us experience such prosocial feelings as compassion, we don't always act on them. Many forces can inhibit altruistic action, including basic tendencies toward self-preservation and fear of embarrassment (for example, if we were to misinterpret a mundane situation as an emergency). When do we act altruistically, and when don't we?

Empathic Concern: A Case of Pure Altruism?

Daniel Batson has made a persuasive case for a selfless, other-oriented state that motivates altruistic behavior like that which inspires Wonder Woman's heroics or was displayed during the Rwandan genocide by Rusesabagina (Batson & Shaw, 1991). Batson begins by proposing that in any altruistic action, several motives are likely to be in play. Two of these motives are essentially selfish (egoistic); a third is more purely oriented toward unselfishly benefiting another person.

The first selfish motive is **social reward**—being esteemed and valued by others in the form of praise, an award, or recognition in the mass media or social media. Those motivated by social rewards act altruistically to enjoy the positive regard of others (Nowak, Page, & Sigmund, 2000). For example, one study

altruism Prosocial behavior that benefits others without regard to consequences for oneself.

"[Sympathy] will have increased through natural selection; for those communities which included the greatest number of the most sympathetic members, would flourish best, and rear the greatest number of offspring."
—CHARLES DARWIN, *THE DESCENT OF MAN* (1871)

social reward A benefit, such as praise, positive attention, something tangible, or gratitude, that may be gained from helping others and thus serves as a motive for altruistic behavior.

EXTRAORDINARY ALTRUISM
New York City ballet dancer Gray Davis jumped on the New York subway tracks to save a fallen man in the face of an oncoming train. He is pictured here (A) in his headshot for the American Ballet Theatre and (B) being recognized for his bravery.

HEROIC ALTRUISM
During the riots in Los Angeles in 1992, Reginald Denny was pulled from his truck and severely beaten. Bobby Green (pictured here) and several other local residents rushed to the scene to rescue Denny.

personal distress A motive for helping others in distress that may arise from a need to reduce one's own distress.

empathic concern Identifying with someone in need, including feeling and understanding what that person is experiencing, accompanied by the intention to help the person.

"Kindness is not an illusion and violence is not a rule. The true resting state of human affairs is not represented by a man hacking his neighbor into pieces with a machete. That is a sick aberration. No, the true state of human affairs is life as it ought to be lived."

—PAUL RUSESABAGINA, *AN ORDINARY MAN: AN AUTOBIOGRAPHY*

found that when prompted to think about enjoying the respect of others, people were more likely to choose environmentally friendly consumer products—efficient dishwashers and cars—over equivalently priced but more desirable luxury products; our desire for the rewards of being respected leads us to sacrifice personal desires for the greater good of the environment (Griskevicius, Tybur, & Van den Bergh, 2010).

Recent neuroscientific studies find that being esteemed by others activates circuits in the brain associated with rewards and personal safety (Inagaki & Eisenberger, 2013). In fact, social rewards can be so powerful that they can trigger arms races of altruism, referred to as competitive altruism (Hardy & van Vugt, 2006; Simpson & Willer, 2015). People will try to outdo one another in their altruistic acts, all in the service of being the most highly esteemed. For example, in many hunter-gatherer cultures, it's the individual who gives away the most food—seal meat among the Inuit of Alaska, yams in hunter-gatherer tribes in New Guinea—who enjoys the greatest status. In laboratory studies, group members will give greater social status to other group members who act altruistically (Hardy & van Vugt, 2006; Nowak & Sigmund, 2005). Social rewards are a powerful motive for altruism, but an egoistic one.

A second selfish motive for helping is **personal distress**; people are motivated to help people in need in order to reduce their *own* distress (Cialdini & Fultz, 1990). Responding with personal distress in encountering others' suffering begins very early in life. In one study, for instance, newborn infants heard a tape recording of their own crying, the crying of another day-old, or the crying of an 11-month-old (Martin & Clark, 1982). The newborns cried the most in response to the cries of another newborn. Later in life, too, when we see someone crying, experiencing physical pain, or stuck in an embarrassing situation, we usually experience our own feelings of personal distress. Neuroscientific studies find that when we watch someone else experience pain, the pain regions of our own brain are activated (Bernhardt & Singer, 2012; Meyer et al., 2013). The resulting feelings lead us to act in ways that return us to a more peaceful state. The most direct way to alleviate our own personal distress in these instances is to reduce the distress of the other person, and helping behavior is one way to do it.

The third motive is **empathic concern**, the feeling people experience when identifying with someone in need, accompanied by the intention to enhance the other person's welfare. When we encounter somebody else in need or in pain, we not only experience our own feelings of distress but also imagine what that person must be experiencing. Taking the other's perspective in this way results in an empathic state of concern, or what we might call sympathy or compassion, which motivates us to help that person address his or her needs and thus enhance that person's welfare, even at our own expense.

According to Batson, this experience of empathic concern is fast and intuitive and produces selfless or other-oriented altruism. It's the split-second feeling of empathy that caused Rusesabagina to risk his life and the lives of his family to help the Tutsis. One recent study examined the reasons extreme altruists gave for

How Selfish Are We?

One of the most widespread assumptions in Western thought is that humans are fundamentally selfish, motivated to achieve their own desires even to the point of dishonesty, theft, and violence. For Sigmund Freud, our actions are motivated by the pleasure principle—we do things that maximize personal pleasure. Niccolò Machiavelli characterized the human race as "fickle, hypocritical, and greedy of gain." Are we hardwired by evolution to maximize our own interests even to the point of harming others? What does social psychology have to say? Something much different.

It Feels Good to Give

In experiments where subjects decide how much of a payment to give to another subject,

39%

people give 39% even though they can give as little as 1%.[1]

71%

of people give between 40% and 50% of their resources.[2]

When asked to decide quickly how much to give to a group they are working with, people give 65% of their resource.

50% | 65%

When asked to deliberate over the decision, they give 50%.[3]

Nearly

70%

of 14-month-olds will spontaneously assist an experimenter trying to pick up a pen.[4]

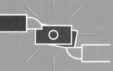

When people give money, the reward circuit of the brain is activated to the same degree as when they receive money.[5]

Trust and Economic Growth

If we assume other people are essentially altruistic and will treat us fairly, we are more likely to cooperate and be generous with our time and resources, and this behavior is likely to benefit our community as a whole. In fact, one study found a strong link between trust and income growth in nations around the world.[6]

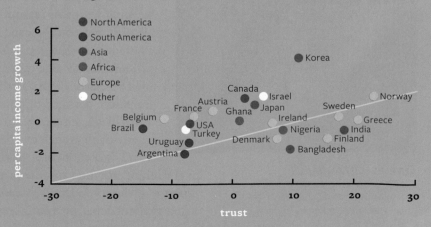

For Critical Thinking

1. Explain the pattern you see in the graph. Can you think of reasons that this relationship might exist between trust and income growth?

2. Think of a few instances where you behaved altruistically. Did certain factors influence you to do so? Who, if anyone, was with you? Did you stand to benefit from your giving behavior?

Sources: 1. Henrich et al., 2001; 2. Fehr & Schmidt, 1999; 3. Rand, Greene, & Nowak, 2012; 4. Warneken & Tomasello, 2007; 5. Harbaugh et al., 2007; 6. Trust and growth: Zak & Knack, 2001.

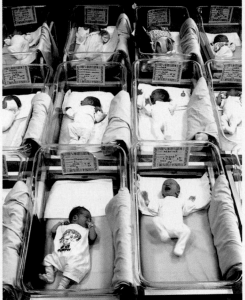

EMPATHY AMONG NEWBORNS
When newborn babies hear another newborn cry, they feel the distress of the other baby and will also begin to cry, as seen in this photo of infants in a hospital nursery.

ALTRUISM IN ANIMALS
Taking care of others is seen in many nonhuman species, such as these elephants helping a younger elephant.

why they risked their own lives to save others (Rand & Epstein, 2014). Most typically, they explained their life-imperiling acts of altruism by referring to an automatic, emotion-like impulse to help others.

EMPATHY VS. PERSONAL DISTRESS Now comes the tricky part: How can researchers document that altruistic action can be motivated by empathic concern alone, independent of the egoistic motive of desiring social rewards or reducing personal distress? To do so, Daniel Batson and his colleagues have carried out studies in which participants encounter another person in distress for whom they feel empathic concern (Batson & Shaw, 1991). At the same time, egoistic motives are manipulated to make helping behavior less likely. In the experiment there may be no social rewards for helping or participants might have the opportunity to reduce their personal distress without helping. If participants still help in these circumstances, it's highly likely that there's an empathy-based form of helping that's not selfishly motivated.

An initial study pitted empathic concern against the selfish motive of reducing personal distress by allowing participants to simply leave the experiment (Batson, O'Quin, Fultz, Vanderplas, & Isen, 1983). Participants were told they'd interact with another participant of the same sex (actually a confederate of the experiment), who would complete several trials of a digit-recall task and receive a shock after each mistake. In the easy-escape condition, the participant had to watch the confederate receive only two of the ten shocks and was then free to leave the experiment while the confederate finished the study. In the difficult-to-escape condition, the participant was told it would be necessary to watch the other person take all ten shocks.

After the first two trials, the confederate, made up to look a little pale, asked for a glass of water, mentioned feelings of discomfort, and recounted a traumatic shock experience from childhood. At this point, participants reported on their current feelings, which were used to divide participants into those who were feeling egoistic distress and those who were feeling empathic concern. The experimenter then asked if the participant would be willing to take some of the confederate's shocks. If there is such a thing as altruism based on empathic concern alone, the researchers reasoned, then they should see substantial levels of altruism (agreeing to sit in for the confederate) on the part of participants who felt empathic concern for the confederate, even when they had the option to simply leave the experiment to escape their distress. In keeping with this reasoning, those participants who mostly felt egoistic distress and could escape the situation took few shocks on behalf of the confederate. Those participants who felt empathic concern, however, volunteered to take more shocks, even when they could leave the study.

Those still skeptical about the possibility of pure altruism based on empathic concern might have a few reservations about this first study. First of all, empathic concern wasn't manipulated; instead, empathic participants were identified according to their self-reports. Perhaps there was a selection bias in this study—that is, the high-empathy participants might just be more helpful in general for reasons other than a selfless response to the confederate in need. Second, the experimenter would know how the participant acted, so a social rewards account of this study can't be ruled out.

Perhaps participants who took more shocks on behalf of the confederate hoped to impress the experimenter or wanted to avoid embarrassing themselves by leaving a person in obvious need. It'd be much more telling to show that there are substantial rates of helping when doing so is completely anonymous. That notion motivated Batson's next study.

ANONYMOUS ALTRUISM In this study, Batson and his colleagues had female participants interact with another person, a communicator, seated in another cubicle (Fultz, Batson, Fortenbach, McCarthy, & Varney, 1986). The communicator, a student confederate who called herself Janet Arnold, wrote two honest and somewhat confessional notes to the participant. The task of the listener (the actual participant) was to form as accurate an impression of Janet as possible. This time, empathic concern was manipulated. In the low-empathy condition, the participant was told to be as objective as possible when reading the notes, to concentrate on the facts at hand. In the high-empathy condition, the participant was told to imagine as vividly as possible how Janet felt. In the first note to the participant, Janet confessed to feeling out of place at her new home at the university. In the second note, Janet expressed a strong need for a friend and asked the participant if she'd like to hang out a bit.

After receiving the second note, the participant was told that Janet had finished and left the study. The experimenter then gave the participant a form that described another "long-term relationship study" and asked whether the participant would like to spend time at some later date with Janet Arnold. In the low-social-evaluation condition, Janet's notes were delivered in sealed envelopes, and the experimenter didn't read them. Similarly, the participant indicated how much time she would spend with Janet on a form enclosed in a sealed envelope to be sent to the professor conducting the study (who was never to meet the participant). Neither the experimenter nor Janet would know of the participant's response. In contrast, in the high-social-evaluation condition, both the experimenter and the participant read Janet's notes, and Janet and the experimenter would know how much time the participant said she would be willing to spend with Janet. The critical dependent measure was the number of hours the participant volunteered to spend with Janet. As **Figure 14.1** shows, participants in the high-empathy condition volunteered to spend more time with her, even when no one would know of their action.

EMPATHIC CONCERN AND VOLUNTEERISM Batson's research shows that feelings of empathic concern and sympathy increase the likelihood that people will act altruistically, helping those who suffer. These feelings are also a primary determinant of other prosocial behaviors. For example, Allen Omoto and Mark Snyder have studied **volunteerism**, which they define as nonmonetary assistance: when people help out with no expectation of receiving any compensation (Omoto & Snyder, 1995; Sturmer, Snyder, & Omoto, 2005). In the United States, estimates indicate that close to 30 percent of the population volunteer in some way, whether providing companionship to older adults, mentoring troubled children, feeding those in poverty, teaching classes in prison, or assisting the sick and dying (Omoto, Malsch, & Barraza, 2009). As with altruism, volunteerism has many motives, including a desire for social rewards and a desire to reduce personal distress. But Omoto and his colleagues have found that self-reports of feelings of empathic concern also predict the likelihood that an individual will

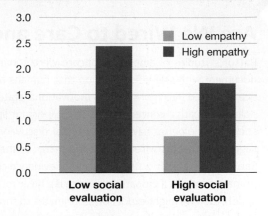

FIGURE 14.1
EMPATHY AND ALTRUISM
This study showed that when participants empathize with someone who is in need, they engage in more altruistic action, even when their sacrifice is anonymous.
Source: Adapted from Fultz et al., 1986.

"I have shewed you all things, how that so labouring ye ought to support the weak, and to remember the words of the Lord Jesus, how he said, It is more blessed to give than to receive."
—ACTS 20:35

volunteerism Assistance a person regularly provides to another person or group with no expectation of compensation.

Are We Wired to Care and Share?

Batson's studies of empathic concern were some of the first to document with scientific precision that humans may act altruistically, guided by a more selfless motivational state—in his terminology, empathic concern. Since this important line of research, social psychologists have made several discoveries that further suggest that we are wired to care and share (Keltner, Kogan, Piff, & Saturn, 2014; Marsh, 2016). One kind of evidence comes from our primate relatives. If empathic concern is a basic motive for human action, then we might expect other primates to show rudimentary forms of altruistic behavior. Indeed, observations of chimpanzees and bonobos find that they do occasionally provide care to those in need, such as fellow primates who have lost their eyesight or who are crippled (de Waal, 1996). They also regularly share food with non-kin in their community, a basic form of altruistic action (de Waal & Lanting, 1997).

If a selfless form of altruism is part of our evolutionary heritage, we might also expect to observe it in young children, much as children reliably show other species-defining tendencies, such as the fear of strangers and the ability to learn language. Work by Felix Warneken and Michael Tomasello provides impressive evidence of the altruistic tendencies of young children (Warneken & Tomasello, 2006). In this research, 18-month-olds encountered adults in need. For example, in one situation, the toddler saw an adult drop a pen and attempt, unsuccessfully, to pick it up from the floor. In another situation, the toddler saw an adult try to open closed doors of a cabinet, again unsuccessfully. In each situation, the toddler could readily offer assistance. In the control conditions, the 18-month-olds encountered the same stimuli—a dropped pen or doors that couldn't be opened—but the adult nearby did not express any need for help. Impressively, across these types of situations, 40–60 percent of the children helped the adult strangers in need, but they did not engage in the helpful actions in the control conditions. These findings suggest that beginning quite early in development, children will respond altruistically to others in need, thus providing still more evidence that we are wired to care and share.

A third kind of evidence in support of the claim that we're wired to be altruistic comes from the study of neurophysiology. That is, are their regions of our nervous system that enable us to act altruistically, much as the human stress response supports fight-or-flight behavior? Indeed, increasingly the case can be made for the "prosocial nervous system" (Keltner et al., 2014). When we feel compassion and are inclined to act altruistically, a distinct part of the frontal lobes is activated (Bernhardt & Singer, 2012). The vagus nerve is the largest bundle of nerves in the human nervous system; it wanders from the brain stem at the top of the spinal cord to muscles in the throat, through the lungs and heart (causing deeper breathing and heart rate deceleration), and eventually to the digestive organs and immune system. When the vagus nerve is activated, it enables vocal communication, eye contact, and the slowing of the stress response and is thus thought to be an ancient physiological system that promotes social connection (Porges, 2001). Recent empirical studies find that it's engaged during feelings of empathic concern, or compassion, and acts of altruism (Eisenberg et al,. 1989; Stellar, Cohen, Oveis, & Keltner, 2015).

engage in volunteerism (Omoto et al., 2009). In fact, people will undergo a great deal of suffering to contribute in charitable ways when such acts provide them with a sense of purpose (Olivola & Shafir, 2013).

Recent evidence suggests that volunteering is good for your health. Stephanie Brown and her colleagues studied 423 elderly married couples over the course of five years and found that volunteerism increases longevity (Brown, Nesse, Vinokur, & Smith, 2003). At the beginning of the study, the participants reported on how often they offered help to other people by doing errands, shopping, or providing childcare for neighbors. To capture how much participants were themselves the beneficiaries of volunteerism, they also indicated how often they received this kind of help from people other than their spouses. Following the participants over the course of five years, the researchers kept track of who died (145 of them did during the study). Remarkably, people who gave more to others were less likely to die during the five years of the study, when controlling for the participant's initial health, gender, and social contacts (see also Konrath,

Fuhrel-Forbis, Lou, & Brown, 2012). And how about the recipients of help? They were no less likely to die than people who didn't receive help. It may indeed be better to give than to receive.

But what cultivates empathic concern in people? What produces the Paul Rusesabaginas of the world or the good-hearted citizens who make sacrifices and volunteer? One answer comes from the remarkable work of the Oliners, who interviewed over 100 rescuers from World War II—individuals who risked their lives to save Jews during the Nazi Holocaust (Oliner & Oliner, 1988). (Samuel Oliner himself was saved by such a person in Poland as a young boy.) In the course of these interviews, rescuers reported that altruism and compassion were highly valued in their homes. Rescuers reported that their parents and grandparents frequently told stories from their own lives and from their culture in which altruism was a theme. Altruism was also a central theme in the books the family read and the teachings they discussed. In their dinnertime conversations about the happenings of the day, they discussed events through the lens of altruism and concern for other people. Altruism was explicitly invoked as an important ethical principle. Empathic concern apparently is a powerful force for good in human societies and can be passed from parents to children.

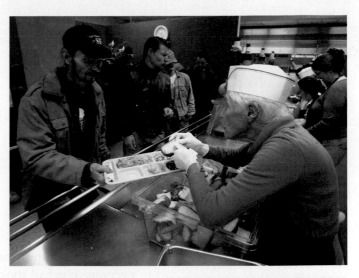

VOLUNTEERING AND BETTER HEALTH
Volunteering, such as serving food to the homeless in soup kitchens, can contribute to improving the volunteer's health.

Situational Determinants of Altruism

People don't always act on the basis of their empathic impulses. Consider the horrifying tragedy that befell Kitty Genovese on March 13, 1964, when Winston Moseley stalked her as she walked home in Queens, New York. He attacked her near her apartment and stabbed her in the back as she ran away. After her initial cries for help, lights went on and windows opened in the surrounding apartments. Moseley left but returned wearing a hat to disguise his face, stalking his victim to a stairwell in her building, then stabbing her eight more times and raping her. New York police got a call 30 minutes after the cries of distress first awakened neighbors. By the time they arrived, Kitty Genovese was beyond help and died in the arms of one neighbor.

Newspaper reports of the Genovese incident shocked the American public. Like Milgram's studies of obedience to authority (see Chapters 1, 5, and 9), the episode raises fundamental questions about human nature. How can so many people be that indifferent to the suffering of others? Accounts of Kitty Genovese's murder moved several social psychologists to attempt to understand the processes that inhibit empathic concern and altruistic action and make people reluctant to intervene during emergencies.

THE PRESENCE OF OTHER PEOPLE One important factor that influences whether people will stop to offer help to others in need is the presence of other people. **Bystander intervention** refers to helping someone when people are witness to an emergency. Studies find that people are less likely to help when other people are around (Latané & Nida, 1981). In part, the presence of other bystanders at emergencies reduces the likelihood of helping because of a **diffusion of responsibility**; knowing that others have seen the situation, each bystander tends

FAILING TO INTERVENE IN AN EMERGENCY
Kitty Genovese was a young woman who was stalked and killed outside her apartment in Queens, New York.

bystander intervention Assistance given by a witness to someone in need.

diffusion of responsibility A reduction of the sense of urgency to help someone in an emergency or dangerous situation, based on the assumption that others who are present will help.

DIFFUSED RESPONSIBILITY
People often fail to help someone in obvious need because they don't interpret the situation as an emergency or because they assume that others will help.

to assume the others will intervene—indeed, may be better positioned to intervene—and thus each person feels less responsibility to help out.

One of the best-known studies on the effect of other people's presence on altruistic behavior was inspired by the Genovese tragedy (Darley & Latané, 1968). College students sat in separate cubicles discussing the problems associated with living in an urban environment. They engaged in this conversation over an intercom system, which allowed only one participant to talk at a time. One of them, a confederate (one of the authors of this book, as it happens), described his difficulties in adjusting to urban life and mentioned he had problems with seizures from time to time, especially when under stress. Then, after everyone else had spoken, the confederate took his second turn. As he did so, he became increasingly loud and incoherent; he choked and gasped. Before falling silent, he uttered the following words:

> If someone could help me out it would it would er er s-s-sure be sure be good . . . because er there er er a cause I er I uh I've got a a one of the er sei-er-er things coming on and and and I could really er use some help so if somebody would er give me a little h-help uh er-er-er-er-er c-could somebody er er help er uh uh uh (choking sounds) . . . I'm gonna die er er I'm gonna die er help er er seizure er (chokes, then quiet). (Darley & Latané, 1968, p. 379)

In one condition, participants were led to believe that their discussion group consisted of only two people (the participant and the victim). In another condition, the conversation was among three people (the participant, the future victim, and another person). And in a final condition, the audience was the largest: the conversation involved six people (the participant, the victim, and four other people). The question, of course, was whether the other students would leave their cubicles to help the victim, who was presumably suffering from a potentially lethal epileptic seizure. The presence of others had a strong effect on helping rates. Eighty-five percent of the participants who were in the two-person condition and hence the only witness to the victim's seizure, left their cubicles to help. In contrast, 62 percent of the participants who were in the three-person condition and 31 percent of those in the six-person condition attempted to help the victim.

In a related vein, several types of studies have examined whether people are less likely to help someone out when other people are around or when they are alone. In these studies, a participant might witness a victim in danger or someone passed out in the subway or a theft occurring in a store (for a review, see Latané & Nida, 1981). Across these kinds of studies, 75 percent of people helped when they were alone compared with 53 percent who helped when they were in the presence of others.

VICTIM CHARACTERISTICS Needless to say, altruism isn't blind, nor is it indiscriminate. People are most likely to help when the harm to the victim is clear and the need is unambiguous (Gaertner & Dovidio, 1977). Researchers have studied altruistic intervention when a person in need either screams

BOX 14.2   FOCUS ON DAILY LIFE

The Likelihood of Being Helped

A typical bystander is less likely to help in an emergency situation if other bystanders are around. But what are the chances of someone receiving help from *any* of the bystanders? When there are more bystanders, there are more people who might help. Consider the "seizure" study described in this chapter. When participants thought they were alone, they helped 85 percent of the time. When they thought there was one other person who might help, they intervened 62 percent of the time. If there really had been two bystanders, each of them with a 62 percent chance of intervening, the victim would have received help 86 percent of the time—virtually identical to the rate of receiving help with one bystander (probability of receiving help = $1 - .38^2 = .86$). When participants thought there were four other people who might offer assistance, they intervened 31 percent of the time. Again, had there really been five bystanders, each of them with a 31 percent chance of intervening, the victim would have received help 84 percent of the time (probability of receiving help = $1 - .69^5 = .84$).

Does this mean it doesn't matter whether there are many or few people around? Not so fast. These studies have also measured how quickly people come to the aid of someone in distress, and they have consistently found that single bystanders act more quickly than the *quickest* person to react in a group of bystanders. And when somebody's in an emergency situation, a lack of speed can be deadly.

---

or remains silent. Bystanders help victims who scream and make their needs known 75–100 percent of the time, but they help silent victims only 20–40 percent of the time.

More enduring characteristics of the victim also influence rates of helping. Most notably, studies find that people are more likely to help others who are similar to them (Dovidio, 1984), including those from their own racial or ethnic group or a similar social class background (Latané & Nida, 1981). In a study by Joan Chiao and her colleagues, African-Americans responded with greater empathy and more altruistic inclinations when viewing the suffering of African-Americans as opposed to European-Americans. Only the suffering of participants' own group members activated a brain region (the medial prefrontal cortex) that's involved in empathic response (Mathur, Harada, Lipke, & Chiao, 2010). In keeping with this theme, studies of charitable contributions find that the wealthy tend to systematically direct their acts of philanthropy to institutions and organizations that benefit largely people like themselves, such as private universities and colleges and arts organizations, rather than social service organizations that benefit the poor (Piff, Kraus, & Keltner, 2017).

Other species appear to respond altruistically to their own group as well. Several nonhuman primates will give up the opportunity to eat and partially starve themselves if their action will terminate a shock that is being administered to a member of their own species—something they won't do for members of other species (Preston & de Waal, 2002).

Construal Processes and Altruism

What would go through your mind if you encountered a person slumped over in a hallway while on your way to a meeting or if you witnessed someone passing out on the subway? What is it about hearing obvious cries of distress or being in

CROSS-SPECIES HELPING
Altruism between different species occurs with surprising frequency. This Rhodesian ridgeback adopted a tiny piglet when it was rejected by its mother and went so far as to feed it with milk from her own body.

the presence of others that influences our inclination to help? In other words, what are the construal processes that influence whether we help or not?

In everyday life, many instances of distress are surprisingly ambiguous. A loud apparent dispute between a man and a woman overheard on the street might be careening toward violence and require intervention. But perhaps it's only a nonthreatening lovers' spat, or just two thespians acting out a dramatic scene from a play. Similarly, a group of adolescent boys could be pummeling a smaller boy—or perhaps they're just playfully wrestling.

HELPING IN AMBIGUOUS SITUATIONS Given the ambiguity of many emergencies, the decision to help means that the potential helper first has to believe that assistance is actually needed based on clues from the victim's behavior. As discussed earlier, when people in need vocalize their distress with loud cries, they're much more likely to be helped because their need for assistance is not ambiguous (Schroeder, Penner, Dovidio, & Piliavin, 1995). Similarly, people are more likely to provide assistance when they are vividly aware of the events that led to the victim's distress (Piliavin, Piliavin, & Broll, 1976). In a study demonstrating this, participants saw a confederate who was unconscious. In the more vivid condition, participants saw the confederate faint and slowly regain consciousness. In the less vivid condition, the participant saw only the aftermath of the incident—a confederate just regaining consciousness. Participants were much more likely to come to the individual's aid (89 percent versus 13 percent) when they saw the entire drama unfold, because they understood the full nature of the problem. It's now believed that one reason many people didn't come to Kitty Genovese's defense is that few people saw the full unfolding of the attack; instead they caught only glimpses of the murder and thus likely didn't understand the degree of harm taking place.

The surrounding social context also influences whether bystanders will think help is needed. A form of pluralistic ignorance occurs when people are unsure about what's happening and assume that nothing is wrong because no one else is responding or appears concerned (see Chapter 4). Staying calm and collected in public, especially during emergencies, is dictated by established social norms. It's embarrassing, after all, to be the one who loses composure when there's no actual danger. When everyone in a potentially dangerous situation behaves as if nothing is wrong, each person will tend to mistake the others' calm demeanor as a sign that there's no emergency (Latané & Darley, 1968).

In one study that examined the role of pluralistic ignorance in bystander intervention, researchers asked participants to fill out a stack of questionnaires (Latané & Darley, 1968). Participants were assigned to one of three conditions in which they carried out this task: alone, in a room with two passive confederates exhibiting the calm demeanor intended to produce pluralistic ignorance, or with two other genuine participants. As participants in these three conditions completed their questionnaires, smoke started to filter in from beneath a door, filling the room. When participants were alone and had no input from other participants as to what was happening, 75 percent of them left the room and reported the smoke to the experimenter. (What could the other 25 percent have been thinking?) In both of the two other conditions, pluralistic ignorance took hold, and participants were less likely to assume that something was amiss. Even in the condition with two other real participants, only 38 percent of the participants left to report the smoke. And remarkably, with two passive confederates showing no signs of concern, only 10 percent reported the smoke to the experimenter.

Anecdotal evidence from this study suggests that participants construed the smoke differently in the three conditions. The students who did report the smoke construed it as a sign of imminent danger. Participants who didn't report the smoke consistently reported that they didn't believe it was dangerous. One participant ventured the hypothesis that it was truth gas!

COMBATING PLURALISTIC IGNORANCE Bystanders are less likely to fall prey to pluralistic ignorance when they can clearly see one another's initial expressions of concern (and before these initial expressions are covered up out of the desire to seem less alarmed). In one study that illustrates this idea, participants had to pass by a worker doing repairs in a hallway on the way to the lab room where the study was being held (Darley, Teger, & Lewis, 1973). Once in the lab room, as part of the experiment, participants had to draw a picture of a horse, either by themselves (the control condition), facing another participant, or turned away from the other participant. As the participants labored over their drawings, they suddenly heard a loud crash and the workman crying out in obvious pain, "Oh, my leg!" An impressive 90 percent of those who were alone, in the control condition, left the room to help the workman. The results of the other two conditions make it clear that seeing others' spontaneous emotional expressions reduces the effects of pluralistic ignorance. While only 20 percent of the participants who were seated back-to-back left to help the workman, demonstrating pluralistic ignorance, a full 80 percent of those who were seated face-to-face left to help. Having others' initial, unguarded reactions to help interpret the incident as a true emergency enabled these participants to overcome pluralistic ignorance and construe the situation as an emergency requiring their help.

So how do you improve the chances of getting help when you need it? According to Darley, who studied the factors affecting bystander intervention for more than a decade, two things are likely to be effective: (1) make your need clear—"I've twisted my ankle and I can't walk; I need help"; and (2) select a specific person—"You there, can you help me?" By doing so, you overcome the two greatest obstacles to intervention: you prevent people from concluding there is no real emergency (thereby eliminating the effect of pluralistic ignorance), and you prevent them from thinking someone else will help (thereby overcoming diffusion of responsibility).

Culture and Altruism

Suppose it's late at night, and you need assistance. Where do you think you'd be more likely to get help: in a large metropolis or a small rural town? In a poor neighborhood or a rich one? Near a church or far away from a place of worship? Each of these questions involves the influence of different kinds of culture—geographical region, social class, and religiousness—on altruism. The prevalence of altruistic behavior varies in dramatic and sometimes surprising ways with these types of cultural influences.

ALTRUISM IN URBAN AND RURAL SETTINGS All across the world, people are moving out of small villages in the country to large cities. And recent studies suggest that the communities they're leaving behind might be kinder and more altruistic. Survey research indicates that people in rural areas report higher levels of empathic concern (Smith, 2009). To investigate whether higher levels of empathic concern lead to more altruistic behavior, Nancy Steblay (1987) reviewed 35 studies that focused on comparisons of helping rates in rural and urban environments. She looked at the helping rates in communities of different sizes, ranging from fewer than 1,000 people to more than 1 million. In all, 17 opportunities to offer assistance were created experimentally, typically in naturalistic settings. Researchers examined whether people would grant simple requests (such as giving the time of day when asked), whether they would intervene to stop a crime, and whether they would help people in need (an injured pedestrian, for instance).

Steblay's analysis showed that strangers are significantly more likely to be helped in rural communities than in urban areas (**Figure 14.2**). The effect of population size was particularly pronounced in towns with populations between 1,000 and 50,000. Thus, you're much more likely to be helped in a town of 1,000 than a town of 5,000; in a town of 5,000 than a town of 10,000; and so on. Once the population rises above 50,000, however, there's little effect of increasing population.

Let's examine this finding a bit. You might ask which matters most for whether a person is likely to offer help: the person's current context or the context in which the person was brought up. For example, if you were brought up in a small rural town but currently live in a big city, which setting is more likely to influence whether you will help someone in need? As it turns out, the current situation wins—hands down. In analyzing the 35 studies, Steblay found that the participant's current context, rural or urban, was a much stronger predictor of helping behavior than the person's rural or urban background (Steblay, 1987). This finding is another nod to the power of the current situation.

What accounts for this rural-urban difference in helping rates? Researchers have offered four explanations. Milgram (1970) attributed it to stimulus overload. The amount of stimulation in modern urban environments is so great that no one can register all of it. As you walk down a city street, for example, the traffic, the construction, the swarms of people are, in combination, too much to take in fully. You narrow your focus, in terms of attention and what circumstances

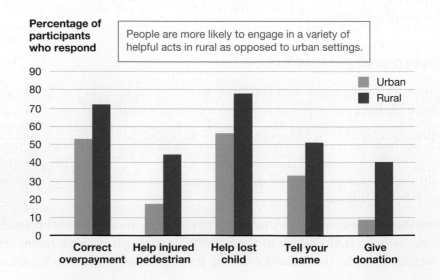

FIGURE 14.2
ALTRUISM IN RURAL AND URBAN ENVIRONMENTS
People in rural communities are more involved in helping others than people in urban settings.
Source: Adapted from Steblay, 1987.

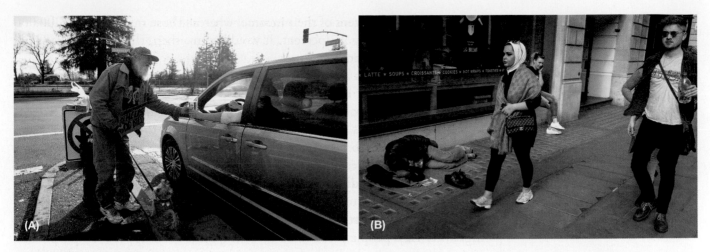

HELPING IN THE COUNTRY
People living in rural settings (A) are more likely to help others than are people in the city (B), as shown here in the different responses to people in need.

you recognize as having a claim on your thoughts, feelings, and actions. There are simply too many inputs, so you shut down a bit and are less likely to attend to the needs of others and thus less likely to act altruistically.

A second explanation might be labeled the diversity hypothesis. Earlier we noted that people are more likely to help others who are similar to themselves. Urban areas, of course, are made up of more diverse populations. Thus, on average, you're more likely to encounter someone similar to yourself in a rural environment than in an urban environment. This factor may also contribute to the observed urban-rural difference in helping rates. A third explanation is that more people are generally around to help in urban areas than in more rural environments, so a diffusion of responsibility could discourage people from helping out in urban settings. Finally, it's probable that in rural settings, people's actions are more likely to be observed by people who know them and who can comment on their reputation to others. Later we'll learn how powerful reputational concerns are as triggers of prosocial behavior.

SOCIAL CLASS AND ALTRUISM In June 2010, Bill Gates, of Microsoft, and investment guru Warren Buffet launched the Giving Pledge, a campaign to encourage the wealthiest people in the world to make a commitment to donate most of their wealth to philanthropic causes. They asked that the richest people in the United States give at least half of their wealth to charity. Buffet, a billionaire, pledged to give away 99 percent of his fortune by the end of his life. More than 170 of America's richest individuals soon followed suit, including Facebook founder Mark Zuckerberg and his wife, pediatrician Priscilla Chan, who pledged $45 billion to fight disease.

How does social class influence levels of altruism? Are the Gateses and Buffets of the world the rule—or the exception to the rule? When it comes to altruism, it turns out that those who have less give more, at least in terms of the proportion of their income that they donate to charity. Nationwide surveys of charitable giving in the United States find that wealthy individuals give away smaller proportions of their income to charity than people who are less well-off (Greve, 2009). For example, a study by the organization Independent Sector (2002) found that people making less than $25,000 per year gave away

"Again I say to you, it is easier for a camel to pass through the eye of a needle, than for a rich man to enter the Kingdom of God."
—MATTHEW 19:25

WEALTH AND CHARITY
Nicki Minaj has an extensive engagement with her philanthropy and has helped pay students' debts and given money to a village in India.

an average of 4.2 percent of their income, whereas those making over $100,000 per year donated only 2.7 percent. It would seem, then, that people like Gates and Buffet are exceptions.

What investigators have learned about empathic concern and altruism sheds light on why the poor may give more than the rich. Specifically, Michael Kraus, Paul Piff, and their colleagues reason that a relative scarcity of resources leads lower-class individuals to be more empathically attuned to others, and they build strong relationships to help them to adapt to their more unpredictable, taxing, and sometimes threatening environments (Kraus, Piff, & Keltner, 2011; see also, Guinote, Cotzia, Sandhu, & Siwa, 2015). Upper-class people, by contrast, enjoy more abundant resources and opportunities that enable them to be more independent but less empathically in tune with others. In keeping with this theorizing, lower-class people prove to be more empathic than upper-class people in a variety of ways: they're better judges of the emotions of a stranger with whom they've just interacted, they're better judges of a friend's emotions, they're more accurate in their inferences about the emotions revealed in photographs (Kraus, Côté, & Keltner, 2010), and they respond with greater empathic concern and compassion-related physiology to the suffering of others (Stellar, Manzo, Kraus, & Keltner, 2012).

Given these social class differences in empathy, are lower-class people more likely to act in a prosocial fashion? Piff and his colleagues have found that they are indeed more altruistic (Piff, Kraus, Côté, Cheng, & Keltner, 2010). In one study, for example, people from different class backgrounds played the dictator game, an economic game in which they received 10 points and were asked to give some portion of those points to a stranger. The number of points the participants had at the end of the experiment determined their chances in a lottery conducted after all participants had completed the study. On average, participants gave away 41 percent of their points, and lower-class participants gave away more of their points to the stranger than did members of the upper class. Subsequent research has found that in contexts in which economic inequality is high, the wealthy share even less (Côté, House, & Willer, 2015) or they choose to share mainly with other wealthy individuals, only augmenting levels of economic inequality (Nishi, Shirado, Rand, & Christakis, 2015).

What, then, might counteract these tendencies? One clear answer is to trigger empathic concern in well-off people. In one study guided by this idea, participants were given the chance to help an obviously distressed confederate who had arrived late for the experiment and therefore needed the participant's assistance to complete required tasks (Piff et al., 2010). Before this opportunity to provide help, participants watched either a neutral film clip (a relatively uninteresting scene from the movie *All the President's Men*) or a moving portrayal of the suffering of children living in poverty. Showing the film about poor children was intended to induce upper-class participants to feel the same level of empathic concern typical of lower-class participants, which the investigators predicted would lead them to help out at higher rates than they otherwise would have. The findings supported these predictions, as shown in **Figure 14.3**: after watching a neutral film clip, lower-class participants offered to spend more time helping

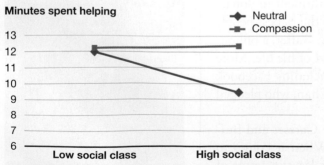

Minutes spent helping

◆ Neutral
■ Compassion

13
12
11
10
9
8
7
6

Low social class   High social class

FIGURE 14.3
SOCIAL CLASS AND ALTRUISM
This study demonstrated that lower-class people help more than upper-class people, except when both groups are made to feel compassion.
Source: Piff et al., 2010.

with the other participant's tasks than upper-class participants did. When upper-class people were made to feel compassion, however, they responded in the same prosocial fashion as their lower-class counterparts.

RELIGION, ETHICS, AND ALTRUISM People throughout the world define themselves in terms of religion—Muslims, Protestants, Methodists, Unitarians, Jews, Catholics, Mormons, Buddhists, Hindus, Sikhs, and so on. Many others who don't have a religious affiliation are spiritual people who believe in forces that transcend the physical laws of nature. Like social class, religion can shape almost every facet of social life, ranging from moral beliefs to marriage partners.

The world's major religions emphasize compassion, altruism, and treating others, even strangers and adversaries, with kindness. This conduct is seen in such religious practices as tithing and tending to those who suffer and in moral codes such as the golden rule: treating others as we would like to be treated ourselves (**Table 14.1**). The golden rule is demonstrated in the texts of the major religions, which encourage a prosocial stance toward others through fables and time-honored passages. Admittedly, many of the world's religions also include stories of taking revenge, putting people to death for seemingly trivial offenses, and treating nonbelievers in cruel ways. Still, these troublesome elements aside, all religions do stress compassion and the need to treat others—at least some others—well.

Does exposure to religious concepts make people more prosocial? Initial studies by Ara Norenzayan and Azim Shariff suggest so (Norenzayan & Shariff, 2008; Shariff, Willard, Anderson, & Norenzayan, 2016). In one study, participants were shown sequences of five words, randomly arranged, and asked to generate sentences using four of those five words. In a religion prime condition, the five words always included at least one word with religious meaning, such as *spirit*, *divine*, *God*, *sacred*, or *prophet*. For example, in this condition participants might read "Felt she eradicate the spirit" and create the sentence "She felt the spirit." In a neutral prime condition, participants did the same task of unscrambling sentences, but none of the words had religious meaning. After this task, participants in both conditions then received 10 Canadian dollars and were asked

TABLE 14.1	THE GOLDEN RULE ACROSS CULTURES AND RELIGIONS
Matthew 7:12	"In everything, therefore, treat people the same way you want them to treat you, for this is the Law and the Prophets." (*New American Standard Bible*, 1995)
Sextus the Pythagorean	"What you wish your neighbors to be to you, you will also be to them."
Buddhism	"Putting oneself in the place of another, one shouldn't kill nor cause another to kill."
Tibetan Buddhism	"If you want others to be happy, practice compassion. If you want to be happy, practice compassion." (Dalai Lama)
Hinduism	"One should never do that to another which one regards as injurious to one's own self." (*Mahabharata*)
Muhammad	"Hurt no one so that no one may hurt you."
Taoism	"He is kind to the kind; he is also kind to the unkind."

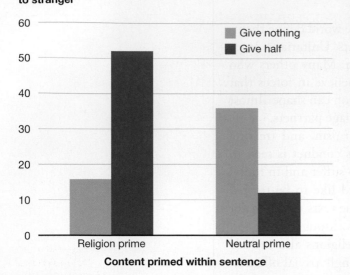

Proportion of participants making gift to stranger

Legend:
- Give nothing
- Give half

(Bar chart showing y-axis from 0 to 60, with x-axis categories "Religion prime" and "Neutral prime")

Content primed within sentence

FIGURE 14.4
RELIGION AND ALTRUISM
As this study showed, being primed with religious concepts leads to greater generosity.
Source: Adapted from Norenzayan & Shariff, 2008.

to give some amount away to a stranger. **Figure 14.4** shows the powerful effect of being primed by religious concepts like "divine" or "sacred." Participants in the neutral prime condition were more than twice as likely to give nothing to a stranger, compared with those in the religion prime condition (36 percent versus 16 percent). By contrast, people who were primed with religious concepts were more than four times as likely to treat a stranger as an equal by giving half of the money to the stranger (52 percent versus 12 percent). Subsequent studies inspired by this work have shown that different kinds of religious priming—reporting on personal religious beliefs, reading passages from religious texts, hearing the Islamic call to prayer in the background, even standing near religious buildings—also increase pro-social behaviors of different kinds (Shariff et al., 2015).

What about secular, nonreligious ideas related to kindness and virtue, of the kind one might learn about from parents, hear about in school, or read about in philosophy or psychology (or even in this chapter)? Shariff and Norenzayan examined whether secular, nonreligious concepts related to kindness and ethical behavior generate similar levels of generosity (Shariff & Norenzayan, 2007). In what they called a "civic" condition, participants unscrambled sentences that included words related to the secular institutions and ideas that build more cooperative societies, such as *civic, jury, court, police,* and *contract.* These words also generated high levels of generosity in the economic game—as much generosity, in fact, as the religious words prompted. It seems the emphasis on fairness and cooperation and equality, seen in both religious traditions and secular treatments of ethics, can do a great deal to elicit prosocial behavior.

Shinobu Kitayama and his colleagues have gathered evidence showing that the sense of being watched, so prominent in religions of different kinds, increases altruism. In fact, so powerful is this effect that it can be achieved by simply seeing three dots arranged to look like the eyes and mouth of a human face. Seeing this arrangement of dots evokes the sense that someone is looking at you and, the reasoning goes, triggers more cooperative behavior. In the relevant study, participants played the dictator game. They were given a sum of money and asked to write down on a sheet of paper the amount they wanted to give to a stranger (Rigdon, Ishii, Watabe, & Kitayama, 2009). On the paper, they saw one of two sets of dots, shown in **Figure 14.5**. In one condition, participants saw the pattern of three dots evocative of the human face (the pattern on the left). In a second condition, participants saw the same dots but configured

FIGURE 14.5
BEING WATCHED
A simple triangular arrangement of dots reminiscent of the human face (the three dots to the left) is associated with a sense of being observed and encourages cooperation more than a triangular arrangement that does not evoke the human face (the three dots to the right).

BOX 14.3   FOCUS ON CULTURE

Prosocial Behavior and the Sense of Being Watched

Common to many religions is the idea that God is watching over people as they carry on with their mundane lives on Earth. The Greeks believed that their gods guided their everyday actions. The same is true for many Christians today, who feel they are being watched by Jesus. And in many religions, this idea of being observed translates directly into religious iconography and architecture. For example, if you travel to Nepal and visit its temples, such as the fifth-century BCE temple Swayambhuntha, you'll have the distinct impression of being watched because of the prominence of the eyes on the surface. You might have a similar experience when visiting the Sistine Chapel, Michelangelo's famous painted ceiling in the Vatican in Rome. There, if you look up into the center of the ceiling, you'll see God looking down upon Adam and Eve in one of the best-known works of art from the Renaissance.

THE SWAYAMBHUNTHA TEMPLE The eyes painted at the top of the temple give visitors the feeling they're being watched.

upside-down (the pattern on the right). When presented with the non-face dots on the response sheet, 40 percent of the participants decided to keep all the money for themselves. This selfish tendency dropped to 25 percent when the dots representing the face were on the response sheet.

Evolution and Altruism

Few behaviors are more difficult to explain from an evolutionary perspective than altruism. Natural selection favors behaviors that increase the likelihood of survival and reproduction. Altruistic behavior, by its very nature, is costly; it devotes precious resources to others that could be used for oneself or one's genetic relatives. The costs of altruism can even include the ultimate sacrifice, as when people risk their lives to save the lives of friends or total strangers. How, then, have evolutionary theorists accounted for altruistic behavior? Two evolutionary explanations have been offered: kin selection and reciprocity.

KIN SELECTION **Kin selection** is an evolutionary strategy that favors behaviors that increase the chance of survival of genetic relatives (Hamilton, 1964). From the perspective of kin selection, people should be more likely to help those who share more of their genes—for example, by helping siblings more than first cousins, first cousins more than second cousins, and so on. By helping relatives survive, people help their own genes pass to future generations.

In keeping with kin selection theory, studies of several nonhuman species find that helping is more likely to be directed toward kin than non-kin. Mockingbirds feed their own hungry nestlings first and then will feed hungry nestlings that are not their own but that are more closely related to them than

kin selection An evolutionary strategy that favors the reproductive success of one's genetic relatives, even at a cost to one's own survival and reproduction.

"A chicken is only an egg's way of making another egg."
—SAMUEL BUTLER, *LIFE AND HABIT*

"An organism is a gene's way of making another gene."
—RICHARD DAWKINS

other hungry nestlings (Curry, 1988). Ground squirrels, when sensing that a predatory coyote or weasel is in the vicinity, are more likely to emit alarm calls (thus putting themselves in danger) to warn a genetic relative or a squirrel they have lived with than to warn unrelated squirrels or squirrels from other areas (Sherman, 1985).

In humans, genetic relatedness influences helping behavior as well. Across many cultures, people report receiving more help from close kin than from more distant relatives or nonrelatives (Essock-Vitale & McGuire, 1985). When hypothetical situations are described to them, people report being more willing to help close relatives (especially those young enough to have children) than to help more distantly related people or strangers (Burnstein, Crandall, & Kitayama, 1994). In a study of kidney donations, donors were about three times as likely to engage in this altruistic act for a relative (73 percent) than for nonrelatives (27 percent) (Borgida, Conner, & Manteufel, 1992). In a puzzle task that required cooperation, identical twins, who share all their genes, were found to cooperate about twice as often (94 percent) as fraternal twins (46 percent), who share only half of their genes (Segal, 1984; see also Burnstein, 2005).

RECIPROCITY How would an evolutionary account make sense of helping non-kin? We often go to great lengths to help friends. We give them money, let them sleep at our apartment and eat out of our refrigerator, help them move, and sometimes even risk our lives for them. Even more compelling, perhaps, is how often we help total strangers. People will dive into icy waters to save people they've never met, donate money anonymously to charities, and engage in all sorts of more ordinary, less costly behaviors, such as giving up a seat on a bus or taking the time to help someone cross a street. Such actions can be accounted for in part by reciprocity and cooperation, which form the basis of the second major evolutionary explanation for altruism.

reciprocal altruism Helping others with the expectation that they will probably return the favor in the future.

In traditional, preliterate societies, individuals living in groups were best able to survive when they cooperated with one another. To explain how cooperation evolved, evolutionary theorists generally use the concept of **reciprocal altruism**—helping other people with the expectation that they'll help in return at some other time (Trivers, 1971). Cooperation among non-kin provides many benefits that increase the chances of survival and reproduction for all parties. Reciprocal altruism reduces the likelihood of dangerous conflict, helps overcome problems arising from scarce resources, and offers a basis for people to form alliances and constrain more dominant individuals (Preston & de Waal, 2002).

There's some evidence in nonhuman species for the mutual helping that's the essence of reciprocal altruism. Vampire bats need blood meals to survive and may starve to death if they don't have a blood meal after 60 hours. Researchers have found that satiated bats will regurgitate blood to feed bats that have given to them in the past, but won't make a donation to a bat that hasn't been a donor itself (Wilkinson, 1990). In his observations of chimpanzees and bonobos, Frans de Waal (1996) has found that primates are disposed to share food with other primates who share with them, to look after each other's offspring, and to systematically groom other primates

RECIPROCAL ALTRUISM
Vampire bats will regurgitate blood to feed starving bats that have given blood to them in the past, but they will not give blood to bats that haven't helped them in the past. Thus, reciprocally altruistic behavior is observed in nonhuman species as well as in humans.

who have groomed them earlier (see also Silk, Brosnan, Henrich, Lambeth, & Shapiro, 2013).

The impulse to reciprocate acts of generosity is a likely human universal (Gouldner, 1960). In hunter-gatherer societies around the world, meat gained from hunts is carefully divided up and shared with others, on the assumption that present acts of generosity will be paid back at some later date (Flannery & Marcus, 2012). In studies using games where players can either cooperate or compete with one another, people are more likely to seek out and cooperate with individuals who have cooperated on the previous round of the game (Rand, Arbesman, & Christakis, 2011).

Perhaps an even more dramatic illustration of our tendency to reciprocate is the following experiment. Researchers mailed Christmas cards to numerous complete strangers. About 20 percent reciprocated by sending their own Christmas cards back to the senders, whom they had never met (Kunz & Wool-cott, 1976). Either the participants had too few friends to accommodate the stacks of Christmas cards they bought or they felt compelled by the norm of reciprocity to respond with a Christmas card to the sender.

Adam Grant and Francesca Gino have made the case that expressions of gratitude act as social rewards and are a powerful trigger of subsequent cooperation, which fits the reciprocal altruism thesis. More specifically, they propose that an act of appreciation functions like a gift; the recipient feels socially valued. Feeling rewarded, the recipient should be more inclined to reciprocate and behave altruistically. In one relevant study, participants helped an experimenter edit a letter online (Grant & Gino, 2010). In the gratitude condition, participants were thanked via e-mail. In the control condition, participants received a polite message of equal length, but without a note of thanks. When asked if they would help the experimenter edit a second letter, those who were thanked responded affirmatively 66 percent of the time compared with 32 percent in the control condition.

FOOD SHARING
In cultures around the world, the sharing of food is a way that people build and maintain cooperative relationships. These women in China share a lunch communally and enjoy the delights of such exchange.

◀ LOOKING BACK

Altruistic tendencies are behaviors that benefit others. People may act altruistically for selfish motives, such as reducing distress or gaining social rewards, but some acts of altruism are based on a more selfless state of empathic concern. Situational determinants influence whether or not people help others. The presence of bystanders may lead to a diffusion of responsibility, in which everyone assumes that someone else will help. People are more likely to help similar others. Construal processes also influence helping; pluralistic ignorance can lead people to be less likely to help. People are more likely to help if they're from rural rather than urban settings or from lower- rather than upper-class backgrounds. Two evolutionary concepts that can account for the existence of altruism are kin selection and reciprocity.

Cooperation

Cooperating with others is part of our evolutionary heritage. The profound vulnerability and dependence of our offspring, who have a long period of complete reliance on adults for food and protection, required cooperative child care; both parents shared the burdens of raising children who were entirely dependent on them (Hrdy, 1999; Konner, 2003). From archaeological studies of the bones of animals our hominid predecessors killed for food, we know that early humans hunted in cooperative groups (Mithen, 1996). The inclination to cooperate for common goals is almost a defining attribute of humans.

One of the most striking aspects of human relations is how quickly adversarial relationships can become cooperative (and vice versa). In World War II, for example, the mortal enemies of the United States were the Germans and Japanese. Shortly after the end of the war, the United States became strong allies with these former enemies. During the Rwandan genocide, Hutus sought to annihilate Tutsis; since then, the two groups have become more collaborative. It's an important lesson of history, how readily people shift from competition and aggression to cooperation.

The Prisoner's Dilemma

Core principles that account for how and why humans cooperate have been examined through the use of an experimental paradigm known as the **prisoner's dilemma**, often structured as a type of economic game. Imagine being ushered into a small cubicle; the experimenter tells you there's another participant (whom you'll never meet) in a cubicle nearby. Both you and the other participant are required to make a simple decision: independently, you must choose to either "cooperate" with each other (do what will benefit both of you) or "defect" (do what will disproportionately benefit only you). The compensation you receive will depend on the choices you make. If both of you cooperate, you'll each receive $5. If both of you defect, you'll each get $2. If one cooperates

COOPERATION BETWEEN WARTIME ENEMIES
During World War I, instances of cooperation took place between enemy soldiers, as during this informal Christmas truce in 1914. Soldiers from both sides emerged from their trenches and fraternized in no-man's-land. This lithograph was published in 1915.

and the other defects, the defector will receive $8 and the cooperator will not receive anything. The experimenter says you'll be paid as soon as each of you makes your choice and reiterates that you and the other person will never meet. What do you do?

To maximize your own self-interest, the best, or "rational," choice is to defect. Whatever your partner does, you make more money by defecting than by cooperating. To see this, consult the summary of payoffs presented in **Figure 14.6**. If your partner cooperates, you receive $8 by defecting but only $5 by cooperating. If your partner defects, you receive $2 by defecting and nothing by cooperating. Defection thus "dominates" cooperation. So why not defect?

Here's the catch: if both players reason this way and choose to defect, they both receive only $2 rather than the $5 that would be theirs through mutual cooperation. The "best" choice for each person (defection) is a terrible choice from the standpoint of the two people in combination.

On the surface, the prisoner's dilemma game seems to hold little promise for teaching anything significant about real human interaction. Unlike many real-world situations, the game offers no range of cooperative to competitive behaviors to choose from; instead, there are only two behaviors—cooperate or defect. In addition, participants aren't allowed to discuss the choices beforehand, and they are never permitted to explain or justify them afterward. Overall it seems too limited, too artificial, to demonstrate anything significant about real-world cooperation and competition.

Looks may be deceiving, however. As simple as the prisoner's dilemma seems, it nevertheless captures the essential features of many significant situations in life (Dawes, 1980; Schelling, 1978). Let's consider a real-world analogue. India and Pakistan have been engaged in an arms race for decades. Like nearly all such struggles, the contest is ultimately futile because its structure is that of the prisoner's dilemma. Each country must decide whether to spend more money on armaments or to stop spending on more arms and enjoy a significant economic "peace dividend," as the United States did following the breakup of the Soviet Union. However, regardless of what the other does, it's "better" to acquire more arms. (In this case, acquiring more arms is akin to choosing to defect in the prisoner's dilemma. If India freezes its acquisition of weapons, Pakistan can achieve an edge by spending more. If India builds up its arsenal, Pakistan has to spend more to avoid vulnerability.) Nonetheless, because the new weapons systems developed by one side are quickly matched by the other, the net effect is waste. The two countries pay dearly for a military balance that was attainable for less expense.

Thus, although the prisoner's dilemma may seem like a sterile and artificial paradigm on the surface, it captures many difficult real-world choices between cooperation and competition. Thousands of studies using the prisoner's dilemma

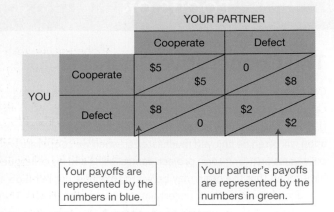

		YOUR PARTNER	
		Cooperate	Defect
YOU	Cooperate	$5 / $5	0 / $8
	Defect	$8 / 0	$2 / $2

Your payoffs are represented by the numbers in blue.

Your partner's payoffs are represented by the numbers in green.

FIGURE 14.6
THE PAYOFF MATRIX FOR THE PRISONER'S DILEMMA GAME

DEVELOPING COOPERATIVE RELATIONSHIPS
Cooperation can emerge between the most violent of enemies and in the most extreme circumstances. Here, members of two rival gangs in El Salvador, MS-13 and 18th Street, stand next to each other in a spirit of cooperation created by a truce signed a year earlier.

BOX 14.4 ▶ FOCUS ON NEUROSCIENCE

The Cooperative Brain

Cooperation is vital to human survival, but as a social strategy it can incur certain costs. For example, when we cooperate, we also risk being exploited by others. In addition, the rewards of cooperation will often be enjoyed much later, as when we cooperate with colleagues on a long-term project. James Rilling and his colleagues have found that the brain may be wired to enable cooperation in the face of these kinds of uncertainties (Rilling et al., 2002). They have shown that during acts of cooperation, our brain fires as if we are receiving rewards.

In their study, 36 women played an online version of prisoner's dilemma with another person. Using fMRI technology, the researchers scanned the brains of the participating women when they cooperated with the online stranger—which was their most common choice. They found that reward-related regions of the brain (the nucleus accumbens, ventral caudate, and ventromedial/orbitofrontal cortex) exhibited increased activation when the women cooperated. These brain regions are rich in dopamine receptors and are activated by all sorts of rewards, such as sweet tastes, pleasant smells, pictures of tropical vacations, and pleasing touches. Cooperation, it seems, is inherently rewarding.

game have yielded some valuable insights about how people make these difficult choices, illuminating why people or groups or countries would be likely to defect or cooperate and suggesting what might be done to foster cooperative relations.

Situational Determinants of Cooperation

The prisoner's dilemma game sets up the simplest of situations: participants are involved in just one round with someone they don't know or even see. Of course, our social lives are much more complex. In real life, we often interact repeatedly over time with certain people—for example, in our careers or in our personal relationships. Are we more cooperative when we interact repeatedly with the same person, compared with a one-shot interaction? Indeed we are. David Rand and Martin Nowak have reviewed numerous studies that varied the number of rounds two people played the prisoner's dilemma game. The evidence is clear: as the likelihood of interacting with someone in the future rises, we become more cooperative (Rand & Nowak, 2013).

In real life we also interact with people face-to-face, allowing us access to various cues about them. Are we more cooperative with people who behave or look a certain way? Indeed we are, and for sensible reasons. A variety of studies suggest that we study others' nonverbal behavior in search of cues that signal that that individual is likely to cooperate; and once those cues are detected, they trigger cooperation on our part in turn. For example, in situations like the prisoner's dilemma game, people are more likely to cooperate with another person who smiles in a friendly fashion, laughs warmly, has a trustworthy-looking face, listens to others attentively, and has a physical appearance that resembles their own appearance (Bachorowski & Owren, 2001; DeBruine, 2002; Kogan et al., 2011; Stirrat & Perrett, 2010). In a similar vein, people also trust and devote resources to other individuals who cooperate quickly and reflexively and in ways that seem spontaneous rather than calculated and strategic (Jordan, Hoffman, Nowak, & Rand, 2016).

In daily life, we also tend to interact with people we know and often whose reputations we know from others. **Reputation** refers to the collective beliefs, evaluations, and impressions about an individual's character that develop within a group or social network (Emler, 1994). Studies of people at work find that they quickly develop reputations for being good citizens (cooperators) or "bad apples" (defectors) and that these reputations spread through the organization and persist over time (Burt, Kilduff, & Tasselli, 2013). Very often, when you interact with someone, say in a dorm or at work, you're likely to know a bit about that person's reputation. Does such knowledge influence levels of cooperation?

To answer this question, some researchers have added a twist to the prisoner's dilemma game: prior to playing, participants are told about their partner's reputation of being someone who cooperates or defects. As you'd expect, participants will readily cooperate and give resources to an interaction partner who has a reputation for cooperation, but they'll defect and choose not to give resources to an interaction partner known to be greedy (Wedekind & Milinski, 2000).

These findings raise an intriguing question: How do we come to know each other's reputation? One idea is that reputations spread through gossiping—something most people are reluctant to admit to doing but often enjoy when they do. Gossip can be defined as a communicative act in which one person comments on the reputation of another who is not present (Feinberg, Willer, Stellar, & Keltner, 2012). One of the primary reasons we gossip is to figure out the reputations of other people; through gossip, we investigate whether other group members are inclined to act in ways that strengthen the group (for example, by being civil, fair, and cooperative) or in ways that might create friction and ill will. This analysis yields what might seem like a counterintuitive prediction—that groups in which gossip takes place might actually be more cooperative. And indeed, that's what Matthew Feinberg and his colleagues have found.

In their study, participants played an economic game in which they could give some money to other people in their group (Feinberg, Willer, & Schultze, 2014). In one condition, they were allowed to gossip about each other's generosity (or lack thereof). In a second condition, no such opportunity to gossip was afforded. Over the course of several iterations, the groups whose members could gossip became more cooperative than the groups who weren't allowed to gossip. The threat of gossip makes people aware of what might happen to their reputations should they choose to act selfishly, thus encouraging more cooperative behavior.

Construal Processes and Cooperation

The way we construe events and situations matters a great deal in shaping interactions toward more cooperative or more competitive outcomes. In particular, the way we explicitly label situations could influence levels of competition and cooperation. If we think of international crises as buildups to war, diplomatic solutions may become less likely. When lawyers treat divorce settlements as adversarial and as opportunities to get their client the best outcome at the expense of the estranged spouse, entrenched bitterness seems inevitable.

In a striking demonstration of the power of labels, Liberman, Samuels, and Ross (2002) conducted a study in which they labeled the prisoner's dilemma game in one of two ways. Half the participants were told they were going to

reputation The collective beliefs, evaluations, and impressions people hold about an individual within a social network.

"It takes many good deeds to build a good reputation, and only one bad deed to lose it."
—BENJAMIN FRANKLIN

BOX 14.5

Not So Fast:
Critical Thinking about Generalizing to the Real World

Much of our discussion about cooperation thus far has come from studies using the prisoner's dilemma and related games, such as the dictator game (collectively known as economic games). Their structure captures a basic tension between cooperating and defecting in relationships of many kinds, from negotiations between adversarial nations to the daily lives of romantic partners. If you're skeptical about the external validity of these games—that is, the extent to which they generalize to cooperative behavior outside the lab—you're not alone.

Critics describe three kinds of doubts about the external validity of economic games (Levitt & List, 2007). First are the stakes involved: people are given money for cooperating or defecting, or they give away money that's been given to them in an experiment. People are dealing with "play" money and not actual money they've earned, which raises the question of whether we would observe similar patterns of cooperation when the money is real, earned, and costly to sacrifice. Second, critics suggest that being in a laboratory makes norms of cooperative behavior more salient. Simply signing up for an experiment, getting there on time, and following instructions from an experimenter are all acts guided by norms of cooperation, again suggesting that patterns of cooperation observed in the lab may diverge from those out in

the real world. Third, in lab studies people are acutely aware of being scrutinized, and scrutiny strengthens the likelihood of cooperative behavior.

The best response to concerns about the external validity of a paradigm is two-fold. First, researchers can ask whether behavior that is observed in the lab, such as cooperation in the prisoner's dilemma game, predicts actual behavior out in the world. On this question, there is mounting evidence that a person's behavior in economic games does indeed predict forms of charity and working to help others (Levit & List, 2007). For example, in one study, participants first played the dictator game (Franzen & Pointner, 2013). They were given 10 euros, and then they chose an amount to give to a stranger, under anonymous conditions. Some 4–5 weeks later, participants got a letter that was made to seem like it was for another student, whom they didn't know. When they opened up the envelope, addressed to them, they discovered a letter from a grandmother to another student, Alexander, congratulating him on doing well academically. Inside the envelope were 10 euros and Alexander's correct address, which gave participants the opportunity to mail the misdirected letter to Alexander. Did the amount the participants shared in the dictator game four weeks earlier predict whether or not they would take time out of their day and

mail the letter to Alexander? Indeed it did. People who gave more in the dictator game were more likely to return the misdirected letter.

A second way to address concerns about the external validity of economic games is with field experiments that seek to replicate findings observed in the lab. Recall that field experiments are studies conducted outside the lab, observing real-world behavior. Here again the evidence supports the principles of cooperation that have been uncovered with economic games. In one study, the researchers wanted to encourage residents in 15 homeowners associations to agree to a more energy-efficient use of their air conditioners (Yoeli, Hoffman, Rand, & Nowak, 2013). They did so by having participants sign up on a sheet posted on a kiosk near the mailboxes for the homes or apartments. In one condition, participants wrote their names on the sheet; in a second condition, they signed up with a numerical code. When people are aware of their own reputations, they're more cooperative in economic games of different kinds. Would this effect of reputation replicate in energy-saving but costly cooperation out in the world? Yes. When participants signed up using their names, they were three times more likely to sign up for the service than when they did so anonymously.

play the "Wall Street" game, and the other half were told it was the "community" game. Everything else about the experiment was the same for the two groups. What might seem to be a trivial change of labels had a dramatic effect on the participants' behavior. Those playing the community game cooperated on the opening round twice as often as those playing the Wall Street game. Moreover, these initial differences were maintained throughout the

BOX 14.6   **FOCUS ON** POSITIVE PSYCHOLOGY

Is Cooperation Contagious?

Popular movies and clever advertisements have used the "pay it forward" concept: when we cooperate, we inspire others to be more cooperative in subsequent situations. Is cooperation contagious? For years, James Fowler and Nicholas Christakis have been gathering evidence on the contagious nature of human behavior and have discovered that smoking, anxiety, happiness, and obesity, for example, spread through communities from one person to another (Christakis & Fowler, 2009). We are a mimetic species, prone to imitating the behaviors of others around us. Using an economic game, Fowler and Christakis found that cooperative acts inspire others to be more cooperative in ensuing situations (Fowler & Christakis, 2010).

In the study, participants played several rounds of an economic game in groups of four; each round involved an entirely new set of participants. In each round, the participant was given 20 money units (MUs) and allowed to give some amount, between 0 and 20, to the group. Each MU the participant gave to the group was translated to an increase of 0.4 MU for each of the four group members. This means that each gift of 1 MU would cost the giver 0.6 MU personally but benefit each other group member. If participants kept all their MUs, they would end the game with 20 MUs. If they each gave all their MUs to the group, each member would end the game with 32 MUs.

This method created the usual dilemma—that behaviors costly to the self are beneficial for the group—and allowed Fowler and Christakis to examine how cooperative gifts to other players by a

player in one round might influence those other players' levels of generosity in subsequent rounds. They found that for every MU a player gave, that player's partners would give 0.19 MU more on average to a *new* set of players in the next round and 0.07 MU on average to still other players in the round after that, two times removed from the original round.

PAYING IT FORWARD The popular movie *Pay It Forward* focuses on the theme of how one person's generosity leads to other acts of generosity.

subsequent rounds of the experiment. The Wall Street label doubtless made the participants adopt a perspective that made maximizing their own profits paramount. In contrast, the community label conjured up a different set of images and motives that increased the appeal of maximizing the participants' joint outcomes.

Culture and Cooperation

Given how labels—and therefore construals—shape levels of cooperation, you might expect cultural factors to have a similar influence on the inclination to either cooperate or defect. To explore this question, Joseph Henrich and his colleagues recruited individuals from 15 small societies around the world to play the ultimatum game, a close relative of the prisoner's dilemma game (Henrich et al., 2001). In the original version of the ultimatum game, one player, the allocator, is given a certain amount of money (say, $10) and chooses to keep a certain amount of that $10 and allocate the rest to a second participant, the responder.

The responder can then choose to either accept or reject the allocator's offer. If the responder accepts the offer, the responder receives what was offered and the allocator keeps the balance. If the responder rejects the offer, neither player receives anything.

The Henrich team conducted a cross-cultural version of the ultimatum game, recruiting participants who were foragers, slash-and-burn farmers, nomadic herders, and individuals in settled, agriculturalist societies in Africa, South America, and Indonesia. What the participants were allowed to offer an anonymous stranger differed. In some cultures it was money, in others a cherished good such as tobacco. In all cases, the researchers attempted to make rewards equal to approximately the same fraction of a daily wage in each culture.

The first finding of note was that in the 15 cultures, allocators offered, on average, 39 percent of the good to anonymous strangers. (In other research across Western cultures, 71 percent of the allocators offered the responder 40–50 percent of the money; Fehr & Schmidt, 1999.) Of course, it's important to bear in mind that there are strategic reasons for participants making such generous offers that have nothing to do with altruistic tendencies. Most notably, they probably anticipated that the respondent would reject unfair, trivial offers. Nevertheless, these results suggest that people are more cooperative and willing to share than one might expect.

Henrich and his colleagues then looked closely at the 15 cultures to determine what cultural factors predict the likelihood of cooperative generosity in the ultimatum game (Henrich et al., 2001). One factor stood out: how much the individuals in a culture depended on one another to survive. The more the members of a culture depended on one another to gather food and meet other needs, the more they offered to a stranger when they were allocators in the ultimatum game. For example, the Machiguenga people of Peru rarely collaborate with members outside of their family to produce food. Their average allocation in the ultimatum game was 26 percent of the resource. The Lamerala of Indonesia, by contrast, fish in highly collaborative groups of individuals from

COOPERATION IN DIFFERENT CULTURES
(A) The Machiguenga of Peru collaborate little with others outside their family and gave little in the ultimatum game (described in the text). (B) The Lamerala of Indonesia collaborate extensively in fishing and gave a lot.

different families. Cooperation is essential to their livelihood and subsistence. Their average gift in the ultimatum game was 58 percent.

This theme, that interdependence fosters cooperation, helps explain other cultural influences on cooperation. Consider, for example, the following findings about cooperation: when people are primed to think about religious concepts, they are more likely to cooperate in the prisoner's dilemma game (Ahmed & Salas, 2011); people from lower socioeconomic backgrounds are more likely to endorse cooperative values (Guinote et al., 2015); and in countries plagued by civil war, such as Sierra Leone and Uganda, it's those individuals who have witnessed violence who are more likely to cooperate in economic games (Bauer et al., 2016). One could argue that religion, being poor, and exposure to violence each create social conditions that require that people depend on one another to survive and that this interdependence prompts greater cooperation.

In keeping with this thinking, even the discipline you choose to study in college and the degree of interdependence it encourages influences cooperation. Take, for example, one of the most popular majors at many American campuses: economics. Economic theory assumes that people are rational actors who always act in self-interested ways, attempting to maximize their own gains independent of the concerns of others. Many people may think that this is a cynical view of the human condition; but in keeping with the ideas of eighteenth-century philosopher Adam Smith, economists have assumed that people and society are best served if individuals are allowed to selfishly pursue their own ends. The storekeeper and restaurateur will succeed to the extent that they serve their patrons well, simultaneously improving their customers' lives and doing well themselves by charging as much as a competitive market will allow.

Does training in the discipline of economics and its axioms of self-interest and independence encourage people to act more selfishly? The results of several studies indicate that it does (Carter & Irons, 1991; Frank, Gilovich, & Regan, 1993; Marwell & Ames, 1981). In one study, undergraduates majoring in economics and in a variety of other disciplines participated in a single-trial prisoner's dilemma game (Frank, Gilovich, et al., 1993). Seventy-two percent of the economics majors defected on their partners, whereas only 47 percent of those majoring in other disciplines defected. In a random sample of over 1,000 professors in 23 disciplines, participants were asked how much money they gave annually to public television, the United Way, and other charitable causes (Frank, Gilovich, et al., 1993). The economists were twice as likely as all the others to take a free ride on the contributions of their fellow citizens—in other words, giving nothing to charity while presumably enjoying services such as public television to the same extent as everyone else. The subculture in which people are immersed appears to powerfully influence their inclination to either cooperate with others or look only after themselves.

Evolution and Cooperation: Tit for Tat

In *The Evolution of Cooperation* (1984), political scientist Robert Axelrod asked how cooperation might emerge in competitive environments governed by the ruthless pursuit of self-interest. In the context of human evolution, how might non-kin begin to act with an eye toward advancing the welfare of others?

"Every individual ... endeavors as much as he can ... to employ his capital in the support of domestic industry, and so to direct that industry that its produce may be of greatest value; every individual necessarily labours to render the annual revenue of the society as great as he can. He ... neither intends to promote the public interest, nor knows how much he is promoting it. By ... directing that industry in such a manner as its produce may be of greatest value, he intends only his own gain, and he is in this, as in many other cases, led by an invisible hand to promote an end which was no part of his intention."
—ADAM SMITH, *THE WEALTH OF NATIONS* (1776)

Axelrod assumed that cooperation was part of our evolutionary heritage, given its universality and its emergence in even the most unlikely of social contexts. For example, in the trenches of World War I, British and French soldiers were separated from their enemies, the Germans, by a few hundred yards of no-man's-land (Axelrod, 1984). Brutal assaults by one side were typically met with equally fierce counterattacks by the other. And yet even here cooperation frequently emerged, allowing soldiers to eat meals peacefully, to enjoy long periods of nonconfrontation, and even to fraternize with one another. The two sides would fly special flags, make verbal agreements, and fire deliberately misguided shots, all to signal and maintain peaceful cooperation between the episodes of attack in which each side was bent on exterminating the other.

Axelrod conducted a study that helps illuminate the evolutionary origins of cooperation. Although simple in design, this study yields profound lessons. Axelrod ran a tournament in which players—academics, prize-winning mathematicians, computer hackers, and common folk—were invited to submit computer programs that specified what choices to make on a round of the prisoner's dilemma game, given what had happened on previous rounds (Axelrod, 1984). In the first tournament, 14 strategies were submitted. Each strategy played 200 rounds of the prisoner's dilemma game with every other strategy. The points were tallied, and the most effective strategy was announced. The winner? It was a so-called tit-for-tat strategy, submitted by mathematical psychologist Anatol Rapaport.

The **tit-for-tat strategy** is disarmingly simple. It cooperates on the first round with every opponent and then reciprocates whatever the opponent did on the previous round. An opponent's cooperation was rewarded with immediate cooperation; defection was punished with immediate defection. In other words, start out cooperatively, and reciprocate your partner's previous move. Axelrod held a second tournament that attracted the submission of 62 strategies. All the entrants knew the results of the first round—that the tit-for-tat strategy had won. In the second tournament, the tit-for-tat strategy again prevailed. Note that the tit-for-tat strategy didn't win every round when pitted against all the different strategies. Instead, it did better overall against the diversity of strategies. What makes the tit-for-tat strategy special, and how might it be relevant to your own life?

Axelrod contends that the tit-for-tat strategy is based on a set of valuable principles that apply when forming friendships, dealing with a difficult personality at work, negotiating with bosses, maintaining long-term romantic relationships, and raising children. Five factors make it an especially compelling strategy: (1) It's cooperative and thus encourages mutually supportive action toward a shared goal. (2) It's not envious; a partner using this strategy can do extremely well without resorting to competitive behavior. (3) It's not exploitable, meaning it's not easily taken advantage of; if you defect on the tit-for-tat, it will defect on you. (4) It's forgiving; that is, it's willing to cooperate at the first cooperative action of the partner, even after long runs of defection and competition. (5) It's easy to read; it shouldn't take long for others to know that the tit-for-tat strategy is being played. Being nice, stalwart, forgiving, and clear—that's a good set of principles to live by.

tit-for-tat strategy A strategy in the prisoner's dilemma game in which the player's first move is cooperative; thereafter, the player mimics the other person's behavior, whether cooperative or competitive. This strategy fares well when used against other strategies.

Cooperation is part of our evolutionary heritage. The prisoner's dilemma game models the many situations in everyday life when defection is the best solution for each person separately but cooperation benefits the two together. Situational factors, such as the likelihood of repeated interactions and whether your reputation is on the line, influence levels of cooperation and competition. So, too, do construal processes: people can be primed to cooperate or defect. Studies of cultures in remote parts of the world reveal that cooperation is a human universal and that cultures characterized by economic interdependence show greater cooperation. The tit-for-tat strategy involves initial cooperation and then reciprocation of an adversary's behavior, encouraging mutual cooperation.

Chapter Review

SUMMARY

Altruism

- People may help others out of selfish motives, including reducing personal distress and gaining social rewards, such as praise, attention, or gratitude.
- A form of pure, undiluted altruism is based on *empathic concern*, the feeling of concern for another person after observing and being moved by that person's needs.
- Empathic concern motivates people to volunteer or otherwise enhance the welfare of others.
- Altruistic behavior is influenced by features of the situation, such as who is present and what sort of need or suffering is observed.
- *Bystander intervention* depends on the number of people observing the person needing help. The presence of others can lead to *diffusion of responsibility*, in which nobody takes responsibility for helping the person in need.
- When people are unsure about an emergency situation, they might do nothing for fear of embarrassment in case nothing is really wrong.
- Victim characteristics that increase the likelihood of being helped include whether the person is similar to potential helpers and whether the victim makes the distress known.

- People who live in rural settings are more likely to help others than people who live in urban settings.
- People from lower-class backgrounds are more empathic than people from upper-class backgrounds and are more likely to give resources to strangers and help people in need.
- Exposure to religious concepts increases levels of altruism, perhaps through the effects of feeling watched.
- From the standpoint of evolution, people's actions should serve to increase the likelihood of survival and reproduction. According to the *kin selection* hypothesis, people will help others to preserve the genes of close kin.
- In *reciprocal altruism*, people help others or grant favors in the belief that such behavior will be reciprocated in the future.

Cooperation

- Cooperation is part of human evolutionary heritage, and it is evident in almost all societies.
- The *prisoner's dilemma* game, used to study cooperation, tempts participants to maximize their own outcomes at the expense of another person by defecting. This strategy backfires if the other person also defects. The optimal outcome is for both to settle for something less than the maximum by cooperating.
- Interacting with people repeatedly over time increases cooperation.
- People look for nonverbal cues that someone will cooperate; if they detect such cues, then they will cooperate in turn.
- Knowing a person's *reputation* as cooperative or competitive influences levels of cooperation in profound ways.
- Gossip is a means of spreading information to other group members about an individual's reputation, and it can increase cooperation in groups.
- Cooperation is widespread in certain cultures, particularly where members are dependent on one another.
- *The tit-for-tat strategy* in the prisoner's dilemma game is a reciprocal strategy that is cooperative, nonenvious, nonexploitable, forgiving, and easy to read. It helps maximize outcomes in potentially competitive situations that occur in real life.

THINK ABOUT IT

1. Someone might argue that as long as you're helping, your motives don't matter. Do you agree? Why or why not? In what situations might motives matter most?

2. Based on what you've learned about bystander intervention and diffusion of responsibility, what actions could you take to increase the likelihood that someone would help you in an emergency that happens in front of a large crowd?

3. Research indicates that lower-class people tend to be more empathic and giving than upper-class people. What factors might explain this difference? How might they relate to what you learned about power and prosocial behavior?

4. According to evolutionary theory, behaviors that optimize survival and reproduction are favored by natural selection and therefore more likely to persist. How, then, can we explain the evolution of altruism, which is by definition costly to the self?

5. After learning about research on gossip, have your feelings about this behavior changed? Under what circumstances might gossip serve a useful purpose?

6. In what ways could the tit-for-tat strategy be relevant in your life, such as in a romantic relationship?

The **answer guidelines** for the think about it questions can be found at the back of the book . . . 👉

ONLINE STUDY MATERIALS

Want to earn a better grade on your test?

Go to **INQUIZITIVE** to learn and review this chapter's content, with personalized feedback along the way.

Social Psychology and Health

MARIE ANTOINETTE, THE NOTORIOUS QUEEN OF FRANCE during the late eighteenth century, was fond of gambling, fine clothes, behind-the-scenes political maneuvers, and extramarital affairs. She was a favorite target of the revolutionaries when they overthrew the monarchy during the French Revolution. Legend has it that after her capture, during the night before her execution by guillotine, Marie Antoinette's hair turned white.

We know it's physiologically impossible for hair to turn white during the course of a day. But excessive levels of stress—in Marie Antoinette's case, her husband's execution, the political upheaval she helped bring about, and her imminent demise—can damage the body. The stress response evolved to help us handle immediate pressures in the short run, but chronic and continuous stress can lead to myriad health problems. For example, physicians now estimate that 1–2 percent of those with the symptoms of a heart attack actually reflect a condition known as apical ballooning syndrome (ABS). ABS arises when stress hormones, such as epinephrine, flood the left ventricle of the heart, causing it to swell to dangerous levels. ABS is often triggered by excessive emotional stress—the death of a child, the loss of a spouse, or exposure to warfare and extreme violence. In 1 percent of cases, ABS can be fatal.

Stress is just one of many emotional and social factors that can affect overall health. Elements of one's culture, such as social class, influence health and well-being, leading people from lower-class backgrounds to suffer more frequently from almost every kind of health problem. Social situations, particularly the richness of social connections, can benefit health. Even certain construal processes—perceptions of control and optimism—can contribute to healthier lives. ■

Evolution and Health: Short-Term and Chronic Stress

Psychological stress results from the sense that our challenges and demands surpass our current capacities, resources, and energies (Lazarus, 1966; Sapolsky, 1994). Not all of them cause equal amounts of stress, however. As a review of over 200 studies reveals, the obligations and expectations that threaten social identity and our connection to others are particularly likely to contribute to our stress levels (Dickerson & Kemeny, 2004). The challenges of daily life often exceed our capacity to meet them, and stress can arise in almost any situation: pressures at work, the loss of a loved one, economic hardship, conflicts with family members, trying times in a marriage. Even positive events can be surprisingly stressful, such as graduation, a new job, planning a wedding, the early stages of marriage. And young children, while introducing incomparable joys for new parents, place new demands and create unexpected sources of stress. In any of these circumstances, we may feel we don't have the energy or skill to handle the challenges effectively; as a result, we experience psychological stress.

How does psychological stress harm physical health? The process begins in a system of the body known as the hypothalamic-pituitary-adrenal (HPA) axis

psychological stress The sense that challenges and demands surpass one's current capacities, resources, and energies.

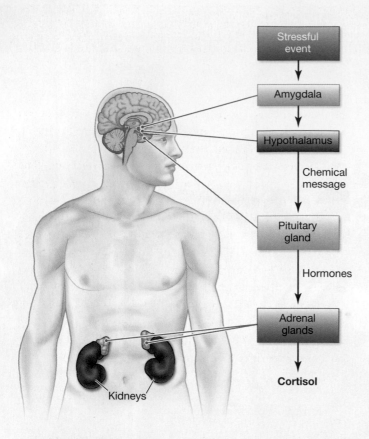

FIGURE A1.1
THE HPA AXIS AND THE
RELEASE OF CORTISOL

and with the stress hormone cortisol (**Figure A1.1**). Stressful events activate the amygdala, a region of the brain that processes information related to threat. The amygdala stimulates the hypothalamus, which sends chemical messages to the pituitary gland to produce adrenocorticotropic hormone (ACTH). ACTH stimulates the adrenal glands (near the kidneys) to release cortisol into the bloodstream.

Cortisol has many effects on the body. Most notably, cortisol increases heart rate and blood pressure, distributing blood to appropriate muscle groups involved in the fight-or-flight response to stress. The hands sweat—a process some think evolved to facilitate grasping. Cortisol suppresses the activity of the immune system, thus keeping resources available for metabolically demanding fight-or-flight behavior. It is also involved in forming flashbulb, stress-related memories in the hippocampus, thereby aiding the recall of sources of danger in the environment.

Activation of the HPA axis and the accompanying release of cortisol into the bloodstream help us respond to short-term stress—immediate threats to survival. During early evolution, this stress response enabled our ancestors to detect an approaching predator or an enraged rival and respond quickly with appropriate action. Today, this same stress response helps us power through lecture notes to study for an exam, avoid danger, or stay up until the wee hours of the morning taking care of a sick friend or child. Not surprisingly, researchers have observed elevated levels of cortisol in race car drivers, parachute jumpers, and students taking exams (Coriell & Adler, 2001).

The normal response to short-term stress is not usually a problem for most of us. Trouble begins when we experience chronic stress, which is frequently the result of **rumination**, the tendency to think about some stressful event over and over again (Nolen-Hoeksema, 1987). When we ruminate, we focus on a specific event, and by thinking of all its deep causes and ramifications, turn it into a continuous source of stress that touches on all facets of our life. Suppose your boss offers some criticism about how to sharpen up a proposal you've been working on. If you were to ruminate about it, you'd take the criticism and elaborate on how that event reflects more general problems you have at work, how you're never living up to expectations, how you'll let your parents down yet again.

Studies have shown that people who ruminate about a negative event experience prolonged stress compared with people who distract themselves from the event (Lyubomirsky & Nolen-Hoeksema, 1995; Morrow & Nolen-Hoeksema, 1990). Through rumination, specific stresses become chronic ones: a marital spat begins to feel like the fast road to divorce; a dip in the economy feels like a prolonged recession; a transient health problem feels like a verdict of deteriorating health.

Moreover, chronic stress can kill. Studies have found that chronic stress can lead to ulcers, heart disease, cancer, and even cell death in the hippocampus and consequent memory loss, in part because chronically high levels of cortisol

rumination The tendency to think about a stressful event repeatedly.

How to Stop Ruminating

One thing you're probably ruminating about right now is how to stop ruminating and avoid the damaging effects of chronic stress. Susan Nolen-Hoeksema, the leading scholar in the study of rumination, offers several tips for reducing the tendency to ruminate (Nolen-Hoeksema, 2003). Here are a few. First, break loose from your pattern of rumination; turn your attention away from those recurring thoughts. Nolen-Hoeksema has documented how engaging in distracting activities during stressful periods—doing a crossword puzzle, knitting, reading a book, or working on a Sudoku problem—quiets the ruminative mind and calms you during stressful times.

A second tip is the stop strategy. Here Nolen-Hoeksema recommends that you simply say "Stop" to yourself, even shout it, when you find yourself ruminating. Shift your attention to other matters in your life rather than the negative thing you're dwelling

on—what you need to do to prepare for grad school, where you might travel in the upcoming years, or friends you need to contact.

Finally, Nolen-Hoeksema recommends that if you're a dyed-in-the-wool ruminator, simply set aside 30 minutes of ruminating time each day, ideally when you're feeling pretty calm. Knowing you've reserved that time period will reduce your tendency to be overcome unexpectedly by rumination at random times throughout the day. Ethan Kross, Ozlem Ayduk, and their colleagues have shown that even for that deliberate period of rumination, it's helpful to engage in **self-distancing**, focusing on your feelings from the perspective of a detached observer (Kross, Ayduk, & Mischel, 2005). Revisiting a situation not from the perspective you initially had, but from the standpoint of a real or imagined observer, lets you reflect on stressful thoughts and feelings without becoming overwhelmed by negativity (Ayduk & Kross, 2008; Kross & Ayduk, 2008).

---

damage different cells and organs in the body (Sapolsky, 1994). Feeling chronically stressed makes people more vulnerable to the common cold (Cohen et al., 2008). Chronic stress can even prematurely age the cells. Elissa Epel and her colleagues found that premenopausal women who reported elevated levels of stress showed shortened telomeres, parts of cells that normally shorten as part of the aging process (Epel et al., 2004). The telomeres of the most stressed women in this study had prematurely aged by ten years.

The message from the literature on stress and cortisol couldn't be clearer. Evolution has equipped us with an immediate stress response, associated with elevated HPA activation and cortisol release, that enables us to respond to pressing problems. However, short-term stresses can sometimes become chronic, triggering excessively high levels of cortisol that damage our health. Ruminating over stressful or negative events can have precisely that effect.

self-distancing The ability to focus on one's feelings from the perspective of a detached observer.

Culture and Health: Class, Stress, and Health Outcomes

In a celebrated but perhaps apocryphal exchange, F. Scott Fitzgerald told Ernest Hemingway, "The rich are different from you and me." Hemingway replied, "Yes, they have more money." Hemingway could have added that the rich also lead healthier and longer lives.

Social psychologists think of wealth in terms of class, or socioeconomic status (SES). We often refer to SES by using such categories as working class and upper class. Researchers measure social class in terms of three variables: family wealth and income, educational achievement (and that of the parents), and the prestige of work or career (and that of the parents) (Oakes & Rossi, 2003; Snibbe & Markus, 2005).

As you've learned throughout this book, social class is an important cultural dimension of one's identity. People of various socioeconomic backgrounds tend to prefer different kinds of music (Snibbe & Markus, 2005), tend to explain economic and political events in different ways (see Chapter 5), and appear to be prone to different levels of altruism (see Chapter 14).

What does social class have to do with physical health? A great deal, it turns out. Dozens of studies have explored the association between social class and indicators of physical health. Just about every health problem is more prevalent in lower-SES people—those of lesser means (Adler et al., 1994; Coriell & Adler, 2001). Lower-SES newborns are more likely to have a low birth weight, which is a major predictor of later health problems. Lower-SES children are more inclined to develop asthma, diabetes, and obesity, other early predictors of health problems later in life. In adulthood, lower-SES people are more likely to suffer from high blood pressure, cardiovascular disease, diabetes, respiratory illness, and poor metabolic functioning related to blood sugar levels. They are also more likely to experience poor health subjectively, with symptoms ranging from stomach upsets to headaches and bad backs (Adler et al., 1994; Gallo, Bogart, Vranceanu, & Matthews, 2005; Lehman, Taylor, Kiefe, & Seeman, 2005; Singh-Manoux, Adler, & Marmot, 2003).

Class, Neighborhood, and Stress

How would you explain these class-based health differences? Your first inclination might be to take a situationist view and think about how the physical environments of poorer people might contribute to health-damaging chronic

THE INFLUENCE OF NEIGHBORHOOD QUALITY ON STRESS
(A) Lower-SES neighborhoods have fewer green spaces and play structures than
(B) higher-SES neighborhoods, which allow for more stress-reducing play and relaxation.

stress. Situations matter, and so does a person's daily environment. For instance, if you live close to someone, you're more likely to become friends (see Chapter 10). Generous acts are more common in rural settings than in urban settings (see Chapter 14). And it's clear that people from lower-SES and upper-SES backgrounds inhabit very different social and physical environments (see Coriell & Adler, 2001).

People living in poorer neighborhoods are more often exposed to air and water pollution, pesticides, and hazardous wastes. Toxins like these harm the nervous system directly, and they can also boost levels of stress. Lower-SES neighborhoods have fewer recreational spaces and parks, so residents have fewer opportunities to exercise, to be outdoors, to relax, or to calm down. It is well known that physical exercise reduces stress and increases general health (Lyubomirsky, 2007). Poorer neighborhoods also have a higher incidence of violent crime, and residents experience more pervasive feelings of threat (Macintyre, Maciver, & Solomon, 1993). And lower-SES neighborhoods tend to have few healthy grocery stores or health care centers—resources that would support a healthier lifestyle.

Class, Rank, and Health

Another explanation for the connection between social class and health has to do with rank, or power (Adler et al., 1994). Lower-SES individuals have fewer resources and more limited access to opportunities, and these play an important role in defining a person's rank in society. Researchers have learned that having subordinate status, in human and nonhuman groups alike, leads to chronic feelings of threat and stress, accompanied by activation of the HPA axis and elevated cortisol. Robert Sapolsky has found, for instance, that subordinate baboons have chronically higher cortisol levels, as well as a variety of health problems, including an increased risk of cardiovascular disease and lower reproductive success (Sapolsky, 1982, 1994).

Social class may influence physical health through perceptions of rank or relative status. Lower-SES people may construe their lives in terms of occupying positions of subordinate status, and it may be this construal that damages their health. To capture this idea, researchers have begun to measure construals of rank with what is known as the ladder measure. Take a look at **Figure A1.2**. Think of the ladder as representing the social class of people in the United States. At the top are those who have the most money, the most education, and the most respected jobs. At the bottom are those who have the least money, the least amount of education, and the least respected job or no job. The higher up you are on this ladder, the closer you are to the people at the very top. The lower you are, the closer you are to the people at the very bottom. Where would you place yourself on this ladder?

What's interesting about this measure is that it's based on subjective construal. A fairly wealthy person living among Fortune 500 CEOs, for example, could indicate a lower rank on this scale—and that would have important health outcomes. With each jump up the ladder of the class hierarchy, people are likely to enjoy better health. In a study of employees of the British Civil Service, those in the lowest-ranked positions (such as janitors) were three times more likely to die over a ten-year period than the highest-ranked administrators (Marmot, Shipley, & Rose, 1984). The experience of subordinate rank clearly can be

FIGURE A1.2
THE LADDER MEASURE
Place a large X on the rung that best represents your socioeconomic rank.

damaging to one's overall health. Conversely, the feeling of being empowered benefits one's sense of agency and self-esteem and therefore general health.

Nancy Adler and her colleagues have found that with each move up the class hierarchy, people are less likely than people just below them to die in infancy, and are less vulnerable to coronary heart disease, lung cancer, bronchitis, respiratory disease, asthma, arthritis, cervical cancer, and neurological disorders (Adler et al., 1994). The experience of subordinate rank, even for people who have a good deal in life (those in the middle or upper middle classes), leads to chronic activation of the HPA axis and the associated health problems.

Situational Factors and Health: Benefits of Social Connection

We are a species that has evolved to connect with other people and to enjoy many kinds of relationships. And when we connect, we are healthier. To explicitly examine the relationship between social connection and health, researchers have measured the strength of social support, using scales like the one in **Table A1.1**. This scale captures the extent to which we can count on friends and family for support and care. With measures like these, researchers have documented that social connections are vital to our physical, mental, and emotional health.

Consider some specific findings. In one study, people who had fewer meaningful connections to others were 1.9 to 3.1 times more likely to have died nine years later (Berkman & Syme, 1979). People who report having strong ties to others live longer (Berkman, 1995; Coriell & Adler, 2001). Janice Kiecolt-Glaser and her colleagues have found that people who report being lonely show higher levels of cortisol, suggesting that strong social connections calm HPA axis activation (Kiecolt-Glaser & Glaser, 1995).

TABLE A1.1 A SOCIAL SUPPORT SCALE

1. There is a special person who is around when I am in need.

2. There is a special person with whom I can share my joys and sorrows.

3. My family really tries to help me.

4. I get the emotional help and support I need from my family.

5. I have a special person who is a real source of comfort for me.

6. My friends really try to help me.

7. I can count on my friends when things go wrong.

8. I can talk about my problems with my family.

9. I have friends with whom I can share my joys and sorrows.

10. There is a special person in my life who cares about my feelings.

11. My family is willing to help me make decisions.

12. I can talk about my problems with my friends.

SOURCE: Adapted from Zimet, Dalhem, Zimet, & Farley, 1988.

These correlational studies raise questions about causation. Do strong relationships promote physical health? Or are physically healthy people more likely to enter into psychologically healthy relationships? Both causal relationships are plausible.

Experimental results indicate that physiological stress is calmed by being with supportive other people. In one study, for example, women performed stressful, challenging tasks either in the presence of a friend or alone. Those accompanied by a friend showed a milder stress-related cardiovascular response to the challenging tasks (Kamarck, Manuch, & Jennings, 1990). In another study, people were required to give a public speech with very little time to prepare, which no doubt caused rattled nerves and elevated cortisol. Those who had a supportive person in the audience, compared with those who did not, had lower blood pressure during the course of the speech (Lepore, Allen, & Evans, 1993). In still other work, participants made a presentation about why each of them would be a good candidate for an administrative job on campus, while two audience members looked on, expressionless, offering few signs of enthusiasm and a great deal of skepticism (Taylor et al., 2008). Before and after the speech, participants' cortisol levels were measured. Those who reported having strong connections with others, a sense of autonomy, and healthy self-esteem showed less intense cortisol responses to the stressful speech.

Perhaps the most dramatic evidence of the health benefits of social connection comes from an influential study by David Spiegel and his colleagues (Spiegel, Bloom, Kraemer, & Gottheil, 1989). Spiegel was interested in whether a sense of social connection would enable more favorable responses to breast cancer. Participants were randomly assigned to one of two conditions. In one condition, they engaged in weekly sessions of emotionally supportive group therapy with other breast cancer patients; in a second condition, participants were assigned to a nonintervention control group. As you can see in **Figure A1.3**, those in the group therapy condition survived 18 months longer (37 months) than women in the nonintervention control group (19 months).

These results support the thesis that social connections lead to positive responses to stress and better health overall. To integrate these findings, Shelley Taylor and her colleagues have offered an influential account of the benefits of a

FIGURE A1.3
HEALTH BENEFITS OF SOCIAL CONNECTION
This study demonstrated that breast cancer survivors live longer thanks to social support.
SOURCE: Adapted from Spiegel et al., 1989.

Tips for Reducing Stress

In her book *The How of Happiness*, Sonja Lyubomirsky summarizes the vast amount of published research and offers some simple recommendations for reducing the effects of stress (Lyubomirsky, 2007). None of them cost much, and all of them yield great health benefits.

1. *Focus on an adaptive coping approach.* Devise specific strategies for responding to your sources of stress, one step at a time, with concrete actions. If you're stressed about how to get into graduate school, write down the specific actions you need to take to get ready to apply—volunteering in a lab, doing extracurricular activities, forming relationships with different professors, preparing for the GREs.

2. *Exercise (the more, the better).* You can get a runner's high not only from jogging, but from many kinds of exercise—dance, pickup basketball, hiking in the mountains, a lunchtime walk with a friend, cross-country skiing. Almost any kind of exercise tends to lower stress levels.

3. *Seek out positive emotions.* Several studies suggest that the more you experience positive emotions, the less stress you'll have. People who experience positive emotions, such as gratitude, love, contentment, and awe, have lower mortality rates (Moskowitz, Epel, & Acree, 2008). When feeling stressed, take a moment to write down something for which you're grateful. If someone has done something to harm you, try to forgive. Go to the movies and see a comedy. Or just take a break and have an outing with friends. All these experiences bring different kinds of positive emotion, which will reduce your stress.

4. *Meditate.* There are many kinds of meditation: focusing on the breath, focusing on different sensations in the body, practicing a kind approach to other people, and being mindful, or aware, of ordinary everyday actions, such as eating and walking. An expanding body of scientific literature shows that meditation reduces levels of cortisol and stress.

"tend-and-befriend" approach to stress (Taylor et al., 2000). Taylor argues that paying attention to the needs of others engages physiological processes in our own body that reduce stress-related HPA axis activation, thus paving the way for better health. A central player in this tend-and-befriend branch of the nervous system is the chemical oxytocin. Oxytocin floats through the brain and bloodstream and fosters feelings of trust, love, and devotion (see Chapter 6). In nonhuman species—from rats to primates—oxytocin increases attachment-related behavior and reduces cortisol levels. When we give, care, and connect, Taylor reasons, we activate oxytocin and this attachment system, thereby moderating our own stress. One of the most important clues to a healthy life, then, is to stay connected.

Construal and Health: Benefits of Perceived Control and Optimism

In the early 1980s, Shelley Taylor began a series of studies of how people live with serious disease (see, for example, Taylor, 1983). In one study, she interviewed women who were being treated for breast cancer. One out of seven women in the United States and Canada suffer from breast cancer during the course of their lives. While the survival rates are improving every year, the psychological ramifications are complex. Upon being diagnosed, women often feel anxiety, fear, shame, and even hostility—just the kinds of emotions that trigger HPA axis activation and cortisol release, thereby causing stress and perhaps worsening the effects of the disease.

In studying the interviews, Taylor found that women with a breast cancer diagnosis did not necessarily accept their condition passively. Instead, they actively constructed narratives about this new dimension to their identity. Many of them found reasons to be grateful in surprising kinds of social comparisons. Women who were diagnosed later in life felt grateful it hadn't happened to them as young women, while they were raising children or starting a career; they appreciated having had the chance to live a full life without cancer. Younger women, by contrast, were grateful they weren't older when they got their diagnosis, for they felt they had the physical robustness to respond strongly to the disease.

One construal process that seems to benefit a person's overall health is developing a sense of control—a feeling of mastery, autonomy, and efficacy in influencing important life outcomes (Shapiro, Schwartz, & Astin, 1996). In Taylor's study of breast cancer patients, perceived control proved to be a source of good health. Taylor found that more than two-thirds of the women reported a sense of control over their situation. They assumed that through diet, exercise, and positive beliefs, they could influence the course of their disease. (People suffering from other conditions, such as HIV/AIDS and coronary problems, have similar feelings.) And the more the patient reported perceived control, the better she responded to the disease, as assessed by her physician (Taylor, Lichtman, & Wood, 1984; Taylor, Wood, & Lichtman, 1983).

In general, people with a more pronounced sense of control enjoy better health and well-being (Cohen & Herbert, 1996). Diseases and other health problems threaten our basic belief about the control we have over our body and our life, and a sense of losing that control is stressful in its own right. Thus, a good dose of perceived control can counter that stress and promote better health.

These findings raise an intriguing possibility: Might introducing a sense of control into the lives of people with declining health improve their health and well-being? That question motivated a striking study by Ellen Langer and Judith Rodin (1976) of nursing home residents. As people age into their later years, they often experience a pronounced loss of control in many realms: the loss of eyesight, muscular coordination, and strength makes simple physical tasks more challenging; the loss of memory can make social interactions difficult. These age-related losses are amplified, many believe, by some of the conditions of certain facilities, where older people forfeit even more control—over their schedules, their meals, and their social activities.

Langer and Rodin did something ingenious. They decided to explore the effects of increasing the sense of control in a particular nursing home (Langer & Rodin, 1976). The participants were all healthy, ambulatory residents, ages 65–90. On one floor, individuals were brought together and led in a discussion, by a young male staff member, about personal responsibility and the various ways they had personal control in their residence, ranging from planning their free time to voicing complaints to the staff. Each participant then received a small plant and was asked to take care of it. In a second condition, on a neighboring floor, participants were told about all the things in the nursing home available to them, with no mention of their personal control. They, too, all received plants but were told the staff would water and care for them.

Before these discussions and again three weeks later, the researchers gathered several measures of how well the elderly residents were faring (**Figure A1.4**, see p. 524). Sure enough, participants on the floor that emphasized personal control

Percentage of
residents rated
by nurses as
having improved

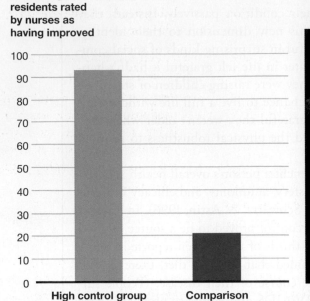

100
90
80
70
60
50
40
30
20
10
0

High control group   Comparison

FIGURE A1.4
PERSONAL CONTROL AND HAPPINESS
The elderly woman in the photo appears to be experiencing little control in her nursing home.
Source: Adapted from Langer & Rodin, 1976.

showed greater increases in happiness compared with those on the neighboring floor. They were more inclined to attend a free movie. They were ten times as likely to participate in a game proposed by the staff. And as rated by the nurses, nearly four times as many of the participants with the uplifted sense of control were judged to have improved in their overall functioning. Having a sense of personal control appears to quiet the emotions that activate the HPA axis.

A second construal that has emerged as quite important in health is optimism (see Chapter 5). Highly optimistic people have positive expectations about the future. They are likely to endorse the statement, "In uncertain times, I usually expect the best," and disagree with the statement, "If something can go wrong for me, it will." Studies have shown that people who are more optimistic tend to have greater happiness and well-being—and they enjoy better health as well. For example, Charles Carver and Michael Scheier found that individuals who report higher levels of optimism respond with greater robustness to coronary artery bypass surgery and breast cancer and recover more quickly (Carver & Scheier, 1982). Researchers have found that self-reports of pessimism predict a more rapid weakening of the immune system (O'Donovan et al., 2009). In a study of men who graduated from college in 1945, those who reported higher levels of optimism at age 21 reported better physical health 35 years later (Peterson, Seligman, & Valliant, 1988).

Taylor and her colleagues have argued that belief in perceived control and optimism benefit health in several ways. With an increased sense of control, people generally respond to stress more effectively. Moreover, people with a heightened sense of control and an optimistic outlook tend to engage in better health practices. In one study, optimistic HIV patients had healthier habits and involvements, including building strong networks of social support (Taylor et al., 1992).

Module Review

SUMMARY

Evolution and Health: Short-Term and Chronic Stress

- *Psychological stress* is the sense that challenges and demands surpass one's capacities, resources, and energies.
- The hypothalamic-pituitary-adrenal (HPA) axis produces the stress hormone cortisol, the continuous release of which results in chronic stress.
- *Rumination*, or repeatedly thinking about some stressful event, can be reduced by *self-distancing*, focusing on feelings from the perspective of a detached observer.

Culture and Health: Class, Stress, and Health Outcomes

- People of lower socioeconomic status have poorer health than higher-SES individuals, in part because they have more stress in daily life.

- The subjective construal of lower rank or status, such as being a subordinate executive, can cause stress-related illnesses.

Situational Factors and Health: Benefits of Social Connection

- People with more meaningful relationships and connections to others are healthier.
- Being accompanied by a sympathetic person when undergoing a stressful experience significantly reduces the potentially damaging physiological and psychological effects.

Construal and Health: Benefits of Perceived Control and Optimism

- Having a sense of perceived control over one's circumstances reduces stress and yields health benefits.
- Having a sense of optimism, a viewpoint that positive outcomes are likely in the future, is associated with better health.

THINK ABOUT IT

1. The experience of psychological stress typically triggers a host of physiological changes, including increased heart rate and blood pressure, sweating, and suppression of the immune system. When might these changes be helpful, and when are they more likely to be harmful?

2. Who is more likely to suffer from health problems, a janitor or a Fortune 500 CEO, and why? How might each person's subjective construal of their position influence their health?

3. According to the tend-and-befriend theory, why might providing social support improve health?

4. Research indicates that optimistic people tend to enjoy better health. Can you conclude from these findings that becoming more optimistic will improve your health? Why or why not? If you were a researcher conducting a study on this topic, what other factors might you want to control for?

The answer guidelines for the Think About It questions can be found at the back of the book . . .

ONLINE STUDY MATERIALS

Want to earn a better grade on your test?

Go to **INQUIZITIVE** to learn and review this application module's content, with personalized feedback along the way.

Social Psychology and Education

OVERHEARD IN PALO ALTO, California: one European-American high school senior said to another, upon hearing of her friend's super-high SAT scores, "Good grief, Jessica, those scores are positively Asian."

On average, the academic achievements of Asian-American students are undeniably impressive, and Asians regularly outperform Americans in math and science. Why do you suppose that is? What could be done to help European-American and African-American students perform at the level of Asian-American students? Or do you think such a change in overall performance is highly unlikely or impossible?

Social psychologists have studied why some students perform better in school than others. More important, they have investigated ways in which research findings might help improve educational outcomes, especially for certain minority students, who often perform below their capacity.

Social psychology has also highlighted excellent tools for improving the critical thinking skills of everyone—and these can be sharpened by certain kinds of educational experiences and by interventions that are remarkably brief but effective. ■

Pygmalion in the Classroom

How much influence does a teacher have on the academic progress of students? The idea that one person can help transform another—even create an extraordinary person from ordinary raw material—has been a theme of literature going back to Greek mythology. A sculptor named Pygmalion made a statue so beautiful that he fell in love with it and, with the help of the goddess Venus, brought

it to life. An updated version of the myth is the musical *My Fair Lady*, about an eccentric English phonetics professor who coaches a lowly flower girl in manners and accent, helping her pass for a lady in British high society.

Social psychologists Robert Rosenthal and Lenore Jacobson published a study in 1968, called *Pygmalion in the Classroom*, that examined the effect of teacher expectations on the intellectual development and achievement of students. The study caused an uproar in the fields of both psychology and education. All students in a particular school took an IQ test. Allegedly on the basis of the test, the researchers told the teachers at the beginning of the school year that some of their students were "late bloomers"—that is, they were expected to show substantial IQ growth over the course of the year. About 20 percent of the children in each classroom were designated—ostensibly on the basis of the test, but in fact by random assignment—as being late bloomers. The investigators reported that the designated late bloomers did indeed achieve substantial IQ gains after a brief time period. The gains for young children were shockingly high—15 points for first-graders and 10 points for second-graders. These increases seemed to indicate that teachers' expectations for children created a powerful self-fulfilling prophecy: if the teacher believed the child was going to gain in intelligence, the teacher behaved toward the child in a way that such a gain was likely to occur (Rosenthal & Jacobson, 1968).

Education critics argued that the results showed that teacher bias, presumably in favor of white middle-class children, was a significant reason these children performed better in school and scored higher on IQ tests. Conversely, the scores of African-American and Hispanic-American children as well as the scores of children of lower socioeconomic status (SES) were being pulled down because of teachers' negative expectations for them.

The furor over the 1968 Rosenthal and Jacobson experiment persists to this day. Claims range from outright accusations of fraud to allegations that the results were an underestimate of what goes on in the classroom all the time. Lee Jussim and Kent Harber (2005) reviewed the almost 400 studies conducted in the first 35 years after the initial report and found several important patterns. (1) When expectations are manipulated, it's clear that teacher expectations sometimes do affect student IQ and academic performance. (If expectations aren't manipulated, a correlation between teacher expectation and student performance could be due simply to accurate assessments of aptitude on the teacher's part: children who are believed to be—and are—more talented do better in school.) (2) The extremely large effects Rosenthal and Jacobson found proved to be exceptional; subsequent investigators almost never documented effects as large. A gain of about 3 IQ points is typical. (3) Teacher expectation effects occur only if expectations are manipulated early in the school year, within the first two weeks. (4) Teacher expectation effects are greater for first-graders and second-graders than for older children. (5) Most important, teacher expectation effects can be genuinely large for low-achieving, lower-SES children and for African-American children.

In light of these findings, a modified version of the original claims appears to be appropriate: a teacher's belief that lower-achieving, lower-SES, and African-American students can do well intellectually and academically can indeed enhance their performance.

Intelligence: Thing or Process?

Self-fulfilling prophecies can result not only from teachers' expectations but also from students' beliefs about their own intellectual abilities. Carol Dweck and her colleagues have shown that people have very different views about the nature of intelligence (Dweck, 2007; Dweck & Leggett, 1988). Some believe intelligence is a malleable quality that can be improved with effort; these researchers call this an **incremental theory of intelligence**. Other people think intelligence is a fixed, predetermined "thing" that people have to one degree or another and that there isn't much they can do to change it; this is the **entity theory of intelligence**.

Incremental theorists believe they can increase their intellectual ability, and they attribute failure to lack of effort or to the difficulty of the task (Henderson & Dweck, 1990). As a result, they work more toward goals that will increase their ability, even at the risk of exposing their ignorance, and less toward goals that would merely tend to document their ability. In contrast, entity theorists are less confident that what they do will make them any smarter. They blame their failures on a lack of intellectual ability, and they're inclined to feel they can do little to improve because they just don't have what it takes. Entity theorists tend to choose tasks that seem likely to indicate they have good intellectual ability, but which provide no opportunity to learn something new. It should be clear

incremental theory of intelligence The belief that intelligence is something people can improve by working at it.

entity theory of intelligence The belief that intelligence is something people are born with and can't change.

How to Tutor: The Five Cs

Social psychologist Mark Lepper made an intriguing discovery while studying college student tutors of elementary school children who were having trouble in math. Some tutors had a big—and fast—impact on their pupils. Others had no effect. Lepper then went to work to determine the difference between the effective and the ineffective tutors. Which of the following behaviors do you think would be helpful, and which unhelpful?

1. When a student starts to make even a minor mistake, stop the student immediately to avoid reinforcing the incorrect behavior.

2. If the student makes a mistake, carefully state the rule the student needs to know to successfully solve the problem.

3. Keep the problems simple to avoid damaging self-esteem.

4. Praise the student often for doing good work.

5. Try to avoid getting emotionally involved with the student's difficulties.

Actually, all these approaches are unhelpful and are shunned by effective tutors. These approaches conflict with one or more of the strategies that characterize the successful tutor. Lepper and his colleagues identified Five Cs for effective tutoring (Lepper & Woolverton, 2001; Lepper, Woolverton, Mumme, & Gurtner, 1993):

1. Control. Foster a sense of control in the student, making the student feel in command of the material.

2. Challenge. Challenge the student—but at a level of difficulty that's within the student's range of capability.

3. Confidence. Instill confidence by maximizing the student's success (assuring the student that the problem the student just solved was a difficult one) and by minimizing failure (providing excuses for mistakes and emphasizing the part of the problem the student got right).

4. Curiosity. Encourage curiosity through Socratic methods (asking leading questions) and by linking the problem to other problems the student has seen that appear on the surface to be different.

5. Contextualize. Place the problem in a real-world context or in a context from a movie or TV show.

Expert tutors have a number of strategies that set them apart. They don't bother to correct minor errors like forgetting to write down a plus sign. If the student is about to make a mistake, they gently suggest a problem-solving path that would prevent it from occurring. Or sometimes they let the student make the mistake when they think it can provide a valuable learning experience. They never dumb down the material for the sake of self-esteem, but instead change the way they present it. Most of what good tutors do is ask questions. They ask students to explain their reasoning. They ask leading questions. They're actually less likely to give *positive* feedback than ineffective tutors are, because, Lepper theorizes, doing so makes the tutoring session feel too evaluative. And finally, expert tutors are always nurturing and empathic.

which attitude tends to result in increased intellectual skills as well as improved self-esteem.

Henderson and Dweck (1990) found that students entering junior high school who were incremental theorists ended up getting better grades than students who were entity theorists. Students who were about equal in their math performance at the beginning of junior high progressively increased their math grades over the course of two years of junior high school if they were incremental theorists, but tended not to improve their grades if they were entity theorists (Blackwell, Trzesniewski, & Dweck, 2007).

But who is right—the entity theorist or the incremental theorist? Neither—or rather, both. If you're an entity theorist, your intellectual skills probably won't improve as much as they could. So you're right: you don't believe your ability is under your control, so in fact it doesn't improve much, and your genes actually exert a greater influence on your ability than they would if you believed otherwise. On the other hand, if you're an incremental theorist, you're also right: you believe your ability is under your control and you act accordingly, thereby building on your genetic strengths and increasing your ability.

Culture and Achievement

Why do Asians—especially Chinese, Japanese, and Koreans and their Asian-American counterparts—tend to perform above average on academic tasks? Are they intrinsically smarter than people of European heritage? Does something about their genes lead to intellectual superiority?

In fact, there is no good evidence that people of Asian heritage have a genetic advantage over Americans of Western origin (Flynn, 2007; Nisbett, 2009; Thomas, 2017). Cross-cultural comparisons of Asians and Westerners find no evidence that Asians have higher IQs, though admittedly it can be difficult to compare IQs across different cultures and languages (Flynn, 1991; Nisbett, 2009). A comparison of the IQs of children starting first grade in Minneapolis, Sendai (Japan), and Taipei (Taiwan) found that the American children had slightly higher IQs than either group of Asian children (Stevenson et al., 1990). Considering the socialization practices of Asians and Americans, this finding shouldn't be surprising: Asians focus on social and emotional growth during the early years, and Americans, especially middle-class and upper-middle-class Americans, are more likely to focus on intellectual skills (Stevenson et al., 1990). By fifth grade, the IQ differences were gone, but the Asian children were far ahead of the Americans in math—partly a result of better teaching of math and longer school years in the Asian countries (Stevenson & Stigler, 1992), but also a result of Asian children tending to work harder at math (Stevenson & Lee, 1996). Asian (and Asian-American) students study many more hours a week on average than European-Americans do, who in turn study many more hours than African-American students.

The best evidence available on ability differences between Asian-Americans and European-Americans comes from a massive study of the high school seniors of the class of 1966 (Flynn, 1991). The IQs of the Asian-Americans were trivially lower than those of the European-Americans—not surprising, given that many of them came from homes where English wasn't the native language. However, Asian-Americans' SAT scores were substantially higher. SAT scores, of course, are partly a reflection of the kinds of skills measured by IQ tests and partly a reflection of the work students have done. Even more striking, when the study participants were adults, fully 55 percent of the Chinese-Americans, the largest group of the Asian-Americans, ended up in professional, technical, or managerial positions (Flynn, 2007). Only a third of European-Americans ended up in those jobs. The Asian-Americans capitalized on their ability to a far greater extent than did the European-Americans.

Blocking Stereotype Threat in the Classroom

Other minority groups, such as African-Americans and Hispanic-Americans, have lower average IQ and academic achievement scores than either Asian-Americans or European-Americans. There are numerous social reasons for these differences. Most of these factors are in flux, however, and in recent years the IQ and achievement gaps have begun to lessen substantially (Nisbett, 2009; Turkheimer, Harden, & Nisbett, 2017a, 2017b).

"If there is no dark and dogged will, there will be no shining accomplishment; if there is no dull and determined effort, there will be no brilliant achievement."

—CHINESE SAYING

Confucius and Theories about Ability

Asian-Americans whose forebears came from the "Confucian cultures," such as China, Japan, and Korea, achieve at levels higher than predicted from their ability scores. Such outcomes could be expected based on ancient theories about talent. The Chinese teacher and philosopher Confucius—the founding father of modern East Asian cultures—said that although some of our ability is a gift from heaven, most of it is due to hard work. For 2,000 years, it was possible for a young person to go from being a poor peasant to being the highest magistrate in China by dint of study and hard work. In no other country until modern times was there that degree of social mobility. It's no surprise that East Asians, and Americans who spring from that region, are devout incremental theorists. They believe, much more than European-Americans, that intellectual achievement is mostly a matter of hard work (Chen & Stevenson, 1995; Choi, Nisbett, & Norenzayan, 1999; Heine et al., 2001; Holloway, 1988; Stevenson et al., 1990). When Japanese and Canadians were told they had either succeeded or failed on a task that presumably measured creativity, the Canadians worked longer on a similar task if they had succeeded on the first one, thereby continuing to regard themselves as good at the task. The Japanese worked longer if they had failed, thus extending their abilities (Heine et al., 2001).

CONFUCIUS

To explore one of the factors suppressing academic success, Claude Steele and Joshua Aronson demonstrated that women and minorities often perform more poorly on ability tests because of stereotype threat, or the fear of confirming stereotypes about their group (see Chapter 11). With Catherine Good and Michael Inzlicht, Aronson decided to see what would happen if poor minority students could be convinced that their abilities were under their control. They performed an intervention with poor Hispanic-American college students in Texas (Good, Aronson, & Inzlicht, 2003). All students in the study were assigned student mentors. Experimental group mentors told their charges that intelligence was changeable and substantially under their control and taught them how the brain can make new connections throughout life. A website reinforced the mentors' message. It showed pictures of the brain, including how neurons make new connections with one another, reflecting the learning that takes place when a person solves new problems. The mentors also helped the students design their own web pages, using their own words and pictures, which reinforced the message of the malleability of intelligence. Control group mentors gave the students cautionary information about drugs and encouraged them to avoid taking them.

The experimental intervention had a very large effect. On a statewide academic achievement test, the boys in the experimental group scored much higher in math than those in the control group. For the girls, who tend to worry that, because of their gender, they're naturally less talented in math, the difference was even greater. In tests of reading skills, both boys and girls in the experimental group did substantially better than students in the control group.

Dweck and her colleagues performed a similar intervention with poor African-American and Latino seventh-grade students in New York City (Blackwell, Trzesniewski, & Dweck, 2007). As in the Texas project, the investigators presented convincing demonstrations of the changes in knowledge and intelligence that are produced by work and study. They taught the students psychological theories about learning, showed them changes in neurotransmission with learning, and showed them the kinds of study skills that would most likely increase their knowledge and intelligence. Junior high is a difficult time for many students, but it seems to be particularly hard for disadvantaged minority children. The math performance of control students in the study grew worse as junior high school went on, but that didn't happen for students in the experimental group. They initially had held entity beliefs about intelligence and feared they were doomed to poor performance because they were incorrigibly unintelligent. Simply being made to believe that their intelligence was under their control had a significant impact on their academic performance.

Daphna Oyserman and her colleagues carried out a different intervention with poor African-American junior high students in Detroit (Oyserman, Bybee, & Terry, 2006). They asked the students to think about what kind of future they wanted to have, what difficulties they might encounter along the way to achieving it, how they could deal with those problems, and which of their friends would be most helpful. The researchers supplemented these sessions by having students work in small groups on how to respond to everyday problems, manage social difficulties and academic issues, and cope with the process of getting to high school graduation. The intervention had a modest effect on grade point average (GPA) and on standardized tests and a very large effect on the likelihood of being held back a grade in school.

A study by Geoffrey Cohen and his colleagues showed that simply having minority students write about their most important values at the beginning of middle school substantially improved their grades (Cohen, Garcia, Apfel, & Master, 2006). The students were enrolled in a mostly middle-class integrated suburban school. As is often true in such schools, the African-American students in the past had had significantly lower grades than the white students. The African-American students were well aware of this, and the social psychologists who conducted the study assumed that these students were subject to worries prompted by stereotype threat. The researchers reasoned that if the students were encouraged to think about their most important values, this self-affirmation in the school context would produce a sense of efficacy and belongingness. In fact, black students who were exposed to the affirmation intervention performed better over the term than black students in the control group (**Figure A2.1**). During the term in which the intervention took place, the students in the affirmation condition reduced the achievement gap with white students by 40 percent, and their likelihood of getting a D or worse was cut in half.

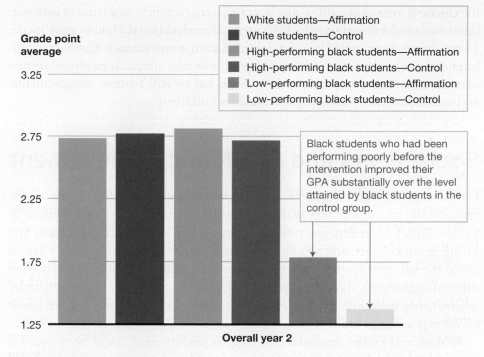

Grade point average

3.25

2.75

2.25

1.75

1.25

Overall year 2

Legend:
- White students—Affirmation
- White students—Control
- High-performing black students—Affirmation
- High-performing black students—Control
- Low-performing black students—Affirmation
- Low-performing black students—Control

Black students who had been performing poorly before the intervention improved their GPA substantially over the level attained by black students in the control group.

FIGURE A2.1
BLOCKING STEREOTYPE THREAT
Mean GPA scores in core courses the year after some students experienced an affirmation intervention (by being asked to write out their most important values). Initially low-performing black students improved their academic performance if exposed to the intervention.
Source: Adapted from Cohen et al., 2009.

It's sad but true that many effective interventions, including educational ones, tend to fade over time. Remarkably, that wasn't true for the self-affirmation intervention. Cohen and his colleagues followed the students over the next two years and found that the effects of the intervention endured (Cohen, Garcia, Purdie-Vaughns, Apfel, & Brzustoski, 2009). The likelihood of needing remediation was reduced from 18 percent to 5 percent. Interestingly, the intervention had no effect on black students who had performed well before entering middle school; presumably, they were sufficiently confident that the affirmation manipulation was unnecessary. Nor did the affirmation manipulation have any effect on white students, whether previously high performing or not.

Still more impressive, Cohen and his colleagues found marked effects of their intervention several years later, after their participants had left high school (Goyer et al., 2017). Black (but not white) students who had been in the experimental group were much more likely to be enrolled in college, and among those in college, experimental group subjects were more likely to be enrolled in prestigious four-year colleges than the control group subjects.

The Cohen group also found very marked effects of their intervention for junior high Latino-American students. Experimental group participants were much more likely to choose college readiness courses than control group participants and half as likely to be enrolled in a remedial clinic.

Why were the Cohen interventions so effective? He and his colleagues argue that the intervention had immediate effects that cascaded to alter the students' life course (Goyer et al., 2017). The intervention gave students a sense of purpose, optimism, and belonging, which changed the educational choices they made. Those choices in turn had beneficial downstream consequences. Cohen and colleagues describe their intervention as having *recursive* effects. It produced immediate improvements in performance, which led to still further improvements, and so on, potentially affecting the students' full life span.

Social Fears and Academic Achievement

Cohen, together with Gregory Walton, explored the effects of other types of concerns on the part of minority students, this time in a college context (Walton & Cohen, 2007). Most first-year undergraduates worry about social acceptance and fitting in on campus, and this is particularly true for minorities. If they fail to make friends, perhaps because of the dearth of minority students and feeling uncomfortable with those from other backgrounds, they may begin to wonder whether they belong on campus. As a result, their motivation may flag, and their GPAs may suffer as well.

Walton and Cohen reasoned that lagging performance could be reversed if minority students knew that worries about social acceptance are common for all students, regardless of ethnicity, and that their experience was likely to improve in the future (Walton & Cohen, 2007). The researchers performed a seemingly modest intervention with black students at a prestigious private university. They invited black and white freshmen to participate in a psychology study at the end of their freshman year. They intended to convince an experimental group that worries about social acceptance were common for students of all ethnicities but tended to vanish as time went on and they made more friends. The experimenters expected that this information would help black students realize that the best way to understand their social difficulties wasn't in terms of their race ("I guess my kind of people don't really belong at this kind of place") but as part of the student experience common to everyone ("I guess everybody has these kinds of problems"). The researchers believed that recognition of the common problem—and that it was likely to get better—would help keep the students from worrying about belonging, thereby enabling them to focus on academic achievement.

To drive the point home, Walton and Cohen had students in the experimental group write an essay about the likelihood that their social situation would improve in the future. Then the students made a videotaped speech allegedly to be shown to new students, so the new students could see what college would be like. This standard dissonance manipulation—getting them to say publicly something different from their own views—was intended to enhance the effects of the persuasive communications they had received.

The researchers measured student behavior related to academic achievement over the next week and recorded student GPAs the subsequent semester. The intervention had a large positive effect on blacks but not on whites. In the period after the intervention, blacks reported studying more, making more contacts with professors, and attending more review sessions and study group meetings. The subsequent term, the grades of the black students in the experimental group reflected these behaviors: their grades were much higher than those of black students in the control group.

College is also a social challenge for first-generation college students—the first in their families to pursue education beyond high school. The attitudes and values they encounter are typically different from those they were exposed to in their families and neighborhoods. Working-class people, for example, are generally more interdependent than middle- and upper-middle-class people. For students of working-class origin, going to college isn't so much an individual achievement as an accomplishment having deep social and interpersonal meaning.

To examine the impact of this difference in prior experience and orientation, Nicole Stephens and her colleagues wrote two different welcome letters for new students (Stephens, Townsend, Markus, & Phillips, 2012). One, modeled on the usual university welcome letter, emphasized independent values such as exploring personal interests, expressing ideas and opinions, and participating in independent research. The other emphasized learning by being part of a community, working with and learning from others, and participating in collaborative research. The students were then asked to give a 5-minute speech about their college goals. The investigators examined the students' stress levels during the speech by measuring blood cortisol (a stress hormone) and by the emotional content of the speech. The cortisol level of first-generation students who had read the independent welcome letter was greater during the speech than it was for those who had read the interdependent letter, whereas the interdependent-themed letter had no effect on the non-first-generation students. The emotional content of the speech reflected more emotional strain for first-generation students who read the independent letter than for those who read the interdependent letter, whereas the manipulation had no effect on the content of other students' speeches. The researchers concluded that there is a mismatch between the values of working-class students and the new college environment—a mismatch that can impair academic performance but which can be combated. A similar intervention by the Stephens group emphasized that working-class origins, although having some disadvantages, also had advantages that could be capitalized on in college (Stephens, Hamedani, & Destin, 2014). Experimental group participants had better academic outcomes than control participants and showed a greater degree of physiological evidence of thriving in the college environment (Stephens, Townsend, Hamedani, Destin, & Manzo, 2015).

Teaching with Entertainment-Education

Which reality television show depicting young people traveling around the countryside featured such contests as how to repel the sexual advances of other young people? And in which states did the show air? You probably don't know. It's *Haath Se Haath Mila* (*Hand in Hand Together*), and it was broadcast in the states of Rajasthan, Haryana, Delhi, Uttar Pradesh, and Uttaranchal—in India. It was designed to alert young people to the risks of HIV/AIDS, which existed in epidemic proportions in that country. The young people in the show, by the way, traveled in separate his-and-hers buses. The program was part of a worldwide network of TV shows collectively called entertainment-education.

Albert Bandura is a learning theorist, a scientist who studies how humans and other animals learn which events signal impending rewards and which

TEACHING WITH TELENOVELAS
These actors are running through a scene on the set of the Mexican telenovela *Heridas de Amor* (*Wounds of Love*).

signal impending punishments. He was one of the first scientists to approach the question of how people learn appropriate and effective social behavior (Bandura, 1973). A fundamental principle of his theory is that people learn what to approach and what to avoid simply by watching relevant others. They observe other people's behavior and its consequences and adopt the behaviors that seem to be successful and avoid those that are punished.

The Mexican television producer Miguel Sabido read about Bandura's principles of social learning and decided to create TV shows that would educate people about effective and rewarding social behaviors and persuade them to avoid dangerous and unproductive ones. He produced the original entertainment-education telenovelas (similar to soap operas) in the 1970s and 1980s.

Sabido's telenovelas are yearlong stories that focus on a specific value. Each one presents three types of characters: positive role models, negative role models, and "doubters," or those who fall in between (Singhal, Rogers, & Brown, 1993). There are typically four positive role models complemented by four negative role models. There is always a character who approves of the value being promoted (and one who disapproves), one who promotes the value (and one who does not), one who exercises the value (and one who does not), and one who validates the value (and one who does not). There are also three doubters. One of the doubters accepts the value about a third of the way through the series, one about two-thirds of the way through, and one never accepts the value. (The third doubter usually dies a painful death.) In general, those who accept the value are immediately rewarded, and those who don't are punished. Throughout the series, epilogues are inserted in which a famous individual speaks to the audience in an effort to reinforce the value.

These broadcasts clearly have an effect on behavior, although much of the early evidence has to be categorized as anecdotal, coming from Bandura's own account of their success (Bandura, 2004). One early telenovela by Sabido urged viewers to enroll in a literacy program. The day after it first appeared, about 25,000 people descended on the distribution center in downtown Mexico City to obtain their reading materials. The result was a monumental traffic jam in the city. The name of the series was *Ven Conmigo* (*Come With Me*), and in the year it aired, enrollment in literacy classes went up tenfold—from about 90,000 to about 900,000. Another drama, *Acompaname* (*Accompany Me*), emphasized family planning. Those who viewed the program were more inclined to think that having fewer children was likely to have social, economic, and psychological benefits. There was a 32 percent increase in new contraceptive users, and national sales of contraceptives went up markedly.

Sabido's telenovelas have been widely imitated. An Indian drama inspired by Sabido's work promoted female rights and family planning. Amazingly, the enrollment of girls in elementary schools rose from 10 percent to 38 percent during the year the series was broadcast. After a family planning telenovela aired in Kenya, contraception practices changed across all socioeconomic levels (Westoff & Rodriguez, 1995).

A radio soap opera designed to combat the spread of HIV in Tanzania spanned four years (Vaughn, Rogers, Singhal, & Swalehe, 2000). The investigators conducted a proper experiment to test for its effects. For the first two years, the soap opera wasn't broadcast in a particular region in Tanzania in order to provide a comparison group. In regions where it was aired, the soap opera resulted in a reduction in the number of sexual partners and increased condom use. The mediating factors that seemed to be crucial in producing these changes were increased self-efficacy, increased communication about HIV, and increased risk awareness. In interviews, listeners said they identified with the characters in the soap opera and tried to emulate them, consistent with the tenets of social learning theory.

Statistics, Social Science Methodology, and Critical Thinking

Consider the following two problems:

1. David is a high school senior choosing between two colleges. He has friends at both. His friends at college A like it a lot on social and academic grounds. His friends at college B aren't as satisfied and are generally unenthusiastic about the college experience. David visits each college for a day. He meets some students at college A who aren't very interesting and a professor who gives him a curt brushoff. He meets several students at college B who are lively and intelligent, and a couple of professors take a personal interest in him. Which college do you think he should go to? Why?

2. Medical research has established that drinking a moderate amount of alcohol is associated with a reduced risk of getting cancer or heart disease. Assume you are a teetotaler on economic and moral grounds. Should you start modest tippling?

Problem 1: If you said that David should go to college B because he has to choose for himself (not let his friends choose for him), you're in good company with most undergraduates. However, you should also have considered the possibility that although David's samples of the two colleges were based on his own personal experience, the samples weren't very large, and the experiences he could expect to have at the two colleges might be very different from his one-day visits. His friends, while they aren't David, at least have the advantage of having much larger samples of what life is like at the two schools. Their opinions ought to give David, and you, pause. Moreover, there may have been an attempt to ensure that David got a biased sample of events at college B. If friends at college B were particularly eager to get David to go there, they might have arranged things to impress David favorably.

Problem 2: If you said it's best to keep your wallet in your pocket and your foot off the bar rail, then you recognized that correlation doesn't establish causation. Indeed, after decades of hearing from researchers that alcohol in moderation is a disease preventive, some scientists are now saying that the association between moderate drinking and health may be a self-selection effect having nothing to do with the effects of alcohol. People who don't drink may avoid it because their health is already poor or because their income discourages them from drinking (and income is strongly correlated with health). And people who drink a lot may be damaging their health. That leaves the middle-of-the-roaders as the healthiest group, but not because alcohol in moderation is making them healthy.

As we've emphasized throughout this book, social psychology promotes the application of statistical and methodological analyses to everyday life events. Taking statistics courses and science courses that emphasize research principles is an excellent way to start using those principles for solving everyday life problems and for critiquing media accounts of scientific research. But courses such as social psychology, which teach those principles in the context of analyzing real-world events, provide an additional boost.

Darrin Lehman and Richard Nisbett (1990) studied the effects of four years of college study in the humanities, the natural sciences, psychology, or the social sciences. Students majoring in psychology and the social sciences showed a 65 percent improvement in their ability to reason using appropriate statistical and methodological principles like the ones just discussed. Students in the humanities and natural sciences improved by only about 25 percent. (Lest you think few advantages in reasoning come from studying the humanities and natural sciences, however, students in those fields improved by 65 percent in various kinds of logical reasoning, and students in psychology and the social sciences improved not at all in those respects.)

Two years of graduate-level training in psychology have a huge impact on people's ability to apply statistical and methodological principles to everyday life—particularly for students in the areas of psychology that deal with ordinary human behavior (Lehman, Lempert, & Nisbett, 1988). This includes the fields of social psychology, developmental psychology, and personality psychology. Improvements are less for students focusing mostly on the fields of biopsychology, cognitive psychology, or cognitive neuroscience, even though students in those fields are trained in basic statistics and methodology. Students of chemistry and law gain absolutely nothing in their ability to apply statistical and methodological reasoning to everyday life events.

Improving one's ability to apply statistical and scientific reasoning doesn't require immersion in higher education. Research by social psychologists shows that statistical and methodological principles, as well as economic concepts such as the cost-benefit principle, can be taught in very brief sessions (Fong, Krantz, & Nisbett, 1986; Larrick, Morgan, & Nisbett, 1990; Larrick, Nisbett, & Morgan, 1993; Nisbett, Fong, Lehman, & Cheng, 1987). In some of these studies, the researchers phoned participants several weeks after the training sessions in the guise of pollsters conducting an "opinion survey." The survey presented various personal and institutional dilemmas for which a grasp of the statistical and methodological principles would dictate a particular answer. Trained participants were more likely to provide answers that conformed to the relevant principles.

You've learned a great deal from this text (and the course you've just taken) about how to think critically about everyday life events and also how to evaluate the thinking of others, including your friends and acquaintances as well as the media. This gift of critical thinking is one that keeps on giving: the more you use these critical thinking principles, the more you're apt to invoke them in an ever-broadening range of circumstances. The effects will be recursive, in other words.

Module Review

SUMMARY

Pygmalion in the Classroom

- Teacher expectations about students can influence their academic achievement. Believing a child is talented or is about to show a spurt in ability may lead to better performance from the child. Expectation effects may be particularly large for lower-SES and minority students.

Intelligence: Thing or Process?

- According to the *incremental theory of intelligence*, people can improve their intelligence by working hard on challenging tasks.
- The *entity theory of intelligence* holds that intelligence is an unchangeable thing (entity) over which people have no control. Entity theorists tend to attribute failures to lack of ability and aren't likely to learn new things by taking on challenges.
- People can shift from being entity theorists to being incremental theorists, thereby improving their academic performance; this is especially true for minority students.

Culture and Achievement

- East Asians tend to be incremental theorists and thereby gain the benefit of hard work and improved ability.

Blocking Stereotype Threat in the Classroom

- When minority group members are persuaded that their ability is under their control, they work harder and perform at higher levels. The same is true when they're asked to think about their goals in life and how to achieve them.

Social Fears and Academic Achievement

- Concerns about social acceptance can hold back minority students from engaging in college life and having academic success. Showing them that social acceptance will improve can result in greater well-being and higher grades.
- Colleges typically emphasize the value of an education in terms of independence goals for personal achievement. When they shift to an emphasis on interdependence values, the performance of first-generation students is likely to benefit.

Teaching with Entertainment-Education

- Entertainment-education, based on Bandura's social learning theory and the success of telenovelas, can have a big impact on the likelihood that people will avoid risky behavior and pursue beneficial goals.

Statistics, Social Science Methodology, and Critical Thinking

- Statistics and social science methodology, including methods used in social psychology, increase critical thinking skills, enabling people to spot the mistakes in reported scientific studies and reduce errors of judgment in their own lives.

THINK ABOUT IT

1. On the first day of summer volleyball camp, if the camp counselors are told that the campers in cabin 1 are on the verge of a growth and strength spurt, compared with the campers in cabin 2, what is likely to happen? How large will the effect of this manipulation probably be? What factors would increase or reduce the impact of this manipulation?

2. Suppose Alex is choosing between two math classes for next semester. She can take either Math 301, which is outside her comfort zone but would teach her new skills, or Math 210, which is well within her domain of knowledge, and she'd probably get an A. If Alex is an entity theorist, which class is she likely to select? Do you think entity versus incremental theorists differ in their overall GPA?

3. How would you change your college's Freshman Welcome program to help reduce achievement differences among students who are traditionally underrepresented in higher education (such as African-American and first-generation college students)?

The **answer guidelines** for the Think About It questions can be found at the back of the book . . . ☞

ONLINE STUDY MATERIALS

Want to earn a better grade on your test?

Go to **INQUIZITIVE** to learn and review this application module's content, with personalized feedback along the way.

Social Psychology and the Law

ON A BRIGHT WINTER DAY IN 1989, 29-year-old Eileen Franklin suddenly recalled a horror. She remembered that 20 years before, she had seen her best friend, 8-year-old Susan Nason, murdered. The murderer, silhouetted by the sun, lifted a heavy rock and crushed Susan Nason's skull. Eileen recalled covering her ears to block the sound of shattering bones. As her memory grew sharper, she realized the murderer had been her own father, George Franklin. In the ensuing days, more details of the incident flooded her mind. She finally went to the police and told them about her recovered memory. Her father was sentenced to life imprisonment based solely on his daughter's testimony, even though some of Eileen's remarkably detailed memories were consistent with botched newspaper accounts rather than the actual facts of the case (Loftus & Ketcham, 1994). Franklin was convicted despite the testimony of psychologist Elizabeth Loftus that "recovered" memories can be utterly mistaken, and people can "remember" things that never happened. In fact, Eileen's memory *was* inaccurate. After serving 6 years in prison, Franklin was proven innocent and released. Loftus's testimony, which was at odds with views about memory held not only by the general public but also by many cognitive psychologists at the time, highlights the important role psychology can play in understanding the procedures that take place in a court of law.

The processes involved in a court case can be separated into three distinct phases: (1) pretrial events, including, in the case of criminal trials, eyewitness identification, attempts to elicit confessions, and efforts to distinguish lies from sincere efforts to tell the truth; (2) issues related to the trial itself, including jury selection, jury deliberation, and jury size; and (3) post-trial events, such as the administration of punishment. Social psychologists have made important contributions

to each of these aspects of jurisprudence, often by identifying flaws in existing practices and suggesting improvements. The criminal justice system has instituted quite a few changes in police practice and judicial procedures in response to social psychological findings—a testimony to how the discoveries of social psychology can be used to improve an important social institution. ■

Before a Case Goes to Trial

You have probably seen many legal dramas on TV and in movies that unfold in a fairly predictable fashion: a crime occurs, the police investigate, witnesses identify one or more suspects, those suspects are interrogated, and the criminal does or does not confess. In real life, however, the process is not always so simple or straightforward.

Eyewitness Testimony

Almost nothing that comes before the jury in a criminal trial is more convincing than a witness who, pointing to the defendant, says, "I'm certain that is the man" (or "the woman," but since the great majority of defendants are men, suspects and defendants are referred to here as men). Every year, 75,000 eyewitnesses testify against suspects in criminal cases in the United States. But their identifications are wrong about a third of the time (Liptak, 2011). In fact, eyewitness errors have been found to be involved in more than half the cases of wrongful conviction (Kovera & Borgida, 2010). In some cases where people have been exonerated by DNA evidence establishing that they could not have been the person who committed the crime, more than one person had wrongly identified the convicted person as the perpetrator.

Social psychologists have studied many factors that can influence the accuracy of eyewitness testimony. Before you continue, however, take the following test. Indicate which of the statements seem to be true and which false. Write a T or F next to each statement to keep yourself honest before you check the answers on page 546. You don't want to fall prey to the "I-knew-it-all-along" effect!

1. Accurate eyewitnesses are generally more confident than inaccurate ones.
2. Witnesses are generally as accurate about identifying perpetrators of a race different from their own as they are in identifying perpetrators of their own race.
3. When the circumstances of a crime are highly stressful and arousing, the memory of an eyewitness is likely to be more accurate than when the events are less arousing.
4. Witnesses with correct memory for many details about the crime context (for example, how many doors were in the room) generally are more accurate in their testimony about perpetrators than witnesses with less correct memory for details.
5. Asking witnesses to help construct a face composite of the perpetrator generally improves the accuracy with which the perpetrator can be identified.
6. Asking witnesses to describe a perpetrator before the witnesses attempt to identify him from photos or a lineup generally increases the accuracy of recognition.

"Memory can change the shape of a room; it can change the color of a car. And memories can be distorted. They're just an interpretation, they're not a record."
—LEONARD SHELBY, PROTAGONIST IN THE FILM *MEMENTO*

THE EFFECT OF MISLEADING QUESTIONS
Participants in this study saw either the picture on the left or the one on the right. Many of those asked about the "stop sign" later reported that they had seen the stop sign even if they had actually seen the yield sign; many of those asked about the "yield sign" reported that they had seen the yield sign even if they had seen the stop sign.
SOURCE: Loftus et al., 1978.

7. Witnesses who rapidly single out an individual from photos or a lineup are generally less accurate than those who take a longer time to consider who they believe to be the perpetrator.
8. Juries are generally capable of distinguishing correct testimony from incorrect testimony.

THE PERSISTENCE OF MEMORY One of the greatest triumphs of the field of psychology is the discovery that memory is not a passive registry of the information a person has encountered. Instead, irrefutable evidence shows that memory is an active, constructive process in which inferences about "what must have been" guide memories of "what was." Through a series of ingenious studies beginning in the late 1970s and early 1980s, researchers have established that memories are inferences, not stored photographs or infallible representations, and they can be affected by all kinds of information that becomes available after an event has occurred.

In one striking demonstration, Loftus and her colleagues showed participants a series of slides of an automobile accident (Loftus, Miller, & Burns, 1978). The image on one of the slides varied slightly from the others. A red Datsun was shown stopped at either a stop sign or a yield sign. Participants were asked questions about the accident they had "witnessed." One crucial question was different for two groups of participants. Participants were asked either "Did another car pass the red Datsun while it was stopped at the stop sign?" or "Did another car pass the red Datsun while it was stopped at the yield sign?" Later, the participants were shown the two pictures and asked which one they had actually seen before. Of those who'd been asked about the sign they had actually seen (stop sign or yield sign), 75 percent identified the correct picture. Of those who had earlier been asked about the sign they hadn't actually seen, only 41 percent identified the correct picture.

In other research, Loftus and her colleagues found that people could be led to think a robber had a mustache when he didn't and that a red light was green (Loftus, 2001). Of course, most of the time when investigators give misleading information to witnesses, they are not deliberately trying to mislead them. Instead, they often operate with patchy or mistaken details and may convey such misinformation to witnesses. In the courtroom, however, attorneys sometimes exercise poetic license in their phraseology in order to lead witnesses in a specific direction.

Research on eyewitness identification is relevant to the claims of psychotherapists that their patients have "recovered" memories that they had forgotten or repressed for decades. People have been convicted of heinous crimes based on reports of adults who have been helped by their therapists to "remember" episodes of abuse or even murder. People are also sometimes convicted of child abuse based solely on the testimony of children who have been questioned by police.

Undoubtedly, some of these recovered memories are valid. But consider a demonstration reported by Loftus and Pickrell (1995), who successfully "implanted" memories in 24 university students. The researchers persuaded the students' relatives to tell the students stories about several events that occurred around the time the student in question was 5 years old. They were also asked to generate a plausible story about that child (the student) having been lost—although the event had not occurred. Six of the participants eventually "recalled" the made-up event, sometimes providing substantial detail over the course of a series of interviews. Thus, 25 percent of randomly selected undergraduates were readily persuaded of the existence of a non-event—and could even provide details about it. Upon being told that one of the episodes never occurred, most of those students could not identify which one it was.

In similar studies with children, Stephen Ceci and Maggie Bruck (1995) asked preschoolers to remember as much as they could, in weekly sessions for ten weeks, about the time they went "to the hospital with a mousetrap on your finger." When they were interviewed later by another adult, 58 percent were able to tell detailed stories about the non-event. One boy remembered that "we went to the hospital, and my mommy, daddy, and Colin drove me there, to the hospital in our van, because it was far away. And the doctor put a bandage on this finger" (Ceci & Bruck, 1995, p. 219). Researchers, including Loftus, Ceci, and their colleagues, have thus established that memories, like perceptions and judgments, should be considered inferences rather than direct readouts of reality.

FACTORS AFFECTING EYEWITNESS ACCURACY Given the generalization that memory is highly imperfect and highly susceptible to information provided after an event (or non-event) occurs, it's not surprising that eyewitness testimony is far from completely reliable. What factors influence whether such testimony is accurate and whether it is believed? Recall the statements about eyewitness testimony you read earlier. If you guessed that each statement was false, you were 100 percent correct. Otherwise, your intuitions fell short to one degree or another.

IMPROVING EYEWITNESS IDENTIFICATION PROCEDURES Fortunately, a massive amount of research by social psychologists on the accuracy of eyewitness testimony has had a significant effect on the law. In the 1990s, a panel of researchers, lawyers, and police from Canada and the United States developed a set of procedures to reduce eyewitness errors. And a landmark decision by the New Jersey Supreme Court, *State v. Henderson* (2011), drawing heavily on the findings of psychological research, established a set of rules judges must follow in evaluating the reliability of eyewitness testimony.

It is a great credit to psychologists that they have produced so much useful knowledge about the reliability of eyewitness testimony and the possible biases of jurors. It's also a great credit to policy makers that this research has been allowed to transform police and judicial practices.

Getting the Truth from Suspects

Guilty offenders sometimes confess their crimes, in which case the trial proceedings are relatively straightforward. Juries and judges simply attempt to arrive at a punishment that fits the admitted crime. But sometimes the guilty party does not admit to committing the crime. In the past, torture was frequently used to elicit confessions from suspects. The assumption was that if people were truly innocent, they would never confess. But in fact people sometimes confess—even without torture—to crimes they did not commit.

FALSE CONFESSIONS In 1989, five teenage boys were arrested for a horrific assault and rape of a woman who had been jogging in Central Park in New York. The woman was beaten nearly to death and was initially not expected to survive, although in a recovery regarded as miraculous she suffered only minor permanent damage. All five of the boys confessed to the crime, and they were given

---

"The best acting I ever did was in juvenile court."
—ACTOR MARK WAHLBERG

Answers to Quiz on pp. 544–545

1. *Confidence and accuracy.* Unless the perpetrator is extremely distinctive looking, confidence bears little relation to accuracy. Nevertheless, jurors are influenced by the degree of certainty expressed by witnesses (Wells, Memon, & Penrod, 2006).

2. *Race and accuracy of identification.* People are generally less accurate at identifying perpetrators of a different race (Brigham, Bennett, Meissner, & Mitchell, 2007; Johnson & Fredrickson, 2005) or age (Wright & Stroud, 2002) from their own.

3. *Stress and accuracy.* In one study, 500 soldiers in mock prisoner-of-war camps were deprived of food and sleep and subjected to interrogations of varying intensity. A day after the camp ended, soldiers subjected to mild stress correctly identified their interrogator

long prison sentences. Thirteen years after the crime, Matias Reyes, who was not one of the five boys, admitted to having been the sole perpetrator of the crime. DNA evidence, which had not been presented at the boys' trial, corroborated Reyes's admission.

Why would the boys have confessed to a crime they had not committed? They'd been up to no good in the park—they had been assaulting people—and during the interrogation they were probably in a state of extreme stress because they knew they were in fact guilty of something. In addition, they were subjected to pretty much standard police procedure. The suspect is placed in a bare, sound-proof room—a situation that has the effect of making the suspect feel alone and helpless. The most widely used manual for police interrogations advises a nine-fold process for questioning suspects in that situation (Inbau, Reid, Buckley, & Jayne, 2001): (1) Insist that the suspect committed the crime; (2) give the suspect helpful excuses for why he might have committed the crime; (3) cut the suspect off when he tries to maintain his innocence; (4) defeat the suspect's objections to the charges; (5) don't let the increasingly silent suspect succeed in ignoring the interrogator; (6) express sympathy for why the suspect might have committed the crime in an effort to get him to admit the crime; (7) offer the suspect an explanation for the crime that would make him feel justified in committing it; (8) if possible, get the suspect to spell out details of the crime; and (9) convert those details into a written confession. If those tactics don't suffice, police may offer sympathy and promise leniency in light of the supposed extenuating circumstances. These procedures often succeed in getting suspects to confess.

The problem, as in the case of the Central Park jogger, is that these police tactics can be altogether too effective, sometimes eliciting false confessions. In fact, in cases where defendants are convicted and later proved innocent by DNA tests, as many as one-fifth had confessed to the crime (Garrett, 2008). The young and inexperienced may be particularly susceptible. The five teenagers in the Central Park jogger case were interrogated for up to 30 hours before they gave their confessions, which were videotaped. The defendants later testified that they had been threatened and that promises of various kinds had been made if they would confess. (These charges were denied by the police.) Because of their naiveté, the boys reported believing they'd be allowed to go home if they just admitted to what they were said to have done.

JURIES AND CONFESSIONS Saul Kassin and Holly Sukel (1997) suspected that confessions made under dubious circumstances might still be taken at face value by jurors. To examine this hypothesis, they presented mock jurors with an account of a murder trial. In one condition, the suspect never admitted committing the crime, and the participants voted guilty 19 percent of the time. In a second condition, it was reported that the suspect had confessed, and the conviction rate rose to 62 percent. In a third condition, the suspect had confessed, but in a situation in which he was afraid and in pain while he was handcuffed behind his back. Although these participants generally recognized that the confession had been coerced, 50 percent of them voted for conviction anyway; they chose to believe the defendant's confession, even if it was forced and even when they were told that the judge ruled it was inadmissible and should be ignored.

Can jurors recognize whether a confession is real or fake when they're allowed to watch a videotape of the interrogation? Not necessarily. In another study, Kassin and his team videotaped prison inmates confessing either to a crime they

62 percent of the time; those subjected to extreme stress were correct only 30 percent of the time (Morgan et al., 2004).

4. *Memory for details and accuracy of perpetrator identification.* The *more* accurate eyewitnesses are about details of the crime scene, the *less* accurate they are about the criminal (Wells & Leippe, 1981). Jurors, however, tend to believe the opposite (Bell & Loftus, 1989).

5. *Constructing a face composite.* The resulting face composite usually doesn't look much like the suspect. More important, the very process of constructing the composite weakens the witness's memory for the actual suspect (Wells, Charman, & Olson, 2005).

6. *Verbally describing a perpetrator.* Witnesses who write a description of the perpetrator tend to be less able later on to spot the correct individual in a photo lineup (Schooler & Engstler-Schooler, 1990).

7. *Speed and accuracy of identification.* Rapid identifications are generally more accurate than slower ones (Dunning & Stern, 1994), especially if the identification from a lineup is made within 12 seconds (Dunning & Perretta, 2002).

8. *Jurors' ability to tell whether eyewitness testimony is accurate.* Wells, Lindsay, and Ferguson (1979) faked thefts and asked participants serving as eyewitnesses to identify the thief from six photos. Other participants serving as jurors rated the testimony as accurate or inaccurate. Eyewitnesses were believed precisely 80 percent of the time—whether they were accurate or not.

Certain, but Wrong

This account is excerpted from a *New York Times* article by Jennifer Thompson.

In 1984 I was a 22-year-old college student. . . . One night someone broke into my apartment, put a knife to my throat and raped me.

During my ordeal . . . I studied every single detail on the rapist's face. I looked at his hairline; I looked for scars, for tattoos, for anything that would help me identify him. When and if I survived the attack, I was going to make sure that he was put in prison and he was going to rot.

. . . Looking at a series of police photos, I identified my attacker. I knew this was the man. I was completely confident. I was sure.

I picked the same man in a lineup. Again, I was sure. I knew it. I had picked the right guy, and he was going to go to jail. If there was the possibility of a death sentence, I wanted him to die. I wanted to flip the switch.

. . . Based on my testimony, Ronald Junior Cotton was sentenced to prison for life. It was the happiest day of my life because I could begin to put it all behind me. . . .

In 1995, 11 years after I had first identified Ronald Cotton, I was asked to provide a blood sample so that DNA tests could be run on evidence from the rape. . . .

I will never forget the day I learned about the DNA results. . . . They [the detective and the prosecuting attorney] told me: "Ronald Cotton didn't rape you. It was Bobby Poole."

RECONCILIATION Ronald Cotton and Jennifer Thompson share a moment after Mr. Cotton served 11 years in prison for a crime he didn't commit, based largely on an inaccurate eyewitness identification by Ms. Thompson.

. . . The man I had identified so emphatically . . . was absolutely innocent.

Ronald Cotton was released from prison after serving 11 years. . . .

Ronald Cotton and I are the same age, so I knew what he had missed during those 11 years. My life had gone on. I had gotten married. I had graduated from college. I worked. I was a parent. Ronald Cotton hadn't gotten to do any of that. . . . (Thompson, 2000)

had actually committed or to one they had not committed (Kassin, Meissner, & Norwick, 2005). College students and police investigators watched the video and indicated whether the inmate had or had not actually committed the crime. Neither the students nor the police were particularly accurate, but the police tended to be quite confident in their judgments.

In response to research like this, some state and local governments now require that the entire interrogation of suspects be videotaped. But as Kassin's research shows, doing so provides no guarantee that confessions are genuine or that jurors can recognize which confessions are genuine and which are not.

Inside the Courtroom

The Sixth Amendment to the U.S. Constitution stipulates: "In all criminal prosecutions, the accused shall enjoy the right to a speedy and public trial, by an impartial jury of the State and district wherein the crime shall have been committed." How does the government in the relevant state and district assemble an impartial jury? And how large should the jury be? We typically think of juries of 12, but would a smaller number suffice? What decision rule should the jury follow in rendering a verdict? A unanimous decision is typically required, but some jurisdictions allow less stringent agreement. How do these differences affect the nature of the jury's deliberation and the kind of verdicts they deliver? Social psychologists have conducted research on all these questions to find out which procedures best serve the cause of justice.

Jury Selection

The first step in creating a jury takes place out of the public eye. Local governments—typically county or municipal courts—use a variety of public records, such as phone books and voter registration rolls, to compile a list of potential jurors. When a trial is coming up, the court randomly selects individuals from this list. Prospective jurors then appear in court and are interviewed by the judge, the prosecuting attorney, and the defense attorney in a jury selection procedure known as **voir dire** (from old French, meaning "to speak the truth"). All three parties ask questions designed to find out whether a prospective juror is reasonably impartial, although the prosecution and defense are usually interested in ensuring that a juror is not biased *against* their side.

To weed out biased jurors, the prosecuting and defense attorneys consult their intuition about human nature and how certain types of people are likely to react to different types of arguments and evidence. Many attorneys believe, for instance, that engineers are stoic (and therefore not inclined to be moved by emotional appeals), that bearded men are unconventional (and therefore unlikely to be swayed by threats to the status quo), or that someone of German descent tends to be strict and conservative. Many attorneys also assume that particular types of jurors have special concerns that might lead them to be prejudiced for or against defendants in certain cases—for example, that mothers are especially sympathetic to claims about crimes involving children, that the rich are sensitive to alleged crimes against property, and that blacks are particularly moved by charges of police misconduct.

Based on the responses of prospective jurors to questions during voir dire, the defense and prosecution can ask the judge to excuse someone "for cause"—that is, because the person would not be impartial. Each side is also allowed a number of *peremptory challenges*—the right to exclude a prospective juror without offering any justification. Although a great deal of time and energy goes into the jury selection process, psychological research shows that neither lawyers' intuitions about certain kinds of people nor jurors' responses to questions during voir dire are reliable guides to the decisions jurors are likely to reach (Kerr, Kramer, Carroll, & Alfini, 1991; Olczak, Kaplan, & Penrod, 1991; Zeisel & Diamond, 1978).

SCIENTIFIC JURY SELECTION Recognizing the limits of their intuitions and the questionable value of prospective jurors' responses during voir dire, attorneys have turned increasingly to the practice of **scientific jury selection**, a statistical approach to selecting (or excluding) jurors likely to be predisposed to certain claims or appeals. Jury selection specialists hired by defense and prosecuting attorneys conduct surveys and compile statistics on how demographic variables—including age, gender, income, and ethnicity—are related to such things as an

voir dire The portion of a trial in U.S. courts in which prospective jurors are questioned about potential biases and a jury is selected.

scientific jury selection A statistical approach to jury selection whereby members of different demographic groups in the community are asked their attitudes toward various issues related to a trial, and defense and prosecuting attorneys try to influence the selection of jurors accordingly.

inclination to trust the government, to admire corporate executives, to care about the environment, or to distrust the police. In scientific jury selection, prospective jurors themselves are not questioned; instead, general associations between certain attitudes and demographic categories are established in the community at large. Scientific jury selection has been used in a great many high-profile trials, including those of former football star O. J. Simpson, television personality Martha Stewart, and hedge fund manager Raj Rajaratnam. Research indicates that the practice can be quite successful (Moran, Cutler, & DeLisa, 1994; Seltzer, 2006), enabling lawyers to know with reasonable accuracy, for instance, whether a prospective juror has a relatively pro-business or anti-business attitude (Hans, 2000). But randomized controlled experiments that would provide the most telling assessment of the practice have not been conducted, and the effectiveness of scientific jury selection is subject to some dispute (Seltzer, 2006).

DEATH-QUALIFIED JURIES As you are surely aware, the death penalty is a highly controversial component of the U.S. penal system. All but 14 states have the death penalty, although opponents question its effectiveness as a deterrent to crime, the consistency with which it is applied, and the very morality of its use. States with the death penalty do not have lower homicide rates than those without. And the homicide rate does not tend to go down when a state adopts the death penalty, nor does it go up when a state abolishes it (Costanzo, 1997; Haney & Logan, 1994). The overwhelming majority of those who are sentenced to death are poor and cannot afford the kind of defense that wealthy defendants use to maximize their chances of acquittal or, barring that, at least receiving a lesser sentence. Moreover, in recent years, DNA evidence has exonerated many individuals who were convicted of capital crimes they did not commit.

In many jurisdictions, the jury decides not only the guilt or innocence of the individual charged with a capital crime, but also whether the death penalty is appropriate. If you were on a jury in a capital case that found the accused guilty, would you be willing to sentence the defendant to death? If the answer is no, should you be excluded from the sentencing phase of the trial? Indeed, should people with profound reservations about the death penalty be allowed to serve as jurors in capital cases at all?

Maintaining that it's not a good idea to have such people serve as jurors in capital cases, the courts allow the practice of death qualification, in which the judge may exclude prospective jurors who say they would never vote for the death sentence. But does the systematic exclusion of people with strong reservations about the death penalty alter the verdicts rendered by **death-qualified juries**? Psychological research indicates that it does indeed.

People who are willing to recommend the death penalty—and hence death-qualified juries as a whole—tend to be more concerned about crime and more trusting of police than people who are unwilling to recommend capital punishment. They also tend to be more skeptical of civil liberty procedures that protect the rights of the accused and to have relatively negative views of defense lawyers (Fitzgerald & Ellsworth, 1984; Haney, Hurtado, & Vega, 1994). In experiments with participants assembled into mock juries who render a hypothetical verdict after looking at a videotape of a real trial, death-qualified juries are more likely to convict than juries in which individuals with

"Please read back that last remark in a more murdery voice."

death-qualified jury A jury from which prospective jurors who would never recommend the death penalty have been excluded.

reservations about the death penalty are not excluded (Cowan, Thompson, & Ellsworth, 1984). In another notable study, merely hearing the questions typically asked in the death qualification part of the voir dire tended to bias the jurors toward conviction, presumably because such questions contain an implication of guilt (Haney, 1984). Given these differences between death-qualified and -unqualified juries, many have questioned whether death-qualified juries really are impartial (Bersoff, 1987). Nevertheless, the U.S. Supreme Court has upheld the permissibility of death-qualified juries, first in *Witherspoon v. Illinois* (1968) and then again in *Lockhart v. McCree* (1986).

"Good news. Your execution was overturned on appeal."

Jury Deliberation

In fictional courtroom dramatizations, it's common for a steadfast and enlightened minority to overcome the impassioned but flawed view of the majority. Although this scenario makes good drama, it rarely happens in real life. In a landmark study of jury decision making, Kalven and Zeisel (1966) interviewed members of 225 juries. In 215 of them, a majority leaned in one direction or the other at the time of the initial straw vote; in 209 of these cases, the jury ended up handing down a verdict consistent with that initial majority. Also, in studies using mock juries, the initial majority almost always wins the day (Kerr, 1981; Stasser & Davis, 1981).

Given what social psychologists have learned about conformity pressures and social influence, it's no surprise that the initial majority so often gets its way. Indeed, studies on the nature of jury deliberation have found that the majority view prevails through the very processes of informational and normative social influence discussed in Chapter 9 (Kaplan & Schershing, 1981; Stasser & Davis, 1981). However, even though a minority rarely succeeds in producing the verdict they initially think is correct, they are able to persuade the majority to move in their direction a bit when it comes to sentencing (Pennington & Hastie, 1990).

JURY DELIBERATION IN FILM In the movie *12 Angry Men*, Henry Fonda plays the only juror who does not vote to convict the accused on the initial ballot. Slowly, employing one deft persuasion move after another, he wins over the other 11 members of the jury and engineers an acquittal.

JURY SIZE Most juries have 12 members, but that number is not specified in the U.S. Constitution, and some states allow smaller juries in noncapital cases. If you were convicted by a 6-person jury, would you think you had received a fair trial? Johnny Williams was in this very situation—convicted of robbery by a 6-person jury in Florida. He understandably thought the outcome might have been different with a larger jury, so he appealed. The Supreme Court, in *Williams v. Florida* (1970), upheld the conviction and affirmed the permissibility of 6-person juries, arguing that "there is no discernible difference between the results reached" by juries of different sizes. Later, in *Ballew v. Georgia* (1978), the Court reaffirmed its earlier opinion but ruled that juries of fewer than 6 people are unconstitutional.

In ruling that there is "no discernible difference" in the verdicts likely to be delivered by 6- and 12-person juries, the Supreme Court based its claim partly on conformity research. One concern of many legal scholars is guarding against the "tyranny of the majority"—that is, a nearly unanimous majority intimidating a slim minority into swallowing their convictions and caving in to the others. The Court maintained that research by Asch (1956) established that the amount of conformity pressure felt by the minority varies with the proportion of majority and minority opinions. By this logic, minorities in a 5-to-1 or a 10-to-2 split are equally likely to give in to the majority. But that's not what Asch found (see Chapter 9). Having an ally makes an enormous difference in allowing the minority to stick to their convictions, so the lone holdout in a 5-to-1 split has a much harder time standing firm than either of the two jurors in a 10-to-2 split. And on purely numerical grounds, someone who dissents from the majority is more likely to have an ally—a bracing partner in dissent—in a group of 12 than in a group of 6. The Supreme Court simply misread the relevant evidence. Indeed, research conducted after the two Supreme Court verdicts has found that 6-person juries are more likely to arrive at unanimous decisions and do so with less deliberation (Saks & Marti, 1997).

JURY DECISION RULE Recall that the Sixth Amendment guarantees anyone accused of a criminal offense "a speedy and public trial." Having juries with fewer than 12 members is one way to try to accelerate the flow of the large number of cases through the courts. Another way to speed up the pace of trials is to allow less than unanimous verdicts. The Supreme Court has twice upheld the permissibility of such decisions in state but not federal criminal trials. In *Apodaca, Cooper, and Madden v. Oregon* (1972), the Court upheld the convictions of three defendants found guilty by a jury operating under a 10-of-12 majority rule. In *Johnson v. Louisiana* (1972), the Court upheld a conviction obtained under a 9-of-12 decision rule. The Court maintained that a "conscientious juror" is concerned with justice, not with simply arriving at a verdict, so having a less-than-unanimous decision rule should not compromise either the length or the vigor of a jury's deliberation. Robust discussion, the Court argued, would continue well after a sufficiently large majority opinion has developed.

At the heart of the Court's ruling, then, was an empirical claim, one that social psychologists quickly set out to test. In one ambitious study, researchers recruited over 800 people and assembled them into 69 mock juries (Hastie, Penrod, & Pennington, 1983). After watching a filmed reenactment of a real-world criminal trial, the mock juries rendered verdicts using one of three different decision rules: unanimous, 10-of-12, or 8-of-12. The results were clear-cut. Although the verdicts rendered by juries operating under different decision rules didn't vary by much, the juries that did not have to achieve unanimity spent much less time discussing the facts of the case and questions of law. The 8-of-12 juries, for example, typically deliberated for less than 5 minutes after reaching a majority of 8 or more. After the criterion was met, in other words, they all but ignored the holdouts, ended discussion, and announced their verdict. Similar results were obtained from an analysis of videotaped civil trials with non-unanimous decision rules in Arizona. Minority opinions were given little attention once a sufficient majority view was reached (Diamond, Rose, & Murphy, 2006).

Note that these differences in how minority views are treated in juries with unanimous versus non-unanimous decision rules are important even if the two types of juries end up making the same decisions (as they often will if the case is relatively straightforward). The mock jurors in the study by Hastie and

"Justice delayed is justice denied."
—BRITISH PRIME MINISTER WILLIAM GLADSTONE

colleagues (1983) later rated the quality of their deliberations, and those required to reach unanimity thought more highly of the thoroughness and seriousness of their discussions. Support for the legal system is enhanced when all participants come away convinced that justice has been served—a sentiment that is much more likely when a unanimous opinion must be reached.

DAMAGE AWARDS Deciding the guilt or innocence of a defendant can sometimes be wrenchingly difficult, but at least there are only a few possible outcomes to consider—guilty versus not guilty, homicide versus manslaughter, and so on. In contrast, jurors in civil trials must often make decisions for which the response options are nearly boundless. For example, jurors must often decide how much a successful plaintiff should be paid in compensatory and punitive damages. How do jurors cope with such complexity, and how effective are they at awarding damages? Psychological research into these questions provides both encouraging and discouraging news (Kahneman, Schkade, & Sunstein, 1998; Sunstein, Kahneman, Schkade, & Ritov, 2002).

A compensatory damage award can be straightforward; it represents the amount the plaintiff should receive to compensate for any loss or harm sustained. The compensatory damages jurors can award are often tightly constrained by economic analyses of the harm done. Punitive damage awards are more subjective; they are designed to deter the defendant and others from acting in a similarly negligent manner or with similar intent in the future, and jurors often have much more discretion in what to award. What amount should a clothing manufacturer pay a child for burns she sustained because her pajamas were not sufficiently flame retardant? How much should a gas company pay if, in playing fast and loose with environmental laws, it contaminated local residents' drinking water?

Research indicates that jurors go about making such decisions by first consulting their sense of outrage at the defendant's behavior. As **Figure A3.1** shows, this sense of outrage tends to be affected by how recklessly the defendant behaved and how much malice seemed to be involved in the defendant's actions (Kahneman, Schkade, & Sunstein, 1998). Jurors then translate their sense of outrage into punitive intent, which is also influenced by the amount of harm the plaintiff experienced and by the plaintiff's identity (harm to children or koalas is likely

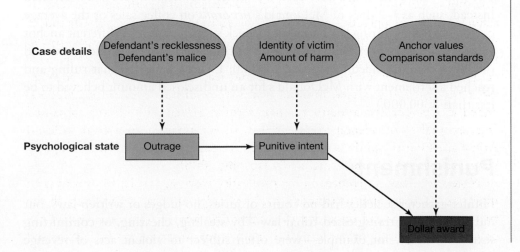

**Figure A3.1
A MODEL OF THE PSYCHOLOGY OF PUNITIVE DAMAGE AWARDS**
When making punitive damage awards, jurors first assess how outraged they are by the facts of the case. Then, considering who the victim is and the amount of harm suffered, they develop a sense of their intent to punish. The translation of punitive intent can be difficult and is often influenced by such extraneous variables as an available anchor value or comparison standards that spring to mind.
SOURCE: Adapted from Kahneman et al., 1998.

to inspire more punitive intent than similar harm to CEOs or hyenas). The difficulty lies in the next step: translating one's sense of punitive intent into an actual dollar figure. How much more should someone pay if you feel strongly that he should be punished rather than merely believing that he should be punished?

The good news is that people tend to agree about how outraged they are about a defendant's actions and their desire to punish. For instance, people generally agree that injuries to children merit more punishment than injuries to healthy retirees, that willful negligence calls for harsher treatment than simple carelessness, and that punishments that might deter the killing of dolphins or whales should be stiffer than those that might inhibit the killing of carp or mollusks.

The bad news is that the last step, translating punitive intent into an actual dollar amount, can be influenced by extraneous variables and therefore can be arbitrary. For example, various standards of comparison that are naturally evoked by a given case might introduce a degree of arbitrariness to the amount of a damage award. Suppose you hear about a company that allowed a toxic chemical to pollute the water supply that served a small nursing home, leading to the early deaths of several residents. You would no doubt be outraged, but your outrage would likely be affected by comparing this incident with other cases of lethal pollution you've heard about—cases involving larger communities and a wider range of victims, including very young children. Such comparisons might lead you to think that this case, though outrageous, is not as serious as some, and therefore the punitive damages should not be as high. In fact, research has shown that people can end up recommending stiffer penalties for harming appealing animals such as dolphins than for harming human beings (Kahneman et al., 1998; Sunstein et al., 2002). Converting our moral sentiments into dollars is a difficult translation, one that is prone to predictable biases.

In certain civil cases an accessible anchor value, or a spontaneously invoked comparison, might influence the compensation awarded. In *Liebeck v. McDonald's Restaurants* (1994), a famous case that inspired calls for reform in civil trials, the jury voted to award 79-year-old Stella Liebeck $2.7 million because she suffered third-degree burns after spilling a cup of McDonald's coffee on her lap. The jury accepted Liebeck's attorneys' argument that McDonald's coffee was too hot (and inadequately labeled as hot), and they appeared to be influenced by her counsel's suggestion that McDonald's should be penalized an amount equal to 1–2 days of its average revenue from the sale of coffee ($1.35 million per day). But what would the award have been if another reasonable figure had been cited instead, such as 1–2 days of McDonald's *net profit* on coffee sales or the average person's earnings during the period of Liebeck's recuperation? A different anchor value would almost certainly have yielded a different result. (The judge reduced the jury's recommended award to $480,000; Liebeck appealed that ruling and reached a settlement with McDonald's for an undisclosed amount believed to be less than $600,000.)

Punishment

Hunter-gatherer societies had no courts or juries, no judges or written laws, but individuals who transgressed tribal law—by stealing, cheating, or committing sexual infidelity, for example—were often subject to violent acts of revenge

(Boehm, 1999). The Middle Ages and Renaissance in Europe were times of spectacularly brutal forms of punishment; beheadings, hangings, drawing and quartering, and whipping were regular practices, often in town squares for all to see. Even minor transgressions were subject to extreme punishment. In parts of Europe, if a baker sold bread that weighed less than advertised, he would receive the equivalent of today's water boarding. In fifteenth-century Scotland, individuals falsely posing as town fools were subject to having their ears nailed to a post or their fingers amputated.

Today, punishment largely has been subsumed by the criminal justice system, which determines the guilt or innocence of an individual alleged to have committed a crime and what the penalty should be if that person is convicted. Within the criminal justice system are people such as police officers, lawyers, judges, and jurors, who make judgments about guilt or innocence and about appropriate punishments. Such judgments are the product of the human mind, and social psychologists have uncovered important underpinnings of people's rationale for punishment—why we punish as we do and what makes punishments seem fair.

Motives and Kinds of Punishment: Just Desserts versus Deterrence

Punishment is referred to as retributive justice, requiring people to make amends for harm and social transgressions. Within the realm of retributive justice, social psychologists differentiate between two motives that govern preferences for different kinds of punishment (Carlsmith, Darley, & Robinson, 2002; Weiner, Graham, & Reyna, 1997). One is the *just desserts* motive, commonly referred to as eye-for-an-eye justice; the goal is to avenge a prior evil deed rather than

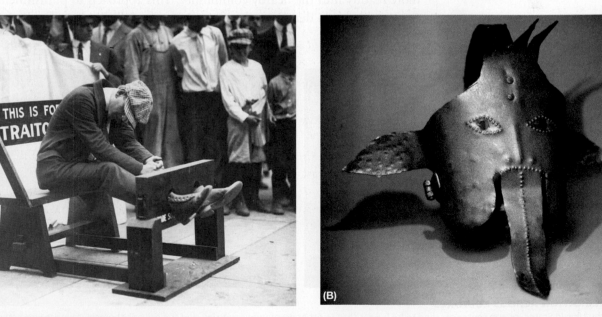

JUST DESSERTS PUNISHMENTS
(A) In earlier times, people who were guilty of various crimes were subjected to public ridicule by being kept in stocks in public venues. (B) Several hundred years ago, people who committed various offenses, such as gossiping too much, might be forced to wear a "shame mask" like this one. These punishments were guided by just desserts—the requirement that the punishment match the crime.

prevent future ones. Such punishments are calibrated to the moral offensiveness of the crime. Empirical studies of U.S. college students find that their recommended punishments closely track their feelings of moral outrage; people prefer punishments that match the perceived severity of the harm caused by the alleged crime (Carlsmith & Darley, 2008).

A second motive that can guide punitive judgments is *deterrence*, the goal of which is to reduce the likelihood of future crimes committed by the criminal or by others. People guided by the motive of deterrence assume that punishments change the cost-benefit analyses of people thinking about committing crimes; they make more salient the costs of committing a crime (such as prison time or fines), which should outweigh any potential benefits, thereby deterring people from committing criminal acts in the future.

Punishments guided by the deterrence motive can take many forms. Incarceration (imprisonment) is an obvious way to prevent a convicted person from committing future crimes. More specific punishments practiced today, as well as those used in the past, reflect the deterrence motive. Lawyers who violate the law or their code of ethics are disbarred—prevented from practicing again. Priests are defrocked for immoral acts. Sex offenders have been castrated. In many countries in the past and present, thieves' hands have been cut off. The underlying logic is that these more specific punishments prevent the perpetrator from committing similar crimes in the future.

An Attributional Account of Punishment

The just desserts and deterrence motives are useful for understanding people's rationale for punishment, and these motives may be at play in the pronounced variation in punishments handed out across different cultures. In Japan and Norway, for example, prisons are much more open, and prisoners are integrated more readily into the nearby community. This approach to punishment appears to be guided by a deterrence-based practice of rehabilitation. The United States,

INCARCERATION ACROSS CULTURES
(A) In the United States, prison sentences tend to be longer than in other developed countries, and the prisons themselves more aggressively segregate prisoners from the rest of the population. (B) In many other countries, such as Norway and Japan, prisoners are more readily integrated into local communities.

by contrast, has much more severe sentencing practices, which might be in part the product of the greater influence of the just desserts motive (although it could readily be argued that severe sentences serve to deter criminals as well). What might account for such cultural variations and, more generally, for preferences for just desserts versus deterrence-oriented punishments?

Bernard Weiner and his colleagues have offered one answer to this question. Their theory draws on the idea that emotion-based intuitions drive different punitive judgments (Weiner, Graham, & Reyna, 1997). According to their account, two attributions lead people to feel anger about a criminal act: (1) the belief that the perpetrator is responsible for the crime and intended it to happen and (2) the belief that the crime reflects a stable part of the perpetrator's character. Numerous studies find that once angered, people prefer just desserts forms of punishment—they want the perpetrator to suffer in proportion to the harm caused (Lerner, Goldberg, & Tetlock, 1998).

A different set of attributions leads people to feel sympathy rather than anger toward the perpetrator of a criminal act. Specifically, people tend to feel sympathy when they believe that (1) situational factors, including the perpetrator's past history (such as being a victim of abuse), led to the crime and (2) the crime does not reflect a stable part of the perpetrator's character. These two attributions reduce the inclination to see the perpetrator suffer in proportion to the harm caused (Rudolph, Roesch, Greitemeyer, & Weiner, 2004). Feeling sympathy also increases forgiveness and makes people prefer punishments that protect the criminal and society, such as forms of rehabilitation (Weiner et al., 1997).

Weiner and his colleagues have tested this framework in studies of teachers' attitudes toward punishing students for breaking rules and U.S. citizens' attitudes toward punishing O. J. Simpson when he was on trial for murdering his wife. The findings are in keeping with their analysis: attributions give rise to feelings of anger or sympathy, and these emotions lead to different punitive judgments. These principles are also at play in the legal strategies typically pursued by the prosecution (focusing on the responsibility and poor character of the defendant) and the defense (focusing on the role of circumstance). The same principles apply in debates about the relevance of a defendant's life history in the courtroom (Toobin, 2011). Many perpetrators of violent acts have suffered profound physical abuse as children, and increasingly this evidence is being considered in trials, particularly in death penalty cases. This kind of information, if allowed at trial, is likely to generate more sympathy for the defendant and therefore more lenient punitive judgments.

Bias in the Criminal Justice System

The United States incarcerates a higher percentage of its citizens than any developed country except Russia. More than 1.5 million Americans are in prison (Bureau of Justice Statistics, 2014). Social scientists have long grappled with a disturbing fact: black and Latino men are represented in higher numbers in U.S. prisons than in the general population. Might this overrepresentation be due in part to bias in the justice system—that is, to people's stereotypes and prejudices about blacks and Latinos?

Social psychologists Jennifer Eberhardt, Phoebe Ellsworth, and Jack Glaser argue that stereotype-based decision making is at least partly responsible for observed biases in the criminal justice system (Eberhardt, Davies, Purdie-Vaughns, & Johnson, 2006; Ellsworth, 2009; Glaser, 2014). Their reasoning is that cultural stereotypes of blacks and Latinos hold that they are more dangerous, more prone to violence, and more likely to use drugs. These stereotypes then guide the many decisions people in the criminal justice system make, thus giving rise to race-related biases in who is convicted and punished for different crimes (Plant & Peruche, 2005). Stereotypes, for example, influence which people police officers pull over and whether they search for drugs or write up a ticket for an offense. For similar reasons, stereotypes may shape how jurors assign responsibility for crimes, the degree to which they feel anger or sympathy, the likelihood of conviction, and sentencing length.

Evidence in support of a stereotype-based account of bias in the criminal justice system is mounting (for a summary, see Glaser, 2014). For example, the Supreme Court gives police officers ample latitude in terms of who they can pull over and search without probable cause. Bureau of Justice statistics indicate that blacks and Latinos are three times more likely to be searched when pulled over, even though these searches are not apt to yield incriminating evidence (Durose, Smith, & Langan, 2007; Plant & Peruche, 2005). Once on trial, blacks and Latinos may not receive treatment equal to that given other defendants; mock jurors are more likely to convict a black defendant than a white defendant in a hypothetical trial for the same crime (Sommers & Ellsworth, 2001). Outside the laboratory, a summary of sentences meted out to 77,000 offenders found that blacks were given longer sentences than whites for similar crimes (Mustard, 2001). A more recent Bureau of Justice Statistics investigation revealed that black men receive sentences 5–10 percent longer than white men for similar crimes (Bureau of Justice Statistics, 2015). Collectively, these findings suggest that racial stereotypes may partly explain racial biases in conviction rates and severity of sentencing.

Perceptions of Fairness of the Criminal Justice System

Theoretically, laws and punishments should instill a sense of order in society. In practice, the U.S. criminal justice system and the influence of its laws and punishments depend critically on another type of justice social psychologists have studied—**procedural justice**, which refers to whether the processes resulting in the administration of rewards and punishments are perceived to be fair. Procedural justice depends on *how* rewards and punishments are determined. The concern with procedural justice is salient, for example, when considering whether employers use the same criteria to give bonuses to different employees, when there are conflicts about which criteria to use for admitting students to colleges and universities, or when there are concerns about whether the likelihood of arrest and the length of prison sentences depend on the race or social class of the individual.

Three factors shape a person's sense of procedural justice, according to social psychologist Tom Tyler (1994). The first involves assessments of the *neutrality* of

procedural justice Assessments of whether the processes leading to legal outcomes are fair.

the authority figure. When figure-skating judges give substantially higher scores to skaters from their own country, their neutrality is clearly in question, and the sense of procedural justice is undermined. With respect to punishment, a citizen's sense of procedural justice will depend critically on whether the legal system is seen as evenhanded. Second, there must be *trust* in the system. The individual must have confidence that authority figures—police officers, lawyers, judges—will be fair, that they will treat everyone according to consistent principles and standards. Third, the individual must feel that everyone is treated with *respect*. Do authority figures meting out justice—police officers giving out traffic tickets or judges delivering sentences, for example—treat those they are punishing politely? Respect on the part of authority figures, Tyler reasons, gives people a sense that the legal system is fair.

Tyler contends that these three facets of procedural justice have as much influence on the sense that outcomes—punishments and rewards in particular—are fair as does the actual content, good or bad, of the outcome itself (Tyler, 1994). In survey research, Tyler and colleagues have contacted people who have had recent experiences with authority figures. In one study, participants had recently received punishment for crimes they had committed, and they indicated what punishment they'd received, such as the length of their prison sentence (Tyler, 1987). Participants also indicated the extent to which they thought the authority figure had been neutral and trustworthy and had treated them with respect. The dependent measure of interest was the participant's feelings about the authority figure's fairness.

Two findings stand out. First, the magnitude of the punishment participants received in their recent experience with the criminal justice system was not correlated with their sense of procedural justice. This is an important finding because it suggests that people separate how the punishment is delivered from the punishment itself. Second, and perhaps more striking, their ratings of neutrality, trust, and respect were stronger determinants of their belief in the fairness of the criminal justice system than the actual punishment they received.

People's sense of justice thus revolves around more than personal gains or losses. People care profoundly about the neutrality of authority figures, the trustworthiness of the system, and the respect they receive from others. On the one hand, we might be encouraged by Tyler's findings. A society can build a sense of justice in groups and communities by ensuring that the distribution of rewards and punishments is neutral, respectful, and carried out by people who can be trusted—and it can do so without changing the allocation of material resources. On the other hand, a more sinister implication of Tyler's findings is that authority figures might be responsible for all sorts of pernicious outcomes, from job layoffs to unwarranted prison sentences, without encountering protest, as long as they deliver them in a neutral, respectful, and trustworthy fashion.

Module Review

SUMMARY

Before a Case Goes to Trial

- Eyewitness testimony can be unreliable; even when trying their best to tell the truth, eyewitnesses can be mistaken when trying to identify perpetrators.
- The guesses of most people about the factors that influence witness accuracy can be wide of the mark. Because police investigators and jurors can't always assess witness accuracy, judicial procedures have recently been developed to minimize the likelihood of conviction due to mistaken identification.
- Suspects' confessions are sometimes false, even when coercion is not great; as a result, certain jurisdictions require videotaping of all interrogations. Jurors are poor judges of whether confessions are false or not.

Inside the Courtroom

- Jury selection begins with the process of *voir dire*, when the judge and the prosecuting and defense attorneys try to determine whether prospective jurors are impartial.
- Using *scientific jury selection*, attorneys accept or reject prospective jurors on the basis of demographic and statistical data.
- Whether only those jurors who would sentence a criminal to death should serve in capital cases is a controversial issue. *Death-qualified juries* are more likely to convict than those in which some jurors have reservations about the death penalty.
- When a minority of jurors dissent from the proposed verdict, the initial majority verdict usually prevails. While juries smaller than 12 people are allowed in some jurisdictions, larger juries are more likely to consider the opinions of a minority of jurors. When verdicts do not need to be unanimous, juries spend less time deliberating after the necessary majority is reached.
- Compensatory damage awards are intended to make up for any loss the plaintiff has suffered; punitive damage awards are intended to deter the defendant and others from acting similarly in the future. Compensatory damages are often straightforward, but punitive damages can be highly subjective and based on arbitrary comparisons and anchor values.

Punishment

- Two motives that guide punishment are the just desserts motive, intended to avenge a crime, and deterrence, intended to prevent the crime from happening again.
- Certain attributions and emotions lead to preferred forms of punishment. Believing that a criminal has acted willfully and is responsible for his actions leads to feelings of anger and a preference for just desserts forms of punishment. Believing that situational factors led, in large part, to the criminal act leads to sympathy and a preference for more deterrence-oriented punishment.
- Social psychological research has yielded evidence of racial bias in the U.S. criminal justice system. Stereotypes about blacks and Latinos being more likely to commit crimes may lead to a greater likelihood that people in those groups will be investigated, convicted, and punished.

Perceptions of Fairness of the Criminal Justice System

- *Procedural justice* refers to people's assessments of whether the processes that result in the distribution of rewards and punishments are fair. If people feel the system is neutral and trustworthy and that they have been treated with respect, they are more likely to believe that outcomes are fair, regardless of the magnitude of the punishment or reward.

THINK ABOUT IT

1. Suppose your laptop is stolen from your dorm room one night, and a few of your neighbors catch a glimpse of a suspect as they are arriving home from a party. Your residence hall advisor (RA) brings in your neighbors individually to ask them about the suspect they saw. How should your RA's questions be posed to get the most accurate eyewitness testimony possible?

2. If you are in charge of establishing rules for jury deliberation, what can you do to increase the likelihood that minority opinions will be adequately considered? What research findings would you cite to back up your decisions?

3. Maria and Tanya are on the jury in a civil court case that has found the defendant guilty. They must now decide how the defendant should be punished. During their deliberations, it becomes clear that Maria is angered by the defendant's behavior, while Tanya feels sympathy. Using what you learned in this module, describe the differing attributions that might have led to Maria's anger compared with Tanya's sympathy. Which kind of punishment do you think each woman is likely to prefer?

4. Thais and Elisa both get speeding tickets and are being punished by their parents. Thais's parents have a system of rules they follow for punishing all their children and calmly but firmly explain to Thais that she will be grounded for a month. Elisa's parents, in contrast, favor her brothers over her, punish their children inconsistently from week to week, and scream at Elisa for her mistake, but only ground her for a week. Who is likely to feel her punishment is more just, and why: Elisa, with her shorter sentence, or Thais, with her longer sentence?

The **answer guidelines** for the Think About It questions can be found at the back of the book . . . ☞

ONLINE STUDY MATERIALS

Want to earn a better grade on your test?

Go to **INQUIZITIVE** to learn and review this module's content, with personalized feedback along the way.

ANSWER GUIDELINES FOR THINK ABOUT IT QUESTIONS

CHAPTER 1

1. How does social psychology differ from related disciplines, like personality psychology and sociology? How might a social psychologist, in contrast to researchers in other disciplines, try to understand the atrocities at Abu Ghraib?

ANSWER: Social psychology can be defined as the scientific study of the feelings, thoughts, and behaviors of individuals in social situations. Whereas personality psychologists study individual differences in behavior and sociologists study aggregate patterns of behavior, social psychologists study the influence of social factors on behavior. When seeking to explain the atrocities at Abu Ghraib, a social psychologist might consider social pressures the abusive guards may have faced from higher-ups, rather than simply assuming that the guards were "bad apples."

2. What does the Milgram experiment on obedience demonstrate about the power of the situation? What features of the experimental situation might have increased the likelihood that participants would continue to shock the learner even after the learner showed signs of pain?

ANSWER: The Milgram experiment demonstrated that, given the right situational factors, a majority of psychologically healthy adults were willing to continue shocking an innocent man even after he screamed and complained of a heart condition. Most of these participants were clearly not sadists, but rather were influenced by a powerful situation, which included the experimenter's insistence that they continue with the shocks, the intimidating setting (a prestigious university), and perhaps even the lack of a clear schema for how to politely discontinue participation.

3. Why are schemas so important for social interaction? What is your schema for being a student in a classroom? What might happen if you didn't have that schema?

ANSWER: To understand and navigate even the most seemingly simple social situations, like ordering food at a restaurant, we rely on complex systems of organized knowledge called schemas. A schema for being a student might consist of the expectation that a teacher will lead the class and that students should sit quietly in their seats, take notes, observe the teacher, and speak only when called upon. Without this schema, a confusing, embarrassing situation might ensue.

4. When trying to understand people's thoughts, feelings, and motivations, why don't researchers just ask them? What does research on automatic versus controlled processing tell us about people's awareness of their own mental states?

ANSWER: People tend to believe they have more conscious access to their mental processes than they really do. Research has shown that most mental processing happens nonconsciously—that is, outside of conscious awareness or control. For this reason, people's self-reports of their beliefs and motivations are not always accurate. Social psychology experiments can be designed in ways that tap into nonconscious processes. For example, one study showed that European-American participants who were reminded of African-Americans and then asked to read a brief description of someone whose race was not specified were more likely to rate that individual as more hostile, suggesting that they might implicitly associate African-Americans with hostility (Devine, 1989b). This was true even for participants who did not openly express negative attitudes toward African-Americans in a questionnaire.

5. How does evolution help explain social behavior? Which types of behaviors seem most likely to be explained by evolution, and which ones seem less likely?

ANSWER: Evolution operates through natural selection, the process whereby animals and plants that possess adaptive traits are more likely to survive and reproduce and therefore pass on the genes that code for those traits to future generations. Many of the adaptive traits that humans almost universally possess, such as the capacity for language and the ability to form affectionate bonds, may have been shaped by natural selection. Traits that vary across cultures and individuals, such as valuing individual accomplishments over group accomplishments, are less likely to be explained by evolutionary theory.

6. What is the naturalistic fallacy, and why is it so important to avoid when considering evolutionary explanations?

ANSWER: The naturalistic fallacy refers to the erroneous claim that the way things are is the way they should be. Evolutionary theory as applied to human behavior is controversial in part because people have at times used evolutionary explanations to justify gender and racial inequality or to promote fascist ideology. The naturalistic fallacy can also lead people to believe that biology is destiny and that there is little they can do to control their behavior. These beliefs are both destructive and inaccurate. Much of human civilization is based on the continual regulation and modification of biological predispositions through medical interventions, education, and law enforcement.

7. How do Western and Eastern countries differ in their beliefs about the role of the self in relation to the group? How might these beliefs lead to different behaviors in an academic setting?

ANSWER: Research suggests that, on average, individuals in independent cultures, such as the United States and Great Britain, tend to focus more on their unique traits and accomplishments, whereas individuals in interdependent cultures, such as China and Korea, tend to focus more on their role within a group and their obligation to that group. In an academic setting, members of a more independent culture might be more likely to strive to stand out among their classmates, whereas members of a more interdependent culture may strive to blend in harmoniously with their peers.

8. Are evolutionary and cultural explanations for behavior compatible? How might these two perspectives complement each other when it comes to explaining gender differences in mate selection?

ANSWER: Evolutionary and cultural explanations for behavior are generally not mutually exclusive; they work together to provide a more complete picture. Evolution has provided humans with a broad array of tools and propensities that can be either cultivated through cultural practices or set aside if they are not useful in a given ecological or economic context. For example, although evolutionary forces may predispose women to prefer mates who have ample resources to support a family, in countries where women have greater financial resources themselves, this preference may no longer be as relevant, and mate preferences may shift.

CHAPTER 2

1. After reading this chapter, do you think it's important for students of social psychology to have a basic understanding of research methods? Why or why not?

ANSWER: Although this question asks for your opinion, it's essential for students of social psychology to have a basic understanding of research methods. This knowledge contributes to your ability both to understand social psychology research (and many other kinds of empirical research) and to think critically about the science involved. For example, without understanding that correlational research does not provide causal information, you might easily believe that certain claims have a causal connection and therefore act on them. Consider parents of overweight children who read that attempts to control their diet will *cause* them to be overweight. If parents new to research methods accepted this finding as fact, it might seem reasonable for them to be overly permissive toward their child's eating habits, with potentially harmful consequences.

2. Recall from Chapter 1 the experiment on nonconscious processing in which participants read a persuasive message in a room with either a fishy smell, an unpleasant smell that was not fishy, or no distinctive smell (Lee & Schwarz, 2012). The researchers measured the degree to which each participant was persuaded by the message and discovered that participants were least likely to be persuaded in the presence of a fishy smell (there was something "fishy" about the message). In this experiment, what was the independent variable? What was the dependent variable?

ANSWER: The independent variable is the variable the researcher manipulates—the hypothesized "cause." In this experiment, it was the smell participants were exposed to, and it had three levels: a fishy smell, an unpleasant smell that was not fishy, and no distinctive smell. The dependent variable is what the researcher measures—the hypothesized "effect." In this experiment, it was the degree to which the message persuaded the participants.

3. Suppose a group of researchers hypothesized that finding your romantic partner physically attractive contributes to feelings of satisfaction in your relationship. To evaluate this hypothesis, the researchers asked 100 participants to complete a survey that included questions assessing their current relationship satisfaction, as well as ratings of how physically attractive they believed their partner to be. The researchers found that the more physically attractive participants rated their partners, the more satisfied they tended to be in their relationship. In this fictitious study, did the researchers employ a correlational or an experimental design? How do you know?

ANSWER: This study is correlational. The researchers evaluated whether a relationship exists between two naturally occurring variables: relationship satisfaction and perceived partner attractiveness. The researchers did not randomly assign participants to levels of the independent variable, so the study cannot be considered an experiment.

4. Consider the hypothetical study in question 3 again. The researchers found a relationship between perceptions of partner physical attractiveness and relationship satisfaction. With these data, can the researchers conclude that perceiving your partner as physically attractive causes you to become more satisfied in your relationship? Are there other potential explanations for these findings?

ANSWER: With these data, the researchers cannot determine a causal relationship between the two variables. For example, perceiving your partner as attractive may cause you to be more satisfied. It is also possible, however, that being in a satisfying relationship causes you to be more attracted to your partner. Perhaps a third variable, such as being a cheerful, optimistic person, causes you to be satisfied in your relationship and causes you to see your partner as attractive (the third-variable problem). To rule out these possibilities, the researchers would have to conduct an experiment.

5. In Chapter 3, you will learn about research on the self, including self-esteem. Suppose the scatterplot below displays the relationship between self-esteem and academic success. How might you interpret this graph? Is the correlation between these two variables positive or negative? Try guessing the correlation coefficient.

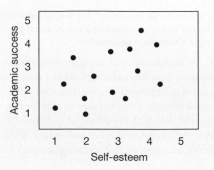

ANSWER: The graph shows that as self-esteem increases, so does academic success. This is a positive correlation. To know the correlation exactly, we would have to evaluate these results with mathematical formulas. It would be reasonable to guess, however, that the correlation is between .30 and .50.

6. In this textbook, you will learn about various studies evaluating social psychological phenomena using functional magnetic resonance imaging (fMRI), which measures activation in the brain while the participant lies immobile in a large metal tube. For example, researchers may measure brain activation while participants experience a social rejection or may look at how brain activation during a stressful experience is affected if a close friend holds the participant's hand. How would you characterize the external validity of such research?

ANSWER: Research using fMRI involves an unusual environment, one unlike any other a participant will experience in everyday life. For that reason, external validity is somewhat low. Unfortunately, questions about the connection between social experiences and reactivity in the brain cannot be answered by field research alone. Nevertheless, a thoughtful researcher can still set up a convincing psychological experience in a scanner. Is a perceived rejection any less real when experienced in the bore of the magnet? Social support from a friend may be particularly valuable in this stressful environment. (Think of a person being comforted by a spouse while undergoing an unusual or frightening medical procedure, not as part of an experiment, but during an actual course of treatment.) Moreover, consensus across studies lends additional support to the conclusion that a set of brain regions is involved under particular social psychological circumstances.

CHAPTER 3

1. According to research on the accuracy of self-knowledge, for what qualities are we the best judges of ourselves? For what qualities are others superior judges of us? How does motivation contribute to this asymmetry?

ANSWER: Although people predict that they are the best judges of themselves, when it comes to predicting behavior, others know us about as well as we know ourselves. However, we are superior judges of ourselves when it comes to private, inner qualities that are not easily observable (like our inner thoughts and feelings), whereas others are superior judges of us when it comes to qualities that are readily displayed in social settings (like our level of talkativeness and enthusiasm). Motivation contributes to the self/other knowledge asymmetry regarding qualities that have a positive or negative connotation. We are strongly motivated to see ourselves favorably, which may give us blind spots about our socially undesirable shortcomings. In these cases, others tend to know us more accurately than we know ourselves. (And thank goodness; you wouldn't want to be fully aware of your every flaw!)

2. Josie is a 13-year-old girl who thinks she's a funny person, and her friends and family generally think Josie is funny too. How would Cooley's notion of the "looking-glass self" explain how Josie's sense of herself as funny developed? Bearing in mind that Josie is an adolescent, what does research suggest is likely occurring in her brain when she thinks about her self-views?

ANSWER: Cooley (1902) would argue that Josie's sense of self developed from the way Josie thinks others perceive her, using others' views as a mirror, or "looking glass," to perceive the self. Research suggests that among young adolescents, brain areas associated with

perspective taking are especially active when contemplating one's self-views, so it seems likely that when Josie thinks about her self-views, regions of her brain that help her take the perspective of others will be activated. Thus, as an adolescent, Josie may be especially prone to incorporate what she thinks other people think of her into her self-concept.

3. How might a female undergraduate's working self-concept regarding her gender shift during a day on campus as she attends her advanced math class (in which she is the only female), has a low-key lunch with a friend, and attends her gender studies class? Will her frequently shifting self-concept undermine her sense of having a coherent self?

ANSWER: The working self-concept shifts with situational cues, such that in a given situation, especially relevant and/or distinctive self-aspects become part of the working self-concept. In her advanced math class, this young woman's gender identity is highly *distinctive* (as she is the only female), and in her gender studies class, her gender identity is highly *relevant* to the situation (discussing gender theory and struggles). Thus, both class contexts should highlight her gender identity in her working self-concept. During lunch, however, it's unlikely that gender will be part of her working self-concept, being neither particularly relevant nor distinctive in that context. Despite these shifts in her working self-concept, she is probably not confused about her identity; she probably has a core set of self-aspects that define who she is regardless of her current working self-concept. Moreover, she is probably used to these fluctuations during her days on campus, since they form a stable pattern of activation and deactivation of her gender in her working self-concept (making her feel especially female in her math and gender studies classes and less so at other times).

4. How do people's daily experiences in their contingent versus noncontingent domains affect their state self-esteem? Over time, how might these experiences translate to trait self-esteem?

ANSWER: Performing well in a contingent domain boosts state self-esteem, whereas performing poorly in a contingent domain diminishes state self-esteem. Performance in noncontingent domains has less influence on state self-esteem. Over time, accumulating experiences of good versus poor performance may influence trait self-esteem. Repeatedly performing poorly in contingent domains (threatening state self-esteem frequently) may ultimately reduce overall trait self-esteem. Similarly, regularly performing well in contingent domains (boosting state self-esteem repeatedly) may ultimately increase overall trait self-esteem. Performance over time in noncontingent domains is unlikely to affect trait self-esteem.

5. Do people from Eastern cultures generally feel worse about themselves than people from Western cultures? How do researchers interpret self-reported self-esteem differences between cultures?

ANSWER: Members of Eastern cultures tend to report lower feelings of self-esteem than members of Western cultures; however, rather than reflecting an overall more negative view of the self, this difference may reflect differing cultural value systems. In East Asian and other non-Western cultures, views of the self are more interwoven with the social context. Accordingly, these cultures prioritize improving the self (perhaps to better fulfill one's obligations and duties in social relationships and systems) and meeting the goals of the group, rather than meeting the goal of being a self-confident and powerful individual (which Western cultures tend to prioritize). Thus, it may not be accurate to conclude that members of Eastern cultures feel worse about themselves than Westerners; they simply feel different about the self as a whole.

6. Should people be more likely to display the better-than-average effect for their own intelligence before or after learning how intelligence is measured in scientific research? How do construals contribute to this process?

ANSWER: According to research on self-serving construals, the better-than-average effect is more prevalent for qualities with ambiguous, or fuzzy, definitions, but dissipates in strength when objective standards become apparent. Thus, before obtaining a clear definition of intelligence, people may be more prone to self-enhance with respect to their intelligence in order to bolster their self-worth. Under these conditions of ambiguity, people may construe different qualities as being more or less important to intelligence, construing their own strengths (perhaps artistic or interpersonal skill) as key to intelligence and construing their weaknesses as less relevant to intelligence. However, once people learn the scientific standards for intelligence, their tendency to display the better-than-average effect should decrease by reducing their freedom to construe their own best qualities as core to intelligence.

7. If you're fairly sure you are scatterbrained, but a friend tells you that you're organized and focused, what will your cognitive reaction likely be? What will your emotional reaction likely be? Which motive—self-enhancement or self-verification—drives which set of reactions?

ANSWER: Self-verification, the need to be seen accurately by others for important self-defining traits, should drive your cognitive reactions to this feedback, making you dubious about the quality of the feedback your friend has provided. In contrast, your emotional system, ruled more by self-enhancement, should register this as positive feedback and lead you to feel good about this feedback, even as your cognitive mind tells you it is inaccurate. Thus, you may think your friend is off-base in her compliment to you (perhaps making you question her competence as a judge of you), but you will still feel emotionally better about it than if she had confirmed your negative self-view of being scatterbrained.

8. Suppose two friends both have an actual self that is relatively happy and a potential self that is extremely happy (happier than their actual self). If this discrepancy in happiness leads one friend to experience agitation and the other friend to experience dejection, what does this tell you? What theory would this evidence support?

ANSWER: Actual selves that are discrepant with ought selves produce agitation, whereas actual selves discrepant with ideal selves produce dejection. This suggests that for the agitated friend, the extremely happy potential self is an ought self, whereas for the dejected friend, the extremely happy potential self is an ideal self. In other words, the first friend feels that she really *should* be happier, whereas the second friend feels she would like to ideally be happier (but it's not a matter of "should"). This pattern of emotional responses would support self-discrepancy theory.

CHAPTER 4

1. How valid are snap judgments? Do brief exposures to a person's physical appearance or "thin slices" of the individual's behavior provide meaningful information about what that person is really like?

ANSWER: Snap judgments often contain a kernel of truth about a person, but not the whole truth. Research described in this chapter showed that snap judgments of a political candidate's competence, based on a brief look at the candidate's photo, were predictive of electoral success, suggesting that these judgments corresponded with the general consensus about the candidate based on larger samples of his or her behavior over time. There is no clear evidence, however, that snap judgments of competence reliably predict *actual* competence, and the same is true for judgments of most other traits. Therefore, it is best to avoid making important decisions solely on the basis of snap judgments.

2. What role might pluralistic ignorance play in the problem of binge drinking on college campuses? What could school administrators do to reduce pluralistic ignorance in this context?

ANSWER: College students who are privately concerned about the dangers of binge drinking may keep quiet because they assume that most other students view binge drinking as acceptable and they don't want to embarrass themselves by speaking out. But it's possible that many other students feel the same way and are not sharing their feelings for similar reasons. To counter this form of pluralistic ignorance, school administrators could launch an information campaign designed to show students that positive attitudes about binge drinking are not as widespread as they may seem.

3. How does the desire to entertain tend to bias the kinds of stories that are reported most frequently in the media? What effects might this bias have on people's beliefs about the world?

ANSWER: The media tend to overreport negative, violent, and sensational events because these types of stories attract viewers' attention more than positive, altruistic, and everyday events. Research shows that 80 percent of the crime reported in the media is violent, whereas in reality only 20 percent of crime is violent. Unfortunately, this bias can lead people to fear victimization and view the world as a terribly dangerous place, especially if they live in an area where crime is more prevalent. This bad news bias can also prevent people from learning about inspiring, altruistic acts, such as relief efforts to help victims of natural disasters and ordinary citizens helping their neighbors through hard times.

4. If you were developing an advertising campaign for a fitness class, what kinds of framing strategies might you use to increase the chances of people signing up for the class? In particular, consider spin framing, positive and negative framing, and temporal framing.

ANSWER: An example of spin framing could be to highlight the low cost of the class: "Sign up now and save $20." An example of positive framing could be to describe the benefits of the class for physical appearance: "Get beach-ready!" An example of negative framing (which generally has greater impact) could be to describe the potential health risks of not exercising: "Inactive people are nearly twice as likely to develop heart disease." An example of temporal framing could be to encourage people to sign up well in advance, before they have a chance to construe the class in potentially less pleasant, concrete terms (sweating, exhaustion, and so on).

5. Suppose you're about to go on a blind date when a mutual friend warns you that your date can be a little cold and unfriendly. According to research on the confirmation bias, how might this information influence the impression you ultimately form about your date?

ANSWER: If you expect your date to be cold and unfriendly, you might be more likely to pick up on behaviors that confirm your expectations; for example, you might notice that your date is short with the waiter. You might also be more likely to ask leading questions that elicit information consistent with your expectations; for example, if your date is a professor, you might ask, "So do your students drive you crazy?" As a result of your biased observations and behavior toward your date, your date may indeed reveal more cold and unfriendly characteristics, and you may consequently form a more negative impression that confirms your initial expectations.

6. Research on priming suggests that it is possible for a stimulus to activate a schema even if a person is not consciously aware of the stimulus. Can you think of ways that you might be able to use priming to influence others' behavior?

ANSWER: To increase creativity, you could have people work in a green or blue environment. To make someone more attracted to you, you could wear red or put a red border around a photo of yourself. To make people behave more honestly, you could put up a poster of something or someone with eyes, which makes people feel like they are being watched. To make people more concerned about preventing climate change, you could make your case about it in an especially hot room.

7. Imagine you're working on a group project with three other students and you are all asked to indicate your individual contribution to the project, relative to the other group members' contributions, in the form of a percentage. If you were to sum the individual percentages reported by each group member, would you expect it to add up to roughly 100 percent? Why or why not?

ANSWER: The sum of estimates would likely be above 100 percent due to the availability heuristic, a mental shortcut that leads people to overestimate their own contributions to joint or group efforts and to underestimate others' contributions. Examples of your own hard work are more available to you because you can experience them firsthand, whereas examples of others' hard work may be harder to bring to mind, making them seem less frequent. As a result, all four group members may estimate their individual contributions as over 25 percent, leading to an impossible total. Research indicates that people tend to overestimate their own contributions even when these contributions are negative (like starting arguments), suggesting that this phenomenon is not explained simply by a motivational bias to present oneself in a favorable light.

CHAPTER 5

1. Carla is the last person to be picked for dodgeball teams in her gym class. She thinks to herself, "Jeez, no one wants me for their team. I'm terrible at dodgeball. In fact, I'm terrible at all sports. No matter how much I work out or how hard I try, I'm never going to get any better." What are the three attribution dimensions that make up a person's explanatory style? Describe where Carla falls on these three dimensions. Overall, what is Carla's explanatory style? How do you know?

ANSWER: The three attribution dimensions that make up explanatory style are internal/external, global/specific, and stable/unstable. In explaining why she gets picked last for the team, Carla says she is terrible at dodgeball. This is an internal attribution. Carla also says that she is terrible at all sports. Carla is going beyond this specific situation and is therefore making a global attribution. Finally, Carla says that no matter how much she works out or how hard she tries, she will never get any better. In this way, Carla is making a stable attribution about her athletic abilities. Overall, Carla is displaying a pessimistic explanatory style. She is explaining a negative event as due to something internal about her, something global (it affects other areas of her life), and something stable (it cannot be changed).

2. Can you think of a time when you committed the fundamental attribution error? What happened? Why do you think you made this mistake?

ANSWER: We are all likely to commit the fundamental attribution error, and probably do so regularly. For example, consider when a friend's new girlfriend comes out with the gang for the first time. If the person is quiet and awkward, it's easy to assume she is an introverted person, thereby attributing her behavior to her disposition. But being the odd person out in a group of close friends will make almost anyone feel a bit shy, right? Why don't we take this into account? The fundamental attribution error occurs for many reasons. For example, according to the just world hypothesis, people want to believe that good things happen to good people. Believing that outcomes are determined by who a person is (her disposition) rather than factors outside of her control (the situation)—the fundamental attribution error, in other words—helps people maintain such just world beliefs. Another reason we commit the fundamental attribution error is that a person's behavior is often more salient or obvious to us than the situational circumstances. We're more likely to notice the new girlfriend's awkward behavior than to be aware of the situation and how it will impact her (particularly because the situation is very different for us—comfortable and familiar). In addition, we know that it's easier to make dispositional attributions; considering the situation takes more energy or effort. We can be lazy, so often the thoughtless dispositional attribution wins out.

3. Curtis, a busy guy with good taste in music, has a friend who raves about a new band. Curtis wants to know whether it's worth his time to listen: Is the band actually awesome (an external attribution) or is his friend not all that discerning about music (an internal attribution)? Curtis recalls that his friend raves about the band every time he listens to them, although none of their other friends rave about the band, and his friend raves about every band. Describe the three components of the covariation principle, and explain how each one applies in this scenario. Based on this information, what should Curtis conclude? Is the band awesome or does his friend simply love all music?

ANSWER: We use the covariation principle to make attributions about a behavior. The three pieces of information we use are consensus (do other people respond similarly when they encounter the situation/stimulus), distinctiveness (does the person respond similarly to other situations/stimuli), and consistency (does the person respond the same way whenever they encounter the situation/stimulus). In this example, there is low consensus (other friends do not rave about the band), low distinctiveness (Curtis's friend raves about every band), and high consistency (Curtis's friend raves about the band every time he listens to them). Using this information, Curtis should conclude that the band is probably not awesome. Rather, his friend raves about the band because he simply loves all music—an internal attribution.

4. Imagine you are single and decide to go to a speed-dating event, in which you will have a series of 5-minute dates with many people. You really care about getting to know what your dates are like. Given this situation, which types of behaviors would strongly signal the type of person your date is? What types of behaviors might you discount, that is, chalk up to the demands of the speed-dating situation? Apply the augmentation and discounting principles in your analysis.

ANSWER: The situational demands in a speed-dating event are strong. For example, in this situation, it's socially appropriate to act friendly, outgoing, and lighthearted. Therefore, if one of your dates acted friendly, outgoing, and lighthearted, it would be hard to tell whether she was truly that kind of person or whether she was acting that way because the situation calls for such traits. This demonstrates the discounting principle, the idea that we should assign less weight to a cause of a behavior (your date's personality) if there are other possible causes that might have produced the behavior, too (the demands of the speed-dating situation). In contrast, acting rude, introverted, or serious goes against the demands of the speed-dating situation. In this way, if one of your dates acted rude, introverted, or serious, it would strongly signal that this is the type of person your date is. This reflects the augmentation principle—the idea that we should assign greater weight to a cause of a behavior (your date's personality) if there are other causes present that normally produce the opposite behavior (the demands of the speed-dating situation).

5. Can you think of other aspects of our identity (besides culture, religion, or social class) that might influence the types of attributions we make? How so?

ANSWER: Many other aspects of our identity—such as political affiliation, gender, and age, to name a few—relate to the ways we make attributions. What about personality variables, like attachment style? In one study, participants imagined their romantic partner engaging in a particular behavior and then made attributions regarding why the partner behaved that way. For example, the scenario "your partner brought you dinner when you were sick" could be attributed to "my partner is a caring and thoughtful person" or "my partner feels guilty about something and is trying to make up for it." Highly avoidant participants, those less comfortable with intimacy in their romantic relationships, were less likely to attribute the partner's behavior to caring intentions.

6. Mary, Travis, and Hussein stand to receive their awards at the National Spelling Bee. Mary, who won first place, receives her trophy with a smile on her face. The second-place winner, Travis, covers his face with his hands and sobs. Eventually, he politely receives his award despite the tears. When Hussein's name is called for the third-place prize, he grins and excitedly claims his award. Using what you learned in this chapter, explain Mary, Travis, and Hussein's (perhaps surprising) reactions to their respective prizes.

ANSWER: As the first-place winner, it's no surprise that Mary receives her award smiling. Travis and Hussein's reactions are more interesting, however. Travis, who won second place, is devastated, whereas Hussein, who won third place, is thrilled. This nicely demonstrates a phenomenon discussed in this chapter regarding counterfactual thinking: considering what could or should have happened if only something small were different. If Travis engages in counterfactual thinking, he's likely to realize he was so close to first place—if only he hadn't made that last mistake. In this way, Travis feels devastated about just missing out. In contrast, if Hussein engages in counterfactual thinking, he's likely to realize that he almost didn't place in the competition. One more slipup and he would have lost altogether. Thus, he is relieved and grateful he won third place.

CHAPTER 6

1. Humans appear to have a coordinated display of embarrassment that resembles appeasement signals in other species. What does this tell us about the function of embarrassment? Why do you feel embarrassed when you trip and fall in a full lecture hall? What effects should your display of embarrassment have on your classmates?

ANSWER: Emotions have myriad social functions, and embarrassment has a particularly interesting role in human relationships, signaling remorse for making social errors (like breaking norms or violating role constraints). Expressing embarrassment tells others in your social network that you're aware you committed a social transgression, recognize you may deserve punishment, and wish to be forgiven. Thus, when you trip and fall in lecture, you have violated an implicit social norm (not to trip and fall but rather to be dignified and composed) and may in turn show a strong blush response and embarrassment display. These automatic signals communicate to your classmates that you know you've blundered and should make them see you as more trustworthy and upstanding, if not especially graceful.

2. The relationship between culture and emotion is complex. Say you're seated at a wedding reception with an older European-American man, who tells you that East Asians never get excited. How would you explain to him that he's mistaken by drawing on the concepts of ideal emotions and display rules?

ANSWER: Excitement is an ideal emotion in Western cultures like America, where it is consistent with American cultural ideals, such as readily expressing the self, and is thus highly valued. In contrast, many East Asian cultures more highly value calmness and contentedness, which are consistent with their cultural ideal of harmony. Moreover, display rules, which regulate expressions of emotion, could also be involved. Thus, even if an American and an East Asian experience the same level of excitement, the American may play up his or her excitement more, augmenting its display, whereas the East Asian may regulate his or her excitement more, minimizing its display. Thus, excitement may simply be more valued and more commonly and readily displayed in America than in East Asia, but it certainly doesn't mean that East Asians never experience or express excitement.

3. Much communication today occurs via electronic text rather than face-to-face, whether in an online chat or text message, an e-mail, or a post on a social media site. Given what you know about the importance of emotions for social relationships, why do you think people frequently use emoticons and emojis in these communications? What social functions do they perform?

ANSWER: Emotion plays an important role in coordinating interactions, communicating our commitments and true feelings, and understanding what others are thinking and feeling. Emoticons and emojis can help us express and signal emotions in the online world, adding a layer of social color and richness to our digital interactions. A smiley face, an uncertain face, a shocked face, or a face of relief can add emotional overtones to otherwise sterile textual conversations, helping us communicate our true intent and understand the nuances of others' statements. Perhaps they even provide social rewards for our conversation partners, and in group texts and conversations, perhaps they help us find and fill our social niche. Although emoticons cannot substitute for the rich language of touch, facial expressions, and vocal expressions of emotions, they may help make up for some of what is lost in a digital context.

4. Suppose you just got into a huge fight with your parents on the phone and are feeling angry. You call up your romantic partner to talk about the fight, but just end up fighting with your partner. Using what you know about emotion's effects on perception, how would you explain this second fight and perpetuated mood states more generally?

ANSWER: Anger makes us more attuned to signals of threat in the environment, making us see more hostile intent in the actions of others. In this situation, the first fight made you angry, which likely colored your perception of the interaction with your romantic partner. Perhaps you saw your romantic partner as more hostile and less understanding than you normally would, which made you quick to respond with even more anger. By altering perception, emotions may thus sometimes perpetuate themselves, leading to extended mood states. For instance, this chapter discusses how happiness makes people more prone to identifying happy words and how fear makes people believe that future threats are more likely; in both cases, the emotion may enhance subsequent experiences of the same emotion.

5. If you were working as a canvasser collecting signatures for a petition to ban same-sex marriage, what strategies could you use to increase your signature count, given what you know about moral foundations theory and the effects of disgust on moral judgment?

ANSWER: Disgust intensifies judgments that impure acts are morally wrong. Gay men and lesbians are, unfortunately, seen as "impure" groups by some people, and same-sex marriage is thus a topic relevant to moral concerns about impurity. To collect more signatures, you might try to target people who are already feeling disgust about another stimulus. For instance, you could try standing next to a smelly garbage can, collecting signatures from people collecting trash on the side of the road. Or you could use a more traditional strategy of simply discussing the supposedly impure aspects of same-sex marriage prior to requesting a signature.

6. Would winning several million dollars in the lottery make you happier? What does research on affective forecasting predict? What does the research on money and happiness have to say? How should you spend your winnings to maximize happiness?

ANSWER: Based on affective forecasting research, although you might predict that winning the lottery would increase your happiness considerably, chances are you'd be less happy after winning the lottery than you'd predicted. This may occur because of focalism, such that you would focus on the salient aspects of winning the lottery (tons of money), but would neglect the possible detractors to this newfound happiness, like complicated taxes, sudden strange fame, and potentially strained relationships with family and friends. The research discussed in this chapter would also suggest that the lottery could indeed increase happiness for some people, but only if they previously had an annual income below $75,000. In other words, money only makes people happier up to a point. To make yourself happiest with your newfound wealth, you should probably spend it on other people and on experiences rather than on yourself and on material goods.

CHAPTER 7

1. Consider an attitude object you feel strongly about, something you love or something you hate. Maybe you're passionate about soccer. Perhaps you are staunchly opposed to capital punishment. Describe this attitude along the three elements of affect, cognition, and behavior.

ANSWER: The three components of an attitude are affect (the degree to which you like or dislike the attitude object), cognition (thoughts, beliefs, memories, and images about the attitude object), and behavior (the tendency to approach or avoid the attitude object). Let's consider soccer as the attitude object from the perspective of someone who is passionate about the sport. With respect to affect, this person strongly likes soccer, or feels positive emotions, such as

excitement, when engaging with soccer. With respect to cognition, this person probably has a large store of knowledge about soccer, including the rules of the game and statistics about players, as well as a host of memories involving soccer. These affective and cognitive components reinforce behavioral tendencies, such as the desire to watch soccer, talk about soccer, and play soccer.

2. Suppose you're an attitude researcher and want to assess participant attitudes about the institution of marriage. Describe three methods you might use in your assessment.

ANSWER: Researchers interested in attitudes toward marriage can use a variety of measurement tools. With surveys, they can ask participants to report on a Likert scale the degree to which they believe marriage contributes to societal functioning. Measuring response latencies can indicate the strength, or accessibility, of an attitude, with participants responding faster to questions about more strongly held attitudes. To evaluate the centrality of attitudes about marriage to someone's belief system, researchers can ask a variety of questions related to the institution of marriage. For example: Do you disapprove of divorce? Do you support traditional gender roles? Finally, researchers can use implicit measures to access nonconscious attitudes toward marriage. For example, they can employ an IAT to determine the association between marriage and good versus bad or look at brain activity when participants respond to marriage-related concepts. The latter implicit measures may be particularly useful if researchers want to study a more controversial aspect of marriage. For example, some participants may not be willing to report their attitudes about same-sex marriage.

3. You have two close friends who you like very much, Tanya and Amanda. Unfortunately, Tanya can't stand Amanda. This makes your life difficult, as the three of you can never spend time together without Tanya getting irritated. Based on what you learned about cognitive dissonance theory, how might you go about getting Tanya to like Amanda more?

ANSWER: One way to make Tanya like Amanda is to get Tanya to behave in ways that suggest she does in fact like Amanda. For example, you might ask Tanya to give Amanda a ride home, to help you plan Amanda's birthday party, or to help out Amanda by picking up her laundry. If her attitude toward Amanda (she doesn't like her) is inconsistent with her behavior toward Amanda (she behaves in a friendly way), Tanya is likely to experience cognitive dissonance and engage in dissonance reduction tactics. Since the friendly behavior has already occurred and cannot be changed, Tanya's best option is to change her attitude. In this way, she may come to hold a more positive attitude toward Amanda than she did before.

4. Although we readily assume that attitudes relate in meaningful ways to behavior, research suggests they don't always match up. Consider the dentist as the attitude object. Why might attitudes toward the dentist not necessarily predict behavioral responses to the dentist?

ANSWER: Attitudes toward the dentist may not predict behavioral responses to the dentist for a variety of reasons. First, attitudes do a poor job predicting behavior if there are other strong determinants of the behavior. Many people have negative attitudes about the dentist but still make dental appointments for maintaining good health and a pleasing smile. Relatedly, attitudes do a poor job predicting behavior if the components of an attitude are in conflict. People may have negative feelings (affect) about the dentist, such as anxiety or fear, but positive thoughts (cognition), such as believing that dentists are critical for maintaining good dental hygiene. Even if a person reports positive attitudes toward the dentist, they may still experience aversion at a gut level, particularly when seeing the drill! Often, these nonconscious or automatic responses to a stimulus are stronger determinants of behavior than more thoughtful, conscious beliefs. Attitudes may also do a poor job predicting behavior if the attitudes are measured at a different level of specificity than the behavior (attitudes about dentists in general and behavior toward a particular dentist).

5. Suppose you're choosing between two vacation spots you think are equally amazing: Greece and Costa Rica. You have to pick one and elect to go to Costa Rica. Following your decision, Costa Rica starts to sound even more fantastic—zip-lining, cloud forests, and incredible wildlife. In contrast, Greece seems a little less special, it's expensive, and the beaches aren't really that nice. Describe a cognitive dissonance account of this change in your attitude following the decision.

ANSWER: Cognitive dissonance theory states that inconsistencies between a person's attitude and behavior can lead to an aversive emotional state called dissonance. After choosing Costa Rica for your vacation you may experience post-decision dissonance, because there is an inconsistency between your attitude (I like Greece) and your behavior (I did not choose Greece). To reduce this dissonance, you will probably change your attitude to better fit your behavior: you did not choose Greece (the behavior), so you must not have liked Greece very much after all (a change in your attitude). In this way, Greece starts to seem less exciting, while Costa Rica starts to seem like an even better choice.

6. Although your son already likes vegetables, you want him to eat even more vegetables. You decide to pay him $1 to spend at the toy store for every portion of vegetables he eats. Given what you learned about self-perception theory, is this a good approach? Why or why not?

ANSWER: You can use rewards and punishments to modify your son's behavior, such as offering him $1 to spend at the toy store for each portion of vegetables he eats. Surely, that would entice him to eat more vegetables, right? However, there is a risk of the overjustification effect when strong rewards are given. According to this phenomenon, we tend to devalue activities we perform in order to get something else. So if you give your son $1 for eating vegetables, he may take notice of his behavior and think, "Hmm, I'm eating more and more veggies," but then recognize, "Oh! But I'm doing it to get the dollar." If your son started out liking vegetables, he will come to perceive himself as someone who eats vegetables—but who does so for the money. Once you stop paying him that dollar, he's likely to stop eating more vegetables, and he's even likely to eat *fewer* vegetables than he did before.

CHAPTER 8

1. A new boutique coffeehouse just opened in your neighborhood featuring coffee sustainably sourced from small organic farms around the world. Design two ads for the coffeehouse, one using the central route to persuasion and one using the peripheral route. How do your ads differ?

ANSWER: The central route to persuasion occurs when the audience thinks carefully about the message's content—that is, when they have the motivation and ability to do so. An ad for the coffeehouse focusing on the central route will include strong arguments in support of the coffee and the shop itself. For example, your ad might state that sustainably sourced coffee is better for the environment, organic coffee is better for your health, in taste tests this coffee is preferred over those sold at other local shops, or the price is better. The peripheral route to persuasion occurs when the audience has low motivation or ability to think critically about the message and they respond to superficial or easy-to-process features, such as the attractiveness or credibility of the message source. For example, you may recruit a famous chef or a trusted community leader to endorse the coffeehouse or simply show an attractive person drinking the coffee. Alternatively, you might include colorful images of the coffee—factors that are easy to process and thus likely to persuade through the peripheral route.

2. Describe the three elements of a persuasive appeal, and give two examples of each element that influence persuasiveness.

ANSWER: The three elements of persuasion are source characteristics, message characteristics, and audience characteristics. Source characteristics are features of the person delivering the message. Attractive sources are more persuasive than unattractive sources. Credible sources, high in expertise and trustworthiness, are more apt to persuade, particularly in the present (less so with a delay—the sleeper effect). Certain or confident sources are also more likely to persuade than uncertain or less confident sources.

In terms of message characteristics, high-quality messages are more persuasive than low-quality messages, particularly if the audience is high in motivation and ability. Explicit messages are more likely to persuade than messages in which the take-home point isn't clear. Messages that overtly refute the opposition are more persuasive, as are messages in which the spokesperson argues in opposition to their own self-interest. Vivid, colorful, interesting, and memorable messages are typically persuasive, as are messages that induce fear to a moderate degree (particularly if coupled with information regarding how to counter the feared outcome). Finally, messages may vary in norms, values, and outlook and may be especially persuasive if they match the cultural background of the target audience.

Audience characteristics are features of the person or group on the receiving end of the message. Audiences vary in their motivation and ability to process the message; those higher in motivation and ability are inclined to be persuaded by strong arguments, whereas people with low motivation and ability are more likely to be persuaded by superficial features of the message. Older participants and those with a stronger need for cognition tend to focus on argument quality when being persuaded. A person's mood can influence persuasion too.

3. Suppose you are part of a global advertising team responsible for creating ads for oatmeal in both South Korea and the United States. Design an ad for each country, and explain why you designed the ads the way you did.

ANSWER: When designing an ad, advertising teams must consider the cultural backdrop for the message. One relevant variable is whether the culture encourages more independent or more interdependent construals of the self. Independent cultures, such as the United States, focus on individual uniqueness and self-actualization. Ads targeting such cultures should focus on the connection between the product and an individual's success or well-being. For example, an oatmeal ad in the United States might emphasize the ability of oatmeal to help *you* grow healthy and strong and become the best version of yourself to achieve your hopes and dreams.

Interdependent cultures, such as South Korea, focus on social harmony. Ads targeting these cultures should focus on the connection between the product and one's social relationships. For example, an oatmeal ad in South Korea might encourage parents to buy oatmeal to help the *family* become healthy and strong.

4. What is the self-validation hypothesis? What aspects about our thoughts, besides the positive-negative direction and number of thoughts we have on a topic, influence whether or not we are persuaded by them?

ANSWER: The self-validation hypothesis states that whether or not we are persuaded is influenced not only by the direction and number of thoughts we have on the issue or topic, but also on how confident we are about our thoughts. The more confident, the more we are likely to be persuaded by them. A few factors are known to influence thought confidence. The more valid we believe our thoughts are, the more easily we are able to come up with our thoughts, and the clearer our thoughts are, the more confident we'll be about our position and the more we are likely to be persuaded.

5. Tyrell and his girlfriend, Shea, have very different views on capital punishment: he opposes it, while she supports it. Even after Tyrell presents evidence that capital punishment is both financially wasteful and ineffective at preventing crime, Shea does not change her views. Using what you know about resistance to persuasion, how might Shea be staving off Tyrell's attempts to persuade her?

ANSWER: Persuasive attempts are often met with strong resistance. Even before Tyrell overtly presents her with counterattitudinal information, Shea is likely to engage in selective attention, tuning in to messages that reinforce her attitudes on capital punishment and tuning out information that contradicts them. She might seek out media outlets that support her perspective and avoid conversations with people who believe the contrary. Shea is also likely to selectively evaluate counterattitudinal messages, such as the information Tyrell presented. She might regard the arguments as weak and their sources as seriously lacking in credibility. Moreover, the more Shea knows about capital punishment, the more she will scrutinize Tyrell's messages in this way. Such processes are especially likely to occur if Shea made prior commitments to her attitudes, such as by joining a pro–capital punishment advocacy group or posting articles that support her beliefs on social media.

CHAPTER 9

1. What two reasons appear to explain why people so often mimic one another?

ANSWER: The two explanations for mimicry are as follows: (1) Because of ideomotor action, we are more likely to do something if it pops into our mind by virtue of witnessing someone else do it. (2) Mimicry enhances rapport and prepares us to have smooth interactions.

2. Suppose your dining hall is having a contest, and you have to guess how many gumballs are in a giant jar (the closest guess wins). You and a few friends walk up to the gumball jar and tell your guesses to the volunteer running the contest. Your friends all say their guesses out loud, and you go last. You find yourself increasing your gumball estimate to be closer to those of your friends. How could each type of social influence (normative and informational) have affected your guess? How could you reduce the normative social influence in this situation?

ANSWER: Given that you're making a judgment about something uncertain (there's not an obvious right answer), you may have used your friends' guesses as a useful source of information, helping you arrive at a judgment that seemed more accurate; this is informational social influence. But given that you're also stating these judgments publicly, there is pressure to state a judgment that is similar to those of your friends, so you won't be seen as odd or clueless; this is normative social influence. You could reduce the normative social influence inherent in this situation by privately submitting your answers on pieces of paper, rather than stating them out loud.

3. In the battle for LGBTQ rights, what kind of social influence can minority LGBTQ groups exert on the majority? Should their goal be to engage public support or private internalization and acceptance of their arguments among members of the majority?

ANSWER: When minority groups influence majority groups to enact social change, it is typically via informational social influence, convincing members of the majority group to hear out their arguments and better understand their perspective. Normative social influence, which typically results in mere public compliance (without any private acceptance of LGBTQ arguments or positions), is a less powerful tool here, as the majority doesn't feel much pressure to conform and avoid public scorn; they largely control the public scorn, after all. Luckily, informational social influence is a powerful force, one that is more likely to result in private acceptance and internalization of the minority perspective among members of the majority, which will likely aid the LGBTQ cause more in the long run.

4. Suppose you want to increase voting rates among millennials (people born in the 1980s and 1990s). Describe one reason-based approach, one emotion-based approach, and one norm-based approach you could use to do so.

ANSWER: Reason-based approach: you could use a foot-in-the-door technique, asking eligible voters to do small volunteering duties for the election, which would highlight their sense of self as a politically engaged individual, hopefully leading to more behavior consistent with that sense of self, such as voting.

Emotion-based approach: you could give away cookies on the street on election day to induce positive emotion before reminding people to vote, which could lead them to construe the act of voting as not terribly inconvenient and make them more inclined to engage in a valued civic act to further or sustain their good mood.

Norm-based approach: you could create flyers that highlight how many people vote in certain neighborhoods and age-groups, but you'd have to be careful not to advertise a norm of *not* voting if rates were low; adding a smiling face along with the numbers could help communicate that high voting rates are desirable.

5. In the context of the Milgram experiment, give an example of "tuning in the learner" and an example of "tuning out the experimenter," and explain how each one affects obedience rates.

ANSWER: "Tuning in the learner" means heightening the salience of the learner and the consequences of the participant's actions for the learner's health and well-being. For example, having participants hold the learner's hand against the shock plate while administering the shocks makes the participants more aware of what they're doing to another person by obeying the instructions of the experimenter, thereby reducing obedience rates. In contrast, "tuning out the experimenter" means reducing the salience of the experimenter, for instance by having the experimenter administer instructions over an intercom rather than in person. This tends to reduce the experimenter's authority and influence over the participant, thus reducing obedience.

CHAPTER 10

1. The need to belong is thought to be a fundamental human drive, similar to physical drives like hunger. When people have their need to belong satisfied, they are unlikely to pursue this drive further. Given this premise, who is more likely to call up a friend to make plans: Betty, who's been spending lots of quality time with her children lately, or Blanche, who tends to stay home by herself?

ANSWER: If the need to belong resembles physical drives like hunger, the less belonging one feels, the more "socially hungry" one should feel, and the more motivated one should be to try to connect with others. This feeling of low belonging is like the feeling of an empty stomach, and it motivates a person to seek social contact. In this scenario, Blanche should be hungrier for social contact and more likely to seek out connection with a friend, compared with Betty, who should have her fill of social contact from spending time with her children.

2. Sean and Mitch are just starting a relationship, but they seem to have different expectations about what each one deserves from a romantic partner. Sean thinks that if his partner doesn't treat him extremely well, then that romantic partner is just not worth his time because there are better guys out there. Mitch, on the other hand, has been in several bad relationships and puts up with just about anything from a partner because he's deeply afraid of being alone. How would you describe Sean and Mitch's respective comparison levels and comparison levels for alternatives? What might the consequences of these levels be?

ANSWER: Sean appears to have a higher comparison level than Mitch, because he believes he deserves better treatment from his romantic partners than Mitch believes he himself does. Sean's comparison level for alternatives in this scenario is high, because he thinks there are better guys out there than a romantic partner who doesn't treat him extremely well. This suggests that Sean sees many potential rewards (high-quality partners) outside of his relationship. Coupled with his high comparison level, Sean may be quick to leave his relationship with Mitch if he doesn't get the treatment he thinks he deserves. Mitch's comparison level for alternatives is low; he sees being alone as an undesirable alternative. This suggests that Mitch may put up with more bad behavior from a partner due to both his low comparison level and his low comparison level for alternatives; he doesn't expect much from his partner and doesn't see many desirable alternatives to being in his current relationship.

3. Jenny feels comfortable relying on and being close to her immediate family members, and she seeks extremely intimate, clingy romantic relationships but keeps her distance from her friends, not disclosing much to them or counting on them. How would you analyze her attachment styles? How would you describe her working models?

ANSWER: It sounds like Jenny has distinct attachment styles for the different types of relationships in her life. She has a secure attachment style with her family, because she feels comfortable trusting them and doesn't seem to worry about being close to them. But with her romantic partners, Jenny wants to be exceedingly close and intimate; this is characteristic of an anxious attachment style. With her friends, Jenny seems avoidant, seeking extreme independence and showing reluctance to be close and dependent. Jenny seems to have multiple attachment working models (corresponding to her three styles of attachment) that become activated and applied differently in various relationships.

4. Robert has a crush on Marilyn, but she doesn't seem to know he exists. What can Robert do to make himself more attractive to Marilyn, based on the principles of proximity and similarity?

ANSWER: If Robert wants to capitalize on proximity, he should find a way to get physically close to Marilyn, such as sitting near her in lecture or moving to an apartment or dorm near hers. The more mere exposure Marilyn experiences with Robert, the more Marilyn should come to like him, so any way he can increase the probability of their paths crossing should help his cause. If he wants to capitalize on similarity, Robert should highlight the ways he and Marilyn are similar, perhaps by altering the style of clothes he wears to more closely resemble hers, playing up the interests they have in common, or taking up new hobbies and causes she enjoys. The more similar Robert appears to be to her, the more rewarding their interactions will be, and the more Marilyn should feel validated about herself.

5. Suppose Alice wants to try an experiment about the halo effect of physical attractiveness on an online dating website. She sets up two profiles for herself, making the content of the profiles identical except for her picture. On one profile, she uses a beautiful photo of herself as her profile photo, but on the other profile, she uses a horrible photo of herself. How might men respond to these two profiles, and how might Alice respond to them in turn?

ANSWER: Based on the halo effect, the high and low attractiveness photos should create self-fulfilling prophecies for Alice's experiences on each profile. When men on the site are interacting with the pretty Alice profile, they may see her content as more charming, interesting, and attractive than the content coming from the ugly Alice profile and in turn may write her more interesting, engaging messages and see her responses to those messages as wittier and funnier. Moreover, Alice's responses could also be affected by the manipulation; she may feel more engaged with the men who are interacting with her pretty profile and actually write better messages. In this way, the heightened expectations men have based on the pretty Alice profile may end up actually eliciting a better side of Alice, compared with Alice's behavior when interacting via the ugly profile.

6. How can the investment model of commitment help explain why people stay in long-term abusive relationships? How might an abusive partner manipulate the factors that contribute to commitment to make an abuse victim stay in the relationship?

ANSWER: In abusive relationships, satisfaction is probably fairly low, since the costs are great. But satisfaction is not the only determinant of commitment; possible alternative partners and investments in the relationship are the other two determinants. Investment in an abusive relationship may be high if the partners are married, financially linked, have children and property together, and have intertwined lives. In any long-term relationship, many resources have been devoted to the relationship over the years. It's possible that an abusive romantic partner would deliberately increase investment on the part of a partner—for instance, by having more children or making more joint commitments (such as loans)—or would find ways to remind the partner of all the investments already made. Alternative partners may also come into play: perhaps partners in abusive relationships feel that there are no other options and that at least having the "good" times with the current partner is better than being alone or with some unknown other. Abusive partners could well manipulate perceptions of alternatives, such as making critical comments that make an abuse victim feel unworthy of love from anyone else. The cycle of abuse is powerful, and leaving is not always determined by something as simple as low satisfaction.

CHAPTER 11

1. Is it possible for people to be prejudiced without being aware of it? How have researchers addressed this question, and what evidence have they found?

ANSWER: Research suggests that it is indeed possible for people to be prejudiced without necessarily being aware of it. Implicit measures, such as the implicit association test (IAT), can reveal subtle, nonconscious prejudice even among those who sincerely believe they are not prejudiced. In research described in this chapter, participants whose IAT scores showed implicit prejudice toward African-Americans were more likely to show activation in a brain area associated with fear when they viewed African-American faces, but they were not more likely to report prejudiced beliefs on the Modern Racism Scale. These results suggest that people may hold attitudes they are either unable or unwilling to acknowledge.

2. Suppose every year, the male CEO of a small company always asks a female employee to take care of organizing the company's holiday party. When one female employee asks the CEO why he always gives this task to women, he says that women are better party planners than men. Is this an example of sexism? Why or why not? What adverse effects might the CEO's positive stereotype regarding women's party planning ability have on the female employees?

ANSWER: The CEO's characterization of women as skilled party planners is an example of benevolent sexism, which refers to positive stereotypes of outgroup members that can nonetheless lead to discrimination and impede social progress. Although the CEO's attitude toward women seems positive, it may also have negative components, such as the belief that women are not as effective as men in more important leadership roles. His attitude may also make his female employees feel they need to conform to traditional female gender roles in order to gain his approval. Another potential cost of the CEO's behavior is that his female employees may have to devote valuable time, which they could be spending on other work, to tasks that are not part of their job description and not helpful for advancing their career.

3. Describe the Robbers Cave experiment, and outline three important points this study revealed about intergroup relations.

ANSWER: After intense screening, the researchers enrolled 22 average boys into their summer camp. The boys were split into two groups and spent the first phase of the study developing a strong group identity through participation in games and activities. In the second phase, the two groups were brought together for a camp competition. The winner of the competition would receive a desirable prize, while the loser would receive nothing. The researchers evaluated intergroup relations and found that hostility between the groups was rampant. Following this competition phase, the researchers brought the groups together under friendlier circumstances. Intergroup conflict did not dissipate. Subsequently, the researchers staged various camp "crises" the boys had to solve by working together. Cooperation, here induced by external demands, did mitigate the conflict between the groups.

This study contributed important insights to the economic perspective, specifically realistic group conflict theory. Three important points from this study include the following. (1) Competition over resources fosters intergroup conflict. During the competition phase, the boys fought over material resources: a medal, along with a highly coveted pocketknife. Here, hostility abounded, involving name-calling, food fights, cabin raids, and challenges to fight. (2) Defusing intergroup conflict cannot be accomplished through contact alone. During the third phase, the boys were brought together under noncompetitive circumstances, but name-calling and fighting persisted. (3) Emphasizing superordinate goals relevant to both groups is necessary for contact to mitigate intergroup conflict. Once the boys worked together to solve the camp crises, including fixing a broken water pipe and pulling a broken-down supply truck with a rope, hostility dissolved and friendships developed among the group members.

4. Imagine that a conversation about race relations in the United States develops during a family dinner. One of your relatives argues that given how ubiquitous stereotypes are, prejudice and discrimination are inevitable. Using research from the cognitive perspective, and controlled and automatic processing in particular, how would you respond to this assertion? Are prejudice and discrimination inevitable? Under which conditions are they more likely to emerge?

ANSWER: As your relative argues, research finds that even nonprejudiced people are aware of cultural stereotypes. Moreover, these stereotypes are likely to be activated automatically, quickly, and reflexively. Research described in this chapter found that participants who were primed (outside of their conscious awareness) with words related to an African-American stereotype were more likely to perceive a target's behavior as hostile in a subsequent task. This automatic stereotyping effect was found even among people who were nonprejudiced, as measured with the Modern Racism Scale. These results, however, do not suggest that prejudice and discrimination are inevitable under all circumstances. If people are motivated and have cognitive resources available, they can still engage in controlled processing to regulate these automatic tendencies. In a subsequent study, participants described characteristics of African-Americans. This task involved controlled processing. Participants had the time and energy to respond as they saw fit. Even though all participants were aware of negative African-American stereotypes (as demonstrated in the first study), nonprejudiced participants listed fewer negative characteristics than prejudiced participants. Collectively, these results suggest that although nonprejudiced people are aware of stereotypes, when controlled processing is possible they will take care not to use them; under such circumstances, prejudice and discrimination are not inevitable, contrary to your relative's argument.

5. Suppose a woman named Taylor was applying for a job at an accounting firm, and applicants had to complete a math test as part of the onsite interview process. If Taylor met her older male interviewer just prior to taking the math test and he (inappropriately) exclaimed, "You're Taylor? I was expecting, well, a man . . .," what impact might that have on Taylor's test performance, interview performance, and eventual likelihood of getting the job?

ANSWER: Taylor will likely experience stereotype threat during her math test, meaning she will become concerned that she will fulfill the stereotype that women are bad at math, and this concern will ultimately detract from her performance on the test, thus fulfilling the stereotype after all. She may also struggle during the interview if she believes that her interviewer is biased against her or if her interviewer is in fact biased against her, treating her differently than he would treat male applicants for the job. This may result in a self-fulfilling prophecy, wherein Taylor and/or her interviewer expects her to do poorly, causing her to do poorly and costing her the job.

6. Suppose you are a social psychologist and have been hired to help reduce prejudice and discrimination among students of different races, classes, cultures, and sexual orientations in a school system. What might you suggest in addressing this concern?

ANSWER: According to the contact hypothesis, bringing together students of different backgrounds is an important first step in reducing prejudice and discrimination. However, research suggests that simple contact between groups is not enough. For example, participants in the Robbers Cave experiment continued to display intergroup hostility after the competition phase, when the groups were brought together under friendlier circumstances. Additional conditions must be met for contact to work. Members of each group must have equal status. Teachers and administrators must not favor one group over another in the classroom or other institutional programs. Moreover, parents, teachers, and community members must support the contact and not endorse it begrudgingly. As the Robbers Cave experiment showed, superordinate goals that prompt cooperation between groups helps to reduce intergroup hostility and catalyzes the development of friendships. You may recommend that teachers institute a jigsaw classroom, in which students from different backgrounds are responsible for different parts of an assignment and must therefore work together to complete the assignment. In addition, one-on-one interactions help people to see others as more than just outgroup members. Assigning students from different backgrounds to work in pairs in the classroom or during other school activities could foster this kind of individualized contact.

CHAPTER 12

1. Open-plan offices, where large communal desks are used in place of private rooms or cubicles, are becoming increasingly popular. From the perspective of Zajonc's social facilitation theory, do you think open-plan offices are likely to facilitate or hinder performance and productivity? Why or why not? How might it depend on the type of work being conducted?

ANSWER: According to Zajonc's social facilitation theory, the presence of others tends to increase physiological arousal, which facilitates performance on well-learned, reflexive tasks but can impair performance on more complex tasks. Open-plan offices may therefore facilitate performance and productivity for employees who work at simple, repetitive tasks, whereas they may hinder performance for those who work on novel, unpredictable, and highly challenging tasks. For the latter group, private rooms may be more beneficial.

2. Can you think of any examples in your own life where groupthink has taken place? What factors contributed to groupthink in these situations? What kinds of safeguards could you put in place in similar future situations to promote better decision making?

ANSWER: Examples relevant to students could involve decisions made by a close group of friends, a student organization, a sports team, or a group working on a project together. Groupthink refers to the tendency for highly cohesive groups to make poor decisions when critical scrutiny of the issues at hand is subverted by social pressures to reach consensus. Factors that can contribute to groupthink include the presence of a strong leader, a sense of invulnerability and moral superiority, a narrow consideration of alternatives, and self-censorship of important information and conflicting viewpoints for fear of disrupting group harmony. Approaches that have been shown to reduce groupthink include designating "devil's advocates" to take alternative positions and point out weaknesses in the plan, welcoming outside input to protect against insularity, and having group leaders refrain from making their opinions or preferences known at the beginning of the discussion.

3. Suppose your company is trying to decide whether to make a risky new hire. Individually, most of the members of the hiring team lean toward hiring the candidate, as it could substantially increase revenues if it works out. When the hiring team gets together to discuss the potential hire, how might you predict that the attitudes of the individuals in the group will shift? What decision is likely to be made?

ANSWER: According to research on group polarization, group decisions tend to be more extreme than those made by individuals, and they tend to be extreme in whatever direction individuals are already leaning. In the hiring decision example, individuals are already leaning in favor of the risky hire, so the group discussion is likely to polarize individuals further in the direction of the hire and increase the likelihood that the hire will be made. Group polarization may be due in part to exposure to additional persuasive arguments from others and in part to the desire to measure up favorably in comparison with others (that is, to appear even more comfortable with risk than others if riskiness is valued).

4. In *The Prince*, Machiavelli argued that people gain power through deception, manipulation, coercion, and the use of fear tactics. How does this perspective compare with research findings about who rises to power?

ANSWER: According to the research, people typically gain power by having knowledge and expertise that is relevant to the goals and identity of the group, by possessing strong social skills and building cooperative alliances among group members, and by demonstrating generosity and fairness. These findings suggest that Machiavelli's perspective may apply on occasion but may not be generally accurate.

5. Do you think it's accurate to say that power corrupts? Why or why not? What factors influence the extent to which power leads to prosocial versus antisocial behavior?

ANSWER: Power involves the freedom to act on one's own wishes, without being constrained by others' wishes. According to the approach/inhibition theory of power, this lack of constraint and inhibition can lead high-power people to make impulsive decisions, stereotype others, feel less empathy, and engage in antisocial behaviors, such as sexual harassment and aggression. Low-power people, by contrast, need to be more cautious and socially attuned because their outcomes are more dependent on others. One factor that can counteract the disinhibiting effects of power is accountability, or a sense of responsibility toward others. Having a child, for example, can make powerful people less likely to engage in reckless behaviors. Another key factor is the extent to which a high-power individual has a communally oriented disposition to begin with: the acquisition of power can lead communally oriented individuals to behave more prosocially, rather than selfishly.

6. What does research on deindividuation show about why crime rates are so high on Halloween?

ANSWER: Deindividuation refers to a reduced sense of individual identity accompanied by diminished self-regulation that can occur in a large group. Deindividuation is fueled by anonymity, diffusion of responsibility, and high levels of arousal, all of which are common on Halloween, when people are disguised in masks and costumes, shrouded in darkness, and likely to move around in large packs. As a result, people might be more prone to engage in destructive and illegal behaviors that they would not otherwise engage in, such as vandalism, theft, or assault.

7. How could you use your knowledge of self-awareness theory to reduce cheating behavior on a test that relies on the honor system?

ANSWER: People are more likely to behave in line with their internal standards and values—and therefore behave more ethically—when they focus attention on themselves. One way to increase self-awareness and thereby reduce cheating could be to put a mirror in the testing room or have students walk by a mirror before taking the test. Another approach could be to display objects that look like eyes or faces in the room so students have the implicit sense that their behavior is being monitored. This approach has been shown to be effective for promoting contributions to an "honest box" in exchange for the use of shared resources, such as coffee in an office setting.

CHAPTER 13

1. Describe the culture of honor, and provide two pieces of evidence that support this characterization. What might be the origin of these cultural tendencies?

ANSWER: A culture of honor, such as the one in parts of the U.S. South, is characterized by strong concerns regarding reputation. Acts of aggression or violence may be used to avenge insults or other threats to one's honor. According to research covered in this chapter, homicides resulting from perceived insult are more common in the South than in the North, and people from the South have been found to react with greater emotion when insulted. This is not the case for other types of crimes. Cultures of honor are believed to grow out of societies that rely on animal herding as a main source of income, where a herder's entire livelihood would be lost if someone stole the herder's animals.

2. According to the research described in this chapter, what kinds of attitudes and behaviors are more likely among men who dehumanize women?

ANSWER: Men who show faster response times to pairings of the concept of "woman" with animal-related words, indicating implicit dehumanization, are more likely to report a willingness to sexually harass and rape women and to believe that women sometimes deserve to be raped.

3. Suppose you're the warden at a prison and can select the temperature setting for the master prison thermostat, but the thermostat doesn't have enough settings, forcing you to choose between an uncomfortably cold setting and an uncomfortably hot setting. Which should you choose, and why?

ANSWER: Given the strong connection between hot temperatures and aggressive behavior, you may want to set the thermostat a bit too cold rather than too hot. If the temperature is too hot, the prisoners might start to exhibit increasingly aggressive behavior (due, perhaps, to attributing their discomfort to their fellow inmates rather than to the prison's temperature), which could result in more fights and potentially spiral into a prison riot. It would be safer, at least in terms of levels of aggression, to err on the side of the prison being too cool.

4. Sometimes people respond to social rejection with physical aggression. How does the fundamental nature of our need for social connectedness help explain this tendency?

ANSWER: Humans are an inherently social species and have evolved a fundamental system to maintain social connectedness, which probably aided our early survival. Because social rejection was a kind of death sentence, we have a basic aversive response to it that activates a threat defense system. This system triggers responses normally cued by physical threats, such as surges in stress hormones, aroused fight-or-flight patterns, and increased defensive aggressive tendencies.

5. Suppose a friend said to you, "Well, men are just biologically hardwired to be more aggressive than women." How would you respond? What nuances might this perspective miss?

ANSWER: First, women do exhibit aggression, but in different ways than men do. Women more commonly express relational aggression, which involves emotional rather than physical forms of harm, such as spreading rumors and damaging a reputation. Second, although some biological factors dictate gender differences in aggression, such as testosterone levels and overall size and strength, cultural factors also play a role. From a very young age, male and female children are treated differently, and aggressive behavior is both more readily perceived and more encouraged among males than among females. Thus, any gender differences in physical aggression may not be purely biologically determined, but may be encouraged by cultural values as well.

6. What kinds of strategies have been shown to be most effective for reducing conflict and promoting peace, and why?

ANSWER: Face-to-face communication involving respectful dialogue and complex reasoning has been shown to facilitate conflict resolution by encouraging participants to find common ground and overcome misperceptions of the other group. It can also be helpful to understand that violence is often motivated not by blood lust but by a genuine sense of moral obligation, misguided as it may be; failure to recognize the motivation behind violence can lead to ineffective military interventions. Formal and informal reconciliation processes involving confession, apology, taking responsibility, and making reparations have been shown to be highly effective; for example, crime victims who participate in restorative justice programs report fewer thoughts of revenge.

CHAPTER 14

1. Someone might argue that as long as you're helping, your motives don't matter. Do you agree? Why or why not? In what situations might motives matter most?

ANSWER: There are three primary motives for helping. Two of them are egoistic (selfish): the desire for social rewards and the desire to reduce personal distress. The third is unselfish: empathic concern. Although the two egoistic motives can lead to helping behavior, they do so less consistently than empathic concern. Getting social rewards or reducing personal distress can be achieved many ways, not all of which involve helping; by contrast, empathic concern has been shown to consistently lead to helping, often at a cost to the self. A person who is motivated by social rewards and distress reduction may help only when rewards are available and when there are no other ways to reduce distress, but may be less likely to help when helping behavior would be anonymous or when it's possible to easily escape the situation.

2. Based on what you've learned about bystander intervention and diffusion of responsibility, what actions could you take to increase the likelihood that someone would help you in an emergency that happens in front of a large crowd?

ANSWER: People are less likely to help when other people are around, presumably because they believe that someone else will help. One way to reduce this diffusion of responsibility could be to single out one person and ask if that person can help you. People hesitate to help when they don't know whether a situation is actually an emergency and when they don't know what to do to help. To address this concern, you could clarify the situation by explicitly calling out and being specific about what you need people to do, such as helping you get up or calling an ambulance.

3. Research indicates that lower-class people tend to be more empathic and giving than upper-class people. What factors might explain this difference? How might they relate to what you learned about power and prosocial behavior?

ANSWER: Lower-class people are more attuned to those around them, in part because social attunement is necessary for adapting to unpredictable, stressful, and at times threatening environments. Upper-class people, by contrast, can be more independent from others because they enjoy greater resources and opportunities. This pattern is similar to that seen in the context of power. High-power people tend to be less empathic. Upper-class people may also be less likely to be regularly exposed to certain forms of suffering, but this can be remedied. Research suggests, for example, that it's possible to increase compassion and prosocial behavior in upper-class people by exposing them to film clips portraying the suffering of children living in poverty.

4. According to evolutionary theory, behaviors that optimize survival and reproduction are favored by natural selection and therefore more likely to persist. How, then, can we explain the evolution of altruism, which is by definition costly to the self?

ANSWER: There are a number of possible evolutionary explanations for altruism, including kin selection, whereby evolution and natural selection favor behaviors that increase the chances of survival of genetic relatives. Kin selection can explain altruism toward relatives, but not toward non-kin. One explanation for altruism toward non-kin is reciprocity, or helping others with the expectation that they will reciprocate in the future. Reciprocal altruism can reduce the likelihood of conflict and facilitate resource sharing.

5. After learning about research on gossip, have your feelings about this behavior changed? Under what circumstances might gossip serve a useful purpose?

ANSWER: Gossip is a communicative act in which someone comments on the reputation of another person who is not present. This communication can be beneficial when it lets people learn about whom to trust and whom to avoid. Research suggests that when people have the opportunity to gossip, they are consequently more cooperative than when they don't. This may be because the threat of gossip serves as a warning that one's reputation could suffer if one behaves selfishly. Not all types of gossip are beneficial, however; mean-spirited comments about someone's appearance will not promote cooperation or goodwill.

6. In what ways could the tit-for-tat strategy be relevant in your life, such as in a romantic relationship?

ANSWER: Tit-for-tat is a strategy to encourage mutual cooperation in the prisoner's dilemma game. This reciprocal strategy is cooperative, nonenvious, nonexploitable, forgiving, and easy to read. It helps maximize outcomes in potentially competitive situations that occur in real life. In the context of a romantic relationship, this strategy could involve being supportive and giving toward your partner initially, and continuing to do so as long as your partner is supportive and giving toward you, but not if your partner mistreats you.

APPLICATION MODULE 1: SOCIAL PSYCHOLOGY AND HEALTH

1. The experience of psychological stress typically triggers a host of physiological changes, including increased heart rate and blood pressure, sweating, and suppression of the immune system. When might these changes be helpful, and when are they more likely to be harmful?

ANSWER: The stress response evolved to help humans respond adaptively to threats in their environment and maximize their chance of survival. Increases in heart rate and blood pressure serve to distribute blood to appropriate muscle groups involved in fight-or-flight behavior, sweating helps regulate body temperature and may facilitate grasping motions, and the suppression of the immune system frees up resources for more pressing tasks. These physiological changes can be helpful for coping with short-term dangers, but when stress is chronic, they can lead to organ damage and the development of ulcers, heart disease, and cancer. Rumination, the tendency to think about a stressful event repeatedly, can contribute to chronic stress and increase health risks.

2. Who is more likely to suffer from health problems, a janitor or a Fortune 500 CEO, and why? How might each person's subjective construal of their position influence their health?

ANSWER: We might expect the janitor to be less healthy than the CEO, based on research showing that lower-SES individuals (having less family wealth and income, less education, and less prestigious jobs) are more likely to have health problems than higher-SES people. This difference can be explained by a number of factors, such as the presence of greater environmental toxins and less access to health care in lower-SES neighborhoods. Another explanation is that lower-SES people are more likely to feel they occupy a subordinate rank in society and therefore experience greater stress. In some cases, however, even someone in an objectively high position, like a CEO, may feel inferior relative to his or her peers and experience stress-related health issues as a result. By the same token, a janitor may enjoy high status within his or her community and experience good health as a result.

3. According to the tend-and-befriend theory, why might providing social support improve health?

ANSWER: When we tend to the needs of other people, the chemical oxytocin is released into our brain and bloodstream. Oxytocin has been shown to increase feelings of trust and love, and to reduce the stress hormone cortisol. Reduced cortisol levels can in turn benefit physical health. This research suggests that people may be able to improve their health by giving support to others, not just by receiving support.

4. Research indicates that optimistic people tend to enjoy better health. Can you conclude from these findings that becoming more optimistic will improve your health? Why or why not? If you were a researcher conducting a study on this topic, what other factors might you want to control for?

ANSWER: No, it is not possible to infer causality from a correlational study design. Optimistic people may enjoy better health in part because they have a better prognosis to begin with, among other reasons unrelated to optimism. As a researcher, it would be important to control for factors such as current health status, disease prognosis, and available financial and social resources. It would also be helpful to experimentally increase optimism in a group of randomly chosen participants and compare this group's health over time with that of a control group.

APPLICATION MODULE 2: SOCIAL PSYCHOLOGY AND EDUCATION

1. On the first day of summer volleyball camp, if the camp counselors are told that the campers in cabin 1 are on the verge of a growth and strength spurt, compared with the campers in cabin 2, what is likely to happen? How large will the effect of this manipulation probably be? What factors would increase or reduce the impact of this manipulation?

ANSWER: Based on the results of studies described in this module, the manipulated expectations should make the camp counselors expect and ultimately elicit stronger performance from the campers in cabin 1. However, the effect might not be particularly strong, as many follow-up studies have demonstrated. The manipulation would have a smaller impact if the counselors were given this information halfway through the summer, but the manipulation could have a larger impact if the campers in cabin 1 were low achieving and/or beginners at volleyball.

2. Suppose Alex is choosing between two math classes for next semester. She can take either Math 301, which is outside her comfort zone but would teach her new skills, or Math 210, which is well within her domain of knowledge, and she'd probably get an A. If Alex is an entity theorist, which class is she likely to select? Do you think entity versus incremental theorists differ in their overall GPA?

ANSWER: As an entity theorist, Alex is likely to choose Math 210, an opportunity to document her existing ability, which she probably thinks of as being relatively fixed. Entity theorists usually don't take on challenging opportunities for growth, because these might indicate lack of adequate skills. If Alex were instead an incremental theorist, she would probably choose the "stretch" class (Math 301) to help her learn new skills, which would be consistent with her concept of her ability. If this pattern played out repeatedly across a student's college years, you could perhaps predict a lower GPA for incremental theorists, who would take on more challenging opportunities for growth, registering for classes that don't guarantee high grades. However, research demonstrates that incremental theorists actually end up with higher grades than entity theorists, perhaps due to greater effort expended on academic work.

3. How would you change your college's Freshman Welcome program to help reduce achievement differences among students who are traditionally underrepresented in higher education (such as African-American and first-generation college students)?

ANSWER: The research reviewed in this module suggests several potentially powerful factors that could help underrepresented students perform at their highest potential. First, teaching new students that they are in control of their performance and that they can grow and change and improve their skill set and intelligence—essentially giving them an incremental mind-set about their abilities—could be very helpful. Second, assuring them that everyone has concerns about fitting in and finding friends on campus could help reduce the fear of not belonging, thus ultimately increasing their confidence and ability to achieve. Third, framing the college experience in a way that resonates with an interdependent mind-set (for example, focusing on community and collaboration) could help to make college a welcoming environment where their learning could be expected to increase their closeness to others.

APPLICATION MODULE 3: SOCIAL PSYCHOLOGY AND THE LAW

1. Suppose your laptop is stolen from your dorm room one night, and a few of your neighbors catch a glimpse of a suspect as they are arriving home from a party. Your residence hall advisor (RA) brings in your neighbors individually to ask them about the suspect they saw. How should your RA's questions be posed to get the most accurate eyewitness testimony possible?

ANSWER: Given the malleability of memory based on prompting, and given that the witnesses only caught a glimpse and may have been inebriated (and thus uncertain about what they saw), your RA should avoid leading the witnesses toward any specific details, such as asking any questions that suggest the perpetrator was of a specific gender, ethnicity, or stature and avoid planting any details about what the person was wearing or carrying. For instance, it would be less problematic to ask "Can you describe the person's clothes?" than to ask a detail-specific question like "Was the person wearing a blue sweatshirt?" Although it could be tempting to prod for such details, especially if another witness provided them initially, research shows that memory is highly suggestible and changeable and that asking leading questions can alter the witnesses' memory significantly.

2. If you are in charge of establishing rules for jury deliberation, what can you do to increase the likelihood that minority opinions will be adequately considered? What research findings would you cite to back up your decisions?

ANSWER: You can require a minimum of 12 rather than 6 jurors, based on research showing that individuals with minority opinions are more likely to stick to their convictions, rather than quickly giving in to the majority view, if they have an ally. Just based on numbers, the likelihood that more than one juror will hold a minority opinion is greater in a group of 12 than in a group of 6. You can also require unanimous verdicts. Research suggests that juries that don't have to reach a unanimous verdict spend significantly less time discussing the case. Once they reach the minimum number of jurors required to come to a verdict, they tend to end their discussion, and minority opinions are no longer considered.

3. Maria and Tanya are on the jury in a civil court case that has found the defendant guilty. They must now decide how the defendant should be punished. During their deliberations, it becomes clear that Maria is angered by the defendant's behavior, while Tanya feels sympathy. Using what you learned in this module, describe the differing attributions that might have led to Maria's anger compared with Tanya's sympathy. Which kind of punishment do you think each woman is likely to prefer?

ANSWER: According to research, the emotion an individual experiences in response to a criminal act, such as anger versus sympathy, drives the type of punishment that person prefers. The emotion depends on the attributions the juror makes about the defendant and his behavior. Maria, for example, is likely to experience anger to the degree that she believes (1) that the defendant is responsible for the crime and intended for the crime to occur and (2) that the crime reflects a stable part of the defendant's character. In contrast, Tanya is likely to experience sympathy to the degree that she believes (1) that situational factors, including the defendant's upbringing and past history, influenced the crime and (2) that the crime does not reflect a stable part of the defendant's character—that is, that the defendant has the potential to change. The emotion a juror experiences in response to the defendant and the crime influences the juror's sense of appropriate punishment. If a juror feels anger, like Maria, she is more likely to prefer just desserts punishment, wanting the defendant to suffer in proportion to the crime. In contrast, if a juror feels sympathy, like Tanya, she is more inclined to prefer deterrence, such as rehabilitation or engagement with the community, punishment that will deter the defendant from committing similar crimes in the future.

4. Thais and Elisa both get speeding tickets and are being punished by their parents. Thais's parents have a system of rules they follow for punishing all their children and calmly but firmly explain to Thais that she will be grounded for a month. Elisa's parents, in contrast, favor her brothers over her, punish their children inconsistently from week to week, and scream at Elisa for her mistake, but only ground her for a week. Who is likely to feel her punishment is more just, and why: Elisa, with her shorter sentence, or Thais, with her longer sentence?

ANSWER: Although Thais receives a harsher penalty, her experience fits better with the principles of procedural justice. Her parents demonstrate neutrality, have a trustworthy system in place whose guidelines they follow impartially and consistently, and treat her with politeness and respect. Thus, Thais should see her punishment as fair, if a little harsh. Elisa, though she is grounded for only a week, probably feels that her punishment is unjust, since her parents do not show neutrality (favoring her brothers), do not have a trustworthy or stable system of guidelines for punishment, and do not treat her with respect. Therefore, even though Thais gets the harsher punishment, she may feel it is more just than Elisa feels about hers.

GLOSSARY

A

actor-observer difference A difference in attribution based on who is making the causal assessment: the actor (who is relatively inclined to make situational attributions) or the observer (who is relatively inclined to make dispositional attributions).

actual self The self that people believe they are. *See also* ideal self, ought self.

affective forecasting Predicting future emotions, such as whether an event will result in happiness or anger or sadness, and for how long.

affect misattribution procedure (AMP) A priming procedure designed to assess people's implicit associations to different stimuli, including their associations to various ethnic, racial, occupational, and lifestyle groups.

agenda control Efforts of the media to select certain events and topics to emphasize, thereby shaping which issues and events people think are important.

altruism Prosocial behavior that benefits others without regard to consequences for oneself.

anxiety dimension of attachment A facet of attachment that captures the degree to which a person is worried about rejection and abandonment by relationship partners. *See also* avoidance dimension of attachment.

applied science Science or research concerned with solving important real-world problems. *See also* basic science.

approach/inhibition theory A theory maintaining that high-power individuals are inclined to go after their goals and make quick (and sometimes rash) judgments, whereas low-power individuals are more likely to constrain their behavior and pay careful attention to others.

attachment theory The idea that early attachments with parents and other caregivers can shape relationships for a person's whole life.

attitude An evaluation of an object in a positive or negative fashion that includes three components: affect, cognition, and behavior.

attitude inoculation Small attacks on people's beliefs that engage their preexisting attitudes, prior commitments, and background knowledge, enabling them to counteract a subsequent larger attack and thus resist persuasion.

attribution theory A set of concepts explaining how people assign causes to the events around them and the effects of these kinds of causal assessments.

audience characteristics Characteristics of those who receive a persuasive message, including need for cognition, mood, and age.

augmentation principle The idea that people will assign greater weight to a particular cause of behavior if other causes are present that normally would produce a different outcome. *See also* discounting principle.

authority Power that derives from institutionalized roles or arrangements.

availability heuristic The process whereby judgments of frequency or probability are based on how readily pertinent instances come to mind. *See also* representativeness heuristic.

avoidance dimension of attachment A facet of attachment that captures the degree to which a person is comfortable with intimacy and dependence on relationship partners. *See also* anxiety dimension of attachment.

B

base-rate information Information about the relative frequency of events or of members of different categories in a population.

basic science Science or research concerned with trying to understand some phenomenon in its own right, with a view toward using that understanding to build valid theories about the nature of some aspect of the world. *See also* applied science.

basking in reflected glory Taking pride in the accomplishments of other people in one's group, such as when sports fans identify with a winning team.

better-than-average effect The finding that most people think they are above average on various personality trait and ability dimensions.

bottom-up processing "Data-driven" mental processing, in which an individual forms conclusions based on the stimuli encountered in the environment. *See also* top-down processes.

broaden-and-build hypothesis The idea that positive emotions broaden thoughts and actions, helping people build social resources.

bystander intervention Assistance given by a witness to someone in need.

C

causal attribution Linking an event to a cause, such as inferring that a personality trait is responsible for a behavior.

central route A route to persuasion wherein people think carefully and deliberately about the content of a persuasive message, attending to its logic and the strength of its arguments, as well as to related evidence and principles. *See also* peripheral route.

cognitive dissonance theory The theory that inconsistency between a person's thoughts, sentiments, and actions creates an aversive emotional state (dissonance) that leads to efforts to restore consistency.

communal relationship A relationship in which the individuals feel a special responsibility for one another and give and receive according to the principle of need. Such relationships are often long term. *See also* exchange relationship.

comparison level Expectations people have about what they think they deserve or expect to get out of a relationship.

comparison level for alternatives Expectations people have about what they can get out of available, alternative relationships.

complementarity The tendency for people to seek out others with characteristics that are different from, and complement, their own.

compliance Responding favorably to an explicit request by another person.

confirmation bias The tendency to test a proposition by searching for evidence that would support it.

conformity Changing one's behavior or beliefs in response to explicit or implicit pressure (real or imagined) from others.

consensus A type of covariation information: whether most people would behave the same way or differently in a given situation. *See also* consistency, distinctiveness.

consistency A type of covariation: whether an individual behaves the same way or differently in a given situation on different occasions. *See also* consensus, distinctiveness.

construal One's interpretation of or inference about the stimuli or situations that one confronts.

construal level theory A theory about the relationship between temporal distance (and other kinds of distance) and abstract or concrete thinking: psychologically distant actions and events are thought about in abstract terms; actions and events that are close at hand are thought about in concrete terms.

contact hypothesis The proposition that prejudice can be reduced by putting members of majority and minority groups in frequent contact with one another.

contingencies of self-worth A perspective maintaining that people's self-esteem is contingent on the successes and failures in domains on which they have based their self-worth.

control condition A condition comparable to the experimental condition in every way except that it lacks the one ingredient hypothesized to produce the expected effect on the dependent variable.

correlational research Research that involves measuring two or more variables and assessing whether there is a relationship between them.

counterfactual thinking Thoughts of what might have, could have, or should have happened "if only" something had occurred differently.

covariation principle The idea that behavior should be attributed to potential causes that occur along with the observed behavior.

D

culture of honor A culture defined by its members' strong concerns about their own and others' reputations, leading to sensitivity to insults and a willingness to use violence to avenge any perceived wrong.

death-qualified jury A jury from which prospective jurors who would never recommend the death penalty have been excluded.

debriefing In preliminary versions of an experiment, asking participants directly if they understood the instructions, found the setup to be reasonable, and so so. In later versions, debriefing is used to educate participants about the questions being studied.

deception research Research in which the participants are misled about the purpose of the research or the meaning of something that is done to them.

dehumanization The attribution of nonhuman characteristics and denial of human qualities to groups other than one's own.

deindividuation A reduced sense of individual identity accompanied by diminished self-regulation that can come over people when they are in a large group.

dependent variable In experimental research, the variable that is measured (as opposed to manipulated); it is hypothesized to be affected by manipulation of the independent variable.

descriptive norm The behavior exhibited by most people in a given context. *See also* prescriptive norm.

diffusion of responsibility A reduction of the sense of urgency to help someone in an emergency or dangerous situation, based on the assumption that others who are present will help.

discounting principle The idea that people will assign reduced weight to a particular cause of behavior if other plausible causes might have produced it. *See also* augmentation principle.

discrimination Favorable or unfavorable treatment of individuals based on their membership in a particular group.

display rule A culturally specific rule that governs how, when, to whom people express emotion.

dispositions Internal factors, such as beliefs, values, personality traits, and abilities, that guide a person's behavior.

distinctiveness A type of covariation information: whether a behavior is unique to a particular situation or occurs in many or all situations. *See also* consensus, consistency.

dominance Behavior enacted with the goal of acquiring or demonstrating power.

dominant response In a person's hierarchy of possible responses in any context, the response that person is most likely to make.

duration neglect Giving relative unimportance of the length of an emotional experience, whether pleasurable or unpleasant, in judging and remembering the overall experience.

E

effort justification The tendency to reduce dissonance by justifying the time, effort, or money devoted to something that turned out to be unpleasant or disappointing.

elaboration likelihood model (ELM) A model of persuasion maintaining that there are two different routes to persuasion: the central route and the peripheral route.

emotion A brief, specific response, both psychological and physiological, that helps people meet goals, many of which are social.

emotional amplification An increase in an emotional reaction to an event that is proportional to how easy it is to imagine the event not happening.

empathic concern Identifying with someone in need, including feeling and understanding what that person is experiencing, accompanied by the intention to help the person.

entity theory of intelligence The belief that intelligence is something people are born with and cannot change. *See also* incremental theory of intelligence.

equity theory The idea that people are motivated to pursue fairness, or equity, in their relationship. A relationship is considered equitable when the benefits are proportionate to the effort both people put into it.

ethnocentrism Glorifying one's own group while vilifying other groups.

evaluation apprehension People's concern about how they might appear in the eyes of others, or be evaluated by them.

exchange relationship A relationship in which individuals feel little responsibility toward one another; giving and receiving are governed by concerns about equity and reciprocity. Such relationships are usually short term. *See also* communal relationship.

experimental research In social psychology, research that randomly assigns people to different conditions, or situations, and that enables researchers to make strong inferences about why a relationship exists or how different situations affect behavior.

explanatory style A person's habitual way of explaining events, typically assessed along three dimensions: internal/external, stable/unstable, and global/specific.

external validity How well the results of an experiment generalize to contexts outside the conditions of the laboratory.

F

face The public image of ourself that we want others to believe.

field experiment An experiment conducted in the real world (not a lab), usually with participants who are not aware they are in a study of any kind.

fluency The feeling of ease (or difficulty) associated with processing information.

focal emotion An emotion that is especially common within a particular culture.

focalism A tendency to focus too much on a central aspect of an event while neglecting the possible impact of associated factors or other events.

foot-in-the-door technique A compliance approach that involves making an initial small request with which nearly everyone complies, followed by a larger request involving the real behavior of interest.

framing effect The influence on judgment resulting from the way information is presented, such as the order of presentation or the wording.

functional distance The influence of an architectural layout to encourage or inhibit certain activities, including contact between people.

fundamental attribution error The failure to recognize the importance of situational influences on behavior, along with the corresponding tendency to overemphasize the importance of dispositions on behavior.

G

Gestalt psychology Based on the German word *gestalt*, meaning "form" or "figure," an approach that stresses the fact that people perceive objects not by means of some automatic registering device but by active, usually nonconscious interpretation of what the object represents as a whole.

group polarization The tendency for group decisions to be more extreme than those made by individuals; whatever way the group as a whole is leaning, group discussion tends to make it lean further in that direction.

groupthink Faulty thinking by members of highly cohesive groups in which the critical scrutiny that should be devoted to the issues at hand is subverted by social pressures to reach consensus.

H

halo effect The common belief (accurate or not) that attractive individuals possess a host of positive qualities beyond their physical appearance.

heuristics Intuitive mental operations, performed quickly and automatically, that provide efficient answers to common problems of judgment.

hindsight bias People's tendency to be overconfident about whether they could have predicted a given outcome.

hostile aggression Behavior intended to harm another, either physically or psychologically, and motivated by feelings of anger and hostility. *See also* instrumental aggression.

hypothesis A prediction about what will happen under particular circumstances.

I

ideal self The self that embodies people's wishes and aspirations. *See also* actual self, ought self.

identifiable victim effect The tendency to be more moved by the vivid plight of a single individual than by a more abstract number of people.

ideomotor action The phenomenon whereby merely thinking about a behavior makes performing it more likely.

illusory correlation The belief that two variables are correlated when in fact they are not.

immune neglect The tendency for people to underestimate their capacity to be resilient in responding to difficult life events, which leads them to overestimate the extent to which life's problems will reduce their personal well-being.

implementation intention An "if-then" plan to engage in a goal-directed behavior ("then") whenever a particular cue ("if") is encountered.

implicit association test (IAT) A technique for revealing nonconscious attitudes toward different stimuli, particularly groups of people.

implicit attitude measure An indirect measure of attitudes that does not involve a self-report.

inclusive fitness According to evolutionary theory, the fitness of an individual is based on reproductive success and the passing of one's own genes and those of relatives to future generations.

incremental theory of intelligence The belief that intelligence is something people can improve by working at it. *See also* entity theory of intelligence.

independent (individualistic) culture A culture in which people tend to think of themselves as distinct social entities, tied to each other by voluntary bonds of affection and organizational memberships but essentially separate from other people and having attributes that exist in the absence of any connection to others. *See also* interdependent (collectivistic) culture.

independent variable In experimental research, the variable that is manipulated; it is hypothesized to be the cause of a particular outcome.

individuation An enhanced sense of individual identity produced by focusing attention on the self, which generally leads people to act carefully and deliberately and in accordance with their sense of propriety and values.

induced (forced) compliance Subtly compelling people to behave in a manner that is inconsistent with their beliefs, attitudes, or values in order to elicit dissonance and therefore a change in their original attitudes or values.

informational social influence The influence of other people that results from taking their comments or actions as a source of information about what is correct, proper, or effective. *See also* normative social influence.

informed consent A person's signed agreement to participate in a procedure or research study after learning all of its relevant aspects.

institutional review board (IRB) A committee that examines research proposals and makes judgments about the ethical appropriateness of the research.

instrumental aggression Behavior intended to harm another in the service of motives other than pure hostility (such as attracting attention, acquiring wealth, or advancing political or ideological causes). *See also* hostile aggression.

interdependent (collectivistic) culture A culture in which people tend to define themselves as part of a collective, inextricably tied to others in their group and placing less importance on individual freedom or personal control over their lives. *See also* independent (individualistic) culture.

internalization Private acceptance of a proposition, orientation, or ideology.

internal validity In experimental research, the likelihood that only the manipulated variable could have produced the results.

intervention An effort to change designed behavior.

investment model of commitment A model of interpersonal relationships maintaining that three determinants make partners more committed to each other: relationship satisfaction, few alternative partners, and investments in the relationship.

J

just world hypothesis The belief that people get what they deserve in life and deserve what they get.

K

kin selection An evolutionary strategy that favors the reproductive success of one's genetic relatives, even at a cost to one's own survival and reproduction.

L

Likert scale A numerical scale used to assess people's attitudes; a scale that includes a set of possible answers with labeled anchors on each extreme.

longitudinal study A study conducted over a long period of time with the same participants.

M

measurement validity The correlation between a measure and some outcome the measure is supposed to predict.

mere exposure effect The idea that repeated exposure to a stimulus, such as an object or a person, leads to greater liking of the stimulus.

message characteristics Aspects, or content, of a persuasive message, including the quality of the evidence and the explicitness of its conclusions.

metacognition Secondary thoughts that are reflections on primary thoughts (cognitions).

minimal group paradigm An experimental paradigm in which researchers create groups based on arbitrary and seemingly meaningless criteria and then examine how the members of these "minimal groups" are inclined to behave toward one another.

modern racism Prejudice directed at racial groups that exists alongside the rejection of explicitly racist beliefs.

moral foundations theory A theory proposing that there are five evolved, universal moral domains in which specific emotions guide moral judgments.

N

natural experiment A naturally occurring event or phenomenon having somewhat different conditions that can be compared with almost as much rigor as in experiments where the investigator manipulates the conditions.

naturalistic fallacy The claim that the way things are is the way they should be.

natural selection An evolutionary process that molds animals and plants so that traits that enhance the probability of survival and reproduction are passed on to subsequent generations.

negative state relief hypothesis The idea that people engage in certain actions, such as agreeing to a request, to relieve their negative feelings and feel better about themselves.

normative social influence The influence of other people that comes from the desire to avoid their disapproval and other social sanctions (ridicule, barbs, ostracism). *See also* informational social influence.

norm of reciprocity A norm dictating that people should provide benefits to those who benefit them.

O

obedience In an unequal power relationship, submitting to the demands of the person in authority.

open science Practices such as sharing data and research materials with anyone in the broader scientific community in an effort to increase the integrity and replicability of scientific research.

ought self The self that is concerned with the duties, obligations, and external demands people feel they are compelled to honor. *See also* actual self, ideal self.

outgroup homogeneity effect The tendency for people to assume that within-group similarity is much stronger for outgroups than for ingroups.

own-race identification bias The tendency for people to be better able to recognize and distinguish faces from their own race than from other races.

P

paired distinctiveness The pairing of two distinctive events that stand out even more because they occur together.

parental investment The evolutionary principle that costs and benefits are associated with reproduction and the nurturing of offspring. Because these costs and benefits are different for males and females, one gender will normally value and invest more in each child than will the other.

peripheral route A route to persuasion wherein people attend to relatively easy-to-process, superficial cues related to a persuasive message, such as its length or the expertise or attractiveness of the source of the message. *See also* central route.

personal distress A motive for helping others in distress that may arise from a need to reduce one's own distress.

pluralistic ignorance Misperception of a group norm that results from observing people who are acting at variance with their private beliefs out of a concern for the social consequences; those actions reinforce the erroneous group norm.

power The ability to control one's own outcomes and those of others; the freedom to act.

precarious manhood hypothesis The idea that a man's gender identity of strength and toughness may be lost under various conditions and that such a loss can trigger aggressive behavior.

prejudice An attitude or affective response (positive or negative) toward a group and its individual members.

prescriptive norm The way a person is supposed to behave in a given context; also called injunctive norm. *See also* descriptive norm.

prevention focus Self-regulation of behavior with respect to ought self standards; a focus on avoiding negative outcomes through avoidance-related behaviors. *See also* promotion focus.

primacy effect A type of order effect: the disproportionate influence on judgment by information presented first in a body of evidence. *See also* recency effect.

priming The presentation of information designed to activate a concept (such as a stereotype) and hence make it accessible. A prime is the stimulus presented to activate the concept in question.

prisoner's dilemma A situation involving payoffs to two people who must decide whether to cooperate or defect. In the end, trust and cooperation lead to higher joint payoffs than mistrust and defection.

procedural justice Assessments of whether the processes leading to legal outcomes are fair.

promotion focus Self-regulation of behavior with respect to ideal self standards; a focus on attaining positive outcomes through approach-related behaviors. *See also* prevention focus.

psychological stress The sense that challenges and demands surpass one's current capacities, resources, and energies.

R

random assignment Assigning participants in experimental research to different groups randomly, so they are as likely to be assigned to one condition as to another.

rape-prone culture A culture in which rape tends to be used as an act of war against enemy women, as a ritual act, or as a threat against women to keep them subservient to men.

reactance theory The idea that people reassert their prerogatives in response to the unpleasant state of arousal they experience when they believe their freedoms are threatened.

reactive devaluation Attaching less value to an offer in a negotiation once the opposing group makes it.

realistic group conflict theory A theory that group conflict, prejudice, and discrimination are likely to arise over competition between groups for limited resources.

recency effect A type of order effect: the disproportionate influence on judgment by information presented last in a body of evidence. *See also* primacy effect.

reciprocal altruism Helping others with the expectation that they will probably return the favor in the future.

reciprocal concessions technique A compliance approach that involves asking someone for a very large favor that will certainly be refused and then following that request with one for a smaller favor (which tends to be seen as a concession the target feels compelled to honor); also called door-in-the-face technique.

reflected self-appraisal A belief about what others think of one's self.

regression effect The statistical tendency, when two variables are imperfectly correlated, for extreme values of one of them to be associated with less extreme values of the other.

regression fallacy The failure to recognize the influence of the regression effect and to offer a causal theory for what is really a simple statistical regularity.

reliability The degree to which the particular way researchers measure a given variable is likely to yield consistent results.

replication Reproduction of research results by the original investigator or by someone else.

representativeness heuristic The process whereby judgments of likelihood are based on assessments of similarity between individuals and group prototypes or between cause and effect. *See also* availability heuristic.

reproductive fitness The capacity to pass one's genes on to subsequent generations.

reputation The collective beliefs, evaluations, and impressions people hold about an individual within a social network.

response latency The amount of time it takes to respond to a stimulus, such as an attitude question.

rumination The tendency to think about a stressful event repeatedly.

S

schema A knowledge structure consisting of any organized body of stored information that is used to help in understanding events.

scientific jury selection A statistical approach to jury selection whereby members of different demographic groups in the community are asked their attitudes toward various issues related to a trial, and defense and prosecuting attorneys try to influence the selection of jurors accordingly.

self-affirmation theory The idea that people can maintain an overall sense of self-worth following psychologically threatening information by affirming a valued aspect of themselves unrelated to the threat.

self-awareness theory A theory maintaining that when people focus their attention inward on themselves, they become concerned with self-evaluation and how their current behavior conforms to their internal standards and values.

self-censorship Withholding information or opinions in group discussions.

self-discrepancy theory A theory that behavior is motivated by standards reflecting ideal and ought selves. Falling short of these standards produces specific emotions: dejection-related emotions in the case of actual-ideal discrepancies and agitation-related emotions in the case of actual-ought discrepancies.

self-distancing The ability to focus on one's feelings from the perspective of a detached observer.

self-enhancement The desire to maintain, increase, or protect one's positive self-views.

self-esteem The overall positive or negative evaluation people have of themselves.

self-fulfilling prophecy The tendency for people to act in ways that bring about the very thing they expect to happen.

self-handicapping The tendency to engage in self-defeating behavior in order to have an excuse ready should one perform poorly or fail.

self-monitoring The tendency to monitor one's behavior to fit the current situation.

self-perception theory The theory that people come to know their own attitudes by looking at their behavior and the context in which it occurred and inferring what their attitudes must be.

self-presentation Presenting the person we would like others to believe we are.

self-regulation Processes by which people initiate, alter, and control their behavior in the pursuit of goals, including the ability to resist short-term rewards that thwart the attainment of long-term goals.

self-schema A cognitive structure, derived from past experience, that represents a person's beliefs and feelings about the self, both in general and in specific situations.

self-selection In correlational research, the situation in which the participant, rather than the researcher, determines the participant's level of each variable (for example, whether they are married or not, or how many hours per day they spend playing video games), thereby creating the problem that it could be these unknown other properties that are responsible for the observed relationship.

self-serving attributional bias The tendency to attribute failure and other bad events to external circumstances and to attribute success and other good events to oneself.

self-validation hypothesis The idea that feeling confident about our thoughts validates those thoughts, making it more likely that we'll be swayed in their direction.

self-verification theory The theory that people sometimes strive for stable, subjectively accurate beliefs about themselves because such self-views give them a sense of coherence and predictability.

sleeper effect An effect that occurs when a persuasive message from an unreliable source initially exerts little influence but later causes attitudes to shift.

social class The amount of wealth, education, and occupational prestige individuals and their families have.

social comparison theory The idea that people compare themselves with other people to obtain an accurate assessment of their own opinions, abilities, and internal states.

social exchange theory A theory based on the idea that how people feel about a relationship depends on their assessments of its costs and rewards.

social facilitation Initially a term for enhanced performance in the presence of others; now a broader term for the effect, positive or negative, of the presence of others on performance.

social identity theory The idea that a person's self-concept and self-esteem derive not only from personal identity and accomplishments, but also from the status and accomplishments of the various groups to which the person belongs.

social influence The many ways people affect one another, including changes in attitudes, beliefs, feelings, and behavior resulting from the comments, actions, or even the mere presence of others. *See also* informational social influence, normative social influence.

social intuitionist model of moral judgment The idea that people first have fast, emotional reactions to morally relevant events, which influence the way they reason to arrive at a judgment of right or wrong.

social loafing The tendency to exert less effort when working on a group task in which individual contributions cannot be monitored.

social psychology The scientific study of the feelings, thoughts, and behaviors of individuals in social situations.

social reward A benefit, such as praise, positive attention, something tangible, or gratitude, that may be gained from helping others and thus serves as a motive for altruistic behavior.

sociometer hypothesis The idea that self-esteem is an internal, subjective index or marker of the extent to which a person is included or looked on favorably by others.

source characteristics Characteristics of the person who delivers a persuasive message, such as attractiveness, credibility, and certainty.

spotlight effect People's conviction that other people are attending to them (to their appearance and behavior) more than they actually are.

statistical significance A measure of the probability that a given result could have occurred by chance.

status The outcome of an evaluation of attributes that produces differences in respect and prominence.

stereotype A belief that certain attributes are characteristic of members of a particular group.

stereotype threat The fear of confirming the stereotypes that others have about one's group.

subliminal Below the threshold of conscious awareness.

subtyping Explaining away exceptions to a given stereotype by creating a subcategory of the stereotyped group that can be expected to differ from the group as a whole.

superordinate goal A goal that transcends the interests of any one group and can be achieved more readily by two or more groups working together.

system justification theory The theory that people are motivated to see the existing sociopolitical system as desirable, fair, and legitimate.

T

terror management theory (TMT) The theory that people deal with the potentially crippling anxiety associated with the knowledge of the inevitability of death by striving for symbolic immortality through preserving valued cultural worldviews and believing they have lived up to the culture's standards.

theory A set of related propositions intended to describe some phenomenon or aspect of the world.

third variable A variable, often measured in correlational research, that can be the true explanation for the relationship between two other variables.

thought polarization hypothesis The hypothesis that more extended thought about a particular issue tends to produce a more extreme, entrenched attitude.

tit-for-tat strategy A strategy in the prisoner's dilemma game in which the player's first move is cooperative; thereafter, the player mimics the other person's behavior, whether cooperative or competitive. This strategy fares well when used against other strategies.

top-down processing "Theory-driven" mental processing, in which an individual filters and interprets new information in light of preexisting knowledge and expectations. *See also* bottom-up processing.

V

voir dire The portion of a trial in U.S. courts in which prospective jurors are questioned about potential biases and a jury is selected.

volunteerism Assistance a person regularly provides to another person or group with no expectation of compensation.

W

working self-concept A subset of self-knowledge that is brought to mind in a particular context.

REFERENCES

Aarts, H., & Dijksterhuis, A. (2003). The silence of the library: Environment, situational norm, and social behavior. *Journal of Personality and Social Psychology, 84,* 18–28.

Abell, G. O. (1981). Astrology. In G. O. Abell & B. Singer (Eds.), *Science and the paranormal: Probing the existence of the supernatural.* New York: Charles Scribner's Sons.

Abrams, D., Viki, G. T., Masser, B., & Bohner, G. (2003). Perceptions of stranger and acquaintance rape: The role of benevolent and hostile sexism in victim blame and rape proclivity. *Journal of Personality and Social Psychology, 84,* 111–125.

Acevedo, B. P., & Aron, A. (2009). Does a long-term relationship kill romantic love? *Review of General Psychology, 13,* 59–65.

Adler, N. E., Boyce, T., Chesney, M. A., Cohen, S., Folkman, S., Kahn, R. L., et al. (1994). Socioeconomic status and health: The challenge of the gradient. *American Psychologist, 49,* 15–24.

Agnew, C. R., Van Lange, P. A. M., Rusbult, C. E., & Langston, C. A. (1998). Cognitive interdependence: Commitment and the mental representation of close relationships. *Journal of Personality and Social Psychology, 74,* 939–954.

Ahmed, A., & Salas, O. (2011). Implicit influence of Christian representations on dictator and prisoner's dilemma game decisions. *Journal of Socio-Economics, 40,* 242–246.

Ainsworth, M. D. S. (1993). Attachment as related to mother-infant interaction. *Advances in Infancy Research, 8,* 1–50.

Ainsworth, M. D. S., Blehar, M., Waters, E., & Wall, S. (1978). *Patterns of attachment.* Hillsdale, NJ: Erlbaum.

Ajzen, I. (1977). Intuitive theories of events and the effects of base-rate information on prediction. *Journal of Personality and Social Psychology, 35,* 303–314.

Ajzen, I. (1987). Attitudes, traits, and actions: Dispositional prediction of behavior in personality and social psychology. In L. Berkowitz (Ed.), *Advances in experimental social psychology* (Vol. 20, pp. 1–63). San Diego, CA: Academic Press.

Akerlof, G. A., Yellen, J. L., & Katz, M. L. (1996). An analysis of out-of-wedlock childbearing in the United States. *Quarterly Journal of Economics, 111,* 277–317.

Akhtar, O., & Wheeler, S. C. (2016). Belief in the immutability of attitudes both increases and decreases advocacy. *Journal of Personality and Social Psychology, 111,* 475–492.

Aknin, L. B., Barrington-Leigh, C. P., Dunn, E. W., Helliwell, J. F., Burns, J., Biswas-Diener, R., et al. (2013). Prosocial spending and well-being: Cross-cultural evidence for a psychological universal. *Journal of Personality and Social Psychology, 104*(4), 635–652.

Albarracin, D., Kumkale, G. T., & Poyner-Del Vento, P. (2017). How people can become persuaded by weak messages presented by credible communicators: Not all sleeper effects are created equal. *Journal of Experimental Social Psychology, 68,* 171–180.

Aldag, R. J., & Fuller, S. R. (1993). Beyond fiasco: A reappraisal of the groupthink phenomenon and a new model of group decision processes. *Psychological Bulletin, 113,* 533–552.

Alicke, M. D., & Govorun, O. (2005). The better-than-average effect. In M. D. Alicke, D. A. Dunning, & J. I. Krueger (Eds.), *The self in social judgment* (pp. 85–106). New York: Psychology Press.

Allan, G. A. (1979). *A sociology of friendship and kinship.* London: Allen & Unwin.

Allcott, H., & Gentzkow, M. (2017). Social media and fake news in the 2016 election. *Journal of Economic Perspectives, 31*(2), 211–236.

Allee, W. C., & Masure, R. H. (1936). A comparison of maze behavior in paired and isolated shell-parakeets (*Melopsittacus undulatus Shaw*) in a two-alley problem box. *Journal of Comparative Psychology, 3,* 159–182.

Allen, M., Emmers-Sommer, T. M., Gebhardt, L., & Giery, M. (1995). Pornography and rape myth acceptance. *Journal of Communication, 45,* 5–26.

Allen, V. L., & Wilder, D. A. (1979). Group categorization and attribution of belief similarity. *Small Group Behavior, 10,* 73–80.

Allport, F. H. (1920). The influence of the group upon association and thought. *Journal of Experimental Psychology, 3,* 159–182.

Alluisi, E. A., & Adams, O. S. (1962). Predicting letter preferences: Aesthetics and filtering in man. *Perceptual and Motor Skills, 14,* 123–131.

Alter, A. L., Oppenheimer, D. M., & Epley, N. (2013). Disfluency prompts analytic thinking—but not always greater accuracy: Response to Thompson et al. (2013). *Cognition, 128,* 252–255.

Alter, A. L., Oppenheimer, D. M., Epley, N., & Eyre, R. N. (2007). Overcoming intuition: Metacognitive difficulty activates analytic reasoning. *Journal of Experimental Psychology: General, 136,* 569–576.

Alterovitz, S. S., & Mendelsohn, G. A. (2009). Partner preferences across the life span: Online dating by older adults. *Psychology and Aging, 24*(2), 513–517.

Amato, P. R., & Keith, B. (1991). Parental divorce and well-being of children. *Psychological Bulletin, 110,* 26–46.

Ambady, N., Hallahan, M., & Conner, B. (1999). Accuracy of judgments of sexual orientation from thin slices of behavior. *Journal of Personality and Social Psychology, 77*(3), 538–547.

Ambady, N., Hallahan, M., & Rosenthal, R. (1995). On judging and being judged in zero-acquaintance situations. *Journal of Personality and Social Psychology, 69,* 518–529.

Ambady, N., & Rosenthal, R. (1993). Haifa minute: Predicting teacher evaluations from thin slices of nonverbal behavior and physical attractiveness. *Journal of Personality and Social Psychology, 64,* 431–441.

Amodio, D. M., & Devine, P. G. (2006). Stereotyping and evaluation in implicit race bias: Evidence for independent constructs and unique effects on behavior. *Journal of Personality and Social Psychology, 91,* 652–661.

Andersen, S. M., & Ross, L. (1984). Self-knowledge and social influence I: The impact of cognitive/affective and behavioral data. *Journal of Personality and Social Psychology, 46,* 280–293.

Anderson, C., & Brown, C. E. (2010). The functions and dysfunctions of hierarchies. *Review of Organizational Behavior, 30,* 55–89.

Anderson, C., Hildreth, J. A. D., & Howland, L. (2015). Is the desire for status a fundamental human motive? A review of the empirical literature. *Psychological Bulletin, 14,* 574–601.

Anderson, C., John, O. P., Keltner, D., & Kring, A. (2001). Social status in naturalistic face-to-face groups: Effects of personality and physical attractiveness in men and women. *Journal of Personality and Social Psychology, 81,* 1108–1129.

Anderson, C., & Kilduff, G. J. (2009). Why do dominant personalities attain influence in face-to-face groups? The competence-signaling effects of trait dominance. *Journal of Personality and Social Psychology, 96,* 491–503.

Anderson, C. A. (1987). Temperature and aggression: Effects on quarterly, yearly, and city rates of violent and nonviolent crime. *Journal of Personality and Social Psychology, 52,* 1161–1173.

Anderson, C. A. (1989). Temperature and aggression: Ubiquitous effects of heat on occurrences of human violence. *Psychological Bulletin, 106,* 74–96.

Anderson, C. A. (1991). How people think about causes: Examination of the typical phenomenal organization of attributions for success and failure. *Social Cognition, 9,* 295–329.

Anderson, C. A., & Bushman, B. J. (2001). Effects of violent video games on aggressive behavior, aggressive cognition, aggressive affect, physiological arousal, and prosocial behavior: A meta-analytic review of the scientific literature. *Psychological Science, 12,* 353–359.

Anderson, C. A., Bushman, B. J., Bartholow, B. D., Cantor, J., Christakis, D., Coyne, S. M., et al. (2017). Screen violence and youth behavior. *Pediatrics, 140*(Supp. 2), S142–S147.

Anderson, C. A., & DeLisi, M. (2011). Implications of global climate change for violence in developed and developing countries. In J. Forgas, A. Kruglanski, & K. Williams (Eds.), *The Psychology of Social Conflict and Aggression* (pp. 249–265). New York: Psychology Press.

Anderson, C. A., & Deuser, W. E. (1993). The primacy of control in causal thinking and attributional style: An attributional functionalism perspective. In G. Weary, F. Gleicher, & K. L. Marsh (Eds.), *Control motivation and social cognition* (pp. 94–121). New York: Springer-Verlag.

Anderson, C. A., John, O. P., & Keltner, D. (2012). The personal sense of power: An interactionist approach. *Journal of Personality, 80,* 313–344.

Anderson, C. A., Krull, D. S., & Weiner, B. (1996). Explanations: Processes and consequences. In E. T. Higgins & A. W. Kruglanski (Eds.), *Social psychology: Handbook of basic principles* (pp. 271–296). New York: Guilford Press.

Anderson, C. A., Sakamoto, A., Gentile, D. A., Ihori, N., Shibuya, A., Yukawa, S., et al. (2008). Longitudinal effects of violent videogames aggression in Japan and the United States, *Pediatrics, 122,* e1067–e1072.

Anderson, C. A., Shibuya, A., Ihori, N., Swing, E. L., Bushman, B. J., Sakamoto, et al. (2010). Violent video game effects on aggression, empathy, and prosocial behavior in Eastern and Western countries. *Psychological Bulletin, 136,* 151–173. doi:10.1037/a0018251

Anderson, J. L., Crawford, C. B., Nadeau, J., & Lindberg, T. (1992). Was the Duchess of Windsor right? A cross-cultural review of the socioecology of ideals of female body shape. *Ethology and Sociobiology, 13,* 197–227.

Andrade, E. B., & Ho, T. (2007). How is the boss's mood today?: I want a raise. *Psychological Science, 18*(8), 668–671.

Antill, J. K. (1983). Sex role complementarity versus similarity in married couples. *Journal of Personality and Social Psychology, 45,* 145–155.

Archer, J. (2006). Cross-cultural differences in physical aggression between partners: A social-role analysis. *Personality and Social Psychology Review, 10,* 133–153.

Archer, J. (2009). Does sexual selection explain human sex differences in aggression? *Behavioral and Brain Sciences, 32*(3–4), 249–311.

Arden, R., Gottfredson, L. S., Miller, G., & Pierce, A. (2008). Intelligence and semen quality are positively correlated [Electronic version]. *Intelligence.* Retrieved from 10.1016/j.intell.2008.11.001

Argyle, M. (1999). Causes and correlates of happiness. In D. Kahneman, E. Diener, & N. Schwarz (Eds.), *Well-being: The foundations of hedonic psychology* (pp. 353–373). New York: Russell Sage.

Arkin, R. M., & Baumgardner, A. H. (1985). Basic issues in attribution theory and research. In J. H. Harvey & G. Weary (Eds.), *Self-handicapping* (pp. 169–202). New York: Academic Press.

Arndt, J., Schimel, J., & Goldenberg, J. L. (2003). Death can be good for your health: Fitness intentions as a proximal and distal defense against mortality salience. *Journal of Applied Social Psychology, 33,* 1726–1746.

Aron, A., & Aron, E. N. (1997). Self-expansion motivation and including the other in self. In S. Duck (Ed.), *Handbook of personal relationships: Theory, research, and interventions* (2nd ed., pp. 251– 270). Chichester, England: Wiley.

Aron, A., Aron, E. N., & Allen, J. (1989). *The motivation for unrequited love: A self-expansion perspective.* Paper presented at the International Conference on Personal Relationships, Iowa City, IA.

Aron, A., Aron, E. N., Tudor, M., & Nelson, G. (1991). Close relationships as including other in self. *Journal of Personality and Social Psychology, 60,* 241–253.

Aron, A., & Fraley, B. (1999). Relationship closeness as including other in the self: Cognitive underpinnings and measures. *Social Cognition, 17,* 140–160.

Aron, A., Norman, C. C., Aron, E. N., McKenna, C., & Heyman, R. E. (2000). Couples' shared participation in novel and arousing activities and experienced relationship quality. *Journal of Personality and Social Psychology, 78,* 273–284.

Aronson, E. (1969). The theory of cognitive dissonance: A current perspective. In L. Berkowitz (Ed.), *Advances in experimental social psychology* (Vol. 4, pp. 1–34). New York: Academic Press.

Aronson, E., & Carlsmith, J. M. (1963). Effect of severity of threat in the devaluation of forbidden behavior. *Journal of Abnormal and Social Psychology, 66,* 584–588.

Aronson, E., Ellsworth, P. C., Carlsmith, J. M., & Gonzalez, M. H. (1990). *Methods of research in social psychology* (2nd ed.). New York: McGraw-Hill.

Aronson, E., Fried, C., & Stone, J. (1991). Overcoming denial and increasing the intention to use condoms through the induction of hypocrisy. *American Journal of Public Health, 81,* 1636–1638.

Aronson, E., & Mills, J. (1959). The effect of severity of initiation on liking for a group. *Journal of Abnormal and Social Psychology, 59,* 177–181.

Aronson, E., Stephan, C., Sikes, J., Blaney, N., & Snapp, M. (1978). *The jigsaw classroom.* Beverly Hills, CA: Sage.

Aronson, E., & Thibodeau, R. (1992). The jigsaw classroom: A co-operative strategy for reducing prejudice. In J. Lynch,

C. Modgil, & S. Modgil (Eds.), *Cultural diversity in the schools* (pp. 110–118). London: Falmer Press.

Aronson, J. M., Lustina, M. J., Good, C., Keough, K., Steele, C. M., & Brown, J. (1999). When white men can't do math: Necessary and sufficient factors in stereotype threat. *Journal of Experimental Social Psychology, 35*, 29–46.

Arriaga, X. B., Kumashiro, M., Simpson, J. A., & Overall, N. C. (2018). Revising working models across time: Relationship situations that enhance attachment security. *Personality and Social Psychology Review, 22*(1), 71–96.

Asch, S. E. (1946). Forming impressions on personality. *Journal of Abnormal and Social Psychology, 41*, 258–290.

Asch, S. E. (1951). Effects of group pressure upon the modification and distortion of judgments. In G. Guetzkow (Ed.), *Groups, leadership, and men* (pp. 177–190). Pittsburgh, PA: Carnegie Press.

Asch, S. E. (1952). *Social psychology.* Englewood Cliffs, NJ: Prentice-Hall.

Asch, S. E. (1956). Studies of independence and conformity: A minority of one against a unanimous majority. *Psychological Monographs, 70* (Whole No. 416).

Asch, S. E., & Zukier, H. (1984). Thinking about persons. *Journal of Personality and Social Psychology, 46*, 1230–1240.

Asendorpf, J. B., Penke, L., & Back, M. D. (2011). From dating to mating and relating: Predictors of initial and long-term outcomes of speed-dating in a community sample. *European Journal of Personality, 25*(1), 16–30.

Ashburn-Nardo, L., Voils, C. I., & Monteith, M. J. (2001). Implicit associations as the seeds of intergroup bias: How easily do they take root? *Journal of Personality and Social Psychology, 81*, 789–799.

Aspinwall, L. G., & Taylor, S. E. (1993). Effects of social comparison direction, threat and self-esteem on affect, evaluation, and expected success. *Journal of Personality and Social Psychology, 64*, 708–722.

Axelrod, R. (1984). *The evolution of cooperation.* New York: Basic Books.

Ayduk, O., Downey, G., Testa, A., Yen, Y., & Shoda, Y. (1999). Does rejection elicit hostility in rejection sensitive women? *Social Cognition, 17*, 245–271.

Ayduk, O., Gyurak, A., & Luerssen, A. (2008). Individual differences in the rejection-aggression link in the hot sauce paradigm: The case of rejection sensitivity. *Journal of Experimental Social Psychology, 44*, 775–782.

Ayduk, O., & Kross, E. (2008). Enhancing the pace of recovery: Differential effects of analyzing negative experiences from a self-distanced vs. self-immersed perspective on blood pressure reactivity. *Psychological Science, 19*, 229–231.

Bachorowski, J. A., & Owren, M. J. (2001). Not all laughs are alike: Voiced but not unvoiced laughter readily elicits positive affect. *Psychological Science, 12*, 252–257.

Back, M. D., Stopfer, J. M., Vazire, S., Gaddis, S., Schmukle, S. C., Egloff, B., & Gosling, S. D. (2010). Facebook profiles reflect actual personality, not self-idealization. *Psychological Science, 21*, 372–374.

Baek, Y. M. (2015). Political mobilization through social network sites: The mobilizing power of political messages received from SNS friends. *Computers in Human Behavior, 44* (March), 12–19.

Bai, Y., Maruskin, L. A., Chen, S., Gordon, A. M., Stellar, J. E., McNeil, G. D., et al. (2017). Awe, the diminished self, and collective engagement: Universals and cultural variations in the small self. *Journal of Personality and Social Psychology, 113*(2), 185–209. .

Bain, L. L., Wilson, T., & Chaikind, E. (1989). Participant perceptions of exercise programs for overweight women. *Research Quarterly for Exercise and Sport, 60*, 134–143.

Baker, L. R., McNulty, J. K., & Vanderdrift, L. E. (2017). Expectations for future relationship satisfaction: Unique sources and critical implications for commitment. *Journal of Experimental Psychology: General, 146*, 700–721.

Baldwin, M. W., Keelan, J. P. R., Fehr, B., Enns, V., & Koh-Rangarajoo, E. (1996). Social-cognitive conceptualizations of attachment working models: Availability and accessibility effects. *Journal of Personality and Social Psychology, 71*, 94–109.

Bamshad, M. J., & Olson, S. E. (2003, December). Does race exist? *Scientific American*, 78–85.

Banaji, M., Hardin, C. C., & Rothman, A. J. (1993). Implicit stereotyping in person judgement. *Journal of Personality and Social Psychology, 65*, 272–281.

Bandura, A. (1973). *Social learning theory.* Englewood Cliffs, NJ: Prentice Hall.

Bandura, A. (2004). Social cognitive theory for personal and social change by enabling media. In M. J. Singhal, E. M. Cody, E. M. Rogers, & M. Sabido (Eds.), *Entertainment education and social change: History, research and practice* (pp. 75–96). Mahwah, NJ: Erlbaum.

Banks, T., & Dabbs, J. M., Jr. (1996). Salivary testosterone and cortisol in delinquents and violent urban culture. *Journal of Social Psychology, 136*, 49–56.

Bapna, R., Ramaprasad, J., Shmueli, G., & Umyarov, A. (2016). One-way mirrors in online dating: A randomized field experiment. *Management Science, 62*, 3100–3122.

Bargh, J. A. (1996). Automaticity in social psychology. In E. T. Higgins & A. W. Kruglanski (Eds.), *Social psychology: Handbook of basic principles* (Vol. 1, pp. 1–40). New York: Guilford Press.

Bargh, J. A., Chaiken, S., Raymond, P., & Hymes, C. (1996). The automatic evaluation effect: Unconditional automatic activation with a pronunciation task. *Journal of Experimental Social Psychology, 31*, 104–128.

Bargh, J. A., Gollwitzer, P. M., Lee-Chai, A., Barndollar, K., & Trotschel, R. (2001). The automated will: Nonconscious activation and pursuit of behavioral goals. *Journal of Personality and Social Psychology, 81*, 1014–1027.

Bargh, J. A., & Pietromonaco, P. (1982). Automatic information processing and social perception: The influence of trait information presented outside of conscious awareness on impression formation. *Journal of Personality and Social Psychology, 43*, 437–449.

Bar-Hillel, M. (1980). The base-rate fallacy in probability judgments. *Acta Psychologica, 44*, 211–233.

Bar-Hillel, M., & Fischhoff, B. (1981). When do base-rates affect predictions? *Journal of Personality and Social Psychology, 41*, 671–680.

Barker, R. G., & Wright, H. F. (1954). *Midwest and its children: The psychological ecology of an American town.* New York: Row, Peterson and Company.

Baron, R. S., Vandello, J. A., & Brunsman, B. (1996). The forgotten variable in conformity research: Impact of task importance on social influence. *Journal of Personality and Social Psychology, 71*, 915–927.

Barsalou, L. W. (2008). Grounded cognition. *Annual Review of Psychology, 59*, 617–645.

Bar-Tal, D. (1990). Causes and consequences of delegitimization: Models of conflict and ethnocentrism. *Journal of Social Issues, 46*, 65–81.

Bar-Tal, D., & Saxe, L. (1976). Perceptions of similarly and dissimilarly attractive couples and individuals. *Journal of Personality and Social Psychology, 33*, 772–781.

Bartholomew, K., & Horowitz, L. M. (1991). Attachment styles among young adults: A test for a four-category model. *Journal of Personality and Social Psychology, 61*, 226–244.

Bartholow, B. D., & Anderson, C. A. (2002). Effects of violent videogames on aggressive behavior: Potential sex differences. *Journal of Experimental Social Psychology, 38*, 283–290.

Bartholow, B. D., Anderson, C. A., Carnagey, N. L., & Benjamin, A. J. (2005). Interactive effects of life experience and situational cues on aggression: The weapons priming effect in hunters and non-hunters. *Journal of Experimental Social Psychology, 41*, 48–60.

Bartholow, B. D., Dickter, C. L., & Sestir, M. A. (2006). Stereotype activation and control of race bias: Cognitive control of inhibition and its impairment by alcohol. *Journal of Personality and Social Psychology, 90*, 272–287.

Bartlett, F. A. (1932). *Remembering: A study in experimental psychology.* Cambridge, England: Cambridge University Press.

Bartsch, R A., Judd, C. M., Louw, D. A., Park, B., & Ryan, C. S. (1997). Cross-national outgroup homogeneity: United States and South African stereotypes. *South African Journal of Psychology, 27*(3), 166–170.

Bartz, J. (2016). Oxytocin and the pharmacological dissection of affiliation. *Current Directions in Psychological Science, 25*, 104–110.

Bateson, M., Nettle, D., & Roberts, G. (2006). Cues of being watched enhance cooperation in a real-world setting. *Biology Letters, 2*(3), 412–414.

Batson, C. D., O'Quin, K., Fultz, J., Vanderplas, M., & Isen, A. (1983). Self-reported distress and empathy and egoistic versus altruistic motivation for helping. *Journal of Personality and Social Psychology, 45*, 706–718.

Batson, C. D., & Shaw, L. L. (1991). Evidence for altruism: Toward a pluralism of prosocial motives. *Psychological Inquiry, 2*, 107–122.

Bauer, M., Blattman, C., Chytilova, J., Henrich, J., Miguel, E., & Mitts., T. (2016). Can war foster cooperation? *Journal of Economic Perspectives, 30*(3), 249–274.

Baumann, J., & DeSteno, D. (2010). Emotion guided threat detection: Expecting guns where there are none. *Journal of Personality and Social Psychology. 99*(4), 595–610. doi:10.1037/a0020665

Baumeister, R. F. (1982). A self-presentational view of social interaction. *Psychological Bulletin, 91*, 3–26.

Baumeister, R. F. (1987). How the self became a problem: A psychological review of historical research. *Journal of Personality and Social Psychology, 52*, 163–176.

Baumeister, R. F., Bratslavsky, E., Finkenauer, C., & Vohs, K. D. (2001). Bad is stronger than good. *Review of General Psychology, 5*, 323–370.

Baumeister, R. F., & Leary, M. R. (1995). The need to belong: Desire for interpersonal attachments as a fundamental human motivation. *Psychological Bulletin, 117*, 497–529.

Beck, S. P., Ward-Hull, C. I., & McLear, P. M. (1976). Variables related to women's somatic preferences of the male and female body. *Journal of Personality and Social Psychology, 34*, 1200–1210.

Becker, E. (1973). *The denial of death.* New York: Simon & Schuster.

Beckman, L. (1970). Effects of students' performance on teachers' and observers' attributions of causality. *Journal of Educational Psychology, 61*, 76–82.

Bell, B. E., & Loftus, E. F. (1989). Trivial persuasion in the courtroom: The power of (a few) minor details. *Journal of Personality and Social Psychology, 56*, 669–679.

Bell, S. T., Kuriloff, P. J., & Lottes, I. (1994). Understanding attributions of blame in stranger-rape and date-rape situations: An examination of gender, race, identification, and students' social perceptions of rape victims. *Journal of Applied Social Psychology, 24*, 1719–1734.

Belsky, G., & Gilovich, T. (1999). *Why smart people make big money mistakes, and how to correct them.* New York: Simon & Schuster.

Bem, D. J. (1967). Self-perception: An alternative interpretation of cognitive dissonance phenomena. *Psychological Review, 74*, 183–200.

Bem, D. J. (1972). Self-perception theory. In L. Berkowitz (Ed.), *Advances in experimental social psychology* (Vol. 6, pp. 1–62). New York: Academic Press.

Bem, S. L. (1993). *The lenses of gender: Transforming the debate on sexual inequality.* New Haven, CT: Yale University Press.

Benet-Martinez, V., Leu, J., Lee, F., & Morris, M. W. (2002). Negotiating biculturalism: Cultural frame switching in biculturals with oppositional versus compatible cultural identities. *Journal of Cross-Cultural Psychology, 33*, 492–516.

Ben-Zeev, T., Fein, S., & Inzlicht, M. (2005). Arousal and stereotype threat. *Journal of Experimental Social Psychology, 41*, 174–181.

Berger, J., Meredith, M., & Wheeler, S. C. (2008). Contextual priming: Where people vote affects how they vote. *Proceedings of the National Academy of Sciences of the USA, 105*(26), 8846–8849.

Berglas, S., & Jones, E. E. (1978). Drug choice as a self-handicapping strategy in response to non-contingent success. *Journal of Personality and Social Psychology, 36*, 405–417.

Berkman, L. F. (1995). The role of social relations in health promotion. *Psychosomatic Medicine, 57*, 245–254.

Berkman, L. F., & Syme, S. L. (1979). Social networks, host resistance, and mortality: A nine-year follow-up study of Alameda County residents. *American Journal of Epidemiology, 100*, 186–204.

Berkowitz, L. (1989). The frustration-aggression hypothesis: An examination and reformulation. *Psychological Bulletin, 106*, 59–73.

Berkowitz, L. (1993). *Aggression.* New York: McGraw-Hill.

Berkowitz, L., & LePage, A. (1967). Weapons as aggression-eliciting stimuli. *Journal of Personality and Social Psychology, 7*, 202–207.

Berman, M., Jonides, J., & Kaplan, S. (2008). The cognitive benefits of interacting with nature. *Psychological Science, 19*, 1207–1212.

Bernhardt, B. C., & Singer, T. (2012). The neural basis of empathy. *Annual Review of Neuroscience, 35*, 1–23.

Bernieri, F. J., Zuckerman, M., Koestner, R., & Rosenthal, R. (1994). Measuring person perception accuracy: Another look at self-other agreement. *Personality and Social Psychology Bulletin, 20*, 367–378.

Bernstein, I. H., Lin, T., & McClellan, P. (1982). Cross- vs. within-racial judgments of attractiveness. *Perception and Psychophysics, 32*, 495–503.

Berry, D. S., & McArthur, L. Z. (1986). Perceiving character in faces: The impact of age-related craniofacial changes in social perception. *Psychological Bulletin, 100*, 3–18.

Berry, D. S., & Zebrowitz-McArthur, L. (1986). Perceiving character in faces: The impact of age-related craniofacial changes in social perception. *Psychological Bulletin, 100*, 3–18.

Berscheid, E. (2010). Love in the fourth dimension. *Annual Review of Psychology, 61*, 1–25.

Berscheid, E., Dion, K., Walster, E., & Walster, G. W. (1971). Physical attractiveness and dating choice: A test of the matching hypothesis. *Journal of Experimental Social Psychology, 7*, 173–189.

Berscheid, E., & Reis, H. T. (1998). Attraction and close relationships. In D. T. Gilbert, S. T. Fiske, & G. Lindzey (Eds.), *The handbook of social psychology* (4th ed., Vol. 2, pp. 193–281). New York: McGraw-Hill.

Bersoff, D. N. (1987). Social science data and the Supreme Court: Lockhart as a case in point. *American Psychologist, 42*, 52–58.

Bessenoff, G. R., & Sherman, J. W. (2000). Automatic and controlled components of prejudice toward fat people: Evaluation versus stereotype activation. *Social Cognition, 18*, 329–353.

Bettencourt, B. A., Brewer, M. B., Croak, M. R., & Miller, N. (1992). Cooperation and the reduction of intergroup bias: The role of reward structure and social orientation. *Journal of Experimental Psychology, 28*, 301–319.

Biernat, M., Manis, M., & Kobrynowicz, D. (1997). Simultaneous assimilation and contrast effects in judgments of self and others. *Journal of Personality and Social Psychology, 73*, 254–269.

Black, M. C., Basile, K. C., Breiding, M. J., Smith, S .G., Walters, M. L., Merrick, et al. (2011). The National Intimate Partner and Sexual Violence Survey: 2010 summary report. Atlanta, GA: Centers for Disease

Control and Prevention, National Center for Injury Prevention and Control. http://www.cdc.gov/ViolencePrevention/pdf/NISVS_Report2010-a.pdf

Blackwell, L., Trzesniewski, K., & Dweck, C. S. (2007). Implicit theories of intelligence predict achievement across an adolescent transition: A longitudinal study and an intervention. *Child Development*, *78*, 246–263.

Blair, I. V., Judd, C. M., & Chapleau, K. M. (2004). The influence of Afrocentric facial features in criminal sentencing. *Psychological Science*, *15*, 674–679.

Blair, I. V., Judd, C. M., & Fallman, J. L. (2004). The automaticity of race and Afrocentric facial features in social judgments. *Journal of Personality and Social Psychology*, *87*, 763–778.

Blair, I. V., Judd, C., Sadler, M. S., & Jenkins, C. (2002). The role of Afrocentric features in person perception: Judging by features and categories. *Journal of Personality and Social Psychology*, *83*, 5–25.

Blair, J., Mitchell, D., & Blair, K. (2005). *The psychopath: Emotion and the brain*. Malden, MA: Blackwell Publishing.

Blanton, H., Buunk, B. P., Gibbons, F. X., & Kuyper, H. (1999). When better-than-others compare upward: Choice of comparison and comparative evaluation as independent predictors of academic performance. *Journal of Personality and Social Psychology*, *76*, 420–430.

Blanco, C., Grant, J., Petry, N. M., Blair Simpson, H., Alegria, A., Liu, S. M., & Hasin, D. (2008). Prevalence and correlates of shoplifting in the United States: Results from the National Epidemiological Survey on Alcohol and Related Conditions (NESARC). *American Journal of Psychiatry*, *165*(2008), 905–913.

Blanton, H., & Jaccard, J. (2008). Unconscious racism: A concept in pursuit of a measure. *Annual Review of Sociology*, *34*, 277–297.

Blascovich, J., Mendes, W. B., Hunter, S. B., & Salomon, K. (1999). Social "facilitation" as challenge and threat. *Journal of Personality and Social Psychology*, *77*, 68–77.

Blass, T. (1999). The Milgram paradigm after 35 years: Some things we now know about obedience to authority. *Journal of Applied Social Psychology*, *29*, 955–978.

Blass, T. (2000). *Obedience to authority: Current perspectives on the Milgram paradigm*. Mahwah, NJ: Erlbaum.

Blass, T. (2004). *The man who shocked the world: The life and legacy of Stanley Milgram*. New York: Basic Books.

Bless, H., Clore, G. L., Schwarz, N., Golisano, V., Rabe, C., & Wölk, M. (1996). Mood and the use of scripts: Does a happy mood really lead to mindlessness? *Journal of Personality and Social Psychology*, *71*(4), 665–679.

Block, J., & Robins, R. W. (1993). A longitudinal study of consistency and change in self-esteem from early adolescence to early adulthood. *Child Development*, *64*, 909–923.

Bodenhausen, G. V. (1988). Stereotypic biases in social decision making and memory: Testing process models of stereotype use. *Journal of Personality and Social Psychology*, *55*, 726–737.

Bodenhausen, G. V. (1990). Stereotypes as judgmental heuristics: Evidence of circadian variations in discrimination. *Psychological Science*, *1*, 319–322.

Bodenhausen, G. V., Macrae, C. N., & Sherman, J. W. (1999). On the dialectics of discrimination: Dual processes in social stereotyping. In S. Chaiken & Y. Trope (Eds.), *Dual process theories in social psychology* (pp. 271–290). New York: Guilford Press.

Boehm, C. (1999). *Hierarchy in the forest: The evolution of egalitarian behavior*. Cambridge, MA: Harvard University Press.

Boehm, J. K., Lyubomirsky, S., & Sheldon, K. M. (2011). A longitudinal experimental study comparing the effectiveness of happiness-enhancing strategies in Anglo Americans and Asian Americans. *Cognition & Emotion*, *25*(7), 1263–1272. doi.org/10.1080/02699931.2010.541227

Boice, R., Quanty, C. B., & Williams, R. C. (1974). Competition and possible dominance in turtles, toads, and frogs. *Journal of Comparative and Physiological Psychology*, *86*, 1116–1131.

Bolkan, S., & Andersen, P. T. (2009). Image induction and social influence: Explication and initial tests. *Basic and Applied Social Psychology*, *31*, 317–324.

Bond, M. H., & Cheung, T. (1983). College students' spontaneous self-concept. *Journal of Cross-Cultural Psychology*, *14*, 154–171.

Bond, R., & Smith, P. B. (1996). Culture and conformity: A meta-analysis of studies using Asch's line judgment task. *Psychological Bulletin*, *119*, 111–137.

Borgida, E., Conner, C., & Manteufel, L. (1992). Understanding living kidney donations: A behavioral decision-making perspective. In S. Spacapan & S. Oskamp (Eds.), *Helping and being helped*. Newbury Park, CA: Sage.

Bornstein, R. F. (1989). Exposure and affect: Overview and meta-analysis of research, 1968–1987. *Psychological Bulletin*, *106*, 265–289.

Bosson, J. K., & Vandello, J. A. (2011). Precarious manhood and its links to action and aggression. *Current Directions in Psychological Science*, *20*, 82–86.

Boster, F. J., & Mongeau, P. (1984). Fear-arousing persuasive messages. In R. N. Bostrom (Ed.), *Communication yearbook* (Vol. 8, pp. 330–375). Beverly Hills, CA: Sage.

Bowlby, J. (1969). *Attachment and loss, Vol. 1: Attachment*. New York: Basic Books.

Bowlby, J. (1973). *Attachment and loss, Vol. 2: Separation*. New York: Basic Books.

Bowlby, J. (1980). *Attachment and loss, Vol. 3: Loss, sadness and depression*. New York: Basic Books.

Bowlby, J. (1982). *Attachment and loss* (2nd ed., Vol. 1). New York: Basic Books.

Boyd, R., & Richerson, P. J. (1985). Frequency-dependent bias and the evolution of cooperation. In R. Boyd & P. J. Richardson (Eds.), *Culture and the evolutionary process* (pp. 204–240). Chicago: University of Chicago Press.

Boyden, T., Carroll, J. S., & Maier, R. A. (1984). Similarity and attraction in homosexual males: The effects of age and masculinity-femininity. *Sex Roles*, *10*, 939–948.

Brackett, M. A., Rivers, S. E. & Salovey, P. (2011), Emotional Intelligence: Implications for Personal, Social, Academic, and Workplace Success. *Social and Personality Psychology Compass*, *5*, 88–103. doi:10.1111/j.1751-9004.2010.00334.x

Bradbury, T. N., & Fincham, F. D. (1990). Attributions in marriage: Review and critique. *Psychological Bulletin*, *107*, 3–33.

Bradfield, A., & Wells, G. L. (2005). Not the same old hindsight bias: Outcome information distorts a broad range of retrospective judgments. *Memory and Cognition*, *33*, 120–130.

Brauer, M., Chambres, P., Niedenthal, P. M., & Chatard-Pannetier, A. (2004). The relationship between expertise and evaluative extremity: The moderating role of experts' task characteristics. *Journal of Personality and Social Psychology*, *86*, 5–18.

Brauer, M., & Er-rafiy, A. (2011). Increasing perceived variability reduces prejudice and discrimination. *Journal of Experimental Social Psychology*, *47*(5), 871–881.

Breckler, S. J. (1984). Empirical validation of affect, behavior, and cognition as distinct components of attitude. *Journal of Personality and Social Psychology*, *47*, 1191–1205.

Brehm, J. W. (1956). Post-decision changes in desirability of alternatives. *Journal of Abnormal and Social Psychology*, *52*, 384–389.

Breines, J. G., & Ayduk, O. (2015). Rejection sensitivity and vulnerability to self-directed hostile cognitions following rejection. *Journal of Personality*, *83*, 1–13.

Breines, J. G., & Chen, S. (2012). Self-compassion increases self-improvement motivation. *Personality and Social Psychology Bulletin*, *38*(9), 1133–1143. https://doi.org/10.1177/0146167212445599

Brendl, C. M., Higgins, E. T., & Lemm, K. M. (1995). Sensitivity to varying gains and losses: The role of self-discrepancies and event framing. *Journal of Personality and Social Psychology*, *69*, 1028–1051.

Brendl, C. M., Markman, A. B., & Messner, C. (2001). How do indirect measures of evaluation work? Evaluating the inference of prejudice in the implicit association test. *Journal of Personality and Social Psychology*, *81*, 760–773.

Brennan, K. A., Clark, C. L., & Shaver, P. R. (1998). Self-report measurement of adult attachment: An integrative overview. In J. A. Simpson & W. S. Rholes (Eds.), *Attachment theory and close relationships* (pp. 46–76). New York: Guilford Press.

Brewer, M. B. (1988). A dual process model of impression formation. In T. K. Srull & R. S. Wyer (Eds.), *Advances in social cognition*. Hillsdale, NJ: Erlbaum.

Brewer, M. B., & Brown, R. J. (1998). Intergroup relations. In D. T. Gilbert, S. T. Fiske, & G. Lindzey (Eds.), *The handbook of social psychology* (4th ed., Vol. 2, pp. 554–594). New York: McGraw-Hill.

Brewer, M. B., & Kramer, R. M. (1985). The psychology of intergroup attitudes and behavior. *Annual Review of Psychology*, *36*, 219–243.

Brewer, M. B., & Miller, N. (1984). Beyond the contact hypothesis: Theoretical perspectives on desegregation. In N. Miller & M. B. Brewer (Eds.), *Groups in contact: The psychology of desegregation* (pp. 281–302). Orlando, FL: Academic Press.

Brewer, M. B., & Miller, N. (1988). Contact and cooperation: When do they work? In P. Katz & D. Taylor (Eds.), *Eliminating racism: Profiles in controversy* (pp. 315–326). New York: Plenum Press.

Brewer, M. B., & Nakamura, G. V. (1984). The nature and functions of schemas. In R. S. Wyer & T. K. Srull (Eds.), *The handbook of social cognition* (Vol. 1). Hillsdale, NJ: Erlbaum.

Briggs, J. L. (1960). *Never in anger: Portrait of an Eskimo family*. Cambridge, MA: Harvard University Press.

Brigham, J. C. (1993). College students' racial attitudes. *Journal of Applied Social Psychology*, *23*, 1933–1967.

Brigham, J. C., Bennett, L., Meissner, C., & Mitchell, T. (2007). The influence of race on eyewitness memory. In R. C. L. Lindsay, D. F. Ross, D. J. Read, & M. P. Toglia (Eds.), *The handbook of eyewitness psychology*. Mahwah, NJ: Erlbaum.

Briñol, P., & DeMarree, K. G. (Eds.). (2012). *Social metacognition*. New York: Psychology Press.

Briñol, P., & Petty, R. E (2003). Overt head movements and persuasion: A self-validation analysis. *Journal of Personality and Social Psychology*, *84*, 1123–1139.

Briñol, P., & Petty, R. E. (2009). Source factors in persuasion: A self-validation approach. *European Review of Social Psychology*, *20*, 49–96.

Brockner, J. (1979). The effects of self-esteem, success-failure, and self-consciousness on task performance. *Journal of Personality and Social Psychology*, *37*, 1732–1741.

Broemer, P., & Diehl, M. (2003). What you think is what you get: Comparative evaluations of close relationships. *Personality and Social Psychology Bulletin*, *29*, 1560–1569.

Brosnan, S. F., & de Waal, F. B. M. (2003). Monkeys reject unequal pay. *Nature*, *425*, 297–299.

Brown, C., & Jantzi, A. (2010). Driving while black. https://courses2.cit.cornell.edu/sociallaw/student_projects/DrivingWhileBlack.htm

Brown, D. E. (1991). *Human universals*. New York: McGraw-Hill.

Brown, J. D. (1998). *The self*. New York: McGraw-Hill.

Brown, J. D., & Dutton, K. A. (1995). The thrill of victory, the complexity of defeat: Self-esteem and people's emotional reactions to success and failure. *Journal of Personality and Social Psychology*, *68*, 712–722.

Brown, K. T., Brown, T. N., Jackson, J. S., Sellers, R. M., & Manuel, W. J. (2003). Teammates on and off the field? Contact with Black teammates and the racial attitudes of White student athletes. *Journal of Applied Social Psychology*, *33*(7), 1379–1403.

Brown, R., & Hewstone, M. (2005). An integrative theory of intergroup contact. In M. P. Zanna (Ed.), *Advances in experimental social psychology* (Vol. 37, pp. 255–343). San Diego, CA: Academic Press.

Brown, S. L., Nesse, R. M., Vinokur, A. D., & Smith, D. M. (2003). Providing social support may be more beneficial than receiving it: Results from a prospective study of mortality. *Psychological Science*, *14*(4), 320–327.

Browning, C. R. (1992). *Ordinary men: Reserve police battalion 101 and the final solution in Poland*. New York: Aaron Asher.

Brownstein, A. L. (2003). Biased predecision processing. *Psychological Bulletin*, *129*, 545–568.

Brownstein, A. L., Read, S. J., & Simon, D. (2004). Bias at the race-track: Effects of individual expertise and task importance on pre-decision reevaluation of alternatives. *Personality and Social Psychology Bulletin*, *57*, 904–915.

Brumberg, J. J. (1997). *The body project: An intimate history of American girls*. New York: Random House.

Bureau of Justice Statistics. (2014). Correctional populations in the United States, 2013. Retrieved from https://www.bjs.gov/index.cfm?ty=pbdetail&iid=5177

Bureau of Justice Statistics. (2015). Federal sentencing disparity: 2005–2012. Retrieved from https://www.bjs.gov/content/pub/pdf/fsd0512_sum.pdf

Burger, J. M. (1981). Motivational biases in the attribution of responsibility for an accident: A meta-analysis of the defensive-attribution hypothesis. *Psychological Bulletin*, *90*, 496–512.

Burger, J. M. (2009). Replicating Milgram: Would people still obey today? *American Psychologist*, *64*, 1–11.

Burger, J. M., Girgis, Z. M., & Manning, C. C. (2011). In their own words: Explaining obedience to authority through an examination of participants' comments. *Social Psychological and Personality Science*, *2*, 460–466.

Burger, J. M., & Guadagno, R. E. (2003). Self-concept clarity and the foot-in-the-door procedure. *Basic and Applied Social Psychology*, *25*, 79–86.

Burger, J. M., Sanchez, J., Imberi, J. E., & Grande, L. R. (2009). The norm of reciprocity as an internalized social norm: Returning favors even when no one finds out. *Social Influence*, *4*, 11–17.

Burgess, E. W., & Wallin, P. (1953). *Engagement and marriage*. Philadelphia: Lippincott.

Burnstein, E. (2005). Kin altruism: The morality of biological systems. In D. M. Buss (Ed.), *The handbook of evolutionary psychology* (pp. 528–551). New York: Wiley.

Burnstein, E., Crandall, C., & Kitayama, S. (1994). Some neo-Darwinian decision rules for altruism: Weighing cues for inclusive fitness as a function of the biological importance of the decision. *Journal of Personality and Social Psychology*, *67*, 773–789.

Burnstein, E., Vinokur, A., & Trope, Y. (1973). Interpersonal comparison versus persuasive argumentation: A more direct test of alternative explanations for group-induced shifts in individual choice. *Journal of Experimental Social Psychology*, *9*, 236–245.

Burt, R., Kilduff, M., & Tasselli, S. (2013). Social Network Analysis: Foundations and Frontiers on Advantage, *Annual Review of Psychology*, *64*, 527–547.

Buss, D. M. (1984). Toward a psychology of person-environment (PE) correlation: The role of spouse selection. *Journal of Personality and Social Psychology*, *47*, 361–377.

Buss, D. M. (1989). Sex differences in human mate preference: Evolutionary hypothesis tested in 37 cultures. *Behavioral and Brain Sciences, 12,* 1–49.

Buss, D. M. (1994). *The evolution of desire: Strategies of human mating.* New York: Basic Books.

Byrne, D. (1961). Interpersonal attraction and attitude similarity. *Journal of Abnormal and Social Psychology, 62,* 713–715.

Byrne, D., Clore, G. L., & Smeaton, G. (1986). The attraction hypothesis: Do similar attitudes predict anything? *Journal of Personality and Social Psychology, 51,* 1167–1170.

Cacioppo, J. T., & Berntson, G. G. (1994). Relationship between attitudes and evaluative space: A critical review with emphasis on the separability of positive and negative substrates. *Psychological Bulletin, 115,* 401–423.

Cacioppo, J. T., Cacioppo, S., Gonzaga, G. C., Ogburn, E. L., & VanderWeele, T. J. (2012). Marital satisfaction and break-ups differ across on-line and off-line meeting venues. *Proceedings of the National Academy of Sciences of the USA, 110,* 10135–10140.

Cacioppo, J. T., Fowler, J. H., & Christakis, N. A. (2009). Alone in the crowd: The structure and spread of loneliness in a large social network. *Journal of Personality and Social Psychology, 97*(6), 977–991. doi:10.1037/a0016076

Cacioppo, J. T., & Gardner, W. L. (1999). Emotion. *Annual Review of Psychology, 50,* 191–214.

Cacioppo, J. T., Petty, R. E., Feinstein, J., & Jarvis, B. (1996). Individual differences in cognitive motivation: The life and times of people varying in need for cognition. *Psychological Bulletin, 119,* 197–253.

Cacioppo, J. T., Petty, R. E., & Morris, K. J. (1983). Effects of need for cognition on message evaluation, recall, and persuasion. *Journal of Personality and Social Psychology, 45,* 805–818.

Cacioppo, J. T., Petty, R. E., & Sidera, J. (1982). The effects of salient self-schema on the evaluation of proattitudinal editorials: Top-down versus bottom-up message processing. *Journal of Experimental Social Psychology, 18,* 324–338.

Cacioppo, J. T., Priester, J. R., & Berntson, G. G. (1993). Rudimentary determinants of attitude. II. Arm flexion and extension have differential effects on attitudes. *Journal of Personality and Social Psychology, 65,* 5–17.

Cadinu, M., Maass, A., Rosabianca, A., & Kiesner, J. (2005). Why do women underperform under stereotype threat? Evidence for the role of negative thinking. *Psychological Science, 16,* 572–578.

Cain, R. (1991). Stigma management and gay identity development. *Social Work, 36,* 67–73.

Calanchini, J., Moons, W. G., & Mackie, D. M. (2016). Angry expressions induce extensive processing of persuasive appeals. *Journal of Experimental Social Psychology, 64,* 88–98.

Camerer, C., Dreber, A., Forsell, E., Ho, T., Huber, J., Johannesson, M., et al. (2016). Evaluating replicability of laboratory experiments in economics. *Science, 351,* 1433–1436.

Cameron, C. D., Brown-Iannuzzi, J. L., & Payne, B. K. (2012). Sequential priming measures of implicit social cognition: A meta-analysis of associations with behavior and explicit attitudes. *Personality and Social Psychology Review, 16,* 330–350.

Cameron, L, & Rutland, A. (2006). Extended contact through story reading in school: Reducing children's prejudice towards the disabled. *Journal of Social Issues, 62,* 469–488.

Campbell, J. D., & Fairey, P. J. (1989). Informational and normative routes to conformity: The effect of faction size as a function of norm extremity and attention to the stimulus. *Journal of Personality and Social Psychology, 57,* 457–468.

Campos, B., Ullman, J., Aguilera, A., & Dunkel Schetter, C. (2014). Familism and psychological health: The intervening role of closeness and social support. *Journal of Cultural Diversity and Ethnic Minority Psychology, 20,* 191–201. doi:10.1037/a0034094

Camposa, L., Ottab, E., & Siqueira, J. (2002). Sex differences in mate selection strategies: Content analyses and responses to personal advertisements in Brazil. *Evolution and Human Behavior, 23,* 395–406.

Carey, R. C., & Markus, H. R. (2016). Understanding consumer psychology in working-class contexts. *Journal of Consumer Psychology, 26,* 568–582.

Carli, L. L. (1999). Cognitive reconstruction, hindsight, and reactions to victims and perpetrators. *Personality and Social Psychology Bulletin, 25,* 966–979.

Carlsmith, J. M., & Gross, A. E. (1969). Some effects of guilt on compliance. *Journal of Personality and Social Psychology, 11,* 232–239.

Carlsmith, K. M., & Darley, J. M. (2008). Psychological aspects of retributive justice. In M. P. Zanna (Ed.), *Advances in experimental social psychology* (Vol. 40, pp. 193–236). San Diego, CA: Academic Press.

Carlsmith, K. M., Darley, J. M., & Robinson, P. H. (2002). Why do we punish? Deterrence and just deserts as motives for punishment. *Journal of Personality and Social Psychology, 83,* 284–299.

Carlson, M., Charlin, V., & Miller, N. (1988). Positive mood and helping behavior: A test of six hypotheses. *Journal of Personality and Social Psychology, 55,* 211–229.

Carlston, D. E., & Skowronski, J. J. (1994). Savings in the relearning of trait information as evidence for spontaneous inference generation. *Journal of Personality and Social Psychology, 66,* 840–880.

Carnevale, P. J., & Isen, A. M. (1986). The influence of positive affect and visual access on the discovery of integrative solutions in bilateral negotiation. *Organizational Behavior and Human Decision Processes, 37,* 1–13.

Carter, J., & Irons, M. (1991). Are economists different, and if so, why? *Journal of Economic Perspectives, 5,* 171–177.

Carter, T., Ferguson, M. J., & Hassin, R. R. (2011). A single exposure to the American flag shifts support toward Republicanism up to 8 months later. *Psychological Science, 22*(8), 341–359.

Carter, T. J., & Gilovich, T. (2010). The relative relativity of material and experiential purchases. *Journal of Personality and Social Psychology, 98*(1), 146–159.

Cartwright, D., & Zander, A. (1968). *Group dynamics: Research and theory.* New York: Harper & Row.

Carver, C. S., DeGregorio, E., & Gillis, R. (1980). Ego-defensive attribution among two categories of observers. *Personality and Social Psychology Bulletin, 6,* 4–50.

Carver, C. S., & Scheier, M. F. (1982). Control theory: A useful conceptual framework for personality-social, clinical, and health psychology. *Psychological Bulletin, 92,* 111–135.

Cash, T. F., & Trimer, C. A. (1984). Sexism and beautyism in women's evaluations of peer performance. *Sex Roles, 10,* 87–98.

Caspi, A., & Herbener, E. S. (1990). Continuity and change: Assortative marriage and the consistency of personality in adulthood. *Journal of Personality and Social Psychology, 58,* 250–258.

Caspi, A., McClay, J., Moffitt, T. E., Mill, J., Martin, J., Craig, I. W., et al. (2002). Role of genotype in the cycle of violence in maltreated children. *Science, 297,* 851–854.

Cate, R. M., Lloyd, S. A., Henton, J. M., & Larson, J. H. (1982). Fairness and reward level as predictors of relationship satisfaction. *Social Psychology Quarterly, 45,* 177–181.

Cavallo, J. V., Holmes, J. G., Fitzsimons, G. M., Murray, S. L., & Wood, J. V. (2012). Managing motivational conflict: How self-esteem and executive resources influence self-regulatory responses to risk. *Journal of Personality and Social Psychology, 103,* 430–451.

Ceci, S. J., & Bruck, M. (1995). *Jeopardy in the courtroom: A scientific analysis of children's testimony.* Washington, DC: American Psychological Association.

Center for Media and Public Affairs. (July–August 2000). The media at the millennium: The networks' top topics, trends, and joke targets of the 1990s. *Media Monitor, 14,* 1–6.

Cha, J.-H., & Nam, K. D. (1985). A test of Kelley's cube theory of attribution: A cross-cultural replication of McArthur's study. *Korean Social Science Journal, 12,* 151–180.

Chagnon, N. A. (1997). *Yanomamö.* New York: Harcourt Brace Jovanovich.

Chaiken, S. (1980). Heuristic versus systematic information processing in the use of source versus message cues in persuasion. *Journal of Personality and Social Psychology, 39,* 752–766.

Chaiken, S., & Baldwin, M. W. (1981). Affective-cognitive consistency and the effect of salient behavioral information on the self-perception of attitudes. *Journal of Personality and Social Psychology, 41,* 1–12.

Chaiken, S., & Eagly, A. H. (1976). Communication modality as a determinant of persuasion: The role of communicator salience. *Journal of Personality and Social Psychology, 45,* 241–256.

Chaiken, S., Liberman, A., & Eagly, A. H. (1989). Heuristic and systematic processing within and beyond the persuasion context. In J. S. Uleman & J. A. Bargh (Eds.), *Unintended thought* (pp. 212–252). New York: Guilford Press.

Chaiken S., & Maheswaran, D. (1994). Heuristic processing can bias systematic processing: Effects of source credibility, argument ambiguity, and task importance on attitude judgment. *Journal of Personality and Social Psychology, 66,* 460–473.

Chapman, L. J., & Chapman, J. (1967). Genesis of popular but erroneous diagnostic observations. *Journal of Abnormal Psychology, 72,* 193–204.

Chartrand, T. L., & Bargh, J. A. (1999). The chameleon effect: The perception-behavior link and social interaction. *Journal of Personality and Social Psychology, 76,* 893–910.

Chen, C., Boucher, H., & Tapias, M. P. (2006). The relational self revealed: Integrative conceptualization and implications for interpersonal life. *Psychological Bulletin, 132*(2), 151–179.

Chen, C., & Stevenson, H. W. (1995). Motivation and mathematics achievement: A comparative study of Asian-American, Caucasian-American and East Asian high school students. *Child Development, 66,* 1215–1234.

Chen, M., & Bargh, J. A. (1999). Consequences of automatic evaluation: Immediate behavioral predispositions to approach or avoid the stimulus. *Personality and Social Psychology Bulletin, 25,* 215–224.

Chen, S., & Chaiken, S. (1999). The heuristic-systematic model in its broader context. In S. Chaiken & Y. Trope (Eds.), *Dual-process theories in social and cognitive psychology* (pp. 73–96). New York: Guilford Press.

Chen, S., Lee-Chai, A. Y., & Bargh, J. A. (2001). Relationship orientation as moderator of the effects of social power. *Journal of Personality and Social Psychology, 80,* 183–187.

Chen, S. C. (1937). Social modification of the activity of ants in nest-building. *Physiological Zoology, 10,* 420–436.

Cheng, J. T., Tracy, J. L., Ho, S., & Henrich, J. (2016). Listen, follow me: Dynamics of vocal signals of dominance predict emergent social rank in humans. *Journal of Experimental Psychology: General, 145,* 536–547.

Cheng, P. W., & Novick, L. R. (1990). A probabilistic contrast model of causal induction. *Journal of Personality and Social Psychology, 58,* 545–567.

Cheryan, S., & Bodenhausen, G. V. (2000). When positive stereotypes threaten intellectual performance: The psychological hazards of "model minority" status. *Psychological Review, 11,* 399–402.

Cheung, F. M., Leung, K., Zhang, J. X., Sun, H. F., Gan, Y. Q., Song, W. Z., & Dong, X. (2001). Indigenous Chinese personality constructs: Is the five-factor model complete? *Journal of Cross-Cultural Psychology, 32,* 407–433.

Choi, I., & Nisbett, R. E. (1998). Situational salience and cultural differences in the correspondence bias and in the actor-observer bias. *Personality and Social Psychology Bulletin, 24,* 949–960.

Choi, I., Nisbett, R. E., & Norenzayan, A. (1999). Causal attribution across cultures: Variation and universality. *Psychological Bulletin, 125,* 47–63.

Choi, J., Laibson, D., & Madrian, B. (2009). Reducing the complexity costs of 401(k) participation through quick enrollment. In D. A. Wise (Ed.), *Research findings in the economics of aging* (pp. 57–82). Chicago: University of Chicago Press.

Chonody, J. M. (2013). Measuring sexual prejudice against gay men and lesbian women: Development of the Sexual Prejudice Scale (SPS). *Journal of Homosexuality, 60*(6), 895–926.

Christakis, N. A., & Fowler, J. H. (2009). *Connected.* New York: Little, Brown.

Christakis, N. A., & Fowler, J. H. (2013). Social contagion theory: Examining dynamic social networks and human behavior," *Statistics in Medicine, 32*(4), 556–577.

Cialdini, R. B. (1984). *Influence: How and why people agree to things.* New York: Quill.

Cialdini, R. B. (2008). *Influence: Science and practice* (5th ed.). New York: Prentice-Hall.

Cialdini, R. B. (2016). *Pre-suasion: A revolutionary way to influence and persuade.* New York: Simon & Schuster.

Cialdini, R. B., Borden, R. J., Thorne, A., Walker, M. R., Freeman, S., & Sloan, L. R. (1976). Basking in reflected glory: Three (football) field studies. *Journal of Personality and Social Psychology, 34,* 366–375.

Cialdini, R. B., Darby, B. L., & Vincent, J. E. (1973). Transgression and altruism: A case for hedonism. *Journal of Experimental Social Psychology, 9,* 502–516.

Cialdini, R. R., Demaine, L. J., Sagarin, B. J., Barrett, D. W., Rhoads, K., & Winters, K. (2006). Activating and aligning social norms for persuasive impact. *Social Influence, 1,* 3–15.

Cialdini, R. B., & Fultz, J. (1990). Interpreting the negative mood-helping literature via "mega" analysis: A contrarian view. *Psychological Bulletin, 107,* 210–214.

Cialdini, R. B., & Goldstein, N. J. (2004). Social influence: Compliance and conformity. *Annual Review of Psychology, 55,* 591–621.

Cialdini, R. B., Kallgren, C. A., & Reno, R. R. (1991). A focus theory of normative conduct: A theoretical refinement and reevaluation of the role of norms in human behavior. In M. P. Zanna (Ed.), *Advances in experimental social psychology* (Vol. 24, pp. 201–234). San Diego, CA: Academic Press.

Cialdini, R. B., Schaller, M., Houlihan, D., Arps, K., Fultz, J., & Beaman, A. L. (1987). Empathy-based helping: Is it selflessly or selfishly motivated? *Journal of Personality and Social Psychology, 52,* 749–758.

Cialdini, R. B., & Trost, M. R. (1998). Social influence: Social norms, conformity, and compliance. In D. T. Gilbert, S. T. Fiske, & G. Lindzey (Eds.), *The handbook of social psychology* (4th ed., Vol. 2, pp. 151–192). New York: McGraw-Hill.

Cialdini, R. B., Vincent, J. E., Lewis, S. K., Catalan, J., Wheeler, D., & Darby, B. L. (1975). Reciprocal concessions procedure for inducing compliance: The door-in-the-face technique. *Journal of Personality and Social Psychology, 31,* 206–215.

Civil Rights Data Collection. (2017). 2013–14 discipline estimations by discipline type. Retrieved from https://ocrdata.ed.gov/StateNational Estimations/Estimations_2013_14

Clancy, S. M., & Dollinger, S. J. (1993). Photographic depictions of the self: Gender and age differences in social connectedness. *Sex Roles, 15,* 145–158.

Clark, M. S. (1992). Research on communal and exchange relationships viewed from a functionalist perspective. In D. A. Owens & M. Wagner (Eds.), *Progress in modern psychology: The legacy of American functionalism* (pp. 241–258). Westport, CT: Praeger.

Clark, M. S., & Aragón, O. R. (2013). Communal (and other) relationships: History, theory development and future directions. In J. Simpson & L. Campbell (Eds.), *The Oxford Handbook of Close Relationships* (pp. 255–280). Oxford, England: Oxford University Press.

Clark, M. S., & Isen, A. M. (1982). Toward understanding the relationship between feeling states and social behavior. In A. H. Hastorf & A. M. Isen (Eds.), *Cognitive social psychology* (pp. 73–108). New York: Elsevier.

Clark, M. S., & Mills, J. R. (1979). Interpersonal attraction in exchange and communal relationships. *Journal of Personality and Social Psychology, 37*, 12–24.

Clark, M. S., & Mills, J. R. (1993). The difference between communal and exchange relationships: What is and is not. *Personality and Social Psychology Bulletin, 19*, 684–691.

Clark, M. S., & Mills, J. R. (2012). A theory of communal (and exchange) relationships. In P.A.M. Van Lange, A. W. Kruglanski, & E. T. Higgins (Eds.), *Handbook of theories of social psychology* (Vol. 2, pp. 232–250). Thousand Oaks, CA: Sage.

Clore, G. L., & Byrne, D. (1974). A reinforcement-effect model of attraction. In T. L. Huston (Ed.), *Foundations of interpersonal attraction* (pp. 143–170). New York: Academic Press.

Clunies-Ross, G, & O'Meara, K. (1989). Changing the attitudes of students towards peers with disabilities. *Australian Psychologist, 24*, 273–284.

Cohen, C. E. (1981). Person categories and social perception: Testing some boundaries of the processing effects of prior knowledge. *Journal of Personality and Social Psychology, 40*, 441–452.

Cohen, D., & Gunz, A. (2002). As seen by the other: Perspectives on the self in the memories and emotional perceptions of Easterners and Westerners. *Psychological Science, 13*(1), 55–59.

Cohen, D., & Nisbett, R. E. (1997). Field experiments examining the culture of honor: The role of institutions in perpetuating norms about violence. *Personality and Social Psychology Bulletin, 23*, 1188–1199.

Cohen, D., Nisbett, R. E., Bowdle, B., & Schwarz, N. (1996). Insult, aggression, and the Southern culture of honor: An "experimental ethnography." *Journal of Personality and Social Psychology, 70*, 945–960.

Cohen, G. L., Garcia, J., Apfel, N., & Master, A. (2006). Reducing the racial achievement gap: A social-psychological intervention. *Science, 313*, 1307–1310.

Cohen, G. L., Garcia, J., Purdie-Vaughns, V., Apfel, N., & Brzustoski, P. (2009). Recursive processes in self-affirmation: Intervening to close the minority achievement gap. *Science, 324*, 400–403.

Cohen, G. L., & Sherman, D. K. (2014). The psychology of change: Self-affirmation and social psychological intervention. *Annual Review in Psychology, 65*, 333–371.

Cohn, N. (2016, November 9). Why Trump won: Working-class whites. *New York Times.* https://www.nytimes.com/2016/11/10/upshot/why-trump-won-working-class-whites.html?_r=0

Cohen, S., Alper, C. M., Doyle, W. J., Adler, N., Treanor, J. J., & Turner, R. B. (2008). Objective and subjective socioeconomic status and susceptibility to the common cold. *Health Psychology, 27*(2), 268–274.

Cohen, S., & Herbert, T. B. (1996). Health psychology: Psychological factors and physical disease from the perspective of human psychoneuroimmunology. *Annual Review of Psychology, 47*, 113–142.

Cohen, S., & Janicki-Deverts, D. (2012). Who's stressed? Distributions of psychological stress in the United States in probability samples from 1983, 2006, and 2009. *Journal of Applied Social Psychology, 42*, 1320–1334.

Cohen, T. R., Montoya, R. M., & Insko, C. A. (2006). Group morality and intergroup relations: Cross-cultural and experimental evidence. *Personality and Social Psychology Bulletin, 32*, 1559–1572.

Coie, J. D., Cillessen, A. H. N., Dodge, K. A., Hubbard, J. A., Schwartz, D., Lemerise, E. D., et al. (1999). It takes two to fight: A test of relational factors and a method for assessing aggressive dyads. *Developmental Psychology, 35*, 1179–1188.

Cole, S. W., Kemeny, M. E., Taylor, S. E., & Visscher, B. R. (1996). Accelerated course of human immunodeficiency virus infection in gay men who conceal their homosexual identity. *Psychosomatic Medicine, 58*(3), 219–231.

Collins, N. L., & Miller, L. C. (1994). Self-disclosure and liking: A meta-analytic review. *Psychological Bulletin, 116*, 457–475.

Collins, N. L., & Read, S. J. (1990). Adult attachment, working models, and relationship quality in dating couples, *Journal of Personality and Social Psychology, 58*, 644–663.

Collins, N. L., & Read, S. J. (1994). Cognitive representations of attachment: The structure and function of working models. In K. Bartholomew & D. Perlman (Eds.), *Attachment processes in adulthood: Advances in personal relationships* (Vol. 5, pp. 53–90). London: Kingsley.

Collins, R. L., Taylor, S. E., Wood, J. V., & Thompson, S. C. (1988). The vividness effect: Elusive or illusory? *Journal of Experimental Social Psychology, 24*, 1–18.

Colvin, C. R., & Block, J. (1994). Do positive illusions foster mental health? An examination of the Taylor and Brown formulation. *Psychological Bulletin, 116*, 3–20.

Colvin, C. R., Block, J., & Funder, D. C. (1995). Overly positive self-evaluations and personality: Negative implications for mental health. *Journal of Personality and Social Psychology, 68*, 1152–1162.

Colvin, C. R., & Griffo, R. (2008). On the psychological costs of self-enhancement. In E. C. Chang (Ed.), *Self-criticism and self-enhancement: Theory, research, and clinical implications* (pp. 123–140). Washington, DC: American Psychological Association.

Condry, J., & Condry, S. (1976). Sex differences: A study of the eye of the beholder. *Child Development, 47*, 812–819.

Conley, T. D., Roesch, S. C., Peplau, L., & Gold, M. S. (2009). A test of positive illusions versus shared reality models of relationship satisfaction among gay, lesbian, and heterosexual couples. *Journal of Applied Social Psychology, 39*(6), 1417–1431.

Connolly, K. (1968). The social facilitation of preening behavior of *Drosophila melanogaster*. *Animal Behavior, 16*, 385–391.

Conway, L. G., & Schaller, M. (2002). On the verifiability of evolutionary psychological theories. *Personality and Social Psychology, 6*, 152–166.

Cooley, C. H. (1902). *Human nature and the social order*. New York: Charles Scribner's Sons.

Coontz, S. (2005). *Marriage, a history: From obedience to intimacy, or how love conquered marriage*. New York: Viking Press.

Cooper, J. (1971). Personal responsibility and dissonance: The role and foreseen consequences. *Journal of Personality and Social Psychology, 18*, 354–363.

Cooper, J., & Worchel, S. (1970). Role of undesired consequences in arousing cognitive dissonance. *Journal of Personality and Social Psychology, 16*, 199–206.

Cooper, M. L., Shaver, P., & Collins, N. L. (1998). Attachment styles, emotion regulation, and adjustment in adolescence. *Journal of Personality and Social Psychology, 74*, 1380–1397.

Cordaro, D. T., Keltner, D., Tshering, S., Wangchuk, D., & Flynn, L. (2016). The voice conveys emotion in ten globalized cultures and one remote village in Bhutan. *Emotion, 16*, 117–128.

Coriell, M., & Adler, N. E. (2001). Social ordering and health. In B. S. McEwen (Vol. Ed.) and H. M. Goodman (Sec. Ed.), *Handbook of physiology. Section 7: The endocrine system* (pp. 533–546). New York: American Physiological Society and Oxford University Press.

Correll, J., & Park, B. (2005). A model of the ingroup as a social resource. *Personality and Social Psychology Review, 9*, 341–359.

Correll, J., Park, B., Judd, C. M., & Wittenbrink, B. (2002). The police officer's dilemma: Using ethnicity to disambiguate potentially threatening individuals. *Journal of Personality and Social Psychology, 83,* 1314–1329.

Correll, J., Park, B., Judd, C. M., Wittenbrink, B., Sadler, M. S., & Keesee, T. (2007). Across the thin blue line: Police officers and racial bias in the decision to shoot. *Journal of Personality and Social Psychology, 92*(6), 1006–1023.

Correll, J., Spencer, S. J., & Zanna, M. (2004). An affirmed self and an open mind: Self-affirmation and sensitivity to argument strength. *Journal of Experimental Social Psychology, 40,* 350–356.

Correll, J., Urland, G. R., & Ito, T. A. (2006). Event-related potentials and the decision to shoot: The role of threat perception and cognitive control. *Journal of Experimental Social Psychology, 42,* 120–128.

Correll, J., Wittenbrink, B., Park, B., Judd, C. M., & Goyle, A. (2011). Dangerous enough: Moderating racial bias with secondary threat cues. *Journal of Experimental Social Psychology, 47,* 184–189.

Cortina, L. M., & Berdahl, J. L. (2008). Sexual harassment in organizations: A decade of research in review. In J. Barling & C. L. Cooper (Eds.), *The SAGE Handbook of Organizational Behavior: Volume I: Micro Approaches* (pp. 469-497). Thousand Oaks, CA: Sage. doi:10.4135/9781849200448.n26

Costanzo, M. (1997). *Just revenge: Costs and consequences of the death penalty.* New York: St. Martin's Press.

Cota, A. A., & Dion, K. L. (1986). Salience of gender and sex composition of ad hoc groups: An experimental test of the distinctiveness theory. *Journal of Personality and Social Psychology, 50,* 770–776.

Côté, S., House, J., & Willer, R. (2015). High economic inequality leads higher-income individuals to be less generous. *Proceedings of the National Academy of Sciences of the USA, 112*(52), 15838–15843. doi:10.1073/pnas.1511536112

Côté, S., & Miners, C. T. H. (2006). Emotional intelligence, cognitive intelligence, and job performance. *Administrative Science Quarterly, 51,* 1–28.

Cotterell, N., Eisenberger, R., & Speicher, H. (1992). Inhibiting effects of reciprocation wariness on interpersonal relationships. *Journal of Personality and Social Psychology, 62,* 658–668.

Cottrell, N. B., Wack, D. L., Sekerak, G. J., & Rittle, R. H. (1968). Social facilitation of dominant responses by the presence of an audience and the mere presence of others. *Journal of Personality and Social Psychology, 9,* 245–250.

Cousins, S. D. (1989). Culture and self-perception in Japan and the United States. *Journal of Personality and Social Psychology, 56,* 124–131.

Cowan, C. L., Thompson, W. C., & Ellsworth, P. C. (1984). The effects of death qualification on jurors' predisposition to convict and on the quality of deliberation. *Law and Human Behavior, 8,* 53–80.

Craig, M.A., & Richeson, J. A. (2014). More diverse yet less tolerant? How the increasingly diverse racial landscape affects White Americans' racial attitudes. *Personality and Social Psychology Bulletin, 40*(6), 750–761.

Crandall, C. S. (1988). Social contagion of binge eating. *Journal of Personality and Social Psychology, 55,* 588–598.

Crandall, C. S., & Eshleman, A. (2003). A justification-suppression model of the expression and experience of prejudice. *Psychological Bulletin, 129,* 414–446.

Crandall, V. C., Katkovsky, W., & Crandall, V. J. (1965). Children's beliefs in their own control of reinforcements in intellectual-academic achievement situations. *Child Development, 36,* 91–109.

Crano, W. D. (1970). Effects of sex, response order, and expertise in conformity: A dispositional approach. *Sociometry, 33,* 239–252.

Critcher, C. R., & Ferguson, M. J. (2013). The costs of keeping it hidden: Decomposing concealment reveals what makes it depleting. *Journal of Experimental Psychology: General, 143,* 721–735.

Crocker, J. (1982). Biased questions in judgment of covariation studies. *Personality and Social Psychology Bulletin, 8,* 214–220.

Crocker, J., Hannah, D. B., & Weber, R. (1983). Person memory and causal attributions. *Journal of Personality and Social Psychology, 44,* 55–66.

Crocker, J., & Luhtanen, R. (1990). Collective self-esteem and ingroup bias. *Journal of Personality and Social Psychology, 58,* 60–67.

Crocker, J., Major, B., & Steele, C. (1998). Social stigma. In D. T. Gilbert, S. T. Fiske, & G. Lindzey (Eds.), *The handbook of social psychology* (4th ed., Vol. 2, pp. 504–553). New York: McGraw-Hill.

Crocker, J., & Park, L. E. (2004). The costly pursuit of self-esteem. *Psychological Bulletin, 130,* 392–414.

Crocker, J., Sommers, S. R., & Luhtanen, R. K. (2002). Hopes dashed and dreams fulfilled: Contingencies of self-worth and graduate school admissions. *Personality and Social Psychology Bulletin, 28,* 1275–1286.

Crocker, J., Voelkl, K., Testa, M., & Major, B. (1991). Social stigma: The affective consequences of attributional ambiguity. *Journal of Personality and Social Psychology, 60,* 218–228.

Crocker, J., & Wolfe, C. T. (2001). Contingencies of self-worth. *sychological Review, 108,* 593–623.

Cross, H. A., Halcomb, C. G., & Matter, W. W. (1967). Imprinting or exposure learning in rats given early auditory stimulation. *Psychonomic Science, 7,* 233–234.

Cross, S. E., & Madson, L. (1997). Models of the self: Self-construals and gender. *Psychological Bulletin, 122,* 5–37.

Cullen, D. (2009). *Columbine.* New York: Twelve Publishing.

Cunningham, M. R., Roberts, A. R., Barbee, A. P., Druen, P. B., & Wu, C. (1995). "Their ideas of beauty are, on the whole, the same as ours": Consistency and variability in the cross-cultural perception of female physical attractiveness. *Journal of Personality and Social Psychology, 68,* 261–279.

Cunningham, W. A., & Brosch, T. (2012). Motivational salience: Amygdala tuning from traits, needs, values, and goals. *Current Directions in Psychological Science, 21,* 54–59.

Curry, R. L. (1988). Influence of kinship on helping behavior in Galápagos mockingbirds. *Behavioral Ecology and Sociobiology, 38,* 181–192.

Cutrona, C. E. (1982). Transition to college: Loneliness and the process of social adjustment. In L. A. Peplau & D. Perlman (Eds.), *Loneliness: A sourcebook of current theory, research, and therapy* (pp. 291–309). New York: Wiley.

Czopp, A. M., & Ashburn-Nardo, L. (2012). Interpersonal confrontations of prejudice. In D. W. Russell & A. Cristel (Eds.), *The psychology of prejudice: Interdisciplinary perspectives on contemporary issues* (pp. 175–201). Hauppauge, NY: Nova Science Publishers.

Czopp, A. M., Kay, A. C., & Cheryan, S. (2015). Positive stereotypes are pervasive and powerful. *Perspectives on Psychological Science, 10,* 451–463.

Czopp, A. M., & Monteith, M. J. (2006). Thinking well of African Americans: Measuring complimentary stereotypes and negative prejudice. *Basic and Applied Social Psychology, 28,* 233–250.

Dabbs, J. M., Jr. (2000). *Heroes, rogues and lovers.* New York: McGraw-Hill.

Dahl, G., & Dellavigna, S. (2009). Does movie violence increase violent crime? *Quarterly Journal of Economics, 124,* 677–734.

Daly, M., & Wilson, M. I. (1988). *Homicide.* New York: De Gruyter.

Daly, M., & Wilson, M. I. (1996). Violence against stepchildren. *Current Directions in Psychological Science, 5,* 77–81.

Daly, M., Wilson, M., & Vasdev, S. (2001). Income inequality and homicide rates in Canada and the United States. *Canadian Journal of Criminology, 43*(2), 219–236.

Daniels, N., Berkman, L., & Kawachi, I. (2000). *Is inequality bad for our health?* Boston: Beacon Press.

Danner, D., Snowdon, D., & Friesen, W. (2001). Positive emotions in early life and longevity: Findings from the nun study. *Journal of Personality and Social Psychology, 80*, 804–813.

Danziger, S., Levav, J., & Avnaim-Pesso, L. (2011). Extraneous factors in judicial decisions. *Proceedings of the National Academy of Sciences of the USA, 108*(17), 6889–6892.

Dardenne, B., Dumont, M., & Bollier T. (2007). Insidious dangers of benevolent sexism: Consequences for women's performance. *Journal of Personality and Social Psychology, 93*(5), 764–779.

Darley, J. M., & Batson, C. D. (1973). From Jerusalem to Jericho: A study of situational and dispositional variables in helping behavior. *Journal of Personality and Social Psychology, 27*, 100–119.

Darley, J. M., & Gross, P. H. (1983). A hypothesis-confirming bias in labeling efects. *Journal of Personality and Social Psychology, 44*, 20–33.

Darley, J. M., & Latané, B. (1968). Bystander intervention in emergencies: Diffusion of responsibility. *Journal of Personality and Social Psychology, 8*, 377–383.

Darley, J. M., Teger, A. I., & Lewis, L. D. (1973). Do groups always inhibit individuals' responses to potential emergencies? *Journal of Personality and Social Psychology, 26*, 395–399.

Darlington, R. B., & Macker, C. E. (1966). Displacement of guilt-produced altruistic behavior. *Journal of Personality and Social Psychology, 4*, 442–443.

Darwin, C. (1871). *The descent of man, and selection in relation to sex.* London: John Murray.

Dasgupta, N., DeSteno, D., Williams, L. A., & Hunsinger, M. (2009). Fanning the flames: The influence of specific incidental emotions on implicit prejudice. *Emotion, 9*, 585–591.

Dashiell, J. F. (1930). An experimental analysis of some group effects. *Journal of Abnormal and Social Psychology, 25*, 190–199.

Davidson, R. J., & Begley, S. (2012). *The emotional life of your brain: How its unique patterns affect the way you think, feel, and live–and how you can change them.* New York: Hudson Street Press.

Davidson, R. J., Kabat-Zinn, J., Schumacher, J., Rosenkranz, M., Muller, D., Santorelli, S. F., et al. (2003). Alterations in brain and immune function produced by mindfulness meditation. *Psychosomatic Medicine, 65*, 564–570.

Davis, M. H., & Franzoi, S. L. (1991). Stability and change in adolescent self-consciousness and empathy. *Journal of Research in Personality, 25*, 70–87.

Dawes, R. M. (1980). Social dilemmas. *Annual Review of Psychology, 31*, 169–193.

Dawes, R. M. (1988). *Rational choice in an uncertain world.* San Diego, CA: Harcourt Brace Jovanovich.

Dawson, E., Gilovich, T., & Regan, D. T. (2002). Motivated reasoning and performance on the Wason selection task. *Personality and Social Psychology Bulletin, 28*, 1379–1387.

Dearing, J. W., & Rogers, E. M. (1996). *Agenda-setting.* Thousand Oaks, CA: Sage.

Deaux, K., & Emswiller, T. (1974). Explanations of successful performance on sex-linked tasks: What is skill for the male is luck for the female. *Journal of Personality and Social Psychology, 29*, 80–85.

Debner, J. A., & Jacoby, L. L. (1994). Unconscious perception: Attention, awareness, and control. *Journal of Experimental Psychology: Learning, Memory and Cognition, 20*, 304–317.

DeBruine, L. M. (2002). Facial resemblance enhances trust. *Proceedings of the Royal Society B: Biological Sciences, 269*, 1307–1312.

Decety, J., & Michalska, K. (2010). Neurodevelopmental changes in the circuits underlying empathy and sympathy from childhood to adulthood. *Developmental Science, 13*, 886–899.

Dechesne, M., Greenberg, J., Arndt, J., & Schimel, J. (2000). Terror management and sports fan affiliation: The effects of mortality salience on fan identification and optimism. *European Journal of Social Psychology, 30*, 813–835.

Dechesne, M., Pyszczynski, T., Arndt, J., Ransom, S., Sheldon, K. M., van Knippenberg, A., et al. (2003). Literal and symbolic immortality: The effect of evidence of literal immortality on self-esteem striving in response to mortality salience. *Journal of Personality and Social Psychology, 84*, 722–737.

Deci, E. L., & Ryan, R. M. (1985). *Intrinsic motivation and self-determination in human behavior.* New York: Plenum Press.

DeCoster, J., & Claypool, H. M. (2004). A meta-analysis of priming effects on impression formation supporting a general model of informational biases. *Personality and Social Psychology Review, 8*, 2–27.

de Dreu, C. K. W., Greer, L. L., Handgraaf, M. J. J., Shalvi, S., van Kleef, G. A., Baas, M., et al. (2010). The neuropeptide oxytocin regulates parochial altruism in intergroup conflict among humans. *Science, 328*(5984), 1408–1411.

Deemer, E. D., Lin, C., & Soto, C. (2015). Stereotype threat and women's science motivation: Examining the disidentification effect. *Journal of Career Assessment, 24*(4), 1–14.

De Freitas, J., Sarkissian, H., Newman, G. E., Grosssman, I., De Brigard, F., Luco, A., & Knobe, J. (2017). Consistent belief in a good true self in misanthropes and three interdependent cultures. *Cognitive Science,* 1–27.

Denes-Raj, V., & Epstein, S. (1994). Conflict between intuitive and rational processing: When people behave against their better judgment. *Journal of Personality and Social Psychology, 66*, 819–829.

de Oliveira, S., & Nisbett, R. E. (2017). Beyond East and West: Cognitive style in Latin America. *Journal of Cross-Cultural Psychology, 48*(10), 1554–1577.

DePaulo, B. M. (2007). *Singled out: How singles are stereotyped, stigmatized, and ignored, and still live happily ever after.* New York: St. Martin's Griffin.

DePaulo, B. M. (2015). *Marriage vs. single life: How science and the media got it so wrong.* CreateSpace Independent Publishing Platform.

DePaulo, B. M., Lanier, K., & Davis, T. (1983). Detecting the deceit of the motivated liar. *Journal of Personality and Social Psychology, 43*, 1096–1103.

Deppe, R. K., & Harackiewicz, J. M. (1996). Self-handicapping and intrinsic motivation: Buffering intrinsic motivation from the threat of failure. *Journal of Personality and Social Psychology, 70*, 868–876.

DeSteno, D., Petty, R., Wegener, D., & Rucker, D. (2000). Beyond valence in the perception of likelihood: The role of emotion specificity. *Journal of Personality and Social Psychology, 78*, 397–416.

Deutsch, M., & Gerard, H. B. (1955). A study of normative and informational social influence upon individual judgment. *Journal of Abnormal and Social Psychology, 51*, 629–636.

Devine, P. G. (1989a). Automatic and controlled processes in prejudice: The roles of stereotypes and personal beliefs. In A. R. Pratkanis, S. J. Breckler, & A. G. Greenwald (Eds.), *Attitude structure and function.* Hillsdale, NJ: Erlbaum.

Devine, P. G. (1989b). Stereotypes and prejudice: Their automatic and controlled components. *Journal of Personality and Social Psychology, 56*, 5–18.

Devine, P. G., & Baker, S. M. (1991). Measurement of racial stereotype subtyping. *Personality and Social Psychology Bulletin, 17*, 44–50.

Devine, P. G., & Elliot, A. J. (1995). Are racial stereotypes really fading? The Princeton trilogy revisited. *Personality and Social Psychology Bulletin, 21*, 1139–1150.

Devine, P. G., Forscher, P. S., Austin, A. J., & Cox, W. T. L. (2012). Long-term reduction in implicit racial bias: A prejudice habit-breaking intervention. *Journal of Experimental Social Psychology, 48*, 1268–1278.

Devine, P. G. , & Malpass, R. S. (1985). Orienting strategies in differential face recognition. *Personality and Social Psychology Bulletin, 11*, 33–40.

Devine, P. G., & Monteith, M. J. (1999). Automaticity and control in stereotyping. In S. Chaiken & Y. Trope (Eds.), *Dual process theories in social psychology* (pp. 339–360). New York: Guilford Press.

Devine, P. G., Monteith, M. J., Zuwerink, J. R., & Elliot, A. J. (1991). Prejudice with and without compunction. *Journal of Personality and Social Psychology, 60*, 817–830.

Devine, P. G., Plant, E. A., Amodio, D. M., Harmon-Jones, E., & Vance, S. L. (2002). Exploring the relationship between implicit and explicit prejudice: The role of motivations to respond without prejudice. *Journal of Personality and Social Psychology, 82*, 835–848.

de Waal, F. B. M. (1986). The integration of dominance and social bonding in primates. *Quarterly Review of Biology, 61*, 459–479.

de Waal, F. B. M. (1996). *Good natured: The origins of right and wrong in humans and other animals.* Cambridge, MA: Harvard University Press.

de Waal, F. B. M., & Lanting, F. (1997). *Bonobo: The forgotten ape.* Berkeley: University of California Press.

DeWall, C. N., Bushman, B. J., Giancola, P. R., & Webster, G. D. (2010). The big, the bad, and the boozed-up: Weight moderates the effect of alcohol on aggression. *Journal of Experimental Social Psychology, 46*, 619–623.

Dhawan, N., Roseman, I. J., Naidu, R. K., Thapa, K., & Rettek, S. I. (1995). Self-concepts across two cultures: India and the United States. *Journal of Cross-Cultural Psychology, 26*, 606–621.

Diamond, L. M. (2003). What does sexual orientation orient? A biobehavioral model distinguishing romantic love and sexual desire. *Psychological Review, 110*, 173–192.

Diamond, S. S., Rose, M. R., & Murphy, B. (2006). Revisiting the unanimity requirement: The behavior of the non-unanimous civil jury. *Northwestern Law Review, 100*, 201–230.

Dickerson, S. S., & Kemeny, M. E. (2004). Acute stressors and cortisol responses: A theoretical integration and synthesis of laboratory research. *Psychological Bulletin, 130*, 355–391.

Diehl, T., Weeks, B. E., & Gil de Zúñiga, H. (2016). Political persuasion on social media: Tracing direct and indirect effects of news use and social interaction. *New Media & Society, 18*(9), 1875–1895.

Diener, E. (1980). Deindividuation: The absence of self-awareness and self-regulation in group members. In P. Paulus (Ed.), *The psychology of group influence* (pp. 209–242). Hillsdale, NJ: Erlbaum.

Diener, E. (2000). Subjective well-being: The science of happiness, and some policy implications. *American Psychologist, 55*, 34–43.

Diener, E., Fraser, S. C., Beaman, A. L., & Kelem, R. T. (1976). Effects of deindividuation variables on stealing among Halloween trick-or-treaters. *Journal of Personality and Social Psychology, 33*, 178–183.

Diener, E., & Wallbom, M. (1976). Effects of self-awareness on antinormative behavior. *Journal of Research in Personality, 10*, 107–111.

Diener, E., Wolsic, B., & Fujita, F. (1995). Physical attractiveness and subjective well-being. *Journal of Personality and Social Psychology, 69*, 207–213.

Dienstbier, R. A., & Munter, P. O. (1971). Cheating as a function of the labeling of natural arousal. *Journal of Personality and Social Psychology, 17*, 208–213.

Dijksterhuis, A., Aarts, H., Bargh, J. A., & van Knippenberg, A. (2000). On the relation between associative strength and automatic behavior. *Journal of Experimental Social Psychology, 36*, 531–544.

Dijksterhuis, A., Aarts, H., & Smith, P. K. (2005). The power of the subliminal: On subliminal persuasion and other potential applications. In R. R. Hassin, J. S. Uleman, & J. A. Bargh (Eds.), *The new unconscious.* New York: Oxford University Press.

Dillard, J. P., Hunter, J. E., & Burgoon, M. (1984). Sequential-request persuasive strategies: Meta-analysis of the foot-in-the-door and door-in-the-face. *Human Communication Research, 10*, 461–488.

Dinero, R. E., Conger, R. D., Shaver, P. R., Widaman, K. F., & Larsen-Rife, D. (2008). Influence of family of origin and adult romantic partners on romantic attachment security. *Journal of Family Psychology, 22*, 622–632.

Dion, K. K., Berscheid, E., & Walster, E. (1972). What is a beautiful good? *Journal of Personality and Social Psychology, 24*, 285–290.

Dion, K. K., & Dion, K. L. (1993). Individualistic and collectivistic perspectives on gender and the cultural context of love and intimacy. *Journal of Social Issues, 49*, 53–69.

Ditto, P. H., Jemmott, J. B., & Darley, J. M. (1988). Appraising the threat of illness: A mental representational approach. *Health Psychology, 7*, 183–200.

Ditto, P. H., & Lopez, D. F. (1992). Motivated skepticism: Use of differential decision criteria for preferred and nonpreferred conclusions. *Journal of Personality and Social Psychology, 63*, 568–584.

Ditzen B., Schaer M., Gabriel B., Bodenmann G., Ehlert U., & Heinrichs M. (2009). Intranasal oxytocin increases positive communication and reduces cortisol levels during couple conflict. *Biological Psychiatry, 65*, 728–731.

Dodge, K. A., & Schwartz, D. (1997). Social information mechanisms in aggressive behavior. In D. M. Stoff & J. Breiling (Eds.), *Handbook of antisocial behavior* (pp. 171–180). New York: Wiley.

Donnellan, M. B., Trzesniewski, K. H., Robins, R. W., Moffitt, T. E., & Caspi, A. (2005). Low self-esteem is related to aggression, antisocial behavior, and delinquency. *Psychological Science, 16*, 328–335.

Donnerstein, E. (1980). Aggressive erotica and violence against women. *Journal of Personality and Social Psychology, 39*, 269–277.

Donnerstein, E., & Berkowitz, L. (1981). Victim reactions in aggressive erotic films as a factor in violence against women. *Journal of Personality and Social Psychology, 41*, 710–724.

Doob, A. N., & MacDonald, G. E. (1979). Television and fear of victimization: Is the relationship causal? *Journal of Personality and Social Psychology, 37*, 170–179.

Dovidio, J. F. (1984). Helping behavior and altruism: An empirical and conceptual overview. In L. Berkowitz (Ed.), *Advances in experimental social psychology* (Vol. 17, pp. 361–427). New York: Academic Press.

Dovidio, J. F. (2001). On the nature of contemporary prejudice: The third wave. *Journal of Social Issues, 57*, 829–849.

Dovidio, J. F., Brigham, J. C., Johnson, B. T., & Gaertner, S. L. (1996). Stereotyping, prejudice and discrimination: Another look. In C. N. Macrae, C. Stangor, & M. Hewstone (Eds.), *Stereotypes and stereotyping* (pp. 276–319). New York: Guilford.

Dovidio, J. F., & Gaertner, S. L. (2004). Aversive racism. In M. P. Zanna (Ed.), *Advances in experimental social psychology* (Vol. 36, pp. 1–52). San Diego, CA: Academic Press.

Dovidio, J. F., Kawakami, K., & Gaertner, S. L. (2002). Implicit and explicit prejudice and interracial interaction. *Journal of Personality and Social Psychology, 82*, 62–68.

Dovidio, J. F., Smith, J. K., Donella, A. G., & Gaertner, S. L. (1997). Racial attitudes and the death penalty. *Journal of Applied Social Psychology, 27*, 1468–1487.

Dovidio, J. F., ten Vergert, M., Stewart, T. L., Gaertner, S. L., Johnson, J. D., Esses, V. M., et al. (2004). Perspective and prejudice: Antecedents and mediating mechanisms. *Personality and Social Psychology Bulletin, 30*, 1537–1549.

Downey, G., & Feldman, S. (1996). Implications of rejection sensitivity for intimate relationships. *Journal of Personality and Social Psychology, 70*, 1327–1343.

Downey, G., Feldman, S., & Ayduk, O. (2000). Rejection sensitivity and male violence in romantic relationships. *Personal Relationships, 7,* 45–61.

Downing, C. J., Sternberg, R. J., & Ross, B. H. (1985). Multicausal inference: Evaluation of evidence in causally complex situations. *Journal of Experimental Psychology: General, 114,* 239–263.

Downing, J. W., Judd, C. M., & Brauer, M. (1992). Effects of repeated expression of attitudes on attitude extremity. *Journal of Personality and Social Psychology, 63,* 17–29.

Draine, S. C., & Greenwald, A. G. (1998). Replicable unconscious semantic priming. *Journal of Experimental Psychology: General, 127,* 286–303.

Druckman, J. N., & Bolsen, T. (2011). Framing, motivated reasoning, and opinions about emergent technologies. *Journal of Communication, 61,* 659–688.

Duflo, E., & Saez, E. (2003). The role of information and social interactions in retirement plan decisions: Evidence from a randomized experiment. *Quarterly Journal of Economics, 118*(3), 815–842.

Duncan, B. L. (1976). Differential social perception and attribution on intergroup violence: Testing the lower limits of stereotyping of blacks. *Journal of Personality and Social Psychology, 34,* 590–598.

Dunn, E. W., Aknin, L. B., & Norton, M. I. (2008). Spending money on others promotes happiness. *Science, 319*(5870), 1687–1688. doi: 10.1126/science.1150952

Dunn, J., & Munn, P. (1985). Becoming a family member: Family conflict and the development of social understanding in the second year. *Child Development, 56,* 480–492.

Dunning, D., Heath, C., & Suls, J. (2004). Flawed self-assessment: Implications for health, education, and the workplace. *Psychological Science in the Public Interest, 5,* 69–106.

Dunning, D., Meyerowitz, J. A., & Holzberg, A. (1989). Ambiguity and self-evaluation: The role of idiosyncratic trait definitions in self-serving assessments of ability. *Journal of Personality and Social Psychology, 57,* 1082–1090.

Dunning, D., & Perretta, S. (2002). Automaticity and eyewitness accuracy: A 10- to 12-second rule for distinguishing accurate from inaccurate positive identifications. *Journal of Applied Psychology, 87,* 951–962.

Dunning, D., & Sherman, D. A. (1997). Stereotypes and tacit inference. *Journal of Personality and Social Psychology, 73,* 459–471.

Dunning, D., & Stern, L. B. (1994). Distinguishing accurate from inaccurate eyewitness identifications via inquiries about decision-making processes. *Journal of Personality and Social Psychology, 67,* 818–835.

Durose, M. R., Smith, E. L., & Langan, P. A. (2007). *Bureau of Justice Statistics Special Report: Contacts between police and the public, 2005.* Washington, DC: U.S. Department of Justice.

Dutton, D. G. (2002). The neurobiology of abandonment homicide. *Aggression and Violent Behavior, 7,* 407–421.

Dutton, D. G., & Aron, A. P. (1974). Some evidence for heightened sexual attraction under conditions of high anxiety. *Journal of Personality and Social Psychology, 30,* 510–517.

Duval, T. S., & Lalwani, N. (1999). Objective self-awareness and causal attributions for self-standard discrepancies: Changing self or changing standards of correctness. *Personality and Social Psychology Bulletin, 25,* 1220–1229.

Duval, T. S., & Wicklund, R. A. (1972). *A theory of objective self-awareness.* New York: Academic Press.

Dweck, C. S. (1975). The role of expectations and attributions in the alleviation of learned helplessness. *Journal of Personality and Social Psychology, 31,* 674–685.

Dweck, C. S. (1986). Motivational processes affecting learning. *American Psychologist, 41,* 1040–1048.

Dweck, C. S. (1999). *Self-theories: Their role in motivation, personality and development.* Philadelphia: Taylor and Francis/Psychology Press.

Dweck, C. S. (2007). *Mindset: The new psychology of success.* New York: Ballantine Books.

Dweck, C. S., Chiu, C., & Hong, Y. (1995). Implicit theories and their role in judgments and reactions: A world from two perspectives. *Psychological Inquiry, 6,* 267–285.

Dweck, C. S., Davidson, W., Nelson, S., & Enna, B. (1978). Sex differences in learned helplessness: (II) The contingencies of evaluative feedback in the classroom and (III) An experimental analysis. *Developmental Psychology, 14,* 268–276.

Dweck, C. S., Hong, Y. Y., & Chiu, C. Y. (1993). Implicit theories and individual differences in the likelihood and meaning of dispositional inference. *Personality and Social Psychology Bulletin, 19,* 644–656.

Dweck, C. S., & Leggett, E. L. (1988). A social-cognitive approach to motivation and personality. *Psychological Review, 95,* 256–273.

Dweck, C. S., & Reppucci, N. D. (1973). Learned helplessness and reinforcement responsibility in children. *Journal of Personality and Social Psychology, 25,* 109–116.

Eagly, A. H. (1987). *Sex differences in social behavior: A social-role interpretation.* Hillsdale, NJ: Erlbaum.

Eagly, A. H., Ashmore, R. D., Makhijani, M. G., & Longo, L. C. (1991). What is beautiful is good, but . . . : A meta-analytic review of research on the physical attractiveness stereotype. *Psychological Bulletin, 110,* 109–128.

Eagly, A. H., & Carli, L. L. (1981). Sex of researchers and sex-typed communications as determinants of sex differences in influence-ability: A meta-analysis of social influence studies. *Psychological Bulletin, 110,* 109–128.

Eagly, A. H., & Chaiken, S. (1993). *The psychology of attitudes.* Fort Worth, TX: Harcourt Brace.

Eagly, A. H., & Chaiken, S. (1998). Attitude structure and function. In D. T. Gilbert, S. T. Fiske, & G. Lindzey (Eds.), *Handbook of social psychology* (4th ed., Vol. 1, pp. 269–322). New York: McGraw-Hill.

Eagly, A. H., & Chrvala, C. (2006). Sex differences in conformity: Status and gender role interpretations. *Psychology of Women Quarterly, 10,* 203–220.

Eagly, A. H., & Wood, W. (1999). The origins of sex differences in human behavior: Evolved dispositions vs. social roles. *American Psychologist, 54,* 408–423.

Eastwick, P. W., & Finkel, E. J. (2008). Sex differences in mate preferences revisited: Do people know what they initially desire in a romantic partner? *Journal of Personality and Social Psychology, 94*(2), 245–264.

Eastwick, P. W., Finkel, E. J., Mochon, D., & Ariely, D. (2007). Selective versus unselective romantic desire: Not all reciprocity is created equal. *Psychological Science, 18,* 317–319.

Eberhardt, J. L., Davies, P. G., Purdie-Vaughns, V. J., & Johnson, S. L. (2006). Looking deathworthy: Perceived stereotypicality of black defendants predicts capital sentencing outcomes. *Psychological Science, 17,* 383–386.

Efran, M. G. (1974). The effect of physical appearance on judgments of guilt, interpersonal attractiveness, and severity of recommended punishment in a simulated jury task. *Journal of Research in Personality, 8,* 45–54.

Ehrlinger, J., Plant, E. A., Eibach, R. P., Columb, C. J., Goplen, J. L., Kunstman, J. W., & Butz, D. A. (2011). How exposure to the Confederate flag affects willingness to vote for Barack Obama. *Political Psychology, 32*(1), 131–146.

Eibach, R. P., Libby, L. K., & Gilovich, T. (2003). When change in the self is mistaken for change in the world. *Journal of Personality and Social Psychology, 84,* 917–931.

Eibach, R. P., & Mock, S. E. (2011). Idealizing parenthood to rationalize parental investments. *Psychological Science, 22,* 203–208.

Eibl-Eibesfeldt, I. (1989). *Human ethology.* New York: Aldine de Gruyter Press.

Eisenberg, N., Fabes, R. A., Miller, P. A., Fultz, J., Shell, R., Mathy, R. M., & Reno, R. R. (1989). Relation of sympathy and personal distress to prosocial behavior: A multimethod study. *Journal of Personality and Social Psychology, 57,* 55–66.

Eisenberg, N., & Lennon, R. (1983). Sex differences in empathy and related capacities. *Psychological Bulletin, 94,* 100–131.

Eisenberger, N. I. (2015). Social pain and the brain: Controversies, questions, and where to go from here. *Annual Review of Psychology, 66,* 601–629.

Eisenberger, N. I., Lieberman, M. D., & Williams, K. D. (2003). Does rejection hurt? An fMRI study of social exclusion. *Science, 302,* 290–292.

Ejima, K. (2017). *Modeling social contagion of obesity.* Paper presented at the AAAS Annual Meeting, Boston, February 19, 2017.

Ekman, P. (1984). Expression and the nature of emotion. In K. Scherer & P. Ekman (Eds.), *Approaches to emotion.* Hillsdale, NJ: Erlbaum.

Ekman, P. (1992). An argument for basic emotions. *Cognition and Emotion, 6,* 169–200.

Ekman, P. (1993). Facial expression and emotion. *American Psychologist, 48,* 384–392.

Ekman, P., & Friesen, W. V. (1969). The repertoire of nonverbal behavior: Categories, origins, usage, and coding. *Semiotica, 1,* 49–98.

Ekman, P., & Friesen, W. V. (1971). Constants across cultures in the face and emotion. *Journal of Personality and Social Psychology, 17,* 124–129.

Ekman, P., & O'Sullivan, M. (1991). Who can catch a liar? *American Psychologist, 46,* 913–920.

Ekman, P., O'Sullivan, M., Friesen, W. V., & Scherer, K. R. (1991). Face, voice and body in detecting deception. *Journal of Nonverbal Behavior, 15,* 125–135.

Ekman, P., Sorenson, E. R., & Friesen, W. V. (1969). Pan cultural elements in facial displays of emotions. *Science, 164,* 86–88.

Elfenbein, H. A., & Ambady, N. (2002). On the universality and cultural specificity of emotion recognition: A meta-analysis. *Psychological Bulletin, 128,* 203–235.

Elfenbein, H. A., & Ambady, N. (2003). Universal and cultural differences in recognizing emotions. *Current Directions in Psychological Science, 12,* 159–164.

Elgar, F. J., & Aitken, N. (2011). Income inequality, trust, and homicide in 33 countries. *European Journal of Public Health, 21*(2), 241–246.

Eliezer, D., Major, B., & Mendes, W. B. (2010). The costs of caring: Gender identification increases threat following exposure to sexism. *Journal of Experimental Social Psychology, 46,* 159–165.

Elliot, A. J., & Devine, P. G. (1994). On the motivational nature of cognitive dissonance: Dissonance as psychological discomfort. *Journal of Personality and Social Psychology, 67,* 382–394.

Elliot, A. J., Kayser, D. N., Greitemeyer, T., Lichtenfeld, S. Gramzow, R. H., Maier, M. A., & Liu, H. (2010). Red, rank, and romance in women viewing men. *Journal of Experimental Psychology: General, 139*(3), 399–417.

Ellis, B. (1992). The evolution of sexual attraction: Evaluative mechanisms in women. In J. H. Barkow, L. Cosmides, & J. Tooby (Eds.), *The adapted mind* (pp. 267–288). New York: Oxford University Press.

Ellsworth, P. C. (2009). Race salience in juror decision-making: Misconceptions, clarifications, and unanswered questions. *Behavioral Science & Law, 27*(4), 599–609.

eMarketer. (2011). Retrieved from www.emarketer.com

eMarketer. (2017, May 1). US adults now spend 12 hours 7 minutes a day consuming media. https://www.emarketer.com/Article/US-Adults-Now-Spend-12-Hours-7-Minutes-Day-Consuming-Media/1015775

Emler, N. (1994). Gossip, reputation, and social adaptatio n. In R. F. Goodman & A. Ben-Ze'ev (Eds.), *Good gossip* (pp. 117–138). Wichita: University Press of Kansas.

English, T., & Chen, S. (2007). Culture and self-concept stability: Consistency across and within contexts among Asian- and European-Americans. *Journal of Personality and Social Psychology, 93,* 478–490.

English, T., John, O. P., & Gross, J. J. (2013). Emotion regulation in relationships. In J. A. Simpson & L. Campbell (Eds.), *Handbook of close relationships* (pp. 500–513). New York: Oxford University Press.

Ensari, N., Christian, J., Kuriyama, D. M., & Miller, N. (2012). The personalization model revisited: An experimental investigation of the role of five personalization-based strategies on prejudice reduction. *Group Processes & Intergroup Relations, 15,* 503–522.

Epel, E. S., Blackburn, E. H., Lin, J., Dhabhar, F. S., Adler, N. E., Morrow, J. D., et al. (2004). Accelerated telomere shortening in response to life stress. *Proceedings of the National Academy of Sciences of the USA, 101,* 17312–17315.

Epley, N., & Dunning, D. (2006). The mixed blessings of self-knowledge in behavioral prediction: Enhanced discrimination but exacerbated bias. *Personality and Social Psychology Bulletin, 32,* 641–655.

Epley, N., & Gilovich, T. (2001). Putting adjustment back in the anchoring and adjustment heuristic: An examination of self-generated and experimenter-provided anchors. *Psychological Science, 12,* 391–396.

Epley, N., & Gilovich, T. (2004). Are adjustments insufficient? *Personality and Social Psychology Bulletin, 30,* 447–460.

Epley, N., Savitsky, K., & Gilovich, T. (2002). Empathy neglect: Reconciling the spotlight effect and the correspondence bias. *Journal of Personality and Social Psychology, 83,* 300–312.

Epstein, S. (1991). Cognitive-experiential self-theory: An integrative theory of personality. In R. Curtis (Ed.), *The self with others: Convergences in psychoanalytic, social, and personality psychology* (pp. 111–137). New York: Guilford Press.

Espinoza, P., Areas da Luz Fontes, A. B., & Arms-Chavez, C. J. (2014). Attributional gender bias: Teachers' ability and effort explanations for students' math performance. *Social Psychology of Education, 17*(1), 105–126.

Esser, J. K. (1998). Alive and well after 25 years: A review of groupthink research. *Organizational Behavior and Human Decision Processes, 73,* 116–141.

Esser, J. K., & Lindoerfer, J. S. (1989). Groupthink and the space shuttle *Challenger* accident: Toward a quantitative case analysis. *Journal of Behavioral Decision Making, 2,* 167–177.

Esses, V. M., Jackson, L. M., & Bennett-AbuAyyash, C. (2010). Intergroup competition. In J. F. Dovidio, M. Hewstone, P. Glick, & V. M. Esses (Eds.), *The SAGE handbook of prejudice, stereotyping, and discrimination* (pp. 225–240). Thousand Oaks, CA: Sage.

Essock-Vitale, S. M., & McGuire, M. T. (1985). Women's lives viewed from an evolutionary perspective II. Patterns of helping. *Ethology and Sociobiology, 6,* 155–173.

Esteban, J., & Schneider, G. (2008). Polarization and conflict: Theoretical and empirical issues. *Journal of Peace Research, 45,* 131–141.

Ettinger, R. F., Marino, C. J., Endler, N. S., Geller, S. H., & Natziuk, T. (1971). Effects of agreement and correctness on relative competence and conformity. *Journal of Personality and Social Psychology, 19,* 204–212.

Evans, J. St. B. T. (2007). *Hypothetical thinking: Dual processes in reasoning and judgment.* New York: Psychology Press.

Evans, R. (1980). *The making of social psychology.* New York: Gardner Press.

Fairchild, K., & Rudman, L. A. (2008). Everyday stranger harassment and women's objectification. *Social Justice Research, 21*(3), 338–357.

Fallon, A. (1990). Culture in the mirror: Sociocultural determinants of body image. In T. F. Cash & T. Pruzinsky (Eds.), *Body images: Development, deviance, and change* (pp. 80–109). New York: Guilford Press.

Fallon, A. E., & Rozin, P. (1985). Sex differences in perceptions of desirable body shape. *Journal of Abnormal Psychology, 94*, 102–105.

Farber, P. D., Khavari, K. A., & Douglass, F. M., IV. (1980). A factor analytic study of reasons for drinking: Empirical validation of positive and negative reinforcement dimensions. *Journal of Consulting and Clinical Psychology, 48*, 780–781.

Fazio, R. H. (1995). Attitudes as object-evaluation associations: Determinants, consequences, and correlates of attitude accessibility. In R. E. Petty & J. A. Krosnick (Eds.), *Attitude strength: Antecedents and consequences* (pp. 247–282). Mahwah, NJ: Erlbaum.

Fazio, R. H., & Hilden, L. E. (2001). Emotional reactions to a seemingly prejudiced response: The role of automatically activated racial attitudes and motivation to control prejudiced reactions. *Personality and Social Psychology Bulletin, 27*, 538–549.

Fazio, R. H., & Olson, M. A. (2003). Implicit measures in social cognition research: Their meaning and use. *Annual Review of Psychology, 54*, 297–327.

Fazio, R. H., Sanbonmatsu, D. M., Powell, M. C., & Kardes, F. R. (1986). On the automatic activation of attitudes. *Journal of Personality and Social Psychology, 50*, 229–238.

Fazio, R. H., & Williams, C. J. (1986). Attitude accessibility as a moderator of the attitude-perception and attitude-behavior relations: An investigation of the 1984 presidential election. *Journal of Personality and Social Psychology, 51*, 505–514.

Fazio, R. H., Zanna, M., & Cooper, J. (1977). Dissonance and self-perception theory: An integrative view of each theory's proper domain of application. *Journal of Experimental Social Psychology, 13*, 464–479.

Feeley, T. H., Anker, A. H., & Aloe, A. M. (2012). The door-in-the-face persuasive message strategy: A meta-analysis of the first 35 years. *Communication Monographs, 79*, 316–343.

Feeney, B. C., & Collins, N. L. (2015). A new look at social support: A theoretical perspective on thriving through relationships. *Personality & Social Psychology Review, 19*, 113–147.

Fehr, B. (1994). Prototype-based assessment of laypeoples' views of love. *Personal Relationships, 1*, 309–331.

Fehr, B., & Russell, J. A. (1991). The concept of love viewed from a prototype perspective. *Journal of Personality and Social Psychology, 60*, 425–438.

Fehr, E., & Gächter, S. (2002). Altruistic punishment in humans. *Nature, 415*, 137–140.

Fehr, E., & Schmidt, K. M. (1999). A theory of fairness, competition, and cooperation. *Quarterly Journal of Economics, 114*(3), 817–868.

Fein, S., & Spencer, S. (1997). Prejudice as a self-esteem maintenance: Affirming the self through derogating others. *Journal of Personality and Social Psychology, 73*, 31–44.

Feinberg, M., & Willer, R. (2013). The moral roots of environmental attitudes. *Psychological Science, 24*, 56–62.

Feinberg, M., Willer, R., & Keltner, D. (2012). Flustered and faithful: Embarrassment as a signal of prosocial behavior. *Journal of Personality and Social Psychology, 102*, 81–97.

Feinberg, M., Willer, R., & Schultze, M. (2014). Gossip and ostracism promote cooperation in groups, *Psychological Science, 25*(3), 656–664.

Feinberg, M., Willer, R., Stellar, J., & Keltner, D. (2012). The virtues of gossip: Reputational information sharing as prosocial behavior. *Journal of Personality and Social Psychology, 102*, 1015.

Feingold, A. (1984). Correlates of physical attractiveness among college students. *Journal of Social Psychology, 122*, 139–140.

Feingold, A. (1990). Gender differences in effects of physical attractiveness on romantic attraction: A comparison across five research paradigms. *Journal of Personality and Social Psychology, 59*, 981–993.

Feingold, A. (1992a). Gender differences in mate selection preferences: A test of the parental investment model. *Psychological Bulletin, 112*, 125–139.

Feingold, A. (1992b). Good-looking people are not what we think. *Psychological Bulletin, 111*, 304–341.

Felson, R. B. (1993). The somewhat social self: How others affect self-appraisals. In J. M. Suls (Ed.), *The self in social perspective* (pp. 1–26). Hillsdale, NJ: Erlbaum.

Fenigstein, A., Scheier, M. F., & Buss, A. H. (1975). Public and private self-consciousness: Assessment and theory. *Journal of Consulting and Clinical Psychology, 43*, 522–527.

Ferguson, C. J., & Kilburn, J. (2010). Much ado about nothing: The misestimation and overinterpretation of violent video game effects in Eastern and Western nations: Comment on Anderson et al. (2010). *Psychological Bulletin, 136*, 174–178. doi:10.1037=a0018566

Ferguson, C. J., San Miguel, C. & Hartley, R.D. (2009). A multivariate analysis of youth violence and aggression: The influence of family, peers, depression, and media violence. *Journal of Pediatrics, 155*, 904–908.

Ferguson, M. J. (2008). On becoming ready to pursue a goal you don't know you have: Effects of nonconscious goals on evaluative readiness. *Journal of Personality and Social Psychology, 95*, 1268–1294.

Ferguson, M. J., & Bargh, J. A. (2008). Evaluative readiness: The motivational nature of automatic evaluation. In A. J. Elliott (Ed.), *Handbook of approach and avoidance motivation* (pp. 289–306). New York: Psychology Press.

Ferguson, M. J., Bargh, J. A., & Nayak, D. (2005). After-affects: How automatic evaluations influence the interpretation of subsequent, unrelated stimuli. *Journal of Experimental Social Psychology, 41*, 182–191.

Ferguson, M. J. & Zayas, V. (2009). Nonconscious evaluation. *Current Directions in Psychological Science, 18*, 362–366.

Festinger, L. (1954). A theory of social comparison processes. *Human Relations, 7*, 117–140.

Festinger, L. (1957). *A theory of cognitive dissonance.* Stanford, CA: Stanford University Press.

Festinger, L. (1964). *Conflict, decision, and dissonance.* Stanford, CA: Stanford University Press.

Festinger, L., & Carlsmith, J. M. (1959). Cognitive consequences of forced compliance. *Journal of Abnormal and Social Psychology, 47*, 382–389.

Festinger, L., Schachter, S., & Back, K. (1950). *Social pressures in informal groups.* Stanford, CA: Stanford University Press.

Fiedler, K. (2000). Illusory correlations: A simple associative algorithm provides a convergent account of seemingly divergent paradigms. *Review of General Psychology, 4*, 25–58.

Fiedler, K. (2007). Construal level theory as an integrative framework for behavioral decision-making research and consumer psychology. *Journal of Consumer Psychology, 17*(2), 101–106.

Fiedler, K., & Freytag, P. (2004). Pseudocontingencies. *Journal of Personality and Social Psychology, 87*, 453–467.

Fiedler, K., Walther, E., & Nickel, S. (1999). Covariation-based attribution: On the ability to assess multiple covariations of an effect. *Personality and Social Psychology Bulletin, 25*, 607–622.

Filindra, A., & Pearson-Merkowitz, S. (2013). Together in good times and bad? How economic triggers condition the effects of intergroup threat. *Social Science Quarterly, 94*, 1328–1345.

Finkel, E. J., Cheung, E. O., Emery, L. F., Carswell, K. L., & Larson, G. M. (2015). The suffocation model: Why marriage in America is becoming an all-or-nothing institution. *Current Directions in Psychological Science, 24,* 238–244.

Finkel, E. J., & Eastwick, P. W. (2008). Speed-dating. *Current Directions in Psychological Science, 17,* 193–197.

Finkel, E. J., Eastwick, P. W., Karney, B. R., Reis, H. T., & Sprecher, S. (2012). Online dating: A critical analysis from the perspective of psychological science. *Psychological Science in the Public Interest, 13,* 3–66.

Finkel, E. J., Rusbult, C. E., Kumashiro, M., & Hannon, P. A. (2002). Dealing with betrayal in close relationships: Does commitment promote forgiveness? *Journal of Personality and Social Psychology, 82,* 956–974.

Finkel, E. J., Simpson, J. A., & Eastwick, P. W. (2017). The psychology of close relationships: Fourteen core principles. *Annual Review of Psychology, 68,* 383–411.

Fischhoff, B., Gonzalez, R., Lerner, J. S., & Small, D. A. (2005). Evolving judgments of terror risks: Foresight, hindsight, and emotion. *Journal of Applied Social Psychology, 23,* 124–139.

Fishbach, A., Friedman, R. S., & Kruglanski, A. W. (2003). Leading us not unto temptation: Momentary allurements elicit overriding goal activation. *Journal of Personality and Social Psychology, 84,* 296–309.

Fishbein, M., & Ajzen, I. (1975). *Belief, attitude, intention, and behavior: An introduction to theory and research.* Reading, MA: Addison-Wesley.

Fisher, B., Cullen, F., & Turner, M. (2000). The sexual victimization of college women (NCJ 182369). Washington, DC: National Institute of Justice, Bureau of Justice Statistics. Retrieved from the National Criminal Justice Reference Service: https://www.ncjrs.gov/pdffiles1/nij/182369.pdf

Fisher, H. E., Aron, A., & Brown, L. L. (2006). Romantic love: A mammalian brain system for mate choice. *Philosophical Transactions of the Royal British Society, 361,* 2173–2186.

Fiske, A. P. (1991). *Structures of social life: The four elementary forms of human relations.* New York: Free Press.

Fiske, A. P. (1992). The four elementary forms of sociality: Framework for a unified theory of social relations. *Psychological Review, 99,* 689–723.

Fiske, A. P., Kitayama, S., Markus, H. R., & Nisbett, R. E. (1998). The cultural matrix of social psychology. In D. T. Gilbert, S. T. Fiske, & G. Lindzey (Eds.), *Handbook of social psychology* (4th ed., pp. 915–981). New York: McGraw-Hill.

Fiske, A. P., & Rai, T. S. (2014). *Virtuous violence.* Cambridge, England.: Cambridge University Press.

Fiske, S. T. (1993). Controlling other people: The impact of power on stereotyping. *American Psychologist, 48*(6), 621–628.

Fiske, S. T. (2010). Interpersonal stratification: Status, power, and subordination. In S. T. Fiske, D. T. Gilbert, & G. Lindzey (Eds.), *Handbook of social psychology* (5th ed., pp. 941–982). New York: Wiley.

Fiske, S. T., & North, M. S. (2015). Measures of stereotyping and prejudice: Barometers of bias. In G. J. Boyle, D. H. Saklofske, & G. Matthews (Eds.), *Measures of personality and social psychological constructs* (pps. 684–718). Amsterdam: Elsevier.

Fiske, S. T., & Taylor, S. E. (1991). *Social cognition.* New York: McGraw-Hill.

Fitzgerald, R., & Ellsworth, P. C. (1984). Due process vs. crime control: Death qualification and jury attitudes. *Law and Human Behavior, 8,* 31–52.

Fivush, R. (1989). Exploring sex differences in the emotional content of mother-child conversations about the past. *Sex Roles, 20,* 675–691.

Fivush, R. (1991). Gender and emotion in mother-child conversations about the past. *Journal of Narrative and Life History, 1,* 325–341.

Fivush, R. (1992). Gender differences in parent-child conversations about past emotions. *Sex Roles, 27,* 683–698.

Flannery, K. V., & Marcus, J. (2012). *The creation of inequality: How our prehistoric ancestors set the stage for monarchy, slavery, and empire.* Cambridge, MA: Harvard University Press.

Flynn, J. R. (1987). Massive IQ gains in 14 nations: What IQ tests really measure. *Psychological Bulletin, 101*(2), 171–191.

Flynn, J. R. (1991). *Asian Americans: Achievement beyond IQ.* Hillsdale, NJ: Erlbaum.

Flynn, J. R. (2007). *What is intelligence? Beyond the Flynn effect.* New York: Cambridge University Press.

Fong, C. (2001). Social preferences, self-interest, and the demand for redistribution. *Journal of Public Economics, 82,* 225–246.

Fong, G. T., Krantz, D. H., & Nisbett, R. E. (1986). The effects of statistical training on thinking about everyday problems. *Cognitive Psychology, 18,* 253–292.

Ford, C. S., & Beach, F. A. (1951). *Patterns of sexual behavior.* New York: Harper & Row.

Ford, T. E., & Kruglanski, A. (1995). Effects of epistemic motivations on the use of momentarily accessible constructs in social judgment. *Personality and Social Psychology Bulletin, 21,* 950–962.

Forgas, J. P. (1998a). Asking nicely? Mood effects on responding to more or less polite requests. *Personality and Social Psychology Bulletin, 24,* 173–185.

Forgas, J. P. (1998b). On being happy and mistaken: Mood effects on the fundamental attribution error. *Journal of Personality and Social Psychology, 75*(2), 318–331.

Forgas, J. P., & Bower, G. H. (1987). Mood effects on person perception judgments. *Journal of Personality and Social Psychology, 53,* 53–60.

Forsterling, F. (1985). Attributional retraining: A review. *Psychological Bulletin, 98,* 495–512.

Forsterling, F. (1989). Models of covariation and attribution: How do they relate to the analogy of analysis of variance? *Journal of Personality and Social Psychology, 57,* 615–625.

Fortune, J. L., & Newby-Clark, I. R. (2008). My friend is embarrassing me: Exploring the guilty by association effect. *Journal of Personality and Social Psychology, 95,* 1440–1449.

Fossett, K. (2017, March 7) The trouble with Trump's immigrant crime list. *Poltico.* http://www.politico.com/magazine/story/2017/03/donald-trump-immigrant-crimes-list-214878

Foushee, M. C. (1984). Dyads and triads at 35,000 feet. *American Psychologist, 39,* 885–893.

Fowler, J., Baker, L. A., & Dawes, C. T. (2008). Genetic variation in political participation. *American Political Science Review, 102,* 233–248.

Fowler, J. H., & Christakis, N. A. (2010). Cooperative behavior cascades in social networks. *Proceedings of the National Academy of Sciences of the USA, 107,* 5334–5338.

Fox, J. A., & Pierce, G. L. (1987). *Supplementary homicide reports 1976–1986* [Machine-readable data file]. Ann Arbor, Michigan.

Fraboni, M., Saltstone, R., & Hughes, S. (1990). The Fraboni Scale of Ageism (FSA): An attempt at a more precise measure of ageism. *Canadian Journal of Aging, 9*(1), 56–66.

Fraley, R. C., Hudson, N. W., Heffernan, M. E., & Segal, N. (2015). Are adult attachment styles categorical or dimensional? A taxometric analysis of general and relationship-specific attachment orientations. *Journal of Personality and Social Psychology, 109*(2), 354–368.

Fraley, R. C., & Spieker, S. J. (2003). Are infant attachment patterns continuously or categorically distributed? A taxometric analysis of strange situation behavior. *Developmental Psychology, 34,* 387–404.

Fraley, R. C., Vicary, A. M., Brumbaugh, C. C., & Roisman, G. I. (2011). Patterns of stability in adult attachment: An empirical test of two models of continuity and change. *Journal of Personality and Social Psychology, 101,* 974–992.

Fraley, R. C., Waller, N. G., & Brennan, K. A. (2000). An item response theory analysis of self-report measures of adult attachment. *Journal of Personality and Social Psychology, 78,* 350–365.

Frank, M. G., & Gilovich, T. (1988). The dark side of self and social perception: Black uniforms and aggression in professional sports. *Journal of Personality and Social Psychology, 54,* 74–85.

Frank, R. H. (1988). *Passions within reason.* New York: Norton.

Frank, R. H., Gilovich, T., & Regan, D. T. (1993). Does studying economics inhibit cooperation? *Journal of Economic Perspectives, 7,* 159–171.

Frank, R. H., Levine, A. S., & Dijk, O. (2014). Expenditure cascades. *Review of Behavioral Economics, 1,* 55–73.

Franzen, A., & Pointner, S. (2013). The external validity of giving in the dictator game. A field experiment using the misdirected letter technique. *Experimental Economics, 16*(2), 155–169.

Frederick, S. (2005). Cognitive reflection and decision making. *Journal of Economic Perspectives, 19,* 24–42.

Fredrickson, B. L. (1998). What good are positive emotions? *Review of General Psychology, 2,* 300–319.

Fredrickson, B. L. (2001). The role of positive emotions in positive psychology: The broaden-and-build theory of positive emotions. *American Psychologist, 56,* 218–226.

Fredrickson, B. L., Cohn, M. A., Coffey, K. A., Pek, J., & Finkel, S. M. (2008). Open hearts build lives: Positive emotions, induced through loving-kindness meditation, build consequential personal resources. *Journal of Personality and Social Psychology, 95*(5), 1045–1062. http://dx.doi.org/10.1037/a0013262

Fredrickson, B. L., & Kahneman, D. (1993). Duration neglect in retrospective evaluations of affective episodes. *Journal of Personality and Social Psychology, 65,* 45–55.

Fredrickson, B. L., & Roberts, T. (1997). Objectification theory: Toward understanding women's lived experiences and mental health risks. *Psychology of Women Quarterly, 21,* 173–206.

Freedman, J. L. (1965). Long-term behavioral effects of cognitive dissonance. *Journal of Experimental Social Psychology, 1,* 145–155.

Freedman, J. L., & Fraser, S. C. (1966). Compliance without pressure: The foot-in-the-door-technique. *Journal of Personality and Social Psychology, 4,* 195–203.

French, J., & Raven, B. (1959). The bases of social power. In D. Cartwright (Ed.), *Studies of social power* (pp. 150–167). Ann Arbor, MI: Institute for Social Research.

Frenkel, O. J., & Doob, A. N. (1976). Post-decision dissonance at the polling booth. *Canadian Journal of Behavioral Science, 8,* 347–350.

Friedman, R. S., & Forster, J. (2000). The effects of approach and avoidance motor actions on the elements of creative thought. *Journal of Personality and Social Psychology, 79,* 477–492.

Friese, M., Hofmann, W., & Schmitt, M. (2008). When and why do implicit measures predict behaviour? Empirical evidence for the moderating role of opportunity, motivation, and process reliance. *European Review of Social Psychology, 19,* 285–338.

Frieze, I. H., Olson, J. E., & Russell, J. (1991). Attractiveness and income for men and women in management. *Journal of Applied Social Psychology, 21,* 1039–1057.

Frijda, N. (1986). *The emotions.* Cambridge, England: Cambridge University Press.

Froming, W. J., Walker, G. R., & Lopyan, K. J. (1982). Public and private self-awareness: When personal attitudes conflict with societal expectations. *Journal of Experimental Social Psychology, 18,* 476–487.

Fujita, K. (2011). On conceptualizing self-control as more than the effortful inhibition of impulses. *Personality and Social Psychology Review, 15,* 352–366.

Fujita, K., Trope, Y., Liberman, N., & Levin-Sagi, M. (2006). Construal levels and self-control. *Journal of Personality and Social Psychology, 90*(3), 351–367.

Fultz, J., Batson, C. D., Fortenbach, V. A., McCarthy, P. M., & Varney, L. (1986). Social evaluation and the empathy-altruism hypothesis. *Journal of Personality and Social Psychology, 50,* 761–769.

Gable, S. L., Gonzaga, G., & Strachman, A. (2006). Will you be there for me when things go right? Social support for positive events. *Journal of Personality and Social Psychology, 91,* 904–917.

Gable, S. L., Reis, H. T., Impett, E. A., & Asher, E. R. (2004). What do you do when things go right? The intrapersonal and interpersonal benefits of sharing positive events. *Journal of Personality and Social Psychology, 87,* 228–245.

Gabrielidis, C., Stephan, W. G., Ybarra, O., Pearson, V. M. D. S., & Villareal, L. (1997). Preferred styles of conflict resolution, Mexico and the United States. *Journal of Cross-Cultural Psychology, 28*(6), 661–677.

Gaertner, L., Iuzzini, J., Witt, M., & Orina, M. M. (2006). Us without them: Evidence for an intragroup origin of positive ingroup regard. *Journal of Personality and Social Psychology, 90,* 426–439.

Gaertner, S. L., & Dovidio, J. F. (1977). The subtlety of white racism, arousal, and helping behavior. *Journal of Personality and Social Psychology, 35,* 691–707.

Gaertner, S. L., & Dovidio, J. F. (1986). The aversive form of racism. In J. F. Dovidio & S. L. Gaertner (Eds.), *Prejudice, discrimination, and racism* (pp. 61–89). Orlando, FL: Academic Press.

Gaertner, S. L., & Dovidio, J. F. (2000). Reducing intergroup bias: The common ingroup identity model. Philadelphia: Psychology Press.

Gaertner, S. L., & Dovidio, J. F. (2009). A common intergroup identity: A categorization-based approach for reducing intergroup bias. In T. D. Nelson (Ed.), *Handbook of prejudice, stereotyping, and discrimination* (pp. 489–505). New York: Psychology Press.

Gaertner, S. L., Dovidio, J. F., Guerra, R., Hehman, E., & Saguy, T. (2016). A common ingroup identity: Categorization, identity, and intergroup relations. In T. D. Nelson (Ed.), *Handbook of prejudice, stereotyping, and discrimination* (2nd ed., pp 433–455). New York: Psychology Press.

Galinsky, A. D., Rucker, D. D., & Magee, J. C. (2016). Power and perspective-taking: A critical examination. *Journal of Experimental Social Psychology, 67,* 91–92.

Galinsky, A. D., Stone, J., & Cooper, J. (2000). The reinstatement of dissonance and psychological discomfort following failed affirmations. *European Journal of Social Psychology, 30,* 123–147.

Gallo, L. C., Bogart, L. M., Vranceanu, A., & Matthews, K. A. (2005). Socioeconomic status, resources, psychological experiences, and emotional responses: A test of the reserve capacity model. *Journal of Personality and Social Psychology, 88*(2), 386–399.

Gandbhir, G., & Foster, B. (2015, March 17). A conversation with my black son. *New York Times.* http://www.theconversationseries.org

Gangestad, S. W., & Snyder, M. (2000). Self-monitoring: Appraisal and reappraisal. *Psychological Bulletin, 126,* 530–555.

Gangestad, S. W., & Thornhill, R. (1998). Menstrual cycle variation in women's preference for the scent of symmetrical men. *Proceedings of the Royal Society of London B, 265,* 727–733.

Garcia-Marques, L., & Hamilton, D. L. (1996). Resolving the apparent discrepancy between the incongruency effect and the expectancy-based illusory correlation effect: The TRAP mode. *Journal of Personality and Social Psychology, 71,* 845–860.

Gardner, W. L., Gabriel, S., & Lee, A. Y. (1999). "I" value freedom, but "we" value relationships: Self-construal priming mirrors cultural differences in judgment. *Psychological Science, 10,* 321–326.

Garner, D. M., Garfinkel, P. E., Schwartz, D., & Thompson, M. (1980). Cultural expectations of thinness in women. *Psychological Reports, 47,* 483–491.

Garofalo, J. (1981). Crime and the mass media: A selective review of research. *Journal of Research in Crime and Delinquency, 18,* 319–350.

Garrett, B. (2008). Judging innocence. *Columbia Law Review, 108,* 55–142.

Gates, G. S. (1924). The effects of an audience upon performance. *Journal of Abnormal and Social Psychology, 18,* 334–342.

Gawronski, B. (2003). Implicational schemata and the correspondence bias: On the diagnostic value of situationally constrained behavior. *Journal of Personality and Social Psychology, 84,* 1154–1171.

Gawronski, B., Cunningham, W. A., LeBel, E. P., & Deutsch, R. (2010). Attentional influences on affective priming: Does categorization influence spontaneous evaluations of multiply categorizable objects? *Cognition and Emotion, 24,* 1008–1025.

Gawronski, B., & Payne, B. K. (Eds.). (2010). *Handbook of implicit social cognition: Measurement, theory, and applications.* New York: Guilford Press.

Geeraert, N. Y., Yzerbyt, V. Y., Corneille, O., & Wigboldus, D. (2004). The return of dispositionalism: On the linguistic consequences of dispositional suppression. *Journal of Experimental Social Psychology, 40,* 264–272.

Gelfand, M. J., Raver, J. L., Nishii, L., Leslie, L. M., Lun, J., Lim, B. C., et al. (2011). Differences between tight and loose cultures: A 33-nation study. *Science, 332,* 1100–1104.

Gelles, D. (2011, July 30). Inside Match.com: It's all about the algorithm. Retrieved from http://www.slate.com/id/2300430/

Gentile, D. A. (2009). Pathological video game use among youth 8 to 18: A national study. *Psychological Science, 20,* 594–602.

Gerard, H. B., Wilhelmy, R. A., & Conolley, E. S. (1968). Conformity and group size. *Journal of Personality and Social Psychology, 8,* 79–82.

Gerber, A. S., & Rogers, T. (2009). Descriptive social norms and motivation to vote: Everyone's voting and so should you. *Journal of Politics, 71,* 178–191.

Gerbner, G., Gross, L., Morgan, M., & Signorielli, N. (1980). The "mainstreaming" of America: Violence profile no. 11. *Journal of Communication, 30,* 10–29.

Gerbner, G., Gross, L., Morgan, M., & Signorielli, N. (1986). Living with television: The dynamics of the cultivation process. In J. Bryant & D. Zillman (Eds.), *Perspectives on media effects* (pp. 17–40). Hillsdale, NJ: Erlbaum.

Gibson, B., & Zielaskowski, K. (2013). Subliminal priming of winning images prompts increased betting in slot machine play. *Journal of Applied Social Psychology, 43,* 106–115.

Gilbert, D. T. (1989). Thinking lightly about others: Automatic components of the social inference process. In J. S. Uleman & J. A. Bargh (Eds.), *Unintended thought.* New York: Guilford Press.

Gilbert, D. T. (2002). Inferential correction. In T. Gilovich, D. W. Griffin, & D. Kahneman (Eds.), *Heuristics and biases: The psychology of intuitive judgment.* New York: Cambridge University Press.

Gilbert, D. T., Brown, R. P., Pinel, E. E., & Wilson, T. D. (2000). The illusion of external agency. *Journal of Personality and Social Psychology, 79,* 690–700.

Gilbert, D. T., & Jones, E. E. (1986). Perceiver-induced constraint: Interpretations of self-generated reality. *Journal of Personality and Social Psychology, 50,* 269–280.

Gilbert, D. T., King, G., Pettigrew, S., & Wilson, T. D. (2016). Comment on "Estimating the reproducibility of psychological science." *Science, 351,* aac6277.

Gilbert, D. T., & Malone, P. S. (1995). The correspondence bias. *Psychological Bulletin, 117,* 21–38.

Gilbert, D. T., Pinel, E. C., Wilson, T. D., Blumberg, S. J., & Wheatley, T. (1998). Immune neglect: A source of durability bias in affective forecasting. *Journal of Personality and Social Psychology, 75,* 617–638.

Gilbert, S. J. (1981). Another look at the Milgram obedience studies: The role of the gradated series of shocks. *Personality and Social Psychology Bulletin, 4,* 690–695.

Gilovich, T. (1983). Biased evaluation and persistence in gambling. *Journal of Personality and Social Psychology, 44,* 1110–1126.

Gilovich, T. (1991). *How we know what isn't so: The fallibility of human reason in everyday life.* New York: Free Press.

Gilovich, T., Griffin, D. W., & Kahneman, D. (Eds.). (2002). *Heuristics and biases: The psychology of intuitive judgment.* New York: Cambridge University Press.

Gilovich, T., Kruger, J., & Medvec, V. H. (2002). The spotlight effect revisited: Overestimating the manifest variability in our actions and appearance. *Journal of Experimental Social Psychology, 38,* 93–99.

Gilovich, T., Kumar, A., & Jampol, L. (2015). A wonderful life: Experiential consumption and the pursuit of happiness. *Journal of Consumer Psychology, 25*(1), 152–165.

Gilovich, T., Medvec, V. H., & Savitsky, K. (2000). The spotlight effect in social judgment: An egocentric bias in estimates of the salience of one's own actions and appearance. *Journal of Personality and Social Psychology, 79,* 211–222.

Gilovich, T., & Savitsky, K. (2002). Like goes with like: The role of representativeness in erroneous and pseudo-scientific beliefs. In T. Gilovich, D. W. Griffin, & D. Kahneman (Eds.), *Heuristics and biases: The psychology of intuitive judgment* (pp. 617–624). New York: Cambridge University Press.

Ginosar, Z., & Trope, Y. (1980). The effects of base rates and individuating information on judgments about another person. *Journal of Experimental Social Psychology, 16,* 228–242.

Gioia, D. A., & Sims, H. P. (1985). Self-serving bias and actor-observer differences in organizations: An empirical analysis. *Journal of Applied Social Psychology, 15,* 547–563.

Givens, D. B. (1983). *Love signals: How to attract a mate.* New York: Crown.

Gladwell, M. (2008). *Outliers.* New York: Little, Brown.

Glanz, J., & Schwartz, J. (2003, September 26). Dogged engineer's effort to assess shuttle damage. *New York Times,* p. Al.

Glaser, J. (2014). *Suspect race: Causes and consequences of racial profiling.* New York: Oxford University Press.

Glasman, L. R., & Albarracín, D. (2006). Forming attitudes that predict future behavior: A meta-analysis of the attitude-behavior relation. *Psychological Bulletin, 132,* 778–822.

Glenn, N. D. (1991). The recent trend in marital success in the United States. *Journal of Marriage and the Family, 53,* 261–270.

Glick, P., & Fiske, S. T. (2001a). Ambivalent sexism. In M. P. Zanna (Ed.), *Advances in experimental social psychology* (Vol. 33, pp. 115–188). Thousand Oaks, CA: Academic Press.

Glick, P., & Fiske, S. T. (2001b). An ambivalent alliance: Hostile and benevolent sexism as complementary justifications of gender inequality. *American Psychologist, 56,* 109–118.

Goethals, G. R., Cooper, J., & Naficy, A. (1979). Role of foreseen, foreseeable, and unforeseeable behavioral consequences in the arousal of cognitive dissonance. *Journal of Personality and Social Psychology, 37,* 1179–1185.

Goff, P. A., Eberhardt, J. L., Williams, M., & Jackson, M. C. (2008). Not yet human: Implicit knowledge, historical dehumanization, and contemporary consequences. *Journal of Personality and Social Psychology, 94,* 292–306.

Goffman, E. (1959). *The presentation of self in everyday life.* Garden City, NY: Doubleday.

Goffman, E. (1966). *Behavior in public places.* New York: Free Press.

Goffman, E. (1967). *Interaction ritual: Essays on face-to-face behavior.* New York: Doubleday.

Goldberg, P. (1968, April). Are women prejudiced against women? *Trans-action: Social Science and Modern Society, 5*, 28–30.

Goldin, C., & Rouse, C. (2000). Orchestrating impartiality: The impact of "blind" auditions on female musicians. *American Economic Review, 90*, 715–741.

Goldman, W., & Lewis, P. (1977). Beautiful is good: Evidence that the physically attractive are more socially skillful. *Journal of Experimental Social Psychology, 13*, 125–130.

Goldstein, N. J., Martin, S. J., & Cialdini, R. B. (2008). *Yes! 50 scientifically proven ways to be persuasive.* New York: Free Press.

Goleman, D. (1985). *Vital lies, simple truths: The psychology of self-deception.* New York: Simon & Schuster.

Gollwitzer, P. M., & Oettingen, G. (2016). Planning promotes goal striving. In K. Vohs, & R. Baumeister (Eds.), *Handbook of self-regulation: Research, theory, and applications* (3rd ed., pp. 223–244). New York: Guilford.

Gollwitzer, P. M., & Sheeran, P. (2006). Implementation intentions and goal achievement: A meta-analysis of effects and processes. In M. P. Zanna (Ed.), *Advances in experimental social psychology* (Vol. 38, pp. 69–119). San Diego, CA: Academic Press.

Gonzaga, G. C., Keltner, D., & Ward, D. (2008). Power in mixed-sex interactions. *Cognition and Emotion, 22*, 1555–1568.

Gonzalez, R., & Griffin, D. (1997). On the statistics of interdependence: Treating dyadic data with respect. In S. Duck (Ed.), *Handbook of personal relationships: Theory, research, and interventions* (2nd ed., pp. 271–302). Chichester, England: Wiley.

Good, C., Aronson, J., & Inzlicht, M. (2003). Improving adolescents' standardized test performance: An intervention to reduce the effects of stereotype threat. *Applied Developmental Psychology, 24*, 645–662.

Good, C., Rattan, A., & Dweck, C. S. (2012). Why do women opt out? Sense of belonging and women's representation in mathematics. *Journal of Personality and Social Psychology, 102*(4), 700–717.

Gordon, A. M., & Chen, S. (2013). Does power help or hurt? The moderating role of self-other focus on power and perspective-taking in romantic relationships. *Personality and Social Psychology Bulletin, 39*, 1097–1110.

Gordon, A. M., Impett, E. A., Kogan, A., Oveis, C., & Keltner, D. (2012). To have and to hold: Gratitude promotes relationship maintenance in intimate bonds. *Journal of Personality and Social Psychology, 103*, 257–274.

Gordon, A. M., Stellar, J. E., Anderson, C. L., McNeil, G. D., Loew, D., & Keltner, D. (2017). The dark side of the sublime: Distinguishing a threat-based variant of awe. *Journal of Personality and Social Psychology, 113*, 310–328.

Gottman, J. M., & Levenson, R. W. (1992). Marital processes predictive of later dissolution: Behavior, physiology, and health. *Journal of Personality and Social Psychology, 63*, 221–233.

Gottman, J. M., & Levenson, R. W. (1999). Rebound from marital conflict and divorce prediction. *Family Processes, 38*, 287–292.

Gottman, J. M., & Levenson, R. W. (2000). The timing of divorce: Predicting when a couple will divorce over a 14-year period. *Journal of Marriage and the Family, 62*, 737–745.

Gouldner, A. W. (1960). The norm of reciprocity: A preliminary statement. *American Sociological Review, 25*, 161–178.

Gourevitch, P. (1998). *We wish to inform you that tomorrow we will be killed with our families.* New York: Picador Press.

Gove, W., Style, C., & Hughes, M. (1990). The effect of marriage on the well-being of adults: A theoretical analysis. *Journal of Family Issues, 11*, 4–35.

Goyer, J. P., Garcia, J., Purdie-Vaughns, V., Binning, K. R., Cook, J. E., Reeves, S. L., et al. (2017). Self-affirmation facilitates minority middle schoolers' progress along college trajectories. *Proceedings of the National Academy of Sciences of the USA, 114*(29): 7594–7599. Retrieved from http://www.pnas.org/content/114/29/7594.full.pdf

Graham, J., Haidt, J., Koleva, S., Motyl, M., Iyer, R., Wojcik, S., & Ditto, P. H. (2013). Moral Foundations Theory: The pragmatic validity of moral pluralism. In P. Devine & A. Plant (Eds.), *Advances in experimental social psychology* (Vol. 47, pp. 55–130). San Diego: Academic Press.

Graham, J., Haidt, J., & Nosek, B. A. (2009). Liberals and conservatives rely on different sets of moral foundations. *Journal of Personality and Social Psychology, 96*(5), 1029.

Grant, A., & Gino, F. (2010). A little thanks goes a long way: Explaining why gratitude expressions motivate prosocial behavior. *Journal of Personality and Social Psychology, 98*(6), 946–955.

Graton, A., Ric, F., & Gonzalez, E. (2016). Reparation or reactance? The influence of guilt on reaction to persuasive communication. *Journal of Experimental Social Psychology, 62*, 40–49.

Green, K., & Keltner, D. (2017, March 1). What happens when we reconnect with nature. *Greater Good.* https://greatergood.berkeley.edu/article/item/what_happens_when_we_reconnect_with_nature

Greenberg, J., Eloul, L., Markus, H. R., & Tsai, J. (2012). *"Neither East nor West": Conformity and self-enhancement in the Muslim Middle East.* Unpublished paper. Stanford, CA: Stanford University.

Greenberg, J., Pyszczynski, T., & Solomon, S. (1982). The self-serving attributional bias: Beyond self-presentation. *Journal of Experimental Social Psychology, 18*, 56–67.

Greenberg, J., Pyszczynski, T., Solomon, S., Rosenblatt, A., Veeder, M., Kirkland, S., et al. (1990). Evidence for terror management theory II: The effects of mortality salience on reactions to those who threaten or bolster the cultural worldview. *Journal of Personality and Social Psychology, 58*, 308–318.

Greenberg, J., Simon, L., Porteus, J., Pyszczynski, T., & Solomon, S. (1995). Evidence of a terror management function of cultural icons: The effects of mortality salience on the inappropriate use of cherished cultural symbols. *Personality and Social Psychology Bulletin, 21*, 1221–1228.

Greene, D., Sternberg, B., & Lepper, M. R. (1976). Overjustification in a token economy. *Journal of Personality and Social Psychology, 34*, 1219–1234.

Greene, J. D. (2013). *Moral tribes: Emotion, reason, and the gap between us and them.* New York: Penguin Press.

Greene, J. D. (2014). The cognitive neuroscience of moral judgment and decision-making. In M. S. Gazzaniga and G. R. Mangun (Eds.), *The cognitive neurosciences* (5th ed., pp. 1013–1024). Cambridge, MA: MIT Press.

Greene, J. D., & Haidt, J. (2002). How (and where) does moral judgment work? *Trends in Cognitive Sciences, 6*, 517–523.

Greene, J. D., Sommerville, R. B., Nystrom, L. E., Darley, J. M., & Cohen, J. D. (2001). An fMRI investigation of emotional engagement in moral judgment. *Science, 293*, 2105–2108.

Greenwald, A. G. (1980). The totalitarian ego: Fabrication and revision of personal history. *American Psychologist, 35*, 603–618.

Greenwald, A. G., & Banaji, M. R. (1995). Implicit social cognition: Attitudes, self-esteem, and stereotypes. *Psychological Review, 102*, 4–27.

Greenwald, A. G., Klinger, M. R., & Liu, T. J. (1989). Unconscious processing of dichotically masked words. *Memory and Cognition, 17*, 35–47.

Greenwald, A. G., McGhee, D. E., & Schwartz, J. L. K. (1998). Measuring individual differences in implicit cognition: The implicit association test. *Journal of Personality and Social Psychology, 74*, 1464–1480.

Greenwald, A. G., Poehlman, T. A., Uhlmann, E. L., & Banaji, M. R. (2009). Understanding and using the Implicit Association Test: III. Meta-analysis of predictive validity. *Journal of Personality and Social Psychology, 97*(1), 17–41.

Greenwald, A. G., Smith, C. T., Sriram, N., Bar-Anan, Y., & Nosek, B. A. (2009). Implicit race attitudes predicted vote in the 2008 U.S. presidential election. *Analyses of Social Issues and Public Policy, 9*(1), 241–253.

Greenwood, M. M., Sorenson, M. E., & Warner, B. R. (2016). Ferguson on Facebook: Political persuasion in a new era of media effects. *Computers in Human Behavior, 57* (April), 1–10.

Greve, F. (2009, May 23). America's poor are its most generous. *The Seattle Times*. Retrieved from http://seattletimes.nwsource.com

Griffitt, W., & Veitch, R. (1974). Preacquaintance attitude similarity and attraction revisited: Ten days in a fall-out shelter. *Sociometry, 37*, 163–173.

Girme, Y. U., Overall, N. C., Faingataa, S., & Sibley, C. G. (2016). Happily single: The link between relationship status and well-being depends on avoidance and approach social goals. *Social Psychological and Personality Science, 7*, 122–130.

Girme, Y. U., Overall, N. C., Simpson, J. A., & Fletcher, G. J. O. (2015). "All or nothing": Attachment avoidance and the curvilinear effects of partner support. *Journal of Personality and Social Psychology, 108*, 450–475.

Griskevicius, V., Tybur, J. M, & Van den Bergh, B. (2010). Going green to be seen: Status, reputation, and conspicuous conservation. *Journal of Personality and Social Psychology, 98*, 392–404.

Grossmann, I., & Kross, E. (2010). The impact of culture on adaptive versus maladaptive self-reflection. *Psychological Science, 21*, 1150–1157. doi:10.1177/0956797610376655

Grossmann, I., & Kross, E. (2014). Exploring "Solomon's paradox": Self-distancing eliminates the self-other asymmetry in wise reasoning about close relations in younger and older adults. *Psychological Science, 25*(8), 1571–1580.

Guéguen, N. (2004). Nonverbal encouragement of participation in a course: The effect of touching. *Social Psychology of Education, 7*(1), 89–98.

Guilbault, R. L., Bryant, F. B., Brockway, J. H., & Posavac, E. J. (2004). A meta-analysis of research on hindsight bias. *Basic and Applied Social Psychology, 26*, 103–117.

Guinote, A. (2007). Power and goal pursuit. *Personality and Social Psychology Bulletin, 33*(8), 1076–1087.

Guinote, A. (2017). How power affects people: Activating, wanting, and goal seeking. *Annual Review of Psychology, 68*, 353–381.

Guinote, A., & Chen, S. (2018). Power as active self: From acquisition to the expression and use of power. In K. Deaux & M. Snyder (Eds.), *Oxford Handbook of Personality and Social Psychology* (2nd ed.). New York: Oxford University Press.

Guinote, A., Cotzia, I., Sandhu, S., & Siwa, P. (2015). Social status modulates prosocial behavior and egalitarianism in preschool children and adults. *Proceedings of the National Academy of Sciences of the USA, 112*, 731–736.

Gunnell, J., & Ceci, S. J. (2010). When emotionality trumps reason: A study of individual processing style and juror bias. *Behavioral Science and the Law, 28*, 850–877.

Gunnthorsdottir, A., McCabe, K. & Smith, V. (2002). Using the Machiavellianism instrument to predict trustworthiness in a bargaining game. *Journal of Economic Psychology, 23*, 49–66,

Gustavsson, L., Johnsson, J. I., & Uller, T. (2008). Mixed support for sexual selection theories of mate preferences in the Swedish population. *Evolutionary Psychology, 6*(4), 575–585.

Haber, S. N., & Knutson, B. (2010). The reward circuit: Linking primate anatomy and human imaging. *Neuropsychopharmacology, 35*, 4–26.

Haberstroh, S., Oyserman, D., Schwarz, N., Kiihnen, U., & Ji, L.-J. (2002). Is the interdependent self more sensitive to question context than the independent self? Self-construal and the observation of conversational norms. *Journal of Experimental Social Psychology, 38*, 323–329.

Haddock, G., Zanna, M. P., & Esses, V. M. (1993). Assessing the structure of prejudicial attitudes: The case of attitudes toward homosexuals. *Journal of Personality and Social Psychology, 65*, 1105–1118.

Haider-Markel, D. P., & Joslyn, M.R. (2008). Beliefs about the origins of homosexuality and support for gay rights: An empirical test of attribution theory. *Public Opinion Quarterly, 72*, 291–310.

Haidt, J. (2001). The emotional dog and its rational tail: A social intuitionist approach to moral judgment. *Psychological Review, 108*, 814–834.

Haidt, J. (2003). The moral emotions. In R. J. Davidson, K. R. Scherer, & H. H. Goldsmith (Eds.), *Handbook of affective sciences* (pp. 852–870). New York: Oxford University Press.

Haidt, J. (2012). *The righteous mind: Why good people are divided by politics and religion*. New York: Pantheon.

Haidt, J., & Joseph, C. (2004). Intuitive ethics: How innately prepared intuitions generate culturally variable virtues. *Daedalus, 133*(4), 55–66, Special issue on human nature.

Halberstam, D. (1969). *The best and the brightest*. New York: Random House.

Haley, K., and Fessler, D. (2005). Nobody's watching? Subtle cues affect generosity in an anonymous economic game. *Evolution and Human Behavior, 26*, 245–256.

Hall, J. A. (1984). *Nonverbal gender differences: Accuracy of communication and expressive style*. Baltimore, MD: Johns Hopkins University Press.

Hamermesh, D. (2011). *Beauty pays: Why attractive people are more successful*. Princeton, NJ: Princeton University Press.

Hamermesh, D., & Biddle, J. (1994). Beauty and the labor market. *American Economic Review, 84*, 1174–1194.

Hamill, R., Wilson, T. D., & Nisbett, R. E. (1980). Insensitivity to sample bias: Generalizing from atypical cases. *Journal of Personality and Social Psychology, 39*, 578–589.

Hamilton, D. L., & Gifford, R. K. (1976). Illusory correlation in interpersonal perception: A cognitive basis of stereotypic judgments. *Journal of Experimental Social Psychology, 12*, 392–407.

Hamilton, D. L., Stroessner, S., & Mackie, D. M. (1993). The influence of affect on stereotyping: The case of illusory correlations. In D. M. Mackie & D. L. Hamilton (Eds.), *Affect, cognition, and stereotyping: Interactive processes in group perception* (pp. 39–61). San Diego, CA: Academic Press.

Hamilton, D. L., & Zanna, M. P. (1974). Context effects in impression formation: Changes in connotative meaning. *Journal of Personality and Social Psychology, 29*, 649–654.

Hamilton, W. D. (1964). The genetical evolution of social behavior. *Journal of Theoretical Biology, 7*, 1–52.

Han, S., & Shavitt, S. (1994). Persuasion and culture: Advertising appeals in individualistic and collectivistic societies. *Journal of Experimental Social Psychology, 30*, 326–350.

Haney, C. (1984). On the selection of capital juries: The biasing effects of the death-qualification process. *Law and Human Behavior, 8*, 121–132.

Haney, C., Banks, C., & Zimbardo, P. G. (1973). Interpersonal dynamics in a simulated prison. *International Journal of Criminology and Penology, 1*, 69–97.

Haney, C., Hurtado, A., & Vega, L. (1994). "Modern" death qualification: New data on its biasing effects. *Law and Human Behavior, 18*, 619–633.

Haney, C., & Logan, D. D. (1994). Broken promise: The Supreme Court's response to social science research on capital punishment. *Journal of Social Issues, 50*, 75–101.

Hanna, J. (1989, September 25). Sexual abandon: The condom is unpopular on the campus. *Maclean's*, p. 48.

Hans, V. P. (2000). *Business on trial: The civil jury and corporate responsibility*. New Haven, CT: Yale University Press.

Harbaugh, W. T., Mayr, U., & Burghart, D. (2007, June). Neural responses to taxation and voluntary giving reveal motives for charitable donations. *Science, 316*(1622), 1622–1625. doi:10.1126/science.1140738

Hardy, C. L., & van Vugt, M. (2006). Nice guys finish first: The competitive altruism hypothesis. *Personality and Social Psychology Bulletin, 32*, 1402–1413.

Hare, R. D. (1991). *The Hare Psychopathy Checklist—Revised*. Toronto: Multi-Health Systems.

Harlow, H. F. (1959). Love in infant monkeys. *Scientific American, 200*, 68–86.

Harmon-Jones, E. (2000). Cognitive dissonance and experienced negative affect: Evidence that dissonance increases experienced negative affect even in the absence of aversive consequences. *Personality and Social Psychology Bulletin, 26*, 1490–1501.

Harmon-Jones, E., Brehm, J. W., Greenberg, J., Simon, L., & Nelson, D. E. (1996). Evidence that the production of aversive consequences is not necessary to create cognitive dissonance. *Journal of Personality and Social Psychology, 70*, 5–16.

Harmon-Jones, E., Price, T. F., & Harmon-Jones, C. (2015). Supine body posture decreases rationalizations: Testing the action-based model of dissonance. *Journal of Experimental Social Psychology, 56*, 228–234.

Harrington, J. R., & Gelfand, M. J. (2014). Tightness-looseness across the 50 united states. *Proceedings of the National Academy of Sciences of the USA, 111*(22), 7990–7995.

Harris, C. R. (2001). Cardiovascular responses of embarassment and effects of emotional suppression in a social setting. *Journal of Personality and Social Psychology, 81*, 886–897.

Harris, R. J., Benson, S. M., & Hall, C. L. (1975). The effects of confession on altruism. *Journal of Social Psychology, 96*, 187–192.

Harris Poll. (2016). Tattoo takeover: Three in ten American have tattoos, and most don't stop at just one. The Harris Poll, February 10, 2016. www.prnewswire.com/news-releases/tattoo-takeover-three-in-ten-americans-have-tattoos-and-most-dont-stop-at-just-one-300217862.html

Hart, D., Lucca-Irizarry, N., & Damon, W. (1986). The development of self-understanding in Puerto Rico and the United States. *Journal of Early Adolescence, 6*, 293–304.

Hart, W., Albarracín, D., Eagly, A. H., Brechan, I., Lindberg, M. J., & Merrill, L. (2009). Feeling validated versus being correct: A meta-analysis of selective exposure to information. *Psychological Bulletin, 135*, 555–588.

Haslam, N., & Loughnan, S. (2014). Dehumanization and infrahumanization. *Annual Review of Psychology, 65*, 399–423.

Hass, R. G., & Linder, D. E. (1972). Counterargument availability and the effects of message structure on persuasion. *Journal of Personality and Social Psychology, 23*, 219–233.

Hassin, R. R., Ferguson, M. J., Shidlovsky, D., & Gross, T. (2007). Waved by invisible flags: The effects of subliminal exposure to flags on political thought and behavior. *Proceedings of the National Academy of Sciences of the USA, 104*, 19757–19761.

Hastie, R. (1981). Schematic principles in human memory. In E. T. Higgins, C. P. Herman, & M. P. Zanna (Eds.), *Social cognition: The Ontario Symposium* (Vol. 1, pp. 39–88). Hillsdale, NJ: Erlbaum.

Hastie, R., Penrod, S. D., & Pennington, N. (1983). *Inside the jury*. Cambridge, MA: Harvard University Press.

Hatala, M., & Prehodka, J. (1996). Content analysis of gay male and lesbian personal advertisements. *Psychological Reports, 78*(2), 371–374.

Hatfield, E., & Rapson, R. L. (2012). Equity theory in close relationships. In P. A. M. Van Lange, A. W. Kruglanski, & E. T. Higgins (Eds), *Handbook of theories of social psychology* (Vol. 2, pp. 200–217). Thousand Oaks, CA: Sage.

Haugtvedt, C. P., & Petty, R. E. (1992). Personality and persuasion: Need for cognition moderates the persistence and resistance of attitude changes. *Journal of Personality and Social Psychology, 63*, 308–319.

Hauser, C. (2004, May 6). Many Iraqis are skeptical of Bush TV appeal. *New York Times*, p. 13.

Havas, D.A., Glenberg, A. M., Gutowski, K. A., Lucarelli, M. J., & Davidson, R. J. (2010). Cosmetic use of botulinum toxin-A affects processing of emotional language. *Psychological Science, 21*, 895–900.

Hazan, C., & Shaver, P. (1987). Romantic love conceptualized as an attachment process. *Journal of Personality and Social Psychology, 52*, 511–524.

Hazan, C., & Shaver, P. (1994). Attachment as an organizational framework for research on close relationships. *Psychological Inquiry, 5*, 1–22.

Heatherton, T. F., & Polivy, J. (1991). Development and validation of a scale for measuring state self-esteem. *Journal of Personality and Social Psychology, 60*, 895–910.

Heatherton, T. F., Wyland, C. L., McCrae, C. N., Demos, K. E., Denny, B. T., & Keley, W. M. (2006). Medial prefrontal activity differentiates self from close others. *Social Cognitive Affective Neuroscience, 1*, 18–25.

Hebl, M. R., Foster, J. B., Mannix, L. M., & Dovidio, J. F. (2002). Formal and interpersonal discrimination: A field study of bias toward homosexual applicants. *Personality and Social Psychology Bulletin, 28*, 815–825.

Hebl, M., & Heatherton, T. F. (1997). The stigma of obesity in women: The difference is black and white. *Personality and Social Psychology Bulletin, 24*, 417–426.

Hedden, T., Ji, L., Jing, Q., Jiao, S., Yao, C., Nisbett, R. E., et al. (2000). *Culture and age differences in recognition memory for social dimensions*. Paper presented at the Cognitive Aging Conference, Atlanta, GA.

Hedden, T., Ketay, S., Aron, A., Markus, H. R., & Gabrieli, J. D. E. (2008). Cultural influences on neural substrates of attentional control. *Psychological Science, 19*, 12–17.

Heider, F. (1958). *The psychology of interpersonal relations*. New York: Wiley.

Heine, S. J. (2005). Constructing good selves in Japan and North America. In R. M. Sorrentino, D. Cohen, J. M. Olson, & M. P. Zanna (Eds.), *Culture and social behavior: The Ontario Symposium* (Vol. 10, pp. 95–116). Hillsdale, NJ: Erlbaum.

Heine, S. J., Kitayama, S., Lehman, D. R., Takata, T., Ide, E., Leung, C., & Matsumoto, H. (2001). Divergent consequences of success and failure in Japan and North America: An investigation of self-improving motivations and malleable selves. *Journal of Personality and Social Psychology, 81*, 599–615.

Heine, S. J., & Lehman, D. R. (1997). Culture, dissonance, and self-affirmation. *Personality and Social Psychology Bulletin, 23*, 389–400.

Heine, S. J., & Lehman, D. R. (2003). Move the body, change the self: Acculturative effects on the self-concept. In M. Schaller & C. S. Crandall (Eds.), *Psychological foundations of culture* (pp. 305–331). Mahwah, NJ: Erlbaum.

Heine, S. J., Lehman, D. R., Markus, H. R., & Kitayama, S. (1999). Is there a universal need for positive self-regard? *Psychological Review, 106*, 766–794.

Helgeson, V. S., & Mickelson, K. D. (1995). Motives for social comparison. *Personality and Social Psychology Bulletin, 21*, 1200–1209.

Helliwell, J. F., & Putnam, R. D. (2004). The social context of well-being. *Philosophical Transactions of the Royal Society B: Biological Sciences, 359*(1449), 1435–1446. doi:10.1098/rstb.2004.1522

Henderson, V. L., & Dweck, C. S. (1990). Achievement and motivation in adolescence: A new model and data. In S. Feldman & G. Elliott (Eds.), *At the threshold: The developing adolescent.* Cambridge, MA: Harvard University Press.

Hendrix, K. S., & Hirt, E. R. (2009). Stressed out over possible failure: The role of regulatory fit on claimed self-handicapping. *Journal of Experimental Social Psychology, 45,* 51–59.

Henningsen, D. D., Henningsen, M. L. M., Eden, J., & Cruz, M. G. (2006). Examining the symptoms of groupthink and retrospective sensemaking. *Small Group Research, 37,* 36–64.

Henrich, J., & Boyd, R. (1998). The evolution of conformist transmission and the emergence of between-group differences. *Evolution and Human Behavior, 19,* 215–242.

Henrich, J., Boyd, R., Bowles, S., Camerer, C., Fehr, E., Gintis, H., et al. (2001). In search of *Homo economicus*: Behavioral experiments in 15 small-scale societies. *American Economic Review, 91*(2), 73–78.

Henrich, J., Heine, S. J., & Norenzayan, A. (2010). The weirdest people in the world? *Behavioral and Brain Sciences, 33,* 61–83.

Herek, G. M. (1998). *Stigma and sexual orientation: Understanding prejudice against lesbians, gay men, and bisexuals.* Thousand Oaks, CA: Sage.

Herr, P. M. (1986). Consequences of priming: Judgment and behavior. *Journal of Personality and Social Psychology, 51,* 1106–1115.

Hertenstein, M. J., Keltner, D., App, B., Bulleit, B. A., & Jaskolka, A. R. (2006). Touch communicates distinct emotions. *Emotion, 6,* 528–533.

Hewstone, M., & Jaspers, J. (1983). A re-examination of the roles of consensus, consistency, & distinctiveness: Kelley's cube revisited. *British Journal of Social Psychology, 22,* 41–50.

Hewstone, M., & Jaspers, J. (1987). Covariation and causal attribution: A logical model of the intuitive analysis of variance. *Journal of Personality and Social Psychology, 53,* 663–672.

Higgins, E. T. (1987). Self discrepancy: A theory relating self and affect. *Psychological Review, 94,* 319–340.

Higgins, E. T. (1996). Ideals, oughts, and regulatory focus: Affect and motivation from distinct pains and pleasures. In P. M. Gollwitzer & J. A. Bargh (Eds.), *The psychology of action: Linking cognition and motivation to behavior* (pp. 91–114). New York: Guilford Press.

Higgins, E. T. (1999). Promotion and prevention as motivational duality: Implications for evaluative processes. In S. Chaiken & Y. Trope (Eds.), *Dual-process theories in social psychology.* New York: Guilford Press.

Higgins, E. T., King, G. A., & Mavin, G. H. (1982). Individual construct accessibility and subjective impressions and recall. *Journal of Personality and Social Psychology, 43,* 35–47.

Higgins, E. T., Rholes, W. S., & Jones, C. R. (1977). Category accessibility and impression formation. *Journal of Experimental Social Psychology, 13,* 141–154.

Higgins, E. T., Shah, J., & Friedman, R. (1997). Emotional responses to goal attainment: Strength of regulatory focus as a moderator. *Journal of Personality and Social Psychology, 72,* 515–525.

Hildreth, J. A. D., & Anderson, C. (2016). Failure at the top: How power undermines collaborative performance. *Journal of Personality and Social Psychology, 110,* 261–286.

Hilton, D. J., & Slugoski, B. R. (1986). Knowledge-based causal attribution: The abnormal conditions focus model. *Psychological Review, 93,* 75–88.

Hilton, D. J., Smith, R. H., & Kim, S. H. (1995). Process of causal explanation and dispositional attribution. *Journal of Personality and Social Psychology, 68,* 377–387.

Hirt, E. R. (1990). Do I see only what I expect? Evidence for an expectancy-guided retrieval model. *Journal of Personality and Social Psychology, 58,* 937–951.

Hirt, E. R., MacDonald, H. E., & Erikson, G. A. (1995). How do I remember thee? The role of encoding set and delay in reconstructive memory processes. *Journal of Experimental Social Psychology, 31,* 379–409.

Hirt, E. R., McCrea, S. M., & Kimble, C. E. (2000). Public self-focus and sex differences in behavioral self-handicapping: Does increasing self-threat still make it just a man's game? *Personality and Social Psychology Bulletin, 26,* 1131–1141.

Hirt, E. R., Zillman, D., Erickson, G. A., & Kennedy, C. (1992). Costs and benefits of allegiance: Changes in fans' self-ascribed competencies after team victory versus defeat. *Journal of Personality and Social Psychology, 63,* 724–738.

Ho, C., & Jackson, J. W. (2001). Attitudes toward Asian Americans: Theory and measurement. *Journal of Applied Social Psychology, 31,* 1553–1581.

Hobart, C. (1991). Conflict in remarriages. *Journal of Divorce and Remarriage, 15,* 69–86.

Hodson, G., Dovidio, J. F., & Gaertner, S. L. (2002). Processes in racial discrimination: Differential weighting of conflicting information. *Personality and Social Psychology Bulletin, 28,* 460–471.

Hoeksema-van Orden, C. Y. D., Gaillard, A. W. K., & Buunk, B. P. (1998). Social loafing under fatigue. *Journal of Personality and Social Psychology, 75,* 1179–1190.

Hofstede, G. (1980). *Culture's consequences: International differences in work-related values.* Beverly Hills, CA: Sage.

Hogue, M., DuBois, C. L. Z., & Fox-Cardamone, L. (2010). Gender differences in pay expectations: The roles of job intention and self-view. *Psychology of Women Quarterly, 34,* 215–227.

Holland, R. W., Hendricks, M., & Aarts, H. (2005). Smells like clean spirit: Nonconscious effects of scent on cognition and behavior. *Psychological Science, 16,* 689–693.

Holloway, S. (1988). Concepts of ability and effort in Japan and the United States. *Review of Educational Research, 58,* 327–345.

Holt-Lunstad, J., Smith, T. B., & Layton, J. B. (2010). Social relationships and mortality risk: A meta-analytic review. *PLoS Med 7*(7), e1000316. doi:10.1371/journal.pmed.1000316

Hong, Y., Chiu, C., & Kung, T. (1997). Bringing culture out in front: Effects of cultural meaning system activation on social cognition. In K. Leung, U. Kim, S. Yamaguchi, & Y. Kashima (Eds.), *Progress in Asian social psychology* (Vol. 1, pp. 135–146). Singapore: Wiley.

Horberg, E. J., Oveis, C., & Keltner, D. (2011). Emotions as moral amplifiers: An appraisal tendency approach to the influences of distinct emotions upon moral judgment. *Emotion Review, 3,* 237–244.

Horberg, E. J., Oveis, C., Keltner, D., & Cohen, A. B. (2009). Disgust and the moralization of purity. *Journal of Personality and Social Psychology, 97,* 963–976.

Hosey, G. R., Wood, M., Thompson, R. J., & Druck, P. L. (1985). Social facilitation in a non-social animal, the centipede *Lithobius forficatus. Behavioral Processes, 10,* 123–130.

Hoshino-Browne, E., Zanna, A. S., Spencer, S. J., & Zanna, M. P. (2004). Investigating attitudes cross-culturally: A case of cognitive dissonance among East Asians and North Americans. In G. Haddock & G. R. Maio (Eds.), *Contemporary perspectives on the psychology of attitudes* (pp. 375–397). East Sussex, England: Psychology Press.

Hovland, C. I., Janis, I. L., & Kelley, H. H. (1953). *Communication and persuasion: Psychological studies of opinion change.* New Haven, CT: Yale University Press.

Hovland, C. J., Lumsdaine, A. A., & Sheffield, F. D. (1949). *Experiments on mass communication*. Princeton, NJ: Princeton University Press.

Hovland, C. J., & Weiss, W. (1951). The influence of source credibility on communication effectiveness. *Public Opinion Quarterly, 15*, 635–660.

Hrdy, S. B. (1999). *Mother nature: A history of mothers, infants, and natural selection*. New York: Pantheon.

Hsiang, S. M., Meng, K. C., & Cane, M. A. (2011). Civil conflicts are associated with the global climate. *Nature, 476*, 438–441.

Hsu, F. L. K. (1953). *Americans and Chinese: Two ways of life*. New York: Schuman.

Huber, M., Van Boven, L., Park, B., & Pizzi, W. T. (2015). Seeing red: Anger increases how much Republication identification predicts partisan attitudes and perceived polarization. *PLoS ONE, 10*(9), e0139193. doi:10.1371/journal.pone.0139193

Huddy, L., & Virtanen, S. (1995). Subgroup differentiation and subgroup bias among Latinos as a function of familiarity and positive distinctiveness. *Journal of Personality and Social Psychology, 68*, 97–108.

Hugenberg, K., Miller, J., & Claypool, H. M. (2007). Categorization and individuation in the cross-race recognition deficit: Toward a solution to an insidious problem. *Journal of Experimental Social Psychology, 43*, 334–340.

Hughes, J. M., Bigler, R. S., & Levy, S. R. (2007). Consequences of learning about historical racism among European American and African American children. *Child Development, 78*, 1689–1705.

Hugo, P., & Dominus, S. (2014, April 6). Portraits of reconciliation. *New York Times Interactive Magazine*.

Humphrey, R. (1985). How work roles influence perception: Structural-cognitive processes and organizational behavior. *American Sociological Review, 50*, 242–252.

Hunter, J. E., & Hunter, R. F. (1984). Validity and utility of alternative predictors of job performance. *Psychological Bulletin, 96*, 72–98.

Hyunh, A. C., Yang, D. Y., & Grossmann, I. (2016). The value of prospective reasoning for close relationships. *Social Psychological and Personality Science, 7*, 893–902.

Inagaki, T. K., & Eisenberger, N. (2013). Shared neural mechanisms underlying social and physical warmth. *Psychological Science, 24*, 2272–2280.

Inbar, Y., Pizarro, D. A., & Bloom, P. (2012). Disgusting smells cause decreased liking of gay men. *Emotion, 12*, 23–27.

Inbau, F. E., Reid, J. E., Buckley, J. P., & Jayne, B. C. (2001). *Criminal interrogation and confessions* (4th ed.). Gaithersburg, MD: Aspen.

Independent Sector. (2002). *Giving and volunteering in the United States*. Washington, DC: Independent Sector.

Insko, C. A., Smith, R. H., Alicke, M. D., Wade, J., & Taylor, S. (1985). Conformity and group size: The concern with being right and the concern with being liked. *Personality and Social Psychology Bulletin, 11*, 41–50.

Inzlicht, M., Aronson, J., & Mendoza-Denton, R. (2009). On being the target of prejudice: Educational implications. In F. Butera & J. Levine (Eds.) *Coping with minority status: Responses to exclusion and inclusion* (pp. 13–37). Cambridge, England: Cambridge University Press.

Inzlicht, M., & Ben-Zeev, T. (2000). A threatening intellectual environment: Why females are susceptible to experiencing problem-solving deficits in the presence of males. *Psychological Science, 11*, 365–371.

Ip, G. W. M., & Bond, M. H. (1995). Culture, values, and the spontaneous self-concept. *Asian Journal of Psychology, 1*, 29–35.

Isen, A. M. (1987). Positive affect, cognitive processes, and social behavior. In L. Berkowitz (Ed.), *Advances in experimental social psychology* (Vol. 20, pp. 203–253). San Diego, CA: Academic Press.

Isen, A. M. (1993). Positive affect and decision making. In M. Lewis & J. M. Haviland-Jones (Eds.), *Handbook of emotions* (pp. 261–278). New York: Guilford Press.

Isen, A. M., Clark, M., & Schwartz, M. F. (1976). Duration of the effect of good mood on helping: Footprints on the sands of time. *Journal of Personality and Social Psychology, 34*, 385–393.

Ito, T. A., Larsen, J. T., Smith, N. K., & Cacioppo, J. T. (1998). Negative information weighs more heavily on the brain: The negativity bias in evaluative categorizations. *Journal of Personality and Social Psychology, 75*, 887–900.

Iyengar, S. (2004). Engineering consent: The renaissance of mass communications research in politics. In J. T. Jost, M. R. Banaji, & D. Prentice (Eds.), *Perspectives in social psychology: The yin and the yang of scientific progress: Perspectives on the social psychology of thought systems*. Washington, DC: APA Press.

Iyengar, S., & Hahn, S. (2009). Red media, blue media: Evidence of ideological selectivity in media use. *Journal of Communication, 59*, 19–39.

Iyengar, S., & Kinder, D. (1987). *News that matters: Television and American opinion*. Chicago: University of Chicago Press.

Iyengar, S., Sood, G., &. Lelkes, Y. (2012). Affect, not ideology: A social identity perspective on polarization. *Public Opinion Quarterly, 76*, 405–431.

Izard, C. E. (1971). *The face of emotion*. New York: Appleton-Century-Crofts.

Izard, C. E. (1994). Innate and universal facial expressions: Evidence from developmental and cross-cultural research. *Psychological Bulletin, 115*, 288–299.

Jacoby, L. L., & Dallas, M. (1981). On the relationship between autobiographical memory and perceptual learning. *Journal of Experimental Psychology, 3*, 306–340.

Jacoby, L. L., Woloshyn, V., & Kelley, C. (1989). Becoming famous without being recognized: Unconscious influences of memory produced by dividing attention. *Journal of Experimental Psychology: General, 118*, 115–125.

Jakobsson, N., & Lindholm, H., (2014). Ethnic preferences in internet dating: A field experiment. *Marriage & Family Review, 50*, 307–317.

Jakubiak, B. K., & Feeney, B. C. (2016). A sense of security: Touch promotes state attachment security. *Social Psychological and Personality Science, 7*, 345–353.

James, W. (1890). *The principles of psychology*. New York: Holt.

Jamieson, J. P., Koslov, K., Nock, M. K., & Mendes, W. B. (2013). Experiencing discrimination increases risk-taking. *Psychological Science, 24*, 131–139.

Janes, L. M., & Olson, J. M. (2000). Jeer pressure: The behavioral effects of observing ridicule of others. *Personality and Social Psychology Bulletin, 26*, 474–485.

Janis, I. L. (1972). *Victims of groupthink*. Boston: Houghton Mifflin.

Janis, I. L. (1982). *Groupthink: Psychological studies of policy decisions and fiascos* (2nd ed.). Boston: Houghton Mifflin.

Janis, I. L., & Mann, L. (1977). *Decision making*. New York: Free Press.

Jenni, K., & Loewenstein, G. (1997). Explaining the identifiable victim effect. *Journal of Risk and Uncertainty, 14*(3), 235–257.

Ji, L., Schwarz, N., & Nisbett, R. E. (2000). Culture, autobiographical memory, and social comparison: Measurement issues in cross-cultural studies. *Personality and Social Psychology Bulletin, 26*, 585–593.

Joel, S., Gordon, A. M., Impett, E. A., MacDonald, G., & Keltner, D. (2013). The things you do for me: Perceptions of a romantic partner's investments promote gratitude and commitment. *Personality and Social Psychology Bulletin, 39*, 1333–1345.

John, O. P., & Robins, R. W. (1994). Accuracy and bias in self-perception: Individual differences in self-enhancement and the role of narcissism. *Journal of Personality and Social Psychology, 66*(1), 206–219.

John-Henderson, N. A., Rheinschmidt, M. L, & Mendoza-Denton, R. (2015). Cytokine response and math performance: The role of stereotype threat and anxiety reappraisals. *Journal of Experimental Social Psychology, 56*, 203–206.

John-Henderson, N. A., Rheinschmidt, M., Mendoza-Denton, R., & Francis, D. D. (2014). Performance and inflammation outcomes predicted by different facets of SES under stereotype threat. *Social Psychological and Personality Science*, 1–9.

Johnson, J. T. (1986). The knowledge of what might have been: Affective and attributional consequences of near outcomes. *Personality and Social Psychology Bulletin, 12*, 51–62.

Johnson, K. J., & Fredrickson, B. L. (2005). We all look the same to me: Positive emotions eliminate the own-race-bias in face recognition. *Psychological Science, 16*, 875–881.

Johnson, S. K., Podratz, K. E., Dipboye, R. L., & Gibbons, E. (2010). Physical attractiveness biases in ratings of employment suitability: Tracking down the "Beauty is Beastly" effect. *Journal of Social Psychology, 150*, 310–318.

Jones, C., & Aronson, E. (1973). Attribution of fault to a rape victim as a function of the respectability of the victim. *Journal of Personality and Social Psychology, 26*, 415–419.

Jones, E. E., & Berglas, S. (1978). Control of attributions about the self through self-handicapping strategies: The appeal of alcohol and the role of underachievement. *Personality and Social Psychology Bulletin, 4*, 200–206.

Jones, E. E., & Davis, K. E. (1965). From acts to dispositions: The attribution process in person perception. In L. Berkowitz (Ed.), *Advances in experimental social psychology* (Vol. 2, pp. 219–266). New York: Academic Press.

Jones, E. E., Farina, A., Hastorf, A. H., Markus, H., Miller, D. T., & Scott, R. A. (1984). *Social stigma: The psychology of marked relationships*. New York: Freeman.

Jones, E. E., & Harris, V. A. (1967). The attribution of attitudes. *Journal of Experimental Social Psychology, 3*, 1–24.

Jones, E. E., & Nisbett, R. E. (1972). The actor and the observer: Divergent perceptions of the causes of behavior. In E. E. Jones, D. E. Kanouse, H. H. Kelley, R. E. Nisbett, S. Valins, & B. Weiner (Eds.), *Attribution: Perceiving the causes of behavior*. Morristown, NJ: General Learning Press.

Jordan, J. J., Hoffman, M., Nowak, M. A., & Rand, D. G. (2016). Uncalculating cooperation is used to signal trustworthiness. *Proceedings of the National Academy of Sciences of the USA, 113*, 8658–8663.

Jost, J. T. (1997). An experimental replication of the depressed entitlement effect among women. *Psychology of Women Quarterly, 21*, 387–393.

Jost, J. T., & Banaji, M. R. (1994). The role of stereotyping in system justification and the production of false consciousness. *British Journal of Social Psychology, 33*, 1–27.

Jost, J. T., Banaji, M. R., & Nosek, B. A. (2004). A decade of system justification theory: Accumulated evidence of conscious and unconscious bolstering of the status quo. *Political Psychology, 25*, 881–919.

Jost, J. T., & Kay, A. C. (2005). Exposure to benevolent sexism and complementary gender stereotypes: Consequences for specific and diffuse forms of system justification. *Journal of Personality and Social Psychology, 88*, 498–509.

Jost, J. T., Pelham, B. W., Sheldon, O., & Sullivan, B. N. (2003). Social inequality and the reduction of ideological dissonance on behalf of the system: Evidence of enhanced system justification among the disadvantaged. *European Journal of Social Psychology, 33*, 13–36.

Jost, J. T., & van der Toorn, J. (2012). System justification theory. In P. A. M. Van Lange, A. W. Kruglanski, & E. T. Higgins (Eds),

Handbook of theories of social psychology (Vol. 2, pp. 313–343). Thousand Oaks, CA: Sage.

Jostmann, N. B., Lakens, D., & Schubert, T. W. (2009). Weight as an embodiment of importance. *Psychological Science, 20*(9), 1169–1174.

Judd, C. M., Blair, I. V., & Chapleau, K. M. (2004). Automatic stereotypes vs. automatic prejudice: Sorting out the possibilities in the Payne (2001) weapon paradigm. *Journal of Experimental Social Psychology, 40*, 75–81.

Judd, C. M., Drake, R. A., Downing, J. W., & Krosnick, J. A. (1991). Some dynamic properties of attitude structures: Context induced responses facilitation and polarization. *Journal of Personality and Social Psychology, 60*, 193–202.

Judd, C. M., & Lusk, C. M. (1984). Knowledge structures and evaluative judgments: Effects of structural variables on judgment extremity. *Journal of Personality and Social Psychology, 46*, 1193–1207.

Judd, C. M., & Park, B. (1993). The assessment of accuracy of social stereotypes. *Psychological Review, 100*, 109–128.

Judge, T. A., Bono, J. E., Hies, R., & Gerhardt, M. W. (2002). Personality and leadership: A qualitative and quantitative review. *Journal of Applied Psychology, 87*, 765–780.

Jussim, L. (1986). Self-fulfilling prophecies: A theoretical and integrative review. *Psychological Review, 93*, 429–445.

Jussim, L. (2012). *Social perception and social reality: Why accuracy dominates bias and self-fulfilling prophecy*. New York: Oxford University Press.

Jussim, L., & Harber, K. (2005). Teacher expectations and self-fulfilling prophecies: Knowns and unknowns, resolved and unresolved controversies. *Personality and Social Psychology Review, 9*, 131–155.

Kahan, D. M. (2012). Why we are poles apart on climate change. *Nature, 488*, 255.

Kahan, D. M., Braman, D., & Jenkins-Smith, H. (2011). Cultural cognition of scientific consensus. *Journal of Risk Research, 14*, 147–174.

Kahneman, D., & Deaton, A. (2010). High income improves evaluation of life but not emotional well-being. *Proceedings of the National Academy of Sciences of the USA, 107*(38), 16489–16493.

Kahneman, D., & Frederick, S. (2002). Representativeness revisited: Attribute substitution in intuitive judgment. In T. Gilovich, D. W. Griffin, & D. Kahneman (Eds.), *Heuristics and biases: The psychology of intuitive judgment* (pp. 49–81). New York: Cambridge University Press.

Kahneman, D., & Miller, D. T. (1986). Norm theory: Comparing reality to its alternatives. *Psychological Review, 93*, 136–153.

Kahneman, D., Schkade, D., & Sunstein, C. R. (1998). Shared outrage and erratic awards: The psychology of punitive damages. *Journal of Risk and Uncertainty, 16*, 49–86.

Kahneman, D., Slovic, P., & Tversky, A. (1982). *Judgment under uncertainty: Heuristics and biases*. New York: Cambridge University Press.

Kahneman, D., & Tversky, A. (1972). Subjective probability: A judgment of representativeness. *Cognitive Psychology, 3*, 430–454.

Kahneman, D., & Tversky, A. (1973a). Availability: A heuristic for judging frequency and probability. *Cognitive Psychology, 4*, 207–232.

Kahneman, D., & Tversky, A. (1973b). On the psychology of prediction. *Psychological Review, 80*, 237–251.

Kahneman, D., & Tversky, A. (1982a). The simulation heuristic. In D. Kahneman, P. Slovic, & A. Tversky (Eds.), *Judgment under certainty: Heuristics and biases* (pp. 201–208). New York: Cambridge University Press.

Kalmijn, M. (2017). The ambiguous link between marriage and health: A dynamic reanalysis of loss and gain effects. *Social Forces, 95*(4), 1607–1636.

Kalven, H., & Zeisel, H. (1966). *The American jury*. Boston: Little, Brown.

Kamarck, T. W., Manuch, S., & Jennings, J. R. (1990). Social support reduces cardiovascular reactivity to psychological challenge: A laboratory model. *Psychosomatic Medicine, 52,* 42–58.

Kaplan, M. F., & Schersching, C. (1981). Juror deliberation: An information integration analysis. In B. Sales (Ed.), *The trial process* (pp. 235–262). New York: Plenum.

Kaplan, R. M., & Kronick, R. G. (2006). Marital status and longevity in the United States population. *Journal of Epidemiology and Community Health, 60,* 760–765.

Karau, S. J., & Williams, K. D. (1995). Social loafing: Research findings, implications, and future directions. *Current Directions in Psychological Science, 4,* 134–140.

Karmarkar, U. R., & Tormala, Z. L. (2010). Believe me, I have no idea what I'm talking about: The effects of source certainty on consumer involvement and persuasion. *Journal of Consumer Research, 36,* 1033–1049.

Karney, B. R., & Bradbury, T. N. (1995). The longitudinal course of marital quality and stability: A review of theory, method, and research. *Psychological Bulletin, 118,* 3–34.

Karney, B. R., & Bradbury, T. N. (1997). Neuroticism, marital interaction, and the trajectory of marital satisfaction. *Journal of Personality and Social Psychology, 72,* 1075–1092.

Karney, B. R., & Bradbury, T. N. (2000). Attributions in marriage: State or trait? A growth curve analysis. *Journal of Personality and Social Psychology, 78,* 295–309.

Karney, B. R., Bradbury, T. N, Fincham, F. D., & Sullivan, K. T. (1994). The role of negative affectivity in the association between attributions and marital satisfaction. *Journal of Personality and Social Psychology, 66,* 413–424.

Karpinski, A., & Hilton, J. L. (2001). Attitudes and the Implicit Association Test. *Journal of Personality and Social Psychology, 81,* 774–788.

Kashima, Y., Siegal, M., Tanaka, K., & Kashima, E. S. (1992). Do people believe behaviours are consistent with attitudes? Towards a cultural psychology of attribution processes. *British Journal of Social Psychology, 37,* 111–124.

Kasof, J. (1993). Sex bias in the naming of stimulus persons. *Psychological Bulletin, 113,* 140–165.

Kasser, T., & Sheldon, K. M. (2000). Of wealth and death: Materialism, mortality salience, and consumption behavior. *Psychological Science, 11,* 348–351.

Kassin, S. (1985). Eyewitness identification: Retrospective self-awareness and the accuracy-confidence correlation. *Journal of Personality and Social Psychology, 49,* 878–893.

Kassin, S. M., Goldstein, C. C., & Savitsky, K. (2003). Behavioral confirmation in the interrogation room: On the dangers of presuming guilt. *Law and Human Behavior, 27*(2), 187–203.

Kassin, S. M., Meissner, C., & Norwick, R. J. (2005). "I'd know a false confession if I saw one": A comparative study of college students and police investigators. *Law and Human Behavior, 29,* 211–227.

Kassin, S. M., & Sukel, H. (1997). Coerced confessions and the jury: An experimental test of the "harmless error" rule. *Law and Human Behavior, 21,* 27–46.

Katz, D., & Braly, K. (1933). Racial stereotypes of one hundred college students. *Journal of Abnormal and Social Psychology, 28,* 280–290.

Kay, A. C., & Jost, J. T. (2003). Complementary justice: Effects of "poor but happy" and "poor but honest" stereotype exemplars on system justification and implicit activation of the justice motive. *Journal of Personality and Social Psychology, 85,* 823–837.

Kay, A. C., Wheeler, S. C., Bargh, J. A., & Ross, L. (2004). Material priming: The influence of mundane physical objects on situation construal and competitive behavioral choice. *Organizational Behavior and Human Decision Processes, 95,* 83–96.

Kelley, H. H. (1967). Attribution theory in social psychology. In D. Levine (Ed.), *Nebraska Symposium on Motivation* (Vol. 15, pp. 192–238). Lincoln: University of Nebraska Press.

Kelley, H. H. (1973). The processes of causal attribution. *American Psychologist, 28,* 107–128.

Kelley, H. H., & Thibaut, J. W. (1978). *Interpersonal relations: A theory of interdependence.* New York: Wiley.

Kelman, H. C. (1958). Compliance, identification, and internalization: Three processes of attitude change. *Journal of Conflict Resolution, 2,* 51–60.

Keltner, D. (1995). The signs of appeasement: Evidence for the distinct displays of embarrassment, amusement, and shame. *Journal of Personality and Social Psychology, 68,* 441–454.

Keltner, D. (2016). *The power paradox: How we gain and lose influence.* New York: Penguin Press.

Keltner, D., & Buswell, B. N. (1997). Embarrassment: Its distinct form and appeasement functions. *Psychological Bulletin, 122,* 250–270.

Keltner, D., Ellsworth, P. C., & Edwards, K. (1993). Beyond simple pessimism: Effects of sadness and anger on social perception. *Journal of Personality and Social Psychology, 64,* 740–752.

Keltner, D., Gruenfeld, D. H., & Anderson, C. A. (2003). Power, approach, and inhibition. *Psychological Review, 110,* 265–284.

Keltner, D., & Haidt, J. (2003). Approaching awe: A moral, spiritual, and aesthetic emotion. *Cognition and Emotion, 17,* 297–314.

Keltner, D., Kogan, A., Piff, P., & Saturn, S. (2014). The sociocultural appraisal, values, and emotions (SAVE) model of prosociality: Core processes from gene to meme. *Annual Review of Psychology, 65,* 425–460.

Keltner, D., Tracy, J., Sauter, D., Cordaro, D. T., & McNeil, G. (2016). Expression of emotions. In L. F. Barrett, M. Lewis, & J. M. Haviland-Jones (Eds.), *Handbook of emotions* (4th ed., pp. 467–482). New York, NY: Guilford Press.

Kenny, D. A., & DePaulo, B. M. (1993). Do people know how others view them? An empirical and theoretical account. *Psychological Bulletin, 114,* 145–161.

Kenrick, D. T., & MacFarlane, S. W. (1984). Ambient temperature and horn-honking: A field study of the heat/aggression relationship. *Environment and Behavior, 18,* 179–191.

Kerr, N. L. (1981). Social transition schemes: Charting the group's road to agreement. *Journal of Personality and Social Psychology, 41,* 684–702.

Kerr, N. L., Kramer, G. P., Carroll, J. S., & Alfini, J. J. (1991). On the effectiveness of voir dire in criminal cases with prejudicial pretrial publicity: An empirical study. *American University Law Review, 40,* 665–701.

Kerr, N. L., MacCoun, R. J., & Kramer, G. P. (1996). Bias in judgment: Comparing individuals and groups. *Psychological Review, 103,* 687–719.

Kiecolt-Glaser, J. K., & Glaser, R. (1995). Psychoneuroimmunology and health consequences: Data and shared mechanisms. *Psychosomatic Medicine, 57,* 269–274.

Kiecolt-Glaser, J. K., Malarkey, W. B., Cacioppo, J. T., & Glaser, R. (1994). Stressful personal relationships: Immune and endocrine function. In R. Glaser & Kiecolt-Glaser (Eds.), *Handbook of human stress and immunity* (pp. 321–339). San Diego, CA: Academic Press.

Kiesler, S. B. (1971). *The psychology of commitment: Experiments linking behavior to belief.* New York: Academic Press.

Kiesler, S. B., & Mathog, R. (1968). The distraction hypothesis in attitude change. *Psychological Reports, 23,* 1123–1133.

Kim, H., & Baron, R. S. (1988). Exercise and illusory correlation: Does arousal heighten stereotypic processes? *Journal of Experimental Social Psychology, 24,* 366–380.

Kim, H., & Markus, H. R. (1999). Deviance or uniqueness, harmony or conformity? A cultural analysis. *Journal of Personality and Social Psychology, 77,* 785–800.

Kimmel, M. S. (2004). *The gendered society* (2nd ed.). New York: Oxford University Press.

Kinder, D. R., & Sears, D. O. (1981). Prejudice and politics: Symbolic racism versus racial threats to the good life. *Journal of Personality and Social Psychology, 40,* 414–431.

King, E. B., Knight, J. L., & Hebl, M. R. (2010). The influence of economic conditions on aspects of stigmatization. *Journal of Social Issues, 66,* 446–460.

King, L. A. (2001) The health benefits of writing about life goals. *Personality and Social Psychology Bulletin, 27*(7), 798–807. https://doi.org/10.1177/0146167201277003

Kitayama, S., Duffy, S., Kawamura, T., & Larsen, J. T. (2002). Perceiving an object in its context in different cultures: A cultural look at the New Look. *Psychological Science, 14,* 201–206.

Kitayama, S., Karasawa, M., & Mesquita, B. (2004). Collective and personal processes in regulating emotions: Emotion and self in Japan and the United States. In P. Philipot & R. S. Feldman (Eds.), *The regulation of emotion* (pp. 251–273). Hillsdale, NJ: Erlbaum.

Kitayama, S., Markus, H. R., Matsumoto, H., & Norasakkunkit, V. (1997). Individual and collective processes in the construction of the self: Self-enhancement in the United States and self-depreciation in Japan. *Journal of Personality and Social Psychology, 72,* 1245–1267.

Kitayama, S., & Masuda, T. (1997). Shaiaiteki ninshiki no bunkateki baikai model: taiousei bias no bunkashinrigakuteki kentou. [Cultural psychology of social inference: The correspondence bias in Japan.] In K. Kashiwagi, S. Kitayama, & H. Azuma (Eds.), *Bunkashinrigaju: riron tojisho. [Cultural psychology: Theory and evidence]*. Tokyo: University of Tokyo Press.

Kitayama, S., Snibbe, A. C., Markus, H. R., & Suzuki, T. (2004). Is there any "free" choice? Self and dissonance in two cultures. *Psychological Science, 15,* 527–533.

Klauer, K. C., & Meiser, T. (2000). A source-monitoring analysis of illusory correlations. *Personality and Social Psychology Bulletin, 26,* 1074–1093.

Klayman, J., & Ha, Y. (1987). Confirmation, disconfirmation, and information in hypothesis testing. *Psychological Review, 94,* 211–228.

Klein, R. A., Ratliff, K. A., Vianello, M., Adams, R. B., Jr., Bahník, Š., Bernstein, M. J., et al. (2014). Investigating variation in replicability: A "many labs" replication project. *Social Psychology, 45*(3), 142–152. http://doi.org/10.1027/1864-9335/a000178

Kleinhesselink, R. R., & Edwards, R. E. (1975). Seeking and avoiding belief-discrepant information as a function of its perceived refutability. *Journal of Personality and Social Psychology, 31,* 787–790.

Klinger, M. R., Burton, P. C., & Pitts, G. S. (2000). Mechanisms of unconscious priming I: Response competition, not spreading activation. *Journal of Experimental Psychology: Learning, Memory, and Cognition, 26,* 441–455.

Klohnen, E. C., & Bera, S. J. (1998). Behavioral and experiential patterns of avoidantly and securely attached women across adulthood: A 30-year longitudinal perspective. *Journal of Personality and Social Psychology, 74,* 211–223.

Kniffin, K. M., & Wilson, D. S. (2004). The effect of nonphysical traits on the perception of physical attractiveness: Three naturalistic studies. *Evolution and Human Behavior, 25,* 88–101.

Knox, R. E., & Inkster, J. A. (1968). Postdecision dissonance at post-time. *Journal of Personality and Social Psychology, 8,* 319–323.

Kogan, A., Saslow, L., Impett, E. A., Oveis, C., Keltner, D., & Saturn, S. (2011). Thin-slicing study of the oxytocin receptor (OXTR) gene and the evaluation and expression of the prosocial disposition. *Proceedings of the National Academy of Sciences of the USA, 108,* 19189–19192.

Kogut. T. (2011). Someone to blame: When identifying a victim decreases helping. *Journal of Experimental Social Psychology, 47,* 748–755.

Kogut T., & Ritov, I. (2005). The "identified victim" effect: An identified group, or just a single individual? *Organizational Behavior and Human Decision Processes, 97,* 106–116.

Kohn, M. L. (1969). Class and conformity: A study in values. Homewood, IL: Dorsey Press.

Kolbert, E. (2009, November 9). The things people say. *The New Yorker,* p. 112.

Konner, M. (2003). *The tangled wing: Biological constraints on the human spirit.* New York: Holt.

Konrath, S. H., Fuhrel-Forbis, A., Lou, A., & Brown, S. (2012). Motives for volunteering are associated with mortality risk in older adults. *Health Psychology, 31,* 87–96.

Koriat, A., Lichtenstein, S., & Fischhoff, B. (1980). Reasons for confidence. *Journal of Experimental Psychology: Human Learning and Memory, 6*(2), 107–118.

Korpela, U., & Kinnunen, K. (2009). How is leisure time interacting with nature related to the need for recovery from work demands? Testing multiple mediators. *Leisure Sciences, 33,* 1–14.

Koslowsky, M., & Schwarzwald, J. (2001). The power interaction model: Theory, methodology, and empirical applications. In A. Y. Lee-Chai & J. A. Bargh (Eds.), *The use and abuse of power: Multiple perspectives on the causes of corruption* (pp. 195–214). Philadelphia: Psychology Press.

Kouchaki, M., & Gino, F. (2016). Memories of unethical actions become obfuscated over time. *Proceedings of the National Academy of Sciences of the USA, 113,* 6166–6171.

Kovera, M. B., & Borgida, E. (2010). Social psychology and law. In D. T. Gilbert and S. T. Fiske (Eds.), *The handbook of social psychology* (5th ed., pp. 1343–1385). Hoboken, NJ: Wiley.

Kowalski, R. M., Giumetti, G. W., Schroeder, A. N., & Lattanner, M. R. (2014). Bullying in the digital age: A critical review and meta-analysis of cyberbullying research among youth. *Psychological Bulletin, 140*(4), 1073–1137.

Krahé, B. (2017). Violence against women. *Current Opinion in Psychology, 19,* 6–10. doi:10.1016/j.copsyc.2017.03.017

Kraus, M. W., Côté, S., & Keltner, D. (2010). Social class, contextualism, and empathic accuracy, *Psychological Science, 21,* 1716–1723.

Kraus, M. W., Huang, C., & Keltner, D. (2010). Tactile communication, cooperation, and performance: An ethological study of the NBA. *Emotion, 10,* 745–749.

Kraus, M. W., & Keltner, D. (2013). Social class rank, essentialism, and punitive judgment. *Journal of Personality and Social Psychology, 105,* 247–261.

Kraus, M. W., Piff, P. K., & Keltner, D. (2009). Social class, sense of control, and social explanation. *Journal of Personality and Social Psychology, 97,* 992–1004.

Kraus, M. W., Piff, P. K., & Keltner, D. (2011). Social class as culture: The convergence of resources and rank in the social realm. *Current Directions in Psychological Science, 100,* 246–250.

Kristof, N. D., & WuDunn, S. (2009). *Half the sky.* New York: Knopf.

Krosch, A. R., & Amodio, D. M. (2014). Economic scarcity alters the perception of race. *Proceedings of the National Academy of Sciences of the USA, 111*(25), 9079–9084.

Krosnick, J. A. (1988). The role of attitude importance in social evaluation: A study of policy preferences, presidential candidate evaluations, and voting behavior. *Journal of Personality and Social Psychology, 55,* 196–210.

Krosnick, J. A., Betz, A. L., Jussim, L. J., & Lynn, A. R. (1992). Subliminal conditioning of attitudes. *Personality and Social Psychology Bulletin, 18,* 152–162.

Krosnick, J. A., & Petty, R. E. (1995). Attitude strength: An overview. In R. E. Petty & J. A. Krosnick (Eds.), *Attitude strength: Antecedents and consequences* (pp. 1–24). Mahwah, NJ: Erlbaum.

Kross, E., & Ayduk, O. (2008). Facilitating adaptive emotional analysis: Distinguishing distanced-analysis of depressive experiences from immersed-analysis and distraction. *Personality and Social Psychology Bulletin, 34*, 924–938.

Kross, E., & Ayduk, O. (2017). Self-distancing: Theory, research and current directions. In J. Olson & M. Zanna (Eds.), *Advances in experimental social psychology* (Vol. 55, pp. 81–136).

Kross, E., Ayduk, O., & Mischel, W. (2005). When asking "why" does not hurt: Distinguishing rumination from reflective processing of negative emotions. *Psychological Science, 16*, 709–715.

Kross, E., Berman, M., Mischel, W., Smith, E. E., & Wager, T. (2011). Social rejection shares somatosensory representations with physical pain. *Proceedings of the National Academy of Sciences of the USA, 108*, 6270–6275.

Kross, E., & Grossmann, I. (2012). Boosting wisdom: Distance from the self enhances wise reasoning, attitudes, and behavior. *Journal of Experimental Psychology: General, 141*(1), 43–48.

Kross, E., Verduyn, P., Demiralp, E., Park, J., Lee, D., Lin, N., et al. (2013). Facebook use predicts declines in subjective well-being in young adults. *PLoS ONE, 8*(8), e69841. https://doi.org/10.1371/journal.pone.0069841

Kruger, J., & Savitsky, K. (2009). On the genesis of inflated (and deflated) judgments of responsibility. *Organizational Behavior and Human Decision Processes, 108*(1), 143–152.

Kruger, J. M., & Dunning, D. (1999). Unskilled and unaware of it: How difficulties in recognizing one's own incompetence lead to inflated self-assessments. *Journal of Personality and Social Psychology, 77*, 1121–1134.

Kruglanski, A. W., Jasko, K., Chernikova, M., Milyavsky, M., Babush, M., Baldner, C., & Pierro, A. (2015). The rocky road from attitudes to behaviors: Charting the goal systemic course of actions. *Psychological Review, 122*, 598–620.

Kruglanski, A. W., & Mayseless, O. (1990). Classic and current social comparison research: Expanding the perspective. *Psychological Bulletin, 108*(2), 195–208.

Kruglanski, A. W., & Webster, D. M. (1991). Group members' reactions to opinion deviates and conformists at varying degrees of proximity to decision deadline and of environmental noise. *Journal of Personality and Social Psychology, 61*, 212–225.

Kruglanski, A. W., & Webster, D. M. (1996). Motivated closing of the mind: "Seizing" and "freezing." *Psychological Review, 103*, 263–283.

Krull, D. S., Loy, M., Lin, J., Wang, C.-F., Chen, S., & Zhao, X. (1996). *The fundamental attribution error: Correspondence bias in independent and interdependent cultures.* Paper presented at the 13th Congress of the International Association for Cross-Cultural Psychology, Montreal, Quebec, Canada.

Kteily, N. S., Sidanius, J., & Levin, S. (2011). Social dominance orientation: Cause or 'mere effect'? Evidence for SDO as a causal predictor of prejudice and discrimination against ethnic and racial outgroups. *Journal of Experimental Social Psychology, 47*, 208–214.

Kuhlmeier, V., Wynn, K., & Bloom, P. (2003). Attribution of dispositional states by 12-month-olds. *Psychological Science, 5*, 402–408.

Kuhn, M. H., & McPartland, T. S. (1954). An empirical investigation of self-attitudes. *American Sociological Review, 19*, 68–76.

Kühnen, U., & Oyserman, D. (2002). *Thinking about the self influences thinking in general: Cognitive consequences of salient self-concept.* Ann Arbor: University of Michigan Press.

Kulik, J. A. (1983). Confirmatory attribution and the perpetuation of social beliefs. *Journal of Personality and Social Psychology, 44*, 1171–1181.

Kunda, Z. (1990). The case for motivated reasoning. *Psychological Bulletin, 108*, 480–496.

Kunda, Z., & Oleson, K. C. (1995). Maintaining stereotypes in the face of disconfirmation: Constructing grounds for subtyping deviants. *Journal of Personality and Social Psychology, 68*, 565–579.

Kunda, Z., & Sherman-Williams, B. (1993). Stereotypes and the construal of individuating information. *Personality and Social Psychology Bulletin, 19*, 90–99.

Kunda, Z., & Thagard, P. (1996). Forming impressions from stereotypes, traits, and behaviors: A parallel-constraint-satisfaction theory. *Psychological Review, 103*, 646–657.

Kunstman, J., & Maner, J. K. (2011). Sexual overperception: Power, mating goals, and biases in social judgment. *Journal of Personality and Social Psychology, 100*, 282–294.

Kunz, P. R., & Woolcott, M. (1976). Season's greetings: From my status to yours. *Social Research, 5*, 269–278.

Kuo, F. E., & Sullivan, W. C. (2001b). Environment and crime in the inner city. Does vegetation reduce crime? *Environment and Behavior, 33*, 343–367.

Kurdek, L. A. (1993). Predicting marital dissolution: A 5-year prospective longitudinal study of newlywed couples. *Journal of Personality and Social Psychology, 64*, 221–242.

Kurtz, L. E., & Algoe, S. B. (2015). Putting laughter in context: Shared laughter as behavioral indicator of relationship well-being. *Personal Relationships, 22*(4), 573–590. doi:10.1111/pere.12095

LaBrie, J. W., Hummer, J. F., Neighbors, C., & Pedersen, E. R. (2008). Live interactive group-specific normative feedback reduces misperceptions and drinking in college students: A randomized cluster trial. *Psychology of Addictive Behaviors, 22*, 141–148.

Lakin, J. L., & Chartrand, T. L. (2003). Using nonconscious behavioral mimicry to create affiliation and rapport. *Psychological Science, 14*, 334–339.

Lakoff, G. (2004). *Don't think of an elephant: Know your values and frame the debate.* White River Junction, VT: Chelsea Green Publishing.

Lakoff, G., & Johnson, M. (1980). *Metaphors we live by.* Chicago: University of Chicago Press.

Lambert, A. J., Burroughs, T., & Nguyen, T. (1999). Perceptions of risk and the buffering hypothesis: The role of just world beliefs and right-wing authoritarianism. *Personality and Social Psychology Bulletin, 25*, 643–656.

Lammers, J., & Maner, J. K. (2016). Power and attraction to the counternormative aspects of infidelity. *Journal of Sex Research, 53*, 54–63.

Lammers, J., Stapel, D. A., & Galinsky, A. D. (2011). Power increases hypocrisy: Moralizing in reasoning, immorality in behavior. *Psychological Science, 21*, 737–744.

Landau, M. J., Solomon, S., Greenberg, J., Cohen, F., & Pyszczynski, T. (2004). Deliver us from evil: The effects of mortality salience and reminders of 9/11 on support for President George W. Bush. *Personality and Social Psychology Bulletin, 30*, 1136–1150.

Lane, K. A., Banaji, M. R., Nosek, B. A., & Greenwald, A. G. (2007). Understanding and using the Implicit Association Test: IV: Procedures and validity. In B. Wittenbrink & N. Schwarz (Eds.), *Implicit measures of attitudes: Procedures and controversies* (pp. 59–102). New York: Guilford Press.

Langer, E. J., & Rodin, J. (1976). The effects of choice and enhanced personal responsibility for the aged: A field experiment in an institutional setting. *Journal of Personality and Social Psychology, 34*, 191–198.

Langlois, J. H., Kalakanis, L., Rubenstein, A. J., Larson, A., Hallam, M., & Smoot, M. (2000). Maxims or myths of beauty? A meta-analytic review and theoretical review. *Psychological Bulletin, 126*, 390–423.

Langlois, J. H., Ritter, J. M., Roggman, L. A., & Vaughn, L. S. (1991). Facial diversity and infant preferences for attractive faces. *Developmental Psychology, 27*, 79–84.

Langlois, J. H., & Roggman, L. A. (1990). Attractive faces are only average. *Psychological Science, 1,* 115–121.

LaPiere, R. T. (1934). Attitudes versus actions. *Social Forces, 13,* 230–237.

Larrick, R. P., Morgan, J. N., & Nisbett, R. E. (1990). Teaching the use of cost-benefit reasoning in everyday life. *Psychological Science, 1,* 362–370.

Larrick, R. P., Nisbett, R. E., & Morgan, J. N. (1993). Who uses the cost-benefit rules of choice? Implications for the normative status of microeconomic theory. *Organizational Behavior and Human Decision Processes, 56,* 331–347.

Larrick, R. P., Timmerman, T. A., Carton, A. M., & Abrevaya, J. (2011). Temper, temperature, and temptation: Heat-related retaliation in baseball. *Psychological Science, 22,* 423–428.

Lassiter, G. D., Geers, A. L., Munhall, P. J., Ploutz-Snyder, R. J., & Breitenbecher, D. L. (2002). Illusory causation: Why it occurs. *Psychological Science, 13,* 299–305.

Latané, B., & Darley, J. M. (1968). Group inhibition of bystander intervention in emergencies. *Journal of Personality and Social Psychology, 10,* 215–221.

Latané, B., & Nida, S. (1981). Ten years of research on group size and helping. *Psychological Bulletin, 89,* 308–324.

Lau, G., Kay, A. C., & Spencer, S. J. (2008). Loving those who justify inequality: The effects of system threat on attraction to women who embody benevolent sexist ideals. *Psychological Science, 19*(1), 20–21.

Lau, R. R., & Russell, D. (1980). Attributions in the sports pages: A field test of some current hypotheses about attribution research. *Journal of Personality and Social Psychology, 39,* 29–38.

Laughlin, P. R., & Ellis, A. L. (1986). Demonstrability and social combination processes on mathematical intellective tasks. *Journal of Experimental Social Psychology, 22,* 177–189.

Laughlin, P. R., Hatch, E. C., Silver, J. S., & Boh, L. (2006). Groups perform better than the best individuals on letters-to-numbers problems: Effects of group size. *Journal of Personality and Social Psychology, 90,* 644–651.

Layous, K., Chancellor, J., & Lyubomirsky, S. (2014). Positive activities as protective factors against mental health conditions. *Journal of Abnormal Psychology, 123,* 3–12.

Lazarus, R. S. (1966). *Psychological stress and the coping process.* New York: McGraw-Hill.

Lea, M., Spears, R., & de Groot, D. (2001). Knowing me, knowing you: Anonymity effects on social identity processes within groups. *Personality and Social Psychology Bulletin, 27,* 526–537.

Leary, M. R. (2007). Motivational and emotional aspects of the self. *Annual Review of Psychology, 58,* 317–344.

Leary, M. R., & Jones, J. L. (1993). The social psychology of tanning and sunscreen use: Self-presentational motives as a predictor of health risk. *Journal of Applied Social Psychology, 23,* 1390–1406.

Leary, M. R., & Kowalski, R. M. (1990). Impression management: A literature review and two-component model. *Psychological Bulletin, 107,* 34–47.

Leary, M. R., Kowalski, R. M., Smith, L., & Phillips, S. (2003). Teasing, rejection, and violence: Case studies of the school shootings. *Aggressive Behavior, 29,* 202–214.

Leary, M. R., Tambor, E. S., Terdal, S. K., & Downs, D. L. (1995). Self-esteem as an interpersonal monitor: The sociometer hypothesis. *Journal of Personality and Social Psychology, 68,* 518–530.

Leary, M. R., Tchividjian, L. R., & Kraxberger, B. E. (1994). Self-presentation can be hazardous to your health: Impression management and health risk. *Health Psychology, 13,* 451–470.

Le Bon, G. (1895). *The crowd.* London: Unwin.

LeDoux, J. E. (1989). Cognitive-emotional interactions in the brain. *Cognition and Emotion, 3,* 267–289.

LeDoux, J. E. (1993). Emotional networks in the brain. In M. Lewis & J. M. Haviland (Eds.), *Handbook of emotions* (pp. 109–118). New York: Guilford Press.

LeDoux, J. E. (1996). *The emotional brain.* New York: Simon & Schuster.

Lee, A., Aaker, J., & Gardner, W. (2000). The pleasures and pains of distinct self-construals: The role of interdependence in regulatory focus. *Journal of Personality and Social Psychology, 78,* 1122–1134.

Lee, F., Hallahan, M., & Herzog, T. (1996). Explaining real-life events: How culture and domain shape attributions. *Personality and Social Psychology Bulletin, 22,* 732–741.

Lee, S. W. S., & Schwarz, N. (2012). Bidirectionality, mediation, and moderation of metaphorical effects: The embodiment of social suspicion and fishy smells. *Journal of Personality and Social Psychology, 103,* 737–749.

Lee, Y., Jussim, L., & McCauley, C. R. (1995). *Stereotype accuracy: Toward appreciating group differences.* Washington, DC: American Psychological Association.

Legate, N., Ryan, R. M., & Weinstein, N. (2012). Is coming out always a "good thing"? Exploring the relations of autonomy support, outness, and wellness for lesbian, gay, and bisexual individuals. *Social Psychological and Personality Science, 3,* 145–152.

Lehman, B. J., Taylor, S. E., Kiefe, C. I., & Seeman, T. E. (2005). Relation of childhood socioeconomic status and family environment to adult metabolic functioning in the CARDIA study. *Psychosomatic Medicine, 67,* 846–854.

Lehman, D. R., Lempert, R. O., & Nisbett, R. E. (1988). The effects of graduate training on reasoning: Formal discipline and thinking about everyday life events. *American Psychologist, 43,* 431–443.

Lehman, D. R., and Nisbett, R. E. (1990). A longitudinal study of the effects of undergraduate education on reasoning. *Developmental Psychology, 26,* 952–960.

Leighton, J., Bird, G., Orsini, C., & Heyes, C. (2010). Social attitudes modulate automatic imitation. *Journal of Experimental Social Psychology, 46,* 905–910.

Leippe, M. R., & Elkin, R. A. (1987). When motives clash: Issue involvement and response involvement as determinants of persuasion. *Journal of Personality and Social Psychology, 52,* 269–278.

Lemay, Jr., E. P. (2016). The forecast model of relationship commitment. *Journal of Personality and Social Psychology, 111,* 34–52.

Lemyre, L., & Smith, P. M. (1985). Intergroup discrimination and self-esteem in the minimal group paradigm. *Journal of Personality and Social Psychology, 49,* 660–670.

Lepore, L., & Brown, R. (1997). Category and stereotype activation: Is prejudice inevitable? *Journal of Personality and Social Psychology, 72,* 275–287.

Lepore, S. J., Allen, K. M., & Evans, G. W. (1993). Social support lowers cardiovascular reactivity to an acute stressor. *Psychosomatic Medicine, 55,* 518–524.

Lepper, M. R. (1973). Dissonance, self-perception, and honesty in children. *Journal of Personality and Social Psychology, 23,* 65–74.

Lepper, M. R., & Greene, D. (1978). *The hidden costs of reward.* Hillsdale, NJ: Erlbaum.

Lepper, M. R., Greene, D., & Nisbett, R. E. (1973). Undermining children's intrinsic interest with extrinsic reward: A test of the overjustification hypothesis. *Journal of Personality and Social Psychology, 28,* 129–137.

Lepper, M. R., Sagotsky, G., Dafoe, J., & Greene, D. (1982). Consequences of superfluous social constraints: Effect on young children's social inferences and subsequent intrinsic interest. *Journal of Personality and Social Psychology, 42,* 51–65.

Lepper, M. R., & Woolverton, M. (2001). The wisdom of practice: Lessons learned from the study of highly effective tutors. In J. Aronson

(Ed.), *Improving academic achievement: Contributions of social psychology*. Orlando, FL: Academic Press.

Lepper, M. R., Woolverton, M., Mumme, D. L., & Gurtner, J.-L. (1993). Motivational techniques of expert human tutors: Lessons for the design of computer-based tutors. In S. P. Lajoie & S. J. Derry (Eds.), *Computers as cognitive tools*. Hillsdale, NJ: Erlbaum.

Lerner, J. S., Goldberg, J. H., & Tetlock, P. E. (1998). Sober second thoughts: The effects of accountability, anger, and authoritarianism on attributions of responsibility. *Personality and Social Psychology Bulletin*, *24*, 563–574.

Lerner, J. S., & Gonzalez, R. M. (2005). Forecasting one's future based on fleeting subjective experiences. *Personality and Social Psychology Bulletin*, *31*(4), 454–466.

Lerner, J. S., Gonzalez, R. M., Small, D. A., & Fischhoff, B. (2003). Effects of fear and anger on perceived risks of terrorism: A national field experiment. *Psychological Science*, *14*(2), 144–150.

Lerner, J. S., Li, Y., Valdesolo, P., & Kassam, K. (2015). Emotion and decision making. *Annual Review of Psychology*, *66*, 799–823.

Lerner, M. J. (1980). *The belief in a just world: A fundamental delusion*. New York: Plenum Press.

Lerner, M. J., & Miller, D. T. (1978). Just world research and the attribution process: Looking back and ahead. *Psychological Bulletin*, *85*, 1030–1051.

Lerner, M. J., & Simmons, C. H. (1966). Observer's reactions to the "innocent victim": Compassion or rejection? *Journal of Personality and Social Psychology*, *4*, 203–210.

Leslie, A. (2000). "Theory of mind" as a mechanism of selective attention. In M. S. Gazzaniga (Ed.), *The new cognitive neurosciences* (pp. 1235–1247). Cambridge, MA: MIT Press.

Levenson, R. W., Ekman, P., & Friesen, W. V. (1990). Voluntary facial action generates emotion-specific autonomic nervous system activity. *Psychophysiology*, *27*, 363–384.

Levenson, R. W., & Gottman, J. M. (1983). Marital interaction: Physiological linkage and affective exchange. *Journal of Personality and Social Psychology*, *45*, 587–597.

Leventhal, H. (Ed.). (1970). *Findings and theory in the study of fear communications*. New York: Academic Press.

Leventhal, H., Singer, R. P., & Jones, S. H. (1965). The effects of fear and specificity of recommendation upon attitudes and behavior. *Journal of Personality and Social Psychology*, *2*, 20–29.

Leventhal, H., Watts, J. C., & Pagano, F. (1967). Effects of fear and instructions on how to cope with danger. *Journal of Personality and Social Psychology*, *6*, 313–321.

Levin, I. P., & Gaeth, G. J. (1988). Framing of attribute information before and after consuming the product. *Journal of Consumer Research*, *15*, 374–378.

Levine, J. M. (1989). Reaction to opinion deviance in small groups. In P. B. Paulus (Ed.), *Psychology of group influence* (2nd ed., pp. 187–231). Hillsdale, NJ: Erlbaum.

Levine, J. M. (1999). Solomon Asch's legacy for group research. *Personality and Social Psychology Review*, *3*, 358–364.

Levine, J. M., Higgins, E. T., & Choi, H. S. (2000). Development of strategic norms in groups. *Organizational Behavior and Human Decision Processes*, *82*, 88–101.

Levine, J. M., & Moreland, R. L. (1990). Progress in small group research. *Annual Review of Psychology*, *41*, 585–634.

Levine, J. M., & Moreland, R. L. (1998). Small groups. In D. T. Gilbert, S. T. Fiske, & G. Lindzey (Eds.), *The handbook of social psychology* (4th ed., Vol. 2, pp. 415–469). New York: McGraw-Hill.

LeVine, R. A., & Campbell, D. T. (1972). *Ethnocentrism*. New York: Wiley.

Levinger, G. (1964). Note on need complementarity in marriage. *Psychological Bulletin*, *61*, 153–157.

Levitt, S., & List, J. (2007). What do laboratory experiments measuring social preferences reveal about the real world? *Journal of Economic Perspectives*, *21*(2), 153–174.

Lewin, K. (1935). The conflict between Aristotelian and Galilean modes of thought in contemporary psychology. *Journal of General Psychology*, *5*, 141–177.

Lewin, K. (1952). Group decision and social change. In G. E. Swanson, T. M. Newcomb, & E. L. Hartley (Eds.), *Readings in social psychology*. New York: Holt.

Lewis, M., & Sullivan, M. W. (2005). The development of self-conscious emotions. In A. J. Elliot & C. S. Dweck (Eds.), *Handbook of competence and motivation* (pp. 185–201). New York: Guilford Press.

Lewis, M. A., & Neighbors, C. (2004). Gender-specific misperceptions of college student drinking norms. *Psychology of Addictive Behaviors*, *18*, 334–339.

Leyens, J. P., Camino, L., Parke, R. D., & Berkowitz, L. (1975). Effects of movie violence on aggression in a field setting as a function of group dominance and cohesion. *Journal of Personality and Social Psychology*, *32*, 346–360.

Leyens, J. P., Cisneros, T., & Hossay, J. F. (1976). Decentration as a means of reducing aggression after exposure to violent stimuli. *European Journal of Social Psychology*, *6*, 459–473.

Leyens, J. P., & Picus, S. (1973). Identification with the winner of a fight and name mediation: Their differential effects upon subsequent aggressive behavior. *British Journal of Social and Clinical Psychology*, *12*, 374–377.

Li, J., Wang, L., & Fischer, K. W. (2004). The organization of Chinese shame concepts. *Cognition and Emotion*, *18*(6), 767–797.

Li, Y., Johnson, E. J., & Zaval, L. (2011). Local warming: Daily temperature change influences belief in global warming. *Psychological Science*, *22*, 454–459.

Li, Y. J., Johnson, K. A., Cohen, A. B., Williams, M. J., Knowles, E. D., & Chen, Z. (2011). Fundamental(ist) attribution error: Protestants are dispositionally focused. *Journal of Personality and Social Psychology*, *102*(2), 281–290

Liberman, N., Sagristano, M., & Trope, Y. (2002). The effect of temporal distance on level of construal. *Journal of Experimental Social Psychology*, *38*, 523–535.

Liberman, N., Trope, Y., & Stephan, E. (2007). Psychological distance. In A. W. Kruglanski & E. T. Higgins (Eds.), *Social psychology: Handbook of basic principles* (2nd ed., pp. 353–381). New York: Guilford Press.

Liberman, V., Samuels, S. M., & Ross, L. (2002). The name of the game: Predictive power of reputations vs. situational labels in determining Prisoner's Dilemma game moves. *Personality and Social Psychology Bulletin*, *30*, 1175–1185.

Lichtenfeld, S., Elliot, A., Maier, M. A., & Pekrun, R. (2012). Fertile green: Green facilitates creative performance. *Personality and Social Psychology Bulletin*, *38*, 784–797.

Lieberman, M. D. (2007). Social cognitive neuroscience: A review of core processes. *Annual Review of Psychology*, *58*, 259–289.

Lieberman, M.D. (2013). *Social: Why our brains are wired to connect*. New York: Crown Publishers.

Linder, D. E., Cooper, J., & Jones, E. E. (1967). Decision freedom as a determinant of the role of incentive magnitude in attitude change. *Journal of Personality and Social Psychology*, *6*, 245–254.

Linville, P. W. (1987). Self-complexity as a cognitive buffer against stress-related illness and depression. *Journal of Personality and Social Psychology*, *52*, 663–676.

Linville, P. W., & Carlston, D. E. (1994). Social cognition of the self. In P. G. Devine, D. L. Hamilton, & T. M. Ostrom (Eds.), *Social Cognition: Impact on Social Psychology* (pp. 143–193). San Diego, CA: Academic Press.

Linville, P. W., Fischer, G. W., & Fischhoff, B. (1993). AIDS risk perceptions and decision biases. In J. B. Pryor and G. D. Reeder (Eds.), *The social psychology of HIV infection* (pp. 5–38). Hillsdale, NJ: Erlbaum.

Linville, P. W., Fischer, G. W., & Salovey, P. (1989). Perceived distributions of the characteristics of in-group and out-group members: Empirical evidence and a computer simulation. *Journal of Personality and Social Psychology, 57*, 165–188.

Lipkus, I. M., Dalbert, C., & Siegler, I. C. (1996). The importance of distinguishing the belief in a just world for self versus for others: Implications for psychological well-being. *Personality and Social Psychology Bulletin, 22*, 666–677.

Lippa, R. A. (2007). The preferred traits of mates in a cross-national study of heterosexual and homosexual men and women: An examination of biological and cultural influences. *Archives of Sexual Behavior, 36*(2), 193–208.

Lippmann, W. (1922). *Public opinion*. New York: Harcourt Brace.

Liptak, A. (2011, August 23). 34 years later, Supreme Court will revisit eyewitness IDs. *New York Times*. Retrieved from http://www.nytimes.com/2011/08/23/us/23bar.html?scp=1&sq=eyewitness%20identification&st=cse

Livingston, R. W., & Brewer, M. B. (2002). What are we really priming? Cue-based versus category-based processing of facial stimuli. *Journal of Personality and Social Psychology, 82*, 5–18.

Livshits, G., & Kobyliansky, E. (1991). Fluctuating asymmetry as a possible measure of developmental homeostasis in humans: A review. *Human Biology, 63*, 441–466.

Lockwood, P. (2002). Could it happen to you? Predicting the impact of downward social comparisons on the self. *Journal of Personality and Social Psychology, 82*, 343–358.

Loersch, C., & Payne, B. K. (2011). The situated inference model: An integrative account of the effects of primes on perception, behavior, and motivation. *Perspectives on Psychological Science, 6*, 234–252.

Loftus, E. F. (1993). The reality of repressed memories. *American Psychologist, 48*, 518–537.

Loftus, E. F. (2001). Imagining the past. *The Psychologist, 14*, 584–587.

Loftus, E. F. (2003). The dangers of memory. In R. J. Sternberg (Ed.), *Psychologists defying the crowd: Stories of those who battled the establishment and won* (pp. 105–117). Washington, DC: American Psychological Association.

Loftus, E. F., & Ketcham, K. (1994). *The myth of repressed memory*. New York: St. Martin's Press.

Loftus, E. F., Miller, D. G., & Burns, H. J. (1978). Semantic integration of verbal information into a visual memory. *Human Learning and Memory, 4*, 19–31.

Loftus, E. F., & Pickrell, J. E. (1995). The formation of false memories. *Psychiatric Annals, 25*, 720–725.

Lord, C. G., Lepper, M. R., & Mackie, D. (1984). Attitude prototypes as determinants of attitude-behavior consistency. *Journal of Personality and Social Psychology, 46*, 1254–1266.

Lord, C. G., Ross, L., & Lepper, M. (1979). Biased assimilation and attitude polarization: The effects of prior theories on subsequently considered evidence. *Journal of Personality and Social Psychology, 37*, 2098–2109.

Lord, C. G., Scott, K. O., Pugh, M. A., & Desforges, D. M. (1997). Leakage beliefs and the correspondence bias. *Personality and Social Psychology Bulletin, 23*, 824–836.

Lorenz, K. (1950/1971). Part and parcel in animal and human societies. In *Studies in animal and human behaviour* (Vol. 2, pp. 115–195). Cambridge, MA: Harvard University Press.

Lott, A. J., & Lott, B. E. (1961). Group cohesiveness, communication level, and conformity. *Journal of Abnormal and Social Psychology, 62*, 408–412.

Lott, A. J., & Lott, B. E. (1974). The role of reward in formation of positive interpersonal attitudes. In T. L. Huston (Ed.), *Foundations of interpersonal attraction* (pp. 171–189). New York: Academic Press.

Lowery, B. S., Unzueta, M. M., Knowles, E. D., & Goff, P. A. (2006). Concern for the ingroup and opposition to affirmative action. *Journal of Personality and Social Psychology, 90*, 961–974.

Lu, L., Yuan, Y. C., & McLeod, P. L. (2012). Twenty-five years of hidden profiles in group decision making: A meta-analysis. *Personality and Social Psychology Review, 16*(1), 54–75.

Luhmann, M., Hofmann, W., Eid, M., & Lucas, R. E. (2012). Subjective well-being and adaptation to life events: A meta-analysis. *Journal of Personality and Social Psychology, 102*, 592–615.

Luo, S., & Zhang, G. (2009). What leads to romantic attraction: Similarity, reciprocity, security, or beauty? Evidence from a speed-dating study. *Journal of Personality, 77*(4), 933–964.

Luttrell, A., Petty, R. E., & Xu, M. (2017). Replicating and fixing failed replications: The case of need for cognition and argument quality. *Journal of Experimental Social Psychology, 69*, 178–183.

Lydon, J., Zanna, M. P., & Ross, M. (1988). Bolstering attitudes by autobiographical recall: Attitude persistence and selective memory. *Personality and Social Psychology Bulletin, 14*, 78–86.

Lynch, J. J. (1979). *The broken heart: The medical consequences of loneliness*. New York: Basic Books.

Lyubomirsky, S. (2007). *The how of happiness*. New York: Penguin Press.

Lyubomirsky, S., King, L., & Diener, E. (2005). The benefits of frequent positive affect: Does happiness lead to success? *Psychological Bulletin, 131*, 803–855.

Lyubomirsky, S., & Layous, K. (2013). How do simple positive activities increase well-being? *Current Directions in Psychological Science, 22*, 57–62.

Lyubomirsky, S., & Nolen-Hoeksema, S. (1995). Effects of self-focused rumination on negative thinking and interpersonal problem solving. *Journal of Personality and Social Psychology, 69*, 176–190.

Ma, D. S., & Correll, J. (2011). Target prototypicality moderates racial bias in the decision to shoot. *Journal of Experimental Social Psychology, 47*, 391–396.

Ma, V., & Schoeneman, T. J. (1997). Individualism versus collectivism: A comparison of Kenyan and American self-concepts. *Basic and Applied Social Psychology, 19*, 261–273.

Maass, A., & Clark, R. D. III (1983). Internalization versus compliance: Different processes underlying minority influence and conformity. *European Journal of Social Psychology, 13*, 197–215.

Maass, A., Salvi, D., Arcuri, L., & Semin, G. (1989). Language use in intergroup contexts: The linguistic intergroup bias. *Journal of Personality and Social Psychology, 57*, 981–993.

Maccoby, E. E. (1990). Gender and relationships: A developmental account. *American Psychologist, 45*, 513–520.

Maccoby, E. E., & Jacklin, C. N. (1974). *The psychology of sex differences*. Stanford, CA: Stanford University Press.

MacCoun, R. (1993). Blaming others to a fault. *Chance, 6*, 31–33.

MacDonald, G., & Leary, M. R. (2005). Why does social exclusion hurt? The relationship between social and physical pain. *Psychological Bulletin, 131*(2), 202–223.

Machiavelli, N. (1532/2003). *The prince* (G. Bull, Trans.). New York: Penguin Classics.

Macintyre, S., Maciver, S., & Solomon, A. (1993). Area, class, and health: Should we be focusing on places or people? *Journal of Social Policy, 22*, 213–234.

Mackie, D. M. (1987). Systematic and nonsystematic processing of majority and minority persuasive communications. *Journal of Personality and Social Psychology, 53*, 41–52.

Macrae, C. N., & Bodenhausen, G. V. (2000). Social cognition: Thinking categorically about others. *Annual Review of Psychology, 51,* 93–120.

Macrae, C. N., Hewstone, M., & Griffiths, R. J. (1993). Processing load and memory for stereotype-based information. *European Journal of Social Psychology, 23,* 77–87.

Macrae, C. N., Milne, A. B., & Bodenhausen, G. V. (1994). Stereotypes as energy-saving devices: A peek inside the cognitive toolbox. *Journal of Personality and Social Psychology, 66,* 37–47.

Macrae, C. N., Stangor, C., & Milne, A. B. (1994). Activating social stereotypes: A functional analysis. *Journal of Experimental Social Psychology, 30,* 370–389.

Madrian, B. C., & Shea, D. F. (2001). The power of suggestion: Inertia in 401(k) participation and savings behavior. *Quarterly Journal of Economics, 116,* 1149–1187.

Magee, J. C., Galinsky, A. D., Inesi, M. E., & Gruenfeld, D. H. (2006). Power and perspectives not taken. *Psychological Science, 17*(12), 1068–1074.

Magnay, J. (2002, November 18). Thorpe straight as the line on the bottom of the pool. *Sydney Morning Herald.* http://www.smh.com.au /articles/2002/11/17/1037490052340.html

Major, B. (1994). From social inequality to personal entitlement: The role of social comparisons, legitimacy appraisals, and group membership. In M. P. Zanna (Ed.), *Advances in experimental social psychology* (Vol. 26, pp. 293–355). San Diego, CA: Academic Press.

Malle, B. F. (1999). How people explain behavior: A new theoretical framework. *Personality and Social Psychology Review, 3,* 23–48.

Malle, B. F. (2001). Folk explanations of intentional actions. In B. F. Malle, L. J. Moses, & D. A. Baldwin (Eds.), *Intentions and intentionality: Foundations of social cognition.* Cambridge, MA: MIT Press.

Malle, B. F. (2004). *How the mind explains behavior: Folk explanations, meaning, and social interaction.* Cambridge, MA: MIT Press.

Malle, B. F. (2006). The actor-observer asymmetry in causal attribution: A (surprising) meta-analysis. *Psychological Bulletin, 132,* 895–919.

Malle, B. F., Moses, L. J., & Baldwin, D. A. (2001). *Intentions and intentionality: Foundations of social cognition.* Cambridge, MA: MIT Press.

Mann, L. (1981). The baiting crowd in episodes of threatened suicide. *Journal of Personality and Social Psychology, 41,* 703–709.

Maret, S. M. (1983). Attractiveness ratings of photographs of blacks by Cruzans and Americans. *Journal of Psychology, 115,* 113–116.

Markow, T. A., & Ricker, J. P. (1992). Male size, developmental stability, and mating success in natural populations of three *Drosophila* species. *Heredity, 69,* 122–127.

Markus, H. R. (1977). Self-schemata and processing information about the self. *Journal of Personality and Social Psychology, 35,* 63–78.

Markus, H. R. (1978). The effect of mere presence on social facilitation. An unobtrusive test. *Journal of Experimental Social Psychology, 14,* 389–397.

Markus, H. R., & Conner, A. (2013). *Clash!: 8 cultural conflicts that make us who we are.* New York: Hudson Street Press.

Markus, H. R., & Kitayama, S. (1991). Culture and the self: Implications for cognition, emotion, and motivation. *Psychological Review, 98,* 224–253.

Markus, H. R., & Wurf, E. (1987). The dynamic self-concept: A social psychological perspective. *Annual Review in Psychology, 38,* 299–337.

Marmot, M. G., Shipley, S., & Rose, G. (1984). Inequalities in death—Specific explanations of a general pattern. *Lancet, 1,* 1003–1006.

Marsh, A. A. (2016). Neural, cognitive, and evolutionary foundations of human altruism. *WIREs Cognitive Science, 7,* 59–71.

Marsh, H. L. (1991). A comparative analysis of crime coverage in newspapers in the United States and other countries from 1960–1989: A review of the literature. *Journal of Criminal Justice, 19,* 67–79.

Marsh, H. W., & Parker, J. W. (1984). Determinants of student self-concept: Is it better to be a relatively large fish in a small pond even if you don't learn to swim as well? *Journal of Personality and Social Psychology, 47,* 213–231.

Martens, J. P., & Tracy, J. L.. (2013). The emotional origins of a social learning bias: Does the pride expression cue copying? *Social Psychological and Personality Science, 4,* 492–499.

Martin, G. G., & Clark, R. D. I. (1982). Distress crying in infants: Species and peer specificity. *Developmental Psychology, 18,* 3–9.

Martin, T., & Bumpass, L. (1989). Recent trends in marital disruption. *Demography, 26,* 37–52.

Martinie, M., Olive, T., Milland, L., Joule, R. & Capa, R. L. (2013). Evidence that dissonance arousal is initially undifferentiated and only later labeled as negative. *Journal of Experimental Social Psychology, 49,* 767–770.

Marwell, G., & Ames, R. (1981). Economists free ride, does anyone else? Experiments on the provision of public goods, IV. *Journal of Public Economics, 15,* 295–310.

Masuda, T., Ellsworth, P. C., Mesquita, B., Leu, J., Tanida, S., & Van de Veerdonk, E. (2008). Placing the face in context: Cultural differences in the perception of facial emotion. *Journal of Personality and Social Psychology, 94,* 365–381.

Mathur, V. A., Harada, T., Lipke, T., & Chiao, J. Y. (2010). Neural basis of extraordinary empathy and altruistic motivation. *Neuroimage, 51,* 1468–1475.

Matsumoto, D., Keltner, D., Shiota, M., O'Sullivan, M., & Frank, M. (2008). Facial expressions of emotion. In M. Lewis, J. Haviland-Jones, & L. F. Barrett (Eds.), *Handbook of Emotions* (pp. 211–234). New York: Guilford Press.

Matsumoto, D., & Willingham, B. (2006). The thrill of victory and the agony of defeat: Spontaneous expressions of medal winners of the 2004 Athens Olympic games. *Journal of Personality and Social Psychology, 91,* 568–581.

Matza, D. (1964). *Delinquency and drift.* New York: Wiley.

Mayer, J. D., Barsade, S. G., & Roberts, R. D. (2008). Human abilities: Emotional intelligence. *Annual Review of Psychology, 59,* 507–536.

McAdams, D. P. (2008). Personal narratives and the life story. In O. P. John, R. Robins, & L. Pervin (Eds.), *Handbook of personality: Theories and research* (3rd ed., pp. 242–262). New York: Guilford Press.

McArthur, L. Z. (1972). The how and what of why: Some determinants and consequences of causal attribution. *Journal of Personality and Social Psychology, 13,* 733–742.

McArthur, L. Z., & Baron, R. M. (1983). Toward an ecological theory of social perception. *Psychological Review, 90,* 215–238.

McCall, C., Tipper, C. M., Blascovich, J., & Grafton, S. T. (2012). Attitudes trigger motor behavior through conditioned associations: Neural and behavioral evidence. *Social Cognitive and Affective Neuroscience, 7,* 841–849.

McCauley, C. (1998). Group dynamics in Janis's theory of groupthink: Backward and forward. *Organizational Behavior and Human Decision Processes, 73,* 142–162.

McClintock, E. A. (2014). Beauty and status: The illusion of exchange in partner selection. *American Sociological Review, 79*(4), 575.

McClure, M. J., Bartz, J. A., & Lydon, J. E. (2013). Uncovering and overcoming ambivalence: The role of chronic and contextually activated attachment in two-person social dilemmas. *Journal of Personality, 81,* 103–117.

McConahay, J. B. (1986). Modern racism, ambivalence, and the modern racism scale. In J. F. Dovidio & S. L. Gaertner (Eds.), *Prejudice, discrimination, and racism* (pp. 91–126). Orlando, FL: Academic Press.

McConahay, J. B., Hardee, B. B., & Batts, V. (1981). Has racism declined in America? It depends upon who is asking and what is asked. *Journal of Conflict Resolution, 25*, 563–579.

McConnell, A. R., & Leibold, J. M. (2001). Relations among the implicit association test, discriminatory behavior, and explicit measures of racial attitudes. *Journal of Experimental Social Psychology, 37*, 435–442.

McCoy, S. K., & Major, B. (2003). Group identification moderates emotional responses to perceived prejudice. *Personality and Social Psychology Bulletin, 29*, 1005–1017.

McCrae, R. R., Costa, P. T., & Yik, M. S. M. (1996). Universal aspects of Chinese personality structure. In M. H. Bond (Ed.), *The handbook of Chinese psychology* (pp. 189–207). Hong Kong: Oxford University Press.

McCullough, M. E. (2008). *Beyond revenge: The evolution of the forgiveness instinct*. New York: Basic Books.

McFayden-Ketchum, M., Bates, S. A., Dodge, K. A., & Pettit, G. S. (1996). Patterns of change in early childhood aggressive-disruptive behavior: Gender differences in predictions from early coercive and affectionate mother-child interactions. *Child Development, 67*, 2417–2433.

McGill, A. L. (1989). Context effects in judgments of causation. *Journal of Personality and Social Psychology, 57*, 189–200.

McGlone, M. S., & Tofighbakhsh, J. (2000). Birds of a feather flock conjointly(?): Rhyme as reason in aphorisms. *Psychological Science, 11*, 424–428.

McGrath, J. (1984). *Groups: Interaction and performance*. Englewood Cliffs, NJ: Prentice-Hall.

McGuire, W. J. (1985). Attitudes and attitude change. In G. Lindzey & E. Aronson (Eds.), *Handbook of social psychology* (3rd ed., Vol. 2, pp. 233–346). New York: Random House.

McGuire, W. J., & Padawer-Singer, A. (1978). Trait salience in the spontaneous self-concept. *Journal of Personality and Social Psychology, 33*, 743–754.

McGuire, W. J., & Papageorgis, D. (1961). The relative efficacy of various types of prior belief-defense in producing immunity against persuasion. *Journal of Abnormal and Social Psychology, 62*, 327–337.

McMahon, D. M. (2006). *Happiness: A history*. New York: Grove Press.

McNeil, B. J., Pauker, S. G., Sox, H. C., & Tversky, A. (1982). On the elicitation of preferences for alternative therapies. *New England Journal of Medicine, 306*, 1259–1262.

McNulty, J. K., & Karney, B. R. (2001). Attributions in marriage: Integrating specific and global evaluations of a relationship. *Personality and Social Psychology Bulletin, 27*, 943–955.

McNulty, J. K., Olson, M. A., Meltzer, A. L., & Shaffer, M. J. (2013). Though they may be unaware, newlyweds implicitly know whether their marriage will be satisfying. *Science, 342*, 1119–1120.

McQueen, A., & Klein, W. (2006). Experimental manipulations of self-affirmation: A systematic review. *Self and Identity, 5*, 289–354.

Mead, G. H. (1934). *Mind, self, and society*. Chicago: University of Chicago Press.

Medcoff, J. W. (1990). PEAT: An integrative model of attribution processes. In M. P. Zanna (Ed.), *Advances in experimental social psychology* (Vol. 23, pp. 111–209). New York: Academic Press.

Medvec, V. H., Madey, S. F., & Gilovich, T. (1995). When less is more: Counterfactual thinking and satisfaction among Olympic medalists. *Journal of Personality and Social Psychology, 69*, 603–610.

Mehrabian, A., & Williams, M. (1969). Nonverbal concomitants of perceived and intended persuasiveness. *Journal of Personality and Social Psychology, 13*, 37–58.

Mehta, P. H., & Josephs, R. A. (2010). Testosterone and cortisol jointly regulate dominance: Evidence for a dual-hormone hypothesis. *Hormones and Behavior, 58*, 898–906.

Mehta, P. H., Mor, S., Yap, A., & Prasad, S. (2015). Dual-hormone changes are related to bargaining performance. *Psychological Science, 26*, 866–876.

Mehta, R., & Zhu, R. J. (2009). Blue or red? Exploring the effect of color on cognitive performances. *Science, 323*, 1226–1229.

Meltzer, A. L., McNulty, J. K., Jackson, G. L., & Karney, B. R. (2014). Men still value physical attractiveness in a long-term mate more than women: Rejoinder to Eastwick, Neff, Finkel, Luchies, and Hunt. *Journal of Personality and Social Psychology, 106*, 435–440.

Merton, R. (1957). *Social theory and social structure*. Glencoe, IL: Free Press.

Mesquita, B., de Leersnyder, J., & Boiger, M. (2016). The cultural psychology of emotions. In L. Feldman Barrett, M. Lewis, & J. Haviland-Jones (Eds.), *Handbook of Emotions* (4th ed., pp. 393–411). New York: Guilford Press.

Mesquita, B., & Leu, J. (2007). The cultural psychology of emotion. In S. Kitayama & D. Cohen (Eds.), *The handbook of cultural psychology* (pp. 734–759). New York: Guilford Press.

Metcalfe, J., & Mischel, W. (1999). A hot/cool system analysis of delay of gratification: Dynamics of willpower. *Psychological Review, 106*(1), 3–19.

Meyer, I. H., & Frost, D. M. (2013). Minority stress and the health of sexual minorities. In C. J. Patterson & A. R. D'Augelli (Eds.), *Handbook of psychology and sexual orientation* (pp. 252–266). New York: Oxford University Press.

Meyer, M. L., Masten, C. L., Ma, Y., Wang, C., Shi, Z., Eisenberger, N. I., & Han, S. (2013). Empathy for the social suffering of friends and strangers recruits distinct patterns of brain activation. *Social Cognitive and Affective Neuroscience, 8*(4), 446–454.

Michaels, J. W., Blommel, J. M., Brocato, R. M., Linkous, R. A., & Rowe, J. S. (1982). Social facilitation and inhibition in a natural setting. *Replications in Social Psychology, 2*, 21–24.

Mikulincer, M. (1998). Attachment working models and the sense of trust: An exploration of interaction goals and affect regulation. *Journal of Personality and Social Psychology, 74*, 1209–1224.

Mikulincer, M., & Shaver, P. R. (2003). The attachment behavioral system in adulthood: Activation, psychodynamics, and interpersonal processes. In M. P. Zanna (Ed.), *Advances in experimental social psychology* (Vol. 35, pp. 53–152). New York: Academic Press.

Mikulincer, M., Shaver, P. R., Gillath, O., & Nitzberg, R. E. (2005). Attachment, caregiving, and altruism: Boosting attachment security increases compassion and helping. *Journal of Personality and Social Psychology, 89*, 817–839.

Milgram, S. (1963). Behavioral study of obedience. *Journal of Abnormal and Social Psychology, 67*, 371–378.

Milgram, S. (1965). Some conditions of obedience and disobedience to authority. *Human Relations, 18*, 57–75.

Milgram, S. (1970). The experience of living in cities. *Science, 167*, 1461–1468.

Milgram, S. (1974). *Obedience to authority: An experimental view*. New York: Harper & Row.

Millar, M., & Tesser, A. (1986). Effects of affective and cognitive focus on the attitude-behavior relation. *Journal of Personality and Social Psychology, 51*, 270–276.

Miller, A. G. (1986). *The obedience experiments: A case study of controversy in social science*. New York: Praeger.

Miller, A. G., Ashton, W., & Mishal, M. (1990). Beliefs concerning the features of constrained behavior: A basis for the fundamental attribution error. *Journal of Personality and Social Psychology, 59*, 635–650.

Miller, A. G., Jones, E. E., & Hinkle, S. (1981). A robust attribution error in the personality domain. *Journal of Experimental Social Psychology, 17*, 587–600.

Miller, D. T., & McFarland, C. (1986). Counterfactual thinking and victim compensation: A test of norm theory. *Personality and Social Psychology Bulletin, 12,* 513–519.

Miller, R. S. (1996). *Embarrassment: Poise and peril in everyday life.* New York: Guilford Press.

Miller, R. S., & Leary, M. R. (1992). Social sources and interactive functions of embarrassment. In M. Clark (Ed.), *Emotion and social behavior.* Newbury Park, CA: Sage.

Miller, S. L., & Maner, J. K. (2010). Scent of a woman: Men's testosterone responses to olfactory ovulation cues. *Psychological Science, 21*(2), 276–283.

Miranda, J., & Storms, M. (1989). Psychological adjustment of lesbians and gay men. *Journal of Counseling & Development, 68,* 41–45.

Mischel, W., & Ayduk, O. (2004). Willpower in a cognitive-affective processing system: The dynamics of delay of gratification. In R. F. Baumeister & K. D. Vohs (Eds.), *Handbook of self-regulation: Research, theory, and applications.* New York: Guildford Press.

Mischel, W., Ebbesen, E. B., & Zeiss, A. R. (1972). Cognitive and attentional mechanisms in delay of gratification. *Journal of Personality and Social Psychology, 21,* 204–218.

Mischel, W., & Shoda, Y. (1995). A cognitive-affective system theory of personality: Reconceptualizing situations, dispositions, dynamics, and invariance in personality structures. *Psychological Review, 102,* 246–268.

Mischel, W., Shoda, Y., & Rodriguez, M. I. (1989). Delay of gratification in children. *Science, 244,* 933–938.

Mithen, S. (1996). *The prehistory of the mind: The cognitive origins of art and science.* London: Thames and Hudson.

Mohr, J. J., Selterman, D., & Fassinger, R. E. (2013). Romantic attachment and relationship functioning in same-sex couples. *Journal of Counseling Psychology, 60*(1), 72–82.

Monteith, M. J., Deneen, N. E., & Tooman, G. (1996). The effect of social norm activation on the expression of opinions concerning gay men and blacks. *Basic & Applied Social Psychology, 18,* 267–288.

Montoya, R. M., Horton, R. S., Vevea, J. L., Citkowicz, M., & Lauber, E. A. (2017). A re-examination of the mere exposure effect: The influence of repeated exposure on recognition, familiarity, and liking. *Psychological Bulletin, 143,* 459–498.

Montoya, R. M., Kershaw, C., & Prosser, J. (in press). A meta-analytic investigation of the relation between interpersonal attraction and enacted behavior. *Psychological Bulletin.*

Moran, G., Cutler, B. L., & De Lisa, A. (1994). Attitudes toward tort reform, scientific jury selection, and juror bias: Verdict inclination in criminal and civil trials. *Law and Psychology Review, 18,* 309–328.

Moran, J. M., Jolly, E., & Mitchell, J. P. (2014). Spontaneous mentalizing predicts the fundamental attribution error. *Journal of Cognitive Neuroscience, 26,* 569–576.

Morelli, G. A., & Rothbaum, F. (2007). Situating the child in context: Attachment relationships and self-regulation in different cultures. In *Handbook of Cultural Psychology* (pp. 500–527). New York: Guilford Press.

Morenoff, J. D., Sampson, R. J., & Raudenbush, S. (2001). Neighborhood inequality, collective efficacy, and the spatial dynamics of urban violence. *Criminology, 39,* 517–560.

Morgan, C. A., III, Hazlett, G., Doran, A., Garrett, S., Hoyt, G., Thomas, P., et al. (2004). Accuracy of eyewitness memory for persons encountered during exposure to highly intense stress. *International Journal of Law and Psychiatry, 27,* 265–279.

Morrow, J., & Nolen-Hoeksema, S. (1990). Effects of responses to depression on the remediation of depressive affect. *Journal of Personality and Social Psychology, 58,* 519–527.

Moscovici, S. (1985). Social influence and conformity. In G. Lindzey & E. Aronson (Eds.), *The handbook of social psychology* (3rd ed., Vol. 2, pp. 347–412). New York: Random House.

Moscovici, S., Lage, E., & Naffrechoux, M. (1969). Influences of a consistent minority on the responses of a majority in a color perception task. *Sociometry, 32,* 365–380.

Moscovici, S., & Zavalloni, M. (1969). The group as a polarizer of attitudes. *Journal of Personality and Social Psychology, 12,* 125–135.

Moskowitz, D. S. (1994). Cross-situational generality and the interpersonal circumplex. *Journal of Personality and Social Psychology, 66,* 921–933.

Moskowitz, D. S. (2010). Quarrelsomeness in daily life. *Journal of Personality, 78,* 39–66.

Moskowitz, J. T., Epel, E. S., & Acree, M. (2008). Positive affect uniquely predicts lower risk of mortality in people with diabetes. *Health Psychology, 27,* 73–82.

Mullen, B., & Riordan, C. A. (1988). Self-serving attributions for performance in naturalistic settings: A meta-analytic review. *Journal of Applied Social Psychology, 18,* 3–22.

Munro, D. (1985). Introduction. In D. Munro (Ed.), *Individualism and holism: Studies in Confucian and Taoist values* (pp. 1–34). Ann Arbor: Center for Chinese Studies, University of Michigan.

Muraven, M. R., & Baumeister, R. F. (2000). Self-regulation and depletion of limited resources: Does self-control resemble a muscle? *Psychological Bulletin, 126,* 247–259.

Murray, S. L., & Holmes, J. G. (1993). Seeing virtues in faults: Negativity and the transformation of interpersonal narratives in close relationships. *Journal of Personality and Social Psychology, 65,* 707–723.

Murray, S. L., & Holmes, J. G. (1997). A leap of faith? Positive illusions in romantic relationships. *Personality and Social Psychology Bulletin, 23,* 586–604.

Murray, S. L., & Holmes, J. G. (1999). The (mental) ties that bind: Cognitive structures that predict relationship resilience. *Journal of Personality and Social Psychology, 77,* 1228–1244.

Murray, S. L., Holmes, J. G., Dolderman, D., & Griffin, D. W. (2000). What the motivated mind sees: Comparing friends' perspectives to married partners' views of each other. *Journal of Experimental Social Psychology, 36,* 600–620.

Murray, S. L., Holmes, J. G., & Griffin, D. W. (1996). The benefits of positive illusions: Idealization and the construction of satisfaction in close relationships. *Journal of Personality and Social Psychology, 70,* 79–98.

Murray, S. L., Holmes, J. G., Griffin, D. W., Bellavia, G., & Rose, P. (2001). The mismeasure of love: How self-doubt contaminates relationship beliefs. *Personality and Social Psychology Bulletin, 27,* 423–436.

Murray, S. L., Holmes, J. G., MacDonald, G., & Ellsworth, P. C. (1998). Through the looking glass darkly? When self-doubts turn into relationship insecurities. *Journal of Personality and Social Psychology, 75,* 1459–1480.

Muscatell, K. A., & Eisenberger, N. I. (2012). A social neuroscience perspective on stress and health. *Social and Personality Psychology Compass, 6,* 890–904.

Mustard, D. B. (2001). Racial, ethnic, and gender disparities in sentencing: Evidence from the U.S. federal courts. *Journal of Law and Economics, 19,* 285–314.

Mwaniki, M. K. (1973). *The relationship between self-concept and academic achievement in Kenyan pupils.* Unpublished doctoral dissertation, Stanford University, California.

Myers, D. G. (2000). *The American paradox.* New Haven: Yale University Press.

Myers, D. G., & Bishop, G. D. (1971). Enhancement of dominant attitudes in group discussion. *Journal of Personality and Social Psychology, 20,* 386–391.

Na, J., & Kitayama, S. (2011). Spontaneous trait inference is culture-specific: Behavioral and neural evidence. *Psychological Science, 22,* 1025–1032.

Nahemow, L., & Lawton, M. P. (1975). Similarity and propinquity in friendship formation. *Journal of Personality and Social Psychology, 32,* 205–213.

Neff, L. A., & Karney, B. R. (2002). Judgments of a relationship partner: Specific accuracy but global enhancement. *Journal of Personality, 70,* 1079–1112.

Neighbors, C., Larimer, M. E., & Lewis, M. A. (2004). Targeting misperceptions of descriptive drinking norms: Efficacy of a computer-delivered personalized normative feedback intervention. *Journal of Consulting and Clinical Psychology, 72,* 434–447.

Neimeyer, R. A., & Mitchell, K. A. (1988). Similarity and attraction: A longitudinal study. *Journal of Social and Personal Relationships, 5,* 131–148.

Nemeroff, C., & Rozin, P. (1989). "You are what you eat": Applying the demand-free "impressions" technique to an unacknowledged belief. *Ethos, 17,* 50–69.

Nemeth, C. (1986). Differential contributions of majority and minority influence. *Psychological Review, 93,* 23–32.

Nesse, R. (1990). Evolutionary explanations of emotions. *Human Nature, 1,* 261–289.

Newcomb, T. M. (1956). The prediction of interpersonal attraction. *American Psychologist, 1,* 575–586.

Newcomb, T. M. (1961). *The acquaintance process.* New York: Holt, Rinehart and Winston.

Newman, L. S. (1991). Why are traits inferred spontaneously? A developmental approach. *Social Cognition, 9,* 221–253.

Newman, L. S. (1993). How individualists interpret behavior: Idiocentrism and spontaneous trait inference. *Social Cognition, 11,* 243–269.

Nickerson, D. W. (2008). Is voting contagious? Evidence from two field experiments. *American Political Science Review, 102,* 49–57.

Niedenthal, P. M., Barsalou, L. W., Winkielman, P., Krauth-Gruber, S., & Ric, F. (2005). Embodiment in attitudes, social perception, and emotion. *Personality and Social Psychology Review, 9,* 184–211.

Niedenthal, P. M., & Setterlund, M. B. (1994). Emotion congruence in perception. *Personality and Social Psychology Bulletin, 20,* 401–410.

Nier, J. A., Gaertner, S. L., Dovidio, J. F., Banker, B. S., & Ward, C. M. (2001). Changing interracial evaluations and behavior: The benefits of a common ingroup identity. *Group Processes and Intergroup Relations, 4,* 299–316.

Nisbett, R. E. (1993). Violence and U.S. regional culture. *American Psychologist, 48,* 441–449.

Nisbett, R. E. (2009). *Intelligence and how to get it: Why schools and cultures count.* New York: Norton.

Nisbett, R. E. (2015). *Mindware: Tools for Smart Thinking.* New York: Farrar, Straus & Giroux.

Nisbett, R. E. (2017). *Mindware: Critical thinking for the information age*: Coursera. https://www.coursera.org/learn/mindware

Nisbett, R. E., Caputo, C., Legant, P., & Maracek, J. (1973). Behavior as seen by the actor and as seen by the observer. *Journal of Personality and Social Psychology, 27,* 154–164.

Nisbett, R. E., & Cohen, D. (1996). *Culture of honor: The psychology of violence in the South.* Boulder, CO: Westview Press.

Nisbett, R. E., Fong, G. T., Lehman, D. R., & Cheng, P. W. (1987). Teaching reasoning. *Science, 238,* 625–631.

Nisbett, R. E., & Ross, L. (1980). *Human inference: Strategies and shortcomings of social judgment.* Englewood Cliffs, NJ: Prentice-Hall.

Nisbett, R. E., & Wilson, T. D. (1977). Telling more than we can know: Verbal reports on mental processes. *Psychological Review, 84,* 231–259.

Nishi, A., Shirado, H., Rand, D. G., & Christakis, N. A. (2015). Inequality and visibility of wealth in experimental social networks. *Nature, 526*(7573), 426–429. doi:10.1038/nature15392

Nolen-Hoeksema, S. (1987). Sex differences in unipolar depression: Evidence and theory. *Psychological Bulletin, 101,* 259–282.

Nolen-Hoeksema, S. (2003). *Women who think too much.* New York: Holt.

Norenzayan, A., Choi, I., & Nisbett, R. E. (1999). Eastern and Western perceptions of causality for social behavior: Lay theories about personalities and social situations. In D. Prentice & D. Miller (Eds.), *Cultural divides: Understanding and overcoming group conflict* (pp. 239–272). New York: Russell Sage Foundation.

Norenzayan, A., & Heine, S. J. (2004). *Psychological universals: What are they and how can we know?* Vancouver: University of British Columbia.

Norenzayan, A., & Shariff, A. F. (2008). The origin and evolution of religious prosociality. *Science, 322,* 58–62.

North, A. C., Hargreaves, D. J., and McKendrick, J. (1999). The influence of in-store music on wine selections. *Journal of Applied Psychology, 84,* 271–276.

Norton, M. I., Mochon, D., & Ariely, D. (2012). The "IKEA effect": When labor leads to love. *Journal of Consumer Psychology, 22*(3), 453–460.

Norton, M. I., Monin, B., Cooper, J., & Hogg, M. (2003). Vicarious dissonance: Attitude change from the inconsistency of others. *Journal of Personality and Social Psychology, 85,* 47–62.

Nosek, B. A., Banaji, M. R., & Greenwald, A. G. (2002). Harvesting implicit group attitudes and beliefs from demonstration web site. *Group Dynamics: Theory, Research, and Practice, 6,* 101–115.

Nosek, B. A., Greenwald, A. G., & Banaji, M. R. (2005). Understanding and using the Implicit Association Test: II. Method variables and construct validity. *Personality and Social Psychology Bulletin, 31,* 166–180.

Nowak, M. A., Page, K. M., & Sigmund, K. (2000). Fairness versus reason in the ultimatum game. *Science, 289,* 1773–1775.

Nowak, M. A., & Sigmund, K. (2005). Evolution of indirect reciprocity. *Nature, 437*(7063), 1291–1298.

Nowland, R., Necka, E. A., & Cacioppo, J. T. (2017). Loneliness and social internet use: Pathways to reconnection in a digital world? *Perspectives on Psychological Science, 13*(1),70–87. doi: 10.1177 /1745691617713052

Nudelman, G., & Shiloh, S. (2011). Who deserves to be sick? An exploration of the relationships between belief in a just world, illness causal attributions and their fairness judgements. *Psychology Health and Medicine, 16,* 675–685. doi:10.1080/13548506.2011. 569730

Oakes, J. M., & Rossi, R. H. (2003). The measurement of SES in health research: Current practice and steps toward a new approach. *Social Science and Medicine, 56,* 769–784.

Oakes, P. J., & Turner, J. C. (1980). Social categorization and intergroup behavior: Does minimal intergroup discrimination make social identity more positive? *European Journal of Social Psychology, 10,* 295–301.

Oatley, K. (1993). Social construction in emotion. In M. Lewis & J. Haviland (Eds.), *Handbook of emotions* (pp. 342–352). New York: Guilford Press.

Oatley, K. (2004). *Emotions: A brief history.* Malden, MA: Blackwell.

Oatley, K., & Johnson-Laird, P. N. (2011). Basic emotions in social relationships, reasoning, and psychological illnesses. *Emotion Review, 3,* 424–433.

O'Brien, L. T, Major, B. N, & Gilbert, P. N. (2012, March). Gender differences in entitlement: The role of system-justifying beliefs. *Basic and Applied Social Psychology, 34*(2), 136–145.

Ochsner, K. N., & Lieberman, M. D. (2001). The emergence of social cognitive neuroscience. *American Psychologist, 56,* 717–734.

O'Donovan, A., Lin, J., Dhabhar, F. S., Wolkowitz, O., Tillie, J. M.,

Blackburn, E., et al. (2009). Pessimism correlates with leukocyte telomere shortness and elevated interleukin-6 in post-menopausal women. *Brain Behavior Immunology, 23*(4), 446–449.

Oishi, S. (2014). Socio-ecological psychology. *Annual Review of Psychology, 65*, 581–609.

Oishi, S., Kesebir, S., & Diener, E. (2011). Income inequality and happiness. *Psychological Science, 22*, 1095–1100.

O'Keefe, D. J., & Figgé, M. (1997). A guilt-based explanation of the door-in-the-face influence strategy. *Human Communication Research, 24*, 64–81.

O'Keefe, D. J., & Hale, S. L. (1998). The door-in-the-face influence strategy: A random-effects meta-analytic review. In M. E. Roloff (Ed.), *Communication yearbook* (Vol. 21, pp. 1–33). Thousand Oaks, CA: Sage.

O'Keefe, D. J., & Hale, S. L. (2001). An odds-ratio-based meta-analysis of research on the door-in-the-face influence strategy. *Communication Reports, 14*, 31–38.

Okonofua, J. A., Paunesku, D., & Walton, G. M. (2016). Brief intervention to encourage empathic discipline cuts suspension rates in half among adolescents. *Proceedings of the National Academy of Sciences of the USA, 113*(19), 5221–5226.

Olczak, P. V., Kaplan, M. F., & Penrod, S. (1991). Attorneys' lay psychology and its effectiveness in selecting jurors: Three empirical studies. *Journal of Social Behavior and Personality, 6*, 431–452.

Oliner, S., & Oliner, P. (1988). *The altruistic personality.* New York: Free Press.

Olivola, C. Y., & Shafir, E. (2013). The martyrdom effect: When pain and effort increase prosocial contributions. *Journal of Behavioral Decision Making, 26*, 91–105.

Omoto, A. M., Malsch, A. M., & Barraza, J. A. (2009). Compassionate acts: Motivations for and correlates of volunteerism among older adults. In B. Fehr, S. Sprecher, & L. G. Underwood (Eds.), *The science of compassionate love: Theory, research, and applications* (pp. 257–282). Malden, MA: Wiley-Blackwell.

Omoto, A. M., & Snyder, M. (1995). Sustained helping without obligation: Motivation, longevity of service, and perceived attitude change among AIDS volunteers. *Journal of Personality and Social Psychology, 68*, 671–686.

Open Science Collaboration. (2015, August). Estimating the reproducibility of psychological science. *Science, 349*(6251), acc4716. doi:10.1126/science.aac4716

Oppenheimer, D. M. (2008). The secret life of fluency. *Trends in Cognitive Sciences, 12*, 237–241.

Ostrom, T. M., & Sedikides, C. (1992). Out-group homogeneity effects in natural and minimal groups. *Psychological Bulletin, 112*, 536–552.

Oswald, F. L., Mitchell., G., Blanton, H., Jaccard, J., & Tetlock, P. E. (2013). Predicting ethnic and racial discrimination: A meta-analysis of IAT criterion studies. *Journal of Personality and Social Psychology, 105*(2), 171–192.

Outten, H. R., Schmitt, M. T., Miller, D. A., & Garcia, A. L. (2012). Feeling threatened about the future: Whites' emotional reactions to anticipated ethnic demographic changes. *Personality and Social Psychology Bulletin, 38*(1), 14–25.

Oxman, T. E., & Hull, J. G. (1997). Social support, depression, and activities of daily living in older heart surgery patients. *Journal of Gerontology: Psychological Sciences, 52*, 1–14.

Oyserman, D., Bybee, D., & Terry, K. (2006). Possible selves and academic outcomes: How and when possible selves impel action. *Journal of Personality and Social Psychology, 91*, 188–204.

PA Consulting Group & UCL (2005). The national safety camera programme: Four-year evaluation report, December 2005. http://www.speedcamerareport.co.uk/4_year_evaluation.pdf

Pallak, M. S., Mueller, M., Dollar, K., & Pallak, J. (1972). Effects of commitment on responsiveness to an extreme consonant communication. *Journal of Personality and Social Psychology, 23*, 429–436.

Paluck E. L. (2009). Reducing intergroup prejudice and conflict using the media: A field experiment in Rwanda. *Journal of Personality and Social Psychology, 96*(3), 574–587.

Paluck, E. L., & Shepherd, H. (2012). The salience of social referents: A field experiment on collective norms and harassment behavior in a school social network. *Journal of Personality and Social Psychology, 103*, 899–915.

Paluck, E. L., Shepherd, H., & Aronow, P. (2016). Changing climates of conflict: A social network driven experiment in 56 schools. *Proceedings of the National Academy of Sciences of the USA, 113*(3), 566–571.

Park, L. E., Troisi, J. D., & Maner, J. K. (2010). Egoistic versus altruistic concerns in communal relationships. *Journal of Social and Personal Relationships, 28*, 315–335.

Park, B., & Judd, C. M. (1990). Measures and models of perceived group variability. *Journal of Personality and Social Psychology, 59*, 173–191.

Parkinson B., & Manstead, A. S. R. (1992). Appraisal as a cause of emotion. *Review of Personality and Social Psychology, 13*, 122–149.

Pascoe, E. A, & Smart Richman, L. (2009). Perceived discrimination and health: A meta-analytic review. *Psychological Bulletin, 135*, 531–554.

Paumgarten, N. (2011, July 4). Looking for someone: Sex, love and loneliness on the Internet. *The New Yorker, 87*, pp. 36–49.

Payne, B. K. (2001). Prejudice and perception: The role of automatic and controlled processes in misperceiving a weapon. *Journal of Personality and Social Psychology, 81*, 181–192.

Payne, B. K. (2006). Weapons bias: Split-second decisions and unintended stereotyping. *Current Directions in Psychological Science, 15*, 287–291.

Payne, B. K., Brown-Iannuzzi, J. L., & Loersch, C. (2016). Replicable effects of primes on human behavior. *Journal of Experimental Psychology: General, 145*(10), 1269–1279.

Payne, B. K., Cheng, C. M., Govorun, O., & Stewart, B. D. (2005). An inkblot for attitudes: Affect misattribution as implicit measurement. *Journal of Personality and Social Psychology, 89*, 277–293.

Payne, B. K., Govorun, O., & Arbuckle, N. L. (2008). Automatic attitudes and alcohol: Does implicit liking predict drinking? *Cognition and Emotion, 22*, 238–271.

Payne, B. K., McClernon, J. F., & Dobbins, I. G. (2007). Automatic affective responses to smoking cues. *Experimental and Clinical Psychopharmacology, 15*, 400–409.

Pearson, C. M., & Porath, C. L. (1999). *Workplace incivility: The target's-eye view.* Paper presented at the Annual Meeting of the Academy of Management, Chicago.

Peng, K., & Knowles, E. (2003). Culture, ethnicity and the attribution of physical causality. *Personality and Social Psychology Bulletin, 29*, 1272–1284.

Pennebaker, J. W., & Roberts, T. A. (1992). Toward a his and hers theory of emotion: Gender differences in visceral perception. *Journal of Social and Clinical Psychology, 11*, 199–212.

Pennington, N., & Hastie, R. (1990). Practical implications of psychological research on juror and jury decision making. *Personality and Social Psychology Bulletin, 16*, 90–105.

Penton-Voak, I. S., Perrett, D. I., Castles, D. L., Kobayashi, T., Burt, D. M., Murray, L. K., et al. (1999). Menstrual cycle alters face preference. *Nature, 399*, 741–742.

Peplau, L. A., & Fingerhut, A. W. (2007). The close relationships of lesbians and gay men. *Annual Review of Psychology, 58*, 405–424.

Peplau, L. A., Frederick, D. A., Yee, C., Maisel, N., Lever, J., & Ghavami, N. (2009). Body image satisfaction in heterosexual, gay, and lesbian adults. *Archives of Sexual Behavior, 38*(5), 713–725.

Pérez-Benítez, C. I., O'Brien, W. H., Carels, R. A., Gordon, A. K., & Chiros, C. E. (2007). Cardiovascular correlates of disclosing homosexual orientation. *Stress and Health, 23*(3), 141–152.

Perissinotto, C. M., Stijacic Cenzer, I., & Covinsky, K. E. (2012). Loneliness in older persons: A predictor of functional decline and death. *Archives of Internal Medicine, 172,* 1078–1083. doi:10.1001/archinternmed.2012.1993 [PubMed: 22710744]

Perkins, H. W., & Craig, D. W. (2006). A successful social norms campaign to reduce alcohol misuse among college student-athletes. *Journal of Studies on Alcohol, 67,* 880–889.

Perkins, H. W., Haines, M. P., & Rice, R. (2005). Misperceiving the college drinking norm and related problems: A nationwide study of exposure to prevention information, perceived norms and student alcohol misuse. *Journal of Studies on Alcohol, 66,* 470–478.

Perner, J., Frith, U., Leslie, A. M., & Leekam, S. R. (1989). Exploration of the autistic child's theory of mind: Knowledge, belief and communication. *Child Development, 60,* 689–700.

Perper, T. (1985). *Sex signals: The biology of love.* Philadelphia: ISI Press.

Perrett, D. I., Lee, K., Penton-Voak, I., Burt, D. M., Rowland, D., Yoshikawa, S., et al. (1998). Sexual dimorphism and facial attractiveness. *Nature, 394,* 884–886.

Perrett, D. I., May, K. A., & Yoshikawa, S. (1994). Facial shape and judgments of female attractiveness. *Nature, 368,* 239–242.

Pessin, J. (1933). The comparative effects of social and mechanical stimulation on memorizing. *American Journal of Psychology, 45,* 263–270.

Pessin, J., & Husband, R. W. (1933). Effect of social stimulation on human maze learning. *Journal of Abnormal and Social Psychology, 28,* 148–154.

Peterson, C. (2000). The future of optimism. *American Psychologist, 55,* 44–55.

Peterson, C., & Barrett, L. C. (1987). Explanatory style and academic performance among university freshmen. *Journal of Personality and Social Psychology, 53,* 603–607.

Peterson, C., Maier, S., & Seligman, M. E. P. (1993). *Learned helplessness.* New York: Oxford University Press.

Peterson, C., Seligman, M. E. P., & Vaillant, G. E. (1988). Pessimistic explanatory style is a risk factor for physical illness: A thirty-five-year longitudinal study. *Journal of Personality and Social Psychology, 55,* 23–27.

Petrocelli, J. V., Tormala, Z. L., & Rucker, D. D. (2007). Unpacking attitude certainty: Attitude clarity and attitude correctness. *Journal of Personality and Social Psychology, 92,* 30–41.

Pettigrew, T. F. (1979). The ultimate attribution error: Extending Allport's cognitive analysis to prejudice. *Personality and Social Psychology Bulletin, 5,* 461–476.

Pettigrew, T. F., & Tropp, L. R. (2000). Does intergroup contact reduce prejudice? Recent meta-analytic findings. In S. Oskamp (Ed.), *Reducing prejudice and discrimination: The Claremont Symposium on Applied Social Psychology* (pp. 93–114). Mahwah, NJ: Erlbaum.

Pettigrew, T. F., & Tropp, L. R. (2006). A meta-analytic test of intergroup contact theory. *Journal of Personality and Social Psychology, 90,* 751–783.

Pettigrew, T. F., & Tropp, L. R. (2008). How does intergroup contact reduce prejudice? Meta-analytic tests of three mediators. *European Journal of Social Psychology, 38,* 922–934.

Petty, R. E. (1997). The evolution of theory and research in social psychology: From single to multiple effect and process models. In C. McGarty & S. A. Haslam (Eds.), *The message of social psychology: Perspectives on mind in society* (pp. 268–290). Oxford, England: Blackwell.

Petty, R. E., & Briñol, P. (2008). Persuasion: From single to multiple to metacognitive processes. *Perspectives on Psychological Science, 3,* 137–147.

Petty, R. E., Briñol, P., & Tormala, Z. L. (2002). Thought confidence as a determinant of persuasion: The self-validation hypothesis. *Journal of Personality and Social Psychology, 82,* 722–741.

Petty, R. E., Briñol, P., Tormala, Z. L., & Wegener, D. T. (2007). The role of metacognition in social judgment. In E. T. Higgins & A. W. Kruglanski, (Eds.), *Social psychology: A handbook of basic principles* (2nd ed., pp. 254–284). New York: Guilford Press.

Petty, R. E., & Cacioppo, J. T. (1979). Issue involvement can increase or decrease persuasion by enhancing message-relevant cognitive responses. *Journal of Personality and Social Psychology, 37,* 1915–1926.

Petty, R. E., & Cacioppo, J. T. (1984). The effects of involvement on responses to argument quantity and quality: Central and peripheral routes to persuasion. *Journal of Personality and Social Psychology, 46,* 69–81.

Petty, R. E., & Cacioppo, J. T. (1986). The elaboration likelihood model of persuasion. In L. Berkowitz (Ed.), *Advances in experimental social psychology* (Vol. 19, pp. 123–205). New York: Academic Press.

Petty, R. E., Cacioppo, J. T., & Goldman, R. (1981). Personal involvement as a determinant of argument-based persuasion. *Journal of Personality and Social Psychology, 41,* 847–855.

Petty, R. E., Cacioppo, J. T., & Schumann, D. W. (1983). Central and peripheral routes to advertising effectiveness: The moderating role of involvement. *Journal of Consumer Research, 10,* 135–146.

Petty, R. E., Haugtvedt, C. P., & Smith, S. M. (1995). Elaboration as a determinant of attitude strength. In R. E. Petty & J. A. Krosnick (Eds.), *Attitude strength: Antecedents and consequences* (pp. 93–130). Mahwah, NJ: Erlbaum.

Petty, R. E., & Wegener, D. (1998). Attitude change: Multiple roles for persuasion variables. In D. T. Gilbert, S. T. Fiske, & G. Lindzey (Eds.), *Handbook of social psychology* (4th ed., pp. 323–390). New York: McGraw-Hill.

Pew Research Center. (2014). Political polarization in the American public. Retrieved from http://www.people-press.org/interactives/political-polarization-1994-2017

Phelps, E. A., O'Connor, K. J., Cunningham, W. A., Funayama, E. S., Gatenby, J. C., Gore, J. C., et al. (2000). Performance on indirect measure of race evaluation predicts amygdala activation. *Journal of Cognitive Neuroscience, 12,* 729–738.

Piedmont, R. L., & Chase, J. H. (1997). Cross-cultural generality of the five-factor model of personality: Development and validation of the NEO-PI-R for Koreans. *Journal of Cross-Cultural Psychology, 28,* 131–155.

Piff, P. K., Dietze, P., Feinberg, M., Stancato, D. M., & Keltner, D. (2015). Awe, the small self, and prosocial behavior. *Journal of Personality and Social Psychology, 108*(6), 883.

Piff, P. K., Kraus, M. W., Côté, S., Cheng, B., & Keltner, D. (2010). Having less, giving more: The influence of social class on prosocial behavior, *Journal of Personality and Social Psychology, 99,* 771–784.

Piff, P. K., Kraus, M. W., & Keltner, D. (2017). Unpacking the inequality paradox: The psychological roots of inequality and social class. In J. Olson (Ed.), *Advances in experimental social psychology* (Vol. 57, pp. 53–124). San Diego, CA: Academic Press.

Piff, P. K., Stancato, D. M., Côté, S., Mendoza-Denton, R., & Keltner, D. (2012). Higher social class predicts increased unethical behavior. *Proceedings of the National Academy of Sciences of the USA, 109,* 4086–4091.

Piliavin, J. A., Piliavin, I. M., & Broll, L. (1976). Time of arousal at an emergency and likelihood of helping. *Personality and Social Psychology Bulletin, 2,* 273–276.

Pinel, E. (1999). Stigma consciousness: The psychological legacy of social stereotypes. *Journal of Personality and Social Psychology, 76,* 114–128.

Pinker, S. (1994). *The language instinct.* New York: HarperCollins.

Pinker, S. (2002). *The blank slate: The modern denial of human nature.* New York: Viking.

Pinker, S. (2007). A history of violence [Electronic version]. *The New Republic Online*. Retrieved March 16, 2009.

Pinker, S. (2011). *The better angels of our nature: Why violence has declined*. New York: Viking.

Plaks, J. E., & Higgins, E. T. (2000). Pragmatic use of stereotyping in teamwork: Social loafing and compensation as a function of inferred partner–situation fit. *Journal of Personality and Social Psychology, 79*, 962–974.

Plant, E. A., Kling, K. C., & Smith, G. L. (2004). The influence of gender and social role on the interpretation of facial expressions. *Sex Roles, 51*, 187–196.

Plant, E. A., & Peruche, B. M. (2005). The consequences of race for police officers' responses to criminal suspects. *Psychological Science, 16*, 180–183.

Plant, E. A., Peruche, B. M., & Butz, D. A. (2005). Eliminating automatic racial bias: Making race non-diagnostic for responses to criminal suspects. *Journal of Experimental Social Psychology, 41*, 141–156.

Platania, J., & Moran, G. P. (2001). Social facilitation as a function of the mere presence of others. *Journal of Social Psychology, 141*, 190–197.

Platt, J. J., & James, W. T. (1966). Social facilitation of eating behavior in young opossums: I. Group vs. solitary feeding. *Psychonomic Science, 6*, 421–422.

Platt, J. J., Yaksh, T., & Darby, C. L. (1967). Social facilitation of eating behavior in armadillos. *Psychological Reports, 20*, 1136.

Platz, S. J., & Hosch, H. M. (1988). Cross-racial/ethnic eyewitness identification: A field study. *Journal of Applied Social Psychology, 18*(11), 972–984.

Plous, S. (1985). Perceptual illusions and military realities. *Journal of Conflict Resolution, 29*, 363–389.

Polak, M. (1993). Parasitic infection increases fluctuating asymmetry of male *Drosophila nigrospiracula*: Implications for sexual selection. *Genetica, 89*, 255–265.

Porges, S. W. (2001). The polyvagal theory: Phylogenetic substrate of a social nervous system. *International Journal of Psychophysiology, 42*, 123–146.

Postmes, T., & Spears, R. (1998). Deindividuation and antinormative behavior: A meta-analysis. *Psychological Bulletin, 123*, 238–259.

Pound, N., Penton-Voak, I. S., & Brown, W. M. (2007). Facial symmetry is positively associated with self-reported extraversion. *Personality and Individual Differences, 43*, 1572–1582.

Pratkanis, A. R., Greenwald, A. G., Leippe, M. R., & Baumgardner, M. H. (1988). In search of reliable persuasion effects: III. The sleeper effect is dead. Long live the sleeper effect. *Journal of Personality and Social Psychology, 54*, 203–218.

Pratto, F., & Bargh, J. A. (1991). Stereotyping based upon apparently individuating information: Trait and global components of sex stereotypes under attention overload. *Journal of Experimental Psychology, 27*, 26–47.

Preciado, P., Snijders, T., Burk, W. J., Stattin, H., & Kerr, M. (2011). Does proximity matter? Distance dependence of adolescent friendships. *Social Networks, 34*, 18–31.

Prentice, D. A. (1990). Familiarity and differences in self- and other-representations. *Journal of Personality and Social Psychology, 59*, 369–383.

Prentice, D. A., & Miller, D. T. (1993). Pluralistic ignorance and alcohol use on campus: Some consequences of misperceiving the social norm. *Journal of Personality and Social Psychology, 64*, 243–256.

Preston, C. E., & Harris, S. (1965). Psychology of drivers in traffic accidents. *Journal of Applied Psychology, 49*, 284–288.

Preston, S. D., & de Waal, F. B. M. (2002). Empathy: Its ultimate and proximate bases. *Behavioral and Brain Sciences, 25*, 1–72.

Preuschoft, S. (1992). "Laughter" and "smile" in Barbary macaques (*Macaca sylvanus*). *Ethology, 91*, 220–236.

Price, K. H., Harrison, D. A., & Gavin, J. H. (2006). Withholding inputs in team contexts: Member composition, interaction processes, evaluation structure, and social loafing. *Journal of Applied Social Psychology, 90*, 197–209.

Price, P. C., & Stone, E. R. (2004). Intuitive evaluation of likelihood judgment producers: Evidence for a confidence heuristic. *Journal of Behavioral Decision Making, 17*, 39–57.

Priester, J. R., Cacioppo, J. T., & Petty, R. E. (1996). The influence of motor processes on attitudes toward novel versus familiar semantic stimuli. *Personality and Social Psychology Bulletin, 22*, 442–447.

Prislin, R., & Crano, W. D. (2012). A history of social influence research. In A. W. Kruglanski & W. Stroebe (Eds.), *Handbook of the history of social psychology* (pp. 321–339). New York: Psychology Press.

Pronin, E., Berger, J., & Molouki, S. (2007). Alone in a crowd of sheep: Asymmetric perceptions of conformity and their roots in an introspection illusion. *Journal of Personality and Social Psychology, 92*, 585–595.

Pronin, E., Gilovich, T., & Ross, L. (2004). Objectivity in the eye of the beholder: Divergent perceptions of bias in self versus others. *Psychological Review, 111*, 781–799.

Pronin, E., Kruger, J., Savitsky, K., & Ross, L. (2001). You don't know me, but I know you: The illusion of asymmetric insight. *Journal of Personality and Social Psychology, 81*, 639–656.

Pronin, E., Lin, D. Y., & Ross, L. (2002). The bias blind spot: Perceptions of bias in self versus others. *Personality and Social Psychology Bulletin, 28*, 369–381.

Pyszczynski, T., & Greenberg, J. (1987). Toward an integration of cognitive and motivational perspectives on social inference: A biased hypothesis-testing model. In L. Berkowitz (Ed.), *Advances in experimental social psychology* (Vol. 20, pp. 297–340). New York: Academic Press.

Quattrociocchi, W., Scala, A., & Sunstein, C.R. (2016). Echo chambers on Facebook. *Social Science Research Network*, posted June 15: https://papers.ssrn.com/sol3/papers.cfm?abstract_id=2795110

Quattrone, G. A., & Jones, E. E. (1980). The perception of variability within in-groups and out-groups: Implications for the law of small numbers. *Journal of Personality and Social Psychology, 38*, 141–152.

Queller, S., & Smith, E. R. (2002). Subtyping versus bookkeeping in stereotype learning and change: Connectionist simulations and empirical findings. *Journal of Personality and Social Psychology, 82*, 300–313.

Rand, D. G., Arbesman, S., & Christakis, N. A. (2011). Dynamic networks promote cooperation in experiments with humans. *Proceedings of the National Academy of Sciences of the USA, 108*, 19193–19198.

Rand, D. G., & Epstein, Z. G. (2014). Risking your life without a second thought: Intuitive decision-making and extreme altruism. *PLoS ONE, 9*, e109687.

Rand, D. G., Greene, J. D., & Nowak, M. A. (2012). Spontaneous giving and calculated greed. *Nature, 489*, 427–430. doi:10.1038/nature11467

Rand, D. G., & Nowak, M. A. (2013) Human cooperation. *Trends in Cognitive Sciences, 17*, 413–425.

Rasinski, H., Geers, A. L., & Czopp, A. M. (2013). "I guess what he said wasn't that bad": Dissonance in nonconfronting targets of prejudice. *Personality and Social Psychology Bulletin, 39*, 856–869.

Read, S. J., & Urada, S. I. (2003). A neural network simulation of the outgroup homogeniety effect. *Personality and Social Psychology Review, 7*, 146–159.

Realo, A., & Allik, J. (1999). A cross-cultural study of collectivism: A comparison of American, Estonian, and Russian students. *Journal of Social Psychology, 139*, 133–142.

Reber, R., Schwarz, N., & Winkielman, P. (2004). Processing fluency and aesthetic pleasure: Is beauty in the perceiver's processing experience? *Personality and Social Psychology Review, 8*, 364–382.

Reber, R., Winkielman, P., & Schwarz, N. (1998). Effects of perceptual fluency on affective judgments. *Psychological Science, 9*, 45–48.

Reed, J. S. (1981). Below the Smith and Wesson line: Reflections on Southern violence. In M. Black & J. Reed (Eds.), *Perspectives on the American South: An annual review of society, politics, and culture.* New York: Gordon and Breach Science Publications.

Reed, J. S. (1990). Billy, the fabulous moolah, and me. In J. S. Reed (Ed.), *Whistling Dixie* (pp. 119–122). San Diego, CA: Harcourt Brace Jovanovich.

Reeder, G. D., Monroe, A. E., & Pryor, J. B. (2008). Impressions of Milgram's obedient teachers: Situational cues inform inferences about motives and traits. *Journal of Personality and Social Psychology, 95*, 1–17.

Reeves, R. A., Baker, G. A., Boyd, J. G., & Cialdini, R. B. (1991). The door-in-the-face technique: Reciprocal concessions vs. self-presentational explanations. *Journal of Social Behavior and Personality, 6*, 645–658.

Regan, D. T. (1971). Effects of a favor and liking on compliance. *Journal of Experimental Social Psychology, 7*, 627–639.

Regan, D. T., & Kilduff, M. (1988). Optimism about elections: Dissonance reduction at the ballot box. *Political Psychology, 9*, 101–107.

Regan, D. T., Williams, M., & Sparling, S. (1972). Voluntary expiation of guilt: A field experiment. *Journal of Personality and Social Psychology, 24*, 42–45.

Reifman, A. S., Larrick, R. P., & Fein, S. (1991). Temper and temperature on the diamond: The heat-aggression relationship in major league baseball. *Personality and Social Psychology Bulletin, 17*, 580–585.

Reis, H. T., & Aron, A. (2008). Love: What is it, why does it matter, and how does it operate? *Perspectives on Psychological Science, 3*, 80–86.

Reis, H. T., Maniaci, M. R., Caprariello, P. A., Eastwick, P. W., & Finkel, E. J. (2011). Familiarity does indeed promote attraction in live interaction. *Journal of Personality and Social Psychology, 101*, 557–570.

Reis, H. T., Smith, S. M., Carmichael, C. L., Caprariello, P. A., Tsai, F., Rodrigues, A., & Maniaci, M. R. (2010). Are you happy for me? How sharing positive events with others provides personal and interpersonal benefits. *Journal of Personality and Social Psychology, 99*, 311–329.

Reis, H. T., Wheeler, L., Speigel, N., Kernis, M. H., Nezlek, J., & Perri, M. (1982). Physical attractiveness in social interaction: 2. Why does appearance affect social experience? *Journal of Personality and Social Psychology, 43*, 979–996.

Remley, A. (1988, October). From obedience to independence. *Psychology Today*, 56–59.

Rhee, E., Uleman, J. S., Lee, H. K., & Roman, R. J. (1995). Spontaneous self-descriptions and ethnic identities in individualistic and collectivist cultures. *Journal of Personality and Social Psychology, 69*, 142–152.

Rhine, R. J., & Severance, L. J. (1970). Ego-involvement, discrepancy, source credibility, and attitude change. *Journal of Personality and Social Psychology, 16*, 175–190.

Rhodes, G., Yoshikawa, S., Clark, A., Lee, K., McKay, R., & Akamatsu, S. (2001). Attractiveness of facial averageness and symmetry in non-Western cultures: In search of biologically based standards of beauty. *Perception, 30*, 611–625.

Rholes, W. S., & Simpson, J. A. (2015). New directions and emerging themes in attachment theory and research. In J. A. Simpson & W. S. Rholes (Eds), *Attachment theory and research: New directions and emerging themes* (pp. 1–7). New York: Guilford.

Richards, Z., & Hewstone, M. (2001). Subtyping and subgrouping: Processes for the prevention and promotion of stereotype change. *Personality and Social Psychology Review, 5*, 52–73.

Rideout, V. (2015). The Common Sense census: Media use by tweens and teens. Common Sense Media. https://www.commonsensemedia.org/sites/default/files/uploads/research/census_researchreport.pdf. Accessed August 24, 2016.

Rigdon, M., Ishii, K., Watabe, M., & Kitayama, S. (2009). Minimal social cues in the dictator game. *Journal of Economic Psychology, 30*, 358–367.

Riggio, R. E., & Friedman, H. S. (1983). Individual differences and cues to deception. *Journal of Personality and Social Psychology, 45*, 899–915.

Rilling, J. K., Gutman, D. A., Zeh, T. R., Pagnoni, G., Berns, G. S., & Kilts, C. D. (2002). A neural basis for cooperation. *Neuron, 35*, 395–405.

Risen, J. L., & Critcher, C. R. (2011). Visceral fit: While in a visceral state, associated states of the world seem more likely. *Journal of Personality and Social Psychology, 100*, 777–785.

Risen, J. L., Gilovich, T., & Dunning, D. (2007). One-shot illusory correlations and stereotyping. *Personality and Social Psychology Bulletin, 33*, 1492–1502.

Ritov, I. & Kogut, T. (2011). Ally or adversary: The effect of identifiability in inter-group conflict situations. *Organizational Behavior and Human Decision Process, 116*, 96–103.

Robberson, M. R., & Rogers, R. W. (1988). Beyond fear appeals: Negative and positive persuasive appeals to health and self-esteem. *Journal of Applied Social Psychology, 18*, 277–287.

Roberts, T. A., & Pennebaker, J. W. (1995). Gender differences in perceiving internal state: Toward a his-and-hers model of perceptual cue use. In M. Zanna (Ed.), *Advances in experimental social psychology* (Vol. 27, pp. 143–176). New York: Academic Press.

Robins, R. W., & Beer, J. S. (2001). Positive illusions about the self: Short-term benefits and long-term costs. *Journal of Personality and Social Psychology, 80*, 340–352.

Robinson, J., & McArthur, L. Z. (1982). Impact of salient vocal qualities on causal attribution for a speaker's behavior. *Journal of Personality and Social Psychology, 43*, 236–247.

Robinson, R., Keltner, D., Ward, A., & Ross, L. (1995). Actual versus assumed differences in construal: "Naive realism" in intergroup perception and conflict. *Journal of Personality and Social Psychology, 68*, 404–417.

Robles, T. F., Slatcher, R. B., Trombello, J. M., & McGinn, M. M. (2014). Marital quality and health: A meta-analytic review. *Psychological Bulletin, 140*, 140–187.

Roddy, S., Stewart, I., & Barnes-Holmes, D. (2010). Anti-fat, pro-slim, or both? Using two reaction-time based measures to assess implicit attitudes to the slim and overweight. *Journal of Health Psychology, 15*(3), 416–425.

Rodeheffer, C. D., Hill, S. E., & Lord, C. G. (2012). Does this recession make me look black? The effect of resource scarcity on the categorization of biracial faces. *Psychological Science, 23*(12), 1476–1478.

Rodriguez-Bailon, R., Bratanova, B., Willis, G. B., Lopez-Rodriguez, L., Sturrock, A., & Loughnan, S. (2017, March). Social class and ideologies of inequality: How they uphold unequal societies. *Journal of Social Issues, 73*(1), 99–116.

Rodriguez Mosquera, P. M., Fischer, A. H., & Manstead, A. S. R. (2000). The role of honor-related values in the elicitation, experience, and communication of pride, shame, and anger: Spain and the Netherlands compared. *Personality and Social Psychology Bulletin, 26*, 833–844.

Rodriguez Mosquera, P. M., Fischer, A. H., & Manstead, A. S. R. (2004). Inside the heart of emotion: On culture and relational concerns. In L. Z. Tiedens & C. W. Leach (Eds.), *The social life of emotions* (pp. 187–202). New York: Cambridge University Press.

Roesch, S. C., & Amirkhan, J. H. (1997). Boundary conditions for self-serving attributions: Another look at the sports pages. *Journal of Applied Social Psychology, 27*, 245–261.

Roese, N. J. (1997). Counterfactual thinking. *Psychological Bulletin, 121*, 133–148.

Roese, N. J., & Olson, J. M. (Eds.). (1995). *What might have been: The social psychology of counterfactual thinking.* Mahwah, NJ: Erlbaum.

Rohrer, J. H., Baron, S. H., Hoffman, E. L., & Swander, D. V. (1954). The stability of autokinetic judgments. *Journal of Abnormal and Social Psychology, 49*, 595–597.

Rose, J. D. (2011). Diverse perspectives on the groupthink theory: A literary review. *Emerging Leadership Journeys, 4*, 37–57.

Rosenberg, L. A. (1961). Group size, prior experience, and conformity. *Journal of Abnormal and Social Psychology, 63*, 436–437.

Rosenberg, M. (1965). *Society and the adolescent self-image.* Princeton, NJ: Princeton University Press.

Rosenblatt, A., Greenberg, J., Solomon, S., Pyszczynski, T., & Lyon, D. (1989). Evidence for terror management theory I: The effects of mortality salience on reactions to those who violate or uphold cultural values. *Journal of Personality and Social Psychology, 57*, 681–690.

Rosenfeld, M. J. (2008). Racial, educational, and religious endogamy in the United States: A comparative historical perspective. *Social Forces, 87*, 1–32.

Rosenfeld, M. J., & Thomas, R. J. (2010). *Meeting online: The rise of the Internet as a social intermediary.* Unpublished manuscript, Department of Sociology, Stanford University, Stanford, CA.

Rosenthal, R., & Jacobson, L. (1968). *Pygmalion in the classroom: Teacher expectation and pupils' intellectual development.* New York: Holt, Rinehart and Winston.

Roseth, C., Johnson, D., & Johnson, R. (2008). Promoting early adolescents' achievement and peer relationships: The effects of cooperative, competitive, and individualistic goal structures. *Psychological Bulletin, 134*(2), 223–246.

Ross, C., Mirowsky, J., & Goldsteen, K. (1990). The impact of the family on health: The decade in review. *Journal of Marriage and the Family, 52*, 1059–1078.

Ross, J. (2017, January 3). Black parents take their kids to school on how to deal with police. *The Washington Post.* https://www.washingtonpost.com/national/black-parents-take-their-kids-to-school-on-how-to-deal-with-police/2017/01/03/86129c1c-c6be-11e6-bf4b-2c064d32a4bf_story.html?utm_term=.73cad1dff93c

Ross, L. (1977). The intuitive psychologist and his shortcomings. In L. Berkowitz (Ed.), *Advances in experimental social psychology* (Vol. 10, pp. 173–220). New York: Academic Press.

Ross, L. (1988). Situationist perspectives on the obedience experiments. *Contemporary Psychology, 33*, 101–104.

Ross, L., Amabile, T. M., & Steinmetz, J. L. (1977). Social roles, social control, and biases on social-perception processes. *Journal of Personality and Social Psychology, 35*, 485–494.

Ross, L., Bierbrauer, G., & Hoffman, S. (1976). The role of attribution process in conformity and dissent: Revisiting the Asch situation. *American Psychologist, 31*, 148–157.

Ross, L., & Stillinger, C. (1991). Barriers to conflict resolution. *Negotiation Journal, 8*, 389–404.

Ross, L., & Ward, A. (1995). Psychological barriers to dispute resolution. In M. P. Zanna (Ed.), *Advances in experimental social psychology* (Vol. 27, pp. 255–304). San Diego, CA: Academic Press.

Ross, L., & Ward, A. (1996). Naive realism in everyday life: Implications for social conflict and misunderstanding. In T. Brown, E. S. Reed, & E. Turiel (Eds.), *Values and knowledge.* The Jean Piaget Symposium Series (pp. 103–135). Hillsdale, NJ: Erlbaum.

Ross, M., & Sicoly, F. (1979). Egocentric biases in availability and attribution. *Journal of Personality and Social Psychology, 32*, 880–892.

Ross, M. W. (1990). The relationship between life events and mental health in homosexual men. *Journal of Clinical Psychology, 46*, 402–411.

Ross, S., & Ross, J. G. (1949). Social facilitation of feeding behavior in dogs: I. Group and solitary feeding. *Journal of Genetic Psychology, 74*, 97–108.

Rothberg, J. M., & Jones, F. D. (1987). Suicide in the U.S. Army: Epidemiological and periodic aspects. *Suicide and Life-Threatening Behavior, 17*, 119–132.

Rozin, P., & Royzman, E. B. (2001). Negativity bias, negativity dominance, and contagion. *Personality and Social Psychology Review, 5*, 296–320.

Rozin, P., & Singh, L. (1999). The moralization of cigarette smoking in America. *Journal of Consumer Behavior, 8*, 321–337.

Rudd, M., Vohs, K. D., & Aaker, J. (2012). Awe expands people's perception of time, alters decision making, and enhances well-being. *Psychological Science, 23*(10), 1130–1136.

Rudman, L. A., & Ashmore, R. D. (2007). Discrimination and the IAT. *Group Processes and Intergroup Relations, 10*, 359–372.

Rudman, L. A., & Borgida, E. (1995). The afterglow of construct accessibility: The behavioral consequences of priming men to view women as sexual objects. *Journal of Experimental Social Psychology, 31*, 493–517.

Rudman, L. A., & Mescher, K. (2012). Of animals and objects: Men's implicit dehumanization of women and male sexual aggression. *Personality and Social Psychology Bulletin, 38*, 734–746.

Rudolph, U., Roesch, S. C., Greitemeyer, T., & Weiner, B. (2004). A meta-analytic review of help giving and aggression from an attributional perspective: Contributions to a general theory of motivation. *Cognition and Emotion, 18*, 815–848.

Rusbult, C. E. (1980). Commitment and satisfaction in romantic associations: A test of the investment model. *Journal of Experimental Social Psychology, 17*, 172–186.

Rusbult, C. E. (1983). A longitudinal test of the investment model: The development (and deterioration) of satisfaction and commitment in heterosexual involvements. *Journal of Personality and Social Psychology, 45*, 101–117.

Rusbult, C. E., Agnew, C. R., & Arriaga, X. B. (2012). The investment model of commitment processes. In P. A. M. Van Lange, A. W. Kruglanski, & E. T. Higgins (Eds.), *Handbook of theories of social psychology* (Vol. 2, pp. 218–231). Los Angeles: Sage.

Rusbult, C. E., Martz, J. M., and Agnew, C. R. (1998). The investment model scale: Measuring commitment level, satisfaction level, quality of alternatives, and investment size. *Personal Relationships, 5*, 357–391.

Rushton, J. P., & Bons, T. A. (2005). Mate choice and friendship in twins: Evidence for genetic similarity. *Psychological Science, 16*, 555–559.

Russell, E. M., DelPriore, D. J, Butterfield, M. E. & Hill, S. E. (2013). Friends with benefits, but without the sex: Straight women and gay men exchange trustworthy mating advice. *Evolutionary Psychology, 11*, 132–147.

Russo, J. E., Meloy, M. G., & Medvec, V. H. (1998). Predecisional distortion of product information. *Journal of Marketing Research, 35*, 438–452.

Russo, J. E., & Shoemaker, P. J. H. (1990). *Decision traps: Ten barriers to brilliant decision-making and how to overcome them.* New York: Doubleday.

Rusting C. I., & Larsen, R. J. (1998). Diurnal patterns of unpleasant mood: Associations with neuroticism, depression, and anxiety. *Journal of Personality, 66*, 85–103.

Ryckman, D. B., & Peckham, P. (1987). Gender differences in attributions for success and failure situations across subject areas. *Journal of Educational Research, 81*, 120–125.

Sabogal, F., Marin, G., Otero-Sabogal, R., VanOss Marin, B., & Perez-Stable, E. J. (1987). Hispanic familism and acculturation: What changes and what doesn't? *Hispanic Journal of Behavioral Sciences, 9*, 397–412. doi:10.1177/07399863870094003

Sagar, H. A., & Schofield, J. W. (1980). Racial and behavioral cues in black and white children's perceptions of ambiguously aggressive acts. *Journal of Personality and Social Psychology, 39*, 590–598.

Said, C. P., & Todorov, A. (2011). A statistical model of facial attractiveness. *Psychological Science, 22*(9), 1183–1190.

Sakai, H. (1981). Induced compliance and opinion change. *Japanese Psychological Research, 23*, 1–8.

Saks, M. J., & Marti, M. W. (1997). A meta-analysis of the effects of jury size. *Law and Human Behavior, 21*, 451–468.

Salancik, G., & Meindl, J. R. (1984). Corporate attributions as strategic illusions of management control. *Administrative Science Quarterly, 29*, 238–254.

Sanchez-Burks, J. (2002). Protestant relational ideology and (in) attention to relational cues in work settings. *Journal of Personality and Social Psychology, 83*(4), 919–929.

Sanchez-Burks, J. (2004). Protestant relational ideology: The cognitive underpinnings and organizational implications of an American anomaly. In B. Staw & R. Kramer (Eds.), *Research in organizational behavior* (Vol. 26, pp. 265–305). San Diego, CA: Elsevier, JAI Press.

Sanchez-Burks, J., Nisbett, R. E., & Ybarra, O. (2000). Cultural styles, relationship schemas, and prejudice against outgroups. *Journal of Personality and Social Psychology, 79*, 174–189.

Sanday, P. R. (1981). The socio-cultural context of rape: A cross-cultural study. *Journal of Social Issues, 37*, 5–27.

Sanday, P. R. (1997). The socio-cultural context of rape: A cross-cultural study. In L. L. O'Toole (Ed.), *Gender violence: Interdisciplinary perspectives*. New York: New York University Press.

Sansone, C., & Harackiewicz, J. M. (Eds.). (2000). *Intrinsic and extrinsic motivation: The search for optimal motivation and performance*. San Diego, CA: Academic Press.

Sapolsky, R. M. (1982). The endocrine stress-response and social status in the wild baboon. *Hormones and Behavior, 16*(3), 279–292.

Sapolsky, R. M. (1994). *Why zebras don't get ulcers*. New York: Freeman.

Sastry, J., & Ross, C. E. (1998). Asian ethnicity and the sense of personal control. *Social Psychology Quarterly, 61*, 101–120.

Saucier, D. A., Miller, C. T., & Doucet, N. (2005). Differences in helping whites and blacks: A meta-analysis. *Personality and Social Psychology Review, 9*, 2–16.

Saulnier, K., & Perlman, D. (1981). The actor-observer bias is alive and well in prison: A sequel to Wells. *Personality and Social Psychology Bulletin, 7*, 559–564.

Savani, K., Markus, H. R., & Conner, A. L. (2008). Let your preference be your guide: Preferences and choices are more tightly linked for North Americans than for Indians. *Journal of Personality and Social Psychology, 95*, 861–876.

Savin-Williams, R. C. (1977). Dominance in a human adolescent group. *Animal Behavior, 25*, 400–406.

Savitsky, K., Adelman, R. M., & Kruger, J. (2012). The feature-positive effect in allocations of responsibility for collaborative tasks. *Journal of Experimental Social Psychology, 48*(3), 791–793.

Savitsky, K., Epley, N., & Gilovich, T. (2001). Is it as bad as we fear? Overestimating the extremity of others' judgments. *Journal of Personality and Social Psychology, 81*, 44–56.

Schachter, S. (1951). Deviation, rejection and communication. *Journal of Abnormal and Social Psychology, 46*, 190–207.

Schachter, S., & Singer, J. E. (1962). Cognitive, social and psychological determinants of emotional state. *Psychological Review, 69*, 379–399.

Schaller, M., Simpson, J. A., & Kenrick, D. T. (2006). *Evolution and social psychology*. New York: Psychology Press.

Schank, R., & Abelson, R. P. (1977). *Scripts, plans, goals, and understanding: An inquiry into human knowledge structures*. Hillsdale, NJ: Erlbaum.

Schaumberg, R., & Flynn, F. (2012). Uneasy lies the head that wears the crown: The link between guilt-proneness and leadership. *Journal of Personality and Social Psychology, 103*, 327–342.

Scheib, J. E., Gangestad, S. W., & Thornhill, R. (1999). Facial attractiveness, symmetry, and cues of good genes. *Proceedings of the Royal Society B: Biological Sciences, 266*, 1913–1917.

Scheier, M. F., Fenigstein, A., & Buss, A. H. (1974). Self-awareness and physical aggression. *Journal of Experimental Social Psychology, 10*, 264–273.

Schelling, T. C. (1978). *Micromotives and macrobehavior*. New York: Norton.

Schick, T., & Vaughn, L. (1995). *How to think about weird things: Critical thinking for a new age*. Mountain View, CA: Mayfield.

Schimmack, U., Oishi, S., & Diener, E. (2002). Cultural influences on the relation between pleasant emotions and unpleasant emotions: Asian dialectic philosophies or individualism-collectivism? *Cognition and Emotion, 16*, 705–719.

Schkade, D. A., & Kahneman, D. (1998). Does living in California make people happy? A focusing illusion in judgments of life satisfaction. *Psychological Science, 9*, 340–346.

Schkade, D. A., Sunstein, C. R., & Hastie, R. (2007). What happened on deliberation day? *California Law Review 95*(3), 915–940. Retrieved from http://www.jstor.org/stable/20439113

Schlenker, B. R. (1980). *Impression management: The self-concept, social identity, and interpersonal relations*. Monterey, CA: Brooks/Cole.

Schlenker, B. R., & Leary, M. R. (1982). Social anxiety and self-presentation: A conceptualization and a model. *Psychological Bulletin, 92*, 641–669.

Schmitt, B. H., Gilovich, T., Goore, N., & Joseph, L. (1986). Mere presence and social facilitation: One more time. *Journal of Experimental Social Psychology, 22*, 242–248.

Schmitt, D. P. (2003). Universal sex differences in the desire for sexual variety: Tests from 52 nations, 6 continents, and 13 islands. *Journal of Personality and Social Psychology, 85*, 85–104.

Schmitt, D. P., & Allik, J. (2005). Simultaneous administration of the Rosenberg Self-Esteem Scale in 53 nations: Exploring the universal and culture-specific features of global self-esteem. *Journal of Personality and Social Psychology, 89*, 623–642.

Schmitt, M. T., Branscombe, N. R., Postmes, T., & Garcia, A. (2014). The consequences of perceived discrimination for psychological well-being: A meta-analytic review. *Psychological Bulletin, 140*, 921–948.

Schnall, E., Wassertheil-Smoller, S., Swencionis, C., Zemon, V., Tinker, L., O'Sullivan, J., et. al. (2008). The relationship between religion and cardiovascular outcomes and all-cause mortality in the women's health initiative observational study. *Psychology & Health, 25*(2), 249–263.

Schoeneman, T. J., & Rubanowitz, D. E. (1985). Attributions in the advice columns: Actors and observers, causes and reasons. *Personality and Social Psychology Bulletin, 11*, 315–325.

Schooler, J. W., & Engstler-Schooler, T. Y. (1990). Verbal overshadowing of visual memories: Some things are better left unsaid. *Cognitive Psychology, 22*, 36–71.

Schroeder, C. M., & Prentice, D. A. (1998). Exposing pluralistic ignorance to reduce alcohol use among college students. *Journal of Applied Social Psychology, 28*, 2150–2180.

Schroeder, D. A., Penner, L. A., Dovidio, J. F., & Piliavin, J. A. (1995). *The psychology of helping and altruism*. New York: McGraw-Hill.

Schroeder, J., Caruso, E. M., & Epley, N. (2016). Many hands make overlooked work: Over-claiming of responsibility increases with group size. *Journal of Experimental Psychology: General, 22*(2), 238–246.

Schroeder, J., & Risen, J. L. (2014). Befriending the enemy: Outgroup friendship longitudinally predicts intergroup attitudes in a co-existence program for Israelis and Palestinians. *Group Processes and Intergroup Relations.* doi:10.1177/1368430214542257

Schultheiss, O. C. (2013). The hormonal correlates of implicit motives. *Social and Personality Psychology Compass, 7*(1), 52–65.

Schultz, P. W., Nolan, J. M., Cialdini, R. B., Goldstein, N. J., & Griskevicius, V. (2007). The constructive, destructive, and reconstructive power of social norms. *Psychological Science, 18*, 429–434.

Schwartz C. R. (2013). Trends and variation in assortative mating: Causes and consequences. *Annual Review of Sociology, 39*, 451–470.

Schwartz, J. (2004, May 6). Simulated prison in '71 showed a fine line between "normal" and "monster." *New York Times*, A14.

Schwarz, N., Bless, H., Strack, F., Klumpp, G., Rittenauer-Schatka, H., & Simons, A. (1991). Ease of retrieval as information: Another look at the availability heuristic. *Journal of Personality and Social Psychology, 61*, 195–202.

Searle, J. R. (1983). *Intentionality: An essay in the philosophy of mind.* Cambridge, England: Cambridge University Press.

Sears, D. O. (1986). College students in the laboratory: Influences of a narrow database on social psychology's view of human nature. *Journal of Personality and Social Psychology, 51*, 515–530.

Sears, D. O. (1988). Symbolic racism. In P. A. Katz & D. A. Taylor (Eds.), *Eliminating racism: Profiles in controversy* (pp. 53–84). New York: Plenum Press.

Sears, D. O., & Henry, P. J. (2005). Over thirty years later: A contemporary look at symbolic racism. In M. P. Zanna (Ed.), *Advances in experimental social psychology* (Vol. 37, pp. 95–150). San Diego, CA: Elsevier.

Sears, D. O., & Kinder, D. R. (1985). Whites' opposition to busing: On conceptualizing and operationalizing group conflict. *Journal of Personality and Social Psychology, 48*, 1141–1147.

Sedikides, C., & Gregg, A. (2008). Self-enhancement: Food for thought. *Perspectives on Psychological Science, 3*, 102–116.

Sedikides, C., & Hepper, E. G. (2009). Self-improvement. *Social and Personality Psychology Compass, 3*, 899–917.

Segal, N. L. (1984). Cooperation, competition, and altruism within twin sets: A reappraisal. *Ethology and Sociobiology, 5*, 163–177.

Seibt, B., & Forster, J. (2004). Stereotype threat and performance: How self-stereotypes influence processing by inducing regulatory foci. *Journal of Personality and Social Psychology, 87*, 38–56.

Seligman, M. E. P. (1988). Boomer blues. *Psychology Today, 22*, 50–53.

Seligman, M. E. P., Maier, S. F., & Geer, J. H. (1968). Alleviation of learned helplessness in the dog. *Journal of Abnormal Psychology, 73*, 256–262.

Seligman, M. E. P., Steen, T. A., Park, N., & Peterson, C. (2005). Positive psychology progress: Empirical validation of interventions. *American Psychologist, 60*(5), 410–421.

Seltzer, R. (2006). Scientific jury selection: Does it work? *Journal of Applied Social Psychology, 36*, 2417–2435.

Sen, A. (1990, January 20). More than 100 million women are missing. *The New York Review of Books.*

Seta, C. E., & Seta, J. J. (1992). Increments and decrements in mean arterial pressure levels as a function of audience composition: An averaging and summation analysis. *Personality and Social Psychology Bulletin, 18*, 173–181.

Shah, A. M., Eisenkraft, N., Bettman, J. R., & Chartrand, T. L. (2016). "Paper or plastic?": How we pay influences post-transaction connection. *Journal of Consumer Research, 42*, 688–708.

Shah, J., & Higgins, E. T. (2001). Regulatory concerns and appraisal efficiency: The general impact of promotion and prevention. *Journal of Personality and Social Psychology, 80*, 693–705.

Shapin, S. (2006, January 16). Eat and run. *The New Yorker*, 76–82.

Shapiro, D. H., Schwartz, C. E., & Astin, J. A. (1996). Controlling ourselves, controlling our world. *American Psychologist, 51*, 1213–1230.

Shariff, A. F., & Norenzayan, A. (2007). God is watching you: Priming God concepts increases prosocial behavior in an anonymous economic game. *Psychological Science, 18*, 803–809.

Shariff, A. F., Willard, A. K., Andersen, T., & Norenzayan, A. (2016). Religious priming: A meta-analysis with a focus on prosociality. *Personality and Social Psychology Review, 20*(1), 27–48.

Shaver, P. R., & Brennan, K. A. (1992). Attachment style and the "big five" of personality traits: Their connections with each other and with romantic relationship outcomes. *Personality and Social Psychology Bulletin, 18*, 536–545.

Shavitt, S., Sanbonmatsu, D. M., Smittipatana, S., & Posavac, S. S. (1999). Broadening the conditions for illusory correlation formation: Implications for judging minority groups. *Basic and Applied Social Psychology, 21*, 263–279.

Shedler, L., & Manis, M. (1986). Can the availability heuristic explain vividness effects? *Journal of Personality and Social Psychology, 51*, 26–36.

Sheley, J. F., & Askins, C. D. (1981). Crime, crime news, and crime views. *Public Opinion Quarterly, 45*, 492–506.

Shelley, H. P. (1965). Eating behavior: Social facilitation or social inhibition. *Psychonomic Science, 3*, 521–522.

Shelton, J. N., Alegre, J. M., & Son, D. (2010). Social stigma and disadvantage: Current themes and future prospects. *Journal of Social Issues, 66*, 618–633.

Shelton, J. N, & Richeson, J. A. (2005). Intergroup contact and pluralistic ignorance. *Journal of Personality and Social Psychology, 88*, 91–107.

Shelton, J. N., Richeson, J. A., & Salvatore, J. (2005). Expecting to be the target of prejudice: Implications for interethnic interactions. *Personality and Social Psychology Bulletin, 31*, 1189–1202.

Shepherd, H., & Paluck, E. L. (2015). Stopping the drama: A field experiment on network signals, gender, and social influence in a high school. *Social Psychology Quarterly, 78*(2), 173–193.

Sherif, M. (1936). *The psychology of social norms.* New York: Harper.

Sherif, M., Harvey, O. J., White, B. J., Hood, W., & Sherif, C. (1961). *Intergroup conflict and cooperation: The Robbers Cave experiment.* Norman: University of Oklahoma Institute of Group Relations.

Sherman, D. A. K., Nelson, L. D., & Steele, C. M. (2000). Do messages about health risks threaten the self? Increasing the acceptance of threatening health messages via self-affirmation. *Personality and Social Psychology Bulletin, 26*, 1046–1058.

Sherman, D. K., & Cohen, G. L. (2006). The psychology of self-defense: Self-affirmation theory. In M. P. Zanna (Ed.), *Advances in experimental social psychology* (Vol. 38, pp. 183–242). San Diego, CA: Academic Press.

Sherman, J. W., Gawronski, B., Gonsalkorale, K., Hugenberg, K., Allen, T. J., & Groom, C. J. (2008). The self-regulation of automatic associations and behavioral impulses. *Psychological Review, 115*, 314–335.

Sherman, L. J., Rice, K., & Cassidy, J. (2015). Infant capacities related to building internal working models of attachment figures: A theoretical and empirical review. *Developmental Review, 37*, 109–141.

Sherman, L. W., & Strang, H. (2007). *Restorative justice: The evidence.* London: Smith Institute.

Sherman, P. W. (1985). Alarm calls of Belding's ground squirrels to aerial predators: Nepotism or self-preservation? *Behavioral Ecology and Sociobiology, 17*, 313–323.

Sherman, S. J., & Gorkin, L. (1980). Attitude bolstering when behavior is inconsistent with central attitudes. *Journal of Experimental Social Psychology, 16*, 388–403.

Sherman, S. J., Mackie, D. M., & Driscoll, D. M. (1990). Priming and the differential use of dimensions in evaluation. *Personality and Social Psychology Bulletin, 16*, 405–418.

Shermer, M. (1997). *Why people believe weird things: Pseudoscience, superstition, and other contusions of our time.* New York: Freeman.

Shih, M., Pittinsky, T. L., & Ambady, N. (1999). Stereotype susceptibility: Identity salience and shifts in quantitative performance. *Psychological Science, 10*(1), 80–83.

Shiota, M. N., Keltner, D., & Mossman, A. (2007). The nature of awe: Elicitors, appraisals, and effects on self-concept. *Cognition and Emotion, 21*(5), 944–963.

Shook, N. J., & Fazio, R. H. (2008). An experimental field test of the contact hypothesis. *Psychological Science, 19*, 717–723.

Showers, C. (1992). Compartmentalization of positive and negative self-knowleldge: Keeping bad apples out of the bunch. *Journal of Personality and Social Psychology, 62*, 1036–1049.

Shrauger, J. S., & Shoeneman, T. J. (1979). Symbolic interactionist view of self-concept: Through the looking glass darkly. *Psychological Bulletin, 86*, 549–573.

Shteynberg, G., Bramlett, J. M., Fles, E. H., & Cameron, J. (2016). The broadcast of shared attention and its impact on political persuasion. *Journal of Personality and Social Psychology, 111*, 665–673.

Shweder, R. A., Jensen, L. A., & Goldstein, W. M. (1995). Who sleeps by whom revisited: A method for extracting moral goods implicit in practice. *New Directions in Child Development, 67*, 21–39.

Sidanius, J., & Pratto, F. (1999). *Social dominance: An intergroup theory of social hierarchy and oppression.* New York: Cambridge University Press.

Sieverding, M., Decker, S., & Zimmermann, F. (2010). Information about low participation in cancer screening demotivates other people. *Psychological Science, 21*, 941–943.

Sigall, H., & Ostrove, N. (1975). Beautiful but dangerous: Effects of offender attractiveness and nature of the crime on juridic judgment. *Journal of Personality and Social Psychology, 31*, 410–414.

Silk, J. B., Brosnan, S. F., Henrich, J., Lambeth, S. P., & Shapiro, S. (2013). Chimpanzees share food for many reasons: The role of kinship, reciprocity, social bonds and harassment on food transfers. *Animal Behaviour, 85*, 941–947.

Silverstein, B., Perdue, L., Peterson, L., & Kelly, E. (1986). The role of the mass media in promoting a thin standard of bodily attractiveness for women. *Sex Roles, 14*, 519–532.

Simon, B., Mlicki, P., Johnston, L., Caetano, A., Warowicki, M., Van Knippenberg, A., et al. (1990). The effects of ingroup and outgroup homogeneity on ingroup favouritism, stereotyping, and overestimation of relative ingroup size. *European Journal of Social Psychology, 20*(6), 519–523.

Simon, D., Krawczyk, D. C., & Holyoak, K. J. (2004). Construction of preferences by constraint satisfaction. *Psychological Science, IS*, 331–336.

Simons, D. J., & Chabris, C. F. (1999). Gorillas in our midst: Sustained inattentional blindness for dynamic events. *Perception, 28*, 1059–1074.

Simpson, B., & Willer, R. (2015). Beyond altruism: Sociological foundations of cooperation and prosocial behavior. *Annual Review of Sociology, 41*, 43–63.

Simpson, G. E., & Yinger, J. M. (1985). *Racial and cultural minorities: An analysis of prejudice and discrimination.* New York: Plenum Press.

Simpson, J. A., & Rholes, W. S. (2017). Adult attachment, stress, and romantic relationships. *Current Opinion in Psychology, 13*, 19–24.

Sinaceur, M., & Tiedens, L. Z. (2006). Get mad and get more than even: When and why anger expression is effective in negotiations. *Journal of Experimental Social Psychology, 42*(3), 314–322.

Sinclair, L., & Kunda, Z. (1999). Reactions to a black professional: Motivated inhibition and activation of conflicting stereotypes. *Journal of Personality and Social Psychology, 77*, 885–904.

Singer, T., & Klimecki, O. (2014). Empathy and compassion. *Current Biology, 24*(18), R875–R878.

Singh, D. (1993). Adaptive significance of female physical attractiveness: Role of waist-to-hip ratio. *Journal of Personality and Social Psychology, 65*, 293–307.

Singhal, A., Rogers, E. M., & Brown, W. J. (1993). Harnessing the potential of entertainment-education telenovelas. *Gazette, 51*, 1–18.

Singh-Manoux, A., Adler, N. E., & Marmot, M. G. (2003). Subjective social status: Its determinants and its association with measures of ill health in the Whitehall II study. *Social Science & Medicine, 56*(6), 1321–1333.

Sistrunk, F., & McDavid, J. W. (1971). Sex variable in conforming behavior. *Journal of Personality and Social Psychology, 17*, 200–207.

Skov, R. B., & Sherman, S. J. (1986). Information-gathering processes: Diagnosticity, hypothesis-confirmatory strategies, and perceived hypothesis confirmation. *Journal of Experimental Social Psychology, 22*, 93–121.

Slatcher, R. B., & Selcuk, E. (2017). A social psycholoical perspective on the links between close relationships and health. *Current Directions in Psychological Science, 26*, 16–21.

Slater, A., von der Shulenburg, C., Brown, E., Badenoch, M., Butterworth, G., Parsons, S., et al. (1998). Newborn infants prefer attractive faces. *Infant Behavior and Development, 21*, 345–354.

Slavin, R. E. (1995). *Cooperative learning: Theory, research, and practice* (2nd ed.). Boston: Allyn & Bacon.

Sloman, S. A. (2002). Two systems of reasoning. In T. Gilovich, D. W. Griffin, & D. Kahneman (Eds.), *Heuristics and biases: The psychology of intuitive judgement* (pp. 379–396). New York: Cambridge University Press.

Slothuus, R., & de Vreese, C. H. (2010). Political parties, motivated reasoning, and issue framing effects. *The Journal of Politics, 72*, 630–645.

Slovic, P., Fischoff, B., & Lichtenstein, S. (1982). Facts versus fears: Understanding perceived risk. In D. Kahneman, P. Slovic, & A. Tversky (Eds.), *Judgment under uncertainty: Heuristics and biases* (pp. 463–489). New York: Cambridge University Press.

Small Arms Survey. (2011). *The Small Arms Survey 2011: States of security.* New York: Cambridge University Press.

Small, D. A., Loewenstein, G. & Slovic, P. (2007). Sympathy and callousness: The impact of deliberative thought on donations to identifiable and statistical victims. *Organizational Behavior and Human Decision Processes, 102*(2), 143–153.

Smith, A. (1776/1998). *The wealth of nations.* Washington, DC: Regnery Publishing.

Smith, A. E., Jussim, L., & Eccles, J. S. (1999). Do self-fulfilling prophecies accumulate, dissipate, or remain stable over time? *Journal of Personality and Social Psychology, 77*, 548–565.

Smith, C., & Ellsworth, P. (1985). Patterns of cognitive appraisal in emotion. *Journal of Personality and Social Psychology, 48*, 813–838.

Smith, E. R., & Miller, F. D. (1979). Salience and the cognitive mediation of attribution. *Journal of Personality and Social Psychology, 37*, 2240–2252.

Smith, E. R., & Zarate, M. A. (1990). Exemplar and prototype use in social categorization. *Social Cognition, 8*, 243–262.

Smith, P. K., Jostmann, N. B., Galinsky, A. D., & van Dijk, W. W (2008). Lacking power impairs executive functions. *Psychological Science, 19*(5), 441–447.

Smith, P. K., & Trope, Y. (2006). You focus on the forest when you're in charge of the trees: Power priming and abstract information processing. *Journal of Personality and Social Psychology, 90*, 578–596.

Smith, S. L., Choueiti, M., Scofield, E., & Pieper, K. (2013). *Gender inequality in 500 popular films: Examining on-screen portrayals and behind-the-scenes employment patterns in motion pictures released between 2007–2012.* Los Angeles: USC Annenberg School for Communication and Journalism.

Smith, S. S., & Richardson, D. (1983). Amelioration of deception and harm in psychological research: The important role of debriefing. *Journal of Personality and Social Psychology, 44*, 1075–1082.

Smith, T. W. (2009). Loving and caring in the United States: Trends and correlates of empathy, altruism, and related constructs. In B. Fehr, S. Sprecher, & L. G. Underwood (Eds.), *The science of compassionate love: Theory, research, and applications* (pp. 81–120). Malden, MA: Wiley-Blackwell.

Snibbe, A. C., & Markus, H. R., (2005). You can't always get what you want: Educational attainment, agency, and choice. *Journal of Personality and Social Psychology, 88*, 703–720.

Snyder, M. (1974). Self-monitoring of expressive behavior. *Journal of Personality and Social Psychology, 30*, 526–537.

Snyder, M. (1979). Self-monitoring processes. In L. Berkowitz (Ed.), *Advances in experimental social psychology* (Vol. 12, pp. 85–128). New York: Academic Press.

Snyder, M., & Swann, W. B. (1978). Hypothesis-testing in social interaction. *Journal of Personality and Social Psychology, 36*, 1202–1212.

Snyder, M., Tanke, E. D., & Berscheid, E. (1977). Social perception and interpersonal behavior: On the self-fulfilling nature of social stereotypes. *Journal of Personality and Social Psychology, 35*, 656–666.

Sommers, S. R. (2006). On racial diversity and group decision making: Identifying multiple effects of racial composition on jury deliberations. *Journal of Personality and Social Psychology, 90*, 597–612.

Sommers, S. R., & Ellsworth, P. C. (2001). White juror bias: An investigation of prejudice against black defendants in the American courtroom. *Psychology and Public Policy & Law, 7*(1), 201–229.

Song, H., & Schwarz, N. (2008). If it's hard to read, it's hard to do. *Psychological Science, 19*, 986–988.

Souchet, L., & Girandola, G. (2013). Double foot-in-the-door, social representations, and environment: Application for energy savings. *Journal of Applied Social Psychology, 43*, 306–315.

Spears, R. (2011). Group identities: The social identity perspective. In S. J. Schwartz, K. Luyckx, & V. L. Vignoles (Eds.), *Handbook of identity theory and research* (Vols. 1 and 2; pp. 201–224). New York: Springer.

Speer, N. K., Reynolds, J. R., Swallow, K. M., & Zacks, J. M. (2009). Reading stories activates neural representations of visual and motor experiences. *Psychological Science, 20*, 989–999.

Spencer, S. J., Steele, C. M., & Quinn, D. M. (1999). Stereotype threat and women's math performance. *Journal of Experimental Social Psychology, 35*, 4–28.

Sperber, D. (1996). *Explaining culture: A naturalistic approach.* Oxford, England: Blackwell.

Spiegel, D., Bloom, J. R., Kraemer, H. C., & Gottheil, E. (1989). Effect of psychosocial treatment on survival of patients with metastatic breast cancer. *Lancet, 2*, 888–891.

Spivey, C. B., & Prentice-Dunn, S. (1990). Assessing the directionality of deindividuated behavior: Effects of deindividuation, modeling, and private self-consciousness on aggressive and pro-social responses. *Basic and Applied Psychology, 11*, 387–403.

Sprecher, S., & Regan, P. C. (1998). Passionate and companionate love in courting and young married couples. *Sociological Inquiry, 68*, 163–185.

Sritharan, R., & Gawronski, B. (2010). Changing implicit and explicit prejudice: Insights from the associative-propositional evaluation model. *Social Psychology, 41*(3), 113–123.

Srull, T. K., & Wyer, R. S. (1979). The role of category accessibility in the interpretation of information about persons: Some determinants and implications. *Journal of Personality and Social Psychology, 37*, 1660–1672.

Srull, T. K., & Wyer, R. S. (1980). Category accessibility and social perception: Some implications for the study of person memory and interpersonal judgments. *Journal of Personality and Social Psychology, 38*, 841–856.

Stangor, C., & Duan, C. (1991). Effects of multiple task demands upon memory for information about social groups. *Journal of Experimental Social Psychology, 27*, 357–378.

Stangor, C., & McMillan, D. (1992). Memory for expectancy-congruent and expectancy-incongruent information: A review of the social and social developmental literatures. *Psychological Bulletin, 111*, 42–61.

Stangor, C., Sechrist, G. B., & Jost, J. T. (2001). Changing racial beliefs by providing consensus information. *Personality and Social Psychology Bulletin, 27*, 484–494.

Stanovich, K. E., & West, R. F. (2002). Individual differences in reasoning: Implications for the rationality debate. In T. Gilovich, D. W. Griffin, & D. Kahneman (Eds.), *Heuristics and biases: The psychology of intuitive judgment* (pp. 421–440). New York: Cambridge University Press.

Stasser, G., & Davis, J. H. (1981). Group decision making and social influence: A social interaction sequence model. *Psychological Review, 88*, 523–551.

Statistics about sexual violence. (2015). Harrisburg, PA: National Sexual Violence Resource Center. https://www.nsvrc.org/

Staub, E. (1989). *The roots of evil: The origins of genocide and other group violence.* Cambridge, England: Cambridge University Press.

Steblay, N. M. (1987). Helping behavior in rural and urban environments: A meta-analysis. *Psychological Bulletin, 102*, 346–356.

Steele, C. M. (1988). The psychology self-affirmation: Sustaining the integrity of the self. In L. Berkowitz (Ed.), *Advances in experimental social psychology* (Vol. 21, pp. 261–302). New York: Academic Press.

Steele, C. M. (1997). A threat in the air: How stereotypes shape intellectual identity and performance. *American Psychologist, 52*, 613–629.

Steele, C. M., & Aronson, J. (1995). Stereotype threat and the intellectual test performance of African Americans. *Journal of Personality and Social Psychology, 69*, 797–811.

Steele, C. M., Spencer, S. J., & Aronson, J. (2002). Contending with group image: The psychology of stereotype and social identity threat. In M. P. Zanna (Ed.), *Advances in experimental social psychology* (Vol. 34, pp. 379–440). San Diego, CA: Academic Press.

Stel, M., van Baaren, R. B., Blascovich, J., van Dijk, E., McCall, C., Pollmann, M. M. H., et al. (2010). Effects of a priori liking on the elicitation of mimicry. *Experimental Psychology, 57*(6), 412–418.

Stellar, J. E., Cohen, A., Oveis, C., & Keltner, D. (2015). Affective and physiological responses to the suffering of others: Compassion and vagal activity. *Journal of Personality and Social Psychology, 108*, 572–585.

Stellar, J. E., Manzo, V. M., Kraus, M. W., & Keltner, D. (2012). Class and compassion: Socioeconomic factors predict responses to suffering. *Emotion, 12*, 449–459.

Stephan, W. G. (1986). The effect of school desegregation: An evaluation 30 years after *Brown.* In M. J. Saks & L. Saxe (Eds.), *Advances in applied social psychology* (Vol. 3, pp. 181–206). Hillsdale, NJ: Erlbaum.

Stephan, W. G., & Stephan, C. W. (1996). *Intergroup relations.* Madison, WI: Brown & Benchmark.

Stephan, W. G., Ybarra, O., & Morrison, K. R. (2009). Intergroup threat theory. In T. D. Nelson, *Handbook of prejudice, stereotyping, and discrimination* (pp. 43–60). New York: Psychology Press,Taylor and Francis Group.

Stephens, N. M., Fryberg, S. A., & Markus, H. R. (2011). When choice does not equal freedom: A sociocultural analysis of agency in working-class American contexts. *Social and Personality Psychology Science, 2*, 33–41.

Stephens, N. M., Fryberg, S., Markus, H. R., Johnson, C., & Covarrubias, R. (2012). Unseen disadvantage: How American universities' focus on independence undermines the academic performance of first-generation college students. *Journal of Personality and Social Psychology, 102,* 1178–1197.

Stephens, N. M., Hamedani, M. G., & Destin, M. (2014). Closing the social-class achievement gap: A difference-education intervention improves first-generation students' academic performance and all students' college transition. *Psychological Science, 25,* 943–953.

Stephens, N. M., Hamedani, M. G., Markus, H. R., Bergsieker, H. B., & Eloul, L. (2009). Why did they "choose" to stay? Perspectives of Hurricane Katrina observers and survivors. *Psychological Science, 20,* 878–886.

Stephens, N. M., Markus, H. R., & Phillips, L. T. (2014). Social class culture cycles: How three gateway contexts shape selves and fuel inequality. *Annual Review of Psychology, 65,* 611–634.

Stephens, N. M., Markus, H. R., & Townsend, S. S. M. (2007). Choice as an act of meaning: The case of social class. *Journal of Personality and Social Psychology, 93,* 814–830.

Stephens, N. M., Townsend, S. S. M., Hamedani, M., Destin, M., & Manzo, V. (2015). A difference-education intervention equips first-generation college students to thrive in the face of stressful college situations. *Psychological Science, 26*(10), 1556–1566.

Stephens, N. M., Townsend, S. S. M., Markus, H. R., & Phillips, L. T. (2012). A cultural mismatch: Independent cultural norms produce greater increases in cortisol and more negative emotions among first-generation college students. *Journal of Experimental Social Psychology, 48,* 1389–1393.

Stephens-Davidowitz, S. (2017). *Everybody lies: Big data, new data, and what the Internet can tell us about who we really are.* New York: HarperCollins.

Stern, C., & West, T. V. (2014). Circumventing anxiety during interpersonal encounters to promote interest in contact: An implementation intention approach. *Journal of Experimental Social Psychology, 50,* 82–93.

Sternberg, R. J. (1986). A triangular theory of love. *Psychological Review, 93,* 119–135.

Stevenson, H. W., & Lee, S. (1996). The academic achievement of Chinese students. In M. H. Bond (Ed.), *The handbook of Chinese psychology* (pp. 124–142). New York: Oxford University Press.

Stevenson, H. W., Lee, S. Y., Chen, C., Stigler, J. W., Hsu, C. C., & Kitamura, S. (1990). Contexts of achievement: A study of American, Chinese and Japanese children. *Monographs of the Society for Research in Child Development, 55,* 1–2, Serial No. 221.

Stevenson, H. W., & Stigler, J. W. (1992). *The learning gap: Why our schools are failing and what we can learn from Japanese and Chinese education.* New York: Summit Books.

Stewart, J. E. (1980). Defendant's attractiveness as a factor in the outcome of criminal trials: An observational study. *Journal of Applied Social Psychology, 10,* 348–361.

Stirrat, M., & Perrett, D. I. (2010). Valid facial cues to cooperation and trust: Male facial width and trustworthiness. *Psychological Science, 21,* 349–354.

Stok, F. M., de Ridder, D. T. D., de Vet, E., & de Wit, J. B. F. (2014). Don't' tell me what I should do, but what others do: The influence of descriptive and injunctive peer norms on fruit consumption in adolescents. *British Journal of Health Psychology, 19,* 52–64.

Stone, J., Lynch, C. I., Sjomeling, M., & Darley, J. M. (1999). Stereotype threat effects on black and white athletic performance. *Journal of Personality and Social Psychology, 77,* 1213–1227.

Stone, J., Perry, Z., & Darley, J. (1997). "White men can't jump": Evidence for perceptual confirmation of racial stereotypes following a basketball game. *Basic and Applied Social Psychology, 19,* 291–306.

Storms, M. D. (1973). Videotape and the attribution process: Reversing actors' and observers' points of view. *Journal of Personality and Social Psychology, 27,* 165–175.

Strack, F., & Deutsch, R. (2004). Reflective and impulsive determinants of social behavior. *Personality and Social Psychology Review, 8,* 220–247.

Strack, F., Martin, L. L., & Schwarz, N. (1988). Priming and communication: The social determinants of information use in judgments of life satisfaction. *European Journal of Social Psychology, 18,* 429–442.

Strahan, E. J., Spencer, S. J., & Zanna, M. P. (2002). Subliminal priming and persuasion: Striking while the iron is hot. *Journal of Experimental Social Psychology, 38,* 556–568.

Strauman, T. J., & Higgins, E. T. (1987). Automatic activation of self-discrepancies and emotional syndromes: When cognitive structures influence affect. *Journal of Personality and Social Psychology, 53,* 1004–1014.

Strickhouser, J. E., & Zell, E. (2015). Self-evaluative effects of dimensional and social comparison. *Journal of Experimental Social Psychology, 59,* 60–66.

Strobel, M. G. (1972). Social facilitation of operant behavior in satiated rats. *Journal of Comparative Physiological Psychology, 80,* 502–508.

Stroebe, K., Spears, R., & Lodewijkx, H. (2007) Contrasting and integrating social identity and interdependence approaches to intergroup discrimination in the minimal group paradigm. In M. Hewstone, H. A. W. Schut, J. B. F. De Wit, K. Van Den Bos, & M. S. Stroebe (Eds.), *The scope of social psychology: Theory and applications* (pp. 173–190). New York: Psychology Press.

Strohmetz, D., Rind, B., Fisher, R. & Lynn, M. (2002). Sweetening the till: The use of candy to increase restaurant tipping. *Journal of Applied Social Psychology, 32,* 300–309.

Stroud, N. J. (2010). Polarization and partisan selective exposure. *Journal of Communication, 60,* 556–576.

Stouffer, S. A., Suchman, E. A., DeVinney, L. C., Star, S. A., & Williams, R. A., Jr. (1949). *The American soldier: Adjustments during Army life.* Princeton, NJ: Princeton University Press.

Sturmer, S., Snyder, M., & Omoto, A. M. (2005). Prosocial emotions and helping: The moderating role of group membership. *Journal of Personality and Social Psychology, 88,* 532–546.

Suedfeld, P., & Tetlock, P. E. (1977). Integrative complexity of communications in international crises. *Journal of Conflict Resolution, 21,* 169–184.

Sugiyama, T., Leslie, E., Giles-Corti, B., & Owen, N. (2008). Associations of neighbourhood greenness with physical and mental health: Do walking, social coherence and local social interaction explain the relationships? *Journal of epidemiology and Public Health, 62,* 238–248.

Suh, E., Diener, E., Oishi, S., & Triandis, H. C. (1998). The shifting basis of life satisfaction judgments across cultures: Emotions versus norms. *Journal of Personality and Social Psychology, 74,* 482–493.

Sulloway, F. J. (1996). *Born to rebel: Birth order, family dynamics, and creative lives.* New York: Pantheon Books.

Sulloway, F. J. (2001). Birth order, sibling competition, and human behavior. In H. R. Halcomb III (Ed.), *Conceptual challenges in evolutionary psychology: Innovative research strategic studies in cognitive systems* (Vol. 27, pp. 39–83). Dordrecht, the Netherlands: Kluwer Academic Publishers.

Suls, J., Martin, R., & Wheeler, L. (2002). Social comparison: Why, with whom and with what effect? *Current Directions in Psychological Science, 11*(5), 159–163.

Suls, J., & Wheeler, L. (2000). *Handbook of social comparison: Theory and research.* New York: Kluwer Academic/Plenum.

Summers, G., & Feldman, N. S. (1984). Blaming the victim versus blaming the perpetrator: An attributional analysis of spouse abuse. *Journal of Applied Social and Clinical Psychology, 2,* 339–347.

Sunstein, C. R., Kahneman, D., Schkade, D., & Ritov, I. (2002). Predictably incoherent judgments. *Stanford Law Review, 54,* 1153–1215.

Svenson, O. (1981). Are we all less risky and more skillful than our fellow drivers? *Acta Psychologica, 47,* 143–148.

Swann, W. B., Jr. (1990). To be adored or to be known: The interplay of self-enhancement and self-verification. In R. M. Sorrentino & E. T. Higgins (Eds.). *Handbook of motivation and cognition* (Vol. 2, pp. 408–448). New York: Guilford Press.

Swann, W. B., Jr., De La Ronde, C., & Hixon, J. G. (1994). Authenticity and positivity strivings in marriage and courtship. *Journal of Personality and Social Psychology, 66,* 857–869.

Swann, W. B., Jr., Griffin, J. J., Predmore, S. C., & Gaines, B. (1987). The cognitive-affective cross: When self-consistency confronts self-enhancement. *Journal of Personality and Social Psychology, 52,* 881–889.

Swann, W. B., Jr., & Read, S. J. (1981). Self-verification processes: How we sustain our self-conceptions. *Journal of Experimental Social Psychology, 17,* 351–372.

Swann, W. B., Jr., Wenzlaff, R. M., Krull, D. S., & Pelham, B. W. (1992). The allure of negative feedback: Self-verification strivings among depressed persons. *Journal of Abnormal Psychology, 101,* 293–306.

Sweeney, P. D., & Gruber, K. L. (1984). Selective exposure: Voter information preferences and the Watergate affair. *Journal of Personality and Social Psychology, 46,* 1208–1221.

Swim, J. K., Aikin, K. J., Hall, W. S., & Hunter, B. A. (1995). Sexism and racism: Old-fashioned and modern prejudices. *Journal of Personality and Social Psychology, 68,* 199–214.

Swim, J. K., & Sanna, L. (1996). He's skilled, she's lucky: A meta-analysis of observers' attributions for women's and men's successes and failures. *Personality and Social Psychology Bulletin, 22,* 507–519.

Szymanski, D. M., Chung, Y., & Balsam, K. F. (2001). Psychosocial correlates of internalized homophobia in lesbians. *Measurement And Evaluation in Counseling and Development, 34*(1), 27–38.

Tajfel, H., & Billig, M. G. (1974). Familiarity and categorization in intergroup behavior. *Journal of Experimental Social Psychology, 10,* 159–170.

Tajfel, H., Billig, M. G., Bundy, R. P., & Flament, C. (1971). Social categorization and intergroup behavior. *European Journal of Social Psychology, 1,* 149–177.

Tajfel, H., & Turner, J. (1979). An integrative theory of intergroup conflict. In W. G. Austin & S. Worchel (Eds.), *The social psychology of intergroup relations*. Monterey, CA: Brooks/Cole.

Tan, D. T. Y., & Singh, R. (1995). Attitudes and attraction: A developmental study of the similarity-attraction dissimilarity-repulsion hypotheses. *Personality and Social Psychology Bulletin, 21,* 975–986.

Tangney, J. P., Miller, R. S., Flicker, L., & Barlow, D. H. (1996). Are shame, guilt, and embarrassment distinct emotions? *Journal of Personality and Social Psychology, 70,* 1256–1264.

Taubman-Ben-Ari, O., Florian, V., & Mikulincer, M. (1999). The impact of mortality salience on reckless driving—A test of terror management mechanisms. *Journal of Personality and Social Psychology, 76,* 35–45.

Taylor, A. F., & Kuo, F. E. (2009). Children with attention deficits concentrate better after a walk in the park. *Journal of Attention Disorders, 12,* 402–409.

Taylor, D. M., & Jaggi, V. (1974). Ethnocentrism and causal attribution in a South Indian context. *Journal of Cross-Cultural Psychology, 5,* 162–171.

Taylor, S. E. (1983). Adjustment to threatening events: A theory of cognitive adaptation. *American Psychologist, 38,* 1161–1173.

Taylor, S. E. (1991). Asymmetrical effects of positive and negative events: The mobilization-minimization hypothesis. *Psychological Bulletin, 110,* 67–85.

Taylor, S. E., & Brown, J. D. (1988). Illusion and well-being: A social psychological perspective on mental health. *Psychological Bulletin, 103,* 193–210.

Taylor, S. E., & Brown, J. D. (1994). Positive illusions and well-being revisited: Separating fact from fiction. *Psychological Bulletin, 116,* 21–27.

Taylor, S. E., Burklund, L. J., Eisenberger, N. I., Lehman, B. J., Hilmert, C. J., & Lieberman, M. D. (2008). Neural bases of moderation of cortisol stress responses by psychosocial resources. *Journal of Personality and Social Psychology, 95,* 197–211.

Taylor, S. E., & Crocker, J. (1981). Schematic bases of social information processing. In E. T. Higgins, C. P. Herman, & M. P. Zanna (Eds.), *Social cognition: The Ontario Symposium* (Vol. 1, pp. 89–134). Hillsdale, NJ: Erlbaum.

Taylor, S. E., & Fiske, S. T. (1975). Point of view and perceptions of causality. *Journal of Personality and Social Psychology, 32,* 439–445.

Taylor, S. E., Kemeny, M., Aspinwall, L. G., Schneider, S. G., Rodriguez, R., & Herbert, M. (1992). Optimism, coping, psychological distress, and high-risk sexual behavior among men at risk for AIDS. *Journal of Personality and Social Psychology, 63,* 460–473.

Taylor, S. E., Klein, L. C., Lewis, B. P., Gruenewal, T. L., Gurung, R. A. R., & Updegraff, J. A. (2000). Biobehavioral responses to stress in females: Tend-and-befriend, not fight-or-flight. *Psychological Review, 107,* 411–429.

Taylor, S. E., Lerner, J. S., Sherman, D. K., Sage, R. M., & McDowell, N. K. (2003). Are self-enhancing cognitions associated with healthy or unhealthy biological profiles? *Journal of Personality and Social Psychology, 85,* 605–615.

Taylor, S. E., Lichtman, R. R., & Wood, J. V. (1984). Attributions, beliefs about control, and adjustment to breast cancer. *Journal of Personality and Social Psychology, 46,* 489–502.

Taylor, S. E., & Thompson, S. C. (1982). Stalking the elusive "vividness" effect. *Psychological Review, 89,* 155–181.

Taylor, S. E., Wood, J. V., & Lichtman, R. R. (1983). It could be worse: Selective evaluation as a response to victimization. *Journal of Social Issues, 39,* 19–40.

Teger, A. I., & Pruitt, D. G. (1967). Components of group risk taking. *Journal of Experimental Social Psychology, 3,* 189–205.

Tenney, E. R., MacCoun, R. J., Spellman, B. A., & Hastie, R. (2007). Calibration trumps confidence as a basis for witness credibility. *Psychological Science, 18,* 46–50.

Tesser, A. (1993). The importance of heritability in psychological research: The case of attitudes. *Psychological Review, 100,* 129–142.

Tesser, A., Campbell, J. D., & Mickler, S. (1983). The role of social pressure, attention to the stimulus, and self-doubt in conformity. *European Journal of Social Psychology, 13,* 217–233.

Tesser, A., & Conlee, M. C. (1975). Some effects of time and thought on attitude polarization. *Journal of Personality and Social Psychology, 31,* 262–270.

Tesser, A., Martin, L., & Mendolia, M. (1995). The impact of thought on attitude extremity and attitude-behavior consistency. In R. E. Petty & J. Krosnick (Eds.), *Attitude strength: Antecedents and consequences*. Mahwah, NJ: Erlbaum.

Tetlock, P. E. (1981). Pre- to post-election shifts in presidential rhetoric: Impression management or cognitive adjustment. *Journal of Personality and Social Psychology, 41,* 207–212.

Tetlock, P. E. (2005). *Expert political judgment: How good is it? How can we know?* Princeton, NJ: Princeton University Press.

Tetlock, P. E., Peterson, R. S., McGuire, C., Chang, S., & Feld, P. (1992). Assessing political group dynamics: A test of the groupthink model. *Journal of Personality and Social Psychology, 20,* 142–146.

Thakerar, J. N., & Iwawaki, S. (1979). Cross-cultural comparisons in interpersonal attraction of females toward males. *Journal of Social Psychology, 108,* 121–122.

Thibaut, J. W., & Kelley, H. H. (1959). *The social psychology of groups*. New York: Wiley.

Thomas, D. (2017). Racial IQ differences among transracial adoptees: Fact or artifact? *Journal of Intelligence, 5*(1). Retrieved from http://www.mdpi.com/search?q=Racial+IQ+differences+among+transracial+adoptees%3A+fact+or+artifact%3F&authors=&article_type=&journal=jintelligence&section=&special_issue=&search=Search doi:10.3390/jintelligence5010001

Thomas, S. L., Skitka, L. J., Christen, S., & Jurgena, M. (2002). Social facilitation and impression formation. *Basic and Applied Social Psychology, 24*, 67–70.

Thompson, J. (2000, June 18). "I was certain, but I was wrong." New York Times, June 18, 2000. Retrieved from http://www.nytimes.com/2000/06/18/opinion/i-was-certain-but-i-was-wrong.html

Thompson, L. (2005). *The heart and mind of the negotiator* (3rd ed.). Upper Saddle River, NJ: Pearson Education.

Thornhill, R., & Gangestad, S. W. (1993). Human facial beauty: Averageness, symmetry, and parasite resistance. *Human Nature, 4*, 237–269.

Thornhill, R., & Gangestad, S. W. (1999). The scent of symmetry: A human sex pheromone that signals fitness? *Evolution and Human Behavior, 20*, 175–201.

Thornhill, R., & Gangestad, S. W. (2005). Facial sexual dimorphism, developmental stability, and susceptibilty to disease in men and women. *Evolution and Human Behavior, 27*, 131–144.

Thornhill, R., Gangestad, S. W., Miller, R., Scheyd, G., McCollough, J., & Franklin, M. (2003). MHC, symmetry and body scent attractiveness in men and women (*Homo sapiens*). *Behavioral Ecology, 14*, 668–768.

Tice, D. M., & Wallace, H. M. (2005). The reflected self: Creating yourself as (you think) others see you. In M. R. Leary & J. P. Tangney (Eds.), *Handbook of self and identity* (pp. 91–105). New York: Guilford Press.

Todorov, A., & Bargh, J. A. (2002). Automatic sources of aggression. *Aggression and Violent Behavior, 7*, 53–68.

Todorov, A., Mandisodza, A. N., Goren, A., & Hall, C. C. (2005). Inferences of competence from faces predict election outcomes. *Science, 308*, 1623–1626.

Todorov, A., Said, C. P., Engell, A. D., & Oosterhof, N. N. (2008). Understanding evaluation of faces on social dimensions. *Trends in Cognitive Sciences, 12*, 455–460.

Todorov, A., & Uleman, J. S. (2003). The efficiency of binding spontaneous trait inferences to actors' faces. *Journal of Experimental Social Psychology, 39*, 549–562.

Toma, C. L. & Hancock, J. T. (2010). Looks and lies: The role of physical attractiveness in online dating self-presentation and deception. *Communication Research, 37*(3), 335–351.

Toma, C. L., Hancock, J. T., & Ellison, N. B. (2008). Separating fact from fiction: An examination of deceptive self-presentation in online dating profiles. *Personality and Social Psychology Bulletin, 34*, 1023–1036.

Tomkins, S. S. (1962). *Affect, imagery, consciousness: I. The positive affects*. New York: Springer.

Tomkins, S. S. (1963). *Affect, imagery, consciousness: II. The negative affects*. New York: Springer.

Toobin, J. (2011, May 9). The mitigator: A new way of looking at the death penalty. *The New Yorker*.

Tooby, J., & Cosmides, L. (1992). The psychological foundations of culture. In J. H. Barkow, L. Cosmides, & J. Tooby (Eds.), *The adapted mind: Evolutionary psychology and the generation of culture*. New York: Oxford University Press.

Tormala, Z. L., Briñol, P., & Petty, R. E. (2007). Multiple roles for source credibility under high elaboration: It's all in the timing. *Social Cognition, 25*, 536–552.

Tormala, Z. L., Petty, R. E., & Briñol, P. (2002). Ease of retrieval effects in persuasion: A self-validation analysis. *Personality and Social Psychology Bulletin, 28*, 1700–1712.

Torrance, E. P. (1955). Some consequences of power differences in decision making in permanent and temporary 3-man groups. In A. P. Hare, E. F. Bogatta, & R. F. Bales (Eds.), *Small groups: Studies in social interaction*. New York: Knopf.

Tourangeau, R., Rasinski, K., & Bradburn, N. (1991). Measuring happiness in surveys: A test of the subtraction hypothesis. *Public Opinion Quarterly, 55*, 255–266.

Tower, R. K., Kelly, C., & Richards, A. (1997). Individualism, collectivism and reward allocation: A cross-cultural study in Russia and Britain. *British Journal of Social Psychology, 36*, 331–345.

Tracy, J. L., & Matsumoto, D. (2008). The spontaneous display of pride and shame: Evidence for biologically innate nonverbal displays. *Proceedings of the National Academy of Sciences of the USA, 105*, 11655–11660.

Tracy, J. L., & Robins, R. W. (2004). Show your pride: Evidence for a discrete emotion expression. *Psychological Science, 15*, 94–97.

Tracy, J. L., & Robins, R. W. (2007). Emerging insights into the nature and function of pride. *Current Directions in Psychological Science, 16*, 147–150.

Travis, L. E. (1925). The effect of a small audience upon eye-hand coordination. *Journal of Abnormal and Social Psychology, 20*, 142–146.

Triandis, H. C. (1987). Individualism and social psychological theory. In C. Kagitcibasi (Ed.), *Growth and progress in cross-cultural psychology* (pp. 78–83). New York: Swets North America.

Triandis, H. C. (1989). The self and social behavior in differing cultural contexts. *Psychological Review, 96*, 269–289.

Triandis, H. C. (1994). *Culture and social behavior*. New York: McGraw-Hill.

Triandis, H. C. (1995). *Individualism and collectivism*. Boulder, CO: Westview Press.

Triandis, H. C., McCusker, C., & Hui, C. H. (1990). Multimethod probes of individualism and collectivism. *Journal of Personality and Social Psychology, 56*, 1006–1020.

Triplett, N. (1898). The dynamogenic factors in pacemaking and competition. *American Journal of Psychology, 9*, 507–533.

Trivers, R. L. (1971). The evolution of reciprocal altruism. *Quarterly Review of Biology, 46*, 35–57.

Trope, Y. (1986). Identification and inferential processes in dispositional attribution. *Psychological Review, 93*, 239–257.

Trope, Y., & Liberman, N. (2003). Temporal construal. *Psychological Review, 110*, 403–421.

Trope, Y., & Liberman, N. (2010). Construal-level theory of psychological distance. *Psychological Review, 117*, 440–463.

Trope, Y., & Liberman, N. (2012). Construal level theory. In P. A. M. Van Lange, A. W. Kruglanski, & E. T. Higgins (Eds.), *Handbook of theories of social psychology* (Vol. 1, pp. 118–134). Thousand Oaks, CA: Sage.

Tsai, J. L. (2007). Ideal affect: Cultural causes and behavioral consequences. *Perspectives on Psychological Science, 2*, 242–259.

Tsai, J. L., Ang, J., Blevins, E., Goernandt, J., Fung, H., Jiang, D., et al. (2016). Leaders' smiles reflect cultural differences in ideal affect. *Emotion, 16*, 183–195.

Tsai, J. L., Knutson, B., & Fung, H. H. (2006). Cultural variation in affect valuation. *Journal of Personality and Social Psychology, 90*, 288–307.

Tsai, J. L., & Levenson, R. W. (1997). Cultural influences on emotional responding: Chinese American and European American dating couples during interpersonal conflict. *Journal of Cross-Cultural Psychology, 28*, 600–625.

Turkheimer, E., Harden, K. P., & Nisbett, R. E. (2017a). Charles Murray is once again peddling junk science about race and IQ. *Vox*.

Retrieved from https://www.vox.com/the-big-idea/2017/5/18/15655638/charles-murray-race-iq-sam-harris-science-free-speech

Turkheimer, E., Harden, K. P., & Nisbett, R. E. (2017b). There's still no reason to believe black-white IQ differences are due to genes. *Vox*. Retrieved from https://www.vox.com/the-big-idea/2017/6/15/15797120/race-black-white-iq-response-critics

Turnbull, C. (1965). *Wayward servants*. New York: Natural History Press.

Tversky, A., & Kahneman, D. (1974). Judgment under uncertainty: Heuristics and biases. *Science, 185*, 1124–1131.

Tversky, A., & Kahneman, D. (1982). Evidential impact of base rates. In D. Kahneman, P. Slovic, & A. Tversky (Eds.), *Judgment under uncertainty: Heuristics and biases* (pp. 153–160). New York: Cambridge University Press.

Twenge, J. M. (2002). Birth cohort, social change, and personality: The interplay of dysphoria and individualism in the 20th century. In D. Cervone & W. Mischel (Eds.), *Advances in personality science*. New York: Guilford Press.

Twenge, J. M., Baumeister, R. F., Tice, D. M., & Stucke, T. S. (2001). If you can't join them, beat them: Effects of social exclusion on aggressive behavior. *Journal of Personality and Social Psychology, 81*, 1058–1069.

Tyler, T. R. (1987). Conditions leading to value-expressive effects in judgments of procedural justice: A test of four models. *Journal of Personality and Social Psychology, 52*, 333–344.

Tyler, T. R. (1994). Psychological models of the justice motive: Antecedents of distributive and procedural justice. *Journal of Personality and Social Psychology, 67*, 850–863.

Uchino, B. N., Cacioppo, J. T., & Kiecolt-Glaser, J. K. (1996). The relationship between social support and physiological process: A review with emphasis on underlying mechanisms and implications for health. *Psychological Bulletin, 119*, 88–531.

Uematsu, T. (1970). Social facilitation of feeding behavior in freshwater fish. I. *Rhodeus, Acheilognathus* and *Rhinogobius*. *Annual of Animal Psychology, 20*, 87–95.

Uleman, J. S. (1987). Consciousness and control: The case of spontaneous trait inferences. *Personality and Social Psychology Bulletin, 13*, 337–354.

Umberson, D., & Hughes, M. (1987). The impact of physical attractiveness on achievement and psychological well-being. *Social Psychology Quarterly, 50*, 227–236.

Unkelbach, C., Forgas, J. P., & Denson, T. F. (2008). The turban effect: The influence of Muslim headgear and induced affect on aggressive responses in the shooter bias paradigm. *Journal of Experimental Social Psychology, 44*, 1409–1413.

UN Women. (2011). Virtual Knowledge Centre to End Violence against Women and Girls. Retrieved from www.endvawnow.org

Updegraff, J. A., & Taylor, S. E. (2000). From vulnerability to growth: Positive and negative effects of stressful life events. In J. H. Harvey & E. D. Miller (Eds.), *Loss and trauma: General and close relationship perspectives* (pp. 3–28). New York: Brunner-Routledge.

Uranowitz, S. W. (1975). Helping and self-attributions: A field experiment. *Journal of Personality and Social Psychology, 31*, 852–854.

U.S. Department of Education. (2015). Student reports of bullying and cyberbullying. Results from the 2013 School Crime Supplement to the National Crime Survey.

Uskul, A. K., Sherman, D. K., & Fitzgibbon, J. (2009). The cultural congruency effect: Culture, regulatory focus, and the effectiveness of gain- vs. loss-framed health messages. *Journal of Experimental Social Psychology, 45*, 535–541.

Vallacher, R. R., & Wegner, D. M. (1987). What do people think they're doing? Action identification and human behavior. *Psychological Review, 94*, 3–15.

Vallone, R. P., Ross, L., & Lepper, M. R. (1985). The hostile media phenomenon: Biased perception and perceptions of media bias in coverage of the Beirut massacre. *Journal of Personality and Social Psychology, 49*, 577–585.

van Baaren, R. B., Holland, R. W., Kawakami, K., & van Knippenberg, A. (2004). Mimicry and pro-social behavior. *Psychological Science, 15*, 71–74.

van Baaren, R. B., Holland, R. W., Steenaert, B., & van Knippenberg, A. (2003). Mimicry for money: Behavioral consequences of imitation. *Journal of Experimental Social Psychology, 39*, 393–398.

Van Boven, L., Campbell, M., & Gilovich, T. (2010). Stigmatizing materialism: On stereotypes and impressions of materialistic versus experiential pursuits. *Personality and Social Psychology Bulletin, 36*, 551–563.

Van Boven, L., Judd, C., & Sherman, D. (2012). Political polarization projection: Social projection of partisan attitude extremity and attitudinal processes. *Journal of Personality and Social Psychology, 103*, 84–100.

Van Boven, L., Kamada, A., & Gilovich, T. (1999). The perceiver as perceived: Everyday intuitions about the correspondence bias. *Journal of Personality and Social Psychology, 77*, 1188–1199.

Van Cappellen, P., & Rimé, B. (2014). Positive emotions and self-transcendence. In V. Saroglou (Ed.), *Religion, personality, and social behavior* (pp. 123–145). New York: Psychology Press.

Vandello, J. A., & Bosson, J. K. (2013). Hard won and easily lost: A review and synthesis of research on precarious manhood. *Psychology of Men & Masculinity, 14*, 101–113.

Vandello, J., & Cohen, D. (1999). Patterns of individualism and collectivism across the United States. *Journal of Personality and Social Psychology, 77*, 279–292.

van der Linden, S., Leiserowitz, A., Rosenthal, S., & Maibach, E. (2017). Inoculating the public against misinformation about climate change. *Global Challenges, 1*, 1–7.

van Dijk, C., de Jong, P. J., & Peters, M. L. (2009). The remedial value of blushing in the context of transgressions and mishaps. *Emotion, 9*, 287–291.

van Kleef, G. A. (2009). How emotions regulate social life: The emotions as social information (EASI) model. *Current Directions in Psychological Science, 18*, 184–188.

van Kleef, G. A., De Dreu, C. K. W., & Manstead, A. S. R. (2010). An interpersonal approach to emotion in social decision making: The emotions as social information model. In M. P. Zanna (Ed.), *Advances in experimental social psychology* (Vol. 42, pp, 45–96). San Diego, CA: Academic Press.

van Kleef, G. A., de Dreu, C. K. W., Pietroni, D., & Manstead, A. S. R. (2006). Power and emotion in negotiation: Power moderates the interpersonal effects of anger and happiness on concession making. *European Journal of Social Psychology* (special issue on social power), *36*, 557–581.

Van Lange, P. A. M., Agnew, C. R., Harinck, F., & Steemers, G. E. M. (1997). From game theory to real life: How social value orientation affects willingness to sacrifice in ongoing close relationships. *Journal of Personality and Social Psychology, 82*, 956–974.

Vanneman, R. D., & Pettigrew, T. F. (1972). Race and relative deprivation in the urban United States. *Race, 13*, 461–486.

Van Zomeren, M., Postmes, T., & Spears, R. (2008). Toward an integrative social identity model of collective action: A quantitative research synthesis of three socio-psychological perspectives. *Psychological Bulletin, 134*(4), 504–535.

Vaughn, A. A., Cronan, S. B., & Beavers, A. J. (2015). Resource effects on in-group boundary formation with respect to sexual identity. *Social Psychological and Personality Science, 6*, 292–299.

Vaughn, P. W., Rogers, E. M., Singhal, A., & Swalehe, R. M. (2000). Entertainment-education and HIV/AIDS prevention: A field experiment in Tanzania. *Journal of Health Communication, 5*, 81–100.

Vazire, S. (2010). Who knows what about a person? The self-other knowledge asymmetry (SOKA) model. *Journal of Personality and Social Psychology, 98,* 281–300.

Vazire, S., & Carlson, E. N. (2011). Others sometimes know us better than we know ourselves. *Current Directions in Psychological Science, 20,* 104–108.

Vazire, S., & Mehl, M. R. (2008). Knowing me, knowing you: The accuracy and unique predictive validity of self-ratings and other-ratings of daily behavior. *Journal of Personality and Social Psychology, 95,* 1202–1216.

Verduyn, P., Lee, D. S., Park, J., Shablack, A. O., Bayer, J., Ybarra, O., et al. (2015). Passive Facebook usage undermines affective well-being: Experimental and longitudinal evidence. *Journal of Experimental Psychology: General, 144,* 480–488.

Vescio, T. K., Gervais, S. J., Heidenreich, S., & Snyder, M. (2006). The effects of prejudice level and social influence strategy on powerful people's responding to racial outgroup members. *European Journal of Social Psychology, 36,* 435–450.

Vescio, T. K., Gervais, S. J., Snyder, M., & Hoover, A. (2005). Power and the creation of patronizing environments: The stereotype-based behaviors of the powerful and their effects on female performance in masculine domains. *Journal of Personality and Social Psychology, 88*(4), 658–672.

Vescio, T. K., Snyder, M., & Butz, D. (2003). Power in stereotypically masculine domains: A social influence strategy ✕ stereotype match model. *Journal of Personality and Social Psychology, 85*(6), 1062–1078.

von Hippel, W., Sekaquaptewa, D., & Vargas, P. (1995). On the role of encoding processes in stereotype maintenance. In M. P. Zanna (Ed.), *Advances in experimental social psychology* (Vol. 27, pp. 177–254). San Diego, CA: Academic Press.

Vonk, R. (1999). Effects of outcome dependency on the correspondence bias. *Personality and Social Psychology Bulletin, 25,* 382–389.

Waggoner, A. S., Smith, E. R., & Collins, E. C. (2009). Person perception by active verses passive perceivers. *Journal of Experimental Social Psychology, 45,* 1028–1031.

Wagner, D. D., Haxby, J. V., & Heatherton, T. F. (2012). The representation of self and person knowledge in the medial prefrontal cortex. *Wiley Interdisciplinary Review: Cognitive Science, 3,* 451–470.

Wagner, R. C. (1975). Complementary needs, role expectations, interpersonal attraction, and the stability of work relationships. *Journal of Personality and Social Psychology, 32,* 116–124.

Wallerstein, J. S., Lewis, J., & Blakeslee, S. (2000). *The unexpected legacy of divorce: The 25-year landmark study.* New York: Hyperion.

Walster, E. (1966). Assignment of responsibility for an accident. *Journal of Personality and Social Psychology, 3,* 73–79.

Walster, E., Aronson, E., & Abrahams, D. (1966). On increasing the persuasiveness of a low prestige communicator. *Journal of Experimental Social Psychology, 2,* 325–342.

Walster, E., Aronson, V., Abrahams, D., & Rottman, L. (1966). Importance of physical attractiveness in dating behavior. *Journal of Personality and Social Psychology, 4,* 508–516.

Walster, E., Walster, G. W., & Berscheid, E. (1978). *Equity: Theory and research.* Boston: Allyn & Bacon.

Walton, G. M., & Cohen, G. L. (2007). A question of belonging: Race, social fit, and achievement. *Journal of Personality and Social Psychology, 92,* 82–96.

Walton, G. M., Logel, C., Peach, J. M., Spencer, S. J., & Zanna, M. P. (2015). Two brief interventions to mitigate a "chilly climate" transform women's experience, relationships, and achievement in engineering. *Journal of Educational Psychology, 107*(2), 468–485.

Wang, F., Peng, K., Chechlacz, M., Humphreys, G., & Sui, J. (2017). The neural basis of independence versus interdependence orientations: A voxel-based morphometric analysis of brain volume. *Psychological Science, 28*(4), 1–11.

Warneken, F., & Tomasello, M. (2006). Altruistic helping in human infants and young chimpanzees. *Science, 311*(5765), 1301–1303.

Warneken, F., & Tomasello, M. (2007). Helping and cooperation at 14 months of age. *Infancy, 11*(3), 271–294.

Waterman, C. K. (1969). The facilitating and interfering effects of cognitive dissonance on simple and complex paired associates learning tasks. *Journal of Experimental Social Psychology, 5,* 31–42.

Watson, D. (1982). The actor and the observer: How are their perceptions of causality divergent? *Psychological Bulletin, 92,* 682–700.

Watson, R. I. (1973). Investigation into deindividuation using a cross-cultural survey technique. *Journal of Personality and Social Psychology, 25,* 342–345.

Waugh, C. E., & Fredrickson, B. L. (2006). Nice to know you: Positive emotions, self-other overlap, and complex understanding in the formation of a new relationship. *Journal of Positive Psychology, 1,* 93–106.

Waytz, A., & Epley, N. (2012). Social connection enables dehumanization. *Journal of Experimental Social Psychology, 48,* 70–76.

Weber, M. (1947). *The theory of social and economic organization* (A. M. Henderson & T. Parsons, Trans.). New York: Oxford University Press.

Weber, R., & Crocker, J. (1983). Cognitive processes in the revision of stereotypic beliefs. *Journal of Personality and Social Psychology, 45,* 961–977.

Wedekind, C., & Milinski, M. (2000). Cooperation through image scoring in humans. *Science, 288,* 850–852.

Wegener, D. T., & Petty, R. E. (1994). Mood management across affective states: The hedonic contingency hypothesis. *Journal of Personality and Social Psychology, 66,* 1034–1048.

Wegener, D. T., Petty, R. E., & Smith, S. M. (1995). Positive mood can increase or decrease message scrutiny: The hedonic contingency view of mood and message processing. *Journal of Personality and Social Psychology, 69,* 5–15.

Wegner, D. M. (1994). Ironic processes of mental control. *Psychological Review, 101,* 34–52.

Wegner, D. M., Ansfield, M., & Pilloff, D. (1998). The putt and the pendulum: Ironic effects of the mental control of action. *Psychological Science, 9,* 196–199.

Weiner, B. (1986). *An attributional theory of achievement and motivation.* New York: Springer-Verlag.

Weiner, B. (2010). The development of an attribution-based theory of motivation: A history of ideas. *Educational Psychologist, 45*(1), 28–36. doi:http://dx.doi.org/10.1080/00461520903433596

Weiner, B., Graham, S., & Reyna, C. (1997). An attributional examination of retributive versus utilitarian philosophies of punishment. *Social Justice Research, 10,* 431–452.

Weingarten, E., Chen, Q., McAdams, M., Yi, J., Hepler, J., & Albarracín, D. (2016). From primed concepts to action: A meta-analysis of the behavioral effects of incidentally presented words. *Psychological Bulletin, 142,* 472–497.

Wellman, H. M. (1990). *The child's theory of mind.* Cambridge, MA: MIT Press.

Wells, G. L., Charman, S. D., & Olson, E. A. (2005). Building face composites can harm lineup identification performance. *Journal of Experimental Psychology, 11,* 147–156.

Wells, G. L., Ferguson, T. J., & Lindsay, R. C. L. (1981). The tractability of eyewitness confidence and its implications for triers of fact. *Journal of Applied Psychology, 66,* 688–696.

Wells, G. L., & Leippe, M. R. (1981). How do triers of fact enter the accuracy of eyewitness identification? *Journal of Applied Psychology, 66,* 682–687.

Wells, G. L., Lindsay, R. C. L., & Ferguson, T. (1979). Accuracy, confidence and juror perceptions in eyewitness identification. *Journal of Applied Psychology, 64*, 440–448.

Wells, G. L., Memon, A., & Penrod, S. D. (2006). Eyewitness evidence: Improving its probative value. *Psychological Science in the Public Interest, 7*, 45–75.

Wells, G. L., & Petty, R. E. (1980). The effects of overt head movements on persuasion: Compatibility and incompatibility of responses. *Basic and Applied Social Psychology, 1*, 219–230.

Welsh, D. T., & Ordonez, L. D. (2014). Conscience without cognition: The effects of subconscious priming on ethical behavior. *Academy of Management Journal, 57*, 723–742.

West, S. G., & Brown, T. J. (1975). Physical attractiveness, the severity of the emergency, and helping: A field experiment and interpersonal simulation. *Journal of Experimental Social Psychology, 11*, 531–538.

West, T. V., Pearson, A. R., Dovidio, J. F., Shelton, J. N., & Trail, T. E. (2009). Superordinate identity and intergroup roommate friendship development. *Journal of Experimental Social Psychology, 45*, 1266–1272.

Westfall, J., Van Boven, L., Chambers, J. R., & Judd, C. M. (2015). Perceiving political polarization in the United States: Party identity strength and attitude extremity exacerbate the perceived partisan divide. *Perspectives on Psychological Science, 10*(2), 145–158.

Westoff, C. F., & Rodriguez, G. (1995). The mass media and family planning in Kenya. *International Family Planning Perspectives, 21*(1), 26–31, 35.

Wetzel, C. G. (1982). Self-serving biases in attribution: A Bayesian analysis. *Journal of Personality and Social Psychology, 43*, 197–209.

Whatley, M. A., Webster, J. M., Smith, R. H., & Rhodes, A. (1999). The effect of a favor on public and private compliance: How internalized is the norm of reciprocity? *Basic and Applied Social Psychology, 21*, 251–259.

Wheeler, L., & Kim, Y. (1997). What is beautiful is culturally good: The physical attractiveness stereotype has different content in collectivistic cultures. *Personality and Social Psychology Bulletin, 23*, 795–800.

Wheeler, L., & Nezlek, J. (1977). Sex differences in social participation. *Journal of Personality and Social Psychology, 35*, 742–754.

White, H. (1997). Longitudinal perspective on alcohol and aggression during adolesence. In M. Galanter (Ed.), *Recent developments in alcoholism: Alcohol and violence: Epidemiology, neurobiology, psychology, and family issues* (Vol. 13, pp. 81–103). New York: Plenum Press.

White, L. K., & Booth, A. (1991). Divorce over the life course: The role of marital happiness. *Review of Personality and Social Psychology, 12*, 265–289.

White, P. A. (2002). Causal attribution from covariation information: The evidential evaluation model. *European Journal of Social Psychology, 32*, 667–684.

Whitley, B. E. (1990). The relationship of heterosexuals' attributions for the causes of homosexuality to attitudes towards lesbians and gay men. *Personality and Social Psychology Bulletin, 16*, 369–377.

Whitley, B. E., & Frieze, I. H. (1985). Children's causal attributions for success and failure in achievement settings: A meta-analysis. *Journal of Educational Psychology, 77*(5), 608–616.

Whittlesea, B. W., & Leboe, J. P. (2000). The heuristic basis of remembering and classification: Fluency, generation, and resemblance. *Journal of Experimental Psychology: General, 129*, 84–106.

Wicker, A. W. (1969). Attitudes versus actions: The relationship of verbal and overt behavioral responses to attitude objects. *Journal of Social Issues, 25*, 41–78.

Wienke, C., & Hill, G. J. (2009). Does the 'marriage benefit' extend to partners in gay and lesbian relationships? Evidence from a random sample of sexually active adults. *Journal of Family Issues, 30*(2), 259–289.

Wigboldus, D. H. J., Sherman, J. W., Franzese, H. L., & van Knippenberg, A. (2004). Capacity and comprehension: Spontaneous stereotyping under cognitive load. *Social Cognition, 22*, 292–309.

Wilder, D. A. (1984). Predictions of belief homogeneity and similarity following social categorization. *British Journal of Social Psychology, 23*, 323–333.

Wilder, D. A. (1986). Social categorization: Implications for creation and reduction of intergroup bias. In L. Berkowitz (Ed.), *Advances in experimental social psychology* (Vol. 19, pp. 291–355). San Diego, CA: Academic Press.

Wiley, M. G., Crittenden, K. S., & Birg, L. D. (1979). Why a rejection? Causal attribution of a career achievement event. *Social Psychology Quarterly, 42*, 214–222.

Wilkinson, F., & Pickett, K. (2009). *Spirit level: Why greater equality makes societies stronger.* New York: Bloomsbury Press.

Wilkinson, G. (1990, February). Food sharing in vampire bats. *Scientific American*, 76–82.

Willer, R. (2009). Groups reward individual sacrifice: The status solution to the collective action problem. *American Sociological Review, 74*, 23–43.

Williams, D. R., & Collins, C. (1995). U.S. socioeconomic and racial differences in health: Patterns and explanations. *Annual Review of Sociology, 21*, 349–386.

Williams, E. F., & Gilovich, T. (2012). The better-than-my-average effect: The relative impact of peak and typical performances in judging the self and others. *Journal of Experimental Social Psychology, 48*, 556–561.

Williams, E. F., Gilovich, T., & Dunning, D. (2012). Being all that you can be: How potential performances influence assessments of self and others. *Personality and Social Psychology Bulletin, 38*(2), 143–154.

Williams, J. R., Insel, T. R., Harbaugh, C. R., & Carter, C. S. (1994). Oxytocin administered centrally facilitates formation of a partner preference in female prairie voles (*Microtus ochrogaster*). *Journal of Neuroendocrinology, 6*, 247–250.

Williams, K. D. (2007). Ostracism. *Annual Review of Psychology, 58*, 425–452.

Williams, K. D., Harkins, S., & Latané, B. (1981). Identifiability as a deterrent to social loafing: Two cheering experiments. *Journal of Personality and Social Psychology, 40*, 303–311.

Willis, J., & Todorov, A. (2006). First impressions: Making up your mind after a 100-ms exposure to a face. *Psychological Science, 17*, 592–598.

Wilson, C., & Moulton, B. (2010). Loneliness among older adults: A national survey of adults 45+. Prepared by Knowledge Networks and Insight Policy Research. Washington, DC: AARP. Retrieved from https://assets.aarp.org/rgcenter/general/loneliness_2010.pdf

Wilson, M. I., Daly, M., & Weghorst, S. J. (1980). Household composition and the risk of child abuse and neglect. *Journal of Biological Science, 12*, 333–340.

Wilson, T. D. (2002). *Strangers to ourselves: Discovering the adaptive unconscious.* Cambridge, MA: Harvard University Press.

Wilson, T. D., & Dunn, D. S. (1986). Effects of introspection on attitude-behavior consistency: Analyzing reasons versus focusing on feelings. *Journal of Experimental Social Psychology, 22*, 249–263.

Wilson, T. D., Dunn, D. S., Bybee, J. A., Hyman, D. B., & Rotondo, J. A. (1984). Effects of analyzing reasons on attitude-behavior consistency. *Journal of Personality and Social Psychology, 47*, 5–16.

Wilson, T. D., & Dunn, E. (2004). Self-knowledge: Its limits, value, and potential for improvement. *Annual Review of Psychology, 55*, 493–518.

Wilson, T. D., Wheatley, T., Kurtz, J., Dunn, & Gilbert, D. T. (2004). When to fire: Anticipatory versus postevent reconstrual of uncontrollable events. *Personality and Social Psychology Bulletin, 30*, 1–12.

Wilson, T. D., Wheatley, T., Meyers, J. M., Gilbert, D. T., & Axson, D. (2000). Focalism: A source of durability bias in affective forecasting. *Journal of Personality and Social Psychology, 78,* 821–836.

Windhauser, J., Seiter, J., & Winfree, T. (1991). Crime news in the Louisiana press. *Journalism Quarterly, 45,* 72–78.

Winkielman, P., & Cacioppo, J. T. (2001). Mind at ease puts a smile on the face: Psychophysiological evidence that processing facilitation increases positive affect. *Journal of Personality and Social Psychology, 81,* 989–1000.

Winter, L., & Uleman, J. S. (1984). When are social judgments made? Evidence for the spontaneousness of trait inferences. *Journal of Personality and Social Psychology, 47,* 237–252.

Wiseman, C. V., Gray, J. J., Mosimann, J. E., & Ahrens, A. H. (1992). Cultural expectations of thinness in women: An update. *International Journal of Eating Disorders, 11,* 85–89.

Wisman, A., and Goldenberg, J. (2005). From the grave to the cradle: Evidence that mortality salience engenders a desire for offspring. *Journal of Personality and Social Psychology, 89,* 46–61.

Wittenbrink, B. (2004). Ordinary forms of prejudice. *Psychological Inquiry, 15,* 306–310.

Wittenbrink, B., & Schwarz, N. (Eds.). (2007). *Implicit measures of attitudes.* New York: Guilford Press.

Wolf, S. (1985). Manifest and latent influence on majorities and minorities. *Journal of Personality and Social Psychology, 48,* 899–908.

Wolfe, T. (1979). *The right stuff.* New York: Farrar, Straus & Giroux.

Wood, J. V. (1996). What is social comparison and how should we study it? *Personality and Social Psychology Bulletin, 22,* 520–537.

Wood, W. (1982). Retrieval of attitude-relevant information from memory: Effects of susceptibility to persuasion and on intrinsic motivation. *Journal of Personality and Social Psychology, 42,* 798–810.

Wood, W., & Eagly, A. H. (2002). A cross-cultural analysis of the behavior of women and men: Implications for the origin of sex differences. *Psychological Bulletin, 126,* 699–727.

Wood, W., & Eagly, A. H. (2015). Two traditions of research on gender identity. *Sex Roles, 73,* 461–473.

Wood, W., & Kallgren, C. A. (1988). Communicator attributes and persuasion: Recipients' access to attitude-relevant information in memory. *Personality and Social Psychology Bulletin, 14,* 172–182.

Wood, W., Kressel, L., Joshi, P. D., & Louie, B. (2014). Meta-analysis of menstrual cycle effects on women's mate preferences. *Emotion Review, 6,* 229–249.

Wood, W., Lundgren, S., Ouellette, J. A., Busceme, S., & Blackstone, T. (1994). Minority influence: A meta-analytic review of social influence processes. *Psychological Bulletin, 115,* 323–345.

Woolley, A. W., Chabris, C. F., Pentland, A., Hashmi, N., & Malone, T. W. (2010, October 29). Evidence for a collective intelligence factor in the performance of human groups. *Science, 330*(6004), 686–688. doi:10.1126/science.1193147)

Woolger, R. J. (1988). *Other lives, other selves: A Jungian psychotherapist discovers past lives.* New York: Bantam.

Word, C. O., Zanna, M. P., & Cooper, J. (1974). The nonverbal mediation of self-fulfilling prophecies in interracial interaction. *Journal of Experimental Social Psychology, 10,* 109–120.

Wright, D. B., & Stroud, J. N. (2002). Age differences in lineup identification accuracy: People are better with their own age. *Law and Human Behavior, 26*(6), 641–654.

Wright, R. (2000). *Nonzero: The logic of human destiny.* New York: Pantheon Books.

Wright, S., Aron, A., McLaughlin-Volpe, T., & Ropp, S. (1997). The extended contact effect: Knowledge of cross-group friendships and prejudice. *Journal of Personality and Social Psychology, 73,* 73–90.

Yamagishi, T., Mifune, N., Liu, J. H., & Pauling, J. (2008). Exchanges of group-based favors: Ingroup bias in the prisoner's dilemma game with minimal groups in Japan and New Zealand. *Asian Journal of Social Psychology, 11*(3), 196–207.

Yang, M. H., & Bond, M. H. (1990). Exploring implicit personality theories with indigenous or imported constructs: The Chinese case. *Journal of Personality and Social Psychology, 58,* 1087–1095.

Yoeli, E., Hoffman, M., Rand, D. G., & Nowak, M. A. (2013) Powering up with indirect reciprocity in a large-scale field experiment. *Proceedings of the National Academy of Sciences of the USA, 110,* 10424–10429.

Yuchida, Y., & Kitayama, S. (2009). *Happiness and unhappiness in East and West.* Kyoto, Japan: Kyoto University.

Yudko, E., Blanchard, D., Henne, J., & Blanchard, R. (1997). Emerging themes in preclinical research on alcohol and aggression. In M. Galanter (Ed.), *Recent developments in alcoholism: Alcohol and violence: Epidemiology, neurobiology, psychology, and family issues* (Vol. 13, pp. 123–138). New York: Plenum Press.

Zadny, J., & Gerard, H. B. (1974). Attributed intentions and informational selectivity. *Journal of Experimental Social Psychology, 10,* 34–52.

Zajonc, R. B. (1965). Social facilitation. *Science, 149,* 269–274.

Zajonc, R. B. (1968). The attitudinal effects of mere exposure. *Journal of Personality and Social Psychology, 9* (monographs), 1–27.

Zajonc, R. B. (2001). Mere exposure: A gateway to the subliminal. *Current Directions in Psychological Science, 10,* 224–228.

Zajonc, R. B. (2002). The zoomorphism of human collective violence. In L. S. Newman & R. Erber (Eds.), *Understanding genocide: The social psychology of the Holocaust* (pp. 222–240). New York: Oxford University Press.

Zajonc, R. B., Adelmann, P. K., Murphy, S. T., & Niedenthal, P. M. (1987). Convergence in the physical appearance of spouses. *Motivation and Emotion, 11,* 335–346.

Zajonc, R. B., Heingartner, A., & Herman, E. M. (1969). Social enhancement and impairment of performance in the cockroach. *Journal of Personality and Social Psychology, 13,* 83–92.

Zak, P. J., & Knack, S. (2001). Trust and growth. *The Economic Journal, 111*(April), 295–321.

Zanna, M. P., & Rempel, J. K. (1988). Attitudes: A new look at an old concept. In D. Bar-Tal & A. W. Kruglanski (Eds.), *The social psychology of knowledge* (pp. 315–334). Cambridge, England: Cambridge University Press.

Zarate, M. A., Uleman, J. S., & Voils, C. I. (2001). Effects of culture and processing goals on the activation and binding of trait concepts. *Social Cognition, 19,* 295–323.

Zebrowitz, L. (1997). *Reading faces: Window to the soul?* Boulder, CO: Westview Press.

Zebrowitz, L. A., & McDonald, S. M. (1991). The impact of litigants' babyfacedness and attractiveness on adjudications in small claims courts. *Law and Human Behavior, 15,* 603–624.

Zebrowitz, L. A., & Montepare, J. M. (2005). Appearance DOES matter. *Science, 308,* 1565–1566.

Zebrowitz, L. A., Tenenbaum, D. R., & Goldstein, L. H. (1991). The impact of job applicants' facial maturity, gender, and academic achievement on hiring recommendations. *Journal of Applied Social Psychology, 21,* 525–548.

Zebrowitz, L. A., Voinescu, L., & Collins, M. A. (1996). "Wide-eyed" and "crooked-faced": Determinants of perceived and real honesty across the life span. *Personality and Social Psychology Bulletin, 22,* 1258–1269.

Zeisel, H., & Diamond, S. (1978). The effect of peremptory challenges on jury and verdict: An experiment in a federal district court. *Stanford Law Review, 30,* 491–531.

Zentner, M., & Mitura, K. (2012). Stepping out of the caveman's shadow: Nations' Gender Gap predicts degree of sex differentiation in mate preferences. *Psychological Science, 23*, 1176–1185.

Zhu, Y., Zhang, L., Fan, J., & Han, S. (2007). Neural basis of cultural influences on self-representation. *Neuroimage, 34*, 1310–1316.

Zimbardo, P. G. (1970). *The human choice: Individuation, reason and order versus deindividuation, impulse and chaos.* Paper presented at the Nebraska Symposium on Motivation (1969), Lincoln, Nebraska.

Zimbardo, P. G. (1990). *Shyness: What it is, what to do about it.* Cambridge, MA: Da Capo Press.

Zimbardo, P. G., & Leippe, M. R. (1991). *The psychology of attitude change and social influence.* New York: McGraw-Hill.

Zimet, G., Dalhem, W., Zimet, S. & Farley, G. (1988). The Multi-dimensional Scale of Perceived Social Support. *Journal of Personality Assessment, 52*(1), 30–41.

Zuber, J. A., Crott, H. W., & Werner, J. (1992). Choice shift and group polarization: An analysis of the status of arguments and social decision schemes. *Journal of Personality and Social Psychology, 62*, 50–61.

Zusne, L., & Jones, W. H. (1982). *Anomalistic psychology.* Hillsdale, NJ: Erlbaum.

Zuwerink, J. R., & Devine, P. G. (1996). Attitude importance and resistance to persuasion: It's not just the thought that counts. *Journal of Personality and Social Psychology, 70*, 931–944.

CREDITS

p. 93 (right): Neilson Barnard/Getty Images; p. 94: PjrStudio/Alamy Stock Photo.

Table 3.1: Morris Rosenberg, "Rosenberg Self Esteem Scale" from *Society and the Adolescent Self-Image*, revised edition. Middletown, CT: Wesleyan University Press (1989). Reprinted with permission of Dr. Florence Rosenberg and the Morris Rosenberg Foundation.

CHAPTER 4

Photos: p. 98 (top left): AP Photo/Eric Michelson; p. 98 (bottom): Jeff Singer/Redux; p. 98 (top left): Jim Purdum/Getty Images; p. 103 (top left): Andy Roberts/Getty Images; p. 103 (top center): Harald Sund/Getty Images; p. 103 (top right): Fuse/Corbis via Getty Images; p. 103 (bottom): Austin Bachand/Daily News-Record via AP; p. 104: Aldo Murillo/Getty Images; p. 105: Richard Cline/The New Yorker Collection/The Cartoon Bank; p. 106: CBS/Photofest; p. 107: David Sipress/The New Yorker Collection/The Cartoon Bank; p. 108: Pete Souza/The White House via AP; p. 110: Jeff Singer/Redux; p. 111: Patti McConville/Alamy Stock Photo p. 112 (left): Jim Purdum/Getty Images; p. 112 (right): YinYang/Getty Images; p. 116: Jonathan Fickies/Getty Images; p. 119: Simons, D. J., & Chabris, C. F. (1999). Gorillas in our midst: Sustained inattentional blindness for dynamic events. Perception, 28, 1059-1074. Figure provided by Daniel Simons (www.dansimons.com, www.theinvisiblegorilla.com); p. 120: Sipa Asia/Sipa USA/Newscom; p. 122: Estelle Johnson/EyeEm/Getty Images; p. 125 (left): Willoughby Owen/Getty Images; p. 125 (right): Courtesy Everett Collection; p. 127: Daniel Leal-Olivas/AFP/Getty Images; p. 128: Hero Images Inc./Alamy Stock Photo; p. 129 (left): Andrea Renault/Polaris Images/Newscom; p. 129 (right): Saul Loeb/AFP/Getty Images; p. 133 (top): Dana Fradon/The New Yorker Collection/The Cartoon Bank; p. 133 (bottom): Sheila Terry/Science Source.

CHAPTER 5

Photos: p. 138 (top left): © Doug Wilson/CORBIS/Corbis via Getty Images; p. 138 (top right): David Silverman/Getty Images; p. 138 (bottom): Al Bello/Getty Images; p. 140 (left): © Doug Wilson/CORBIS/Corbis via Getty Images; p. 140 (right): Mark Graham/AFP/Getty Images; p. 141: Moodboard/Getty Images; p. 142 (left): Antonio Guillem/Shutterstock; p. 142 (right): AlpamayoPhoto/Getty Images; p. 144: Bettmann/Getty Images; p. 145: Leo Cullum/The New Yorker Collection/The Cartoon Bank; p. 147: John M. Heller/Getty Images; p. 149 (top): Al Bello/Getty Images; p. 149 (bottom left): Ben Pipe Sports/Alamy Stock Photo; p. 149 (bottom right): David Silverman/Getty Images; p. 151 (top): Frank Cotham/The New Yorker Collection/The Cartoon Bank; p. 151 (bottom): David Sipress/The New Yorker Collection/The Cartoon Bank; p. 153 (left): LG Patterson/MLB Photos via Getty Images; p. 153 (right): AP Photo/Gene J. Puskar; p. 154: Marco Secchi/Corbis via Getty Images; p. 156: Leo Cullum/The New Yorker Collection/The Cartoon Bank; p. 157 (left): Joe Raedle/Getty Images; p. 157 (right): Robert Galbraith/REUTERS/Newscom; p. 159: Image Source Salsa/Alamy Stock Photo; p. 160: Ariel Skelly/Getty Images; p. 164 (left): Jerome Madramootoo/ShutterQuill/Alamy Stock Photo; p. 164 (right): The Asahi Shimbun via Getty Images; p. 166 (left): Tupungato/Getty Images; p. 166 (center left): RichLegg/Getty Images; p. 166 (center right): DeiMosz/Shutterstock; p. 166 (right): Chris Heller/Corbis via Getty Images; p. 168: Sipa via AP Images.

CHAPTER 6

Photos: p. 172 (bottom): © Walt Disney Co./Courtesy Everett Collection; p. 172 (top): Daniel Milchev/Getty Images; p. 172 (center): Cultura Creative/Alamy Stock Photo; p. 174: Pete Docter; p. 175 (left): Laura Romin & Larry Dalton/Alamy Stock Photo; p. 175 (right): Tauseef Mustafa/AFP/GettyImages; p. 177: Wade Eakle/

Getty Images; p. 178 (top): From The Expression of the Emotions in Man and Animals by Charles Darwin; p. 178 (center): From The Expression of the Emotions in Man and Animals by Charles Darwin; p. 178 (bottom): Pictorial Press Ltd/Alamy Stock Photo; p. 179 (top a–d): Adapted from Ekman, Sorenson, & Friesen (1969); p. 179 (bottom a–f): Photographs courtesy Professor Dacher Keltner; p. 180 (top left): Steve Bloom Images/Alamy Stock Photo; p. 180 (top right): M. Watson/ardea.com; p. 180 (bottom): Bettmann/Getty Images; p. 181 (left): © Radius Images/Corbis; p. 181 (right): Photo courtesy of Frans de Waal; p. 183 (bottom left): Courtesy Dr. Alex Kogan; p. 183 (bottom right): Courtesy Dr. Alex Kogan; p. 183 (row 1, left): Courtesy Matt Jones; p. 183 (row 1, right): Courtesy Sam Hood; p. 183 (row 2, left): Courtesy Matt Jones; p. 183 (row 2, right): Courtesy Sam Hood; p. 183 (row 3, left): Courtesy Matt Jones; p. 183 (row 3, right): Courtesy Sam Hood; p. 184 (top): Daniel Milchev/Getty Images; p. 184 (bottom): Ole Spata/Picture-Alliance/dpa/AP Images; p. 185: Morsa Images/Getty Images; p. 186 (top): Cultura Creative/Alamy Stock Photo; p. 186 (bottom): With permission by NU LIFE, www.pheromax.com; p. 188 (top): Pierre Lahalle/Corbis/VCG via Getty Images; p. 188 (bottom): Mike Twohy/The New Yorker Collection/The Cartoon Bank; p. 190: AP Photo/The Sacramento Bee, Randall Benton; p. 193: Joel Angel Juarez/Anadolu Agency/Getty Images; p. 195: Andresr/Getty Images; p. 198: BERKO85/Getty Images; p. 200: Wade Davis/Getty Images; p. 201: Ruslan Dashinsky/iStockphoto/Getty Images.

Fig. 6.4: Figure 1a from Barbara L. Fredrickson and Christine Branigan, "Positive emotions broaden the scope of attention and thought-action repertoires," *Cogn Emot.* 2005 May 1; 19(3): 313–332. Copyright © 2005 Routledge. Reproduced by permission of Taylor & Francis LLC (http://www.tandfonline.com); **Fig. 6.5:** Graham, Haidt & Nosek, Figure 1 from "Liberals and conservatives use different sets of moral foundations," *Journal of Personality and Social Psychology 96,* 1029-1046. Copyright © 2009, American Psychological Association.

CHAPTER 7

Photos: p. 204 (bottom right): Everett Collection Historical/Alamy Stock Photo; p. 204 (top): Ron Haviv/VII/Redux; p. 204 (bottom left): Bill Frakes/Sports Illustrated/Getty Images; p. 206 (left): Bettmann/Getty Images; p. 206 (right): AP/World Wide Photos; p. 207: Pakhnyushchy/Shutterstock; p. 209: Animals Animals/Superstock; p. 210: Looper5920; p. 211: Timothy A. Clary/AFP/Getty Images; p. 212: Rebecca Nowalski/Polaris/Newscom; p. 213: Ron Chapple/Getty Images; p. 214: ROGERS © Pittsburgh Post-Gazette. Reprinted by permission of ANDREWS MCMEEL SYNDICATION. All rights reserved.; p. 215 (top): Kevin R. Morris/Corbis/VCG/Getty Images; p. 215 (bottom): 1982 Karen Zebuion, Courtesy New School Public Relations Department; p. 216: Kim Warp/The New Yorker Collection/The Cartoon Bank; p. 218: Photo courtesy of Terp Weekly Edition; p. 222: Universal Images Group/Superstock; p. 223: DILBERT © 1999 Scott Adams. Used by permission of ANDREWS MCMEEL SYNDICATION. All rights reserved.; p. 224: The Washington Post/Getty Images; p. 228 (left): Steve D. Starr/Corbis via Getty Images; p. 228 (right): Sunshine Pics/Alamy Stock Photo; p. 229: Bill Frakes/Sports Illustrated/Getty Images; p. 231: Apex News and Pictures Agency/Alamy Stock Photo; p. 233: Hero Images/Getty Images; p. 234 (top): Bill Woodman/The New Yorker Collection/The Cartoon Bank; p. 234 (bottom): Ron Haviv/VII/Redux.

CHAPTER 8

Photos: p. 238 (bottom left): Jesse Mendoza/Valley Morning Star/Harlingen, Texas; p. 238 (top): Central Press/Getty Images; p. 238 (bottom right): Cindy Ord/Getty Images for Sony Pictures; p. 240:

CHAPTER 13

CHAPTER 14

APPLICATION MODULE 1

APPLICATION MODULE 2

APPLICATION MODULE 3

NAME INDEX

Material in figures or tables is indicated by italic page numbers.

Hamilton, W. D., 499
Han, S., 74, 251
Hancock, J. T., 95, 329
Haney, C., 409, 550, 551
Hanna, J., 94
Hannah, D. B., 387
Hannon, P. A., 348
Hans, V. P., 550
Harackiewicz, J. M., 93, 231
Harada, T., 491
Harbaugh, C. R., 186
Harbaugh, W. T., 485
Harber, K., 528
Hardee, B. B., 365
Harden, K. P., 530
Hardin, C. C., 368
Hardy, C. L., 484
Hare, R. D., 470
Hargreaves, D. J., 121
Harinck, F., 348
Harkins, S., 418
Harlow, H. F., 314
Harmon-Jones, C., 207
Harmon-Jones, E., 15, 207, 228
Harrington, J. R., 283
Harris, C. R., 180
Harris, E., 450, 451, 452
Harris, K., 387
Harris, R. J., 292
Harris, S., 83
Harris, V. A., 164
Harrison, D. A., 418
Harris Poll, 269
Hart, D., 165
Hart, W., 260
Hartley, R. D., 452
Harvey, O. J., 271
Hashmi, N., 423
Haslam, N., 459
Hass, R. G., 248
Hassin, R. R., 121
Hastie, R., 118, 248, 425, 551, 552
Hatala, M., 341
Hatch, E. C., 419
Hatfield, E., 318
Haugtvedt, C. P., 245, 252, 263
Hauser, C., 5
Havas, D. A., 231
Haxby, J. V., 23
Hazan, C., 319, 320
Heath, C., 86
Heatherton, T. F., 23, 74, 79, 336
Hebl, M., 336
Hebl, M. R., 370, 387
Hedden, T., 162, 163
Hefferman, M. E., 321
Hehman, E., 405
Heidenreich, S., 430
Heider, F., 145, 168
Heine, S. J., 24, 26, 81, 81, 82, 85, 225, 531
Heingartner, A., 414
Heinrich, J., 468
Helgeson, V. S., 76
Helliwell, J. F., 198
Hemingway, E., 517
Henderson, V. L., 59, 528, 529
Hendricks, M., 121
Hendrix, K. S., 93
Henne, J., 447
Henningsen, D. D., 420
Henningsen, M. L. M., 420
Henrich, J., 24, 272, 485, 501, 507, 508
Henry, P. J., 363
Henton, J. M., 347
Hepburn, A., 314

Hepper, E. G., 76
Herbener, E. S., 328
Herbert, T. B., 523
Herek, G. M., 396
Herman, E. M., 414
Herr, P. M., 121
Hertenstein, M. J., 187, 187
Herzog, T., 164
Hewstone, M., 146, 147, 384, 387, 405
Heyes, C., 274
Heyman, R. E., 352
Hies, R., 427
Higgins, E. T., 88, 120, 121, 122, 276, 418
Hilden, L. E., 368
Hildreth, J. A. D., 332, 421
Hill, G. J., 314
Hill, S. E., 318, 370, 397
Hilton, D. J., 145, 147
Hilton, J. L., 368
Hinkle, S., 153
Hirt, E. R., 79, 93, 119, 122, 379
Hitler, A., 9, 252, 429, 458, 473
Hixon, J. G., 86
Ho, C., 364
Ho, S., 468
Ho, T., 290
Hobart, C., 466
Hobbes, T., 22
Hodson, G., 364
Hoeksema-van Orden, C. Y. D., 418
Hoffman, E. L., 275
Hoffman, M., 504, 506
Hoffman, S., 280
Hofmann, W., 315, 369
Hofstede, G., 25
Hogg, M., 228
Hogue, J., 91, 92
Hogue, M., 233
Holland, R. W., 121, 274
Holloway, S., 531
Holmes, J. G., 333, 349, 353, 354
Holmes, O. W., 281
Holt-Lunstad, J., 314, 317
Holyoak, K. J., 215
Holzberg, A., 83
Hong, Y., 59, 165, 168
Hood, W., 370
Hoover, A., 430
Horberg, E. J., 193
Horowitz, L. M., 321
Horton, R. S., 326
Hosch, H. M., 391
Hosey, G. R., 412
Hoshino-Browne, E., 226
Hossay, J. F., 449
House, J., 496
Hovland, C. I., 246
Hovland, C. J., 247, 248
Howland, L., 332
Hrdy, S. B., 319, 502
Hsiang, S. M., 449
Hsu, F. L. K., 25, 26
Huang, C., 187
Huber, M., 457
Huddy, L., 390
Hudson, N. W., 321
Huffington, A., 78
Hugenberg, K., 391
Hughes, J. M., 402
Hughes, M., 314, 335
Hughes, S., 365
Hugo, P., 476
Hui, C. H., 26
Hull, J. G., 315
Hume, D., 189

Hummer, J. F., 295
Humphrey, R., 155
Humphreys, G., 26
Hunsinger, M., 193
Hunter, B. A., 363
Hunter, J. E., 160, 289
Hunter, R. F., 160
Hunter, S. B., 415
Hurtado, A., 550
Husband, R. W., 412
Hussein, S., 429
Hyman, D. B., 211
Hymes, C., 207
Hyunh, A. C., 460

I

Ihori, N., 449
Imberi, J. E., 287
Impett, E. A., 347, 352
Inagaki, T. K., 484
Inbar, Y., 193
Inbau, F. E., 547
Independent Sector, 495
Inesi, M. E., 430
Inkster, J. A., 214
Insel, T. R., 186
Insko, C. A., 279, 459
Inzlicht, M., 396, 397, 400, 414, 531
Ip, G. W. M., 73
Irons, M., 509
Isen, A., 486
Isen, A. M., 190, 191, 290, 291, 291
Ishii, K., 498
Ito, T. A., 208, 394
Iuzzini, J., 362
Iwawaki, S., 336
Iyengar, S., 257, 258, 471, 472
Izard, C. E., 178, 179

J

Jaccard, J., 368
Jacklin, C. N., 74
Jackson, G. L., 336
Jackson, J. S., 403
Jackson, J. W., 364
Jackson, L. A., 336
Jackson, L. M., 370
Jackson, M. C., 459
Jacobson, L., 104, 527, 528
Jacoby, L. L., 122, 128
Jaggi, V., 388
Jakobsson, N., 329
Jakubiak, B. K., 323
James, J., 371
James, W., 64, 273, 313
James, W. T., 412
Jamieson, J. P., 453
Janes, L. M., 279
Janicki-Deverts, D., 33
Janis, I. L., 246, 420, 421
Jantzi, A., 359
Jarvis, B., 252
Jaskolka, A. R., 187
Jaspers, J., 146, 147
Jayne, B. C., 547
Jefferson, T., 122
Jemmott, J. B., 261
Jenkins, C., 397
Jenkins, P., 481
Jenkins-Smith, H., 261
Jenni, K., 249
Jennings, J. R., 521
Jensen, L. A., 323
Jergena, M., 415
Ji, L., 162
Ji, L. J., 109

Joel, S., 347
John, O. P., 84, 185, 426
John-Henderson, N. A., 400, 453
Johnson, B. T., 365
Johnson, C., 75
Johnson, D., 374
Johnson, E. J., 232
Johnson, J. T., 148
Johnson, K. J., 546
Johnson, L. B., 205, 206
Johnson, M., 345
Johnson, R., 374
Johnson, S. L., 397, 558
Johnson-Laird, P. N., 189
Johnsson, J. I., 341
Jolly, E., 159
Jones, C., 157
Jones, C. R., 120
Jones, E. E., 93, 94, 145, 153, 154, 161, 162, 164, 168, 222, 390, 396
Jones, F. D., 314
Jones, J. L., 94
Jones, S. H., 10
Jones, W. H., 133
Jonides, J., 455
Jordan, J. J., 504
Joseph, C., 192
Joseph, L., 418
Josephs, R. A., 468
Joshi, P. D., 342
Jost, J. T., 232, 233, 402
Jostmann, N. B., 121, 431
Joule, R., 228
Judd, C., 472
Judd, C. M., 16, 107, 263, 362, 390, 393, 394, 472
Judge, T. A., 427
Jurgena, M., 415
Jussim, L., 104, 361, 383, 528
Jussim, L. J., 243

K

Kahan, D. M., 261
Kahneman, D., 5, 53, 124, 125, 126, 129, 130, 131, 148, 161, 196, 197, 198, 553, 553, 554
Kallgren, C. A., 246, 277
Kalmijn, M., 315
Kalven, H., 551
Kamada, A., 154
Kamarck, T. W., 521
Kaplan, M. F., 549, 551
Kaplan, R. M., 314
Kaplan, S., 455
Karasawa, M., 182, 195
Karau, S. J., 418
Kardes, F. R., 207
Karmarkar, U. R., 248
Karney, B. R., 312, 329, 336, 349, 351, 353
Karpinski, A., 368
Kashima, E. S., 74
Kashima, Y., 74
Kasof, J., 366
Kassam, K., 189
Kasser, T., 235
Kassin, S., 248
Kassin, S. M., 104, 547, 548
Katkovsky, W., 144
Katz, D., 365
Katz, M. L., 292
Kawachi, I., 456
Kawakami, K., 274, 368
Kawamura, T., 163
Kay, A. C., 121, 233, 364, 365
Keelan, J. P. R., 319

SUBJECT INDEX

Material in figures or tables is indicated by italic page numbers.

influence of exceptions *vs.* routines, 150
intentions of actors and, 168–169
internal/external dimension, 168–169, 171
perceptual salience and, 158
pervasiveness and importance of, 141–142
priming cultures, 165–166
processes of, 145–150, 170
role of imagined outcomes in, 148
self-serving attributional bias, 150–152, *152*, 170
social class and, 166–167, 170
stable/unstable dimension, 142
tutoring experiment, 151–152
see also fundamental attribution error
cause and effect, resemblance between, 131–132
celebrity endorsements, persuasion and, 246
central (systematic) route to persuasion, 241, *241*, 242, *244*, 257, 266
see also persuasion
certainty, source characteristics and, 248
Challenger space shuttle, 420
channel factors, 10–11
child labor, 284
children
  advertising and, 254
  aggressive behavior and watching television, 50
  empathic concern, 488
  sleeping arrangements of, 323
chimpanzees, 180
Chinese, expatriate, 361
Chrysler Building, 334
civil rights and race relations
  Brown v. Board of Education of Topeka, 402
  see also discrimination; prejudice; stereotypes
Civil Rights Movement, 360, 370
class differences *see* social class
climate change, 193–194
  selective evaluation and, 261
  see also global warming
coacting, 414
cognition
  attribution and, 158–159
  embodied nature of, 229–232
cognitive consistency theories, 213, 222
  see also cognitive dissonance theory; rationalization
cognitive dissonance theory, 41
  cultural differences, 225–226, *226*
  decisions and dissonance, 214–215
  dissonance reduction, 228
  effort justification, 215–217, 219
  "forbidden toy" paradigm, 220–221, *221*
  forseeability and dissonance, 224
  fraternity hazing, 218
  free choice and dissonance, 222–223, 225
  group initiation and liking for the group, 216, *216*
  induced compliance and attitude change, 219–220, *220*
  induced compliance and extinguishing undesired behavior, 220–221
  insufficient justification and dissonance, 223
  negative consequences and dissonance, 223–224
  reconciling with self-perception theory, 227–229
  self-affirmation and dissonance, 224–225
  testing for arousal, 227–228
  why inconsistency produces dissonance, 221–224
  see also attitudes; self-perception theory
cognitive fluency, 328, 334
cognitive perspective on prejudice and discrimination, 381–395
  automatic and controlled processing, 391–395
  concrete *vs.* abstract construal, 388–389
  construal processes and biased assessments, 383–389
  expectations and biased information processing, 385–386

explaining away exceptions, 387–389
illusory correlations, 383–385
ingroup similarity and outgroup difference assumptions, 389–390
outgroup homogeneity effect, 390–391, 407
overview, 361
stereotypes and conservation of cognitive resources, 381–382, *382*
stereotype subtyping, 387
see also discrimination; prejudice
Cognitive Reflection Test, 128
collective intelligence, 423
collectivistic culture, 26, 34
collectivistic cultures *see* interdependent cultures
Columbia space shuttle, 420
Columbine High School shootings, 450, 452, 454
commitment in romantic relationships, 185–186, 346–348, 356
communal relationships, 316, 356
  culture, 316
communication
  conflict and, 474, 478
  emotional communication through touch, 186–188, *187*
  face-to-face communication, 476
  flirtation and nonverbal display, 186
  intergroup conflict and, 474–476
community support and prejudice reduction, 403
companionate love, 345
comparison and self-enhancement, 83–84
comparison level, 318
comparison level for alternatives, 318
compassion and prosocial behavior, 488, 495
compassionate love, 345, 356
compensatory awards in civil trials, 553–554, 560
competition
  quiz-show competition, 154–155, *155*
  in Robbers Cave experiment, 371–372, 402–403
  shifts between competition and cooperation, 372–373, 374, 403
  social facilitation and, 411–412, *413*
competitive altruism, 484
complementarity, 330–332
  social status, 332
  status exchange hypothesis, 332
compliance, 271
  descriptive norms, 295–296, 308
  door-in-the-face (reciprocal concessions) technique, 288–289, 308
  emotion-based approaches, 290–292, 296
  foot-in-the-door technique, 289–290, 308
  negative mood and, 291–292
  negative state relief hypothesis, 292, 308
  norm-based approaches, 292–296
  overview, 286
  positive mood and, 290–291, *291*
  prescriptive (injunctive) norms, 295–296, 308
  reason-based approaches, 287–290
  see also conformity; induced compliance; social influence
Computer Center Corporation (CCC), 139
computer science, founder of, 3
concrete *vs.* abstract construal, 112–113
confirmation bias, 113–117, *114*, 136
conflict and peacemaking, 471–477
conflict discussion task approach, with married couples, 349
conformity, 271–286
  anonymity, effect of, 281
  automatic mimicry, 272–274
  construal and, 280
  evolution and, 271–272
  expertise and status, effect of, 281–282
  factors affecting conformity pressure, 279–284
  free speech and, 281
  gender differences, 284

group size effect, *279*, 279–280
ideomotor action and, 273
interdependent *vs.* independent cultures, 282, 308
interpretive context of, disagreement and, 280
jury deliberations, 551–554
minority opinion influence on the majority, 284–286
overview, 271
pressures in daily life, 271
Sherif's conformity experiment, 274–276, *275*
tight and loose cultures, 283–284
unanimity, effect of, 280–281, *281*, 308
see also Asch's conformity experiment; compliance; social influence
Con Man (Moss), 91
consensus and covariation information, 146–147
conservative political views, 425
conservatives, moral foundations theory and, 193–194, *194*
consistency and covariation information, 147
consistency theories, 209–210, 213
  see also cognitive dissonance theory; rationalization
conspiracy theories, 116–117
construal, 5, 11–15, 34, 100
  abstract *vs.* concrete, 112–113
  aggression and, 457, 459–460, 478
  alternative, 380
  altruism and construal processes, 491–493
  automatic processing, 15
  better-than-average effect, 83
  breast cancer and, 522–523
  in conflict and peacemaking, 471
  conformity and, 280
  construal level theory, 112
  cooperation and, 505–507
  expectations and biased information processing, 385–386
  gestalt principles, *11,* 12–13
  health and, 522–524
  high-level, 89–90
  illusory correlations, 133–134, 137, 383–385, *384*
  independent self-construal, 71–72, 74, *74,* 75
  ingroup similarity and outgroup difference assumptions, 390
  interdependent self-construal, 71–72, 74, *74,* 75
  judgments about social world and, 11–12, 13
  low-level, 89–90
  in Milgram experiment, 13
  outgroup homogeneity effect, 390–391, 407
  prisoner's dilemma game, 505–507
  romantic partners, 346, *346,* 351–352
  schemas and, 13–14, 119–120
  self-construal and gender, 74, 76
  in self-control, 89–90
  self-serving construals, 83
  shifts in, 89–90
  socioeconomic status, *519,* 519–520
  stereotypes, concrete *vs.* abstract construal, 388–389
  stereotypes and, 14
  stereotypes and biased assessments, 383–389
  visual perception and, *11, 12,* 12–13
construal level theory, 112
contact hypothesis, 402–403, 405
contamination, 209
contempt in romantic relationships, 350, *350,* 356, 359
contingencies of self-worth, 79–80, 82, 96
controlled processing, 391–393
  attitudes toward outgroups, 391
  automatic processing *vs.,* 15–17, 34
  explicit attitudes and beliefs, 15
  stereotypes and prejudice, 391–395, 407
  see also automatic processing

convenience sampling, 42, *43*
cooperation, 502–511
  brain and, 504
  construal processes and, 505–507
  contagious nature of, 507
  culture and, 507–509, 512
  evolution and, 509–510, 512
  prosocial behavior and, 477
  reputation and, 505, 512
  shifts between competition and, 475
  situational determinants of, 504–505
  ultimatum game, 505–507
  between World War I enemies, 510
  see also prisoner's dilemma game
correlational research, 60
  causation and correlation, 44–46, 218
  illusory correlations, 133–134
  longitudinal studies, 47, 452
  reverse causation, 44
  scatterplots and correlations, 45, *45*
  secular trends, 439
  self-selection, 44
  strength of relationships, 45
  value of correlational findings, 45–46
cortisol
  benefits of social connection, 520–521
  in culture of honor, 463
  effects on the body, 516, 535
  fight-or-flight behavior, 516
  hypothalamic-pituitary-adrenal (HPA) axis,
    515–516, *516*, 517, 520, 522, 525
  meditation and, 522
  oxytocin and, 522
  self-enhancement and, 84
  social rejection and, 453
  subordinate status and, 519
cost-benefit analysis, 222
cost-benefit principle, 539
counterfactual emotions, on Olympic podium,
  149–150
counterfactual thoughts, 150, 170
  emotional effects of, 148–150
courtroom events and procedures
  compensatory awards, 553–554, 560
  damage awards in civil trials, 553–554
  death-qualified juries, 550–551, 560
  jury decision rule, 552–553
  jury deliberation, 551–554
  jury selection, 549–551
  jury size, 551–552
  overview, 542–543
  punitive awards, 553–554
  scientific jury selection, 549–550, 560
  voir dire, 549, 551, 560
  see also criminal justice system; pretrial events
covariation principle, 146–147, 150, 153, 170
credibility, source characteristics and, 246–247
criminal justice system, 543–560
  death-qualified juries, 550–551, 560
  DNA evidence, 547, 550
  eyewitness testimony, 543–545
  false confessions, 546–547
  juries and confession, 547–548
  jury deliberation, 551–554
  jury selection, 549–551
  perceptions of fairness of, 558–559
  police interrogation procedures, 547
  procedural justice, 558, 560
  racial bias in, 557–558, 560
  restorative justice, 476
  scientific jury selection, 549–550, 560
  Sixth Amendment to the U.S. Constitution,
    548–549, 552
  stereotypical facial features and death penalty,
    397
  voir dire, 549, 551, 560
  see also courtroom events and procedures;
    pretrial events; punishment

critical thinking
  finding proper comparison, 366
  social psychology and, 31–32, 35
criticism in romantic relationships, 349, 350, 356
Cuban missile crisis, 422, 474
cultural differences
  aggression, 461–465, 478
  altruism and, 493–499, 512
  among African groups, 73
  attention to action *vs.* relationships, *27*
  causal attribution and, 162–168, 170
  children's readers, 27, *27*
  class differences, 27–28
  cognitive dissonance, 225–226
  conformity, 282, 308
  cooperation, 505–507, 512
  display rules, 182
  dissonance and, 225–226, *226*, 236
  educational achievement and IQ, 530, 540
  emoji, 183
  emotional expression, 178–179, 181–184
  focal emotions, 182–184
  framed line task, 163, *163*
  fundamental attribution error, 164–165
  gender and mating preferences, 341
  gender roles, 29–30, 34–35
  gender socialization, 29
  Golden Rule across cultures and religions,
    497
  halo effect of physical attractiveness, 335, 356
  homosexuality, 29
  ideal emotions, 182–184
  independent *vs.* interdependent societies,
    overview, *25*, 25–28
  marriage, 344, 354–355, 356
  persuasion and, *251*, 251–252
  positive illusions and, 85
  predictions by tribes, 132–133
  priming cultures, 165–166
  promotion *vs.* prevention focus, 89, 251–252
  rape-prone cultures, 464–465
  regional and subcultural qualifications, 28
  self-definition and self-understanding, 24–26
  self-esteem, 80–82, *81*
  sexual mores, 29–30, 34–35
  sleeping arrangements of children, 323
  social class, 27–28
  in social relations and self-understanding,
    24–26
  social self and culture, 71–74
  tight *vs.* loose cultures, 283–284
  use in understanding situations, 30
  "Who Am I" test, 73–74
cultural supremacy
  ethnocentrism, 370
culture of honor
  anger, 182
  attitudes toward violence, 43–44, 478
  dueling tradition, *38*
  herding cultures and, 43–44
  homicides and, 41–42
  honor experiments, 47–49
  insult-related homicides, 47, *462*, 462–463
  Southern *vs.* Northern regions, 37–38, 42,
    43–44, 47–49, 462–463
cyberbullying, 468

D

danger, alerting to, 23
Darfur massacres (Sudan), 302, 360, 464
Darwin, Charles
  on emotions, 176, 178
  on evolution, 18, 41
  Galápagos Islands, 18, 41
  HMS *Beagle*, 176
  on natural selection, 18, 41
  on principle of serviceable habits, 178

death, biased assessments of perceived causes of,
  126, *127*
death penalty
  motivated confirmation bias and, 117
  stereotypical facial features and, 397
debriefing, 58, 60
deception research, 58
Declaration of Independence, 71, 195
defensiveness in romantic relationships, 349,
  350, 356
dehumanization, 459–460, 471, 478
deindividuation
  diffusion of responsibility, 435
  emergent properties of groups, 434
  empirical tests of model, 436–438
  group mind, 434–435
  at Halloween, 438
  impulsivity and, 436, 438, 442
  suicide baiting, 436–437
  theoretical model of, *435*
  transgression and, 438, *438*
  "Twinkie defense," 433
  in warfare, 437–438
  Zimbardo's model of deindividuation,
    overview, 435–436
  see also individuation; mob psychology
Democrats
  groupthink, 425
  snap judgment of, 102
"denial of death," 233
dependent variables, 47, 48, 51, 54, 60
descriptive norms, 295–296, 308
deterrence motive, 556, 560
dictator game, 496, 506
diffusion of responsibility, 489, 512
  altruism and helping others, 489–490, 493,
    495, 512
  deindividuation, 435
disabled children, prejudice reduction of, 402
discounting principle, 148, 158, 170
discrimination
  cost of concealment, 400–401
  definition, 362
  economic perspective on prejudice and dis-
    crimination, 369–374
  elderly, 360
  gays and lesbians, 360
  racial basis in criminal justice system, 359–360
  reducing, 401, 407
  theoretical perspectives, 360–361, 406
  women, 360
  see also cognitive perspective on prejudice and
    discrimination; prejudice
disfluency, 128
disgust, 191, 192
disidentification, 400
display rules, 183, 202
dispositional attribution, 147
dispositions, 10
  dispositional inference and attribution,
    158–159, *159*
  flexibility of, 167–168
  fundamental attribution error, 10, 158–159,
    159
dissonance *see* cognitive dissonance theory
distancing from aggression, 460–461
distinctiveness
  covariation information, 146–147
  paired distinctiveness, 383–385
  sense of self and, 69–70
distinctiveness hypothesis, 69–70
diversification principle, 68
diversity hypothesis, 495
DNA evidence in criminal trials, 544, 547, 550
dominance, 20, 428
  definition, 428
dominance dimension, judgment of faces, *101*,
  101–102

eyewitness testimony
    effect of misleading questions, 545
    eyewitness errors, 544–545, 546, 560
    improving eyewitness identification procedures,
        546
    overview, 543–545
    persistence of memory, 545–546
    recovered memories, 542, 545–546

F

face, 96
Facebook, 32, 94–95, 116–117, 495
    news of opposing viewpoints, 107
    persuasion and, 257–258
    social comparison, 77
facial expressions
    blind and sighted individuals, 178, 181
    cultural differences, 178–179
    Darwin on, 178
    universality of, 20, 178–181
    see also emotions
Fairness and Accuracy in Reporting (FAIR), 259
fairness/cheating moral domain, 192–193
fake news, 106–108, 259
Fame, The (Lady Gaga), 63
familialism, 27
family, origins of sense of self and, 67–69
fatalities, biased assessments of risk, 126, *127*
fear and persuasiveness, 250, *250*
female infanticide, 463
field experiments, 50–51, 60
Filipinos in Gulf countries, 370
Finch emoji, 183
firsthand information, 103–105
Five Cs for effective tutoring, 529
flirtation and nonverbal display, 186
fluency, 127–128, 137, 328, 334
focal emotions, 182–184, 202
focalism, 197
food sharing, 20
footbridge dilemma, 192
foot-in-the-door technique, 289–290, 308
"forbidden toy" paradigm, 220–221, *221*
Fore tribe (Papua New Guinea), 178–179
"Four Horsemen of the Apocalypse," 349–350
Fraboni Scale of Ageism, 365
framing effects, 110–111, 136
    construal level theory, 112
    order effects, 109–110
    positive and negative framing, 110–111
    primacy effects, 109
    recency effects, 109–110
    spin framing, 110–111
    temporal framing, 111–113
fraternity hazing, 218
free speech and conformity, 281
French Revolution, 514
friendship
    diversity and, 326
    emotions in, 184–188
    evolution and, 313
    limitation number of close friends, 313
    proximity and, 324–326, *325*, 333
    similarity and, 328–330
    Westgate West apartment friendship research,
        324–326, *325*
functional distance, 325, 356
functional magnetic resonance imaging (fMRI),
    22, 163, 192, 354, 504
fundamental attribution error, *11*, 34
    altruistic *vs.* selfish response, 153–154, *154*
    automatic characterizations, 159
    cognition and attribution, 158–159
    consequences of, 159–160
    critical thinking about, 157
    cultural differences, 164–165
    derogation of victims, 156–157
    dispositions and, 9–10, 158–159, *159*

experimental demonstrations of, 153–154
Hurricane Katrina and, 157
just world hypothesis, 156–157, 170
Milgram study of obedience, 153
motivational influences, 156–157
perception about advantage and disadvantage,
    154–156, *155*
perceptual salience, 158
quiz-show competition, *154*, 154–155
salience of people *vs.* situations, 158–159
salient situations, 159
see also causal attribution

G

gaydar, 102
gay marriage *see* same-sex marriage
gay rights, 284
gays
    discrimination, 360
    overturning of "don't ask, don't tell" in the
        military, 3–4
    see also homosexuality
gender
    aggression and, 467–470, 478
    attribution style and, 144
    differences in social self, 74, 76
    effect on conformity, 284
    impact of physical attractiveness, 336,
        341–342
    nameism and, 366
    sex differences in mate preferences, 342–344
    stereotype threat and, 397
gender roles
    cultural differences, 29–30, 34–35
    evolution and, 21
    gender socialization, 29, 74
    lifetime monogamy, 29
    parental investment and, 21, 34
    polyandry, 21, 29–30
    polygyny, 21, 29
    serial monogamy, 29
    social self and, 74, 76
genetics and political allegiances, 262, 263
genocide
    aftermath of social upheavals, 305
    Armenians, 361
    Bosnia, 302, 464
    Cambodia, 302
    Darfur (Sudan), 302, 360, 464
    despotic leaders and, 429
    expatriate Chinese, 361
    Jews, 307, 361, 473
    reconciliation, 476
    Rohingya (Myanmar), 445
    Rwanda, 302, 305, 445, 446, 459, 464, 471,
        482–483, 502
    Somalia, 360
    step-to-step guide to genocide, 307
    Urganda, 445
    see also Holocaust
Genovese, Kitty, murder, 489, 490
gestalt psychology, 12–13
Giving Pledge, 495
globalization, 477
global warming
    heat and aggression, 448–449
    persuasion and, 240, 250, 254
    room temperature effect on global warming
        relief, 231–232
    steps to control carbon emissions, 240, 250,
        254
goals and implementation intentions, 90–91
Golden Gate Bridge, 334
Golden Rule across cultures and religions, *497*
Good Samaritan study with seminarians, 9, *9*, 49
gossip, 505, 512
Granville Market Letter, 104
gratitude, 198

green spaces and aggression, 455
group living, evolution, 20–21, 410, 442
group polarization
    in homogeneous groups, 425
    in modern life, 424
    persuasive arguments account, 423–424, 442
    politics, 425
    risk and, 424
    risky shift, 424
    social comparison interpretation account, 424,
        442
groups, 409–443
    being a member of a stigmatized group,
        396–401, 407
    dehumanization and, 459
    emergent properties of, 434
    emotion and knowing our place in, 188
    evolution of group living, 410
    group decision making, 419–426, 442
    measuring attitudes about groups, 365–369
    nature and purpose of group living, 410–411
    risky shift, 424
    social identity theory, 381
    spotlight effect, 440, *440,* 442
    see also group polarization; groupthink;
        intergroup conflict; mob psychology; power;
        social facilitation
groupthink
    Bay of Pigs decision making, 420, 421
    Challenger space shuttle, 420
    Columbia space shuttle, 420
    Democrats, 425
    devil's advocate role, 422
    Janis's groupthink hypothesis, 419–420, *421*
    Johnson administration and Vietnam war, 420
    overview, 419–420
    Pearl Harbor attack, 420
    prevention, 421–422
    Republicans, 425
    self-censorship, 421, 442
    social determinants, 423
    strong leaders and, 427–428
    symptoms and sources of, 420–421
    see also groups; social facilitation
guilt
    compliance and, 292
    moral judgment and, 191
    shame-or guilt-prone cultures, 182
gun control study
    selective framing and, 261

H

Haath Se Haath Mila (Hand in Hand Together),
    535
Halloween, 438
halo effect, 335–336, 356
handguns and automatic stereotyping, 393–394
Hannibal (movie), 450
happiness, 33, 195–201
    affective forecasting, 196, 202
    awe, 201
    components of, 195
    creativity and positive emotions, 195
    cultivating, 198–201
    effects of romantic breakups, 196, *196*
    emotional well-being, 195
    environmental factors, 201
    life satisfaction, 195
    marriage and, 44, 49
    meaning of, 195
    meditation and, 200
    money and, 198–199
    Olympic medal winners, 149–150
    optimism and, *143*
    predicting happiness, 195–197, 202
    pursuing, 198–201
    recalling happy moments, 197
    relationships and, 198

interventions, 59
interviews, fallibility of, 160
intimacy in romantic relationships, 346
introspection, 211–212
intuition, 123–124, *124*, 136
    reason and, *123*
    see also heuristics
Inuit of Alaska, 461, 484
investment model of commitment, 346–348
IQ test validity, 52
ISIS, 364, 464, 473
Islamic State of Iraq and Syria *see* ISIS
Israelis, 360, 369, 404

J

Janis's groupthink hypothesis, 419–420, *421*
Japan and Japanese
    cognitive dissonance, 225–226, 236
    context and causal attribution, 163
    gender and the social self, 74
    self-esteem and everyday experiences, 81–82
Jews, 361, 489
"jigsaw" classrooms, 374
Jim Crow laws, 397
Johnson v. Louisiana, 552
joint projects, biased estimates of contributions
    to, 126–127
Judas Priest rock band, 243
juries
    Apodaca, Cooper, and Madden v. Oregon, 552
    Ballew v. Georgia, 551
    compensatory awards, 553–554, 560
    confessions and, 546–548
    damage awards in civil trials, 553–554, 560
    death-qualified juries, 550–551
    Johnson v. Louisiana, 552
    jury decision rule, 552–553
    jury deliberation, 551–554
    jury selection, 549–551
    jury size, 551–552
    Liebeck v. McDonald's Restaurants, 554
    Lockhart v. McCree, 551
    peremptory challenges, 549
    punitive awards, *553,* 553–554
    scientific jury selection, 549–550, 560
    voir dire, 549, 551, 560
    Williams v. Florida, 551
    Witherspoon v. Illinois, 551
just desserts motive, 555–556, 557
justice, anger and restoration of, 175
just world hypothesis, 156–157, 170

K

Kanizsa triangle, *11,* 11–12
kin selection, 499–501, 512
knowledge, resistance and, 263–264
Korea and Koreans
    consensus information and, 165
    fundamental attribution error and, 164–165
    halo effect, 335
    interdependent culture, 26
    on malleability of personality, 167–168
Ku Klux Klan, 364

L

ladder measure, *519,* 519–520
Lamerala of Indonesia, 508–509
language, evolution and, 20–21
Latino-Americans and interdependent culture, 27
Latinos
    academic achievement and, 532–533
    criminal justice system and, 557
law and social psychology, 542–561
    see also courtroom events and procedures;
        criminal justice system; pretrial events
leaders, characteristics of, 427–428
leadership, 426–432, 442
    see also groups; power

legal system *see* criminal justice system
lesbians and discrimination, 360
liberal political views, 425
liberals, moral foundations theory and, 193–194,
    194
Lie to Me, 249
life satisfaction, 195
Likert scale, 207, 236
Literary Digest, 42
Lockhart v. McCree, 551
loneliness
    age, 317
    health effects, 317
    social media, 317
longitudinal studies, 47, 322, 452
"looking-glass self," 68
loose cultures, tight cultures *vs.,* 283–284
Lou Gehrig's disease, 240
love
    brain and, 354
    companionate love, 356
    compassionate love, 356
    expressed in emoji, 183
    nonverbal signs of romantic love, 345
    oxytocin and, 185–186
    passionate love, 356
    sympathy maps and, *183*
    types of, 344–346
    see also romantic relationships
low-level construals, 89–90
loyalty/betrayal moral domain, 193
lying, 249

M

Machiguenga of Peru, 508
malleability, in the social self, 70
mammals, reciprocity and grooming among, 287
marijuana, legalization arguments, 260–261
marketing
    message characteristics, 248–252
    spin framing in, 110–111
    subliminal advertising, 243, *243*
marriage
    arranged marriages, 354–355
    cultural differences, 344, 354–355, 356
    divorce frequency, 348
    "Four Horsemen of the Apocalypse," 349–350
    happiness and, 44, 49
    marital dissatisfaction, 348–351
    marriage benefit, 314
    marriage equality, support for, 4
    predictors of divorce, 349
math performance
    stereotype threat, 398
Mbuti Pygmies, 465
measurement validity, 52, 60
media
    agenda control, 258
    aggression and media violence, 449–450, 478
    bias, 259
    body image problems of women and, 337
    conceptions of social reality and, 258–260
    effects of bad-news bias, 106
    focus on bad news in entertainment, 106
    hostile media phenomenon, 259
    persuasion and, 257–260
    power of, 257–258
    public service announcements, 246
    shared attention, 257
    violence in movies and television, 449–450,
        478
    violent TV, children and later violence, 451
    weak affects on attitudes and behaviors,
        262–263
medial prefrontal cortex, 74, 491
medical condition study, selective evaluation
    and, 261
meditation, 200, 522

memory
    eyewitness testimony, 543–546
    as inference, not infallible record, 545, 546
    persistence of, 545–546
    recovered memories, 542, 545–546
    schemas and retrieval of, 119
menstrual cycle and male attractiveness to
    women, 342–343, *343*
mental health and casual sex, 44
mentalizing network, 23
mere exposure effect, 326–328, *328,* 334, 356
mere presence, testing for, 417–418
message characteristics and persuasion, 248–252
    culture, 251–252
    fear, 250
message quality, 248
    vividness, 248–249
metacognition
    defined, 254
    persuasion and, 254–256, 266
methods of social psychology, 37–61
    applied science, 58–59
    archival research, 41–42, 60
    basic science, 58–59
    convenience sampling, 42, *43*
    correlational research, 44–47, 60
    debriefing, 58
    deception research, 58
    dependent variables, 47, 60
    ethical concerns, 58
    experimental research, 44, 47–49, 60
    external validity in experiments, 50–51
    field experiments, 50–51
    hypotheses, formation from theory, 40–41
    hypotheses, testing, 39–40
    independent variables, 47, 60
    informed consent, 58
    institutional review boards (IRBs), 57
    internal validity in experiments, 51–52
    measurement validity, 52
    observational research, 41
    participant observation, 41, 60
    predicting results of social psychology studies,
        39, 40
    random sampling, 42–43, *43,* 60
    reliability, 52
    replication, 54
    statistical significance, 54
    statistics, social science methodology, and
        critical thinking, 537–539, 540
    surveys, 42–44, 60
    see also scientific method
Mexican-Americans and fundamental attribution
    error, 165
Microsoft, 139, 140
Middle East, 360
Milgram study of obedience, 297–298, 300,
    308, 489
    awareness of learner's suffering, 8–9, 298,
        304
    Burger's near replication of experiment, 303
    construal and, 13
    effects of legitimacy of experiment, 302, 304
    ethical concerns, 57–58, 298
    exceptionalist explanation, 302
    explanations and interpretations of results, 9
    external validity, 50
    forces for terminating participation, 298
    fundamental attribution error, 153
    ineffective and indecisive disobedience, 304
    moral imperative to stop suffering, 298
    motivating forces affecting participants, 298
    normalist explanation, 302
    normative social influence, 298, 308
    opposing forces, 298, 300
    parallels to Nazi Germany, 302, 306
    power of social situations, 7–9
    procedure, 308

proximity version of experiment, 300, *300*
release of participants from responsibility, 305–306, 308
remote-feedback version of experiment, 300, *300*
role of construal, 13
setup of experiments, 297–298
step-by-step involvement, 307
touch-proximity version of experiment, 300, *300*
tuning in the learner, *300,* 300–301
tuning out the experimenter, 301, *302*
tuning out victims with military technologies, *300,* 301
variations in experiment, 303
voice-feedback version of experiment, 300, *300*
see also obedience; social influence
military and racial integration, 402, 403
mimicry *see* automatic mimicry
minimal group paradigm, 375–376, *376,* 406
misperceptions in intergroup conflict, 471–472
mistaken judgment, intuitive processing and, *124*
mob psychology
deindividuation, definition, 435
deindividuation in warfare, 437–438
emergent properties of groups, 434
empirical tests of deindividuation model, 436–438
group mind, 434–435
at Halloween, 438
impulsivity and, 436, 438
rioting after Dan White sentencing, San Francisco, 433–434
rioting after Super Bowl win, San Francisco, 434
suicide baiting, 436–437
theoretical model of deindividuation model, *435*
Zimbardo's model of deindividuation, overview, 435–436
see also groups
Modern Family, 311–312
Modern Racism Scale, 365, 392
monoamine oxidase A (MAOA) gene, 447
monogamy, 29
mood maintenance, 291, 308
moods, emotions *vs.,* 174
moral foundations theory, 192–193, *194,* 202
moral judgment, 23
Mark and Julie's relationship, 191
moral murders, 473
mortality and loneliness, 317
mortality salience
nationalism and, 234–235
presidential candidates and, 234–235, *235*
Mortal Kombat, 451
motivated confirmation bias, 117
motivation, persuasion and role of, 242–245
motivational perspective on prejudice and discrimination
basking in reflected glory, 378–379
ingroup favoritism, 376–377
minimal group paradigm, 375–376, *376,* 406
overview, 360–361, 375
self-esteem and boosting ingroup status, 377–378
self-esteem and denigrating outgroups, *379,* 379–381
social identity theory, 376–381, 406
see also discrimination; prejudice
motive, 156
Müller-Lyer illusion, *274,* 274–276
murders, moral, 473
musical preference, repeated exposure and, 327, *328*
Myanmar upheaval, 32
My Fair Lady, 527

N

"naïve realism," 13, 259
narcissism, self-esteem and, 84
narratives
about causes of emotions, 177
happiness and, 197
women diagnosed with breast cancer, 522–523
nationalism, mortality salience and, 234–235
natural experiments, 49, 313
naturalistic fallacy, 22, 34
natural selection, 18, 34, 41, 466
Nazi Germany
dehumanization, 459
deportations in freight trains, 306
persuasion and effect of mood, 252
Polish occupation, 304
step-to-step guide to genocide, 307
negative framing, positive framing *vs.,* 110–111
negative mood, compliance and, 291–292
negative state relief hypothesis, 292, 308
neocortex, 23
neuroscience
age and, 23
amygdala and attitudes, 209
amygdala and emotions, 354
amygdala and IAT response, 368
amygdala and stress, 516
amygdala and threats, 516
anterior cingulate and pain, 453
attitudes and motor cortex activation, 207
cooperation, 504
culture and the social self in the brain, 74
empathic concern, 488
evolution and, 22–23
functional magnetic resonance imaging (fMRI), 22, 163, 192, 354, 504
meditation effects, 200
moral brain, 192
orbitofrontal cortex, 504
personal distress at other's pain, 484
prefrontal cortex, 23
romantic love, 354
social neuroscience, 22–23
social rejection and pain response, 453
strength of negative and positive stimuli, 209
stress-related brain regions, 515–516
ventral striatum and rewards, 354
see also brain
news about politics, 106, 107
newspapers with selective reporting of sources, 108
news shows with selective reporting of sources, 108
nonconscious attitudes, 208
nonconscious processing
functions of, 17
types of, 16–17
normal distribution, 53
normal distribution: bell curve, 53, *53*
normative social influence, 276–277, *277,* 285
anonymity, effect of, 281
Asch's conformity experiment, 276–279
in bulimia, 278
group size effect, 279–280
in jury deliberations, 551
Milgram study of obedience, 298, 308
status, effect of, 281–282
see also informational social influence; social influence
norm-based appeals, effective, 293–295
norm of reciprocity, 287–288, 308
nucleus accumbens, *22, 23*
cooperation and, 504
nudges, 10–11
nursing home patients, personal control study, 523–524, *524*

O

obedience, 271
ineffective and indecisive disobedience, 304
overview, 296
see also Milgram study of obedience; social influence
obesity, 337
social influence network, 269
objectivist view of beauty, 334
observational research, 41
Olympic medalists and counterfactual thinking, 149–150
online dating, 329
online social networking sites, online self and, 94–95, 96
open science, 56–57
optimism
benefits of perceived control and, 524, 525
leading to happiness, *143*
orbitofrontal cortex, 504
order effects, 109–110
Organization Man, The (Whyte), 325
organ transplant, channel factors and, 11
Origin of Species (Darwin), 18
ought self, 88, 96
outgroup
homogeneity effect, 390–391, 407
own-race identification bias, 391
Outside magazine, 42
"Outside Your Bubble" app, 107
overjustification effect, 230–231, *231*
own-race identification bias, 391
oxytocin
commitment and, 185–186
cortisol and, 522
social connections and, 522

P

pair bonding, 185–186
paired distinctiveness, 383–385, 406
Pakistan-India arms race, 503
Palestinians, 360, 369, 404
palio competition, concrete and abstract construals during, 388–389
parental investment, 21, 34, 339–340, 356, 466
participant observation, 41, 60
passion in romantic relationships, 345–346
Passion of the Christ (movie), 450
peacemaking, conflict and, 471–477
peak moments, 197
Pearl Harbor attack, 420
People magazine, 42–43
perception, emotions and influence on, 189–190, 194
perceptual fluency, 334
perceptual psychologists, 100
performance-contingent rewards, 230–231
peripheral route to persuasion, *241,* 241–242, 244–245, 266
personal distress motive in altruism, 484, 487
personality
"Big Five" personality dimensions, 167
inferring from physical appearance, 100–102
personalization, 404
persuasion, 239–267
ability and, 242–245
attentional biases and resistance, 260–261
attitude inoculation, 264–265, 267
audience age and, 253–254, 266
audience characteristics, 252–254
central (systematic) route, 241, *241,* 244–245, 266
certainty, 248
changes in attitude certainty, 264–265
culture and, 251–252
dual-process approaches to, 240–245, *241,* 266
elements of, 246–254
embodiment and confidence, 255–256

persuasion (*Continued*)
  Facebook and, 257–258
  fear and, 250, *250*
  global warming, 240, 250, 254
  heuristic-systematic model, 241–242
  identifiable victim effect, 249–250
  knowledge and resistance, 263–264
  lying as persuasion, 249
  media and, 257–260, 266
  message characteristics, 248–252
  message quality and, 248
  message targeting to particular cultures, 251–252
  message vividness and, 248–249, 266
  metacognition and, 254–256, 266
  mood and, 252–253
  motivation and ability, 242–245
  need for cognition and, 252–254
  peripheral (heuristic) route, *241*, 241–242, 244–245, 266
  previous commitments and resistance, 262–263
  public commitments and, 262
  public service announcements, 246
  resistance to, 240, 260–265, 266–267
  self-validation hypothesis and, 244, 266
  shared attention, 257
  sleeper effect, 246–247, 266
  social media and, 257–258
  source attractiveness and, 246
  source credibility and, 246–247
  subliminal cues, 243, *243*
  thought polarization hypothesis, 262, 267
  timing and, 253
  see also attitudes; elaboration likelihood model (ELM) of persuasion
Petrified Forest National Park, 296
PGA Tournament Golf, 451
physical appearance, inferring personality from, 100–102
physical attractiveness, 332–339
  attraction and, overview, 332–333
  of average faces, 338–339
  bilateral symmetry and, 334, 339
  biology and, 338, 342–344, *343*
  body weight, 337
  evolutionary theory, 338–339
  gender and, 336, 341–342
  halo effect, 335–336, 356
  impact of, 333
  reproductive fitness, 338
  universality of, 336–337, 338
pilot training, 53
pituitary gland, stress, HPA axis, and, *516*
playfulness in romantic relationships, 352–353
pleasure, recollections of, 197
pleasure principle, 485
pluralistic ignorance, 103–104, 136, 294, *294*, 492–493
poker face, 184
police's treatment of African Americans, 359
political allegiances and genetics, 262, 263
political candidates, snap judgment of, 102
political conservatism, 193–194
politics
  group polarization, 425
  news about, 106, 107
polyandry, 21, 29–30
polygyny, 21, 29
positive emotions, 522
positive framing, negative framing *vs.,* 110–111
positive illusions about the self, 84–85
positive mood, compliance and, 290–291, *291*
possible selves, 87–88
power
  accountability, and, 431
  antisocial behavior and, 431–432
  approach/inhibition theory, 429–430, 442

definition, 428
disinhibition of high-power people, 431–432, 442
effect on social perception, 429–430
elements of, 428
ethical behavior, *432*
health and, 519–520
influence on behavior, 429–432
inhibition of low-power people, 430–431
leadership and, 426–432, 442
Machiavelli on, 427
overview, 426–427
reduced empathy with power, *430*, 430–431
sexually inappropriate behavior, 431
see also groups
Pravda, 247
precarious manhood hypothesis, 469, 478
predicting research results, 39, 40
prefrontal cortex, *22, 23*
prejudice
  affect misattribution procedure (AMP), 369
  attributional ambiguity and, 396–397
  automatic and controlled processing and, 15–16, 391–395
  automatic stereotyping, *395*
  being a member of a stigmatized group, 396–401, 407
  benevolent racism and sexism, 364–365, 406
  definition, 362
  economic perspective on prejudice and discrimination, 369–374
  Implicit Association Test (IAT), 365, *367,* 367–368, 406
  measuring, 365
  measuring attitudes about groups, 365, 367–369
  modern racism, 362–364, 392, 406
  motivational perspective on, 375–381
  own-race identification bias, 391
  priming and implicit prejudice, 368–369, *369*, 406
  reducing, 401–403, 407
  self-esteem and boosting ingroup status, 377–378
  self-esteem and denigrating outgroups, *379*, 379–381
  self-esteem and racial prejudice, 379–381, *380*
  theoretical perspectives, 360–361, 406
  see also cognitive perspective on prejudice and discrimination; stereotypes
prejudice reduction
  community support, 403
  contact hypothesis, 402–403
  individual approaches to, 401–402
  intergroup approaches to, 402–403
prescriptive (injunctive) norms, 295–296, 308
presidential election, U.S., 1984, 208
presidential election, U.S., 2012, 107
presidential election, U.S., 2016, 106, 107, 116, 257, 259
presidential election, U.S. and selective attention, 261
pretrial events
  eyewitness testimony, 543–545
  false confessions, 546–547
  juries and confessions, 547–548
  police interrogation procedures, 547
  see also courtroom events and procedures; criminal justice system
prevention focus, 88, 96, 251–252
  East Asians and, 89, 251–252
previous commitments, resistance and, 262–263
Pride and Prejudice (Austen), 340
primacy effects, 109, 136
priming, 120–121, 136
  affect misattribution procedure (AMP), 369
  cultures, 165–166
  implicit prejudice, 368–369, *369*, 392, 406
  power, 431

in prisoner's dilemma game, 505
religion and altruism, 497–498, *498*
schemas, 122
subliminal, 120–121
primogeniture, 30
Prince, The (Machiavelli), 427
principle of serviceable habits, 178
Principles of Psychology, The (James), 64
prisoner's dilemma game
  competitive player, 505–507
  construal, 505–507
  cooperative players, 503, *503*
  defecting strategy, 503, 512
  economics majors as players, 509
  overview, 502–503
  priming, 505
  reputation of players, 505
  tit-for-tat strategy, 509–510, 512
  "Wall Street" game, 506–507
  see also cooperation
prisons
  Abu Ghraib prisoner abuse, 5–6
  cultural differences, 556–557
  Zimbardo prison study, 6
prison sentence lengths, 248
procedural justice, 558, 560
professors' performance, snap judgment of, 102
projective tests, 133–134
promotion focus, 88, 96
propaganda on attitude change, 59
prosocial behavior, sense of being watched and, *498*, 498–499
prosocial nervous system, 488
Protestants
  dispositional attributions, 166, 168
  murdering Catholics, 473
proximity
  anticipation of interactions, 325
  attraction, 329
  friendship, 324–326, *325*, 333
  functional distance, 325
  mere exposure effect, 326–328, *328*, 334
  proximity version of Milgram experiment, 300, *300*
  studies of attraction and, 324–326
  touch-proximity version of Milgram experiment, 300, *300*
  Westgate West apartment houses, 324–325, *325*
pseudo-recognition test, 416
pseudoscience, 133
psycholinguists, 100
psychological immune system, 196
psychological stress, 515, 525
psychopaths and psychopathologies, 470
public commitments and persuasion, 262
public self and self-presentation, 92
public service announcements (PSAs), 246
Puerto Ricans and fundamental attribution error, 165
punishment
  attributional account of, 556–557
  death penalty, 550, 551, 557
  deterrence motive, 556
  just desserts motive, 555–556
  overview, 554–555
  sympathy, effect on judgment, 557
punitive awards in civil trials, *553*, 553–554, 560
punitive mindset, 399
purity/degradation moral domain, 193
"Pygmalion in the Classroom," 526–528, 540
Pygmalion in the Classroom (Rosenthal and Jacobson), 527

R

race
  disparities in school system, 399
  military integration, 402, 403
  school suspensions, 399

racism, 399
  Attitudes toward Blacks Scale, 363–364, 365
  benevolent, 364–365, 406
  modern, 362–364, 406
  Modern Racism Scale, 368, 392
  racial bias in criminal justice system, 557–558,
    560
  see also civil rights and race relations;
    discrimination; prejudice; stereotypes
random assignment, 47–48
random sampling, 42–43, 43, 60
rape, dehumanization and, 459
rape-prone cultures, 464–465, 478
rationalization
  after making decisions, 215–217, 219
  dissonance reduction, 215
  before making decisions, 215–217, 219–220
  sweet lemons rationalization, 215–216
  see also cognitive dissonance theory
rational system and reason, 124, 124–125, 136
reactance theory, 298
reactive devaluation, 472
realistic group conflict theory, 370, 406
reason
  intuition and, 123
  rational system and, 124, 125–126, 136
receiver characteristics, 252–254
recency effects, 109–110, 136
reciprocal concessions (door-in-the-face)
    technique, 288–289, 308
reciprocity
  among animals, 500
  door-in-the-face (reciprocal concessions)
    technique, 288–289, 308
  norm of reciprocity, 287–288, 308
  reciprocal altruism, 500–501, 512
recovered memories, 542, 545–546
reflected self-appraisals, 68–69, 96
regression effect, 132
  traffic safety, 132
regression fallacy, 132
regression to the mean, 53
relational aggression, 467
relational self, 315, 318–319
relationships, 311–357
  biology and the need to belong, 313–315
  characterizing, 312–323
  communal and exchange relationships, 316,
    356
  communal relationships, 316
  culture, 316
  effect of past on current interactions, 322–323
  equity theory, 318, 324
  evidence for the need to belong, 314–315
  evolutionary basis, 319
  exchange relationships, 316
  extended families, 311–312
  human health risks without relationships, 314
  importance of, 313–315
  longitudinal studies, 313, 322
  online dating, 329
  relational self, 315, 318–319
  research methods and challenges, 312–313
  reward framework for relationships, 316–317
  sense of self and, 313–315
  social exchange theory, 316, 356
  universality of, 314
  see also attachment; attraction; romantic
    relationships
reliability, 52, 60
religion, altruism and, 497, 497–499, 498
replication, 54, 60
  scientific findings, 56–57
representativeness heuristic, 129–135, 137
  academic disciplines and, 131
  base-rate information and, 129, 130, 137
  in health and medicine, 133–134
  predictions by tribes, 132–133

pseudoscience, 133
regression effect, 132
resemblance between cause and effect, 131–132
resemblance between members and categories,
    129–131
  use of, overview, 129
  see also heuristics
reproductive fitness, 338, 356
Republicans
  groupthink, 425
  snap judgment of, 102
reputation, 505, 506, 512
research methods see methods of social
    psychology
response cries, 92
response latency, 208, 236
restorative justice, 476
retirement plan, channel factors and, 11
retributive justice see punishment
reward circuit, 23
rewards
  in induced compliance, 219–220
  overjustification effect, 230–231, 231
  performance-contingent rewards, 230–231
  reward framework for relationships, 316–317
  romantic relationships, 346
  self-control and, 89–90
  social exchange theory and, 316–317
  social rewards motive in altruism, 483–484
  task-contingent rewards, 230–231
  ventral striatum and, 354
rhesus monkey "mother surrogates" research, 314
rhetoric
  conflict and complexity of, 472–473, 474
  simplistic reasoning and, 472–474, 474
risk, biased assessment of, 126, 127
risk aversion, 424
risk seeking, 424
risky shift, 424
Robbers Cave experiment, 374
  competition and intergroup conflict, 371–373
  ingroup solidarity and, 375
  "jigsaw" classroom and, 374
  overview, 371–373
  reducing intergroup conflict through
    superordinate goals, 372–374, 403, 406
Rohingya massacre (Myanmar), 445
romantic relationships, 344–355, 356
  attitudes and, 211
  blame, 351–352, 356
  capitalizing on the good, 352, 356
  commitment, 346–348
  companionate love, 345
  contempt in, 349, 350, 350, 356
  creating stronger romantic bonds, 352–354
  criticism in, 349, 350, 356
  cultural differences in marriage, 354–355, 356
  defensiveness in, 349, 350, 356
  effects of romantic breakups on happiness,
    196, 196
  evolution, 313
  forgiveness, 348
  "Four Horsemen of the Apocalypse," 349–350
  illusions and idealization in, 353–354
  intimacy in, 346
  investment model of commitment, 346–348,
    356
  marital dissatisfaction, 348–351, 356
  measuring commitment determinants in,
    347–348, 348
  measuring relationship satisfaction, 351
  nonverbal signs of romantic love, 345
  passionate, 345–346
  playfulness in, 352–353, 356
  predictors of divorce, 349
  satisfaction, 347
  stonewalling, 349, 350, 356
  see also attraction; relationships

Rorschach inkblots, 133–134
rumination, 516, 517, 525
Rusbult's investment model, 346–347, 348
Rwanda
  altruism, 482–483
  dehumanization, 459
  genocide, 305, 360, 445, 446, 471, 502
  ideological distortion, 305–306
  rapes, 464
  reconciliation, 471, 476

S

same-sex marriage, 284
  legalization of, 360
  support for, 4
Sandy Hook Elementary School shootings, 454
scatterplots and correlations, 45, 45
schemas, 118–122
  activation, consciousness of, 122
  activation, recent, 121
  activation, subliminal, 120–121
  activation and behavior, 121–122
  activation by expectation, 122
  chronic accessibility, 121–122
  in construal, 13–14, 34, 119–120
  expectations, 122
  frequent activation of, 121–122
  influence on attention, 118
  influence on behavior, 120–122
  influence on memory, 119
  priming, 120–121
  stereotypes and, 119
  top-down processes, 118–122
  see also social cognition
schools and racial disparities, 399
school suspensions per racial group, 399
SchuelerVZ, 94
Science magazine, 56
scientific findings, replicating, 56–57
scientific jury selection, 549–550, 560
scientific method
  Albert Einstein on, 39
  attitude inoculation, 264, 264–265
  correlations and, 45
  counterfactual thinking by Olympic medalists,
    149–150
  induced compliance and attitude change, 220
  normative social influence, 277
  power of situation and helping, 9
  social facilitation on simple and complex tasks,
    415
  see also experimental research; methods of social
    psychology
secondhand information, 105–108
  see also eyewitness testimony
secular trends, 439
secure attachment style, 319, 321, 321, 322, 323
Seeds of Peace, 404
selective attention, 260–261
  U.S. presidential elections and, 261
selective evaluation, 260–261, 261, 262
  climate change and, 261
selective framing, 261
self-affirmation, 83–84, 224–225
self-affirmation theory, 83–84
self-agency, 26
self-assessment, accurate, cognitive barrier to, 86
self-awareness, 23
self-awareness theory, 438, 442
  see also individuation; spotlight effect
self-censorship, 421, 442
self-concept
  differences in African groups, 73
  gender and self-concept, 74, 76
  independent vs. interdependent societies, 25,
    26–28
  "Who Am I" test, 73–74
  working self-concept, 69, 70, 319

self-control, 89–91, 96
  construals, 89–90
  rewards and, 89–90
self-defeating behavior, 93
self-definition, *72*
self-discrepancy theory, 87–88, 96
self-distancing, 517, 525
self-enhancement
  adaptive value of positive illusions, 84–85
  affirmations, 83–84
  better-than-average effect, 83
  comparison and reflecting, 83–84
  integrating self-verification perspective with, 86–87
  self-serving construals, 83
  well-being and, 84–85
self-esteem, 64, 78–82
  boosting ingroup status and, 377–378
  California self-esteem task force, 78
  contingencies of self worth, 79–80, 82
  culture and, 80–82, *81*
  denigrating outgroups and, *379*, 379–381
  downward social comparisons and, 76, 79
  forces driving self-evaluation, 81–82
  gender differences, 79
  good or bad outcomes of high self-esteem, 81–82
  mortality salience, 235
  narcissism and, 84
  racial prejudice and, 387
  self-esteem movement, 78
  self-esteem scale, *79*
  self-improvement efforts *vs.* self-esteem, 81, 82
  self-serving construals, 83
  self-verification, 85–87
  situationism, 69–70
  social acceptance and, 80
  sociometer hypothesis, 80, 82
  state self-esteem, 79–80, 82
  terror management theory, 234, 235
  trait self-esteem, 78–79, 82, 96
  see also self-concept; self-enhancement; social self
self-evaluation, motives driving, 82–87, 96
self-fulfilling prophecies, 104–105, 136, 386–387, 527
self-handicapping, 93–94, 95, 96
self-insight, lack of, 65–66
selfish, 485
self-knowledge
  accuracy of, 65–66
  differences in African groups, 73
  distinctiveness and the sense of self, 69–70, *70*
  family and other socialization agents, 67–69
  independent self-construal, 71, *71*
  interdependent self-construal, 71, *71*
  malleability and stability of the self, 70
  organization of, 66–67
  origins of, 65–66
  prefrontal cortex and, 74
  reflected self-appraisals, 68–69
  self-discrepancy theory, 87–88, 96
  self-schemas, 66–67, 96
  self-verification theory, 85–87
  social comparison theory, 76–77
  social me and, 65–66
  "Who Am I" test, 73–74
  working self-concept, 69, 70, 319
  see also self-concept
self-monitoring, 92–93, 95, 96
self-perception theory, 236
  embodied cognition and emotion, 229–232
  inferring our own attitudes, 226–227
  overjustification effect, 230–231, *231*
  reconciling with dissonance theory, 227–229, 232
  testing for arousal, 227–228
  see also attitudes; cognitive dissonance theory

self-presentation, 91–93, 94–95, 96
  on social media, 94–95
self-regulation
  automatic self-control strategies, 90–91
  possible selves, 87–88
  prevention focus, 89
  promotion focus, 89
  self-discrepancy theory, 87–88
  self-handicapping, 93–94
  self-monitoring, 92–93
self-schemas, 66–67, 96
self-selection, 44, 60, 312, 350
self-serving attributional bias, 150–152, *152*, 162, 170
self-serving construals, 83
self-understanding, 24–26
self-validation hypothesis, 255, 257, 266
self-verification and integrating self-enhancement perspective, 86–87
self-verification theory, 85–87
seminarians as Good Samaritans, 9, *9*, 49
serial monogamy, 29
sex, casual and mental health, 44
sexism
  benevolent, 364–365
  nameism and, 366
sexually inappropriate behavior and power, 431
sexual orientation
  cost of concealment, 400–401
  snap judgment of, 102
Sexual Prejudice Scale, 365
sexual trafficking, 463
sexual violence, cultural differences, 463–465
shame, 182
shared attention, 257
Sherif's conformity experiment, 274–276, *275*
  see also Asch's conformity experiment
Shia Muslims, 360
shooting and automatic stereotyping, 393–395
sibling dynamics and birth order, 68
Sierra Club, 455
signaling intentions, *178*
similarity
  attraction, 329
  attraction and, overview, 328
  complementarity *vs.*, 330–332
  of couples, 330
  explanation for increased attraction, 330
  studies on attraction and, 328–330
Sistine Chapel, 499
situational attribution, 147
situations
  aggression, situational determinants, 446–456, 478
  altruism, situational determinants, 489–491
  competition, situational determinants, 504
  cooperation, situational determinants, 504–505
  cultural differences and, 30
  evolution and, 30
  explaining behavior with social psychology, 5–7
  fundamental attribution error, 9–10
  lateness and helping behaviors of seminarians, 9, *9*
  Milgram experiment and social situations, 7–9
  power to affect behavior, 7–11, 34
  salience of people *vs.* situations, 158
  situationism and the social self, 69–70
  social connection and health, 520–522, 525
  social self and, 69–70
  subtle situational influence, 123
  working self-concept, 69, 70, 319
60 Minutes, 303
Skype, 477
Slate poll, 43
Slave Market with Disappearing Bust of Voltaire (Dali), *12*
slavery, 284

sleeper effect, 246–247, 266
smiling muscle (zygomaticus major), 334
smoking
  anti-smoking persuasion and advertising, 250, *250*
  arguing against self-interest, *248*
  attitude inoculation and, 265
  health risks, 260
  resistance to anti-smoking efforts, 260
  Surgeon General's Report on Smoking and Health, 260
snap judgments
  accuracy, 102
  consensus opinion prediction, 100–101
  dominance assessment of faces, *101*, 101–102
  facial trait judgments, effect of time constraints, 101, *101*
  inferring personality from appearance, 100–102
  trustworthiness assessment of faces, *101*, 101–102
sneaky bookers, 94
social acceptance, self-esteem and, 80
social attribution *see* causal attribution
social class
  academic achievement and, 75
  altruism and, 495–497, *496*, 512, 518
  attribution and, 166–167
  causal attribution and, 170
  health and, 517–520, 525
  independence, 251
  independence *vs.* interdependence, 27–28
  ladder measure, *519*, 519–520
  social fears of working-class students, 535
  social self and, 75, *75*
  see also socioeconomic status (SES)
social cognition
  bad-news bias, 106
  bottom-up processes, 118, 136
  confirmation bias, 113–117
  emotions and moral judgment, 191–194
  emotions influence perception, 189–190
  emotions *vs.* reason in decision making, 190–191
  facial trait judgments, effect of time constraints, 101, *101*
  fake news, 106–108
  footbridge dilemma, 192
  framing effects in, 110–111, 136
  Haidt's two-system theory of moral judgment, 191–192
  how information is presented, 109–113
  ideological distortions, 105
  inferring personality from physical appearance, 100–102
  information available for, 100–108, 136
  misleading firsthand information, 104–105
  misleading secondhand information, 105–108
  motivated confirmation bias, 117
  order effects in, 109–110
  overview, 99–100
  pluralistic ignorance, 103–104
  primacy effects, 109, 136
  recency effects, 109–110, 136
  response to infantile features, 101–102
  snap judgments, 101–102
  studying, 100, 136
  temporal framing in, 111–113
  top-down processes, 118–122, 136
  trolley dilemma, 192
  trustworthiness assessment of faces, *101*, 101–102
  see also heuristics; schemas
social comparisons, 96
  on Facebook, 77
  on social media, 77
social comparison theory, 76–77
social connection, benefits of, 520–522, 525

social context
  aspects of self that are distinctive in, 60–70
  aspects of self that are relevant in, 69–70
social determinants of social intelligence, 423
social exchange theory, 318
  comparison level, 318
  comparison level for alternatives, 318
social facilitation
  coacting and, 414
  dominant responses, 413, *418*
  early research, 411–412
  evaluation apprehension, *416*, 416–417, 442
  mere presence effect, 414, *415*, 442
  overview, 411
  social loafing and, 418, 442
  Zajonc's model of social facilitation, *413*,
    413–415
  see also groups
social fears and academic achievement, 534–535,
    540
social hierarchies, 426–427
social identity theory, 376–381, 406
  groups, 381
social influence, 269–309
  bulimia and, 278
  informational, and Sherif 's conformity
    experiment, *275*, 275–276
  networks, 269–270, *270*
  normative, 276–277, *277*, 285, 308
  overview, 269–271
  resisting, 299
  tattoos and, 269
  see also compliance; conformity; informational
    social influence; Milgram study of obedience;
    normative social influence; obedience
social intuitionist model of moral judgment,
    192, 202
socialization agents, 67–69
social learning theory, 540
social loafing, 418, 442
social me, 64
social media
  loneliness, 317
  magnifying fake news, 107
  news about politics, 107
  persuasion and, 257–258
  self-presentation, 94–95
  social comparison on, 77
  uses and abuses, 32
social neuroscience, 22–23
social psychology, general
  characterizing, 5–7
  critical thinking and, 31–32, 35
  explaining behavior with social psychology, 5–7
  see also methods of social psychology
social psychology research, value of, 38–39, 60
social reality, media and conceptions of, 258–260
social rejection and aggression, 451–454, 478
social relations, cultural differences in, 24–26
social rewards motive in altruism, 483–484
social self, 63–97
  actual self, 88
  automatic self-control strategies, 90–91
  construals and the self, 71–72
  cultural differences, 71–74, *73*, *74*
  culture and, 71–74
  distinctiveness and sense of self, 69–70, *70*
  dramaturgic perspective on, 92
  face, 92–93
  gender and, 74, 76
  health risks and, 94
  ideal self, 88
  malleability and stability of, 70
  nature of the social self, 64
  online presence, 94–95, 96
  ought self, 88
  possible selves, 87–88
  presenting self online, 94–95

prevention focus, 91, 96
promotion focus, 91, 96
protecting others' face, 92–93
reflected self-appraisals, 68–69
self-construal and gender, 74, 76
self-control, 96
self-discrepancy theory, 87–88, 96
self-enhancement, 82–85
self-handicapping, 93–94, 96
self-monitoring, 92, 96
self-presentation, 91–93, 96
self-regulation, 87–88, 96
sibling dynamics, 68
situationism and, 69–70
social class and, 75, *85*
social comparison theory, 76–77
working self-concept, 69, 70
see also self-esteem; self-knowledge
social support scale, 520, *520*
socioeconomic status (SES)
  academic achievement and, 383
  in arranged marriages, 354–355
  causal attribution and, 166–167, 170
  construal and, *519*, 519–520
  divorce and, 349
  health and, 517–520, 525
  ladder measure, *519*, 519–520
  see also social class
sociometer hypothesis, 80, 82
Somalia, 360
source characteristics and persuasion, 246–248
  attractiveness, 246
  certainty, 248
  credibility, 246–247
source credibility, thought confidence and,
    255–256
South Africa and divestment movement, 472
Spanish Inquisition, 476
spin framing, 110–111
Sports Illustrated jinx, 132
sport teams, 405
spotlight effect, 440, *440*, 442
  see also self-awareness theory
Sri Lankans in Gulf countries, 370
stability, in the social self, 70
state self-esteem, 79–80, 82, 96
State v. Henderson, 546
statistical significance, 54, 60
status
  anger and, 188
  definition, 428
  hierarchies, 188
  role negotiation within groups, 188
  social influence and, 277
  see also socioeconomic status (SES)
status exchange hypothesis, 332
STEM (science, technology, engineering and
    mathematics), 400
stepfamilies and violence, 466–467, 478
stereotypes, 34
  of African Americans, 359
  attributional ambiguity and, 396–397
  automatic, 393–395
  automatic and controlled processes, 15–16
  bias in criminal justice system, 557–558, 560
  categorization and, 393–394
  coining of term, 381
  concrete *vs.* abstract construal, 388–389
  conservation of cognitive resources and,
    381–383
  construal and, 14
  construal processes and biased assessments,
    383–389
  disconfirmation, 387
  expectations and biased information process-
    ing, 385–386
  explaining away exceptions, 387–389
  facial features and criminal sentences, 397

illusory correlations, 383–385
ingroup similarity and outgroup difference
    assumptions, 390
outgroup homogeneity effect, 390–391, 406
physical attractiveness and social skills,
    335–336
reducing, 401, 407
representativeness heuristic and, 129
schemas and, 119
self-fulfilling prophecies, 386–387
stereotype threat, 397–400, *398*, 407,
    530–534, 540
subtyping, 387
system justification theory, 233
theoretical perspectives, 360–361, 406
"typical" gay man, 212–213
see also discrimination; prejudice
stereotype threat, 397–400, *398*, 407, 530–534,
    540
  African Americans, 400
  arousal, 400
  disidentification, 400
  math performance, 398
stonewalling in romantic relationships, 349, 350,
    356
Strange Situation, 319–320
stress, 33
  biological responses to, 515–516
  brain regions related to, 515–516, *516*
  cardiovascular arousal and, 514
  chronic stress, 516–517
  cortisol and, 516, *516*, 517
  hypothalamic-pituitary-adrenal (HPA) axis,
    515–516, *516*, 517, 520–521, 522, 525
  Marie Antoinette, 514
  marital conflict and, 348
  neighborhoods and, 518–519
  participants in Milgram study, 298, 300
  psychological stress, 515, 525
  rumination, 516, 517, 525
  self-enhancement and, 84
  self-esteem and, 84
  short-term stress, 515–516
  social class and, 517–520
  soothing effect of touch, 187–188
  "tend-and-befriend" approach to, 522
  tips for reducing stress, 522
  see also health
Stroop task, 431
StudiVZ, 94
subjectivist view of beauty, 334
subliminal stimuli, 120–121, 122, 243, *243*
submission, 20
subtle situational influence, 123
subtyping, 387
success, 26
suicide baiting, 436–437
suicide *vs.* homicide rates, 126
Sunni Muslims, 360
superordinate goals, 372–374, 403
surveys, 42–44
Swayamghuntha Temple, 499
sweet lemons justification, 215–216
sympathy, 487
  love maps and, *183*
Syria, 360
systematic route *see* central (systematic) route to
    persuasion
system justification theory, 232–233, 237

T

task-contingent rewards, 230–231
tattoos, 269
telenovelas, 536–537, 540
television watching
  anxiety and, 46
  children watching aggressive behavior, 50
telomeres, 517

temporal framing, 111–113
temptations and goals, 90–91
terrorist attacks on 9/11, 370
terror management theory, 233–234, 237
    certainty of death, 233
    mortality salience, 234–235
    symbolic immortality, 233, 234
    see also attitudes
testosterone, 48, 447, 463, 468–469
tetanus inoculations, channel factors and, 10–11
thalamus, 209
theory of mind, 20–21, 34
thinness and physical attractiveness, 337
thought confidence
    self-validation hypothesis and, 255
    source credibility and, 255–256
thought experiment, 39
thought polarization hypothesis, 262, 267
threat defense system, 515–516
tight cultures, loose cultures *vs.*, 283–284
time-constrained trait judgments, correlations
    between unconstrained trait judgments and,
    101
TIME magazine, 44, 46
timing and persuasion, 253
tit-for-tat strategy, 509–510, 512
token economy program, 230
toothbrushing and attitude inoculation, 264
top-down processes, 118, 136
    see also schemas
touch, emotion communicated through, *187*,
    187–188
traffic safety, 132
trait self-esteem, 78–79, 82, 96
transcendentalists, 455
trolley dilemma, 192
Trump Tower, 116
trust and economic growth, *485*
trustworthiness dimension, judgment of faces,
    101, 101–102
tutoring effectiveness, Five Cs of, 529
Tutsis, 445, 446, 459, 471, 482–483, 484, 502
"Twinkie defense," 433
two-system theory of moral judgment, 191–192

U

Ukraine, 360
ultimatum game, 505–507

unconscious processing *see* automatic processing
unconstrained trait judgments, correlations
    between time-constrained trait judgments
    and, *101*
uniqueness, personal, 26, 28
United Way, 509
universals
    attractiveness, 336–337, 338
    evolution and, 19–20
    facial expressions, 20, 178–181
    reciprocity, 501
    universal behaviors, reactions, and institutions,
    19
Up movie, 173
upward social comparisons, 76–77
U.S. Constitution, 80
U.S. News and World Report, 44
U.S. presidential election, 1984, 208
U.S. presidential election, 2012, 107
U.S. presidential election, 2016, 106, 107, 116,
    257, 259
Utku Inuit (Eskimos), lack of anger, 182

V

vagus nerve, 488
validity coefficients, 52
vampire bats, 500
Ven Conmigo (Come With Me), 537
ventral caudate, cooperation and, 504
ventral striatum, 354
ventromedial/orbitofrontal cortex, cooperation
    and, 504
ventromedial prefrontal cortex, 26
video games
    aggression and video game violence, 450–451,
    478
    Columbine High School shootings and, 450
    Doom, 450
    Mortal Kombat, 451
    PGA Tournament Golf, 451
Vietnam War, 205–206
violence, attitudes toward, 22
    dueling tradition, *38*
    insult-related homicides, 47, 462–463
    job applicant with felony conviction, 37–38,
    51
    South *vs.* Northern regions, 42, 43–44, 47–49,
    51, *462,* 462–463

survey questions, 43
violence on TV and fear of victimization, 106
    see also aggression; attitudes
Virtuous Violence (Fiske and Rai), 473
visual perception, construal and, *11, 12,* 13
voir dire, 549, 551, 560
volunteerism, 487–489
voting, channel factors and, 11

W

well-being, self-enhancement and, 84–85
Westgate West apartment friendship research,
    324–325, *325*
"Who Am I" test, 73–74
Williams v. Florida, 551
Witherspoon v. Illinois, 551
Wizard of Oz, The, 125, 126
woman suffrage, 284
women
    aggression, 467–468
    discrimination, 360
    gender differences in social self, 74, 76
    male attractiveness during menstrual cycle,
    342–343, *343*
    in STEM (science, technology, engineering and
    mathematics), 400
Wonder Woman, 481–482
working self-concept, 69, 70, 319
World War I
    conflict and complexity of rhetoric,
    474, *474*
    cooperation between enemies, 510
World War II
    ally formation with former enemies, 502
    altruism, 489
    Jewish genocide, 307, 361, 473
    Pearl Harbor attack, 420
    see also Holocaust

Y

Yale University, 246
Yanomami, 461
Yemen, 360

Z

Zajonc's model of social facilitation, *413,*
    413–415
Zimbardo prison study, 6